REPORT OF
THE PRESIDENT'S COMMISSION
ON THE ASSASSINATION OF
PRESIDENT KENNEDY

JOHN FITZGERALD KENNEDY
35th President of the United States
May 29, 1917–November 22, 1963

THE WARREN COMMISSION REPORT

Report of President's Commission on the Assassination of President John F. Kennedy

ST. MARTIN'S PRESS
NEW YORK

Photo credits:

Page 66 & 67: Thomas C. Dillard/*Dallas Morning News*
Pages 100, 101, 102, 103, 108 & 114 (Zapruder stills): © 1963, 1967 LMH Company c/o
James Silverberg, Esq., Washington, D.C.
Page 108 (Nix still): © 1963, 1964–1991 Nix c/o James Silverberg, Esq., Washington, D.C.
Page 113: AP/Wide World
Page 126: Detroit Free Press
Page 177: Hill Exhibit B/National Archives
Pages 203, 205, 214, 218, 223: KRLD-TV/CBS
Pages 220, 232, 341: WBAP-TV/NBC
Page 356: AP/Wide World
All other photos and illustrations courtesy of the National Archives

ISBN 0-312-08256-8 (hc.)
ISBN 0-312-08257-6 (pbk.)

PRESIDENT'S COMMISSION
ON THE
ASSASSINATION OF PRESIDENT KENNEDY

CHIEF JUSTICE EARL WARREN, *Chairman*

SENATOR RICHARD B. RUSSELL

SENATOR JOHN SHERMAN COOPER

REPRESENTATIVE HALE BOGGS

REPRESENTATIVE GERALD R. FORD

MR. ALLEN W. DULLES

MR. JOHN J. McCLOY

J. LEE RANKIN, *General Counsel*

Assistant Counsel

FRANCIS W. H. ADAMS

JOSEPH A. BALL

DAVID W. BELIN

WILLIAM T. COLEMAN, Jr.

MELVIN ARON EISENBERG

BURT W. GRIFFIN

LEON D. HUBERT, Jr.

ALBERT E. JENNER, Jr.

WESLEY J. LIEBELER

NORMAN REDLICH

W. DAVID SLAWSON

ARLEN SPECTER

SAMUEL A. STERN

HOWARD P. WILLENS*

Staff Members

PHILLIP BARSON

EDWARD A. CONROY

JOHN HART ELY

ALFRED GOLDBERG

MURRAY J. LAULICHT

ARTHUR MARMOR

RICHARD M. MOSK

JOHN J. O'BRIEN

STUART POLLAK

ALFREDDA SCOBEY

CHARLES N. SHAFFER, Jr.

LLOYD L. WEINREB

---

*Mr. Willens also acted as liaison between the Commission and the Department of Justice.

PRESIDENT'S COMMISSION
ON THE
ASSASSINATION OF PRESIDENT KENNEDY

200 Maryland Ave. N.E.
Washington, D.C. 20002
Telephone 543-1400

EARL WARREN,
  Chairman
RICHARD B. RUSSELL
JOHN SHERMAN COOPER
HALE BOGGS
GERALD R. FORD
JOHN J. McCLOY
ALLEN W. DULLES

J. LEE RANKIN,
  General Counsel

September 24, 1964

The President
The White House
Washington, D. C.

Dear Mr. President:

Your Commission to investigate the assassination of President Kennedy on November 22, 1963, having completed its assignment in accordance with Executive Order No. 11130 of November 29, 1963, herewith submits its final report.

Respectfully,

Earl Warren
Earl Warren, Chairman

Richard B. Russell
Richard B. Russell

John Sherman Cooper
John Sherman Cooper

Hale Boggs
Hale Boggs

Gerald R. Ford
Gerald R. Ford

Allen W. Dulles
Allen W. Dulles

John J. McCloy
John J. McCloy

Foreword

PRESIDENT LYNDON B. JOHNSON, by Executive Order No. 11130 dated November 29, 1963,[1] created this Commission to investigate the assassination on November 22, 1963, of John Fitzgerald Kennedy, the 35th President of the United States. The President directed the Commission to evaluate all the facts and circumstances surrounding the assassination and the subsequent killing of the alleged assassin and to report its findings and conclusions to him.[2]

The subject of the Commission's inquiry was a chain of events which saddened and shocked the people of the United States and of the world. The assassination of President Kennedy and the simultaneous wounding of John B. Connally, Jr., Governor of Texas, had been followed within an hour by the slaying of Patrolman J. D. Tippit of the Dallas Police Department. In the United States and abroad, these events evoked universal demands for an explanation.

Immediately after the assassination, State and local officials in Dallas devoted their resources to the apprehension of the assassin. The U.S. Secret Service, which is responsible for the protection of the President, and the Federal Bureau of Investigation began an investigation at the direction of President Johnson. Within 35 minutes of the killing of Patrolman Tippit, Lee Harvey Oswald was arrested by the Dallas police as a suspect in that crime. Based on evidence provided by Federal, State, and local agencies, the State of Texas arraigned Oswald within 12 hours of his arrest, charging him with the assassination of President Kennedy and the murder of Patrolman Tippit. On November 24, 1963, less than 48 hours after his arrest, Oswald was fatally shot in the basement of the Dallas Police Department by Jack Ruby, a Dallas nightclub owner. This shooting took place in full view of a national television audience.

The events of these 2 days were witnessed with shock and disbelief by a Nation grieving the loss of its young leader. Throughout the world, reports on these events were disseminated in massive detail. Theories and speculations mounted regarding the assassination. In many instances, the intense public demand for facts was met by partial and frequently conflicting reports from Dallas and elsewhere. After Oswald's arrest and his denial of all guilt, public attention focused both on the extent of the evidence against him and the possibility of a conspiracy, domestic or foreign. His subsequent death heightened public interest and stimulated additional suspicions and rumors.

THE COMMISSION AND ITS POWERS

After Lee Harvey Oswald was shot by Jack Ruby, it was no longer possible to arrive at the complete story of the assassination through normal judicial procedures during a trial of the alleged assassin. Alternative means for instituting a complete investigation were widely discussed. Federal and State officials conferred on the possibility of initiating a court of inquiry before a State magistrate in Texas. An investigation by the grand jury of Dallas County also was considered. As speculation about the existence of a foreign or domestic conspiracy became widespread, committees in both Houses of Congress weighed the desirability of congressional hearings to discover all the facts relating to the assassination.

By his order of November 29 establishing the Commission, President Johnson sought to avoid parallel investigations and to concentrate factfinding in a body having the broadest national mandate. As Chairman of the Commission, President Johnson selected Earl Warren, Chief Justice of the United States, former Governor and attorney general of the State of California. From the U.S. Senate, he chose Richard B. Russell, Democratic Senator from Georgia and chairman of the Senate Armed Services Committee, former Governor of, and county attorney in, the State of Georgia, and John Sherman Cooper, Republican Senator from Kentucky, former county and circuit judge, State of Kentucky, and U.S. Ambassador to India. Two members of the Commission were drawn from the U.S. House of Representatives: Hale Boggs, Democratic U.S. Representative from Louisiana and majority whip, and Gerald R. Ford, Republican, U.S. Representative from Michigan and chairman of the House Republican Conference. From private life, President Johnson selected two lawyers by profession, both of whom have served in the administrations of Democratic and Republican Presidents: Allen W. Dulles, former Director of Central Intelligence, and John J. McCloy, former President of the International Bank for Reconstruction and Development, former U.S. High Commissioner for Germany, and during World War II, the Assistant Secretary of War.

From its first meeting on December 5, 1963, the Commission viewed the Executive order as an unequivocal Presidential mandate to conduct a thorough and independent investigation. Because of the numerous rumors and theories, the Commission concluded that the public interest in insuring that the truth was ascertained could not be met by merely accepting the reports or the analyses of Federal or State agencies. Not only were the premises and conclusions of those reports critically reassessed, but all assertions or rumors relating to a possible conspiracy, or the complicity of others than Oswald, which have come to the attention of the Commission, were investigated.

On December 13, 1963, Congress enacted Senate Joint Resolution 137 (Public Law 88–202) [3] empowering the Commission to issue subpoenas requiring the testimony of witnesses and the production of evidence relating to any matter under its investigation. In addition, the resolution authorized the Commission to compel testimony from witnesses claiming the privilege against self-incrimination under the fifth amendment to the U.S. Constitution by providing for the grant of immunity to persons testifying under such compulsion. Immunity under these provisions was not granted to any witness during the Commission's investigation.

The Commission took steps immediately to obtain the necessary staff to fulfill its assignment. J. Lee Rankin, former Solicitor General of the United States, was sworn in as general counsel for the Commission on December 16, 1963. Additional members of the legal staff were selected during the next few weeks. The Commission has been aided by 14 assistant counsel with high professional qualifications, selected by it from widely separated parts of the United States. This staff undertook the work of the Commission with a wealth of legal and investigative experience and a total dedication to the determination of the truth. The Commission has been assisted also by highly qualified personnel from several Federal agencies, assigned to the Commission at its request. This group included lawyers from the Department of Justice, agents of the Internal Revenue Service, a senior historian from the Department of Defense, an editor from the Department of State, and secretarial and administrative staff supplied by the General Services Administration and other agencies.

In addition to the assistance afforded by Federal agencies, the Commission throughout its inquiry had the cooperation of representatives of the city of Dallas and the State of Texas. The attorney general of Texas, Waggoner Carr, aided by two distinguished lawyers of that State, Robert G. Storey of Dallas, retired dean of the Southern Methodist University Law School and former president of the American Bar Association, and Leon Jaworski of Houston, former president of the Texas State Bar Association, has been fully informed at all times as to the progress of the investigation, and has advanced such suggestions as he and his special assistants considered helpful to the accomplishment of the Commission's assignment. Attorney General Carr has promptly supplied the Commission with pertinent information possessed by Texas officials. Dallas officials, particularly those from the police department, have fully complied with all requests made by the Commission.

THE INVESTIGATION

During December and early January the Commission received an increasing volume of reports from Federal and State investigative agencies. Of principal importance was the five-volume report of the Federal Bureau of Investigation, submitted on December 9, 1963, which summarized the results of the investigation conducted by the Bureau immediately after the assassination. After reviewing this report, the Commission requested the Federal Bureau of Investigation to furnish the underlying investigative materials relied upon in the summary report. The first investigative reports submitted in response to this request were delivered to the Commission on December 20, 1963. On December 18, the Secret Service submitted a detailed report on security precautions taken before President Kennedy's trip to Texas and a summary of the events of November 22, as witnessed by Secret Service agents. A few days later the Department of State submitted a report relating to Oswald's defection to the Soviet Union in 1959, and his return to the United States in 1962. On January 7 and 11, 1964, the attorney general of Texas submitted an extensive set of investigative materials, largely Dallas police reports, on the assassination of President Kennedy and the killing of Oswald.

As these investigative reports were received, the staff began analyzing and summarizing them. The members of the legal staff, divided into teams, proceeded to organize the facts revealed by these investigations, determine the issues, sort out the unresolved problems, and recommend additional investigation by the Commission. Simultaneously, to insure that no relevant information would be overlooked, the Commission directed requests to the 10 major departments of the Federal Government, 14 of its independent agencies or commissions, and 4 congressional committees for all information relating to the assassination or the background and activities of Lee Harvey Oswald and Jack Ruby.

After reviewing the accumulating materials, the Commission directed numerous additional requests to Federal and State investigative agencies. The Federal Bureau of Investigation and the Secret Service executed the detailed requests for statements of witnesses and examinations of physical evidence with dispatch and thoroughness. All these reports were reviewed and analyzed by the Commission. Additional investigative requests, where appropriate, were handled by Internal Revenue Service, Department of State, and the military intelligence agencies with comparable skill. Investigative analyses of particular significance and sensitivity in the foreign areas were contributed by the Central Intelligence Agency. On occasion the Commission used independent experts from State and city governments to supplement or verify information. During the investigation the Commission on several occasions visited the scene of the assassination and other places in the Dallas area pertinent to the inquiry.

The scope and detail of the investigative effort by the Federal and State agencies are suggested in part by statistics from the Federal Bureau of Investigation and the Secret Service. Immediately after the assassination more than 80 additional FBI personnel were transferred to the Dallas office on a temporary basis to assist in the investigation. Beginning November 22, 1963, the Federal Bureau of Investigation conducted approximately 25,000 interviews and reinterviews of persons having information of possible relevance to the investigation and by September 11, 1964, submitted over 2,300 reports totaling approximately 25,400 pages to the Commission. During the same period the Secret Service conducted approximately 1,550 interviews and submitted 800 reports totaling some 4,600 pages.

Because of the diligence, cooperation, and facilities of Federal investigative agencies, it was unnecessary for the Commission to employ investigators other than the members of the Commission's legal staff. The Commission recognized, however, that special measures were required whenever the facts or rumors called for an appraisal of the acts of the agencies themselves. The staff reviewed in detail the actions of several Federal agencies, particularly the Federal Bureau of Investigation, the Secret Service, the Central Intelligence Agency, and the Department of State. Initially the Commission requested the agencies to furnish all their reports relating to the assassination and their relationships with Oswald or Ruby. On the basis of these reports, the Commission submitted specific questions to the agency involved. Members of the staff followed up the answers by reviewing the relevant files of each agency for additional information. In some instances, members of the Commission also reviewed the files in person. Finally, the responsible officials of these agencies were called to testify under oath. Dean Rusk, Secretary of State; C. Douglas Dillon, Secretary of the Treasury; John A. McCone, Director of the Central Intelligence Agency; J. Edgar Hoover, Director of the Federal Bureau of Investigation; and James J. Rowley, Chief of the Secret Service, appeared as witnesses and testified fully regarding their agencies' participation in the matters under scrutiny by the Commission.

COMMISSION HEARINGS

In addition to the information resulting from these investigations, the Commission has relied primarily on the facts disclosed by the sworn testimony of the principal witnesses to the assassination and related events. Beginning on February 3, 1964, the Commission and its staff has taken the testimony of 552 witnesses. Of this number, 94 appeared before members of the Commission; 395 were questioned by members of the Commission's legal staff; 61 supplied sworn affidavits; and 2 gave statements.[4] Under Commission procedures, all witnesses were advised that they had the right to the presence and the advice of their lawyer during the interrogation, with the corollary rights to raise objections to any questions asked, to make any clarifying statement on the record after the interrogation, and to purchase a copy of their testimony.[5]

Commission hearings were closed to the public unless the witness appearing before the Commission requested an open hearing. Under these procedures, testimony of one witness was taken in a public hearing on two occasions. No other witness requested a public hearing. The Commission concluded that the premature publication by it of testimony regarding the assassination or the subsequent killing of Oswald might interfere with Ruby's rights to a fair and impartial trial on the charges filed against him by the State of Texas. The Commission also recognized that testimony would be presented before it which would be inadmissible in judicial proceedings and might prejudice innocent parties if made public out of context. In addition to the witnesses who appeared before the Commission, numerous others provided sworn depositions, affidavits, and statements upon which the Commission has relied. Since this testimony, as well as that taken before the Commission, could not always be taken in logical sequence, the Commission concluded that partial publication of testimony as the investigation progressed was impractical and could be misleading.

THE COMMISSION'S FUNCTION

The Commission's most difficult assignments have been to uncover all the facts concerning the assassination of President Kennedy and to determine if it was in any way directed or encouraged by unknown persons at home or abroad. In this process, its objective has been to identify the person or persons responsible for both the assassination of President Kennedy and the killing of Oswald through an examination of the evidence. The task has demanded unceasing appraisal of the evidence by the individual members of the Commission in their effort to discover the whole truth.

The procedures followed by the Commission in developing and assessing evidence necessarily differed from those of a court conducting a criminal trial of a defendant present before it, since under our system there is no provision for a posthumous trial. If Oswald had lived he could have had a trial by American standards of justice where he would have been able to exercise his full rights under the law. A judge and jury would have presumed him innocent until proven guilty beyond a reasonable doubt. He might have furnished information which could have affected the course of his trial. He could have participated in and guided his defense. There could have been an examination to determine whether he was sane under prevailing legal standards. All witnesses, including possibly the defendant, could have been subjected to searching examination under the adversary system of American trials.

The Commission has functioned neither as a court presiding over an adversary proceeding nor as a prosecutor determined to prove a case, but as a factfinding agency committed to the ascertainment of the truth. In the course of the investigation of the facts and rumors surrounding these matters, it was necessary to explore hearsay and other sources of information not admissible in a court proceeding obtained from persons who saw or heard and others in a position to observe what occurred. In fairness to the alleged assassin and his family, the Commission on February 25, 1964, requested Walter E. Craig, president of the American Bar Association, to participate in the investigation and to advise the Commission whether in his opinion the proceedings conformed to the basic principles of American justice. Mr. Craig accepted this assignment and participated fully and without limitation. He attended Commission hearings in person or through his appointed assistants. All working papers, reports, and other data in Commission files were made available, and Mr. Craig and his associates were given the opportunity to cross-examine witnesses, to recall any witness heard prior to his appointment, and to suggest witnesses whose testimony they would like to have the Commission hear. This procedure was agreeable to counsel for Oswald's widow.

THE COMMISSION'S REPORT

In this report the Commission submits the results of its investigation. Each member of the Commission has given careful consideration to the entire report and concurs in its findings and conclusions. The report consists of an initial chapter summarizing the Commission's basic findings and conclusions, followed by a detailed analysis of the facts and the issues raised by the events of November 22, 1963, and the 2 following days. Individual chapters consider the trip to Dallas, the shots from the Texas School Book Depository, the identity of the assassin, the killing of Lee Harvey Oswald, the possibility of a conspiracy, Oswald's background and possible motive, and arrangements for the protection of the President. In these chapters, rather than rely on cross references, the Commission on occasion has repeated certain testimony in order that the reader might have the necessary information before him while examining the conclusions of the Commission on each important issue.

With this report the Commission is submitting the complete testimony of all the witnesses who appeared before the Commission or gave sworn depositions or affidavits, the accompanying documentary exhibits, and other investigative materials which are relied upon in this report. The Commission is committing all of its reports and working papers to the National Archives, where they can be permanently preserved under the rules and regulations of the National Archives and applicable Federal law.

Contents

CHAPTER I

Summary and Conclusions

THE ASSASSINATION of John Fitzgerald Kennedy on November 22, 1963, was a cruel and shocking act of violence directed against a man, a family, a nation, and against all mankind. A young and vigorous leader whose years of public and private life stretched before him was the victim of the fourth Presidential assassination in the history of a country dedicated to the concepts of reasoned argument and peaceful political change. This Commission was created on November 29, 1963, in recognition of the right of people everywhere to full and truthful knowledge concerning these events. This report endeavors to fulfill that right and to appraise this tragedy by the light of reason and the standard of fairness. It has been prepared with a deep awareness of the Commission's responsibility to present to the American people an objective report of the facts relating to the assassination.

NARRATIVE OF EVENTS

At 11:40 a.m., c.s.t., on Friday, November 22, 1963, President John F. Kennedy, Mrs. Kennedy, and their party arrived at Love Field, Dallas, Tex. Behind them was the first day of a Texas trip planned 5 months before by the President, Vice President Lyndon B. Johnson, and John B. Connally, Jr., Governor of Texas. After leaving the White House on Thursday morning, the President had flown initially to San Antonio where Vice President Lyndon B. Johnson joined the party and the President dedicated new research facilities at the U.S. Air Force School of Aerospace Medicine. Following a testimonial dinner in Houston for U.S. Representative Albert Thomas, the President flew to Fort Worth where he spent the night and spoke at a large breakfast gathering on Friday.

Planned for later that day were a motorcade through downtown Dallas, a luncheon speech at the Trade Mart, and a flight to Austin where the President would attend a reception and speak at a Democratic fundraising dinner. From Austin he would proceed to the Texas ranch of the Vice President. Evident on this trip were the

1

varied roles which an American President performs—Head of State, Chief Executive, party leader, and, in this instance, prospective candidate for reelection.

The Dallas motorcade, it was hoped, would evoke a demonstration of the President's personal popularity in a city which he had lost in the 1960 election. Once it had been decided that the trip to Texas would span 2 days, those responsible for planning, primarily Governor Connally and Kenneth O'Donnell, a special assistant to the President, agreed that a motorcade through Dallas would be desirable. The Secret Service was told on November 8 that 45 minutes had been allotted to a motorcade procession from Love Field to the site of a luncheon planned by Dallas business and civic leaders in honor of the President. After considering the facilities and security problems of several buildings, the Trade Mart was chosen as the luncheon site. Given this selection, and in accordance with the customary practice of affording the greatest number of people an opportunity to see the President, the motorcade route selected was a natural one. The route was approved by the local host committee and White House representatives on November 18 and publicized in the local papers starting on November 19. This advance publicity made it clear that the motorcade would leave Main Street and pass the intersection of Elm and Houston Streets as it proceeded to the Trade Mart by way of the Stemmons Freeway.

By midmorning of November 22, clearing skies in Dallas dispelled the threat of rain and the President greeted the crowds from his open limousine without the "bubbletop," which was at that time a plastic shield furnishing protection only against inclement weather. To the left of the President in the rear seat was Mrs. Kennedy. In the jump seats were Governor Connally, who was in front of the President, and Mrs. Connally at the Governor's left. Agent William R. Greer of the Secret Service was driving, and Agent Roy H. Kellerman was sitting to his right.

Directly behind the Presidential limousine was an open "followup" car with eight Secret Service agents, two in the front seat, two in the rear, and two on each running board. These agents, in accordance with normal Secret Service procedures, were instructed to scan the crowds, the roofs, and windows of buildings, overpasses, and crossings for signs of trouble. Behind the "followup" car was the Vice-Presidential car carrying the Vice President and Mrs. Johnson and Senator Ralph W. Yarborough. Next were a Vice-Presidential "followup" car and several cars and buses for additional dignitaries, press representatives, and others.

The motorcade left Love Field shortly after 11:50 a.m., and proceeded through residential neighborhoods, stopping twice at the President's request to greet well-wishers among the friendly crowds. Each time the President's car halted, Secret Service agents from the "followup" car moved forward to assume a protective stance near the President and Mrs. Kennedy. As the motorcade reached Main Street, a principal east-west artery in downtown Dallas, the welcome became

2

tumultuous. At the extreme west end of Main Street the motorcade turned right on Houston Street and proceeded north for one block in order to make a left turn on Elm Street, the most direct and convenient approach to the Stemmons Freeway and the Trade Mart. As the President's car approached the intersection of Houston and Elm Streets, there loomed directly ahead on the intersection's northwest corner a seven-story, orange brick warehouse and office building, the Texas School Book Depository. Riding in the Vice President's car, Agent Rufus W. Youngblood of the Secret Service noticed that the clock atop the building indicated 12:30 p.m., the scheduled arrival time at the Trade Mart.

The President's car which had been going north made a sharp turn toward the southwest onto Elm Street. At a speed of about 11 miles per hour, it started down the gradual descent toward a railroad overpass under which the motorcade would proceed before reaching the Stemmons Freeway. The front of the Texas School Book Depository was now on the President's right, and he waved to the crowd assembled there as he passed the building. Dealey Plaza—an open, landscaped area marking the western end of downtown Dallas—stretched out to the President's left. A Secret Service agent riding in the motorcade radioed the Trade Mart that the President would arrive in 5 minutes.

Seconds later shots resounded in rapid succession. The President's hands moved to his neck. He appeared to stiffen momentarily and lurch slightly forward in his seat. A bullet had entered the base of the back of his neck slightly to the right of the spine. It traveled downward and exited from the front of the neck, causing a nick in the left lower portion of the knot in the President's necktie. Before the shooting started, Governor Connally had been facing toward the crowd on the right. He started to turn toward the left and suddenly felt a blow on his back. The Governor had been hit by a bullet which entered at the extreme right side of his back at a point below his right armpit. The bullet traveled through his chest in a downward and forward direction, exited below his right nipple, passed through his right wrist which had been in his lap, and then caused a wound to his left thigh. The force of the bullet's impact appeared to spin the Governor to his right, and Mrs. Connally pulled him down into her lap. Another bullet then struck President Kennedy in the rear portion of his head, causing a massive and fatal wound. The President fell to the left into Mrs. Kennedy's lap.

Secret Service Agent Clinton J. Hill, riding on the left running board of the "followup" car, heard a noise which sounded like a firecracker and saw the President suddenly lean forward and to the left. Hill jumped off the car and raced toward the President's limousine. In the front seat of the Vice-Presidential car, Agent Youngblood heard an explosion and noticed unusual movements in the crowd. He vaulted into the rear seat and sat on the Vice President in order to protect him. At the same time Agent Kellerman in the front seat of the Presidential limousine turned to observe the President. Seeing that the President was struck, Kellerman instructed the driver, "Let's get out of here; we are hit." He radioed ahead to the lead car, "Get us to the hospital immediately." Agent Greer immediately accelerated the Presidential car. As it gained speed, Agent Hill managed to pull himself onto the back of the car where Mrs. Kennedy had climbed. Hill pushed her back into the rear seat and shielded the stricken President and Mrs. Kennedy as the President's car proceeded at high speed to Parkland Memorial Hospital, 4 miles away.

At Parkland, the President was immediately treated by a team of physicians who had been alerted for the President's arrival by the Dallas Police Department as the result of a radio message from the motorcade after the shooting. The doctors noted irregular breathing movements and a possible heartbeat, although they could not detect a pulsebeat. They observed the extensive wound in the President's head and a small wound approximately one-fourth inch in diameter in the lower third of his neck. In an effort to facilitate breathing, the physicians performed a tracheotomy by enlarging the throat wound and inserting a tube. Totally absorbed in the immediate task of trying to preserve the President's life, the attending doctors never turned the President over for an examination of his back. At 1 p.m., after all heart activity ceased and the Last Rites were administered by a priest, President Kennedy was pronounced dead. Governor Connally underwent surgery and ultimately recovered from his serious wounds.

Upon learning of the President's death, Vice President Johnson left Parkland Hospital under close guard and proceeded to the Presidential plane at Love Field. Mrs. Kennedy, accompanying her husband's body, boarded the plane shortly thereafter. At 2:38 p.m., in the central compartment of the plane, Lyndon B. Johnson was sworn in as the 36th President of the United States by Federal District Court Judge Sarah T. Hughes. The plane left immediately for Washington, D.C., arriving at Andrews AFB, Md., at 5:58 p.m., e.s.t. The President's body was taken to the National Naval Medical Center, Bethesda, Md., where it was given a complete pathological examination. The autopsy disclosed the large head wound observed at Parkland and the wound in the front of the neck which had been enlarged by the Parkland doctors when they performed the tracheotomy. Both of these wounds were described in the autopsy report as being "presumably of exit." In addition the autopsy revealed a small wound of entry in the rear of the President's skull and another wound of entry near the base of the back of the neck. The autopsy report stated the cause of death as "Gunshot wound, head," and the bullets which struck the President were described as having been fired "from a point behind and somewhat above the level of the deceased."

At the scene of the shooting, there was evident confusion at the outset concerning the point of origin of the shots. Witnesses differed in their accounts of the direction from which the sound of the shots emanated. Within a few minutes, however, attention centered on the Texas School Book Depository Building as the source of the shots. The building was occupied by a private corporation, the Texas School

4

Book Depository Co., which distributed school textbooks of several publishers and leased space to representatives of the publishers. Most of the employees in the building worked for these publishers. The balance, including a 15-man warehousing crew, were employees of the Texas School Book Depository Co. itself.

Several eyewitnesses in front of the building reported that they saw a rifle being fired from the southeast corner window on the sixth floor of the Texas School Book Depository. One eyewitness, Howard L. Brennan, had been watching the parade from a point on Elm Street directly opposite and facing the building. He promptly told a policeman that he had seen a slender man, about 5 feet 10 inches, in his early thirties, take deliberate aim from the sixth-floor corner window and fire a rifle in the direction of the President's car. Brennan thought he might be able to identify the man since he had noticed him in the window a few minutes before the motorcade made the turn onto Elm Street. At 12:34 p.m., the Dallas police radio mentioned the Depository Building as a possible source of the shots, and at 12:45 p.m., the police radio broadcast a description of the suspected assassin based primarily on Brennan's observations.

When the shots were fired, a Dallas motorcycle patrolman, Marrion L. Baker, was riding in the motorcade at a point several cars behind the President. He had turned right from Main Street onto Houston Street and was about 200 feet south of Elm Street when he heard a shot. Baker, having recently returned from a week of deer hunting, was certain the shot came from a high-powered rifle. He looked up and saw pigeons scattering in the air from their perches on the Texas School Book Depository Building. He raced his motorcycle to the building, dismounted, scanned the area to the west and pushed his way through the spectators toward the entrance. There he encountered Roy Truly, the building superintendent, who offered Baker his help. They entered the building, and ran toward the two elevators in the rear. Finding that both elevators were on an upper floor, they dashed up the stairs. Not more than 2 minutes had elapsed since the shooting.

When they reached the second-floor landing on their way up to the top of the building, Patrolman Baker thought he caught a glimpse of someone through the small glass window in the door separating the hall area near the stairs from the small vestibule leading into the lunchroom. Gun in hand, he rushed to the door and saw a man about 20 feet away walking toward the other end of the lunchroom. The man was emptyhanded. At Baker's command, the man turned and approached him. Truly, who had started up the stairs to the third floor ahead of Baker, returned to see what had delayed the patrolman. Baker asked Truly whether he knew the man in the lunchroom. Truly replied that the man worked in the building, whereupon Baker turned from the man and proceeded, with Truly, up the stairs. The man they encountered had started working in the Texas School Book Depository Building on October 16, 1963. His fellow workers described him as very quiet—a "loner." His name was Lee Harvey Oswald.

Within about 1 minute after his encounter with Baker and Truly, Oswald was seen passing through the second-floor offices. In his hand was a full "Coke" bottle which he had purchased from a vending machine in the lunchroom. He was walking toward the front of the building where a passenger elevator and a short flight of stairs provided access to the main entrance of the building on the first floor. Approximately 7 minutes later, at about 12:40 p.m., Oswald boarded a bus at a point on Elm Street seven short blocks east of the Depository Building. The bus was traveling west toward the very building from which Oswald had come. Its route lay through the Oak Cliff section in southwest Dallas, where it would pass seven blocks east of the roominghouse in which Oswald was living, at 1026 North Beckley Avenue. On the bus was Mrs. Mary Bledsoe, one of Oswald's former landladies who immediately recognized him. Oswald stayed on the bus approximately 3 or 4 minutes, during which time it proceeded only two blocks because of the traffic jam created by the motorcade and the assassination. Oswald then left the bus.

A few minutes later he entered a vacant taxi four blocks away and asked the driver to take him to a point on North Beckley Avenue several blocks beyond his roominghouse. The trip required 5 or 6 minutes. At about 1 p.m. Oswald arrived at the roominghouse. The housekeeper, Mrs. Earlene Roberts, was surprised to see Oswald at midday and remarked to him that he seemed to be in quite a hurry. He made no reply. A few minutes later Oswald emerged from his room zipping up his jacket and rushed out of the house.

Approximately 14 minutes later, and just 45 minutes after the assassination, another violent shooting occurred in Dallas. The victim was Patrolman J. D. Tippit of the Dallas police, an officer with a good record during his more than 11 years with the police force. He was shot near the intersection of 10th Street and Patton Avenue, about nine-tenths of a mile from Oswald's roominghouse. At the time of the assassination, Tippit was alone in his patrol car, the routine practice for most police patrol cars at this time of day. He had been ordered by radio at 12:45 p.m. to proceed to the central Oak Cliff area as part of a concentration of patrol car activity around the center of the city following the assassination. At 12:54 Tippit radioed that he had moved as directed and would be available for any emergency. By this time the police radio had broadcast several messages alerting the police to the suspect described by Brennan at the scene of the assassination—a slender white male, about 30 years old, 5 feet 10 inches and weighing about 165 pounds.

At approximately 1:15 p.m., Tippit was driving slowly in an easterly direction on East 10th Street in Oak Cliff. About 100 feet past the intersection of 10th Street and Patton Avenue, Tippit pulled up alongside a man walking in the same direction. The man met the general description of the suspect wanted in connection with the assassination. He walked over to Tippit's car, rested his arms on the door on the right-hand side of the car, and apparently exchanged words with Tippit through the window. Tippit opened the door on the left side and started to walk around the front of his car. As he reached the front wheel on the driver's side, the man on the sidewalk drew a revolver and fired several shots in rapid succession, hitting Tippit four times and killing him instantly. An automobile repairman, Domingo Benavides, heard the shots and stopped his pickup truck on the opposite side of the street about 25 feet in front of Tippit's car. He observed the gunman start back toward Patton Avenue, removing the empty cartridge cases from the gun as he went. Benavides rushed to Tippit's side. The patrolman, apparently dead, was lying on his revolver, which was out of its holster. Benavides promptly reported the shooting to police headquarters over the radio in Tippit's car. The message was received shortly after 1:16 p.m.

As the gunman left the scene, he walked hurriedly back toward Patton Avenue and turned left, heading south. Standing on the northwest corner of 10th Street and Patton Avenue was Helen Markham, who had been walking south on Patton Avenue and had seen both the killer and Tippit cross the intersection in front of her as she waited on the curb for traffic to pass. She witnessed the shooting and then saw the man with a gun in his hand walk back toward the corner and cut across the lawn of the corner house as he started south on Patton Avenue.

In the corner house itself, Mrs. Barbara Jeanette Davis and her sister-in-law, Mrs. Virginia Davis, heard the shots and rushed to the door in time to see the man walk rapidly across the lawn shaking a revolver as if he were emptying it of cartridge cases. Later that day each woman found a cartridge case near the house. As the gunman turned the corner he passed alongside a taxicab which was parked on Patton Avenue, a few feet from 10th Street. The driver, William W. Scoggins, had seen the slaying and was now crouched behind his cab on the street side. As the gunman cut through the shrubbery on the lawn, Scoggins looked up and saw the man approximately 12 feet away. In his hand was a pistol and he muttered words which sounded to Scoggins like "poor dumb cop" or "poor damn cop."

After passing Scoggins, the gunman crossed to the west side of Patton Avenue and ran south toward Jefferson Boulevard, a main Oak Cliff thoroughfare. On the east side of Patton, between 10th Street and Jefferson Boulevard, Ted Callaway, a used car salesman, heard the shots and ran to the sidewalk. As the man with the gun rushed past, Callaway shouted "What's going on?" The man merely shrugged, ran on to Jefferson Boulevard and turned right. On the next corner was a gas station with a parking lot in the rear. The assailant ran into the lot, discarded his jacket and then continued his flight west on Jefferson.

In a shoe store a few blocks farther west on Jefferson, the manager, Johnny Calvin Brewer, heard the siren of a police car moments after the radio in his store announced the shooting of the police officer in Oak Cliff. Brewer saw a man step quickly into the entranceway of the store and stand there with his back toward the street. When the police car made a **U**-turn and headed back in the direction of the Tippit shooting, the man left and Brewer followed him. He saw the man enter the Texas Theatre, a motion picture house about 60 feet away, without buying a ticket. Brewer pointed this out to the cashier, Mrs. Julia Postal, who called the police. The time was shortly after 1:40 p.m.

At 1:29 p.m., the police radio had noted the similarity in the descriptions of the suspects in the Tippit shooting and the assassination. At 1:45 p.m., in response to Mrs. Postal's call, the police radio sounded the alarm: "Have information a suspect just went in the Texas Theatre on West Jefferson." Within minutes the theater was surrounded. The house lights were then turned up. Patrolman M. N. McDonald and several other policemen approached the man, who had been pointed out to them by Brewer.

McDonald ordered the man to his feet and heard him say, "Well, it's all over now." The man drew a gun from his waist with one hand and struck the officer with the other. McDonald struck out with his right hand and grabbed the gun with his left hand. After a brief struggle McDonald and several other police officers disarmed and handcuffed the suspect and drove him to police headquarters, arriving at approximately 2 p.m.

Following the assassination, police cars had rushed to the Texas School Book Depository in response to the many radio messages reporting that the shots had been fired from the Depository Building. Inspector J. Herbert Sawyer of the Dallas Police Department arrived at the scene shortly after hearing the first of these police radio messages at 12:34 p.m. Some of the officers who had been assigned to the area of Elm and Houston Streets for the motorcade were talking to witnesses and watching the building when Sawyer arrived. Sawyer entered the building and rode a passenger elevator to the fourth floor, which was the top floor for this elevator. He conducted a quick search, returned to the main floor and, between approximately 12:37 and 12:40 p.m., ordered that no one be permitted to leave the building.

Shortly before 1 p.m. Capt. J. Will Fritz, chief of the homicide and robbery bureau of the Dallas Police Department, arrived to take charge of the investigation. Searching the sixth floor, Deputy Sheriff Luke Mooney noticed a pile of cartons in the southeast corner. He squeezed through the boxes and realized immediately that he had discovered the point from which the shots had been fired. On the floor were three empty cartridge cases. A carton had apparently been placed on the floor at the side of the window so that a person sitting on the carton could look down Elm Street toward the overpass and scarcely be noticed from the outside. Between this carton and the half-open window were three additional cartons arranged at such an angle that a rifle resting on the top carton would be aimed directly at the motorcade as it moved away from the building. The high stack of boxes, which first attracted Mooney's attention, effectively screened a person at the window from the view of anyone else on the floor.

8

Mooney's discovery intensified the search for additional evidence on the sixth floor, and at 1:22 p.m., approximately 10 minutes after the cartridge cases were found, Deputy Sheriff Eugene Boone turned his flashlight in the direction of two rows of boxes in the northwest corner near the staircase. Stuffed between the two rows was a bolt-action rifle with a telescopic sight. The rifle was not touched until it could be photographed. When Lt. J. C. Day of the police identification bureau decided that the wooden stock and the metal knob at the end of the bolt contained no prints, he held the rifle by the stock while Captain Fritz ejected a live shell by operating the bolt. Lieutenant Day promptly noted that stamped on the rifle itself was the serial number "C2766" as well as the markings "1940" "MADE ITALY" and "CAL. 6.5." The rifle was about 40 inches long and when disassembled it could fit into a handmade paper sack which, after the assassination, was found in the southeast corner of the building within a few feet of the cartridge cases.

As Fritz and Day were completing their examination of this rifle on the sixth floor, Roy Truly, the building superintendent, approached with information which he felt should be brought to the attention of the police. Earlier, while the police were questioning the employees, Truly had observed that Lee Harvey Oswald, 1 of the 15 men who worked in the warehouse, was missing. After Truly provided Oswald's name, address, and general description, Fritz left for police headquarters. He arrived at headquarters shortly after 2 p.m. and asked two detectives to pick up the employee who was missing from the Texas School Book Depository. Standing nearby were the police officers who had just arrived with the man arrested in the Texas Theatre. When Fritz mentioned the name of the missing employee, he learned that the man was already in the interrogation room. The missing School Book Depository employee and the suspect who had been apprehended in the Texas Theatre were one and the same—Lee Harvey Oswald.

The suspect Fritz was about to question in connection with the assassination of the President and the murder of a policeman was born in New Orleans on October 18, 1939, 2 months after the death of his father. His mother, Marguerite Claverie Oswald, had two older children. One, John Pic, was a half-brother to Lee from an earlier marriage which had ended in divorce. The other was Robert Oswald, a full brother to Lee and 5 years older. When Lee Oswald was 3, Mrs. Oswald placed him in an orphanage where his brother and half-brother were already living, primarily because she had to work.

In January 1944, when Lee was 4, he was taken out of the orphanage, and shortly thereafter his mother moved with him to Dallas, Tex., where the older boys joined them at the end of the school year. In May of 1945 Marguerite Oswald married her third husband, Edwin A. Ekdahl. While the two older boys attended a military boarding school, Lee lived at home and developed a warm attachment to Ekdahl, occasionally accompanying his mother and stepfather on business trips around the country. Lee started school in Benbrook, Tex., but in the fall of 1946, after a separation from Ekdahl, Marguerite Oswald reentered Lee in the first grade in Covington, La. In January 1947, while Lee was still in the first grade, the family moved to Fort Worth, Tex., as the result of an attempted reconciliation between Ekdahl and Lee's mother. A year and a half later, before Lee was 9, his mother was divorced from her third husband as the result of a divorce action instituted by Ekdahl. Lee's school record during the next 5½ years in Fort Worth was average, although generally it grew poorer each year. The comments of teachers and others who knew him at that time do not reveal any unusual personality traits or characteristics.

Another change for Lee Oswald occurred in August 1952, a few months after he completed the sixth grade. Marguerite Oswald and her 12-year-old son moved to New York City where Marguerite's oldest son, John Pic, was stationed with the Coast Guard. The ensuing year and one-half in New York was marked by Lee's refusals to attend school and by emotional and psychological problems of a seemingly serious nature. Because he had become a chronic school truant, Lee underwent psychiatric study at Youth House, an institution in New York for juveniles who have had truancy problems or difficulties with the law, and who appear to require psychiatric observation, or other types of guidance. The social worker assigned to his case described him as "seriously detached" and "withdrawn" and noted "a rather pleasant, appealing quality about this emotionally starved, affectionless youngster." Lee expressed the feeling to the social worker that his mother did not care for him and regarded him as a burden. He experienced fantasies about being all powerful and hurting people, but during his stay at Youth House he was apparently not a behavior problem. He appeared withdrawn and evasive, a boy who preferred to spend his time alone, reading and watching television. His tests indicated that he was above average in intelligence for his age group. The chief psychiatrist of Youth House diagnosed Lee's problem as a "personality pattern disturbance with schizoid features and passive-aggressive tendencies." He concluded that the boy was "an emotionally, quite disturbed youngster" and recommended psychiatric treatment.

In May 1953, after having been at Youth House for 3 weeks, Lee Oswald returned to school where his attendance and grades temporarily improved. By the following fall, however, the probation officer reported that virtually every teacher complained about the boy's behavior. His mother insisted that he did not need psychiatric assistance. Although there was apparently some improvement in Lee's behavior during the next few months, the court recommended further treatment. In January 1954, while Lee's case was still pending, Marguerite and Lee left for New Orleans, the city of Lee's birth.

Upon his return to New Orleans, Lee maintained mediocre grades but had no obvious behavior problems. Neighbors and others who knew him outside of school remembered him as a quiet, solitary and introverted boy who read a great deal and whose vocabulary made him quite articulate. About 1 month after he started the 10th grade and 11 days before his 16th birthday in October 1955, he brought to school a note purportedly written by his mother, stating that the family was moving to California. The note was written by Lee. A few days later he dropped out of school and almost immediately tried to join the Marine Corps. Because he was only 16, he was rejected.

After leaving school Lee worked for the next 10 months at several jobs in New Orleans as an office messenger or clerk. It was during this period that he started to read communist literature. Occasionally, in conversations with others, he praised communism and expressed to his fellow employees a desire to join the Communist Party. At about this time, when he was not yet 17, he wrote to the Socialist Party of America, professing his belief in Marxism.

Another move followed in July 1956 when Lee and his mother returned to Fort Worth. He reentered high school but again dropped out after a few weeks and enlisted in the Marine Corps on October 24, 1956, 6 days after his 17th birthday. On December 21, 1956, during boot camp in San Diego, Oswald fired a score of 212 for record with the M–1 rifle—2 points over the minimum for a rating of "sharpshooter" on a marksman/sharpshooter/expert scale. After his basic training, Oswald received training in aviation fundamentals and then in radar scanning.

Most people who knew Oswald in the Marines described him as a "loner" who resented the exercise of authority by others. He spent much of his free time reading. He was court-martialed once for possessing an unregistered privately owned weapon and, on another occasion, for using provocative language to a noncommissioned officer. He was, however, generally able to comply with Marine discipline, even though his experiences in the Marine Corps did not live up to his expectations.

Oswald served 15 months overseas until November 1958, most of it in Japan. During his final year in the Marine Corps he was stationed for the most part in Santa Ana, Calif., where he showed a marked interest in the Soviet Union and sometimes expressed politically radical views with dogmatic conviction. Oswald again fired the M–1 rifle for record on May 6, 1959, and this time he shot a score of 191 on a shorter course than before, only 1 point over the minimum required to be a "marksman." According to one of his fellow marines, Oswald was not particularly interested in his rifle performance, and his unit was not expected to exhibit the usual rifle proficiency. During this period he expressed strong admiration for Fidel Castro and an interest in joining the Cuban army. He tried to impress those around him as an intellectual, but his thinking appeared to some as shallow and rigid.

Oswald's Marine service terminated on September 11, 1959, when at his own request he was released from active service a few months ahead of his scheduled release. He offered as the reason for his release the ill health and economic plight of his mother. He returned to Fort Worth, remained with his mother only 3 days and left for New

Orleans, telling his mother he planned to get work there in the shipping or import-export business. In New Orleans he booked passage on the freighter SS *Marion Lykes*, which sailed from New Orleans to Le Havre, France, on September 20, 1959.

Lee Harvey Oswald had presumably planned this step in his life for quite some time. In March of 1959 he had applied to the Albert Schweitzer College in Switzerland for admission to the spring 1960 term. His letter of application contained many blatant falsehoods concerning his qualifications and background. A few weeks before his discharge he had applied for and obtained a passport, listing the Soviet Union as one of the countries which he planned to visit. During his service in the Marines he had saved a comparatively large sum of money, possibly as much as $1,500, which would appear to have been accomplished by considerable frugality and apparently for a specific purpose.

The purpose of the accumulated fund soon became known. On October 16, 1959, Oswald arrived in Moscow by train after crossing the border from Finland, where he had secured a visa for a 6-day stay in the Soviet Union. He immediately applied for Soviet citizenship. On the afternoon of October 21, 1959, Oswald was ordered to leave the Soviet Union by 8 p.m. that evening. That same afternoon in his hotel room Oswald, in an apparent suicide attempt, slashed his left wrist. He was hospitalized immediately. On October 31, 3 days after his release from the hospital, Oswald appeared at the American Embassy, announced that he wished to renounce his U.S. citizenship and become a Russian citizen, and handed the Embassy officer a written statement he had prepared for the occasion. When asked his reasons, Oswald replied, "I am a Marxist." Oswald never formally complied with the legal steps necessary to renounce his American citizenship. The Soviet Government did not grant his request for citizenship, but in January 1960 he was given permission to remain in the Soviet Union on a year-to-year basis. At the same time Oswald was sent to Minsk where he worked in a radio factory as an unskilled laborer. In January 1961 his permission to remain in the Soviet Union was extended for another year. A few weeks later, in February 1961, he wrote to the American Embassy in Moscow expressing a desire to return to the United States.

The following month Oswald met a 19-year-old Russian girl, Marina Nikolaevna Prusakova, a pharmacist, who had been brought up in Leningrad but was then living with an aunt and uncle in Minsk. They were married on April 30, 1961. Throughout the following year he carried on a correspondence with American and Soviet authorities seeking approval for the departure of himself and his wife to the United States. In the course of this effort, Oswald and his wife visited the U.S. Embassy in Moscow in July of 1961. Primarily on the basis of an interview and questionnaire completed there, the Embassy concluded that Oswald had not lost his citizenship, a decision subsequently ratified by the Department of State in Washington, D.C. Upon their return to Minsk, Oswald and his wife filed with the Soviet authorities for permission to leave together. Their formal application was made in July 1961, and on December 25, 1961, Marina Oswald was advised it would be granted.

A daughter was born to the Oswalds in February 1962. In the months that followed they prepared for their return to the United States. On May 9, 1962, the U.S. Immigration and Naturalization Service, at the request of the Department of State, agreed to waive a restriction under the law which would have prevented the issuance of a United States visa to Oswald's Russian wife until she had left the Soviet Union. They finally left Moscow on June 1, 1962, and were assisted in meeting their travel expenses by a loan of $435.71 from the U.S. Department of State. Two weeks later they arrived in Fort Worth, Tex.

For a few weeks Oswald, his wife and child lived with Oswald's brother Robert. After a similar stay with Oswald's mother, they moved into their own apartment in early August. Oswald obtained a job on July 16 as a sheet metal worker. During this period in Fort Worth, Oswald was interviewed twice by agents of the FBI. The report of the first interview, which occurred on June 26, described him as arrogant and unwilling to discuss the reasons why he had gone to the Soviet Union. Oswald denied that he was involved in Soviet intelligence activities and promised to advise the FBI if Soviet representatives ever communicated with him. He was interviewed again on August 16, when he displayed a less belligerent attitude and once again agreed to inform the FBI of any attempt to enlist him in intelligence activities.

In early October 1962 Oswald quit his job at the sheet metal plant and moved to Dallas. While living in Forth Worth the Oswalds had been introduced to a group of Russian-speaking people in the Dallas-Fort Worth area. Many of them assisted the Oswalds by providing small amounts of food, clothing, and household items. Oswald himself was disliked by almost all of this group whose help to the family was prompted primarily by sympathy for Marina Oswald and the child. Despite the fact that he had left the Soviet Union, disillusioned with its Government, Oswald seemed more firmly committed than ever to his concepts of Marxism. He showed disdain for democracy, capitalism, and American society in general. He was highly critical of the Russian-speaking group because they seemed devoted to American concepts of democracy and capitalism and were ambitious to improve themselves economically.

In February 1963 the Oswalds met Ruth Paine at a social gathering. Ruth Paine was temporarily separated from her husband and living with her two children in their home in Irving, Tex., a suburb of Dallas. Because of an interest in the Russian language and sympathy for Marina Oswald, who spoke no English and had little funds, Ruth Paine befriended Marina and, during the next 2 months, visited her on several occasions.

On April 6, 1963, Oswald lost his job with a photography firm. A few days later, on April 10, he attempted to kill Maj. Gen. Edwin

A. Walker (Resigned, U.S. Army), using a rifle which he had ordered by mail 1 month previously under an assumed name. Marina Oswald learned of her husband's act when she confronted him with a note which he had left, giving her instructions in the event he did not return. That incident and their general economic difficulties impelled Marina Oswald to suggest that her husband leave Dallas and go to New Orleans to look for work.

Oswald left for New Orleans on April 24, 1963. Ruth Paine, who knew nothing of the Walker shooting, invited Marina Oswald and the baby to stay with her in the Paines' modest home while Oswald sought work in New Orleans. Early in May, upon receiving word from Oswald that he had found a job, Ruth Paine drove Marina Oswald and the baby to New Orleans to rejoin Oswald.

During the stay in New Orleans, Oswald formed a fictitious New Orleans Chapter of the Fair Play for Cuba Committee. He posed as secretary of this organization and represented that the president was A. J. Hidell. In reality, Hidell was a completely fictitious person created by Oswald, the organization's only member. Oswald was arrested on August 9 in connection with a scuffle which occurred while he was distributing pro-Castro leaflets. The next day, while at the police station, he was interviewed by an FBI agent after Oswald requested the police to arrange such an interview. Oswald gave the agent false information about his own background and was evasive in his replies concerning Fair Play for Cuba activities. During the next 2 weeks Oswald appeared on radio programs twice, claiming to be the spokesman for the Fair Play for Cuba Committee in New Orleans.

On July 19, 1963, Oswald lost his job as a greaser of coffee processing machinery. In September, after an exchange of correspondence with Marina Oswald, Ruth Paine drove to New Orleans and on September 23, transported Marina, the child, and the family belongings to Irving, Tex. Ruth Paine suggested that Marina Oswald, who was expecting her second child in October, live at the Paine house until after the baby was born. Oswald remained behind, ostensibly to find work either in Houston or some other city. Instead, he departed by bus for Mexico, arriving in Mexico City on September 27, where he promptly visited the Cuban and Russian Embassies. His stated objective was to obtain official permission to visit Cuba, on his way to the Soviet Union. The Cuban Government would not grant his visa unless the Soviet Government would also issue a visa permitting his entry into Russia. Oswald's efforts to secure these visas failed, and he left for Dallas, where he arrived on October 3, 1963.

When he saw his wife the next day, it was decided that Oswald would rent a room in Dallas and visit his family on weekends. For 1 week he rented a room from Mrs. Bledsoe, the woman who later saw him on the bus shortly after the assassination. On October 14, 1963, he rented the Beckley Avenue room and listed his name as O. H. Lee. On the same day, at the suggestion of a neighbor, Mrs. Paine phoned the Texas School Book Depository and was told that there was a job opening. She informed Oswald who was interviewed the following day at the Depository and started to work there on October 16, 1963.

On October 20 the Oswalds' second daughter was born. During October and November Oswald established a general pattern of weekend visits to Irving, arriving on Friday afternoon and returning to Dallas Monday morning with a fellow employee, Buell Wesley Frazier, who lived near the Paines. On Friday, November 15, Oswald remained in Dallas at the suggestion of his wife who told him that the house would be crowded because of a birthday party for Ruth Paine's daughter. On Monday, November 18, Oswald and his wife quarreled bitterly during a telephone conversation, because she learned for the first time that he was living at the roominghouse under an assumed name. On Thursday, November 21, Oswald told Frazier that he would like to drive to Irving to pick up some curtain rods for an apartment in Dallas. His wife and Mrs. Paine were quite surprised to see him since it was a Thursday night. They thought he had returned to make up after Monday's quarrel. He was conciliatory, but Marina Oswald was still angry.

Later that evening, when Mrs. Paine had finished cleaning the kitchen, she went into the garage and noticed that the light was burning. She was certain that she had not left it on, although the incident appeared unimportant at the time. In the garage were most of the Oswalds' personal possessions. The following morning Oswald left while his wife was still in bed feeding the baby. She did not see him leave the house, nor did Ruth Paine. On the dresser in their room he left his wedding ring which he had never done before. His wallet containing $170 was left intact in a dresser-drawer.

Oswald walked to Frazier's house about half a block away and placed a long bulky package, made out of wrapping paper and tape, into the rear seat of the car. He told Frazier that the package contained curtain rods. When they reached the Depository parking lot, Oswald walked quickly ahead. Frazier followed and saw Oswald enter the Depository Building carrying the long bulky package with him.

During the morning of November 22, Marina Oswald followed President Kennedy's activities on television. She and Ruth Paine cried when they heard that the President had been shot. Ruth Paine translated the news of the shooting to Marina Oswald as it came over television, including the report that the shots were probably fired from the building where Oswald worked. When Marina Oswald heard this, she recalled the Walker episode and the fact that her husband still owned the rifle. She went quietly to the Paine's garage where the rifle had been concealed in a blanket among their other belongings. It appeared to her that the rifle was still there, although she did not actually open the blanket.

At about 3 p.m. the police arrived at the Paine house and asked Marina Oswald whether her husband owned a rifle. She said that he did and then led them into the garage and pointed to the rolled up blanket. As a police officer lifted it, the blanket hung limply over either side of his arm. The rifle was not there.

Meanwhile, at police headquarters, Captain Fritz had begun questioning Oswald. Soon after the start of the first interrogation, agents of the FBI and the U.S. Secret Service arrived and participated in the questioning. Oswald denied having anything to do with the assassination of President Kennedy or the murder of Patrolman Tippit. He claimed that he was eating lunch at the time of the assassination, and that he then spoke with his foreman for 5 to 10 minutes before going home. He denied that he owned a rifle and when confronted, in a subsequent interview, with a picture showing him holding a rifle and pistol, he claimed that his face had been superimposed on someone else's body. He refused to answer any questions about the presence in his wallet of a selective service card with his picture and the name "Alek J. Hidell."

During the questioning of Oswald on the third floor of the police department, more than 100 representatives of the press, radio, and television were crowded into the hallway through which Oswald had to pass when being taken from his cell to Captain Fritz' office for interrogation. Reporters tried to interview Oswald during these trips. Between Friday afternoon and Sunday morning he appeared in the hallway at least 16 times. The generally confused conditions outside and inside Captain Fritz' office increased the difficulty of police questioning. Advised by the police that he could communicate with an attorney, Oswald made several telephone calls on Saturday in an effort to procure representation of his own choice and discussed the matter with the president of the local bar association, who offered to obtain counsel. Oswald declined the offer saying that he would first try to obtain counsel by himself. By Sunday morning he had not yet engaged an attorney.

At 7:10 p.m. on November 22, 1963, Lee Harvey Oswald was formally advised that he had been charged with the murder of Patrolman J. D. Tippit. Several witnesses to the Tippit slaying and to the subsequent flight of the gunman had positively identified Oswald in police lineups. While positive firearm identification evidence was not available at the time, the revolver in Oswald's possession at the time of his arrest was of a type which could have fired the shots that killed Tippit.

The formal charge against Oswald for the assassination of President Kennedy was lodged shortly after 1:30 a.m., on Saturday, November 23. By 10 p.m. of the day of the assassination, the FBI had traced the rifle found on the sixth floor of the Texas School Book Depository to a mailorder house in Chicago which had purchased it from a distributor in New York. Approximately 6 hours later the Chicago firm advised that this rifle had been ordered in March 1963 by an A. Hidel for shipment to post office box 2915, in Dallas, Tex., a box rented by Oswald. Payment for the rifle was remitted by a money order signed by A. Hidell. By 6:45 p.m. on November 23, the FBI was able to advise the Dallas police that, as a result of handwriting analysis of the documents used to purchase the rifle, it had concluded that the rifle had been ordered by Lee Harvey Oswald.

Throughout Friday and Saturday, the Dallas police released to the public many of the details concerning the alleged evidence against Oswald. Police officials discussed important aspects of the case, usually in the course of impromptu and confused press conferences in the third-floor corridor. Some of the information divulged was erroneous. Efforts by the news media representatives to reconstruct the crime and promptly report details frequently led to erroneous and often conflicting reports. At the urgings of the newsmen, Chief of Police Jesse E. Curry, brought Oswald to a press conference in the police assembly room shortly after midnight of the day Oswald was arrested. The assembly room was crowded with newsmen who had come to Dallas from all over the country. They shouted questions at Oswald and flashed cameras at him. Among this group was a 52-year-old Dallas nightclub operator—Jack Ruby.

On Sunday morning, November 24, arrangements were made for Oswald's transfer from the city jail to the Dallas County jail, about 1 mile away. The news media had been informed on Saturday night that the transfer of Oswald would not take place until after 10 a.m. on Sunday. Earlier on Sunday, between 2:30 and 3 a.m., anonymous telephone calls threatening Oswald's life had been received by the Dallas office of the FBI and by the office of the county sheriff. Nevertheless, on Sunday morning, television, radio, and newspaper representatives crowded into the basement to record the transfer. As viewed through television cameras, Oswald would emerge from a door in front of the cameras and proceed to the transfer vehicle. To the right of the cameras was a "down" ramp from Main Street on the north. To the left was an "up" ramp leading to Commerce Street on the south.

The armored truck in which Oswald was to be transferred arrived shortly after 11 a.m. Police officials then decided, however, that an unmarked police car would be preferable for the trip because of its greater speed and maneuverability. At approximately 11:20 a.m. Oswald emerged from the basement jail office flanked by detectives on either side and at his rear. He took a few steps toward the car and was in the glaring light of the television cameras when a man suddenly darted out from an area on the right of the cameras where newsmen had been assembled. The man was carrying a Colt .38 revolver in his right hand and, while millions watched on television, he moved quickly to within a few feet of Oswald and fired one shot into Oswald's abdomen. Oswald groaned with pain as he fell to the ground and quickly lost consciousness. Within 7 minutes Oswald was at Parkland Hospital where, without having regained consciousness, he was pronounced dead at 1:07 p.m.

The man who killed Oswald was Jack Ruby. He was instantly arrested and, minutes later, confined in a cell on the fifth floor of the Dallas police jail. Under interrogation, he denied that the killing of Oswald was in any way connected with a conspiracy involving the assassination of President Kennedy. He maintained that he had killed Oswald in a temporary fit of depression and rage over the

President's death. Ruby was transferred the following day to the county jail without notice to the press or to police officers not directly involved in the transfer. Indicted for the murder of Oswald by the State of Texas on November 26, 1963, Ruby was found guilty on March 14, 1964, and sentenced to death. As of September 1964, his case was pending on appeal.

CONCLUSIONS

This Commission was created to ascertain the facts relating to the preceding summary of events and to consider the important questions which they raised. The Commission has addressed itself to this task and has reached certain conclusions based on all the available evidence. No limitations have been placed on the Commission's inquiry; it has conducted its own investigation, and all Government agencies have fully discharged their responsibility to cooperate with the Commission in its investigation. These conclusions represent the reasoned judgment of all members of the Commission and are presented after an investigation which has satisfied the Commission that it has ascertained the truth concerning the assassination of President Kennedy to the extent that a prolonged and thorough search makes this possible.

1. The shots which killed President Kennedy and wounded Governor Connally were fired from the sixth floor window at the southeast corner of the Texas School Book Depository. This determination is based upon the following:

(a) Witnesses at the scene of the assassination saw a rifle being fired from the sixth floor window of the Depository Building, and some witnesses saw a rifle in the window immediately after the shots were fired.

(b) The nearly whole bullet found on Governor Connally's stretcher at Parkland Memorial Hospital and the two bullet fragments found in the front seat of the Presidential limousine were fired from the 6.5-millimeter Mannlicher-Carcano rifle found on the sixth floor of the Depository Building to the exclusion of all other weapons.

(c) The three used cartridge cases found near the window on the sixth floor at the southeast corner of the building were fired from the same rifle which fired the above-described bullet and fragments, to the exclusion of all other weapons.

(d) The windshield in the Presidential limousine was struck by a bullet fragment on the inside surface of the glass, but was not penetrated.

(e) The nature of the bullet wounds suffered by President Kennedy and Governor Connally and the location of the car at the time of the shots establish that the bullets were fired from above and behind the Presidential limousine, striking the President and the Governor as follows:

(1) President Kennedy was first struck by a bullet which entered at the back of his neck and exited through the lower front portion of his neck, causing a wound which would not necessarily have been lethal. The President was struck a second time by a bullet which entered the right-rear portion of his head, causing a massive and fatal wound.

(2) Governor Connally was struck by a bullet which entered on the right side of his back and traveled downward through the right side of his chest, exiting below his right nipple. This bullet then passed through his right wrist and entered his left thigh where it caused a superficial wound.

(f) There is no credible evidence that the shots were fired from the Triple Underpass, ahead of the motorcade, or from any other location.

2. The weight of the evidence indicates that there were three shots fired.

3. Although it is not necessary to any essential findings of the Commission to determine just which shot hit Governor Connally, there is very persuasive evidence from the experts to indicate that the same bullet which pierced the President's throat also caused Governor Connally's wounds. However, Governor Connally's testimony and certain other factors have given rise to some difference of opinion as to this probability but there is no question in the mind of any member of the Commission that all the shots which caused the President's and Governor Connally's wounds were fired from the sixth floor window of the Texas School Book Depository.

4. The shots which killed President Kennedy and wounded Governor Connally were fired by Lee Harvey Oswald. This conclusion is based upon the following:

(a) The Mannlicher-Carcano 6.5-millimeter Italian rifle from which the shots were fired was owned by and in the possession of Oswald.

(b) Oswald carried this rifle into the Depository Building on the morning of November 22, 1963.

(c) Oswald, at the time of the assassination, was present at the window from which the shots were fired.

(d) Shortly after the assassination, the Mannlicher-Carcano rifle belonging to Oswald was found partially hidden between some cartons on the sixth floor and the improvised paper bag in which Oswald brought the rifle to the Depository was found close by the window from which the shots were fired.

(e) Based on testimony of the experts and their analysis of films of the assassination, the Commission has concluded that a rifleman of Lee Harvey Oswald's capabilities could have fired the shots from the rifle used in the assassination within the elapsed time of the shooting. The Commission has concluded further that Oswald possessed the capability with a rifle which enabled him to commit the assassination.

(f) Oswald lied to the police after his arrest concerning important substantive matters.

(g) Oswald had attempted to kill Maj. Gen. Edwin A. Walker (Resigned, U.S. Army) on April 10, 1963, thereby demonstrating his disposition to take human life.

5. Oswald killed Dallas Police Patrolman J. D. Tippit approximately 45 minutes after the assassination. This conclusion upholds the finding that Oswald fired the shots which killed President Kennedy and wounded Governor Connally and is supported by the following:

(a) Two eyewitnesses saw the Tippit shooting and seven eyewitnesses heard the shots and saw the gunman leave the scene with revolver in hand. These nine eyewitnesses positively identified Lee Harvey Oswald as the man they saw.

(b) The cartridge cases found at the scene of the shooting were fired from the revolver in the possession of Oswald at the time of his arrest to the exclusion of all other weapons.

(c) The revolver in Oswald's possession at the time of his arrest was purchased by and belonged to Oswald.

(d) Oswald's jacket was found along the path of flight taken by the gunman as he fled from the scene of the killing.

6. Within 80 minutes of the assassination and 35 minutes of the Tippit killing Oswald resisted arrest at the theatre by attempting to shoot another Dallas police officer.

7. The Commission has reached the following conclusions concerning Oswald's interrogation and detention by the Dallas police:

(a) Except for the force required to effect his arrest, Oswald was not subjected to any physical coercion by any law enforcement officials. He was advised that he could not be compelled to give any information and that any statements made by him might be used against him in court. He was advised of his right to counsel. He was given the opportunity to obtain counsel of his own choice and was offered legal assistance by the Dallas Bar Association, which he rejected at that time.

(b) Newspaper, radio, and television reporters were allowed uninhibited access to the area through which Oswald had to pass when he was moved from his cell to the interrogation room and other sections of the building, thereby subjecting Oswald to harassment and creating chaotic conditions which were not conducive to orderly interrogation or the protection of the rights of the prisoner.

(c) The numerous statements, sometimes erroneous, made to the press by various local law enforcement officials, during this period of confusion and disorder in the police station, would have presented serious obstacles to the obtaining of a fair trial for Oswald. To the extent that the information was erroneous or misleading, it helped to create doubts, speculations, and fears in the mind of the public which might otherwise not have arisen.

8. The Commission has reached the following conclusions concerning the killing of Oswald by Jack Ruby on November 24, 1963:

(*a*) Ruby entered the basement of the Dallas Police Department shortly after 11:17 a.m. and killed Lee Harvey Oswald at 11:21 a.m.

(*b*) Although the evidence on Ruby's means of entry is not conclusive, the weight of the evidence indicates that he walked down the ramp leading from Main Street to the basement of the police department.

(*c*) There is no evidence to support the rumor that Ruby may have been assisted by any members of the Dallas Police Department in the killing of Oswald.

(*d*) The Dallas Police Department's decision to transfer Oswald to the county jail in full public view was unsound. The arrangements made by the police department on Sunday morning, only a few hours before the attempted transfer, were inadequate. Of critical importance was the fact that news media representatives and others were not excluded from the basement even after the police were notified of threats to Oswald's life. These deficiencies contributed to the death of Lee Harvey Oswald.

9. The Commission has found no evidence that either Lee Harvey Oswald or Jack Ruby was part of any conspiracy, domestic or foreign, to assassinate President Kennedy. The reasons for this conclusion are:

(*a*) The Commission has found no evidence that anyone assisted Oswald in planning or carrying out the assassination. In this connection it has thoroughly investigated, among other factors, the circumstances surrounding the planning of the motorcade route through Dallas, the hiring of Oswald by the Texas School Book Depository Co. on October 15, 1963, the method by which the rifle was brought into the building, the placing of cartons of books at the window, Oswald's escape from the building, and the testimony of eyewitnesses to the shooting.

(*b*) The Commission has found no evidence that Oswald was involved with any person or group in a conspiracy to assassinate the President, although it has thoroughly investigated, in addition to other possible leads, all facets of Oswald's associations, finances, and personal habits, particularly during the period following his return from the Soviet Union in June 1962.

(*c*) The Commission has found no evidence to show that Oswald was employed, persuaded, or encouraged by any foreign government to assassinate President Kennedy or that he was an agent of any foreign government, although the Commission has reviewed the circumstances surrounding Oswald's defection to the Soviet Union, his life there from October of 1959 to June of 1962 so far as it can be reconstructed, his known contacts with the Fair Play for Cuba Committee, and his visits to the Cuban and Soviet Embassies in Mexico City during his trip to Mexico from

September 26 to October 3, 1963, and his known contacts with the Soviet Embassy in the United States.

(*d*) The Commission has explored all attempts of Oswald to identify himself with various political groups, including the Communist Party, U.S.A., the Fair Play for Cuba Committee, and the Socialist Workers Party, and has been unable to find any evidence that the contacts which he initiated were related to Oswald's subsequent assassination of the President.

(*e*) All of the evidence before the Commission established that there was nothing to support the speculation that Oswald was an agent, employee, or informant of the FBI, the CIA, or any other governmental agency. It has thoroughly investigated Oswald's relationships prior to the assassination with all agencies of the U.S. Government. All contacts with Oswald by any of these agencies were made in the regular exercise of their different responsibilities.

(*f*) No direct or indirect relationship between Lee Harvey Oswald and Jack Ruby has been discovered by the Commission, nor has it been able to find any credible evidence that either knew the other, although a thorough investigation was made of the many rumors and speculations of such a relationship.

(*g*) The Commission has found no evidence that Jack Ruby acted with any other person in the killing of Lee Harvey Oswald.

(*h*) After careful investigation the Commission has found no credible evidence either that Ruby and Officer Tippit, who was killed by Oswald, knew each other or that Oswald and Tippit knew each other.

Because of the difficulty of proving negatives to a certainty the possibility of others being involved with either Oswald or Ruby cannot be established categorically, but if there is any such evidence it has been beyond the reach of all the investigative agencies and resources of the United States and has not come to the attention of this Commission.

10. In its entire investigation the Commission has found no evidence of conspiracy, subversion, or disloyalty to the U.S. Government by any Federal, State, or local official.

11. On the basis of the evidence before the Commission it concludes that Oswald acted alone. Therefore, to determine the motives for the assassination of President Kennedy, one must look to the assassin himself. Clues to Oswald's motives can be found in his family history, his education or lack of it, his acts, his writings, and the recollections of those who had close contacts with him throughout his life. The Commission has presented with this report all of the background information bearing on motivation which it could discover. Thus, others may study Lee Oswald's life and arrive at their own conclusions as to his possible motives.

The Commission could not make any definitive determination of Oswald's motives. It has endeavored to isolate factors which contributed to his character and which might have influenced his decision to assassinate President Kennedy. These factors were:

(a) His deep-rooted resentment of all authority which was expressed in a hostility toward every society in which he lived;

(b) His inability to enter into meaningful relationships with people, and a continuous pattern of rejecting his environment in favor of new surroundings;

(c) His urge to try to find a place in history and despair at times over failures in his various undertakings;

(d) His capacity for violence as evidenced by his attempt to kill General Walker;

(e) His avowed commitment to Marxism and communism, as he understood the terms and developed his own interpretation of them; this was expressed by his antagonism toward the United States, by his defection to the Soviet Union, by his failure to be reconciled with life in the United States even after his disenchantment with the Soviet Union, and by his efforts, though frustrated, to go to Cuba.

Each of these contributed to his capacity to risk all in cruel and irresponsible actions.

12. The Commission recognizes that the varied responsibilities of the President require that he make frequent trips to all parts of the United States and abroad. Consistent with their high responsibilities Presidents can never be protected from every potential threat. The Secret Service's difficulty in meeting its protective responsibility varies with the activities and the nature of the occupant of the Office of President and his willingness to conform to plans for his safety. In appraising the performance of the Secret Service it should be understood that it has to do its work within such limitations. Nevertheless, the Commission believes that recommendations for improvements in Presidential protection are compelled by the facts disclosed in this investigation.

(a) The complexities of the Presidency have increased so rapidly in recent years that the Secret Service has not been able to develop or to secure adequate resources of personnel and facilities to fulfill its important assignment. This situation should be promptly remedied.

(b) The Commission has concluded that the criteria and procedures of the Secret Service designed to identify and protect against persons considered threats to the president, were not adequate prior to the assassination.

(1) The Protective Research Section of the Secret Service, which is responsible for its preventive work, lacked sufficient trained personnel and the mechanical and technical assistance needed to fulfill its responsibility.

(2) Prior to the assassination the Secret Service's criteria dealt with direct threats against the President. Although the Secret Service treated the direct threats against the President adequately, it failed to recognize the necessity of identifying

23

other potential sources of danger to his security. The Secret Service did not develop adequate and specific criteria defining those persons or groups who might present a danger to the President. In effect, the Secret Service largely relied upon other Federal or State agencies to supply the information necessary for it to fulfill its preventive responsibilities, although it did ask for information about direct threats to the President.

(c) The Commission has concluded that there was insufficient liaison and coordination of information between the Secret Service and other Federal agencies necessarily concerned with Presidential protection. Although the FBI, in the normal exercise of its responsibility, had secured considerable information about Lee Harvey Oswald, it had no official responsibility, under the Secret Service criteria existing at the time of the President's trip to Dallas, to refer to the Secret Service the information it had about Oswald. The Commission has concluded, however, that the FBI took an unduly restrictive view of its role in preventive intelligence work prior to the assassination. A more carefully coordinated treatment of the Oswald case by the FBI might well have resulted in bringing Oswald's activities to the attention of the Secret Service.

(d) The Commission has concluded that some of the advance preparations in Dallas made by the Secret Service, such as the detailed security measures taken at Love Field and the Trade Mart, were thorough and well executed. In other respects, however, the Commission has concluded that the advance preparations for the President's trip were deficient.

(1) Although the Secret Service is compelled to rely to a great extent on local law enforcement officials, its procedures at the time of the Dallas trip did not call for well-defined instructions as to the respective responsibilities of the police officials and others assisting in the protection of the President.

(2) The procedures relied upon by the Secret Service for detecting the presence of an assassin located in a building along a motorcade route were inadequate. At the time of the trip to Dallas, the Secret Service as a matter of practice did not investigate, or cause to be checked, any building located along the motorcade route to be taken by the President. The responsibility for observing windows in these buildings during the motorcade was divided between local police personnel stationed on the streets to regulate crowds and Secret Service agents riding in the motorcade. Based on its investigation the Commission has concluded that these arrangements during the trip to Dallas were clearly not sufficient.

(e) The configuration of the Presidential car and the seating arrangements of the Secret Service agents in the car did not afford the Secret Service agents the opportunity they should have had to be of immediate assistance to the President at the first sign of danger.

(*f*) Within these limitations, however, the Commission finds that the agents most immediately responsible for the President's safety reacted promptly at the time the shots were fired from the Texas School Book Depository Building.

RECOMMENDATIONS

Prompted by the assassination of President Kennedy, the Secret Service has initiated a comprehensive and critical review of its total operations. As a result of studies conducted during the past several months, and in cooperation with this Commission, the Secret Service has prepared a planning document dated August 27, 1964, which recommends various programs considered necessary by the Service to improve its techniques and enlarge its resources. The Commission is encouraged by the efforts taken by the Secret Service since the assassination and suggests the following recommendations.

1. A committee of Cabinet members including the Secretary of the Treasury and the Attorney General, or the National Security Council, should be assigned the responsibility of reviewing and overseeing the protective activities of the Secret Service and the other Federal agencies that assist in safeguarding the President. Once given this responsibility, such a committee would insure that the maximum resources of the Federal Government are fully engaged in the task of protecting the President, and would provide guidance in defining the general nature of domestic and foreign dangers to Presidential security.

2. Suggestions have been advanced to the Commission for the transfer of all or parts of the Presidential protective responsibilities of the Secret Service to some other department or agency. The Commission believes that if there is to be any determination of whether or not to relocate these responsibilities and functions, it ought to be made by the Executive and the Congress, perhaps upon recommendations based on studies by the previously suggested committee.

3. Meanwhile, in order to improve daily supervision of the Secret Service within the Department of the Treasury, the Commission recommends that the Secretary of the Treasury appoint a special assistant with the responsibility of supervising the Secret Service. This special assistant should have sufficient stature and experience in law enforcement, intelligence, and allied fields to provide effective continuing supervision, and to keep the Secretary fully informed regarding the performance of the Secret Service. One of the initial assignments of this special assistant should be the supervision of the current effort by the Secret Service to revise and modernize its basic operating procedures.

4. The Commission recommends that the Secret Service completely overhaul its facilities devoted to the advance detection of potential threats against the President. The Commission suggests the following measures.

(a) The Secret Service should develop as quickly as possible more useful and precise criteria defining those potential threats to the President which should be brought to its attention by other agencies. The criteria should, among other additions, provide for prompt notice to the Secret Service of all returned defectors.

(b) The Secret Service should expedite its current plans to utilize the most efficient data-processing techniques.

(c) Once the Secret Service has formulated new criteria delineating the information it desires, it should enter into agreements with each Federal agency to insure its receipt of such information.

5. The Commission recommends that the Secret Service improve the protective measures followed in the planning, and conducting of Presidential motorcades. In particular, the Secret Service should continue its current efforts to increase the precautionary attention given to buildings along the motorcade route.

6. The Commission recommends that the Secret Service continue its recent efforts to improve and formalize its relationships with local police departments in areas to be visited by the President.

7. The Commission believes that when the new criteria and procedures are established, the Secret Service will not have sufficient personnel or adequate facilities. The Commission recommends that the Secret Service be provided with the personnel and resources which the Service and the Department of the Treasury may be able to demonstrate are needed to fulfill its important mission.

8. Even with an increase in Secret Service personnel, the protection of the President will continue to require the resources and cooperation of many Federal agencies. The Commission recommends that these agencies, specifically the FBI, continue the practice as it has developed, particularly since the assassination, of assisting the Secret Service upon request by providing personnel or other aid, and that there be a closer association and liaison between the Secret Service and all Federal agencies.

9. The Commission recommends that the President's physician always accompany him during his travels and occupy a position near the President where he can be immediately available in case of any emergency.

10. The Commission recommends to Congress that it adopt legislation which would make the assassination of the President and Vice President a Federal crime. A state of affairs where U.S. authorities have no clearly defined jurisdiction to investigate the assassination of a President is anomalous.

11. The Commission has examined the Department of State's handling of the Oswald matters and finds that it followed the law

throughout. However, the Commission believes that the Department in accordance with its own regulations should in all cases exercise great care in the return to this country of defectors who have evidenced disloyalty or hostility to this country or who have expressed a desire to renounce their American citizenship and that when such persons are so returned, procedures should be adopted for the better dissemination of information concerning them to the intelligence agencies of the Government.

12. The Commission recommends that the representatives of the bar, law enforcement associations, and the news media work together to establish ethical standards concerning the collection and presentation of information to the public so that there will be no interference with pending criminal investigations, court proceedings, or the right of individuals to a fair trial.

CHAPTER II

The Assassination

THIS CHAPTER describes President Kennedy's trip to Dallas, from its origin through its tragic conclusion. The narrative of these events is based largely on the recollections of the participants, although in many instances documentary or other evidence has also been used by the Commission. Beginning with the advance plans and Secret Service preparations for the trip, this chapter reviews the motorcade through Dallas, the fleeting moments of the assassination, the activities at Parkland Memorial Hospital, and the return of the Presidential party to Washington. An evaluation of the procedures employed to safeguard the President, with recommendations for improving these procedures, appears in chapter VIII of the report.

PLANNING THE TEXAS TRIP

President Kennedy's visit to Texas in November 1963 had been under consideration for almost a year before it occurred. He had made only a few brief visits to the State since the 1960 Presidential campaign and in 1962 he began to consider a formal visit.[1] During 1963, the reasons for making the trip became more persuasive. As a political leader, the President wished to resolve the factional controversy within the Democratic Party in Texas before the election of 1964.[2] The party itself saw an opportunity to raise funds by having the President speak at a political dinner eventually planned for Austin.[3] As Chief of State, the President always welcomed the opportunity to learn, firsthand, about the problems which concerned the American people.[4] Moreover, he looked forward to the public appearances which he personally enjoyed.[5]

The basic decision on the November trip to Texas was made at a meeting of President Kennedy, Vice President Johnson, and Governor Connally on June 5, 1963, at the Cortez Hotel in El Paso, Tex.[6] The President had spoken earlier that day at the Air Force Academy in Colorado Springs, Colo., and had stopped in El Paso to discuss the proposed visit and other matters with the Vice President and the Governor.[7] The three agreed that the President would come to Texas in late November 1963.[8] The original plan called for the President to spend only 1 day in the State, making whirlwind visits to Dallas, Fort Worth, San Antonio, and Houston.[9] In September, the White House decided to permit further visits by the President and extended the trip to run from the afternoon of November 21 through the evening of Friday, November 22.[10] When Governor Connally called at the White House on October 4 to discuss the details of the visit, it was agreed that the planning of events in Texas would be left largely to the Governor.[11] At the White House, Kenneth O'Donnell, special assistant to the President, acted as coordinator for the trip.[12]

Everyone agreed that, if there was sufficient time, a motorcade through downtown Dallas would be the best way for the people to see their President. When the trip was planned for only 1 day, Governor Connally had opposed the motorcade because there was not enough time.[13] The Governor stated, however, that "once we got San Antonio moved from Friday to Thursday afternoon, where that was his initial stop in Texas, then we had the time, and I withdrew my objections to a motorcade."[14] According to O'Donnell, "we had a motorcade wherever we went," particularly in large cities where the purpose was to let the President be seen by as many people as possible.[15] In his experience, "it would be automatic" for the Secret Service to arrange a route which would, within the time allotted, bring the President "through an area which exposes him to the greatest number of people."[16]

ADVANCE PREPARATIONS FOR THE DALLAS TRIP

Advance preparations for President Kennedy's visit to Dallas were primarily the responsibility of two Secret Service agents: Special Agent Winston G. Lawson, a member of the White House detail who acted as the advance agent, and Forrest V. Sorrels, special agent in charge of the Dallas office.[17] Both agents were advised of the trip on November 4.[18] Lawson received a tentative schedule of the Texas trip on November 8 from Roy H. Kellerman, assistant special agent in charge of the White House detail, who was the Secret Service official responsible for the entire Texas journey.[19] As advance agent working closely with Sorrels, Lawson had responsibility for arranging the timetable for the President's visit to Dallas and coordinating local activities with the White House staff, the organizations directly concerned with the visit, and local law enforcement officials.[20] Lawson's most important responsibilities were to take preventive action against anyone in Dallas considered a threat to the President, to select the luncheon site and motorcade route, and to plan security measures for the luncheon and the motorcade.

Preventive Intelligence Activities

The Protective Research Section (PRS) of the Secret Service maintains records of people who have threatened the President or so conducted themselves as to be deemed a potential danger to him. On November 8, 1963, after undertaking the responsibility for advance preparations for the visit to Dallas, Agent Lawson went to the PRS offices in Washington. A check of the geographic indexes there revealed no listing for any individual deemed to be a potential danger to the President in the territory of the Secret Service regional office which includes Dallas and Fort Worth.[21]

To supplement the PRS files, the Secret Service depends largely on local police departments and local offices of other Federal agencies which advise it of potential threats immediately before the visit of the President to their community. Upon his arrival in Dallas on November 12 Lawson conferred with the local police and the local office of the Federal Bureau of Investigation about potential dangers to the President. Although there was no mention in PRS files of the demonstration in Dallas against Ambassador Adlai Stevenson on October 24, 1963, Lawson inquired about the incident and obtained through the local police photographs of some of the persons involved.[22] On November 22 a Secret Service agent stood at the entrance to the Trade Mart, where the President was scheduled to speak, with copies of these photographs. Dallas detectives in the lobby of the Trade Mart and in the luncheon area also had copies of these photographs. A number of people who resembled some of those in the photographs were placed under surveillance at the Trade Mart.[23]

The FBI office in Dallas gave the local Secret Service representatives the name of a possibly dangerous individual in the Dallas area who was investigated. It also advised the Secret Service of the circulation on November 21 of a handbill sharply critical of President Kennedy,[24] discussed in chapter VI of this report. Shortly before, the Dallas police had reported to the Secret Service that the handbill had appeared on the streets of Dallas. Neither the Dallas police nor the FBI had yet learned the source of the handbill.[25] No one else was identified to the Secret Service through local inquiry as potentially dangerous, nor did PRS develop any additional information between November 12, when Lawson left Washington, and November 22. The adequacy of the intelligence system maintained by the Secret Service at the time of the assassination, including a detailed description of the available data on Lee Harvey Oswald and the reasons why his name had not been furnished to the Secret Service, is discussed in chapter VIII.

The Luncheon Site

An important purpose of the President's visit to Dallas was to speak at a luncheon given by business and civic leaders. The White House staff informed the Secret Service that the President would arrive and depart from Dallas' Love Field; that a motorcade through the downtown area of Dallas to the luncheon site should be arranged; and that following the luncheon the President would return to the airport by the most direct route. Accordingly, it was important to determine the luncheon site as quickly as possible, so that security could be established at the site and the motorcade route selected.

On November 4, Gerald A. Behn, agent in charge of the White House detail, asked Sorrels to examine three potential sites for the luncheon.[26] One building, Market Hall, was unavailable for November 22. The second, the Women's Building at the State Fair Grounds, was a one-story building with few entrances and easy to make secure, but it lacked necessary food-handling facilities and had certain unattractive features, including a low ceiling with exposed conduits and beams. The third possibility, the Trade Mart, a handsome new building with all the necessary facilities, presented security problems. It had numerous entrances, several tiers of balconies surrounding the central court where the luncheon would be held, and several catwalks crossing the court at each level. On November 4, Sorrels told Behn he believed security difficulties at the Trade Mart could be overcome by special precautions.[27] Lawson also evaluated the security hazards at the Trade Mart on November 13.[28] Kenneth O'Donnell made the final decision to hold the luncheon at the Trade Mart; Behn so notified Lawson on November 14.[29]

Once the Trade Mart had been selected, Sorrels and Lawson worked out detailed arrangements for security at the building. In addition to the preventive measures already mentioned, they provided for controlling access to the building, closing off and policing areas around it, securing the roof and insuring the presence of numerous police officers inside and around the building. Ultimately more than 200 law enforcement officers, mainly Dallas police but including 8 Secret Service agents, were deployed in and around the Trade Mart.[30]

The Motorcade Route

On November 8, when Lawson was briefed on the itinerary for the trip to Dallas, he was told that 45 minutes had been allotted for a motorcade procession from Love Field to the luncheon site.[31] Lawson was not specifically instructed to select the parade route, but he understood that this was one of his functions.[32] Even before the Trade Mart had been definitely selected, Lawson and Sorrels began to consider the best motorcade route from Love Field to the Trade Mart. On November 14, Lawson and Sorrels attended a meeting at Love Field and on their return to Dallas drove over the route which Sorrels believed best suited for the proposed motorcade.[33] This route, eventually selected for the motorcade from the airport to the Trade Mart, measured 10 miles and could be driven easily within the allotted 45 minutes.[34] From Love Field the route passed through a portion of suburban Dallas, through the downtown area along Main Street and then to the Trade Mart via Stemmons Freeway. For the President's return to Love Field following the luncheon, the agents selected the most direct route, which was approximately 4 miles.[35]

After the selection of the Trade Mart as the luncheon site, Lawson and Sorrels met with Dallas Chief of Police Jesse E. Curry, Assistant

Chief Charles Batchelor, Deputy Chief N. T. Fisher, and several other command officers to discuss details of the motorcade and possible routes.[36] The route was further reviewed by Lawson and Sorrels with Assistant Chief Batchelor and members of the local host committee on November 15. The police officials agreed that the route recommended by Sorrels was the proper one and did not express a belief that any other route might be better.[37] On November 18, Sorrels and Lawson drove over the selected route with Batchelor and other police officers, verifying that it could be traversed within 45 minutes. Representatives of the local host committee and the White House staff were advised by the Secret Service of the actual route on the afternoon of November 18.[38]

The route impressed the agents as a natural and desirable one. Sorrels, who had participated in Presidential protection assignments in Dallas since a visit by President Franklin D. Roosevelt in 1936,[39] testified that the traditional parade route in Dallas was along Main Street, since the tall buildings along the street gave more people an opportunity to participate.[40] The route chosen from the airport to Main Street was the normal one, except where Harwood Street was selected as the means of access to Main Street in preference to a short stretch of the Central Expressway, which presented a minor safety hazard and could not accommodate spectators as conveniently as Harwood Street.[41] According to Lawson, the chosen route seemed to be the best.

> It afforded us wide streets most of the way, because of the buses that were in the motorcade. It afforded us a chance to have alternative routes if something happened on the motorcade route. It was the type of suburban area a good part of the way where the crowds would be able to be controlled for a great distance, and we figured that the largest crowds would be downtown, which they were, and that the wide streets that we would use downtown would be of sufficient width to keep the public out of our way.[42]

Elm Street, parallel to Main Street and one block north, was not used for the main portion of the downtown part of the motorcade because Main Street offered better vantage points for spectators.

To reach the Trade Mart from Main Street the agents decided to use the Stemmons Freeway (Route No. 77), the most direct route. The only practical way for westbound traffic on Main Street to reach the northbound lanes of the Stemmons Freeway is via Elm Street, which Route No. 77 traffic is instructed to follow in this part of the city. (See Commission Exhibit No. 2113, p. 34.) Elm Street was to be reached from Main by turning right at Houston, going one block north and then turning left onto Elm. On this last portion of the journey, only 5 minutes from the Trade Mart, the President's motorcade would pass the Texas School Book Depository Building on the northwest corner of Houston and Elm Streets. The building overlooks Dealey Plaza,

DEALEY PLAZA -- DALLAS, TEXAS

1. TEXAS SCHOOL BOOK DEPOSITORY
2. DAL-TEX BUILDING
3. DALLAS COUNTY RECORDS BUILDING
4. DALLAS COUNTY CRIMINAL COURTS BUILDING
5. OLD COURT HOUSE
6. NEELEY BRYAN HOUSE
7. DALLAS COUNTY GOVERNMENT CENTER (UNDER CONSTRUCTION)
8. UNITED STATES POST OFFICE BUILDING
9. PERGOLAS
10. PERISTYLES AND REFLECTING POOLS
11. RAILROAD OVERPASS (TRIPLE UNDERPASS)

COMMISSION EXHIBIT No. 876

FREEWAY CONVERGENCE AT TRIPLE UNDERPASS
DALLAS, TEXAS

Commission Exhibit 2113

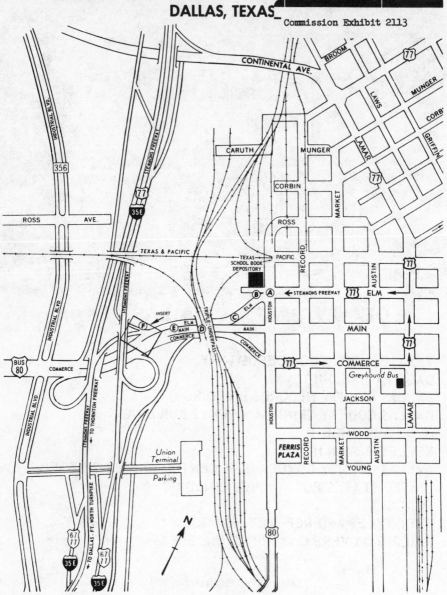

COMMISSION EXHIBIT No. 2113

A — LOOKING TOWARD ENTRANCE TO DEALEY PLAZA FROM INTERSECTION OF HOUSTON AND ELM STS.

B — LOOKING WEST THROUGH DEALEY PLAZA ALONG ELM ST.

C — LOOKING WEST THROUGH TRIPLE UNDERPASS

D — LOOKING WEST TOWARD COMMERCE ST. FROM TRIPLE UNDERPASS

COMMISSION EXHIBIT No. 2114

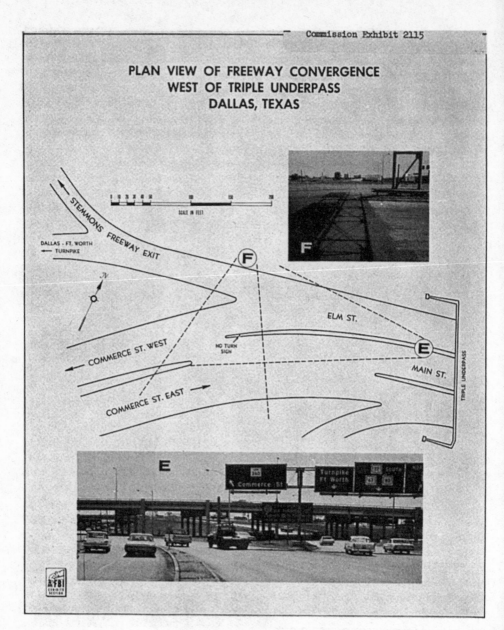

PLAN VIEW OF FREEWAY CONVERGENCE
WEST OF TRIPLE UNDERPASS
DALLAS, TEXAS

COMMISSION EXHIBIT No. 2115

AERIAL VIEW (500 FT. ALTITUDE) OF FREEWAY CONVERGENCE WEST OF TRIPLE UNDERPASS, DALLAS, TEXAS

COMMISSION EXHIBIT No. 2116

COMMISSION EXHIBIT No. 2967

Traffic sign on Main Street which directs westbound traffic to turn right at Houston Street to gain access to the Dallas-Fort Worth Turnpike.

an attractively landscaped triangle of 3 acres. (See Commission Exhibit No. 876, p. 33.) From Houston Street, which forms the base of the triangle, three streets—Commerce, Main, and Elm—trisect the plaza, converging at the apex of the triangle to form a triple underpass beneath a multiple railroad bridge almost 500 feet from Houston Street.[43] Elm Street, the northernmost of the three, after intersecting Houston curves in a southwesterly arc through the underpass and leads into an access road, which branches off to the right and is used by traffic going to the Stemmons Freeway and the Dallas-Fort Worth Turnpike. (See Commission Exhibits Nos. 2113–2116, pp. 34–37.)

The Elm Street approach to the Stemmons Freeway is necessary in order to avoid the traffic hazards which would otherwise exist if right turns were permitted from both Main and Elm into the freeway. To create this traffic pattern, a concrete barrier between Main and Elm Streets presents an obstacle to a right turn from Main across Elm to the access road to Stemmons Freeway and the Dallas-Fort Worth Turnpike. This concrete barrier extends far enough beyond the access road to make it impracticable for vehicles to turn right from Main directly to the access road. A sign located on this barrier instructs Main Street traffic not to make any turns.[45] (See Commission Exhibits Nos. 2114–2116, pp. 35–37.) In conformity with these arrangements, traffic proceeding west on Main is directed to turn right at Houston in order to reach the Dallas-Fort Worth Turnpike, which has the same access road from Elm Street as does the Stemmons Freeway.[46] (See Commission Exhibit No. 2967, p. 38.)

The planning for the motorcade also included advance preparations for security arrangements along the route. Sorrels and Lawson reviewed the route in cooperation with Assistant Chief Batchelor and other Dallas police officials who took notes on the requirements for controlling the crowds and traffic, watching the overpasses, and providing motorcycle escort.[47] To control traffic, arrangements were made for the deployment of foot patrolmen and motorcycle police at various positions along the route.[48] Police were assigned to each overpass on the route and instructed to keep them clear of unauthorized persons.[49] No arrangements were made for police or building custodians to inspect buildings along the motorcade route since the Secret Service did not normally request or make such a check.[50] Under standard procedures, the responsibility for watching the windows of buildings was shared by local police stationed along the route and Secret Service agents riding in the motorcade.[51]

As the date for the President's visit approached, the two Dallas newspapers carried several reports of his motorcade route. The selection of the Trade Mart as the possible site for the luncheon first appeared in the Dallas Times-Herald on November 15, 1963.[52] The following day, the newspaper reported that the Presidential party "apparently will loop through the downtown area, probably on Main Street, en route from Dallas Love Field" on its way to the Trade

Mart.[53] On November 19, the Times-Herald afternoon paper detailed the precise route:

> From the airport, the President's party will proceed to Mockingbird Lane to Lemmon and then to Turtle Creek, turning south to Cedar Springs.
> The motorcade will then pass through downtown on Harwood and then west on Main, turning back to Elm at Houston and then out Stemmons Freeway to the Trade Mart.[54]

Also on November 19, the Morning News reported that the President's motorcade would travel from Love Field along specified streets, then "Harwood to Main, Main to Houston, Houston to Elm, Elm under the Triple Underpass to Stemmons Freeway, and on to the Trade Mart." [55] On November 20 a front page story reported that the streets on which the Presidential motorcade would travel included "Main and Stemmons Freeway." [56] On the morning of the President's arrival, the Morning News noted that the motorcade would travel through downtown Dallas onto the Stemmons Freeway, and reported that "the motorcade will move slowly so that crowds can 'get a good view' of President Kennedy and his wife." [57]

DALLAS BEFORE THE VISIT

The President's intention to pay a visit to Texas in the fall of 1963 aroused interest throughout the State. The two Dallas newspapers provided their readers with a steady stream of information and speculation about the trip, beginning on September 13, when the Times-Herald announced in a front page article that President Kennedy was planning a brief 1-day tour of four Texas cities—Dallas, Fort Worth, San Antonio, and Houston.[58] Both Dallas papers cited White House sources on September 26 as confirming the President's intention to visit Texas on November 21 and 22, with Dallas scheduled as one of the stops.[59]

Articles, editorials, and letters to the editor in the Dallas Morning News and the Dallas Times-Herald after September 13 reflected the feeling in the community toward the forthcoming Presidential visit. Although there were critical editorials and letters to the editors, the news stories reflected the desire of Dallas officials to welcome the President with dignity and courtesy. An editorial in the Times-Herald of September 17 called on the people of Dallas to be "congenial hosts" even though "Dallas didn't vote for Mr. Kennedy in 1960, may not endorse him in '64." [60] On October 3 the Dallas Morning News quoted U.S. Representative Joe Pool's hope that President Kennedy would receive a "good welcome" and would not face demonstrations like those encountered by Vice President Johnson during the 1960 campaign.[61]

Increased concern about the President's visit was aroused by the incident involving the U.S. Ambassador to the United Nations, Adlai E. Stevenson. On the evening of October 24, 1963, after addressing a meeting in Dallas, Stevenson was jeered, jostled, and spat upon by hostile demonstrators outside the Dallas Memorial Auditorium Theater.[62] The local, national, and international reaction to this incident evoked from Dallas officials and newspapers strong condemnations of the demonstrators. Mayor Earle Cabell called on the city to redeem itself during President Kennedy's visit.[63] He asserted that Dallas had shed its reputation of the twenties as the "Southwest hate capital of Dixie." [64] On October 26 the press reported Chief of Police Curry's plans to call in 100 extra off-duty officers to help protect President Kennedy.[65] Any thought that the President might cancel his visit to Dallas was ended when Governor Connally confirmed on November 8 that the President would come to Texas on November 21–22, and that he would visit San Antonio, Houston, Fort Worth, Dallas, and Austin.[66]

During November the Dallas papers reported frequently on the plans for protecting the President, stressing the thoroughness of the preparations. They conveyed the pleas of Dallas leaders that citizens not demonstrate or create disturbances during the President's visit. On November 18 the Dallas City Council adopted a new city ordinance prohibiting interference with attendance at lawful assemblies.[67] Two days before the President's arrival Chief Curry warned that the Dallas police would not permit improper conduct during the President's visit.[68]

Meanwhile, on November 17 the president of the Dallas Chamber of Commerce referred to the city's reputation for being the friendliest town in America and asserted that citizens would "greet the President of the United States with the warmth and pride that keep the Dallas spirit famous the world over." [69] Two days later, a local Republican leader called for a "civilized nonpartisan" welcome for President Kennedy, stating that "in many respects Dallas County has isolated itself from the main stream of life in the world in this decade." [70]

Another reaction to the impending visit—hostile to the President— came to a head shortly before his arrival. On November 21 there appeared on the streets of Dallas the anonymous handbill mentioned above. It was fashioned after the "wanted" circulars issued by law enforcement agencies. Beneath two photographs of President Kennedy, one fullface and one profile, appeared the caption, "Wanted for Treason," followed by a scurrilous bill of particulars that constituted a vilification of the President.[71] And on the morning of the President's arrival, there appeared in the Morning News a full page, black-bordered advertisement headed "Welcome Mr. Kennedy to Dallas," sponsored by the American Factfinding Committee, which the sponsor later testified was an ad hoc committee "formed strictly for the purpose of having a name to put in the paper." [72] The "welcome" consisted of a series of statements and questions critical of the

President and his administration.[73]   (See Commission Exhibit No. 1031, p. 294.)

VISITS TO OTHER TEXAS CITIES

The trip to Texas began with the departure of President and Mrs. Kennedy from the White House by helicopter at 10:45 a.m., e.s.t., on November 21, 1963, for Andrews AFB.   They took off in the Presidential plane, *Air Force One*, at 11 a.m., arriving at San Antonio at 1:30 p.m., c.s.t.   They were greeted by Vice President Johnson and Governor Connally, who joined the Presidential party in a motorcade through San Antonio.[74]   During the afternoon, President Kennedy dedicated the U.S. Air Force School of Aerospace Medicine at Brooks AFB.[75]   Late in the afternoon he flew to Houston where he rode through the city in a motorcade, spoke at the Rice University Stadium, and attended a dinner in honor of U.S. Representative Albert Thomas.[76]

At Rice Stadium a very large, enthusiastic crowd greeted the President.[77]   In Houston, as elsewhere during the trip, the crowds showed much interest in Mrs. Kennedy.   David F. Powers of the President's staff later stated that when the President asked for his assessment of the day's activities, Powers replied "that the crowd was about the same as the one which came to see him before but there were 100,000 extra people on hand who came to see Mrs. Kennedy." [78]   Late in the evening, the Presidential party flew to Fort Worth where they spent the night at the Texas Hotel.[79]

On the morning of November 22, President Kennedy attended a breakfast at the hotel and afterward addressed a crowd at an open parking lot.[80]   The President liked outdoor appearances because more people could see and hear him.[81]   Before leaving the hotel, the President, Mrs. Kennedy, and Kenneth O'Donnell talked about the risks inherent in Presidential public appearances.[82]   According to O'Donnell, the President commented that "if anybody really wanted to shoot the President of the United States, it was not a very difficult job—all one had to do was get a high building someday with a telescopic rifle, and there was nothing anybody could do to defend against such an attempt." [83]   Upon concluding the conversation, the President prepared to depart for Dallas.

ARRIVAL AT LOVE FIELD

In Dallas the rain had stopped, and by midmorning a gloomy overcast sky had given way to the bright sunshine that greeted the Presidential party when *Air Force One* touched down at Love Field at 11:40 a.m., c.s.t.[84]   Governor and Mrs. Connally and Senator Ralph W. Yarborough had come with the President from Fort Worth.[85]   Vice President Johnson's airplane, *Air Force Two*, had arrived at Love

Field at approximately 11:35 a.m., and the Vice President and Mrs. Johnson were in the receiving line to greet President and Mrs. Kennedy.[86]

After a welcome from the Dallas reception committee, President and Mrs. Kennedy walked along a chain-link fence at the reception area greeting a large crowd of spectators that had gathered behind it.[87] Secret Service agents formed a cordon to keep the press and photographers from impeding their passage and scanned the crowd for threatening movements.[88] Dallas police stood at intervals along the fence and Dallas plainclothesmen mixed in the crowd.[89] Vice President and Mrs. Johnson followed along the fence, guarded by four members of the Vice-Presidential detail.[90] Approximately 10 minutes after the arrival at Love Field, the President and Mrs. Kennedy went to the Presidential automobile to begin the motorcade.[91]

ORGANIZATION OF THE MOTORCADE

Secret Service arrangements for Presidential trips, which were followed in the Dallas motorcade, are designed to provide protection while permitting large numbers of people to see the President.[92] Every effort is made to prevent unscheduled stops, although the President may, and in Dallas did, order stops in order to greet the public.[93] When the motorcade slows or stops, agents take positions between the President and the crowd.[94]

The order of vehicles in the Dallas motorcade was as follows:

Motorcycles.—Dallas police motorcycles preceded the pilot car.[95]

The pilot car.—Manned by officers of the Dallas Police Department, this automobile preceded the main party by approximately a quarter of a mile. Its function was to alert police along the route that the motorcade was approaching and to check for signs of trouble.[96]

Motorcycles.—Next came four to six motorcycle policemen whose main purpose was to keep the crowd back.[97]

The lead car.—Described as a "rolling command car," this was an unmarked Dallas police car, driven by Chief of Police Curry and occupied by Secret Service Agents Sorrels and Lawson and by Dallas County Sheriff J. E. Decker. The occupants scanned the crowd and the buildings along the route. Their main function was to spot trouble in advance and to direct any necessary steps to meet the trouble. Following normal practice, the lead automobile stayed approximately four to five car lengths ahead of the President's limousine.[98]

The Presidential limousine.—The President's automobile was a specially designed 1961 Lincoln convertible with two collapsible jump seats between the front and rear seats.[99] (See Commission Exhibit No. 346, p. 44.) It was outfitted with a clear plastic bubbletop which was neither bulletproof nor bullet resistant.[100] Because the skies had cleared in Dallas, Lawson directed that the top not be used for the day's activities. He acted on instructions he had re-

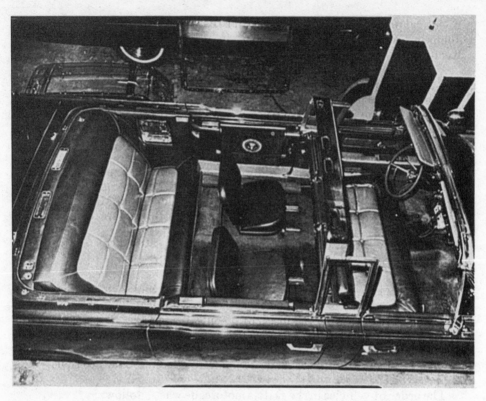

COMMISSION EXHIBIT No. 346

Interior of Presidential limousine used on November 22, 1963.

ceived earlier from Assistant Special Agent in Charge Roy H. Kellerman, who was in Fort Worth with the President.[101] Kellerman had discussed the matter with O'Donnell, whose instructions were, "If the weather is clear and it is not raining, have that bubbletop off." [102] Elevated approximately 15 inches above the back of the front seat was a metallic frame with four handholds that riders in the car could grip while standing in the rear seat during parades.[103] At the rear on each side of the automobile were small running boards, each designed to hold a Secret Service agent, with a metallic handle for the rider to grasp.[104] The President had frequently stated that he did not want agents to ride on these steps during a motorcade except when necessary. He had repeated this wish only a few days before, during his visit to Tampa, Fla.[105]

President Kennedy rode on the right-hand side of the rear seat with Mrs. Kennedy on his left.[106] Governor Connally occupied the right jump seat, Mrs. Connally the left.[107] Driving the Presidential limousine was Special Agent William R. Greer of the Secret Service; on his right sat Kellerman.[108] Kellerman's responsibilities included maintaining radio communications with the lead and followup cars, scanning the route, and getting out and standing near the President when the cars stopped.

Motorcycles.—Four motorcycles, two on each side, flanked the rear of the Presidential car. They provided some cover for the President, but their main purpose was to keep back the crowd.[109] On previous occasions, the President had requested that, to the extent possible, these flanking motorcycles keep back from the sides of his car.[110]

Presidential followup car.—This vehicle, a 1955 Cadillac eight-passenger convertible especially outfitted for the Secret Service, followed closely behind the President's automobile.[111] It carried eight Secret Service agents—two in the front seat, two in the rear, and two on each of the right and left running boards.[112] Each agent carried a .38-caliber pistol, and a shotgun and automatic rifle were also available.[113] Presidential Assistants David F. Powers and Kenneth O'Donnell sat in the right and left jump seats, respectively.[114]

The agents in this car, under established procedure, had instructions to watch the route for signs of trouble, scanning not only the crowds but the windows and roofs of buildings, overpasses, and crossings.[115] They were instructed to watch particularly for thrown objects, sudden actions in the crowd, and any movements toward the Presidential car.[116] The agents on the front of the running boards had directions to move immediately to positions just to the rear of the President and Mrs. Kennedy when the President's car slowed to a walking pace or stopped, or when the press of the crowd made it impossible for the escort motorcycles to stay in position on the car's rear flanks.[117] The two agents on the rear of the running boards were to advance toward the front of the President's car whenever it stopped or slowed down sufficiently for them to do so.[118]

Vice-Presidential car.—The Vice-Presidential automobile, a four-door Lincoln convertible obtained locally for use in the motor-

45

cade, proceeded approximately two to three car lengths behind the President's followup car.[119] This distance was maintained so that spectators would normally turn their gaze from the President's automobile by the time the Vice President came into view.[120] Vice President Johnson sat on the right-hand side of the rear seat, Mrs. Johnson in the center, and Senator Yarborough on the left.[121] Rufus W. Youngblood, special agent in charge of the Vice President's detail, occupied the right-hand side of the front seat, and Hurchel Jacks of the Texas State Highway patrol was the driver.[122]

Vice-Presidential followup car.—Driven by an officer of the Dallas Police Department, this vehicle was occupied by three Secret Service agents and Clifton C. Carter, assistant to the Vice President.[123] These agents performed for the Vice President the same functions that the agents in the Presidential followup car performed for the President.

Remainder of motorcade.—The remainder of the motorcade consisted of five cars for other dignitaries, including the mayor of Dallas and Texas Congressmen, telephone and Western Union vehicles, a White House communications car, three cars for press photographers, an official party bus for White House staff members and others, and two press buses. Admiral George G. Burkley, physician to the President, was in a car following those "containing the local and national representatives." [124]

Police car and motorcycles.[125]—A Dallas police car and several motorcycles at the rear kept the motorcade together and prevented unauthorized vehicles from joining the motorcade.

Communications in the motorcade.[126]—A base station at a fixed location in Dallas operated a radio network which linked together the lead car, Presidential car, Presidential followup car, White House communications car, Trade Mart, Love Field, and the Presidential and Vice-Presidential airplanes. The Vice-Presidential car and Vice-Presidential followup car used portable sets with a separate frequency for their own car-to-car communication.

THE DRIVE THROUGH DALLAS

The motorcade left Love Field shortly after 11:50 a.m. and drove at speeds up to 25 to 30 miles an hour through thinly populated areas on the outskirts of Dallas.[127] At the President's direction, his automobile stopped twice, the first time to permit him to respond to a sign asking him to shake hands.[128] During this brief stop, agents in the front positions on the running boards of the Presidential followup car came forward and stood beside the President's car, looking out toward the crowd, and Special Agent Kellerman assumed his position next to the car.[129] On the other occasion, the President halted the motorcade to speak to a Catholic nun and a group of small children.[130]

In the downtown area, large crowds of spectators gave the President a tremendous reception.[131] The crowds were so dense

COMMISSION EXHIBIT No. 698

Presidential limousine in Dallas motorcade.

that Special Agent Clinton J. Hill had to leave the left front running board of the President's followup car four times to ride on the rear of the President's limousine.[132] (See Commission Exhibit No. 698, p. 47.) Several times Special Agent John D. Ready came forward from the right front running board of the Presidential followup car to the right side of the President's car.[133] Special Agent Glen A. Bennett once left his place inside the followup car to help keep the crowd away from the President's car. When a teenage boy ran toward the rear of the President's car,[134] Ready left the running board to chase the boy back into the crowd. On several occasions when the Vice President's car was slowed down by the throng, Special Agent Youngblood stepped out to hold the crowd back.[135]

According to plan, the President's motorcade proceeded west through downtown Dallas on Main Street to the intersection of Houston Street, which marks the beginning of Dealey Plaza.[136] From Main Street the motorcade turned right and went north on Houston Street, passing tall buildings on the right, and headed toward the Texas School Book Depository Building.[137] The spectators were still thickly congregated in front of the buildings which lined the east side of Houston Street, but the crowd thinned abruptly along Elm Street, which curves in a southwesterly direction as it proceeds downgrade toward the Triple Underpass and the Stemmons Freeway.[138]

As the motorcade approached the intersection of Houston and Elm Streets, there was general gratification in the Presidential party about the enthusiastic reception. Evaluating the political overtones, Kenneth O'Donnell was especially pleased because it convinced him that the average Dallas resident was like other American citizens in respecting and admiring the President.[139] Mrs. Connally, elated by the reception, turned to President Kennedy and said, "Mr. President, you can't say Dallas doesn't love you." The President replied, "That is very obvious." [140]

THE ASSASSINATION

At 12:30 p.m., c.s.t., as the President's open limousine proceeded at approximately 11 miles per hour along Elm Street toward the Triple Underpass, shots fired from a rifle mortally wounded President Kennedy and seriously injured Governor Connally. One bullet passed through the President's neck; a subsequent bullet, which was lethal, shattered the right side of his skull. Governor Connally sustained bullet wounds in his back, the right side of his chest, right wrist, and left thigh.

The Time

The exact time of the assassination was fixed by the testimony of four witnesses. Special Agent Rufus W. Youngblood observed that the large electric sign clock atop the Texas School Book Depository Building showed the numerals "12:30" as the Vice-Presidential automobile proceeded north on Houston Street, a few seconds before the shots were fired.[141] Just prior to the shooting, David F. Powers, riding in the Secret Service followup car, remarked to Kenneth O'Donnell that it was 12:30 p.m., the time they were due at the Trade Mart.[142] Seconds after the shooting, Roy Kellerman, riding in the front seat of the Presidential limousine, looked at his watch and said "12:30" to the driver, Special Agent Greer.[143] The Dallas police radio log reflects that Chief of Police Curry reported the shooting of the President and issued his initial orders at 12:30 p.m.[144]

Speed of the Limousine

William Greer, operator of the Presidential limousine, estimated the car's speed at the time of the first shot as 12 to 15 miles per hour.[145] Other witnesses in the motorcade estimated the speed of the President's limousine from 7 to 22 miles per hour.[146] A more precise determination has been made from motion pictures taken on the scene by an amateur photographer, Abraham Zapruder. Based on these films, the speed of the President's automobile is computed at an average speed of 11.2 miles per hour. The car maintained this average speed over a distance of approximately 136 feet immediately preceding the shot which struck the President in the head. While the car traveled this distance, the Zapruder camera ran 152 frames. Since the camera operates at a speed of 18.3 frames per second, it was calculated that the car required 8.3 seconds to cover the 136 feet. This represents a speed of 11.2 miles per hour.[147]

In the Presidential Limousine

Mrs. John F. Kennedy, on the left of the rear seat of the limousine, looked toward her left and waved to the crowds along the route. Soon after the motorcade turned onto Elm Street, she heard a sound similar to a motorcycle noise and a cry from Governor Connally, which caused her to look to her right. On turning she saw a quizzical look on her husband's face as he raised his left hand to his throat. Mrs. Kennedy then heard a second shot and saw the President's skull torn open under the impact of the bullet. As she cradled her mortally wounded husband, Mrs. Kennedy cried, "Oh, my God, they have shot my husband. I love you, Jack." [148]

Governor Connally testified that he recognized the first noise as a rifle shot and the thought immediately crossed his mind that it was an assassination attempt. From his position in the right jump seat immediately in front of the President, he instinctively turned to his right because the shot appeared to come from over his right shoulder. Unable to see the President as he turned to the right, the Governor started to look back over his left shoulder, but he never completed the turn because he felt something strike him in the back.[149] In his testimony before the Commission, Governor Connally was certain that he was hit by the second shot, which he stated he did not hear.[150]

Mrs. Connally, too, heard a frightening noise from her right. Looking over her right shoulder, she saw that the President had both hands at his neck but she observed no blood and heard nothing. She watched as he slumped down with an empty expression on his face.[151] Roy Kellerman, in the right front seat of the limousine, heard a report like a firecracker pop. Turning to his right in the direction of the noise, Kellerman heard the President say "My God, I am hit," and saw both of the President's hands move up toward his neck. As he told the driver, "Let's get out of here; we are hit," Kellerman grabbed his microphone and radioed ahead to the lead car, "We are hit. Get us to the hospital immediately." [152]

The driver, William Greer, heard a noise which he took to be a backfire from one of the motorcycles flanking the Presidential car. When he heard the same noise again, Greer glanced over his shoulder and saw Governor Connally fall. At the sound of the second shot he realized that something was wrong, and he pressed down on the accelerator as Kellerman said, "Get out of here fast." [153] As he issued his instructions to Greer and to the lead car, Kellerman heard a "flurry of shots" within 5 seconds of the first noise. According to Kellerman, Mrs. Kennedy then cried out: "What are they doing to you?" Looking back from the front seat, Kellerman saw Governor Connally in his wife's lap and Special Agent Clinton J. Hill lying across the trunk of the car.[154]

Mrs. Connally heard a second shot fired and pulled her husband down into her lap.[155] Observing his blood-covered chest as he was pulled into his wife's lap, Governor Connally believed himself mortally wounded. He cried out, "Oh, no, no, no. My God, they are going to kill us all." [156] At first Mrs. Connally thought that her husband had been killed, but then she noticed an almost imperceptible movement and knew that he was still alive. She said, "It's all right. Be still." [157] The Governor was lying with his head on his wife's lap when he heard a shot hit the President.[158] At that point, both Governor and Mrs. Connally observed brain tissue splattered over the interior of the car.[159] According to Governor and Mrs. Connally, it was after this shot that Kellerman issued his emergency instructions and the car accelerated.[160]

Reaction by Secret Service Agents

From the left front running board of the President's followup car, Special Agent Hill was scanning the few people standing on the south side of Elm Street after the motorcade had turned off Houston Street. He estimated that the motorcade had slowed down to approximately 9 or 10 miles per hour on the turn at the intersection of Houston and Elm Streets and then proceeded at a rate of 12 to 15 miles per hour with the followup car trailing the President's automobile by approximately 5 feet.[161] Hill heard a noise, which seemed to be a firecracker, coming from his right rear. He immediately looked to his right, "and, in so doing, my eyes had to cross the Presidential limousine and I saw President Kennedy grab at himself and lurch forward and to the left." [162] Hill jumped from the followup car and ran to the President's automobile. At about the time he reached the President's automobile, Hill heard a second shot, approximately 5 seconds after the first, which removed a portion of the President's head.[163]

At the instant that Hill stepped onto the left rear step of the President's automobile and grasped the handhold, the car lurched forward, causing him to lose his footing. He ran three or four steps, regained his position and mounted the car. Between the time he originally seized the handhold and the time he mounted the car, Hill recalled that—

> Mrs. Kennedy had jumped up from the seat and was, it appeared to me, reaching for something coming off the right rear bumper of the car, the right rear tail, when she noticed that I was trying to climb on the car. She turned toward me and I grabbed her and put her back in the back seat, crawled up on top of the back seat and lay there.[164]

David Powers, who witnessed the scene from the President's followup car, stated that Mrs. Kennedy would probably have fallen off the rear end of the car and been killed if Hill had not pushed her back into the Presidential automobile.[165] Mrs. Kennedy had no recollection of climbing onto the back of the car.[166]

Special Agent Ready, on the right front running board of the Presidential followup car, heard noises that sounded like firecrackers and ran toward the President's limousine. But he was immediately called back by Special Agent Emory P. Roberts, in charge of the followup car, who did not believe that he could reach the President's car at the speed it was then traveling.[167] Special Agent George W. Hickey, Jr., in the rear seat of the Presidential followup car, picked up and cocked an automatic rifle as he heard the last shot. At this point the cars were speeding through the underpass and had left the scene of the shooting, but Hickey kept the automatic weapon ready as the car raced to the hospital.[168] Most of the other Secret Service agents in the motorcade had drawn their sidearms.[169] Roberts noticed that the Vice President's car was approximately one-half block behind the Presidential followup car at the time of the shooting and signaled for it to move in closer.[170]

Directing the security detail for the Vice President from the right front seat of the Vice-Presidential car, Special Agent Youngblood recalled:

> As we were beginning to go down this incline, all of a sudden there was an explosive noise. I quickly observed unnatural movement of crowds, like ducking or scattering, and quick movements in the Presidential followup car. So I turned around and hit the Vice President on the shoulder and hollered, get down, and then looked around again and saw more of this movement, and so I proceeded to go to the back seat and get on top of him. [171]

Youngblood was not positive that he was in the rear seat before the second shot, but thought it probable because of President Johnson's statement to that effect immediately after the assassination.[172] President Johnson emphasized Youngblood's instantaneous reaction after the first shot:

> I was startled by the sharp report or explosion, but I had no time to speculate as to its origin because Agent Youngblood turned in a flash, immediately after the first explosion, hitting me on the shoulder, and shouted to all of us in the back seat to get down. I was pushed down by Agent Youngblood. Almost in the same moment in which he hit or pushed me, he vaulted over the back seat and sat on me. I was bent over under the weight of Agent Youngblood's body, toward Mrs. Johnson and Senator Yarborough.[173]

Clifton C. Carter, riding in the Vice President's followup car a short distance behind, reported that Youngblood was in the rear seat using his body to shield the Vice President before the second and third shots were fired.[174]

Other Secret Service agents assigned to the motorcade remained at their posts during the race to the hospital. None stayed at the scene of the shooting, and none entered the Texas School Book Depository Building at or immediately after the shooting. Secret Service procedure requires that each agent stay with the person being protected and not be diverted unless it is necessary to accomplish the protective assignment.[175] Forrest V. Sorrels, special agent in charge of the Dallas office, was the first Secret Service agent to return to the scene of the assassination, approximately 20 or 25 minutes after the shots were fired.[176]

PARKLAND MEMORIAL HOSPITAL

The Race to the Hospital

In the final instant of the assassination, the Presidential motorcade began a race to Parkland Memorial Hospital, approximately 4 miles from the Texas School Book Depository Building.[177] On receipt of the radio message from Kellerman to the lead car that the President had been hit, Chief of Police Curry and police motorcyclists at the head of the motorcade led the way to the hospital.[178] Meanwhile, Chief Curry ordered the police base station to notify Parkland Hospital that the wounded President was en route.[179] The radio log of the Dallas Police Department shows that at 12:30 p.m. on November 22 Chief Curry radioed, "Go to the hospital—Parkland Hospital. Have them stand by." A moment later Curry added, "Looks like the President has been hit. Have Parkland stand by." The base station replied, "They have been notified."[180] Traveling at speeds estimated at times to be up to 70 or 80 miles per hour down the Stemmons Freeway and Harry Hines

Boulevard, the Presidential limousine arrived at the emergency entrance of the Parkland Hospital at about 12:35 p.m.[181] Arriving almost simultaneously were the President's followup car, the Vice President's automobile, and the Vice President's followup car. Admiral Burkley, the President's physician, arrived at the hospital "between 3 and 5 minutes following the arrival of the President," since the riders in his car "were not exactly aware what had happened" and the car went on to the Trade Mart first.[182]

When Parkland Hospital received the notification, the staff in the emergency area was alerted and trauma rooms 1 and 2 were prepared.[183] These rooms were for the emergency treatment of acutely ill or injured patients.[184] Although the first message mentioned an injury only to President Kennedy, two rooms were prepared.[185] As the President's limousine sped toward the hospital, 12 doctors rushed to the emergency area: surgeons, Drs. Malcolm O. Perry, Charles R. Baxter, Robert N. McClelland, Ronald C. Jones; the chief neurologist, Dr. William Kemp Clark; 4 anesthesiologists, Drs. Marion T. Jenkins, Adolph H. Giesecke, Jr., Jackie H. Hunt, Gene C. Akin; a urological surgeon, Dr Paul C. Peters; an oral surgeon, Dr. Don T. Curtis; and a heart specialist, Dr. Fouad A. Bashour.[186]

Upon arriving at Parkland Hospital, Lawson jumped from the lead car and rushed into the emergency entrance, where he was met by hospital staff members wheeling stretchers out to the automobile.[187] Special Agent Hill removed his suit jacket and covered the President's head and upper chest to prevent the taking of photographs.[188] Governor Connally, who had lost consciousness on the ride to the hospital, regained consciousness when the limousine stopped abruptly at the emergency entrance. Despite his serious wounds, Governor Connally tried to get out of the way so that medical help could reach the President. Although he was reclining in his wife's arms, he lurched forward in an effort to stand upright and get out of the car, but he collapsed again. Then he experienced his first sensation of pain, which became excruciating.[189] The Governor was lifted onto a stretcher and taken into trauma room 2.[190] For a moment, Mrs. Kennedy refused to release the President, whom she held in her lap, but then Kellerman, Greer, and Lawson lifted the President onto a stretcher and pushed it into trauma room 1.[191]

Treatment of President Kennedy

The first physician to see the President at Parkland Hospital was Dr. Charles J. Carrico, a resident in general surgery.[192] Dr. Carrico was in the emergency area, examining another patient, when he was notified that President Kennedy was en route to the hospital.[193] Approximately 2 minutes later, Dr. Carrico saw the President on his back, being wheeled into the emergency area.[194] He noted that the President was blue-white or ashen in color; had slow, spasmodic, agonal respiration without any coordination; made no voluntary movements; had his eyes open with the pupils dilated without any reaction

53

to light; evidenced no palpable pulse; and had a few chest sounds which were thought to be heart beats.[195] On the basis of these findings, Dr. Carrico concluded that President Kennedy was still alive.[196]

Dr. Carrico noted two wounds: a small bullet wound in the front lower neck, and an extensive wound in the President's head where a sizable portion of the skull was missing.[197] He observed shredded brain tissue and "considerable slow oozing" from the latter wound, followed by "more profuse bleeding" after some circulation was established.[198] Dr. Carrico felt the President's back and determined that there was no large wound there which would be an immediate threat to life.[199] Observing the serious problems presented by the head wound and inadequate respiration, Dr. Carrico directed his attention to improving the President's breathing.[200] He noted contusions, hematoma to the right of the larynx, which was deviated slightly to the left, and also ragged tissue which indicated a tracheal injury.[201] Dr. Carrico inserted a cuffed endotracheal tube past the injury, inflated the cuff, and connected it to a Bennett machine to assist in respiration.[202]

At that point, direction of the President's treatment was undertaken by Dr. Malcolm O. Perry, who arrived at trauma room 1 a few moments after the President.[203] Dr. Perry noted the President's back brace as he felt for a femoral pulse, which he did not find.[204] Observing that an effective airway had to be established if treatment was to be effective, Dr. Perry performed a tracheotomy, which required 3 to 5 minutes.[205] While Dr. Perry was performing the tracheotomy, Drs. Carrico and Ronald Jones made cutdowns on the President's right leg and left arm, respectively, to infuse blood and fluids into the circulatory system.[206] Dr. Carrico treated the President's known adrenal insufficiency by administering hydrocortisone.[207] Dr. Robert N. McClelland entered at that point and assisted Dr. Perry with the tracheotomy.[208]

Dr. Fouad Bashour, chief of cardiology, Dr. M. T. Jenkins, chief of anesthesiology, and Dr. A. H. Giesecke, Jr., then joined in the effort to revive the President.[209] When Dr. Perry noted free air and blood in the President's chest cavity, he asked that chest tubes be inserted to allow for drainage of blood and air. Drs. Paul C. Peters and Charles R. Baxter initiated these procedures.[210] As a result of the infusion of liquids through the cutdowns, the cardiac massage, and the airway, the doctors were able to maintain peripheral circulation as monitored at the neck (carotid) artery and at the wrist (radial) pulse. A femoral pulse was also detected in the President's leg.[211] While these medical efforts were in progress, Dr. Clark noted some electrical activity on the cardiotachyscope attached to monitor the President's heart responses.[212] Dr. Clark, who most closely observed the head wound, described a large, gaping wound in the right rear part of the head, with substantial damage and exposure of brain tissue, and a considerable loss of blood.[213] Dr. Clark did not see any other hole or wound on the President's head. According to Dr. Clark, the small bullet hole on the right rear of the President's head discovered during the subsequent autopsy "could have easily been hidden in the blood and hair." [214]

In the absence of any neurological, muscular, or heart response, the doctors concluded that efforts to revive the President were hopeless.[215] This was verified by Admiral Burkley, the President's physician, who arrived at the hospital after emergency treatment was underway and concluded that "my direct services to him at that moment would have interfered with the action of the team which was in progress." [216] At approximately 1 p.m., after last rites were administered to the President by Father Oscar L. Huber, Dr. Clark pronounced the President dead. He made the official determination because the ultimate cause of death, the severe head injury, was within his sphere of specialization.[217] The time was fixed at 1 p.m., as an approximation, since it was impossible to determine the precise moment when life left the President.[218] President Kennedy could have survived the neck injury, but the head wound was fatal.[219] From a medical viewpoint, President Kennedy was alive when he arrived at Parkland Hospital; the doctors observed that he had a heart beat and was making some respiratory efforts.[220] But his condition was hopeless, and the extraordinary efforts of the doctors to save him could not help but to have been unavailing.

Since the Dallas doctors directed all their efforts to controlling the massive bleeding caused by the head wound, and to reconstructing an airway to his lungs, the President remained on his back throughout his medical treatment at Parkland.[221] When asked why he did not turn the President over, Dr. Carrico testified as follows:

A. This man was in obvious extreme distress and any more thorough inspection would have involved several minutes—well, several—considerable time which at this juncture was not available. A thorough inspection would have involved washing and cleansing the back, and this is not practical in treating an acutely injured patient. You have to determine which things, which are immediately life threatening and cope with them, before attempting to evaluate the full extent of the injuries.

Q. Did you ever have occasion to look at the President's back?

A. No, sir. Before—well, in trying to treat an acutely injured patient, you have to establish an airway, adequate ventilation and you have to establish adequate circulation. Before this was accomplished the President's cardiac activity had ceased and closed cardiac massage was instituted, which made it impossible to inspect his back.

Q. Was any effort made to inspect the President's back after he had expired?

A. No, sir.

Q. And why was no effort made at that time to inspect his back?

A. I suppose nobody really had the heart to do it.[222]

Moreover, the Parkland doctors took no further action after the President had expired because they concluded that it was beyond the scope of their permissible duties.[223]

Treatment of Governor Connally

While one medical team tried to revive President Kennedy, a second performed a series of operations on the bullet wounds sustained by Governor Connally.[224] Governor Connally was originally seen by Dr. Carrico and Dr. Richard Dulany.[225] While Dr. Carrico went on to attend the President, Dr. Dulany stayed with the Governor and was soon joined by several other doctors.[226] At approximately 12:45 p.m., Dr. Robert Shaw, chief of thoracic surgery, arrived at trauma room 2, to take charge of the care of Governor Connally, whose major wound fell within Dr. Shaw's area of specialization.[227]

Governor Connally had a large sucking wound in the front of the right chest which caused extreme pain and difficulty in breathing. Rubber tubes were inserted between the second and third ribs to reexpand the right lung, which had collapsed because of the opening in the chest wall.[228] At 1:35 p.m., after Governor Connally had been moved to the operating room, Dr. Shaw started the first operation by cutting away the edges of the wound on the front of the Governor's chest and suturing the damaged lung and lacerated muscles.[229] The elliptical wound in the Governor's back, located slightly to the left of the Governor's right armpit approximately five-eighths inch (a centimeter and a half) in its greatest diameter, was treated by cutting away the damaged skin and suturing the back muscle and skin.[230] This operation was concluded at 3:20 p.m.[231]

Two additional operations were performed on Governor Connally for wounds which he had not realized he had sustained until he regained consciousness the following day.[232] From approximately 4 p.m. to 4:50 p.m. on November 22, Dr. Charles F. Gregory, chief of orthopedic surgery, operated on the wounds of Governor Connally's right wrist, assisted by Drs. William Osborne and John Parker.[233] The wound on the back of the wrist was left partially open for draining, and the wound on the palm side was enlarged, cleansed, and closed. The fracture was set, and a cast was applied with some traction utilized.[234] While the second operation was in progress, Dr. George T. Shires, assisted by Drs. Robert McClelland, Charles Baxter, and Ralph Don Patman, treated the gunshot wound in the left thigh.[235] This punctuate missile wound, about two-fifths inch in diameter (1 centimeter) and located approximately 5 inches above the left knee, was cleansed and closed with sutures; but a small metallic fragment remained in the Governor's leg.[236]

Vice President Johnson at Parkland

As President Kennedy and Governor Connally were being removed from the limousine onto stretchers, a protective circle of Secret Service agents surrounded Vice President and Mrs. Johnson and escorted them into Parkland Hospital through the emergency entrance.[237] The agents moved a nurse and patient out of a nearby room, lowered the shades, and took emergency security measures to protect the Vice President.[238] Two men from the President's followup car were detailed to help protect the Vice President. An agent was stationed at the entrance to stop anyone who was not a member of the Presidential party. U.S. Representatives Henry B. Gonzalez, Jack Brooks, Homer Thornberry, and Albert Thomas joined Clifton C. Carter and the group of special agents protecting the Vice President.[239] On one occasion Mrs. Johnson, accompanied by two Secret Service agents, left the room to see Mrs. Kennedy and Mrs. Connally.[240]

Concern that the Vice President might also be a target for assassination prompted the Secret Service agents to urge him to leave the hospital and return to Washington immediately.[241] The Vice President decided to wait until he received definitive word of the President's condition.[242] At approximately 1:20 p.m., Vice President Johnson was notified by O'Donnell that President Kennedy was dead.[243] Special Agent Youngblood learned from Mrs. Johnson the location of her two daughters and made arrangements through Secret Service headquarters in Washington to provide them with protection immediately.[244]

When consulted by the Vice President, O'Donnell advised him to go to the airfield immediately and return to Washington.[245] It was decided that the Vice President should return on the Presidential plane rather than on the Vice-Presidential plane because it had better communication equipment.[246] The Vice President conferred with White House Assistant Press Secretary Malcolm Kilduff and decided that there would be no release of the news of the President's death until the Vice President had left the hospital.[247] When told that Mrs. Kennedy refused to leave without the President's body, the Vice President said that he would not leave Dallas without her.[248] On the recommendation of the Secret Service agents, Vice President Johnson decided to board the Presidential airplane, *Air Force One*, and wait for Mrs. Kennedy and the President's body.[249]

Secret Service Emergency Security Arrangements

Immediately after President Kennedy's stretcher was wheeled into trauma room 1, Secret Service agents took positions at the door of the small emergency room. A nurse was asked to identify hospital personnel and to tell everyone, except necessary medical staff members, to leave the emergency room. Other Secret Service agents posted themselves in the corridors and other areas near the emergency room. Special Agent Lawson made certain that the Dallas police kept the public and press away from the immediate area of the hospital.[250] Agents Kellerman and Hill telephoned the head of the White House detail, Gerald A. Behn, to advise him of the assassination. The telephone line to Washington was kept open throughout the remainder of the stay at the hospital.[251]

Secret Service agents stationed at later stops on the President's itinerary of November 22 were redeployed. Men at the Trade Mart were driven to Parkland Hospital in Dallas police cars.[252] The Secret Service group awaiting the President in Austin were instructed to return to Washington.[253] Meanwhile, the Secret Service agents in charge of security at Love Field started to make arrangements for departure. As soon as one of the agents learned of the shooting, he asked the officer in charge of the police detail at the airport to institute strict security measures for the Presidential aircraft, the airport terminal, and the surrounding area. The police were cautioned to prevent picture taking. Secret Service agents working with police cleared the areas adjacent to the aircraft, including warehouses, other terminal buildings and the neighboring parking lots, of all people.[254] The agents decided not to shift the Presidential aircraft to the far side of the airport because the original landing area was secure and a move would require new measures.[255]

When security arrangements at the airport were complete, the Secret Service made the necessary arrangements for the Vice President to leave the hospital. Unmarked police cars took the Vice President and Mrs. Johnson from Parkland Hospital to Love Field. Chief Curry drove one automobile occupied by Vice President Johnson, U.S. Representatives Thomas and Thornberry, and Special Agent Youngblood. In another car Mrs. Johnson was driven to the airport accompanied by Secret Service agents and Representative Brooks. Motorcycle policemen who escorted the automobiles were requested by the Vice President and Agent Youngblood not to use sirens. During the drive Vice President Johnson, at Youngblood's instruction, kept below window level.[256]

Removal of the President's Body

While the team of doctors at Parkland Hospital tried desperately to save the life of President Kennedy, Mrs. Kennedy alternated between watching them and waiting outside.[257] After the President was pronounced dead, O'Donnell tried to persuade Mrs. Kennedy to leave the area, but she refused. She said that she intended to stay with her husband.[258] A casket was obtained and the President's body was prepared for removal.[259] Before the body could be taken from the hospital, two Dallas officials informed members of the President's staff that the body could not be removed from the city until an autopsy was performed. Despite the protests of these officials, the casket was wheeled out of the hospital, placed in an ambulance, and transported to the airport shortly after 2 p.m.[260] At approximately 2:15 p.m. the casket was loaded, with some difficulty because of the narrow airplane door, onto the rear of the Presidential plane where seats had been removed to make room.[261] Concerned that the local officials might try to prevent the plane's departure, O'Donnell asked that the pilot take off immediately. He was informed that takeoff would be delayed until Vice President Johnson was sworn in.[262]

THE END OF THE TRIP

Swearing in of the New President

From the Presidential airplane, the Vice President telephoned Attorney General Robert F. Kennedy, who advised that Mr. Johnson take the Presidential oath of office before the plane left Dallas.[263] Federal Judge Sarah T. Hughes hastened to the plane to administer the oath.[264] Members of the Presidential and Vice-Presidential parties filled the central compartment of the plane to witness the swearing in. At 2:38 p.m., c.s.t., Lyndon Baines Johnson took the oath of office as the 36th President of the United States.[265] Mrs. Kennedy and Mrs. Johnson stood at the side of the new President as he took the oath of office.[266] Nine minutes later, the Presidential airplane departed for Washington, D.C.[267]

Return to Washington, D.C.

On the return flight, Mrs. Kennedy sat with David Powers, Kenneth O'Donnell, and Lawrence O'Brien.[268] At 5:58 p.m., e.s.t., *Air Force One* landed at Andrews AFB, where President Kennedy had begun his last trip only 31 hours before.[269] Detailed security arrangements had been made by radio from the President's plane on the return flight.[270] The public had been excluded from the base, and only Government officials and the press were permitted near the landing area. Upon arrival, President Johnson made a brief statement over television and radio. President and Mrs. Johnson were flown by helicopter to the White House, from where Mrs. Johnson was driven to her residence under Secret Service escort. The President then walked to the Executive Office Building, where he worked until 9 p.m.[271]

The Autopsy

Given a choice between the National Naval ·Medical Center at Bethesda, Md., and the Army's Walter Reed Hospital, Mrs. Kennedy chose the hospital in Bethesda for the autopsy because the President had served in the Navy.[272] Mrs. Kennedy and the Attorney General, with three Secret Service agents, accompanied President Kennedy's body on the 45-minute automobile trip from Andrews AFB to the Hospital.[273] On the 17th floor of the Hospital, Mrs. Kennedy and the Attorney General joined other members of the Kennedy family to await the conclusion of the autopsy.[274] Mrs. Kennedy was guarded by Secret Service agents in quarters assigned to her in the naval hospital.[275] The Secret Service established a communication system with the White House and screened all telephone calls and visitors.[276]

The hospital received the President's body for autopsy at approximately 7:35 p.m.[277] X-rays and photographs were taken preliminarily and the pathological examination began at about 8 p.m.[278] The autopsy report noted that President Kennedy was 46 years of age, 72½ inches tall, weighed 170 pounds, had blue eyes and reddish-brown hair. The body was muscular and well developed with no gross skeletal abnormalities except for those caused by the gunshot wounds. Under "Pathological Diagnosis" the cause of death was set forth as "Gunshot wound, head." [279] (See app. IX.)

The autopsy examination revealed two wounds in the President's head. One wound, approximately one-fourth of an inch by five-eighths of an inch (6 by 15 millimeters), was located about an inch (2.5 centimeters) to the right and slightly above the large bony protrusion (external occipital protuberance) which juts out at the center of the lower part of the back of the skull. The second head wound measured approximately 5 inches (13 centimeters) in its greatest diameter, but it was difficult to measure accurately because multiple crisscross fractures radiated from the large defect.[280] During the autopsy examination, Federal agents brought the surgeons three pieces of bone recovered from Elm Street and the Presidential automobile. When put together, these fragments accounted for approximately three-quarters of the missing portion of the skull.[281] The surgeons observed, through X-ray analysis, 30 or 40 tiny dustlike fragments of metal running in a line from the wound in the rear of the President's head toward the front part of the skull, with a sizable metal fragment lying just above the right eye.[282] From this head wound two small irregularly shaped fragments of metal were recovered and turned over to the FBI.[283]

The autopsy also disclosed a wound near the base of the back of President Kennedy's neck slightly to the right of his spine. The doctors traced the course of the bullet through the body and, as information was received from Parkland Hospital, concluded that the bullet had emerged from the front portion of the President's neck that had been cut away by the tracheotomy at Parkland.[284] The nature and characteristics of this neck wound and the two head wounds are discussed fully in the next chapter.

After the autopsy was concluded at approximately 11 p.m., the President's body was prepared for burial. This was finished at approximately 4 a.m.[285] Shortly thereafter, the President's wife, family and aides left Bethesda Naval Hospital.[286] The President's body was taken to the East Room of the White House where it was placed under ceremonial military guard.

CHAPTER III

The Shots From the Texas School Book Depository

I N THIS chapter the Commission analyzes the evidence and sets forth its conclusions concerning the source, effect, number and timing of the shots that killed President Kennedy and wounded Governor Connally. In that connection the Commission has evaluated (1) the testimony of eyewitnesses present at the scene of the assassination; (2) the damage to the Presidential limousine; (3) the examination by qualified experts of the rifle and cartridge cases found on the sixth floor of the Texas School Book Depository and the bullet fragments found in the Presidential limousine and at Parkland Hospital; (4) the wounds suffered by President Kennedy and Governor Connally; (5) wound ballistics tests; (6) the examination by qualified experts of the clothing worn by President Kennedy and Governor Connally; and (7) motion-picture films and still photographs taken at the time of the assassination.

THE WITNESSES

As reflected in the previous chapter, passengers in the first few cars of the motorcade had the impression that the shots came from the rear and from the right, the general direction of the Texas School Book Depository Building, although none of these passengers saw anyone fire the shots. Some spectators at Houston and Elm Streets, however, did see a rifle being fired in the direction of the President's car from the easternmost window of the sixth floor on the south side of the building. Other witnesses saw a rifle in this window immediately after the assassination. Three employees of the Depository, observing the parade from the fifth floor, heard the shots fired from the floor immediately above them. No credible evidence suggests that the shots were fired from the railroad bridge over the Triple Underpass, the nearby railroad yards or any place other than the Texas School Book Depository Building.

COMMISSION EXHIBIT No. 477

Position of Howard L. Brennan on November 22, 1963. (Photograph taken on March 20, 1964, and marked by Brennan during his testimony to show the window (A) in which he saw a man with a rifle, and the window (B) on the fifth floor in which he saw people watching the motorcade.)

Near the Depository

Eyewitnesses testified that they saw a man fire a weapon from the sixth-floor window. Howard L. Brennan, a 45-year-old steamfitter, watched the motorcade from a concrete retaining wall at the southwest corner of Elm and Houston, where he had a clear view of the south side of the Depository Building.[1] (See Commission Exhibit No. 477, p. 62.) He was approximately 107 feet from the Depository entrance and 120 feet from the southeast corner window of the sixth floor.[2] Brennan's presence and vantage point are corroborated by a motion picture of the motorcade taken by amateur photographer Abraham Zapruder, which shows Brennan, wearing gray khaki work clothes and a gray work helmet, seated on the retaining wall.[3] Brennan later identified himself in the Zapruder movie.[4] While waiting about 7 minutes for the President to arrive, he observed the crowd on the street and the people at the windows of the Depository Building.[5] He noticed a man at the southeast corner window of the sixth floor, and observed him leave the window "a couple of times."[6]

Brennan watched the President's car as it turned the corner at Houston and Elm and moved down the incline toward the Triple Underpass. Soon after the President's car passed, he heard an explosion like the backfire of a motorcycle.[7] Brennan recalled:

> Well, then something, just right after this explosion, made me think that it was a firecracker being thrown from the Texas Book Store. And I glanced up. And this man that I saw previous was aiming for his last shot.

*   *   *   *   *   *   *

> Well, as it appeared to me he was standing up and resting against the left window sill, with gun shouldered to his right shoulder, holding the gun with his left hand and taking positive aim and fired his last shot. As I calculate a couple of seconds. He drew the gun back from the window as though he was drawing it back to his side and maybe paused for another second as though to assure hisself that he hit his mark, and then he disappeared.[8]

Brennan stated that he saw 70 to 85 percent of the gun when it was fired and the body of the man from the waist up.[9] The rifle was aimed southwesterly down Elm Street toward the underpass.[10] Brennan saw the man fire one shot and he remembered hearing a total of only two shots. When questioned about the number of shots, Brennan testified:

> I don't know what made me think that there was firecrackers throwed out of the Book Store unless I did hear the second shot, because I positively thought the first shot was a backfire, and subconsciously I must have heard a second shot, but I do not recall it. I could not swear to it.[11]

Brennan quickly reported his observations to police officers.[12] Brennan's description of the man he saw is discussed in the next chapter.

Amos Lee Euins, a 15-year-old ninth grade student, stated that he was facing the Depository as the motorcade turned the corner at Elm and Houston. He recalled:

> Then I was standing here, and as the motorcade turned the corner, I was facing, looking dead at the building. And so I seen this pipe thing sticking out the window. I wasn't paying too much attention to it. Then when the first shot was fired, I started looking around, thinking it was a backfire. Everybody else started looking around. Then I looked up at the window, and he shot again.[13]

After witnessing the first shots, Euins hid behind a fountain bench and saw the man shoot again from the window in the southeast corner of the Depository's sixth floor.[14] According to Euins, the man had one hand on the barrel and the other on the trigger. Euins believed that there were four shots.[15] Immediately after the assassination, he reported his observations to Sgt. D. V. Harkness of the Dallas Police Department and also to James Underwood of station KRLD–TV of Dallas.[16] Sergeant Harkness testified that Euins told him that the shots came from the last window of the floor "under the ledge" on the side of the building they were facing.[17] Based on Euins' statements, Harkness radioed to headquarters at 12:36 p.m. that "I have a witness that says that it came from the fifth floor of the Texas Book Depository Store."[18] Euins accurately described the sixth floor as the floor "under the ledge." Harkness testified that the error in the radio message was due to his own "hasty count of the floors."[19]

Other witnesses saw a rifle in the window after the shots were fired. Robert H. Jackson, staff photographer, Dallas Times Herald, was in a press car in the Presidential motorcade, eight or nine cars from the front. On Houston Street about halfway between Main and Elm, Jackson heard the first shot.[20] As someone in the car commented that it sounded like a firecracker, Jackson heard two more shots.[21] He testified:

> Then we realized or we thought that it was gunfire, and then we could not at that point see the President's car. We were still moving slowly, and after the third shot the second two shots seemed much closer together than the first shot, than they were to the first shot. Then after the last shot, I guess all of us were just looking all around and I just looked straight up ahead of me which would have been looking at the School Book Depository and I noticed two Negro men in a window straining to see directly above them, and my eyes followed right on up to the window above them and I saw the rifle or what looked like a rifle approximately half of the weapon, I guess I saw, and just as I looked

at it, it was drawn fairly slowly back into the building, and I saw no one in the window with it.

I didn't even see a form in the window.[22]

In the car with Jackson were James Underwood, television station KRLD–TV; Thomas Dillard, chief photographer, Dallas Morning News; Malcolm O. Couch and James Darnell, television newsreel cameramen. Dillard, Underwood, and the driver were in the front seat, Couch and Darnell were sitting on top of the back seat of the convertible with Jackson. Dillard, Couch, and Underwood confirmed that Jackson spontaneously exclaimed that he saw a rifle in the window.[23] According to Dillard, at the time the shots were fired he and his fellow passengers "had an absolutely perfect view of the School Depository from our position in the open car."[24] Dillard immediately took two pictures of the building: one of the east two-thirds of the south side and the other of the southeast corner, particularly the fifth- and sixth-floor windows.[25] These pictures show three Negro men in windows on the fifth floor and the partially open window on the sixth floor directly above them. (See Dillard Exhibits C and D, pp. 66–67.) Couch also saw the rifle in the window, and testified:

> And after the third shot, Bob Jackson, who was, as I recall, on my right, yelled something like, "Look up in the window! There's the rifle!"
> And I remember glancing up to a window on the far right, which at the time impressed me as the sixth or seventh floor, and seeing about a foot of a rifle being—the barrel brought into the window.[26]

Couch testified he saw people standing in other windows on the third or fourth floor in the middle of the south side, one of them being a Negro in a white T-shirt leaning out to look up at the windows above him.[27]

Mayor and Mrs. Earle Cabell rode in the motorcade immediately behind the Vice-Presidential followup car.[28] Mrs. Cabell was seated in the back seat behind the driver and was facing U.S. Representative Ray Roberts on her right as the car made the turn at Elm and Houston. In this position Mrs. Cabell "was actually facing" the seven-story Depository when the first shot rang out.[29] She "jerked" her head up immediately and saw a "projection" in the first group of windows on a floor which she described both as the sixth floor and the top floor.[30] According to Mrs. Cabell, the object was "rather long looking," but she was unable to determine whether it was a mechanical object or a person's arm.[31] She turned away from the window to tell her husband that the noise was a shot, and "just as I got the words out * * * the second two shots rang out."[32] Mrs. Cabell did not look at the sixth-floor window when the second and third shots were fired.[33]

Tom C. Dillard   Exhibit C

DILLARD EXHIBIT C
Enlargement of photograph taken by Thomas C. Dillard on November 22, 1963.

DILLARD EXHIBIT D
Photograph taken by Thomas C. Dillard on November 22, 1963.

James N. Crawford and Mary Ann Mitchell, two deputy district clerks for Dallas County, watched the motorcade at the southeast corner of Elm and Houston. After the President's car turned the corner, Crawford heard a loud report which he thought was backfire coming from the direction of the Triple Underpass.[34] He heard a second shot seconds later, followed quickly by a third. At the third shot, he looked up and saw a "movement" in the far east corner of the sixth floor of the Depository, the only open window on that floor.[35] He told Miss Mitchell "that if those were shots they came from that window." When asked to describe the movement more exactly, he said,

> * * * I would say that it was a profile, somewhat from the waist up, but it was a very quick movement and rather indistinct and it was very light colored. * * *

> *   *   *   *   *   *   *

> When I saw it, I automatically in my mind came to the conclusion that it was a person having moved out of the window. * * * [36]

He could not state whether the person was a man or a woman.[37] Miss Mitchell confirmed that after the third shot Crawford told her, "Those shots came from that building." [38] She saw Crawford pointing at a window but was not sure at which window he was pointing.[39]

On the Fifth Floor

Three Depository employees shown in the picture taken by Dillard were on the fifth floor of the building when the shots were fired: James Jarman, Jr., age 34, a wrapper in the shipping department; Bonnie Ray Williams, age 20, a warehouseman temporarily assigned to laying a plywood floor on the sixth floor; and Harold Norman, age 26, an "order filler." Norman and Jarman decided to watch the parade during the lunch hour from the fifth-floor windows.[40] From the ground floor they took the west elevator, which operates with push-button controls, to the fifth floor.[41] Meanwhile, Williams had gone up to the sixth floor where he had been working and ate his lunch on the south side of that floor. Since he saw no one around when he finished his lunch, he started down on the east elevator, looking for company. He left behind his paper lunch sack, chicken bones and an empty pop bottle.[42] Williams went down to the fifth floor, where he joined Norman and Jarman at approximately 12:20 p.m.[43]

Harold Norman was in the fifth-floor window in the southeast corner, directly under the window where witnesses saw the rifle. (See Commission Exhibit No. 485, p. 69.) He could see light through the ceiling cracks between the fifth and sixth floors.[44] As the motorcade went by, Norman thought that the President was saluting with his right arm,

COMMISSION EXHIBIT No. 485

Positions occupied by Depository employees on fifth floor on November 22, 1963.

* * * and I can't remember what the exact time was but I know I heard a shot, and then after I heard the shot, well, it seems as though the President, you know, slumped or something, and then another shot and I believe Jarman or someone told me, he said, "I believe someone is shooting at the President," and I think I made a statement "It is someone shooting at the President, and I believe it came from up above us."

Well, I couldn't see at all during the time but I know I heard a third shot fired, and I could also hear something sounded like the shell hulls hitting the floor and the ejecting of the rifle * * *.[45]

Williams said that he "really did not pay any attention" to the first shot—

* * * because I did not know what was happening. The second shot, it sounded like it was right in the building, the second and third shot. And it sounded—it even shook the building, the side we were on. Cement fell on my head.

Q. You say cement fell on your head?

A. Cement, gravel, dirt, or something, from the old building, because it shook the windows and everything. Harold was sitting next to me, and he said it came right from over our head.[46]

Williams testified Norman said "I can even hear the shell being ejected from the gun hitting the floor." [47]

When Jarman heard the first sound, he thought that it was either a backfire—

* * * or an officer giving a salute to the President. And then at that time I didn't, you know, think too much about it. * * *

*   *   *   *   *   *   *

Well, after the third shot was fired, I think I got up and I run over to Harold Norman and Bonnie Ray Williams, and told them, I said, I told them that it wasn't a backfire or anything, that somebody was shooting at the President.[48]

Jarman testified that Norman said "that he thought the shots had come from above us, and I noticed that Bonnie Ray had a few debris in his head. It was sort of white stuff, or something." [49] Jarman stated that Norman said "that he was sure that the shot came from inside the building because he had been used to guns and all that, and he said it didn't sound like it was too far off anyway." [50] The three men ran to the west side of the building, where they could look toward the Triple Underpass to see what had happened to the motorcade.[51]

After the men had gone to the window on the west side of the building, Jarman "got to thinking about all the debris on Bonnie Ray's head" and said, "That shot probably did come from upstairs, up over us." [52] He testified that Norman said, "I know it did, because I could hear the action of the bolt, and I could hear the cartridges drop on the floor." [53] After pausing for a few minutes, the three men ran downstairs. Norman and Jarman ran out of the front entrance of the building, where they saw Brennan, the construction worker who had seen the man in the window firing the gun, talking to a police officer, and they then reported their own experience. [54]

On March 20, 1964, preceding their appearance before the Commission, these witnesses were interviewed in Dallas. At that time members of the Commission's legal staff conducted an experiment. Norman, Williams, and Jarman placed themselves at the windows of the fifth floor as they had been on November 22. A Secret Service agent operated the bolt of a rifle directly above them at the southeast corner window of the sixth floor. At the same time, three cartridge shells were dropped to the floor at intervals of about 3 seconds. According to Norman, the noise outside was less on the day of the assassination than on the day of the test. [55] He testified, "Well, I heard the same sound, the sound similar. I heard three something that he dropped on the floor and then I could hear the rifle or whatever he had up there." [56] The experiment with the shells and rifle was repeated for members of the Commission on May 9, 1964, on June 7, 1964, and again on September 6, 1964. All seven of the Commissioners clearly heard the shells drop to the floor.

At the Triple Underpass

In contrast to the testimony of the witnesses who heard and observed shots fired from the Depository, the Commission's investigation has disclosed no credible evidence that any shots were fired from anywhere else. When the shots were fired, many people near the Depository believed that the shots came from the railroad bridge over the Triple Underpass or from the area to the west of the Depository. [57] In the hectic moments after the assassination, many spectators ran in the general direction of the Triple Underpass or the railroad yards northwest of the building. Some were running toward the place from which the sound of the rifle fire appeared to come, others were fleeing the scene of the shooting. [58] None of these people saw anyone with a rifle, and the Commission's inquiry has yielded no evidence that shots were fired from the bridge over the Triple Underpass or from the railroad yards.

On the day of the motorcade, Patrolman J. W. Foster stood on the east side of the railroad bridge over the Triple Underpass and Patrolman J. C. White stood on the west side. [59] Patrolman Joe E. Murphy was standing over Elm Street on the Stemmons Freeway overpass, west of the railroad bridge farther away from the Depository. [60] Two other officers were stationed on Stemmons Freeway to control traffic as the motorcade entered the Freeway. [61] Under the advance preparations worked out between the Secret Service and the Dallas Police Department, the policemen were under instructions to keep "unauthorized" people away from these locations. [62] When the motorcade reached the intersection of Elm and Houston Streets, there were no spectators on Stemmons Freeway where Patrolman Murphy was stationed.[63] Patrolman Foster estimated that there were 10 or 11 people on the railroad bridge where he was assigned; [64] another witness testified that there were between 14 and 18 people there as the motorcade came into view.[65] Investigation has disclosed 15 persons who were on the railroad bridge at this time, including 2 policemen, 2 employees of the Texas-Louisiana Freight Bureau and 11 employees of the Union Terminal Co.[66] In the absence of any explicit definition of "unauthorized" persons, the policemen permitted these employees to remain on the railroad bridge to watch the motorcade. (See chapter VIII, pp. 446–447.) At the request of the policemen, S. M. Holland, signal supervisor for Union Terminal Co., came to the railroad bridge at about 11:45 a.m. and remained to identify those persons who were railroad employees.[67] In addition, Patrolman Foster checked credentials to determine if persons seeking access to the bridge were railroad employees.[68] Persons who were not railroad employees were ordered away, including one news photographer who wished only to take a picture of the motorcade.[69]

Another employee of the Union Terminal Co., Lee E. Bowers, Jr., was at work in a railroad tower about 14 feet above the tracks to the north of the railroad bridge and northwest of the corner of Elm and Houston, approximately 50 yards from the back of the Depository.[70] (See Commission Exhibit No. 2218, p. 73.) From the tower he could view people moving in the railroad yards and at the rear of the Depository. According to Bowers, "Since approximately 10 o'clock in the morning traffic had been cut off into the area so that anyone moving around could actually be observed." [71] During the 20 minutes prior to the arrival of the motorcade, Bowers noticed three automobiles which entered his immediate area; two left without discharging any passengers and the third was apparently on its way out when last observed by Bowers.[72] Bowers observed only three or four people in the general area, as well as a few bystanders on the railroad bridge over the Triple Underpass.[73]

As the motorcade proceeded toward the Triple Underpass, the spectators were clustered together along the east concrete wall of the railroad bridge facing the oncoming procession.[74] (See Commission Exhibit No. 2215, p. 75.) Patrolman Foster stood immediately behind them and could observe all of them.[75] Secret Service agents in the lead car of the motorcade observed the bystanders and the police officer on the bridge.[76] Special Agent Winston G. Lawson motioned through the windshield in an unsuccessful attempt to instruct Patrolman Foster to move the people away from their position directly over the path of the motorcade.[77] Some distance away, on the Stemmons Freeway overpass above Elm Street, Patrolman Murphy also had the group on the railroad bridge within view.[78] When he heard the shots, Foster rushed to the wall of the railroad bridge over the Triple Underpass and looked toward the street.[79] After the third shot, Foster ran toward the Depository and shortly thereafter informed

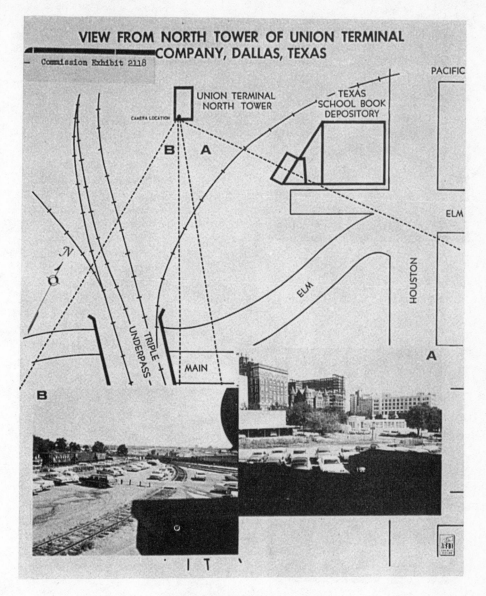

VIEW FROM NORTH TOWER OF UNION TERMINAL COMPANY, DALLAS, TEXAS

COMMISSION EXHIBIT No. 2118

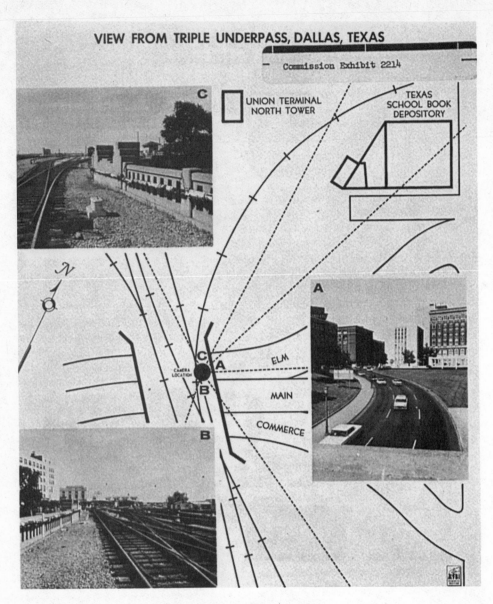

VIEW FROM TRIPLE UNDERPASS, DALLAS, TEXAS

Commission Exhibit 2214

COMMISSION EXHIBIT No. 2214

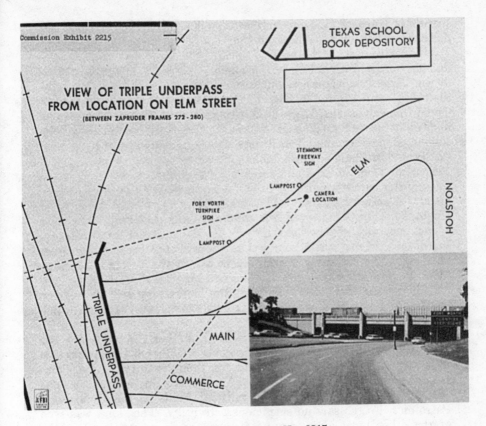

COMMISSION EXHIBIT No. 2215

Inspector Herbert J. Sawyer of the Dallas Police Department that he thought the shots came from the vicinity of Elm and Houston.[80]

Other witnesses on the railroad bridge had varying views concerning the source and number of the shots. Austin L. Miller, employed by the Texas-Louisiana Freight Bureau, heard three shots and thought that they came from the area of the Presidential limousine itself.[81] One of his coworkers, Royce G. Skelton, thought he heard four shots, but could not tell their exact source.[82] Frank E. Reilly, an electrician at Union Terminal, heard three shots which seemed to come from the trees "On the north side of Elm Street at the corner up there." [83] According to S. M. Holland, there were four shots which sounded as though they came from the trees on the north side of Elm Street where he saw a puff of smoke.[84] Thomas J. Murphy, a mail foreman at Union Terminal Co., heard two shots and said that they came from a spot just west of the Depository.[85] In the railroad tower, Bowers heard three shots, which sounded as though they came either from the Depository Building or near the mouth of the Triple Underpass. Prior to November 22, 1963, Bowers had noted the similarity of the sounds coming from the vicinity of the Depository and those from the Triple Underpass, which he attributed to "a reverberation which takes place from either location." [86]

Immediately after the shots were fired, neither the policemen nor the spectators on the railroad bridge over the Triple Underpass saw anything suspicious on the bridge in their vicinity. (See Commission Exhibit No. 2214, p. 74.) No one saw anyone with a rifle. As he ran around through the railroad yards to the Depository, Patrolman Foster saw no suspicious activity.[87] The same was true of the other bystanders, many of whom made an effort after the shooting to observe any unusual activity. Holland, for example, immediately after the shots, ran off the overpass to see if there was anyone behind the picket fence on the north side of Elm Street, but he did not see anyone among the parked cars.[88] Miller did not see anyone running across the railroad tracks or on the plaza west of the Depository.[89] Bowers and others saw a motorcycle officer dismount hurriedly and come running up the incline on the north side of Elm Street.[90] The motorcycle officer, Clyde A. Haygood, saw no one running from the railroad yards.[91]

THE PRESIDENTIAL AUTOMOBILE

After the Presidential car was returned to Washington on November 22, 1963, Secret Service agents found two bullet fragments in the front seat. One fragment, found on the seat beside the driver, weighed 44.6 grains and consisted of the nose portion of a bullet.[92] The other fragment, found along the right side of the front seat, weighed 21.0 grains and consisted of the base portion of a bullet.[93] During the course of an examination on November 23, agents of the Federal Bureau of Investigation found three small lead particles, weighing between seven-tenths and nine-tenths of a grain each, on the rug underneath the left jump seat which had been occupied by Mrs. Connally.[94] During this examination, the Bureau agents noted a small residue of lead on the inside surface of the laminated windshield and a very small pattern of cracks on the outer layer of the windshield immediately behind the lead residue.[95] There was a minute particle of glass missing from the outside surface, but no penetration. The inside layer of glass was not broken.[96] The agents also observed a dent in the strip of chrome across the top of the windshield, located to the left of the rear view mirror support.[97]

The lead residue on the inside of the windshield was compared under spectrographic analysis by FBI experts with the bullet fragments found on and alongside the front seat and with the fragments under the left jump seat. It was also compared with bullet fragments found at Parkland Hospital. All these bullet fragments were found to be similar in metallic composition, but it was not possible to determine whether two or more of the fragments came from the same bullet.[98] It is possible for the fragments from the front seat to have been a part of the same bullet as the three fragments found near the left jump seat,[99] since a whole bullet of this type weighs 160–161 grains.[100] (See app. X, pp. 555–558.)

The physical characteristics of the windshield after the assassination demonstrate that the windshield was struck on the inside surface. The windshield is composed of two layers of glass with a very thin layer of plastic in the middle "which bonds them together in the form of safety glass." [101] The windshield was extracted from the automobile and was examined during a Commission hearing.[102] (See Commission Exhibit No. 350, p. 78.) According to Robert A. Frazier, FBI firearms expert, the fact that cracks were present on the outer layer of glass showed that the glass had been struck from the inside. He testified that the windshield

> could not have been struck on the outside surface because of the manner in which the glass broke and further because of the lead residue on the inside surface. The cracks appear in the outer layer of the glass because the glass is bent outward at the time of impact which stretches the outer layer of the glass to the point where these small radial or wagon spoke, wagon wheel spoke-type cracks appear on the outer surface.[103]

Although there is some uncertainty whether the dent in the chrome on the windshield was present prior to the assassination,[104] Frazier testified that the dent "had been caused by some projectile which struck the chrome on the inside surface." [105] If it was caused by a shot during the assassination, Frazier stated that it would not have been caused by a bullet traveling at full velocity, but rather by a fragment traveling at "fairly high velocity." [106] It could have been caused by either fragment found in the front seat of the limousine.[107]

COMMISSION EXHIBIT No. 350

Windshield of Presidential limousine.

EXPERT EXAMINATION OF RIFLE, CARTRIDGE CASES, AND BULLET FRAGMENTS

On the sixth floor of the Depository Building, the Dallas police found three spent cartridges and a rifle. A nearly whole bullet was discovered on the stretcher used to carry Governor Connally at Parkland Hospital. As described in the preceding section, five bullet fragments were found in the President's limousine. The cartridge cases, the nearly whole bullet and the bullet fragments were all subjected to firearms identification analysis by qualified experts. It was the unanimous opinion of the experts that the nearly whole bullet, the two largest bullet fragments and the three cartridge cases were definitely fired in the rifle found on the sixth floor of the Depository Building to the exclusion of all other weapons.

Discovery of Cartridge Cases and Rifle

Shortly after the assassination, police officers arrived at the Depository Building and began a search for the assassin and evidence.[108] Around 1 p.m. Deputy Sheriff Luke Mooney noticed a pile of cartons in front of the window in the southeast corner of the sixth floor.[109] (See Commission Exhibit No. 723, p. 80.) Searching that area he found at approximately 1:12 p.m. three empty cartridge cases on the floor near the window.[110] When he was notified of Mooney's discovery, Capt. J. W. Fritz, chief of the homicide bureau of the Dallas Police Department, issued instructions that nothing be moved or touched until technicians from the police crime laboratory could take photographs and check for fingerprints.[111] Mooney stood guard to see that nothing was disturbed.[112] A few minutes later, Lt. J. C. Day of the Dallas Police Department arrived and took photographs of the cartridge cases before anything had been moved.[113]

At 1:22 p.m. Deputy Sheriff Eugene Boone and Deputy Constable Seymour Weitzman found a bolt-action rifle with a telescopic sight between two rows of boxes in the northwest corner near the staircase on the sixth floor.[114] No one touched the weapon or otherwise disturbed the scene until Captain Fritz and Lieutenant Day arrived and the weapon was photographed as it lay on the floor.[115] After Lieutenant Day determined that there were no fingerprints on the knob of the bolt and that the wooden stock was too rough to take fingerprints, he picked the rifle up by the stock and held it that way while Captain Fritz opened the bolt and ejected a live round.[116] Lieutenant Day retained possession of the weapon and took it back to the police department for examination.[117] Neither Boone nor Weitzman handled the rifle.[118]

Discovery of Bullet at Parkland Hospital

A nearly whole bullet was found on Governor Connally's stretcher at Parkland Hospital after the assassination. After his arrival at the hospital the Governor was brought into trauma room No. 2 on a

COMMISSION EXHIBIT No. 723

Shield of cartons around sixth floor southeast corner window.

stretcher, removed from the room on that stretcher a short time later, and taken on an elevator to the second-floor operating room.[119] On the second floor he was transferred from the stretcher to an operating table which was then moved into the operating room, and a hospital attendant wheeled the empty stretcher into an elevator.[120] Shortly afterward, Darrell C. Tomlinson, the hospital's senior engineer, removed this stretcher from the elevator and placed it in the corridor on the ground floor, alongside another stretcher wholly unconnected with the care of Governor Connally.[121] A few minutes later, he bumped one of the stretchers against the wall and a bullet rolled out.[122]

Although Tomlinson was not certain whether the bullet came from the Connally stretcher or the adjacent one, the Commission has concluded that the bullet came from the Governor's stretcher. That conclusion is buttressed by evidence which eliminated President Kennedy's stretcher as a source of the bullet. President Kennedy remained on the stretcher on which he was carried into the hospital while the doctors tried to save his life.[123] He was never removed from the stretcher from the time he was taken into the emergency room until his body was placed in a casket in that same room.[124] After the President's body was removed from that stretcher, the linen was taken off and placed in a hamper and the stretcher was pushed into trauma room No. 2, a completely different location from the site where the nearly whole bullet was found.[125]

Description of Rifle

The bolt-action, clip-fed rifle found on the sixth floor of the Depository, described more fully in appendix X, is inscribed with various markings, including "MADE ITALY," "CAL. 6.5," "1940" and the number C2766.[126] (See Commission Exhibit Nos. 1303, 541(2) and 541(3), pp. 82–83.) These markings have been explained as follows: "MADE ITALY" refers to its origin; "CAL. 6.5" refers to the rifle's caliber; "1940" refers to the year of manufacture; and the number C2766 is the serial number. This rifle is the only one of its type bearing that serial number.[127] After review of standard reference works and the markings on the rifle, it was identified by the FBI as a 6.5-millimeter model 91/38 Mannlicher-Carcano rifle.[128] Experts from the FBI made an independent determination of the caliber by inserting a Mannlicher-Carcano 6.5-millimeter cartridge into the weapon for fit, and by making a sulfur cast of the inside of the weapon's barrel and measuring the cast with a micrometer.[129] From outward appearance, the weapon would appear to be a 7.35-millimeter rifle, but its mechanism had been rebarreled with a 6.5-millimeter barrel.[130] Constable Deputy Sheriff Weitzman, who only saw the rifle at a glance and did not handle it, thought the weapon looked like a 7.65 Mauser bolt-action rifle.[131] (See chapter V, p. 235.)

The rifle is 40.2 inches long and weighs 8 pounds.[132] The minimum length broken down is 34.8 inches, the length of the wooden stock.[133]

COMMISSION EXHIBIT No. 1303

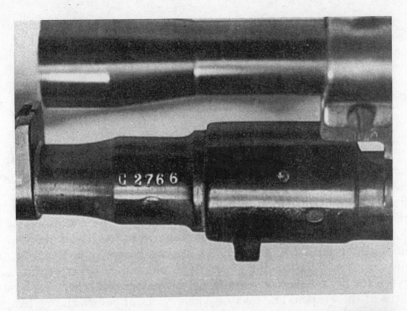

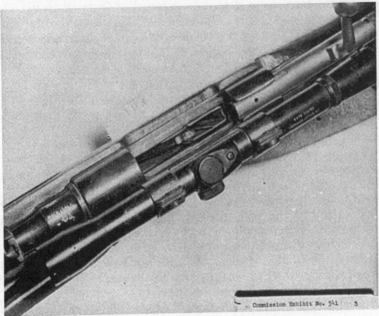

COMMISSION EXHIBITS Nos. 541(2) AND 541(3)
Photograph of markings on C2766 Mannlicher-Carcano rifle.

(See Commission Exhibit No. 1304, p. 132.) Attached to the weapon is an inexpensive four-power telescopic sight, stamped "Optics Ordnance Inc./Hollywood California," and "Made in Japan." [134] The weapon also bears a sling consisting of two leather straps. The sling is not a standard rifle sling but appears to be a musical instrument strap or a sling from a carrying case or camera bag. [135]

Expert Testimony

Four experts in the field of firearms identification analyzed the nearly whole bullet, the two largest fragments and the three cartridge cases to determine whether they had been fired from the C2766 Mannlicher-Carcano rifle found on the sixth floor of the Depository. Two of these experts testified before the Commission. One was Robert A. Frazier, a special agent of the FBI assigned to the FBI Laboratory in Washington, D.C. Frazier has worked generally in the field of firearms identification for 23 years, examining firearms of various types for the purpose of identifying the caliber and other characteristics of the weapons and making comparisons of bullets and cartridge cases for the purpose of determining whether or not they were fired in a particular weapon. [136] He estimated that he has made "in the neighborhood of 50,000 to 60,000" firearms comparisons and has testified in court on about 400 occasions. [137] The second witness who testified on this subject was Joseph D. Nicol, superintendent of the bureau of criminal identification and investigation for the State of Illinois. Nicol also has had long and substantial experience since 1941 in firearms identification, and estimated that he has made thousands of bullet and cartridge case examinations. [138]

In examining the bullet fragments and cartridge cases, these experts applied the general principles accepted in the field of firearms identification, which are discussed in more detail in appendix X at pages 547–553. In brief, a determination that a particular bullet or cartridge case has been fired in a particular weapon is based upon a comparison of the bullet or case under examination with one or more bullets or cases known to have been fired in that weapon. When a bullet is fired in any given weapon, it is engraved with the characteristics of the weapon. In addition to the rifling characteristics of the barrel which are common to all weapons of a given make and model, every weapon bears distinctive microscopic markings on its barrel, firing pin and bolt face. [139] These markings arise initially during manufacture, since the action of the manufacturing tools differs microscopically from weapon to weapon and since, in addition, the tools change microscopically while being used. As a weapon is used further distinctive markings are introduced. Under microscopic examination a qualified expert may be able to determine whether the markings on a bullet known to have been fired in a particular weapon and the markings on a suspect bullet are the same and, therefore, whether both bullets were fired in the same weapon to the exclusion of all other weapons. Similarly, firearms identification experts are able to compare the markings left upon the base of cartridge cases and thereby determine whether both cartridges were fired by the same weapon to the exclusion of all other weapons. According to Frazier, such an identification "is made on the presence of sufficient individual microscopic characteristics so that a very definite pattern is formed and visualized on the two surfaces." [140] Under some circumstances, as where the bullet or cartridge case is seriously mutilated, there are not sufficient individual characteristics to enable the expert to make a firm identification. [141]

After making independent examinations, both Frazier and Nicol positively identified the nearly whole bullet from the stretcher and the two larger bullet fragments found in the Presidential limousine as having been fired in the C2766 Mannlicher-Carcano rifle found in the Depository to the exclusion of all other weapons. [142] Each of the two bullet fragments had sufficient unmutilated area to provide the basis for an identification. [143] However, it was not possible to determine whether the two bullet fragments were from the same bullet or from two different bullets. [144] With regard to the other bullet fragments discovered in the limousine and in the course of treating President Kennedy and Governor Connally, however, expert examination could demonstrate only that the fragments were "similar in metallic composition" to each other, to the two larger fragments and to the nearly whole bullet. [145] After examination of the three cartridge cases found on the sixth floor of the Depository, Frazier and Nicol concluded that they had been fired in the C2766 Mannlicher-Carcano rifle to the exclusion of all other weapons. [146] Two other experts from the Federal Bureau of Investigation, who made independent examinations of the nearly whole bullet, bullet fragments and cartridge cases, reached the identical conclusions. [147]

THE BULLET WOUNDS

In considering the question of the source of the shots fired at President Kennedy and Governor Connally, the Commission has also evaluated the expert medical testimony of the doctors who observed the wounds during the emergency treatment at Parkland Hospital and during the autopsy at Bethesda Naval Hospital. It paid particular attention to any wound characteristics which would be of assistance in identifying a wound as the entrance or exit point of a missile. Additional information regarding the source and nature of the injuries was obtained by expert examination of the clothes worn by the two men, particularly those worn by President Kennedy, and from the results of special wound ballistics tests conducted at the Commission's request, using the C2766 Mannlicher-Carcano rifle with ammunition of the same type as that used and found on November 22, 1963.

The President's Head Wounds

The detailed autopsy of President Kennedy performed on the night of November 22 at the Bethesda Naval Hospital led the three examining pathologists to conclude that the smaller hole in the rear of the President's skull was the point of entry and that the large opening on the right side of his head was the wound of exit.[148] The smaller hole on the back of the President's head measured one-fourth of an inch by five-eighths of an inch (6 by 15 millimeters).[149] The dimensions of that wound were consistent with having been caused by a 6.5-millimeter bullet fired from behind and above which struck at a tangent or an angle causing a 15-millimeter cut. The cut reflected a larger dimension of entry than the bullet's diameter of 6.5 millimeters, since the missile, in effect, sliced along the skull for a fractional distance until it entered.[150] The dimension of 6 millimeters, somewhat smaller than the diameter of a 6.5-millimeter bullet, was caused by the elastic recoil of the skull which shrinks the size of an opening after a missile passes through it.[151]

Lt. Col. Pierre A. Finck, Chief of the Wound Ballistics Pathology Branch of the Armed Forces Institute of Pathology, who has had extensive experience with bullet wounds, illustrated the characteristics which led to his conclusions about the head wound by a chart prepared by him. This chart, based on Colonel Finck's studies of more than 400 cases, depicted the effect of a perforating missile wound on the human skull.[152] When a bullet enters the skull (cranial vault) at one point and exits at another, it causes a beveling or cratering effect where the diameter of the hole is smaller on the impact side than on the exit side. Based on his observations of that beveling effect on the President's skull, Colonel Finck testified: "President Kennedy was, in my opinion, shot from the rear. The bullet entered in the back of the head and went out on the right side of his skull * * * he was shot from above and behind." [153]

Comdr. James J. Humes, senior pathologist and director of laboratories at the Bethesda Naval Hospital, who acted as chief autopsy surgeon, concurred in Colonel Finck's analysis. He compared the beveling or coning effect to that caused by a BB shot which strikes a pane of glass, causing a round or oval defect on the side of the glass where the missile strikes and a belled-out or coned-out surface on the opposite side of the glass.[154] Referring to the bullet hole on the back of President Kennedy's head, Commander Humes testified: "The wound on the inner table, however, was larger and had what in the field of wound ballistics is described as a shelving or coning effect." [155] After studying the other hole in the President's skull, Commander Humes stated: "* * * we concluded that the large defect to the upper right side of the skull, in fact, would represent a wound of exit." [156] Those characteristics led Commander Humes and Comdr. J. Thornton Boswell, chief of pathology at Bethesda Naval Hospital, who assisted in the autopsy, to conclude that the bullet penetrated the rear of the President's head and exited through a large wound on the right side of his head.[157]

Ballistics experiments (discussed more fully in app. X, pp. 585–586) showed that the rifle and bullets identified above were capable of producing the President's head wound. The Wound Ballistics Branch of the U.S. Army laboratories at Edgewood Arsenal, Md., conducted an extensive series of experiments to test the effect of Western Cartridge Co. 6.5-millimeter bullets, the type found on Governor Connally's stretcher and in the Presidential limousine, fired from the C2766 Mannlicher-Carcano rifle found in the Depository. The Edgewood Arsenal tests were performed under the immediate supervision of Alfred G. Olivier, a doctor who had spent 7 years in wounds ballistics research for the U.S. Army.[158]

One series of tests, performed on reconstructed inert human skulls, demonstrated that the President's head wound could have been caused by the rifle and bullets fired by the assassin from the sixth-floor window. The results of this series were illustrated by the findings on one skull which was struck at a point closely approximating the wound of entry on President Kennedy's head. That bullet blew out the right side of the reconstructed skull in a manner very similar to the head wound of the President.[159] As a result of these tests, Dr. Olivier concluded that a Western Cartridge Co. 6.5 bullet fired from the C2766 Mannlicher-Carcano rifle at a distance of 90 yards would make the same type of wound as that found on the President's head. Referring to the series of tests, Dr. Olivier testified:

> It disclosed that the type of head wounds that the President received could be done by this type of bullet. This surprised me very much, because this type of stable bullet I didn't think would cause a massive head wound, I thought it would go through making a small entrance and exit, but the bones of the skull are enough to deform the end of this bullet causing it to expend a lot of energy and blowing out the side of the skull or blowing out fragments of the skull.[160]

After examining the fragments of the bullet which struck the reconstructed skull, Dr. Olivier stated that—

> the recovered fragments were very similar to the ones recovered on the front seat and on the floor of the car.
> This, to me, indicates that those fragments did come from the bullet that wounded the President in the head.[161]

The President's Neck Wounds

During the autopsy at Bethesda Naval Hospital another bullet wound was observed near the base of the back of President Kennedy's neck slightly to the right of his spine which provides further enlightenment as to the source of the shots. The hole was located approximately 5½ inches (14 centimeters) from the tip of the right shoulder joint and approximately the same distance below the tip of the right mastoid process, the bony point immediately behind the ear.[162] The wound was approximately one-fourth by one-seventh of an inch (7 by 4 millimeters), had clean edges, was sharply delineated, and had margins similar in all respects to those of the entry wound in the skull.[163] Commanders Humes and Boswell agreed with Colonel Finck's testimony that this hole—

> * * * is a wound of entrance. * * * The basis for that conclusion is that this wound was relatively small with clean edges. It was not a jagged wound, and that is what we see in wound of entrance at a long range.[164]

The autopsy examination further disclosed that, after entering the President, the bullet passed between two large muscles, produced a contusion on the upper part of the pleural cavity (without penetrating that cavity), bruised the top portion of the right lung and ripped the windpipe (trachea) in its path through the President's neck.[165] The examining surgeons concluded that the wounds were caused by the bullet rather than the tracheotomy performed at Parkland Hospital. The nature of the bruises indicated that the President's heart and lungs were functioning when the bruises were caused, whereas there was very little circulation in the President's body when incisions on the President's chest were made to insert tubes during the tracheotomy.[166] No bone was struck by the bullet which passed through the President's body.[167] By projecting from a point of entry on the rear of the neck and proceeding at a slight downward angle through the bruised interior portions, the doctors concluded that the bullet exited from the front portion of the President's neck that had been cut away by the tracheotomy.[168]

Concluding that a bullet passed through the President's neck, the doctors at Bethesda Naval Hospital rejected a theory that the bullet lodged in the large muscles in the back of his neck and fell out through the point of entry when external heart massage was applied at Parkland Hospital. In the earlier stages of the autopsy, the surgeons were unable to find a path into any large muscle in the back of the neck. At that time they did not know that there had been a bullet hole in the front of the President's neck when he arrived at Parkland Hospital because the tracheotomy incision had completely eliminated that evidence.[169] While the autopsy was being performed, surgeons learned that a whole bullet had been found at Parkland Hospital on a stretcher which, at that time, was thought to be the stretcher occupied by the President. This led to speculation that the bullet might have penetrated a short distance into the back of the neck and then dropped out onto the stretcher as a result of the external heart massage.[170]

Further exploration during the autopsy disproved that theory. The surgeons determined that the bullet had passed between two large strap muscles and bruised them without leaving any channel, since the bullet

88

merely passed between them.[171]   Commander Humes, who believed that a tracheotomy had been performed from his observations at the autopsy, talked by telephone with Dr. Perry early on the morning of November 23, and learned that his assumption was correct and that Dr. Perry had used the missile wound in the neck as the point to make the incision.[172]   This confirmed the Bethesda surgeons' conclusion that the bullet had exited from the front part of the neck.

The findings of the doctors who conducted the autopsy were consistent with the observations of the doctors who treated the President at Parkland Hospital.   Dr. Charles S. Carrico, a resident surgeon at Parkland, noted a small wound approximately one-fourth of an inch in diameter (5 to 8 millimeters) in the lower third of the neck below the Adam's apple.[173]   Dr. Malcolm O. Perry, who performed the tracheotomy, described the wound as approximately one-fifth of an inch in diameter (5 millimeters) and exuding blood which partially hid edges that were "neither cleancut, that is, punched out, nor were they very ragged." [174]   Dr. Carrico testified as follows:

Q. Based on your observations on the neck wound alone did you have a sufficient basis to form an opinion as to whether it was an entrance or an exit wound?
A. No, sir; we did not.   Not having completely evaluated all the wounds, traced out the course of the bullets, this wound would have been compatible with either entrance or exit wound depending upon the size, the velocity, the tissue structure and so forth.[175]

The same response was made by Dr. Perry to a similar query:

Q. Based on the appearance of the neck wound alone, could it have been either an entrance or an exit wound?
A. It could have been either.[176]

Then each doctor was asked to take into account the other known facts, such as the autopsy findings, the approximate distance the bullet traveled and tested muzzle velocity of the assassination weapon.   With these additional factors, the doctors commented on the wound on the front of the President's neck as follows:

Dr. CARRICO. With those facts and the fact as I understand it no other bullet was found this would be, this was, I believe, was an exit wound.[177]
Dr. PERRY. A full jacketed bullet without deformation passing through skin would leave a similar wound for an exit and entrance wound and with the facts which you have made available and with these assumptions, I believe that it was an exit wound.[178]

Other doctors at Parkland Hospital who observed the wound prior to the tracheotomy agreed with the observations of Drs. Perry and Carrico.[179]   The bullet wound in the neck could be seen for only a short time, since Dr. Perry eliminated evidence of it when he performed

730-900 O-64—8

the tracheotomy. He selected that spot since it was the point where such an operation was customarily performed, and it was one of the safest and easiest spots from which to reach the trachea. In addition, there was possibly an underlying wound to the muscles in the neck, the carotid artery or the jugular vein, and Dr. Perry concluded that the incision, therefore, had to be low in order to maintain respiration.[180]

Considerable confusion has arisen because of comments attributed to Dr. Perry concerning the nature of the neck wound. Immediately after the assassination, many people reached erroneous conclusions about the source of the shots because of Dr. Perry's observations to the press. On the afternoon of November 22, a press conference was organized at Parkland Hospital by members of the White House press staff and a hospital administrator. Newsmen with microphones and cameras were crowded into a room to hear statements by Drs. Perry and William Kemp Clark, chief neurosurgeon at Parkland, who had attended to President Kennedy's head injury. Dr. Perry described the situation as "bedlam." [181] The confusion was compounded by the fact that some questions were only partially answered before other questions were asked.[182]

At the news conference, Dr. Perry answered a series of hypothetical questions and stated to the press that a variety of possibilities could account for the President's wounds. He stated that a single bullet could have caused the President's wounds by entering through the throat, striking the spine, and being deflected upward with the point of exit being through the head.[183] This would have accounted for the two wounds he observed, the hole in the front of the neck and the large opening in the skull. At that time, Dr. Perry did not know about either the wound on the back of the President's neck or the small bullet-hole wound in the back of the head. As described in chapter II, the President was lying on his back during his entire time at Parkland. The small hole in the head was also hidden from view by the large quantity of blood which covered the President's head. Dr. Perry said his answers at the press conference were intended to convey his theory about what could have happened, based on his limited knowledge at the time, rather than his professional opinion about what did happen.[184] Commenting on his answers at the press conference, Dr. Perry testified before the Commission:

> I expressed it [his answers] as a matter of speculation that this was conceivable. But, again, Dr. Clark [who also answered questions at the conference] and I emphasized that we had no way of knowing.[185]

Dr. Perry's recollection of his comments is corroborated by some of the news stories after the press conference. The New York Herald Tribune on November 23, 1963, reported as follows:

> Dr. Malcolm Perry, 34, attendant surgeon at Parkland Hospital who attended the President, said he saw two wounds—

one below the Adam's apple, the other at the back of the head. He said he did not know if two bullets were involved. It is possible, he said, that the neck wound was the entrance and the other the exit of the missile.[186]

According to this report, Dr. Perry stated merely that it was "possible" that the neck wound was a wound of entrance. This conforms with his testimony before the Commission, where he stated that by themselves the characteristics of the neck wound were consistent with being either a point of entry or exit.

Wound ballistics tests.—Experiments performed by the Army Wound Ballistics experts at Edgewood Arsenal, Md. (discussed in app. X, p. 582) showed that under simulated conditions entry and exit wounds are very similar in appearance. After reviewing the path of the bullet through the President's neck, as disclosed in the autopsy report, the experts simulated the neck by using comparable material with a thickness of approximately 5½ inches (13½ to 14½ centimeters), which was the distance traversed by the bullet. Animal skin was placed on each side, and Western Cartridge Co. 6.5 bullets were fired from the C2766 Mannlicher-Carcano rifle from a distance of 180 feet. The animal skin on the entry side showed holes which were regular and round. On the exit side two holes were only slightly elongated, indicating that the bullet had become only a little unstable at the point of exit.[187] A third exit hole was round, although not quite as regular as the entry holes.[188] The exit holes, especially the one most nearly round, appeared similar to the descriptions given by Drs. Perry and Carrico of the hole in the front of the President's neck.[189]

The autopsy disclosed that the bullet which entered the back of the President's neck hit no bony structure and proceeded in a slightly downward angle. The markings on the President's clothing indicate that the bullet moved in a slight right to left lateral direction as it passed through the President's body.[190] After the examining doctors expressed the thought that a bullet would have lost very little velocity in passing through the soft tissue of the neck, wound ballistics experts conducted tests to measure the exit velocity of the bullet.[191] The tests were the same as those used to create entry and exit holes, supplemented by the use of break-type screens which measured the velocity of bullets. The entrance velocity of the bullet fired from the rifle averaged 1,904 feet per second after it traveled 180 feet. The exit velocity averaged 1,772 to 1,798 feet per second, depending upon the substance through which the bullet passed. A photograph of the path of the bullet traveling through the simulated neck showed that it proceeded in a straight line and was stable.[192]

Examination of clothing.—The clothing worn by President Kennedy on November 22 had holes and tears which showed that a missile entered the back of his clothing in the vicinity of his lower neck and exited through the front of his shirt immediately behind his tie, nicking the knot of his tie in its forward flight.[193] Although the caliber of the bullet could not be determined and some of the clothing items precluded a positive determination that some tears were made by a bullet, all the defects could have been caused by a 6.5-millimeter bullet entering the back of the President's lower neck and exiting in the area of the knot of his tie.[194]

An examination of the suit jacket worn by the President by FBI Agent Frazier revealed a roughly circular hole approximately one-fourth of an inch in diameter on the rear of the coat, 5⅜ inches below the top of the collar and 1¾ inches to the right of the center back seam of the coat.[195] The hole was visible on the upper rear of the coat slightly to the right of center. Traces of copper were found in the margins of the hole and the cloth fibers around the margins were pushed inward.[196] Those characteristics established that the hole was caused by an entering bullet.[197] Although the precise size of the bullet could not be determined from the hole, it was consistent with having been made by a 6.5-millimeter bullet.[198]

The shirt worn by the President contained a hole on the back side 5¾ inches below the top of the collar and 1⅛ inches to the right of the middle of the back of the shirt.[199] The hole on the rear of the shirt was approximately circular in shape and about one-fourth of an inch in diameter, with the fibers pressed inward.[200] These factors established it as a bullet entrance hole.[201] The relative position of the hole in the back of the suit jacket to the hole in the back of the shirt indicated that both were caused by the same penetrating missile.[202]

On the front of the shirt, examination revealed a hole seven-eighths of an inch below the collar button and a similar opening seven-eighths of an inch below the buttonhole. These two holes fell into alinement on overlapping positions when the shirt was buttoned.[203] Each hole was a vertical, ragged slit approximately one-half of an inch in height, with the cloth fibers protruding outward. Although the characteristics of the slit established that the missile had exited to the front, the irregular nature of the slit precluded a positive determination that it was a bullet hole.[204] However, the hole could have been caused by a round bullet although the characteristics were not sufficiently clear to enable the examining expert to render a conclusive opinion.[205]

When the President's clothing was removed at Parkland Hospital, his tie was cut off by severing the loop immediately to the wearer's left of the knot, leaving the knot in its original condition.[206] The tie had a nick on the left side of the knot.[207] The nick was elongated horizontally, indicating that the tear was made by some object moving horizontally, but the fibers were not affected in a manner which would shed light on the direction or the nature of the missile.[208]

The Governor's Wounds

While riding in the right jump seat of the Presidential limousine on November 22, Governor Connally sustained wounds of the back, chest, right wrist and left thigh. Because of the small size and clean-cut edges of the wound on the Governor's back, Dr. Robert Shaw concluded that it was an entry wound.[209] The bullet traversed the Governor's chest in a downward angle, shattering his fifth rib, and exited below the right nipple.[210] The ragged edges of the 2-inch (5 centimeters) opening on the front of the chest led Dr. Shaw to conclude that it was the exit point of the bullet.[211] When Governor Connally testified before the Commission 5 months after the assassination, on April 21, 1964, the Commission observed the Governor's chest wounds, as well as the injuries to his wrist and thigh and watched Dr. Shaw measure with a caliper an angle of declination of 25° from the point of entry on the back to the point of exit on the front of the Governor's chest.[212]

At the time of the shooting, Governor Connally was unaware that he had sustained any injuries other than his chest wounds.[213] On the back of his arm, about 2 inches (5 centimeters) above the wrist joint on the thumb side, Dr. Charles F. Gregory observed a linear perforating wound approximately one-fifth of an inch (one-half centimeter) wide and 1 inch (2½ centimeters) long.[214] During his operation on this injury, the doctor concluded that this ragged wound was the point of entry because thread and cloth had been carried into the wound to the region of the bone.[215] Dr. Gregory's conclusions were also based upon the location in the Governor's wrist, as revealed by X-ray, of small fragments of metal shed by the missile upon striking the firm surface of the bone.[216] Evidence of different amounts of air in the tissues of the wrist gave further indication that the bullet passed from the back to the front of the wrist.[217] An examination of the palm surface of the wrist showed a wound approximately one-fifth of an inch (one-half centimeter) long and approximately three-fourths of an inch (2 centimeters) above the crease of the right wrist.[218] Dr. Shaw had initially believed that the missile entered on the palm side of the Governor's wrist and exited on the back side.[219] After reviewing the factors considered by Dr. Gregory, however, Dr. Shaw withdrew his earlier opinion. He deferred to the judgment of Dr. Gregory, who had more closely examined that wound during the wrist operation.[220]

In addition, Governor Connally suffered a puncture wound in the left thigh that was approximately two-fifths of an inch (1 centimeter) in diameter and located approximately 5 or 6 inches above the Governor's left knee.[221] On the Governor's leg, very little soft-tissue damage was noted, which indicated a tangential wound or the penetration of a larger missile entering at low velocity and stopping after entering the skin.[222] X-ray examination disclosed a tiny metallic fragment embedded in the Governor's leg.[223] The surgeons who attended the Governor concluded that the thigh wound was not caused by the small fragment in the thigh but resulted from the impact of a larger missile.[224]

Examination of clothing.—The clothing worn by Governor Connally on November 22, 1963, contained holes which matched his wounds. On the back of the Governor's coat, a hole was found 1⅛ inches from the seam where the right sleeve attached to the coat and 7¼ inches to the right of the midline.[225] This hole was elongated in a horizontal direction approximately five-eighths of an inch in length and one-fourth of an inch in height.[226] The front side of the Governor's coat contained a circular hole three-eighths of an inch in diameter, located 5 inches to the right of the front right edge of the coat slightly above the top button.[227] A rough hole approximately five-eighths of an inch in length and three-eighths of an inch in width was found near the end of the right sleeve.[228] Each of these holes could have been caused by a bullet, but a positive determination of this fact or the direction of the missile was not possible because the garment had been cleaned and pressed prior to any opportunity for a scientific examination.[229]

An examination of the Governor's shirt disclosed a very ragged tear five-eighths of an inch long horizontally and one-half of an inch vertically on the back of the shirt near the right sleeve 2 inches from the line where the sleeve attaches.[230] Immediately to the right was another small tear, approximately three-sixteenths of an inch long.[231] The two holes corresponded in position to the hole in the back of the Governor's coat.[232] A very irregular tear in the form of an "H" was observed on the front side of the Governor's shirt, approximately 1½ inches high, with a crossbar tear approximately 1 inch wide, located 5 inches from the right side seam and 9 inches from the top of the right sleeve.[233] Because the shirt had been laundered, there were insufficient characteristics for the expert examiner to form a conclusive opinion on the direction or nature of the object causing the holes.[234] The rear hole could have been caused by the entrance of a 6.5-millimeter bullet and the front hole by the exit of such a bullet.[235]

On the French cuff of the right sleeve of the Governor's shirt was a ragged, irregularly shaped hole located 1½ inches from the end of the sleeve and 5½ inches from the outside cuff-link hole.[236] The characteristics after laundering did not permit positive conclusions but these holes could have been caused by a bullet passing through the Governor's right wrist from the back to the front sides.[237] The Governor's trousers contained a hole approximately one-fourth of an inch in diameter in the region of the left knee.[238] The roughly circular shape of the hole and the slight tearing away from the edges gave the hole the general appearance of a bullet hole but it was not possible to determine the direction of the missile which caused the hole.[239]

Course of bullet.—Ballistics experiments and medical findings established that the missile which passed through the Governor's wrist and penetrated his thigh had first traversed his chest. The Army Wound Ballistics experts conducted tests which proved that the Governor's wrist wound was not caused by a pristine bullet. (See app. X, pp. 582–585.) A bullet is pristine immediately on exiting from a rifle muzzle when it moves in a straight line with a spinning motion and maintains its uniform trajectory with but a minimum of nose surface striking the air through which it passes.[240] When the straight line of flight of a bullet is deflected by striking some object, it starts to wobble or become irregular in flight, a condition called yaw.[241] A bullet with yaw has a greater surface exposed to the striking material or air, since the target or air is struck not only by the nose of the bullet, its smallest striking surface, but also by the bullet's sides.[242]

The ballistics experts learned the exact nature of the Governor's wrist wound by examining Parkland Hospital records and X-rays and conferring with Dr. Gregory. The C2766 Mannlicher-Carcano rifle found in the Depository was fired with bullets of the same type as the bullet found on the Governor's stretcher and the fragments found in the Presidential limousine. Shots were fired from a distance of 70 yards at comparable flesh and bone protected by material similar to the clothing worn by the Governor.[243] One of the test shots wounded the comparable flesh and bone structure in virtually the same place and from the same angle as the wound inflicted on Governor Connally's wrist. An X-ray and photograph of the simulated wrist confirmed the similarity.[244] The bullet which inflicted that injury during the tests had a nose which was substantially flattened from striking the material.[245] The striking velocity at 70 yards of seven shots fired during the tests averaged 1,858 feet per second; the average exit velocity of five shots was 1,776 feet per second.[246]

The conclusion that the Governor's wrist was not struck by a pristine bullet was based upon the following: (1) greater damage was inflicted on the test material than on the Governor's wrist; [247] (2) the test material had a smaller entry wound and a larger exit wound, characteristic of a pristine bullet, while the Governor's wrist had a larger entry wound as compared with its exit wound, indicating a bullet which was tumbling; [248] (3) cloth was carried into the wrist wound, which is characteristic of an irregular missile; [249] (4) the partial cutting of a radial nerve and tendon leading to the Governor's thumb further suggested that the bullet which struck him was not pristine, since such a bullet would merely push aside a tendon and nerve rather than catch and tear them; [250] (5) the bullet found on the Governor's stretcher probably did not pass through the wrist as a pristine bullet because its nose was not considerably flattened, as was the case with the pristine bullet which struck the simulated wrist; [251] and (6) the bullet which caused the Governor's thigh injury and then fell out of the wound had a "very low velocity," whereas the pristine bullets fired during the tests possessed a very high exit velocity.[252]

All the evidence indicated that the bullet found on the Governor's stretcher could have caused all his wounds. The weight of the whole bullet prior to firing was approximately 160–161 grains and that of the recovered bullet was 158.6 grains.[253] An X-ray of the Governor's wrist showed very minute metallic fragments, and two or three of these fragments were removed from his wrist.[254] All these fragments were sufficiently small and light so that the nearly whole bullet found on the stretcher could have deposited those pieces of metal as it tumbled through his wrist.[255] In their testimony, the three doctors who attended Governor Connally at Parkland Hospital expressed independently their opinion that a single bullet had passed through his chest; tumbled through his wrist with very little exit velocity, leaving small metallic fragments from the rear portion of the bullet; punctured his left thigh after the bullet had lost virtually all of its velocity; and had fallen out of the thigh wound.[256]

Governor Connally himself thought it likely that all his wounds were caused by a single bullet. In his testimony before the Commission, he repositioned himself as he recalled his position on the jump seat, with his right palm on his left thigh, and said:

I * * * wound up the next day realizing I was hit in three places, and I was not conscious of having been hit but by one bullet, so I tried to reconstruct how I could have been hit in three places by the same bullet, and I merely, I know it penetrated from the back through the chest first.

I assumed that I had turned as I described a moment ago, placing my right hand on my left leg, that it hit my wrist, went out the center of the wrist, the underside, and then into my leg, but it might not have happened that way at all.[257]

The Governor's posture explained how a single missile through his body would cause all his wounds. His doctors at Parkland Hospital had recreated his position, also, but they placed his right arm somewhat higher than his left thigh although in the same alinement.[258] The wound ballistics experts concurred in the opinion that a single bullet caused all the Governor's wounds.[259]

THE TRAJECTORY

The cumulative evidence of eyewitnesses, firearms and ballistic experts and medical authorities demonstrated that the shots were fired from above and behind President Kennedy and Governor Connally, more particularly, from the sixth floor of the Texas School Book Depository Building. In order to determine the facts with as much precision as possible and to insure that all data were consistent with the shots having been fired from the sixth floor window, the Commission requested additional investigation, including the analysis of motion picture films of the assassination and onsite tests. The facts developed through this investigation by the FBI and Secret Service confirmed the conclusions reached by the Commission regarding the source and trajectory of the shots which hit the President and the Governor. Moreover, these facts enabled the Commission to make certain approximations regarding the locations of the Presidential limousine at the time of the shots and the relevant time intervals.

Films and Tests

When the shots rang out the Presidential limousine was moving beyond the Texas School Book Depository Building in a southwesterly direction on Elm Street between Houston Street and the Triple Underpass.[260] The general location of the car was described and marked on maps by eyewitnesses as precisely as their observations and recollections permitted.[261] More exact information was provided by motion pictures taken by Abraham Zapruder, Orville O. Nix and Mary Muchmore, who were spectators at the scene.[262] Substantial light has been shed on the assassination sequence by viewing these motion pictures, particularly the Zapruder film, which was the most complete and from which individual 35-millimeter slides were made of each motion picture frame.[263]

Examination of the Zapruder motion picture camera by the FBI established that 18.3 pictures or frames were taken each second, and therefore, the timing of certain events could be calculated by allowing 1/18.3 seconds for the action depicted from one frame to the next.[264] The films and slides made from individual frames were viewed by Governor and Mrs. Connally, the Governor's doctors, the autopsy surgeons, and the Army wound ballistics scientists in order to apply the knowledge of each to determine the precise course of events.[265] Tests of the assassin's rifle disclosed that at least 2.3 seconds were required between shots.[266] In evaluating the films in the light of these timing guides, it was kept in mind that a victim of a bullet wound may not react immediately and, in some situations, according to experts, the victim may not even know where he has been hit, or when.[267]

On May 24, 1964, agents of the FBI and Secret Service conducted a series of tests to determine as precisely as possible what happened on November 22, 1963. Since the Presidential limousine was being remodeled and was therefore unavailable, it was simulated by using the Secret Service followup car, which is similar in design.[268] Any differences were taken into account. Two Bureau agents with approximately the same physical characteristics sat in the car in the same relative positions as President Kennedy and Governor Connally had occupied. The back of the stand-in for the President was marked with chalk at the point where the bullet entered. The Governor's model had on the same coat worn by Governor Connally when he was shot, with the hole in the back circled in chalk.[269]

To simulate the conditions which existed at the assassination scene on November 22, the lower part of the sixth-floor window at the southeast corner of the Depository Building was raised halfway, the cardboard boxes were repositioned, the C2766 Mannlicher-Carcano rifle found on the sixth floor of the Depository was used, and mounted on that rifle was a camera which recorded the view as was seen by the assassin.[270] In addition, the Zapruder, Nix, and Muchmore cameras were on hand so that photographs taken by these cameras from the same locations where they were used on November 22, 1963, could be compared with the films of that date.[271] The agents ascertained that the foliage of an oak tree that came between the gunman and his target along the motorcade route on Elm Street was approximately the same as on the day of the assassination.[272]

The First Bullet That Hit

The position of President Kennedy's car when he was struck in the neck was determined with substantial precision from the films and onsite tests. The pictures or frames in the Zapruder film were marked by the agents, with the number "1" given to the first frame where the motorcycles leading the motorcade came into view on Houston Street.[273] The numbers continue in sequence as Zapruder filmed the Presidential limousine as it came around the corner and proceeded down Elm. The President was in clear view of the assassin as he rode up Houston Street and for 100 feet as he proceeded down Elm Street, until he came to a point denoted as frame 166 on the Zapruder film.[274] These facts were determined in the test by placing the car and men on Elm Street in the exact spot where they were when each frame of the Zapruder film was photographed. To pinpoint their locations, a man stood at Zapruder's position and directed the automobile and both models to the positions shown on each frame, after which a Bureau photographer crouched at the sixth-floor window and looked through a camera whose lens recorded the view through the telescopic sight of the C2766 Mannlicher-Carcano rifle.[275] (See Commission Exhibit No. 887, p. 99.) Each position was measured to determine how far President Kennedy had gone down Elm from a point, which was designated as station C, on a line drawn along the west curbline of Houston Street.[276]

Based on these calculations, the agents concluded that at frame 166 of the Zapruder film the President passed beneath the foliage of the large oak tree and the point of impact on the President's back disappeared from the gunman's view as seen through the telescopic lens.[277] (See Commission Exhibit No. 889, p. 100.) For a fleeting instant, the President came back into view in the telescopic lens at frame 186 as he appeared in an opening among the leaves.[278] (See Commission Exhibit No. 891, p. 101.) The test revealed that the next point at which the rifleman had a clear view through the telescopic sight of the point where the bullet entered the President's back was when the car emerged from behind the tree at frame 210.[279] (See Commission Exhibit No. 893, p. 102.) According to FBI Agent Lyndal L. Shaneyfelt, "There is no obstruction from the sixth floor window from the time they leave the tree until they disappear down toward the triple overpass." [280]

As the President rode along Elm Street for a distance of about 140 feet, he was waving to the crowd. [281] Shaneyfelt testified that the waving is seen on the Zapruder movie until around frame 205, when a road sign blocked out most of the President's body from Zapruder's view through the lens of his camera. However, the assassin continued to have a clear view of the President as he proceeded down Elm.[282] When President Kennedy again came fully into view in the Zapruder film at frame 225, he seemed to be reacting to his neck wound by raising his hands to his throat.[283] (See Commission Exhibit No. 895, p. 103.) According to Shaneyfelt the reaction was "clearly apparent in 226 and barely apparent in 225." [284] It is probable that the President was not shot before frame 210, since it is unlikely that the assassin would deliberately have shot at him with a view obstructed by the oak tree when he was about to have a clear opportunity. It is

COMMISSION EXHIBIT No. 887

Photograph taken during reenactment showing C2766 rifle with camera attached.

PHOTOGRAPH FROM ZAPRUDER FILM

PHOTOGRAPH FROM RE-ENACTMENT

PHOTOGRAPH THROUGH RIFLE SCOPE

DISTANCE TO STATION C .... 95.6 FT.

DISTANCE TO RIFLE IN WINDOW ..... 138.2 FT.

ANGLE TO RIFLE IN WINDOW .... 26°52'

DISTANCE TO OVERPASS .... 391.5 FT.

ANGLE TO OVERPASS .... 0°07'

FRAME 166

COMMISSION EXHIBIT No. 889

PHOTOGRAPH FROM ZAPRUDER FILM

PHOTOGRAPH FROM RE-ENACTMENT

PHOTOGRAPH THROUGH RIFLE SCOPE

DISTANCE TO STATION C .... 116.3 FT.

DISTANCE TO RIFLE IN WINDOW ..... 156.3 FT.

ANGLE TO RIFLE IN WINDOW .... 24°03'

DISTANCE TO OVERPASS .... 371.7 FT.

ANGLE TO OVERPASS .... +0°03'

FRAME 186

COMMISSION EXHIBIT NO. 891

PHOTOGRAPH FROM ZAPRUDER FILM

PHOTOGRAPH FROM RE-ENACTMENT

PHOTOGRAPH THROUGH RIFLE SCOPE

DISTANCE TO STATION C .... 138.9 FT.

DISTANCE TO RIFLE IN WINDOW .... 176.9 FT.

ANGLE TO RIFLE IN WINDOW .... 21°34'

DISTANCE TO OVERPASS .... 348.8 FT.

ANGLE TO OVERPASS .... +0°22'

FRAME 210

COMMISSION EXHIBIT No. 893

PHOTOGRAPH FROM ZAPRUDER FILM

PHOTOGRAPH FROM RE-ENACTMENT

PHOTOGRAPH THROUGH RIFLE SCOPE

DISTANCE TO STATION C	153.8 FT.
DISTANCE TO RIFLE IN WINDOW	190.8 FT.
ANGLE TO RIFLE IN WINDOW	20°11'
DISTANCE TO OVERPASS	334.0 FT.
ANGLE TO OVERPASS	+0°26'

FRAME 225

COMMISSION EXHIBIT No. 895

COMMISSION EXHIBIT No. 697

Photograph of Presidential limousine taken during motorcade.

also doubtful that even the most proficient marksman would have hit him through the oak tree. In addition, the President's reaction is "barely apparent" in frame 225, which is 15 frames or approximately eight-tenths second after frame 210, and a shot much before 210 would assume a longer reaction time than was recalled by eyewitnesses at the scene. Thus, the evidence indicated that the President was not hit until at least frame 210 and that he was probably hit by frame 225. The possibility of variations in reaction time in addition to the obstruction of Zapruder's view by the sign precluded a more specific determination than that the President was probably shot through the neck between frames 210 and 225, which marked his position between 138.9 and 153.8 feet west of station C.[285]

According to Special Agent Robert A. Frazier, who occupied the position of the assassin in the sixth-floor window during the reenactment, it is likely that the bullet which passed through the President's neck, as described previously, then struck the automobile or someone else in the automobile.[286] The minute examination by the FBI inspection team, conducted in Washington between 14 and 16 hours after the assassination, revealed no damage indicating that a bullet struck any part of the interior of the Presidential limousine, with the exception of the cracking of the windshield and the dent on the windshield chrome.[287] Neither of these points of damage to the car could have been caused by the bullet which exited from the President's neck at a velocity of 1,772 to 1,779 feet per second.[288] If the trajectory had permitted the bullet to strike the windshield, the bullet would have penetrated it and traveled a substantial distance down the road unless it struck some other object en route.[289] Had that bullet struck the metal framing, which was dented, it would have torn a hole in the chrome and penetrated the framing, both inside and outside the car.[290] At that exit velocity, the bullet would have penetrated any other metal or upholstery surface of the interior of the automobile.[291]

The bullet that hit President Kennedy in the back and exited through his throat most likely could not have missed both the automobile and its occupants. Since it did not hit the automobile, Frazier testified that it probably struck Governor Connally.[292] The relative positions of President Kennedy and Governor Connally at the time when the President was struck in the neck confirm that the same bullet probably passed through both men. Pictures taken of the President's limousine on November 22, 1963, showed that the Governor sat immediately in front of the President.[293] Even though the precise distance cannot be ascertained, it is apparent that President Kennedy was somewhat to the Governor's right. The President sat on the extreme right, as noted in the films and by eyewitnesses, while the right edge of the jump seat in which the Governor sat is 6 inches from the right door.[294] (See Commission Exhibit No. 697, p. 104.) The President wore a back brace which tended to make him sit up straight, and the Governor also sat erect since the jump seat gave him little leg room.[295]

Based on his observations during the reenactment and the position of Governor Connally shown in the Zapruder film after the car emerged from behind the sign, Frazier testified that Governor Connally was in a position during the span from frame 207 to frame 225 to receive a bullet which would have caused the wounds he actually suffered.[296] Governor Connally viewed the film and testified that he was hit between frames 231 and 234.[297] According to Frazier, between frames 235 and 240 the Governor turned sharply to his right, so that by frame 240 he was too far to the right to have received his injuries at that time.[298] At some point between frames 235 and 240, therefore, is the last occasion when Governor Connally could have received his injuries, since in the frames following 240 he remained turned too far to his right.[299] If Governor Connally was hit by a separate shot between frames 235 and 240 which followed the shot which hit the President's neck, it would follow that: (1) the assassin's first shot, assuming a minimum firing time of 2.3 seconds (or 42 frames), was fired between frames 193 and 198 when his view was obscured by the oak tree; (2) President Kennedy continued waving to the crowd after he was hit and did not begin to react for about 1½ seconds; and (3) the first shot, although hitting no bones in the President's body, was deflected after its exit from the President's neck in such a way that it failed to hit either the automobile or any of the other occupants.

Viewed through the telescopic sight of the C2766 Mannlicher-Carcano rifle from the sixth-floor window during the test, the marks that simulated the entry wounds on the stand-ins for the President and the Governor were generally in a straight line. That alinement became obvious to the viewer through the scope as the Governor's model turned slightly to his right and assumed the position which Governor Connally had described as his position when he was struck. Viewing the stand-ins for the President and the Governor in the sight of the C2766 Mannlicher-Carcano rifle at the location depicted in frames 207 and 210, Frazier testified: "They both are in direct alinement with the telescopic sight at the window. The Governor is immediately behind the President in the field of view." [300] (See Commission Exhibit No. 893, p. 102.) A surveyor then placed his sighting equipment at the precise point of entry on the back of the President's neck, assuming that the President was struck at frame 210, and measured the angle to the end of the muzzle of the rifle positioned where it was believed to have been held by the assassin.[301] That angle measured 21°34'.[302] From the same points of reference, the angle at frame 225 was measured at 20°11', giving an average angle of 20°52'30" from frame 210 to frame 225.[303] Allowing for a downward street grade of 3°9', the probable angle through the President's body was calculated at 17°43'30", assuming that he was sitting in a vertical position.[304]

That angle was consistent with the trajectory of a bullet passing through the President's neck and then striking Governor Connally's back, causing the wounds which were discussed above. Shortly after that angle was ascertained, the open car and the stand-ins were taken by the agents to a nearby garage where a photograph was taken to determine through closer study whether the angle of that shot could have accounted for the wounds in the President's neck and the Gov-

ernor's back.[305] A rod was placed at an angle of 17°43'30'' next to
the stand-ins for the President and the Governor, who were seated in
the same relative positions.[306] The wounds of entry and exit on the
President were approximated based on information gained from the
autopsy reports and photographs.[307] The hole in the back of the jacket
worn by the Governor and the medical description of the wound on his
back marked that entry point.[308] That line of fire from the sixth floor
of the Depository would have caused the bullet to exit under the Governor's right nipple just as the bullet did. Governor Connally's
doctors measured an angle of declination on his body from the entry
wound on his back to the exit on the front of his chest at about 25°
when he sat erect.[309] That difference was explained by either a slight
deflection of the bullet caused by striking the fifth rib or the Governor's
leaning slightly backward at the time he was struck. In addition,
the angle could not be fixed with absolute precision, since the large
wound on the front of his chest precluded an exact determination of
the point of exit.[310]

The alinement of the points of entry was only indicative and not
conclusive that one bullet hit both men. The exact positions of the
men could not be re-created; thus, the angle could only be approximated.[311] Had President Kennedy been leaning forward or backward,
the angle of declination of the shot to a perpendicular target would
have varied. The angle of 17°43'30'' was approximately the angle
of declination reproduced in an artist's drawing.[312] That drawing,
made from data provided by the autopsy surgeons, could not reproduce
the exact line of the bullet, since the exit wound was obliterated by the
tracheotomy. Similarly, if the President or the Governor had been
sitting in a different lateral position, the conclusion might have
varied. Or if the Governor had not turned in exactly the way calculated, the alinement would have been destroyed.

Additional experiments by the Army Wound Ballistics Branch
further suggested that the same bullet probably passed through both
President Kennedy and Governor Connally. (See app. X, pp.
582–585.) Correlation of a test simulating the Governor's chest wound
with the neck and wrist experiments indicated that course. After
reviewing the Parkland Hospital medical records and X-rays of
the Governor and discussing his chest injury with the attending
surgeon, the Army ballistics experts virtually duplicated the wound
using the assassination weapon and animal flesh covered by cloth.[313]
The bullet that struck the animal flesh displayed characteristics similar
to the bullet found on Governor Connally's stretcher.[314] Moreover,
the imprint on the velocity screen immediately behind the animal
flesh showed that the bullet was tumbling after exiting from the flesh,
having lost a total average of 265 feet per second.[315] Taking into
consideration the Governor's size, the reduction in velocity of a
bullet passing through his body would be approximately 400 feet per
second.[316]

Based upon the medical evidence on the wounds of the Governor
and the President and the wound ballistics tests performed at Edge-

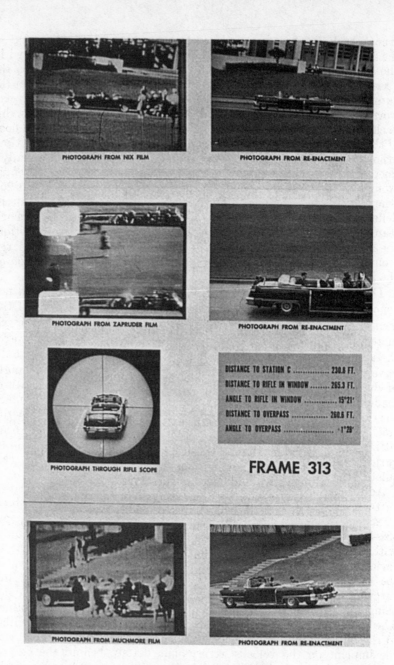

PHOTOGRAPH FROM NIX FILM

PHOTOGRAPH FROM RE-ENACTMENT

PHOTOGRAPH FROM ZAPRUDER FILM

PHOTOGRAPH FROM RE-ENACTMENT

PHOTOGRAPH THROUGH RIFLE SCOPE

DISTANCE TO STATION C .... 230.8 FT.
DISTANCE TO RIFLE IN WINDOW .... 265.3 FT.
ANGLE TO RIFLE IN WINDOW .... 15°21'
DISTANCE TO OVERPASS .... 260.6 FT.
ANGLE TO OVERPASS .... 1°28'

FRAME 313

PHOTOGRAPH FROM MUCHMORE FILM

PHOTOGRAPH FROM RE-ENACTMENT

COMMISSION EXHIBIT No. 902

wood Arsenal, Drs. Olivier and Arthur J. Dziemian, chief of the Army Wound Ballistics Branch, who had spent 17 years in that area of specialization, concluded that it was probable that the same bullet passed through the President's neck and then inflicted all the wounds on the Governor.[317] Referring to the President's neck wound and all the Governor's wounds, Dr. Dziemian testified: "I think the probability is very good that it is, that all the wounds were caused by one bullet." [318] Both Drs. Dziemian and Olivier believed that the wound on the Governor's wrist would have been more extensive had the bullet which inflicted that injury merely passed through the Governor's chest, exiting at a velocity of approximately 1,500 feet per second.[319] Thus, the Governor's wrist wound suggested that the bullet passed through the President's neck, began to yaw in the air between the President and the Governor, and then lost more velocity than 400 feet per second in passing through the Governor's chest. A bullet which was yawing on entering into the Governor's back would lose substantially more velocity in passing through his body than a pristine bullet.[320] In addition, the bullet that struck the animal flesh was flattened to a greater extent than the bullet which presumably struck the Governor's rib,[321] which suggests that the bullet which entered the Governor's chest had already lost velocity by passing through the President's neck. Moreover, the large wound on the Governor's back would be explained by a bullet which was yawing, although that type of wound might also be accounted for by a tangential striking.[322]

Dr. Frederick W. Light, Jr., the third of the wound ballistics experts, who has been engaged in that specialty at Edgewood Arsenal since 1951, testified that the anatomical findings were insufficient for him to formulate a firm opinion as to whether the same bullet did or did not pass through the President's neck first before inflicting all the wounds on Governor Connally.[323] Based on the other circumstances, such as the relative positions of the President and the Governor in the automobile, Dr. Light concluded that it was probable that the same bullet traversed the President's neck and inflicted all the wounds on Governor Connally.[324]

The Subsequent Bullet That Hit

After a bullet penetrated President Kennedy's neck, a subsequent shot entered the back of his head and exited through the upper right portion of his skull. The Zapruder, Nix and Muchmore films show the instant in the sequence when that bullet struck. (See Commission Exhibit No. 902, p. 108.) That impact was evident from the explosion of the President's brain tissues from the right side of his head. The immediately preceding frame from the Zapruder film shows the President slumped to his left, clutching at his throat, with his chin close to his chest and his head tilted forward at an angle.[325] Based upon information provided by the doctors who conducted the autopsy, an artist's drawing depicted the path of the bullet through the President's head, with his head being in the same approximate position.[326]

By using the Zapruder, Nix and Muchmore motion pictures, the President's location at the time the bullet penetrated his head was fixed with reasonable precision. A careful analysis of the Nix and Muchmore films led to fixing the exact location of these cameramen. The point of impact of the bullet on the President's head was apparent in all of the movies. At that point in the Nix film a straight line was plotted from the camera position to a fixed point in the background and the President's location along this line was marked on a plat map.[327] A similar process was followed with the Muchmore film. The President's location on the plat map was identical to that determined from the Nix film.[328] The President's location, established through the Nix and Muchmore films, was confirmed by comparing his position on the Zapruder film. This location had hitherto only been approximated, since there were no landmarks in the background of the Zapruder frame for alinement purposes other than a portion of a painted line on the curb.[329] Through these procedures, it was determined that President Kennedy was shot in the head when he was 230.8 feet from a point on the west curbline on Houston Street where it intersected with Elm Street.[330] The President was 265.3 feet from the rifle in the sixth-floor window and at that position the approximate angle of declination was 15°21'.[331]

NUMBER OF SHOTS

The consensus among the witnesses at the scene was that three shots were fired.[332] However, some heard only two shots,[333] while others testified that they heard four and perhaps as many as five or six shots.[334] The difficulty of accurate perception of the sound of gunshots required careful scrutiny of all of this testimony regarding the number of shots. The firing of a bullet causes a number of noises: the muzzle blast, caused by the smashing of the hot gases which propel the bullet into the relatively stable air at the gun's muzzle; the noise of the bullet, caused by the shock wave built up ahead of the bullet's nose as it travels through the air; and the noise caused by the impact of the bullet on its target.[335] Each noise can be quite sharp and may be perceived as a separate shot. The tall buildings in the area might have further distorted the sound.

The physical and other evidence examined by the Commission compels the conclusion that at least two shots were fired. As discussed previously, the nearly whole bullet discovered at Parkland Hospital and the two larger fragments found in the Presidential automobile, which were identified as coming from the assassination rifle, came from at least two separate bullets and possibly from three.[336] The most convincing evidence relating to the number of shots was provided by the presence on the sixth floor of three spent cartridges which were demonstrated to have been fired by the same rifle that fired the bullets which caused the wounds. It is possible that the assassin carried an empty shell in the rifle and fired only two shots, with the witnesses hearing multiple noises made by the same shot. Soon after the three

110

empty cartridges were found, officials at the scene decided that three shots were fired, and that conclusion was widely circulated by the press. The eyewitness testimony may be subconsciously colored by the extensive publicity given the conclusion that three shots were fired. Nevertheless, the preponderance of the evidence, in particular the three spent cartridges, led the Commission to conclude that there were three shots fired.

THE SHOT THAT MISSED

From the initial findings that (*a*) one shot passed through the President's neck and then most probably passed through the Governor's body, (*b*) a subsequent shot penetrated the President's head, (*c*) no other shot struck any part of the automobile, and (*d*) three shots were fired, it follows that one shot probably missed the car and its occupants. The evidence is inconclusive as to whether it was the first, second, or third shot which missed.

The First Shot

If the first shot missed, the assassin perhaps missed in an effort to fire a hurried shot before the President passed under the oak tree, or possibly he fired as the President passed under the tree and the tree obstructed his view. The bullet might have struck a portion of the tree and been completely deflected. On the other hand, the greatest cause for doubt that the first shot missed is the improbability that the same marksman who twice hit a moving target would be so inaccurate on the first and closest of his shots as to miss completely, not only the target, but the large automobile.

Some support for the contention that the first shot missed is found in the statement of Secret Service Agent Glen A. Bennett, stationed in the right rear seat of the President's followup car, who heard a sound like a firecracker as the motorcade proceeded down Elm Street. At that moment, Agent Bennett stated:

> * * * I looked at the back of the President. I heard another firecracker noise and saw that shot hit the President about four inches down from the right shoulder. A second shot followed immediately and hit the right rear high of the President's head.[337]

Substantial weight may be given Bennett's observations. Although his formal statement was dated November 23, 1963, his notes indicate that he recorded what he saw and heard at 5:30 p.m., November 22, 1963, on the airplane en route back to Washington, prior to the autopsy, when it was not yet known that the President had been hit in the back.[338] It is possible, of course, that Bennett did not observe the hole in the President's back, which might have been there immediately after the first noise.

111

Governor Connally's testimony supports the view that the first shot missed, because he stated that he heard a shot, turned slightly to his right, and, as he started to turn back toward his left, was struck by the second bullet.[339] He never saw the President during the shooting sequence, and it is entirely possible that he heard the missed shot and that both men were struck by the second bullet. Mrs. Connally testified that after the first shot she turned and saw the President's hands moving toward his throat, as seen in the films at frame 225.[340] However, Mrs. Connally further stated that she thought her husband was hit immediately thereafter by the second bullet.[341] If the same bullet struck both the President and the Governor, it is entirely possible that she saw the President's movements at the same time as she heard the second shot. Her testimony, therefore, does not preclude the possibility of the first shot having missed.

Other eyewitness testimony, however, supports the conclusion that the first of the shots fired hit the President. As discussed in chapter II, Special Agent Hill's testimony indicates that the President was hit by the first shot and that the head injury was caused by a second shot which followed about 5 seconds later. James W. Altgens, a photographer in Dallas for the Associated Press, had stationed himself on Elm Street opposite the Depository to take pictures of the passing motorcade. Altgens took a widely circulated photograph which showed President Kennedy reacting to the first of the two shots which hit him. (See Commission Exhibit No. 900, p. 113.) According to Altgens, he snapped the picture "almost simultaneously" with a shot which he is confident was the first one fired.[342] Comparison of his photograph with the Zapruder film, however, revealed that Altgens took his picture at approximately the same moment as frame 255 of the movie, 30 to 45 frames (approximately 2 seconds) later than the point at which the President was shot in the neck.[343] (See Commission Exhibit No. 901, p. 114.) Another photographer, Phillip L. Willis, snapped a picture at a time which he also asserts was simultaneous with the first shot. Analysis of his photograph revealed that it was taken at approximately frame 210 of the Zapruder film, which was the approximate time of the shot that probably hit the President and the Governor. If Willis accurately recalled that there were no previous shots, this would be strong evidence that the first shot did not miss.[344]

If the first shot did not miss, there must be an explanation for Governor Connally's recollection that he was not hit by it. There was, conceivably, a delayed reaction between the time the bullet struck him and the time he realized that he was hit, despite the fact that the bullet struck a glancing blow to a rib and penetrated his wrist bone. The Governor did not even know that he had been struck in the wrist or in the thigh until he regained consciousness in the hospital the next day. Moreover, he testified that he did not hear what he thought was the second shot, although he did hear a subsequent shot which coincided with the shattering of the President's head.[345] One possibility, therefore, would be a sequence in which the Governor heard the first shot, did not immediately feel the penetration of the bullet,

PHOTOGRAPH BY AP PHOTOGRAPHER

PHOTOGRAPH FROM RE-ENACTMENT

Commission Exhibit No. 900

PHOTOGRAPH FROM ZAPRUDER FILM

PHOTOGRAPH FROM RE-ENACTMENT

PHOTOGRAPH THROUGH RIFLE SCOPE

DISTANCE TO STATION C .... 181.9 FT.

DISTANCE TO RIFLE IN WINDOW .... 218.0 FT.

ANGLE TO RIFLE IN WINDOW .... 18°03'

DISTANCE TO OVERPASS .... 307.1 FT.

ANGLE TO OVERPASS .... +0°44'

FRAME 255

COMMISSION EXHIBIT No. 901

then felt the delayed reaction of the impact on his back, later heard the shot which shattered the President's head, and then lost consciousness without hearing a third shot which might have occurred later.

The Second Shot

The possibility that the second shot missed is consistent with the elapsed time between the two shots that hit their mark. From the timing evidenced by the Zapruder films, there was an interval of from 4.8 to 5.6 seconds between the shot which struck President Kennedy's neck (between frames 210 to 225) and the shot which struck his head at frame 313.[346] Since a minimum of 2.3 seconds must elapse between shots, a bullet could have been fired from the rifle and missed during this interval.[347] This possibility was buttressed by the testimony of witnesses who claimed that the shots were evenly spaced, since a second shot occurring within an interval of approximately 5 seconds would have to be almost exactly midway in this period. If Altgens' recollection is correct that he snapped his picture at the same moment as he heard a shot, then it is possible that he heard a second shot which missed, since a shot fired 2.3 seconds before he took his picture at frame 255 could have hit the President at about frame 213.

On the other hand, a substantial majority of the witnesses stated that the shots were not evenly spaced. Most witnesses recalled that the second and third shots were bunched together, although some believed that it was the first and second which were bunched.[348] To the extent that reliance can be placed on recollection of witnesses as to the spacing of the shots, the testimony that the shots were not evenly spaced would militate against a second shot missing. Another factor arguing against the second shot missing is that the gunman would have been shooting at very near the minimum allowable time to have fired the three shots within 4.8 to 5.6 seconds, although it was entirely possible for him to have done so. (See ch. IV, pp. 188–194.)

The Third Shot

The last possibility, of course, is that it was the third shot which missed. This conclusion conforms most easily with the probability that the assassin would most likely have missed the farthest shot, particularly since there was an acceleration of the automobile after the shot which struck the President's head. The limousine also changed direction by following the curve to the right, whereas previously it had been proceeding in almost a straight line with a rifle protruding from the sixth-floor window of the Depository Building.

One must consider, however, the testimony of the witnesses who described the head shot as the concluding event in the assassination sequence. Illustrative is the testimony of Associated Press photographer Altgens, who had an excellent vantage point near the President's car. He recalled that the shot which hit the President's head "was the last shot—that much I will say with a great degree of certainty." [349]   On the other hand, Emmett J. Hudson, the grounds-keeper of Dealey Plaza, testified that from his position on Elm Street, midway between Houston Street and the Triple Underpass, he heard a third shot after the shot which hit the President in the head.[350]   In addition, Mrs. Kennedy's testimony indicated that neither the first nor the second shot missed.   Immediately after the first noise she turned, because of the Governor's yell, and saw her husband raise his hand to his forehead.   Then the second shot struck the President's head.[351]

Some evidence suggested that a third shot may have entirely missed and hit the turf or street by the Triple Underpass.   Royce G. Skelton, who watched the motorcade from the railroad bridge, testified that after two shots "the car came on down close to the Triple Underpass" and an additional shot "hit in the left front of the President's car on the cement." [352]   Skelton thought that there had been a total of four shots, either the third or fourth of which hit in the vicinity of the underpass.[353]   Dallas Patrolman J. W. Foster, who was also on the Triple Underpass, testified that a shot hit the turf near a manhole cover in the vicinity of the underpass.[354]   Examination of this area, however, disclosed no indication that a bullet struck at the locations indicated by Skelton or Foster.[355]

At a different location in Dealey Plaza, the evidence indicated that a bullet fragment did hit the street.   James T. Tague, who got out of his car to watch the motorcade from a position between Commerce and Main Streets near the Triple Underpass, was hit on the cheek by an object during the shooting.[356]   Within a few minutes Tague reported this to Deputy Sheriff Eddy R. Walthers, who was examining the area to see if any bullets had struck the turf.[357]   Walthers immediately started to search where Tague had been standing and located a place on the south curb of Main Street where it appeared a bullet had hit the cement.[358]   According to Tague, "There was a mark quite obviously that was a bullet, and it was very fresh." [359]   In Tague's opinion, it was the second shot which caused the mark, since he thinks he heard the third shot after he was hit in the face.[360]   This incident appears to have been recorded in the contemporaneous report of Dallas Patrol-man L. L. Hill, who radioed in around 12:40 p.m.: "I have one guy that was possibly hit by a richochet from the bullet off the concrete." [361]   Scientific examination of the mark on the south curb of Main Street by FBI experts disclosed metal smears which, "were spectrographically determined to be essentially lead with a trace of antimony." [362]   The mark on the curb could have originated from the lead core of a bullet but the absence of copper precluded "the possibility that the mark on the curbing section was made by an unmutilated military full metal-jacketed bullet such as the bullet from Governor Connally's stretcher." [363]

It is true that the noise of a subsequent shot might have been drowned out by the siren on the Secret Service followup car immediately after the head shot, or the dramatic effect of the head shot might have caused so much confusion that the memory of subsequent events was blurred.

Nevertheless, the preponderance of the eyewitness testimony that the head shot was the final shot must be weighed in any determination as to whether it was the third shot that missed. Even if it were caused by a bullet fragment, the mark on the south curb of Main Street cannot be identified conclusively with any of the three shots fired. Under the circumstances it might have come from the bullet which hit the President's head, or it might have been a product of the fragmentation of the missed shot upon hitting some other object in the area.[364] Since he did not observe any of the shots striking the President, Tague's testimony that the second shot, rather than the third, caused the scratch on his cheek, does not assist in limiting the possibilities.

The wide range of possibilities and the existence of conflicting testimony, when coupled with the impossibility of scientific verification, precludes a conclusive finding by the Commission as to which shot missed.

TIME SPAN OF SHOTS

Witnesses at the assassination scene said that the shots were fired within a few seconds, with the general estimate being 5 to 6 seconds.[365] That approximation was most probably based on the earlier publicized reports that the first shot struck the President in the neck, the second wounded the Governor and the third shattered the President's head, with the time span from the neck to the head shots on the President being approximately 5 seconds. As previously indicated, the time span between the shot entering the back of the President's neck and the bullet which shattered his skull was 4.8 to 5.6 seconds. If the second shot missed, then 4.8 to 5.6 seconds was the total time span of the shots. If either the first or third shots missed, then a minimum of 2.3 seconds (necessary to operate the rifle) must be added to the time span of the shots which hit, giving a minimum time of 7.1 to 7.9 seconds for the three shots. If more than 2.3 seconds elapsed between a shot that missed and one that hit, then the time span would be correspondingly increased.

CONCLUSION

Based on the evidence analyzed in this chapter, the Commission has concluded that the shots which killed President Kennedy and wounded Governor Connally were fired from the sixth-floor window at the southeast corner of the Texas School Book Depository Building. Two bullets probably caused all the wounds suffered by President Kennedy and Governor Connally. Since the preponderance of the evidence indicated that three shots were fired, the Commission concluded that one shot probably missed the Presidential limousine and its occupants, and that the three shots were fired in a time period ranging from approximately 4.8 to in excess of 7 seconds.

117

CHAPTER IV

The Assassin

THE PRECEDING chapter has established that the bullets which killed President Kennedy and wounded Governor Connally were fired from the southeast corner window of the sixth floor of the Texas School Book Depository Building and that the weapon which fired these bullets was a Mannlicher-Carcano 6.5-millimeter Italian rifle bearing the serial number C2766. In this chapter the Commission evaluates the evidence upon which it has based its conclusion concerning the identity of the assassin. This evidence includes (1) the ownership and possession of the weapon used to commit the assassination, (2) the means by which the weapon was brought into the Depository Building, (3) the identity of the person present at the window from which the shots were fired, (4) the killing of Dallas Patrolman J. D. Tippit within 45 minutes after the assassination, (5) the resistance to arrest and the attempted shooting of another police officer by the man (Lee Harvey Oswald) subsequently accused of assassinating President Kennedy and killing Patrolman Tippit, (6) the lies told to the police by Oswald, (7) the evidence linking Oswald to the attempted killing of Maj. Gen. Edwin A. Walker (Resigned, U.S. Army) on April 10, 1963, and (8) Oswald's capability with a rifle.

OWNERSHIP AND POSSESSION OF ASSASSINATION WEAPON

Purchase of Rifle by Oswald

Shortly after the Mannlicher-Carcano rifle was found on the sixth floor of the Texas School Book Depository Building,[1] agents of the FBI learned from retail outlets in Dallas that Crescent Firearms, Inc., of New York City, was a distributor of surplus Italian 6.5-millimeter military rifles.[2] During the evening of November 22, 1963, a review of the records of Crescent Firearms revealed that the firm had shipped an Italian carbine, serial number C2766, to Klein's Sporting Goods Co., of Chicago, Ill.[3] After searching their records from 10 p.m. to 4 a.m. the officers of Klein's discovered that a rifle bearing serial number C2766 had been shipped to one A. Hidell,

Post Office Box 2915, Dallas, Tex., on March 20, 1963.[4]   (See Waldman Exhibit No. 7, p. 120.)

According to its microfilm records, Klein's received an order for a rifle on March 13, 1963, on a coupon clipped from the February 1963 issue of the American Rifleman magazine. The order coupon was signed, in handprinting, "A. Hidell, P. O. Box 2915, Dallas, Texas." (See Commission Exhibit No. 773, p. 120.)   It was sent in an envelope bearing the same name and return address in handwriting. Document examiners for the Treasury Department and the FBI testified unequivocally that the bold printing on the face of the mail-order coupon was in the handprinting of Lee Harvey Oswald and that the writing on the envelope was also his.[5]   Oswald's writing on these and other documents was identified by comparing the writing and printing on the documents in question with that appearing on documents known to have been written by Oswald, such as his letters, passport application, and endorsements of checks.[6]   (See app. X, p. 568–569.)

In addition to the order coupon the envelope contained a U.S. postal money order for $21.45, purchased as No. 2,202,130,462 in Dallas, Tex., on March 12, 1963.[7]   The canceled money order was obtained from the Post Office Department. Opposite the printed words "Pay To" were written the words "Kleins Sporting Goods," and opposite the printed word "From" were written the words "A. Hidell, P. O. Box 2915 Dallas, Texas." These words were also in the handwriting of Lee Harvey Oswald.[8]   (See Commission Exhibit No. 788, p. 120.)

From Klein's records it was possible to trace the processing of the order after its receipt.   A bank deposit made on March 13, 1963, included an item of $21.45.   Klein's shipping order form shows an imprint made by the cash register which recorded the receipt of $21.45 on March 13, 1963.   This price included $19.95 for the rifle and the scope, and $1.50 for postage and handling.   The rifle without the scope cost only $12.78.[9]

According to the vice president of Klein's, William Waldman, the scope was mounted on the rifle by a gunsmith employed by Klein's, and the rifle was shipped fully assembled in accordance with customary company procedures.[10]   The specific rifle shipped against the order had been received by Klein's from Crescent on February 21, 1963. It bore the manufacturer's serial number C2766.   On that date, Klein's placed an internal control number VC836 on this rifle.[11]   According to Klein's shipping order form, one Italian carbine 6.5 X–4× scope, control number VC836, serial number C2766, was shipped parcel post to "A. Hidell, P. O. Box 2915, Dallas, Texas," on March 20, 1963.[12] Information received from the Italian Armed Forces Intelligence Service has established that this particular rifle was the only rifle of its type bearing serial number C2766.[13]   (See app. X, p. 554.)

The post office box to which the rifle was shipped was rented to "Lee H. Oswald" from October 9, 1962, to May 14, 1963.[14]   Experts on handwriting identification from the Treasury Department and the

DOCUMENTS ESTABLISHING
PURCHASE OF RIFLE BY LEE HARVEY OSWALD

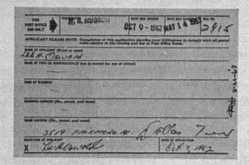

↑ APPLICATION FOR
POST OFFICE BOX
(COMMISSION EXHIBIT 791)

↑ PURCHASE ORDER
(COMMISSION EXHIBIT 773)

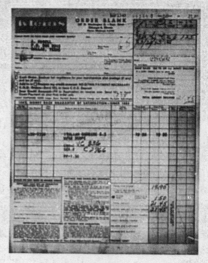

↑ MONEY ORDER
(COMMISSION EXHIBIT 788)

↑ KLEIN'S SHIPPING ORDER
(WALDMAN'S EXHIBIT 7)

FBI testified that the signature and other writing on the application for that box were in the handwriting of Lee Harvey Oswald,[15] as was a change-of-address card dated May 12, 1963,[16] by which Oswald requested that mail addressed to that box be forwarded to him in New Orleans, where he had moved on April 24.[17] Since the rifle was shipped from Chicago on March 20, 1963, it was received in Dallas during the period when Oswald rented and used the box. (See Commission Exhibit No. 791, p. 120.)

It is not known whether the application for post office box 2915 listed "A. Hidell" as a person entitled to receive mail at this box. In accordance with postal regulations, the portion of the application which lists names of persons, other than the applicant, entitled to receive mail was thrown away after the box was closed on May 14, 1963.[18] Postal Inspector Harry D. Holmes of the Dallas Post Office testified, however, that when a package is received for a certain box, a notice is placed in that box regardless of whether the name on the package is listed on the application as a person entitled to receive mail through that box. The person having access to the box then takes the notice to the window and is given the package. Ordinarily, Inspector Holmes testified, identification is not requested because it is assumed that the person with the notice is entitled to the package.[19]

Oswald's use of the name "Hidell" to purchase the assassination weapon was one of several instances in which he used this name as an alias. When arrested on the day of the assassination, he had in his possession a Smith & Wesson .38 caliber revolver [20] purchased by mail-order coupon from Seaport-Traders, Inc., a mail-order division of George Rose & Co., Los Angeles. The mail-order coupon listed the purchaser as "A. J. Hidell Age 28" with the address of post office box 2915 in Dallas.[21] Handwriting experts from the FBI and the Treasury Department testified that the writing on the mail-order form was that of Lee Harvey Oswald.[22]

Among other identification cards in Oswald's wallet at the time of his arrest were a Selective Service notice of classification, a Selective Service registration certificate,[23] and a certificate of service in the U.S. Marine Corps,[24] all three cards being in his own name. Also in his wallet at that time were a Selective Service notice of classification and a Marine certificate of service in the name of Alek James Hidell.[25] On the Hidell Selective Service card there appeared a signature, "Alek J. Hidell," and the photograph of Lee Harvey Oswald.[26] Experts on questioned documents from the Treasury Department and the FBI testified that the Hidell cards were counterfeit photographic reproductions made by photographing the Oswald cards, retouching the resulting negatives, and producing prints from the retouched negatives. The Hidell signature on the notice of classification was in the handwriting of Oswald.[27] (See app. X, p. 572.)

In Oswald's personal effects found in his room at 1026 North Beckley Avenue in Dallas was a purported international certificate of vaccination signed by "Dr. A. J. Hideel," Post Office Box 30016, New

121

Orleans.[28] It certified that Lee Harvey Oswald had been vaccinated for smallpox on June 8, 1963. This, too, was a forgery. The signature of "A. J. Hideel" was in the handwriting of Lee Harvey Oswald.[29] There is no "Dr. Hideel" licensed to practice medicine in Louisiana.[30] There is no post office box 30016 in the New Orleans Post Office but Oswald had rented post office box 30061 in New Orleans [31] on June 3, 1963, listing Marina Oswald and A. J. Hidell as additional persons entitled to receive mail in the box.[32] The New Orleans postal authorities had not discarded the portion of the application listing the names of those, other than the owner of the box, entitled to receive mail through the box. Expert testimony confirmed that the writing on this application was that of Lee Harvey Oswald.[33]

Hidell's name on the post office box application was part of Oswald's use of a nonexistent Hidell to serve as president of the so-called New Orleans Chapter of the Fair Play for Cuba Committee. (As discussed below in ch.VI, p. 292.) Marina Oswald testified that she first learned of Oswald's use of the fictitious name "Hidell" in connection with his pro-Castro activities in New Orleans.[34] According to her testimony, he compelled her to write the name "Hidell" on membership cards in the space designated for the signature of the "Chapter President." [35] The name "Hidell" was stamped on some of the "Chapter's" printed literature and on the membership application blanks.[36] Marina Oswald testified, "I knew there was no such organization. And I know Hidell is merely an altered Fidel, and I laughed at such foolishness." [37] Hidell was a fictitious president of an organization of which Oswald was the only member.[38]

When seeking employment in New Orleans, Oswald listed a "Sgt. Robt. Hidell" as a reference on one job application [39] and "George Hidell" as a reference on another.[40] Both names were found to be fictitious.[41] Moreover, the use of "Alek" as a first name for Hidell is a further link to Oswald because "Alek" was Oswald's nickname in Russia.[42] Letters received by Marina Oswald from her husband signed "Alek" were given to the Commission.[43]

Oswald's Palmprint on Rifle Barrel

Based on the above evidence, the Commission concluded that Oswald purchased the rifle found on the sixth floor of the Depository Building. Additional evidence of ownership was provided in the form of palmprint identification which indicated that Oswald had possession of the rifle he had purchased.

A few minutes after the rifle was discovered on the sixth floor of the Depository Building [44] it was examined by Lt. J. C. Day of the identification bureau of the Dallas police. He lifted the rifle by the wooden stock after his examination convinced him that the wood was too rough to take fingerprints. Capt. J. W. Fritz then ejected a cartridge by operating the bolt, but only after Day viewed the knob on the bolt through a magnifying glass and found no prints.[45] Day continued to examine the rifle with the magnifying glass, looking for possible fingerprints. He applied fingerprint powder to the side of the metal housing near the trigger, and noticed traces of two prints.[46] At 11:45 p.m. on November 22, the rifle was released to the FBI and forwarded to Washington where it was examined on the morning of November 23 by Sebastian F. Latona, supervisor of the Latent Fingerprint Section of the FBI's Identification Division.[47]

In his testimony before the Commission, Latona stated that when he received the rifle, the area where prints were visible was protected by cellophane.[48] He examined these prints, as well as photographs of them which the Dallas police had made, and concluded that:

> * * * the formations, the ridge formations and characteristics, were insufficient for purposes of either effecting identification or a determination that the print was not identical with the prints of people. Accordingly, my opinion simply was that the latent prints which were there were of no value.[49]

Latona then processed the complete weapon but developed no identifiable prints.[50] He stated that the poor quality of the wood and the metal would cause the rifle to absorb moisture from the skin, thereby making a clear print unlikely.[51]

On November 22, however, before surrendering possession of the rifle to the FBI Laboratory, Lieutenant Day of the Dallas Police Department had "lifted" a palmprint from the underside of the gun barrel "near the firing end of the barrel about 3 inches under the woodstock when I took the woodstock loose." [52] "Lifting" a print involves the use of adhesive material to remove the fingerprint powder which adheres to the original print. In this way the powdered impression is actually removed from the object.[53] The lifting had been so complete in this case that there was no trace of the print on the rifle itself when it was examined by Latona. Nor was there any indication that the lift had been performed.[54] Day, on the other hand, believed that sufficient traces of the print had been left on the rifle barrel, because he did not release the lifted print until November 26, when he received instructions to send "everything that we had" to the FBI.[55] The print arrived in the FBI Laboratory in Washington on November 29, mounted on a card on which Lieutenant Day had written the words "off underside gun barrel near end of foregrip C2766." [56] The print's positive identity as having been lifted from the rifle was confirmed by FBI Laboratory tests which established that the adhesive material bearing the print also bore impressions of the same irregularities that appeared on the barrel of the rifle.[57]

Latona testified that this palmprint was the right palmprint of Lee Harvey Oswald.[58] At the request of the Commission, Arthur Mandella, fingerprint expert with the New York City Police Department, conducted an independent examination and also determined that this was the right palmprint of Oswald.[59] Latona's findings were also confirmed by Ronald G. Wittmus, another FBI fingerprint expert.[60]   In the opinion of these experts, it was not possible to estimate the time which elapsed between the placing of the print on the rifle and the date of the lift.[61]

Experts testifying before the Commission agreed that palmprints are as unique as fingerprints for purposes of establishing identification.[62]   Oswald's palmprint on the underside of the barrel demonstrates that he handled the rifle when it was disassembled.   A palmprint could not be placed on this portion of the rifle, when assembled, because the wooden foregrip covers the barrel at this point.[63]   The print is additional proof that the rifle was in Oswald's possession.

Fibers on Rifle

In a crevice between the butt plate of the rifle and the wooden stock was a tuft of several cotton fibers of dark blue, gray-black, and orange-yellow shades.[64]   On November 23, 1963, these fibers were examined by Paul M. Stombaugh, a special agent assigned to the Hair and Fiber Unit of the FBI Laboratory.[65]   He compared them with the fibers found in the shirt which Oswald was wearing when arrested in the Texas Theatre.[66]   This shirt was also composed of dark blue, gray-black and orange-yellow cotton fibers.   Stombaugh testified that the colors, shades, and twist of the fibers found in the tuft on the rifle matched those in Oswald's shirt.[67]   (See app. X, p. 592.)

Stombaugh explained in his testimony that in fiber analysis, as distinct from fingerprint or firearms identification, it is not possible to state with scientific certainty that a particular small group of fibers come from a certain piece of clothing to the exclusion of all others because there are not enough microscopic characteristics present in fibers.[68]   Judgments as to probability will depend on the number and types of matches.[69]   He concluded, "There is no doubt in my mind that these fibers could have come from this shirt.   There is no way, however, to eliminate the possibility of the fibers having come from another identical shirt." [70]

Having considered the probabilities as explained in Stombaugh's testimony, the Commission has concluded that the fibers in the tuft on the rifle most probably came from the shirt worn by Oswald when he was arrested, and that this was the same shirt which Oswald wore on the morning of the assassination.   Marina Oswald testified that she thought her husband wore this shirt to work on that day.[71]   The testimony of those who saw him after the assassination was inconclusive about the color of Oswald's shirt,[72] but Mary Bledsoe, a former landlady of Oswald, saw him on a bus approximately 10 minutes after the assassination and identified the shirt as being the one worn by Oswald primarily because of a distinctive hole in the shirt's right elbow.[73]   Moreover, the bus transfer which he obtained as he left the bus was still in the pocket when he was arrested.[74]   Although Oswald returned to his roominghouse after the assassination and when questioned by the police, claimed to have changed his shirt,[75] the evidence indicates that he continued wearing the same shirt which he was wearing all morning and which he was still wearing when arrested.

In light of these findings the Commission evaluated the additional testimony of Stombaugh that the fibers were caught in the crevice of the rifle's butt plate "in the recent past." [76] Although Stombaugh was unable to estimate the period of time the fibers were on the rifle he said that the fibers "were clean, they had good color to them, there was no grease on them and they were not fragmented. They looked as if they had just been picked up." [77] The relative freshness of the fibers is strong evidence that they were caught on the rifle on the morning of the assassination or during the preceding evening. For 10 days prior to the eve of the assassination Oswald had not been present at Ruth Paine's house in Irving, Tex.,[78] where the rifle was kept.[79] Moreover, the Commission found no reliable evidence that Oswald used the rifle at any time between September 23, when it was transported from New Orleans, and November 22, the day of the assassination.[80] The fact that on the morning of the assassination Oswald was wearing the shirt from which these relatively fresh fibers most probably originated, provides some evidence that they were placed on the rifle that day since there was limited, if any, opportunity for Oswald to handle the weapon during the 2 months prior to November 22.

On the other hand Stombaugh pointed out that fibers might retain their freshness if the rifle had been "put aside" after catching the fibers. The rifle used in the assassination probably had been wrapped in a blanket for about 8 weeks prior to November 22.[81] Because the relative freshness of these fibers might be explained by the continuous storage of the rifle in the blanket, the Commission was unable to reach any firm conclusion as to when the fibers were caught in the rifle. The Commission was able to conclude, however, that the fibers most probably came from Oswald's shirt. This adds to the conviction of the Commission that Oswald owned and handled the weapon used in the assassination.

Photograph of Oswald With Rifle

During the period from March 2, 1963, to April 24, 1963, the Oswalds lived on Neely Street in Dallas in a rented house which had a small back yard.[82] One Sunday, while his wife was hanging diapers, Oswald asked her to take a picture of him holding a rifle, a pistol and issues of two newspapers later identified as the Worker and the Militant.[83] Two pictures were taken. The Commission has concluded that the rifle shown in these pictures is the same rifle which was found on the sixth floor of the Depository Building on November 22, 1963. (See Commission Exhibits Nos. 133–A and 133–B, p. 126.)

One of these pictures, Exhibit No. 133–A, shows most of the rifle's configuration.[84] Special Agent Lyndal L. Shaneyfelt, a photography expert with the FBI, photographed the rifle used in the assassination, attempting to duplicate the position of the rifle and the lighting in Exhibit No. 133–A.[85] After comparing the rifle in the simulated

PHOTOGRAPHS OF OSWALD HOLDING RIFLE

COMMISSION EXHIBIT NO. 133-A   COMMISSION EXHIBIT NO. 133-B

COMMISSION EXHIBIT NO. 134
(Enlargement of Commission Exhibit No. 133-A)

photograph with the rifle in Exhibit No. 133–A, Shaneyfelt testified, "I found it to be the same general configuration. All appearances were the same." He found "one notch in the stock at this point that appears very faintly in the photograph." He stated, however, that while he "found no differences" between the rifles in the two photographs, he could not make a "positive identification to the exclusion of all other rifles of the same general configuration." [86]

The authenticity of these pictures has been established by expert testimony which links the second picture, Commission Exhibit No. 133–B, to Oswald's Imperial Reflex camera, with which Marina Oswald testified she took the pictures. [87] The negative of that picture, Commission Exhibit No. 133–B, was found among Oswald's possessions. [88] Using a recognized technique of determining whether a picture was taken with a particular camera, Shaneyfelt compared this negative with a negative which he made by taking a new picture with Oswald's camera. [89] He concluded that the negative of Exhibit No. 133–B was exposed in Oswald's Imperial Reflex camera to the exclusion of all other cameras. [90] He could not test Exhibit No. 133–A in the same way because the negative was never recovered. [91] Both pictures, however, have identical backgrounds and lighting and, judging from the shadows, were taken at the same angle. They are photographs of the same scene. [92] Since Exhibit No. 133–B was taken with Oswald's camera, it is reasonably certain that Exhibit No. 133–A was taken by the same camera at the same time, as Marina Oswald testified. Moreover, Shaneyfelt testified that in his opinion the photographs were not composites of two different photographs and that Oswald's face had not been superimposed on another body. [93]

One of the photographs taken by Marina Oswald was widely published in newspapers and magazines, and in many instances the details of these pictures differed from the original, and even from each other, particularly as to the configuration of the rifle. The Commission sought to determine whether these photographs were retouched prior to publication. Shaneyfelt testified that the published photographs appeared to be based on a copy of the original which the publications had each retouched differently. [94] Several of the publications furnished the Commission with the prints they had used, or described by correspondence the retouching they had done. This information enabled the Commission to conclude that the published pictures were the same as the original except for retouching done by these publications, apparently for the purpose of clarifying the lines of the rifle and other details in the picture. [95]

The dates surrounding the taking of this picture and the purchase of the rifle reinforce the belief that the rifle in the photograph is the rifle which Oswald bought from Klein's. The rifle was shipped from Klein's in Chicago on March 20, 1963, at a time when the Oswalds were living on Neely Street. [96] From an examination of one of the photographs, the Commission determined the dates of the issues of the Militant and the Worker which Oswald was holding in his hand.

By checking the actual mailing dates of these issues and the time it usually takes to effect delivery to Dallas, it was established that the photographs must have been taken sometime after March 27.[97] Marina Oswald testified that the photographs were taken on a Sunday about 2 weeks before the attempted shooting of Maj. Gen. Edwin A. Walker on April 10, 1963.[98] By Sunday, March 31, 1963, 10 days prior to the Walker attempt, Oswald had undoubtedly received the rifle shipped from Chicago on March 20, the revolver shipped from Los Angeles on the same date,[99] and the two newspapers which he was holding in the picture.

Rifle Among Oswald's Possessions

Marina Oswald testified that the rifle found on the sixth floor of the Depository Building was the "fateful rifle of Lee Oswald." [100] Moreover, it was the only rifle owned by her husband following his return from the Soviet Union in June 1962.[101] It had been purchased in March 1963, and taken to New Orleans where Marina Oswald saw it in their rented apartment during the summer of 1963.[102] It appears from his wife's testimony that Oswald may have sat on the screened-in porch at night practicing with the rifle by looking through the telescopic sight and operating the bolt.[103] In September 1963, Oswald loaded their possessions into a station wagon owned by Ruth Paine, who had invited Marina Oswald and the baby to live at her home in Irving,[104] Tex. Marina Oswald has stated that the rifle was among these possessions,[105] although Ruth Paine testified that she was not aware of it.[106]

From September 24, 1963, when Marina Oswald arrived in Irving from New Orleans, until the morning of the assassination, the rifle was, according to the evidence, stored in a green and brown blanket in the Paines' garage among the Oswalds' other possessions.[107] About 1 week after the return from New Orleans, Marina Oswald was looking in the garage for parts to the baby's crib and thought that the parts might be in the blanket. When she started to open the blanket, she saw the stock of the rifle.[108] Ruth and Michael Paine both noticed the rolled-up blanket in the garage during the time that Marina Oswald was living in their home.[109] On several occasions, Michael Paine moved the blanket in the garage.[110] He thought it contained tent poles, or possibly other camping equipment such as a folding shovel.[111] When he appeared before the Commission, Michael Paine lifted the blanket with the rifle wrapped inside and testified that it appeared to be the same approximate weight and shape as the package in his garage.[112]

About 3 hours after the assassination, a detective and deputy sheriff saw the blanket-roll, tied with a string, lying on the floor of the Paines' garage. Each man testified that he thought he could detect the outline of a rifle in the blanket, even though the blanket was empty.[113] Paul M. Stombaugh, of the FBI Laboratory, examined the blanket and discovered a bulge approximately 10 inches long midway in the blanket. This bulge was apparently caused by a hard protruding object which had stretched the blanket's fibers. It could have been caused by the telescopic sight of the rifle which was approximately 11 inches long.[114] (See Commission Exhibit No. 1304, p. 132.)

Conclusion

Having reviewed the evidence that (1) Lee Harvey Oswald purchased the rifle used in the assassination, (2) Oswald's palmprint was on the rifle in a position which shows that he had handled it while it was disassembled, (3) fibers found on the rifle most probably came from the shirt Oswald was wearing on the day of the assassination, (4) a photograph taken in the yard of Oswald's apartment showed him holding this rifle, and (5) the rifle was kept among Oswald's possessions from the time of its purchase until the day of the assassination, the Commission concluded that the rifle used to assassinate President Kennedy and wound Governor Connally was owned and possessed by Lee Harvey Oswald.

THE RIFLE IN THE BUILDING

The Commission has evaluated the evidence tending to show how Lee Harvey Oswald's Mannlicher-Carcano rifle, serial number C2766, was brought into the Depository Building, where it was found on the sixth floor shortly after the assassination. In this connection the Commission considered (1) the circumstances surrounding Oswald's return to Irving, Tex., on Thursday, November 21, 1963, (2) the disappearance of the rifle from its normal place of storage, (3) Oswald's arrival at the Depository Building on November 22, carrying a long and bulky brown paper package, (4) the presence of a long handmade brown paper bag near the point from which the shots were fired, and (5) the palmprint, fiber, and paper analyses linking Oswald and the assassination weapon to this bag.

The Curtain Rod Story

During October and November of 1963, Lee Harvey Oswald lived in a roominghouse in Dallas while his wife and children lived in Irving, at the home of Ruth Paine,[115] approximately 15 miles from Oswald's place of work at the Texas School Book Depository. Oswald traveled between Dallas and Irving on weekends in a car driven by a neighbor of the Paines, Buell Wesley Frazier, who also worked at the Depository.[116] Oswald generally would go to Irving on Friday afternoon and return to Dallas Monday morning. According to the testimony of Frazier, Marina Oswald, and Ruth Paine, it appears that Oswald never returned to Irving in midweek prior to November 21, 1963, except on Monday, October 21, when he visited his wife in the hospital after the birth of their second child.[117]

During the morning of November 21, Oswald asked Frazier whether he could ride home with him that afternoon. Frazier, surprised, asked

129

him why he was going to Irving on Thursday night rather than Friday. Oswald replied, "I'm going home to get some curtain rods * * * [to] put in an apartment." [118] The two men left work at 4:40 p.m. and drove to Irving. There was little conversation between them on the way home.[119] Mrs. Linnie Mae Randle, Frazier's sister, commented to her brother about Oswald's unusual midweek return to Irving. Frazier told her that Oswald had come home to get curtain rods.[120]

It would appear, however, that obtaining curtain rods was not the purpose of Oswald's trip to Irving on November 21. Mrs. A. C. Johnson, his landlady, testified that Oswald's room at 1026 North Beckley Avenue had curtains and curtain rods,[121] and that Oswald had never discussed the subject with her.[122] In the Paines' garage, along with many other objects of a household character, there were two flat lightweight curtain rods belonging to Ruth Paine but they were still there on Friday afternoon after Oswald's arrest.[123] Oswald never asked Mrs. Paine about the use of curtain rods,[124] and Marina Oswald testified that Oswald did not say anything about curtain rods on the day before the assassination.[125] No curtain rods were known to have been discovered in the Depository Building after the assassination.[126] In deciding whether Oswald carried a rifle to work in a long paper bag on November 22, the Commission gave weight to the fact that Oswald gave a false reason for returning home on November 21, and one which provided an excuse for the carrying of a bulky package the following morning.

The Missing Rifle

Before dinner on November 21, Oswald played on the lawn of the Paines' home with his daughter June.[127] After dinner Ruth Paine and Marina Oswald were busy cleaning house and preparing their children for bed.[128] Between the hours of 8 and 9 p.m. they were occupied with the children in the bedrooms located at the extreme east end of the house.[129] On the west end of the house is the attached garage, which can be reached from the kitchen or from the outside.[130] In the garage were the personal belongings of the Oswald family including, as the evidence has shown, the rifle wrapped in the old brown and green blanket.[131]

At approximately 9 p.m., after the children had been put to bed, Mrs. Paine, according to her testimony before the Commission, "went out to the garage to paint some children's blocks, and worked in the garage for half an hour or so. I noticed when I went out that the light was on." [132] Mrs. Paine was certain that she had not left the light on in the garage after dinner.[133] According to Mrs. Paine, Oswald had gone to bed by 9 p.m.; [134] Marina Oswald testified that it was between 9 and 10 p.m.[135] Neither Marina Oswald nor Ruth Paine saw Oswald in the garage.[136] The period between 8 and 9 p.m., however, provided ample opportunity for Oswald to prepare the rifle for his departure the next morning. Only if disassembled could the rifle fit into the paper bag found near the window [137] from which the shots were fired. A firearms expert with the FBI assembled the rifle in 6 minutes using a 10-cent coin as a tool, and he could disassemble it more rapidly.[138] While the rifle may have already been disassembled when Oswald arrived home on Thursday, he had ample time that evening to disassemble the rifle and insert it into the paper bag.

On the day of the assassination, Marina Oswald was watching television when she learned of the shooting. A short time later Mrs. Paine told her that someone had shot the President "from the building in which Lee is working." Marina Oswald testified that at that time "My heart dropped. I then went to the garage to see whether the rifle was there and I saw that the blanket was still there and I said 'Thank God.'" She did not unroll the blanket. She saw that it was in its usual position and it appeared to her to have something inside.[139]

Soon afterward, at about 3 p.m., police officers arrived and searched the house. Mrs. Paine pointed out that most of the Oswalds' possessions were in the garage.[140] With Ruth Paine acting as an interpreter, Detective Rose asked Marina whether her husband had a rifle. Mrs. Paine, who had no knowledge of the rifle, first said "No," but when the question was translated, Marina Oswald replied "Yes." [141] She pointed to the blanket which was on the floor very close to where Ruth Paine was standing. Mrs. Paine testified:

> As she [Marina] told me about it I stepped onto the blanket roll. * * * And she indicated to me that she had peered into this roll and saw a portion of what she took to be a gun she knew her husband to have, a rifle. And I then translated this to the officers that she knew that her husband had a gun that he had stored in here. * * * I then stepped off of it and the officer picked it up in the middle and it bent so. * * * [142]

Mrs. Paine had the actual blanket before her as she testified and she indicated that the blanket hung limp in the officer's hand.[143] Marina Oswald testified that this was her first knowledge that the rifle was not in its accustomed place.[144]

The Long and Bulky Package

On the morning of November 22, 1963, Lee Harvey Oswald left the Paine house in Irving at approximately 7:15 a.m., while Marina Oswald was still in bed.[145] Neither she nor Mrs. Paine saw him leave the house.[146] About half-a-block away from the Paine house was the residence of Mrs. Linnie Mae Randle, the sister of the man with whom Oswald drove to work—Buell Wesley Frazier. Mrs. Randle stated that on the morning of November 22, while her brother was eating breakfast, she looked out the breakfast-room window and saw Oswald cross the street and walk toward the driveway where her brother parked his car near the carport. He carried a "heavy brown bag." [147] Oswald

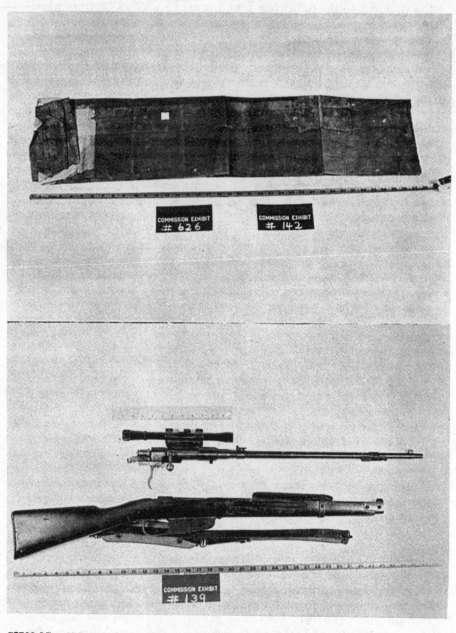

C2766 Mannlicher-Carcano rifle and paper bag found on the sixth floor of the Texas School Book Depository.

COMMISSION EXHIBIT NO. 1304

gripped the bag in his right hand near the top. "It tapered like this as he hugged it in his hand. It was * * * more bulky toward the bottom" than toward the top.[148] She then opened the kitchen door and saw Oswald open the right rear door of her brother's car and place the package in the back of the car.[149] Mrs. Randle estimated that the package was approximately 28 inches long and about 8 inches wide.[150] She thought that its color was similar to that of the bag found on the sixth floor of the School Book Depository after the assassination.[151]

Frazier met Oswald at the kitchen door and together they walked to the car.[152] After entering the car, Frazier glanced over his shoulder and noticed a brown paper package on the back seat. He asked, "What's the package, Lee?" Oswald replied, "curtain rods." [153] Frazier told the Commission "* * * the main reason he was going over there that Thursday afternoon when he was to bring back some curtain rods, so I didn't think any more about it when he told me that." [154] Frazier estimated that the bag was 2 feet long "give and take a few inches," and about 5 or 6 inches wide.[155] As they sat in the car, Frazier asked Oswald where his lunch was, and Oswald replied that he was going to buy his lunch that day.[156] Frazier testified that Oswald carried no lunch bag that day. "When he rode with me, I say he always brought lunch except that one day on November 22 he didn't bring his lunch that day." [157]

Frazier parked the car in the company parking lot about 2 blocks north of the Depository Building. Oswald left the car first, picked up the brown paper bag, and proceeded toward the building ahead of Frazier. Frazier walked behind and as they crossed the railroad tracks he watched the switching of the cars. Frazier recalled that one end of the package was under Oswald's armpit and the lower part was held with his right hand so that it was carried straight and parallel to his body. When Oswald entered the rear door of the Depository Building, he was about 50 feet ahead of Frazier. It was the first time that Oswald had not walked with Frazier from the parking lot to the building entrance.[158] When Frazier entered the building, he did not see Oswald.[159] One employee, Jack Dougherty, believed that he saw Oswald coming to work, but he does not remember that Oswald had anything in his hands as he entered the door.[160] No other employee has been found who saw Oswald enter that morning.[161]

In deciding whether Oswald carried the assassination weapon in the bag which Frazier and Mrs. Randle saw, the Commission has carefully considered the testimony of these two witnesses with regard to the length of the bag. Frazier and Mrs. Randle testified that the bag which Oswald was carrying was approximately 27 or 28 inches long,[162] whereas the wooden stock of the rifle, which is its largest component, measured 34.8 inches.[163] The bag found on the sixth floor was 38 inches long.[164] (See Commission Exhibit No. 1304, p. 132.) When Frazier appeared before the Commission and was asked to demonstrate how Oswald carried the package, he said, "Like I said, I remember that I didn't look at the package very much * * * but when I did look at it he did have his hands on the package like that," [165] and at this point Frazier placed the upper part of the package under his armpit and attempted to cup his right hand beneath the bottom of the bag. The disassembled rifle was too long to be carried in this manner. Similarly, when the butt of the rifle was placed in Frazier's hand, it extended above his shoulder to ear level.[166] Moreover, in an interview on December 1, 1963, with agents of the FBI, Frazier had marked the point on the back seat of his car which he believed was where the bag reached when it was laid on the seat with one edge against the door. The distance between the point on the seat and the door was 27 inches.[167]

Mrs. Randle said, when shown the paper bag, that the bag she saw Oswald carrying "wasn't that long, I mean it was folded down at the top as I told you. It definitely wasn't that long." [168] And she folded the bag to a length of about 28½ inches. Frazier doubted whether the bag that Oswald carried was as wide as the bag found on the sixth floor,[169] although Mrs. Randle testified that the width was approximately the same.[170]

The Commission has weighed the visual recollection of Frazier and Mrs. Randle against the evidence here presented that the bag Oswald carried contained the assassination weapon and has concluded that Frazier and Randle are mistaken as to the length of the bag. Mrs. Randle saw the bag fleetingly and her first remembrance is that it was held in Oswald's right hand "and it almost touched the ground as he carried it." [171] Frazier's view of the bag was from the rear. He continually advised that he was not paying close attention.[172] For example, he said,

> * * * I didn't pay too much attention the way he was walking because I was walking along there looking at the railroad cars and watching the men on the diesel switch them cars and I didn't pay too much attention on how he carried the package at all.[173]

Frazier could easily have been mistaken when he stated that Oswald held the bottom of the bag cupped in his hand with the upper end tucked into his armpit.

Location of Bag

A handmade bag of wrapping paper and tape [174] was found in the southeast corner of the sixth floor alongside the window from which the shots were fired.[175] (See Commission Exhibit No. 2707, p. 142.) It was not a standard type bag which could be obtained in a store and it was presumably made for a particular purpose. It was the appropriate size to contain, in disassembled form, Oswald's Mannlicher-Carcano rifle, serial No. C2766, which was also found on the sixth floor.[176] Three cartons had been placed at the window apparently to act as a gun rest and a fourth carton was placed behind those at the window.[177] (See Commission Exhibit No. 1301,

p. 138.) A person seated on the fourth carton could assemble the rifle without being seen from the rest of the sixth floor because the cartons stacked around the southeast corner would shield him.[178] (See Commission Exhibit No. 723, p. 80.) The presence of the bag in this corner is cogent evidence that it was used as the container for the rifle. At the time the bag was found, Lieutenant Day of the Dallas police wrote on it, "Found next to the sixth floor window gun fired from. May have been used to carry gun. Lt. J. C. Day." [179]

Scientific Evidence Linking Rifle and Oswald to Paper Bag

Oswald's fingerprint and palmprint found on bag.—Using a standard chemical method involving silver nitrates [180] the FBI Laboratory developed a latent palmprint and latent fingerprint on the bag. (See app. X, p. 565.) Sebastian F. Latona, supervisor of the FBI's Latent Fingerprint Section, identified these prints as the left index fingerprint and right palmprint of Lee Harvey Oswald.[181] The portion of the palm which was identified was the heel of the right palm, i.e., the area near the wrist, on the little finger side.[182] These prints were examined independently by Ronald G. Wittmus of the FBI,[183] and by Arthur Mandella, a fingerprint expert with the New York City Police Department.[184] Both concluded that the prints were the right palm and left index finger of Lee Oswald. No other identifiable prints were found on the bag.[185]

Oswald's palmprint on the bottom of the paper bag indicated, of course, that he had handled the bag. Furthermore, it was consistent with the bag having contained a heavy or bulky object when he handled it since a light object is usually held by the fingers.[186] The palmprint was found on the closed end of the bag. It was from Oswald's right hand, in which he carried the long package as he walked from Frazier's car to the building.[187]

Materials used to make bag.—On the day of the assassination, the Dallas police obtained a sample of wrapping paper and tape from the shipping room of the Depository and forwarded it to the FBI Laboratory in Washington.[188] James C. Cadigan, a questioned-documents expert with the Bureau, compared the samples with the paper and tape in the actual bag. He testified, "In all of the observations and physical tests that I made I found * * * the bag * * * and the paper sample * * * were the same." [189]

Among other tests, the paper and tape were submitted to fiber analysis and spectrographic examination.[190] In addition the tape was compared to determine whether the sample tape and the tape on the bag had been taken from the tape dispensing machine at the Depository. When asked to explain the similarity of characteristics, Cadigan stated : [191]

Well, briefly, it would be the thickness of both the paper and the tape, the color under various lighting conditions of both the paper and the tape, the width of the tape, the knurled markings on the surface of the fiber, the texture of the fiber, the felting pattern * * *

    *   *   *   *   *   *   *

I found that the paper sack found on the sixth floor * * * and the sample * * * had the same observable characteristics both under the microscope and all the visual tests that I could conduct.

    *   *   *   *   *   *   *

The papers I also found were similar in fiber composition, therefore, in addition to the visual characteristics, microscopic and UV [ultra violet] characteristics.

Mr. Cadigan concluded that the paper and tape from the bag were identical in all respects to the sample paper and tape taken from the Texas School Book Depository shipping room on November 22, 1963.[192]

On December 1, 1963, a replica bag was made from materials found on that date in the shipping room. This was done as an investigatory aid since the original bag had been discolored during various laboratory examinations and could not be used for valid identification by witnesses.[193] Cadigan found that the paper used to make this replica sack had different characteristics from the paper in the original bag.[194] The science of paper analysis enabled him to distinguish between different rolls of paper even though they were produced by the same manufacturer.[195]

Since the Depository normally used approximately one roll of paper every 3 working days,[196] it was not surprising that the replica sack made on December 1, 1963, had different characteristics from both the actual bag and the sample taken on November 22. On the other hand, since two rolls could be made from the same batch of paper, one cannot estimate when, prior to November 22, Oswald made the paper bag. However, the complete identity of characteristics between the paper and tape in the bag found on the sixth floor and the paper and tape found in the shipping room of the Depository on November 22 enabled the Commission to conclude that the bag was made from these materials. The Depository shipping department was on the first floor to which Oswald had access in the normal performance of his duties filling orders.[197]

Fibers in paper bag matched fibers in blanket.—When Paul M. Stombaugh of the FBI Laboratory examined the paper bag, he found, on the inside, a single brown delustered viscose fiber and several light green cotton fibers.[198] The blanket in which the rifle was stored was composed of brown and green cotton, viscose and woolen fibers.[199]

The single brown viscose fiber found in the bag matched some of the brown viscose fibers from the blanket in all observable characteristics.[200] The green cotton fibers found in the paper bag matched some of the green cotton fibers in the blanket "in all observable microscopic characteristics." [201] Despite these matches, however, Stombaugh was unable to render an opinion that the fibers which he found in the bag had probably come from the blanket, because other types of fibers present in the blanket were not found in the bag. He concluded:

> All I would say here is that it is possible that these fibers could have come from this blanket, because this blanket is composed of brown and green woolen fibers, brown and green delustered viscose fibers, and brown and green cotton fibers. * * * We found no brown cotton fibers, no green viscose fibers, and no woolen fibers.
> So if I found all of these then I would have been able to say these fibers probably had come from this blanket. But since I found so few, then I would say the possibility exists, these fibers could have come from this blanket.[202]

Stombaugh confirmed that the rifle could have picked up fibers from the blanket and transferred them to the paper bag.[203] In light of the other evidence linking Lee Harvey Oswald, the blanket, and the rifle to the paper bag found on the sixth floor, the Commission considered Stombaugh's testimony of probative value in deciding whether Oswald carried the rifle into the building in the paper bag.

Conclusion

The preponderance of the evidence supports the conclusion that Lee Harvey Oswald (1) told the curtain rod story to Frazier to explain both the return to Irving on a Thursday and the obvious bulk of the package which he intended to bring to work the next day; (2) took paper and tape from the wrapping bench of the Depository and fashioned a bag large enough to carry the disassembled rifle; (3) removed the rifle from the blanket in the Paines' garage on Thursday evening; (4) carried the rifle into the Depository Building, concealed in the bag; and, (5) left the bag alongside the window from which the shots were fired.

OSWALD AT WINDOW

Lee Harvey Oswald was hired on October 15, 1963, by the Texas School Book Depository as an "order filler." [204] He worked principally on the first and sixth floors of the building, gathering books listed on orders and delivering them to the shipping room on the first floor.[205] He had ready access to the sixth floor,[206] from the southeast corner window of which the shots were fired. [207] The Commission evaluated the physical evidence found near the window after the assassination and the testimony of eyewitnesses in deciding whether Lee Harvey Oswald was present at this window at the time of the assassination.

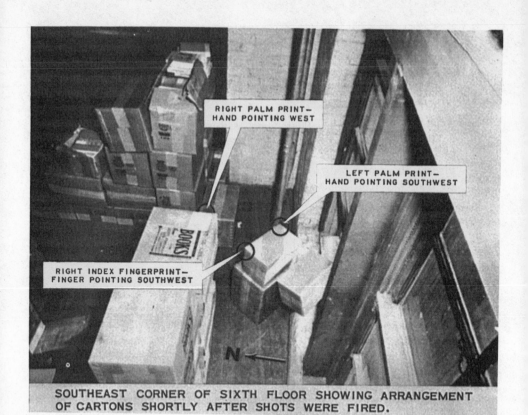

RIGHT PALM PRINT—
HAND POINTING WEST

LEFT PALM PRINT—
HAND POINTING SOUTHWEST

RIGHT INDEX FINGERPRINT—
FINGER POINTING SOUTHWEST

BOOKS

N

SOUTHEAST CORNER OF SIXTH FLOOR SHOWING ARRANGEMENT OF CARTONS SHORTLY AFTER SHOTS WERE FIRED.

COMMISSION EXHIBIT No. 1301

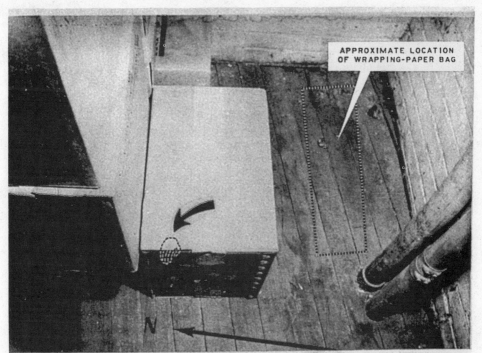

APPROXIMATE LOCATION OF WRAPPING-PAPER BAG AND LOCATION OF PALM PRINT ON CARTON NEAR WINDOW IN SOUTHEAST CORNER. (HAND POSITION SHOWN BY DOTTED LINE ON BOX)

COMMISSION EXHIBIT No. 1302

Palmprints and Fingerprints on Cartons and Paper Bag

Below the southeast corner window on the sixth floor was a large carton of books measuring approximately 18 by 12 by 14 inches which had been moved from a stack along the south wall.[208]   Atop this carton was a small carton marked "Rolling Readers," measuring approximately 13 by 9 by 8 inches.[209]   In front of this small carton and resting partially on the windowsill was another small "Rolling Readers" carton.[210]   These two small cartons had been moved from a stack about three aisles away.[211]   The boxes in the window appeared to have been arranged as a convenient gun rest.[212]   (See Commission Exhibit No. 1301, p. 138.)   Behind these boxes was another carton placed on the floor on which a man sitting could look southwesterly down Elm Street over the top of the "Rolling Readers" cartons.[213]   Next to these cartons was the handmade paper bag, previously discussed, on which appeared the print of the left index finger and right palm of Lee Harvey Oswald.[214]   (See Commission Exhibit No. 1302, p. 139.)

The cartons were forwarded to the FBI in Washington.   Sebastian F. Latona, supervisor of the Latent Fingerprint Section, testified that 20 identifiable fingerprints and 8 palmprints were developed on these cartons.[215]   The carton on the windowsill and the large carton below the window contained no prints which could be identified as being those of Lee Harvey Oswald.[216]   The other "Rolling Readers" carton, however, contained a palmprint and a fingerprint which were identified by Latona as being the left palmprint and right index fingerprint of Lee Harvey Oswald.[217]   (See app. X, p. 566.)

The Commission has considered the possibility that the cartons might have been moved in connection with the work that was being performed on the sixth floor on November 22.   Depository employees were laying a new floor at the west end and transferring books from the west to the east end of the building.[218]   The "Rolling Readers" cartons, however, had not been moved by the floor layers and had apparently been taken to the window from their regular position for some particular purpose.[219]   The "Rolling Readers" boxes contained, instead of books, light blocks used as reading aids.[220]   They could be easily adjusted and were still solid enough to serve as a gun rest.

The box on the floor, behind the three near the window, had been one of these moved by the floor layers from the west wall to near the east side of the building in preparation for the laying of the floor.[221]   During the afternoon of November 22, Lieutenant Day of the Dallas police dusted this carton with powder and developed a palmprint on the top edge of the carton on the side nearest the window.[222]   The position of this palmprint on the carton was parallel with the long axis of the box, and at right angles with the short axis; the bottom of the palm rested on the box.[223]   Someone sitting on the box facing the window would have his palm in this position if he placed his hand alongside his right hip.   (See Commission Exhibit No. 1302, p. 139.)   This print which had been cut out of the box was also forwarded to the FBI and Latona identified it as Oswald's right palmprint.[224]   In Latona's opinion "not too long" a time had elapsed between the time that the print was placed on the carton and the time that it had been developed by the Dallas police.[225]   Although Bureau experiments had shown that 24 hours was a likely maximum time, Latona stated that he could only testify with certainty that the print was less than 3 days old.[226]

The print, therefore, could have been placed on the carton at any time within this period.   The freshness of this print could be estimated only because the Dallas police developed it through the use of powder.   Since cartons absorb perspiration, powder can successfully develop a print on such material [227] only within a limited time. When the FBI in Washington received the cartons, the remaining prints, including Oswald's on the Rolling Readers carton, were developed by chemical processes.   The freshness of prints developed in this manner [228] cannot be estimated, so no conclusions can be drawn as to whether these remaining prints preceded or followed the print developed in Dallas by powder.   Most of the prints were found to have been placed on the cartons by an FBI clerk and a Dallas police officer after the cartons had been processed with powder by the Dallas Police.[229]   (See ch. VI, p. 249; app. X, p. 566.)

In his independent investigation, Arthur Mandella of the New York City Police Department reached the same conclusion as Latona that the prints found on the cartons were those of Lee Harvey Oswald.[229]   In addition, Mandella was of the opinion that the print taken from the carton on the floor was probably made within a day or a day and a half of the examination on November 22.[230]   Moreover, another expert with the FBI, Ronald G. Wittmus, conducted a separate examination and also agreed with Latona that the prints were Oswald's.[231]

In evaluating the significance of these fingerprint and palmprint identifications, the Commission considered the possibility that Oswald handled these cartons as part of his normal duties.   Since other identifiable prints were developed on the cartons, the Commission requested that they be compared with the prints of the 12 warehouse employees who, like Oswald, might have handled the cartons.   They were also compared with the prints of those law enforcement officials who might have handled the cartons.   The results of this investigation are fully discussed in chapter VI, page 249.   Although a person could handle a carton and not leave identifiable prints, none of these employees except Oswald left identifiable prints on the cartons.[232]   This finding, in addition to the freshness of one of the prints and the presence of Oswald's prints on two of the four cartons and the paper bag led the Commission to attach some probative value to the fingerprint and palmprint identifications in reaching the conclusion that Oswald was at the window from which the shots were fired, although the prints do not establish the exact time he was there.

141

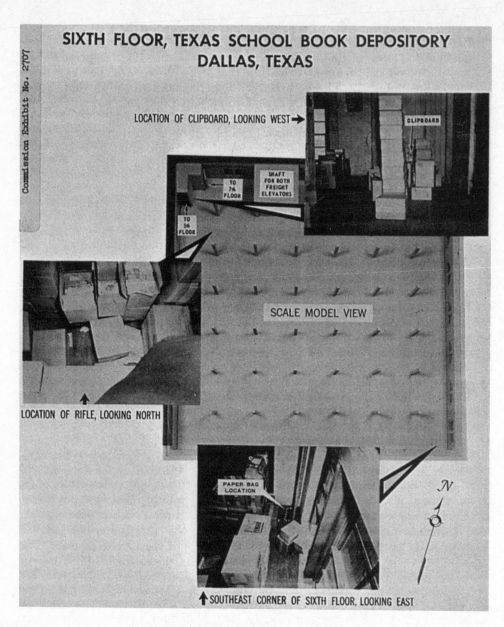

SIXTH FLOOR, TEXAS SCHOOL BOOK DEPOSITORY
DALLAS, TEXAS

LOCATION OF CLIPBOARD, LOOKING WEST→

CLIPBOARD

TO 7th FLOOR

SHAFT FOR BOTH FREIGHT ELEVATORS

TO 5th FLOOR

SCALE MODEL VIEW

LOCATION OF RIFLE, LOOKING NORTH

PAPER BAG LOCATION

N

↑SOUTHEAST CORNER OF SIXTH FLOOR, LOOKING EAST

COMMISSION EXHIBIT No. 2707

Oswald's Presence on Sixth Floor Approximately 35 Minutes Before the Assassination

Additional testimony linking Oswald with the point from which the shots were fired was provided by the testimony of Charles Givens, who was the last known employee to see Oswald inside the building prior to the assassination. During the morning of November 22, Givens was working with the floor-laying crew in the southwest section of the sixth floor.[233] At about 11:45 a.m. the floor-laying crew used both elevators to come down from the sixth floor. The employees raced the elevators to the first floor.[234] Givens saw Oswald standing at the gate on the fifth floor as the elevator went. by.[235] Givens testified that after reaching the first floor, "I discovered I left my cigarettes in my jacket pocket upstairs, and I took the elevator back upstairs to get my jacket with my cigarettes in it." [236] He saw Oswald, a clipboard in hand, walking from the southeast corner of the sixth floor toward the elevator.[237] (See Commission Exhibit No. 2707, p. 142.) Givens said to Oswald, "Boy are you going downstairs? * * * It's near lunch time." Oswald said, "No, sir. When you get downstairs, close the gate to the elevator." [238] Oswald was referring to the west elevator which operates by pushbutton and only with the gate closed.[239] Givens said, "Okay," and rode down in the east elevator. When he reached the first floor, the west elevator—the one with the gate—was not there. Givens thought this was about 11:55 a.m.[240] None of the Depository employees is known to have seen Oswald again until after the shooting.[241]

The significance of Givens' observation that Oswald was carrying his clipboard became apparent on December 2, 1963, when an employee, Frankie Kaiser, found a clipboard hidden by book cartons in the northwest corner of the sixth floor at the west wall a few feet from where the rifle had been found.[242] This clipboard had been made by Kaiser and had his name on it.[243] Kaiser identified it as the clipboard which Oswald had appropriated from him when Oswald came to work at the Depository.[244] Three invoices on this clipboard, each dated November 22, were for Scott-Foresman books, located on the first and sixth floors.[245] Oswald had not filled any of the three orders.[246]

Eyewitness Identification of Assassin

Howard L. Brennan was an eyewitness to the shooting. As indicated previously the Commission considered his testimony as probative in reaching the conclusion that the shots came from the sixth floor, southeast corner window of the Depository Building.[247] (See ch. III, pp. 61–68.) Brennan also testified that Lee Harvey Oswald, whom he viewed in a police lineup on the night of the assassination, was the man he saw fire the shots from the sixth-floor window of the Depository Building.[248] When the shots were fired, Brennan was in an excellent position to observe anyone in the window. He was sitting on a concrete wall on the southwest corner of Elm and Houston Streets, looking north at the Depository Building which was directly in front of him.[249] The window was approximately 120 feet away.[250] (See Commission Exhibit No. 477, p. 62.)

In the 6- to 8-minute period before the motorcade arrived,[251] Brennan saw a man leave and return to the window "a couple of times."[252] After hearing the first shot, which he thought was a motorcycle back-fire, Brennan glanced up at the window. He testified that "this man I saw previously was aiming for his last shot * * * as it appeared to me he was standing up and resting against the left window sill * * *.[253]

Brennan saw the man fire the last shot and disappear from the window. Within minutes of the assassination, Brennan described the man to the police.[254] This description most probably led to the radio alert sent to police cars at approximately 12:45 p.m., which described the suspect as white, slender, weighing about 165 pounds, about 5'10" tall, and in his early thirties.[255] In his sworn statement to the police later that day, Brennan described the man in similar terms, except that he gave the weight as between 165 and 175 pounds and the height was omitted.[256] In his testimony before the Commission, Brennan described the person he saw as "* * * a man in his early thirties, fair complexion, slender, but neat, neat slender, possible 5 foot 10 * * * 160 to 170 pounds."[257] Oswald was 5'9", slender and 24 years old. When arrested, he gave his weight as 140 pounds.[258] On other occasions he gave weights of both 140 and 150 pounds.[259] The New Orleans police records of his arrest in August of 1963 show a weight of 136 pounds.[260] The autopsy report indicated an estimated weight of 150 pounds.[261]

Brennan's description should also be compared with the eyewitness description broadcast over the Dallas police radio at 1:22 p.m. of the man who shot Patrolman J. D. Tippit. The suspect was described as "a white male about 30, 5'8", black hair, slender. * * *"[262] At 1:29 p.m. the police radio reported that the description of the suspect in the Tippit shooting was similar to the description which had been given by Brennan in connection with the assassination.[263] Approximately 7 or 8 minutes later the police radio reported that "an eyeball witness" described the suspect in the Tippit shooting as "a white male, 27, 5'11", 165 pounds, black wavy hair."[264] As will be discussed fully below, the Commission has concluded that this suspect was Lee Harvey Oswald.

Although Brennan testified that the man in the window was standing when he fired the shots,[265] most probably he was either sitting or kneeling. The half-open window,[266] the arrangement of the boxes,[267] and the angle of the shots virtually preclude a standing position.[268] It is understandable, however, for Brennan to have believed that the man with the rifle was standing. A photograph of the building taken seconds after the assassination shows three employees looking out of the fifth-floor window directly below the window from which the shots were fired. Brennan testified that they were standing,[269] which is their apparent position in the photograph.[270] (See Dillard Exhibits Nos. C and D, pp. 66–67.) But the testimony of these employees,[271] together with photographs subsequently taken of them at the scene of the assassination,[272] establishes that they were either squatting or kneeling. (See Commission Exhibit No. 485, p. 69.) Since the window ledges in the Depository Building are lower than in most buildings,[273] a person squatting or kneeling exposes more of his body than would normally be the case. From the street, this creates the impression that the person is standing. Brennan could have seen enough of the body of a kneeling or squatting person to estimate his height.

Shortly after the assassination Brennan noticed two of these employees leaving the building and immediately identified them as having been in the fifth-floor windows.[274] When the three employees appeared before the Commission, Brennan identified the two whom he saw leave the building.[275] The two men, Harold Norman and James Jarman, Jr., each confirmed that when they came out of the building, they saw and heard Brennan describing what he had seen.[276] Norman stated, "* * * I remember him talking and I believe I remember seeing him saying that he saw us when we first went up to the fifth-floor window, he saw us then." [277] Jarman heard Brennan "talking to this officer about that he had heard these shots and he had seen the barrel of the gun sticking out the window, and he said that the shots came from inside the building." [278]

During the evening of November 22, Brennan identified Oswald as the person in the lineup who bore the closest resemblance to the man in the window but he said he was unable to make a positive identification.[279] Prior to the lineup, Brennan had seen Oswald's picture on television and he told the Commission that whether this affected his identification "is something I do not know." [280] In an interview with FBI agents on December 17, 1963, Brennan stated that he was sure that the person firing the rifle was Oswald.[281] In another interview with FBI agents on January 7, 1964, Brennan appeared to revert to his earlier inability to make a positive identification,[282] but, in his testimony before the Commission, Brennan stated that his remarks of January 7 were intended by him merely as an accurate report of what he said on November 22.[283]

Brennan told the Commission that he could have made a positive identification in the lineup on November 22 but did not do so because he felt that the assassination was "a Communist activity, and I felt like there hadn't been more than one eyewitness, and if it got to be a known fact that I was an eyewitness, my family or I, either one, might not be safe." [284] When specifically asked before the Commission whether or not he could positively identify the man he saw in the sixth-floor window as the same man he saw in the police station, Brennan stated, "I could at that time—I could, with all sincerity, identify him as being the same man." [285]

Although the record indicates that Brennan was an accurate observer, he declined to make a positive identification of Oswald when he first saw him in the police lineup.[286] The Commission, therefore, does not base its conclusion concerning the identity of the assassin on Brennan's subsequent certain identification of Lee Harvey Oswald as the man he saw fire the rifle. Immediately after the assassination, however, Brennan described to the police the man he saw in the window and then identified Oswald as the person who most nearly resembled the man he saw. The Commission is satisfied that, at the least, Brennan saw a man in the window who closely resembled Lee Harvey Oswald, and that Brennan believes the man he saw was in fact Lee Harvey Oswald.

Two other witnesses were able to offer partial descriptions of a man they saw in the southeast corner window of the sixth floor approximately 1 minute before the assassination, although neither witness saw the shots being fired.[287] Ronald Fischer and Robert Edwards were standing on the curb at the southwest corner of Elm and Houston Streets,[288] the same corner where Brennan was sitting on a concrete wall.[289] Fischer testified that about 10 or 15 seconds before the motorcade turned onto Houston Street from Main Street, Edwards said, "Look at that guy there in that window." [290]

Fischer looked up and watched the man in the window for 10 or 15 seconds and then started watching the motorcade, which came into view on Houston Street.[291] He said that the man held his attention until the motorcade came because the man:

> * * * appeared uncomfortable for one, and secondly, he wasn't watching * * * he didn't look like he was watching for the parade. He looked like he was looking down toward the Trinity River and the Triple Underpass down at the end—toward the end of Elm Street. And * * * all the time I watched him, he never moved his head, he never—he never moved anything. Just was there transfixed.[292]

Fischer placed the man in the easternmost window on the south side of the Depository Building on either the fifth or the sixth floor.[293] He said that he could see the man from the middle of his chest to the top of his head, and that as he was facing the window the man was in the lower right-hand portion of the window and "seemed to be sitting a little forward." [294] The man was dressed in a light-colored, open-neck shirt which could have been either a sports shirt or a T-shirt, and he had brown hair, a slender face and neck with light complexion, and looked to be 22 or 24 years old.[295] The person in the window was a white man and "looked to me like he was looking straight at the Triple Underpass" down Elm Street.[296] Boxes and cases were stacked behind him.[297]

Approximately 1 week after the assassination, according to Fischer, policemen showed him a picture of Oswald.[298] In his testimony he said, "I told them that that could have been the man. * * * That that could have been the man that I saw in the window in the School Book Depository Building, but that I was not sure." [299] Fischer described the man's hair as some shade of brown—"it wasn't dark and it wasn't light." [300] On November 22, Fischer had apparently described the man as "light-headed." [301] Fischer explained that he did not mean by the earlier statement that the man was blond, but rather that his hair was not black.[302]

Robert Edwards said that, while looking at the south side of the Depository Building shortly before the motorcade, he saw nothing of importance "except maybe one individual who was up there in the corner room of the sixth floor which was crowded in among boxes." [303] He said that this was a white man about average in size, "possibly thin," and that he thought the man had light-brown hair.[304] Fischer and Edwards did not see the man clearly enough or long enough to identify him. Their testimony is of probative value, however, because their limited description is consistent with that of the man who has been found by the Commission, based on other evidence, to have fired the shots from the window.

Another person who saw the assassin as the shots were fired was Amos L. Euins, age 15, who was one of the first witnesses to alert the police to the Depository as the source of the shots, as has been discussed in chapter III.[305] Euins, who was on the southwest corner of Elm and Houston Streets,[306] testified that he could not describe the man he saw in the window. According to Euins, however, as the man lowered his head in order to aim the rifle down Elm Street, he appeared to have a white bald spot on his head.[307] Shortly after the assassination, Euins signed an affidavit describing the man as "white," [308] but a radio reporter testified that Euins described the man to him as "colored." [309] In his Commission testimony, Euins stated that he could not ascertain the man's race and that the statement in the affidavit was intended to refer only to the white spot on the man's head and not to his race.[310] A Secret Service agent who spoke to Euins approximately 20 to 30 minutes after the assassination confirmed that Euins could neither describe the man in the window nor indicate his race.[311] Accordingly, Euins' testimony is considered probative as to the source of the shots but is inconclusive as to the identity of the man in the window.

In evaluating the evidence that Oswald was at the southeast corner window of the sixth floor at the time of the shooting, the Commission has considered the allegation that Oswald was photographed standing in front of the building when the shots were fired. The picture which gave rise to these allegations was taken by Associated Press Photographer James W. Altgens, who was standing on the south side of Elm Street between the Triple Underpass and the Depository Building.[312] As the motorcade started its descent down Elm Street, Altgens snapped a picture of the Presidential limousine with the entrance to the Depository Building in the background.[313] Just before snapping the picture Altgens heard a noise which sounded like the popping of a firecracker. Investigation has established that Altgens' picture was taken approximately 2 seconds after the firing of the shot which entered the back of the President's neck.[314]

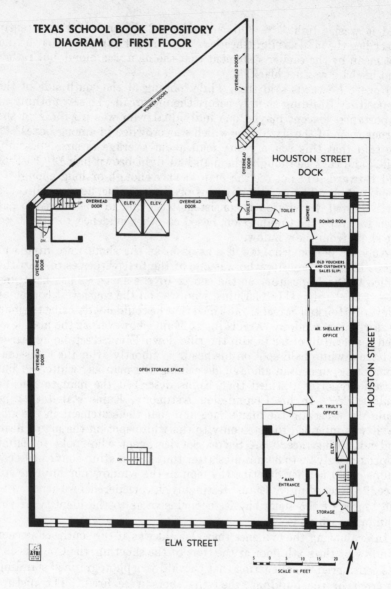

TEXAS SCHOOL BOOK DEPOSITORY
DIAGRAM OF FIRST FLOOR

WOODEN DOORS

OVERHEAD DOORS

UP

OVERHEAD DOOR

HOUSTON STREET
DOCK

UP OVERHEAD DOOR ELEV. ELEV. OVERHEAD DOOR

TOILET TOILET SHOWER

DN. DOMINO ROOM

OVERHEAD DOOR

OLD VOUCHERS AND CUSTOMER'S SALES SLIP

MR. SHELLEY'S OFFICE

OVERHEAD DOOR

OPEN STORAGE SPACE

HOUSTON STREET

MR. TRULY'S OFFICE

ELEV.

DN.

UP

MAIN ENTRANCE

STORAGE

ELM STREET

N

5   0   5   10   15   20
SCALE IN FEET

COMMISSION EXHIBIT No. 1061

148

In the background of this picture were several employees watching the parade from the steps of the Depository Building. One of these employees was alleged to resemble Lee Harvey Oswald.[315] The Commission has determined that the employee was in fact Billy Nolan Lovelady, who identified himself in the picture.[316] Standing alongside him were Buell Wesley Frazier[317] and William Shelley,[318] who also identified Lovelady. The Commission is satisfied that Oswald does not appear in this photograph. (See Commission Exhibit No. 900, p. 113.)

Oswald's Actions in Building After Assassination

In considering whether Oswald was at the southeast corner window at the time the shots were fired, the Commission has reviewed the testimony of witnesses who saw Oswald in the building within minutes after the assassination. The Commission has found that Oswald's movements, as described by these witnesses, are consistent with his having been at the window at 12:30 p.m.

The encounter in the lunchroom.—The first person to see Oswald after the assassination was Patrolman M. L. Baker of the Dallas Police Department. Baker was riding a two-wheeled motorcycle behind the last press car of the motorcade.[319] As he turned the corner from Main onto Houston at a speed of about 5 to 10 miles per hour,[320] a strong wind blowing from the north almost unseated him.[321] At about this time he heard the first shot.[322] Having recently heard the sounds of rifles while on a hunting trip, Baker recognized the shots as that of a high-powered rifle; "it sounded high and I immediately kind of looked up, and I had a feeling that it came from the building, either right in front of me [the Depository Building] or of the one across to the right of it."[323] He saw pigeons flutter upward. He was not certain, "but I am pretty sure they came from the building right on the northwest corner."[324] He heard two more shots spaced "pretty well even to me."[325] After the third shot, he "revved that motorcycle up," drove to the northwest corner of Elm and Houston, and parked approximately 10 feet from the traffic signal.[326] As he was parking he noted that people were "falling, and they were rolling around down there * * * grabbing their children" and rushing about.[327] A woman screamed, "Oh, they have shot that man, they have shot that man."[328] Baker "had it in mind that the shots came from the top of this building here," so he ran straight to the entrance of the Depository Building.[329]

Baker testified that he entered the lobby of the building and "spoke out and asked where the stairs or elevator was * * * and this man, Mr. Truly, spoke up and says, it seems to me like he says, 'I am a building manager. Follow me, officer, and I will show you.'"[330] Baker and building superintendent Roy Truly went through a second set of doors[331] and stopped at a swinging door where Baker bumped into Truly's back.[332] They went through the swinging door and continued at "a good trot" to the northwest corner of the floor where Truly hoped to find one of the two freight elevators. (See Commission

149

TEXAS SCHOOL BOOK DEPOSITORY
DIAGRAM OF SECOND FLOOR
SHOWING ROUTE OF OSWALD

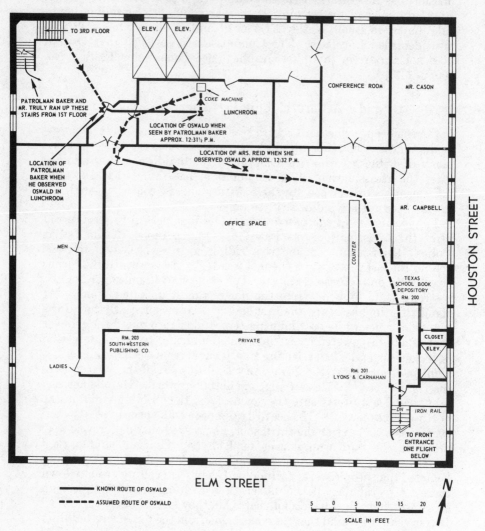

COMMISSION EXHIBIT No. 1118

150

Exhibit No. 1061, p. 148.) Neither elevator was there.[333] Truly pushed the button for the west elevator which operates automatically if the gate is closed.[334] He shouted twice, "Turn loose the elevator." [335] When the elevator failed to come, Baker said, "let's take the stairs," and he followed Truly up the stairway, which is to the west of the elevator.[336]

The stairway is located in the northwest corner of the Depository Building. The stairs from one floor to the next are "L-shaped," with both legs of the "L" approximately the same length. Because the stairway itself is enclosed, neither Baker nor Truly could see anything on the second-floor hallway until they reached the landing at the top of the stairs.[337] On the second-floor landing there is a small open area with a door at the east end. This door leads into a small vestibule, and another door leads from the vestibule into the second-floor lunch-room.[338] (See Commission Exhibit No. 1118, p. 150.) The lunchroom door is usually open, but the first door is kept shut by a closing mechanism on the door.[339] This vestibule door is solid except for a small glass window in the upper part of the door.[340] As Baker reached the second floor, he was about 20 feet from the vestibule door.[341] He intended to continue around to his left toward the stairway going up but through the window in the door he caught a fleeting glimpse of a man walking in the vestibule toward the lunchroom.[342]

Since the vestibule door is only a few feet from the lunchroom door,[343] the man must have entered the vestibule only a second or two before Baker arrived at the top of the stairwell. Yet he must have entered the vestibule door before Truly reached the top of the stair-well, since Truly did not see him.[344] If the man had passed from the vestibule into the lunchroom, Baker could not have seen him. Baker said:

> He [Truly] had already started around the bend to come to the next elevator going up, I was coming out this one on the second floor, and I don't know, I was kind of sweeping this area as I come up, I was looking from right to left and as I got to this door here I caught a glimpse of this man, just, you know, a sudden glimpse * * * and it looked to me like he was going away from me. * * *
>
> I can't say whether he had gone on through that door [the lunchroom door] or not. All I did was catch a glance at him, and evidently he was—this door might have been, you know, closing and almost shut at that time. [345]

With his revolver drawn, Baker opened the vestibule door and ran into the vestibule. He saw a man walking away from him in the lunchroom. Baker stopped at the door of the lunchroom and commanded, "Come here." [346] The man turned and walked back toward Baker.[347] He had been proceeding toward the rear of the lunch-room.[348] Along a side wall of the lunchroom was a soft drink vending machine,[349] but at that time the man had nothing in his hands.[350]

Meanwhile, Truly had run up several steps toward the third floor. Missing Baker, he came back to find the officer in the doorway to the lunchroom "facing Lee Harvey Oswald."[351] Baker turned to Truly and said, "Do you know this man, does he work here?"[352] Truly replied, "Yes."[353] Baker stated later that the man did not seem to be out of breath; he seemed calm. "He never did say a word or nothing. In fact, he didn't change his expression one bit."[354] Truly said of Oswald: "He didn't seem to be excited or overly afraid or anything. He might have been a bit startled, like I might have been if somebody confronted me. But I cannot recall any change in expression of any kind on his face."[355] Truly thought that the officer's gun at that time appeared to be almost touching the middle portion of Oswald's body. Truly also noted at this time that Oswald's hands were empty.[356]

In an effort to determine whether Oswald could have descended to the lunchroom from the sixth floor by the time Baker and Truly arrived, Commission counsel asked Baker and Truly to repeat their movements from the time of the shot until Baker came upon Oswald in the lunchroom. Baker placed himself on a motorcycle about 200 feet from the corner of Elm and Houston Streets where he said he heard the shots.[357] Truly stood in front of the building.[358] At a given signal, they reenacted the event. Baker's movements were timed with a stopwatch. On the first test, the elapsed time between the simulated first shot and Baker's arrival on the second-floor stair landing was 1 minute and 30 seconds. The second test run required 1 minute and 15 seconds.[359]

A test was also conducted to determine the time required to walk from the southeast corner of the sixth floor to the second-floor lunchroom by stairway. Special Agent John Howlett of the Secret Service carried a rifle from the southeast corner of the sixth floor along the east aisle to the northeast corner. He placed the rifle on the floor near the site where Oswald's rifle was actually found after the shooting. Then Howlett walked down the stairway to the second-floor landing and entered the lunchroom. The first test, run at normal walking pace, required 1 minute, 18 seconds;[360] the second test, at a "fast walk" took 1 minute, 14 seconds.[361] The second test followed immediately after the first. The only interval was the time necessary to ride in the elevator from the second to the sixth floor and walk back to the southeast corner. Howlett was not short winded at the end of either test run.[362]

The minimum time required by Baker to park his motorcycle and reach the second-floor lunchroom was within 3 seconds of the time needed to walk from the southeast corner of the sixth floor down the stairway to the lunchroom. The time actually required for Baker and Truly to reach the second floor on November 22 was probably longer than in the test runs. For example, Baker required 15 seconds after the simulated shot to ride his motorcycle 180 to 200 feet, park it, and run 45 feet to the building.[363] No allowance was made for the special conditions which existed on the day of the assassination—possible delayed reaction to the shot, jostling with the crowd of people on

152

the steps and scanning the area along Elm Street and the parkway.[364] Baker said, "We simulated the shots and by the time we got there, we did everything that I did that day, and this would be the minimum, because I am sure that I, you know, it took me a little longer." [365] On the basis of this time test, therefore, the Commission concluded that Oswald could have fired the shots and still have been present in the second-floor lunchroom when seen by Baker and Truly.

That Oswald descended by stairway from the sixth floor to the second-floor lunchroom is consistent with the movements of the two elevators, which would have provided the other possible means of descent. When Truly, accompanied by Baker, ran to the rear of the first floor, he was certain that both elevators, which occupy the same shaft,[366] were on the fifth floor.[367] Baker, not realizing that there were two elevators, thought that only one elevator was in the shaft and that it was two or three floors above the second floor.[368] In the few seconds which elapsed while Baker and Truly ran from the first to the second floor, neither of these slow elevators could have descended from the fifth to the second floor. Furthermore, no elevator was at the second floor when they arrived there.[369] Truly and Baker continued up the stairs after the encounter with Oswald in the lunchroom. There was no elevator on the third or fourth floor. The east elevator was on the fifth floor when they arrived; the west elevator was not. They took the east elevator to the seventh floor and ran up a stairway to the roof where they searched for several minutes.[370]

Jack Dougherty, an employee working on the fifth floor, testified that he took the west elevator to the first floor after hearing a noise which sounded like a backfire.[371] Eddie Piper, the janitor, told Dougherty that the President had been shot,[372] but in his testimony Piper did not mention either seeing or talking with Dougherty during these moments of excitement.[373] Both Dougherty and Piper were confused witnesses. They had no exact memory of the events of that afternoon. Truly was probably correct in stating that the west elevator was on the fifth floor when he looked up the elevator shaft from the first floor. The west elevator was not on the fifth floor when Baker and Truly reached that floor, probably because Jack Dougherty took it to the first floor while Baker and Truly were running up the stairs or in the lunchroom with Oswald. Neither elevator could have been used by Oswald as a means of descent.

Oswald's use of the stairway is consistent with the testimony of other employees in the building. Three employees—James Jarman, Jr., Harold Norman, and Bonnie Ray Williams—were watching the parade from the fifth floor, directly below the window from which the shots were fired. They rushed to the west windows after the shots were fired and remained there until after they saw Patrolman Baker's white helmet on the fifth floor moving toward the elevator.[374] While they were at the west windows their view of the stairwell was completely blocked by shelves and boxes.[375] This is the period during which Oswald would have descended the stairs. In all likelihood Dougherty took the elevator down from the fifth floor after Jarman,

Norman, and Williams ran to the west windows and were deciding what to do. None of these three men saw Dougherty, probably because of the anxiety of the moment and because of the books which may have blocked the view.[376] Neither Jarman, Norman, Williams, or Dougherty saw Oswald.[377]

Victoria Adams, who worked on the fourth floor of the Depository Building, claimed that within about 1 minute following the shots she ran from a window on the south side of the fourth floor,[378] down the rear stairs to the first floor, where she encountered two Depository employees—William Shelley and Billy Lovelady.[379] If her estimate of time is correct, she reached the bottom of the stairs before Truly and Baker started up, and she must have run down the stairs ahead of Oswald and would probably have seen or heard him. Actually she noticed no one on the back stairs. If she descended from the fourth to the first floor as fast as she claimed in her testimony, she would have seen Baker or Truly on the first floor or on the stairs, unless they were already in the second-floor lunchroom talking to Oswald. When she reached the first floor, she actually saw Shelley and Lovelady slightly east of the east elevator.

Shelley and Lovelady, however, have testified that they were watching the parade from the top step of the building entrance when Gloria Calverly, who works in the Depository Building, ran up and said that the President had been shot.[380] Lovelady and Shelley moved out into the street.[381] About this time Shelley saw Truly and Patrolman Baker go into the building.[382] Shelley and Lovelady, at a fast walk or trot, turned west into the railroad yards and then to the west side of the Depository Building. They reentered the building by the rear door several minutes after Baker and Truly rushed through the front entrance.[383] On entering, Lovelady saw a girl on the first floor who he believes was Victoria Adams.[384] If Miss Adams accurately recalled meeting Shelley and Lovelady when she reached the bottom of the stairs, then her estimate of the time when she descended from the fourth floor is incorrect, and she actually came down the stairs several minutes after Oswald and after Truly and Baker as well.

Oswald's departure from building.—Within a minute after Baker and Truly left Oswald in the lunchroom, Mrs. R. A. Reid, clerical supervisor for the Texas School Book Depository, saw him walk through the clerical office on the second floor toward the door leading to the front stairway. Mrs. Reid had watched the parade from the sidewalk in front of the building with Truly and Mr. O. V. Campbell, vice president of the Depository.[385] She testified that she heard three shots which she thought came from the building.[386] She ran inside and up the front stairs into the large open office reserved for clerical employees. As she approached her desk, she saw Oswald.[387] He was walking into the office from the back hallway, carrying a full bottle of Coca-Cola in his hand,[388] presumably purchased after the encounter with Baker and Truly. As Oswald passed Mrs. Reid she said, "Oh, the President has been shot, but maybe they didn't hit him." [389] Oswald mumbled something and walked by.[390] She paid no more attention to him. The only exit from the office in the direction Oswald was moving was through the door to the front stairway.[391] (See Commission Exhibit 1118, p. 150.) Mrs. Reid testified that when she saw Oswald, he was wearing a T-shirt and no jacket.[392] When he left home that morning, Marina Oswald, who was still in bed, suggested that he wear a jacket.[393] A blue jacket, later identified by Marina Oswald as her husband's,[394] was subsequently found in the building,[395] apparently left behind by Oswald.

Mrs. Reid believes that she returned to her desk from the street about 2 minutes after the shooting.[396] Reconstructing her movements, Mrs. Reid ran the distance three times and was timed in 2 minutes by stopwatch.[397] The reconstruction was the minimum time.[398] Accordingly, she probably met Oswald at about 12:32, approximately 30–45 seconds after Oswald's lunchroom encounter with Baker and Truly. After leaving Mrs. Reid in the front office, Oswald could have gone down the stairs and out the front door by 12:33 p.m.[399]—3 minutes after the shooting. At that time the building had not yet been sealed off by the police.

While it was difficult to determine exactly when the police sealed off the building, the earliest estimates would still have permitted Oswald to leave the building by 12:33. One of the police officers assigned to the corner of Elm and Houston Streets for the Presidential motorcade, W. E. Barnett, testified that immediately after the shots he went to the rear of the building to check the fire escape. He then returned to the corner of Elm and Houston where he met a sergeant who instructed him to find out the name of the building. Barnett ran to the building, noted its name, and then returned to the corner.[400] There he was met by a construction worker—in all likelihood Howard Brennan, who was wearing his work helmet.[401] This worker told Barnett that the shots had been fired from a window in the Depository Building, whereupon Barnett posted himself at the front door to make certain that no one left the building. The sergeant did the same thing at the rear of the building.[402] Barnett estimated that approximately 3 minutes elapsed between the time he heard the last of the shots and the time he started guarding the front door. According to Barnett, "there were people going in and out" during this period.[403]

Sgt. D. V. Harkness of the Dallas police said that to his knowledge the building was not sealed off at 12:36 p.m. when he called in on police radio that a witness (Amos Euins) had seen shots fired from a window of the building.[404] At that time, Inspector Herbert V. Sawyer's car was parked in front of the building.[405] Harkness did not know whether or not two officers with Sawyer were guarding the doors.[406] At 12:34 p.m. Sawyer heard a call over the police radio that the shots had come from the Depository Building.[407] He then entered the building and took the front passenger elevator as far as it would go—the fourth floor.[408] After inspecting this floor, Sawyer returned to the street about 3 minutes after he entered the building.[409] After he returned to the street he directed Sergeant Harkness to station two patrolmen at the front door and not let anyone in or out;

he also directed that the back door be sealed off.[410] This was no earlier than 12:37 p.m.[411] and may have been later. Special Agent Forrest V. Sorrels of the Secret Service, who had been in the motorcade, testified that after driving to Parkland Hospital, he returned to the Depository Building about 20 minutes after the shooting, found no police officers at the rear door and was able to enter through this door without identifying himself.[412]

Although Oswald probably left the building at about 12:33 p.m., his absence was not noticed until at least one-half hour later. Truly, who had returned with Patrolman Baker from the roof, saw the police questioning the warehouse employees. Approximately 15 men worked in the warehouse [413] and Truly noticed that Oswald was not among those being questioned.[414] Satisfying himself that Oswald was missing, Truly obtained Oswald's address, phone number, and description from his employment application card. The address listed was for the Paine home in Irving. Truly gave this information to Captain Fritz who was on the sixth floor at the time.[415] Truly estimated that he gave this information to Fritz about 15 or 20 minutes after the shots,[416] but it was probably no earlier than 1:22 p.m., the time when the rifle was found. Fritz believed that he learned of Oswald's absence after the rifle was found.[417] The fact that Truly found Fritz in the northwest corner of the floor, near the point where the rifle was found, supports Fritz' recollection.

Conclusion

Fingerprint and palmprint evidence establishes that Oswald handled two of the four cartons next to the window and also handled a paper bag which was found near the cartons. Oswald was seen in the vicinity of the southeast corner of the sixth floor approximately 35 minutes before the assassination and no one could be found who saw Oswald anywhere else in the building until after the shooting. An eyewitness to the shooting immediately provided a description of the man in the window which was similar to Oswald's actual appearance. This witness identified Oswald in a lineup as the man most nearly resembling the man he saw and later identified Oswald as the man he observed. Oswald's known actions in the building immediately after the assassination are consistent with his having been at the southeast corner window of the sixth floor at 12:30 p.m. On the basis of these findings the Commission has concluded that Oswald, at the time of the assassination, was present at the window from which the shots were fired.

THE KILLING OF PATROLMAN J. D. TIPPIT

After leaving the Depository Building at approximately 12:33 p.m., Lee Harvey Oswald proceeded to his roominghouse by bus and taxi. He arrived at approximately 1 p.m. and left a few minutes later. At about 1:16 p.m., a Dallas police officer, J. D. Tippit, was shot less than 1 mile from Oswald's roominghouse. In deciding whether Oswald killed Patrolman Tippit the Commission considered the following: (1) positive identification of the killer by two eyewitnesses who saw the shooting and seven eyewitnesses who heard the shots and saw the gunman flee the scene with the revolver in his hand, (2) testimony of firearms identification experts establishing the identity of the murder weapon, (3) evidence establishing the ownership of the murder weapon, (4) evidence establishing the ownership of a zipper jacket found along the path of flight taken by the gunman from the scene of the shooting to the place of arrest.

Oswald's Movements After Leaving Depository Building

The bus ride.—According to the reconstruction of time and events which the Commission found most credible, Lee Harvey Oswald left the building approximately 3 minutes after the assassination. He probably walked east on Elm Street for seven blocks to the corner of Elm and Murphy where he boarded a bus which was heading back in the direction of the Depository Building, on its way to the Oak Cliff section of Dallas. (See Commission Exhibit 1119–A, p. 158.)

When Oswald was apprehended, a bus transfer marked for the Lakewood-Marsalis route was found in his shirt pocket.[418] The transfer was dated "Fri. Nov. 22, '63" and was punched in two places by the busdriver. On the basis of this punchmark, which was distinctive to each Dallas driver, the transfer was conclusively identified as having been issued by Cecil J. McWatters, a busdriver for the Dallas Transit Co.[419] On the basis of the date and time on the transfer, McWatters was able to testify that the transfer had been issued by him on a trip which passed a check point at St. Paul and Elm Streets at 12:36 p.m., November 22, 1963.[420]

McWatters was sure that he left the checkpoint on time and he estimated that it took him 3 to 4 minutes to drive three blocks west from the checkpoint to Field Street, which he reached at about 12:40 p.m.[421] McWatters' recollection is that he issued this transfer to a man who entered his bus just beyond Field Street, where a man beat on the front door of the bus, boarded it and paid his fare.[422] About two blocks later, a woman asked to get off to make a 1 o'clock train at Union Station and requested a transfer which she might use if she got through the traffic.

* * * So I gave her a transfer and opened the door and she was going out the gentleman I had picked up about two blocks [back] asked for a transfer and got off at the same place in the middle of the block where the lady did.
* * * It was the intersection near Lamar Street, it was near Poydras and Lamar Street.[423]

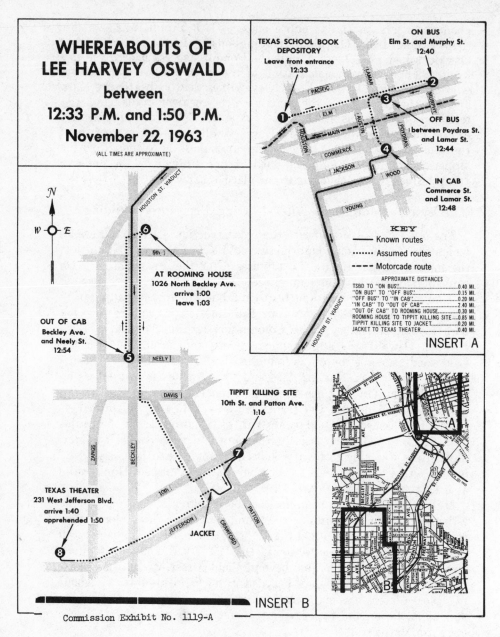

WHEREABOUTS OF LEE HARVEY OSWALD
between
12:33 P.M. and 1:50 P.M.
November 22, 1963
(ALL TIMES ARE APPROXIMATE)

TEXAS SCHOOL BOOK DEPOSITORY
Leave front entrance
12:33

ON BUS
Elm St. and Murphy St.
12:40

OFF BUS
between Poydras St. and Lamar St.
12:44

IN CAB
Commerce St. and Lamar St.
12:48

KEY
—— Known routes
······· Assumed routes
- - - Motorcade route

APPROXIMATE DISTANCES
TSBD TO "ON BUS"..............................0.40 MI.
"ON BUS" TO "OFF BUS"......................0.15 MI.
"OFF BUS" TO "IN CAB"......................0.20 MI.
"IN CAB" TO "OUT OF CAB"...............2.40 MI.
"OUT OF CAB" TO ROOMING HOUSE........0.30 MI.
ROOMING HOUSE TO TIPPIT KILLING SITE....0.85 MI.
TIPPIT KILLING SITE TO JACKET...............0.20 MI.
JACKET TO TEXAS THEATER...................0.40 MI.

INSERT A

N
W ─●─ E
S

AT ROOMING HOUSE
1026 North Beckley Ave.
arrive 1:00
leave 1:03

OUT OF CAB
Beckley Ave. and Neely St.
12:54

TIPPIT KILLING SITE
10th St. and Patton Ave.
1:16

TEXAS THEATER
231 West Jefferson Blvd.
arrive 1:40
apprehended 1:50

INSERT B

Commission Exhibit No. 1119-A

COMMISSION EXHIBIT No. 1119–A

158

The man was on the bus approximately 4 minutes.[424]

At about 6:30 p.m. on the day of the assassination, McWatters viewed four men in a police lineup. He picked Oswald from the lineup as the man who had boarded the bus at the "lower end of town on Elm around Houston," and who, during the ride south on Marsalis, had an argument with a woman passenger.[425] In his Commission testimony, McWatters said he had been in error and that a teenager named Milton Jones was the passenger he had in mind.[426] In a later interview, Jones confirmed that he had exchanged words with a woman passenger on the bus during the ride south on Marsalis.[427] McWatters also remembered that a man received a transfer at Lamar and Elm Streets and that a man in the lineup was about the size of this man.[428] However, McWatters' recollection alone was too vague to be a basis for placing Oswald on the bus.

Riding on the bus was an elderly woman, Mary Bledsoe, who confirmed the mute evidence of the transfer. Oswald had rented a room from Mrs. Bledsoe about 6 weeks before, on October 7,[429] but she had asked him to leave at the end of a week. Mrs. Bledsoe told him "I am not going to rent to you any more." [430] She testified, "I didn't like his attitude. * * * There was just something about him I didn't like or want him. * * * Just didn't want him around me." [431] On November 22, Mrs. Bledsoe came downtown to watch the Presidential motorcade. She boarded the Marsalis bus at St. Paul and Elm Streets to return home.[432] She testified further:

> And, after we got past Akard, at Murphy—I figured it out. Let's see. I don't know for sure. Oswald got on. He looks like a maniac. His sleeve was out here. * * * His shirt was undone.
>
> *   *   *   *   *   *   *
>
> Was a hole in it, hole, and he was dirty, and I didn't look at him. I didn't want to know I even seen him * * *
>
> *   *   *   *   *   *   *
>
> * * * he looked so bad in his face, and his face was so distorted.
>
> *   *   *   *   *   *   *
>
> * * * Hole in his sleeve right here.[433]

As Mrs. Bledsoe said these words, she pointed to her right elbow.[434] When Oswald was arrested in the Texas Theatre, he was wearing a brown sport shirt with a hole in the right sleeve at the elbow.[435] Mrs. Bledsoe identified the shirt as the one Oswald was wearing and she stated she was certain that it was Oswald who boarded the bus.[436] Mrs. Bledsoe recalled that Oswald sat halfway to the rear of the bus which moved slowly and intermittently as traffic became heavy.[437] She heard a passing motorist tell the driver that the President had been shot.[438] People on the bus began talking about it. As the bus neared Lamar Street, Oswald left the bus and disappeared into the crowd.[439]

The Marsalis bus which Oswald boarded traveled a route west on Elm, south on Houston, and southwest across the Houston viaduct to service the Oak Cliff area along Marsalis.[440] A Beckley bus which also served the Oak Cliff area, followed the same route as the Marsalis bus through downtown Dallas, except that it continued west on Elm, across Houston in front of the Depository Building, past the Triple Underpass into west Dallas, and south on Beckley.[441] Marsalis Street is seven blocks from Beckley.[442] Oswald lived at 1026 North Beckley.[443] He could not reach his roominghouse on the Marsalis bus, but the Beckley bus stopped across the street.[444] According to McWatters, the Beckley bus was behind the Marsalis bus, but he did not actually see it.[445] Both buses stopped within one block of the Depository Building. Instead of waiting there, Oswald apparently went as far away as he could and boarded the first Oak Cliff bus which came along rather than wait for one which stopped across the street from his roominghouse.

In a reconstruction of this bus trip, agents of the Secret Service and the FBI walked the seven blocks from the front entrance of the Depository Building to Murphy and Elm three times, averaging 6½ minutes for the three trips.[446] A bus moving through heavy traffic on Elm from Murphy to Lamar was timed at 4 minutes.[447] If Oswald left the Depository Building at 12:33 p.m., walked seven blocks directly to Murphy and Elm, and boarded a bus almost immediately, he would have boarded the bus at approximately 12:40 p.m. and left it at approximately 12:44 p.m. (See Commission Exhibit No. 1119–A, p. 158.)

Roger D. Craig, a deputy sheriff of Dallas County, claimed that about 15 minutes after the assassination he saw a man, whom he later identified as Oswald,[448] coming from the direction of the Depository Building and running down the hill north of Elm Street toward a light-colored Rambler station wagon, which was moving slowly along Elm toward the underpass.[449] The station wagon stopped to pick up the man and then drove off.[450] Craig testified that later in the afternoon he saw Oswald in the police interrogation room and told Captain Fritz that Oswald was the man he saw.[451] Craig also claimed that when Fritz pointed out to Oswald that Craig had identified him, Oswald rose from his chair, looked directly at Fritz, and said, "Everybody will know who I am now." [452]

The Commission could not accept important elements of Craig's testimony. Captain Fritz stated that a deputy sheriff whom he could not identify did ask to see him that afternoon and told him a similar story to Craig's.[453] Fritz did not bring him into his office to identify Oswald but turned him over to Lieutenant Baker for questioning. If Craig saw Oswald that afternoon, he saw him through the glass windows of the office. And neither Captain Fritz nor any other officer can remember that Oswald dramatically arose from his chair and said,

"Everybody will know who I am now." [454]   If Oswald had made such a statement, Captain Fritz and others present would probably have remembered it.   Craig may have seen a person enter a white Rambler station wagon 15 or 20 minutes after the shooting and travel west on Elm Street, but the Commission concluded that this man was not Lee Harvey Oswald, because of the overwhelming evidence that Oswald was far away from the building by that time.

The taxicab ride.—William Whaley, a taxicab driver, told his employer on Saturday morning, November 23, that he recognized Oswald from a newspaper photograph as a man whom he had driven to the Oak Cliff area the day before. [455]   Notified of Whaley's statement, the police brought him to the police station that afternoon.   He was taken to the lineup room where, according to Whaley, five young teenagers, all handcuffed together, were displayed with Oswald. [456]   He testified that Oswald looked older than the other boys. [457]   The police asked him whether he could pick out his passenger from the lineup.   Whaley picked Oswald.   He said,

> * * * you could have picked him out without identifying him by just listening to him because he was bawling out the policeman, telling them it wasn't right to put him in line with these teenagers and all of that and they asked me which one and I told them.   It was him all right, the same man.
>
> *   *   *   *   *   *   *
>
> He showed no respect for the policemen, he told them what he thought about them.   They knew what they were doing and they were trying to railroad him and he wanted his lawyer. [458]

Whaley believes that Oswald's conduct did not aid him in his identification "because I knew he was the right one as soon as I saw him." [459]

Whaley's memory of the lineup is inaccurate.   There were four men altogether, not six men, in the lineup with Oswald. [460]   Whaley said that Oswald was the man under No. 2. [461]   Actually Oswald was under No. 3.   Only two of the men in the lineup with Oswald were teenagers: John T. Horn, aged 18, was No. 1; David Knapp, aged 18, was No. 2; Lee Oswald was No. 3; and Daniel Lujan, aged 26, was No. 4. [462]

When he first testified before the Commission, Whaley displayed a trip manifest [463] which showed a 12 o'clock trip from Travis Hotel to the Continental bus station, unloaded at 12:15 p.m., a 12:15 p.m. pickup at Continental to Greyhound, unloaded at 12:30 p.m., and a pickup from Greyhound (bus station) at 12:30 p.m., unloaded at 500 North Beckley at 12:45 p.m.   Whaley testified that he did not keep an accurate time record of his trips but recorded them by the quarter hour, and that sometimes he made his entry right after a trip while at other times he waited to record three or four trips. [464]   As he unloaded his Continental bus station passenger in front of Greyhound, he started to get out to buy a package of cigarettes.[465] He saw a man walking south on Lamar from Commerce. The man was dressed in faded blue color khaki work clothes, a brown shirt, and some kind of work jacket that almost matched his pants.[466] The man asked, "May I have the cab?", and got into the front seat.[467] Whaley described the ensuing events as follows:

> And about that time an old lady, I think she was an old lady, I don't remember nothing but her sticking her head down past him in the door and said, "Driver, will you call me a cab down here?"
>
> She had seen him get this cab and she wanted one, too, and he opened the door a little bit like he was going to get out and he said, "I will let you have this one," and she says, "No, the driver can call me one."
>
>   *   *   *   *   *   *   *
>
> * * * I asked him where he wanted to go. And he said, "500 North Beckley."
>
> Well, I started up, I started to that address, and the police cars, the sirens was going, running crisscrossing everywhere, just a big uproar in that end of town and I said, "What the hell. I wonder what the hell is the uproar?"
>
> And he never said anything. So I figured he was one of these people that don't like to talk so I never said any more to him.
>
> But when I got pretty close to 500 block at Neches and North Beckley which is the 500 block, he said, "This will do fine," and I pulled over to the curb right there. He gave me a dollar bill, the trip was 95 cents. He gave me a dollar bill and didn't say anything, just got out and closed the door and walked around the front of the cab over to the other side of the street [east side of the street]. Of course, the traffic was moving through there and I put it in gear and moved on, that is the last I saw of him.[468]

Whaley was somewhat imprecise as to where he unloaded his passenger. He marked what he thought was the intersection of Neches and Beckley on a map of Dallas with a large "X." [469] He said, "Yes, sir; that is right, because that is the 500 block of North Beckley." [470] However, Neches and Beckley do not intersect. Neches is within one-half block of the roominghouse at 1026 North Beckley where Oswald was living. The 500 block of North Beckley is five blocks south of the roominghouse.[471]

After a review of these inconsistencies in his testimony before the Commission, Whaley was interviewed again in Dallas. The route of the taxicab was retraced under the direction of Whaley.[472] He directed the driver of the car to a point 20 feet north of the northwest corner of the intersection of Beckley and Neely, the point at which he said his passenger alighted.[473] This was the 700 block of North

Beckley.[474] The elapsed time of the reconstructed run from the Greyhound Bus Station to Neely and Beckley was 5 minutes and 30 seconds by stopwatch.[475] The walk from Beckley and Neely to 1026 North Beckley was timed by Commission counsel at 5 minutes and 45 seconds.[476]

Whaley testified that Oswald was wearing either the gray zippered jacket or the heavy blue jacket.[477] He was in error, however. Oswald could not possibly have been wearing the blue jacket during the trip with Whaley, since it was found in the "domino" room of the Depository late in November.[478] Moreover, Mrs. Bledsoe saw Oswald in the bus without a jacket and wearing a shirt with a hole at the elbow.[479] On the other hand, Whaley identified Commission Exhibit No. 150 (the shirt taken from Oswald upon arrest) as the shirt his passenger was wearing.[480] He also stated he saw a silver identification bracelet on his passenger's left wrist.[481] Oswald was wearing such a bracelet when he was arrested.[482]

On November 22, Oswald told Captain Fritz that he rode a bus to a stop near his home and then walked to his roominghouse.[483] When queried the following morning concerning a bus transfer found in his possession at the time of his arrest, he admitted receiving it.[484] And when interrogated about a cab ride, Oswald also admitted that he left the slow-moving bus and took a cab to his roominghouse.[485]

The Greyhound Bus Station at Lamar and Jackson Streets, where Oswald entered Whaley's cab, is three to four short blocks south of Lamar and Elm.[486] If Oswald left the bus at 12:44 p.m. and walked directly to the terminal, he would have entered the cab at 12:47 or 12:48 p.m. If the cab ride was approximately 6 minutes, as was the reconstructed ride, he would have reached his destination at approximately 12:54 p.m. If he was discharged at Neely and Beckley and walked directly to his roominghouse, he would have arrived there about 12:59 to 1 p.m. From the 500 block of North Beckley, the walk would be a few minutes longer, but in either event he would have been in the roominghouse at about 1 p.m. This is the approximate time he entered the roominghouse, according to Earlene Roberts, the housekeeper there.[487] (See Commission Exhibit No. 1119–A, p. 158.)

Arrival and departure from roominghouse.—Earlene Roberts, housekeeper for Mrs. A. C. Johnson at 1026 North Beckley, knew Lee Harvey Oswald under the alias of O. H. Lee. She first saw him the day he rented a room at that address on October 14, 1963.[488] He signed his name as O. H. Lee on the roominghouse register.[489]

Mrs. Roberts testified that on Thursday, November 21, Oswald did not come home. On Friday, November 22, about 1 p.m., he entered the house in unusual haste. She recalled that it was subsequent to the time the President had been shot. After a friend had called and told her, "President Kennedy has been shot," she turned on the television. When Oswald came in she said, "Oh, you are in a hurry," but Oswald did not respond. He hurried to his room and stayed no longer than 3 or 4 minutes. Oswald had entered the house in his shirt sleeves,

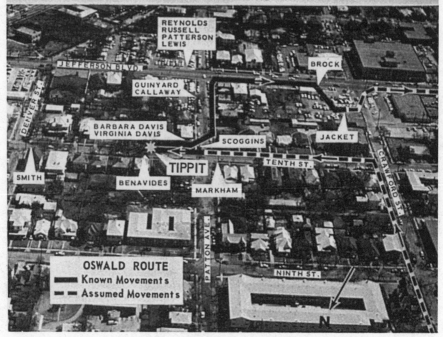

COMMISSION EXHIBIT No. 1968

but when he left, he was zipping up a jacket. Mrs. Roberts saw him a few seconds later standing near the bus stop in front of the house on the east side of Beckley.[490]

Oswald was next seen about nine-tenths of a mile away at the southeast corner of 10th Street and Patton Avenue, moments before the Tippit shooting. (See Commission Exhibit No. 1119–A, p. 158.) If Oswald left his roominghouse shortly after 1 p.m. and walked at a brisk pace, he would have reached 10th and Patton shortly after 1:15 p.m.[491] Tippit's murder was recorded on the police radio tape at about 1:16 p.m.[492]

Description of Shooting

Patrolman J. D. Tippit joined the Dallas Police Department in July 1952.[493] He was described by Chief Curry as having the reputation of being "a very fine, dedicated officer." [494] Tippit patroled district No. 78 in the Oak Cliff area of Dallas during daylight hours. He drove a police car painted distinctive colors with No. 10 prominently displayed on each side. Tippit rode alone, as only one man was normally assigned to a patrol car in residential areas during daylight shifts.[495]

At about 12:44 p.m. on November 22, the radio dispatcher on channel 1 ordered all downtown patrol squads to report to Elm and Houston, code 3 (emergency).[496] At 12:45 p.m. the dispatcher ordered No. 78 (Tippit) to "move into central Oak Cliff area." [497] At 12:54 p.m., Tippit reported that he was in the central Oak Cliff area at Lancaster and Eighth. The dispatcher ordered Tippit to be: "* * * at large for any emergency that comes in." [498] According to Chief Curry, Tippit was free to patrol the central Oak Cliff area.[499] Tippit must have heard the description of the suspect wanted for the President's shooting; it was broadcast over channel 1 at 12:45 p.m., again at 12:48 p.m., and again at 12:55 p.m.[500] The suspect was described as a "white male, approximately 30, slender build, height 5 foot 10 inches, weight 165 pounds." [501] A similar description was given on channel 2 at 12:45 p.m.[502]

At approximately 1:15 p.m., Tippit, who was cruising east on 10th Street, passed the intersection of 10th and Patton, about eight blocks from where he had reported at 12:54 p.m. About 100 feet past the intersection Tippit stopped a man walking east along the south side of Patton. (See Commission Exhibit No. 1968, p. 164.) The man's general description was similar to the one broadcast over the police radio. Tippit stopped the man and called him to his car. He approached the car and apparently exchanged words with Tippit through the right front or vent window. Tippit got out and started to walk around the front of the car. As Tippit reached the left front wheel the man pulled out a revolver and fired several shots. Four bullets hit Tippit and killed him instantly. The gunman started back toward Patton Avenue, ejecting the empty cartridge cases before reloading with fresh bullets.

At least 12 persons saw the man with the revolver in the vicinity of the Tippit crime scene at or immediately after the shooting. By the evening of November 22, five of them had identified Lee Harvey Oswald in police lineups as the man they saw. A sixth did so the next day. Three others subsequently identified Oswald from a photograph. Two witnesses testified that Oswald resembled the man they had seen. One witness felt he was too distant from the gunman to make a positive identification. (See Commission Exhibit No. 1968, p. 164.)

A taxi driver, William Scoggins, was eating lunch in his cab which was parked on Patton facing the southeast corner of 10th Street and Patton Avenue a few feet to the north.[503] A police car moving east on 10th at about 10 or 12 miles an hour passed in front of his cab. About 100 feet from the corner the police car pulled up alongside a man on the sidewalk. This man, dressed in a light-colored jacket, approached the car. Scoggins lost sight of him behind some shrubbery on the southeast corner lot, but he saw the policeman leave the car, heard three or four shots, and then saw the policeman fall. Scoggins hurriedly left his seat and hid behind the cab as the man came back toward the corner with gun in hand. The man cut across the yard through some bushes, passed within 12 feet of Scoggins, and ran south on Patton. Scoggins saw him and heard him mutter either "Poor damn cop" or "Poor dumb cop." [504] The next day Scoggins viewed a lineup of four persons and identified Oswald as the man whom he had seen the day before at 10th and Patton.[505] In his testimony before the Commission, Scoggins stated that he thought he had seen a picture of Oswald in the newspapers prior to the lineup identification on Saturday. He had not seen Oswald on television and had not been shown any photographs of Oswald by the police.[506]

Another witness, Domingo Benavides, was driving a pickup truck west on 10th Street. As he crossed the intersection a block east of 10th and Patton, he saw a policeman standing by the left door of the police car parked along the south side of 10th. Benavides saw a man standing at the right side of the parked police car. He then heard three shots and saw the policeman fall to the ground. By this time the pickup truck was across the street and about 25 feet from the police car. Benavides stopped and waited in the truck until the gunman ran to the corner. He saw him empty the gun and throw the shells into some bushes on the southeast corner lot.[507] It was Benavides, using Tippit's car radio, who first reported the killing of Patrolman Tippit at about 1:16 p.m.: "We've had a shooting out here." [508] He found two empty shells in the bushes and gave them to Patrolman J. M. Poe who arrived on the scene shortly after the shooting.[509] Benavides never saw Oswald after the arrest. When questioned by police officers on the evening of November 22, Benavides told them that he did not think that he could identify the man who fired the shots. As a result, they did not take him to the police station.

He testified that the picture of Oswald which he saw later on television bore a resemblance to the man who shot Officer Tippit.[510]

Just prior to the shooting, Mrs. Helen Markham, a waitress in downtown Dallas, was about to cross 10th Street at Patton. As she waited on the northwest corner of the intersection for traffic to pass,[511] she noticed a young man as he was "almost ready to get up on the curb"[512] at the southeast corner of the intersection, approximately 50 feet away. The man continued along 10th Street. Mrs. Markham saw a police car slowly approach the man from the rear and stop alongside of him. She saw the man come to the right window of the police car. As he talked, he leaned on the ledge of the right window with his arms. The man appeared to step back as the policeman "calmly opened the car door" and very slowly got out and walked toward the front of the car. The man pulled a gun. Mrs. Markham heard three shots and saw the policeman fall to the ground near the left front wheel. She raised her hands to her eyes as the man started to walk back toward Patton.[513] She peered through her fingers, lowered her hands, and saw the man doing something with his gun. "He was just fooling with it. I didn't know what he was doing. I was afraid he was fixing to kill me."[514] The man "in kind of a little trot" headed down Patton toward Jefferson Boulevard, a block away. Mrs. Markham then ran to Officer Tippit's side and saw him lying in a pool of blood.[515]

Helen Markham was screaming as she leaned over the body.[516] A few minutes later she described the gunman to a policeman.[517] Her description and that of other eyewitnesses led to the police broadcast at 1:22 p.m. describing the slayer as "about 30, 5'8'', black hair, slender."[518] At about 4:30 p.m., Mrs. Markham, who had been greatly upset by her experience, was able to view a lineup of four men handcuffed together at the police station.[519] She identified Lee Harvey Oswald as the man who shot the policeman.[520] Detective L. C. Graves, who had been with Mrs. Markham before the lineup testified that she was "quite hysterical" and was "crying and upset."[521] He said that Mrs. Markham started crying when Oswald walked into the lineup room.[522] In testimony before the Commission, Mrs. Markham confirmed her positive identification of Lee Harvey Oswald as the man she saw kill Officer Tippit.[523]

In evaluating Mrs. Markham's identification of Oswald, the Commission considered certain allegations that Mrs. Markham described the man who killed Patrolman Tippit as "short, a little on the heavy side," and having "somewhat bushy" hair.[524] The Commission reviewed the transcript of a phone conversation in which Mrs. Markham is alleged to have provided such a description.[525] A review of the complete transcript has satisfied the Commission that Mrs. Markham strongly reaffirmed her positive identification of Oswald and denied having described the killer as short, stocky and having bushy hair. She stated that the man weighed about 150 pounds.[526] Although she used the words "a little bit bushy" to describe the gunman's hair, the transcript establishes that she was referring to the uncombed state of his hair, a description fully supported by a photograph of Oswald taken at the time of his arrest. (See Pizzo Exhibit No. 453–C, p. 177.) Although in the phone conversation she described the man as "short," [527] on November 22, within minutes of the shooting and before the lineup, Mrs. Markham described the man to the police as 5'8" tall.[528]

During her testimony Mrs. Markham initially denied that she ever had the above phone conversation.[529] She has subsequently admitted the existence of the conversation and offered an explanation for her denial.[530] Addressing itself solely to the probative value of Mrs. Markham's contemporaneous description of the gunman and her positive identification of Oswald at a police lineup, the Commission considers her testimony reliable. However, even in the absence of Mrs. Markham's testimony, there is ample evidence to identify Oswald as the killer of Tippit.

Two young women, Barbara Jeanette Davis and Virginia Davis, were in an apartment of a multiple-unit house on the southeast corner of 10th and Patton when they heard the sound of gunfire and the screams of Helen Markham. They ran to the door in time to see a man with a revolver cut across their lawn and disappear around a corner of the house onto Patton.[531] Barbara Jeanette Davis assumed that he was emptying his gun as "he had it open and was shaking it." [532] She immediately called the police. Later in the day each woman found an empty shell on the ground near the house. These two shells were delivered to the police.[533]

On the evening of November 22, Barbara Jeanette and Virginia Davis viewed a group of four men in a lineup and each one picked Oswald as the man who crossed their lawn while emptying his pistol.[534] Barbara Jeanette Davis testified that no one had shown her a picture of Oswald before the identification and that she had not seen him on television. She was not sure whether she had seen his picture in a newspaper on the afternoon or evening of November 22 prior to the lineup.[535] Her reaction when she saw Oswald in the lineup was that "I was pretty sure it was the same man I saw. When they made him turn sideways, I was positive that was the one I seen." [536] Similarly, Virginia Davis had not been shown pictures of anyone prior to the lineup and had not seen either television or the newspapers during the afternoon.[537] She identified Oswald, who was the No. 2 man in the lineup,[538] as the man she saw running with the gun: she testified, "I would say that was him for sure." [539] Barbara Jeanette Davis and Virginia Davis were sitting alongside each other when they made their positive identifications of Oswald.[540] Each woman whispered Oswald's number to the detective. Each testified that she was the first to make the identification.[541]

William Arthur Smith was about a block east of 10th and Patton when he heard shots. He looked west on 10th and saw a man running to the west and a policeman falling to the ground. Smith failed to make himself known to the police on November 22. Several days later he reported what he had seen and was questioned by FBI agents.[542] Smith subsequently told a Commission staff member that he saw Oswald on television the night of the murder and thought that Oswald was the man he had seen running away from the shooting.[543] On television Oswald's hair looked blond, whereas Smith remembered that the man who ran away had hair that was brown or brownish black. Later, the FBI showed Smith a picture of Oswald. In the picture the hair was brown.[544] According to his testimony, Smith told the FBI, "It looked more like him than it did on television." He stated further that from "What I saw of him" the man looked like the man in the picture.[545]

Two other important eyewitnesses to Oswald's flight were Ted Callaway, manager of a used-car lot on the northeast corner of Patton Avenue and Jefferson Boulevard, and Sam Guinyard, a porter at the lot. They heard the sound of shots to the north of their lot.[546] Callaway heard five shots, and Guinyard three. Both ran to the sidewalk on the east side of Patton at a point about a half a block south of 10th. They saw a man coming south on Patton with a revolver held high in his right hand. According to Callaway, the man crossed to the west side of Patton.[547] From across the street Callaway yelled, "Hey, man, what the hell is going on?" He slowed down, halted, said something, and then kept on going to the corner, turned right, and continued west on Jefferson.[548] Guinyard claimed that the man ran down the east side of Patton and passed within 10 feet of him before crossing to the other side.[549] Guinyard and Callaway ran to 10th and Patton and found Tippit lying in the street beside his car.[550] Apparently he had reached for his gun; it lay beneath him outside of the holster. Callaway picked up the gun.[551] He and Scoggins attempted to chase down the gunman in Scoggin's taxicab,[552] but he had disappeared. Early in the evening of November 22, Guinyard and Callaway viewed the same lineup of four men from which Mrs. Markham had earlier made her identification of Lee Harvey Oswald. Both men picked Oswald as the man who had run south on Patton with a gun in his hand.[553] Callaway told the Commission: "So they brought four men in. I stepped to the back of the room, so I could kind of see him from the same distance which I had seen him before. And when he came out I knew him." [554] Guinyard said, "I told them that was him right there. I pointed him out right there." [555] Both Callaway and Guinyard testified that they had not been shown any pictures by the police before the lineup.[556]

The Dallas Police Department furnished the Commission with pictures of the men who appeared in the lineups with Oswald,[557] and the Commission has inquired into general lineup procedures used by the Dallas police as well as the specific procedures in the lineups involving Oswald.[558] The Commission is satisfied that the lineups were conducted fairly.

As Oswald ran south on Patton Avenue toward Jefferson Boulevard he was moving in the direction of a used-car lot located on the southeast corner of this intersection.[559] Four men—Warren Reynolds,[560]

169

REVOLVER USED IN TIPPIT KILLING

COMMISSION EXHIBIT No. 143

Harold Russell,[561] Pat Patterson,[562] and L. J. Lewis [563]—were on the lot at the time, and they saw a white male with a revolver in his hands running south on Patton. When the man reached Jefferson, he turned right and headed west. Reynolds and Patterson decided to follow him. When he reached a gasoline service station one block away he turned north and walked toward a parking area in the rear of the station. Neither Reynolds nor Patterson saw the man after he turned off Jefferson at the service station.[564] These four witnesses were interviewed by FBI agents 2 months after the shooting. Russell and Patterson were shown a picture of Oswald and they stated that Oswald was the man they saw on November 22, 1963. Russell confirmed this statement in a sworn affidavit for the Commission.[565] Patterson, when asked later to confirm his identification by affidavit said he did not recall having been shown the photograph. He was then shown two photographs of Oswald and he advised that Oswald was "unquestionably" the man he saw.[566] Reynolds did not make a positive identification when interviewed by the FBI, but he subsequently testified before a Commission staff member and, when shown two photographs of Oswald, stated that they were photographs of the man he saw.[567] L. J. Lewis said in an interview that because of the distance from which he observed the gunman he would hesitate to state whether the man was identical with Oswald.[568]

Murder Weapon

When Oswald was arrested, he had in his possession a Smith & Wesson .38 Special caliber revolver, serial number V510210. (See Commission Exhibit No. 143, p. 170). Two of the arresting officers placed their initials on the weapon and a third inscribed his name. All three identified Exhibit No. 143 as the revolver taken from Oswald when he was arrested.[569] Four cartridge cases were found in the shrubbery on the corner of 10th and Patton by three of the eyewitnesses—Domingo Benavides, Barbara Jeanette Davis, and Virginia Davis.[570] It was the unanimous and unequivocal testimony of expert witnesses before the Commission that these used cartridge cases were fired from the revolver in Oswald's possession to the exclusion of all other weapons. (See app. X, p. 559.)

Cortlandt Cunningham, of the Firearms Identification Unit of the FBI Laboratory, testified that he compared the four empty cartridge cases found near the scene of the shooting with a test cartridge fired from the weapon in Oswald's possession when he was arrested. Cunningham declared that this weapon fired the four cartridges to the exclusion of all other weapons. Identification was effected through breech face marks and firing pin marks.[571] Robert A. Frazier and Charles Killion, other FBI firearms experts, independently examined the four cartridge cases and arrived at the same conclusion as Cunningham.[572] At the request of the Commission, Joseph D. Nicol, superintendent of the Illinois Bureau of Criminal Identification Investigation, also examined the four cartridge cases found near the site of the homicide and compared them with the test cartridge cases fired from the Smith & Wesson revolver taken from Oswald. He concluded that all of these cartridges were fired from the same weapon.[573]

Cunningham compared four lead bullets recovered from the body of Patrolman Tippit with test bullets fired from Oswald's revolver.[574] He explained that the bullets were slightly smaller than the barrel of the pistol which had fired them. This caused the bullets to have an erratic passage through the barrel and impressed upon the lead of the bullets inconsistent individual characteristics which made identification impossible. Consecutive bullets fired from the revolver by the FBI experts could not be identified as having been fired from that revolver.[575] (See app. X, p. 559.) Cunningham testified that all of the bullets were mutilated, one being useless for comparison purposes. All four bullets were fired from a weapon with five lands and grooves and a right twist [576] which were the rifling characteristics of the revolver taken from Oswald. He concluded, however, that he could not say whether the four bullets were fired from the revolver in Oswald's possession.[577] "The only thing I can testify is they could have on the basis of the rifling characteristics—they could have been." [578]

Nicol differed with the FBI experts on one bullet taken from Tippit's body. He declared that this bullet [579] was fired from the same weapon that fired the test bullets to the exclusion of all other weapons. But he agreed that because the other three bullets were mutilated, he could not determine if they had been fired from the same weapon as the test bullets.[580]

The examination and testimony of the experts enabled the Commission to conclude that five shots may have been fired, even though only four bullets were recovered. Three of the bullets recovered from Tippit's body were manufactured by Winchester-Western, and the fourth bullet by Remington-Peters, but only two of the four discarded cartridge cases found on the lawn at 10th Street and Patton Avenue were of Winchester-Western manufacture.[581] Therefore, one cartridge case of this type was not recovered. And though only one bullet of Remington-Peters manufacture was recovered, two empty cartridge cases of that make were retrieved. Therefore, either one bullet of Remington-Peters manufacture is missing or one used Remington-Peters cartridge case, which may have been in the revolver before the shooting, was discarded along with the others as Oswald left the scene. If a bullet is missing, five were fired. This corresponds with the observation and memory of Ted Callaway,[582] and possibly Warren Reynolds, but not with the other eyewitnesses who claim to have heard from two to four shots.

Ownership of Revolver

By checking certain importers and dealers after the assassination of President Kennedy and slaying of Officer Tippit, agents of the FBI determined that George Rose & Co. of Los Angeles was a major dis-

172

REVOLVER PURCHASE AND SHIPPING DOCUMENTS

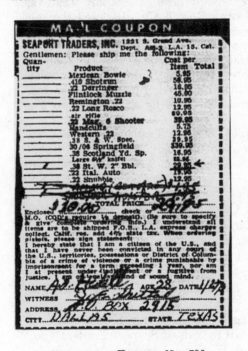

MA·L COUPON

SEAPORT TRADERS, INC. 1221 S. Grand Ave.
Dept. AM-3 L.A. 15. Cat.
Gentlemen: Please ship me the following:

Quan-tity	Product	Cost per Item	Total
	Mexican Bowie	5.95	
	.410 Shotgun	26.95	
	.22 Derringer	14.95	
	Flintlock Muzzle	45.00	
	Remington .22	10.95	
	.22 Long Rosco	12.95	
	air rifle	$9.95	
	.22 Mag. 6 Shooter	39.95	
	Handcuffs	5.75	
	Western .22	12.95	
	.38 S. & W. Spec.	29.95	
	30/06 Springfield	$39.95	
	.38 Scotland Yd. Sp.	16.95	
	Large 8½ knife	13.95	
	.38 St. W. 2" Bbl.	29.95	
	.22 Ital. Auto	19.95	
	.22 Snubble	12.95	

COMMISSION EXHIBIT No. 790

MICHAELIS EXHIBIT No. 2

MICHAELIS EXHIBIT No. 5

MICHAELIS EXHIBIT No. 4

tributor of this type of revolver.[583]   Records of Seaport Traders, Inc., a mail-order division of George Rose & Co., disclosed that on January 3, 1963, the company received from Empire Wholesale Sporting Goods, Ltd., Montreal, a shipment of 99 guns in one case. Among these guns was a .38 Special caliber Smith & Wesson revolver, serial No. V510210, the only revolver made by Smith & Wesson with this serial number.[584]   When first manufactured, it had a 5-inch barrel. George Rose & Co. had the barrel shortened by a gunsmith to 2¼ inches.[585]

Sometime after January 27, 1963, Seaport Traders, Inc., received through the mail a mail-order coupon for one ".38 St. W. 2" Bbl.," cost $29.95.   Ten dollars in cash was enclosed.   The order was signed in ink by "A. J. Hidell, aged 28." [586]   (See Commission Exhibit No. 790, p. 173.)   The date of the order was January 27 (no year shown), and the return address was Post Office Box 2915, Dallas, Tex.   Also on the order form was an order, written in ink, for one box of ammunition and one holster, but a line was drawn through these items.   The mail-order form had a line for the name of a witness to attest that the person ordering the gun was a U.S. citizen and had not been convicted of a felony.   The name written in this space was D. F. Drittal.[587]

Heinz W. Michaelis, office manager of both George Rose & Co., Inc., and Seaport Traders, Inc., identified records of Seaport Traders, Inc., which showed that a ".38 S and W Special two-inch Commando, serial number V510210" was shipped on March 20, 1963, to A. J. Hidell, Post Office Box 2915, Dallas, Tex.   The invoice was prepared on March 13, 1963; the revolver was actually shipped on March 20 by Railway Express.   The balance due on the purchase was $19.95. Michaelis furnished the shipping copy of the invoice, and the Railway Express Agency shipping documents, showing that $19.95, plus $1.27 shipping charge, had been collected from the consignee, Hidell.[588] (See Michaelis Exhibits Nos. 2, 4, 5, p. 173.)

Handwriting experts, Alwyn Cole of the Treasury Department and James C. Cadigan of the FBI, testified before the Commission that the writing on the coupon was Oswald's.   The signature of the witness, D. F. Drittal, who attested that the fictitious Hidell was an American citizen and had not been convicted of a felony, was also in Oswald's handwriting.[589]   Marina Oswald gave as her opinion that the mail-order coupon was in Oswald's handwriting.[590]   When shown the revolver, she stated that she recognized it as the one owned by her husband.[591]   She also testified that this appeared to be the revolver seen in Oswald's belt in the picture she took in late March or early April 1963 when the family was living on Neely Street in Dallas.[592]   Police found an empty revolver holster when they searched Oswald's room on Beckley Avenue after his arrest.[593]   Marina Oswald testified that this was the holster which contained the revolver in the photographs taken on Neely Street.[594]

Oswald's Jacket

Approximately 15 minutes before the shooting of Tippit, Oswald was seen leaving his roominghouse.[595] He was wearing a zipper jacket which he had not been wearing moments before when he had arrived home.[596] When Oswald was arrested, he did not have a jacket.[597] Shortly after Tippit was slain, policemen found a light-colored zipper jacket along the route taken by the killer as he attempted to escape.[598] (See Commission Exhibit No. 1968, p. 164.)

At 1:22 p.m. the Dallas police radio described the man wanted for the murder of Tippit as "a white male about thirty, five foot eight inches, black hair, slender, wearing a white jacket, white shirt and dark slacks." [599] According to Patrolman Poe this description came from Mrs. Markham and Mrs. Barbara Jeanette Davis.[600] Mrs. Markham told Poe that the man was a "white male, about 25, about five feet eight, brown hair, medium," and wearing a "white jacket." Mrs. Davis gave Poc the same general description: a "white male in his early twenties, around five foot seven inches or eight inches, about 145 pounds," and wearing a white jacket.

As has been discussed previously, two witnesses, Warren Reynolds and B. M. Patterson, saw the gunman run toward the rear of a gasoline service station on Jefferson Boulevard. Mrs. Mary Brock, the wife of a mechanic who worked at the station, was there at the time and she saw a white male, "5 feet, 10 inches * * * wearing light clothing * * * a light-colored jacket" walk past her at a fast pace with his hands in his pocket. She last saw him in the parking lot directly behind the service station. When interviewed by FBI agents on January 21, 1964, she identified a picture of Oswald as being the same person she saw on November 22. She confirmed this interview by a sworn affidavit.[601]

At 1:24 p.m., the police radio reported, "The suspect last seen running west on Jefferson from 400 East Jefferson." [602] Police Capt. W. R. Westbrook and several other officers concentrated their search along Jefferson Boulevard.[603] Westbrook walked through the parking lot behind the service station [604] and found a light-colored jacket lying under the rear of one of the cars.[605] Westbrook identified Commission Exhibit No. 162 as the light-colored jacket which he discovered underneath the automobile.[606]

This jacket belonged to Lee Harvey Oswald. Marina Oswald stated that her husband owned only two jackets, one blue and the other gray.[607] The blue jacket was found in the Texas School Book Depository [608] and was identified by Marina Oswald as her husband's.[609] Marina Oswald also identified Commission Exhibit No. 162, the jacket found by Captain Westbrook, as her husband's second jacket.[610]

The eyewitnesses vary in their identification of the jacket. Mrs. Earlene Roberts, the housekeeper at Oswald's roominghouse and the last person known to have seen him before he reached 10th Street and Patton Avenue, said that she may have seen the gray zipper jacket but she was not certain. It seemed to her that the jacket Oswald wore was darker than Commission Exhibit No. 162.[611] Ted Callaway, who saw the gunman moments after the shooting, testified that Commission Exhibit No. 162 looked like the jacket he was wearing but "I thought it had a little more tan to it." [612] Two other witnesses, Sam Guinyard and William Arthur Smith, testified that Commission Exhibit No. 162 was the jacket worn by the man they saw on November 22. Mrs. Markham and Barbara Davis thought that the jacket worn by the slayer of Tippit was darker than the jacket found by Westbrook.[613] Scoggins thought it was lighter.[614]

There is no doubt, however, that Oswald was seen leaving his roominghouse at about 1 p.m. wearing a zipper jacket, that the man who killed Tippit was wearing a light-colored jacket, that he was seen running along Jefferson Boulevard, that a jacket was found under a car in a lot adjoining Jefferson Boulevard, that the jacket belonged to Lee Harvey Oswald, and that when he was arrested at approximately 1:50 p.m., he was in shirt sleeves. These facts warrant the finding that Lee Harvey Oswald disposed of his jacket as he fled from the scene of the Tippit killing.

Conclusion

The foregoing evidence establishes that (1) two eyewitnesses who heard the shots and saw the shooting of Dallas Police Patrolman J. D. Tippit and seven eyewitnesses who saw the flight of the gunman with revolver in hand positively identified Lee Harvey Oswald as the man they saw fire the shots or flee from the scene, (2) the cartridge cases found near the scene of the shooting were fired from the revolver in the possession of Oswald at the time of his arrest, to the exclusion of all other weapons, (3) the revolver in Oswald's possession at the time of his arrest was purchased by and belonged to Oswald, and (4) Oswald's jacket was found along the path of flight taken by the gunman as he fled from the scene of the killing. On the basis of this evidence the Commission concluded that Lee Harvey Oswald killed Dallas Police Patrolman J. D. Tippit.

OSWALD'S ARREST

The Texas Theatre is on the north side of Jefferson Boulevard, approximately eight blocks from the scene of the Tippit shooting and six blocks from where several witnesses last saw Oswald running west on Jefferson Boulevard.[615] (See Commission Exhibit No. 1968, p. 164.) Shortly after the Tippit murder, police sirens sounded along Jefferson Boulevard. One of the persons who heard the sirens was Johnny Calvin Brewer, manager of Hardy's Shoestore, a few doors east of the Texas Theatre. Brewer knew from radio broadcasts that the President had been shot and that a patrolman had also been shot in Oak Cliff.[616] When he heard police sirens, he "looked up and

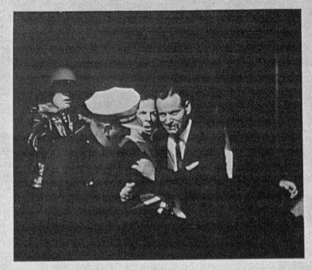

OSWALD IN FRONT OF
TEXAS THEATER
(HILL EXHIBIT B)

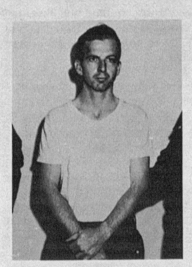

OSWALD AT DALLAS POLICE DEPARTMENT

(FRANK PIZZO EXHIBIT 453-C)   COMMISSION EXHIBIT NO. 1797

saw the man enter the lobby," a recessed area extending about 15 feet between the sidewalk and the front door of his store.[617] A police car made a U-turn, and as the sirens grew fainter, the man in the lobby "looked over his shoulder and turned around and walked up West Jefferson towards the theatre."[618] The man wore a T-shirt beneath his outer shirt and he had no jacket.[619] Brewer said, "He just looked funny to me. * * * His hair was sort of messed up and looked like he had been running, and he looked scared, and he looked funny."[620]

Mrs. Julia Postal, selling tickets at the box office of the Texas Theatre, heard police sirens and then saw a man as he "ducked into" the outer lobby space of the theatre near the ticket office.[621] Attracted by the sound of the sirens, Mrs. Postal stepped out of the box office and walked to the curb.[622] Shortly thereafter, Johnny Brewer, who had come from the nearby shoestore, asked Mrs. Postal whether the fellow that had ducked in had bought a ticket.[623] She said, "No; by golly, he didn't," and turned around, but the man was nowhere in sight.[624] Brewer told Mrs. Postal that he had seen the man ducking into his place of business and that he had followed him to the theatre.[625] She sent Brewer into the theatre to find the man and check the exits, told him about the assassination, and said "I don't know if this is the man they want * * * but he is running from them for some reason."[626] She then called the police.[627]

At 1:45 p.m., the police radio stated, "Have information a suspect just went in the Texas Theatre on West Jefferson."[628] Patrol cars bearing at least 15 officers converged on the Texas Theatre.[629] Patrolman M. N. McDonald, with Patrolmen R. Hawkins, T. A. Hutson, and C. T. Walker, entered the theatre from the rear.[630] Other policemen entered the front door and searched the balcony.[631] Detective Paul L. Bentley rushed to the balcony and told the projectionist to turn up the house lights.[632] Brewer met McDonald and the other policemen at the alley exit door, stepped out onto the stage with them [633] and pointed out the man who had come into the theatre without paying.[634] The man was Oswald. He was sitting alone in the rear of the main floor of the theatre near the right center aisle.[635] About six or seven people were seated on the theatre's main floor and an equal number in the balcony.[636]

McDonald first searched two men in the center of the main floor, about 10 rows from the front.[637] He walked out of the row up the right center aisle.[638] When he reached the row where the suspect was sitting, McDonald stopped abruptly and told the man to get on his feet.[639] Oswald rose from his seat, bringing up both hands.[640] As McDonald started to search Oswald's waist for a gun, he heard him say, "Well, it's all over now."[641] Oswald then struck McDonald between the eyes with his left fist; with his right hand he drew a gun from his waist.[642] McDonald struck back with his right hand and grabbed the gun with his left hand.[643] They both fell into the seats.[644] Three other officers, moving toward the scuffle, grabbed Oswald from the front, rear and side.[645] As McDonald fell into the seat with his left hand on the gun, he felt something graze across his hand and heard what sounded like the snap of the hammer.[646] McDonald felt the pistol scratch his cheek as he wrenched it away from Oswald.[647] Detective Bob K. Carroll, who was standing beside McDonald, seized the gun from him.[648]

The other officers who helped subdue Oswald corroborated McDonald in his testimony except that they did not hear Oswald say, "It's all over now." Deputy Sheriff Eddy R. Walthers recalled such a remark but he did not reach the scene of the struggle until Oswald had been knocked to the floor by McDonald and the others.[649] Some of the officers saw Oswald strike McDonald with his fist.[650] Most of them heard a click which they assumed to be a click of the hammer of the revolver.[651] Testimony of a firearms expert before the Commission established that the hammer of the revolver never touched the shell in the chamber.[652] Although the witnesses did not hear the sound of a misfire, they might have heard a snapping noise resulting from the police officer grabbing the cylinder of the revolver and pulling it away from Oswald while he was attempting to pull the trigger.[653] (See app. X, p. 560.)

Two patrons of the theatre and John Brewer testified regarding the arrest of Oswald, as did the various police officers who participated in the fight. George Jefferson Applin, Jr., confirmed that Oswald fought with four or five officers before he was handcuffed.[654] He added that one officer grabbed the muzzle of a shotgun, drew back, and hit Oswald with the butt end of the gun in the back.[655] No other theatre patron or officer has testified that Oswald was hit by a gun. Nor did Oswald ever complain that he was hit with a gun, or injured in the back. Deputy Sheriff Walthers brought a shotgun into the theatre but laid it on some seats before helping subdue Oswald.[656] Officer Ray Hawkins said that there was no one near Oswald who had a shotgun and he saw no one strike Oswald in the back with a rifle butt or the butt of a gun.[657]

John Gibson, another patron in the theatre, saw an officer grab Oswald, and he claims that he heard the click of a gun misfiring.[658] He saw no shotgun in the possession of any policeman near Oswald.[659] Johnny Brewer testified he saw Oswald pull the revolver and the officers struggle with him to take it away but that once he was subdued, no officer struck him.[660] He further stated that while fists were flying he heard one of the officers say "Kill the President, will you." [661] It is unlikely that any of the police officers referred to Oswald as a suspect in the assassination. While the police radio had noted the similarity in description of the two suspects, the arresting officers were pursuing Oswald for the murder of Tippit.[662] As Oswald, handcuffed, was led from the theatre, he was, according to McDonald, "cursing a little bit and hollering police brutality." [663] At 1:51 p.m., police car 2 reported by radio that it was on the way to headquarters with the suspect.[664]

Captain Fritz returned to police headquarters from the Texas School Book Depository at 2:15 after a brief stop at the sheriff's office.[665]   When he entered the homicide and robbery bureau office, he saw two detectives standing there with Sgt. Gerald L. Hill, who had driven from the theatre with Oswald.[666]   Hill testified that Fritz told the detective to get a search warrant, go to an address on Fifth Street in Irving, and pick up a man named Lee Oswald.   When Hill asked why Oswald was wanted, Fritz replied, "Well, he was employed down at the Book Depository and he had not been present for a roll call of the employees."[667]   Hill said, "Captain, we will save you a trip * * * there he sits."[668]

STATEMENTS OF OSWALD DURING DETENTION

Oswald was questioned intermittently for approximately 12 hours between 2:30 p.m., on November 22, and 11 a.m., on November 24. Throughout this interrogation he denied that he had anything to do either with the assassination of President Kennedy or the murder of Patrolman Tippit.   Captain Fritz of the homicide and robbery bureau did most of the questioning, but he kept no notes and there were no stenographic or tape recordings.   Representatives of other law enforcement agencies were also present, including the FBI and the U.S. Secret Service.   They occasionally participated in the questioning.   The reports prepared by those present at these interviews are set forth in appendix XI.   A full discussion of Oswald's detention and interrogation is presented in chapter V of this report.

During the evening of November 22, the Dallas Police Department performed paraffin tests on Oswald's hands and right cheek in an apparent effort to determine, by means of a scientific test, whether Oswald had recently fired a weapon.   The results were positive for the hands and negative for the right cheek.[669]   Expert testimony before the Commission was to the effect that the paraffin test was unreliable [670] in determining whether or not a person has fired a rifle or revolver.[671] The Commission has, therefore, placed no reliance on the paraffin tests administered by the Dallas police.   (See app. X, pp. 561–562.)

Oswald provided little information during his questioning.   Frequently, however, he was confronted with evidence which he could not explain, and he resorted to statements which are known to be lies.[672]   While Oswald's untrue statements during interrogation were not considered items of positive proof by the Commission, they had probative value in deciding the weight to be given to his denials that he assassinated President Kennedy and killed Patrolman Tippit. Since independent evidence revealed that Oswald repeatedly and blatantly lied to the police, the Commission gave little weight to his denials of guilt.

Denial of Rifle Ownership

From the outset, Oswald denied owning a rifle.   On November 23, Fritz confronted Oswald with the evidence that he had purchased a rifle under the fictitious name of "Hidell."   Oswald said that this was not true. Oswald denied that he had a rifle wrapped up in a blanket in the Paine garage. Oswald also denied owning a rifle and said that since leaving the Marine Corps he had fired only a small bore .22 rifle.[673] On the afternoon of November 23, Officers H. M. Moore, R. S. Stovall, and G. F. Rose obtained a search warrant and examined Oswald's effects in the Paine garage. They discovered two photographs, each showing Oswald with a rifle and a pistol.[674] These photographs were shown to Oswald on the evening of November 23 and again on the morning of the 24th. According to Fritz, Oswald sneered, saying that they were fake photographs, that he had been photographed a number of times the day before by the police, that they had superimposed upon the photographs a rifle and a revolver.[675] He told Fritz a number of times that the smaller photograph was either made from the larger, or the larger photograph was made from the smaller and that at the proper time he would show that the pictures were fakes. Fritz told him that the two small photographs were found in the Paine garage. At that point, Oswald refused to answer any further questions.[676] As previously indicated, Marina Oswald testified that she took the two pictures with her husband's Imperial Reflex camera when they lived on Neely Street. Her testimony was fully supported by a photography expert who testified that in his opinion the pictures were not composites.[677]

The Revolver

At the first interrogation, Oswald claimed that his only crime was carrying a gun and resisting arrest. When Captain Fritz asked him why he carried the revolver, he answered, "Well, you know about a pistol. I just carried it." [678] He falsely alleged that he bought the revolver in Fort Worth,[679] when in fact he purchased it from a mail-order house in Los Angeles.[680]

The Aliases "Hidell" and "O. H. Lee"

The arresting officers found a forged selective service card with a picture of Oswald and the name "Alek J. Hidell" in Oswald's billfold.[681] On November 22 and 23, Oswald refused to tell Fritz why this card was in his possession,[682] or to answer any questions concerning the card.[683] On Sunday morning, November 24, Oswald denied that he knew A. J. Hidell. Captain Fritz produced the selective service card bearing the name "Alek J. Hidell." Oswald became angry and said, "Now, I've told you all I'm going to tell you about that card in my billfold—you have the card yourself and you know as much about it as I do." [684] At the last interrogation on November 24, Oswald admitted to Postal Inspector Holmes that he had rented post office box 2915, Dallas, but denied that he had received a package in this box addressed to Hidell. He also denied that he had received the rifle through this box.[685] Holmes reminded Oswald that A. J.

Hidell was listed on post office box 30061, New Orleans, as one entitled to receive mail. Oswald replied, "I don't know anything about that."[686]

When asked why he lived at his roominghouse under the name O. H. Lee, Oswald responded that the landlady simply made a mistake, because he told her that his name was Lee, meaning his first name.[687] An examination of the roominghouse register revealed that Oswald actually signed the name O. H. Lee.[688]

The Curtain Rod Story

In concluding that Oswald was carrying a rifle in the paper bag on the morning of November 22, 1963, the Commission found that Oswald lied when he told Frazier that he was returning to Irving to obtain curtain rods. When asked about the curtain rod story, Oswald lied again. He denied that he had ever told Frazier that he wanted a ride to Irving to get curtain rods for an apartment.[689] He explained that a party for the Paine children had been planned for the weekend and he preferred not to be in the Paine house at that time; therefore, he made his weekly visit on Thursday night.[690] Actually, the party for one of the Paine's children was the preceding weekend, when Marina Oswald suggested that Oswald remain in Dallas.[691] When told that Frazier and Mrs. Randle had seen him carrying a long heavy package, Oswald replied, "Well, they was mistaken. That must have been some other time he picked me up." [692] In one interview, he told Fritz that the only sack he carried to work that day was a lunch sack which he kept on his lap during the ride from Irving to Dallas.[693] Frazier testified before the Commission that Oswald carried no lunch sack that day.[694]

Actions During and After Shooting

During the first interrogation on November 22, Fritz asked Oswald to account for himself at the time the President was shot. Oswald told him that he ate lunch in the first-floor lunchroom and then went to the second floor for a Coke which he brought downstairs. He acknowledged the encounter with the police officer on the second floor. Oswald told Fritz that after lunch he went outside, talked with Foreman Bill Shelley for 5 or 10 minutes and then left for home. He said that he left work because Bill Shelley said that there would be no more work done that day in the building.[695] Shelley denied seeing Oswald after 12 noon or at any time after the shooting.[696] The next day, Oswald added to his story. He stated that at the time the President was shot he was having lunch with "Junior" but he did not give Junior's last name.[697] The only employee at the Depository Building named "Junior" was James Jarman, Jr. Jarman testified that he ate his lunch on the first floor around 5 minutes to 12, and that he neither ate lunch with nor saw Oswald.[698] Jarman did talk to Oswald that morning:

* * * he asked me what were the people gathering around on the corner for and I told him that the President was supposed to pass that morning, and he asked me did I know which way he was coming, and I told him, yes, he probably come down Main and turn on Houston and then back again on Elm. Then he said, "Oh, I see," and that was all.[699]

PRIOR ATTEMPT TO KILL

The Attempt on the Life of Maj. Gen. Edwin A. Walker

At approximately 9 p.m., on April 10, 1963, in Dallas, Tex., Maj. Gen. Edwin A. Walker, an active and controversial figure on the American political scene since his resignation from the U.S. Army in 1961, narrowly escaped death when a rifle bullet fired from outside his home passed near his head as he was seated at his desk.[700] There were no eyewitnesses, although a 14-year-old boy in a neighboring house claimed that immediately after the shooting he saw two men, in separate cars, drive out of a church parking lot adjacent to Walker's home.[701] A friend of Walker's testified that two nights before the shooting he saw "two men around the house peeking in windows." [702] General Walker gave this information to the police before the shooting, but it did not help solve the crime. Although the bullet was recovered from Walker's house (see app. X, p. 562), in the absence of a weapon it was of little investigatory value. General Walker hired two investigators to determine whether a former employee might have been involved in the shooting.[703] Their results were negative. Until December 3, 1963, the Walker shooting remained unsolved.

The Commission evaluated the following evidence in considering whether Lee Harvey Oswald fired the shot which almost killed General Walker: (1) A note which Oswald left for his wife on the evening of the shooting, (2) photographs found among Oswald's possessions after the assassination of President Kennedy, (3) firearm identification of the bullet found in Walker's home, and (4) admissions and other statements made to Marina Oswald by Oswald concerning the shooting.

Note left by Oswald.—On December 2, 1963, Mrs. Ruth Paine turned over to the police some of the Oswalds' belongings, including a Russian volume entitled "Book of Useful Advice." [704] In this book was an undated note written in Russian. In translation, the note read as follows:

1. This is the key to the mailbox which is located in the main post office in the city on Ervay Street. This is the same street where the drugstore, in which you always waited is located. You will find the mailbox in the post office which is located 4 blocks from the drugstore on that street. I paid for the box last month so don't worry about it.

2. Send the information as to what has happened to me to the Embassy and include newspaper clippings (should there be anything about me in the newspapers). I believe that the Embassy will come quickly to your assistance on learning everything.

3. I paid the house rent on the 2d so don't worry about it.

4. Recently I also paid for water and gas.

5. The money from work will possibly be coming. The money will be sent to our post office box. Go to the bank and cash the check.

6. You can either throw out or give my clothing, etc. away. Do not keep these. However, I prefer that you hold on to my personal papers (military, civil, etc.).

7. Certain of my documents are in the small blue valise.

8. The address book can be found on my table in the study should need same.

9. We have friends here. The Red Cross also will help you. (Red Cross in English). [sic]

10. I left you as much money as I could, $60 on the second of the month. You and the baby [apparently] can live for another 2 months using $10 per week.

11. If I am alive and taken prisoner, the city jail is located at the end of the bridge through which we always passed on going to the city (right in the beginning of the city after crossing the bridge).[705]

James C. Cadigan, FBI handwriting expert, testified that this note was written by Lee Harvey Oswald.[706]

Prior to the Walker shooting on April 10, Oswald had been attending typing classes on Monday, Tuesday, and Thursday evenings. He had quit these classes at least a week before the shooting, which occurred on a Wednesday night.[707] According to Marina Oswald's testimony, on the night of the Walker shooting, her husband left their apartment on Neely Street shortly after dinner. She thought he was attending a class or was "on his own business." [708] When he failed to return by 10 or 10:30 p.m., Marina Oswald went to his room and discovered the note. She testified: "When he came back I asked him what had happened. He was very pale. I don't remember the exact time, but it was very late. And he told me not to ask him any questions. He only told me he had shot at General Walker." [709] Oswald told his wife that he did not know whether he had hit Walker; according to Marina Oswald when he learned on the radio and in the newspapers the next day that he had missed, he said that he "was very sorry that he had not hit him." [710] Marina Oswald's testimony was fully supported by the note itself which appeared to be the work of a man expecting to be killed, or imprisoned, or to disappear. The last paragraph directed her to the jail and the other paragraphs instructed her on the disposal of Oswald's personal effects and the management of her affairs if he should not return.

It is clear that the note was written while the Oswalds were living in Dallas before they moved to New Orleans in the spring of 1963.

The references to house rent and payments for water and gas indicated that the note was written when they were living in a rented apartment; therefore it could not have been written while Marina Oswald was living with the Paines. Moreover, the reference in paragraph 3 to paying "the house rent on the 2d" would be consistent with the period when the Oswalds were living on Neely Street since the apartment was rented on March 3, 1963. Oswald had paid the first month's rent in advance on March 2, 1963, and the second month's rent was paid on either April 2 or April 3.[711] The main post office "on Ervay Street" refers to the post office where Oswald rented box 2915 from October 9, 1962, to May 14, 1963.[712] Another statement which limits the time when it could have been written is the reference "you and the baby," which would indicate that it was probably written before the birth of Oswald's second child on October 20, 1963.

Oswald had apparently mistaken the county jail for the city jail. From Neely Street the Oswalds would have traveled downtown on the Beckley bus, across the Commerce Street viaduct and into downtown Dallas through the Triple Underpass.[713] Either the viaduct or the underpass might have been the "bridge" mentioned in the last paragraph of the note. The county jail is at the corner of Houston and Main Streets "right in the beginning of the city" after one travels through the underpass.

Photographs.—In her testimony before the Commission in February 1964, Marina Oswald stated that when Oswald returned home on the night of the Walker shooting, he told her that he had been planning the attempt for 2 months. He showed her a notebook 3 days later containing photographs of General Walker's home and a map of the area where the house was located.[714] Although Oswald destroyed the notebook,[715] three photographs found among Oswald's possessions after the assassination were identified by Marina Oswald as photographs of General Walker's house.[716] Two of these photographs were taken from the rear of Walker's house.[717] The Commission confirmed, by comparison with other photographs, that these were, indeed, photographs of the rear of Walker's house.[718] An examination of the window at the rear of the house, the wall through which the bullet passed, and the fence behind the house indicated that the bullet was fired from a position near the point where one of the photographs was taken.[719]

The third photograph identified by Marina Oswald depicts the entrance to General Walker's driveway from a back alley.[720] Also seen in the picture is the fence on which Walker's assailant apparently rested the rifle.[721] An examination of certain construction work appearing in the background of this photograph revealed that the picture was taken between March 8 and 12, 1963, and most probably on either March 9 or March 10.[722] Oswald purchased the money order for the rifle on March 12, the rifle was shipped on March 20,[723] and the shooting occurred on April 10. A photography expert with the FBI was able to determine that this picture was taken with the Imperial Reflex camera owned by Lee Harvey Oswald.[724] (See app. X, p. 596.)

185

A fourth photograph, showing a stretch of railroad tracks, was also identified by Marina Oswald as having been taken by her husband, presumably in connection with the Walker shooting.[725] Investigation determined that this photograph was taken approximately seven-tenths of a mile from Walker's house.[726] Another photograph of railroad tracks found among Oswald's possessions was not identified by his wife, but investigation revealed that it was taken from a point slightly less than half a mile from General Walker's house.[727] Marina Oswald stated that when she asked her husband what he had done with the rifle, he replied that he had buried it in the ground or hidden it in some bushes and that he also mentioned a railroad track in this connection. She testified that several days later Oswald recovered his rifle and brought it back to their apartment.[728]

Firearms identification.—In the room beyond the one in which General Walker was sitting on the night of the shooting the Dallas police recovered a badly mutilated bullet which had come to rest on a stack of paper.[729] The Dallas City-County Investigation Laboratory tried to determine the type of weapon which fired the bullet. The oral report was negative because of the battered condition of the bullet.[730] On November 30, 1963, the FBI requested the bullet for ballistics examination; the Dallas Police Department forwarded it on December 2, 1963.[731]

Robert A. Frazier, an FBI ballistics identification expert, testified that he was "unable to reach a conclusion" as to whether or not the bullet recovered from Walker's house had been fired from the rifle found on the sixth floor of the Texas School Book Depository Building. He concluded that "the general rifling characteristics of the rifle * * * are of the same type as those found on the bullet * * * and, further, on this basis * * * the bullet could have been fired from the rifle on the basis of its land and groove impressions." [732] Frazier testified further that the FBI avoids the category of "probable" identification. Unless the missile or cartridge case can be identified as coming from a particular weapon to the exclusion of all others, the FBI refuses to draw any conclusion as to probability.[733] Frazier testified, however, that he found no microscopic characteristics or other evidence which would indicate that the bullet was not fired from the Mannlicher-Carcano rifle owned by Lee Harvey Oswald. It was a 6.5-millimeter bullet and, according to Frazier, "relatively few" types of rifles could produce the characteristics found on the bullet.[734]

Joseph D. Nicol, superintendent of the Illinois Bureau of Criminal Identification and Investigation, conducted an independent examination of this bullet and concluded "that there is a fair probability" that the bullet was fired from the rifle used in the assassination of President Kennedy.[735] In explaining the difference between his policy and that of the FBI on the matter of probable identification, Nicol said:

I am aware of their position. This is not, I am sure, arrived at without careful consideration. However, to say that because one does not find sufficient marks for identification that it is a negative,

I think is going overboard in the other direction. And for purposes of probative value, for whatever it might be worth, in the absence of very definite negative evidence, I think it is permissible to say that in an exhibit such as 573 there is enough on it to say that it could have come, and even perhaps a little stronger, to say that it probably came from this, without going so far as to say to the exclusion of all other guns. This I could not do.[736]

Although the Commission recognizes that neither expert was able to state that the bullet which missed General Walker was fired from Oswald's rifle to the exclusion of all others, this testimony was considered probative when combined with the other testimony linking Oswald to the shooting.

Additional corroborative evidence.—The admissions made to Marina Oswald by her husband are an important element in the evidence that Lee Harvey Oswald fired the shot at General Walker. As shown above, the note and the photographs of Walker's house and of the nearby railroad tracks provide important corroboration for her account of the incident. Other details described by Marina Oswald coincide with facts developed independently of her statements. She testified that her husband had postponed his attempt to kill Walker until that Wednesday because he had heard that there was to be a gathering at the church next door to Walker's house on that evening. He indicated that he wanted more people in the vicinity at the time of the attempt so that his arrival and departure would not attract great attention.[737] An official of this church told FBI agents that services are held every Wednesday at the church except during the month of August.[738] Marina Oswald also testified that her husband had used a bus to return home.[739] A study of the bus routes indicates that Oswald could have taken any one of several different buses to Walker's house or to a point near the railroad tracks where he may have concealed the rifle.[740] It would have been possible for him to take different routes in approaching and leaving the scene of the shooting.

Conclusion.—Based on (1) the contents of the note which Oswald left for his wife on April 10, 1963, (2) the photographs found among Oswald's possessions, (3) the testimony of firearms identification experts, and (4) the testimony of Marina Oswald, the Commission has concluded that Lee Harvey Oswald attempted to take the life of Maj. Gen. Edwin A. Walker (Resigned, U.S. Army) on April 10, 1963. The finding that Lee Harvey Oswald attempted to murder a public figure in April 1963 was considered of probative value in this investigation, although the Commission's conclusion concerning the identity of the assassin was based on evidence independent of the finding that Oswald attempted to kill General Walker.

Richard M. Nixon Incident

Another alleged threat by Oswald against a public figure involved former Vice President Richard M. Nixon. In January 1964, Marina Oswald and her business manager, James Martin, told Robert Oswald,

Lee Harvey Oswald's brother, that Oswald had once threatened to shoot former Vice President Richard M. Nixon.[741] When Marina Oswald testified before the Commission on February 3–6, 1964, she had failed to mention the incident when she was asked whether Oswald had ever expressed any hostility toward any official of the United States.[742] The Commission first learned of this incident when Robert Oswald related it to FBI agents on February 19, 1964,[743] and to the Commission on February 21.[744]

Marina Oswald appeared before the Commission again on June 11, 1964, and testified that a few days before her husband's departure from Dallas to New Orleans on April 24, 1963, he finished reading a morning newspaper "* * * and put on a good suit. I saw that he took a pistol. I asked him where he was going, and why he was getting dressed. He answered 'Nixon is coming. I want to go and have a look.' " He also said that he would use the pistol if the opportunity arose.[745] She reminded him that after the Walker shooting he had promised never to repeat such an act. Marina Oswald related the events which followed:

> I called him into the bathroom and I closed the door and I wanted to prevent him and then I started to cry. And I told him that he shouldn't do this, and that he had promised me.

*   *   *   *   *   *   *

> I remember that I held him. We actually struggled for several minutes and then he quieted down.[746]

She stated that it was not physical force which kept him from leaving the house. "I couldn't keep him from going out if he really wanted to." [747] After further questioning she stated that she might have been confused about shutting him in the bathroom, but that "there is no doubt that he got dressed and got a gun." [748]

Oswald's revolver was shipped from Los Angeles on March 20, 1963,[749] and he left for New Orleans on April 24, 1963.[750] No edition of either Dallas newspaper during the period January 1, 1963, to May 15, 1963, mentioned any proposed visit by Mr. Nixon to Dallas.[751] Mr. Nixon advised the Commission that the only time he was in Dallas in 1963 was on November 20–21, 1963.[752] An investigation failed to reveal any invitation extended to Mr. Nixon during the period when Oswald's threat reportedly occurred.[753] The Commission has concluded, therefore, that regardless of what Oswald may have said to his wife he was not actually planning to shoot Mr. Nixon at that time in Dallas.

On April 23, 1963, Vice President Lyndon B. Johnson was in Dallas for a visit which had been publicized in the Dallas newspapers throughout April.[754] The Commission asked Marina Oswald whether she might have misunderstood the object of her husband's threat. She stated, "there is no question that in this incident it was a question of Mr. Nixon." [755] When asked later whether it might have been

Mr. Johnson, she said, "Yes, no. I am getting a little confused with so many questions. I was absolutely convinced it was Nixon and now after all these questions I wonder if I am right in my mind." [756] She stated further that Oswald had only mentioned Nixon's name once during the incident. [757] Marina Oswald might have misunderstood her husband. Mr. Johnson was the then Vice President and his visit took place on April 23d. [758] This was 1 day before Oswald left for New Orleans and Marina appeared certain that the Nixon incident "wasn't the day before. Perhaps 3 days before." [759]

Marina Oswald speculated that the incident may have been unrelated to an actual threat. She said,

> * * * It might have been that he was just trying to test me. He was the kind of person who could try and wound somebody in that way. Possibly he didn't want to go out at all but was just doing this all as a sort of joke, not really as a joke but rather to simply wound me, to make me feel bad. [760]

In the absence of other evidence that Oswald actually intended to shoot someone at this time, the Commission concluded that the incident, as described by Marina Oswald, was of no probative value in the Commission's decision concerning the identity of the assassin of President Kennedy.

OSWALD'S RIFLE CAPABILITY

In deciding whether Lee Harvey Oswald fired the shots which killed President Kennedy and wounded Governor Connally, the Commission considered whether Oswald, using his own rifle, possessed the capability to hit his target with two out of three shots under the conditions described in chapter III. The Commission evaluated (1) the nature of the shots, (2) Oswald's Marine training in marksmanship, (3) his experience and practice after leaving the Marine Corps, and (4) the accuracy of the weapon and the quality of the ammunition.

The Nature of the Shots

For a rifleman situated on the sixth floor of the Texas School Book Depository Building the shots were at a slow-moving target proceeding on a downgrade in virtually a straight line with the alinement of the assassin's rifle, at a range of 177 to 266 feet. [761] An aerial photograph of Dealey Plaza shows that Elm Street runs at an angle so that the President would have been moving in an almost straight line away from the assassin's rifle. [762] (See Commission Exhibit No. 876, p. 33.) In addition, the 3° downward slope of Elm Street was of assistance in eliminating at least some of the adjustment which is ordinarily required when a marksman must raise his rifle as a target moves farther away. [763]

Four marksmanship experts testified before the Commission. Maj. Eugene D. Anderson, assistant head of the Marksmanship Branch of the U.S. Marine Corps, testified that the shots which struck the President in the neck and in the head were "not * * * particularly difficult." [764] Robert A. Frazier, FBI expert in firearms identification and training, said:

> From my own experience in shooting over the years, when you shoot at 175 feet or 260 feet, which is less than 100 yards, with a telescopic sight, you should not have any difficulty in hitting your target.

>   *   *   *   *   *   *   *

> I mean it requires no training at all to shoot a weapon with a telescopic sight once you know that you must put the crosshairs on the target and that is all that is necessary.[765]

Ronald Simmons, chief of the U.S. Army Infantry Weapons Evaluation Branch of the Ballistics Research Laboratory, said: "Well, in order to achieve three hits, it would not be required that a man be an exceptional shot. A proficient man with this weapon, yes." [766]

The effect of a four-power telescopic sight on the difficulty of these shots was considered in detail by M. Sgt. James A. Zahm, noncommissioned officer in charge of the Marksmanship Training Unit in the Weapons Training Battalion of the Marine Corps School at Quantico, Va.[767] Referring to a rifle with a four-power telescope, Sergeant Zahm said:

> * * * this is the ideal type of weapon for moving targets * * * [768]

>   *   *   *   *   *   *   *

> * * * Using the scope, rapidly working a bolt and using the scope to relocate your target quickly and at the same time when you locate that target you identify it and the crosshairs are in close relationship to the point you want to shoot at, it just takes a minor move in aiming to bring the crosshairs to bear, and then it is a quick squeeze.[769]

>   *   *   *   *   *   *   *

> I consider it a real advantage, particularly at the range of 100 yards, in identifying your target. It allows you to see your target clearly, and it is still of a minimum amount of power that it doesn't exaggerate your own body movements. It just is an aid in seeing in the fact that you only have the one element, the crosshair, in relation to the target as opposed to iron sights with aligning the sights and then aligning them on the target.[770]

Characterizing the four-power scope as "a real aid, an extreme aid" in rapid fire shooting, Sergeant Zahm expressed the opinion that the shot which struck President Kennedy in the neck at 176.9 to 190.8 feet was "very easy" and the shot which struck the President in the head at a distance of 265.3 feet was "an easy shot." [771] After viewing photographs depicting the alinement of Elm Street in relation to the Texas School Book Depository Building, Zahm stated further:

> This is a definite advantage to the shooter, the vehicle moving directly away from him and the downgrade of the street, and he being in an elevated position made an almost stationary target while he was aiming in, very little movement if any.[772]

Oswald's Marine Training

In accordance with standard Marine procedures, Oswald received extensive training in marksmanship.[773] During the first week of an intensive 3-week training period he received instruction in sighting, aiming, and manipulation of the trigger.[774] He went through a series of exercises called dry firing where he assumed all positions which would later be used in the qualification course.[775] After familiarization with live ammunition in the .22 rifle and .22 pistol, Oswald, like all Marine recruits, received training on the rifle range at distances up to 500 yards, firing 50 rounds each day for five days.[776]

Following that training, Oswald was tested in December of 1956, and obtained a score of 212, which was 2 points above the minimum for qualifications as a "sharpshooter" in a scale of marksman—sharpshooter—expert.[777] In May of 1959, on another range, Oswald scored 191, which was 1 point over the minimum for ranking as a "marksman." [778] The Marine Corps records maintained on Oswald further show that he had fired and was familiar with the Browning Automatic rifle, .45 caliber pistol, and 12-gage riot gun.[779]

Based on the general Marine Corps ratings, Lt. Col. A. G. Folsom, Jr., head, Records Branch, Personnel Department, Headquarters U.S. Marine Corps, evaluated the sharpshooter qualification as a "fairly good shot" and a low marksman rating as a "rather poor shot." [780]

When asked to explain the different scores achieved by Oswald on the two occasions when he fired for record, Major Anderson said:

> * * * when he fired that [212] he had just completed a very intensive preliminary training period. He had the services of an experienced highly trained coach. He had high motivation. He had presumably a good to excellent rifle and good ammunition. We have nothing here to show under what conditions the B course was fired. It might well have been a bad day for firing the rifle— windy, rainy, dark. There is little probability that he had a good, expert coach, and he probably didn't have as high a motivation because he was no longer in recruit training and under the care of the drill instructor. There is some possibility that the rifle he was firing might not have been as good a rifle as the rifle that he was firing in his A course firing, because [he] may well have carried this rifle for quite some time, and it got banged around in normal usage.[781]

Major Anderson concluded:

> I would say that as compared to other Marines receiving the same type of training, that Oswald was a good shot, somewhat better than or equal to—better than the average let us say. As compared to a civilian who had not received this intensive training, he would be considered as a good to excellent shot.[782]

When Sergeant Zahm was asked whether Oswald's Marine Corps training would have made it easier to operate a rifle with a four-power scope, he replied:

> Based on that training, his basic knowledge in sight manipulation and trigger squeeze and what not, I would say that he would be capable of sighting that rifle in well, firing it, with 10 rounds.[783]

After reviewing Oswald's marksmanship scores, Sergeant Zahm concluded:

> I would say in the Marine Corps he is a good shot, slightly above average, and as compared to the average male of his age throughout the civilian, throughout the United States, that he is an excellent shot.[784]

Oswald's Rifle Practice Outside the Marines

During one of his leaves from the Marines, Oswald hunted with his brother Robert, using a .22 caliber bolt-action rifle belonging either to Robert or Robert's in-laws.[785] After he left the Marines and before departing for Russia, Oswald, his brother, and a third companion went hunting for squirrels and rabbits.[786] On that occasion Oswald again used a bolt-action .22 caliber rifle; and according to Robert, Lee Oswald exhibited an average amount of proficiency with that weapon.[787] While in Russia, Oswald obtained a hunting license, joined a hunting club and went hunting about six times, as discussed more fully in chapter VI.[788] Soon after Oswald returned from the Soviet Union he again went hunting with his brother, Robert, and used a borrowed .22 caliber bolt-action rifle.[789] After Oswald purchased the Mannlicher-Carcano rifle, he told his wife that he practiced with it.[790] Marina Oswald testified that on one occasion she saw him take the rifle, concealed in a raincoat, from the house on Neely Street. Oswald told her he was going to practice with it.[791] According to George De Mohrenschildt, Oswald said that he went target shooting with that rifle.[792]

Marina Oswald testified that in New Orleans in May of 1963, she observed Oswald sitting with the rifle on their screened porch at night, sighting with the telescopic lens and operating the bolt.[793] Examination of the cartridge cases found on the sixth floor of the Depository

Building established that they had been previously loaded and ejected from the assassination rifle, which would indicate that Oswald practiced operating the bolt.[794]

Accuracy of Weapon

It will be recalled from the discussion in chapter III that the assassin in all probability hit two out of the three shots during the maximum time span of 4.8 to 5.6 seconds if the second shot missed, or, if either the first or third shots missed, the assassin fired the three shots during a minimum time span of 7.1 to 7.9 seconds.[795] A series of tests were performed to determine whether the weapon and ammunition used in the assassination were capable of firing the shots which were fired by the assassin on November 22, 1963. The ammunition used by the assassin was manufactured by Western Cartridge Co. of East Alton, Ill. In tests with the Mannlicher-Carcano C2766 rifle, over 100 rounds of this ammunition were fired by the FBI and the Infantry Weapons Evaluation Branch of the U.S. Army. There were no misfires.[796]

In an effort to test the rifle under conditions which simulated those which prevailed during the assassination, the Infantry Weapons Evaluation Branch of the Ballistics Research Laboratory had expert riflemen fire the assassination weapon from a tower at three silhouette targets at distances of 175, 240, and 265 feet. The target at 265 feet was placed to the right of the 240-foot target which was in turn placed to the right of the closest silhouette.[797] Using the assassination rifle mounted with the telescopic sight, three marksmen, rated as master by the National Rifle Association, each fired two series of three shots. In the first series the firers required time spans of 4.6, 6.75, and 8.25 seconds respectively. On the second series they required 5.15, 6.45, and 7 seconds. None of the marksmen had any practice with the assassination weapon except for exercising the bolt for 2 or 3 minutes on a dry run. They had not even pulled the trigger because of concern about breaking the firing pin.[798]

The marksmen took as much time as they wanted for the first target and all hit the target.[799] For the first four attempts, the firers missed the second shot by several inches.[800] The angle from the first to the second shot was greater than from the second to the third shot and required a movement in the basic firing position of the marksmen.[801] This angle was used in the test because the majority of the eyewitnesses to the assassination stated that there was a shorter interval between shots two and three than between shots one and two.[802] As has been shown in chapter III, if the three shots were fired within a period of from 4.8 to 5.6 seconds, the shots would have been evenly spaced and the assassin would not have incurred so sharp an angular movement.[803]

Five of the six shots hit the third target where the angle of movement of the weapon was small.[804] On the basis of these results, Simmons testified that in his opinion the probability of hitting the targets at the relatively short range at which they were hit was very high.[805]

Considering the various probabilities which may have prevailed during the actual assassination, the highest level of firing performance which would have been required of the assassin and the C2766 rifle would have been to fire three times and hit the target twice within a span of 4.8 to 5.6 seconds. In fact, one of the firers in the rapid fire test in firing his two series of three shots, hit the target twice within a span of 4.6 and 5.15 seconds. The others would have been able to reduce their times if they had been given the opportunity to become familiar with the movement of the bolt and the trigger pull.[806] Simmons testified that familiarity with the bolt could be achieved in dry practice and, as has been indicated above, Oswald engaged in such practice.[807] If the assassin missed either the first or third shot, he had a total of between 4.8 and 5.6 seconds between the two shots which hit and a total minimum time period of from 7.1 to 7.9 seconds for all three shots. All three of the firers in these tests were able to fire the rounds within the time period which would have been available to the assassin under those conditions.

Three FBI firearms experts tested the rifle in order to determine the speed with which it could be fired. The purpose of this experiment was not to test the rifle under conditions which prevailed at the time of the assassination but to determine the maximum speed at which it could be fired. The three FBI experts each fired three shots from the weapon at 15 yards in 6, 7, and 9 seconds, and one of these agents, Robert A. Frazier, fired two series of three shots at 25 yards in 4.6 and 4.8 seconds.[808] At 15 yards each man's shots landed within the size of a dime.[809] The shots fired by Frazier at the range of 25 yards landed within an area of 2 inches and 5 inches respectively.[810] Frazier later fired four groups of three shots at a distance of 100 yards in 5.9, 6.2, 5.6, and 6.5 seconds. Each series of three shots landed within areas ranging in diameter from 3 to 5 inches.[811] Although all of the shots were a few inches high and to the right of the target, this was because of a defect in the scope which was recognized by the FBI agents and which they could have compensated for if they were aiming to hit a bull's-eye.[812] They were instead firing to determine how rapidly the weapon could be fired and the area within which three shots could be placed. Frazier testified that while he could not tell when the defect occurred, but that a person familiar with the weapon could compensate for it.[813] Moreover, the defect was one which would have assisted the assassin aiming at a target which was moving away. Frazier said, "The fact that the crosshairs are set high would actually compensate for any lead which had to be taken. So that if you aimed with this weapon as it actually was received at the laboratory, it would not be necessary to take any lead whatsoever in order to hit the intended object. The scope would accomplish the lead for you." Frazier added that the scope would cause a slight miss to the right. It should be noted, however, that the President's car was curving slightly to the right when the third shot was fired.

Based on these tests the experts agreed that the assassination rifle was an accurate weapon. Simmons described it as "quite accurate," in fact, as accurate as current military rifles.[814]   Frazier testified that the rifle was accurate, that it had less recoil than the average military rifle and that one would not have to be an expert marksman to have accomplished the assassination with the weapon which was used.[815]

Conclusion

The various tests showed that the Mannlicher-Carcano was an accurate rifle and that the use of a four-power scope was a substantial aid to rapid, accurate firing. Oswald's Marine training in marksmanship, his other rifle experience and his established familiarity with this particular weapon show that he possessed ample capability to commit the assassination. Based on the known facts of the assassination, the Marine marksmanship experts, Major Anderson and Sergeant Zahm, concurred in the opinion that Oswald had the capability to fire three shots, with two hits, within 4.8 and 5.6 seconds.[816]   Concerning the shots which struck the President in the back of the neck, Sergeant Zahm testified: "With the equipment he [Oswald] had and with his ability I consider it a very easy shot." [817]   Having fired this shot the assassin was then required to hit the target one more time within a space of from 4.8 to 5.6 seconds. On the basis of Oswald's training and the accuracy of the weapon as established by the tests, the Commission concluded that Oswald was capable of accomplishing this second hit even if there was an intervening shot which missed. The probability of hitting the President a second time would have been markedly increased if, in fact, he had missed either the first or third shots thereby leaving a time span of 4.8 to 5.6 seconds between the two shots which struck their mark. The Commission agrees with the testimony of Marine marksmanship expert Zahm that it was "an easy shot" to hit some part of the President's body, and that the range where the rifleman would be expected to hit would include the President's head.[818]

CONCLUSION

On the basis of the evidence reviewed in this chapter, the Commission has found that Lee Harvey Oswald (1) owned and possessed the rifle used to kill President Kennedy and wound Governor Connally, (2) brought this rifle into the Depository Building on the morning of the assassination, (3) was present, at the time of the assassination, at the window from which the shots were fired, (4) killed Dallas Police Officer J. D. Tippit in an apparent attempt to escape, (5) resisted arrest by drawing a fully loaded pistol and attempting to shoot another police officer, (6) lied to the police after his arrest concerning important substantive matters, (7) attempted, in April 1963, to kill Maj. Gen. Edwin A. Walker, and (8) possessed the capability with a rifle which would have enabled him to commit the assassination. On the basis of these findings the Commission has concluded that Lee Harvey Oswald was the assassin of President Kennedy.

CHAPTER V

Detention and Death of Oswald

LEE HARVEY OSWALD spent almost all of the last 48 hours of his life in the Police and Courts Building, a gray stone structure in downtown Dallas that housed the headquarters of the Dallas Police Department and the city jail. Following his arrest early Friday afternoon, Oswald was brought immediately to this building and remained there until Sunday morning, November 24, when he was scheduled to be transferred to the county jail. At 11:21 that morning, in full view of millions of people watching on television, Oswald was fatally wounded by Jack Ruby, who emerged suddenly from the crowd of newsmen and policemen witnessing the transfer and fired a single shot at Oswald.

Whether the killing of Oswald was part of a conspiracy involving the assassination of President Kennedy is considered in chapter VI. Aside from that question, the occurrences within the Police and Courts Building between November 22 and 24 raise other important issues concerning the conduct of law enforcement officials, the responsibilities of the press, the rights of accused persons, and the administration of criminal justice in the United States. The Commission has therefore deemed it necessary to determine the facts concerning Oswald's detention and death and to evaluate the actions and responsibilities of the police and press involved in these events.

TREATMENT OF OSWALD IN CUSTODY

The focal center of the Police and Courts Building during Oswald's detention was the third floor, which housed the main offices of the Dallas Police Department. The public elevators on this floor opened into a lobby midpoint of a corridor that extended along the length of the floor for about 140 feet. At one end of this 7-foot-wide corridor were the offices occupied by Chief of Police Jesse E. Curry and his immediate subordinates; at the other end was a small pressroom that could accommodate only a handful of reporters. Along this corridor were other police offices, including those of the major detective bureaus. Between the pressroom and the lobby was the complex of offices

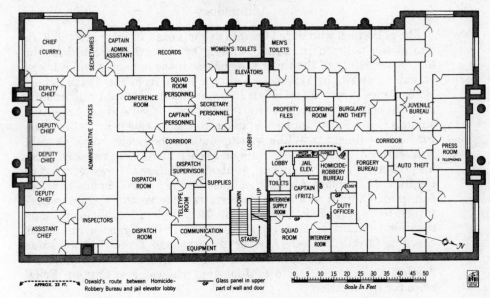

THIRD FLOOR PLAN
DALLAS POLICE DEPARTMENT
DALLAS, TEXAS

COMMISSION EXHIBIT No. 2175

197

belonging to the homicide and robbery bureau, headed by Capt. J. Will Fritz.[1] (See Commission Exhibit No. 2175, p. 197.)

Chronology

The policemen who seized Oswald at the Texas Theatre arrived with him at the police department building at about 2 p.m. and brought him immediately to the third floor offices of the homicide and robbery bureau to await the arrival of Captain Fritz from the Texas School Book Depository.   After about 15 or 20 minutes Oswald was ushered into the office of Captain Fritz for the first of several interrogation sessions.[2]   At 4:05 p.m. he was taken to the basement assembly room for his first lineup.[3]   While waiting outside the lineup room, Oswald was searched, and five cartridges and other items were removed from his pockets.[4]   After the lineup, at about 4:20, Oswald was returned to Captain Fritz' office for further questioning.[5]   Two hours later, at 6:20 p.m., Oswald was taken downstairs for a second lineup and returned to Captain Fritz' office within 15 minutes for additional interrogation.[6]   Shortly after 7 p.m., Captain Fritz signed a complaint charging Oswald with the murder of Patrolman Tippit.   Oswald was formally arraigned, i.e., advised of the charges, at 7:10 p.m., before Justice of the Peace David L. Johnston, who came to Captain Fritz' office for the occasion.[7]

After a third lineup at about 7:40 p.m., Oswald was returned to Fritz' office.[8]   About an hour later, after further questioning, Oswald's fingerprints and palmprints were taken and a paraffin test (see app. XI) administered in Fritz' office, after which the questioning resumed.[9]   At 11:26 p.m. Fritz signed the complaint charging Oswald with the murder of President Kennedy.[10]   Shortly after midnight, detectives took Oswald to the basement assembly room for an appearance of several minutes before members of the press.[11]   At about 12:20 a.m. Oswald was delivered to the jailer who placed him in a maximum security cell on the fifth floor.[12]   His cell was the center one in a block of three cells that were separated from the remainder of the jail area. The cells on either side of Oswald were empty and a guard was nearby whenever Oswald was present.[13]   Shortly after 1:30 a.m. Oswald was brought to the identification bureau on the fourth floor and arraigned before Justice of the Peace Johnston, this time for the murder of President Kennedy.[14]

Questioning resumed in Fritz' office on Saturday morning at about 10:25 a.m., and the session lasted nearly an hour and 10 minutes.[15] Oswald was then returned to his cell for an hour, and at 12:35 p.m. he was brought back to Fritz' office for an additional half-hour of questioning.[16]   From 1:10 to 1:30 p.m., Oswald's wife and mother visited him in the fourth floor visiting area; [17] at 1:40 p.m. he attempted to call an attorney in New York.[18]   He appeared in another lineup at 2:15 p.m.[19]   At 2:45 p.m., with Oswald's consent, a member of the identification bureau obtained fingernail scrapings and specimens of hair from him.[20]   He returned to the fourth floor at 3:30

p.m. for a 10-minute visit with his brother, Robert.[21]   Between 4 and
4:30 p.m., Oswald made two telephone calls to Mrs. Ruth Paine [22] at
her home in Irving; at about 5:30 p.m. he was visited by the president
of the Dallas Bar Association [23] with whom he spoke for about 5
minutes.   From 6 to 7:15 p.m. Oswald was interrogated once again in
Captain Fritz' office and then returned to his cell.[24]   At 8 p.m. he
called the Paine residence again and asked to speak to his wife, but
Mrs. Paine told him that his wife was no longer there.[25]

Oswald was signed out of jail at 9:30 a.m. on Sunday, November
24, and taken to Captain Fritz' office for a final round of questioning.[26]
The transfer party left Fritz' office at about 11:15 a.m.; [27] at 11:21
a.m. Oswald was shot.[28]   He was declared dead at Parkland Hospital
at 1:07 p.m.[29]

Interrogation Sessions

During the period between 2:30 p.m. on Friday afternoon and 11:15
a.m. Sunday morning, Oswald was interrogated for a total of approximately 12 hours.[30]   Though subject to intermittent questioning for
more than 7 hours on Friday, Oswald was given 8 to 9 hours to rest
that night.   On Saturday he was questioned for a total of only 3 hours
during three interrogation sessions, and on Sunday he was questioned
for less than 2 hours.[31]   (These interrogations are discussed in ch. IV.)

Captain Fritz' office, within which the interrogations took place, was
a small room, 14 feet by 9½ feet in size.[32]   In addition to the policemen guarding the prisoner, those present usually included Dallas
detectives, investigators from the FBI and the Secret Service, and
occasionally other officials, particularly a post office inspector and the
U.S. marshal.   (See statements in app. XI.)   As many as seven or
eight people crowded into the small office.[33]   In all, more than 25
different persons participated in or were present at some time during
interrogations.   Captain Fritz, who conducted most of the interrogations, was frequently called from the room.   He said, "I don't believe
there was any time when I went through a very long period without
having to step to the door, or step outside, to get a report from some
pair of officers, or to give them additional assignments." [34]   In his
absence, others present would occasionally question Oswald.[35]

The interrogators differ on whether the confusion prevailing in
the main third floor corridor penetrated Fritz' office and affected the
atmosphere within.[36]   Oswald's processions through the third floor
corridor, described more fully below, tended, in Fritz' opinion, to keep
Oswald upset, and the remarks and questions of newsmen sometimes
caused him to become annoyed.   Despite the confusion that frequently
prevailed, Oswald remained calm most of the time during the interrogations.[37]   According to Captain Fritz:

> You know I didn't have trouble with him.   If we would just
> talk to him quietly like we are talking right now, we talked all
> right until I asked him a question that meant something, every

time I asked him a question that meant something, that would produce evidence he immediately told me he wouldn't tell me about it and he seemed to anticipate what I was going to ask.[38]

Special Agent James W. Bookhout, who represented the FBI at most of the interrogations, stated, "I think generally you might say anytime that you asked a question that would be pertinent to the investigation, that would be the type of question he would refuse to discuss." [39]

The number of people in the interrogation room and the tumultuous atmosphere throughout the third floor made it difficult for the interrogators to gain Oswald's confidence and to encourage him to be truthful. As Chief Curry has recognized in his testimony, "we were violating every principle of interrogation * * * it was just against all principles of good interrogation practice." [40]

Oswald's Legal Rights

All available evidence indicates that Oswald was not subjected to any physical hardship during the interrogation sessions or at any other time while he was in custody. He was fed and allowed to rest. When he protested on Friday against being handcuffed from behind, the cuffs were removed and he was handcuffed in front.[41] Although he made remarks to newsmen about desiring a shower and demanding his "civil rights," Oswald did not complain about his treatment to any of the numerous police officers and other persons who had much to do with him during the 2 days of his detention.[42] As described in chapter IV, Oswald received a slight cut over his right eye and a bruise under his left eye during the scuffle in the Texas Theatre with the arresting officers, three of whom were injured and required medical treatment. These marks were visible to all who saw him during the 2 days of his detention and to millions of television viewers.[43]

Before the first questioning session on Friday afternoon, Fritz warned Oswald that he was not compelled to make any statement and that statements he did make could be used against him.[44] About 5 hours later, he was arraigned for the Tippit murder and within an additional 6½ hours he was arraigned for the murder of President Kennedy. On each occasion the justice of the peace advised Oswald of his right to obtain counsel and the right to remain silent.[45]

Throughout the period of detention, however, Oswald was not represented by counsel. At the Friday midnight press conference in the basement assembly room, he made the following remarks:

OSWALD. Well, I was questioned by Judge ———— [Johnston]. However, I protested at that time that I was not allowed legal representation during that very short and sweet hearing. I really don't know what the situation is about. Nobody has told me anything except that I am accused of, of, murdering a police-

man. I know nothing more than that and I do request someone
to come forward to give me legal assistance.

Q. Did you kill the President?

A. No. I have not been charged with that. In fact nobody has
said that to me yet. The first thing I heard about it was when
the newspaper reporters in the hall asked me that question.

*   *   *   *   *   *   *

Q. Mr. Oswald, how did you hurt your eye?

A. A policeman hit me.[46]

At this time Oswald had been arraigned only for the murder of Patrolman Tippit, but questioning by Captain Fritz and others had been
substantially concerned with Oswald's connection with the assassination.[47]

On Friday evening, representatives of the American Civil Liberties
Union visited the police department to determine whether Oswald
was being deprived of counsel. They were assured by police officials
and Justice of the Peace Johnston that Oswald had been informed of
his rights and was being allowed to seek a lawyer.[48] On Saturday
Oswald attempted several times to reach John Abt, a New York lawyer, by telephone, but with no success.[49] In the afternoon, he called
Ruth Paine and asked her to try to reach Abt for him, but she too
failed.[50] Later in the afternoon, H. Louis Nichols, president of the
Dallas Bar Association, visited Oswald in his cell and asked him
whether he wanted the association to obtain a lawyer for him. Oswald
declined the offer, stating a first preference for Abt and a second
preference for a lawyer from the American Civil Liberties Union.[51]
As late as Sunday morning, according to Postal Inspector Harry D.
Holmes, Oswald said that he preferred to get his own lawyer.[52]

ACTIVITY OF NEWSMEN

Within an hour of Oswald's arrival at the police department on
November 22, it became known to newsmen that he was a possible
suspect in the slaying of President Kennedy as well as in the murder
of Patrolman Tippit. At least as early as 3:26 p.m. a television report carried this information. Reporters and cameramen flooded
into the building and congregated in the corridor of the third floor,
joining those few who had been present when Oswald first arrived.[53]

On the Third Floor

Felix McKnight, editor of the Dallas Times-Herald, who handled
press arrangements for the President's visit, estimated that within
24 hours of the assassination more than 300 representatives of news
media were in Dallas, including correspondents from foreign newspapers and press associations.[54] District Attorney Henry M. Wade

thought that the crowd in the third floor hallway itself may have numbered as many as 300.[55] Most estimates, including those based on examination of video tapes, place upwards of 100 newsmen and cameramen in the third floor corridor of the police department by the evening of November 22.[56] (See Commission Exhibit No. 2633, p. 203.)

In the words of an FBI agent who was present, the conditions at the police station were "not too much unlike Grand Central Station at rush hour, maybe like the Yankee Stadium during the World Series games. * * *"[57] In the lobby of the third floor, television cameramen set up two large cameras and floodlights in strategic positions that gave them a sweep of the corridor in either direction. Technicians stretched their television cables into and out of offices, running some of them out of the windows of a deputy chief's office and down the side of the building. Men with newsreel cameras, still cameras, and microphones, more mobile than the television cameramen, moved back and forth seeking information and opportunities for interviews. Newsmen wandered into the offices of other bureaus located on the third floor, sat on desks, and used police telephones; indeed, one reporter admits hiding a telephone behind a desk so that he would have exclusive access to it if something developed.[58]

By the time Chief Curry returned to the building in the middle of the afternoon from Love Field where he had escorted President Johnson from Parkland Hospital, he found that "there was just pandemonium on the third floor."[59] The news representatives, he testified:

> * * * were jammed into the north hall of the third floor, which are the offices of the criminal investigation division. The television trucks, there were several of them around the city hall. I went into my administrative offices, I saw cables coming through the administrative assistant office and through the deputy chief of traffic through his office, and running through the hall they had a live TV set up on the third floor, and it was a bedlam of confusion.[60]

According to Special Agent Winston G. Lawson of the Secret Service:

> At least by 6 or 7 o'clock * * * [the reporters and cameramen] were quite in evidence up and down the corridors, cameras on the tripods, the sound equipment, people with still cameras, motion picture-type hand cameras, all kinds of people with tape recorders, and they were trying to interview people, anybody that belonged in police headquarters that might know anything about Oswald * * *.[61]

The corridor became so jammed that policemen and newsmen had to push and shove if they wanted to get through, stepping over cables,

COMMISSION EXHIBIT No. 2633

Scene in third floor corridor.

wires, and tripods.[62] The crowd in the hallway was so dense that District Attorney Wade found it a "strain to get the door open" to get into the homicide office.[63] According to Lawson, "You had to literally fight your way through the people to get up and down the corridor." [64] A witness who was escorted into the homicide offices on Saturday afternoon related that he

> tried to get by the reporters, stepping over television cables and you couldn't hardly get by, they would grab you and wanted to know what you were doing down here, even with the detectives one in front and one behind you.[65]

The television cameras continued to record the scene on the third floor as some of the newsmen kept vigil through the night.[66]

Such police efforts as there were to control the newsmen were unavailing. Capt. Glen D. King, administrative assistant to Chief Curry, witnessed efforts to clear an aisle through the hallway, but related that "this was a constant battle because of the number of newsmen who were there. They would move back into the aisleway that had been cleared. They interfered with the movement of people who had to be there." [67] According to one detective, "they would be asked to stand back and stay back but it wouldn't do much good, and they would push forward and you had to hold them off physically." The detective recalled that on one occasion when he was escorting a witness through the corridor he "stopped * * * and looked down and there was a joker had a camera stuck between * * * [his] legs taking pictures. * * * " [68] Forrest V. Sorrels of the Secret Service had the impression that the "press and the television people just * * * took over." [69]

Police control over the access of other than newsmen to the third floor was of limited but increasing effectiveness after Oswald's arrival at the police department. Initially no steps were taken to exclude unauthorized persons from the third floor corridor, but late Friday afternoon Assistant Chief Charles Batchelor stationed guards at the elevators and the stairway to prevent the admission of such persons. He also directed the records room in the basement to issue passes, after verification by the bureaus involved, to people who had legitimate business on the third floor.[70] Throughout the 3 days of Oswald's detention, the police were obliged to continue normal business in all five bureaus located along the third floor hallway. Thus many persons—relatives of prisoners, complainants, witnesses [71]—had occasion to visit police offices on the third floor on business unrelated to the investigation of the assassination.

Newsmen seeking admission to the third floor were required to identify themselves by their personal press cards; however, the department did not follow its usual procedure of checking the authenticity of press credentials.[72] Captain King felt that this would have been impossible in light of "the atmosphere that existed over there, the tremendous pressures that existed, the fact that telephones were ringing constantly,

COMMISSION EXHIBIT No. 2631

Oswald being moved through third floor corridor.

that there were droves of people in there * * * the fact that the method by which you positively identify someone * * * it's not easy." [73]

Police officers on the third floor testified that they carefully checked all persons for credentials, and most newsmen indicated that after Batchelor imposed security they were required to identify themselves by their press cards.[74] Special Agent Sorrels of the Secret Service stated that he was requested to present credentials on some of his visits to the third floor.[75] However, other newsmen apparently went unchallenged during the entire period before Oswald was killed, although some of them were wearing press badges on their lapels and some may have been known to the police officers.[76]

According to some reporters and policemen, people who appeared to be unauthorized were present on the third floor after security procedures were instituted, and video tapes seem to confirm their observations.[77] Jack Ruby was present on the third floor on Friday night.[78] Assistant Chief of Police N. T. Fisher testified that even on Saturday "anybody could come up with a plausible reason for going to one of the third floor bureaus and was able to get in." [79]

Oswald and the Press

When the police car bringing Oswald from the Texas Theatre drove into the basement of police headquarters at about 2 p.m. on Friday, some reporters and cameramen, principally from local papers and stations, were already on hand. The policemen formed a wedge around Oswald and conducted him to the elevator, but several newsmen crowded into the elevator with Oswald and the police. When the elevator stopped at the third floor, the cameramen ran ahead down the corridor, and then turned around and backed up, taking pictures of Oswald as he was escorted toward the homicide and robbery bureau office. According to one escorting officer, some six or seven reporters followed the police into the bureau office.[80]

From Friday afternoon, when Oswald arrived in the building, until Sunday, newspaper reporters and television cameras focused their attention on the homicide office. In full view and within arm's length of the assembled newsmen, Oswald traversed the 20 feet of corridor between the homicide office and the locked door leading to the jail elevator at least 15 times after his initial arrival. The jail elevator, sealed off from public use, took him to his fifth floor cell and to the assembly room in the basement for lineups and the Friday night news conference.[81]

On most occasions, Oswald's escort of three to six detectives and policemen had to push their way through the newsmen who sought to surround them. (See Commission Exhibit No. 2631, p. 205.) Although the Dallas press normally did not take pictures of a prisoner without first obtaining permission of the police, who generally asked the prisoner, this practice was not followed by any of the newsmen with Oswald.[82] Generally when Oswald appeared the newsmen turned their cameras on him, thrust microphones at his face, and shouted

OSWALD AT PRESS CONFERENCE IN
ASSEMBLY ROOM, FRIDAY NIGHT
(COMMISSION EXHIBIT 2965)

questions at him. Sometimes he answered. Reporters in the forefront of the throng would repeat his answers for the benefit of those behind them who could not hear. On Saturday, however in response to police admonitions, the reporters exercised more restraint and shouted fewer questions at Oswald when he passed through the corridor.[83]

Oswald's most prolonged exposure occurred at the midnight press conference on Friday night. In response to demands of newsmen, District Attorney Wade, after consulting with Chief Curry and Captain Fritz, had announced shortly before midnight that Oswald would appear at a press conference in the basement assembly room.[84] An estimated 70 to 100 people, including Jack Ruby, and other unauthorized persons, crowded into the small downstairs room. No identification was required.[85] The room was so packed that Deputy Chief M. W. Stevenson and Captain Fritz who came down to the basement after the crowd had assembled could not get in and were forced to remain in the doorway.[86]

Oswald was brought into the room shortly after midnight.[87] Curry had instructed policemen not to permit newsmen to touch Oswald or get close to him, but no steps were taken to shield Oswald from the crowd.[88] Captain Fritz had asked that Oswald be placed on the platform used for lineups so that he could be more easily removed "if anything happened." [89] Chief Curry, however, insisted that Oswald stand on the floor in front of the stage, where he was also in front of the one-way nylon-cloth screen customarily used to prevent a suspect from seeing those present in the room. This was done because cameramen had told Curry that their cameras would not photograph well through the screen.[90]

Curry had instructed the reporters that they were not to "ask any questions and try to interview * * * [Oswald] in any way," but when he was brought into the room, "immediately they began to shoot questions at him and shove microphones into his face." [91] It was difficult to hear Oswald's answers above the uproar. Cameramen stood on the tables to take pictures and others pushed forward to get close-ups. (See Commission Exhibit No. 2965, p. 207.) The noise and confusion mounted as reporters shouted at each other to get out of the way and camermen made frantic efforts to get into position for pictures.[92] After Oswald had been in the room only a few minutes, Chief Curry intervened and directed that Oswald be taken back to the jail because, he testified, the newsmen "tried to overrun him." [93]

THE ABORTIVE TRANSFER

In Dallas, after a person is charged with a felony, the county sheriff ordinarily takes custody of the prisoner and assumes responsibility for his safekeeping. Normally, the Dallas Police Department notifies the sheriff when a prisoner has been charged with a felony and the sheriff dispatches his deputies to transport the accused to the county jail. This is usually done within a few hours after the complaint has been filed. In cases of unusual importance, however, the Dallas city police sometimes transport the prisoners to the county jail.[94]

The decision to move Oswald to the county jail on Sunday morning was reached by Chief Curry the preceding evening. Sometime after 7:30 Saturday evening, according to Assistant Chief Batchelor, two reporters told him that they wanted to go out to dinner but that "they didn't want to miss anything if we were going to move the prisoner." Curry came upon them at that point and told the two newsmen that if they returned by 10 o'clock in the morning, they wouldn't "miss anything."[95] A little later, after checking with Captain Fritz, Curry made a similar announcement to the assembled reporters. Curry reported the making of his decision to move Oswald as follows:

> Then, I talked to Fritz about when he thought he would transfer the prisoner, and he didn't think it was a good idea to transfer him at night because of the fact you couldn't see, and if anybody tried to cause them any trouble, they needed to see who they were and where it was coming from and so forth, and he suggested that we wait until daylight, so this was normal procedure, I mean, for Fritz to determine when he is going to transfer his prisoners, so I told him "Okay." I asked him, I said, "What time do you think you will be ready tomorrow?" And he didn't know exactly and I said, "Do you think about 10 o'clock," and he said, "I believe so," and then is when I went out and told the newspaper people * * * "I believe if you are back here by 10 o'clock you will be back in time to observe anything you care to observe."[96]

During the night, between 2:30 and 3 a.m., the local office of the FBI and the sheriff's office received telephone calls from an unidentified man who warned that a committee had decided "to kill the man that killed the President."[97] Shortly after, an FBI agent notified the Dallas police of the anonymous threat. The police department and ultimately Chief Curry were informed of both threats.[98]

Immediately after his arrival at the building on Sunday morning between 8:30 and 8:45 a.m., Curry spoke by telephone with Sheriff J. E. Decker about the transfer. When Decker indicated that he would leave to Curry the decision on whether the sheriff's office or the police would move Oswald, Curry decided that the police would handle it because "we had so much involved here, we were the ones that were investigating the case and we had the officers set up downstairs to handle it."[99]

After talking with Decker, Curry began to discuss plans for the transfer. With the threats against Oswald in mind, Curry suggested to Batchelor and Deputy Chief Stevenson that Oswald be transported to the county jail in an armored truck, to which they agreed. While Batchelor made arrangements to have an armored truck brought to the building, Curry and Stevenson tentatively agreed on the route the armored truck would follow from the building to the county jail.[100]

Curry decided that Oswald would leave the building via the basement. He stated later that he reached this decision shortly after his arrival at the police building Sunday morning, when members of the press had already begun to gather in the basement. There is no evidence that anyone opposed this decision.[101] Two members of the Dallas police did suggest to Captain Fritz that Oswald be taken from the building by another exit, leaving the press "waiting in the basement and on Commerce Street, and we could be to the county jail before anyone knew what was taking place."[102] However, Fritz said that he did not think Curry would agree to such a plan because he had promised that Oswald would be transferred at a time when newsmen could take pictures.[103] Forrest Sorrels also suggested to Fritz that Oswald be moved at an unannounced time when no one was around, but Fritz again responded that Curry "wanted to go along with the press and not try to put anything over on them."[104]

Preliminary arrangements to obtain additional personnel to assist with the transfer were begun Saturday evening. On Saturday night, the police reserves were requested to provide 8 to 10 men on Sunday, and additional reservists were sought in the morning.[105] Capt. C. E. Talbert, who was in charge of the patrol division for the city of Dallas on the morning of November 24, retained a small number of policemen in the building when he took charge that morning and later ordered other patrolmen from several districts to report to the basement.[106] At about 9 a.m. Deputy Chief Stevenson instructed all detectives within the building to remain for the transfer.[107] Sheriff Decker testified that his men were ready to receive Oswald at the county jail from the early hours of Sunday morning.[108]

With the patrolmen and reserve policemen available to him, Captain Talbert, on his own initiative, undertook to secure the basement of the police department building. He placed policemen outside the building at the top of the Commerce Street ramp to keep all spectators on the opposite side of Commerce Street. Later, Talbert directed that patrolmen be assigned to all street intersections the transfer vehicle would cross along the route to the county jail.[109] His most significant security precautions, however, were steps designed to exclude unauthorized persons from the basement area.

The spacious basement of the Police and Courts Building contains, among other things, the jail office and the police garage. (See Commission Exhibit No. 2179, p. 211.) The jail office, into which the jail elevator opens, is situated on the west side of an auto ramp cutting across the length of the basement from Main Street, on the north side of the building, to Commerce Street, on the south side. From the foot of this ramp, on the east side, midway through the basement, a decline runs down a short distance to the L-shaped police garage. In addition to the auto ramp, five doors to the garage provide access to the basement from the Police and Courts Building on the west side of the garage and the attached Municipal Building on the east. Three of these five doors provide access to three elevators opening into the garage, two for passengers near the central part of the garage and

BASEMENT
DALLAS POLICE DEPARTMENT, DALLAS, TEXAS

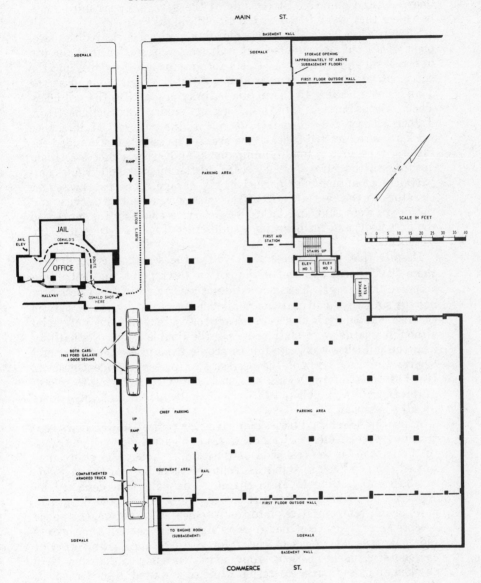

COMMISSION EXHIBIT No. 2179

one for service at the east end of the garage. A fourth door near the passenger elevator opens into the municipal building; the fifth door, at the Commerce Street side of the garage, opens into a sub-basement that is connected with both buildings.[110]

Shortly after 9 o'clock Sunday morning, policemen cleared the basement of all but police personnel. Guards were stationed at the top of the Main and Commerce Streets auto ramps leading down into the basement, at each of the five doorways into the garage, and at the double doors leading to the public hallway adjacent to the jail office. Then, Sgt. Patrick T. Dean, acting under instructions from Talbert, directed 14 men in a search of the garage. Maintenance workers were directed to leave the area. The searchers examined the rafters, tops of air conditioning ducts, and every closet and room opening off the garage. They searched the interior and trunk compartment of automobiles parked in the garage. The two passenger elevators in the central part of the garage were not in service and the doors were shut and locked; the service elevator was moved to the first floor, and the operator was instructed not to return it to the basement.[111]

Despite the thoroughness with which the search was conducted, there still existed one and perhaps two weak points in controlling access to the garage. Testimony did not resolve positively whether or not the stairway door near the public elevators was locked both from the inside and outside as was necessary to secure it effectively.[112] And although guards were stationed near the double doors, the hallway near the jail office was accessible to people from inside the Police and Courts Building without the necessity of presenting identification. Until seconds before Oswald was shot, newsmen hurrying to photograph Oswald were able to run without challenge through those doors into the basement.[113]

After the search had been completed, the police allowed news representatives to reenter the basement area and gather along the entrance to the garage on the east side of the ramp. Later, the police permitted the newsmen to stand in front of the railing on the east side of the ramp leading to Main Street. The policemen deployed by Talbert and Dean had instructions to allow no one but identified news media representatives into the basement. As before, the police accepted any credentials that appeared authentic, though some officers did make special efforts to check for pictures and other forms of corroborating identification. Many newsmen reported that they were checked on more than one occasion while they waited in the basement. A small number did not recall that their credentials were ever checked.[114]

Shortly after his arrival on Sunday morning, Chief Curry issued instructions to keep reporters and cameramen out of the jail office and to keep television equipment behind the railing separating the basement auto ramp from the garage. Curry observed that in other respects Captain Talbert appeared to have security measures in hand and allowed him to proceed on his own initiative. Batchelor and

Stevenson checked progress in the basement during the course of the morning, and the officials were generally satisfied with the steps Talbert had taken.[115]

At about 11 a.m., Deputy Chief Stevenson requested that Capt. O. A. Jones of the forgery bureau bring all available detectives from the third floor offices to the basement. Jones instructed the detectives who accompanied him to the basement to line the walls on either side of the passageway cleared for the transfer party.[116] According to Detective T. D. McMillon,

> * * * Captain Jones explained to us that, when they brought the prisoner out, that he wanted two lines formed and we were to keep these two lines formed, you know, a barrier on either side of them, kind of an aisle * * * for them to walk through, and when they came down this aisle, we were to keep this line intact and move along with them until the man was placed in the car.[117]

With Assistant Chief Batchelor's permission, Jones removed photographers who had gathered once again in the basement jail office. Jones recalled that he instructed all newsmen along the Main Street ramp to remain behind an imaginary line extending from the southeast corner of the jail office to the railing on the east side of the ramp; other officers recalled that Jones directed the newsmen to move away from the foot of the Main Street ramp and to line up against the east railing. In any event, newsmen were allowed to congregate along the foot of the ramp after Batchelor observed that there was insufficient room along the east of the ramp to permit all the news representatives to see Oswald as he was brought out.[118]

By the time Oswald reached the basement, 40 to 50 newsmen and 70 to 75 police officers were assembled there. Three television cameras stood along the railing and most of the newsmen were congregated in that area and at the top of the adjacent decline leading into the garage. A group of newsmen and police officers, best estimated at about 20, stood strung across the bottom of the Main Street ramp. Along the south wall of the passageway outside the jail office door were about eight detectives, and three detectives lined the north wall. Two officers stood in front of the double doors leading into the passageway from the corridor next to the jail office.[119] (See Commission Exhibit No. 2634, p. 214.)

Beginning Saturday night, the public had been kept informed of the approximate time of the transfer. At approximately 10:20 a.m. Curry told a press conference that Oswald would be moved in an armored truck and gave a general description of other security precautions.[120] Apparently no newsmen were informed of the transfer route, however, and the route was not disclosed to the driver of the armored truck until the truck arrived at the Commerce Street exit at about 11:07 a.m.[121] When they learned of its arrival, many of the remaining newsmen who had waited on the third floor descended to the basement. Shortly after, newsmen may have had another indication

213

COMMISSION EXHIBIT No. 2634

Scene in areaway outside jail office immediately before shooting
(Sunday, November 24).

214

that the transfer was imminent if they caught a glimpse through the glass windows of Oswald putting on a sweater in Captain Fritz' office.[122]

Because the driver feared that the truck might stall if it had to start from the bottom of the ramp and because the overhead clearance appeared to be inadequate, Assistant Chief Batchelor had it backed only into the entranceway at the top of the ramp. Batchelor and others then inspected the inside of the truck.[123]

When Chief Curry learned that the truck had arrived, he informed Captain Fritz that security controls were in effect and inquired how long the questioning of Oswald would continue. At this point, Fritz learned for the first time of the plan to convey Oswald by armored truck and immediately expressed his disapproval. He urged the use of an unmarked police car driven by a police officer, pointing out that this would be better from the standpoint of both speed and maneuverability. Curry agreed to Fritz' plan; the armored truck would be used as a decoy. They decided that the armored truck would leave the ramp first, followed by a car which would contain only security officers. A police car bearing Oswald would follow. After proceeding one block, the car with Oswald would turn off and proceed directly to the county jail; the armored truck would follow a lead car to the jail along the previously agreed upon and more circuitous route.[124]

Captain Fritz instructed Detectives C. W. Brown and C. N. Dhority and a third detective to proceed to the garage and move the followup car and the transfer car into place on the auto ramp. He told Lt. Rio S. Pierce to obtain another automobile from the basement and take up a lead position on Commerce Street.[125] Deputy Chief Stevenson went back to the basement to inform Batchelor and Jones of the change in plans.[126] Oswald was given his sweater, and then his right hand was handcuffed to the left hand of Detective J. R. Leavelle.[127] Detective T. L. Baker called the jail office to check on security precautions in the basement and notify officials that the prisoner was being brought down.[128]

On arriving in the basement, Pierce asked Sgts. James A. Putnam and Billy Joe Maxey to accompany him in the lead car. Since the armored truck was blocking the Commerce Street ramp, it would be necessary to drive out the Main Street ramp and circle the block to Commerce Street. Maxey sat on the back seat of Pierce's car, and Putnam helped clear a path through reporters on the ramp so that Pierce could drive up toward Main Street. When the car passed by the reporters at about 11:20 a.m., Putnam entered the car on the right front side. Pierce drove to the top of the Main Street ramp and slowed momentarily as Patrolman Roy E. Vaughn stepped from his position at the top of the ramp toward the street to watch for traffic.[129] After Pierce's car left the garage area, Brown drove another police car out of the garage, moved part way up the Commerce Street ramp, and began to back down into position to receive Oswald. Dhority also proceeded to drive the followup car into position ahead of Brown.[130]

As Pierce's car started up the ramp at about 11:20 a.m., Oswald, accompanied by Captain Fritz and four detectives, arrived at the jail office. Cameramen in the hallway of the basement took pictures of Oswald through the interior glass windows of the jail office as he was led through the office to the exit.[131] Some of these cameramen then ran through the double doors near the jail office and squeezed into the line which had formed across the Main Street ramp.[132] Still others remained just inside the double doors or proceeded through the double doors after Oswald and his escort emerged from the jail office.[133] (See Commission Exhibit No. 2177, p. 217.)

When Fritz came to the jail office door, he asked if everything was ready, and a detective standing in the passageway answered yes.[134] Someone shouted, "Here he comes!"; additional spotlights were turned on in the basement, and the din increased. A detective stepped from the jail office and proceeded toward the transfer car. Seconds later Fritz and then Oswald, with Detective Leavelle at his right, Detective L. C. Graves at his left, and Detective L. D. Montgomery at his rear, came through the door. Fritz walked to Brown's car, which had not yet backed fully into position; Oswald followed a few feet behind. Newsmen near the double door moved forward after him.[135] Though movie films and video tapes indicate that the front line of newsmen along the Main Street ramp remained fairly stationary, it was the impression of many who were close to the scene that with Oswald's appearance the crowd surged forward. According to Detective Montgomery, who was walking directly behind Oswald, "as soon as we came out this door * * * this bunch here just moved in on us." [136] To Detective B. H. Combest, standing on the Commerce Street side of the passageway from the jail office door, it appeared that

> Almost the whole line of people pushed forward when Oswald started to leave the jail office, the door, the hall—all the newsmen were poking their sound mikes across to him and asking questions, and they were everyone sticking their flashbulbs up and around and over him and in his face.[137]

After Oswald had moved about 10 feet from the door of the jail office, Jack Ruby passed between a newsman and a detective at the edge of the straining crowd on the Main Street ramp. With his right hand extended and holding a .38 caliber revolver, Ruby stepped quickly forward and fired a single fatal bullet into Oswald's abdomen.[138] (See Commission Exhibit No. 2636, p. 218.)

POSSIBLE ASSISTANCE TO JACK RUBY IN ENTERING THE BASEMENT

The killing of Lee Harvey Oswald in the basement of police headquarters in the midst of more than 70 police officers gave rise to im-

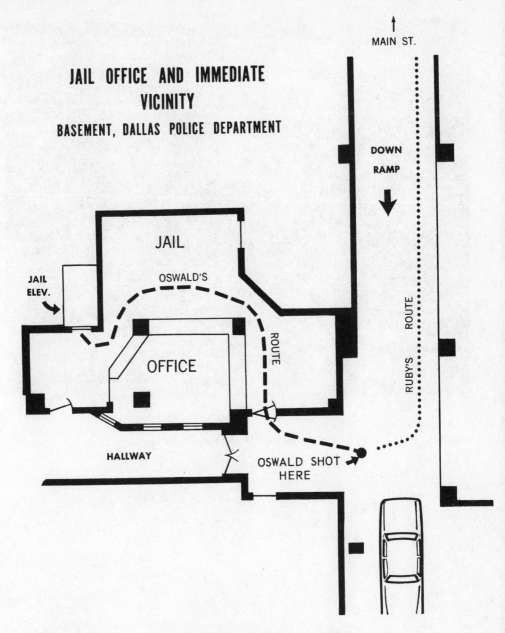

JAIL OFFICE AND IMMEDIATE
VICINITY

BASEMENT, DALLAS POLICE DEPARTMENT

MAIN ST.

DOWN
RAMP

JAIL

OSWALD'S

JAIL
ELEV.

ROUTE

OFFICE

RUBY'S ROUTE

HALLWAY

OSWALD SHOT
HERE

COMMISSION EXHIBIT No. 2177

217

COMMISSION EXHIBIT No. 2636

Ruby shooting Oswald (Sunday, November 24).

mediate speculation that one or more members of the police department provided Jack Ruby assistance which had enabled him to enter the basement and approach within a few feet of the accused Presidential assassin. In chapter VI, the Commission has considered whether there is any evidence linking Jack Ruby with a conspiracy to kill the President. At this point, however, it is appropriate to consider whether there is evidence that Jack Ruby received assistance from Dallas policemen or others in gaining access to the basement on the morning of November 24. An affirmative answer would require that the evidence be evaluated for possible connection with the assassination itself. While the Commission has found no evidence that Ruby received assistance from any person in entering the basement, his means of entry is significant in evaluating the adequacy of the precautions taken to protect Oswald.

Although more than a hundred policemen and newsmen were present in the basement of police headquarters during the 10 minutes before the shooting of Oswald, none has been found who definitely observed Jack Ruby's entry into the basement. After considering all the evidence, the Commission has concluded that Ruby entered the basement unaided, probably via the Main Street ramp, and no more than 3 minutes before the shooting of Oswald.

Ruby's account of how he entered the basement by the Main Street ramp merits consideration in determining his means of entry. Three Dallas policemen testified that approximately 30 minutes after his arrest, Ruby told them that he had walked to the top of the Main Street ramp from the nearby Western Union office and that he walked down the ramp at the time the police car driven by Lieutenant Pierce emerged into Main Street.[139] This information did not come to light immediately because the policemen did not report it to their superiors until some days later.[140] Ruby refused to discuss his means of entry in interrogations with other investigators later on the day of his arrest.[141] Thereafter, in a lengthy interview on December 21 and in a sworn deposition taken after his trial, Ruby gave the same explanation he had given to the three policemen.[142]

The Commission has been able to establish with precision the time of certain events leading up to the shooting. Minutes before Oswald appeared in the basement, Ruby was in the Western Union office located on the same block of Main Street some 350 feet from the top of the Main Street ramp. The time stamp on a money order which he sent and on the receipt found in his pocket establish that the order was accepted for transmission at almost exactly 11:17 a.m. Ruby was then observed to depart the office walking in the direction of the police building.[143] Video tapes taken without interruption before the shooting establish that Lieutenant Pierce's car cleared the crowd at the foot of the ramp 55 seconds before the shooting. They also show Ruby standing at the foot of the ramp on the Main Street side before the shooting.[144] (See Commission Exhibit No. 2635, p. 220.) The shooting occurred very close to 11:21 a.m. This time has been established by observing the time on a clock appearing in motion pictures

Commission Exhibit No. 2635

COMMISSION EXHIBIT No. 2635

Ruby in basement (extreme right) immediately before shooting (Sunday, November 24).

of Oswald in the basement jail office, and by records giving the time of Oswald's departure from the city jail and the time at which an ambulance was summoned for Oswald.[145]

The Main Street ramp provided the most direct route to the basement from the Western Union office. At normal stride, it requires approximately 1 minute to walk from that office to the top of the Main Street ramp and about 20–25 seconds to descend the ramp.[146] It is certain, therefore, that Ruby entered the basement no more than 2–3 minutes before the shooting. This timetable indicates that a little more than 2 of the 4 minutes between Ruby's departure from the Western Union office and the time of the shooting are unaccounted for. Ruby could have consumed this time in loitering along the way, at the top of the ramp, or inside the basement. However, if Ruby is correct that he passed Pierce's car at the top of the ramp, he could have been in the basement no more than 30 seconds before the shooting.[147]

The testimony of two witnesses partially corroborates Ruby's claim that he entered by the Main Street ramp. James Turner, an employee of WBAP–TV Fort Worth, testified that while he was standing near the railing on the east side of the Main Street ramp, perhaps 30 seconds before the shooting, he observed a man he is confident was Jack Ruby moving slowly down the Main Street ramp about 10 feet from the bottom.[148] Two other witnesses testified that they thought they had seen Ruby on the Main Street side of the ramp before the shooting.[149]

One other witness has testified regarding the purported movements of a man on the Main Street ramp, but his testimony merits little credence. A former police officer, N. J. Daniels, who was standing at the top of the ramp with the single patrolman guarding this entrance, R. E. Vaughn, testified that "3 or 4 minutes, I guess"[150] before the shooting, a man walked down the Main Street ramp in full view of Vaughn but was not stopped or questioned by the officer. Daniels did not identify the man as Ruby. Moreover, he gave a description which differed in important respects from Ruby's appearance on November 24, and he has testified that he doesn't think the man was Ruby.[151] On November 24, Vaughn telephoned Daniels to ask him if he had seen anybody walk past him on the morning of the 24th and was told that he had not; it was not until November 29 that Daniels came forward with the statement that he had seen a man enter.[152]

Although the sum of this evidence tends to support Ruby's claim that he entered by the Main Street ramp, there is other evidence not fully consistent with Ruby's story. Patrolman Vaughn stated that he checked the credentials of all unknown persons seeking to enter the basement, and his testimony was supported by several persons.[153] Vaughn denied that the emergence of Lieutenant Pierce's car from the building distracted him long enough to allow Ruby to enter the ramp unnoticed, and neither he nor any of the three officers in Lieutenant Pierce's car saw Ruby enter.[154]

Despite Vaughn's denial the Commission has found no credible evidence to support any other entry route. Two Dallas detectives believed they observed three men pushing a WBAP–TV camera into the basement minutes before the shooting, while only two were with the camera after Oswald had been shot.[155] However, films taken in the basement show the WBAP–TV camera being pushed past the detectives by only two men.[156] The suspicion of the detectives is probably explained by testimony that a third WBAP–TV employee ran to help steady the incoming camera as it entered the basement, probably just before the camera became visible on the films.[157] Moreover, since the camera entered the basement close to 4 minutes before the shooting,[158] it is virtually impossible that Ruby could have been in the basement at that time.

The possibility that Ruby entered the basement by some other route has been investigated, but the Commission has found no evidence to support it. Ruby could have walked from the Western Union office to the Commerce Street ramp on the other side of the building in about 2½ minutes.[159] However, during the minutes preceding the shooting video tapes show the armored truck in the entranceway to this ramp with only narrow clearance on either side. (See Commission Exhibit No. 2710, p. 223.) Several policemen were standing near the truck and a large crowd of spectators was gathered across the street.[160] It is improbable that Ruby could have squeezed past the truck without having been observed. If Ruby entered by any other means, he would have had to pass first through the Police and Courts Building or the attached Municipal Building, and then secondly through one of the five doors into the basement, all of which, according to the testimony of police officers, were secured. The testimony was not completely positive about one of the doors.[161]

There is no evidence to support the speculations that Ruby used a press badge to gain entry to the basement or that he concealed himself in a police car. Police found no form of press card on Ruby's person after his apprehension, nor any discarded badges within the basement.[162] There is no evidence that any police officer admitted Ruby on the pretense that he was a member of the press or any other pretense.[163]

Police vehicles in the basement were inspected during the course of the search supervised by Sergeant Dean.[164] According to Patrolman Vaughn, the only vehicles that entered the basement while he was at the top of the Main Street ramp were two patrol cars, one of which entered twice, and a patrol wagon which was searched by another policeman after it entered the basement. All entered on official police business and considerably more than 4 minutes before Oswald was shot.[165] None of the witnesses at the top of the Main Street ramp recalled any police car entering the basement in the 4-minute period after Ruby left the Western Union office and preceding the shooting.[166] The possibility that Ruby could have entered the basement in a car may therefore be completely discounted.

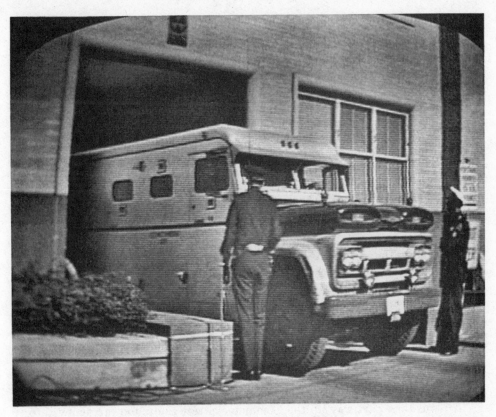

COMMISSION EXHIBIT No. 2710

The Dallas Police Department, concerned at the failure of its security measures, conducted an extensive investigation that revealed no information indicating complicity between any police officer and Jack Ruby.[167] Ruby denied to the Commission that he received any form of assistance.[168] The FBI interviewed every member of the police department who was on duty in the basement on November 24, and Commission staff members took sworn depositions from many. With few exceptions, newsmen who were present in the basement at the time also gave statements and/or depositions. As the record before the Commission indicated, Ruby had had rather free access to the Dallas police quarters during the period subsequent to the assassination, but there was no evidence that implicated the police or newsmen in Ruby's actions on that day.[169]

Ruby was known to have a wide acquaintanceship with Dallas policemen and to seek their favor. According to testimony from many sources, he gave free coffee at his clubs to many policemen while they were on duty and free admittance and discounts on beverages when they were off duty.[170] Although Chief Curry's estimate that approximately 25 to 50 of the 1,175 men in the Dallas Police Department knew Ruby [171] may be too conservative, the Commission found no evidence of any suspicious relationships between Ruby and any police officer.

The Commission found no substantial evidence that any member of the Dallas Police Department recognized Jack Ruby as an unauthorized person in the basement prior to the time Sgt. P. T. Dean, according to his testimony, saw Ruby dart forward toward Oswald. But Dean was then part way up the Commerce Street ramp, too far removed to act.[172] Patrolman W. J. Harrison, Capt. Glen King, and reserve officers Capt. C. O. Arnett and Patrolman W. M. Croy were among those in front of Ruby at the time Dean saw him. They all faced away from Ruby, toward the jail office.[173] Video tapes show that Harrison turned in the direction of the ramp at the time Lieutenant Pierce's car passed, and once again 25 seconds later, but there is no indication that he observed or recognized Ruby.[174] The policemen standing on the south side of the passageway from the jail office, who might have been looking in Ruby's direction, had the glare of television and photographer's lights in their eyes.[175]

The Commission also considered the possibility that a member of the police department called Ruby at his apartment and informed him, either intentionally or unintentionally, of the time of the planned transfer. From at least 10:19 a.m., until close to 11 a.m., on Sunday, Ruby was at his apartment,[176] where he could have received a call that the transfer was imminent. He apparently left his apartment between 10:45 and 11 a.m.[177] However, the drive from Ruby's apartment to the Western Union office takes approximately 15 minutes.[178] Since the time of the contemplated transfer could not have been known to anyone until a few minutes before 11:15 a.m., a precise time could not have been conveyed to Ruby while he was at his apartment. Moreover, the television and radio publicized the transfer plans throughout the morning, obviating the need for Ruby to obtain information surreptitiously.

ADEQUACY OF SECURITY PRECAUTIONS

The shooting of Lee Harvey Oswald obviously resulted from the failure of the security precautions which the Dallas Police Department had taken to protect their prisoner. In assessing the causes of the security failure, the Commission has not overlooked the extraordinary circumstances which prevailed during the days that the attention of the world was turned on Dallas. Confronted with a unique situation, the Dallas police took special security measures to insure Oswald's safety. Unfortunately these did not include adequate control of the great crowd of newsmen that inundated the police department building.

The Dallas police had in custody a man whose alleged act had brought upon him immediate and universal opprobrium. There were many possible reasons why people might have attempted to kill him if given the opportunity. Concerned that there might be an attempt on Oswald's life, FBI Director J. Edgar Hoover sent a message to Chief Curry on November 22 through Special Agent Manning C. Clements of the FBI's Dallas office, urging that Oswald be afforded the utmost security. Curry does not recall receiving the message.[179]

Although the presence of a great mass of press representatives created an extraordinary security problem in the building, the police department pursued its normal policy of admitting the press. That policy, set forth in General Order No. 81 of the Dallas Police Department, provided—

> * * * that members of this Department render every assistance, except such as obviously may seriously hinder or delay the proper functioning of the Department, to the accredited members of the official news-gathering agencies and this includes newspaper, television cameramen and news-reel photographers.[180]

In a letter to all members of the police department, dated February 7, 1963, Chief Curry explained the general order, in part, as follows:

> The General Order covering this subject is not merely permissive. It does not state that the Officer may, if he so chooses, assist the press. It rather places on him a responsibility to lend active assistance.
>
> *   *   *   *   *   *   *
>
> * * * as a Department we deal with public affairs. It is the right of the public to know about these affairs, and one of the most accurate and useful avenues we have of supplying this information is through the newspapers and radio and television stations.
>
> Implied in the General Order is a prohibition for the Officer to improperly attempt to interfere with the news media representa-

tive, who is functioning in his capacity as such. Such activity on the part of any Police Officer is regarded by the press as an infringement of rights, and the Department shares this view.[181]

Under this policy, news representatives ordinarily had access to the Police and Courts Building. The first newsmen to arrive on Friday afternoon were admitted in accordance with the policy; others who came later simply followed behind them. Shortly after Oswald arrived, Captain King granted permission to bring television cameras to the third floor.[182] By the time the unwieldy proportions of the crowd of newsmen became apparent, it had already become well entrenched on the third floor. No one suggested reversing the department's policy expressed in General Order No. 81. Chief Curry testified that at no time did he consider clearing the crowd from the building; he "saw no particular harm in allowing the media to observe the prisoner."[183] Captain King later stated candidly that he simply became "accustomed to the idea of them being out there."[184]

The general policy of the Dallas police recognized that the rule of full cooperation did not apply when it might jeopardize an investigation.[185] In retrospect, most members of the department believed that the general rule allowing admittance of the press to the police quarters should not have been followed after the assassination. Few, if any, thought this at the time.[186] By failing to exclude the press from the building on Friday and Saturday, the Dallas police made it possible for the uncontrolled crowd to nearly surround Oswald on the frequent occasions that he moved through the third floor corridor. The decision to allow newsmen to observe the transfer on Sunday followed naturally the policy established during these first 2 days of Oswald's detention.

The reporters and cameramen descended upon the third floor of the Police and Courts Building in such numbers that the pressroom on the third floor proved wholly inadequate. Rather than the "two or three or maybe a half dozen reporters" who normally appeared to cover local police stories,[187] the police were faced with upward of 100. Bringing with them cameras, microphones, cables, and spotlights, the newsmen inevitably spilled over into areas where they interfered with the transaction of police business and the maintenance of security.[188]

Aside from numbers, the gathering of reporters presented a problem because most of them were representatives of the national and foreign press, rather than the local press.[189] These newsmen carried individual press cards rather than identification cards issued by the Dallas police. Therefore, it was impossible for the police to verify quickly the identity of this great number of unfamiliar people who appeared almost simultaneously.[190] Because of the close physical proximity of the milling mass of insistent newsmen to the prisoner, the failure to authenticate press credentials subjected the prisoner to a serious security risk.

Although steps were taken on Friday afternoon to insure that persons seeking entry to the third floor were there for a legitimate purpose, reasons could be fabricated. Moreover, because of the large crowd, it was easier for unauthorized persons to slip by those guarding the entrances. Jack Ruby, for one, was able to gain entry to the third-floor corridor on Friday night.[191]

The third-floor corridor provided the only passageway between the homicide and robbery bureau and the jail elevator. No thought seems to have been given, however, to the possibility of questioning Oswald on some other floor.[192] Moreover, Oswald's most extended exposure to the press, at the Friday evening press conference, was unrelated to any phase of the investigation and was motivated primarily by the desire to satisfy the demands of the news media to see the prisoner.[193] The risks attendant upon this appearance were emphasized by the presence of unauthorized persons, including Jack Ruby, at the press conference in the basement assembly room.[194]

Although Oswald was repeatedly exposed to possible assaults on Friday and Saturday, he met his death on Sunday, when police took the most extensive security precautions. The assembly of more than 70 police officers, some of them armed with tear gas, and the contemplated use of an armored truck, appear to have been designed primarily to repel an attempt of a mob to seize the prisoner.[195] Chief Curry's own testimony indicated that such a focus resulted not from any appraisal of the varied risks to Oswald's life but came about in response to the telephone threat Sunday morning that a hundred men were going to attack Oswald.[196]

A more balanced appraisal would have given thought to protection against any attack. For example, the acceptance of inadequate press credentials posed a clear avenue for a one-man assault. The likelihood of an unauthorized person obtaining entry by such means is confirmed not alone by the fact that Jack Ruby managed to get by a guard at one entrance. Several newsmen related that their credentials were not checked as they entered the basement Sunday morning. Seconds before Oswald was shot, the double doors from the hallway next to the jail office afforded a means of entry to the basement without presentation of credentials earlier demanded of newsmen.[197]

The swarm of newspeople in the basement also substantially limited the ability of the police to detect an unauthorized person once he had entered the basement. While Jack Ruby might have been easily spotted if only police officers had been in the basement,[198] he remained apparently unnoticed in the crowd of newsmen until he lunged forward toward Oswald. The near-blinding television and motion picture lights which were allowed to shine upon the escort party further increased the difficulty of observing unusual movements in the basement.

Moreover, by making public the plans for the transfer, the police attracted to the city jail many persons who otherwise might not have learned of the move until it had been completed. This group included the onlookers gathered on Commerce Street and a few people on Main Street. Also, continuous television and radio coverage of the activities in the basement might have resulted in compromise of the transfer operation.

These risks to Oswald's safety, growing in part out of adherence to the general policy of the police department, were also accepted for other reasons. Many members of the police department believed that the extraordinary public attention aroused by the tragic death of President Kennedy obliged them to make special efforts to accommodate the press. Captain King carefully articulated one reason why the newsmen were permitted

> * * * to remain in the hallways, * * * to view the investigation and to keep in constant touch with progress of the investigation.
>
> *   *   *   *   *   *   *
>
> We realized that if we arrested a suspect, that if we brought him into the police station and then conducted all of our investigations behind closed doors, that if we gave no reports on the progress of our investigation and did not permit the newsmen to see the suspect—if we excluded them from it—we would leave ourselves open not only to criticisms that we were fabricating a suspect and were attempting to pin something on someone, but even more importantly, we would cause people to lose faith in our fairness and, through losing faith in our fairness, to lose faith to a certain extent in the processes of law.
>
> We felt it was mandatory that as many people knew about it as possible. We knew, too, that if we did exclude the newsmen, we would be leaving ourselves open to a charge that we were using improper action, duress, physical abuse, all of these things.[199]

While Oswald was in custody, the Dallas police kept the press informed about the treatment Oswald was receiving. The public could have been assured that the prisoner was not mistreated and that his rights were fully respected by the police, without each one of hundreds of cameramen and reporters being permitted to satisfy himself that the police had not abused the prisoner. This result could have been accomplished by obtaining reports from members of the family who visited him, or by a committee of the bar or other substantial citizens of the community. When it became known on Saturday that Oswald did not have an attorney, the president of the Dallas Bar Association visited him to inquire whether he wished assistance in obtaining counsel.[200]

Moreover, the right of the public to know does not give the press license to interfere with the efficient operation of law-enforcement agencies. Permitting the press to remain on the third floor of the building served no valid purpose that could not have been met if the press had been excluded from the third floor, as it was from the fourth and fifth floors, and informed of developments either through press releases or at press conferences elsewhere in the building.

Having failed to exclude the mass of the press from the basement during the transfer of Oswald, the police department's security measures could not be completely effective. Despite the pressures that prevailed, planning and coordination of security arrangements could have been more thorough and precise. No single member of the Dallas Police Department ever assumed full responsibility for the details of Oswald's transfer.[201] Chief Curry participated in some of the planning, but he felt that primary authority for the transfer should be Fritz', since Fritz had charge of the investigation. According to Chief Curry—

> Fritz and I, I think, discussed this briefly, the possibility of getting that prisoner out of the city hall during the night hours and by another route and slipping him to the jail, but actually Fritz was not too much in favor of this and I more or less left this up to Fritz as to when and how this transfer would be made, because he has in the past transferred many of his prisoners to the county jail and I felt that since it was his responsibility, the prisoner was, to let him decide when and how he wanted to transfer this prisoner.[202]

Fritz, on the other hand, felt that Curry was directing the transfer arrangements: "I was transferring him like the chief told me to transfer him." [203] When Capt. W. B. Frazier notified Fritz by telephone early Sunday morning about the threats to Oswald's life, Fritz replied that Curry should be notified, since he was handling the transfer.[204] When urged to modify the transfer plans to avoid the press, as he later testified he would have preferred to do, Fritz declined on the ground that Curry had already decided to the contrary.[205] Hence, if the recollection of both officials is accurate, the basic decision to move Oswald at an announced time and in the presence of the news media was never carefully thought through by either man. Curry and Fritz had agreed Saturday evening that Oswald should not be moved at night, but their discussion apparently went little further.[206]

Perhaps the members of the Dallas Police Department were, as many testified, accustomed to working together so that formal instructions were sometimes unnecessary. On the other hand, it is clear, at least in retrospect, that this particular occasion demanded more than the usual informal unspoken understandings. The evidence indicates that no member of the department at any time considered fully the implications of moving Oswald through the basement. Nor did any single official or group of officials coordinate and direct where the transfer vehicle would be stationed to accept Oswald, where the press would stand, and the number and positioning of police officers in the basement. Captain Jones indicated that there were to be two solid lines of policemen from the jail office door to the transfer vehicle,[207] but lines were formed only along the walls of the areaway between the jail office door and the ramp. The newsmen were not kept east of the auto ramp where a railing would have separated them from Oswald. No strong ranks of policemen were ever placed in front of the newsmen once they were allowed to gather in the area of the Main Street ramp.[208] Many policemen in the basement did not know the function they were supposed to perform. No instructions were given that certain policemen should watch the crowd rather than Oswald.[209] Apparently no one gave any thought to the blinding effect of television and other camera lights upon the escort party.

Largely on his own initiative, Captain Talbert undertook to secure the basement, with only minimal coordination with those responsible for and familiar with the route Oswald would take through the basement. Several officials recalled that Lt. Woodrow Wiggins was directed to clear the basement jail office, but Wiggins testified that he received no such assignment.[210] In any event, less than 20 minutes before the transfer, Captain Jones observed newsmen in the jail office and had them removed. But no official removed news personnel from the corridor beside the jail office; indeed, cameramen took pictures through the glass windows of the jail office as Oswald walked through it toward the basement, and then approached to within 20 feet of Oswald from the rear at the same time that Jack Ruby moved toward Oswald from the front.[211]

A clear example of the inadequacy of coordination was the last-minute change in plans to transfer Oswald in an unmarked police car rather than by armored truck.[212] The plan to use an armored vehicle was adopted without informing Fritz. When Fritz was told of the arrangement shortly after 11 o'clock, he objected, and hurried steps were taken to modify the arrangements. Fritz was then prematurely informed that the basement arrangements were complete. When Oswald and the escorting detectives entered the basement, the transfer car had not yet been backed into position, nor had the policemen been arranged to block the newsmen's access to Oswald's path.[213] If the transfer car had been carefully positioned between the press and Oswald, Ruby might have been kept several yards from his victim and possibly without a clear view of him. Detective Leavelle, who accompanied Oswald into the basement, testified:

> * * * I was surprised when I walked to the door and the car was not in the spot it should have been, but I could see it was in back, and backing into position, but had it been in position where we were told it would be, that would have eliminated a lot of the area in which anyone would have access to him, because it would have been blocked by the car. In fact, if the car had been sitting where we were told it was going to be, see—it would have been sitting directly upon the spot where Ruby was standing when he fired the shot.[214]

Captain Jones described the confusion with which Oswald's entry into the basement was in fact received:

Then the change—going to put two cars up there. There is no reason why that back car can't get all the way back to the jail office. The original plan would be that the line of officers would be from the jail door to the vehicle. Then they say, "Here he comes." * * * It is too late to get the people out of the way of the car and form the line. I am aware that Oswald is already coming because of the furor, so, I was trying to keep everybody out of the way and keep the way clear and I heard a shot.[215]

Therefore, regardless of whether the press should have been allowed to witness the transfer, security measures in the basement for Oswald's protection could and should have been better organized and more thorough. These additional deficiencies were directly related to the decision to admit newsmen to the basement. The Commission concludes that the failure of the police to remove Oswald secretly or to control the crowd in the basement at the time of the transfer were the major causes of the security breakdown which led to Oswald's death.

NEWS COVERAGE AND POLICE POLICY

Consistent with its policy of allowing news representatives to remain within the working quarters of the Police and Courts Building, the police department made every effort to keep the press fully informed about the progress of the investigation. As a result, from Friday afternoon until after the killing of Oswald on Sunday, the press was able to publicize virtually all of the information about the case which had been gathered until that time. In the process, a great deal of misinformation was disseminated to a worldwide audience. (For some examples see app. XII.)

As administrative assistant to Chief Curry, Captain King also handled departmental press relations and issued press releases. According to King, it was "the responsibility of each member of the department to furnish to the press information on incidents in which they, themselves, were involved, except on matters which involved * * * personnel policies of the department, or * * * unless it would obviously interfere with an investigation underway." [216] In Oswald's case, Chief Curry released most of the information to the press. He and Assistant Chief Batchelor agreed on Friday that Curry would make all announcements to the press.[217] However, there is no evidence that this decision was ever communicated to the rest of the police force. The chief consequence appears to have been that Batchelor refrained from making statements to the news media during this period.

Most of the information was disclosed through informal oral statements or answers to questions at impromptu and clamorous press conferences in the third floor corridor. Written press releases were not employed. The ambulatory press conference became a familiar sight during these days. Whenever Curry or other officials appeared in the

COMMISSION EXHIBIT No. 2632

Press interview with Chief Curry in third floor corridor.

hallway, newsmen surrounded them, asking questions and requesting statements. Usually the officials complied. (See Commission Exhibit No. 2632, p. 232.)

Curry appeared in interviews on television and radio at least a dozen times during November 22–24. He did not attend any of the interrogations of Oswald in Captain Fritz' office except at the beginning and toward the end of Sunday morning's session; he received his information through Captain Fritz and other sources.[218] Nevertheless, in sessions with the newsmen on Friday and Saturday he gave detailed information on the progress of the case against Oswald. Recorded statements of television and radio interviews with Curry and other officials in Dallas during November 22–24 have been transcribed and included in the record compiled by the Commission.[219] An example of these interviews is the following transcript of remarks made by Curry to newsmen on Saturday:

Q. Chief Curry, I understand you have some new information in this case. Could you relate what that is?

A. Yes, we've just been informed by the Federal Bureau of Investigation, that they, the FBI, have the order letter from a mail order house, and the order was sent to their laboratory in Washington and the writing on this order was compared with known samples of our suspect, Oswald's handwriting and found to be the same.

Q. This order was for the rifle?

A. This order was for the rifle to a mail order house in Chicago. It was [inaudible]. The return address was to Dallas, Texas, to the post office box under the name of A. Hidell, H-I-D-E-double L. This is the post office box of our suspect. This gun was mailed parcel post March 20, 1963. I understand he left Dallas shortly after this and didn't come back until I think about two months ago.

Q. Do you know again on what date this rifle was ordered and are you able to link it definitely as the rifle which you confiscated at the School Book Depository?

A. That we have not done so far. If the FBI has been able to do it I have not been informed of it yet. We do know that this man ordered a rifle of the type that was used in the assassination of the President from this mail order house in Chicago and the FBI has definitely identified the writing as that of our suspect.

Q. On another subject—I understand you have photographs of the suspect, Oswald, with a rifle like that used. Could you describe that picture?

A. This is the picture of Oswald standing facing a camera with a rifle in his hand which is very similar to the rifle that we have in our possession. He also had a pistol strapped on his hip. He was holding two papers in his hand, with one of them seemed to be The Worker and the other says Be Militant—I don't know whether that was headlines or the name of the paper.

Q. How much did the gun cost from the mail order house?

A. I understand the gun was advertised for $12.78, I believe.

Q. Have you received any results on the ballistics test conducted on the gun and on Oswald?

A. They're going to be favorable. I don't have a formal report yet.

Q. But you are sure at this time they will be favorable?

A. Yes.

Q. Do you feel now that you have the case completely wrapped up, or are you continuing?

A. We will continue as long as there is a shred of evidence to be gathered. We have a strong case at this time.

Q. I believe you said earlier this afternoon that you have a new development which does wrap up the case—the first time you said the case definitely is secure. Is that correct?

A. That was this morning. This additional evidence just makes a stronger case.

Q. But this is not the same evidence you were referring to then?

A. No, that's true.

Q. Would you be willing to say what that evidence was?

A. No, sir. I don't wish to reveal it. It might jeopardize our case.

Commentator: Thank you very much Chief Jesse Curry of the Dallas Police Department.[220]

Although Captain Fritz permitted himself to be interviewed by the news media less frequently than did Chief Curry, he nevertheless answered questions and ventured opinions about the progress of the investigation. On Saturday he told reporters that he was convinced beyond a doubt that Oswald had killed the President. He discussed some of the evidence in the case, especially the rifle, but his contribution to the knowledge of the reporters was small compared with that of Chief Curry.[221]

Many other members of the police department, including high officials, detectives, and patrolmen, were also interviewed by news representatives during these days.[222] Some of these men had participated in specific aspects of the case, such as the capture of Oswald at the Texas Theatre and the search for evidence at the Texas School Book Depository Building. Few, if any, seemed reluctant to submit to questions and to being televised. It seemed to District Attorney Wade that the newsmen "just followed everybody everywhere they went * * * they interviewed some of your patrolmen * * * on the corner * * * they were interviewing anybody." [223]

Wade himself also made several statements to the press. He visited police headquarters twice on Friday, twice on Saturday, and twice on Sunday. On most of these occasions he was interviewed by the press and appeared on television.[224] After Oswald had appeared before the press on Friday night, Wade held an impromptu conference with reporters in the overflowing assembly room.[225] Wade told the press on Saturday that he would not reveal any evidence because it might prejudice the selection of a jury.[226] On other occasions, however, he mentioned some items of evidence and expressed his opinions regarding Oswald's guilt. He told the press on Friday night that Oswald's wife had told the police that her husband had a rifle in the garage at the house in Irving and that it was missing the morning of the assassination. On one occasion he repeated the error that the murder rifle had been a Mauser. Another time, he stated his belief that Oswald had prepared for the assassination months in advance, including what he would tell the police. He also said that Oswald had practiced with the rifle to improve his marksmanship.[227]

The running commentary on the investigation by the police inevitably carried with it the disclosure of many details that proved to be erroneous. In their efforts to keep the public abreast of the investigation, the police reported hearsay items and unverified leads; further investigation proved many of these to be incorrect or inaccurate. For example, the rifle found on the sixth floor of the Texas School Book Depository Building was initially identified as a Mauser 7.65 rather than a Mannlicher-Carcano 6.5 because a deputy constable who was one of the first to see it thought it looked like a Mauser. He neither handled the weapon nor saw it at close range.[228]

Police sources were also responsible for the mistaken notion that the chicken bones found on the sixth floor were the remains of Oswald's lunch. They had in fact been left by another employee who ate his lunch there at least 15 minutes before the assassination.[229] Curry repeated the erroneous report that a Negro had picked up Oswald near the scene of the assassination and driven him across town.[230] It was also reported that the map found in Oswald's room contained a marked route of the Presidential motorcade when it actually contained markings of places where Oswald may have applied for jobs, including, of course, the Texas School Book Depository.[231]

Concern about the effects of the unlimited disclosures was being voiced by Saturday morning. According to District Attorney Wade, he received calls from lawyers in Dallas and elsewhere expressing concern about providing an attorney for Oswald and about the amount of information being given to the press by the police and the district attorney.[232] Curry continued to answer questions on television and radio during the remainder of the day and Sunday morning.[233]

FBI Director J. Edgar Hoover became concerned because "almost as soon as * * * [FBI Laboratory reports] would reach the Dallas Police Department, the chief of police or one of the representatives of the department would go on TV or radio and relate findings of the FBI, giving information such as the identification of the gun and other items of physical evidence." [234] On Sunday, after Oswald was shot, Hoover dispatched a personal message to Curry requesting him

"not to go on the air any more until this case * * * [is] resolved."
Hoover testified later that Curry agreed not to make any more
statements.[235]

The shooting of Oswald shocked the Dallas police, and after the
interviews that immediately followed the shooting they were disposed
to remain silent. Chief Curry made only one more television appearance after the shooting. At 1:30 p.m., he descended to the assembly
room where, tersely and grimly, he announced Oswald's death. He
refused to answer any of the questions shouted at him by the persistent
reporters, concluding the conference in less than a minute.[236]

District Attorney Wade also held one more press conference.
Before doing so on Sunday evening, he returned once more to the
police station and held a meeting with "all the brass" except Curry.
Wade told them that "people are saying * * * you had the wrong
man and you all were the one who killed him or let him out here to
have him killed intentionally." Wade told the police that "somebody
ought to go out in television and lay out the evidence that you had on
Oswald, and tell them everything." He sat down and listed from
memory items of evidence in the case against Oswald. According to
Wade, Chief Curry refused to make any statements because he had
told an FBI inspector that he would say no more. The police refused
to furnish Wade with additional details of the case.[237]

Wade nonetheless proceeded to hold a lengthy formal press conference that evening, in which he attempted to list all of the evidence
that had been accumulated at that point tending to establish Oswald
as the assassin of President Kennedy. Unfortunately, at that time,
as he subsequently testified, he lacked a thorough grasp of the evidence and made a number of errors.[238] He stated that Oswald had
told a woman on a bus that the President had been killed, an error
apparently caused by the busdriver having confused Oswald with
another passenger who was on the bus after Oswald had left. Wade
also repeated the error about Oswald's having a map marked with the
route of the motorcade. He told reporters that Oswald's description
and name "went out by the police to look for him." [239] The police
never mentioned Oswald's name in their broadcast descriptions before
his arrest.[240]

Wade was innocent of one error imputed to him since November 24.
The published transcript of part of the press conference furnished to newspapers by the Associated Press represented Wade
as having identified the cabdriver who took Oswald to North Beckley
Avenue after the shooting, as one named "Darryl Click." The transcript as it appeared in the New York Times and the Washington
Post of November 26, reads:

A. [Wade] a lady. He then—the bus, he asked the bus driver
to stop, got off at a stop, caught a taxicab driver, Darryl Click. I
don't have his exact place—and went to his home in Oak Cliff,
changed his clothes hurriedly, and left.[241]

236

The correct transcript of the press conference, taken from an audio tape supplied by station WBAP, Fort Worth, is as follows:

A. [Wade] A lady. He then—the bus, he asked the bus driver to stop, got off at a stop, caught a taxicab driver.
Q. Where?
A. In Oak Cliff. I don't have the exact place—and went to his home in Oak Cliff, changed his clothes hurriedly and left.[242]

In this manner, a section of Dallas, "Oak Cliff," became a non-existent taxicab driver, "Darryl Click." Wade did not mention the cabdriver by name at any time. In transcribing the conference from the sound tape, a stenographer apparently made an error that might have become permanently imbedded in the literature of the event but for the preservation and use of an original sound tape.

Though many of the inaccuracies were subsequently corrected by the police and are negated by findings of the Commission included elsewhere in this report, the publicizing of unchecked information provided much of the basis for the myths and rumors that came into being soon after the President's death. The erroneous disclosures became the basis for distorted reconstructions and interpretations of the assassination. The necessity for the Dallas authorities to correct themselves or to be corrected by other sources gave rise not only to criticism of the police department's competence but also to doubts regarding the veracity of the police. Skeptics sought to cast doubt on much of the correct evidence later developed and to find support for their own theories in these early police statements.

The immediate disclosure of information by the police created a further risk of injuring innocent citizens by unfavorable publicity. This was the unfortunate experience of Joe R. Molina, a Dallas-born Navy veteran who had been employed by the Texas School Book Depository since 1947 and on November 22, 1963, held the position of credit manager. Apparently because of Molina's employment at the Depository and his membership in a veterans' organization, the American G.I. Forum, that the Dallas police considered possibly subversive, Dallas policemen searched Molina's home with his permission, at about 1:30 a.m., Saturday, November 23. During the day Molina was intermittently interrogated at police headquarters for 6 or 7 hours, chiefly about his membership in the American G.I. Forum, and also about Oswald. He was never arrested, charged, or held in custody.[243]

While Molina was being questioned, officials of the police department made statements or answered questions[244] that provided the basis for television reports about Molina during the day. These reports spoke of a "second suspect being picked up," insinuated that the Dallas police had reason to suspect another person who worked in the Texas School Book Depository, stated that the suspect had been arrested and his home searched, and mentioned that Molina may have been identified by the U.S. Department of Justice as a possible subversive.[245]

No evidence was ever presented to link Molina with Oswald except as a fellow employee of the Texas School Book Depository. According to Molina, he had never spoken to Oswald.[246] The FBI notified the Commission that Molina had never been the subject of an investigation by it and that it had never given any information about Molina to the Dallas police concerning any alleged subversive activities by him.[247] The Dallas police explained in a statement to the FBI that they had never had a file on Molina, but that they did have one on the American G.I. Forum.[248]

Molina lost his his job in December. He felt that he was being discharged because of the unfavorable publicity he had received, but officials of the Depository claimed that automation was the reason. Molina testified that he had difficulty in finding another position, until finally, with the help of a fellow church member, he secured a position at a lower salary than his previous one.[249]

If Oswald had been tried for his murders of November 22, the effects of the news policy pursued by the Dallas authorities would have proven harmful both to the prosecution and the defense. The misinformation reported after the shootings might have been used by the defense to cast doubt on the reliability of the State's entire case. Though each inaccuracy can be explained without great difficulty, the number and variety of misstatements issued by the police shortly after the assassination would have greatly assisted a skillful defense attorney attempting to influence the attitudes of jurors.

A fundamental objection to the news policy pursued by the Dallas police, however, is the extent to which it endangered Oswald's constitutional right to a trial by an impartial jury. Because of the nature of the crime, the widespread attention which it necessarily received, and the intense public feelings which it aroused, it would have been a most difficult task to select an unprejudiced jury, either in Dallas or elsewhere. But the difficulty was markedly increased by the divulgence of the specific items of evidence with which the police linked Oswald to the two killings. The disclosure of evidence encouraged the public, from which a jury would ultimately be impaneled, to prejudge the very questions that would be raised at trial.

Moreover, rules of law might have prevented the prosecution from presenting portions of this evidence to the jury. For example, though expressly recognizing that Oswald's wife could not be compelled to testify against him, District Attorney Wade revealed to the Nation that Marina Oswald had affirmed her husband's ownership of a rifle like that found on the sixth floor of the Texas School Book Depository.[250] Curry stated that Oswald had refused to take a lie detector test, although such a statement would have been inadmissible in a trial.[251] The exclusion of such evidence, however, would have been meaningless if jurors were already familiar with the same facts from previous television or newspaper reports. Wade might have influenced prospective jurors by his mistaken statement that the paraffin test showed that Oswald had fired a gun. The tests merely showed that he had nitrate traces on his hands, which did not necessarily mean that he had fired either a rifle or a pistol.[252]

The disclosure of evidence was seriously aggravated by the statements of numerous responsible officials that they were certain of Oswald's guilt. Captain Fritz said that the case against Oswald was "cinched." Curry reported on Saturday that "we are sure of our case." [253] Curry announced that he considered Oswald sane, and Wade told the public that he would ask for the death penalty.[254]

The American Bar Association declared in December 1963 that "widespread publicizing of Oswald's alleged guilt, involving statements by officials and public disclosures of the details of 'evidence,' would have made it extremely difficult to impanel an unprejudiced jury and afford the accused a fair trial." [255] Local bar associations expressed similar feelings.[256] The Commission agrees that Lee Harvey Oswald's opportunity for a trial by 12 jurors free of preconception as to his guilt or innocence would have been seriously jeopardized by the premature disclosure and weighing of the evidence against him.

The problem of disclosure of information and its effect on trials is, of course, further complicated by the independent activities of the press in developing information on its own from sources other than law enforcement agencies. Had the police not released the specific items of evidence against Oswald, it is still possible that the other information presented on television and in the newspapers, chiefly of a biographical nature, would itself have had a prejudicial effect on the public.

In explanation of the news policy adopted by the Dallas authorities, Chief Curry observed that "it seemed like there was a great demand by the general public to know what was going on." [257] In a prepared statement, Captain King wrote:

> At that time we felt a necessity for permitting the newsmen as much latitude as possible. We realized the magnitude of the incident the newsmen were there to cover. We realized that not only the nation but the world would be greatly interested in what occurred in Dallas. We believed that we had an obligation to make as widely known as possible everything we could regarding the investigation of the assassination and the manner in which we undertook that investigation.[258]

The Commission recognizes that the people of the United States, and indeed the world, had a deep-felt interest in learning of the events surrounding the death of President Kennedy, including the development of the investigation in Dallas. An informed public provided the ultimate guarantee that adequate steps would be taken to apprehend those responsible for the assassination and that all necessary precautions would be taken to protect the national security. It was therefore proper and desirable that the public know which agencies were participating in the investigation and the rate at which their work was progressing. The public was also entitled to know that Lee Harvey Oswald had been apprehended and that the State had gathered sufficient evidence to arraign him for the murders of the President and Patrolman Tippit, that he was being held pending action of the grand jury, that the investigation was continuing, and that the law enforcement agencies had discovered no evidence which tended to show that any other person was involved in either slaying.

However, neither the press nor the public had a right to be contemporaneously informed by the police or prosecuting authorities of the details of the evidence being accumulated against Oswald. Undoubtedly the public was interested in these disclosures, but its curiosity should not have been satisfied at the expense of the accused's right to a trial by an impartial jury. The courtroom, not the newspaper or television screen, is the appropriate forum in our system for the trial of a man accused of a crime.

If the evidence in the possession of the authorities had not been disclosed, it is true that the public would not have been in a position to assess the adequacy of the investigation or to apply pressures for further official undertakings. But a major consequence of the hasty and at times inaccurate divulgence of evidence after the assassination was simply to give rise to groundless rumors and public confusion. Moreover, without learning the details of the case, the public could have been informed by the responsible authority of the general scope of the investigation and the extent to which State and Federal agencies were assisting in the police work.

RESPONSIBILITY OF NEWS MEDIA

While appreciating the heavy and unique pressures with which the Dallas Police Department was confronted by reason of the assassination of President Kennedy, primary responsibility for having failed to control the press and to check the flow of undigested evidence to the public must be borne by the police department. It was the only agency that could have established orderly and sound operating procedures to control the multitude of newsmen gathered in the police building after the assassination.

The Commission believes, however, that a part of the responsibility for the unfortunate circumstances following the President's death must be borne by the news media. The crowd of newsmen generally failed to respond properly to the demands of the police. Frequently without permission, news representatives used police offices on the third floor, tying up facilities and interfering with normal police operations. Police efforts to preserve order and to clear passageways in the corridor were usually unsuccessful. On Friday night the reporters completely ignored Curry's injunction against asking Oswald questions in the assembly room and crowding in on him. On Sunday morning, the newsmen were instructed to direct no questions at Oswald; nevertheless, several reporters shouted questions at him when he appeared in the basement.[259]

Moreover, by constantly pursuing public officials, the news representatives placed an insistent pressure upon them to disclose information. And this pressure was not without effect, since the police attitude toward the press was affected by the desire to maintain satisfactory relations with the news representatives and to create a favorable image of themselves. Chief Curry frankly told the Commission that

> I didn't order them out of the building, which if I had it to do over I would. In the past like I say, we had always maintained very good relations with our press, and they had always respected us. * * * [260]

Curry refused Fritz' request to put Oswald behind the screen in the assembly room at the Friday night press conference because this might have hindered the taking of pictures.[261] Curry's subordinates had the impression that an unannounced transfer of Oswald to the county jail was unacceptable because Curry did not want to disappoint the newsmen; he had promised that they could witness the transfer.[262] It seemed clear enough that any attempt to exclude the press from the building or to place limits on the information disclosed to them would have been resented and disputed by the newsmen, who were constantly and aggressively demanding all possible information about anything related to the assassination.

Although the Commission has found no corroboration in the video and audio tapes, police officials recall that one or two representatives of the press reinforced their demands to see Oswald by suggesting that the police had been guilty of brutalizing him. They intimated that unless they were given the opportunity to see him, these suggestions would be passed on to the public.[263] Captain King testified that he had been told that

> A short time after Oswald's arrest one newsman held up a photograph and said, "This is what the man charged with the assassination of the President looks like. Or at least this is what he did look like. We don't know what he looks like after an hour in the custody of the Dallas Police Department." [264]

City Manager Elgin Crull stated that when he visited Chief Curry in his office on the morning of November 23, Curry told him that he "felt it was necessary to cooperate with the news media representatives, in order to avoid being accused of using Gestapo tactics in connection with the handling of Oswald." Crull agreed with Curry.[265] The Commission deems any such veiled threats to be absolutely without justification.

The general disorder in the Police and Courts Building during November 22–24 reveals a regrettable lack of self-discipline by the newsmen. The Commission believes that the news media, as well as the police authorities, who failed to impose conditions more in keeping with the orderly process of justice, must share responsibility for the failure of law enforcement which occurred in connection with the death of Oswald. On previous occasions, public bodies have voiced the need for the exercise of self-restraint by the news media in periods when the demand for information must be tempered by other fundamental requirements of our society.

At its annual meeting in Washington in April 1964, the American Society of Newspaper Editors discussed the role of the press in Dallas immediately after President Kennedy's assassination. The discussion revealed the strong misgivings among the editors themselves about the role that the press had played and their desire that the press display more self-discipline and adhere to higher standards of conduct in the future.[266] To prevent a recurrence of the unfortunate events which followed the assassination, however, more than general concern will be needed. The promulgation of a code of professional conduct governing representatives of all news media would be welcome evidence that the press had profited by the lesson of Dallas.

The burden of insuring that appropriate action is taken to establish ethical standards of conduct for the news media must also be borne, however, by State and local governments, by the bar, and ultimately by the public. The experience in Dallas during November 22–24 is a dramatic affirmation of the need for steps to bring about a proper balance between the right of the public to be kept informed and the right of the individual to a fair and impartial trial.

CHAPTER VI

Investigation of Possible Conspiracy

THIS chapter sets forth the findings of the Commission as to whether Lee Harvey Oswald had any accomplices in the planning or execution of the assassination. Particularly after the slaying of Oswald by Jack Ruby under the circumstances described in the preceding chapter, rumors and suspicions developed regarding the existence of a conspiracy to assassinate President Kennedy. As discussed in appendix XII, many of these rumors were based on a lack of information as to the nature and extent of evidence that Oswald alone fired the shots which killed President Kennedy and wounded Governor Connally. Others of the more widely publicized rumors maintained that Oswald must have received aid from one or more persons or political groups, ranging from the far left to the far right of the political spectrum, or from a foreign government, usually either the Castro regime in Cuba or the Soviet Union.

The Commission faced substantial difficulties in determining whether anyone conspired with or assisted the person who committed the assassination. Prior to his own death Oswald had neither admitted his own involvement nor implicated any other persons in the assassination of the President. The problem of determining the existence or nonexistence of a conspiracy was compounded because of the possibility of subversive activity by a foreign power. Witnesses and evidence located in other countries were not subject to subpena, as they would have been if they had been located in the United States. When evidence was obtained from a foreign nation, it could not be appraised as effectively as if it had been derived from a domestic source. The Commission has given the closest scrutiny to all available evidence which related or might have related to a foreign country. All such evidence was tested, whenever possible, against the contingency that it had been fabricated or slanted to mislead or confuse.

In order to meet its obligations fully, the Commission has investigated each rumor and allegation linking Oswald to a conspiracy which has come to its attention, regardless of source. In addition, the Commission has explored the details of Lee Harvey Oswald's activities and life, especially in the months immediately preceding the assassination, in order to develop any investigative lead relevant to the issue of conspiracy. All of Oswald's known writings or other possessions which might have been used for code or other espionage purposes have been examined by either the Federal Bureau of Investigation or the National Security Agency, or both agencies, to determine whether they were so used.[1]

In setting forth the results of this investigation, the first section of this chapter reviews the facts related to the assassination itself, previously considered in more detail in chapter IV. If any conspiracy did exist, it might have manifested itself at some point during Oswald's preparation for the shooting, his execution of the plan, or his escape from the scene of the assassination. The Commission has therefore studied the precise means by which the assassination occurred for traces of evidence that Oswald received any form of assistance in effecting the killing.

The second section of the chapter deals more broadly with Oswald's life since 1959. During the period following his discharge from the Marines in 1959, Oswald engaged in several activities which demand close scrutiny to determine whether, through these pursuits, he developed any associations which were connected with the planning or execution of the assassination. Oswald professed commitment to Marxist ideology; he defected to the Soviet Union in 1959; he attempted to expatriate himself and acquire Soviet citizenship; and he resided in the Soviet Union until June of 1962. After his return to the United States he sought to maintain contacts with the Communist Party, Socialist Workers Party, and the Fair Play for Cuba Committee; he associated with various Russian-speaking citizens in the Dallas-Fort Worth area—some of whom had resided in Russia; he traveled to Mexico City where he visited both the Cuban and Soviet Embassies 7 weeks before the assassination; and he corresponded with the Soviet Embassy in Washington, D.C. In view of these activities, the Commission has instituted a thorough investigation to determine whether the assassination was in some manner directed or encouraged through contacts made abroad or through Oswald's politically oriented activities in this country. The Commission has also considered whether any connections existed between Oswald and certain right-wing activity in Dallas which, shortly before the assassination, led to the publication of hostile criticism of President Kennedy.

The final section of this chapter considers the possibility that Jack Ruby was part of a conspiracy to assassinate President Kennedy. The Commission explored Ruby's background and his activities in the months prior to the assassination, and especially his activities in the 2 days after the assassination, in an effort to determine whether there was any indication that Ruby was implicated in that event. The Commission also sought to ascertain the truth or falsity of assertions that Oswald and Ruby were known to one another prior to the assassination.

In considering the question of foreign involvement, the Commission has received valuable assistance from the Department of State, the Central Intelligence Agency, the Federal Bureau of Investigation, and other Federal agencies with special competence in the field of foreign investigation. Some of the information furnished by these agencies is of a highly confidential nature. Nevertheless, because the disclosure of all facts relating to the assassination of President Kennedy is of great public importance, the Commission has included in this report all information furnished by these agencies which the Commission relied upon in coming to its conclusions, or which tended to contradict those conclusions. Confidential sources of information, as contrasted with the information itself, have, in a relatively few instances, been withheld.

CIRCUMSTANCES SURROUNDING THE ASSASSINATION

Earlier chapters have set forth the evidence upon which the Commission concluded that President Kennedy was fired upon from a single window in the southeast corner of the sixth floor of the Texas School Book Depository, and that Lee Harvey Oswald was the person who fired the shots from this point. As reflected in those chapters, a certain sequence of events necessarily took place in order for the assassination to have occurred as it did. The motorcade traveled past the Texas School Book Depository; Oswald had access to the sixth floor of the building; Oswald brought the rifle into the building; the cartons were arranged at the sixth-floor window; and Oswald escaped from the building before the police had sealed off the exits. Accordingly, the Commission has investigated these circumstances to determine whether Oswald received help from any other person in planning or performing the shooting.

Selection of Motorcade Route

The factors involved in the choice of the motorcade route by the Secret Service have been discussed in chapter II of this report.[2] It was there indicated that after passing through a portion of suburban Dallas, the motorcade was to travel west on Main Street, and then to the Trade Mart by way of the Stemmons Freeway, the most direct route from that point. This route would take the motorcade along the traditional parade route through downtown Dallas; it allowed the maximum number of persons to observe the President; and it enabled the motorcade to cover the distance from Love Field to the Trade Mart in the 45 minutes allocated by members of the White House staff planning the President's schedule in Dallas. No member of the Secret Service, the Dallas Police Department, or the local host committee who was consulted felt that any other route would be preferable.

To reach Stemmons Freeway from Main Street, it was determined that the motorcade would turn right from Main Street onto Houston Street for one block and then left onto Elm Street, proceeding through the Triple Underpass to the Stemmons Freeway access road. This route took the motorcade past the Texas School Book Depository

Building on the northwest corner of Elm and Houston Streets. Because of the sharp turn at this corner, the motorcade also reduced its speed. The motorcade would have passed approximately 90 yards further from the Depository Building and made no turn near the building if it had attempted to reach the Stemmons Freeway directly from Main Street. The road plan in Dealey Plaza, however, is designed to prevent such a turn. In order to keep motorists from reaching the freeway from Main Street, a concrete barrier has been erected between Main and Elm Streets extending beyond the freeway entrance. (See Commission Exhibits Nos. 2114–2116, pp. 35–37.) Hence, it would have been necessary for the motorcade either to have driven over this barrier or to have made a sharp S-turn in order to have entered the freeway from Main Street. Selection of the motorcade route was thus entirely appropriate and based on such legitimate considerations as the origin and destination of the motorcade, the desired opportunity for the President to greet large numbers of people, and normal patterns of traffic.

Oswald's Presence in the Depository Building

Oswald's presence as an employee in the Texas School Book Depository Building was the result of a series of happenings unrelated to the President's trip to Dallas. He obtained the Depository job after almost 2 weeks of job hunting which began immediately upon his arrival in Dallas from Mexico on October 3, 1963.[3] At that time he was in poor financial circumstances, having arrived from Mexico City with approximately $133 or less,[4] and with his unemployment compensation benefits due to expire on October 8.[5] Oswald and his wife were expecting the birth of their second child, who was in fact born on October 20.[6] In attempting to procure work, Oswald utilized normal channels, including the Texas Employment Commission.[7]

On October 4, 1963, Oswald applied for a position with Padgett Printing Corp., which was located at 1313 Industrial Boulevard, several blocks from President Kennedy's parade route.[8] Oswald favorably impressed the plant superintendent who checked his prior job references, one of which was Jaggars-Chiles-Stovall, the firm where Oswald had done photography work from October 1962 to April 1963.[9] The following report was written by Padgett's plant superintendent on the reverse side of Oswald's job application: "Bob Stovall does not recommend this man. He was released because of his record as a troublemaker.—Has Communistic tendencies."[10] Oswald received word that Padgett Printing had hired someone else.[11]

Oswald's employment with the Texas School Book Depository came about through a chance conversation on Monday, October 14, between Ruth Paine, with whom his family was staying while Oswald was living in a roominghouse in Dallas, and two of Mrs. Paine's neighbors.[12] During a morning conversation over coffee, at which Marina Oswald was present, Oswald's search for employment was mentioned. The neighbors suggested several places where Oswald might apply for work. One of the neighbors present, Linnie Mae Randle, said that her brother had recently been hired as a schoolbook order filler at the Texas School Book Depository and she thought the Depository might need additional help. She testified, "and of course you know just being neighborly and everything, we felt sorry for Marina because her baby was due right away as we understood it, and he didn't have any work * * *." [13]

When Marina Oswald and Mrs. Paine returned home, Mrs. Paine promptly telephoned the Texas School Book Depository and spoke to Superintendent Roy Truly, whom she did not know.[14] Truly agreed to interview Oswald, who at the time was in Dallas seeking employment. When Oswald called that evening, Mrs. Paine told him of her conversation with Truly.[15] The next morning Oswald went to the Texas School Book Depository where he was interviewed and hired for the position of order filler.[16]

On the same date, the Texas Employment Commission attempted to refer Oswald to an airline company which was looking for baggage and cargo handlers at a salary which was $100 per month higher than that offered by the Depository Co.[17] The Employment Commission tried to advise Oswald of this job at 10:30 a.m. on October 16, 1963. Since the records of the Commission indicate that Oswald was then working,[18] it seems clear that Oswald was hired by the Depository Co. before the higher paying job was available. It is unlikely that he ever learned of this second opportunity.

Although publicity concerning the President's trip to Dallas appeared in Dallas newspapers as early as September 13, 1963, the planning of the motorcade route was not started until after November 4, when the Secret Service was first notified of the trip.[19] A final decision as to the route could not have been reached until November 14, when the Trade Mart was selected as the luncheon site.[20] Although news reports on November 15 and November 16 might have led a person to believe that the motorcade would pass the Depository Building, the route was not finally selected until November 18; it was announced in the press on November 19, only 3 days before the President's arrival.[21] Based on the circumstances of Oswald's employment and the planning of the motorcade route, the Commission has concluded that Oswald's employment in the Depository was wholly unrelated to the President's trip to Dallas.

Bringing Rifle Into Building

On the basis of the evidence developed in chapter IV the Commission concluded that Lee Harvey Oswald carried the rifle used in the assassination into the Depository Building on Friday, November 22, 1963, in the handmade brown paper bag found near the window from which the shots were fired.[22] The arrangement by which Buell Wesley Frazier drove Oswald between Irving and Dallas was an innocent one, having commenced when Oswald first started working at the Depository.[23] As noted above, it was Frazier's sister, Linnie May Randle, who had suggested to Ruth Paine that Oswald might be able

247

to find employment at the Depository. When Oswald started working there, Frazier, who lived only a half block away from the Paines, offered to drive Oswald to and from Irving whenever he was going to stay at the Paines' home.[24] Although Oswald's request for a ride to Irving on Thursday, November 21, was a departure from the normal weekend pattern, Oswald gave the explanation that he needed to obtain curtain rods for an "apartment" in Dallas.[25] This served also to explain the long package which he took with him from Irving to the Depository Building the next morning.[26] Further, there is no evidence that Ruth Paine or Marina Oswald had reason to believe that Oswald's return was in any way related to an attempt to shoot the President the next day. Although his visit was a surprise, since he arrived on Thursday instead of Friday for his usual weekend visit, both women testified that they thought he had come to patch up a quarrel which he had with his wife a few days earlier when she learned that he was living in Dallas under an assumed name.[27]

It has also been shown that Oswald had the opportunity to work in the Paines' garage on Thursday evening and prepare the rifle by disassembling it, if it were not already disassembled, and packing it in the brown bag.[28] It has been demonstrated that the paper and tape from which the bag was made came from the shipping room of the Texas School Book Depository and that Oswald had access to this material.[29] Neither Ruth Paine nor Marina Oswald saw the paper bag or the paper and tape out of which the bag was constructed.[30] If Oswald actually prepared the bag in the Depository out of materials available to him there, he could have concealed it in the jacket or shirt which he was wearing.[31] The Commission has found no evidence which suggests that Oswald required or in fact received any assistance in bringing the rifle into the building other than the innocent assistance provided by Frazier in the form of the ride to work.

Accomplices at the Scene of the Assassination

The arrangement of boxes at the window from which the shots were fired was studied to determine whether Oswald required any assistance in moving the cartons to the window. Cartons had been stacked on the floor, a few feet behind the window, thus shielding Oswald from the view of anyone on the sixth floor who did not attempt to go behind them.[32] (See Commission Exhibit No. 723, p. 80.) Most of those cartons had been moved there by other employees to clear an area for laying a new flooring on the west end of the sixth floor.[33] Superintendent Roy Truly testified that the floor-laying crew moved a long row of books parallel to the windows on the south side and had "quite a lot of cartons" in the southeast corner of the building.[34] He said that there was not any particular pattern that the men used in putting them there. "They were just piled up there more or less at that time." [35] According to Truly, "several cartons" which had been in the extreme southeast corner had been placed on top of the ones that had been piled in front of the southeast corner window.[36]

248

The arrangement of the three boxes in the window and the one on which the assassin may have sat has been described previously.[37] Two of these four boxes, weighing approximately 55 pounds each, had been moved by the floor-laying crew from the west side of the floor to the area near the southwest corner.[38] The carton on which the assassin may have sat might not even have been moved by the assassin at all. A photograph of the scene depicts this carton on the floor alongside other similar cartons. (See Commission Exhibit No. 1301, p. 138.) Oswald's right palmprint on this carton may have been placed there as he was sitting on the carton rather than while carrying it. In any event both of these 55-pound cartons could have been carried by one man. The remaining two cartons contained light block-like reading aids called "Rolling Readers" weighing only about 8 pounds each.[39] Although they had been moved approximately 40 feet [40] from their normal locations at the southeast corner window, it would appear that one man could have done this in a matter of seconds.

In considering the possibility of accomplices at the window, the Commission evaluated the significance of the presence of fingerprints other than Oswald's on the four cartons found in and near the window. Three of Oswald's prints were developed on two of the cartons.[41] In addition a total of 25 identifiable prints were found on the 4 cartons.[42] Moreover, prints were developed which were considered as not identifiable, i.e., the quality of the print was too fragmentary to be of value for identification purposes.[43]

As has been explained in chapter IV, the Commission determined that none of the warehouse employees who might have customarily handled these cartons left prints which could be identified.[44] This was considered of some probative value in determining whether Oswald moved the cartons to the window. All but 1 of the 25 definitely identifiable prints were the prints of 2 persons—an FBI employee and a member of the Dallas Police Department who had handled the cartons during the course of the investigation.[45] One identifiable palmprint was not identified.[46]

The presence on these cartons of unidentified prints, whether or not identifiable, does not appear to be unusual since these cartons contained commercial products which had been handled by many people throughout the normal course of manufacturing, warehousing, and shipping. Unlike other items of evidence such as, for example, a ransom note in a kidnaping, these cartons could contain the prints of many people having nothing to do with the assassination. Moreover, the FBI does not maintain a filing system for palmprints because, according to the supervisor of the Bureau's latent fingerprint section, Sebastian F. Latona, the problems of classification make such a system impracticable.[47] Finally, in considering the significance of the unidentified prints, the Commission gave weight to the opinion of Latona to the effect that people could handle these cartons without leaving prints which were capable of being developed.[48]

Though the fingerprints other than Oswald's on the boxes thus provide no indication of the presence of an accomplice at the window, two Depository employees are known to have been present briefly on the sixth floor during the period between 11:45 a.m., when the floor-laying crew stopped for lunch, and the moment of the assassination. One of these was Charles Givens, a member of the floor-laying crew, who went down on the elevator with the others and then, returned to the sixth floor to get his jacket and cigarettes.[49] He saw Oswald walking away from the southeast corner, but saw no one else on the sixth floor at that time. He then took one of the elevators back to the first floor at approximately 11:55 a.m.[50]

Bonnie Ray Williams, who was also working with the floor-laying crew, returned to the sixth floor at about noon to eat his lunch and watch the motorcade.[51] He looked out on Elm Street from a position in the area of the third or fourth set of windows from the east wall.[52] At this point he was approximately 20–30 feet away from the southeast corner window. He remained for about "5, 10, maybe 12 minutes" eating his lunch which consisted of chicken and a bottle of soda pop.[53] Williams saw no one on the sixth floor during this period, although the stacks of books prevented his seeing the east side of the building.[54] After finishing his lunch Williams took the elevator down because no one had joined him on the sixth floor to watch the motorcade.[55] He stopped at the fifth floor where he joined Harold Norman and James Jarman, Jr., who watched the motorcade with him from a position on the fifth floor directly below the point from which the shots were fired. Williams left the remains of his lunch, including chicken bones and a bottle of soda, near the window where he was eating.[56]

Several witnesses outside the building claim to have seen a person in the southeast corner window of the sixth floor. As has already been indicated, some were able to offer better descriptions than others and one, Howard L. Brennan, made a positive identification of Oswald as being the person at the window.[57] Although there are differences among these witnesses with regard to their ability to describe the person they saw, none of these witnesses testified to seeing more than one person in the window.[58]

One witness, however, offered testimony which, if accurate, would create the possibility of an accomplice at the window at the time of the assassination. The witness was 18-year-old Arnold Rowland, who testified in great detail concerning his activities and observations on November 22, 1963. He and his wife were awaiting the motorcade, standing on the east side of Houston Street between Maine and Elm,[59] when he looked toward the Depository Building and noticed a man holding a rifle standing back from the southwest corner window on the sixth floor. The man was rather slender in proportion to his size and of light complexion with dark hair.[60] Rowland said that his wife was looking elsewhere at the time and when they looked back to the window the man "was gone from our vision."[61] They thought the man was most likely someone protecting the President. After the assassination Rowland signed an affidavit in which he told of seeing this man, although Rowland was unable to identify him.[62]

When Rowland testified before the Commission on March 10, 1964, he claimed for the first time to have seen another person on the sixth floor. Rowland said that before he had noticed the man with the rifle on the southwest corner of the sixth floor he had seen an elderly Negro man "hanging out that window" on the southeast corner of the sixth floor.[63] Rowland described the Negro man as "very thin, an elderly gentleman, bald or practically bald, very thin hair if he wasn't bald," between 50 and 60 years of age, 5 feet 8 inches to 5 feet 10 inches tall, with fairly dark complexion.[64] Rowland claimed that he looked back two or three times and noticed that the man remained until 5 or 6 minutes prior to the time the motorcade came. Rowland did not see him thereafter. He made no mention of the Negro man in his affidavit.[65] And, while he said he told FBI agents about the man in the southeast corner window when interviewed on the Saturday and Sunday following the assassination,[66] no such statement appears in any FBI report.[67]

Mrs. Rowland testified that her husband never told her about seeing any other man on the sixth floor except the man with the rifle in the southwest corner that he first saw. She also was present during Rowland's interview with representatives of the FBI[68] and said she did not hear him make such a statement,[69] although she also said that she did not hear everything that was discussed.[70] Mrs. Rowland testified that after her husband first talked about seeing a man with the rifle, she looked back more than once at the Depository Building and saw no person looking out of any window on the sixth floor.[71] She also said that "At times my husband is prone to exaggerate."[72] Because of inconsistencies in Rowland's testimony and the importance of his testimony to the question of a possible accomplice, the Commission requested the FBI to conduct an inquiry into the truth of a broad range of statements made by Rowland to the Commission. The investigation showed that numerous statements by Rowland concerning matters about which he would not normally be expected to be mistaken—such as subjects he studied in school, grades he received, whether or not he had graduated from high school, and whether or not he had been admitted to college—were false.[73]

The only possible corroboration for Rowland's story is found in the testimony of Roger D. Craig, a deputy sheriff of Dallas County, whose testimony on other aspects of the case has been discussed in chapter IV. Craig claimed that about 10 minutes after the assassination he talked to a young couple, Mr. and Mrs. Rowland,

> * * * and the boy said he saw two men on the sixth floor of the Book Depository Building over there; one of them had a rifle with a telescopic sight on it—but he thought they were Secret Service agents or guards and didn't report it. This was about—oh, he said, 15 minutes before the motorcade ever arrived.[74]

According to Craig, Rowland said that he looked back a few minutes later and "the other man was gone, and there was just one man—the man with the rifle." [75] Craig further testified that Rowland told him that when he first saw the two men, they were walking back and forth in front of the window for several minutes. They were both white men and one of them had a rifle with a scope on it.[76] This report by Craig is contradicted by the testimony of both the Rowlands, and by every recorded interview with them conducted by law enforcement agencies after the assassination.

As part of its investigation of Rowland's allegation and of the general question of accomplices at the scene of the assassination, the Commission undertook an investigation of every person employed in the Texas School Book Depository Building. Two employees might possibly fit the general description of an elderly Negro man, bald or balding. These two men were on the first floor of the building during the period before and during the assassination.[77] Moreover, all of the employees were asked whether they saw any strangers in the building on the morning of November 22.[78] Only one employee saw a stranger whom he described as a feeble individual who had to be helped up the front steps of the building. He went to a public restroom and left the building 5 minutes later, about 40 minutes before the assassination.[79]

Rowland's failure to report his story despite several interviews until his appearance before the Commission, the lack of probative corroboration, and the serious doubts about his credibility, have led the Commission to reject the testimony that Rowland saw an elderly balding Negro man in the southeast corner window of the sixth floor of the Depository Building several minutes before the assassination.

Oswald's Escape

The Commission has analyzed Oswald's movements between the time of the assassination and the shooting of Patrolman Tippit to determine whether there is any evidence that Oswald had assistance in his flight from the building. Oswald's activities during this period have been traced through the testimony of seven witnesses and discussed in detail in chapter IV.[80] (See Commission Exhibit No. 1119–A, p. 158 and Commission Exhibit No. 1118, p. 150.) Patrolman M. L. Baker and Depository superintendent Roy Truly saw him within 2 minutes of the assassination on the second floor of the building. Mrs. R. A. Reid saw him less than 1 minute later walking through the second-floor offices toward the front of the building. A busdriver, Cecil J. McWatters, and Oswald's former landlady, Mrs. Mary Bledsoe, saw him board a bus at approximately 12:40 p.m., and get off about 4 minutes later. A cabdriver, William W. Whaley, drove Oswald from a cabstand located a few blocks from where Oswald left the bus to a point in Oak Cliff about four blocks from his roominghouse; and Earlene Roberts, the housekeeper at Oswald's roominghouse, saw him enter the roominghouse at about 1 p.m. and leave a few minutes later. When seen by these seven witnesses Oswald was always alone.

Particular attention has been directed to Oswald's departure from the Depository Building in order to determine whether he could have left the building within approximately 3 minutes of the assassination without assistance. As discussed more fully in chapter IV, the building was probably first sealed off no earlier than 12:37 by Inspector Herbert Sawyer.[81] The shortest estimate of the time taken to seal off the building comes from Police Officer W. E. Barnett, one of the officers assigned to the corner of Elm and Houston Streets for the Presidential motorcade, who estimated that approximately 3 minutes elapsed between the time he heard the last of the shots and the time he started guarding the front door.[82] According to Barnett, "there were people going in and out" during this period.[83] The evidence discussed in chapter IV shows that 3 minutes would have been sufficient time for Oswald to have descended from the sixth floor and left the building without assistance.[84]

One witness, James R. Worrell, Jr., claims to have seen a man running from the rear of the building shortly after the assassination, but in testimony before the Commission he stated that he could not see his face.[85] Two other witnesses who watched the rear of the building during the first 5 minutes after the shooting saw no one leave.[86] The claim of Deputy Sheriff Roger Craig that he saw Oswald leave the Depository Building approximately 15 minutes after the assassination has been discussed in chapter IV.[87] Although Craig may have seen someone enter a station wagon 15 minutes after the assassination, the person he saw was not Lee Harvey Oswald, who was far removed from the building at that time.

The possibility that accomplices aided Oswald in connection with his escape was suggested by the testimony of Earlene Roberts, the housekeeper at the 1026 North Beckley roominghouse.[88] She testified that at about 1 p.m. on November 22, after Oswald had returned to the roominghouse, a Dallas police car drove slowly by the front of the 1026 North Beckley premises and stopped momentarily; she said she heard its horn several times.[89] Mrs. Roberts stated that the occupants of the car were not known to her even though she had worked for some policemen who would occasionally come by.[90] She said the policeman she knew drove car No. 170 and that this was not the number on the police car that honked on November 22. She testified that she first thought the car she saw was No. 106 and then said that it was No. 107.[91] In an FBI interview she had stated that she looked out the front window and saw police car No. 207.[92] Investigation has not produced any evidence that there was a police vehicle in the area of 1026 North Beckley at about 1 p.m. on November 22.[93] Squad car 207 was at the Texas School Book Depository Building, as was car 106. Squad cars 170 and 107 were sold in April 1963 and their numbers were not reassigned until February 1964.[94]

Whatever may be the accuracy of Mrs. Roberts' recollection concerning the police car, it is apparent from Mrs. Roberts' further testimony that she did not see Oswald enter a car when he hurriedly left the house. She has stated that when she last saw Oswald, shortly after

1 p.m., he was standing at a bus stop in front of the house.[95]   Oswald was next seen less than 1 mile away, at the point where he shot Patrolman Tippit. Oswald could have easily reached this point on foot by about 1:16 p.m., when Tippit was shot. Finally, investigation has produced no evidence that Oswald had prearranged plans for a means to leave Dallas after the assassination or that any other person was to have provided him assistance in hiding or in departing the city.

BACKGROUND OF LEE HARVEY OSWALD

Finding no evidence in the circumstances immediately surrounding the assassination that any person other than Lee Harvey Oswald was involved in the killing of the President, the Commission directed an intensive investigation into his life for the purpose, among others, of detecting any possible traces that at some point he became involved in a conspiracy culminating in the deed of November 22, 1963. As a product of this investigation, the Commission has compiled a detailed chronological biography of Oswald which is set forth as appendix XIII. Study of the period from Oswald's birth in 1939 to his military service from 1956 to 1959 has revealed no evidence that he was associated with any type of sinister or subversive organization during that period. Though his personality and political views took shape during these early years, the events of that period are significant primarily to an understanding of the personality of Lee Harvey Oswald and are discussed in that connection in chapter VII. Beginning with his preparation for defection to the Soviet Union in 1959, however, Oswald engaged in several activities which required close scrutiny by the Commission. In an appraisal of Oswald's actions since 1959 for the purpose of determining whether he was part of a conspiracy, several aspects of his background and character must be borne in mind. He was young, inexperienced, and had only a limited education. As will be more fully discussed in chapter VII, he was unable to establish relationships with others and had a resentment for authority and any discipline flowing from it. While he demonstrated the ability to act secretively and alone, without regard to the consequences to himself, as in his defection to the Soviet Union, he does not appear to have been the kind of person whom one would normally expect to be selected as a conspirator.

Residence in the Soviet Union

Lee Harvey Oswald was openly committed to Marxist ideology, he defected to the Soviet Union in 1959, and resided there until June of 1962, eventually returning to the United States with a Russian wife. In order to evaluate rumors and speculations [96] that Oswald may have been an agent of the Soviet Union, the Commission investigated the facts surrounding Oswald's stay in Russia. The Commission was thus fulfilling its obligation to probe all facts of possible relevance to the assassination, and does not suggest by this investigation that the rulers of the Soviet Union believed that their political interests would be advanced by the assassination of President Kennedy. On this question, the Secretary of State testified before the Commission on June 10, 1964 as follows:

I have seen no evidence that would indicate to me that the Soviet Union considered that it had an interest in the removal of President Kennedy or that it was in any way involved in the removal of President Kennedy.

* * * * * * *

I have not seen or heard of any scrap of evidence indicating that the Soviet Union had any desire to eliminate President Kennedy 'nor in any way participated in any such event.

Now, standing back and trying to look at that question objectively despite the ideological differences between our two great systems, I can't see how it could be to the interest of the Soviet Union to make any such effort.

* * * * * * *

I do think that the Soviet Union, again objectively considered, has an interest in the correctness of state relations. This would be particularly true among the great powers, with which the major interests of the Soviet Union are directly engaged.

* * * * * * *

I think that although there are grave differences between the Communist world and the free world, between the Soviet Union and other major powers, that even from their point of view there needs to be some shape and form to international relations, that it is not in their interest to have this world structure dissolve into complete anarchy, that great states and particularly nuclear powers have to be in a position to deal with each other, to transact business with each other, to try to meet problems with each other, and that requires the maintenance of correct relations and access to the leadership on all sides.

I think also that although there had been grave differences between Chairman Khrushchev and President Kennedy, I think there were evidences of a certain mutual respect that had developed over some of the experiences, both good and bad, through which these two men had lived.

I think both of them were aware of the fact that any Chairman of the Soviet Union, and any President of the United States, necessarily bear somewhat special responsibility for the general peace of the world. Indeed without exaggeration, one could almost say the existence of the northern hemisphere in this nuclear age.

* * * * * * *

So that it would be an act of rashness and madness for Soviet leaders to undertake such an action as an active policy. Because everything would have been put in jeopardy or at stake in connection with such an act.

It has not been our impression that madness has characterized the actions of the Soviet leadership in recent years.[97]

The Commission accepts Secretary Rusk's estimate as reasonable and objective, but recognizes that a precise assessment of Soviet intentions or interests is most difficult. The Commission has thus examined all the known facts regarding Oswald's defection, residence in the Soviet Union, and return to the United States. At each step the Commission sought to determine whether there was any evidence which supported a conclusion that Soviet authorities may have directly or indirectly influenced Oswald's actions in assassinating the President.

Oswald's entry into the Soviet Union.—Although the evidence is inconclusive as to the factors which motivated Oswald to go to the Soviet Union, there is no indication that he was prompted to do so by agents of that country. He may have begun to study the Russian language when he was stationed in Japan, which was intermittently from August 1957 to November 1958.[98] After he arrived in Moscow in October 1959 he told several persons that he had been planning his defection for 2 years, which suggests that the decision was made while he was in the Far East.[99] George De Mohrenschildt, who met Oswald after his return from the Soviet Union, testified that Oswald once told him much the same thing: "I met some Communists in Japan and they got me excited and interested, and that was one of my inducements in going to Soviet Russia, to see what goes on there."[100] This evidence, however, is somewhat at variance with Oswald's statements made to two American newspaper reporters in Moscow shortly after his defection in 1959,[101] and to other people in the United States after his return in 1962.[102] Though his remarks were not inconsistent as to the time he decided to defect, to these people he insisted that before going to the Soviet Union he had "never met a Communist" and that the intent to defect derived entirely from his own reading and thinking. He said much the same to his brother in a letter he wrote to him from Russia explaining why he had defected.[103] Which of Oswald's statements was· the more accurate remains unknown.

There is no evidence that Oswald received outside assistance in financing his trip to the Soviet Union. After he arrived in Moscow, Oswald told a newspaper correspondent, Aline Mosby, that he had saved $1,500 out of his Marine Corps salary to finance his defection,[104] although the news story based upon Oswald's interview with Aline Mosby unaccountably listed the sum of $1,600 instead of $1,500.[105] After this article had appeared, Marguerite Oswald also related the $1,600 figure to an FBI agent.[106] Either amount could have been accumulated out of Oswald's earnings in the Marine Corps; during his 2 years and 10 months of service he received $3,452.20, after all taxes, allotments and other deductions.[107] Moreover Oswald could certainly have made the entire trip on less than $1,000. The ticket on the ship he took from New Orleans to Le Havre, France, cost $220.75;[108] it cost him about $20 to reach London from Le Havre; his plane fare from London to Helsinki, where he received his visa, cost him $111.90; he probably purchased Russian "tourist vouchers" normally good for room and board for 10 days for $300; his train fare from Helsinki to Moscow was about $44; in Moscow he paid only $1.50 to $3 a night for his room and very little for his meals after his tourist vouchers ran out;[109] and apparently he did not pay his hotel bill at all after November 30, 1959.[110] Oswald's known living habits indicate that he could be extraordinarily frugal when he had reason to be, and it seems clear that he did have a strong desire to go to the Soviet Union.

While in Atsugi, Japan, Oswald studied the Russian language, perhaps with some help from an officer in his unit who was interested in Russian and used to "talk about it" with Oswald occasionally.[111] He studied by himself a great deal in late 1958 and early 1959 after he was transferred from Japan to California.[112] He took an Army aptitude test in Russian in February 1959 and rated "Poor."[113] When he reached the Soviet Union in October of the same year he could barely speak the language.[114] During the period in Moscow while he was awaiting decision on his application for citizenship, his diary records that he practiced Russian 8 hours a day.[115] After he was sent to Minsk in early January 1960 he took lessons from an interpreter assigned to him for that purpose by the Soviet Government.[116] Marina Oswald said that by the time she met him in March 1961 he spoke the language well enough so that at first she thought he was from one of the Baltic areas of her country, because of his accent. She stated that his only defects were that his grammar was sometimes incorrect and that his writing was never good.[117]

Thus, the limited evidence provides no indication that Oswald was recruited by Soviet agents in the Far East with a view toward defection and eventual return to the United States. Moreover, on its face such a possibility is most unlikely. If Soviet agents had communicated with Oswald while he was in the Marine Corps, one of the least probable instructions they would have given him would have been to defect. If Oswald had remained a Marine radar specialist, he might at some point have reached a position of value as a secret agent. However, his defection and the disloyal statements he made publicly in connection with it eliminated the possibility that he would ever gain access to confidential information or programs of the United States. The very fact that he defected, therefore, is itself persuasive evidence that he was not recruited as an agent prior to his defection.

The Commission has investigated the circumstances under which Oswald obtained a visa to enter the Soviet Union for possible evidence that he received preferential treatment in being permitted to enter the country. Oswald left New Orleans, La., for Europe on September 20, 1959,[118] having been released from active duty in the Marine Corps on

September 11, 1959.[119]   He went directly to Helsinki, Finland, by way of Le Havre, France, and London, England, arriving at Helsinki on Saturday, October 10, 1959.[120]   Oswald probably arrived in Helsinki too late in the evening to have applied for a visa at the Soviet Union consulate that night.[121]   In light of the rapidity with which he made connections throughout his entire trip,[122] he probably applied for a visa early on Monday, October 12.   On October 14, he was issued Soviet Tourist Visa No. 403339, good for one 6-day visit in the U.S.S.R.[123]   He left Helsinki on a train destined for Moscow on October 15.[124]

The Department of State has advised the Commission that it has some information that in 1959 it usually took an American tourist in Helsinki 1 to 2 weeks to obtain a visa,[125] and that it has other information that the normal waiting period during the past 5 years has been a week or less.[126]   According to the Department's information, the waiting period has always varied frequently and widely, with one confirmed instance in 1963 of a visa routinely issued in less than 24 hours.[127]   The Central Intelligence Agency has indicated that visas during the 1964 tourist season were being granted in about 5 to 7 days.[128]

This information from the Department of State and the Central Intelligence Agency thus suggests that Oswald's wait for a visa may have been shorter than usual but not beyond the range of possible variation.   The prompt issuance of Oswald's visa may have been merely the result of normal procedures, due in part to the fact that the summer rush had ended.   It might also mean that Oswald was unusually urgent in his demands that his visa be issued promptly.   Oswald himself told officials at the American Embassy in Moscow on October 31, when he appeared to renounce his citizenship, that he had said nothing to the Soviets about defecting until he arrived in Moscow.[129]   In any event, the Commission has found nothing in the circumstances of Oswald's entry into the Soviet Union which indicates that he was at the time an agent of the U.S.S.R.

Defection and admission to residence.—Two months and 22 days elapsed from Oswald's arrival in Moscow until he left that city to take up residence in Minsk.   The Commission has considered the possibility that Oswald was accepted for residence in the Soviet Union and sent to Minsk unusually soon after he arrived, either because he had been expected or because during his first weeks in Moscow he developed an undercover relationship with the Soviet Government.   In doing so, the Commission has attempted to reconstruct the events of those months, though it is, of course, impossible to account for Oswald's activities on every day of that period.

Oswald's "Historic Diary," [130] which commences on October 16, 1959, the date Oswald arrived in Moscow, and other writings he later prepared,[131] have provided the Commission with one source of information about Oswald's activities throughout his stay in the Soviet Union. Even assuming the diary was intended to be a truthful record, it is not

258

an accurate guide to the details of Oswald's activities. Oswald seems not to have been concerned about the accuracy of dates and names,[132] and apparently made many of his entries subsequent to the date the events occurred. Marina Oswald testified that she believed that her husband did not begin to keep the diary until he reached Minsk, 3 months after his arrival in Russia,[133] and scraps of paper found in Oswald's possession, containing much the same information as appears in his diary,[134] suggest that he transcribed the entries into the diary at a later time. The substance of Oswald's writings has been carefully examined for consistency with all other related information available to the Commission. In addition, the writings have been checked for handwriting,[135] and for consistency of style, grammar, and spelling with earlier and later writings which are known to be his.[136] No indication has been found that entries were written or coached by other persons.[137]

However, the most reliable information concerning the period Oswald spent in Moscow in the latter part of 1962 comes from the records of the American Embassy in Moscow,[138] the testimony of Embassy officials,[139] and the notes of two American newspaper reporters, Aline Mosby [140] and Priscilla Johnson,[141] who interviewed Oswald during this period. Oswald's correspondence with his brother and mother has also been relied upon for some relatively minor information. The findings upon which the Commission based its conclusion concerning Soviet involvements in the assassination were supported by evidence other than material provided by the Soviet Union [142] or Oswald's writings. The Central Intelligence Agency has also contributed data on the normal practices and procedures of the Soviet authorities in handling American defectors.

The "Historic Diary" indicates that on October 16, 1959, the day Oswald arrived in Moscow, he told his Intourist guide, Rima Shirokova, that he wished to renounce his American citizenship and become a Soviet citizen. The same day, the guide reportedly helped Oswald prepare a letter to the Soviet authorities requesting citizenship.[143] The diary indicates, however, that on October 21 he was informed that his visa had expired and that he would be required to leave Moscow within 2 hours.[144] During the preceding days, according to the diary, he had been interviewed once and perhaps twice by Soviet officials.[145] During this period the KGB,* the agency with

---

*The Committee for State Security, best known by its Russian initials, "KGB," is a lineal descendant of the revolutionary ChEKA and has passed through numerous changes of name since 1917 with little change of function. Presently the KGB handles all Soviet counterintelligence operations and is the instrument for various types of subversive activities. It is responsible for the internal security of the Soviet state and the safety of its leaders. In addition it shares responsibility for foreign espionage activities with the intelligence component of the Ministry of Defense, the "GRU." The KGB would have the primary responsibility for keeping track of a defector such as Oswald.

The Ministry of Internal Affairs or "MVD" was for many years the designation of the organization responsible for civil law enforcement and administration of prisons and forced labor camps in the Soviet Union. During a part of its history it also directed vast economic combines. In January 1960, the central or all-union MVD was abolished and its powers transferred to the MVD's of the several Soviet republics. A further change took place in the summer of 1962, when the republic MVD's were renamed Ministries for the Preservation of Public Order and Safety. In the past few years the republic MVD's

primary responsibility for examining defectors arriving in Russia, undoubtedly investigated Oswald as fully as possible. In 1959, virtually all Intourist guides were KGB informants, and there is no reason to believe that this was not true of Oswald's guide.[146]

According to Oswald's diary he attempted suicide when he learned his application for citizenship had been denied.[147] If true, this would seem to provide strong evidence that, at least prior to October 21, there was no undercover relationship between Oswald and the Soviet Government. Though not necessarily conclusive, there is considerable direct evidence which indicates that Oswald did slash his wrist. Oswald's autopsy showed that he had a scar on his left wrist and that it was of the kind which could have been caused by a suicide attempt.[148] The medical records from the Botkinskaya Hospital in Moscow, furnished by the Soviet Government, reveal that from October 21 to October 28 he was treated there for a self-inflicted wound on the left wrist.[149] The information contained in these records is consistent with the facts disclosed by the autopsy examination relating to Oswald's wrist and to other facts known about Oswald. Although no witness recalled Oswald mentioning a suicide attempt,[150] Marina Oswald testified that when she questioned her husband about the scar on his wrist, he became "very angry," and avoided giving her a reply.[151] Oswald's character, discussed in the following chapter, does not seem inconsistent with a suicide or feigned suicide attempt, nor with his having failed to disclose the suicide attempt. Many witnesses who testified before the Commission observed that he was not an "open" or trusting person, had a tendency toward arrogance, and was not the kind of man who would readily admit weaknesses.[152]

Oswald appeared at the American Embassy in Moscow on October 31, 1959, 3 days after his release from the Botkinskaya Hospital.[153] He did not give the officials at the Embassy any indication that he had recently received medical treatment.[154] Oswald's appearance was the first notification to the American Government that he was in Russia, since he had failed to inform the Embassy upon his arrival,[155] as most American tourists did at the time.[156] In appendix XV, Oswald's dealings with the Embassy in 1959 until his return to the United States in 1962 are described in full, and all action taken by the American officials on his case is evaluated. His conduct at the Embassy has also been considered by the Commission for any indication it may provide as to whether or not Oswald was then acting under directions of the Soviet Government.

At the Embassy, Oswald declared that he wished to renounce his U.S. citizenship,[157] but the consul to whom he spoke, Richard E.

have been gradually divesting themselves of their economic functions. When Lee Harvey Oswald was in the Soviet Union though, the MVD still carried on substantial economic activities. For example, inmates of the MVD-administered "corrective labor colonies" engaged in brickmaking, heavy construction work, and lumbering.

In the Commission's report, the term KGB will be used, as above, to describe the principal Soviet counterintelligence and espionage service. Oswald often inaccurately referred to the "secret police" as the MVD; and in any quotations from him, the Commission will reproduce his actual words. Whenever the Commission refers to the MVD, it will be referring to it as defined in this footnote.

NOTE HANDED BY OSWALD TO·THE AMERICAN
EMBASSY IN MOSCOW ON OCT. 31, 1959

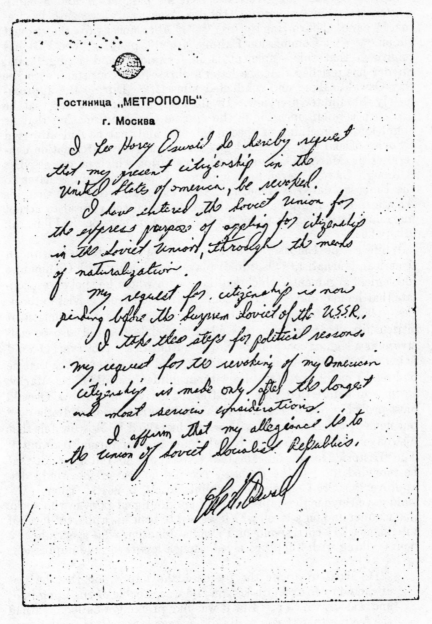

Гостиница „МЕТРОПОЛЬ"
   г. Москва

I Lee Harvy Oswald do hereby request
that my present citizenship in the
United States of america, be revoked.

   I have entered the Soviet Union for
the express purpose of appling for citizenship
in the Soviet Union, through the means
of naturalization.

   my request for citizenship is now
pending before the Supreme Soviet of the U.S.S.R.

   I take these steps for political reasons.
my request for the revoking of my american
citizenship is made only after the longest
and most serious considerations.

   I affirm that my allegiance is to
the union of Soviet Socialist Republics.

COMMISSION EXHIBIT No. 913

Snyder, refused to accept his renunciation at that time, telling him that he would have to return to complete the necessary papers.[158] However, Oswald did give the consul his passport [159] and a hand-written statement requesting that his American citizenship be "re-voked" and "affirm[ing] [his] * * * allegiance" to the Soviet Union.[160] (See Commission Exhibit No. 913, p. 261.) The FBI has confirmed that this statement is in Oswald's handwriting,[161] and Snyder has testified that the letter's phrases are consistent with the way Oswald talked and conducted himself.[162] During the approximately 40-minute interview, Oswald also informed Snyder that he had been a radar operator in the Marine Corps, intimating that he might know something of special interest, and that he had informed a Soviet official that he would give the Soviets any information concerning the Marine Corps and radar operation which he possessed.[163] Although Oswald never filed a formal renunciation, in a letter to the Embassy dated November 3, 1959, he again requested that his American citizenship be revoked and protested the refusal to accept his renunciation on October 31.[164] (See Commission Exhibit No. 912, p. 263.)

While at the Embassy,[165] and in a subsequent interview with an American journalist,[166] Oswald displayed familiarity with Communist ideological arguments, which led those with whom he spoke to speculate that he may have received some instruction from Soviet authorities. Oswald's familiarity with the law regarding renunciation of citizenship, observed by both Embassy officials,[167] could also be construed as a sign of coaching by Soviet authorities. However, Oswald is known to have been an avid reader [168] and there is evidence that he had read Communist literature without guidance while in the Marine Corps and before that time.[169] After his arrival in Moscow, Oswald most probably had discussions with his Intourist guide and others,[170] but none of the Americans with whom he talked in Moscow felt that his conversations necessarily revealed any type of formal training.[171] The "Historic Diary" indicates that Oswald did not tell his guide that he intended to visit the Embassy because he feared she would disapprove.[172] (See Commission Exhibit No. 24, p. 264.) Though Oswald gave Snyder the impression "of an intelligent person who spoke in a manner and on a level, which seemed to befit his apparent level of intelligence," [173] correspondent Priscilla Johnson, who spent about 5 hours talking with him,[174] received a much less favorable impression:

He liked to create the pretense, the impression that he was attracted to abstract discussion and was capable of engaging in it, and was drawn to it. But it was like pricking a balloon. I had the feeling that if you really did engage him on this ground, you very quickly would discover that he didn't have the capacity for a logical sustained argument about an abstract point on economics or on noneconomic, political matters or any matter, philosophical.[175]

LETTER MAILED BY OSWALD TO THE AMERICAN EMBASSY IN MOSCOW

Nov. 3 1959

CONSULAR SECTION
TAKEN

I, Lee Harvey Oswald, do hereby request that my present United States citizenship be revoked.

I appeared in person, at the consulate office of the United States Embassy, Moscow, on Oct 31st, for the purpose of signing the formal papers to this effect. This legal right I was refused at that time.

I wish to protest against this action, and against the conduct of the official of the United States consular service who acted on behalf of the United States government.

My application, requesting that I be considered for citizenship in the Soviet Union is now pending before the Supreme Soviet of the U.S.S.R..

In the event of acceptance, I will request my government to lodge a formal protest regarding this incident.

EMBASSY OF THE UNITED STATES
OF AMERICA

NOV. 06. 1959

MOSCOW

Lee Harvey Oswald

COMMISSION EXHIBIT No. 912

OSWALD'S OWN ACCOUNT OF HIS MEETING AT THE AMERICAN EMBASSY IN MOSCOW OCT. 31, 1959

Excerpts from his "Historic Diary"

COMMISSION EXHIBIT NO. 24

A comparison of the formal note Oswald handed Snyder [176] and his letter of November 3 [177] with the provisions of section 349(a) of the Immigration and Nationality Act [178] suggests that Oswald had read the statute but understood it imperfectly; he apparently was trying to use three out of the four ways set out in the statute to surrender his citizenship, but he succeeded in none.

Moreover, persuasive evidence that Oswald's conduct was not carefully coached by Soviet agents is provided by some of his actions at the Embassy. The single statement which probably caused Oswald the most future trouble was his declaration that he had already volunteered to a Soviet official that he would, if asked, tell the Soviet Government all that he knew about his job in radar as a Marine. Certainly a statement of this type would prejudice any possibility of his being an effective pro-Communist agent.

Further, though unquestionably evidencing anti-American sentiments, Oswald's behavior at the Embassy, which brought him exceedingly close to expatriation, was unlikely to have increased his value in any capacity to the Soviet Union. Richard E. Snyder, the official who interviewed Oswald on October 31, testified that he "had every reason to believe" that Oswald would have carried through a formal—and therefore effective—renunciation of his American citizenship immediately if he had let him.[179] However, as a defector, Oswald could have had considerable propaganda value without expatriating himself; and if he had expatriated himself his eventual return to the United States would have been much more difficult and perhaps impossible. If Snyder's assessment of Oswald's intentions is accurate, it thus tends to refute the suggestion that Oswald was being coached by the Soviets. In addition, reporters noticed Oswald's apparent ambivalence in regard to renouncing his citizenship—stormily demanding that he be permitted to renounce while failing to follow through by completing the necessary papers [180]— behavior which might have detracted from his propaganda value.

According to Oswald's "Historic Diary" [181] and the documents furnished to the Commission by the Soviet Government,[182] Oswald was not told that he had been accepted as a resident of the Soviet Union until about January 4, 1960. Although on November 13 and 16 Oswald informed Aline Mosby [183] and Priscilla Johnson [184] that he had been granted permission to remain in the country indefinitely, the diary indicates that at that time he had been told only that he could remain "until some solution is found with what to do with me." [185] The diary is more consistent with the letter Oswald wrote to his brother Robert on December 17, saying that he was then, more than a month after he saw Johnson and Mosby, about to leave his hotel,[186] and with some later correspondence with his mother. Oswald mailed a short note to his mother which she received in Texas on January 5; that same day she mailed a money order to him in Moscow, but it apparently got there too late, because she received it back, unopened, on February 25.[187] Oswald's conflicting statement to the correspondents also seems reconcilable with his very apparent desire to appear important to others.

Moreover, so long as Oswald continued to stay in a hotel in Moscow, the inference is that the Soviet authorities had not yet decided to accept him.[188] This inference is supported by information supplied by the CIA on the handling of other defectors in the Soviet Union.[189]

Thus, the evidence is strong that Oswald waited at least until November 16, when he saw Miss Johnson, and it is probable that he was required to wait until January 4, a little over 2½ months from October 16, before his application to remain in Russia was granted. In mid-November Miss Johnson asked Oswald whether the Russians were encouraging his defection, to which Oswald responded: "The Russians are treating it like a legal formality. They don't encourage you and they don't discourage you." [190] And, when the Soviet Government finally acted, Oswald did not receive Soviet citizenship, as he had requested, but merely permission to reside in Russia on a year-to-year basis.[191]

Asked to comment upon the length of time, 2 months and 22 days, that probably passed before Oswald was granted the right to remain in the Soviet Union, the CIA has advised that "when compared to five other defector cases, this procedure seems unexceptional." [192] Similarly, the Department of State reports that its information "indicated that a 2-month waiting period is not unusual." [193] The full response of the CIA is as follows:

> Oswald said that he asked for Soviet citizenship on 16 October 1959. According to his diary, he received word a month later that he could stay in the USSR pending disposition of his request, but it was another month and a half before he was given his stateless passport.
>
> When compared to five other defector cases, this procedure seems unexceptional. Two defectors from US Army intelligence units in West Germany appear to have been given citizenship immediately, but both had prior KGB connections and fled as a result of Army security checks. Of the other three cases, one was accepted after not more than five weeks and given a stateless passport apparently at about the same time. The second was immediately given permission to stay for a while, and his subsequent request for citizenship was granted three months later. The third was allowed to stay after he made his citizenship request, but almost two months passed before he was told that he had been accepted. Although the Soviet Ministry of Foreign Affairs soon after told the US Embassy that he was a Soviet citizen, he did not receive his document until five or six months after initial application. We know of only one case in which an American asked for Soviet citizenship but did not take up residence in the USSR. In that instance, the American changed his mind and voluntarily returned to the United States less than three weeks after he had requested Soviet citizenship.[194]

The Department of State has commented as follows:

The files of the Department of State reflect the fact that Oswald first applied for permission to remain in Russia permanently, or at least for a long period, when he arrived in Moscow, and that he obtained permission to remain within one or two months.

A. Is the fact that he obtained permission to stay within this period of time usual?

Answer—Our information indicates that a two months waiting period is not unusual. In the case of [name withheld] the Supreme Soviet decided within two months to give Soviet citizenship and he was thereafter, of course, permitted to stay.

B. Can you tell us what the normal procedures are under similar circumstances?

Answer—It is impossible for us to state any "normal" procedures. The Soviet Government never publicizes the proceedings in these cases or the reasons for its action. Furthermore, it is, of course, extremely unusual for an American citizen to defect.[195]

The information relating to Oswald's suicide attempt indicates that his application to remain in the Soviet Union was probably rejected about 6 days after his arrival in Moscow. Since the KGB is the Soviet agency responsible for the initial handling of all defectors,[196] it seems likely that the original decision not to accept Oswald was made by the KGB. That Oswald was permitted to remain in Moscow after his release from the hospital suggests that another ministry of the Soviet Government may have intervened on his behalf. This hypothesis is consistent with entries in the "Historic Diary" commenting that the officials Oswald met after his hospital treatment were different from those with whom he had dealt before.[197] The most plausible reason for any such intervention may well have been apprehension over the publicity that would follow the rejection of a devout convert to the Communist cause.

Oswald's Life in Minsk.—According to the "Historic Diary"[198] and documents received from the Soviet Government,[199] Oswald resided in the city of Minsk from January 1960 until June 1962. Oswald's life in Minsk is the portion of his life concerning which the least is known. The primary sources of information are Oswald's own writings and the testimony of Marina Oswald. Other evidence, however, establishes beyond doubt that Oswald was in fact located in Minsk on at least two occasions. The Commission has obtained two photographs which were taken by American tourists in Minsk in August 1961 in which Oswald appears.[200] The tourists did not know Oswald, nor did they speak with him; they remembered only that several men gathered near their car.[201] (See Kramer Exhibit 1, p. 268.) In addition, Oswald was noticed in Minsk by a student who was traveling with

OSWALD, MAN STANDING ON RIGHT IN FIGURED SHIRT.
PHOTOGRAPH TAKEN IN MINSK, U.S.S.R. BY AN AMERICAN
TOURIST IN AUGUST, 1961.
(KRAMER DEPOSITION 1)

the University of Michigan band on a tour of Russia in the spring of 1961.[202] Oswald corresponded with the American Embassy in Moscow from Minsk,[203] and wrote letters from Minsk to his family in the United States.[204] Oswald and his wife have many photographs taken of themselves which show Minsk backgrounds and persons who are identifiable as residents of Minsk.[205] After he returned to the United States, Oswald conversed about the city with Russian-born American citizens who were familiar with it.[206] Marina Oswald is also familiar with the city.[207] The Commission has also been able independently to verify the existence in Minsk of many of the acquaintances of Oswald and his wife whom they said they knew there.[208] (See Commission Exhibits Nos. 1392, 1395, 2606, 2609, 2612 and 2623, pp. 270–271.)

Once he was accepted as a resident alien in the Soviet Union, Oswald was given considerable benefits which ordinary Soviet citizens in his position in society did not have. The "Historic Diary" recites that after Oswald was informed that he could remain in the Soviet Union and was being sent to Minsk he was given 5,000 rubles* ($500) by the "Red Cross, * * * for expenses." He used 2,200 rubles to pay his hotel bill, and another 150 rubles to purchase a train ticket. With the balance of slightly over 2,500 rubles, Oswald felt, according to the diary, like a rich man.[209] Oswald did not receive free living quarters, as the diary indicates the "Mayor" of Minsk promised him,[210] but about 6 weeks after his arrival he did receive an apartment, very pleasant by Soviet standards, for which he was required to pay only 60 rubles ($6.00) a month. Oswald considered the apartment "almost rent free."[211] Oswald was given a job in the "Byelorussian Radio and Television Factory," where his pay on a per piece basis ranged from 700 to 900 rubles ($70–$90) a month.[212] According to his wife, this rate of pay was average for people in his occupation but good by Soviet standards generally.[213] She explained that piecework rates throughout the Soviet Union have generally grown out of line with compensation for other jobs.[214] The CIA has confirmed that this condition exists in many areas and occupations in the Soviet Union.[215] In addition to his salary, Oswald regularly received 700 rubles ($70) per month from the Soviet "Red Cross."[216] The well-paying job, the monthly subsidy, and the "almost rent-free" apartment combined to give Oswald more money than he needed. The only complaint recorded in the "Historic Diary" is that there was "no place to spend the money."[217]

The Commission has found no basis for associating Oswald's preferred income with Soviet undercover activity. Marina Oswald testified that foreign nationals are commonly given special treatment in the Soviet Union,[218] and the Central Intelligence Agency has confirmed that it is standard practice in the Soviet Union for Americans and other foreign defectors from countries with high standards of living to be "subsidized."[219] Apparently it is Soviet practice

---

*About a year after Oswald received this money, the ruble was revalued to about 10 times its earlier value.

PHOTOGRAPHS OF THE OSWALDS IN MINSK, U.S.S.R.

OSWALD AND MARINA ON A BRIDGE IN MINSK (COMMISSION EXHIBIT 1392)

UNCLE VASILY AKSIONOV AND AUNT LUBOVA AKSIONOVA, WITH THE OSWALDS (COMMISSION EXHIBIT 2623)

MARINA WAITING FOR BUS (COMMISSION EXHIBIT 1395)

PHOTOGRAPHS OF OSWALDS
IN U. S. S. R.

ROSA KUZNETSOVA, ELLA GERMAN,
LEE HARVEY OSWALD, AND
PAVEL GOLOVACHEV
(COMMISSION EXHIBIT 2609)

OSWALD AND ALFRED (LAST NAME UNKNOWN),
A HUNGARIAN FRIEND OF ANITA ZIGER
(COMMISSION EXHIBIT 2612)

VIEW OVERLOOKING THE SVISLOCH
RIVER FROM THE BALCONY OF
THE OSWALDS' APARTMENT
IN MINSK
(COMMISSION EXHIBIT 2606)

271

to attempt to make life sufficiently pleasant for a foreign defector so that he will not become disillusioned and return to his native country. The Commission has also assumed that it is customary for Soviet intelligence agencies to keep defectors under surveillance during their residence in the Soviet Union, through periodic interviews of neighbors and associates of the defector.[220] Oswald once mentioned that the Soviet police questioned his neighbors occasionally.[221]

Moreover, it is from Oswald's personal writings alone that the Commission has learned that he received supplementary funds from the Soviet "Red Cross." In the notes he made during the return trip to the United States Oswald recognized that the "Red Cross" subsidy had nothing to do with the well-known International Red Cross. He frankly stated that the money was paid to him for having "denounced" the United States and that it had come from the "MVD." [222] Oswald's papers reveal that the "Red Cross" subsidy was terminated as soon as he wrote the American Embassy in Moscow in February 1961 asking that he be permitted to return.[223] (See Commission Exhibit No. 25, p. 273.) Marina Oswald's testimony confirmed this; she said that when she knew Oswald he no longer was receiving the monthly grant but still retained some of the savings accumulated in the months when he had been receiving it.[224] Since she met Oswald in March and married him in April of 1961, her testimony was consistent with his records.

The nature of Oswald's employment while in Minsk has been examined by the Commission. The factory in which he worked was a large plant manufacturing electronic parts and radio and television sets. Marina Oswald has testified that he was an "apprentice machinist" and "ground small metallic parts for radio receivers, on a lathe." [225] So far as can be determined, Oswald never straightforwardly described to anyone else in the United States exactly what his job was in the Soviet Union.[226] Some of his acquaintances in Dallas and Fort Worth had the impression that he was disappointed in having been given a menial job and not assigned to an institution of higher learning in the Soviet Union.[227] Marina Oswald confirmed this and also testified that her husband was not interested in his work and not regarded at the factory as a very good worker.[228] The documents furnished to the Commission by the Soviet government were consistent with her testimony on this point, since they included a report from Oswald's superior at the factory which is critical of his performance on the job.[229] Oswald's employment and his job performance are thus consistent with his known occupational habits in this country and otherwise afford no ground for suspicion.

Oswald's membership in a hunting club while he was in the Soviet Union has been a matter of special interest to the Commission. One Russian emigre testified that this was a suspicious circumstance because no one in the Soviet Union is permitted to own a gun for pleasure.[230] The Commission's investigation, however, has established that this is not so. The Central Intelligence Agency has advised the Commission that hunting societies such as the one to

EXCERPTS FROM A SPEECH OSWALD NEVER DELIVERED, WHICH HE PROBABLY WROTE ABOARD THE SHIP WHILE RETURNING FROM THE U. S. S. R. WITH HIS FAMILY

(COMMISSION EXHIBIT 25)

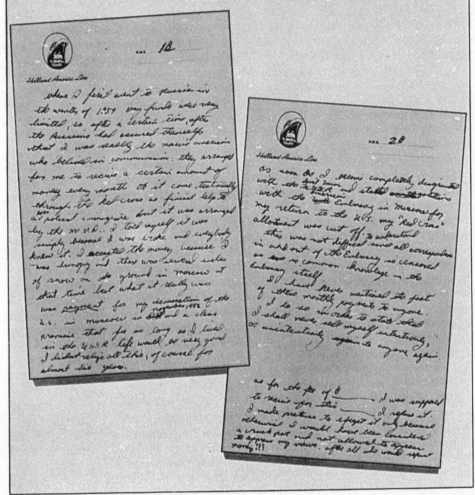

which Oswald belonged are very popular in the Soviet Union.[231] They are frequently sponsored by factories for their employees, as was Oswald's.[232] Moreover, Soviet citizens (or foreigners residing in the Soviet Union) are permitted to own shotguns, but not rifles, without joining a society; all that is necessary is that the gun be registered at the local militia office immediately after it has been purchased.[233] Experts from the Central Intelligence Agency have examined Oswald's club membership certificate and gun permit and expressed the opinion that its terms and numbers are consistent with other information the CIA has about the Soviet Union.[234]

Marina Oswald testified that her husband went hunting only on one occasion during the time of their marriage.[235] However, Oswald apparently joined the Byelorussian Society of Hunters and Fishermen in the summer of 1960 [236] and did not marry until April 30, 1961,[237] so he could have been more active while he was still a bachelor. Oswald made no secret of his membership in the hunting club. He mentioned it on occasion to friends after he returned to the United States; [238] discussed it at some length in a speech at a Jesuit Seminary in Mobile, Ala., in the summer of 1962; [239] included it in his correspondence with his brother Robert; [240] and kept his membership certificate [241] and gun permit [242] until the day he was killed. In view of these facts, it is unlikely that Oswald's membership in a hunting club was contrived to conceal some sort of secret training. Moreover, the CIA has informed the Commission that it is in possession of considerable information on the location of secret Soviet training institutions and that it knows of no such institution in or near Minsk during the time Oswald was there.[243]

Oswald's marriage to Marina Prusakova on April 30, 1961,[244] is itself a fact meriting consideration. A foreigner living in Russia cannot marry without the permission of the Soviet Government.[245] It seems unlikely that the Soviet authorities would have permitted Oswald to marry and to take his wife with him to the United States if they were contemplating using him alone as an agent. The fact that he had a Russian wife would be likely, in their view, to increase any surveillance under which he would be kept by American security agencies, would make him even more conspicuous to his neighbors as "an ex-Russian," and would decrease his mobility. A wife's presence in the United States would also constitute a continuing risk of disclosure. On the other hand, Marina Oswald's lack of English training and her complete ignorance of the United States and its customs [246] would scarcely recommend her to the Soviet authorities as one member of an "agent team" to be sent to the United States on a difficult and dangerous foreign enterprise.

Oswald's departure from the Soviet Union.—On February 13, 1961, the American Embassy in Moscow received a letter from Oswald postmarked Minsk, February 5, asking that he be readmitted to the United States.[247] This was the first time that the Embassy had heard from or about Oswald since November 16, 1959.[248] The end of the 15-month silence came only a few days after the Department of State in Washington had forwarded a request to the Moscow Embassy on February 1, 1961, informing the Embassy that Oswald's mother was worried about him, and asking that he get in touch with her if possible.[249] The simultaneity of the two events was apparently coincidental. The request from Marguerite Oswald went from Washington to Moscow by sealed diplomatic pouch and there was no evidence that the seal had been tampered with.[250] The officer of the Department of State who carried the responsibility for such matters has testified that the message was not forwarded to the Russians after it arrived in Moscow.[251]

Oswald's letter does not seem to have been designed to ingratiate him with the Embassy officials. It starts by incorrectly implying that he had written an earlier letter that was not answered, states that he will return to the United States only if he can first "come to some agreement" on there being no legal charges brought against him, and ends with a reminder to the officials at the Embassy that they have a responsibility to do everything they can to help him, since he is an American citizen.[252]

The Embassy's response to this letter was to invite Oswald to come personally to Moscow to discuss the matter.[253] Oswald at first protested because of the difficulty of obtaining Soviet permission.[254] He wrote two more protesting letters during the following 4 months,[255] but received no indication that the Embassy would allow him to handle the matter by mail.[256] While the Department of State was clarifying its position on this matter,[257] Oswald unexpectedly appeared in Moscow on Saturday, July 8, 1961.[258] On Sunday, Marina Oswald flew to Moscow,[259] and was interviewed by officials in the American Embassy on Tuesday.[260]

The Commission asked the Department of State and the Central Intelligence Agency to comment on whether the Oswalds' travel to Moscow without permission signified special treatment by the Soviet Union. From their responses, it appears that since Marina Oswald possessed a Soviet citizen's internal passport, she did not require prior approval to make the trip.[261] Although Soviet law did require her husband, as the holder of a "stateless passport," to obtain advance permission for the trip, his failure to do so would not normally have been considered a serious violation. In this respect, the CIA has advised the Commission as follows:

OSWALD'S travel from Minsk to Moscow and return in July 1961 would normally have required prior authorization. Bearers of a Soviet "passport for foreigners" (*vid na zhitelstov v. SSSR dlya innostrantsa*) are required to obtain travel authorization from the Visa and Registration Department (OVIR) (or Passport Registration Department (PRO) in smaller towns) if they desire to leave the city (or oblast) where they are domiciled. This same requirement is believed to apply to persons, such as OSWALD, holding Soviet "stateless passports" (*vid na zhitelstvo v. SSSR dlya lits bez grazhdanstva*).

The practicality of even "unauthorized" travel was demonstrated by events related by a United States citizen who defected in 1960, and subsequently was sent to Kiev to study. After repatriating this defector told U.S. authorities he had made a total of seven unauthorized trips from Kiev during his stay in the USSR. He was apprehended on two of his flights and was returned to Kiev each time, the second time under escort. On both occasions he was merely reprimanded by the deputy chief of the institute at which he was studying. Since Marina had a Soviet citizen's internal passport there would have been no restrictions against her making the trip to Moscow.[262]

The answers of the Department of State, together with the Commission's specific questions, are as follows:

B. Could resident foreigners normally travel in this manner without first obtaining such permission?

Answer—There are only a few U.S. nationals now living in the Soviet Union. They include an American Roman Catholic priest, an American Protestant minister, a number of correspondents, some students and technical advisers to Soviet businesses. We know that the priest, the minister, the correspondents and the students must obtain permission from Soviet authorities before taking any trips. The technical advisers notify officials of their project before they travel and these officials personally inform the militia.

C. If travel of this type was not freely permitted, do you believe that Oswald normally would have been apprehended during the attempt or punished after the fact for traveling without permission?

Answer—Based on the information we have, we believe that if Oswald went to Moscow without permission, and this was known to the Soviet authorities, he would have been fined or reprimanded. Oswald was not, of course, an average foreign resident. He was a defector from a foreign country and the bearer of a Soviet internal "stateless" passport * * * during the time when he was contemplating the visit to Moscow to come to the Embassy * * *

The Soviet authorities probably knew about Oswald's trip even if he did not obtain advance permission, since in most instances the Soviet militia guards at the Embassy ask for the documents of unidentified persons entering the Embassy grounds * * *

An American citizen who, with her American citizen husband, went to the Soviet Union to live permanently and is now trying to obtain permission to leave, informed the Embassy that she had been fined for not getting permission to go from Odessa to Moscow on a recent trip to visit the Embassy.

D. Even if such travel did not have to be authorized, do you have any information or observations regarding the practicality of such travel by Soviet citizens or persons in Oswald's status?

Answer—It is impossible to generalize in this area. We understand from interrogations of former residents in the Soviet Union who were considered "stateless" by Soviet authorities that they were not permitted to leave the town where they resided without permission of the police. In requesting such permission they were required to fill out a questionnaire giving the reason for travel, length of stay, addresses of individuals to be visited, etc.

Notwithstanding these requirements, we know that at least one "stateless" person often traveled without permission of the authorities and stated that police stationed at railroad stations usually spotchecked the identification papers of every tenth traveler, but that it was an easy matter to avoid such checks. Finally, she stated that persons who were caught evading the registration requirements were returned to their home towns by the police and sentenced to short jail terms and fined. These sentences were more severe for repeated violations.[263]

When Oswald arrived at the Embassy in Moscow, he met Richard E. Snyder, the same person with whom he had dealt in October of 1959.[264] Primarily on the basis of Oswald's interview with Snyder on Monday, July 10, 1961, the American Embassy concluded that Oswald had not expatriated himself.[265] (See app. XV, pp. 752–760.) On the basis of this tentative decision, Oswald was given back his American passport, which he had surrendered in 1959.[266] The document was due to expire in September 1961,[267] however, and Oswald was informed that its renewal would depend upon the ultimate decision by the Department of State on his expatriation.[268] On July 11, Marina Oswald was interviewed at the Embassy and the steps necessary for her to obtain an American visa were begun.[269] In May 1962, after 15 months of dealings with the Embassy, Oswald's passport was ultimately renewed and permission for his wife to enter the United States was granted.[270]

The files on Oswald and his wife compiled by the Department of State and the Immigration and Naturalization Service contain no indication of any expert guidance by Soviet authorities in Oswald's dealings with the Department or the Service. For example, the letters from Minsk to the Embassy in Moscow,[271] which are in his handwriting,[272] display the arrogant attitude which was characteristic of him both before and after he lived in Russia, and, when compared with other letters that were without doubt composed and written by him,[273] show about the same low level of sophistication, fluency, and spelling. The Department officer who most frequently dealt with Oswald when he began negotiations to return to the United States, Richard E. Snyder, testified that he can recall nothing that indicated Oswald was being guided or assisted by a third party when he appeared at the Embassy in July 1961.[274] On the contrary, the arrogant and presumptuous attitude which Oswald displayed in his correspondence with the Embassy from early 1961 until June 1962,[275] when he finally departed from Russia, undoubtedly hindered his attempts to return to the United States. Snyder has testified that although he made a sincere effort to treat Oswald's application objectively, Oswald's attitude made this very difficult.[276]

In order to leave Russia, it was also necessary for the Oswalds to obtain permission from the Soviet Government. The timing and circumstances under which the Oswalds obtained this permission have also been considered by the Commission. Marina Oswald, although her memory is not clear on the point, said that she and Oswald first made their intentions to go to the United States known to Soviet officials in Minsk in May, even before coming to Moscow in July for the conference at the American Embassy.[277] The Oswalds' correspondence with the Embassy and the documents furnished the Commission by the Soviet Government show that the Oswalds made a series of formal applications to the Soviets from July 15 to August 21.[278] Presumably the most difficult question for the Soviet authorities was whether to allow Marina Oswald to accompany her husband. She was called to the local passport office in Minsk on December 25, 1961, and told that authority had been received to issue exit visas to her and Oswald.[279] Obtaining the permission of the Soviet Government to leave may have been aided by a conference which Marina Oswald had, at her own request, with a local MVD official, Colonel Aksenov, sometime in late 1961. She testified that she applied for the conference at her husband's urging, after he had tried unsuccessfully to arrange such a conference for himself.[280] She believed that it may have been granted her because her uncle with whom she had lived in Minsk before her marriage was also an MVD official.[281]

The correspondence with the American Embassy at this time reflected that the Oswalds did not pick up their exit visas immediately.[282] On January 11, 1962, Marina Oswald was issued her Soviet exit visa. It was marked valid until December 1, 1962.[283] The Oswalds did not leave Russia until June 1962, but the additional delay was caused by problems with the U.S. Government and by the birth of a child in February.[284] Permission of the Soviet authorities to leave, once given, was never revoked. Oswald told the FBI in July 1962, shortly after he returned to the United States, that he had been interviewed by the MVD twice, once when he first came to the Soviet Union and once just before he departed.[285] His wife testified that the second interview did not occur in Moscow but that she and her husband dealt with the MVD visa officials frequently in Minsk.[286]

Investigation of the circumstances, including the timing, under which the Oswalds obtained permission from the Soviet Government to leave Russia for the United States show that they differed in no discernible manner from the normal. The Central Intelligence Agency has informed the Commission that normally a Soviet national would not be permitted to emigrate if he might endanger Soviet national security once he went abroad.[287] Those persons in possession of confidential information, for example, would constitute an important category of such "security risks." Apparently Oswald's predeparture interview by the MVD was part of an attempt to ascertain whether he or his wife had access to any confidential information. Marina Oswald's reported interview with the MVD in late 1961, which was arranged at her request, may have served the same purpose. The Commission's awareness of both interviews derives entirely from Oswald's and his wife's statements and letters to the American Embassy, which afford additional evidence that the conferences carried no subversive significance.

It took the Soviet authorities at least 5½ months, from about July 15, 1961, until late December, to grant permission for the Oswalds to leave the country. When asked to comment upon the alleged rapidity of the Oswalds' departure, the Department of State advised the Commission:

> * * * In the immediate post-war period there were about fifteen marriages in which the wife had been waiting for many years for a Soviet exit permit. After the death of Stalin the Soviet Government showed a disposition to settle these cases. In the summer of 1953 permission was given for all of this group of Soviet citizen wives to accompany their American citizen husbands to the United States.
>
> Since this group was given permission to leave the Soviet Union, there have been from time to time marriages in the Soviet Union of American citizens and Soviet citizens. With one exception, it is our understanding that all of the Soviet citizens involved have been given permission to emigrate to the United States after waiting periods which were, in some cases from three to six months and in others much longer.[288]

Both the Department of State and the Central Intelligence Agency compiled data for the Commission on Soviet wives of American citizens who received exit visas to leave the Soviet Union, where the relevant information was available. In both cases the data were consistent with the above conclusion of the State Department. The Department of State had sufficient information to measure the timespan in 14 cases. The Department points out that it has information on the dates of application for and receipt of Soviet exit visas only on those cases that have been brought to its attention. A common reason for bringing a case to the attention of the Department is that the granting of the exit visa by the Soviet Union has been delayed, so that the American spouse seeks the assistance of his own government. It therefore appears that the sampling data carry a distinct bias toward lengthy waiting periods. Of the 14 cases tested, 6 involve women who applied for visas after 1953, when the liberalized post-Stalin policy was in effect. The approximate waiting periods for these wives were, in decreasing order, 13 months, 6 months, 3 months, 1 month, and 10 days.[289] Of the 11 cases examined by the Central Intelligence Agency in which the time period is known or can be inferred, the Soviet wives had to wait from 5 months to a year to obtain exit visas.[290]

In his correspondence with the American Embassy and his brother while he was in Russia,[291] in his diary,[292] and in his conversations with people in the United States after he returned,[293] Oswald claimed that his wife had been subjected to pressure by the Soviet Government in an effort to induce her not to emigrate to the United States. In the Embassy correspondence, Oswald claimed that the pressure had been so intense that she had to be hospitalized for 5 days for "nervous exhaustion." [294] Marina Oswald testified that her husband exaggerated and that no such hospitalization or "nervous exhaustion" ever occurred.[295] However, she did testify that she was questioned on the matter occasionally and given the impression that her government was not pleased with her decision.[296] Her aunt and uncle in Minsk did not speak to her "for a long time"; she also stated that she was dropped from membership in the Communist Youth Organization (Komsomol) when the news of her visit to the American Embassy in Moscow reached that organization.[297] A student who took Russian lessons from her in Texas testified that she once referred to the days when the pressure was applied as "a very horrible time." [298] Despite all this Marina Oswald testified that she was surprised that their visas were granted as soon as they were—and that hers was granted at all.[299] This evidence thus indicates that the Soviet authorities, rather than facilitating the departure of the Oswalds, first tried to dissuade Marina Oswald from going to the United States and then, when she failed to respond to the pressure, permitted her to leave without undue delay. There are indications that the Soviet treatment of another recent defector who left the Soviet Union to return to the United States resembled that accorded to the Oswalds.[300]

On the basis of all the foregoing evidence, the Commission concluded that there was no reason to believe that the Oswalds received unusually favorable treatment in being permitted to leave the Soviet Union.

Associations in the Dallas-Fort Worth Community

The Russian-speaking community.—Shortly after his return from Russia in June 1962, Oswald and his family settled in Fort Worth, Tex., where they met a group of Russian-born or Russian-speaking persons in the Dallas-Fort Worth area.[301] The members of this community were attracted to each other by common background, language, and culture. Many of them were well-educated, accomplished, and industrious people, several being connected with the oil exploration, production, and processing industry that flourishes in the Dallas-Fort Worth area.[302] As described more fully in chapter VII and in appendix XIII, many of these persons assisted the Oswalds in various ways. Some provided the Oswalds with gifts of such things as food, clothing, and baby furniture.[303] Some arranged appointments and transportation for medical and dental treatment, and assumed the cost in some instances.[304] When Oswald undertook to look for employment in Dallas in early October of 1962 and again when marital difficulties arose between the Oswalds in November of the same year, Marina Oswald and their child were housed at times in the homes of various members of the group.[305] The Commission has examined the background of many of these individuals and has thoroughly investigated Oswald's relationship with them.

There is no basis to suppose that Oswald came to Fort Worth upon his return from Russia for the purpose of establishing contacts with the Russian-speaking community located in that area. Oswald had spent several of his grammar-school years in Fort Worth.[306] In 1962, his brother Robert lived in Fort Worth and his mother resided in nearby Vernon, Tex. In January of that year, Oswald indicated to American officials in Russia that he intended to stay with his mother upon his return to the United States; however, sometime after mid-February, he received an invitation to stay with Robert and his family until he became settled, and he did spend the first several weeks after his return at Robert's home.[307] In July, Oswald's mother moved to Fort Worth and Oswald and his wife and child moved into an apartment with her.[308] While in that apartment, Oswald located a job in Fort Worth and then rented and moved with his family into an apartment on Mercedes Street.[309]

Upon his arrival in 1962, Oswald did not know any members of the relatively small and loosely knit Russian-speaking community.[310] Shortly after his arrival Oswald obtained the name of two Russian-speaking persons in Fort Worth from the office of the Texas Employment Commission in that city.[311] Attempts to arrange a prompt visit with one of them failed.[312] The second person, Peter Paul Gregory, was a consulting petroleum engineer and part-time Russian-language instructor at the Fort Worth Public Library. Oswald contacted him in order to obtain a letter certifying to his proficiency in Russian and Marina Oswald later tutored his son in the Russian language.[313] Gregory introduced the Oswalds to George Bouhe and Anna Meller, both of whom lived in Dallas and became interested in the welfare of Marina Oswald and her child.[314] Through them, other members of the Russian community became acquainted with the Oswalds.[315]

The Oswalds met some 30 persons in the Russian-speaking community, of whom 25 testified before the Commission or its staff; others were interviewed on behalf of the Commission.[316] This range of testimony has disclosed that the relationship between Lee Harvey Oswald and the Russian-speaking community was short lived and generally quite strained.[317] During October and November of 1962 Marina Oswald lived at the homes of some of the members of the Russian-speaking community.[318] She stayed first with Elena Hall while Oswald was looking for work in Dallas.[319] In early November, Marina Oswald and the baby joined Oswald in Dallas, but soon thereafter, she spent approximately 2 weeks with different Russian-speaking friends during another separation.[320] Oswald openly resented the help Marina's "Russian friends" gave to him and his wife and the efforts of some of them to induce Marina to leave him.[321] George

Bouhe attempted to dissuade Marina from returning to her husband in November 1962, and when she rejoined him, Bouhe became displeased with her as well.[322] Relations between the Oswalds and the members of the Russian community had practically ceased by the end of 1962. Katherine Ford, one of the members of the group, summed up the situation as it existed at the end of January 1963: "So it was rather, sort of, Marina and her husband were dropped at that time, nobody actually wanted to help. * * *"[323]

In April of 1963, Oswald left Fort Worth for New Orleans, where he was later joined by his wife and daughter, and remained until his trip to Mexico City in late September and his subsequent return to the Dallas-Fort Worth area in early October of 1963.[324] With only minor exceptions,[325] there is no evidence that any member of the Russian-speaking community had further contact with Oswald or his family after April.[326] In New Orleans, Oswald made no attempt to make new Russian-speaking acquaintances for his wife and there is no evidence that he developed any friendships in that city.[327] Similarly, after the return from New Orleans, there seems to have been no communication between the Oswalds and this group until the evening of November 22, 1963, when the Dallas Police enlisted Ilya Mamantov to serve as an interpreter for them in their questioning of Marina Oswald.[328]

George De Mohrenschildt and his wife, both of whom speak Russian as well as several other languages, however, did continue to see the Oswalds on occasion up to about the time Oswald went to New Orleans on April 24, 1963. De Mohrenschildt was apparently the only Russian-speaking person living in Dallas for whom Oswald had appreciable respect, and this seems to have been true even though De Mohrenschildt helped Marina Oswald leave her husband for a period in November of 1962.[329]

In connection with the relations between Oswald and De Mohrenschildt, the Commission has considered testimony concerning an event which occurred shortly after Oswald shot at General Walker. The De Mohrenschildts came to Oswald's apartment on Neely Street for the first time on the evening of April 13, 1963, apparently to bring an Easter gift for the Oswald child.[330] Mrs. De Mohrenschildt testified that while Marina Oswald was showing her the apartment, she saw a rifle with a scope in a closet. Mrs. De Mohrenschildt then told her husband, in the presence of the Oswalds, that there was a rifle in the closet.[331] Mrs. De Mohrenschildt testified that "George, of course, with his sense of humor—Walker was shot at a few days ago, within that time. He said, 'Did you take a pot shot at Walker by any chance?' "[332] At that point, Mr. De Mohrenschildt testified, Oswald "sort of shriveled, you see, when I asked this question. * * * made a peculiar face * * * [and] changed the expression on his face" and remarked that he did target shooting.[333] Marina Oswald testified that the De Mohrenschildts came to visit a few days after the Walker incident and that when De Mohrenschildt made his reference to Oswald's possibly shooting at Walker, Oswald's "face changed, * * * he almost became speechless."[334] According to the De Mohrenschildts, Mr. De Mohrenschildt's remark was intended as a joke, and he had no knowledge of Oswald's involvement in the attack on Walker.[335] Nonetheless, the remark appears to have created an uncomfortable silence, and the De Mohrenschildts left "very soon afterwards." They never saw either of the Oswalds again.[336] They left in a few days on a trip to New York City and did not return until after Oswald had gone to New Orleans.[337] A postcard from Oswald to De Mohrenschildt was apparently the only contact they had thereafter.[338] The De Mohrenschildts left in early June for Haiti on a business venture, and they were still residing there at the time they testified on April 23, 1964.[339]

Extensive investigation has been conducted into the background of both De Mohrenschildts.[340] The investigation has revealed that George De Mohrenschildt is a highly individualistic person of varied interests. He was born in the Russian Ukraine in 1911 and fled Russia with his parents in 1921 during the civil disorder following the revolution. He was in a Polish cavalry military academy for 1½ years. Later he studied in Antwerp and attended the University of Liege from which he received a doctor's degree in international commerce in 1928. Soon thereafter, he emigrated to the United States; he became a U.S. citizen in 1949.[341] De Mohrenschildt eventually became interested in oil exploration and production; he entered the University of Texas in 1944 and received a master's degree in petroleum geology and petroleum engineering in 1945.[342] He has since become active as a petroleum engineer throughout the world.[343] In 1960, after the death of his son, he and his wife made an 8-month hike from the United States-Mexican border to Panama over primitive jungle trails. By happenstance they were in Guatemala City at the time of the Bay of Pigs invasion.[344] A lengthy film and complete written log was prepared by De Mohrenschildt and a report of the trip was made to the U.S. Government.[345] Upon arriving in Panama they journeyed to Haiti where De Mohrenschildt eventually became involved in a Government-oriented business venture in which he has been engaged continuously since June 1963 until the time of this report.[346]

The members of the Dallas-Fort Worth Russian community and others have variously described De Mohrenschildt as eccentric, outspoken, and a strong believer in individual liberties and in the U.S. form of government, but also of the belief that some form of undemocratic government might be best for other peoples.[347] De Mohrenschildt frankly admits his provocative personality.[348]

Jeanne De Mohrenschildt was born in Harbin, China, of White Russian parents. She left during the war with Japan, coming to New York in 1938 where she became a successful ladies dress and sportswear apparel designer. She married her present husband in 1959.[349]

The Commission's investigation has developed no signs of subversive or disloyal conduct on the part of either of the De Mohrenschildts. Neither the FBI, CIA, nor any witness contacted by the

Commission has provided any information linking the De Mohren-schildts to subversive or extremist organizations.[350] Nor has there been any evidence linking them in any way with the assassination of President Kennedy.

The Commission has also considered closely the relations between the Oswalds and Michael and Ruth Paine of Irving, Tex. The Paines were not part of the Russian community which has been discussed above. Ruth Paine speaks Russian, however, and for this reason was invited to a party in February of 1963 at which she became acquainted with the Oswalds.[351] The host had met the Oswalds through the De Mohrenschildts.[352] Marina Oswald and Ruth Paine subsequently became quite friendly, and Mrs. Paine provided considerable assistance to the Oswalds.[353] Marina Oswald and her child resided with Ruth Paine for a little over 2 weeks while Oswald sought a job in New Orleans in late April and early May 1963.[354] In May, she transported Marina Oswald to New Orleans, paying all of the traveling and other expenses.[355] While the Oswalds were in New Orleans, the two women corresponded.[356] Mrs. Paine came to New Orleans in late September and took Marina Oswald and her child to her home in Irving.[357]

Since Oswald left for Mexico City promptly after Mrs. Paine and his family departed New Orleans,[358] the Commission has considered whether Ruth Paine's trip to New Orleans was undertaken to assist Oswald in this venture, but the evidence is clear that it was not. In her letters to Ruth Paine during the summer of 1963, Marina Oswald confided that she was having continuing difficulties with her husband, and Mrs. Paine urged Marina Oswald to live with her in Irving; the letters of the two women prior to Mrs. Paine's arrival in New Orleans on September 20, 1963, however, contain no mention that Oswald was planning a trip to Mexico City or elsewhere.[359] In New Orleans, Mrs. Paine was told by Oswald that he planned to seek employment in Houston, or perhaps Philadelphia. Though Marina Oswald knew this to be false, she testified that she joined in this deception.[360] At no time during the entire weekend was Mexico City mentioned.[361] Corroboration for this testimony is found in a letter Mrs. Paine wrote her mother shortly after she and Marina Oswald had returned to Irving on September 24, in which she stated that Marina Oswald was again living with her temporarily and that Oswald was job-hunting.[362] When Oswald arrived at the Paine home on October 4, he continued his deception by telling Mrs. Paine, in his wife's presence, that he had been unsuccessful in finding employment.[363] At Oswald's request, Marina Oswald remained silent.[364]

Marina Oswald lived with Ruth Paine through the birth of her second daughter on October 20, 1963, and until the assassination of President Kennedy.[365] During this period, Oswald obtained a room in Dallas and found employment in Dallas, but spent weekends with his family at the Paine home.[366] On November 1 and 5, Ruth Paine was interviewed by agents of the FBI who were investigating Oswald's activities since his return from the Soviet Union, as set forth in greater detail in chapter VIII. She did not then know Oswald's address in Dallas.[367] She was not asked for, nor did she volunteer, Oswald's telephone number in Dallas, which she did know.[368] She advised the Bureau agent to whom she spoke of Oswald's periodic weekend visits, and she informed him that Oswald was employed at the Texas School Book Depository Building.[369]

On November 10, Ruth Paine discovered a draft of Oswald's letter written the day before to the Soviet Embassy in Washington, in which he indicated that he had journeyed to Mexico City and conferred with a "comrade Kostine in the Embassy of the Soviet Union, Mexico City, Mexico." [370] (This letter is discussed later in this chapter.) Mr. and Mrs. Paine testified that although they initially assumed the letter was a figment of Oswald's imagination, the letter gave Mrs. Paine considerable misgivings.[371] She determined that if the FBI agents returned she would deliver to them the copy of a draft of the letter which, unknown to Oswald, she had made.[372] However, the agents did not return before the assassination.[373] On November 19, Mrs. Paine learned that Oswald was living in his Dallas rooming-house under an assumed name.[374] She did not report this to the FBI because, as she testified, she "had no occasion to see them, and * * * did not think it important enough to call them after that until the 23d of November." [375]

The Commission has thoroughly investigated the background of both Paines. Mrs. Paine was born Ruth Hyde in New York City on September 3, 1932. Her parents moved to Columbus, Ohio, in the late 1930's.[376] They were divorced in 1961.[377] Ruth Paine graduated from Antioch College in 1955.[378] While in high school she first became interested in Quaker activities; she and her brother became Quakers in 1951.[379] In 1952, following completion of her sophomore year at Antioch College, she was a delegate to two Friends conferences in England.[380]

At the time the Paines met in 1955, Mrs. Paine was active in the work of the Young Friends Committee of North America, which, with the cooperation of the Department of State, was making an effort to lessen the tensions between Soviet Russia and the United States by means of the stimulation of contacts and exchange of cultures between citizens of the two nations through "pen-pal" correspondence and exchanges of young Russians and Americans.[381] It was during this period that Mrs. Paine became interested in the Russian language.[382] Mrs. Paine participated in a Russian-American student exchange program sponsored by the Young Friends Committee of North America, and has participated in the "pen-pal" phase of the activities of the Young Friends Committee.[383] She has corresponded until recently with a schoolteacher in Russia.[384] Although her active interest in the Friends' program for the lessening of East-West tensions ceased upon her marriage in December 1957, she has continued to hold to the tenets of the Quaker faith.[385]

Michael Paine is the son of George Lyman Paine and Ruth Forbes Paine, now Ruth Forbes Young, wife of Arthur Young of Philadelphia, Pa.[386] His parents were divorced when he was 4 years of age. His father, George Lyman Paine, is an architect and resides in California.[387] Michael Paine testified that during his late grammar and early high school days his father participated actively in the Trotskyite faction of the Communist movement in the United States and that he attended some of those meetings.[388] He stated that his father, with whom he has had little contact throughout most of his life, has not influenced his political thinking. He said that he has visited his father four or five times in California since 1959, but their discussions did not include the subject of communism.[389] Since moving to Irving, Tex., in 1959, he has been a research engineer for Bell Helicopter Co. in Fort Worth.[390] Mr. Paine has security clearance for his work.[391] He has been a long-time member of the American Civil Liberties Union.[392] Though not in sympathy with rightist political aims, he has attended a few meetings of far-right organizations in Dallas for the purpose, he testified, of learning something about those organizations and because he "was interested in seeing more communication between the right and the left." [393]

The Commission has conducted a thorough investigation of the Paines' finances and is satisfied that their income has been from legitimate and traceable sources, and that their expenditures were consistent with their income and for normal purposes. Although in the course of their relationship with the Oswalds, the Paines assumed expenses for such matters as food and transportation, with a value of approximately $500, they made no direct payments to, and received no moneys or valuables from, the Oswalds.[394]

Although prior to November 22, Mrs. Paine had information relating to Oswald's use of an alias in Dallas, his telephone number, and his correspondence with the Soviet Embassy, which she did not pass on to the FBI,[395] her failure to have come forward with this information must be viewed within the context of the information available to her at that time. There is no evidence to contradict her testimony that she did not then know about Oswald's attack on General Walker, the presence of the rifle on the floor of her garage, Oswald's ownership of a pistol, or the photographs of Oswald displaying the firearms.[396] She thus assumed that Oswald, though a difficult and disturbing personality, was not potentially violent, and that the FBI was cognizant of his past history and current activities.[397]

Moreover, it is from Mrs. Paine herself that the Commission has learned that she possessed the information which she did have. Mrs. Paine was forthright with the agent of the FBI with whom she spoke in early November 1963, providing him with sufficient information to have located Oswald at his job if he had deemed it necessary to do so,[398] and her failure to have taken immediate steps to notify the Bureau of the additional information does not under the circumstances appear unusual. Throughout the Commission's investigation, Ruth Paine has been completely cooperative, voluntarily producing all correspondence, memoranda, and other written communications in her possession that had passed between her and Marina Oswald both before and after November 22, 1963.[399]   The Commission has had the benefit of Mrs. Paine's 1963 date book and calendar and her address book and telephone notation book, in both of which appear many entries relating to her activities with the Oswalds.[400]   Other material of a purely personal nature was also voluntarily made available.[401]   The Commission has found nothing in the Paines' background, activities, or finances which suggests disloyalty to the United States,[402] and it has concluded that Ruth and Michael Paine were not involved in any way with the assassination of President Kennedy.

A fuller narrative of the social contacts between the Oswalds and the various persons of the Dallas-Fort Worth community is incorporated in chapter VII and appendix XIII, and the testimony of all members of the group who testified before the Commission is included in the printed record which accompanies the report.   The evidence establishes that the Oswalds' contacts with these people were originated and maintained under normal and understandable circumstances.   The files maintained by the FBI contain no information indicating that any of the persons in the Dallas-Fort Worth community with whom Oswald associated were affiliated with any Communist, Fascist, or other subversive organization.[403]   During the course of this investigation, the Commission has found nothing which suggests the involvement of any member of the Russian-speaking community in Oswald's preparations to assassinate President Kennedy.

Political Activities Upon Return to the United States

Upon his return from the Soviet Union, Oswald had dealings with the Communist Party, U.S.A., the Socialist Workers Party, and the Fair Play for Cuba Committee, and he also had minor contacts with at least two other organizations with political interests.   For the purpose of determining whether Oswald received any advice, encouragement, or assistance from these organizations in planning or executing the assassination of President Kennedy, the Commission has conducted a full investigation of the nature and extent of Oswald's relations with them.   The Commission has also conducted an investigation to determine whether certain persons and organizations expressing hostility to President Kennedy prior to the assassination had any connection with Lee Harvey Oswald or with the shooting of the President.

Communist Party, U.S.A.; Socialist Workers Party.—In August of 1962, Oswald subscribed to the Worker, a publication of the Communist Party, U.S.A.[404]   He also wrote the Communist Party to obtain pamphlets and other literature which, the evidence indicates, were sent to him as a matter of course.[405]

Oswald also attempted to initiate other dealings with the Communist Party, U.S.A., but the organization was not especially responsive. From New Orleans, he informed the party of his activities in connection with the Fair Play for Cuba Committee, discussed below, submitting membership cards in his fictitious chapter to several party officials.[406] In a letter from Arnold S. Johnson, director of the information and lecture bureau of the party, Oswald was informed that although the Communist Party had no "organizational ties" with the committee, the party issued much literature which was "important for anybody who is concerned about developments in Cuba." [407] In September 1963 Oswald inquired how he might contact the party when he relocated in the Baltimore-Washington area, as he said he planned to do in October, and Johnson suggested in a letter of September 19 that he "get in touch with us here [New York] and we will find some way of getting in touch with you in that city [Baltimore]." [408] However, Oswald had also written asking whether, "handicapped as it were, by * * * [his] past record," he could "still * * * compete with antiprogressive forces, above ground or whether in your opinion * * * [he] should always remain in the background, i.e., underground," and in the September 19 letter received the reply that "often it is advisable for some people to remain in the background, not underground." [409]

In a letter postmarked November 1, Oswald informed the party that he had moved to Dallas, and reported his attendance at a meeting at which General Walker had spoken, and at a meeting of the American Civil Liberties Union; he asked Johnson for the party's "general view" of the latter organization and "to what degree, if any, [he] should attempt to highten its progressive tendencies." According to Johnson, this letter was not received by the Communist Party until after the assassination.[410] At different times, Oswald also wrote the Worker and the Hall-Davis Defense Committee, enclosing samples of his photographic work and offering to assist in preparing posters; he was told that "his kind offer [was] most welcomed and from time to time we shall call on you," but he was never asked for assistance.[411] The correspondence between Oswald and the Communist Party, and with all other organizations, is printed in the record accompanying this report.

When Oswald applied for a visa to enter Cuba during his trip to Mexico City, discussed below,[412] Senora Silvia Duran, the Cuban consular employee who dealt with Oswald, wrote on the application that Oswald said he was a member of the Communist Party and that he had "displayed documents in proof of his membership." [413] When Oswald went to Mexico, he is believed to have carried his letters from the Soviet Embassy in Washington and from the Communist Party in the United States, his 1959 passport, which contained stamps showing that he had lived in Russia for 2½ years, his Russian work permit, his Russian marriage certificate, membership cards and newspaper clippings purporting to show his role in the Fair Play for Cuba Committee, and a prepared statement of his qualifications as a "Marxist." [414] Because of the mass of papers Oswald did present showing his affinity for communism, some in the Russian language, which was foreign to Senora Duran, and because further investigation, discussed below, indicated that Oswald was not a member of the party, Senora Duran's notation was probably inaccurate.

Upon his arrest after the assassination, Oswald attempted to contact John J. Abt, a New York attorney, to request Abt to represent him. Abt was not in New York at the time, and he was never reached in connection with representing Oswald. Abt has testified that he at no time had any dealings with Oswald and that prior to the assassination he had never heard of Lee Harvey Oswald.[415]

After his return from the Soviet Union, Oswald also carried on a limited correspondence with the Socialist Workers Party. In October of 1962 he attempted to join the party, but his application was not accepted since there was then no chapter in the Dallas area.[416] Oswald also wrote the Socialist Workers Party offering his assistance in preparing posters. From this organization too he received the response that he might be called upon if needed. He was asked for further information about his photographic skills, which he does not appear to have ever provided.[417] Oswald did obtain literature from the Socialist Workers Party, however, and in December 1962 he entered a subscription to the affiliated publication, the Militant.[418] Apparently in March of 1963 Oswald wrote the party of his activities and submitted a clipping with his letter. In response, he was told that his name was being sent to the Young Socialist Alliance for further correspondence, but the files of the alliance apparently contain no reference to Oswald. Neither the letter nor the clipping which Oswald sent has been located.[419]

Investigation by the Commission has produced no plausible evidence that Lee Harvey Oswald had any other significant contacts with the Communist Party, U.S.A., the Socialist Workers Party, or with any other extreme leftist political organization. The FBI and other Federal security agencies have made a study of their records and files and contacted numerous confidential informants of the agencies and have produced no such evidence.[420] The Commission has questioned persons who, as a group, knew Oswald during virtually every phase of his adult life, and from none of these came any indication that Oswald maintained a surreptitious relationship with any organization. Arnold S. Johnson, of the American Communist Party; James T. Tormey, executive secretary of the Hall-Davis Defense Committee; and Farrell Dobbs, secretary of the Socialist Workers Party, voluntarily appeared before the Commission and testified under oath that Oswald was not a member of these organizations and that a thorough search of their files had disclosed no records relating to Oswald other than those which they produced for the Commission.[421] The material that has been disclosed is in all cases consistent with other data in the possession of the Commission.

Socialist Labor Party.—Oswald also wrote to the Socialist Labor Party in New York in November 1962 requesting literature. Horace Twiford, a national committeeman at large for the party in the State of Texas, was informed by the New York headquarters in July 1963 of Oswald's request, and on September 11, 1963, he did mail literature to Oswald at his old post office box in Dallas.[422] On his way to Mexico City in September 1963, Oswald attempted to contact Twiford at his home in Houston; Oswald spoke briefly with Twiford's wife, identifying himself as a member of the Fair Play for Cuba Committee, but since Twiford was out of town at the time, Oswald was unable to speak with him.[423] Arnold Peterson, national secretary and treasurer of the Socialist Labor Party, has stated that a search of the records of the national headquarters reveals no record pertaining to Oswald; he explained that letters requesting literature are routinely destroyed.[424] The Socialist Party-Social Democratic Federation has also advised that a review of its records fails to reflect any information or correspondence pertaining to Oswald.[425]

Fair Play for Cuba Committee.—During the period Oswald was in New Orleans, from the end of April to late September 1963, he was engaged in activity purportedly on behalf of the now defunct Fair Play for Cuba Committee (FPCC), an organization centered in New York which was highly critical of U.S. policy toward the Cuban Government under Fidel Castro. In May 1963, after having obtained literature from the FPCC,[426] Oswald applied for and was granted membership in the organization.[427] When applying for membership, Oswald wrote national headquarters that he had

> * * * been thinking about renting a small office at my own expense for the purpose of forming a F.P.C.C. branch here in New Orleans.
> Could you give me a charter? [428]

With his membership card, Oswald apparently received a copy of the constitution and bylaws for FPCC chapters, and a letter, dated May 29, which read in part as follows (with spelling as in original):

> It would be hard to concieve of a chapter with as few members as seem to exist in the New Orleans area. I have just gone through our files and find that Louisiana seams somewhat restricted for Fair Play activities. However, with what is there perhaps you could build a larger group if a few people would undertake the disciplined responsibility of concrete organizational work.
> We certainly are not at all adverse to a very small Chapter but certainly would expect that there would be at least twice the amount needed to conduct a legal executive board for the Chapter. Should this be reasonable we could readily issue a charter for a New Orleans Chapter of FPCC. In fact, we would be very, very pleased to see this take place and would like to do everything possible to assist in bringing it about.
>
> *   *   *   *   *   *   *

You must realize that you will come under tremendous pressures with any attempt to do FPCC work in that area and that you will not be able to operate in the manner which is conventional here in the north-east. Even most of our big city Chapters have been forced to Abandon the idea of operating an office in public. * * * Most Chapters have discovered that it is easier to operate semi-privately out of a home and maintain a P.O. Box for all mailings and public notices. (A P.O. Box is a must for any Chapter in the organization to guarnatee the continued contact with the national even if an individual should move or drop out.) We do have a serious and often violent opposition and this proceedure helps prevent many unnecessary incidents which frighten away prospective supporters. I definitely would not recommend an office, at least not one that will be easily identifyable to the lunatic fringe in your community. Certainly, I would not recommend that you engage in one at the very beginning but wait and see how you can operate in the community through several public experiences.[429]

Thereafter Oswald informed national headquarters that he had opened post office box No. 30061, and that against its advice he had decided "to take an office from the very beginning"; he also submitted copies of a membership application form and a circular headed "Hands Off Cuba!" which he had had printed, and informed the headquarters that he intended to have membership cards for his chapter printed, which he subsequently did.[430] He wrote three further letters to the New York office to inform it of his continued activities.[431] In one he reported that he had been evicted from the office he claimed to have opened, so that he "worked out of a post office box and by useing street demonstrations and some circular work * * * sustained a great deal of interest but no new members."[432]

Oswald did distribute the handbills he had printed on at least three occasions.[433] Once, while doing so, he was arrested and fined for being involved in a disturbance with anti-Castro Cuban refugees,[434] one of whom he had previously met by presenting himself as hostile to Premier Castro in an apparent effort to gain information about anti-Castro organizations operating in New Orleans.[435] When arrested, he informed the police that his chapter had 35 members.[436] His activities received some attention in the New Orleans press, and he twice appeared on a local radio program representing himself as a spokesman for the Fair Play for Cuba Committee.[437] After his return to Dallas, he listed the FPCC as an organization authorized to receive mail at his post office box.[438]

Despite these activities, the FPCC chapter which Oswald purportedly formed in New Orleans was entirely fictitious. Vincent T. Lee, formerly national director of the Fair Play for Cuba Committee, has testified that the New York office did not authorize the creation of a New Orleans chapter, nor did it provide Oswald with funds to support his activities there.[439] The national office did not write

Oswald again after its letter of May 29. As discussed more fully in chapter VII, Oswald's later letters to the national office purporting to inform it of his progress in New Orleans contained numerous exaggerations about the scope of his activities and the public reaction to them.[440] There is no evidence that Oswald ever opened an office as he claimed to have done. Although a pamphlet taken from him at the time of his arrest in New Orleans contains the rubber stamp imprint "FPCC, 544 CAMP ST., NEW ORLEANS, LA.," investigation has indicated that neither the Fair Play for Cuba Committee nor Lee Harvey Oswald ever maintained an office at that address.[441] The handbills and other materials bearing the name of the Fair Play for Cuba Committee were printed commercially by Oswald without the approval of the national headquarters.[442] Oswald's membership card in the "New Orleans chapter" of the committee carried the signature of "A. J. Hidell," purportedly the president of the chapter, but there is no evidence that an "A. J. Hidell" existed and, as pointed out in chapter IV, there is conclusive evidence that the name was an alias which Oswald used on various occasions. Marina Oswald herself wrote the name "Hidell" on the membership card at her husband's insistence.[443]

No other member of the so-called New Orleans chapter of the committee has ever been found. The only occasion on which anyone other than Oswald was observed taking part in these activities was on August 9, 1963, when Oswald and two young men passed out leaflets urging "Hands Off Cuba!" on the streets of New Orleans. One of the two men, who was 16 years old at the time, has testified that Oswald approached him at the Louisiana State Employment Commission and offered him $2 for about an hour's work. He accepted the offer but later, when he noticed that television cameras were being focused on him, he obtained his money and left. He testified that he had never seen Oswald before and never saw him again. The second individual has never been located; but according to the testimony of the youth who was found, he too seemed to be someone not previously connected with Oswald.[444] Finally, the FBI has advised the Commission that its information on undercover Cuban activities in the New Orleans area reveals no knowledge of Oswald before the assassination.[445]

Right-wing groups hostile to President Kennedy.—The Commission also considered the possibility that there may have been a link between Oswald and certain groups which had bitterly denounced President Kennedy and his policies prior to the time of the President's trip to Dallas. As discussed in chapter II, two provocative incidents took place concurrently with President Kennedy's visit and a third but a month prior thereto. The incidents were (1) the demonstration against the Honorable Adlai E. Stevenson, U.S. Ambassador to the United Nations, in late October 1963, when he came to Dallas on United Nations Day; (2) the publication in the Dallas Morning News on November 22 of the full page, black-bordered paid advertisement entitled, "Welcome Mr. Kennedy"; and (3) the distribution of a throwaway handbill entitled "Wanted for Treason" throughout Dallas on November 20 and 21. Oswald was aware of the Stevenson incident; there is no evidence that he became aware of either the "Welcome Mr. Kennedy" advertisement or the "Wanted for Treason" handbill, though neither possibility can be precluded.

The only evidence of interest on Oswald's part in rightist groups in Dallas was his alleged attendance at a rally at the Dallas Auditorium the evening preceding Ambassador Stevenson's address on United Nations Day, October 24, 1963. On the evening of October 25, 1963, at the invitation of Michael Paine, Oswald attended a monthly meeting of the Dallas chapter of the American Civil Liberties Union in which he was later to seek membership.[446] During the course of the discussion at this meeting, a speaker mentioned Maj. Gen. Edwin A. Walker (Resigned, U.S. Army). Oswald arose in the midst of the meeting to remark that a "night or two nights before" he had attended a meeting at which General Walker had spoken in terms that led Oswald to assert that General Walker was both anti-Catholic and anti-Semitic.[447] General Walker testified that he had been the speaker at a rally the night before Ambassador Stevenson's appearance, but that he did not know and had never heard of Oswald prior to the announcement of his name on radio and television on the afternoon of November 22.[448] Oswald confirmed his attendance at the U.S. Day rally in an undated letter he wrote to Arnold Johnson, director of the information and lecture bureau of the Communist Party, mailed November 1, 1963, in which he reported:

> On October 23rd, I had attended a ultra-right meeting headed by General Edwin a. Walker, who lives in Dallas.
> This meeting preceded by one day the attack on a. e. Stevenson at the United Nations Day meeting at which he spoke.
> As you can see, political friction between 'left' and 'right' is very great here.[449]

In the light of Oswald's attack upon General Walker on the evening of April 10, 1963, discussed in chapter IV,[450] as well as Oswald's known political views,[451] his asserted attendance at the political rally at which General Walker spoke may have been induced by many possible motives. However, there is no evidence that Oswald attended any other rightist meetings or was associated with any politically conservative organizations.

While the black-bordered "Welcome Mr. Kennedy" advertisement in the November 22 Dallas Morning News, which addressed a series of critical questions to the President, probably did not come to Oswald's attention, it was of interest to the Commission because of its appearance on the day of the assassination and because of an allegation made before the Commission concerning the person whose name appeared as the chairman of the committee sponsoring the advertisement. The black-bordered advertisement was purported to be sponsored by "The American Fact-Finding Committee," which was described as "An unaffiliated and nonpartisan group of citizens who wish truth." Bernard Weissman was listed as "Chairman" and a

WELCOME MR. KENNEDY

TO DALLAS...

...A CITY so disgraced by a recent Liberal smear attempt that its citizens here just elected two more Conservative Americans to public office.

...A CITY that is an economic "boom town," not because of Federal handouts, but through conservative economic and business practices.

...A CITY that will continue to grow and prosper despite efforts by you and your administration to penalize it for its non-conformity to "New Frontierism."

...A CITY that rejected your philosophy and policies in 1960 and will do so again in 1964—even more emphatically than before.

MR. KENNEDY, despite contentions on the part of your administration, the State Department, the Mayor of Dallas, the Dallas City Council, and members of your party, we free-thinking and America-thinking citizens of Dallas still have, through a Constitution largely ignored by you, the right to address our grievances, to question you, to disagree with you, and to criticize you.

In asserting this constitutional right, we wish to ask you publicly the following questions—indeed, questions of paramount importance and interest to all free peoples everywhere—which we trust you will answer ... in public, without sophistry. These questions are:

WHY is Latin America turning either anti-American or Communistic, or both, despite increased U. S. foreign aid, State Department policy, and your own Ivy-Tower pronouncements?

WHY do you say we have built a "wall of freedom" around Cuba when there is no freedom in Cuba today? Because of your policy, thousands of Cubans have been imprisoned, are starving and being persecuted—with thousands already murdered and thousands more awaiting execution and, in addition, the entire population of almost 7,000,000 Cubans are living in slavery.

WHY have you approved the sale of wheat and corn to our enemies when you know the Communist soldiers "travel on their stomachs" just as ours do? Communist soldiers are daily wounding and/or killing American soldiers in South Viet Nam.

WHY did you host, salute and entertain Tito — Moscow's Trojan Horse — just a short time after our sworn enemy, Khrushchev, embraced the Yugoslav dictator as a great hero and leader of Communism?

WHY have you urged greater aid, comfort, recognition, and understanding for Yugoslavia, Poland, Hungary, and other Communist countries, while turning your back on the pleas of Hungarian, East German, Cuban and other anti-Communist freedom fighters?

WHY did Cambodia kick the U.S. out of its country after we poured nearly 400 Million Dollars of aid into its ultra-leftist government?

WHY has Gus Hall, head of the U.S. Communist Party praised almost every one of your policies and announced that the party will endorse and support your re-election in 1964?

WHY have you banned the showing at U.S. military bases of the film "Operation Abolition"—the movie by the House Committee on Un-American Activities exposing Communism in America?

WHY have you ordered or permitted your brother Bobby, the Attorney General, to go soft on Communists, fellow-travelers, and ultra-leftists in America, while permitting him to persecute loyal Americans who criticize you, your administration, and your leadership?

WHY are you in favor of the U.S. continuing to give economic aid to Argentina, in spite of that fact that Argentina has just seized almost 400 Million Dollars of American private property?

WHY has the Foreign Policy of the United States degenerated to the point that the C.I.A. is arranging coups and having staunch Anti-Communist Allies of the U.S. bloodily exterminated.

WHY have you scrapped the Monroe Doctrine in favor of the "Spirit of Moscow"?

MR. KENNEDY, as citizens of these United States of America, we DEMAND answers to these questions, and we want them NOW.

THE AMERICAN FACT-FINDING COMMITTEE

"An unaffiliated and non-partisan group of citizens who wish truth"

BERNARD WEISSMAN,
Chairman

Commission Exhibit No. 1031

P.O. Box 1792 — Dallas 21, Texas

COMMISSION EXHIBIT No. 1031

post office box in Dallas was the only address. (See Commission Exhibit No. 1031, p. 294.)

The Commission has conducted a full investigation into the genesis of this advertisement and the background of those responsible for it. Three of the four men chiefly responsible, Bernard W. Weissman, William B. Burley III, and Larrie H. Schmidt, had served together in the U.S. Army in Munich, Germany, in 1962. During that time they had with others devised plans to develop two conservative organizations, one political and the other business. The political entity was to be named Conservatism—USA, or CUSA, and the business entity was to be named American Business, or AMBUS.[452] While in Munich, according to Weissman, they attempted to develop in their "own minds * * * ways to build up various businesses that would support us and at the same time support our political activities."[453] According to a subsequent letter from Schmidt to Weissman, "Cusa was founded for patriotic reasons rather than for personal gain—even though, as a side effect, Ambus was to have brought great return, as any business endeavor should."[454] To establish their organizations, Weissman testified that they:

> * * * had planned while in Munich that in order to accomplish our goals, to try to do it from scratch would be almost impossible, because it would be years before we could even get the funds to develop a powerful organization. So we had planned to infiltrate various rightwing organizations and by our own efforts become involved in the hierarchy of these various organizations and eventually get ourselves elected or appointed to various higher offices in these organizations, and by doing this bring in some of our own people, and eventually take over the leadership of these organizations, and at that time having our people in these various organizations, we would then, you might say, call a conference and have them unite, and while no one knew of the existence of CUSA aside from us, we would then bring them all together, unite them, and arrange to have it called CUSA.[455]

Schmidt was the first to leave the service; settling in Dallas in October 1962, he became a life insurance salesman and quickly engaged in numerous political activities in pursuit of the objectives devised in Munich.[456] He became affiliated with several organizations and prepared various political writings.[457]

Upon their release from the military, Weissman and Burley did not immediately move to Dallas, though repeatedly urged to do so by Schmidt.[458] On October 1, 1963, Schmidt wrote Weissman: "Adlai Stevenson is scheduled here on the 24th on UN Day. Kennedy is scheduled in Dallas on Nov. 24th. There are to be protests. All the big things are happening *now*—if we don't get in right now we may as well forget it."[459] The day of the Stevenson demonstration, Schmidt telephoned Weissman, again urging him to move to Dallas. Recalling that conversation with Schmidt, Weissman testified:

And he said, "If we are going to take advantage of the situation * * * you better hurry down here and take advantage of the publicity, and at least become known among these various right-wingers, because this is the chance we have been looking for to infiltrate some of these organizations and become known," in other words, go along with the philosophy we had developed in Munich.[460]

Five days later he wrote to Weissman and Burley to report that as the "only organizer of the demonstration to have publicly identified himself," he had "become, overnight, a 'fearless spokesman' and 'leader' of the rightwing in Dallas. What I worked so hard for in one year—and nearly failed—finally came through one incident in one night!" He ended, "Politically, CUSA is set. It is now up to you to get Ambus going." [461]

Weissman and Burley accepted Schmidt's prompting and traveled to Dallas, arriving on November 4, 1963.[462] Both obtained employment as carpet salesmen. At Schmidt's solicitation they took steps to join the John Birch Society, and through Schmidt they met the fourth person involved in placing the November 22 advertisement, Joseph P. Grinnan, Dallas independent oil operator and a John Birch Society coordinator in the Dallas area.[463]

Within a week to 10 days after Weissman and Burley had arrived in Dallas, the four men began to consider plans regarding President Kennedy's planned visit to Dallas.[464] Weissman explained the reason for which it was decided that the ad should be placed:

> * * * after the Stevenson incident, it was felt that a demonstration would be entirely out of order, because we didn't want anything to happen in the way of physical violence to President Kennedy when he came to Dallas. But we thought that the conservatives in Dallas—I was told—were a pretty downtrodden lot after that, because they were being oppressed by the local liberals, because of the Stevenson incident. We felt we had to do something to build up the morale of the conservative element, in Dallas. So we hit upon the idea of the ad.[465]

Weissman, Schmidt, and Grinnan worked on the text for the advertisement.[466] A pamphlet containing 50 questions critical of American policy was employed for this purpose, and was the source of the militant questions contained in the ad attacking President Kennedy's administration.[467] Grinnan undertook to raise the $1,465 needed to pay for the ad.[468] He employed a typed draft of the advertisement to support his funds solicitation.[469] Grinnan raised the needed money from three wealthy Dallas businessmen: Edgar R. Crissey, Nelson Bunker Hunt, and H. R. Bright, some of whom in turn collected contributions from others.[470] At least one of the contributors would not make a contribution unless a question he suggested was inserted.[471] Weissman, believing that Schmidt, Grinnan, and the contributors were active members of the John Birch Society, and that Grinnan eventually took charge of the project, expressed the opinion that the advertisement was the creation of the John Birch Society,[472] though Schmidt and Grinnan have maintained that they were acting "solely as individuals." [473]

A fictitious sponsoring organization was invented out of whole cloth.[474] The name chosen for the supposed organization was The American Fact-Finding Committee.[475] This was "Solely a name," Weissman testified; "* * * As a matter of fact, when I went to place the ad, I could not remember the name * * * I had to refer to a piece of paper for the name." [476] Weissman's own name was used on the ad in part to counter charges of anti-Semitism which had been leveled against conservative groups in Dallas.[477] Weissman conceived the idea of using a black border,[478] and testified he intended it to serve the function of stimulating reader attention.[479] Before accepting the advertisement, the Dallas Morning News apparently submitted it to its attorneys for their opinion as to whether its publication might subject them to liability.[480]

Weissman testified that the advertisement drew 50 or 60 mailed responses.[481] He took them from the post office box early on Sunday morning, November 24.[482] He said that those postmarked before the attack on President Kennedy were "favorable" in tone; [483] those of later postmark were violently unfavorable, nasty, and threatening; [484] and, according to a report from Schmidt, those postmarked some weeks later were again of favorable tone.[485]

The four promoters of the ad deny that they had any knowledge of or familiarity with Lee Harvey Oswald prior to November 22, or Jack Ruby prior to November 24.[486] Each has provided a statement of his role in connection with the placement of the November 22 advertisement and other matters, and investigation has revealed no deception. The Commission has found no evidence that any of these persons was connected with Oswald or Ruby, or was linked to a conspiracy to assassinate President Kennedy.

The advertisement, however, did give rise to one allegation concerning Bernard Weissman which required additional investigation. On March 4, 1964, Mark Lane, a New York attorney, testified before the Commission that an undisclosed informant had told him that Weissman had met with Jack Ruby and Patrolman J. D. Tippit at Ruby's Carousel Club on November 14, 1963. Lane declined to state the name of his informant but said that he would attempt to obtain his informant's permission to reveal his name.[487] On July 2, 1964, after repeated requests by the Commission that he disclose the name of his informant, Lane testified a second time concerning this matter, but declined to reveal the information, stating as his reason that he had promised the individual that his name would not be revealed without his permission.[488] Lane also made this allegation during a radio appearance, whereupon Weissman twice demanded that Lane reveal the name of the informant.[489] As of the date of this report Lane has failed to reveal the name of his informant and has offered no evidence to support his allegation. The Commission has investigated the allegation of a Weissman-Ruby-Tippit meeting and has found no evidence that such a meeting took place anywhere at any time. The investigation into this matter is discussed in a later section of this chapter dealing with possible conspiracies involving Jack Ruby.

A comparable incident was the appearance of the "Wanted for Treason" handbill on the streets of Dallas 1 to 2 days before President Kennedy's arrival. These handbills bore a reproduction of a front and profile photograph of the President and set forth a series of inflammatory charges against him.[490] Efforts to locate the author and the lithography printer of the handbill at first met with evasive responses [491] and refusals to furnish information.[492] Robert A. Surrey was eventually identified as the author of the handbill.[493] Surrey, a 38-year-old printing salesman employed by Johnson Printing Co. of Dallas, Tex., has been closely associated with General Walker for several years in his political and business activities.[494] He is president of American Eagle Publishing Co. of Dallas, in which he is a partner with General Walker.[495] Its office and address is the post office box of Johnson Printing Co. Its assets consist of cash and various printed materials composed chiefly of General Walker's political and promotional literature,[496] all of which is stored at General Walker's headquarters.[497]

Surrey prepared the text for the handbill and apparently used Johnson Printing Co. facilities to set the type and print a proof.[498] Surrey induced Klause, a salesman employed by Lettercraft Printing Co. of Dallas,[499] whom Surrey had met when both were employed at Johnson Printing Co.,[500] to print the handbill "on the side." [501] According to Klause, Surrey contacted him initially approximately 2 or 2½ weeks prior to November 22.[502] About a week prior to November 22, Surrey delivered to Klause two slick paper magazine prints of photographs of a front view and profile of President Kennedy,[503] together with the textual page proof.[504] Klause was unable to make the photographic negative of the prints needed to prepare the photographic printing plate,[505] so that he had this feature of the job done at a local shop.[506] Klause then arranged the halftone front and profile representations of President Kennedy at the top of the textual material he had received from Surrey so as to simulate a "man wanted" police placard. He then made a photographic printing plate of the picture.[507] During the night, he and his wife surreptitiously printed approximately 5,000 copies on Lettercraft Printing Co. offset printing equipment without the knowledge of his employers.[508] The next day he arranged with Surrey a meeting place, and delivered the handbills.[509] Klause's charge for the printing of the handbills was, including expenses, $60.[510]

At the outset of the investigation Klause stated to Federal agents that he did not know the name of his customer, whom he incorrectly described; [511] he did say, however, that the customer did not resemble either Oswald or Ruby.[512] Shortly before he appeared before the

Commission, Klause disclosed Surrey's identity.[513]   He explained that no record of the transaction had been made because "he saw a chance to make a few dollars on the side." [514]

Klause's testimony receives some corroboration from Bernard Weissman's testimony that he saw a copy of one of the "Wanted for Treason" handbills on the floor of General Walker's station wagon shortly after November 22.[515]   Other details of the manner in which the handbills were printed have also been verified.[516]   Moreover, Weissman testified that neither he nor any of his associates had anything to do with the handbill or were acquainted with Surrey, Klause, Lettercraft Printing Co., or Johnson Printing Co.[517]   Klause and Surrey, as well as General Walker, testified that they were unacquainted with Lee Harvey Oswald and had not heard of him prior to the afternoon of November 22.[518]   The Commission has found no evidence of any connection between those responsible for the handbill and Lee Harvey Oswald or the assassination.

Contacts With the Cuban and Soviet Embassies in Mexico City and the Soviet Embassy in Washington, D.C.

Eight weeks before the assassination, Oswald traveled to Mexico City where he visited both the Cuban and Soviet Embassies.*   Oswald's wife knew of this trip before he went,[519] but she denied such knowledge until she testified before the Commission.[520]   The Commission undertook an intensive investigation to determine Oswald's purpose and activities on this journey, with specific reference to reports that Oswald was an agent of the Cuban or Soviet Governments. As a result of its investigation, the Commission believes that it has been able to reconstruct and explain most of Oswald's actions during this time.   A detailed chronological account of this trip appears in appendix XIII.

Trip to Mexico.—Oswald was in Mexico from September 26, 1963, until October 3, 1963.[521]   (See Commission Exhibits Nos. 2478, 2481, p. 300.)   Marina Oswald testified that Oswald had told her that the purpose of the trip was to evade the American prohibition on travel to Cuba and to reach that country.[522]   He cautioned her that the trip and its purpose were to be kept strictly secret.[523]   She testified that he had earlier laid plans to reach Cuba by hijacking an airliner flying out of New Orleans, but she refused to cooperate and urged him to give it up, which he finally did.[524]   Witnesses who spoke with Oswald while he was on a bus going to Mexico City also testified that Oswald told them he intended to reach Cuba by way of Mexico, and that he hoped to meet Fidel Castro after he arrived.[525]   When Oswald spoke to the Cuban and Soviet consular officials in Mexico City, he represented that he intended to travel to the Soviet Union and requested

---

*The Soviet Embassy in Mexico City includes consular as well as diplomatic personnel in a single building.   The Cuban Embassy and Cuban Consulate in Mexico City, though in separate buildings, are in the same compound.   Both the Soviet and the Cuban establishments will be referred to throughout the report simply as Embassies.

OSWALD'S MEXICAN TOURIST CARD AND APPLICATION

APPLICATION FOR TOURIST CARD

(COMMISSION EXHIBIT 2481)

TOURIST CARD

(COMMISSION EXHIBIT 2478)

an "in-transit" Cuban visa to permit him to enter Cuba on September 30 on the way to the Soviet Union. Marina Oswald has testified that these statements were deceptions designed to get him to Cuba.[526] Thus, although it is possible that Oswald intended to continue on to Russia from Cuba, the evidence makes it more likely that he intended to remain in Cuba.[527]

Oswald departed from New Orleans probably about noon on September 25 and arrived in Mexico City at about 10 a.m. on September 27.[528] In Mexico City he embarked on a series of visits to the Soviet and Cuban Embassies, which occupied most of his time during the first 2 days of his visit. At the Cuban Embassy, he requested an "in-transit" visa to permit him to visit Cuba on his way to the Soviet Union.[529] Oswald was informed that he could not obtain a visa for entry into Cuba unless he first obtained a visa to enter the U.S.S.R.,[530] and the Soviet Embassy told him that he could not expect an answer on his application for a visa for the Soviet Union for about 4 months.[531] Oswald carried with him newspaper clippings, letters and various documents, some of them forged or containing false information, purporting to show that he was a "friend" of Cuba.[532] With these papers and his record of previous residence in the Soviet Union and marriage to a Soviet national, he tried to curry favor with both Embassies.[533] Indeed, his wife testified that in her opinion Oswald's primary purpose in having engaged in Fair Play for Cuba Committee activities was to create a public record that he was a "friend" of Cuba.[534] He made himself especially unpopular at the Cuban Embassy by persisting in his demands that as a sympathizer in Cuban objectives he ought to be given a visa. This resulted in a sharp argument with the consul, Eusebio Azque.[535]

By Saturday, September 28, 1963, Oswald had failed to obtain visas at both Embassies.[536] From Sunday, September 29, through Wednesday morning, October 2, when he left Mexico City on a bus bound for the United States, Oswald spent considerable time making his travel arrangements, sightseeing and checking again with the Soviet Embassy to learn whether anything had happened on his visa application.[537] Marina Oswald testified that when she first saw him after his return to the United States he was disappointed and discouraged at his failure to reach Cuba.[538]

The general outlines of Oswald's activities in Mexico, particularly the nature and extent of his contacts at the Cuban Embassy, were learned very early in the investigation. An important source of information relating to his business at the Cuban Embassy was Senora Silvia Tirado de Duran, a Mexican national employed in the visa section of the Cuban Embassy, who was questioned intensively by Mexican authorities soon after the assassination.[539] An excerpt from the report of the Mexican Government summarized the crucial portion of Senora Duran's recollection of Oswald. In translation it reads as follows:

* * * she remembered * * * [that Lee Harvey Oswald] was the name of an American who had come to the Cuban Consulate to

obtain a visa to travel to Cuba in transit to Russia, the latter part of September or the early part of October of this year, and in support of his application had shown his passport, in which it was noted that he had lived in that country for a period of three years; his labor card from the same country written in the Russian language; and letters in that same language. He had presented evidence that he was married to a Russian woman, and also that he was apparently the leader of an organization in the city of New Orleans called "Fair * * * [Play] for Cuba," claiming that he should be accepted as a "friend" of the Cuban Revolution. Accordingly, the declarant, complying with her duties, took down all of the information and completed the appropriate application form; and the declarant, admittedly exceeding her responsibilities, informally telephoned the Russian consulate, with the intention of doing what she could to facilitate issuance of the Russian visa to Lee Harvey Oswald. However, they told her that there would be a delay of about four months in processing the case, which annoyed the applicant since, according to his statement, he was in a great hurry to obtain visas that would enable him to travel to Russia, insisting on his right to do so in view of his background and his loyalty and his activities in behalf of the Cuban movement. The declarant was unable to recall accurately whether or not the applicant told her he was a member of the Communist Party, but he did say that his wife * * * was then in New York City, and would follow him, * * * [Senora Duran stated] that when Oswald understood that it was not possible to give him a Cuban visa without his first having obtained the Russian visa, * * * he became very excited or angry, and accordingly, the affiant called Consul Ascue [sic], * * * [who] came out and began a heated discussion in English with Oswald, that concluded by Ascue telling him that "if it were up to him, he would not give him the visa," and "a person of his type was harming the Cuban Revolution rather than helping it," it being understood that in their conversation they were talking about the Russian Socialist Revolution and not the Cuban. Oswald maintained that he had two reasons for requesting that his visa be issued promptly, and they were: one, that his tourist permit in Mexico was about to expire; and the other, that he had to get to Russia as quickly as possible. Despite her annoyance, the declarant gave Oswald a paper * * * in which she put down her name, "Silvia Durán," and the number of the telephone at the consulate, which is "11–28–47" and the visa application was processed anyway. It was sent to the Ministry of [Foreign] Relations of Cuba; from which a routine reply was received some fifteen to thirty days later, approving the visa, but on the condition that the Russian visa be obtained first, although she does not recall whether or not Oswald later telephoned her at the Consulate number that she gave him.[540]

OSWALD'S APPLICATION FOR A VISA FOR TRAVEL TO CUBA AND THE REPLY OF THE CUBAN GOVERNMENT

(COMMISSION EXHIBIT 2564)

OSWALD'S APPLICATION

CUBAN REPLY

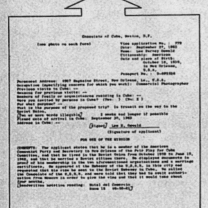

TRANSLATION

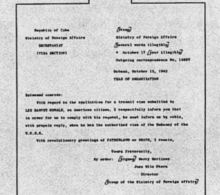

TRANSLATION

BOTH DOCUMENTS FURNISHED BY THE GOVERNMENT OF CUBA.

With the dates of Oswald's entry into and departure from Mexico, which had been obtained from the records of the Mexican Immigration Service very shortly after the assassination, the Government of Mexico initiated a thorough investigation to uncover as much information as possible on Oswald's trip.[541] Representatives of U.S. agencies worked in close liaison with the Mexican law enforcement authorities. The result of this investigative effort was to corroborate the statements of Senora Duran and to verify the essentials of Oswald's activities in Mexico as outlined above.

Senora Duran is a well-educated native of Mexico, who was 26 years old at the time of her interrogation. She is married to Senor Horacio Duran Navarro, a 40-year-old industrial designer, and has a young child. Although Senora Duran denies being a member of the Communist Party or otherwise connected with it, both Durans have been active in far left political affairs in Mexico, believe in Marxist ideology, and sympathize with the government of Fidel Castro,[542] and Senor Duran has written articles for El Dia, a pro-Communist newspaper in Mexico City.[543] The Commission has reliable evidence from a confidential source that Senora Duran as well as other personnel at the Cuban Embassy were genuinely upset upon receiving news of President Kennedy's death. Senora Duran's statements were made to Mexican officials soon after the assassination,[544] and no significant inaccuracies in them have been detected. Documents fitting the description given by Senora Duran of the documents Oswald had shown her, plus a notation which she said she had given him, were found among his possessions after his arrest.[545]

The Cuban Government was asked to document and confirm the essentials of Senora Duran's testimony. Its response, which has been included in its entirety in this Report, included a summary statement of Oswald's activities at the Cuban Embassy;[546] a photograph of the application for a visa he completed there,[547] and a photograph of the communication from Havana rejecting the application unless he could first present a Soviet visa.[548] (See Commission Exhibit No. 2564, p. 306.) The information on these documents concerning Oswald's date of birth, American passport number and activities and statements at the Embassy is consistent with other information available to the Commission.[549] CIA experts have given their opinion that the handwriting on the visa application which purports to be Oswald's is in fact his and that, although the handwritten notations on the bottom of the document are too brief and faint to permit a conclusive determination, they are probably Senora Duran's.[550] The clothes which Oswald was wearing in the photograph which appears on the application appear to be the same as some of those found among his effects after the assassination, and the photograph itself appears to be from the same negative as a photograph found among his effects.[551] Nothing on any of the documents raises a suspicion that they might not be authentic.

By far the most important confirmation of Senora Duran's testimony, however, has been supplied by confidential sources of extremely high reliability available to the United States in Mexico. The information from these sources establishes that her testimony was truthful and accurate in all material respects. The identities of these sources cannot be disclosed without destroying their future usefulness to the United States.

The investigation of the Commission has produced considerable testimonial and documentary evidence establishing the precise time of Oswald's journey, his means of transportation, the hotel at which he stayed in Mexico City, and a restaurant at which he often ate. All known persons whom Oswald may have met while in Mexico, including passengers on the buses he rode,[552] and the employees and guests of the hotel where he stayed,[553] were interviewed. No credible witness has been located who saw Oswald with any unidentified person while in Mexico City; to the contrary, he was observed traveling alone to and from Mexico City,[554] at his hotel,[555] and at the nearby restaurant where he frequently ate.[556] A hotel guest stated that on one occasion he sat down at a table with Oswald at the restaurant because no empty table was available, but that neither spoke to the other because of the language barrier.[557] Two Australian girls who saw Oswald on the bus to Mexico City relate that he occupied a seat next to a man who has been identified as Albert Osborne, an elderly itinerant preacher.[558] Osborne denies that Oswald was beside him on the bus.[559] To the other passengers on the bus it appeared that Osborne and Oswald had not previously met,[560] and extensive investigation of Osborne has revealed no further contact between him and Oswald. Osborne's responses to Federal investigators on matters unrelated to Oswald have proved inconsistent and unreliable, and, therefore, based on the contrary evidence and Osborne's lack of reliability, the Commission has attached no credence to his denial that Oswald was beside him on the bus. Investigation of his background and activities, however, disclose no basis for suspecting him of any involvement in the assassination.[561]

Investigation of the hotel at which Oswald stayed has failed to uncover any evidence that the hotel is unusual in any way that could relate to Oswald's visit. It is not especially popular among Cubans, and there is no indication that it is used as a meeting place for extremist or revolutionary organizations.[562] Investigation of other guests of the hotel who were there when Oswald was has failed to uncover anything creating suspicion.[563] Oswald's notebook which he carried with him to Mexico City contained the telephone number of the Cuban Airlines Office in Mexico City; [564] however, a Cuban visa is required by Mexican authorities before an individual may enplane for Cuba,[565] and a confidential check of the Cuban Airlines Office uncovered no evidence that Oswald visited their offices while in the city.[566]

Allegations of conspiracy.—Literally dozens of allegations of a conspiratorial contact between Oswald and agents of the Cuban Government have been investigated by the Commission. Among the claims made were allegations that Oswald had made a previous trip to

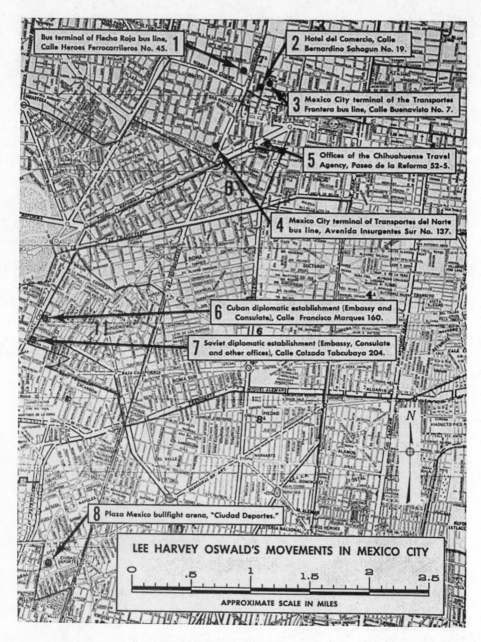

1 Bus terminal of Flecha Roja bus line, Calle Heroes Ferrocarrileros No. 45.

2 Hotel del Comercio, Calle Bernardino Sahagun No. 19.

3 Mexico City terminal of the Transportes Frontera bus line, Calle Buenavista No. 7.

5 Offices of the Chihuahuense Travel Agency, Paseo de la Reforma 52-5.

4 Mexico City terminal of Transportes del Norte bus line, Avenida Insurgentes Sur No. 137.

6 Cuban diplomatic establishment (Embassy and Consulate), Calle Francisco Marques 160.

7 Soviet diplomatic establishment (Embassy, Consulate and other offices), Calle Calzada Tabcubaya 204.

8 Plaza Mexico bullfight arena, "Ciudad Deportes."

LEE HARVEY OSWALD'S MOVEMENTS IN MEXICO CITY

APPROXIMATE SCALE IN MILES

COMMISSION EXHIBIT No. 1400

306

Mexico City in early September to receive money and orders for the assassination,[567] that he had been flown to a secret airfield somewhere in or near the Yucatan Peninsula,[568] that he might have made contacts in Mexico City with a Communist from the United States shortly before the assassination,[569] and that Oswald assassinated the President at the direction of a particular Cuban agent who met with him in the United States and paid him $7,000.[570] A letter was received from someone in Cuba alleging the writer had attended a meeting where the assassination had been discussed as part of a plan which would soon include the death of other non-Communist leaders in the Americas.[571] The charge was made in a Cuban expatriate publication that in a speech he delivered 5 days after the assassination, while he was under the influence of liquor, Fidel Castro made a slip of the tongue and said, "The first time Oswald was in Cuba," thereby giving away the fact that Oswald had made one or more surreptitious trips to that country.[572]

Some stories linked the assassination to anti-Castro groups who allegedly were engaged in obtaining illicit firearms in the United States, one such claim being that these groups killed the President as part of a bargain with some illicit organizations who would then supply them with firearms as payment.[573] Other rumors placed Oswald in Miami, Fla., at various times, allegedly in pro-Cuban activities there.[574] The assassination was claimed to have been carried out by Chinese Communists operating jointly with the Cubans.[575] Oswald was also alleged to have met with the Cuban Ambassador in a Mexico City restaurant and to have driven off in the Ambassador's car for a private talk.[576] Castro himself, it was alleged, 2 days after the assassination called for the files relating to Oswald's dealings with two members of the Cuban diplomatic mission in the Soviet Union; the inference drawn was that the "dealings" had occurred and had established a secret subversive relationship which continued through Oswald's life.[577] Without exception, the rumors and allegations of a conspiratorial contact were shown to be without any factual basis, in some cases the product of mistaken identification.

Illustrative of the attention given to the most serious allegations is the case of "D," a young Latin American secret agent who approached U.S. authorities in Mexico shortly after the assassination and declared that he saw Lee Harvey Oswald receiving $6,500 to kill the President. Among other details, "D" said that at about noon on September 18, waiting to conduct some business at the Cuban consulate, he saw a group of three persons conversing in a patio a few feet away. One was a tall, thin Negro with reddish hair, obviously dyed, who spoke rapidly in both Spanish and English, and another was a man he said was Lee Harvey Oswald. A tall Cuban joined the group momentarily and passed some currency to the Negro. The Negro then allegedly said to Oswald in English, "I want to kill the man." Oswald replied, "You're not man enough, I can do it." The Negro then said in Spanish, "I can't go with you, I have a lot to do." Oswald replied, "The people are waiting for me back there." The

Negro then gave Oswald $6,500 in large-denomination American bills, saying, "This isn't much." After hearing this conversation, "D" said that he telephoned the American Embassy in Mexico City several times prior to the assassination in an attempt to report his belief that someone important in the United States was to be killed, but was finally told by someone at the Embassy to stop wasting his time.

"D" and his allegations were immediately subjected to intensive investigation. His former employment as an agent for a Latin American country was confirmed, although his superiors had no knowledge of his presence in Mexico or the assignment described by "D." Four days after "D" first appeared the U.S. Government was informed by the Mexican authorities that "D" had admitted in writing that his whole narrative about Oswald was false. He said that he had never seen Oswald anyplace, and that he had not seen anybody paid money in the Cuban Embassy. He also admitted that he never tried to telephone the American Embassy in September and that his first call to the Embassy was after the assassination. "D" said that his motive in fabricating the story was to help get himself admitted into the United States so that he could there participate in action against Fidel Castro. He said that he hated Castro and hoped that the story he made up would be believed and would cause the United States to "take action" against him.

Still later, when questioned by American authorities, "D" claimed that he had been pressured into retracting his statement by the Mexican police and that the retraction, rather than his first statement, was false. A portion of the American questioning was carried on with the use of a polygraph machine, with the consent of "D." When told that the machine indicated that he was probably lying, "D" said words to the effect that he "must be mistaken." Investigation in the meantime had disclosed that the Embassy extension number "D" said he had called would not have given him the person he said he spoke to, and that no one at the Embassy—clerks, secretaries, or officers— had any recollection of his calls. In addition, Oswald spoke little, if any, Spanish. That he could have carried on the alleged conversation with the red-headed Negro in the Cuban Embassy, part of which was supposed to have been in Spanish, was therefore doubtful. "D" now said that he was uncertain as to the date when he saw "someone who looked like Oswald" at the Cuban Embassy, and upon reconsideration, he now thought it was on a Tuesday, September 17, rather than September 18. On September 17, however, Oswald visited the Louisiana State Unemployment Commission in New Orleans and also cashed a check from the Texas Employment Commission at the Winn-Dixie Store No. 1425 in New Orleans. On the basis of the retractions made by "D" when he heard the results of the polygraph examination, and on the basis of discrepancies which appeared in his story, it was concluded that "D" was lying.[578]

The investigation of the Commission has thus produced no evidence that Oswald's trip to Mexico was in any way connected with the assassination of President Kennedy, nor has it uncovered evidence that the

Cuban Government had any involvement in the assassination. To the contrary, the Commission has been advised by the CIA and FBI that secret and reliable sources corroborate the statements of Senora Duran in all material respects, and that the Cuban Government had no relationship with Lee Harvey Oswald other than that described by Senora Duran. Secretary of State Rusk also testified that after the assassination "there was very considerable concern in Cuba as to whether they would be held responsible and what the effect of that might be on their own position and their own safety." [579]

Contacts with the Soviet Embassy in the United States.—Soon after the Oswalds reached the United States in June 1962 they wrote to the Soviet Embassy in Washington, D.C. Oswald requested information about subscriptions to Russian newspapers and magazines and ultimately did subscribe to several Russian journals. Soviet law required Marina Oswald, as a Soviet citizen living abroad, to remain in contact with her nation's Embassy and to file various papers occasionally.[580] In 1963, after Oswald had experienced repeated employment difficulties, there were further letters when the Oswalds sought permission to return to the Soviet Union. The first such request was a letter written by Marina Oswald on February 17, 1963. She wrote that she wished to return to Russia but that her husband would stay in the United States because "he is an American by nationality." [581] She was informed on March 8, 1963, that it would take from 5 to 6 months to process the application.[582] The Soviet Union made available to the Commission what purports to be the entire correspondence between the Oswalds and the Russian Embassy in the United States.[583] This material has been checked for codes and none has been detected.[584] With the possible exception of a letter which Oswald wrote to the Soviet Embassy after his return from Mexico City, discussed below, there is no material which gives any reason for suspicion. The implications of all of this correspondence for an understanding of Lee Harvey Oswald's personality and motivation is discussed in the following chapter.

Oswald's last letter to the Soviet Embassy in Washington, D.C., dated November 9, 1963, began by stating that it was written "to inform you of recent events since my meetings with Comrade Kostin in the Embassy of the Soviet Union, Mexico City, Mexico." [585] The envelope bears a postmark which appears to be November 12, 1963.[586] Ruth Paine has testified that Oswald spent the weekend at her home working on the letter and that she observed one preliminary draft.[587] A piece of paper which was identified as one of these drafts was found among Oswald's effects after the assassination. (See Commission Exhibits Nos. 15, 103, p. 311.) According to Marina Oswald, her husband retyped the envelope 10 times.[588]

Information produced for the Commission by the CIA is to the effect that the person referred to in the letter as "comrade Kostin" was probably Valeriy Vladimirovich Kostikov, a member of the consular staff of the Soviet Union in Mexico City. He is also one of the KGB officers stationed at the Embassy.[589] It is standard Soviet procedure for KGB officers stationed in embassies and in consulates to carry on the normal duties of such a position in addition to the undercover activities.[590] The Commission has identified the Cuban consul referred to in Oswald's letter as Senor Eusebio Azque (also "Ascue"), the man with whom Oswald argued at the Cuban Embassy, who was in fact replaced. The CIA advised the Commission:

> We surmise that the references in Oswald's 9 November letter to a man who had since been replaced must refer to Cuban Consul Eusebio Azque, who left Mexico for Cuba on permanent transfer on 18 November 1963, four days before the assassination. Azque had been in Mexico for 18 years and it was known as early as September 1963 that Azque was to be replaced. His replacement did arrive in September. Azque was scheduled to leave in October but did not leave until 18 November.
>
> We do not know who might have told Oswald that Azque or any other Cuban had been or was to be replaced, but we speculate that Silvia Duran or some Soviet official might have mentioned it if Oswald complained about Azque's altercation with him.[591]

When asked to explain the letter, Marina Oswald was unable to add anything to an understanding of its contents.[592] Some light on its possible meaning can be shed by comparing it with the early draft. When the differences between the draft and the final document are studied, and especially when crossed-out words are taken into account, it becomes apparent that Oswald was intentionally beclouding the true state of affairs in order to make his trip to Mexico sound as mysterious and important as possible.

For example, the first sentence in the second paragraph of the letter reads, "I was unable to remain in Mexico indefinily because of my mexican visa restrictions which was for I5 days only." The same sentence in the draft begins, before the words are crossed out, "I was unable to remain in Mexico City because I considered useless * * *" As already mentioned, the Commission has good evidence that Oswald's trip to Mexico was indeed "useless" and that he returned to Texas with that conviction. The first draft, therefore, spoke the truth; but Oswald rewrote the sentence to imply that he had to leave because his visa was about to expire. This is false; Oswald's tourist card still had a full week to run when he departed from Mexico on October 3.[593]

The next sentence in the letter reads, "I could not take a chance on reqesting a new visa unless I used my real name, so I returned to the United States." The fact is that he did use his real name for his tourist card, and in all dealings with the Cuban Embassy, the Russian Embassy and elsewhere. Oswald did use the name of "Lee" on the trip, but as indicated below, he did so only sporadically and probably as the result of a clerical error. In the opinion of the Commission, based upon its knowledge of Oswald, the letter constitutes no more than a clumsy effort to ingratiate himself with the Soviet Embassy.

OSWALD'S LETTER TO THE
EMBASSY U. S. S. R., WASHINGTON, D. C.

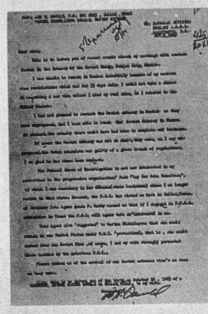

COMMISSION
EXHIBIT
15

PRELIMINARY DRAFT
(COMMISSION EXHIBIT 103)

Investigation of Other Activities

Oswald's use of post office boxes and false names.—After his return from the Soviet Union, Lee Harvey Oswald is known to have received his mail at post office boxes and to have used different aliases on numerous occasions. Since either practice is susceptible of use for clandestine purposes, the Commission has directed attention to both for signs that Oswald at some point made undercover contact with other persons who might have been connected with the assassination.

Oswald is known to have opened three post office boxes during 1962 and 1963. On October 9, 1962, the same day that he arrived in Dallas from Fort Worth, and before establishing a residence there, he opened box No. 2915 at the Dallas General Post Office. This box was closed on May 14, 1963, shortly after Oswald had moved to New Orleans.[594] That portion of the post office box application listing the names of those persons other than the applicant entitled to receive mail at the box was discarded in accordance with postal regulations after the box was closed; hence, it is not known what names other than Oswald's were listed on that form.[595] However, as discussed in chapter IV, Oswald is known to have received the assassination rifle under the name of A. Hidell and his Smith & Wesson revolver under the name of A. J. Hidell at that box.[596] On June 3, 1963, Oswald opened box No. 30061 at the Lafayette Square Substation in New Orleans. Marina Oswald and A. J. Hidell were listed as additional persons entitled to receive mail at this box.[597] Immediately before leaving for Mexico City in late September, Oswald submitted a request to forward his mail to the Paines' address in Irving, and the box was closed on September 26.[598] On November 1, 1963, he opened box No. 6225 at the Dallas Post Office Terminal Annex. The Fair Play for Cuba Committee and the American Civil Liberties Union were listed as also being entitled to receive mail at this box.[599]

Oswald's use of post office boxes is consistent with other information known about him. His frequent changes of address and receipt of Communist and other political literature would appear to have provided Oswald reason to have rented postal boxes. These were the explanations for his use of the boxes which he provided Postal Inspector H. D. Holmes on November 24.[600] Moreover, on October 14, 1963, he had moved into a room on Beckley Avenue under the name of O. H. Lee [601] and it would have been extremely difficult for Oswald to have received his mail at that address without having disclosed his true name. The boxes cost Oswald only $1.50 or less per month.[602]

Although the possibilities of investigation in this area are limited, there is no evidence that any of the three boxes was ever used for the surreptitious receipt of messages or was used by persons other than Oswald or his family. No unexplainable notes were found among Oswald's possessions after his arrest. Oswald's box on the day of the assassination, No. 6225, was kept under constant personal surveillance by postal inspectors from about 5 p.m. November 22 until midnight November 24. A modified surveillance was maintained thereafter. No one called for mail out of this box; indeed the only mail in the box was a Russian magazine addressed to Oswald. The single outstanding key was recovered from Oswald immediately after he was taken in custody.[603]

In appraising the import of Oswald's rental of post office boxes, it is significant that he was not secretive about their use. All three boxes were rented by Oswald using his true name.[604] His application for box No. 2915 showed his home address as that of Alexandra De Mohrenschildt (Taylor), whose husband had agreed to allow Oswald to use his address.[605] His application for the New Orleans box listed his address as 657 French Street; his aunt, Lillian Murret, lived at 757 French Street.[606] On the application for box No. 6225, Oswald gave an incorrect street number, though he did show Beckley Avenue, where he was then living.[607] He furnished the box numbers to his brother, to an employer, to Texas and New Orleans unemployment commissions, and to others.[608] Based on all the facts disclosed by its investigation, the Commission has attached no conspiratorial significance to Oswald's rental of post office boxes.

Oswald's use of aliases is also well established. In chapter IV, the evidence relating to his repeated use of the name "A. J. Hidell," and close variants thereof, is set forth.[609] Because Oswald's use of this pseudonym became known quickly after the assassination, investigations were conducted with regard to persons using the name Hidell or names similar to it. Subversive files, public carrier records, telegraph company records, banking and other commercial records, and other matters investigated and persons interviewed have been examined with regard to Oswald's true name and his known alias.[610] No evidence has been produced that Oswald ever used the name Hidell as a means of making undercover contact with any person. Indeed, though Oswald did prepare a counterfeit selective service card and other identification using this name, he commonly used "Hidell" to represent persons other than himself, such as the president of his nonexistent Fair Play for Cuba Committee chapter, the doctor whose name appeared on his counterfeit international certificate of vaccination, and as references on his job applications.[611]

Alwyn Cole, questioned document expert for the Treasury Department, testified that the false identification found on Oswald upon his arrest could have been produced by employing elementary techniques used in a photographic printing plant.[612] (See app. X, pp. 571–578.) Though to perform the necessary procedures would have been difficult without the use of expensive photographic equipment, such equipment and the needed film and photographic paper were available to Oswald when he was employed from October 1962 through early April 1963 at Jaggars-Chiles-Stovall, a commercial advertising photography firm in Dallas.[613] While so employed, Oswald is known to have become familiar with the mechanics of photographic enlargements, contraction, and image distortion that would have been necessary to produce his false identification, and to have used the facilities of his employer for some personal work.[614] Cole testified that the cards in Oswald's wallet did not exhibit a great deal of skill, pointing out various errors that had been committed.[615] Oswald's supervisor at Jaggars-Chiles-Stovall has stated that Oswald seemed unable to perform photographic work with precision, which was one of the main reasons for which he was ultimately discharged.[616] The retouched negatives used to make Oswald's counterfeit certificate of service identification were found among Oswald's personal effects after his arrest, as was a rubber stamping kit apparently employed to produce his spurious international certificate of vaccination.[617] There is strong evidence, therefore, that Oswald himself made the various pieces of counterfeit identification which he carried, and there is no reason to believe that he received assistance from any person in establishing his alias.

Oswald also used incorrect names other than Hidell, but these too appear unconnected with any form of conspiracy. Oswald's last name appears as "Lee" in three places in connection with his trip to Mexico City, discussed above. His tourist card was typed by the Mexican consulate in New Orleans, "Lee, Harvey Oswald." [618] However, the comma seems to have been a clerical error, since Oswald signed both the application and the card itself, "Lee H. Oswald." Moreover, Oswald seems originally to have also printed his name, evenly spaced, as "Lee H Oswald," but, noting that the form instructed him to "Print full name. No initials," printed the remainder of his middle name after the "H." The clerk who typed the card thus saw a space after "Lee," followed by "Harvey Oswald" crowded together, and probably assumed that "Lee" was the applicant's last name. (See Commission Exhibit 2481, p. 300.) The clerk who prepared Oswald's bus reservation for his return trip wrote "H. O. Lee." He stated that he did not remember the occasion, although he was sure from the handwriting and from other facts that he had dealt with Oswald. He surmised that he probably made out the reservation directly from the tourist card, since Oswald spoke no Spanish, and, seeing the comma, wrote the name "H. O. Lee." [619] Oswald himself signed the register at the hotel in Mexico City as "Lee, Harvey Oswald," [620] but since the error is identical to that on the tourist card and since he revealed the remainder of his name, "Harvey Oswald," it is possible that Oswald inserted the comma to conform to the tourist card, or that the earlier mistake suggested a new pseudonym to Oswald which he decided to continue.

In any event, Oswald used his correct name in making reservations for the trip to Mexico City, in introducing himself to passengers on the bus, and in his dealings with the Cuban and Soviet Embassies.[621] When registering at the Beckley Avenue house in mid-October, Oswald perpetuated the pseudonym by giving his name as "O. H. Lee," [622] though he had given his correct name to the owner of the previous roominghouse where he had rented a room after his return from Mexico City.[623] Investigations of the Commission have been conducted with regard to persons using the name "Lee," and no evidence has been found that Oswald used this alias for the purpose of making any type of secret contacts.

Oswald is also known to have used the surname "Osborne" in ordering Fair Play for Cuba Committee handbills in May 1963.[624] He also used the false name D. F. Drittal as a certifying witness on the mail-order coupon with which he purchased his Smith & Wesson revolver.[625] He used the name Lt. J. Evans as a reference on an employment application in New Orleans.[626]

Oswald's repeated use of false names is probably not to be disassociated from his antisocial and criminal inclinations. No doubt he purchased his weapons under the name of Hidell in attempt to prevent their ownership from being traced. Oswald's creation of false names and ficititious personalities is treated in the discussion of possible motives set forth in chapter VII. Whatever its significance in that respect may be, the Commission has found no indication that Oswald's use of aliases was linked with any conspiracy with others.

Ownership of a second rifle.—The Commission has investigated a report that, during the first 2 weeks of November 1963, Oswald had a telescopic sight mounted and sighted on a rifle at a sporting goods store in Irving, Tex. The main evidence that Oswald had such work performed for him is an undated repair tag bearing the name "Oswald" from the Irving Sports Shop in Irving, Tex. On November 25, 1963, Dial D. Ryder, an employee of the Irving Sports Shop, presented this tag to agents of the FBI, claiming that the tag was in his handwriting. The undated tag indicated that three holes had been drilled in an unspecified type of rifle and a telescopic sight had been mounted on the rifle and boresighted.[627]

As discussed in chapter IV, the telescopic sight on the C2766 Mannlicher-Carcano rifle was already mounted when shipped to Oswald, and both Ryder and his employer, Charles W. Greener, feel certain that they never did any work on this rifle.[628] If the repair tag actually represented a transaction involving Lee Harvey Oswald, therefore, it would mean that Oswald owned another rifle. Although this would not alter the evidence which establishes Oswald's ownership of the rifle used to assassinate President Kennedy, the possession of a second rifle warranted investigation because it would indicate that a possibly important part of Oswald's life had not been uncovered.

Since all of Oswald's known transactions in connection with firearms after his return to the United States were undertaken under an assumed name,[629] it seems unlikely that if he did have repairs made at the sports shop he would have used his real name Investigation has revealed that the authenticity of the repair tag bearing Oswald's name is indeed subject to grave doubts. Ryder testified that he found the repair tag while cleaning his workbench on November 23, 1963.[630] However, Ryder spoke with Greener repeatedly during the period between November 22–28 and, sometime prior to November 25, he discussed with him the possibility that Oswald had been in the store. Neither he nor Greener could remember that he had been. But despite these conversations with Greener, it is significant that Ryder never called the repair tag to his employer's attention. Greener did not learn about the tag until November 28, when he was called by TV reporters after the story had appeared in the Dallas Times-Herald.[631] The peculiarity of Ryder's silence is compounded by the fact that, when speaking to the FBI on November 25, Ryder fixed the period during which the tag had been issued as November 1–14, 1963, yet, from his later testimony, it appears that he did so on the basis that it must have occurred when Greener was on vacation since Greener did not remember the transaction.[632] Moreover, the FBI had been directed to the Irving Sports Shop by anonymous telephone calls received by its Dallas office and by a local television station. The anonymous male who telephoned the Bureau attributed his information to an unidentified sack boy at a specified supermarket in Irving, but investigation has failed to verify this source.[633]

Neither Ryder nor Greener claimed that Lee Harvey Oswald had ever been a customer in the Irving Sports Shop. Neither has any recollection of either Oswald or his Mannlicher-Carcano rifle, nor does either recall the transaction allegedly represented by the repair tag or the person for whom the repair was supposedly made.[634] Although Ryder stated to the FBI that he was "quite sure" that he had seen Oswald and that Oswald may have been in the store at one time, when shown a photograph of Oswald during his deposition, Ryder testified he knew the picture to be of Oswald, "as the pictures in the paper, but as far as seeing the guy personally, I don't think I ever have." [635]

Subsequent events also reflect on Ryder's credibility. In his deposition, Ryder emphatically denied that he talked to any reporters about this matter prior to the time a story about it appeared in the November 28, 1963, edition of the Dallas Times-Herald.[636] Earlier, however, he told an agent of the U.S. Secret Service that the newspaper had misquoted him.[637] Moreover, a reporter for the Dallas Times-Herald has testified that on November 28, 1963, he called Ryder at his home and obtained from him all of the details of the alleged transaction, and his story is supported by the testimony of a second reporter who overheard one end of the telephone conversation.[638] No other person by the name of Oswald in the Dallas-Fort Worth area has been found who had a rifle repaired at the Irving Sports Shop.[639]

Possible corroboration for Ryder's story is provided by two women, Mrs. Edith Whitworth, who operates the Furniture Mart, a furniture store located about 1½ blocks from the Irving Sports Shop, and Mrs. Gertrude Hunter, a friend of Mrs. Whitworth. They testified that in early November of 1963, a man who they later came to believe was Oswald drove up to the Furniture Mart in a two-tone blue and white 1957 Ford automobile, entered the store and asked about a part for a gun, presumably because of a sign that appeared in the building advertising a gunsmith shop that had formerly occupied part of the premises. When he found that he could not obtain the part, the man allegedly returned to his car and then came back into the store with a woman and two young children to look at furniture, remaining in the store for about 30 to 40 minutes.[640]

Upon confronting Marina Oswald, both women identified her as the woman whom they had seen in the store on the occasion in question, although Mrs. Hunter could not identify a picture of Lee Harvey Oswald and Mrs. Whitworth identified some pictures of Oswald but not others. Mrs. Hunter purported to identify Marina Oswald by her eyes, and did not observe the fact that Marina Oswald had a front tooth missing at the time she supposedly saw her.[641] After a thorough inspection of the Furniture Mart, Marina Oswald testified that she had never been on the premises before.[642]

The circumstances surrounding the testimony of the two women are helpful in evaluating the weight to be given to their testimony, and the extent to which they lend support to Ryder's evidence. The women previously told newspaper reporters that the part for which the man was looking was a "plunger," which the Commission has been advised is a colloquial term used to describe a firing pin.[643] This work was completely different from the work covered by Ryder's repair tag, and the firing pin of the assassination weapon does not appear to have been recently replaced.[644] At the time of their depositions, neither woman was able to recall the type of work which the man wanted done.[645]

Mrs. Whitworth related to the FBI that the man told her that the younger child with him was born on October 20, 1963, which was in fact Rachel Oswald's birthday.[646] In her testimony before the Commission, however, Mrs. Whitworth could not state that the man had told her the child's birthdate was October 20, 1963, and in fact expressed uncertainty about the birthday of her own grandchild, which she had previously used as a guide to remembering the birthdate of the younger child in the shop.[647] Mrs. Hunter thought that the man she and Mrs. Whitworth believed was Oswald drove the car to and from the store; [648] however, Lee Harvey Oswald apparently was not able to drive an automobile by himself and does not appear to have had access to a car.[649]

The two women claimed that Oswald was in the Furniture Mart on a weekday, and in midafternoon. However, Oswald had reported to work at the Texas School Book Depository on the dates referred to by the women and there is no evidence that he left his job during business hours.[650] In addition, Ruth Paine has stated that she always accompanied Marina Oswald whenever Marina left the house with her children and that they never went to the Furniture Mart, either with or without Lee Harvey Oswald, at any time during October or November of 1963.[651] There is nothing to indicate that in November the Oswalds were interested in buying furniture.[652]

Finally, investigation has produced reason to question the credibility of Mrs. Hunter as a witness. Mrs. Hunter stated that one of the reasons she remembers the description of the car in which Oswald supposedly drove to the furniture store was that she was awaiting the arrival of a friend from Houston, who drove a similar automobile.[653] However, the friend in Houston has advised that in November 1963, she never visited or planned to visit Dallas, and that she told no one that she intended to make such a trip. Moreover the friend added, according to the FBI interview report, that Mrs. Hunter has "a strange obsession for attempting to inject herself into any big event which comes to her attention" and that she "is likely to claim some personal knowledge of any major crime which receives much publicity." [654] She concluded that "the entire family is aware of these 'tall tales' Mrs. Hunter tells and they normally pay no attention to her." [655]

Another allegation relating to the possible ownership of a second rifle by Oswald comes from Robert Adrian Taylor, a mechanic at a service station in Irving. Some 3 weeks after the assassination, Taylor reported to the FBI that he thought that, in March or April of 1963, a man he believed to be Oswald had been a passenger in an automobile that stopped at his station for repairs; since neither the driver nor the passenger had sufficient funds for the repair work, the person believed to be Oswald sold a U.S. Army rifle to Mr. Taylor, using the proceeds to pay for the repairs.[656] However, a second employee at the service station, who recalled the incident, believed that, despite a slight resemblance, the passenger was not Oswald.[657] Upon reflection, Taylor himself stated that he is very doubtful that the man was Oswald.[658]

Rifle practice.—Several witnesses believed that in the weeks preceding the assassination, they observed a man resembling Oswald practicing with a rifle in the fields and wooded areas surrounding Dallas, and at rifle ranges in that area. Some witnesses claimed Oswald was alone, while others said he was accompanied by one or more other persons. In most instances, investigation has disclosed that there is no substantial basis for believing that the person reported by the various witnesses was Oswald.[659]

One group of witnesses, however, believed that they observed Lee Harvey Oswald at the Sports Drome Rifle Range in Dallas at various times from September through November of 1963. In light of the number of witnesses, the similarity of the descriptions of the man they saw, and the type of weapon they thought the individual was shooting, there is reason to believe that these witnesses did see the same person at the firing range, although the testimony of none of these witnesses is fully consistent with the reported observations of the other witnesses.

The witnesses who claimed to have seen Oswald at the firing range had more than a passing notice of the person they observed. Malcolm H. Price, Jr., adjusted the scope on the individual's rifle on one occasion; [660] Garland G. Slack had an altercation with the individual on another occasion because he was shooting at Slack's target; [661] and Sterling C. Wood, who on a third date was present at the range with his father, Dr. Homer Wood, spoke with his father and very briefly with the man himself about the individual's rifle.[662] All three of these persons, as well as Dr. Wood, expressed confidence that the man they saw was Oswald.[663] Two other persons believed they saw a person resembling Oswald firing a similar rifle at another range near Irving 2 days before the assassination.[664]

Although the testimony of these witnesses was partially corroborated by other witnesses,[665] there was other evidence which prevented the Commission from reaching the conclusion that Lee Harvey Oswald was the person these witnesses saw. Others who were at the firing range remembered the same individual but, though noting a similarity to Oswald, did not believe that the man was Oswald; [666] others either were unable to state whether the man was Oswald or did not recall seeing anybody who they feel may have been Oswald.[667] Moreover, when interviewed on December 2, 1963, Slack recalled that the individual whom he saw had blond hair,[668] and on December 3, 1963, Price stated that on several occasions when he saw the individual, he was wearing a "Bulldogger Texas style" hat and had bubble gum or chewing tobacco in his cheek.[669] None of these characteristics match those known about Lee Harvey Oswald.

Moreover, the date on which Price adjusted the scope for the unknown person was September 28, 1963, but Oswald is known to have been in Mexico City at that time; [670] since a comparison of the events testified to by Price and Slack strongly suggests that they were describing the same man,[671] there is reason to believe that Slack was also describing a man other than Oswald. In addition, Slack believed he saw the same person at the rifle range on November 10 [672] and there is persuasive evidence that on November 10, Oswald was at the Paine's home in Irving and did not leave to go to the rifle range.[673] Finally, the man whom Price assisted on September 28 drove an old car, possibly a 1940 or 1941 Ford.[674] However, there is evidence that Oswald could not drive at that time, and there is no indication that Oswald ever had access to such a car.[675] Neither Oswald's name nor any of his known aliases was found in the sign-in register maintained at the Sports Drome Rifle Range, though many customers did not sign this register.[676] The allegations pertaining to the companions who reportedly accompanied the man believed to be Oswald are also inconsistent among themselves [677] and conform to no other credible information ascertained by the Commission. Several witnesses noticed a bearded man at the club when the person believed to be Oswald was there, although only one witness thought the two men were together; [678] the bearded gentleman was located, and he was not found to have any connection with Oswald.[679]

It seems likely that the identification of Price, Slack, and the Woods was reinforced in their own minds by the belief that the man whom they saw was firing a rifle perhaps identical to Oswald's Mannlicher-Carcano. The witnesses agreed that the man they observed was firing a Mauser-type bolt-action rifle with the ammunition clip immediately in front of the trigger action, and that a scope was mounted on the rifle.[680] These features are consistent with the rifle Oswald used for the assassination.[681] The witnesses agreed that the man had accurate aim with the rifle.[682]

However, the evidence demonstrated that the weapon fired by the man they observed was different from the assassination rifle. The witnesses agreed that the barrel of the gun which the individual was firing had been shortened in the process of "sporterizing" the weapon.[683] In addition, Price and Slack recalled that certain pieces were missing from the top of the weapon,[684] and Dr. Wood and his son, and others, remembered that the weapon spouted flames when fired.[685] None of these characteristics correspond with Oswald's Mannlicher-Carcano.[686] Price and Slack believed that the gun did not have a sling, but the assassination weapon did have one. Sterling Wood, on the other hand, recalled that the rifle which he saw had a sling.[687] Price also recalled that he examined the rifle briefly for some indication as to where it had been manufactured, but saw nothing, whereas the words "MADE ITALY" are marked on the top of Oswald's Mannlicher-Carcano.[688]

The scope on the rifle observed at the firing range does not appear to be the same as the one on the assassination weapon. Price remembered that the individual told him that his scope was Japanese, that he had paid $18 for it, and that he had it mounted in a gunshop in Cedar Hills, though apparently no such shop exists in that area.[689] The scope on the Mannlicher-Carcano was of Japanese origin but it was worth a little more than $7 and was already mounted when he received the rifle from a mail-order firm in Chicago.[690] Sterling Wood and Slack agreed that the scope had a somewhat different appearance from the scope on the assassination rifle.[691]

Though the person believed to be Oswald retained his shell casings, presumably for reuse,[692] all casings recovered from areas where it is believed that Oswald may have practiced have been examined by the FBI Laboratory, and none has been found which was fired from Oswald's rifle.[693] Finally, evidence discussed in chapter IV tends to prove that Oswald brought his rifle to Dallas from the home of the Paines in Irving on November 22, and there is no other evidence which indicates that he took the rifle or a package which might have contained the rifle out of the Paine's garage, where it was stored, prior to that date.[694]

Automobile demonstration.—The testimony of Albert Guy Bogard has been carefully evaluated because it suggests the possibility that Oswald might have been a proficient automobile driver and, during November 1963, might have been expecting funds with which to purchase a car. Bogard, formerly an automobile salesman with a Lincoln-Mercury firm in Dallas, testified that in the early afternoon of November 9, 1963, he attended a prospective customer who he believes was Lee Harvey Oswald. According to Bogard, the customer, after test driving an automobile over the Stemmons Freeway at 60 to 70 miles per hour, told Bogard that in several weeks he would have the money to make a purchase. Bogard asserted that the customer gave his name as "Lee Oswald," which Bogard wrote on a business card. After Oswald's name was mentioned on the radio on November 22, Bogard assertedly threw the card in a trash can, making the comment to coemployees that he supposed Oswald would no longer wish to buy a car.[695]

Bogard's testimony has received corroboration.[696] The assistant sales manager at the time, Frank Pizzo, and a second salesman, Eugene M. Wilson, stated that they recall an instance when the customer described by Bogard was in the showroom.[697] Another salesman, Oran Brown, recalled that Bogard asked him to assist the customer if he appeared during certain evenings when Bogard was away from the showroom. Brown stated that he too wrote down the customer's name and both he and his wife remember the name "Oswald" as being on a paper in his possession before the assassination.[698]

However, doubts exist about the accuracy of Bogard's testimony. He, Pizzo, and Wilson differed on important details of what is supposed to have occurred when the customer was in the showroom. Whereas Bogard stated that the customer said he did not wish credit and wanted to purchase a car for cash,[699] Pizzo and Wilson both indicated that the man did attempt to purchase on credit.[700] According to Wilson, when the customer was told that he would be unable to purchase a car without a credit rating, substantial cash or a lengthy employment record, he stated sarcastically, "Maybe I'm going to have to go back to Russia to buy a car." [701] While it is possible that Oswald would have made such a remark, the statement is not consistent with Bogard's story. Indeed, Bogard has made no mention that the customer ever spoke with Wilson while he was in the showroom.[702] More important, on November 23, a search through the showroom's refuse was made, but no paper bearing Oswald's name was found.[703] The paper on which Brown reportedly wrote Oswald's name also has never been located.[704]

The assistant sales manager, Mr. Pizzo, who saw Bogard's prospect on November 9 and shortly after the assassination felt that Oswald may have been this man, later examined pictures of Oswald and expressed serious doubts that the person with Bogard was in fact Oswald. While noting a resemblance, he did not believe that Oswald's hairline matched that of the person who had been in the showroom on November 9.[705] Wilson has stated that Bogard's customer was only about 5 feet tall.[706] Several persons who knew Oswald have testified that he was unable to drive,[707] although Mrs. Paine, who was giving Oswald driving lessons, stated that Oswald was showing some improvement by November.[708] Moreover, Oswald's whereabouts on November 9, as testified to by Marina Oswald and Ruth Paine, would have made it impossible for him to have visited the automobile showroom as Mr. Bogard claims.[709]

Alleged association with various Mexican or Cuban individuals.— The Commission has examined Oswald's known or alleged contacts and activities in an effort to ascertain whether or not he was involved in any conspiracy may be seen in the investigation it conducted as a result of the testimony given by Mrs. Sylvia Odio. The Commission investigated her statements in connection with its consideration of the testimony of several witnesses suggesting that Oswald may have been seen in the company of unidentified persons of Cuban or Mexican background. Mrs. Odio was born in Havana in 1937 and remained in Cuba until 1960; it appears that both of her parents are political prisoners of the Castro regime. Mrs. Odio is a member of the Cuban Revolutionary Junta (JURE), an anti-Castro organization.[710] She testified that late in September 1963, three men came to her apartment in Dallas and asked her to help them prepare a letter soliciting funds for JURE activities. She claimed that the men, who exhibited personal familiarity with her imprisoned father, asked her if she were "working in the underground," and she replied that she was not.[711] She testified that two of the men appeared to be Cubans, although they also had some characteristics that she associated with Mexicans. Those two men did not state their full names, but identified themselves only by their fictitious underground "war names." Mrs. Odio remembered the name of one of the Cubans as "Leopoldo." [712] The third man, an American, allegedly was introduced to Mrs. Odio as "Leon Oswald," and she was told that he was very much interested in the Cuban cause.[713] Mrs. Odio said that the men told her that they had just come from New Orleans and that they were then about to leave on a trip.[714] Mrs. Odio testified that the next day Leopoldo called her on the telephone and told her that it was his idea to introduce the American into the underground "because he is great, he is kind of nuts." [715] Leopoldo also said that the American had been in the Marine Corps and was an excellent shot, and that the American said the Cubans "don't have any guts * * * because President Kennedy should have been assassinated after the Bay of Pigs, and some Cubans should have done that, because he was the one that was holding the freedom of Cuba actually." [716]

Although Mrs. Odio suggested doubts that the men were in fact members of JURE, [717] she was certain that the American who was introduced to her as Leon Oswald was Lee Harvey Oswald.[718] Her sister, who was in the apartment at the time of the visit by the three men, and who stated that she saw them briefly in the hallway when answering the door, also believed that the American was Lee Harvey Oswald.[719] By referring to the date on which she moved from her former apartment, October 1, 1963, Mrs. Odio fixed the date of the alleged visit on the Thursday or Friday immediately preceding that date, i.e., September 26 or 27. She was positive that the visit occurred prior to October 1.[720]

During the course of its investigation, however, the Commission concluded that Oswald could not have been in Dallas on the evening of either September 26 or 27, 1963. It also developed considerable evidence that he was not in Dallas at any time between the beginning of September and October 3, 1963. On April 24, Oswald left Dallas for New Orleans, where he lived until his trip to Mexico City in late September and his subsequent return to Dallas. Oswald is known to have been in New Orleans as late as September 23, 1963, the date on which Mrs. Paine and Marina Oswald left New Orleans for Dallas.[721] Sometime between 4 p.m. on September 24 and 1 p.m. on September 25, Oswald cashed an unemployment compensation check at a store in New Orleans;[722] under normal procedures this check would not have reached Oswald's postal box in New Orleans until at least 5 a.m. on September 25.[723] The store at which he cashed the check did not open until 8 a.m.[724] Therefore, it appeared that Oswald's presence in New Orleans until sometime between 8 a.m. and 1 p.m. on September 25 was quite firmly established.

Although there is no firm evidence of the means by which Oswald traveled from New Orleans to Houston, on the first leg of his Mexico City trip, the Commission noted that a Continental Trailways bus leaving New Orleans at 12:30 p.m. on September 25 would have brought Oswald to Houston at 10:50 p.m. that evening.[725] His presence on this bus would be consistent with other evidence before the Commission.[726] There is strong evidence that on September 26, 1963, Oswald traveled on Continental Trailways bus No. 5133 which left Houston at 2:35 a.m. for Laredo, Tex. Bus company records disclose that one ticket from Houston to Laredo was sold during the night shift on September 25–26, and that such ticket was the only one of its kind sold in the period of September 24 through September 26. The agent who sold this ticket has stated that Oswald could have been the purchaser.[727] Two English passengers, Dr. and Mrs. John B. McFarland, testified that they saw Oswald riding alone on this bus shortly after they awoke at 6 a.m.[728] The bus was scheduled to arrive in Laredo at 1:20 p.m. on September 26, and Mexican immigration records show that Oswald in fact crossed the border at Laredo to Nuevo Laredo, Mexico, between 6 a.m. and 2 p.m. on that day.[729] Evidence set out in appendix XIII establishes that Oswald did not leave Mexico until October 3, and that he arrived in Dallas the same day.

The Commission noted that the only time not strictly accounted for during the period that Mrs. Odio thought Oswald might have visited her is the span between the morning of September 25 and 2:35 a.m. on September 26. The only public means of transportation by which Oswald could have traveled from New Orleans to Dallas in time to catch his bus from Houston to Laredo, would have been the airlines. Investigation disclosed no indication that he flew between these points.[730] Moreover, it did not seem probable that Oswald would speed from New Orleans, spend a short time talking to Sylvia Odio, and then travel from Dallas to Mexico City and back on the bus. Automobile travel in the time available, though perhaps possible, would have been difficult.[731] The Commission noted, however, that if Oswald had reached Dallas on the evening of September 25, he could have traveled by bus to Alice, Tex., and there caught the bus which had left Houston for Laredo at 2:35 a.m. on September 26, 1963.[732] Further investigation in that regard indicated, however, that no tickets were sold, during the period September 23–26, 1963 for travel from

Dallas to Laredo or points beyond by the Dallas office of Continental Trailways, the only bus line on which Oswald could have made connections with the bus on which he was later seen. Furthermore, if Oswald had traveled from Dallas to Alice, he would not have reached the Houston to Laredo bus until after he was first reportedly observed on it by the McFarlands.[733] Oswald had also told passengers on the bus to Laredo that he had traveled from New Orleans by bus, and made no mention of an intervening trip to Dallas.[734] In addition, the Commission noted evidence that on the evening of September 25, 1963, Oswald made a telephone call to a party in Houston proposing to visit a resident of Houston that evening [735] and the fact that such a call would appear to be inconsistent with Oswald's having been in Dallas at the time. It thus appeared that the evidence was persuasive that Oswald was not in Dallas on September 25, and, therefore, that he was not in that city at the time Mrs. Odio said she saw him.

In spite of the fact that it appeared almost certain that Oswald could not have been in Dallas at the time Mrs. Odio thought he was, the Commission requested the FBI to conduct further investigation to determine the validity of Mrs. Odio's testimony.[736] The Commission considered the problems raised by that testimony as important in view of the possibility it raised that Oswald may have had companions on his trip to Mexico.[737] The Commission specifically requested the FBI to attempt to locate and identify the two men who Mrs. Odio stated were with the man she thought was Oswald.[738] In an effort to do that the FBI located and interviewed Manuel Ray, a leader of JURE who confirmed that Mrs. Odio's parents were political prisoners in Cuba, but stated that he did not know anything about the alleged Oswald visit.[739] The same was true of Rogelio Cisneros,[740] a former anti-Castro leader from Miami who had visited Mrs. Odio in June of 1962 in connection with certain anti-Castro activities.[741] Additional investigation was conducted in Dallas and in other cities in search of the visitors to Mrs. Odio's apartment.[742] Mrs. Odio herself was reinterviewed.[743]

On September 16, 1964, the FBI located Loran Eugene Hall in Johnsandale, Calif.[744] Hall has been identified as a participant in numerous anti-Castro activities.[745] He told the FBI that in September of 1963 he was in Dallas, soliciting aid in connection with anti-Castro activities. He said he had visited Mrs. Odio. He was accompanied by Lawrence Howard, a Mexican-American from East Los Angeles and one William Seymour from Arizona. He stated that Seymour is similar in appearance to Lee Harvey Oswald; he speaks only a few words of Spanish,[746] as Mrs. Odio had testified one of the men who visited her did.[747] While the FBI had not yet completed its investigation into this matter at the time the report went to press, the Commission has concluded that Lee Harvey Oswald was not at Mrs. Odio's apartment in September of 1963.

The Commission has also noted the testimony of Evaristo Rodriguez, a bartender in the Habana Bar in New Orleans, to the effect that he saw Oswald in that bar in August of 1963 in the company of a

Latin-appearing man.[748]   Rodriguez' description of the man accompanying the person he thought to be Oswald was similar in respects to the description given by Sylvia Odio since both testified that the man may have been of either Cuban or Mexican extraction, and had a slight bald spot on the forepart of his hairline.[749]   Rodriguez' identification of Oswald was uncorroborated except for the testimony of the owner of the bar, Orest Pena; according to Rodriguez, Pena was not in a position to observe the man he thought later to have been Oswald.[750] Although Pena has testified that he did observe the same person as did Rodriguez, and that this person was Oswald,[751] an FBI interview report indicated that a month earlier Pena had stated that he "could not at this time or at any time say whether or not the person was identical with Lee Harvey Oswald." [752]   Though when testifying, Pena identified photographs of Oswald, the FBI report also recorded that Pena "stated the only reason he was able to recognize Oswald was because he had seen Oswald's picture in the news media so often after the assassination of President John F. Kennedy." [753]   When present at Pena's bar, Oswald was supposed to have been intoxicated to the extent that he became ill,[754] which is inconsistent with other evidence that Oswald did not drink alcoholic beverages to excess.[755]

The Commission has also noted the testimony of Dean Andrews, an attorney in New Orleans.   Andrews stated that Oswald came to his office several times in the summer of 1963 to seek advice on a less than honorable discharge from the Armed Forces, the citizenship status of his wife and his own citizenship status.   Andrews, who believed that he was contacted on November 23 to represent Oswald, testified that Oswald was always accompanied by a Mexican and was at times accompanied by apparent homosexuals.[756]   Andrews was able to locate no records of any of Oswald's alleged visits, and investigation has failed to locate the person who supposedly called Andrews on November 23, at a time when Andrews was under heavy sedation.[757]   While one of Andrews' employees felt that Oswald might have been at his office, his secretary has no recollection of Oswald being there.[758]

Oswald Was Not an Agent for the U.S. Government

From the time of his release from the Marine Corps until the assassination, Lee Harvey Oswald dealt in various transactions with several agencies of the U.S. Government.   Before departing the United States for the Soviet Union in 1959, he obtained an American passport, which he returned to the Embassy in Moscow in October 1959 when he attempted to renounce his U.S. citizenship.   Thereafter, while in the Soviet Union, Oswald had numerous contacts with the American Embassy, both in person and through correspondence.   Two years later, he applied for the return and renewal of his passport, which was granted him.   His application concerning the admittance of his wife to this country was passed upon by the Immigration and Naturalization Service of the Department of Justice in addition to the State Department.   And before returning to this country, he secured a loan from the State Department to help cover his transportation costs from Moscow to New York. These dealings with the Department of State and the Immigration and Naturalization Service have been reviewed earlier in this chapter and are considered in detail in appendix XV. After his return, Oswald was interviewed on three occasions by agents of the FBI, and Mrs. Paine was also questioned by the FBI about Oswald's activities. Oswald obtained a second passport in June of 1963. And both the FBI and the CIA took note of his Fair Play for Cuba Committee activities in New Orleans and his appearance at the Soviet consulate in Mexico City. For reasons which will be discussed fully in chapter VIII, Oswald's name was never given to the U.S. Secret Service.

These dealings have given rise to numerous rumors and allegations that Oswald may have been a paid informant or some type of undercover agent for a Federal agency, usually the FBI or the CIA. The Commission has fully explored whether Oswald had any official or unofficial relationship with any Federal agency beyond that already described.

Oswald's mother, Mrs. Marguerite Oswald, testified before the Commission that she believes her son went to Russia and returned as an undercover agent for the U.S. Government.[759] Mrs. Oswald mentioned the belief that her son was an agent to a State Department representative whom she visited in January 1961, when she was trying to locate her son.[760] She had been interviewed earlier by FBI Agent John W. Fain, within some 6 months of Oswald's departure for Russia, and did not at that time suggest such an explanation for Oswald's departure.[761] Though provided the opportunity to present any material she considered pertinent, Mrs. Oswald was not able to give the Commission any reasonable basis for her speculation.[762] As discussed later in this chapter, the Commission has investigated Marguerite Oswald's claim that an FBI agent showed her a picture of Jack Ruby after the assassination but before Lee Harvey Oswald had been killed; this allegation was inaccurate, since the picture was not of Ruby.

After the assassination it was reported that in 1962 Oswald had told Pauline Bates, a public stenographer in Fort Worth, Tex., that he had become a "secret agent" of the U.S. Government and that he was soon going back to Russia "for Washington." [763] Mrs. Bates in her sworn testimony denied that Oswald ever told her anything to that effect.[764] She testified that she had stated "that when he first said that he went to Russia and had gotten a visa that I thought—it was just a thought—that maybe he was going over under the auspices of the State Department—as a student or something." [765]

In order to evaluate the nature of Oswald's dealings with the Department of State and the Immigration and Naturalization Service, the Commission has obtained the complete files of both the Department and the Service pertaining to Lee Harvey Oswald. Officials who were directly involved in dealing with the Oswald case on these matters have testified before the Commission. A critical evaluation of the manner in which they were handled by these organizations is set forth in appendix XV. The record establishes that Oswald received no preferential treatment and that his case involved no impropriety on the part of any Government official.

Director John A. McCone and Deputy Director Richard Helms of the Central Intelligence Agency testified before the Commission that no one connected with the CIA had ever interviewed Oswald or communicated with him in any way.[766] In his supplementing affidavit, Director McCone stated unequivocally that Oswald was not an agent, employee, or informant of the CIA, that the Agency never communicated with him in any manner or furnished him any compensation, and that Oswald was never directly or indirectly associated with the CIA.[767] The Commission has had access to the full CIA file on Oswald which is entirely consistent with Director McCone's statements.

The Director of the FBI, J. Edgar Hoover, Assistant to the Director Alan H. Belmont, FBI Agents John W. Fain and John L. Quigley, who interviewed Oswald, and FBI Agent James P. Hosty, Jr., who was in charge of his case at the time of the assassination, have also testified before the Commission. All declared, in substance, that Oswald was not an informant or agent of the FBI, that he did not act in any other capacity for the FBI, and that no attempt was made to recruit him in any capacity.[768] Director Hoover and each Bureau agent, who according to the FBI would have been responsible for or aware of any attempt to recruit Oswald as an informant, have also provided the Commission with sworn affidavits to this effect.[769] Director Hoover has sworn that he caused a search to be made of the records of the Bureau, and that the search discloses that Oswald "was never an informant of the FBI, and never assigned a symbol number in that capacity, and was never paid any amount of money by the FBI in any regard." [770] This testimony is corroborated by the Commission's independent review of the Bureau files dealing with the Oswald investigation.

The Commission also investigated the circumstances which led to the presence in Oswald's address book of the name of Agent Hosty together with his office address, telephone number, and license number.[771] Hosty and Mrs. Paine testified that on November 1, 1963, Hosty left his name and phone number with Mrs. Paine so that she could advise Hosty when she learned where Oswald was living in Dallas.[772] Mrs. Paine and Marina Oswald have testified that Mrs. Paine handed Oswald the slip of paper on which Hosty had written this information.[773] In accordance with prior instructions from Oswald,[774] Marina Oswald noted Hosty's license number which she gave to her husband.[775] The address of the Dallas office of the FBI could have been obtained from many public sources.

Thus, close scrutiny of the records of the Federal agencies involved and the testimony of the responsible officials of the U.S. Government establish that there was absolutely no type of informant or undercover relationship between an agency of the U.S. Government and Lee Harvey Oswald at any time.

Oswald's Finances

In search of activities or payments demonstrating the receipt of unexplained funds, the Commission undertook a detailed study of Oswald's receipts and expenditures starting with the date of his return from the Soviet Union on June 13, 1962, and continuing to the date of his arrest on November 22, 1963. In appendix XIV there appears a table listing Oswald's estimated receipts and expenditures on a monthly basis during this period.

The Commission was assisted in this phase of the investigation by able investigators of the Internal Revenue Service of the Department of the Treasury and by agents of the FBI. The investigation extended far beyond interrogation of witnesses who appeared before the Commission. At banks in New Orleans, La.; Fort Worth, Dallas, Houston, and Laredo, Tex., inquiries were made for any record of a checking, savings, or loan accounts or a safe deposit box rented in the names of Lee Harvey Oswald, his known aliases, or members of his immediate family. In many cases a photograph of Oswald was exhibited to bank officials who were in a position to see a person in the safe deposit box area of their banks. No bank account or safe deposit boxes were located which could be identified with Oswald during this period of his life, although evidence was developed of a bank account which he had used prior to his trip to the Soviet Union in 1959. Telegraph companies were checked for the possibility of money orders that may have been sent to Oswald. All known locations where Oswald cashed checks which he received were queried as to the possibility of his having cashed other checks there. Further inquiries were made at Oswald's places of employment, his residences and with local credit associations, hospitals, utility companies, State and local government offices, post offices, periodicals, newspapers, and employment agencies.[776]

Marina Oswald testified that she knew of no sources of income Oswald other than his wages and his unemployment compensation.[777] No evidence of other cash income has been discovered. The Commission has found that the funds known to have been available to Oswald during the period June 13, 1962, through November 22, 1963, were sufficient to cover all of his known expenditures during this period. Including cash on hand of $63 when he arrived from the Soviet Union, the Oswalds received a total of $3,665.89 in cash from wages, unemployment compensation benefits, loans, and gifts from acquaintances. His cash disbursements during this period were estimated at $3,501.79, leaving a balance of $164.10. (See app. XIV.) This estimated balance is within $19 of the $183.87 in cash which was actually in Oswald's possession at the time of his arrest, consisting of $13.87 on his person and $170 in his wallet left at the Paine house.[778]

In computing Oswald's expenditures, estimates were made for food, clothing, and incidental expenses. The incidental expenses included telephone calls, the cost of local newspapers, money order and check-cashing fees, postage, local transportation costs, personal care goods and services, and other such small items. All of these expenses, including food and clothing, were estimated at a slightly higher figure than would be normal for a family with the income of the Oswalds, and probably higher than the Oswalds actually spent on such items.[779] This was done in order to be certain that even if some of Oswald's minor expenditures are not known, he had adequate funds to cover his known expenditures.

During the 17-month period preceding his death, Oswald's pattern of living was consistent with his limited income. He lived with his family in furnished apartments whose cost, including utilities, ranged from about $60 to $75 per month.[780] Witnesses testified to his wife's disappointment and complaints and to their own shock and misgivings about several of the apartments in which the Oswalds lived during the period.[781] Moreover, the Oswalds, particularly Marina, frequently lived with relatives and acquaintances at no cost. Oswald and his family lived with his brother Robert and then with Marguerite Oswald from June until sometime in August 1962.[782] As discussed previously, Marina Oswald lived with Elena Hall and spent a few nights at the Taylors' house during October of 1962;[783] in November of that same year, Marina Oswald lived with two families.[784] When living away from his family Oswald rented rooms for $7 and $8 per week or stayed at the YMCA in Dallas where he paid $2.25 per day.[785] During late April and early May 1963, Oswald lived with relatives in New Orleans, while his wife lived with Ruth Paine in Irving, Tex.[786] From September 24, 1963, until November 22, Marina Oswald stayed with Ruth Paine, while Oswald lived in roominghouses in Dallas.[787] During the period Marina Oswald resided with others, neither she nor her husband made any contribution to her support.[788]

The Oswalds owned no major household appliances, had no automobile, and resorted to dental and hospital clinics for medical care.[789] Acquaintances purchased baby furniture for them, and paid dental bills in one instance.[790] After his return to the United States, Oswald did not smoke or drink, and he discouraged his wife from doing so.[791] Oswald spent much of his time reading books which he obtained from the public library, and periodicals to which he subscribed.[792] He resided near his place of employment and used buses to travel to and from work.[793] When he visited his wife and the children on weekends in October and November 1963, he rode in a neighbor's car, making no contribution for gasoline or other expenses.[794] Oswald's personal wardrobe was also very modest. He customarily wore T-shirts, cheap slacks, well-worn sweaters, and well-used zipper jackets. Oswald owned one suit, of Russian make and purchase, poor fitting and of heavy fabric which, despite its unsuitability to the climates of Texas and Louisiana and his obvious discomfort, he wore on the few occasions that required dress.[795]

Food for his family was extremely meager. Paul Gregory testified that during the 6 weeks that Marina Oswald tutored him he took the Oswalds shopping for food and groceries on a number of occasions and that he was "amazed at how little they bought."[796] Their friends in the Dallas-Fort Worth area frequently brought them food and groceries.[797] Marina testified that her husband ate "very little." He "never had breakfast. He just drank coffee and that is all. Not because he was trying to economize. Simply he never liked to eat." She estimated that when he was living by himself in a roominghouse, he would spend "about a dollar, $1.30" for dinner and have a sandwich and soft drink for lunch.[798]

The thrift which Oswald exercised in meeting his living expenses allowed him to accumulate sufficient funds to meet other expenses which he incurred after his return from the Soviet Union. From his return until January of 1963, Oswald repaid the $435.71 he had borrowed from the State Department for travel expenses from Moscow, and the $200 loan he had obtained from his brother Robert to fly from New York to Dallas upon his return to this country. He completed the retirement of the debt to his brother in October 1962.[799] His cash receipts from all sources from the day of his arrival in Fort Worth through October 1962 aggregated $719.94; it is estimated that he could have made the repayments to Robert and met his other known expenses and still have been left with savings of $122.06 at the end of the month. After making initial $10 monthly payments to the State Department, Oswald paid the Government $190 in December and $206 in January, thus liquidating that debt.[800] From his net earning of $805.96 from November through January plus his prior savings, Oswald could have made these payments to the State Department, met his other known expenses, and still have had a balance of $8.59 at the end of January 1963. In discussing the repayment of these debts, Marina Oswald testified: "Of course we did not live in luxury. We did not buy anything that was not absolutely needed, because Lee had to pay his debt to Robert and to the Government. But it was not particularly difficult." [801]

Included in the total figure for Oswald's disbursements were $21.45 for the rifle used in the assassination and $31.22 for the revolver with which Oswald shot Officer Tippit. The major portion of the purchase price for these weapons was paid in March 1963, when Oswald had finished paying his debts, and the purchases were compatible with the total funds then available to him.[802] During May, June, and July of 1963, Oswald spent approximately $23 for circulars, application blanks, and membership cards for his one-man New Orleans chapter of the Fair Play for Cuba Committee.[803] In August he paid $2 to one and possibly two young men to assist in passing out circulars and then paid a $10 court fine after pleading guilty to a charge of disturbing the peace.[804] Although some of these expenses were incurred after Oswald lost his job on July 19, 1963, his wages during June and July, and his unemployment compensation thereafter, provided sufficient funds to enable him to finance these activities out of his own resources.[805]

Although Oswald paid his own busfare to New Orleans on April 24, 1963, his wife and the baby were taken there, at no cost to Oswald, by Ruth Paine.[806] Similarly, Ruth Paine drove to New Orleans in

September and brought Marina Oswald and the baby back to Irving, Tex.[807] Oswald's uncle, Charles Murret, also paid for the short trip taken by Oswald and his family from New Orleans to Mobile, Ala., on July 27, 1963.[808] It is estimated that when Oswald left for Mexico City in September 1963, he had accumulated slightly over $200. Marina Oswald testified that when he left for Mexico City he had "a little over $100," though she may not have taken into account the $33 unemployment compensation check which Oswald collected after her departure from New Orleans.[809] In any event, expenses in Mexico have been estimated as approximately $85, based on transportation costs of $50 and a hotel expense of about $1.28 per day. Oswald ate inexpensively and, allowing $15 for entertainment and miscellaneous items, it would appear that he had the funds available to finance the trip.[810]

The Commission has considered the testimony of Leonard E. Hutchison, proprietor of Hutch's Market in Irving, in connection with Oswald's finances. Hutchison has testified that on a Friday during the first week in November, a man he believes to have been Lee Harvey Oswald attempted to cash a "two-party," or personal check for $189, but that he refused to cash the check since his policy is to cash personal checks for no more than $25.[811] Oswald is not known to have received a check for this amount from any source.

On Friday, November 1, Oswald did cash a Texas Unemployment Commission check for $33 at another supermarket in Irving,[812] so that a possible explanation of Hutchison's testimony is that he refused to cash this $33 check for Oswald and is simply in error as to the amount of the instrument. However, since the check cashed at the supermarket was issued by the State comptroller of Texas, it is not likely that Hutchison could have confused it with a personal check.

Examination of Hutchison's testimony indicates that a more likely explanation is that Oswald was not in his store at all. Hutchison testified that the man who attempted to cash the check was a customer in his store on previous occasions; in particular, Hutchison recalled that the man, accompanied by a woman he believes was Marina Oswald and an elderly woman, were shopping in his store in October or November of 1963 on a night he feels certain was a Wednesday evening.[813] Oswald, however, is not known to have been in Irving on any Wednesday evening during this period.[814] Neither of the two checkers at the market recall such a visit by a person matching the description provided by Hutchison, and both Marina Oswald and Marguerite Oswald deny that they were ever in Hutchison's store.[815] Hutchison further stated that the man made irregular calls at his grocery between 7:20 a.m. and 7:45 a.m. on weekday mornings, and always purchased cinnamon rolls and a full gallon of milk.[816] However, the evidence indicates that except for rare occasions Oswald was in Irving only on weekends; moreover, Buell Wesley Frazier, who drove Oswald to and from Irving on these occasions, testified that on Monday mornings he picked Oswald up at a point which is many blocks from Hutchison's store and ordinarily by 7:20 a.m.[817]

Hutchison also testified that Ruth Paine was an occasional customer in his store; [818] however, Mrs. Paine indicated that she was not in the store as often as Hutchison testified; [819] and her appearance is dissimilar to the description of the woman Hutchison stated was Mrs. Paine.[820] In light of the strong reasons for doubting the correctness of Hutchison's testimony and the absence of any other sign that Oswald ever possessed a personal check for $189, the Commission was unable to conclude that he ever received such a check.

The Commission has also examined a report that, not long before the assassination, Oswald may have received unaccounted funds through money orders sent to him in Dallas. Five days after the assassination, C. A. Hamblen, early night manager for the Western Union Telegraph Co. in Dallas, told his superior that about 2 weeks earlier he remembered Oswald sending a telegram from the office to Washington, D.C., possibly to the Secretary of the Navy, and that the application was completed in an unusual form of hand printing.[821] The next day Hamblen told a magazine correspondent who was in the Western Union office on other business that he remembered seeing Oswald in the office on prior occasions collecting money orders for small amounts of money.[822] Soon thereafter Hamblen signed a statement relating to both the telegram and the money orders, and specifying two instances in which he had seen the person he believed to be Oswald in the office; in each instance the man had behaved disagreeably and one other Western Union employee had become involved in assisting him.[823]

During his testimony, Hamblen did not recall with clarity the statements he had previously made, and was unable to state whether the person he reportedly had seen in the Western Union office was or was not Lee Harvey Oswald.[824] Investigation has disclosed that a second employee does recall one of the occurrences described by Hamblen, and believes that the money order in question was delivered "to someone at the YMCA"; however, he is unable to state whether or not the man involved was Oswald.[825] The employee referred to by Hamblen in connection with the second incident feels certain that the unusual episode described by Hamblen did not occur, and that she at no time observed Oswald in the Western Union office.[826]

At the request of Federal investigators, officers of Western Union conducted a complete search of their records in Dallas and in other cities, for the period from June through November 1963, for money orders payable to Lee Harvey Oswald or his known aliases and for telegrams sent by Oswald or his known aliases. In addition, all money orders addressed to persons at the YMCA in Dallas during October and November 1963 were inspected, and all telegrams handled from November 1 through November 22 by the employee who Hamblen assertedly saw service Oswald were examined, as were all telegrams sent from Dallas to Washington during November. No indication of any such money order or telegram was found in any of these records.[827] Hamblen himself participated in this search, and was "unab'e * * * to pin down any of these telegrams or money orders that would indicate it was Oswald." [828]   Hamblen's superiors have concluded "that this whole thing was a figment of Mr. Hamblen's imagination," [829] and the Commission accepts this assessment.

POSSIBLE CONSPIRACY INVOLVING JACK RUBY

Jack Ruby shot Lee Harvey Oswald at 11:21 a.m., on Sunday, November 24, 1963, shortly after Ruby entered the basement of the Dallas Police Department. Almost immediately, speculation arose that Ruby had acted on behalf of members of a conspiracy who had planned the killing of President Kennedy and wanted to silence Oswald. This section of chapter VI sets forth the Commission's investigation into the possibility that Ruby, together with Oswald or with others, conspired to kill the President, or that Ruby, though not part of any such conspiracy, had accomplices in the slaying of Oswald. Presented first are the results of the Commission's detailed inquiry into Ruby's actions from November 21 to November 24. In addition, this section analyzes the numerous rumors and suspicions that Ruby and Oswald were acquainted and examines Ruby's background and associations for evidence of any conspiratorial relationship or motive. A detailed life of Ruby is given in appendix XVI which provides supplemental information about Ruby and his associations.

Ruby's Activities From November 21 to November 24, 1963

The Commission has attempted to reconstruct as precisely as possible the movements of Jack Ruby during the period November 21–November 24, 1963. It has done so on the premise that, if Jack Ruby were involved in a conspiracy, his activities and associations during this period would, in some way, have reflected the conspiratorial relationship. The Commission has not attempted to determine the time at which Ruby first decided to make his attack on Lee Harvey Oswald, nor does it purport to evaluate the psychiatric and related legal questions which have arisen from the assault upon Oswald. Ruby's activities during this 3-day period have been scrutinized, however, for the insight they provide into whether the shooting of Oswald was grounded in any form of conspiracy.

The eve of the President's visit.—On Thursday, November 21, Jack Ruby was attending to his usual duties as the proprietor of two Dallas night spots—the Carousel Club, a downtown nightclub featuring striptease dancers, and the Vegas Club, a rock-and-roll establishment in the Oaklawn section of Dallas. Both clubs opened for business each day in the early evening and continued 7 days a week until after midnight.[830] Ruby arrived at the Carousel Club at about 3 p.m. Thursday afternoon, as was his custom,[831] and remained long enough to chat with a friend and receive messages from Larry Crafard, a handyman and helper who lived at the Carousel.[832] Earlier in the day Ruby had visited with a young lady who was job hunting in Dallas,[833] paid his rent for the Carousel premises,[834] conferred about a peace bond he had been obliged to post as a result of a fight with one of his striptease dancers,[835] consulted with an attorney about problems he was having with Federal tax authorities,[836] distributed membership cards for the Carousel Club,[837] talked with Dallas County Assistant District Attorney William F. Alexander about insufficient fund checks which a friend had passed,[838] and submitted advertising copy for his nightclubs to the Dallas Morning News.[839]

Ruby's evening activities on Thursday, November 21, were a combination of business and pleasure. At approximately 7:30 p.m., he drove Larry Crafard to the Vegas Club which Crafard was overseeing because Ruby's sister, Eva Grant, who normally managed the club, was convalescing from a recent illness.[840] Thereafter, Ruby returned to the Carousel Club and conversed for about an hour with Lawrence Meyers, a Chicago businessman.[841] Between 9:45 and 10:45 p.m., Ruby had dinner with Ralph Paul, his close friend and financial backer. While dining Ruby spoke briefly with a Dallas Morning News employee, Don Campbell, who suggested that they go to the Castaway Club, but Ruby declined.[842] Thereafter, Ruby returned to the Carousel Club where he acted as master of ceremonies for his show and peacefully ejected an unruly patron.[843] At about midnight Ruby rejoined Meyers at the Bon Vivant Room of the Dallas Cabana where they met Meyers' brother and sister-in-law.[844] Neither Ralph Paul nor Lawrence Meyers recalled that Ruby mentioned the President's trip to Dallas.[845] Leaving Meyers at the Cabana after a brief visit, Ruby returned to close the Carousel Club and obtain the night's receipts.[846] He then went to the Vegas Club which he helped Larry Crafard close for the night; [847] and, as late as 2:30 a.m., Ruby was seen eating at a restaurant near the Vegas Club.[848]

Friday morning at the Dallas Morning News.—Jack Ruby learned of the shooting of President Kennedy while in the second-floor advertising offices of the Dallas Morning News, five blocks from the Texas School Book Depository, where he had come Friday morning to place regular weekend advertisements for his two nightclubs.[849] On arriving at the newspaper building at about 11 or 11:30 a.m., he talked briefly with two newspaper employees concerning some diet pills he had recommended to them.[850] Ruby then went to the office of Morning News columnist, Tony Zoppi, where he states he obtained a brochure on his new master of ceremonies that he wanted to use in preparing copy for his advertisements.[851] Proceeding to the advertising department, he spoke with advertising employee Don Campbell from about noon until 12:25 p.m. when Campbell left the office.[852] In addition to the business at hand, much of the conversation concerned Ruby's unhappiness over the financial condition of his clubs and his professed ability to handle the physical fights which arose in connection with the clubs.[583] According to Campbell, Ruby did not mention the Presidential motorcade nor did he display any unusual behavior.[854]

About 10 minutes after the President had been shot but before word had spread to the second floor, John Newnam, an advertising department employee, observed Ruby sitting at the same spot where Campbell had left him. At that time Ruby had completed the advertisement, which he had apparently begun to compose when Campbell departed, and was reading a newspaper.[855] To Newnam, Ruby voiced criticism of the black-bordered advertisement entitled "Welcome, Mr. Kennedy" appearing in the morning paper and bearing the name of Bernard Weissman as the chairman of the committee sponsoring the advertisement.[856] (See Commission Exhibit No. 1031, p. 294.) According to Eva Grant, Ruby's sister, he had telephoned her earlier in the morning to call her attention to the ad.[857] At about 12:45 p.m., an employee entered the office and announced that shots had been fired at the President. Newnam remembered that Ruby responded with a look of "stunned disbelief." [858]

Shortly afterward, according to Newnam, "confusion reigned" in the office as advertisers telephoned to cancel advertising they had placed for the weekend.[859] Ruby appears to have believed that some of those cancellations were motivated by the Weissman advertisement.[860] After Newnam accepted a few telephone calls, he and Ruby walked toward a room where other persons were watching television.[861] One of the newspaper employees recalled that Ruby then appeared "obviously shaken, and an ashen color—just very pale * * *" [362] showed little disposition to converse,[863] and sat for a while with a dazed expression in his eyes.[864]

After a few minutes, Ruby placed telephone calls to Andrew Armstrong, his assistant at the Carousel Club, and to his sister, Mrs. Grant. He told Armstrong, "If anything happens we are going to close the club" and said he would see him in about 30 minutes.[865] During the call to his sister, Ruby again referred to the Weissman advertisement; at one point he put the telephone to Newnam's ear, and Newnam heard Mrs. Grant exclaim, "My God, what do they want?" It was Newnam's recollection that Ruby tried to calm her.[866]

Ruby testified that after calling his sister he said, "John, I will have to leave Dallas." [867] Ruby explained to the Commission:

> I don't know why I said that, but it is a funny reaction that you feel; the city is terribly let down by the tragedy that happened. And I said, "John, I am not opening up tonight."
> And I don't know what else transpired. I know people were just heartbroken * * *.
> I left the building and I went down and I got in my car and I couldn't stop crying. * * * [868]

Newnam estimated that Ruby departed from the Morning News at about 1:30 p.m., but other testimony indicated that Ruby may have left earlier.[869]

Ruby's alleged visit to Parkland Hospital.—The Commission has investigated claims that Jack Ruby was at Parkland Hospital at about 1:30 p.m., when a Presidential press secretary, Malcolm Kilduff, announced that President Kennedy was dead. Seth Kantor, a newspaperman who had previously met Ruby in Dallas, reported and later testified that Jack Ruby stopped him momentarily inside the main entrance to Parkland Hospital some time between 1:30 and 2 p.m., Friday, November 22, 1963.[870] The only other person besides Kantor who recalled seeing Ruby at the hospital did not make known her observation until April 1964, had never seen Ruby before, allegedly saw him only briefly then, had an obstructed view, and was uncertain of the time.[871] Ruby has firmly denied going to Parkland and has stated that he went to the Carousel Club upon leaving the Morning News.[872] Video tapes of the scene at Parkland do not show Ruby there, although Kantor can be seen.[873]

Investigation has limited the period during which Kantor could have met Ruby at Parkland Hospital on Friday to a few minutes before and after 1:30 p.m. Telephone company records and the testimony of Andrew Armstrong established that Ruby arrived at the Carousel Club no later than 1:45 p.m. and probably a few minutes earlier.[874] Kantor was engaged in a long-distance telephone call to his Washington office from 1:02 p.m. until 1:27 p.m.[875] Kantor testified that, after completing that call, he immediately left the building from which he had been telephoning, traveled perhaps 100 yards, and entered the main entrance of the hospital. It was there, as he walked through a small doorway, that he believed he saw Jack Ruby, who, Kantor said, tugged at his coattails and asked, "Should I close my places for the next three nights, do you think?" Kantor recalled that he turned briefly to Ruby and proceeded to the press conference at which the President's death was announced. Kantor was certain he encountered Ruby at Parkland but had doubts about the exact time and place.[876]

Kantor probably did not see Ruby at Parkland Hospital in the few minutes before or after 1:30 p.m., the only time it would have been possible for Kantor to have done so. If Ruby immediately returned to the Carousel Club after Kantor saw him, it would have been necessary for him to have covered the distance from Parkland in approximately 10 or 15 minutes in order to have arrived at the club before 1:45 p.m., when a telephone call was placed at Ruby's request to his entertainer, Karen Bennett Carlin.[877] At a normal driving speed under normal conditions the trip can be made in 9 or 10 minutes.[878] However, it is likely that congested traffic conditions on November 22 would have extended the driving time.[879] Even if Ruby had been able to drive from Parkland to the Carousel in 15 minutes, his presence at the Dallas Morning News until after 1 p.m., and at the Carousel prior to 1:45 p.m., would have made his visit at Parkland exceedingly brief. Since Ruby was observed at the Dallas Police Department during a 2 hour period after 11 p.m. on Friday,[880] when Kantor was also present, and since Kantor did not remember seeing Ruby there,[881] Kantor may have been mistaken about both the time and the place that he saw Ruby. When seeing Ruby, Kantor was preoccupied with the important event that a press conference represented. Both Ruby and Kantor were present at another important event, a press conference held about midnight, November 22, in the assembly room of the Dallas Police Department. It is conceivable that Kantor's encounter with Ruby occurred at that time, perhaps near the small doorway there.[882]

Ruby's decision to close his clubs.—Upon arriving at the Carousel Club shortly before 1:45 p.m., Ruby instructed Andrew Armstrong, the Carousel's bartender, to notify employees that the club would be closed that night.[883] During much of the next hour Ruby talked by telephone to several persons who were or had been especially close to him, and the remainder of the time he watched television and spoke with Armstrong and Larry Crafard about the assassination.[884] At 1:51 p.m., Ruby telephoned Ralph Paul in Arlington, Tex., to say that he was going to close his clubs. He urged Paul to do likewise with his drive-in restaurant.[885] Unable to reach Alice Nichols, a former girl friend, who was at lunch, Ruby telephoned his sister, Eileen Kaminsky, in Chicago.[886] Mrs. Kaminsky described her brother as completely unnerved and crying about President Kennedy's death.[887] To Mrs. Nichols, whose return call caused Ruby to cut short his conversation with Mrs. Kaminsky, Ruby expressed shock over the assassination.[888] Although Mrs. Nichols had dated Ruby for nearly 11 years, she was surprised to hear from him on November 22 since they had not seen one another socially for some time.[889] Thereafter, Ruby telephoned at 2:37 p.m. to Alex Gruber, a boyhood friend from Chicago who was living in Los Angeles.[890] Gruber recalled that in their 3-minute conversation Ruby talked about a dog he had promised to send Gruber, a carwash business Gruber had considered starting, and the assassination.[891] Ruby apparently lost his self-control during the conversation and terminated it.[892] However, 2 minutes after that call ended, Ruby telephoned again to Ralph Paul.[893]

Upon leaving the Carousel Club at about 3:15 p.m., Ruby drove to Eva Grant's home but left soon after he arrived, to obtain some weekend food for his sister and himself.[894] He first returned to the Carousel Club and directed Larry Crafard to prepare a sign indicating that the club would be closed; however, Ruby instructed Crafard not to post the sign until later in the evening to avoid informing his competitors that he would be closed.[895] (See Commission Exhibit 2427, p. 339.) Before leaving the club, Ruby telephoned Mrs. Grant who reminded him to purchase food.[896] As a result he went to the Ritz Delicatessen, about two blocks from the Carousel Club, and bought a great quantity of cold cuts.[897]

Ruby probably arrived a second time at his sister's home close to 5:30 p.m. and remained for about 2 hours. He continued his rapid rate of telephone calls, ate sparingly, became ill, and attempted to get some rest.[898] While at the apartment, Ruby decided to close his clubs for 3 days. He testified that after talking to Don Saffran, a columnist for the Dallas Times-Herald:

> I put the receiver down and talked to my sister, and I said, "Eva, what shall we do?"
> And she said, "Jack, let's close for the 3 days." She said, "We don't have anything anyway, but we owe it to—" (chokes up.)

So I called Don Saffran back immediately and I said, "Don, we decided to close for Friday, Saturday, and Sunday."

And he said, "Okay." [899]

Ruby then telephoned the Dallas Morning News to cancel his advertisement and, when unable to do so, he changed his ad to read that his clubs would be closed for the weekend.[900]   Ruby also telephoned Cecil Hamlin, a friend of many years.   Sounding very "broken up," he told Hamlin that he had closed the clubs since he thought most people would not be in the mood to visit them and that he felt concern for President Kennedy's "kids." [901]   Thereafter he made two calls to ascertain when services at Temple Shearith Israel would be held.[902]   He placed a second call to Alice Nichols to tell her of his intention to attend those services [903] and phoned Larry Crafard at the Carousel to ask whether he had received any messages.[904]   Eva Grant testified:

When he was leaving, he looked pretty bad.   This I remember. I can't explain it to you.   He looked too broken, a broken man already.   He did make the remark, he said, "I never felt so bad in my life, even when Ma or Pa died."

So I said, "Well, Pa was an old man.   He was almost 89 years. * * *" [905]

Friday evening.—Ruby is uncertain whether he went directly from his sister's home to his apartment or possibly first to his club.[906]   At least 5 witnesses recall seeing a man they believe was Ruby on the third floor of police headquarters at times they have estimated between 6 and 9 p.m.; [907] however, it is not clear that Ruby was present at the Police and Courts Building before 11 p.m.   With respect to three of the witnesses, it is doubtful that the man observed was Ruby. Two of those persons had not known Ruby previously and described wearing apparel which differed both from Ruby's known dress that night and from his known wardrobe.[908]   The third, who viewed from the rear the person he believed was Ruby, said the man unsuccessfully attempted to enter the homicide office.[909]   Of the police officers on duty near homicide at the time of the alleged event, only one remembered the episode, and he said the man in question definitely was not Ruby.[910]   The remaining witnesses knew or talked with Ruby, and their testimony leaves little doubt that they did see him on the third floor at some point on Friday night; however the possibility remains that they observed Ruby later in the evening, when his presence is conclusively established.[911]   Ruby has denied being at the police department Friday night before approximately 11:15 p.m.[912]

In any event, Ruby eventually returned to his own apartment before 9 p.m.   There he telephoned Ralph Paul but was unable to persuade Paul to join him at synagogue services.[913]   Shortly after 9 p.m., Ruby called the Chicago home of his oldest brother, Hyman Rubenstein, and two of his sisters, Marion Carroll and Ann Volpert.[914]   Hyman Rubenstein testified that, during the call, his brother was so disturbed

"CLOSED" SIGN POSTED IN THE WINDOW OF THE CAROUSEL CLUB AND RUBY'S NEWSPAPER ADVERTISEMENT ANNOUNCING THAT THE VEGAS AND CAROUSEL CLUBS WILL BE CLOSED

(COMMISSION EXHIBIT 2427)

DALLAS TIMES HERALD
SATURDAY, NOV. 23, 1963
PAGE A-13

about the situation in Dallas that he mentioned selling his business and returning to Chicago.[915] From his apartment, Ruby drove to Temple Shearith Israel, arriving near the end of a 2-hour service which had begun at 8 p.m.[916] Rabbi Hillel Silverman, who greeted him among the crowd leaving the services [917] was surprised that Ruby, who appeared depressed, mentioned only his sister's recent illness and said nothing about the assassination.[918]

Ruby related that, after joining in the postservice refreshments,[919] he drove by some night clubs, noticing whether or not they had been closed as his were.[920] He testified that, as he drove toward town, a radio announcement that the Dallas police were working overtime prompted the thought that he might bring those at police headquarters something to eat.[921] At about 10:30 p.m., he stopped at a delicatessen near the Vegas Club and purchased 8 kosher sandwiches and 10 soft drinks.[922] From the delicatessen, he called the police department but was told that the officers had already eaten.[923] He said he then tried to offer the food to employees at radio station KLIF but failed in several attempts to obtain the private night line number to the station.[924] On three occasions between phone calls, Ruby spoke with a group of students whom he did not know, lamenting the President's death, teasing one of the young men about being too young for his clubs, borrowing their copy of the Dallas Times Herald to see how his advertisements had been run, and stating that his clubs were the only ones that had closed because of the assassination. He also expressed the opinion, as he had earlier in the day, that the assassination would be harmful to the convention business in Dallas.[925] Upon leaving the delicatessen with his purchases, Ruby gave the counterman as a tip a card granting free admission to his clubs.[926] He drove downtown to the police station where he has said he hoped to find an employee from KLIF who could give him the "hot line" phone number for the radio station.[927]

The third floor of police headquarters.—Ruby is known to have made his way, by about 11:30 p.m., to the third floor of the Dallas Police Department where reporters were congregated near the homicide bureau.[928] Newsman John Rutledge, one of those who may well have been mistaken as to time, gave the following description of his first encounter with Ruby at the police station:

> I saw Jack and two out-of-state reporters, whom I did not know, leave the elevator door and proceed toward those television cameras, to go around the corner where Captain Fritz's office was. Jack walked between them. These two out-of-state reporters had big press cards pinned on their coats, great big red ones, I think they said "President Kennedy's Visit to Dallas—Press", or something like that. And Jack didn't have one, but the man on either side of him did. And they walked pretty rapidly from the elevator area past the policeman, and Jack was bent over like this—writing on a piece of paper, and talking to one of the reporters, and pointing to something on the piece of paper, he was kind of hunched over.[929]

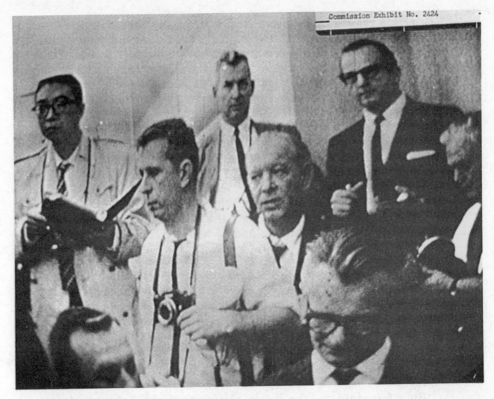

Jack Ruby at press conference in basement assembly room about midnight November 22, 1963. (Jack Ruby is the individual in the dark suit, back row, right-hand side, wearing horn-rimmed glasses.)

COMMISSION EXHIBIT No. 2424

Detective Augustus M. Eberhardt, who also recalled that he first saw Ruby earlier in the evening, said Ruby carried a note pad and professed to be a translator for the Israeli press. He remembered Ruby's remarking how unfortunate the assassination was for the city of Dallas and that it was "hard to realize that a complete nothing, a zero like that, could kill a man like President Kennedy * * *." [930]

Video tapes confirm Ruby's statement that he was present on the third floor when Chief Jesse E. Curry and District Attorney Henry M. Wade announced that Oswald would be shown to the newsmen at a press conference in the basement. [931] Though he has said his original purpose was only to locate a KLIF employee, Ruby has stated that while at the police station he was "carried away with the excitement of history." [932] He accompanied the newsmen to the basement to observe Oswald. His presence at the midnight news conference is established by television tapes and by at least 12 witnesses. [933] When Oswald arrived, Ruby, together with a number of newsmen, was standing atop a table on one side of the room. [934] (See Commission Exhibit No. 2424, p. 341.) Oswald was taken from the room after a brief appearance, and Ruby remained to hear reporters question District Attorney Wade. During the press conference, Wade stated that Oswald would probably be moved to the county jail at the beginning of the next week. [935] In answer to one question, Wade said that Oswald belonged to the "Free Cuba Committee." A few reporters spoke up correcting Wade and among the voices was that of Jack Ruby. [936]

Ruby later followed the district attorney out of the press conference, walked up to him and, according to Wade, said "Hi Henry * * * Don't you know me? * * * I am Jack Ruby, I run the Vegas Club. * * *" [937] Ruby also introduced himself to Justice of the Peace David L. Johnston, shook his hand, gave Johnston a business card to the Carousel Club, and, upon learning Johnston's official position, shook Johnston's hand again. [938] After talking with Johnston, he gave another card to Icarus M. Pappas, a reporter for New York radio station WNEW. [939] From a representative of radio station KBOX in Dallas, Ruby obtained the "hot line" telephone number to KLIF. [940] He then called the station and told one of the employees that he would like to come up to distribute the sandwiches and cold drinks he had purchased. [941] Observing Pappas holding a telephone line open and attempting to get the attention of District Attorney Wade, Ruby directed Wade to Pappas, who proceeded to interview the district attorney. [942] Ruby then called KLIF a second time and offered to secure an interview with Wade; he next summoned Wade to his phone, whereupon KLIF recorded a telephone interview with the district attorney. [943] A few minutes later, Ruby encountered Russ Knight, a reporter from KLIF who had left the station for the police department at the beginning of Ruby's second telephone call. Ruby directed Knight to Wade and waited a short distance away while the reporter conducted another interview with the district attorney. [944]

At radio station KLIF.—When Ruby left police headquarters, he drove to radio station KLIF, arriving at approximately 1:45 a.m. and remaining for about 45 minutes.[945] After first distributing his sandwiches and soft drinks, Ruby settled in the newsroom for the 2 a.m. newscast in which he was credited with suggesting that Russ Knight ask District Attorney Wade whether or not Oswald was sane.[946] After the newscast, Ruby gave a Carousel card to one KLIF employee, although another did not recall that Ruby was promoting his club as he normally did.[947] When speaking with KLIF's Danny Patrick McCurdy, Ruby mentioned that he was going to close his clubs for the weekend and that he would rather lose $1,200 or $1,500 than remain open at that time in the Nation's history. McCurdy remembered that Ruby "looked rather pale to me as he was talking to me and he kept looking at the floor." [948] To announcer Glen Duncan, Ruby expressed satisfaction that the evidence was mounting against Oswald. Duncan said that Ruby did not appear to be grieving but, instead, seemed pleased about the personal contact he had had with the investigation earlier in the evening.[949]

Ruby left the radio station accompanied by Russ Knight. Engaging Knight in a short conversation, Ruby handed him a radio script entitled "Heroism" from a conservative radio program called "Life Line." It was apparently one of the scripts that had come into Ruby's hands a few weeks before at the Texas Products Show when Hunt Foods were including such scripts with samples of their products.[950] The script extolled the virtues of those who embark upon risky business ventures and stand firmly for causes they believe to be correct.[951] Ruby asked Knight's views on the script and suggested that there was a group of "radicals" in Dallas which hated President Kennedy and that the owner of the radio station should editorialize against this group. Knight could not clearly determine whether Ruby had reference to persons who sponsored programs like "Life Line" or to those who held leftwing views.[952] Knight gained the impression that Ruby believed such persons, whoever they might be, were partially responsible for the assassination.[953]

Early morning of November 23.—At about 2:30 a.m., Ruby entered his automobile and departed for the Dallas Times-Herald Building. En route, he stopped for about an hour to speak with Kay Helen Coleman, one of his dancers, and Harry Olsen, a member of the Dallas Police Department, who had hailed him from a parking garage at the corner of Jackson and Field Streets. The couple were crying and extremely upset over the assassination. At one point, according to Ruby, the police officer remarked that "they should cut this guy [Oswald] inch by inch into ribbons," and the dancer said that "in England they would drag him through the streets and would have hung him." [954] Although Ruby failed to mention this episode during his first two FBI interviews,[955] he later explained that his reason for failing to do so was that he did not "want to involve them in anything, because it was supposed to be a secret that he [the police officer] was going with this young lady." [956] About

6 weeks after the assassination, Olsen left the Dallas Police Department and married Miss Coleman. Both Olsen and his wife testified that they were greatly upset during their lengthy conversation with Ruby early Saturday morning; but Mrs. Olsen denied and Olsen did not recall the remarks ascribed to them.[957] The Olsens claimed instead that Ruby had cursed Oswald.[958] Mrs. Olsen also mentioned that Ruby expressed sympathy for Mrs. Kennedy and her children.[959]

From Jackson and Field Streets, Ruby drove to the Dallas Times-Herald, where he talked for about 15 minutes with composing room employee Roy Pryor, who had just finished a shift at 4 a.m. Ruby mentioned that he had seen Oswald earlier in the night, that he had corrected Henry Wade in connection with the Fair Play for Cuba Committee, and that he had set up a telephone interview with Wade. Pryor testified that Ruby explicitly stated to him that he believed he was in good favor with the district attorney.[960] Recalling that Ruby described Oswald as a "little weasel of a guy" and was emotionally concerned about the President's wife and children, Pryor also was impressed by Ruby's sorrowful mood and remembered that, as he talked, Ruby shook a newspaper to emphasize his concern over the assassination.[961]

When Pryor left the composing room, Ruby remained and continued speaking with other employees, including Arthur Watherwax and the foreman, Clyde Gadash. Ruby, who often visited the Times-Herald at that early morning hour in connection with his ads, sought Watherwax's views on his decision to close his clubs and indicated he was going to attempt to persuade other club owners to do likewise. Watherwax described Ruby as "pretty shaken up" about the assassination and at the same time "excited" that he had attended Oswald's Friday night press conference.[962]

While at the Times-Herald, Ruby displayed to the composing room employees a "twistboard" he had previously promised to Gadash.[963] The twistboard was an exercising device consisting of two pieces of hardened materials joined together by a lazy susan bearing so that one piece could remain stationary on the floor while a person stood atop it and swiveled to and fro.[964] Ruby had been trying to promote sales of the board in the weeks before President Kennedy was killed.[965] Considerable merriment developed when one of the women employees at the Times-Herald demonstrated the board, and Ruby himself, put on a demonstration for those assembled.[966] He later testified: "* * * not that I wanted to get in with the hilarity of frolicking, but he [Gadash] asked me to show him, and the other men gathered around." [967] Gadash agreed that Ruby's general mood was one of sorrow.[968]

At about 4:30 a.m., Ruby drove from the Dallas Times-Herald to his apartment where he awakened his roommate George Senator.[969] During his visit in the composing room Ruby had expressed the view that the Weissman advertisement was an effort to discredit the Jews.[970] Senator testified that when Ruby returned to the apartment, he began to discuss the Weissman advertisement and also a signboard he had seen in Dallas urging that Chief Justice Earl Warren be impeached.[971] Shortly thereafter, Ruby telephoned Larry Crafard at the Carousel Club.[972] He told Crafard to meet him and Senator at the Nichols Garage adjacent to the Carousel Club and to bring a Polaroid camera kept in the club.[973] After Crafard joined Ruby and Senator, the three men drove to the "Impeach Earl Warren" sign near Hall Avenue and Central Expressway in Dallas. There Ruby instructed Crafard to take three photographs of the billboard. Believing that the sign and the Weissman newspaper ad might somehow be connected, Ruby noted on the back of an envelope a name and post office box number that appeared on the sign.[974] According to George Senator:

> * * * when he was looking at the sign and taking pictures of it, and the newspaper ad, * * * this is where he really wanted to know the whys or why these things had to be out. He is trying to combine these two together, which I did hear him say, "This is the work of the John Birch Society or the Communist Party or maybe a combination of both." [975]

Pursuing a possible connection between the billboard and the newspaper advertisement, Ruby drove to the post office and asked a postal employee for the name of the man who had rented the box indicated on the billboard, but the employee said that he could not provide such information. Ruby inspected the box, however, and was upset to find it stuffed with mail.[976] The three men then drove to a coffeeshop where Ruby continued to discuss the two advertisements. After about 30 minutes, they left the coffeeshop. Crafard was taken to the Carousel Club; Ruby and Senator returned to their apartment,[977] and Ruby retired at about 6 a.m.[978]

The morning and afternoon of November 23.—At 8 or 8:30 a.m. Crafard, who had been asked to feed Ruby's dogs, telephoned Ruby at his apartment to inquire about food for the animals.[979] Ruby forgot that he had told Crafard he did not plan to go to bed and reprimanded Crafard for waking him.[980] A few hours thereafter Crafard assembled his few belongings, took from the Carousel cash register $5 of money due him from Ruby, left a receipt and thank-you note, and began hitchhiking to Michigan. Later that day, Andrew Armstrong found the note and telephoned Ruby.[981]

Ruby apparently did not return to bed following Crafard's call. During the morning hours, he watched a rabbi deliver on television a moving eulogy of President Kennedy.[982] According to Ruby, the rabbi:

> went ahead and eulogized that here is a man that fought in every battle, went to every country, and had to come back to his own country to be shot in the back [starts crying] * * *. That created a tremendous emotional feeling for me, the way he said that. Prior to all the other times, I was carried away.[983]

An employee from the Carousel Club who telephoned Ruby during the morning remembered that his "voice was shaking" when he spoke of the assassination.[984]

Ruby has stated that, upon leaving his apartment some time between noon and 1:30 p.m., he drove to Dealey Plaza where a police officer, who noted Ruby's solemnity, pointed out to him the window from which the rifleshots had been fired the day before.[985] Ruby related that he inspected the wreaths that had been placed in memory of the President and became filled with emotion while speaking with the police officer.[986] Ruby introduced himself to a reporter for radio station KRLD who was working inside a mobile news unit at the plaza; the newsman mentioned to Ruby that he had heard of Ruby's help to KLIF in obtaining an interview with Henry Wade, and Ruby pointed out to the reporter that Capt. J. Will Fritz and Chief Curry were then in the vicinity. Thereafter, the newsman interviewed and photographed the officers.[987] Ruby said that he next drove home and returned downtown to Sol's Turf Bar on Commerce Street.[988]

The evidence indicated, however, that sometime after leaving Dealey Plaza, Ruby went to the Nichols Parking Garage adjacent to the Carousel Club, where he was seen by Garnett C. Hallmark, general manager of the garage, and Tom Brown, an attendant. Brown believed that at about 1:30 p.m. he heard Ruby mention Chief Curry's name in a telephone conversation from the garage. Brown also recalled that, before finally departing, Ruby asked him to inform acquaintances whom he expected to stop by the garage that the Carousel would be closed.[989] Hallmark testified that Ruby drove into the garage at about 3 p.m., walked to the telephone, inquired whether or not a competing burlesque club would be closed that night, and told Hallmark that he (Ruby) was "acting like a reporter."[990] Hallmark then heard Ruby address someone at the other end of the telephone as "Ken" and caught portions of a conversation concerning the transfer of Oswald.[991] Hallmark said Ruby never called Oswald by name but used the pronoun "he" and remarked to the recipient of the call, "you know I'll be there."[992]

Ken Dowe, a KLIF announcer, to whom Ruby made at least two telephone calls within a short span of time Saturday afternoon, confirmed that he was probably the person to whom Hallmark and Brown overheard Ruby speaking. In one call to Dowe, Ruby asked whether the station knew when Oswald would be moved; and, in another, he stated he was going to attempt to locate Henry Wade.[993] After Ruby finished his calls, he walked onto Commerce Street, passed the Carousel Club, and returned a few minutes later to get his car.[994]

Ruby's comment that he was "acting like a reporter" and that he would be at the Oswald transfer suggests that Ruby may have spent part of Saturday afternoon shuttling back and forth from the Police and Courts Building to Dealey Plaza. Such activity would explain the fact that Tom Brown at the Nichols Garage believed he saw Ruby at 1:30 p.m. while Garnett Hallmark placed Ruby at the garage at 3 p.m. It would also explain Ken Dowe's receiving two phone calls from Ruby. The testimony of five news reporters supports the possibility that Ruby was at the Police and Courts Building Saturday afternoon.[995] One stated that Ruby provided sandwiches for newsmen on duty there Saturday afternoon, although no news representative has mentioned personally receiving such sandwiches.[996] Another testified that he received a card to the Carousel Club from Ruby about 4 p.m. that day at the police station.[997] A third believed he saw Ruby enter an office in which Henry Wade was working, but no one else reported a similar event.[998] The remaining two witnesses mentioned no specific activities.[999] None of the persons who believed they saw Ruby at the police department on Saturday had known him previously, and no police officer has reported Ruby's presence on that day. Ruby has not mentioned such a visit. The Commission, therefore, reached no firm conclusion as to whether or not Ruby visited the Dallas Police Department on Saturday.

Shortly after 3 p.m. Ruby went to Sol's Turf Bar on Commerce Street where he remained for about 45 minutes. Ruby, a nondrinker, stated that he visited Sol's for the purpose of talking with his accountant, who customarily prepared the bar's payroll on Saturday afternoon. The accountant testified, however, that he saw Ruby only briefly and mentioned no business conversation with Ruby.[1000] Ruby was first noticed at the Turf Bar by jeweler Frank Bellochio, who, after seeing Ruby, began to berate the people of Dallas for the assassination.[1001] Ruby disagreed and, when Bellochio said he might close his jewelry business and leave Dallas, Ruby attempted to calm him, saying that there were many good citizens in Dallas.[1002] In response, Bellochio pointed to a copy of the Bernard Weissman advertisement.[1003] To Bellochio's bewilderment, Ruby then said he believed that the advertisement was the work of a group attempting to create anti-Semitic feelings in Dallas and that he had learned from the Dallas Morning News that the ad had been paid for partly in cash.[1004] Ruby thereupon produced one of the photographs he had taken Saturday morning of the "Impeach Earl Warren" sign and excitedly began to rail against the sign as if he agreed with Bellochio's original criticism of Dallas.[1005] He "seemed to be taking two sides—he wasn't coherent," Bellochio testified.[1006] When Bellochio saw Ruby's photographs, which Bellochio thought supported his argument against Dallas, he walked to the front of the bar and showed them to Tom Apple, with whom he had been previously arguing. In Apple's presence, Bellochio asked Ruby for one of the pictures but Ruby refused, mentioning that he regarded the pictures as a scoop.[1007] Bellochio testified: "I spoke to Tom and said a few more words to Tom, and Ruby was gone—never said 'Goodbye' or 'I'll be seeing you.'" [1008]

Ruby may have left in order to telephone Stanley Kaufman, a friend and attorney who had represented him in civil matters.[1009] Kaufman testified that, at approximately 4 p.m., Ruby called him about the Bernard Weissman advertisement. According to Kaufman, "Jack was particularly impressed with the [black] border as being a tipoff of some sort—that this man knew the President was going to be assassinated * * *." [1010]   Ruby told Kaufman that he had tried to locate Weissman by going to the post office and said that he was attempting to be helpful to law enforcement authorities.[1011]

Considerable confusion exists as to the place from which Ruby placed the call to Kaufman and as to his activities after leaving Sol's Turf Bar. Eva Grant stated that the call was made from her apartment about 4 p.m.[1012]   Ruby, however, believed it was made from the Turf Bar. He stated that from the Turf Bar he went to the Carousel and then home and has not provided additional details on his activities during the hours from about 4 to 9:30 p.m.[1013]   Robert Larkin saw him downtown at about 6 p.m.[1014] and Andrew Armstrong testified that Ruby visited the Carousel Club between 6 and 7 p.m. and remained about an hour.[1015]

At Eva Grant's apartment Saturday evening.—Eva Grant believed that, for most of the period from 4 until 8 p.m., Ruby was at her apartment. Mrs. Grant testified that her brother was still disturbed about the Weissman advertisement when he arrived, showed her the photograph of the Warren sign, and recounted his argument with Bellochio about the city of Dallas. Still curious as to whether or not Weissman was Jewish, Mrs. Grant asked her brother whether he had been able to find the name Bernard Weissman in the Dallas city directory, and Ruby said he had not. Their doubts about Weissman's existence having been confirmed, both began to speculate that the Weissman ad and the Warren sign were the work of either "Commies or the Birchers," and were designed to discredit the Jews.[1016]   Apparently in the midst of that conversation Ruby telephoned Russ Knight at KLIF and, according to Knight, asked who Earl Warren was.[1017]

Mrs. Grant has testified that Ruby eventually retired to her bedroom where he made telephone calls and slept.[1018]   About 8:30 p.m., Ruby telephoned to Thomas J. O'Grady, a friend and former Dallas police officer who had once worked for Ruby as a bouncer. To O'Grady, Ruby mentioned closing the Carousel Club, criticized his competitors for remaining open, and complained about the "Impeach Earl Warren" sign.[1019]

Saturday evening at Ruby's apartment.—By 9:30 p.m., Ruby had apparently returned to his apartment where he received a telephone call from one of his striptease dancers, Karen Bennett Carlin, who, together with her husband, had been driven from Fort Worth to Dallas that evening by another dancer, Nancy Powell.[1020]   All three had stopped at the Colony Club, a burlesque nightclub which competed with the Carousel.[1021]   Mrs. Carlin testified that, in need of money, she telephoned Ruby, asked whether the Carousel would be open that night, and requested part of her salary.[1022]   According to Mrs. Carlin, Ruby became angry at the suggestion that the Carousel Club might be open for business but told her he would come to the Carousel in about an hour.[1023]

Thereafter, in a depressed mood, Ruby telephoned his sister Eva Grant, who suggested he visit a friend.[1024]   Possibly in response to that suggestion, Ruby called Lawrence Meyers, a friend from Chicago with whom he had visited two nights previously.[1025] Meyers testified that, during their telephone conversation, Ruby asked him what he thought of this "terrible thing." Ruby then began to criticize his competitors, Abe and Barney Weinstein, for failing to close their clubs on Saturday night. In the course of his conversation about the Weinsteins and the assassination, Ruby said "I've got to do something about this."[1026] Meyers initially understood that remark to refer to the Weinsteins. Upon reflection after Oswald was shot, Meyers was uncertain whether Ruby was referring to his competitors, or to the assassination of President Kennedy; for Ruby had also spoken at length about Mrs. Kennedy and had repeated "those poor people, those poor people."[1027] At the conclusion of their conversation, Meyers declined Ruby's invitation to join him for a cup of coffee but invited Ruby to join him at the motel. When Ruby also declined, the two agreed to meet for dinner the following evening.[1028]

Meanwhile, Karen Carlin and her husband grew anxious over Ruby's failure to appear with the money they had requested.[1029] After a substantial wait, they returned together to the Nichols Garage where Mr. Carlin telephoned to Ruby.[1030] Carlin testified that he told Ruby they needed money in order to return to Fort Worth [1031] although Nancy Powell testified that she drove the Carlins home that evening.[1032] Agreeing to advance a small sum, Ruby asked to speak to Mrs. Carlin, who claimed that Ruby told her that if she needed more money she should call him on Sunday.[1033] Thereafter, at Ruby's request, garage attendant Huey Reeves gave Mrs. Carlin $5, and she signed with her stage name "Little Lynn" a receipt which Reeves time-stamped 10:33 p.m., November 23.[1034] (See Commission Exhibit No. 1476, p. 351.)

Inconsistent testimony was developed regarding Ruby's activities during the next 45 minutes. Eva Grant testified that she did not see her brother on Saturday night after 8 p.m. and has denied calling Ralph Paul herself that night.[1035] Nonetheless, telephone company records revealed that at 10:44 p.m. a call was made to Ralph Paul's Bull Pen Drive-In in Arlington, Tex., from Mrs. Grant's apartment.[1036] It was the only call to Paul from her apartment on Friday or Saturday; [1037] she recalled her brother making such a call that weekend; [1038] and Ralph Paul has testified that Ruby telephoned him Saturday night from Eva Grant's apartment and said he and his sister were there crying.[1039]

Nineteen-year-old Wanda Helmick, a former waitress at the Bull Pen Drive-In, first reported in June, 1964 that some time during the evening she saw the cashier answer the Bull Pen's pay telephone and heard her call out to Paul, "It is for you. It is Jack."[1040] Mrs. Helmick claimed she overheard Paul, speaking on the telephone, mention something about a gun which, she understood from Paul's conversation, the caller had in his possession. She said she also heard Paul exclaim "Are you crazy?"[1041] She provided no other details of the conversation. Mrs. Helmick claimed that on Sunday, November 24,

349

after Oswald had been shot, she heard Paul repeat the substance of the call to other employees as she had related it and that Paul said Ruby was the caller.[1042] Ralph Paul denied the allegations of Mrs. Helmick.[1043] Both Paul and Mrs. Helmick agreed that Paul went home soon after the call, apparently about 11 p.m.[1044]

Shortly after 11 p.m., Ruby arrived at the Nichols Garage where he repaid Huey Reeves and obtained the receipt Mrs. Carlin had signed.[1045] Outside the Carousel, Ruby exchanged greetings with Police Officer Harry Olsen and Kay Coleman, whom he had seen late the previous night.[1046] Going upstairs to the club, Ruby made a series of five brief long-distance phone calls, the first being to the Bull Pen Drive-In at 11:18 p.m. and lasting only 1 minute.[1047] Apparently unable to reach Paul there, Ruby telephoned Paul's home in Arlington, Tex., for 3 minutes.[1048] A third call was placed at 11:36 p.m. for 2 minutes, again to Paul's home.[1049] At 11:44 p.m. Ruby telephoned Breck Wall, a friend and entertainer who had gone to Galveston, Tex., when his show in Dallas suspended its performance out of respect to President Kennedy. The call lasted 2 minutes.[1050] Thereafter, Ruby immediately placed a 1-minute phone call to Paul's home.[1051]

Although Ruby has mentioned those calls, he has not provided details to the Commission; however, he has denied ever indicating to Paul or Wall that he was going to shoot Oswald and has said he did not consider such action until Sunday morning.[1052] Ralph Paul did not mention the late evening calls in his interview with FBI agents on November 24, 1963.[1053] Later Paul testified that Ruby called him from downtown to say that nobody was doing any business.[1054] Breck Wall testified that Ruby called him to determine whether or not the American Guild of Variety Artists (AGVA), which represented striptease dancers in Dallas, had met concerning a dispute Ruby was having with the union.[1055] Ruby's major difference with AGVA during the preceding 2 weeks had involved what Ruby considered to be AGVA's failure to enforce against his 2 competitors, Abe and Barney Weinstein, AGVA's ban on "striptease contests" and performances by "amateurs." [1056] As recently as Wednesday, November 20, Ruby had telephoned an AGVA representative in Chicago about that complaint and earlier in November he had unsuccessfully sought to obtain assistance from a San Francisco gambler and a Chicagoan reputed for his heavyhanded union activities.[1057] Wall testified that Ruby "was very upset the President was assassinated and he called Abe Weinstein or Bernie Weinstein * * * some names for staying open * * * ." Wall added, "he was very upset * * * that they did not have the decency to close on such a day and he thought out of respect they should close." [1058]

Ruby's activities after midnight.—After completing the series of calls to Paul and Wall at 11:48 p.m., Ruby went to the Pago Club, about a 10-minute drive from the Carousel Club.[1059] He took a table near the middle of the club and, after ordering a Coke, asked the waitress in a disapproving tone, "Why are you open?" [1060] When Robert

350

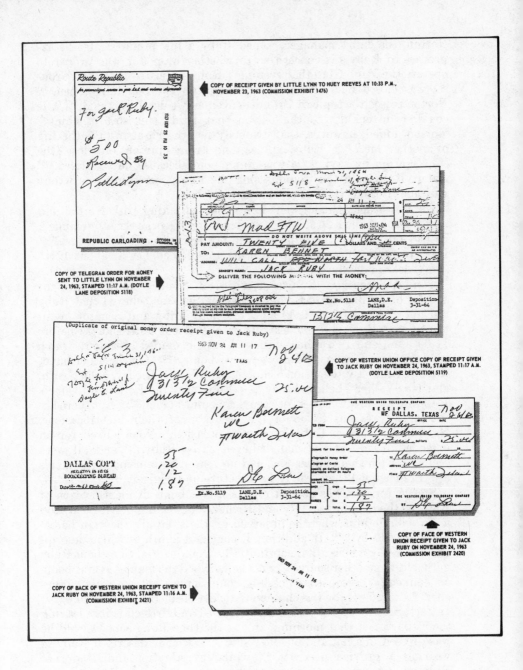

COPY OF RECEIPT GIVEN BY LITTLE LYNN TO HUEY REEVES AT 10:33 P.M., NOVEMBER 23, 1963 (COMMISSION EXHIBIT 1476)

COPY OF TELEGRAM ORDER FOR MONEY SENT TO LITTLE LYNN ON NOVEMBER 24, 1963, STAMPED 11:17 A.M. (DOYLE LANE DEPOSITION 5118)

COPY OF WESTERN UNION OFFICE COPY OF RECEIPT GIVEN TO JACK RUBY ON NOVEMBER 24, 1963, STAMPED 11:17 A.M. (DOYLE LANE DEPOSITION 5119)

COPY OF FACE OF WESTERN UNION RECEIPT GIVEN TO JACK RUBY ON NOVEMBER 24, 1963 (COMMISSION EXHIBIT 2420)

COPY OF BACK OF WESTERN UNION RECEIPT GIVEN TO JACK RUBY ON NOVEMBER 24, 1963, STAMPED 11:16 A.M. (COMMISSION EXHIBIT 2421)

351

Norton, the club's manager, joined Ruby a few minutes later he expressed to Ruby his concern as to whether or not it was proper to operate the Pago Club that evening. Ruby indicated that the Carousel was closed but did not criticize Norton for remaining open.[1061] Norton raised the topic of President Kennedy's death and said, "[W]e couldn't do enough to the person that [did] this sort of thing." Norton added, however, that "Nobody has the right to take the life of another one." [1062] Ruby expressed no strong opinion, and closed the conversation by saying he was going home because he was tired.[1063] Later, Ruby told the Commission: "he knew something was wrong with me in the certain mood I was in." [1064]

Ruby testified that he went home after speaking with Norton and went to bed about 1:30 a.m.[1065] By that time, George Senator claimed, he had retired for the night and did not remember Ruby's return.[1066] Eva Grant testified that her brother telephoned her at about 12:45 a.m. to learn how she was feeling.[1067]

Sunday morning.—Ruby's activities on Sunday morning are the subject of conflicting testimony. George Senator believed that Ruby did not rise until 9 or 9:30 a.m.; [1068] both Ruby and Senator maintained that Ruby did not leave their apartment until shortly before 11:00 a.m., and two other witnesses have provided testimony which supports that account of Ruby's whereabouts.[1069] On the other hand, three WBAP–TV television technicians—Warren Richey, John Smith, and Ira Walker—believed they saw Ruby near the Police and Courts Building at various times between 8 a.m. and 11 a.m.[1070] But there are substantial reasons to doubt the accuracy of their identifications. None had ever seen Ruby on a prior occasion. None looked for an extended period at the man believed to be Ruby,[1071] and all were occupied with their duties and had no reason to remember the man's appearance until they saw Ruby's picture on television.[1072]

Smith, for one, was not entirely positive about his identification of Ruby as the man he saw; [1073] and Richey was looking down from atop a TV mobile unit when he observed on the sidewalk the man he believed was Ruby.[1074] In addition, Richey and Smith provided descriptions of Ruby which differ substantially from information about Ruby gathered from other sources. Smith described the man he saw as being an "unkempt person that possibly could have slept with his clothes on * * *." [1075] Ruby was characteristically clean and well groomed.[1076] In fact, Senator testified that Ruby shaved and dressed before leaving their apartment that morning, and at the time Ruby shot Oswald he was dressed in a hat and business suit.[1077] Richey described Ruby as wearing a grayish overcoat,[1078] while investigation indicated that Ruby did not own an overcoat and was not wearing one at the time of the shooting.[1079] (See Pappas Deposition Exhibit No. 1, p. 356.) Although Walker's identification of Ruby is the most positive, his certainty must be contrasted with the indefinite identification made by Smith, who had seen the man on one additional occasion.[1080] Both Smith and Walker saw a man resembling Ruby when the man, on two occasions, looked through the window of their mobile news unit and once asked whether Oswald had been transferred. Both saw only the man's head, and Smith was closer to the window; yet Smith would not state positively that the man was Ruby.[1081] Finally, video tapes of scenes on Sunday morning near the NBC van show a man close to the Commerce Street entrance who might have been mistaken for Ruby.[1082]

George Senator said that when he arose, before 9 a.m., he began to do his laundry in the basement of the apartment building while Ruby slept.[1083] During Senator's absence, Ruby received a telephone call from his cleaning lady, Mrs. Elnora Pitts, who testified that she called sometime between 8:30 and 9 a.m. to learn whether Ruby wanted her to clean his apartment that day.[1084] Mrs. Pitts remembered that Ruby "sounded terrible strange to me." She said that "there was something wrong with him the way he was talking to me." [1085] Mrs. Pitts explained that, although she had regularly been cleaning Ruby's apartment on Sundays, Ruby seemed not to comprehend who she was or the reason for her call and required her to repeat herself several times.[1086] As Senator returned to the apartment after the call, he was apparently mistaken for Ruby by a neighbor, Sidney Evans, Jr. Evans had never seen Ruby before but recalled observing a man resembling Ruby, clad in trousers and T-shirt, walk upstairs from the "washateria" in the basement of their building and enter Ruby's suite with a load of laundry. Later in the morning, Malcolm Slaughter who shared an apartment with Evans, saw an individual, similarly clad, on the same floor as Ruby's apartment.[1087] Senator stated that it was not Ruby's custom to do his own washing and that Ruby did not do so that morning.[1088]

While Senator was in the apartment, Ruby watched television, made himself coffee and scrambled eggs, and received, at 10:19 a.m., a telephone call from his entertainer, Karen Carlin.[1089] Mrs. Carlin testified that in her telephone conversation she asked Ruby for $25 inasmuch as her rent was delinquent and she needed groceries.[1090] She said that Ruby, who seemed upset, mentioned that he was going downtown anyway and that he would send the money from the Western Union office.[1091] According to George Senator, Ruby then probably took a half hour or more to bathe and dress.[1092]

Supporting the accounts given by Mrs. Carlin and Mrs. Pitts of Ruby's emotional state, Senator testified that during the morning Ruby:

> * * * was even mumbling, which I didn't understand. And right after breakfast he got dressed. Then after he got dressed he was pacing the floor from the living room to the bedroom, from the bedroom to the living room, and his lips were going. What he was jabbering I don't know. But he was really pacing.[1093]

Ruby has described to the Commission his own emotions of Sunday morning as follows:

* * * Sunday morning * * * [I] saw a letter to Caroline, two columns about a 16-inch area. Someone had written a letter to Caroline. The most heartbreaking letter. I don't remember the contents. * * * alongside that letter on the same sheet of paper was a small comment in the newspaper that, I don't know how it was stated, that Mrs. Kennedy may have to come back for the trial of Lee Harvey Oswald. * * *

I don't know what bug got ahold of me. I don't know what it is, but I am going to tell the truth word for word.

I am taking a pill called Preludin. It is a harmless pill, and it is very easy to get in the drugstore. It isn't a highly prescribed pill. I use it for dieting.

I don't partake of that much food. I think that was a stimulus to give me an emotional feeling that suddenly I felt, which was so stupid, that I wanted to show my love for our faith, being of the Jewish faith, and I never used the term and I don't want to go into that—suddenly the feeling, the emotional feeling came within me that someone owed this debt to our beloved President to save her the ordeal of coming back. I don't know why that came through my mind.[1084]

(See Commission Exhibit No. 2426, p. 355.)

Sunday morning trip to police department.—Leaving his apartment a few minutes before 11 a.m., Ruby went to his automobile taking with him his dachshund, Sheba, and a portable radio.[1095] He placed in his pocket a revolver which he routinely carried in a bank moneybag in the trunk of his car.[1096] Listening to the radio, he drove downtown, according to his own testimony, by a route that took him past Dealey Plaza where he observed the scattered wreaths. Ruby related that he noted the crowd that had gathered outside the county jail and assumed that Oswald had already been transferred. However, when he passed the Main Street side of the Police and Courts Building, which is situated on the same block as the Western Union office, he also noted the crowd that was gathered outside that building.[1097] Normal driving time for the trip from his apartment would have been about 15 minutes, but Ruby's possible haste and the slow movement of traffic through Dealey Plaza make a reliable estimate difficult.[1098]

Ruby parked his car in a lot directly across the street from the Western Union office. He apparently placed his keys and billfold in the trunk of the car, then locked the trunk, which contained approximately $1,000 in cash, and placed the trunk key in the glove compartment of the car. He did not lock the car doors.[1099]

With his revolver, more than $2,000 in cash, and no personal identification, Ruby walked from the parking lot across the street to the Western Union office where he filled out forms for sending $25 by telegraph to Karen Carlin.[1100] After waiting in line while one other Western Union customer completed her business,[1101] Ruby paid for the telegram and retained as a receipt one of three time-stamped docu-

BEDROOM OF JACK RUBY'S APARTMENT
(COMMISSION EXHIBIT 2426)

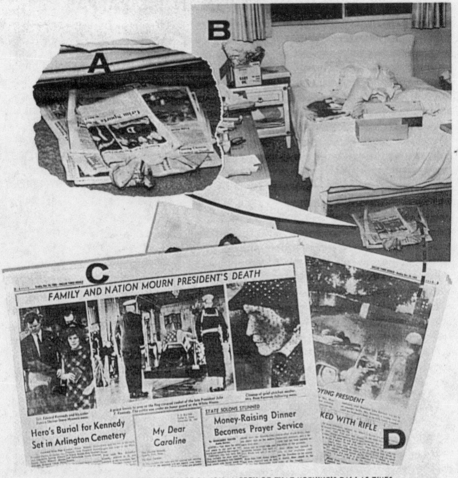

ON SUNDAY AFTERNOON NOVEMBER 24, 1963, A COPY OF THAT MORNING'S DALLAS TIMES HERALD WAS FOUND AT THE FOOT OF JACK RUBY'S BED (B). AS REVEALED IN THE BLOW-UP (A), THE PAPER WAS OPEN TO PAGE A-3 (A AND D). THE FACING PAGE, 2-A, BORE A LETTER TO CAROLINE KENNEDY (C) WHICH JACK RUBY TESTIFIED THAT HE READ THAT MORNING BEFORE SHOOTING LEE HARVEY OSWALD.

JACK RUBY MOVING TOWARD OSWALD
IN FRONT OF NEWSMAN IKE PAPPAS

PAPPAS DEPOSITION EXHIBIT 1

PAPPAS DEPOSITION EXHIBIT 2

ments which show that the transaction was completed at almost exactly 11:17 a.m., c.s.t.[1102] (See Commission Exhibits Nos. 1476, 2420, 2421; D. Lane Deposition Exhibits Nos. 5118, 5119, p. 351.) The Western Union clerk who accepted Ruby's order recalls that Ruby promptly turned, walked out of the door onto Main Street, and proceeded in the direction of the police department one block away.[1103] The evidence set forth in chapter V indicates that Ruby entered the police basement through the auto ramp from Main Street and stood behind the front rank of newsmen and police officers who were crowded together at the base of the ramp awaiting the transfer of Oswald to the county jail.[1104] As Oswald emerged from a basement office at approximately 11:21 a.m., Ruby moved quickly forward and, without speaking,[1105] fired one fatal shot into Oswald's abdomen before being subdued by a rush of police officers.[1106]

Evaluation of activities.—Examination of Ruby's activities immediately preceding and following the death of President Kennedy revealed no sign of any conduct which suggests that he was involved in the assassination. Prior to the tragedy, Ruby's activities were routine. Though persons who saw him between November 22 and 24 disagree as to whether or not he appeared more upset than others around him, his response to the assassination appears to have been one of genuine shock and grief. His indications of concern over the possible effects of the assassination upon his businesses seem consistent with other evidence of his character.[1107] During the course of the weekend, Ruby seems to have become obsessed with the possibility that the Impeach Earl Warren sign and the Bernard Weissman ad were somehow connected and related to the assassination. However, Ruby's interest in these public notices was openly expressed and, as discussed below, the evidence reveals no connection between him and any political organization.

Examination of Larry Crafard's sudden departure from Dallas shortly before noon on November 23 does not suggest that Ruby was involved in a conspiracy. To be sure, Crafard started hitchhiking to Michigan, where members of his family lived, with only $7 in his pocket.[1108] He made no attempt to communicate with law enforcement officials after Oswald's death;[1109] and a relative in Michigan recalled that Crafard spoke very little of his association with Ruby.[1110] When finally located by the FBI 6 days later, he stated that he left Ruby's employ because he did not wish to be subjected to further verbal abuse by Ruby and that he went north to see his sister, from whom he had not heard in some time.[1111]

An investigation of Crafard's unusual behavior confirms that his departure from Dallas was innocent. After Oswald was shot, FBI agents obtained from the Carousel Club an unmailed letter drafted by Crafard to a relative in Michigan at least a week before the assassination.[1112] The letter revealed that he was considering leaving Dallas at that time.[1113] On November 17, Crafard, who had been receiving only room, board, and incidental expenses, told Ruby he wanted to stop working for him; however, Crafard agreed to remain when Ruby promised a salary.[1114]   Then on the morning of November 23, Ruby and Crafard had a minor altercation over the telephone.[1115]   Although Crafard did not voluntarily make known to the authorities his associations with Ruby, he spoke freely and with verifiable accuracy when questioned.   The automobile driver who provided Crafard his first ride from Dallas has been located; his statement generally conforms with Crafard's story; and he did not recall any unusual or troubled behavior by Crafard during that ride.[1116]

Although Crafard's peremptory decision to leave Dallas might be unusual for most persons, such behavior does not appear to have been uncommon for him.   His family residence had shifted frequently among California, Michigan, and Oregon.[1117]   During his 22 years, he had earned his livelihood picking crops, working in carnivals, and taking other odd jobs throughout the country.[1118]   According to his testimony, he had previously hitchhiked across the country with his then wife and two infant children.[1119]   Against such a background, it is most probable that the factors motivating Crafard's departure from Dallas on November 23 were dissatisfaction with his existence in Ruby's employ, which he had never considered more than temporary, Ruby's decision to close his clubs for 3 days, the argument on Saturday morning, and his own desire to see his relatives in Michigan.   There is no evidence to suggest any connection between Crafard's departure and the assassination of the President or the shooting of Oswald.

The allegations of Wanda Helmick raised speculation that Ruby's Saturday night phone calls to Ralph Paul and Breck Wall might have concerned the shooting of Oswald, but investigation has found nothing to indicate that the calls had conspiratorial implications.   Paul was a close friend, business associate, and adviser to Jack Ruby.   Ruby normally kept in close telephone contact with Paul, who had a substantial sum of money committed to the Carousel Club.[1120]   Paul explained that Ruby called him Saturday evening once to point out his ads, another time to say that nobody seemed to be doing any business in downtown Dallas, and a third time to relate that both he and his sister were crying over the assassination.[1121]   Between two of those phone calls to Paul, Ruby telephoned to Galveston, Tex., to speak with Wall, a friend and former business associate who was an official of the American Guild of Variety Artists.   Wall related that during that call Ruby criticized the Weinsteins for failing to close their clubs.

Having earlier made the same complaint to Lawrence Meyers to whom he mentioned a need "to do something about this" it would have been characteristic for Ruby to want to direct Breck Wall's attention, as an AGVA official, to what he regarded as the Weinsteins' improper conduct.   The view that the calls to Wall and Paul could have had conspiratorial implications also is belied in large measure by the conduct of both men before and after the events of November 22–24.   A check of long-distance telephone records reveals no suspicious activity by either man.[1122]   Paul, in fact, is not known to have visited Dallas during the weekend of the assassination except to appear openly in an effort to arrange counsel for Ruby within a few hours of the attack on Oswald. Neither the FBI nor the CIA has been able to provide any information that Ralph Paul or Breck Wall ever engaged in any form of subversive activity.[1123]

Moreover, Mrs. Helmick's reliability is undermined by her failure to report her information to any investigative official until June 9, 1964.[1124] Although a sister-in-law confirms that Mrs. Helmick wrote her "something about a gun" shortly after the shooting,[1125] the only mention of any statement by Paul which was included in a letter written by Mrs. Helmick after the Ruby trial was that Paul believed Ruby was "not in his right mind." [1126] No corroborating witness named by Mrs. Helmick has been found who remembers the conversations she mentioned.[1127] Both Ruby and Paul have denied that anything was said, as Mrs. Helmick suggests, about a gun or an intent to shoot Oswald, and Wall has stated that Ruby did not discuss such matters with him.[1128] Even if Mrs. Helmick is accurate the statements ascribed to Paul indicate only that he may have heard of a possible reference by Ruby to shooting Oswald. According to her, Paul's response was to exclaim "Are you crazy?" But under no circumstances does the report of Mrs. Helmick or any other fact support a belief that Paul or Wall was involved in the shooting of Oswald.

The Commission has conducted an investigation of the telephone call Ruby received from Karen Carlin at 10:19 Sunday morning to determine whether that call was prearranged for the purpose of conveying information about the transfer of Oswald or to provide Ruby an excuse for being near the police department. The Commission has examined the records of long-distance telephone calls on Sunday morning for Jack Ruby,[1129] the Carlins,[1130] the Dallas police,[1131] and several other persons [1132] and has found no sign of any indirect communication to Ruby through Mr. or Mrs. Carlin. No other evidence showing any link between the Carlins and the shooting of Oswald has been developed.

Ruby and Oswald Were Not Acquainted

The possibility of a prior acquaintanceship between Ruby and Oswald has been suggested by some persons who viewed the shooting on television and believed that a look of recognition appeared on Oswald's face as Ruby moved toward him in the jail basement. The Commission has examined the television tapes and movie films which were made as Oswald moved through the basement and has observed no facial expressions which can be interpreted as signifying recognition of Ruby by Oswald. It is doubtful even that Oswald could have seen Ruby sufficiently clearly to discern his identity since Oswald was walking from a dark corridor into "the flash from the many cameras" and the lights of TV cameramen which were "blinding." [1133] In addition to such generalized suspicion, there have been numerous specific allegations that Oswald was seen in the company of Ruby prior to November 22, often at Ruby's Carousel Club. All such allegations have been investigated, but the Commission has found none which merits credence. In all but a few instances where the Commission was able to trace the claim to its source, the person responsible for the report either denied making it or admitted that he had no basis for the original allegations.[1134] Frequently those responsible for the allegations have proved to be persons of erratic memory or dubious mental stability.[1135] In a few instances, the source of the story has remained unidentified, and no person has come forward to substantiate the rumor.[1136]

The testimony of a few witnesses who claim to have seen Ruby with a person who they feel may have been Oswald warrants further comment. One such witness, Robert K. Patterson, a Dallas electronics salesman, has stated that on a date established from sales records as November 1, 1963, Ruby, accompanied by a man who resembled Oswald, purchased some equipment at his business establishment.[1137] However, Patterson did not claim positively that the man he saw was Oswald,[1138] and two of his associates who were also present at the time could not state that the man was Oswald.[1139] Other evidence indicates that Ruby's companion was Larry Crafard. Crafard, who lived at the Carousel Club while working for Ruby from mid-October until November 23, 1963, stated that sometime in late October or early November he accompanied Ruby to an electronics store in connection with the purchase of electronics equipment.[1140] Ruth Paine testified that Crafard's photograph bears a strong resemblance to Oswald; and employment records of the Texas School Book Depository show that Oswald worked a full day on November 1, 1963.[1141]

William D. Crowe, Jr., a young nightclub master of ceremonies who had worked for Ruby on three occasions and had begun a 4- or 5-week engagement at the Carousel Club on November 11, 1963, was the first person who reported a possible association between Ruby and Oswald.[1142] While attempting to enter the Carousel Club on November 24, shortly after Oswald was shot, Crowe encountered two news media representatives who were gathering information on Jack Ruby.[1143] At that time, Crowe, who included a memory act in his repertoire,[1144] mentioned the "possibility" that he had seen Oswald at the Carousel Club.[1145] As a result he was asked to appear on television. In Crowe's own words, the story "started snowballing." He testified:

> They built up the memory thing and they built up the bit of having seen Oswald there, and I never stated definitely, positively, and they said that I did, and all in all, what they had in the paper was hardly even close to what I told them.[1146]

Crowe added that his memory act involved a limited system which did not, in fact, improve his memory and that his memory might not even be as good as that of the average person. When asked how certain he was that the man he saw was Oswald, Crowe testified: "* * * the face seemed familiar as some faces do, and I had associated him with a patron that I had seen in the club a week before. That was about it." [1147]

A possible explanation for Crowe's belief that Oswald's face seemed familiar was supplied by a freelance photographer, Eddie Rocco, who had taken pictures at the Carousel Club for Ruby at about the time Crowe was employed there. Rocco produced one of those photographs which depicted a man who might have been mistaken for Oswald by persons having no reason to remember the man at the time they saw him.[1148] When shown the Rocco photograph, Crowe said that there was as strong a possibility that the man he recalled seeing was the man in the photograph as there was that he was Oswald.[1149] Crowe's uncertainty was further underscored by his failure initially to provide his information about Oswald to David Hoy, a news-media friend whom Crowe telephoned in Evansville, Ind., less than 20 minutes after Oswald was shot.[1150] By then the possible recognition had occurred to Crowe,[1151] and Hoy said he was quite surprised that Crowe had given the information first to other news representatives instead of telling him in that early conversation.[1152]

After Crowe's identification had been publicized, four other persons also reported seeing Oswald at the Carousel Club. One man said he saw Ruby and Oswald seated at a table together and recalled that the man resembling Oswald was addressed by a blond-haired waitress as "Bettit" or "Pettit." The witness was unable to give any description of "Pettit" except that he was the man who had been shot by Ruby. He could not describe the inside of the Carousel and was unable to give a precise location for the club.[1153] Another witness, a resident of Tennessee, related seeing a man resembling Oswald at the Carousel Club on November 10.[1154] Ruth Paine has testified, however, that Oswald spent the entire holiday weekend of November 9, 10, and 11 at her home in Irving, Tex.[1155] Two of Ruby's former employees, Karen Carlin and Billy Joe Willis, also believed they had seen a person who resembled Oswald. Willis believed he saw the man at the Carousel Club but did not think the man was Oswald.[1156] Mrs. Carlin likewise was not certain that the man was Oswald nor was she sure where she had seen him.[1157] Neither reported any connection between the man and Ruby. No other employees recalled seeing Oswald or a person resembling him at the Carousel Club.[1158]

Wilbryn Waldon (Robert) Litchfield II also claimed to have seen at the Carousel Club a man resembling Oswald. Litchfield stated that during a visit to the Carousel Club in late October or early November 1963, he saw such a man enter Ruby's office, apparently to confer with Ruby.[1159] Although there is substantial evidence that Litchfield did see Ruby at the Carousel Club about that time,[1160] there is strong reason to believe that Litchfield did not see Lee Harvey Oswald. Litchfield described the man he saw as having pockmarks on the right side of his chin; [1161] Oswald did not have such identifying marks.[1162] Moreover, the Commission has substantial doubts concerning Litchfield's credibility. Although present at an FBI interview of another witness on November 29, Litchfield made no mention of his observation to public officials until December 2, 1963.[1163] Litchfield, who had twice been convicted for offenses involving forged checks,[1164] testified that he first recalled that Oswald resembled the visitor he saw at the Carousel Club while watching a television showing on Sunday morning, November 24, of the shooting by Ruby.[1165] At that time Litchfield was playing poker with three friends, and he testified that he promptly informed them of the resemblance he observed.[1166] However, none of the three poker companions remembered Litchfield's making such a remark; and two added that Litchfield's statements were often untrustworthy.[1167]

With regard to all of the persons who claimed to have seen Ruby and Oswald together, it is significant that none had particular reason to pay close attention to either man, that substantial periods of time elapsed before the events they assertedly witnessed became meaningful, and that, unlike the eyewitnesses who claimed to have seen Oswald on November 22, none reported their observations soon after Oswald was arrested. In the course of its investigation, the Commission has encountered numerous clear mistakes of identification. For example, at least four persons, other than Crafard, are known to have been mistaken for Oswald.[1168] Other persons have been misidentified as Jack Ruby.[1169] Under all the available evidence there is no substantial likelihood that the person the various witnesses claimed to have seen with Ruby was in fact Oswald.

In addition to probing the reported evidence that Ruby and Oswald had been seen together, the Commission has examined other circumstances for signs that the two men were acquainted. From the time Oswald returned from Mexico, both he and Jack Ruby lived in the Oak Cliff section of Dallas, slightly more than a mile apart. Numerous neighbors of both Oswald and Ruby were interviewed, and none knew of any association between the two.[1170] Oswald's work began at 8 each weekday morning and terminated at 4:45 each afternoon.[1171] Jack Ruby usually remained in his apartment until past 9 a.m. each day.[1172] Although both men worked in downtown Dallas, they normally traveled to their places of employment by different routes. Ruby owned an automobile, and the shortest route downtown from his home was via a freeway adjacent to his apartment.[1173] Oswald did not own a car and had, at best, a rudimentary ability to drive.[1174] From his roominghouses on North Beckley Avenue and on Marsalis Street, he normally took public transportation which did not bring him within six blocks of either Ruby's apartment or his downtown nightclub, nor did Oswald's route from the bus stop to home or work bring him near Ruby's home or business.[1175] Persons at Oswald's roominghouse testified that he regularly came home promptly after work and remained in his room.[1176] While in Dallas, he is not known to have visited any nightclub.[1177] Ruby was generally at the Carousel Club from 9 o'clock each evening until after 1 a.m.[1178] In a few instances, Ruby and Oswald patronized the same stores, but no indication has been found that they ever met at such stores.[1179] Ruby at one time frequented a restaurant where Oswald occasionally ate breakfast, but the times of their patronage were widely separated and restaurant employees knew of no acquaintance between Ruby and Oswald.[1180]

Likewise, Ruby has held various memberships in the Dallas YMCA and Oswald lived there for brief periods; however, there is no indication that they were there at the same time.[1181]

Both Ruby and Oswald maintained post office boxes at the terminal annex of the U.S. post office in Dallas, but there is no indication that those facts were more than coincidental. On November 1, 1963, Oswald rented box No. 6225, his third since October 1962.[1182] Oswald's possible purpose has been discussed previously in this chapter. On November 7, 1963, Jack Ruby rented post office box No. 5475 because he hoped to receive mail responses to advertisements for the twistboard exercise device which he was then promoting.[1183] Although it is conceivable that Oswald and Ruby coincidentally encountered one another while checking their boxes, the different daily schedules of the two men render even this possibility unlikely. Moreover, Oswald's withdrawn personality makes it improbable that the two would have spoken if their paths had crossed.

The Commission has also examined the known friends and acquaintances of Ruby and Oswald for evidence that the two were acquainted, but it has found very few possible links. One conceivable association was through John Carter, a boarder at 1026 North Beckley Avenue while Oswald lived there. Carter was friendly with Wanda Joyce Killam, who had known Jack Ruby since shortly after he moved to Dallas in 1947 and worked for him from July 1963 to early November 1963. Mrs. Killam, who volunteered the information about Carter's residence during an interview with an agent of the FBI, has stated that she did not believe Carter ever visited the Carousel Club and that she did not think Carter knew Ruby.[1184] Carter stated that he had not heard of Ruby until Oswald was shot, had talked briefly with Oswald only once or twice, and had never heard Oswald mention Ruby or the Carousel Club.[1185] The Commission has no reason to disbelieve either Mrs. Killam or Mr. Carter.

A second possible link between Oswald and Ruby was through Earlene Roberts, the housekeeper at 1026 North Beckley Avenue. Bertha Cheek, the sister of Mrs. Roberts, is known to have visited Jack Ruby at the Carousel Club during the afternoon of November 18, 1963. Mrs. Cheek testified that she had met with Ruby and a person whom Ruby represented to be an interior decorator for the purpose of discussing the possibility of financially backing Ruby in a new nightclub which he planned to open. Mrs. Cheek said she had met Ruby only once, a few years before, and that she had not heard of Oswald until he shot President Kennedy.[1186] Mr. Frank Boerder, the decorator who was present at the November 18 meeting, confirmed the substance of the discussion reported by Mrs. Cheek,[1187] and other witnesses establish that Ruby was, in fact, seeking an associate for a new nightclub venture.[1188] There is no evidence that Jack Ruby ever associated with Earlene Roberts, nor is there any indication that Mrs. Cheek knew of Lee Harvey Oswald prior to November 22.[1189]

Oswald's trips to the home of Mrs. Ruth Paine at 2115 West Fifth Street in Irving, Tex., presented another possible link to Ruby.

While Oswald's family resided with Mrs. Paine, William F. Simmons, pianoplayer in the musical combo which worked at the Carousel Club from September 17, 1963, until November 21, 1963, lived at 2539 West Fifth Street, in Irving. Simmons has stated that his only relationship to Ruby was as an employee, that Ruby never visited him, that he did not know Oswald, and that he had never seen Oswald at the Carousel Club.[1190] Other persons in the neighborhood knew of no connection between Ruby and Oswald.[1191]

The Commission has investigated rumors that Jack Ruby and Lee Harvey Oswald were both homosexuals and, thus, might have known each other in that respect. However, no evidence has been uncovered to support the rumors, the closest acquaintances of both men emphatically deny them,[1192] and Ruby's nightclubs were not known to have been frequented by homosexuals.[1193]

A final suggestion of a connection between Jack Ruby and Lee Harvey Oswald arises from the testimony of Oswald's mother, Marguerite Oswald. When appearing before the Commission, Mrs. Oswald related that on November 23, 1963, before Ruby shot Oswald, FBI Agent Bardwell D. Odum showed her a picture of a man she believed was Jack Ruby, and asked whether the man shown was familiar to her. Odum had first attempted to see Marina Oswald, but Marguerite refused to allow Marina to be disturbed at that time.[1194] In the course of Marguerite's testimony, the Commission asked the FBI for a copy of the photograph displayed by Odum to her. When Marguerite viewed the photograph provided the Commission, she stated that the picture was different from the one she saw in November, in part because the "top two corners" were cut differently and because the man depicted was not Jack Ruby.[1195]

The Commission has investigated this matter and determined that Special Agent Odum did show a picture to Marguerite Oswald for possible identification but that the picture was not of Jack Ruby. On November 22 the CIA had provided the FBI with a photograph of a man who, it was thought at the time, might have been associated with Oswald. To prevent the viewer from determining precisely where the picture had been taken, FBI Agent Odum had trimmed the background from the photograph by making a series of straight cuts which reduced the picture to an irregular hexagonal shape.[1196] The picture which was displayed by the Commission to Marguerite Oswald was a copy of the same picture shown her by Agent Odum; however, in supplying a duplicate photograph for Commission use the FBI had cropped the background by cutting along the contours of the body of the man shown,[1197] resulting in a photograph without any background, unlike the first photograph Marguerite viewed on November 23. Affidavits obtained from the CIA and from the two FBI agents who trimmed the photographs established that the one shown to Mrs. Oswald before the Commission, though trimmed differently from the one shown her on November 23, was a copy of the same picture. Neither picture was of Jack Ruby.[1198] The original photograph had been taken by the CIA outside of the United States sometime between

July 1, 1963, and November 22, 1963, during all of which time Ruby was within the country.[1199]

Ruby's Background and Associations

In addition to examining in detail Jack Ruby's activities from November 21 to November 24 and his possible acquaintanceship with Lee Harvey Oswald, the Commission has considered whether or not Ruby had ties with individuals or groups that might have obviated the need for any direct contact near the time of the assassination. Study of Jack Ruby's background, which is set out more fully in appendix XVI, leads to the firm conclusion that he had no such ties.

Business activities.—Ruby's entire life is characteristic of a rigorously independent person. He moved from his family home soon after leaving high school at age 16, although a "family" residence has been maintained in Chicago throughout the years.[1200]   Later, in 1947, he moved from Chicago to Dallas and maintained only sporadic contact with most of his family.[1201]   For most of his working years and continuously since 1947, Jack Ruby was self-employed.[1202]   Although he had partners from time to time, the partnerships were not lasting, and Ruby seems to have preferred to operate independently.

Ruby's main sources of income were his two nightclubs—the Carousel Club and the Vegas Club—although he also frequently pursued a number of independent, short-lived business promotions. (Ruby's business dealings are described in greater detail in app. XVI.)   At the time of the assassination, the United States claimed approximately $44,000 in delinquent taxes, and he was in substantial debt to his brother Earl and to his friend Ralph Paul.[1203]   However, there are no indications that Earl Ruby or Ralph Paul was exerting pressure for payment or that Ruby's tax liabilities were not susceptible to an acceptable settlement.   Ruby operated his clubs on a cash basis, usually carrying large amounts of cash on his person; thus there is no particular significance to the fact that approximately $3,000 in cash was found on his person and in his automobile when arrested. Nor do his meager financial records reflect any suspicious activities. He used his bank accounts only infrequently, with no unexplained large transactions; and no entries were made to Ruby's safe-deposit boxes in over a year prior to the shooting of Oswald.[1204]   There is no evidence that Ruby received any sums after his arrest except royalties from a syndicated newspaper article on his life and small contributions for his defense from friends, sympathizers, and family members.[1205]

Ruby's political activities.—Jack Ruby considered himself a Democrat, perhaps in part because his brother Hyman had been active in Democratic ward politics in Chicago.[1206]   When Ruby was arrested, police officers found in his apartment, 10 political cards urging the election of the "Conservative Democratic slate," [1207] but the Commission has found no evidence that Ruby had distributed that literature and he is not known ever to have campaigned for any political candidates.[1208]   None of his friends or associates expressed any knowledge that he belonged to any groups interested in political issues, nor did they remember that he had discussed political problems except on rare occasions.[1209]

As a young man, Ruby participated in attacks upon meetings of the German-American Bund in Chicago, but the assaults were the efforts of poolhall associates from his predominantly Jewish neighborhood rather than the work of any political group. His only other known activities which had any political flavor possessed stronger overtones of financial self-interest. In early 1942 he registered a copyright for a placard which displayed an American flag and bore the inscription "Remember Pearl Harbor." The placard was never successfully promoted. At other times, he is reported to have attempted to sell busts of President Franklin D. Roosevelt.[1210]   The rabbi of Ruby's synagogue expressed the belief that Ruby was too unsophisticated to grasp or have a significant interest in any political creed.[1211]   Although various views have been given concerning Ruby's attitude toward President Kennedy prior to the assassination, the overwhelming number of witnesses reported that Ruby had considerable respect for the President, and there has been no report of any hostility toward him.[1212]

There is also no reliable indication that Ruby was ever associated with any Communist or radical causes. Jack Ruby's parents were born in Poland in the 1870's and his father served in the Czarist Russian army from 1893–98. Though neither parent became a citizen after emigrating to the United States in the early 1900's, the evidence indicates that neither Ruby nor his family maintained any ties with relatives in Europe.[1213]   Jack Ruby has denied ever being connected with any Communist activities. The FBI has reported that, prior to the shooting of Oswald, its nationwide files contained no information of any subversive activities by Ruby.[1214]   In addition, a Commission staff member has personally examined all subversive activities reports from the Dallas-Fort Worth office of the FBI for the year 1963 and has found no reports pertaining to Jack Ruby or any of his known acquaintances.[1215]

The Commission has directed considerable attention to an allegation that Jack Ruby was connected with Communist Party activities in Muncie, Ind. On the day after Oswald's death, a former resident of Muncie claimed that between 1943 and 1947 a Chicagoan resembling Ruby and known to him as Jack Rubenstein was in Muncie on three occasions and associated with persons who the witness suspected were Communists. The witness stated that the man resembling Ruby visited Muncie during these years as a guest of the son-in-law of a now-deceased jeweler for whom the witness worked.[1216]   A second son-in-law of the jewelry store owner suggested that he may have known Ruby while the two resided in Chicago,[1217] but the son-in-law whom Ruby allegedly visited disclaimed any acquaintanceship with Ruby.[1218]   Both sons-in-law denied any Communist activities and the Commission has found no contrary evidence other than the testimony of the witness.

On the first two occasions on which Ruby is alleged to have been in Muncie, military records show him to have been on active military duty in the South.[1219] The witness also said that the man he knew as Rubenstein owned or managed a nightclub when he met him, but the Commission has no reliable evidence that Jack Ruby ever owned or worked in any nightclubs when he lived in Chicago.[1220] The witness further stated that on one occasion he found the name of Jack Rubenstein, or perhaps a similar name, together with the names of others he believed were Communists, on a list which had been left in a room above the jewelry store after a meeting held there. The witness said he gave the list to his wife's cousin, now deceased, who was then the chief of detectives in Muncie.[1221] However, neither the list nor a person identifiable as Jack Ruby has been located after a thorough search by the FBI of its own files and those of the Muncie Police Department, the Indiana State Police, and other agencies.[1222] The witness did not recall seeing Rubenstein in Muncie during the period of that meeting, and he had never heard Rubenstein say anything which would indicate he was a Communist.[1223]

The FBI has interviewed all living persons who the witness stated were involved with Ruby in Communist activities in Muncie. One person named by the witness was known previously to have been involved in Communist Party activities, but subversive activities files have revealed no such activities for any of the others.[1224] The admitted former Communist denied knowing Ruby and stated that the jewelry store owner was not known to him as a Communist and that Communist meetings were never held above the store.[1225] All other Muncie residents named by the witness as possible associates of Ruby denied knowing Ruby.[1226] Similarly, fellow employees of the witness whom he did not claim were Communists knew of no Communist activities connected with the jewelry store owner or any visits of Jack Ruby, and FBI informants familiar with Communist activities in Indiana and Chicago did not know of any participation by Ruby.[1227] Finally, the witness testified that even though he believed as early as 1947 that all of the persons named by him were Communists he had never brought his information to the attention of any authority investigating such activities, except for providing the alleged list to his cousin.[1228] The Commission finds no basis for accepting the witness's testimony.

The Commission has also investigated the possibility that Ruby was associated with ultraconservative political endeavors in Dallas. Upon his arrest, there were found in Ruby's possession two radio scripts of a right-wing program promoted by H. L. Hunt, whose political views are highly conservative. Ruby had acquired the scripts a few weeks earlier at the Texas Products Show, where they were enclosed in bags of Hunt food products. Ruby is reported to have become enraged when he discovered the scripts, and threatened to send one to "Kennedy." [1229] He is not known to have done anything with them prior to giving one to a radio announcer on November 23; and on that day he seemed to confuse organizations of the extreme right with those of the far left.[1230] On November 21, Ruby drove Connie Trammel, a young college graduate whom he had met some months previously, to the office of Lamar Hunt, the son of H. L. Hunt, for a job interview. Although Ruby stated that he would like to meet Hunt, seemingly to establish a business connection, he did not enter Hunt's office with her.[1231]

An allegation that Ruby was a visitor at the home of Maj. Gen. Edwin A. Walker (Resigned, U.S. Army) appears totally unfounded. The allegation was made in late May 1964 to an agent of the U.S. Secret Service by William McEwan Duff. Duff, who was discharged from military service in June 1964 because of a fraudulent enlistment, disclaimed any knowledge of Ruby or Oswald when questioned by FBI agents in January 1964.[1232]

Another allegation connecting Jack Ruby with right-wing activities was Mark Lane's assertion, mentioned previously, that an unnamed informant told him of a meeting lasting more than 2 hours in the Carousel Club on November 14, 1963, between Jack Ruby, Patrolman J. D. Tippit, and Bernard Weissman.[1233] Although the name of Lane's informant has never been revealed to the Commission, an investigation has been conducted in an effort to find corroboration for the claimed Tippit, Weissman, and Ruby meeting. No employee of the Carousel Club has any knowledge of the meeting described by Lane.[1234] Ruby and Weissman both deny that such a meeting occurred, and Officer Tippit's widow has no knowledge that her late husband ever went to the Carousel Club.[1235]

Some confusion has arisen, however, because early Friday afternoon, November 22, Ruby remarked that he knew the Tippit who had been shot by Oswald. Later Ruby stated that he did not know J. D. Tippit but that his reference was to G. M. Tippit, a member of the special services bureau of the Dallas Police Department who had visited Ruby establishments occasionally in the course of his official duties.[1236] Larry Crafard was unable to recognize photographs of J. D. Tippit and had no recollection of a Tippit, Weissman, and Ruby meeting at any time.[1237] However, uncertainty was introduced when Crafard identified a photograph of Bernard Weissman as resembling a man who had visited the Carousel Club and had been referred to by Ruby as "Weissman." [1238] In a subsequent interview Crafard stated that he believed Weissman was a detective on the Dallas Police Department, that his first name may have been Johnny, and that he was in his late thirties or early forties.[1239] As set forth previously, Bernard Weissman was a 26-year-old New York carpet salesman. Crafard added "I could have my recollection of a Mr. Weissman mixed up with someone else".[1240]

Ruby's conduct on November 22 and 23, 1963, corroborates his denial that he knew Bernard Weissman. Ruby expressed hostility to the November 22 full-page advertisement to many persons. To none did he give any indication that he was familiar with the person listed as responsible for the advertisement.[1241] His attempt on November 23 to trace the holder of the post office box shown on the "Impeach Earl Warren" sign and to locate Weissman's name in a Dallas city directory [1242] also tends to indicate that in fact he was not familiar with Weissman. Had he been involved in some type of unlawful activity with Weissman, it is highly unlikely that Ruby would have called attention to Weissman as he did.

Investigation has disclosed no evidence that Officer J. D. Tippit was acquainted with either Ruby or Oswald. Neither Tippit's wife nor his close friends knew of such an acquaintanceship.[1243] Tippit was not known to frequent nightclubs [1244] and he had no reason during the course of his police duties to enter Ruby's clubs.[1245] Although at the time of the assassination Tippit was working weekends in a Dallas restaurant owned by a member of the John Birch Society, the restaurant owner stated that he never discussed politics with Tippit.[1246] Persons close to Tippit related that Tippit rarely discussed political matters with any person and that he was a member of no political organization.[1247] Telephone records for the period following September 26, 1963, revealed no suspicious long-distance calls from the Tippit household.[1248]

Tippit's encounter with Oswald following the shooting of the President is indicative of no prior association between the two men. Police radio logs show that, as part of general directions issued to all officers immediately after the assassination, Tippit was specifically directed to patrol the Oak Cliff area where he came upon Oswald.[1249] His movement from the area which he had been patrolling into the central Oak Cliff area was also in conformity with the normal procedure of the Dallas Police Department for partol cars to cover nearby districts when the patrol cars in that district became otherwise engaged, as occurred after the assassination.[1250] Oswald fit the general description, which, 15 minutes after the assassination, was broadcast to all police cars of a suspect described by a bystander who had seen Oswald in the sixth-floor window of the Texas School Book Depository.[1251] There is thus no basis for any inference that, in approaching Oswald, Tippit was acting other than in the line of police duty.

Allegations of Cuban activity.—No substantiation has been found for rumors linking Ruby with pro- or anti-Castro Cuban activities,[1252] except for one incident in January 1959 when Ruby made preliminary inquiries, as a middleman, concerning the possible sale to Cuba of some surplus jeeps located in Shreveport, La., and asked about the possible release of prisoners from a Cuban prison. No evidence has been developed that the project ever became more than a "possibility". Ruby explained that in early 1959 United States sentiment toward Cuba was still favorable and that he was merely pursuing a money-making opportunity.[1253]

During the period of the "jeep sale", R. D. Matthews, a gambler and a "passing acquaintance" of Ruby, returned to Dallas from Havana where he had been living. In mid-1959, he returned to Cuba until mid-1960.[1254] On October 3, 1963, a telephone call was made from the Carousel Club to Matthews' former wife in Shreveport.[1255] No evidence has been uncovered that Matthews was associated with the sale of jeeps or the release of prisoners or that he knew of Oswald prior to the assassination.[1256] Matthews' ex-wife did not recall the phone call in October of 1963, and she asserted that she did not know Jack Ruby or anybody working for him.[1257]

In September 1959, Ruby traveled to Havana as a guest of a close friend and known gambler, Lewis J. McWillie. Both Ruby and McWillie state the trip was purely social.[1258] In January 1961, McWillie left Cuba with strong feelings of hostility to the Castro regime. In early 1963, Ruby purchased a pistol which he shipped to McWillie in Nevada, but McWillie did not accept the package.[1259] The Commission has found no evidence that McWillie has engaged in any activities since leaving Cuba that are related to pro- or anti-Castro political movements or that he was involved in Ruby's abortive jeep transaction.

The Commission has also received evidence that in April 1962, a telegram sent to Havana, Cuba, was charged to the business telephone of Earl Ruby, brother of Jack Ruby.[1260] Earl Ruby stated that he was unable to recall that telegram but testified that he had never traveled to Cuba nor had any dealings with persons in Cuba.[1261] Jack Ruby is not known to have visited his brother at that time, and during that period Earl and Jack did not maintain a close relationship.[1262] Earl Ruby is not known to have been involved in any subversive activities.[1263]

Finally, examination of FBI information relative to Cuban groups in the Dallas-Fort Worth area for the year 1963 fails to disclose any person who might provide a link between Ruby and such groups.[1264] The Central Intelligence Agency has no information suggesting that Jack Ruby or any of his closest associates have been involved in any type of revolutionary or subversive Cuban activity.[1265]

Possible underworld connections.—The Commission has investigated Ruby's possible criminal activities, looking with particular concern for evidence that he engaged in illegal activities with members of the organized underworld or that, on his own, he was a promoter of illegal endeavors. The results of that investigation are more fully detailed in appendix XVI. Ruby was reared in a Chicago neighborhood where he became acquainted with local criminals and with persons who later became criminals. Throughout his life, Ruby's friendships with persons of that character were limited largely to professional gamblers, although his night club businesses brought him in contact with persons who had been convicted of other offenses. There is no credible evidence that Ruby, himself, gambled on other than a social basis or that he had any unpaid gambling debts.[1266] He had never been charged with a felony prior to his attack on Oswald; his only encounters in Chicago stemmed from ticket scalping and the unauthorized sale of copyrighted music; and, in Dallas, his law violations, excluding traffic charges, resulted from the operation of his clubs or outbursts of temper.[1267] Ruby has disclaimed that he was associated with organized criminal activities, and law enforcement agencies have confirmed that denial.[1268]

Investigation of George Senator.—In addition to examining Ruby's own activities and background, the Commission has paid careful attention to the activities and background of George Senator, Ruby's roommate and one of his closest friends in Dallas. Senator was interrogated by staff members over a 2-day period; he provided a detailed account of his own life and cooperated fully in all aspects of the Commission's inquiry into the activities of Jack Ruby.

Senator was 50 years old at the time Ruby shot Oswald. He had been born September 4, 1913, in Gloversville, N.Y., and had received an eighth grade education. Upon leaving school, he worked in Gloversville and New York City until about age 25. For the next few years he worked in various restaurants and cafeterias in New York and Florida until enlisting in the Army in August 1941.[1269] After his honorable discharge in September 1945, Senator was employed for most of the next 13 years selling inexpensive dresses throughout the South and Southwest. In the course of that employment he moved to Dallas where he met Jack Ruby while visiting Ruby's Vegas Club in about 1955 or 1956.[1270] Ruby was one of many who helped Senator when he encountered financial difficulties during the years 1958 to 1962. For a while in 1962, Ruby provided room and board in exchange for Senator's help in his clubs and apartment. In August 1963, Senator was unable to maintain his own apartment alone following his roommate's marriage. Ruby again offered to help and on November 1, 1963, Senator moved into Ruby's apartment.[1271] The Commission has found no evidence that Senator ever engaged in any political activities. [1272]

Against this background the Commission has evaluated Senator's account of his own activities on November 22, 23, and 24. When questioned by Dallas and Federal authorities hours after the shooting of Oswald, Senator omitted mention of having accompanied Ruby to photograph the "Impeach Earl Warren" sign on Saturday morning. Senator stated to Commission staff members that in the interviews of November 24 he omitted the incident because of oversight.[1273] However, he spoke freely about it in his sworn testimony and no inaccuracies have been noted in that portion of his testimony. Senator also failed to mention to the Commission and to previous interrogators that, shortly after Ruby left their apartment Sunday morning, he called friends, Mr. and Mrs. William Downey, and offered to visit their apartment and make breakfast for them.[1274] Downey stated, in June 1964, that Senator said he was alone and that, after Downey declined the offer, Senator remarked that he would then go downtown for breakfast.[1275] When told of Downey's account, Senator denied it and explained that the two were not friendly by the time Senator left Dallas about six weeks after the assassination.[1276]

The Commission also experienced difficulty in ascertaining the activities of Senator on November 22 and 23. He was unable to account specifically for large segments of time when he was not with

Ruby.[1277] And, as to places and people Senator says he visited on those days prior to the time Oswald was shot, the Commission has been unsuccessful in obtaining verification.[1278] Senator admitted that he had spent much of that time drinking but denied that he was intoxicated.[1279]

It is difficult to know with complete certainty whether Senator had any foreknowledge of the shooting of Oswald. Ruby testified that at about 10:15 a.m. on Sunday morning, November 24, he said, in Senator's presence, "If something happened to this person, that then Mrs. Kennedy won't have to come back for the trial." [1280] According to Ruby, this is the most explicit statement he made concerning Oswald that morning.[1281] Senator denies any knowledge of Ruby's intentions.[1282]

Senator's general response to the shooting was not like that of a person seeking to conceal his guilt. Shortly before it was known that Ruby was the slayer of Oswald, Senator visited the Eatwell Restaurant in downtown Dallas. Upon being informed that Ruby was the attacker, Senator exclaimed, "My God," in what appeared to be a genuinely surprised tone.[1283] He then ran to a telephone, returned to gulp down his coffee, and quickly departed.[1284] He drove promptly to the home of James Martin, an attorney and friend. Martin recalled that Senator's concern was for his friend Ruby and not for himself.[1285] Martin and Senator drove to the Dallas Police Department where Senator voluntarily submitted himself to police questioning, and gave interviews to newspaper and television reporters.[1286] The Commission has concluded, on the basis of its investigation into Senator's background, activities, and reaction to the shooting, that Senator did not aid or conspire with Jack Ruby in the killing of Oswald.

Ruby's activities preceding President's trip.—In addition to the broad investigation into Ruby's background and associations, the Commission delved particularly into Ruby's pattern of activities during the 2 months preceding President Kennedy's visit to Dallas in order to determine whether there was unusual conduct which might be linked to the President's forthcoming trip.

The Commission has been able to account specifically for Jack Ruby's presence in Dallas on every day after September 26, 1963, except five—September 29, 30 and October 11, 14, and 24—and there is no evidence that he was out of the Dallas-Fort Worth area on those days.[1287] The report of one person who saw Ruby on September 28 indicates that Ruby probably remained in Dallas on September 29 and 30,[1288] when Oswald was in Mexico City. The Commission has looked for but has found no evidence that Ruby traveled to Mexico at that time.[1289] Both Ruby and Ralph Paul have stated that Ruby did not leave the Dallas-Fort Worth area during September, October, or November 1963.[1290]

During October and November of 1963, Jack Ruby maintained his usual vigorous pace of business activities. In particular, he directed considerable attention to his two nightclubs and to other business promotions.[1291] During the final month before the Kennedy trip, his time was increasingly occupied with personnel problems at both his clubs. There is no indication that he devoted less than full attention to these matters or that he appeared preoccupied with other affairs. His acquaintances did feel that Ruby seemed depressed and concerned that his friends were deserting him.[1292] However, there were no signs of secretive conduct.

Scrutiny of Ruby's activities during the several days preceding the President's arrival in Dallas has revealed no indication of any unusual activity. Ruby is remembered to have discussed the President's impending trip with only two persons and only briefly.[1293] Two newspapers containing a description of the expected motorcade routes through Dallas and Fort Worth were found in Ruby's car at the time of this arrest. However, such papers circulated widely in Dallas, and Ruby's car, like his apartment, was so cluttered with other newspapers, notebooks, brochures, cards, clothing, and personal items [1294] that there is no reason to attach any significance to the papers.

Aside from the results of the Commission's investigation reported above, there are other reasons to doubt that Jack Ruby would have shot Oswald as he did if he had been involved in a conspiracy to carry out the assassination, or that he would have been delegated to perform the shooting of Oswald on behalf of others who were involved in the slaying of the President. By striking in the city jail, Ruby was certain to be apprehended. An attempt to silence Oswald by having Ruby kill him would have presented exceptionally grave dangers to any other persons involved in the scheme. If the attempt had failed, Oswald might have been moved to disclose his confederates to the authorities. If it succeeded, as it did, the additional killing might itself have produced a trail to them. Moreover, Ruby was regarded by most persons who knew him as moody and unstable—hardly one to have encouraged the confidence of persons involved in a sensitive conspiracy.[1295]

Since his apprehension, Jack Ruby has provided the Federal authorities with several detailed accounts of his activities both preceding and following the assassination of President Kennedy. Ruby has shown no reluctance to answer any questions addressed to him. The accounts provided by Ruby are consistent with evidence available to the Commission from other sources.

These additional considerations are thus fully consistent with the results of the Commission's investigation. Rumors of a connection between Ruby and Oswald have proved groundless, while examination of Ruby's background and associations, his behavior prior to the assassination, and his activities during the November 22–24 weekend has yielded no evidence that Ruby conspired with anyone in planning or executing the killing of Lee Harvey Oswald. Whatever the legal culpability of Jack Ruby for his act of November 24, the evidence is persuasive that he acted independently in shooting Oswald.

CONCLUSION

Based upon the investigation reviewed in this chapter, the Commission concluded that there is no credible evidence that Lee Harvey Oswald was part of a conspiracy to assassinate President Kennedy. Examination of the facts of the assassination itself revealed no indication that Oswald was aided in the planning or execution of his scheme. Review of Oswald's life and activities since 1959, although productive in illuminating the character of Lee Harvey Oswald (which is discussed in the next chapter), did not produce any meaningful evidence of a conspiracy. The Commission discovered no evidence that the Soviet Union or Cuba were involved in the assassination of President Kennedy. Nor did the Commission's investigation of Jack Ruby produce any grounds for believing that Ruby's killing of Oswald was part of a conspiracy. The conclusion that there is no evidence of a conspiracy was also reached independently by Dean Rusk, the Secretary of State; Robert S. McNamara, the Secretary of Defense; C. Douglas Dillon, the Secretary of the Treasury; Robert F. Kennedy, the Attorney General; J. Edgar Hoover, the Director of the FBI; John A. McCone, the Director of the CIA; and James J. Rowley, the Chief of the Secret Service, on the basis of the information available to each of them.[1296]

CHAPTER VII

Lee Harvey Oswald: Background and Possible Motives

THE EVIDENCE reviewed above identifies Lee Harvey Oswald as the assassin of President Kennedy and indicates that he acted alone in that event. There is no evidence that he had accomplices or that he was involved in any conspiracy directed to the assassination of the President. There remains the question of what impelled Oswald to conceive and to carry out the assassination of the President of the United States. The Commission has considered many possible motives for the assassination, including those which might flow from Oswald's commitment to Marxism or communism, the existence of some personal grievance, a desire to effect changes in the structure of society or simply to go down in history as a well publicized assassin. None of these possibilities satisfactorily explains Oswald's act if it is judged by the standards of reasonable men. The motives of any man, however, must be analyzed in terms of the character and state of mind of the particular individual involved. For a motive that appears incomprehensible to other men may be the moving force of a man whose view of the world has been twisted, possibly by factors of which those around him were only dimly aware. Oswald's complete state of mind and character are now outside of the power of man to know. He cannot, of course, be questioned or observed by those charged with the responsibility for this report or by experts on their behalf. There is, however, a large amount of material available in his writings and in the history of his life which does give some insight into his character and, possibly, into the motives for his act.

Since Oswald is dead, the Commission is not able to reach any definite conclusions as to whether or not he was "sane" under prevailing legal standards. Under our system of justice no forum could properly make that determination unless Oswald were before it. It certainly could not be made by this Commission which, as has been pointed out above, ascertained the facts surrounding the assassination but did not draw conclusions concerning Oswald's legal guilt.

Indications of Oswald's motivation may be obtained from a study of the events, relationships and influences which appear to have been significant in shaping his character and in guiding him. Perhaps the most outstanding conclusion of such a study is that Oswald was profoundly alienated from the world in which he lived. His life was characterized by isolation, frustration, and failure. He had very few, if any, close relationships with other people and he appeared to have great difficulty in finding a meaningful place in the world. He was never satisfied with anything. When he was in the United States he resented the capitalist system which he thought was exploiting him and others like him. He seemed to prefer the Soviet Union and he spoke highly of Cuba.[1] When he was in the Soviet Union, he apparently resented the Communist Party members, who were accorded special privileges and who he thought were betraying communism, and he spoke well of the United States.[2] He accused his wife of preferring others to himself and told her to return to the Soviet Union without him but without a divorce. At the same time he professed his love for her and said that he could not get along without her.[3] Marina Oswald thought that he would not be happy anywhere, "Only on the moon, perhaps." [4]

While Oswald appeared to most of those who knew him as a meek and harmless person, he sometimes imagined himself as "the Commander" [5] and, apparently seriously, as a political prophet—a man who said that after 20 years he would be prime minister.[6] His wife testified that he compared himself with great leaders of history. Such ideas of grandeur were apparently accompanied by notions of oppression.[7] He had a great hostility toward his environment, whatever it happened to be, which he expressed in striking and sometimes violent acts long before the assassination. There was some quality about him that led him to act with an apparent disregard for possible consequences.[8] He defected to the Soviet Union, shot at General Walker, tried to go to Cuba and even contemplated hijacking an airplane to get there. He assassinated the President, shot Officer Tippit, resisted arrest and tried to kill another policeman in the process.

Oswald apparently started reading about communism when he was about 15. In the Marines, he evidenced a strong conviction as to the correctness of Marxist doctrine, which one associate described as "irrevocable," but also as "theoretical"; that associate did not think that Oswald was a Communist.[9] Oswald did not always distinguish between Marxism and communism.[10] He stated several times that he was a Communist but apparently never joined any Communist Party.[11]

His attachment to Marxist and Communist doctrine was probably, in some measure, an expression of his hostility to his environment. While there is doubt about how fully Oswald understood the doctrine which he so often espoused, it seems clear that his commitment to Marxism was an important factor influencing his conduct during his adult years. It was an obvious element in his decision to go to Russia and later to Cuba and it probably influenced his decision to shoot at General Walker. It was a factor which contributed to his character and thereby might have influenced his decision to assassinate President Kennedy.

The discussion below will describe the events known to the Commission which most clearly reveals the formation and nature of Oswald's character. It will attempt to summarize the events of his early life, his experience in New York City and in the Marine Corps, and his interest in Marxism. It will examine his defection to the Soviet Union in 1959, his subsequent return to the United States and his life here after June of 1962. The review of the latter period will evaluate his personal and employment relations, his attempt to kill General Walker, his political activities, and his unsuccessful attempt to go to Cuba in late September of 1963. Various possible motives will be treated in the appropriate context of the discussion outlined above.

The Early Years

Significant in shaping the character of Lee Harvey Oswald was the death of his father, a collector of insurance premiums. This occurred 2 months before Lee was born in New Orleans on October 18, 1939.[12] That death strained the financial fortunes of the remainder of the Oswald family. It had its effect on Lee's mother, Marguerite, his brother Robert, who had been born in 1934, and his half-brother John Pic, who had been born in 1932 during Marguerite's previous marriage.[13] It forced Marguerite Oswald to go to work to provide for her family.[14] Reminding her sons that they were orphans and that the family's financial condition was poor, she placed John Pic and Robert Oswald in an orphans' home.[15] From the time Marguerite Oswald returned to work until December 26, 1942, when Lee too was sent to the orphans' home, he was cared for principally by his mother's sister, by babysitters and by his mother, when she had time for him.[16]

Marguerite Oswald withdrew Lee from the orphans' home and took him with her to Dallas when he was a little over 4 years old.[17] About 6 months later she also withdrew John Pic and Robert Oswald.[18] Apparently that action was taken in anticipation of her marriage to Edwin A. Ekdahl, which took place in May of 1945.[19] In the fall of that year John Pic and Robert Oswald went to a military academy where they stayed, except for vacations, until the spring of 1948.[20] Lee Oswald remained with his mother and Ekdahl,[21] to whom he became quite attached. John Pic testified that he thought Lee found in Ekdahl the father that he never had.[22] That situation, however, was short-lived, for the relations between Marguerite Oswald and Ekdahl were stormy and they were finally divorced, after several separations and reunions, in the summer of 1948.[23]

After the divorce Mrs. Oswald complained considerably about how unfairly she was treated, dwelling on the fact that she was a widow with three children. John Pic, however, did not think her position was worse than that of many other people.[24] In the fall of 1948 she told John Pic and Robert Oswald that she could not afford to send them back to the military school and she asked Pic to quit school entirely to help support the family, which he did for 4 months in the fall of 1948.[25] In order to supplement their income further she falsely swore that Pic was 17 years old so that he could join the Marine Corps Reserves.[26] Pic did turn over part of his income to his mother, but he returned to high school in January of 1949, where he stayed until 3 days before he was scheduled to graduate, when he left school in order to get into the Coast Guard.[27] Since his mother did not approve of his decision to continue school he accepted the responsibility for that decision himself and signed his mother's name to all his own excuses and report cards.[28]

Pic thought that his mother overstated her financial problems and was unduly concerned about money. Referring to the period after the divorce from Ekdahl, which was apparently caused in part by Marguerite's desire to get more money from him, Pic said: "Lee was brought up in this atmosphere of constant money problems, and I am sure it had quite an effect on him, and also Robert." [29] Marguerite Oswald worked in miscellaneous jobs after her divorce from Ekdahl.[30] When she worked for a time as an insurance saleslady, she would sometimes take Lee with her, apparently leaving him alone in the car while she transacted her business.[31] When she worked during the school year, Lee had to leave an empty house in the morning, return to it for lunch and then again at night, his mother having trained him to do that rather than to play with other children.[32]

An indication of the nature of Lee's character at this time was provided in the spring of 1950, when he was sent to New Orleans to visit the family of his mother's sister, Mrs. Lillian Murret, for 2 or 3 weeks. Despite their urgings, he refused to play with the other children his own age.[33] It also appears that Lee tried to tag along with his older brothers but apparently was not able to spend as much time with them as he would have liked, because of the age gaps of 5 and 7 years, which became more significant as the children grew older.[34]

New York City

Whatever problems may have been created by Lee's home life in Louisiana and Texas, he apparently adjusted well enough there to have had an average, although gradually deteriorating, school record with no behavior or truancy problems. That was not the case, however, after he and his mother moved to New York in August of 1952, shortly before Lee's 13th birthday. They moved shortly after Robert joined the Marines; they lived for a time with John Pic who was stationed there with the Coast Guard.[35] Relations soon became strained, however,[36] so in late September Lee and his mother moved to their own apartment in the Bronx.[37] Pic and his wife would have been happy to have kept Lee, however, who was becoming quite a disciplinary problem for his mother, having struck her on at least one occasion.[38]

The short-lived stay with the Pics was terminated after an incident in which Lee allegedly pulled out a pocket knife during an argument and threatened to use it on Mrs. Pic. When Pic returned home, Mrs. Oswald tried to play down the event but Mrs. Pic took a different view and asked the Oswalds to leave. Lee refused to discuss the matter with Pic, whom he had previously idolized, and their relations were strained thereafter.[39]

On September 30, 1952, Lee enrolled in P.S. 117,[40] a junior high school in the Bronx, where the other children apparently teased him because of his "western" clothes and Texas accent.[41] He began to stay away from school, preferring to read magazines and watch television at home by himself.[42] This continued despite the efforts of the school authorities and, to a lesser extent, of his mother to have him return to school.[43] Truancy charges were brought against him alleging that he was "beyond the control of his mother insofar as school attendance is concerned."[44] Lee Oswald was remanded for psychiatric observation to Youth House, an institution in which children are kept for psychiatric observation or for detention pending court appearance or commitment to a child-caring or custodial institution such as a training school.[45] He was in Youth House from April 16 to May 7, 1953,[46] during which time he was examined by its Chief Psychiatrist, Dr. Renatus Hartogs, and interviewed and observed by other members of the Youth House staff.[47]

Marguerite Oswald visited her son at Youth House, where she recalled that she waited in line "with Puerto Ricans and Negroes and everything."[48] She said that her pocketbook was searched "becaus the children in this home were such criminals, dope fiends, and had been in criminal offenses, that anybody entering this home had to be searched in case the parents were bringing cigarettes or narcotics or anything."[49] She recalled that Lee cried and said, "Mother, I want to get out of here. There are children in here who have killed people, and smoke. I want to get out."[50] Marguerite Oswald said that she had not realized until then in what kind of place her son had been confined.[51]

On the other hand, Lee told his probation officer, John Carro, that "while he liked Youth House he miss[ed] the freedom of doing what he wanted. He indicated that he did not miss his mother."[52] Mrs. Evelyn Strickman Siegel, a social worker who interviewed both Lee and his mother while Lee was confined in Youth House, reported that Lee "confided that the worse thing about Youth House was the fact that he had to be with other boys all the time, was disturbed about disrobing in front of them, taking showers with them etc."[53]

Contrary to reports that appeared after the assassination, the psychiatric examination did not indicate that Lee Oswald was a potential assassin, potentially dangerous, that "his outlook on life had strongly paranoid overtones" or that he should be institutionalized.[54] Dr. Hartogs did find Oswald to be a tense, withdrawn, and evasive boy who intensely disliked talking about himself and his feelings. He noted that Lee liked to give the impression that he did not care for other people but preferred to keep to himself, so that he was not bothered and did not have to make the effort of communicating. Oswald's withdrawn tendencies and solitary habits were thought to be the result of "intense anxiety, shyness, feelings of awkwardness and insecurity." [55] He was reported to have said "I don't want a friend and I don't like to talk to people" and "I dislike everybody." [56] He was also described as having a "vivid fantasy life, turning around the topics of omnipotence and power, through which he tries to compensate for his present shortcomings and frustrations." [57] Dr. Hartogs summarized his report by stating:

> This 13 year old well built boy has superior mental resources and functions only slightly below his capacity level in spite of chronic truancy from school which brought him into Youth House. No finding of neurological impairment or psychotic mental changes could be made. Lee has to be diagnosed as "personality pattern disturbance with schizoid features and passive—aggressive tendencies." Lee has to be seen as an emotionally, quite disturbed youngster who suffers under the impact of really existing emotional isolation and deprivation, lack of affection, absence of family life and rejection by a self involved and conflicted mother.[58]

Dr. Hartogs recommended that Oswald be placed on probation on condition that he seek help and guidance through a child guidance clinic. There, he suggested, Lee should be treated by a male psychiatrist who could substitute for the lack of a father figure. He also recommended that Mrs. Oswald seek "psychotherapeutic guidance through contact with a family agency." The possibility of commitment was to be considered only if the probation plan was not successful.[59]

Lee's withdrawal was also noted by Mrs. Siegel, who described him as a "seriously detached, withdrawn youngster." [60] She also noted that there was "a rather pleasant, appealing quality about this emotionally starved, affectionless youngster which grows as one speaks to him." [61] She thought that he had detached himself from the world around him because "no one in it ever met any of his needs for love." [62] She observed that since Lee's mother worked all day, he made his own meals and spent all his time alone because he didn't make friends with the boys in the neighborhood. She thought that he "withdrew into a completely solitary and detached existence where he did as he wanted and he didn't have to live by any rules or come into contact with people." [63] Mrs. Siegel concluded that Lee "just felt that his mother never gave a damn for him. He always felt like a burden that she simply just had to tolerate." [64] Lee confirmed some of those observations by saying that he felt almost as if there were a veil between him and other people through which they could not reach him, but that he preferred the veil to remain intact. He admitted to fantasies about being powerful and sometimes hurting and killing people, but refused to elaborate on them. He took the position that such matters were his own business.[65]

A psychological human figure-drawing test corroborated the interviewer's findings that Lee was insecure and had limited social contacts. Irving Sokolow, a Youth House psychologist reported that:

> The Human Figure Drawings are empty, poor characterizations of persons approximately the same age as the subject. They reflect a considerable amount of impoverishment in the social and emotional areas. He appears to be a somewhat insecure youngster exhibiting much inclination for warm and satisfying relationships to others. There is some indication that he may relate to men more easily than to women in view of the more mature conceptualisation. He appears slightly withdrawn and in view of the lack of detail within the drawings this may assume a more significant characteristic. He exhibits some difficulty in relationship to the maternal figure suggesting more anxiety in this area than in any other.[66]

Lee scored an IQ of 118 on the Wechsler Intelligence Scale for Children. According to Sokolow, this indicated a "present intellectual functioning in the upper range of bright normal intelligence." [67] Sokolow said that although Lee was "presumably disinterested in school subjects he operates on a much higher than average level." [68] On the Monroe Silent Reading Test, Lee's score indicated no retardation in reading speed and comprehension; he had better than average ability in arithmetical reasoning for his age group.[69]

Lee told Carro, his probation officer, that he liked to be by himself because he had too much difficulty in making friends.[70] The reports of Carro and Mrs. Siegel also indicate an ambivalent attitude toward authority on Oswald's part. Carro reported that Lee was disruptive in class after he returned to school on a regular basis in the fall of 1953. He had refused to salute the flag and was doing very little, if any, work. It appears that he did not want to do any of the things which the authorities suggested in their efforts to bring him out of the shell into which he appeared to be retreating.[71] He told Mrs. Siegel that he would run away if sent to a boarding school. On the other hand he also told her that he wished his mother had been more firm with him in her attempts to get him to return to school.[72]

The reports of the New York authorities indicate that Lee's mother gave him very little affection and did not serve as any sort of substitute for a father. Furthermore she did not appear to understand her own relationship to Lee's psychological problems. After her interview with Mrs. Oswald, Mrs. Siegel described her as a "smartly dressed, gray haired woman, very self-possessed and alert and superficially affable," but essentially a "defensive, rigid, self-involved person who had real difficulty in accepting and relating to people" and who had "little understanding" of Lee's behavior and of the "protective shell he has drawn around himself." [73] Dr. Hartogs reported that Mrs. Oswald did not understand that Lee's withdrawal was a form of "violent but silent protest against his neglect by her and represents his reaction to a complete absence of any real family life." [74] Carro reported that when questioned about his mother Lee said, "well I've got to live with her. I guess I love her." [75] It may also be significant that, as reported by John Pic, "Lee slept with my mother until I joined the service in 1950. This would make him approximately 10, well, almost 11 years old." [76]

The factors in Lee Oswald's personality which were noted by those who had contact with him in New York indicate that he had great difficulty in adapting himself to conditions in that city. His usual reaction to the problems which he encountered there was simply withdrawal. Those factors indicated a severe inability to enter into relationships with other people. In view of his experiences when he visited his relatives in New Orleans in the spring of 1950, and his other solitary habits, Lee had apparently been experiencing similar problems before going to New York, and as will be shown below, this failure to adapt to his environment was a dominant trait in his later life.

It would be incorrect, however, to believe that those aspects of Lee's personality which were observed in New York could have led anyone to predict the outburst of violence which finally occurred. Carro was the only one of Oswald's three principal observers who recommended that he be placed in a boy's home or similar institution.[77] But Carro was quite specific that his recommendation was based primarily on the adverse factors in Lee's environment—his lack of friends, the apparent unavailability of any agency assistance and the ineffectualness of his mother—and not on any particular mental disturbance in the boy himself.[78] Carro testified that:

> There was nothing that would lead me to believe when I saw him at the age of 12 that there would be seeds of destruction for somebody. I couldn't in all honesty sincerely say such a thing.[79]

Mrs. Siegel concluded her report with the statement that:

> Despite his withdrawal, he gives the impression that he is not so difficult to reach as he appears and patient, prolonged effort in a sustained relationship with one therapist might bring results. There are indications that he has suffered serious personality damage but if he can receive help quickly this might be repaired to some extent.[80]

Lee Oswald never received that help. Few social agencies even in New York were equipped to provide the kind of intensive treatment that he needed, and when one of the city's clinics did find room to handle him, for some reason the record does not show, advantage was never taken of the chance afforded to Oswald. When Lee became a disciplinary problem upon his return to school in the fall of 1953, and when his mother failed to cooperate in any way with school authorities, authorities were finally forced to consider placement in a home for boys. Such a placement was postponed, however, perhaps in part at least because Lee's behavior suddenly improved. Before the court took any action, the Oswalds left New York [81] in January of 1954, and returned to New Orleans where Lee finished the ninth grade before he left school to work for a year.[82] Then in October of 1956, he joined the Marines.[83]

Return to New Orleans and Joining the Marine Corps

After his return to New Orleans Oswald was teased at school because of the northern accent which he had acquired.[84] He concluded that school had nothing to offer him.[85] His mother exercised little control over him and thought he could decide for himself whether to go on in school.[86] Neighbors and others who knew him at that time recall an introverted boy who read a great deal.[87] He took walks and visited museums, and sometimes rode a rented bicycle in the park on Saturday mornings.[88] Mrs. Murret believes that he talked at length with a girl on the telephone, but no one remembers that he had any dates.[89] A friend, Edward Voebel, testified that "he was more bashful about girls than anything else." [90]

Several witnesses testified that Lee Oswald was not aggressive.[91] He was, however, involved in some fights. Once a group of white boys beat him up for sitting in the Negro section of a bus, which he apparently did simply out of ignorance.[92] Another time, he fought with two brothers who claimed that he had picked on the younger of them, 3 years Oswald's junior. Two days later, "some big guy, probably from a high school—he looked like a tremendous football player" accosted Oswald on the way home from school and punched him in the mouth, making his lip bleed and loosening a tooth. Voebel took Oswald back to the school to attend to his wounds, and their "mild friendship" stemmed from that incident.[93] Voebel also recalled that Oswald once outlined a plan to cut the glass in the window of a store on Rampart Street and steal a pistol, but he was not sure then that Oswald meant to carry out the plan, and in fact they never did. Voebel said that Oswald "wouldn't start any fights, but if you wanted to start one with him, he was going to make sure that he ended it, or you were going to really have one, because he wasn't going to take anything from anybody." [94] In a space for the names of "close friends" on the ninth grade personal history record, Oswald first wrote "Edward Vogel," an obvious misspelling of Voebel's name, and "Arthor Abear," most likely Arthur Hebert, a classmate who has said that he did not know Oswald well. Oswald erased those names, however, and indicated that he had no close friends.[95]

It has been suggested that this misspelling of names, apparently on a phonetic basis, was caused by a reading-spelling disability from which Oswald appeared to suffer.[96] Other evidence of the existence of such a disability is provided by the many other misspellings that appear in Oswald's writings, portions of which are quoted below.

Sometime during this period, and under circumstances to be discussed more fully below, Oswald started to read Communist literature, which he obtained from the public library.[97]   One of his fellow employees, Palmer McBride, stated that Oswald said he would like to kill President Eisenhower because he was exploiting the working class.[98]   Oswald praised Khrushchev and suggested that he and McBride join the Communist Party "to take advantage of their social functions." [99]   Oswald also became interested in the New Orleans Amateur Astronomy Association, an organization of high school students.   The association's then president, William E. Wulf, testified that he remembered an occasion when Oswald

> * * * started expounding the Communist doctrine and saying that he was highly interested in communism, that communism was the only way of life for the worker, et cetera, and then came out with a statement that he was looking for a Communist cell in town to join but he couldn't find any.   He was a little dismayed at this, and he said that he couldn't find any that would show any interest in him as a Communist, and subsequently, after this conversation, my father came in and we were kind of arguing back and forth about the situation, and my father came in the room, heard what we were arguing on communism, and that this boy was loud-mouthed, boisterous, and my father asked him to leave the house and politely put him out of the house, and that is the last I have seen or spoken with Oswald.[100]

Despite this apparent interest in communism, Oswald tried to join the Marines when he was 16 years old.[101]   This was 1 year before his actual enlistment and just a little over 2½ years after he left New York.   He wrote a note in his mother's name to school authorities in New Orleans saying that he was leaving school because he and his mother were moving to San Diego.   In fact, he had quit school in an attempt to obtain his mother's assistance to join the Marines.[102]   While he apparently was able to induce his mother to make a false statement about his age he was nevertheless unable to convince the proper authorities that he was really 17 years old.[103]   There is evidence that Oswald was greatly influenced in his decision to join the Marines by the fact that his brother Robert had done so approximately 3 years before.[104]   Robert Oswald had given his Marine Corps manual to his brother Lee, who studied it during the year following his unsuccessful attempt to enlist until "He knew it by heart." [105]   According to Marguerite Oswald, "Lee lived for the time that he would become 17 years old to join the Marines—that whole year." [106]   In John Pic's view, Oswald was motivated to join the Marines in large part by a desire "to get from out and under * * * the yoke of oppression from my mother." [107]

Oswald's inability or lack of desire to enter into meaningful relationships with other people continued during this period in New Orleans (1954–56).[108]   It probably contributed greatly to the general dissatisfaction which he exhibited with his environment, a dissatisfaction which seemed to find expression at this particular point in his intense desire to join the Marines and get away from his surroundings and his mother. His study of Communist literature, which might appear to be inconsistent with his desire to join the Marines, could have been another manifestation of Oswald's rejection of his environment.[109]

His difficulty in relating to other people and his general dissatisfaction with the world around him continued while he was in the Marine Corps. Kerry Thornley, a marine associate, who, shortly after Oswald's defection, wrote an as yet unpublished novel based in considerable part on Oswald's life, testified that "definitely the Marine Corps was not what he had expected it to be when he joined." He said that Oswald "seemed to guard against developing real close friendships." [110]   Daniel Powers, another marine who was stationed with Oswald for part of his marine career, testified that Oswald seemed "always [to be] striving for a relationship, but whenever he did * * * his general personality would alienate the group against him." [111] Other marines also testified that Oswald had few friends and kept very much to himself.[112]

While there is nothing in Oswald's military records to indicate that he was mentally unstable or otherwise psychologically unfit for duty in the Marine Corps,[113] he did not adjust well to conditions which he found in that service.[114]   He did not rise above the rank of private first class, even though he had passed a qualifying examination for the rank of corporal.[115]   His Marine career was not helped by his attitude that he was a man of great ability and intelligence and that many of his superiors in the Marine Corps were not sufficiently competent to give him orders.[116]   While Oswald did not seem to object to authority in the abstract, he did think that he should be the one to exercise it.   John E. Donovan, one of his former officers, testified that Oswald thought "that authority, particularly the Marine Corps, ought to be able to recognize talent such as his own, without a given magic college degree, and put them in positions of prominence." [117]

Oswald manifested this feeling about authority by baiting his officers. He led them into discussions of foreign affairs about which they often knew less than he did, since he had apparently devoted considerable time to a study of such matters.[118]   When the officers were unable to discuss foreign affairs satisfactorily with him, Oswald regarded them as unfit to exercise command over him.[119]   Nelson Delgado, one of Oswald's fellow Marines, testified that Oswald tried to "cut up anybody that was high ranking" in those arguments "and make himself come out top dog." [120]   Oswald probably engaged his superiors in arguments on a subject that he had studied in an attempt to attract attention to himself and to support his exaggerated idea of his own abilities.

Thornley also testified that he thought that Oswald's extreme personal sloppiness in the Marine Corps "fitted into a general personality pattern of his: to do whatever was not wanted of him, a recalcitrant trend in his personality." [121]   Oswald "seemed to be a person who would go out of his way to get into trouble" [122] and then used the "special treatment" he received as an example of the way in which he was being picked on and "as a means of getting or attempting to get sympathy." [123] In Thornley's view, Oswald labored under a persecution complex which he strove to maintain and "felt the Marine Corps kept a pretty close watch on him because of his 'subversive' activities." Thornley added: "I think it was kind of necessary to him to believe that he was being picked on. It wasn't anything extreme. I wouldn't go as far as to call it, call him a paranoid, but a definite tendency there was in that direction, I think." [124]

Powers considered Oswald to be meek and easily led,[125] an "individual that you would brainwash, and quite easy * * * [but] I think once he believed in something * * * he stood in his beliefs." [126] Powers also testified that Oswald was reserved and seemed to be "somewhat the frail, little puppy in the litter." [127] He had the nickname "Ozzie Rabbit." [128]

Oswald read a good deal, said Powers, but "he would never be reading any of the shoot-em-up westerns or anything like that. Normally, it would be a good type of literature; and the one that I recall was 'Leaves of Grass,' by Walt Whitman." [129] According to Powers, Oswald said: " 'All the Marine Corps did was to teach you to kill' and after you got out of the Marines you might be good gangsters." [130] Powers believed that when Oswald arrived in Japan he acquired a girlfriend, "finally attaining a male status or image in his own eyes." [131] That apparently caused Oswald to become more self-confident, aggressive and even somewhat pugnacious, although Powers "wouldn't say that this guy is a troublemaker." [132] Powers said "now he was Oswald the man rather than Oswald the rabbit." [133] Oswald once told Powers that he didn't care if he returned to the United States at all.[134]

While in Japan, Oswald's new found apparent self confidence and pugnaciousness led to an incident in which he spilled a drink on one of his sergeants and abusively challenged him to fight.[135] At the court-martial hearing which followed, Oswald admitted that he had been rather drunk when the incident occurred. He testified that he had felt the sergeant had a grudge against him and that he had unsuccessfully sought a transfer from the sergeant's unit. He said that he had simply wanted to discuss the question with the sergeant and the drink had been spilled accidentally. The hearing officer agreed with the latter claim but found Oswald guilty of wrongfully using provoking words and sentenced him to 28 days, canceling the suspension of a 20-day sentence that Oswald had received in an earlier court-martial for possessing an unauthorized pistol with which he had accidentally shot himself.[136]

At his own request, Oswald was transferred from active duty to the Marine Corps Reserve under honorable conditions in September of 1959, 3 months prior to his regularly scheduled separation date,[137] ostensibly to care for his mother who had been injured in an accident at her work.[138] He was undesirably discharged from the Marine Corps Reserve, to which he had been assigned on inactive status following his transfer from active duty, after it was learned that he had defected to the Soviet Union.[139]   In an attempt to have this discharge reversed, Oswald wrote to then Secretary of the Navy Connally on January 30, 1962, stating that he would "employ all means to right this gross mistake or injustice." [140]

Governor Connally had just resigned to run for Governor of Texas, so he advised Oswald that he had forwarded the letter to his successor.[141] It is thus clear that Oswald knew that Governor Connally was never directly concerned with his discharge and he must have known that President Kennedy had had nothing to do with it.   In that connection, it does not appear that Oswald ever expressed any dissatisfaction of any kind with either the President or Governor Connally.[142] Marina Oswald testified that she "had never heard anything bad about Kennedy from Lee. And he never had anything against him." [143] Mrs. Oswald said that her husband did not say anything about Governor Connally after his return to the United States. She testified: "But while we were in Russia he spoke well of him. * * * Lee said that when he would return to the United States he would vote for him [for Governor]." [144] Oswald must have already learned that the Governor could not help him with his discharge because he was no longer Secretary of the Navy, at the time he made that remark.

Even though Oswald apparently did not express any hostility against the President or Governor Connally, he continued to be concerned about his undesirable discharge.[145] It is clear that he thought he had been unjustly treated. Probably his complaint was due to the fact that his discharge was not related to anything he had done while on active duty and also because he had not received any notice of the original discharge proceedings, since his whereabouts were not known.[146] He continued his efforts to reverse the discharge by petitioning the Navy Discharge Review Board, which finally declined to modify the discharge and so advised him in a letter dated July 25, 1963.[147]

Governor Connally's connection with the discharge, although indirect, caused the Commission to consider whether he might have been Oswald's real target. In that connection, it should be noted that Marina Oswald testified on September 6, 1964, that she thought her husband "was shooting at Connally rather than President Kennedy." In support of her conclusion Mrs. Oswald noted her husband's undesirable discharge and that she could not think of any reason why Oswald would want to kill President Kennedy.[148] It should be noted, however, that at the time Oswald fired the shots at the Presidential limousine the Governor occupied the seat in front of the President, and it would have been almost impossible for Oswald to have hit the Governor without hitting the President first. Oswald could have shot the Governor as the car approached the Depository or as it was making the turn onto Elm Street. Once it had started down Elm Street toward the Triple Underpass, however, the President almost completely blocked Oswald's view of the Governor prior to the time the first shot struck the President.[150] Furthermore, Oswald would have had other and more favorable opportunities to strike at the Governor than on this occasion when, as a member of the President's party, he had more protection than usual. It would appear, therefore, that to the extent Oswald's undesirable discharge affected his motivation, it was more in terms of a general hostility against the government and its representatives rather than a grudge against any particular person.

Interest in Marxism

As indicated above, Oswald started to read Communist literature after he and his mother left New York and moved to New Orleans.[151] He told Aline Mosby, a reporter who interviewed him after he arrived in Moscow:

> I'm a Marxist, * * * I became interested about the age of 15. From an ideological viewpoint. An old lady handed me a pamphlet about saving the Rosenbergs. * * * I looked at that paper and I still remember it for some reason, I don't know why.[152]

Oswald studied Marxism after he joined the Marines and his sympathies in that direction and for the Soviet Union appear to have been widely known, at least in the unit to which he was assigned after his return from the Far East. His interest in Russia led some of his associates to call him "comrade"[153] or "Oswaldskovitch."[154] He always wanted to play the red pieces in chess because, as he said in an apparently humorous context, he preferred the "Red Army."[155] He studied the Russian language,[156] read a Russian language newspaper[157] and seemed interested in what was going on in the Soviet Union.[158] Thornley, who thought Oswald had an "irrevocable conviction" that his Marxist beliefs were correct, testified:

> I think you could sit down and argue with him for a number of years * * * and I don't think you could have changed his mind on that unless you knew why he believed it in the first place. I certainly don't. I don't think with any kind of formal argument you could have shaken that conviction. And that is why I say irrevocable. It was just—never getting back to looking at things from any other way once he had become a Marxist, whenever that was.[159]

Thornley also testified about an incident which grew out of a combination of Oswald's known Marxist sympathies and George Orwell's book "1984," one of Oswald's favorite books which Thornley read at Oswald's suggestion. Shortly after Thornley finished reading that book the Marine unit to which both men were assigned was required to take part in a Saturday morning parade in honor of some retiring noncommissioned officers, an event which they both approached with little enthusiasm. While waiting for the parade to start they talked briefly about "1984" even though Oswald seemed to be lost in his own thoughts. After a brief period of silence Oswald remarked on the stupidity of the parade and on how angry it made him, to which Thornley replied: "Well, comes the revolution you will change all that." Thornley testified:

> At which time he looked at me like a betrayed Caesar and screamed, screamed definitely, "Not you, too, Thornley." And I remember his voice cracked as he said this. He was definitely disturbed at what I had said and I didn't really think I had said that much. * * * I never said anything to him again and he never said anything to me again.[160]

Thornley said that he had made his remark only in the context of "1984" and had not intended any criticism of Oswald's political views which is the way in which, Thornley thought, Oswald took his remarks.[161]

Lieutenant Donovan testified that Oswald thought that "there were many grave injustices concerning the affairs in the international situation." He recalled that Oswald had a specific interest in Latin America, particularly Cuba, and expressed opposition to the Batista regime and sympathy for Castro, an attitude which, Donovan said, was "not * * * unpopular" at that time. Donovan testified that he never heard Oswald express a desire personally to take part in the elimination of injustices anywhere in the world and that he "never heard him in any way, shape or form confess that he was a Communist, or that he ever thought about being a Communist." [162] Delgado testified that Oswald was "a complete believer that our way of government was not quite right" and believed that our Government did not have "too much to offer," but was not in favor of "the Communist way of life." Delgado and Oswald talked more about Cuba than Russia, and sometimes imagined themselves as leaders in the Cuban Army or Government, who might "lead an expedition to some of these other islands and free them too." [163]

Thornley also believed that Oswald's Marxist beliefs led to an extraordinary view of history under which:

> He looked upon the eyes of future people as some kind of tribunal, and he wanted to be on the winning side so that 10,000 years from now people would look in the history books and say, "Well, this man was ahead of his time." * * * The eyes of the future became * * * the eyes of God. * * * He was concerned with his image in history and I do think that is why he chose * * * the particular method [of defecting] he chose and did it in the way he did. It got him in the newspapers. It did broadcast his name out.[164]

Thornley thought that Oswald not only wanted a place in history but also wanted to live comfortably in the present. He testified that if Oswald could not have that "degree of physical comfort that he expected or sought, I think he would then throw himself entirely on the other thing he also wanted, which was the image in history. * * *

I think he wanted both if he could have them. If he didn't, he wanted to die with the knowledge that, or with the idea that he was somebody." [165]

Oswald's interest in Marxism led some people to avoid him, even though as his wife suggested, that interest may have been motivated by a desire to gain attention.[166] He used his Marxist and associated activities as excuses for his difficulties in getting along in the world, which were usually caused by entirely different factors. His use of those excuses to present himself to the world as a person who was being unfairly treated is shown most clearly by his employment relations after his return from the Soviet Union. Of course, he made his real problems worse to the extent that his use of those excuses prevented him from discovering the real reasons for and attempting to overcome his difficulties. Of greater importance, Oswald's commitment to Marxism contributed to the decisions which led him to defect to the Soviet Union in 1959, and later to engage in activities on behalf of the Fair Play for Cuba Committee in the summer of 1963, and to attempt to go to Cuba late in September of that year.

Defection to the Soviet Union

After Oswald left the Marine Corps in September of 1959, ostensibly to care for his mother, he almost immediately left for the Soviet Union where he attempted to renounce his citizenship. At the age of 19, Oswald thus committed an act which was the most striking indication he had yet given of his willingness to act on his beliefs in quite extraordinary ways.

While his defection resulted in part from Oswald's commitment to Marxism, it appears that personal and psychological factors were also involved. On August 17, 1963, Oswald told Mr. William Stuckey, who had arranged a radio debate on Oswald's activities on behalf of the Fair Play for Cuba Committee, that while he had begun to read Marx and Engels at the age of 15,

the conclusive thing that made him decide that Marxism was the answer was his service in Japan. He said living conditions over there convinced him something was wrong with the system, and that possibly Marxism was the answer. He said it was in Japan that he made up his mind to go to Russia and see for himself how a revolutionary society operates, a Marxist society.[167]

On the other hand, at least one person who knew Oswald after his return thought that his defection had a more personal and psychological basis.[168] The validity of the latter observation is borne out by some of the things Oswald wrote in connection with his defection indicating that his motivation was at least in part a personal one. On November 26, 1959, shortly after he arrived in the Soviet Union, and probably before Soviet authorities had given him permission to stay indefinitely, he wrote to his brother Robert that the Soviet Union

390

was a country which "I have always considered * * * to be my own" and that he went there "only to find freedom. * * * I could never have been personally happy in the U.S." [169] He wrote in another letter that he would "never return to the United States which is a country I hate." [170] His idea that he was to find "freedom" in the Soviet Union was to be rudely shattered.

Whatever Oswald's reasons for going to the Soviet Union might have been, however, there can be little doubt that his desire to go was quite strong. In addition to studying the Russian language while he was in the Marines, Oswald had managed to save enough money to cover the expenses of his forthcoming trip. While there is no proof that he saved $1,500, as he claimed, it would have taken considerable discipline to save whatever amount was required to finance his defection out of the salary of a low ranking enlisted man.[171]

The extent of Oswald's desire to go to the Soviet Union and of his initial commitment to that country can best be understood, however, in the context of his concomitant hatred of the United States, which was most clearly expressed in his November 26, 1959, letter to his brother Robert. Addressing himself to the question of why "I and my fellow workers and communist's would like to see the present capitalist government of the U.S. overthrown" Oswald stated that that government supported an economic system "which exploits all its workers" and under which "art, culture and the sprit of man are subjected to commercial enterpraising, [and] religion and education are used as a tool to surpress what would otherwise be a population questioning their government's unfair economic system and plans for war." [172]

He complained in his letter about segregation, unemployment, automation, and the use of military forces to suppress other populations. Asking his brother why he supported the American Government and what ideals he put forward, Oswald wrote:

Ask me and I will tell you I fight for *communism*. * * * I will not say your grandchildren will live under communism, look for yourself at history, look at a world map! America is a dieing country, I do not wish to be a part of it, nor do I ever again wish to be used as a tool in its military aggressions.

This should answewer your question, and also give you a glimpse of my way of thinking.

So you speak of advantages. Do you think that is why I am here? For personal, material advantages? Happiness is not based on oneself, it does not consist of a small home, of taking and getting, Happiness is taking part in the struggle, where there is no borderline between one's own personal world, and the world in general. I never believed I would find more material advantages at *this* stage of development in the Soviet Union than I might of had in the U.S.

* * * * * * *

I have been a pro-communist for years and yet I have never met a communist, instead I kept silent and observed, and what I observed plus my Marx'ist learning brought me here to the Soviet Union. I have always considered this country to be my own.[173]

Responding to Robert's statement that he had not "renounced" him, Oswald told his brother "on what terms I want this arrangement." He advised Robert that:

1. In the event of war I would kill *any* american who put a uniform on in defence of the american government—any american.
2. That in my own mind I have no attachment's of any kind in the U.S.
3. That I want to, and I shall, live a normal happy and peacful life here in the Soviet Union *for the rest of my life*.
4. that my mother and you are (in spite of what the newspaper said) *not* objects of affection, but only examples of workers in the U.S.[174]

Despite this commitment to the Soviet Union Oswald met disappointments there just as he had in the past. At the outset the Soviets told him that he could not remain. It seems that Oswald immediately attempted suicide—a striking indication of how much he desired to remain in the Soviet Union.[175] It shows how willing he was to act dramatically and decisively when he faced an emotional crisis with few readily available alternatives at hand. He was shocked to find that the Soviet Union did not accept him with open arms. The entry in his self-styled "Historic Diary" for October 21, 1959, reports:

I am shocked ! ! My dreams! * * * I have waited for 2 year to be accepted. My fondes dreams are shattered because of a petty offial, * * * I decide to end it. Soak rist in cold water to numb the pain, Than slash my leftwrist. Than plaug wrist into bathtum of hot water. * * * Somewhere, a violin plays, as I wacth my life whirl away. I think to myself "How easy to Die" and "A Sweet Death, (to violins) * * *[176]

Oswald was discovered in time to thwart his attempt at suicide.[177] He was taken to a hospital in Moscow where he was kept until October 28, 1959.[178]

Still intent, however, on staying in the Soviet Union, Oswald went on October 31, to the American Embassy to renounce his U.S. citizenship. Mr. Richard E. Snyder, then Second Secretary and senior consular official at the Embassy, testified that Oswald was extremely sure of himself and seemed "to know what his mission was. He took charge, in a sense, of the conversation right from the beginning."[179] He presented the following signed note:

I Lee Harvey Oswald do hereby request that my present citizenship in the United States of America, be revoked.

I have entered the Soviet Union for the express purpose of
appling for citizenship in the Soviet Union, through the means of
naturalization.

My request for citizenship is now pending before the Surprem
Soviet of the U.S.S.R. .

I take these steps for political reasons. My request for the revoking of my American citizenship is made only after the longest
and most serious considerations.

I affirm that my allegiance is to the Union of Soviet Socialist
Republics.[180] (See Commission Exhibit 913, p. 261.)

As his "principal reason" for renouncing his citizenship Oswald
stated: "I am a Marxist."[181] He also alluded to hardships endured
by his mother as a worker, referring to them as experiences that he did
not intend to have himself,[182] even though he stated that he had never
held a civilian job.[183] He said that his Marine service in Okinawa
and elsewhere had given him "a chance to observe 'American imperialism.'" but he also displayed some sensitivity at not having reached
a higher rank in the Marine Corps.[184] He stated that he had
volunteered to give Soviet officials any information that he had concerning Marine Corps operations,[185] and intimated that he might know
something of special interest.[186] Oswald's "Historic Diary" describes the event in part as follows:

I leave Embassy, elated at this showdown, returning to my
hotel I feel now my enorgies are not spent in vain. I'm sure
Russians will except me after this sign of my faith in them.[187]

The Soviet authorities finally permitted Oswald to remain in their
country.[188] No evidence has been found that they used him for any
particular propaganda or other political or informational purposes.
They sent him to Minsk to work in a radio and television factory as a
metal worker.[189] The Soviet authorities denied Oswald permission to
attend a university in Moscow,[190] but they gave him a monthly allowance of 700 rubles a month (old exchange rate)[191] in addition to his
factory salary of approximately equal amount[192] and considerably better living quarters than those accorded to Soviet citizens of equal age
and station.[193] The subsidy, apparently similar to those sometimes
given to foreigners allowed to remain in the Soviet Union, together
with his salary, gave Oswald an income which he said approximated
that of the director of the factory in which he worked.[194]

Even though he received more money and better living quarters
than other Russians doing similar work, he envied his wife's uncle, a
colonel in the MVD, because of the larger apartment in which he
lived. Reminiscent of his attitude toward his superiors in the Marine
Corps, Oswald apparently resented the exercise of authority over him
and the better treatment afforded to Communist Party officials.[195]
After he returned to the United States he took the position that the
Communist Party officials in the Soviet Union were opportunists who

were betraying their positions for personal gain. He is reported to have expressed the conclusion that they had "fat stinking politicians over there just like we have over here." [196]

Oswald apparently continued to have personal difficulties while he was in Minsk. Although Marina Oswald told the Commission that her husband had good personal relationships in the Soviet Union,[197] Katherine Ford, one of the members of the Russian community in Dallas with which the Oswalds became acquainted upon their arrival in the United States, stated that Mrs. Oswald told her everybody in Russia "hated him." [198] Jeanne De Mohrenschildt, another member of that group, said that Oswald told her that he had returned because "I didn't find what I was looking for." [199] George De Mohrenschildt thought that Oswald must have become disgusted with life in the Soviet Union as the novelty of the presence of an American wore off and he began to be less the center of attention.[200]

The best description of Oswald's state of mind, however, is set forth in his own "Historic Diary." Under the entry for May 1, 1960, he noted that one of his acquaintances "relats many things I do not know about the U.S.S.R. . I begin to feel uneasy inside, its true!" [201] Under the entry for August–September of that year he wrote:

> As my Russian improves I become increasingly concious of just what sort of a sociaty I live in. Mass gymnastics, complusory afterwork meeting, usually political information meeting. Complusory attendence at lectures and the sending of the entire shop collective (except me) to pick potatoes on a Sunday, at a state collective farm: A "patroict duty" to bring in the harvest. The opions of the workers (unvoiced) are that its a great pain in the neck: they don't seem to be esspicialy enthusiastic about any of the "collective" duties a natural feeling. I am increasingly aware of the presence, in all thing, of Lebizen, shop party secretary, fat, fortyish, and jovial on the outside. He is a no-nonsense party regular.[202]

Finally, the entry of January 4–31 of 1961:

> I am stating to reconsider my disire about staying the work is drab the money I get has nowhere to be spent. No night clubs or bowling allys no places of recreation acept the trade union dances I have have had enough.[203]

Shortly thereafter, less than 18 months after his defection, about 6 weeks before he met Marina Prusakova, Oswald opened negotiations with the U.S. Embassy in Moscow looking toward his return to the United States.[204]

Return to the United States

In view of the intensity of his earlier commitment to the Soviet Union, a great change must have occurred in Oswald's thinking to induce him to return to the United States. The psychological effects of that change must have been highly unsettling. It should be remembered that he was not yet 20 years old when he went to the Soviet Union with such high hopes and not quite 23 when he returned bitterly disappointed. His attempt to renounce his citizenship had been an open expression of hostility against the United States and a profound rejection of his early life. The dramatic break with society in America now had to be undone. His return to the United States publicly testified to the utter failure of what had been the most important act of his life.

Marina Oswald confirmed the fact that her husband was experiencing psychological difficulties at the time of his return. She said that "immediately after coming to the United States Lee changed. I did not know him as such a man in Russia." [205] She added that while he helped her as he had done before, he became more of a recluse, that "[he] was very irritable, sometimes for a trifle" and that "Lee was very unrestrained and very explosive" during the period from November 19, 1962 to March of 1963.[206]

After the assassination she wrote that:

> In general, our family life began to deteriorate after we arrived in America. Lee was always hot-tempered, and now this trait of character more and more prevented us from living together in harmony. Lee became very irritable, and sometimes some completely trivial thing would drive him into a rage. I myself do not have a particularly quiet disposition, but I had to change my character a great deal in order to maintain a more or less peaceful family life.[207]

Marina Oswald's judgment of her husband's state of mind may be substantiated by comparing material which he wrote in the Soviet Union with what he wrote while on the way back to the United States and after his return. While in the Soviet Union he wrote his longest and clearest piece of work, "The Collective." This was a fairly coherent description of life in that country, basically centered around the radio and television factory in which he worked.[208] While it was apparently intended for publication in the United States, and is in many respects critical of certain aspects of life in the Soviet Union, it appears to be the work of a fairly well organized person. Oswald prefaced his manuscript with a short autobiographical sketch which reads in part as follows:

> Lee Harvey Oswald was born in Oct 1939 in New Orleans La. the son of a Insuraen Salesmen whose early death left a far mean streak of indepence brought on by negleck. entering the US Marine corp at 17 this streak of independence was strengthed by exotic journeys to Japan the Philipines and the scores of odd Islands in the Pacific immianly after serving out his 3 years

COMMISSION EXHIBIT 2891

COMMISSION EXHIBIT 2892

PHOTOGRAPH OF LEE HARVEY OSWALD
TAKEN AFTER HIS RETURN FROM THE SOVIET UNION

(COMMISSION EXHIBIT 2788)

in the USMC he abonded his american life to seek a new life in the USSR. full of optimism and hope he stood in red square in the fall of 1959 vowing to see his chosen course through, after, however, two years and alot of growing up I decided to return to the USA. * * * [209]

"The Collective" contrasts sharply with material which Oswald seems to have written after he left the Soviet Union,[210] which appears to be more an expression of his own psychological condition than of a reasoned analysis. The latter material expresses great hostility to both communism and capitalism. He wrote, that to a person knowing both of those systems, "their can be no mediation between those systems as they exist to-day and that person. He must be opposed to their basic foundations and representatives" [211]

and yet it is imature to take the sort of attitude which says "a curse on both your houses!"
their are two great represenative of power in the world, simply expressed, the left and right, and their ~~offspring~~ factions and concers.
any practical attempt at one alternative must have as its nuclus the triditionall ideological best of both systems, and yet be utterly opposed to both systems.[212]

Such an alternative was to be opposed both to capitalism and communism because:

No man, having known, having lived, under the Russian Communist and American capitalist system, could possibly make a choice between them, there is no choice, one offers oppresstion the other poverty. Both offer imperilistic injustice, tinted with two brands of slavery.[213]

Oswald actually did attempt to formulate such an alternative [214] which he planned to "put forward" himself.[215] He thought the new alternative would have its best chance to be accepted after "conflict between the two world systems leaves the ~~world~~ country without defense or foundation of goverment," [216] after which the survivors would "seek a alturnative ~~opposed~~ to those systems which have brough them misery." [217] Oswald realized that "their thinking and education will be steeped in the traiditions of those systems [and] they would never except a 'new order' complete beyond their understanding." [218] As a result he thought it would be "neccary to oppose the old systems but at the same time support their cherised trations." [219]
Expanding on his ideas on how his alternative to communism and capitalism might be introduced, he wrote of a "readily foreseeable * * * economic, political or military crisis, internal or external, [which] will bring about the final destrution of the capitalist system," [220] and indicated that "preparation in a special party could safeguard an inde-

pendant course of action after the debacle," [221] which would achieve the goal, which was:

> The emplacement of a separate, democratic, pure communist sociaty * * * but one with union-communes, democratic socializing of production and without regard to the twisting apart of ~~Marxism~~ Marxist Communism by other powers.[222]

While "[r]esoufualniss and patient working towards the aforesaid goal's are prefered rather than loud and useless manifestation's of protest," [223] Oswald went on to note:

> But these prefered tactics now, may prove to be too limited in the near future, they should not be confused with slowness, indesision or fear, only the intellectualy fearless could even be remotly attracted too our doctrine, and yet this doctrine requirers the ~~uptmost~~ utmost restraint, a state of being in itself majustic in power.[224]

Oswald's decided rejection of both capitalism and communism seemed to place him in a situation in which he could not live with satisfaction either in the United States or in the Soviet Union. The discussion above has already set forth examples of his expression of hatred for the United States. He also expressed hatred of the Soviet Union and of the Communist Party, U.S.A., even though he later referred to the latter as "trusted long time fighters for progress." [225] He wrote:

> The Communist Party of the United States has betrayed itself!
> it has turned itself into the tradional lever of a foreign power to overthrow the goverment of the United States; not in the name of freedow or high ideals, but in servile conformity to the wishes of the Soviet Union and in anticipation of Soviet Russia's complete domination of the American continent.[226]
>
> *   *   *   *   *   *   *
>
> There can be no sympathy for those who have turned the idea of communism into a vill curse to western man.
> The Soviets have committed crimes unsurpassed even by their early day capitalist counterparts, the imprisonment of their own peoples, with the mass extermination so typical of Stalin, and the individual surpresstion and regimentation under Krushchev.
> The deportations, the purposefull curtailment of diet in the consumer slighted population of Russia, the murder of history, the prositution of art and culture.[227]

A suggestion that Oswald hated more than just capitalism and communism is provided by the following, which was apparently written either on the ship coming back, or after his return from the Soviet Union:

I have offen wondered why it is that the communist, ~~anarchist~~ capitatist and even the fasist and anarchist elements in american, allways profess patrotistism toward the land and the people, if not the goverment; although their ~~ideals~~ movements must surly lead to the bitter destruction of all and everything.

I am quite sure these people must hate not only the goverment but ~~our~~ the ~~peop~~ culture, ~~traditions~~, heritage and very people itself, and yet they stand up and piously pronouce themselfs patriots, displaying their war medles, that they gained in conflicts ~~long past~~ between themselfs.

*   *   *   *   *   *   *

I wonder what would happen it somebody was to stand up and say he was utterly opposed not only to the goverments, but to the people, too the entire land and complete foundations of his socially.[228]

Oswald demonstrated his thinking in connection with his return to the United States by preparing two sets of identical questions of the type which he might have thought he would be asked at a press conference when he returned. With either great ambivalence or cold calculation he prepared completely different answers to the same questions. Judged by his other statements and writings, however, he appears to have indicated his true feelings in the set of answers first presented and to have stated in the second what he thought would be least harmful to him as he resumed life in the United States. For example, in response to his questions about his decision to go to the Soviet Union, his first draft answered "as a mark of dicuss and protest against american political policies in foriengn countrys, my personal sign of discontent and horror at the misguided line of resoning of the U.S. Goverment." [229] His second answer was that he "went as a citizen of the U.S. (as a tourist) residing in a forieng conutry which I have a perfect right to do. I went there to see the land, the people and how their system works." [230]

To the question of "Are you a communits?" he first answered "Yes, basically, allthough I hate the USSR and socialist system I still *think* marxism can work under different circumstances." [231] His second answer to this question was, "No of course not, I have never even know a communist, outside of the ones in the USSR but you can't help that." [232] His first set of questions and answers indicated his belief that there were no outstanding differences between the Soviet Union and the United States, "except in the US. the living standard is a little higher. freedoms are about the same, medical aid and the educational system in the USSR is better than in the USA." [233] In the second simulated transcript which ended with the statement "Newspapers, thank you sir; you are a *real* patriot ! !" he apparently concluded that the United States offered "freedom of speech travel outspoken opposition to unpopular policies freedom to believe in god," while the Soviet Union did not.[234]

Despite the hatred that Oswald expressed toward the Soviet Union after his residence there, he continued to be interested in that country after he returned to the United States. Soon after his arrival he wrote to the Soviet Embassy in Washington requesting information on how to subscribe to Russian newspapers and magazines and asked for "any periodicals or bulletins which you may put out for the beneifit of your citizens living, for a time, in the U.S.A.." [235] Oswald subsequently did subscribe to several Soviet journals. [236] While Marina Oswald tried to obtain permission to return to the Soviet Union she testified that she did so at her husband's insistence. [237]

In July of 1963, Oswald also requested the Soviet Union to provide a visa for his return to that country. [238] In August of 1963, he gave the New Orleans police as a reason for refusing to permit his family to learn English, that "he hated America and he did not want them to become 'Americanized' and that his plans were to go back to Russia." [239] Even though his primary purpose probably was to get to Cuba, he sought an immediate grant of visa on his trip to Mexico City in late September of 1963. [240] He also inquired about visas for himself and his wife in a letter which he wrote to the Soviet Embassy in Washington on November 9, 1963. [241]

Personal Relations

Apart from his relatives, Oswald had no friends or close associates in Texas when he returned there in June of 1962, and he did not establish any close friendships or associations, although it appears that he came to respect George De Mohrenschildt. [242] Somewhat of a nonconformist, [243] De Mohrenschildt was a peripheral member of the so-called Russian community, with which Oswald made contact through Mr. Peter Gregory, a Russian-speaking petroleum engineer whom Oswald met as a result of his contact with the Texas Employment Commission office in Fort Worth. [244] Sóme of the members of that group saw a good deal of the Oswalds through the fall of 1963, and attempted to help Mrs. Oswald particularly, in various ways. [245] In general, Oswald did not like the members of the Russian community. [246] In fact, his relations with some of them, particularly George Bouhe, became quite hostile. [247] Part of the problem resulted from the fact that, as Jeanne De Mohrenschildt testified, Oswald was "very, very disagreeable and disappointed." [248] He also expressed considerable resentment at the help given to his wife by her Russian-American friends. Jeanne De Mohrenschildt said:

> Marina had a hundred dresses given to her * * * [and] he objected to that lavish help, because Marina was throwing it into his face.
>
> *   *   *   *   *   *   *
>
> He was offensive with the people. And I can understand why, * * * because that hurt him. He could never give her what the

people were showering on her. * * * no matter how hard he worked—and he worked very hard.[249]

The relations between Oswald and his wife became such that Bouhe wanted to "liberate" her from Oswald.[250] While the exact sequence of events is not clear because of conflicting testimony, it appears that De Mohrenschildt and his wife actually went to Oswald's apartment early in November of 1962 and helped to move the personal effects of Marina Oswald and the baby. Even though it appears that they may have left Oswald a few days before, it seems that he resisted the move as best he could. He even threatened to tear up his wife's dresses and break all the baby things. According to De Mohrenschildt, Oswald submitted to the inevitable, presumably because he was "small, you know, and he was rather a puny individual." [251] De Mohrenschildt said that the whole affair made him nervous since he was "interfering in other people's affairs, after all." [252]

Oswald attempted to get his wife to come back and, over Bouhe's protest, De Mohrenschildt finally told him where she was. De Mohrenschildt admitted that:

> if somebody did that to me, a lousy trick like that, to take my wife away, and all the furniture, I would be mad as hell, too. I am surprised that he didn't do something worse.[253]

After about a 2-week separation, Marina Oswald returned to her husband.[254] Bouhe thoroughly disapproved of this and as a result almost all communication between the Oswalds and members of the Russian community ceased. Contacts with De Mohrenschildt and his wife did continue and they saw the Oswalds occasionally until the spring of 1963.[255]

Shortly after his return from the Soviet Union, Oswald severed all relations with his mother; he did not see his brother Robert from Thanksgiving of 1962 until November 23, 1963.[256] At the time of his defection, Oswald had said that neither his brother, Robert, nor his mother were objects of his affection, "but only examples of workers in the U.S." He also indicated to officials at the American Embassy in Moscow that his defection was motivated at least in part by so-called exploitation of his mother by the capitalist system.[257] Consistent with this attitude he first told his wife that he did not have a mother, but later admitted that he did but that "he didn't love her very much." [258]

When they arrived from the Soviet Union, Oswald and his family lived at first with his brother Robert. The latter testified that they "were just together again," as if his brother "had not been to Russia." He also said that he and his family got along well with Marina Oswald and enjoyed showing her American things.[259] After about a month with his brother, Oswald and his family lived for a brief period with his mother at her urging, but Oswald soon decided to move out.[260]

Marguerite Oswald visited her son and his family at the first apartment which he rented after his return, and tried to help them get settled there. After she had bought some clothes for Marina Oswald and a highchair for the baby, Oswald emphatically told her to stop. As Marguerite Oswald testified, "he strongly put me in my place about buying things for his wife that he himself could not buy." [261] Oswald objected to his mother visiting the apartment and became quite incensed with his wife when she would open the door for her in spite of his instructions to the contrary.[262] Oswald moved to Dallas on about October 8, 1962, without telling his mother where he was going. He never saw or communicated with her in any way again until she came to see him after the assassination.[263]

Even though Oswald cut off relations with his mother, he attempted for the first time to learn something about his family background when he went to New Orleans in April of 1963. He visited some of his father's elderly relatives and the cemetery where his father was buried in an effort to develop the facts of his genealogy.[264] While it does not appear that he established any new relationships as a result of his investigation, he did obtain a large picture of his father from one of the elderly relatives with whom he spoke.[265] Oswald's interest in such things presents a sharp contrast with his attitude at the time of his defection, when he evidenced no interest in his father and hardly mentioned him, even when questioned.[266]

Employment

Oswald's defection, his interest in the Soviet Union, and his activities on behalf of the Fair Play for Cuba Committee not only caused him difficulties in his employment relations, but they also provided him with excuses for employment failures which were largely of his own making. Oswald experienced some difficulty finding employment. Perhaps this was partially because of his lack of any specific skill or training.[267] Some of his acquaintances, feeling that Oswald tried to impress people with the fact that he had lived and worked in Russia, were led to the belief that his employment difficulties were caused by his telling prospective employers that he had last been employed in Minsk.[268] While he might have expected difficulty from such an approach, in fact the evidence indicates that Oswald usually told his prospective employers and employment counselors that he had recently been discharged from the Marine Corps.[269]

Oswald obtained a job in July of 1962 as a sheet metal worker with a company in Fort Worth. His performance for that company was satisfactory.[270] Even though he told his wife that he had been fired, he voluntarily left on October 8, 1962, and moved to Dallas.[271]

On October 9, 1962 he went to the Dallas office of the Texas Employment Commission where he expressed a reluctance to work in the industrial field.[272] He indicated an interest in writing. An employment counselor testified, on the basis of a general aptitude test Oswald had taken, that he had some aptitude in that area, "because the verbal score is high and the clerical score is high." [273] While that counselor found that he was qualified to handle many different types of jobs, because of his need for immediate employment she attempted to obtain for him any job that was available at the time. Oswald made qualifying marks in 19 of 23 categories included on the general aptitude examination and scored 127 on the verbal test, as compared with 50 percent of the people taking it who score less than 100. The counselor testified that there was some indication that Oswald was capable of doing college work and noted that Oswald's verbal and clerical potential was "outstanding." [274] Employment Commission records concerning Oswald stated: "Well-groomed & spoken, business suit, alert replies—Expresses self extremely well." [275] Oswald said that he hoped eventually to develop qualifications for employment as a junior executive through a work-study program at a local college. He indicated, however, that he would have to delay that program because of his immediate financial needs and responsibilities.[276]

On October 11, 1962, the Employment Commission referred Oswald to a commercial advertising photography firm in Dallas,[277] where he was employed as a trainee starting October 12, 1962.[278] Even though Oswald indicated that he liked photographic work,[279] his employer found that he was not an efficient worker. He was not able to produce photographic work which adhered with sufficient precision to the job specifications and as a result too much of his work had to be redone.[280] He also had difficulty in working with the other employees. This was at least in part because of the close physical confines in which some of the work had to be done.[281] He did not seem to be able to make the accommodations necessary when people work under such conditions and as a result became involved in conflicts, some of which were fairly heated, with his fellow employees.[282]

In February or March of 1963, it began to appear that Oswald was having considerable difficulty doing accurate work and in getting along with the other employees. It appears that his discharge was hastened by the fact that he brought a Russian language newspaper to work.[283] It is not possible to tell whether Oswald did this to provide an excuse for his eventual discharge, or whether he brought the Russian language newspaper with him one day after his other difficulties became clear. It is possible that his immediate supervisor noticed the newspaper at that time because his attention had otherwise been drawn more directly to Oswald. In any event, Oswald was discharged on April 6, 1963, ostensibly because of his inefficiency and difficult personality. His supervisor admitted, however, that while he did not fire Oswald because of the newspaper incident or even weigh it heavily in his decision, "it didn't do his case any good." [284]

Upon moving to New Orleans on April 24, 1963, Oswald's employment problems became more difficult. He left his wife and child at the home of a friend, Mrs. Ruth Paine, of Irving, Tex.[285] In New Orleans he obtained work as a greaser and oiler of coffee processing machines for the William B. Reily Co., beginning May 10, 1963.[286]

After securing this job and an apartment, Oswald asked his wife to join him. Mrs. Paine brought Oswald's family to New Orleans.[287] Refusing to admit that he could only get work as a greaser, Oswald told his wife and Mrs. Paine that he was working as a commercial photographer.[288] He lost his job on July 19, 1963, because his work was not satisfactory [289] and because he spent too much time loitering in the garage next door, where he read rifle and hunting magazines.[290] Oswald apparently concluded that his Fair Play for Cuba Committee activities were not related to his discharge.[291] The correctness of that conclusion is supported by the fact that he does not seem to have been publicly identified with that organization until August 9, 1963, almost a month after he lost his job.[292]

His Fair Play for Cuba Committee activities, however, made it more difficult for him to obtain other employment. A placement interviewer of the Louisiana Department of Labor who had previously interviewed Oswald, saw him on television and heard a radio debate in which he engaged on August 21, 1963. He consulted with his supervisor and "it was determined that we should not undertake to furnish employment references for him." [293] Ironically, he failed to get a job in another photographic firm after his return to Dallas in October of 1963, because the president of the photographic firm for which he had previously worked told the prospective employer that Oswald was "kinda peculiar sometimes and that he had some knowledge of the Russian language," and that he "may be a damn Communist. I can't tell you. If I was you, I wouldn't hire him." [294] The plant superintendent of the new firm testified that one of the employees of the old firm "implied that Oswald's fellow employees did not like him because he was propagandizing and had been seen reading a foreign newspaper." As a result Oswald was not hired.[295] He subsequently found a job with the Texas School Book Depository for which he performed his duties satisfactorily.[296]

Attack on General Walker

The Commission has concluded that on April 10, 1963, Oswald shot at Maj. Gen. Edwin A. Walker (Resigned, U.S. Army), demonstrating once again his propensity to act dramatically and, in this instance violently, in furtherance of his beliefs. The shooting occurred 2 weeks before Oswald moved to New Orleans and a few days after he had been discharged by the photographic firm. As indicated in chapter IV, Oswald had been planning his attack on General Walker for at least 1 [297] and perhaps as much as 2 months.[298] He outlined his plans in a notebook and studied them at considerable length before his attack.[299] He also studied Dallas bus schedules to prepare for his later use of buses to travel to and from General Walker's house.[300] Sometime after March 27, but according to Marina Oswald, prior to April 10, 1963,[301] Oswald posed for two pictures with his recently acquired rifle and pistol, a copy of the March 24, 1963, issue of the Worker, and the March 11, 1963, issue of the

404

Militant.[302] He told his wife that he wanted to send the pictures to the Militant and he also asked her to keep one of the pictures for his daughter, June.[303]

Following his unsuccessful attack on Walker, Oswald returned home. He had left a note for his wife telling her what to do in case he were apprehended, as well as his notebook and the pictures of himself holding the rifle.[304] She testified that she was agitated because she had found the note in Oswald's room, where she had gone, contrary to his instructions, after she became worried about his absence.[305] She indicated that she had no advance knowledge of Oswald's plans, that she became quite angry when Oswald told her what he had done, and that she made him promise never to repeat such a performance. She said that she kept the note to use against him "if something like that should be repeated again."[306] When asked if Oswald requested the note back she testified that:

> He forgot about it. But apparently after he thought that what he had written in his book might be proof against him, and he destroyed it. [the book][307]

She later gave the following testimony [*indicates that the witness answered without using the interpreter]:

> Q. After he brought the rifle home, then, he showed you the book?
> *A. Yes.
> Q. And you said it was not a good idea to keep this book?
> *A. Yes.
> Q. And then he burned the book?
> *A. Yes.
> Q. Did you ask him why he had not destroyed the book before he actually went to shoot General Walker?
> A. It never came to me, myself, to ask him that question.[308]

Marina Oswald's testimony indicates that her husband was not particularly concerned about his continued possession of the most incriminating sort of evidence.[309] If he had been successful and had been apprehended even for routine questioning, his apartment would undoubtedly have been searched, and his role would have been made clear by the evidence which he had left behind. Leaving the note and picture as he did would seem to indicate that he had considered the possibility of capture. Possibly he might have wanted to be caught, and wanted his involvement made clear if he was in fact apprehended. Even after his wife told him to destroy the notebook he removed at least some of the pictures which had been pasted in it and saved them among his effects, where they were found after the assassination.[310] His behavior was entirely consistent with his wife's testimony that:

405

I asked him what for he was making all these entries in the book and he answered that he wanted to leave a complete record so that all the details would be in it.

*   *   *   *   *   *   *

I am guessing that perhaps he did it to appear to be a brave man in case he were arrested, but that is my supposition. * * * [311]

The attempt on General Walker's life deserves close attention in any consideration of Oswald's possible motive for the assassination and the trail of evidence he left behind him on that occasion. While there are differences between the two events as far as Oswald's actions and planning are concerned, there are also similarities that should be considered. The items which Oswald left at home when he made his attack on Walker suggest a strong concern for his place in history. If the attack had succeeded and Oswald had been caught, the pictures showing him with his rifle and his Communist and Socialist Worker's Party newspapers would probably have appeared on the front pages of newspapers or magazines all over the country, as, in fact, one of them did appear after the assassination.[312] The circumstances of the attack on Walker coupled with other indications that Oswald was concerned about his place in history [313] and with the circumstances surrounding the assassination, have led the Commission to believe that such concern is an important factor to consider in assessing possible motivation for the assassination.

In any event, the Walker incident indicates that in spite of the belief among those who knew him that he was apparently not dangerous,[314] Oswald did not lack the determination and other traits required to carry out a carefully planned killing of another human being and was willing to consummate such a purpose if he thought there was sufficient reason to do so. Some idea of what he thought was sufficient reason for such an act may be found in the nature of the motive that he stated for his attack on General Walker. Marina Oswald indicated that her husband had compared General Walker to Adolph Hitler. She testified that Oswald said that General Walker "was a very bad man, that he was a fascist, that he was the leader of a fascist organization, and when I said that even though all of that might be true, just the same he had no right to take his life, he said if someone had killed Hitler in time it would have saved many lives." [315]

Political Activities

Oswald's political activities after his return to the United States center around his interest in Cuba and in the Fair Play for Cuba Committee. Although, as indicated above, the Commission has been unable to find any credible evidence that he was involved in any conspiracy, his political activities do provide insight into certain aspects of Oswald's character and into his possible motivation for the assassination. While it appears that he may have distributed

Fair Play for Cuba Committee materials on one uneventful occasion in Dallas sometime during the period April 6–24, 1963,[316] Oswald's first public identification with that cause was in New Orleans. There, in late May and early June of 1963, under the name Lee Osborne, he had printed a handbill headed in large letters "Hands Off Cuba," an application form for, and a membership card in, the New Orleans branch of the Fair Play for Cuba Committee.[317] He first distributed his handbills and other material uneventfully in the vicinity of the U.S.S. *Wasp*, which was berthed at the Dumaine Street wharf in New Orleans, on June 16, 1963.[318] He distributed literature in downtown New Orleans on August 9, 1963, and was arrested because of a dispute with three anti-Castro Cuban exiles, and again on August 16, 1963.[319] Following his arrest, he was interviewed by the police, and at his own request, by an agent of the FBI.[320] On August 17, 1963, he appeared briefly on a radio program [321] and on August 21, 1963, he debated over radio station WDSU, New Orleans, with Carlos Bringuier, one of the Cuban exiles who had been arrested with him on August 9.[322] Bringuier claimed that on August 5, 1963, Oswald had attempted to infiltrate an anti-Castro organization with which he was associated.[323]

While Oswald publicly engaged in the activities described above, his "organization" was a product of his imagination.[324] The imaginary president of the nonexistent chapter was named A. J. Hidell,[325] the name that Oswald used when he purchased the assassination weapon.[326] Marina Oswald said she signed that name, apparently chosen because it rhymed with "Fidel," [327] to her husband's membership card in the New Orleans chapter. She testified that he threatened to beat her if she did not do so.[328] The chapter had never been chartered by the national FPCC organization.[329] It appears to have been a solitary operation on Oswald's part in spite of his misstatements to the New Orleans police that it had 35 members, 5 of which were usually present at meetings which were held once a month.[330]

Oswald's Fair Play for Cuba activities may be viewed as a very shrewd political operation in which one man single handedly created publicity for his cause or for himself. It is also evidence of Oswald's reluctance to describe events accurately and of his need to present himself to others as well as to himself in a light more favorable than was justified by reality. This is suggested by his misleading and sometime untruthful statements in his letters to Mr. V. T. Lee, then national director of FPCC. In one of those letters, dated August 1, 1963, Oswald wrote that an office which he had previously claimed to have rented for FPCC activities had been "promply closed 3 days later for some obsure reasons by the renters, they said something about remodeling ect., I'm sure you understand." [331] He wrote that "thousands of circulars were distrubed" [332] and that he continued to receive inquiries through his post office box which he endeavored "to keep ansewering to the best of my ability." [333] In his letter to V. T. Lee, he stated that he was then alone in his efforts on behalf of FPCC, but he attributed his lack of support to an attack by Cuban exiles in a street demonstration and being "officialy cautioned" by the police, events which "robbed me of what support I had leaving me alone." [334]

In spite of those claims, the Commission has not been able to uncover any evidence that anyone ever attacked any street demonstration in which Oswald was involved, except for the Bringuier incident mentioned above, which occurred 8 days after Oswald wrote the above letter to V. T. Lee.[335] Bringuier, who seemed to be familiar with many anti-Castro activities in New Orleans, was not aware of any such incident.[336] Police reports also fail to reflect any activity on Oswald's part prior to August 9, 1963, except for the uneventful distribution of literature at the Dumaine Street wharf in June.[337] Furthermore, the general tenor of Oswald's next letter to V. T. Lee, in which he supported his report on the Bringuier incident with a copy of the charges made against him and a newspaper clipping reporting the event, suggests that his previous story of an attack by Cuban exiles was at least greatly exaggerated.[338] While the legend "FPCC 544 Camp St. NEW ORLEANS, LA." was stamped on some literature that Oswald had in his possession at the time of his arrest in New Orleans, extensive investigation was not able to connect Oswald with that address, although it did develop the fact that an anti-Castro organization had maintained offices there for a period ending early in 1962.[339] The Commission has not been able to find any other indication that Oswald had rented an office in New Orleans. In view of the limited amount of public activity on Oswald's part before August 9, 1963, there also seems to be no basis for his claim that he had distributed "thousands" of circulars, especially since he had claimed to have printed only 2,000 and actually had only 1,000 printed. In addition, there is no evidence that he received any substantial amount of materials from the national headquarters.[340]

In another letter to V. T. Lee, dated August 17, 1963, Oswald wrote that he had appeared on Mr. William Stuckey's 15-minute television program over WDSU–TV called "Latin American Focus" as a result of which he was "flooded with callers and invitations to debate's ect. as well as people interested in joining the F.P.C.C. New Orleans branch." [341] WDSU has no program of any kind called "Latin American Focus." [342] Stuckey had a radio program called "Latin Listening Post," on which Oswald was heard for less than 5 minutes on August 17, 1963.[343] It appears that Oswald had only one caller in response to all of his FPCC activities, an agent of Bringuier's attempting to learn more about the true nature of the alleged FPCC "organization" in New Orleans.[344]

Oswald's statements suggest that he hoped to be flooded with callers and invitations to debate. This would have made him a real center of attention as he must have been when he first arrived in the Soviet Union and as he was to some extent when he returned to the United States. The limited notoriety that Oswald received as a result of the street fracas and in the subsequent radio debate was apparently not enough to satisfy him. He exaggerated in his letters to V. T. Lee in an appar-

OSWALD DISTRIBUTING FAIR PLAY FOR CUBA HANDBILLS IN NEW ORLEANS, AUGUST 16, 1963 -- INSETS SHOW SAMPLES OF HIS HAND-BILLS ON WHICH HE HAD STAMPED HIS NAME AND THE NAME OF "A J HIDELL"

GARNER DEPOSITION EXHIBIT 1

ent attempt to make himself and his activities appear far more important than they really were.

His attempt to express himself through his Fair Play for Cuba activities, however, was greatly impeded by the fact that the radio debate over WDSU on August 21, 1963, brought out the history of his defection to the Soviet Union.[345] The basic facts of the event were uncovered independently by William Stuckey, who arranged the debate, and Edward Butler, executive director of the Information Council of the Americas, who also appeared on the program.[346] Oswald was confronted with those facts at the beginning of the debate and was so thrown on the defensive by this that he was forced to state that Fair Play for Cuba was "not at all Communist controlled regardless of the fact that I had the experience of living in Russia."[347]

Stuckey testified that uncovering Oswald's defection was very important:

> I think that we finished him on that program. * * * because we had publicly linked the Fair Play for Cuba Committee with a fellow who had lived in Russia for 3 years and who was an admitted Marxist.
>
> The interesting thing, or rather the danger involved, was the fact that Oswald seemed like such a nice, bright boy and was extremely believable before this. We thought the fellow could probably get quite a few members if he was really indeed serious about getting members. We figured after this broadcast of August 21, why, that was no longer possible.[348]

In spite of the fact that Oswald had been surprised and was on the defensive throughout the debate, according to Stuckey: "Mr. Oswald handled himself very well, as usual."[349] Stuckey thought Oswald "appeared to be a very logical, intelligent fellow," and "was arrested by his cleancutness."[350] He did not think Oswald looked like the "type" that he would have expected to find associating with a group such as the Fair Play for Cuba Committee.[351] Stuckey thought that Oswald acted very much as would a young attorney.[352]

Following the disclosure of his defection, Oswald sought advice from the Communist Party, U.S.A., concerning his Fair Play for Cuba activity.[353] He had previously sent, apparently unsolicited, to the Party newspaper, the Worker, samples of his photographic work, offering to contribute that sort of service without charge.[354] The Worker replied: "Your kind offer is most welcomed and from time to time we shall call on you."[355] He later wrote to another official of the Worker, seeking employment, and mentioning the praise he had received for submitting his photographic work.[356] He presented Arnold Johnson, Gus Hall, and Benjamin J. Davis honorary membership cards in his nonexistent New Orleans chapter of the Fair Play for Cuba Committee, and advised them of some of his activities on behalf of the organization.[357] Arnold Johnson, director of the information and lecture bureau of the Communist Party, U.S.A., replied stating:

> It is good to know that movements in support of fair play for Cuba has developed in New Orleans as well as in other cities. We do not have any organizational ties with the Committee, and yet there is much material that we issue from time to time that is important for anybody who is concerned about developments in Cuba.[358]

Marina Oswald said that such correspondence from people he considered important meant much to Oswald. After he had begun his Cuban activity in New Orleans "he received a letter from somebody in New York, some Communist—probably from New York—I am not sure from where—from some Communist leader and he was very happy, he felt that this was a great man that he had received the letter from." [359] Since he seemed to feel that no one else understood his political views, the letter was of great value to him for it "was proof * * * that there were people who understood his activity." [360]

He anticipated that the full disclosure of his defection would hinder him in "the struggle for progress and freedom in the United States" [361] into which Oswald, in his own words, had "thrown" himself. He sought advice from the central committee of the Communist Party, U.S.A., in a letter dated August 28, 1963, about whether he could "continue to fight, handicapped as it were, by my past record * * * [and] compete with anti-progressive forces, aboveground or weather in your opion I should always remain in the background, i.e. underground." [362] Stating that he had used his "position" with what he claimed to be the local branch of the Fair Play for Cuba Committee to "foster communist ideals," Oswald wrote that he felt that he might have compromised the FPCC and expressed concern lest "Our opponents could use my background of residence in the U.S.S.R. against any cause which I join, by association, they could say the organization of which I am a member, is Russian controled, ect." [363] In reply Arnold Johnson advised Oswald that, while as an American citizen he had a right to participate in such organizations as he wished, "there are a number of organizations, including possibly Fair Play, which are of a very broad character, and often it is advisable for some people to remain in the background, not underground." [364]

By August of 1963, after a short 3 months in New Orleans, the city in which he had been born and had lived most of his early life, Oswald had fallen on difficult times. He had not liked his job as a greaser of coffee processing machinery and he held it for only a little over 2 months.[365] He had not found another job. His wife was expecting their second child in October and there was concern about the cost which would be involved.[366] His brief foray on behalf of the Fair Play for Cuba Committee had failed to win any support. While he had drawn some attention to himself and had actually appeared on two radio programs, he had been attacked by Cuban exiles and arrested, an event which his wife thought upset him and as a result of which "he became less active, he cooled off a little." [367] More seriously, the facts of his defection had become known, leaving him open to almost unanswerable attack by those who opposed his views. It would not have been possible to have followed Arnold Johnson's advice to remain in the background, since there was no background to the New Orleans FPCC "organization," which consisted solely of Oswald. Furthermore, he had apparently not received any letters from the national headquarters of FPCC since May 29, 1963,[368] even though he had written four detailed letters since that time to Mr. V. T. Lee [369] and had also kept the national headquarters informed of each of his changes of mailing address.[370] Those events no doubt had their effects on Oswald.

Interest in Cuba

By August of 1963, Oswald had for some time been considering the possibility of leaving the United States again. On June 24, 1963, he applied for a new passport [371] and in late June or early July he told his wife that he wanted to return to the Soviet Union with her. She said that he was extremely upset, very unhappy, and that he actually wept when he told her that.[372] He said that nothing kept him in the United States, that he would not lose anything if he returned to the Soviet Union, that he wanted to be with her and that it would be better to have less and not have to be concerned about tomorrow.[373]

As a result of that conversation, Marina Oswald wrote the Soviet Embassy in Washington concerning a request she had first made on February 17, 1963, for permission for herself and June to return to the Soviet Union.[374] While that first request, made according to Marina Oswald at her husband's insistence, specifically stated that Oswald was to remain in the United States, she wrote in her letter of July 1963, that "things are improving due to the fact that my husband expresses a sincere wish to return together with me to the USSR." [375] Unknown to his wife, however, Oswald apparently enclosed a note with her letter of July in which he requested the Embassy to rush his wife's entrance visa because of the impending birth of the second child but stated that: "As for my return entrance visa please consider it *separatably*." [376]

Thus, while Oswald's real intentions, assuming that they were known to himself, are not clear, he may not have intended to go to the Soviet Union directly, if at all.[377] It appears that he really wanted to go to Cuba. In his wife's words:

> I only know that his basic desire was to get to Cuba by any means, and that all the rest of it was window dressing for that purpose.[378]

Marina Oswald testified that her husband engaged in Fair Play for Cuba Committee activities "primarily for purposes of self-advertising. He wanted to be arrested. I think he wanted to get into the newspapers, so that he would be known." [379] According to Marina Oswald, he thought that would help him when he got to Cuba. [380] He asked his wife to help him to hijack an airplane to get there, but gave up that scheme when she refused. [381]

During this period Oswald may have practiced opening and closing the bolt on his rifle in a screened porch in his apartment. [382] In September he began to review Spanish. [383] He approved arrangements for his family to return to Irving, Tex., to live with Mrs. Ruth Paine. [384] On September 20, 1963, Mrs. Paine and her two children arrived in New Orleans from a trip to the East Coast [385] and left for Irving with Marina Oswald and June and most of the Oswalds' effects 3 days later. [386] While Marina Oswald knew of her husband's plan to go to Mexico and thence to Cuba if possible, [387] Mrs. Paine was told that Oswald was going to Houston and possibly to Philadelphia to look for work. [388]

Oswald left for Mexico City on September 25, 1963, and arrived on September 27, 1963. He went almost directly to the Cuban Embassy and applied for a visa to Cuba in transit to Russia. [389] Representing himself as the head of the New Orleans branch of the "organization called 'Fair Play for Cuba,' he stated his desire that he should be accepted as a 'friend' of the Cuban Revolution." [390] He apparently based his claim for a visa in transit to Russia on his previous residence, his work permit for that country, and several unidentified letters in the Russian language. The Cubans would not, however, give him a visa until he had received one from the Soviets, which involved a delay of several months. When faced with that situation Oswald became greatly agitated, and although he later unsuccessfully attempted to obtain a Soviet visa at the Soviet Embassy in Mexico City, he insisted that he was entitled to the Cuban visa because of his background, partisanship, and personal activities on behalf of the Cuban movement. He engaged in an angry argument with the consul who finally told him that "as far as he was concerned he would not give him a visa" and that "a person like him [Oswald] in place of aiding the Cuban Revolution, was doing it harm." [391]

Oswald must have been thoroughly disillusioned when he left Mexico City on October 2, 1963. In spite of his former residence in the Soviet Union and his Fair Play for Cuba Committee activities he had been rebuffed by the officials of both Cuba and the Soviet Union in Mexico City. Now there appeared to be no chance to get to Cuba, where he had thought he might find his communist ideal. The U.S. Government would not permit travel there and as far as the performance of the Cubans themselves was concerned, he was "disappointed at not being able to get to Cuba, and he didn't have any great desire to do so any more because he had run into, as he himself said—into bureaucracy and red tape." [392]

Oswald's attempt to go to Cuba was another act which expressed his hostility toward the United States and its institutions as well as a concomitant attachment to a country in which he must have thought were embodied the political principles to which he had been committed for so long. It should be noted that his interest in Cuba seems to have increased along with the sense of frustration which must have developed as he experienced successive failures in his jobs, in his political activity, and in his personal relationships. In retrospect his attempt to go to Cuba or return to the Soviet Union may well have been Oswald's last escape hatch, his last gambit to extricate himself from the mediocrity and defeat which plagued him throughout most of his life.

Oswald's activities with regard to Cuba raise serious questions as to how much he might have been motivated in the assassination by a desire to aid the Castro regime, which President Kennedy so outspokenly criticized. For example, the Dallas Times Herald of November 19, 1963, prominently reported President Kennedy as having "all but invited the Cuban people today to overthrow Fidel Castro's Communist regime and promised prompt U.S. aid if they do." [393] The Castro regime severely attacked President Kennedy in connection with the Bay of Pigs affair, the Cuban missile crisis, the ban on travel to Cuba, the economic embargo against that country, and the general policy of the United States with regard to Cuba. An examination of the Militant, to which Oswald subscribed,[394] for the 3-month period prior to the assassination reflects an extremely critical attitude toward President Kennedy and his administration concerning Cuban policy in general as well as on the issues of automation and civil rights, issues which appeared to concern Oswald a great deal.[395] The Militant also reflected a critical attitude toward President Kennedy's attempts to reduce tensions between the United States and the Soviet Union. It also dealt with the fear of the Castro regime that such a policy might result in its abandonment by the Soviet Union.

The October 7, 1963, issue of the Militant reported Castro as saying Cuba could not accept a situation where at the same time the United States was trying to ease world tensions it also "was increasing its efforts to 'tighten the noose' around Cuba." [396] Castro's opposition to President Kennedy's attempt to reduce world tensions was also reported in the October 1, 1963, issue of the Worker, to which Oswald also subscribed.[397] In this connection it should be noted that in speaking of the Worker, Oswald told Michael Paine, apparently in all seriousness, that "you could tell what they wanted you to do * * * by reading between the lines, reading the thing and doing a little reading between the lines." [398]

The general conflict of views between the United States and Cuba was, of course, reflected in other media to such an extent that there can be no doubt that Oswald was aware generally of the critical attitude that Castro expressed about President Kennedy. Oswald was asked during the New Orleans radio debate in which he engaged on August 21, 1963, whether or not he agreed with Castro that President

Kennedy was a "ruffian and a thief." He replied that he "would not agree with that particular wording." [399] It should also be noted, however, that one witness testified that shortly before the assassination Oswald had expressed approval of President Kennedy's active role in the area of civil rights. [400]

Although Oswald could possibly have been motivated in part by his sympathy for the Castro government, it should be remembered that his wife testified that he was disappointed with his failure to get to Cuba and had lost his desire to do so because of the bureaucracy and red tape which he had encountered. [401] His unhappy experience with the Cuban consul seems thus to have reduced his enthusiasm for the Castro regime and his desire to go to Cuba.

While some of Castro's more severe criticisms of President Kennedy might have led Oswald to believe that he would be well received in Cuba after he had assassinated the American President, it does not appear that he had any plans to go there. Oswald was carrying only $13.87 at the time of his arrest, although he had left, apparently by design, $170 in a wallet in his wife's room in Irving. [402] If there was no conspiracy which would help him escape, the possibility of which has been considered in chapter VI, it is unlikely that a reasoning person would plan to attempt to travel from Dallas, Tex., to Cuba with $13.87 when considerably greater resources were available to him. The fact that Oswald left behind the funds which might have enabled him to reach Cuba suggests the absence of any plan to try to flee there and raises serious questions as to whether or not he ever expected to escape.

Possible Influence of Anti-Kennedy Sentiment in Dallas

It has been suggested that one of the motivating influences operating on Lee Oswald was the atmosphere in the city of Dallas, especially an atmosphere of extreme opposition to President Kennedy that was present in some parts of the Dallas community and which received publicity there prior to the assassination. [403] Some of that feeling was expressed in the incident involving then vice-presidential candidate Johnson during the 1960 campaign, in the treatment of Ambassador Adlai Stevenson late in October of 1963 and in the extreme anti-Kennedy newspaper advertisement and handbills that appeared in Dallas at the time of the President's visit there. [404]

The Commission has found no evidence that the extreme views expressed toward President Kennedy by some rightwing groups centered in Dallas or any other general atmosphere of hate or rightwing extremism which may have existed in the city of Dallas had any connection with Oswald's actions on November 22, 1963. There is, of course, no way to judge what the effect of the general political ferment present in that city might have been, even though Oswald was aware of it. His awareness is shown by a letter that he wrote to Arnold Johnson of the Communist Party U.S.A., which Johnson said he did not receive until after the assassination. The letter said in part:

On October 23rd, I had attened a ultra-right meeting headed by General Edwin A. Walker, who lives in Dallas.

This meeting preceded by one day the attack on A. E. Stevenson at the United Nations Day meeting at which he spoke

As you can see, political friction between "left" and "right" is very great here.

Could you advise me as to the general view we have on the American Civil Liberties Union? [405]

In any event, the Commission has been unable to find any credible evidence that Oswald had direct contact or association with any of the personalities or groups epitomizing or representing the so-called rightwing, even though he did, as he told Johnson, attend a meeting at which General Walker spoke to approximately 1,300 persons.[406] Oswald's writings and his reading habits indicate that he had an extreme dislike of the rightwing, an attitude most clearly reflected by his attempt to shoot General Walker.

Relationship With Wife

The relations between Lee and Marina Oswald are of great importance in any attempt to understand Oswald's possible motivation. During the period from Oswald's return from Mexico to the assassination, he and his wife spent every weekend but one together at the Irving, Tex., home of Mrs. Ruth Paine, who was then separated from her husband. The sole exception was the weekend of November 16–17, 1963, the weekend before the assassination, when his wife asked Oswald not to come to Irving. During the week, Oswald lived in a roominghouse in Dallas, but he usually called his wife on the telephone twice a day.[407] She testified that after his return from Mexico Oswald "changed for the better. He began to treat me better. * * * He helped me more—although he always did help. But he was more attentive." [408] Marina Oswald attributed that to their living apart and to the imminent birth of their second child. She testified that Oswald "was very happy" about the birth of the child.[409]

While those considerations no doubt had an effect on Oswald's attitude toward his family it would seem that the need for support and sympathy after his recent rebuffs in Mexico City might also have been important to him. It would not have been the first time that Oswald sought closer ties with his family in time of adversity.[410]

His past relationships with his wife had been stormy, however, and it did not seem that she respected him very much. They had been married after a courtship of only about 6 weeks, a part of which Oswald spent in the hospital. Oswald's diary reports that he married his wife shortly after his proposal of marriage to another girl had been rejected. He stated that the other girl rejected him partly because he was an American, a fact that he said she had exploited. He stated that "In spite of fact I married Marina to hurt Ella [the girl that had rejected him] I found myself in love with Marina." [411]

416

Many of the people with whom the Oswalds became acquainted after their arrival in the United States thought that Marina Oswald had married her husband primarily in the hope that she would be able to leave the Soviet Union. Marina Oswald has denied this.[412]

Marina Oswald expressed one aspect of her husband's attitude toward her when she testified that:

> * * * Lee wanted me to go to Russia, and I told him that if he wanted me to go then that meant that he didn't love me, and that in that case what was the idea of coming to the United States in the first place. Lee would say that it would be better for me if I went to Russia. I did not know why. I did not know what he had in mind. He said he loved me but that it would be better for me if I went to Russia, and what he had in mind I don't know.[413]

On the other hand, Oswald objected to the invitation that his wife had received to live with Mrs. Ruth Paine, which Mrs. Paine had made in part to give her an alternative to returning to the Soviet Union.[414] Marina Oswald wrote to Mrs. Paine that: "Many times he [Oswald] has recalled this matter to me and said that I am just waiting for an opportunity to hurt him. It has been the cause of many of our arguments."[415] Oswald claimed that his wife preferred others to him.[416] He said this about members of the Russian-speaking group in the Dallas-Ft. Worth area, whom she said he tried to forbid her from seeing,[417] and also about Mrs. Paine.[418] He specifically made that claim when his wife refused to come to live with him in Dallas as he asked her to do on the evening of November 21, 1963.[419]

The instability of their relations was probably a function of the personalities of both people. Oswald was overbearing in relations with his wife. He apparently attempted to be "the Commander" by dictating many of the details of their married life.[420] While Marina Oswald said that her husband wanted her to learn English,[421] he made no attempt to help her and there are other indications that he did not want her to learn that language. Oswald apparently wished to continue practicing his own Russian with her.[422] Lieutenant Martello of the New Orleans police testified that Oswald stated that he did not speak English in his family because he did not want them to become Americanized.[423] Marina Oswald's inability to speak English also made it more difficult for her to have an independent existence in this country. Oswald struck his wife on occasion,[424] did not want her to drink, smoke or wear cosmetics [425] and generally treated her with lack of respect in the presence of others.[426]

The difficulties which Oswald's problems would have caused him in any relationship were probably not reduced by his wife's conduct. Katherine Ford, with whom Marina Oswald stayed during her separation from her husband in November of 1962, thought that Marina Oswald was immature in her thinking and partly responsible for the difficulties that the Oswalds were having at that time.[427] Mrs. Ford said that Marina Oswald admitted that she provoked Oswald on occasion.[428] There can be little doubt that some provocation existed. Oswald once struck his wife because of a letter which she wrote to a former boy friend in Russia. In the letter Marina Oswald stated that her husband had changed a great deal and that she was very lonely in the United States. She was "sorry that I had not married him [the Russian boy friend] instead, that it would have been much easier for me." [429] The letter fell into Oswald's hands when it was returned to his post office box because of insufficient postage, which apparently resulted from an increase in postal rates of which his wife had been unaware.[430] Oswald read the letter, but refused to believe that it was sincere, even though his wife insisted to him that it was. As a result Oswald struck her, as to which she testified: "Generally, I think that was right, for such things that is the right thing to do. There was some grounds for it.[431]

Although she denied it in some of her testimony before the Commission,[432] it appears that Marina Oswald also complained that her husband was not able to provide more material things for her.[433] On that issue George De Mohrenschildt, who was probably as close to the Oswalds as anyone else during their first stay in Dallas, said that:

> She was annoying him all the time—"Why don't you make some money?" * * * Poor guy was going out of his mind. * * * We told her she should not annoy him—poor guy, he is doing his best, "Don't annoy him so much." * * * [434]

The De Mohrenschildts also testified that "right in front" of Oswald Marina Oswald complained about Oswald's inadequacy as a husband.[435] Mrs. Oswald told another of her friends that Oswald was very cold to her, that they very seldom had sexual relations and that Oswald "was not a man." [436] She also told Mrs. Paine that she was not satisfied with her sexual relations with Oswald.[437]

Marina Oswald also ridiculed her husband's political views, thereby tearing down his view of his own importance. He was very much interested in autobiographical works of outstanding statesmen of the United States, to whom his wife thought he compared himself.[438] She said he was different from other people in "At least his imagination, his fantasy, which was quite unfounded, as to the fact that he was an outstanding man." [439] She said that she "always tried to point out to him that he was a man like any others who were around us. But he simply could not understand that." [440] Jeanne De Mohrenschildt, however, thought that Marina Oswald "said things that will hurt men's pride." [441] She said that if she ever spoke to her husband the way Marina Oswald spoke to her husband, "we would not last long." [442] Mrs. De Mohrenschildt thought that Oswald, whom she compared to "a puppy dog that everybody kicked," [443] had a lot of good qualities, in spite of the fact that "Nobody said anything good about him." [444] She had "the impression that he was just pushed, pushed, pushed, and she [Marina Oswald] was probably nagging, nagging, nagging." [445] She thought that he might not have become involved in the assassination if people had been kinder to him.[446]

In spite of these difficulties, however, and in the face of the economic problems that were always with them, things apparently went quite smoothly from the time Oswald returned from Mexico until the weekend of November 16–17, 1963.[447] Mrs. Paine was planning a birthday party for one of her children on that weekend and her husband, Michael, was to be at the house. Marina Oswald said that she knew her husband did not like Michael Paine and so she asked him not to come out that weekend, even though he wanted to do so. She testified that she told him "that he shouldn't come every week, that perhaps it is not convenient for Ruth that the whole family be there, live there." She testified that he responded: "As you wish. If you don't want me to come, I won't." [448] Ruth Paine testified that she heard Marina Oswald tell Oswald about the birthday party.[449]

On Sunday, November 17, 1963, Ruth Paine and Marina Oswald decided to call Oswald [450] at the place where he was living, unbeknownst to them, under the name of O. H. Lee.[451] They asked for Lee Oswald who was not called to the telephone because he was known by the other name.[452] When Oswald called the next day his wife became very angry about his use of the alias.[453] He said that he used it because "he did not want his landlady to know his real name because she might read in the paper of the fact that he had been in Russia and that he had been questioned." [454] Oswald also said that he did not want the FBI to know where he lived "Because their visits were not very pleasant for him and he thought that he loses jobs because the FBI visits the place of his employment." [455] While the facts of his defection had become known in New Orleans as a result of his radio debate with Bringuier,[456] it would appear to be unlikely that his landlady in Dallas would see anything in the newspaper about his defection, unless he engaged in activities similar to those which had led to the disclosure of his defection in New Orleans. Furthermore, even though it appears that at times Oswald was really upset by visits of the FBI, it does not appear that he ever lost his job because of its activities, although he may well not have been aware of that fact.[457]

While Oswald's concern about the FBI had some basis in fact, in that FBI agents had interviewed him in the past and had renewed their interest to some extent after his Fair Play for Cuba Committee activities had become known, he exaggerated their concern for him. Marina Oswald thought he did so in order to emphasize his importance.[458] For example, in his letter of November 9, 1963, to the Soviet Embassy in Washington, he asked about the entrance visas for which he and his wife had previously applied. He absolved the Soviet Embassy in Mexico City of any blame for his difficulties there. He advised the Washington Embassy that the FBI was "not now" interested in his Fair Play for Cuba Committee activities, but noted that the FBI "has visited us here in Dallas, Texas, on November 1. Agent James P. Hasty warned me that if I engaged in F.P.C.C. activities in Texas

419

the F.B.I. will again take an 'interrest' in me." [459]   Neither Hosty nor any other agent of the FBI spoke to Oswald on any subject from August 10, 1963, to the time of the assassination.[460] The claimed warning was one more of Oswald's fabrications. Hosty had come to the Paine residence on November 1 and 5, 1963, but did not issue any such warning or suggest that Marina Oswald defect from the Soviet Union and remain in the United States under FBI protection, as Oswald went on to say.[461] In Oswald's imagination "I and my wife strongly protested these tactics by the notorious F.B.I." [462] In fact, his wife testified that she only said that she would prefer not to receive any more visits from the Bureau because of the "very exciting and disturbing effect" they had upon her husband,[463] who was not even present at that time.[464]

The arguments he used to justify his use of the alias suggest that Oswald may have come to think that the whole world was becoming involved in an increasingly complex conspiracy against him. He may have felt he could never tell when the FBI was going to appear on the scene or who else was going to find out about his defection and use it against him as had been done in New Orleans.[465] On the other hand, the concern he expressed about the FBI may have been just another story to support the objective he sought in his letter.

Those arguments, however, were not persuasive to Marina Oswald, to whom "it was nothing terrible if people were to find out that he had been in Russia." [466] She asked Oswald: "After all, when will all your foolishness come to an end? All of these comedies. First one thing and then another. And now this fictitious name." [467] She said: "On Monday [November 18, 1963] he called several times, but after I hung up on him and didn't want to talk to him he did not call again. He then arrived on Thursday [November 21, 1963]." [468]

The events of that evening can best be appreciated through Marina Oswald's testimony:

Q. Did your husband give any reason for coming home on Thursday?

A. He said that he was lonely because he hadn't come the preceding weekend, and he wanted to make his peace with me.

Q. Did you say anything to him then?

A. He tried to talk to me but I would not answer him, and he was very upset. ·

Q. Were you upset with him?

A. I was angry, of course. He was not angry—he was upset. I was angry. He tried very hard to please me. He spent quite a bit of time putting away diapers and played with the children on the street.

Q. How did you indicate to him that you were angry with him?

A. By not talking to him.

Q. And how did he show that he was upset?

A. He was upset over the fact that I would not answer him. He tried to start a conversation with me several times, but I would not answer. And he said that he didn't want me to be angry at him because this upsets him.

On that day, he suggested that we rent an apartment in Dallas. He said that he was tired of living alone and perhaps the reason for my being so angry was the fact that we were not living together. That if I want to he would rent an apartment in Dallas tomorrow—that he didn't want me to remain with Ruth any longer, but wanted me to live with him in Dallas.

He repeated this not once but several times, but I refused. And he said that once again I was preferring my friends to him, and that I didn't need him.

Q. What did you say to that?

A. I said it would be better if I remained with Ruth until the holidays, he would come, and we would all meet together. That this was better because while he was living alone and I stayed with Ruth, we were spending less money. And I told him to buy me a washing machine, because two children it became too difficult to wash by hand.

Q. What did he say to that?

A. He said he would buy me a washing machine.

Q. What did you say to that?

A. Thank you. That it would be better if he bought something for himself—that I would manage.[469]

That night Oswald went to bed before his wife retired. She did not speak to him when she joined him there, although she thought that he was still awake. The next morning he left for work before anyone else arose.[470] For the first time he left his wedding ring in a cup on the dresser in his room.[471] He also left $170 in a wallet in one of the dresser drawers. He took with him $13.87 [472] and the long brown package that Frazier and Mrs. Randle saw him carry and which he was to take to the School Book Depository.[473]

The Unanswered Questions

No one will ever know what passed through Oswald's mind during the week before November 22, 1963. Instead of returning to Irving on November 15 for his customary weekend visit, he remained in Dallas at his wife's suggestion because of the birthday party. He had argued with her over the use of an alias and had not called her after that argument, although he usually telephoned once or twice a day. Then on Thursday morning, November 21, he asked Frazier for a ride to Irving that night, stating falsely that he wanted to pick up some curtain rods to put in an apartment.[474]

He must have planned his attack at the very latest prior to Thursday morning when he spoke to Frazier. There is, of course, no way to determine the degree to which he was committed to his plan at that time. While there is no way to tell when he first began to think specifically of assassinating the President it should be noted that mention of the Trade Mart as the expected site of the Presidential luncheon appeared in The Dallas Times Herald on November 15, 1963.[475] The next day that paper announced the final approval of the Trade Mart as the luncheon site and stated that the motorcade "apparently will loop through the downtown area, probably on Main Street, en route from Dallas Love Field" on its way to the Trade Mart on Stemmons Freeway.[476] Anyone who was familiar with that area of Dallas would have known that the motorcade would probably pass the Texas School Book Depository to get from Main Street onto the Stemmons Freeway. That fact was made precisely clear in subsequent news stories on November 19, 20, and 22.[477]

On November 15, 1963, the same day that his wife told him not to come to Irving, Oswald could have assumed that the Presidential motorcade would pass in front of his place of work. Whether he thought about assassinating the President over the weekend can never be known, but it is reasonably certain that over the weekend he did think about his wife's request that he not come to Irving, which was prompted by the birthday party being held at the Paine home. Oswald had a highly exaggerated sense of his own importance, but he had failed at almost everything he had ever tried to do. He had great difficulty in establishing meaningful relations with other people. Except for his family he was completely alone. Even though he had searched—in the Marine Corps, in his ideal of communism, in the Soviet Union and in his attempt to get to Cuba—he had never found anything to which he felt he could really belong.

After he returned from his trip to Mexico where his application to go to Cuba had been sharply rejected, it must have appeared to him that he was unable to command even the attention of his family. He could not keep them with him in Dallas, where at least he could see his children whom, several witnesses testified, he seemed to love.[478] His family lived with Mrs. Paine, ostensibly because Oswald could not afford to keep an apartment in Dallas, but it was also, at least in part, because his wife did not want to live there with him.[479] Now it appeared that he was not welcome at the Paine home, where he had spent every previous weekend since his return from Mexico and his wife was once again calling into question his judgment, this time concerning his use of an alias.

The conversation on Monday, November 18, 1963, ended when Marina Oswald hung up and refused to talk to him. Although he may long before have decided on the course he was to follow and may have told his wife the things he did on the evening of November 21, 1963, merely to disarm her and to provide a justification of sorts, both she and Mrs. Paine thought he had come home to make up after the fight on Monday.[480] Thoughts of his personal difficulties must have been at least partly on his mind when he went to Irving on Thursday night and told his wife that he was lonely, that he wanted to make peace with her and bring his family to Dallas where they could live with him again.

The Commission does not believe that the relations between Oswald and his wife caused him to assassinate the President. It is unlikely that the motivation was that simple. The feelings of hostility and aggression which seem to have played such an important part in Oswald's life were part of his character long before he met his wife and such a favorable opportunity to strike at a figure as great as the President would probably never have come to him again.

Oswald's behavior after the assassination throws little light on his motives. The fact that he took so little money with him when he left Irving in the morning indicates that he did not expect to get very far from Dallas on his own and suggests the possibility, as did his note to his wife just prior to the attempt on General Walker, that he did not expect to escape at all. On the other hand, he could have traveled some distance with the money he did have and he did return to his room where he obtained his revolver. He then killed Patrolman Tippit when that police officer apparently tried to question him after he had left his roominghouse and he vigorously resisted arrest when he was finally apprehended in the Texas Theatre. Although it is not fully corroborated by others who were present, two officers have testified that at the time of his arrest Oswald said something to the effect that "it's all over now." [481]

Oswald was overbearing and arrogant throughout much of the time between his arrest and his own death.[482] He consistently refused to admit involvement in the assassination or in the killing of Patrolman Tippit.[483] While he did become enraged at at least one point in his interrogation, the testimony of the officers present indicates that he handled himself with considerable composure during his questioning. He admitted nothing that would damage him but discussed other matters quite freely.[484] His denials under questioning, which have no probative value in view of the many readily demonstrable lies he told at that time [485] and in the face of the overwhelming evidence against him which has been set forth above, only served to prolong the period during which he was the center of the attention of the entire world.

Conclusion

Many factors were undoubtedly involved in Oswald's motivation for the assassination, and the Commission does not believe that it can ascribe to him any one motive or group of motives. It is apparent, however, that Oswald was moved by an overriding hostility to his environment. He does not appear to have been able to establish meaningful relationships with other people. He was perpetually discontented with the world around him. Long before the assassination he expressed his hatred for American society and acted in protest against it. Oswald's search for what he conceived to be the perfect society was doomed from the start. He sought for himself a place in history—a role as the "great man" who would be recognized as having been in advance of his times. His commitment to Marxism and communism appears to have been another important factor in his motivation. He also had demonstrated a capacity to act decisively and without regard to the consequences when such action would further his aims of the moment. Out of these and the many other factors which may have molded the character of Lee Harvey Oswald there emerged a man capable of assassinating President Kennedy.

CHAPTER VIII

The Protection of the President

I N THE 100 years since 1865 four Presidents of the United States have been assassinated—Abraham Lincoln, James A. Garfield, William McKinley, and John F. Kennedy. During this same period there were three other attacks on the life of a President, a President-elect, and a candidate for the Presidency, which narrowly failed: on Theodore Roosevelt while campaigning in October of 1912; on President-elect Franklin Delano Roosevelt, when visiting Miami on February 15, 1933; and on President Harry S. Truman on November 1, 1950, when his temporary residence, Blair House, was attacked by Puerto Rican Nationalists.[1] One out of every five Presidents since 1865 has been assassinated; there have been attempts on the lives of one out of every three.

Prompted by these dismaying statistics, the Commission has inquired into the problems and methods of Presidential protection in effect at the time of President Kennedy's assassination. This study has led the Commission to conclude that the public interest might be served by any contribution it can make to the improvement of protective arrangements. The Commission has not undertaken a comprehensive examination of all facets of this subject; rather, it has devoted its time and resources to those broader aspects of Presidential protection to which the events of last November called attention.

In this part of its inquiry the Commission has had full access to a major study of all phases of protective activities prepared by the Secret Service for the Secretary of the Treasury following the assassination. As a result of this study, the Secretary of the Treasury has prepared a planning document dated August 27, 1964, which recommends additional personnel and facilities to enable the Secret Service to expand its protection capabilities. The Secretary of the Treasury submitted this planning document on August 31, 1964, to the Bureau of the Budget for review and approval. This planning document has been made a part of the Commission's published record; the underlying staff and consultants' reports reviewed by the Commission have not, since a disclosure of such detailed information relating to protective measures might undermine present methods of protecting the President. However, all information considered by the Commission which pertains to the protective function as it was carried out in Dallas has been published as part of this report.

The protection of the President of the United States is an immensely difficult and complex task. It is unlikely that measures can be devised to eliminate entirely the multitude of diverse dangers that may arise, particularly when the President is traveling in this country or abroad. The protective task is further complicated by the reluctance of Presidents to take security precautions which might interfere with the performance of their duties, or their desire to have frequent and easy access to the people. The adequacy of existing procedures can fairly be assessed only after full consideration of the difficulty of the protective assignment, with particular attention to the diverse roles which the President is expected to fill. After reviewing this aspect of the matter this chapter will set forth the Commission's conclusions regarding certain protective measures in force at the time of the Dallas trip and propose recommendations for improvements.

THE NATURE OF THE PROTECTIVE ASSIGNMENT

The President is Head of State, Chief Executive, Commander in Chief, and leader of a political party. As the ceremonial head of the Government the President must discharge a wide range of public duties, not only in Washington but throughout the land. In this role he appears to the American people, in the words of William Howard Taft, as "the personal embodiment and representative of their dignity and majesty." [2] As Chief Executive, the President controls the exercise of the vast, almost incalculable powers of the executive branch of the Federal Government. As Commander in Chief of the Armed Forces, he must maintain ultimate authority over the development and disposition of our military power. Finally, in accordance with George Washington's maxim that Americans have a government "of accommodation as well as a government of laws," [3] it is the President's right and duty to be the active leader of his party, as when he seeks to be reelected or to maintain his party in power.

In all of these roles the President must go to the people. Exposure of the President to public view through travel among the people of this country is a great and historic tradition of American life. Desired by both the President and the public, it is an indispensable means of communication between the two. More often than not, Presidential journeys have served more than one purpose at the same time: ceremonial, administrative, political.

From George Washington to John F. Kennedy, such journeys have been a normal part of the President's activities. To promote nationwide acceptance of his administration Washington made grand tours that served also to excite interest in the Presidency.[4] In recent years, Presidential journeys have been frequent and extensive, partly because of the greater speed and comfort of travel and partly because of the greater demands made on the President. It is now possible for Presidents to travel the length and breadth of a land far larger than the United States in 1789 in less time than it took George Washington to travel from New York to Mount Vernon or Thomas Jefferson from Washington to Monticello. During his Presidency, Franklin D. Roosevelt made almost 400 journeys and traveled more than 350,000 miles.[5] Since 1945, Roosevelt's successors have ranged the world, and their foreign journeys have come to be accepted as normal rather than extraordinary.

John F. Kennedy's journey to Texas in November 1963 was in this tradition. His friend and Special Assistant Kenneth O'Donnell, who accompanied him on his last visit to Dallas, stated the President's views of his responsibilities with simplicity and clarity:

> The President's views of his responsibilities as President of the United States were that he meet the people, that he go out to their homes and see them, and allow them to see him, and discuss, if possible, the views of the world as he sees it, the problems of the country as he sees them. And he felt that leaving Washington for the President of the United States was a most necessary—not only for the people, but for the President himself, that he expose himself to the actual basic problems that were disturbing the American people. It helped him in his job here, he was able to come back here with a fresh view of many things. I think he felt very strongly that the President ought to get out of Washington, and go meet the people on a regular basis.[6]

Whatever their purpose, Presidential journeys have greatly enlarged and complicated the task of protecting the President. The Secret Service and the Federal, State, and local law enforcement agencies which cooperate with it, have been confronted in recent years with increasingly difficult problems, created by the greater exposure of the President during his travels and the greater diversity of the audiences he must face in a world torn by conflicting ideologies.

If the sole goal were to protect the life of the President, it could be accomplished with reasonable assurance despite the multiple roles he must play. But his very position as representative of the people prevents him from effectively shielding himself from the people. He cannot and will not take the precautions of a dictator or a sovereign. Under our system, measures must be sought to afford security without impeding the President's performance of his many functions. The protection of the President must be thorough but inconspicuous to avoid even the suggestion of a garrison state. The rights of private individuals must not be infringed. If the protective job is well done, its performance will be evident only in the unexceptional fact of its success. The men in charge of protecting the President, confronted by complex problems and limited as they are in the measures they may

427

employ, must depend upon the utmost cooperation and understanding from the public and the President.

The problem and the reasonable approach to its solution were ably stated in a memorandum prepared by FBI Director J. Edgar Hoover for the President soon after the assassination:

> The degree of security that can be afforded the President of the United States is dependent to a considerable extent upon the degree of contact with the general public desired by the President. Absolute security is neither practical nor possible. An approach to complete security would require the President to operate in a sort of vacuum, isolated from the general public and behind impregnable barriers. His travel would be in secret; his public appearances would be behind bulletproof glass.
>
> A more practical approach necessitates compromise. Any travel, any contact with the general public, involves a calculated risk on the part of the President and the men responsible for his protection. Such risks can be lessened when the President recognizes the security problem, has confidence in the dedicated Secret Service men who are ready to lay down their lives for him and accepts the necessary security precautions which they recommend. Many Presidents have been understandably impatient with the security precautions which many years of experience dictate because these precautions reduce the President's privacy and the access to him of the people of the country. Nevertheless the procedures and advice should be accepted if the President wishes to have any security.[7]

EVALUATION OF PRESIDENTIAL PROTECTION AT THE TIME OF THE ASSASSINATION OF PRESIDENT KENNEDY

The history of Presidential protection shows growing recognition over the years that the job must be done by able, dedicated, thoroughly professional personnel, using the best technical equipment that can be devised.[8] The assassination of President Kennedy demands an examination of the protective measures employed to safeguard him and an inquiry whether improvements can be made which will reduce the risk of another such tragedy. This section considers first the means used to locate potential sources of danger to the President in time to take appropriate precautions. In this connection the information available to Federal agencies about Lee Harvey Oswald is set out and the reasons why this information was not furnished to the Secret Service appraised. Second, the adequacy of other advance preparations for the security of the President during his visit to Dallas, largely measures taken by the Secret Service, is considered. Finally, the performance of those charged with the immediate responsibility of protecting the President on November 22 is reviewed.

428

Intelligence Functions Relating to Presidential Protection at the Time of the Dallas Trip

A basic element of Presidential protection is the identification and elimination of possible sources of danger to the President before the danger becomes actual. The Secret Service has attempted to perform this function through the activities of its Protective Research Section and requests to other agencies, Federal and local, for useful information. The Commission has concluded that at the time of the assassination the arrangements relied upon by the Secret Service to perform this function were seriously deficient.

Adequacy of preventive intelligence operations of the Secret Service.—The main job of the Protective Research Section (PRS) is to collect, process, and evaluate information about persons or groups who may be a danger to the President. In addition to this function, PRS is responsible for such tasks as obtaining clearance of some categories of White House employees and all tradesmen who service the White House, the security processing of gifts sent to the President, and technical inspections against covert listening devices.[9] At the time of the assassination PRS was a very small group, comprised of 12 specialists and 3 clerks.[10]

Many persons call themselves to the attention of PRS by attempting to visit the President for bizarre reasons or by writing or in some other way attempting to communicate with him in a threatening or abusive manner or with undue persistence. Robert I. Bouck, special agent in charge of PRS, estimated that most of the material received by his office originated in this fashion or from the occasional investigations initiated by the Secret Service, while the balance was furnished to PRS by other Federal agencies, with primary source being the FBI.[11] The total volume of information received by PRS has risen steadily. In 1943 PRS received approximately 9,000 items of information; in 1953 this had increased to more than 17,000 items; in 1963 the total exceeded 32,000 items.[12] Since many items may pertain to a single case, these figures do not show the caseload. In the period from November 1961 to November 1963, PRS received items in 8,709 cases.[13]

Before the assassination of President Kennedy, PRS expressed its interest in receiving information on suspects in very general terms. For example, PRS instructed the White House mailroom, a source of much PRS data, to refer all communications on identified existing cases and, in addition, any communication "that in any way indicates anyone may have possible intention of harming the President."[14] Slightly more specific criteria were established for PRS personnel processing White House mail referred by the White House mailroom, but again the standards were very general.[15] These instructions to PRS personnel appear to be the only instance where an effort was made to reduce the criteria to writing.[16] When requested to provide a specific statement of the standards employed by PRS in deciding what information to seek and retain, the Secret Service responded:

The criteria in effect prior to November 22, 1963, for determining whether to accept material for the PRS general files were broad and flexible. All material is and was desired, accepted, and filed if it indicated or tended to indicate that the safety of the President is or might be in danger, either at the present or in the future. * * * There are many actions, situations, and incidents that may indicate such potential danger. Some are specific, such as threats; danger may be implied from others, such as membership or activity in an organization which believes in assassination as a political weapon. All material received by PRS was separately screened and a determination made as to whether the information might indicate possible harm to the President. If the material was evaluated as indicating some potential danger to the President—no matter how small—it was indexed in the general PRS files under the name of the individual or group of individuals to whom that material related.[17]

The general files of PRS consist of folders on individuals, card indexed by name. The files are manually maintained, without use of any automatic data-processing techniques.[18] At the time of the assassination, the active PRS general files contained approximately 50,000 cases accumulated over a 20-year period,[19] some of which included more than one individual. A case file was established if the information available suggested that the subject might be a danger to the President. Many of these cases were not investigated by PRS. The case file served merely as a repository for information until enough had accumulated to warrant an investigation.[20] During the period November 1961 to November 1963, PRS investigated 34 newly established or reactivated cases concerning residents of Texas.[21] Most of these cases involved persons who used threatening language in communications to or about the President. An additional 115 cases concerning Texas residents were established but not investigated.[22]

When PRS learns of an individual whose conduct warrants scrutiny, it requests an investigation by the closest Secret Service field office,[23] of which there are 65 throughout the country. If the field office determines that the case should be subject to continuing review, PRS establishes a file which requires a checkup at least every 6 months.[24] This might involve a personal interview or interviews with members of the person's household.[25] Wherever possible, the Secret Service arranges for the family and friends of the individual, and local law enforcement officials, to advise the field office if the subject displays signs of increased danger or plans to leave his home area. At the time of the assassination there were approximately 400 persons throughout the country who were subject to periodic review.[26]

If PRS concludes after investigation that an individual presents a significant danger to the life of the President, his name is placed in a "trip index file" which is maintained on a geographical field office basis.[27] At the time of the assassination the names of about 100 persons were in this index, all of whom were included in the group of

400 being reviewed regularly.[28] PRS also maintains an album of photographs and descriptions of about 12 to 15 individuals who are regarded as clear risks to the President and who do not have a fixed place of residence.[29] Members of the White House detail of the Secret Service have copies of this album.[30]

Individuals who are regarded as dangerous to the President and who are in penal or hospital custody are listed only in the general files of PRS, but there is a system for the immediate notification of the Secret Service by the confining institution when a subject is released or escapes.[31] PRS attempts to eliminate serious risks by hospitalization or, where necessary, the prosecution of persons who have committed an offense such as threatening the President.[32] In June 1964 PRS had arrangements to be notified about the release or escape of approximately 1,000 persons.[33]

In summary, at the time of the assassination PRS had received, over a 20-year period, basic information on some 50,000 cases; it had arrangements to be notified about release from confinement in roughly 1,000 cases; it had established periodic regular review of the status of 400 individuals; it regarded approximately 100 of these 400 cases as serious risks and 12 to 15 of these cases as highly dangerous risks. Members of the White House detail were expected to familiarize themselves with the descriptions and photographs of the highest risk cases. The cases subject to periodic review and the 100 or so cases in the higher risk category were filed on a geographic basis, and could conveniently be reviewed by a Secret Service agent preparing for a Presidential trip to a particular part of the country. These were the files reviewed by PRS on November 8, 1963, at the request of Special Agent Lawson, advance agent for President Kennedy's trip to Dallas.[34] The general files of PRS were not indexed by geographic location and were of little use in preparing for a Presidential visit to a specific locality.

Secret Service requests to other agencies for intelligence information were no more specific than the broad and general instructions to its own agents and the White House mailroom. The head of PRS testified that the Secret Service requested other agencies to provide "any and all information that they may come in contact with that would indicate danger to the President." [35] These requests were not communicated in writing by the Secret Service; rather, the Service depended on the personal liaison maintained by PRS with the headquarters of the Federal intelligence agencies, particularly the FBI, and at the working level with personnel of the field offices of the various agencies.[36] The Service frequently participated in the training programs of other law enforcement agencies, and agents from other agencies attended the regular Secret Service training schools. Presidential protection was an important topic in these training programs.[37]

In the absence of more specific instructions, other Federal agencies interpreted the Secret Service's informal requests to relate principally to overt threats to harm the President or other specific manifestations of hostility. For example, at the time of the assassination, the FBI

Handbook, which is in the possession of every Bureau special agent, provided:

> Threats against the President of the U.S., members of his immediate family, the President-elect, and the Vice-President

> Investigation of threats against the President of the United States, members of his immediate family, the President-Elect, and the Vice-President is within the exclusive jurisdiction of the U.S. Secret Service. Any information indicating the possibility of an attempt against the person or safety of the President, members of the immediate family of the President, the President-Elect or the Vice-President must be referred immediately by the most expeditious means of communication to the nearest office of the U.S. Secret Service. Advise the Bureau at the same time by teletype of the information so furnished to the Secret Service and the fact that it has been so disseminated. The above action should be taken without delay in order to attempt to verify the information and no evaluation of the information should be attempted. When the threat is in the form of a written communication, give a copy to local Secret Service and forward the original to the Bureau where it will be made available to Secret Service headquarters in Washington. The referral of the copy to local Secret Service should not delay the immediate referral of the information by the fastest available means of communication to Secret Service locally.[38]

The State Department advised the Secret Service of all crank and threat letter mail or crank visitors and furnished reports concerning any assassination or attempted assassination of a ruler or other major official anywhere in the world.[39] The several military intelligence agencies reported crank mail and similar threats involving the President.[40] According to Special Agent in Charge Bouck, the Secret Service had no standard procedure for the systematic review of its requests for and receipt of information from other Federal agencies.[41]

The Commission believes that the facilities and procedures of the Protective Research Section of the Secret Service prior to November 22, 1963, were inadequate. Its efforts appear to have been too largely directed at the "crank" threat. Although the Service recognized that its advance preventive measures must encompass more than these most obvious dangers, it made little effort to identify factors in the activities of an individual or an organized group, other than specific threats, which suggested a source of danger against which timely precautions could be taken. Except for its special "trip index" file of 400 names, none of the cases in the PRS general files was available for systematic review on a geographic basis when the President planned a particular trip.

As reported in chapter II, when the special file was reviewed on November 8, it contained the names of no persons from the entire

432

Dallas-Fort Worth area, notwithstanding the fact that Ambassador Stevenson had been abused by pickets in Dallas less than a month before. Bouck explained the failure to try to identify the individuals involved in the Stevenson incident after it occurred on the ground that PRS required a more direct indication of a threat to the President, and that there was no such indication until the President's scheduled visit to that area became known.[42] Such an approach seriously undermines the precautionary nature of PRS work; if the presence in Dallas of the Stevenson pickets might have created a danger for the President on a visit to that city, PRS should have investigated and been prepared to guard against it.

Other agencies occasionally provided information to the Secret Service concerning potentially dangerous political groups. This was done in the case of the Nationalist Party of Puerto Rico, for example, but only after members of the group had resorted to political violence.[43] However, the vague requests for information which the Secret Service made to Federal intelligence and law enforcement agencies were not well designed to elicit information from them about persons other than those who were obvious threats to the President. The requests shifted the responsibility for evaluating difficult cases from the Service, the agency most responsible for performing that task, to the other agencies. No specific guidance was provided. Although the CIA had on file requests from the Treasury Department for information on the counterfeiting of U.S. currency and certain smuggling matters,[44] it had no written specification of intelligence information collected by CIA abroad which was desired by the Secret Service in advance of Presidential trips outside the United States.

Information known about Lee Harvey Oswald prior to the assassination.—No information concerning Lee Harvey Oswald appeared in PRS files before the President's trip to Dallas. Oswald was known to other Federal agencies with which the Secret Service maintained intelligence liaison. The FBI had been interested in him, to some degree at least, since the time of his defection in October 1959. It had interviewed him twice shortly after his return to the United States, again a year later at his request and was investigating him at the time of the assassination. The Commission has taken the testimony of Bureau agents who interviewed Oswald after his return from the Soviet Union and prior to November 22, 1963, the agent who was assigned his case at the time of the assassination, the Director of the FBI, and the Assistant to the Director in charge of all investigative activities under the Director and Associate Director.[45] In addition, the Director and Deputy Director for Plans of the CIA testified concerning that Agency's limited knowledge of Oswald before the assassination.[46] Finally, the Commission has reviewed the complete files on Oswald, as they existed at the time of the assassination, of the Department of State, the Office of Naval Intelligence, the FBI, and the CIA. The information known to the FBI is summarized below.

433

From defection to return to Fort Worth.—The FBI opened a file on Oswald in October 1959,[47] when news reports appeared of his defection to the Soviet Union.[48] The file was opened "for the purpose of correlating information inasmuch as he was considered a possible security risk in the event he returned to this country."[49] Oswald's defection was also the occasion for the opening of files by the Department of State, CIA, and the Office of Naval Intelligence. Until April 1960, FBI activity consisted of placing in Oswald's file information regarding his relations with the U.S. Embassy in Moscow and background data relating largely to his prior military service, provided by other agencies. In April 1960, Mrs. Marguerite Oswald and Robert Oswald were interviewed in the course of a routine FBI investigation of transfers of small sums of money from Mrs. Oswald to her son in Russia.[50]

During the next 2 years the FBI continued to accumulate information, and kept itself informed on Oswald's status by periodic reviews of State Department and Office of Naval Intelligence files. In this way, it learned that when Oswald had arrived in the Soviet Union he had attempted to renounce his U.S. citizenship and applied for Soviet citizenship, had described himself as a Marxist, had said he would give the Soviet Union any useful information he had acquired as a marine radar technician and had displayed an arrogant and aggressive attitude at the U.S. Embassy; it learned also that Oswald had been discharged from the Marine Corps Reserve as undesirable in August 1960.[51] In June 1962, the Bureau was advised by the Department of State of Oswald's plan to return to the United States. The Bureau made arrangements to be advised by immigration authorities of his return, and instructed the Dallas office to interview him when he got back to determine whether he had been recruited by a Soviet intelligence service.[52] Oswald's file at the Department of State Passport Office was reviewed in June 1962. It revealed his letter of January 30, 1962, to Secretary of the Navy Connally, in which he protested his discharge and declared that he would use "all means" to correct it. The file reflected the Department's determination that Oswald had not expatriated himself.[53]

From return to Fort Worth to move to New Orleans.—Oswald was first interviewed by FBI Agents John W. Fain and B. Tom Carter on June 26, 1962, in Fort Worth.[54] Agent Fain reported to headquarters that Oswald was impatient and arrogant, and unwilling to answer questions regarding his motive for going to the Soviet Union. Oswald "denied that he had ever denounced his U.S. citizenship, and * * * that he had ever applied for Soviet citizenship specifically."[55] Oswald was, however, willing to discuss his contacts with Soviet authorities. He denied having any involvement with Soviet intelligence agencies and promised to advise the FBI if he heard from them.[56]

Agent Fain was not satisfied by this interview and arranged to see Oswald again on August 16, 1962.[57] According to Fain's contemporaneous memorandum and his present recollection, while Oswald remained somewhat evasive at this interview, he was not antagonistic

and seemed generally to be settling down.[58] (Marina Oswald, however, recalled that her husband was upset by this interview.)[59]
Oswald again agreed to advise the FBI if he were approached under suspicious circumstances; however, he deprecated the possibility of this happening, particularly since his employment did not involve any sensitive information.[60] Having concluded that Oswald was not a security risk or potentially dangerous or violent, Fain determined that nothing further remained to be done at that time and recommended that the case be placed in a closed status.[61] This is an administrative classification indicating that no further work has been scheduled. It does not preclude the agent in charge of the case from reopening it if he feels that further work should be done.[62]

From August 1962 until March 1963, the FBI continued to accumulate information regarding Oswald but engaged in no active investigation. Agent Fain retired from the FBI in October 1962, and the closed Oswald case was not reassigned.[63] However, pursuant to a regular Bureau practice of interviewing certain immigrants from Iron Curtain countries, Fain had been assigned to see Marina Oswald at an appropriate time.[64] This assignment was given to Agent James P. Hosty, Jr. of the Dallas office upon Fain's retirement. In March 1963, while attempting to locate Marina Oswald, Agent Hosty was told by Mrs. M. F. Tobias, a former landlady of the Oswalds at 602 Elsbeth Street in Dallas, that other tenants had complained because Oswald was drinking to excess and beating his wife.[65] This information led Hosty to review Oswald's file, from which he learned that Oswald had become a subscriber to the Worker, a Communist Party publication. Hosty decided that the Lee Harvey Oswald case should be reopened because of the alleged personal difficulties and the contact with the Worker, and his recommendation was accepted.[66] He decided, however, not to interview Marina Oswald at that time, and merely determined that the Oswalds were living at 214 Neely Street in Dallas.[67]

On April 21, 1963, the FBI field office in New York was advised that Oswald was in contact with the Fair Play for Cuba Committee in New York, and that he had written to the committee stating that he had distributed its pamphlets on the streets of Dallas.[68] This information did not reach Agent Hosty in Dallas until June.[69] Hosty considered the information to be "stale" by that time, and did not attempt to verify Oswald's reported statement.[70] Under a general Bureau request to be on the alert for activities of the Fair Play for Cuba Committee, Hosty had inquired earlier and found no evidence that it was functioning in the Dallas area.[71]

In New Orleans.—In the middle of May of 1963, Agent Hosty checked Oswald's last known residence and found that he had moved.[72] Oswald was tentatively located in New Orleans in June, and Hosty asked the New Orleans FBI office to determine Oswald's address and what he was doing.[73] The New Orleans office investigated and located Oswald, learning his address and former place of employment on August 5, 1963.[74] A confidential informant advised the FBI that Oswald was not known to be engaged in Communist Party activities in New Orleans.[75]

On June 24, Oswald applied in New Orleans for a passport, stating that he planned to depart by ship for an extended tour of Western European countries, the Soviet Union, Finland, and Poland. The Passport Office of the Department of State in Washington had no listing for Oswald requiring special treatment, and his application was approved on the following day.[76] The FBI had not asked to be informed of any effort by Oswald to obtain a passport, as it might have under existing procedures, and did not know of his application.[77] According to the Bureau,

> We did not request the State Department to include Oswald on a list which would have resulted in advising us of any application for a passport inasmuch as the facts relating to Oswald's activities at that time did not warrant such action. Our investigation of Oswald had disclosed no evidence that Oswald was acting under the instructions or on behalf of any foreign government or instrumentality thereof.[78]

On August 9, 1963, Oswald was arrested and jailed by the New Orleans Police Department for disturbing the peace, in connection with a street fight which broke out when he was accosted by anti-Castro Cubans while distributing leaflets on behalf of the Fair Play for Cuba Committee. On the next day, he asked the New Orleans police to arrange for him to be interviewed by the FBI. The police called the local FBI office and an agent, John L. Quigley, was sent to the police station.[79] Agent Quigley did not know of Oswald's prior FBI record when he interviewed him, inasmuch as the police had not given Oswald's name to the Bureau when they called the office.[80]

Quigley recalled that Oswald was receptive when questioned about his general background but less than completely truthful or cooperative when interrogated about the Fair Play for Cuba Committee. Quigley testified:

> When I began asking him specific details with respect to his activities in the Fair Play for Cuba Committee in New Orleans as to where meetings were held, who was involved, what occurred, he was reticent to furnish information, reluctant and actually as far as I was concerned, was completely evasive on them.[81]

In Quigley's judgment, Oswald "was probably making a self-serving statement in attempting to explain to me why he was distributing this literature, and for no other reason, and when I got to questioning him further then he felt that his purpose had been served and he wouldn't say anything further." [82]

During the interview Quigley obtained background information from Oswald which was inconsistent with information already in the Bureau's possession. When Quigley returned to his office, he learned that another Bureau agent, Milton R. Kaack, had been conducting a background investigation of Oswald at the request of Agent Hosty in Dallas. Quigley advised Kaack of his interview and gave him a detailed memorandum.[83] Kaack was aware of the facts known to the FBI and recognized Oswald's false statements.[84] For example, Oswald claimed that his wife's maiden name was Prossa and that they had been married in Fort Worth and lived there until coming to New Orleans.[85] He had told the New Orleans arresting officers that he had been born in Cuba.[86]

Several days later, the Bureau received additional evidence that Oswald had lied to Agent Quigley. On August 22, it learned that Oswald had appeared on a radio discussion program on August 21.[87] William Stuckey, who had appeared on the radio program with Oswald, told the Bureau on August 30 that Oswald had told him that he had worked and been married in the Soviet Union.[88] Neither these discrepancies nor the fact that Oswald had initiated the FBI interview was considered sufficiently unusual to necessitate another interview.[89] Alan H. Belmont, Assistant to the Director of the FBI, stated the Bureau's reasoning in this way:

> Our interest in this man at this point was to determine whether his activities constituted a threat to the internal security of the country. It was apparent that he had made a self-serving statement to Agent Quigley. It became a matter of record in our files as a part of the case, and if we determined that the course of the investigation required us to clarify or face him down with this information, we would do it at the appropriate time.
>
> In other words, he committed no violation of the law by telling us something that wasn't true, and unless this required further investigation at that time, we would handle it in due course, in accord with the whole context of the investigation.[90]

On August 21, 1963, Bureau headquarters instructed the New Orleans and Dallas field offices to conduct an additional investigation of Oswald in view of the activities which had led to his arrest.[91] FBI informants in the New Orleans area, familiar with pro-Castro or Communist Party activity there, advised the Bureau that Oswald was unknown in such circles.[92]

In Dallas.—In early September 1963 the FBI transferred the principal responsibility for the Oswald case from the Dallas office to the New Orleans office.[93] Soon after, on October 1, 1963, the FBI was advised by the rental agent for the Oswalds' apartment in New Orleans that they had moved again.[94] According to the information received by the Bureau they had vacated their apartment, and Marina Oswald had departed with their child in a station wagon with Texas registration.[95] On October 3, Hosty reopened the case in Dallas to assist the New Orleans office.[96] He checked in Oswald's old neighborhood and throughout the Dallas-Fort Worth area but was unable to locate Oswald.[97]

437

The next word about Oswald's location was a communication from the CIA to the FBI on October 10, advising that an individual tentatively identified as Oswald had been in touch with the Soviet Embassy in Mexico City in early October of 1963.[98] The Bureau had had no earlier information suggesting that Oswald had left the United States. The possible contact with the Soviet Embassy in Mexico intensified the FBI's interest in learning Oswald's whereabouts.[99] The FBI representative in Mexico City arranged to follow up this information with the CIA and to verify Oswald's entry into Mexico.[100] The CIA message was sent also to the Department of State where it was reviewed by personnel of the Passport Office, who knew from Oswald's file that he had sought and obtained a passport on June 25, 1963.[101] The Department of State did not advise either the CIA or the FBI of these facts.[102]

On October 25, the New Orleans office of the FBI learned that in September Oswald had given a forwarding address of 2515 West Fifth Street, Irving, Tex.[103] After receiving this information on October 29, Agent Hosty attempted to locate Oswald. On the same day Hosty interviewed neighbors on Fifth Street and learned that the address was that of Mrs. Ruth Paine.[104] He conducted a limited background investigation of the Paines, intending to interview Mrs. Paine and ask her particularly about Oswald's whereabouts.[105]

Having determined that Mrs. Paine was a responsible and reliable citizen, Hosty interviewed her on November 1. The interview lasted about 20–25 minutes.[106] In response to Hosty's inquiries, Mrs. Paine

* * * readily admitted that Mrs. Marina Oswald and Lee Oswald's two children were staying with her. She said that Lee Oswald was living somewhere in Dallas. She didn't know where. She said it was in the Oak Cliff area but she didn't have his address.

I asked her if she knew where he worked. After a moment's hesitation, she told me that he worked at the Texas School Book Depository near the downtown area of Dallas. She didn't have the exact address, and it is my recollection that we went to the phone book and looked it up, found it to be 411 Elm Street.[107]

Mrs. Paine told Hosty also that Oswald was living alone in Dallas because she did not want him staying at her house, although she was willing to let Oswald visit his wife and children.[108] According to Hosty, Mrs. Paine indicated that she thought she could find out where Oswald was living and would let him know.[109] At this point in the interview, Hosty gave Mrs. Paine his name and office telephone number on a piece of paper.[110] At the end of the interview, Marina Oswald came into the room. When he observed that she seemed "quite alarmed" about the visit, Hosty assured her, through Mrs. Paine as interpreter, that the FBI would not harm or harass her.[111]

On November 4, Hosty telephoned the Texas School Book Depository and learned that Oswald was working there and that he had given as his address Mrs. Paine's residence in Irving.[112]   Hosty took the necessary steps to have the Dallas office of the FBI, rather than the New Orleans office, reestablished as the office with principal responsibility.[113]   On November 5, Hosty was traveling near Mrs. Paine's home and took the occasion to stop by to ask whether she had any further information.   Mrs. Paine had nothing to add to what she had already told him, except that during a visit that past weekend, Oswald had said that he was a "Trotskyite Communist," and that she found this and similar statements illogical and somewhat amusing.[114]   On this occasion Hosty was at the Paine residence for only a few minutes.[115]

During neither interview did Hosty learn Oswald's address or telephone number in Dallas.   Mrs. Paine testified that she learned Oswald's telephone number at the Beckley Street roominghouse in the middle of October shortly after Oswald rented the room on October 14.   As discussed in chapter VI, she failed to report this to Agent Hosty because she thought the FBI was in possession of a great deal of information and certainly would find it very easy to learn where Oswald was living.[116]

Hosty did nothing further in connection with the Oswald case until after the assassination.   On November 1, 1963, he had received a copy of the report of the New Orleans office which contained Agent Quigley's memorandum of the interview in the New Orleans jail on August 10,[117] and realized immediately that Oswald had given false biographic information.[118]   Hosty knew that he would eventually have to investigate this, and "was quite interested in determining the nature of his contact with the Soviet Embassy in Mexico City." [119]   When asked what his next step would have been, Hosty replied:

> Well, as I had previously stated, I have between 25 and 40 cases assigned to me at any one time.   I had other matters to take care of.   I had now established that Lee Oswald was not employed in a sensitive industry.   I can now afford to wait until New Orleans forwarded the necessary papers to me to show me I now had all the information.   It was then my plan to interview Marina Oswald in detail concerning both herself and her husband's background.
>
> Q. Had you planned any steps beyond that point?
> A. No.   I would have to wait until I had talked to Marina to see what I could determine, and from there I could make my plans.
> Q. Did you take any action on this case between November 5 and November 22?
> A. No, sir.[120]

The official Bureau files confirm Hosty's statement that from November 5 until the assassination, no active investigation was conducted.[121]   On November 18 the FBI learned that Oswald recently had been in communication with the Soviet Embassy in Washington and so advised the Dallas office in the ordinary course of business.

Hosty received this information on the afternoon of November 22, 1963.[122]

Nonreferral of Oswald to the Secret Service.—The Commission has considered carefully the question whether the FBI, in view of all the information concerning Oswald in its files, should have alerted the Secret Service to Oswald's presence in Dallas prior to President Kennedy's visit. The Secret Service and the FBI differ as to whether Oswald fell within the category of "threats against the President" which should be referred to the Service.

Robert I. Bouck, special agent in charge of the Protective Research Section, testified that the information available to the Federal Government about Oswald before the assassination would, if known to PRS, have made Oswald a subject of concern to the Secret Service.[123] Bouck pointed to a number of characteristics besides Oswald's defection the cumulative effect of which would have been to alert the Secret Service to potential danger:

> I would think his continued association with the Russian Embassy after his return, his association with the Castro groups would have been of concern to us, a knowledge that he had, I believe, been courtmartialed for illegal possession of a gun, of a hand gun in the Marines, that he had owned a weapon and did a good deal of hunting or use of it, perhaps in Russia, plus a number of items about his disposition and unreliability of character, I think all of those, if we had had them altogether, would have added up to pointing out a pretty bad individual, and I think that, together, had we known that he had a vantage point would have seemed somewhat serious to us, even though I must admit that none of these in themselves would be—would meet our specific criteria, none of them alone.
>
> But it is when you begin adding them up to some degree that you begin to get criteria that are meaningful.[124]

Mr. Bouck pointed out, however, that he had no reason to believe that any one Federal agency had access to all this information, including the significant fact that Oswald was employed in a building which overlooked the motorcade route.[125]

Agent Hosty testified that he was fully aware of the pending Presidential visit to Dallas. He recalled that the special agent in charge of the Dallas office of the FBI, J. Gordon Shanklin, had discussed the President's visit on several occasions, including the regular biweekly conference on the morning of November 22:

> Mr. Shanklin advised us, among other things, that in view of the President's visit to Dallas, that if anyone had any indication of any possibility of any acts of violence or any demonstrations against the President, or Vice President, to immediately notify the Secret Service and confirm it in writing. He had made the

440

same statement about a week prior at another special conference which we had held. I don't recall the exact date. It was about a week prior.[126]

In fact, Hosty participated in transmitting to the Secret Service two pieces of information pertaining to the visit.[127]   Hosty testified that he did not know until the evening of Thursday, November 21, that there was to be a motorcade, however, and never realized that the motorcade would pass the Texas School Book Depository Building.   He testified that he did not read the newspaper story describing the motorcade route in detail, since he was interested only in the fact that the motorcade was coming up Main Street, "where maybe I could watch it if I had a chance." [128]

Even if he had recalled that Oswald's place of employment was on the President's route, Hosty testified that he would not have cited him to the Secret Service as a potential threat to the President.[129] Hosty interpreted his instructions as requiring "some indication that the person planned to take some action against the safety of the President of the United States or the Vice President." [130]   In his opinion, none of the information in the FBI files—Oswald's defection, his Fair Play for Cuba activities in New Orleans, his lies to Agent Quigley, his recent visit to Mexico City—indicated that Oswald was capable of violence.[131]   Hosty's initial reaction on hearing that Oswald was a suspect in the assassination, was "shock, complete surprise," because he had no reason to believe that Oswald "was capable or potentially an assassin of the President of the United States." [132]

Shortly after Oswald was apprehended and identified, Hosty's superior sent him to observe the interrogation of Oswald.[133]   Hosty parked his car in the basement of police headquarters and there met an acquaintance, Lt. Jack Revill of the Dallas police force.   The two men disagree about the conversation which took place between them.   They agree that Hosty told Revill that the FBI had known about Oswald and, in particular, of his presence in Dallas and his employment at the Texas School Book Depository Building.[134]   Revill testified that Hosty said also that the FBI had information that Oswald was "capable of committing this assassination." [135]   According to Revill, Hosty indicated that he was going to tell this to Lieutenant Wells of the homicide and robbery bureau.[136]   Revill promptly made a memorandum of this conversation in which the quoted statement appears.[137]   His secretary testified that she prepared such a report for him that afternoon [138] and Chief of Police Jesse E. Curry and District Attorney Henry M. Wade both testified that they saw it later that day.[139]

Hosty has unequivocally denied, first by affidavit and then in his testimony before the Commission, that he ever said that Oswald was capable of violence, or that he had any information suggesting this.[140] The only witness to the conversation was Dallas Police Detective V. J. Brian, who was accompanying Revill.   Brian did not hear Hosty make any statement concerning Oswald's capacity to be an

441

assassin but he did not hear the entire conversation because of the commotion at police headquarters and because he was not within hearing distance at all times.[141]

Hosty's interpretation of the prevailing FBI instructions on referrals to the Secret Service was defended before the Commission by his superiors. After summarizing the Bureau's investigative interest in Oswald prior to the assassination, J. Edgar Hoover concluded that "There was nothing up to the time of the assassination that gave any indication that this man was a dangerous character who might do harm to the President or to the Vice President." [142]   Director Hoover emphasized that the first indication of Oswald's capacity for violence was his attempt on General Walker's life, which did not become known to the FBI until after the assassination.[143]   Both Director Hoover and his assistant, Alan H. Belmont, stressed also the decision by the Department of State that Oswald should be permitted to return to the United States.[144]   Neither believed that the Bureau investigation of him up to November 22 revealed any information which would have justified referral to the Secret Service. According to Belmont, when Oswald returned from the Soviet Union,

> * * * he indicated that he had learned his lesson, was disenchanted with Russia, and had a renewed concept—I am paraphrasing, a renewed concept—of the American free society.
>
> We talked to him twice. He likewise indicated he was disenchanted with Russia. We satisfied ourselves that we had met our requirement, namely to find out whether he had been recruited by Soviet intelligence. The case was closed.
>
> We again exhibited interest on the basis of these contacts with The Worker, Fair Play for Cuba Committee, which are relatively inconsequential.
>
> His activities for the Fair Play for Cuba Committee in New Orleans, we knew, were not of real consequence as he was not connected with any organized activity there.
>
> The interview with him in jail is not significant from the standpoint of whether he had a propensity for violence.
>
> Q. This is the Quigley interview you are talking about?
>
> A. Yes; it was a self-serving interview.
>
> The visits with the Soviet Embassy were evidently for the purpose of securing a visa, and he had told us during one of the interviews that he would probably take his wife back to Soviet Russia some time in the future. He had come back to Dallas. Hosty had established that he had a job, he was working, and had told Mrs. Paine that when he got the money he was going to take an apartment when the baby was old enough, he was going to take an apartment, and the family would live together.
>
> He gave evidence of settling down. Nowhere during the course of this investigation or the information that came to us from other agencies was there any indication of a potential for violence on his part.

Consequently, there was no basis for Hosty to go to Secret Service and advise them of Oswald's presence. * * * [145]

As reflected in this testimony, the officials of the FBI believed that there was no data in its files which gave warning that Oswald was a source of danger to President Kennedy. While he had expressed hostility at times toward the State Department, the Marine Corps, and the FBI as agents of the Government,[146] so far as the FBI knew he had not shown any potential for violence. Prior to November 22, 1963, no law enforcement agency had any information to connect Oswald with the attempted shooting of General Walker. It was against this background and consistent with the criteria followed by the FBI prior to November 22 that agents of the FBI in Dallas did not consider Oswald's presence in the Texas School Book Depository Building overlooking the motorcade route as a source of danger to the President and did not inform the Secret Service of his employment in the Depository Building.

The Commission believes, however, that the FBI took an unduly restrictive view of its responsibilities in preventive intelligence work, prior to the assassination. The Commission appreciates the large volume of cases handled by the FBI (636,371 investigative matters during fiscal year 1963).[147] There were no Secret Service criteria which specifically required the referral of Oswald's case to the Secret Service; nor was there any requirement to report the names of defectors. However, there was much material in the hands of the FBI about Oswald: the knowledge of his defection, his arrogance and hostility to the United States, his pro-Castro tendencies, his lies when interrogated by the FBI, his trip to Mexico where he was in contact with Soviet authorities, his presence in the School Book Depository job and its location along the route of the motorcade. All this does seem to amount to enough to have induced an alert agency, such as the FBI, possessed of this information to list Oswald as a potential threat to the safety of the President. This conclusion may be tinged with hindsight, but it stated primarily to direct the thought of those responsible for the future safety of our Presidents to the need for a more imaginative and less narrow interpretation of their responsibilities.

It is the conclusion of the Commission that, even in the absence of Secret Service criteria which specifically required the referral of such a case as Oswald's to the Secret Service, a more alert and carefully considered treatment of the Oswald case by the Bureau might have brought about such a referral. Had such a review been undertaken by the FBI, there might conceivably have been additional investigation of the Oswald case between November 5 and November 22. Agent Hosty testified that several matters brought to his attention in late October and early November, including the visit to the Soviet Embassy in Mexico City, required further attention. Under proper procedures knowledge of the pending Presidential visit might have prompted Hosty to have made more vigorous efforts to locate

Oswald's roominghouse address in Dallas and to interview him regarding these unresolved matters.

The formal FBI instructions to its agents outlining the information to be referred to the Secret Service were too narrow at the time of the assassination. While the Secret Service bears the principal responsibility for this failure, the FBI instructions did not reflect fully the Secret Service's need for information regarding potential threats. The handbook referred thus to "the possibility of an attempt against the person or safety of the President." [148] It is clear from Hosty's testimony that this was construed, at least by him, as requiring evidence of a plan or conspiracy to injure the President.[149] Efforts made by the Bureau since the assassination, on the other hand, reflect keen awareness of the necessity of communicating a much wider range of intelligence information to the Service.[150]

Most important, notwithstanding that both agencies have professed to the Commission that the liaison between them was close and fully sufficient,[151] the Commission does not believe that the liaison between the FBI and the Secret Service prior to the assassination was as effective as it should have been. The FBI Manual of Instructions provided:

Liaison With Other Government Agencies

To insure adequate and effective liaison arrangements, each SAC should specifically designate an Agent (or Agents) to be responsible for developing and maintaining liaison with other Federal Agencies. This liaison should take into consideration FBI-agency community of interests, location of agency headquarters, and the responsiveness of agency representatives. In each instance, liaison contacts should be developed to include a close friendly relationship, mutual understanding of FBI and agency jurisdictions, and an indicated willingness by the agency representative to coordinate activities and to discuss problems of mutual interest. Each field office should determine those Federal agencies which are represented locally and with which liaison should be conducted.[152]

The testimony reveals that liaison responsibilities in connection with the President's visit were discussed twice officially by the special agent in charge of the FBI office in Dallas. As discussed in chapter II, some limited information was made available to the Secret Service.[153] But there was no fully adequate liaison between the two agencies. Indeed, the Commission believes that the liaison between all Federal agencies responsible for Presidential protection should be improved.

Other Protective Measures and Aspects of Secret Service Performance

The President's trip to Dallas called into play many standard operating procedures of the Secret Service in addition to its preventive

444

intelligence operations. Examination of these procedures shows that in most respects they were well conceived and ably executed by the personnel of the Service. Against the background of the critical events of November 22, however, certain shortcomings and lapses from the high standards which the Commission believes should prevail in the field of Presidential protection are evident.

Advance preparations.—The advance preparations in Dallas by Agent Winston G. Lawson of the White House detail have been described in chapter II. With the assistance of Agent in Charge Sorrels of the Dallas field office of the Secret Service, Lawson was responsible for working out a great many arrangements for the President's trip. The Service prefers to have two agents perform advance preparations. In the case of Dallas, because President Kennedy had scheduled visits to five Texas cities and had also scheduled visits to other parts of the country immediately before the Texas trip, there were not enough men available to permit two agents to be assigned to all the advance work. Consequently, Agent Lawson did the advance work alone from November 13 to November 18, when he was joined by Agent David B. Grant, who had just completed advance work on the President's trip to Tampa.

The Commission concludes that the most significant advance arrangements for the President's trip were soundly planned. In particular, the Commission believes that the motorcade route selected by Agent Lawson, upon the advice of Agent in Charge Sorrels and with the concurrence of the Dallas police, was entirely appropriate, in view of the known desires of the President. There were far safer routes via freeways directly to the Trade Mart, but these routes would not have been in accordance with the White House staff instructions given the Secret Service for a desirable motorcade route.[154] Much of Lawson's time was taken with establishing adequate security over the motorcade route and at the two places where the President would stop, Love Field and the Trade Mart. The Commission concludes that the arrangements worked out at the Trade Mart by these Secret Service agents with the cooperation of the Dallas police and other local law enforcement agents, were carefully executed. Since the President was to be at the Trade Mart longer than at any other location in Dallas and in view of the security hazards presented by the building, the Secret Service correctly gave particular attention in the advance preparations to those arrangements. The Commission also regards the security arrangements worked out by Lawson and Sorrels at Love Field as entirely adequate.

The Commission believes, however, that the Secret Service has inadequately defined the responsibilities of its advance agents, who have been given broad discretion to determine what matters require attention in making advance preparations and to decide what action to take. Agent Lawson was not given written instructions concerning the Dallas trip or advice about any peculiar problems which it might involve; all instructions from higher authority were communicated to him orally. He did not have a checklist of the tasks he was expected to accomplish, either by his own efforts or with the cooperation of local authorities.[155]   The only systematic supervision of the activities of the advance agent has been that provided by a requirement that he file interim and final reports on each advance assignment.   The interim report must be in the hands of the agent supervising the protective group traveling with the President long enough before his departure to apprise him of any particular problems encountered and the responsive action taken.[156]   Agent Lawson's interim report was received by Agent Kellerman on November 20, the day before departure on the Texas trip.[157]

The Secret Service has advised the Commission that no unusual precautions were taken for the Dallas trip, and that "the precautions taken for the President's trip were the usual safeguards employed on trips of this kind in the United States during the previous year." [158] Special Agent in Charge Sorrels testified that the advance preparations followed on this occasion were "pretty much the same" as those followed in 1936 during a trip to Dallas by President Roosevelt, which was Sorrels' first important assignment in connection with Presidential work.[159]

In view of the constant change in the nature of threats to the President and the diversity of the dangers which may arise in the various cities within the United States, the Commission believes that standard procedures in use for many years and applied in all parts of the country may not be sufficient.   There is, for example, no Secret Service arrangement for evaluating before a trip particular difficulties that might be anticipated, which would bring to bear the judgment and experience of members of the White House detail other than the advance agent.   Constant reevaluation of procedures, with attention to special problems and the development of instructions specific to particular trips, would be a desirable innovation.

   Liaison with local law enforcement authorities.—In the description of the important aspects of the advance preparations, there have been references to the numerous discussions between Secret Service representatives and the Dallas Police Department.   The wholehearted support of these local authorities was indispensable to the Service in carrying out its duties.   The Service had 28 agents participating in the Dallas visit.[160]   Agent Lawson's advance planning called for the deployment of almost 600 members of the Dallas Police Department, Fire Department, County Sheriff's Department, and the Texas Department of Public Safety.[161]   Despite this dependence on local authorities, which would be substantially the same on a visit by the President to any large city, the Secret Service did not at the time of the assassination have any established procedure governing its relationships with them.[162]   It had no prepared checklist of matters to be covered with local police on such visits to metropolitan areas and no written description of the role the local police were expected to perform.   Discussions with the Dallas authorities and requests made of them were entirely informal.

446

The Commission believes that a more formal statement of assigned responsibilities, supplemented in each case to reflect the peculiar conditions of each Presidential trip, is essential. This would help to eliminate varying interpretations of Secret Service instructions by different local law enforcement representatives. For example, while the Secret Service representatives in Dallas asked the police to station guards at each overpass to keep "unauthorized personnel" off, this term was not defined. At some overpasses all persons were excluded, while on the overpass overlooking the assassination scene railroad and yard terminal workmen were permitted to remain under police supervision, as discussed in chapter III.[163] Assistant Chief Batchelor of the Dallas police noted the absence of any formal statement by the Secret Service of specific work assigned to the police and suggested the desirability of such a statement.[164] Agent Lawson agreed that such a procedure would assist him and other agents in fulfilling their responsibilities as advance agents.[165]

Check of buildings along route of motorcade.—Agent Lawson did not arrange for a prior inspection of buildings along the motorcade route, either by police or by custodians of the buildings, since it was not the usual practice of the Secret Service to do so.[166] The Chief of the Service has provided the Commission a detailed explanation of this policy:

Except for inauguration or other parades involving foreign dignitaries accompanied by the President in Washington, it has not been the practice of the Secret Service to make surveys or checks of buildings along the route of a Presidential motorcade. For the inauguration and certain other parades in Washington where the traditional route is known to the public long in advance of the event, buildings along the route can be checked by teams of law enforcement officers, and armed guards are posted along the route as appropriate. But on out-of-town trips where the route is decided on and made public only a few days in advance, buildings are not checked either by Secret Service agents or by any other law enforcement officers at the request of the Secret Service. With the number of men available to the Secret Service and the time available, surveys of hundreds of buildings and thousands of windows is not practical.

In Dallas the route selected necessarily involved passing through the principal downtown section between tall buildings. While certain streets thought to be too narrow could be avoided and other choices made, it was not practical to select a route where the President could not be seen from roofs or windows of buildings. At the two places in Dallas where the President would remain for a period of time, Love Field and the Trade Mart, arrangements were made for building and roof security by posting police officers where appropriate. Similar arrangements for a motorcade of ten miles, including many blocks of tall commercial buildings is not practical. Nor is it practical to prevent

447

people from entering such buildings, or to limit access in every building to those employed or having business there. Even if it were possible with a vastly larger force of security officers to do so, many observers have felt that such a procedure would not be consistent with the nature and purpose of the motorcade to let the people see their President and to welcome him to their city.

In accordance with its regular procedures, no survey or other check was made by the Secret Service, or by any other law enforcement agency at its request, of the Texas School Book Depository Building or those employed there prior to the time the President was shot.[167]

This justification of the Secret Service's standing policy is not persuasive. The danger from a concealed sniper on the Dallas trip was of concern to those who had considered the problem. President Kennedy himself had mentioned it that morning,[168] as had Agent Sorrels when he and Agent Lawson were fixing the motorcade route.[169] Admittedly, protective measures cannot ordinarily be taken with regard to all buildings along a motorcade route. Levels of risk can be determined, however, as has been confirmed by building surveys made since the assassination for the Department of the Treasury.[170] An attempt to cover only the most obvious points of possible ambush along the route in Dallas might well have included the Texas School Book Depository Building.

Instead of such advance precautions, the Secret Service depended in part on the efforts of local law enforcement personnel stationed along the route. In addition, Secret Service agents riding in the motorcade were trained to scan buildings as part of their general observation of the crowd of spectators.[171] These substitute measures were of limited value. Agent Lawson was unable to state whether he had actually instructed the Dallas police to scan windows of buildings lining the motorcade route, although it was his usual practice to do so.[172] If such instructions were in fact given, they were not effectively carried out. Television films taken of parts of the motorcade by a Dallas television station show the foot patrolmen facing the passing motorcade, and not the adjacent crowds and buildings, as the procession passed.[173]

Three officers from the Dallas Police Department were assigned to the intersection of Elm and Houston during the morning of November 22 prior to the motorcade.[174] All received their instructions early in the morning from Capt. P. W. Lawrence of the traffic division.[175] According to Captain Lawrence:

I then told the officers that their primary duty was traffic and crowd control and that they should be alert for any persons who might attempt to throw anything and although it was not a violation of the law to carry a placard, that they were not to tolerate any actions such as the Stevenson incident and arrest any person who might attempt to throw anything or try to get at the President and his party; paying particular attention to the crowd for any unusual activity. I stressed the fact that this was our President and he should be shown every respect due his position and that it was our duty to see that this was done.[176]

Captain Lawrence was not instructed to have his men watch buildings along the motorcade route and did not mention the observation of buildings to them.[177] The three officers confirm that their primary concern was crowd and traffic control, and that they had no opportunity to scan the windows of the Depository or any other building in the vicinity of Elm and Houston when the motorcade was passing. They had, however, occasionally observed the windows of buildings in the area before the motorcade arrived, in accordance with their own understanding of their function.[178]

As the motorcade approached Elm Street there were several Secret Service agents in it who shared the responsibility of scanning the windows of nearby buildings. Agent Sorrels, riding in the lead car, did observe the Texas School Book Depository Building as he passed by, at least for a sufficient number of seconds to gain a "general impression" of the lack of any unusual activity.[179] He was handicapped, however, by the fact that he was riding in a closed car whose roof at times obscured his view.[180] Lawson, also in the lead car, did not scan any buildings since an important part of his job was to look backward at the President's car.[181] Lawson stated that he "was looking back a good deal of the time, watching his car, watching the sides, watching the crowds, giving advice or asking advice from the Chief and also looking ahead to the known hazards like overpasses, underpasses, railroads, et cetera." [182] Agent Roy H. Kellerman, riding in the front seat of the Presidential car, stated that he scanned the Depository Building, but not sufficiently to be alerted by anything in the windows or on the roof.[183] The agents in the followup car also were expected to scan adjacent buildings. However, the Commission does not believe that agents stationed in a car behind the Presidential car, who must concentrate primarily on the possibility of threats from crowds along the route, provide a significant safeguard against dangers in nearby buildings.

Conduct of Secret Service agents in Fort Worth on November 22.— In the early morning hours on November 22, 1963, in Fort Worth, there occurred a breach of discipline by some members of the Secret Service who were officially traveling with the President. After the President had retired at his hotel, nine agents who were off duty went to the nearby Fort Worth Press Club at midnight or slightly thereafter, expecting to obtain food; they had had little opportunity to eat during the day.[184] No food was available at the Press Club. All of the agents stayed for a drink of beer, or in several cases, a mixed drink. According to their affidavits, the drinking in no case amounted to more than three glasses of beer or 1½ mixed drinks, and others who were present say that no agent was inebriated or acted improperly. The statements of the agents involved are supported by statements of members of the Fort Worth press who accompanied or observed them and by a Secret Service investigation.[185]

According to their statements, the agents remained at the Press Club for periods varying from 30 minutes to an hour and a half, and the last agent left the Press Club by 2 a.m.[186] Two of the nine agents returned to their rooms. The seven others proceeded to an establishment called the Cellar Coffee House, described by some as a beatnik place and by its manager as "a unique show place with continuous light entertainment all night [serving] only coffee, fruit juices and no hard liquors or beer." [187] There is no indication that any of the agents who visited the Cellar Coffee House had any intoxicating drink at that establishment.[188] Most of the agents were there from about 1:30 or 1:45 a.m. to about 2:45 or 3 a.m.; one agent was there from 2 until 5 a.m.[189]

The lobby of the hotel and the areas adjacent to the quarters of the President were guarded during the night by members of the midnight to 8 a.m. shift of the White House detail. These agents were each relieved for a half hour break during the night.[190] Three members of this shift separately took this opportunity to visit the Cellar Coffee House.[191] Only one stayed as long as a half hour, and none had any beverage there.[192] Chief Rowley testified that agents on duty in such a situation usually stay within the building during their relief, but that their visits to the Cellar were "neither consistent nor inconsistent" with their duty.[193]

Each of the agents who visited the Press Club or the Cellar Coffee House (apart from the three members of the midnight shift) had duty assignments beginning no later than 8 a.m. that morning. President Kennedy was scheduled to speak across the street from his hotel in Fort Worth at 8:30 a.m.,[194] and then at a breakfast, after which the entourage would proceed to Dallas. In Dallas, one of the nine agents was assigned to assist in security measures at Love Field, and four had protective assignments at the Trade Mart. The remaining four had key responsibilities as members of the complement of the followup car in the motorcade. Three of these agents occupied positions on the running boards of the car, and the fourth was seated in the car.[195]

The supervisor of each of the off-duty agents who visited the Press Club or the Cellar Coffee House advised, in the course of the Secret Service investigation of these events, that each agent reported for duty on time, with full possession of his mental and physical capabilities and entirely ready for the performance of his assigned duties.[196] Chief Rowley testified that, as a result of the investigation he ordered, he was satisfied that each of the agents performed his duties in an entirely satisfactory manner, and that their conduct the night before did not impede their actions on duty or in the slightest way prevent them from taking any action that might have averted the tragedy.[197] However, Chief Rowley did not condone the action of the off-duty agents, particularly since it violated a regulation of the Secret Service, which provides:

Liquor, use of.—a. Employees are strictly enjoined to refrain from the use of intoxicating liquor during the hours they are officially employed at their post of duty, or when they may reasonably expect that they may be called upon to perform an official duty. During entire periods of travel status, the special agent is officially employed and should not use liquor, until the completion of all of his official duties for the day, after which time a very moderate use of liquor will not be considered a violation. However, all members of the White House Detail and special agents cooperating with them on Presidential and similar protective assignments are considered to be subject to call for official duty at any time while in travel status. Therefore, the use of intoxicating liquor of any kind, including beer and wine, by members of the White House Detail and special agents cooperating with them, or by special agents on similar assignments, while they are in a travel status, is prohibited.[198]

The regulations provide further that "violation or slight disregard" of these provisions "will be cause for removal from the Service." [199]

Chief Rowley testified that under ordinary circumstances he would have taken disciplinary action against those agents who had been drinking in clear violation of the regulation. However, he felt that any disciplinary action might have given rise to an inference that the violation of the regulation had contributed to the tragic events of November 22. Since he was convinced that this was not the case, he believed that it would be unfair to the agents and their families to take explicit disciplinary measures. He felt that each agent recognized the seriousness of the infraction and that there was no danger of a repetition.[200]

The Commission recognizes that the responsibilities of members of the White House detail of the Secret Service are arduous. They work long, hard hours, under very great strain, and must travel frequently. It might seem harsh to circumscribe their opportunities for relaxation. Yet their role of protecting the President is so important to the well-being of the country that it is reasonable to expect them to meet very high standards of personal conduct, so that nothing can interfere with their bringing to their task the finest qualities and maximum resources of mind and body. This is the salutary goal to which the Secret Service regulation is directed, when it absolutely forbids drinking by any agent accompanying the President on a trip. Nor is this goal served when agents remain out until early morning hours, and lose the opportunity to get a reasonable amount of sleep. It is conceivable that those men who had little sleep, and who had consumed alcoholic beverages, even in limited quantities, might have been more alert in the Dallas motorcade if they had retired promptly in Fort Worth. However, there is no evidence that these men failed to take any action in Dallas within their power that would have averted the tragedy. As will be seen, the instantaneous and heroic response to the assassination of some of the agents concerned was in the finest tradition of Government service.

The motorcade in Dallas.—Rigorous security precautions had been arranged at Love Field with the local law enforcement authorities by Agents Sorrels and Lawson. These precautions included reserving a ceremonial area for the Presidential party, stationing police on the rooftops of all buildings overlooking the reception area, and detailing police in civilian clothes to be scattered throughout the sizable crowd.[201] When President and Mrs. Kennedy shook hands with members of the public along the fences surrounding the reception area, they were closely guarded by Secret Service agents who responded to the unplanned event with dispatch.[202]

As described in chapter II, the President directed that his car stop on two occasions during the motorcade so that he could greet members of the public.[203] At these stops, agents from the Presidential follow-up car stood between the President and the public, and on one occasion Agent Kellerman left the front seat of the President's car to take a similar position. The Commission regards such impromptu stops as presenting an unnecessary danger, but finds that the Secret Service agents did all that could have been done to take protective measures.

The Presidential limousine.—The limousine used by President Kennedy in Dallas was a convertible with a detachable, rigid plastic "bubble" top which was neither bulletproof nor bullet resistant.[204] The last Presidential vehicle with any protection against small-arms fire left the White House in 1953. It was not then replaced because the state of the art did not permit the development of a bulletproof top of sufficiently light weight to permit its removal on those occasions when the President wished to ride in an open car. The Secret Service believed that it was very doubtful that any President would ride regularly in a vehicle with a fixed top, even though transparent.[205] Since the assassination, the Secret Service, with the assistance of other Federal agencies and of private industry, has developed a vehicle for the better protection of the President.[206]

Access to passenger compartment of Presidential car.—On occasion the Secret Service has been permitted to have an agent riding in the passenger compartment with the President. Presidents have made it clear, however, that they did not favor this or any other arrangement which interferes with the privacy of the President and his guests. The Secret Service has therefore suggested this practice only on extraordinary occasions.[207] Without attempting to prescribe or recommend specific measures which should be employed for the future protection of Presidents, the Commission does believe that there are aspects of the protective measures employed in the motorcade at Dallas which deserve special comment.

The Presidential vehicle in use in Dallas, described in chapter II, had no special design or equipment which would have permitted the Secret Service agent riding in the driver's compartment to move into the passenger section without hindrance or delay. Had the vehicle been so designed it is possible that an agent riding in the front seat could have reached the President in time to protect him from the second and fatal shot to hit the President. However, such access to the President was interfered with both by the metal bar some 15 inches above the back of the front seat and by the passengers in the jump seats. In contrast, the Vice Presidential vehicle, although not specially designed for that purpose, had no passenger in a jump seat between Agent Youngblood and Vice President Johnson to interfere with Agent Youngblood's ability to take a protective position in the passenger compartment before the third shot was fired.[208]

The assassination suggests that it would have been of prime importance in the protection of the President if the Presidential car permitted immediate access to the President by a Secret Service agent at the first sign of danger. At that time the agents on the running boards of the followup car were expected to perform such a function. However, these agents could not reach the President's car when it was traveling at an appreciable rate of speed. Even if the car is traveling more slowly, the delay involved in reaching the President may be crucial. It is clear that at the time of the shots in Dallas, Agent Clinton J. Hill leaped to the President's rescue as quickly as humanly possible. Even so, analysis of the motion picture films taken by amateur photographer Zapruder reveals that Hill first placed his hand on the Presidential car at frame 343, 30 frames and therefore approximately 1.6 seconds after the President was shot in the head.[209] About 3.7 seconds after the President received this wound, Hill had both feet on the car and was climbing aboard to assist President and Mrs. Kennedy.[210]

Planning for motorcade contingencies.—In response to inquiry by the Commission regarding the instructions to agents in a motorcade of emergency procedures to be taken in a contingency such as that which actually occurred, the Secret Service responded:

> The Secret Service has consistently followed two general principles in emergencies involving the President. All agents are so instructed. The first duty of the agents in the motorcade is to attempt to cover the President as closely as possible and practicable and to shield him by attempting to place themselves between the President and any source of danger. Secondly, agents are instructed to remove the President as quickly as possible from known or impending danger. Agents are instructed that it is not their responsibility to investigate or evaluate a present danger, but to consider any untoward circumstances as serious and to afford the President maximum protection at all times. No responsibility rests upon those agents near the President for the identification or arrest of any assassin or an attacker. Their primary responsibility is to stay with and protect the President.
>
> Beyond these two principles the Secret Service believes a detailed contingency or emergency plan is not feasible because the variations possible preclude effective planning. A number of steps are taken, however, to permit appropriate steps to be taken

in an emergency. For instance, the lead car always is manned by Secret Service agents familiar with the area and with local law enforcement officials; the radio net in use in motorcades is elaborate and permits a number of different means of communication with various local points. A doctor is in the motorcade.[211]

This basic approach to the problem of planning for emergencies is sound. Any effort to prepare detailed contingency plans might well have the undesirable effect of inhibiting quick and imaginative responses. If the advance preparation is thorough, and the protective devices and techniques employed are sound, those in command should be able to direct the response appropriate to the emergency.

The Commission finds that the Secret Service agents in the motorcade who were immediately responsible for the President's safety reacted promptly at the time the shots were fired. Their actions demonstrate that the President and the Nation can expect courage and devotion to duty from the agents of the Secret Service.

RECOMMENDATIONS

The Commission's review of the provisions for Presidential protection at the time of President Kennedy's trip to Dallas demonstrates the need for substantial improvements. Since the assassination, the Secret Service and the Department of the Treasury have properly taken the initiative in reexamining major aspects of Presidential protection. Many changes have already been made and others are contemplated, some of them in response to the Commission's questions and informal suggestions.

Assassination a Federal Crime

There was no Federal criminal jurisdiction over the assassination of President Kennedy. Had there been reason to believe that the assassination was the result of a conspiracy, Federal jurisdiction could have been asserted; it has long been a Federal crime to conspire to injure any Federal officer, on account of, or while he is engaged in, the lawful discharge of the duties of his office.[212] Murder of the President has never been covered by Federal law, however, so that once it became reasonably clear that the killing was the act of a single person, the State of Texas had exclusive jurisdiction.

It is anomalous that Congress has legislated in other ways touching upon the safety of the Chief Executive or other Federal officers, without making an attack on the President a crime. Threatening harm to the President is a Federal offense,[213] as is advocacy of the overthrow of the Government by the assassination of any of its officers.[214] The murder of Federal judges, U.S. attorneys and marshals, and a number of other specifically designated Federal law enforcement officers is a Federal crime.[215] Equally anomalous are statutory provisions which specifically authorize the Secret Service to protect the President, without authorizing it to arrest anyone who harms him. The same provisions authorize the Service to arrest without warrant persons committing certain offenses, including counterfeiting and certain frauds involving Federal checks or securities.[216] The Commission agrees with the Secret Service [217] that it should be authorized to make arrests without warrant for all offenses within its jurisdiction, as are FBI agents and Federal marshals.[218]

There have been a number of efforts to make assassination a Federal crime, particularly after the assassination of President McKinley and the attempt on the life of President-elect Franklin D. Roosevelt.[219] In 1902 bills passed both Houses of Congress but failed of enactment when the Senate refused to accept the conference report.[220] A number of bills were introduced immediately following the assassination of President Kennedy.[221]

The Commission recommends to the Congress that it adopt legislation which would:

> Punish the murder or manslaughter of, attempt or conspiracy to murder, kidnaping of and assault upon
>
> the President, Vice President, or other officer next in the order of succession to the Office of President, the President-elect and the Vice-President-elect,
>
> whether or not the act is committed while the victim is in the performance of his official duties or on account of such performance.

Such a statute would cover the President and Vice President or, in the absence of a Vice President, the person next in order of succession. During the period between election and inauguration, the President-elect and Vice-President-elect would also be covered. Restricting the coverage in this way would avoid unnecessary controversy over the inclusion or exclusion of other officials who are in the order of succession or who hold important governmental posts. In addition, the restriction would probably eliminate a need for the requirement which has been urged as necessary for the exercise of Federal power, that the hostile act occur while the victim is engaged in or because of the performance of official duties.[222] The governmental consequences of assassination of one of the specified officials give the United States ample power to act for its own protection.[223] The activities of the victim at the time an assassination occurs and the motive for the assassination bear no relationship to the injury to the United States which follows from the act. This point was ably made in the 1902 debate by Senator George F. Hoar, the sponsor of the Senate bill:

> * * * what this bill means to punish is the crime of interruption of the Government of the United States and the destruction of its security by striking down the life of the person who is actually in the exercise of the executive power, or of such persons as have been

constitutionally and lawfully provided to succeed thereto in case of a vacancy. It is important to this country that the interruption shall not take place for an hour * * * [224]

Enactment of this statute would mean that the investigation of any of the acts covered and of the possibility of a further attempt would be conducted by Federal law enforcement officials, in particular, the FBI with the assistance of the Secret Service.[225] At present, Federal agencies participate only upon the sufferance of the local authorities. While the police work of the Dallas authorities in the early identification and apprehension of Oswald was both efficient and prompt, FBI Director J. Edgar Hoover, who strongly supports such legislation, testified that the absence of clear Federal jurisdiction over the assassination of President Kennedy led to embarrassment and confusion in the subsequent investigation by Federal and local authorities.[226] In addition, the proposed legislation will insure that any suspects who are arrested will be Federal prisoners, subject to Federal protection from vigilante justice and other threats.[227]

Committee of Cabinet Officers

As our Government has become more complex, agencies other than the Secret Service have become involved in phases of the overall problem of protecting our national leaders. The FBI is the major domestic investigating agency of the United States, while the CIA has the primary responsibility for collecting intelligence overseas to supplement information acquired by the Department of State. The Secret Service must rely in large part upon the investigating capacity and experience of these and other agencies for much of its information regarding possible dangers to the President. The Commission believes that it is necessary to improve the cooperation among these agencies and to emphasize that the task of Presidential protection is one of broad national concern.

The Commission suggests that consideration might be given to assigning to a Cabinet-level committee or the National Security Council (which is responsible for advising the President respecting the coordination of departmental policies relating to the national security)[228] the responsibility to review and oversee the protective activities of the Secret Service and the other Federal agencies that assist in safeguarding the President. The Committee should include the Secretary of the Treasury and the Attorney General, and, if the Council is used, arrangements should be made for the attendance of the Secretary of the Treasury and the Attorney General at any meetings which are concerned with Presidential protection.[229] The Council already includes, in addition to the President and Vice President, the Secretaries of State and Defense and has a competent staff.

The foremost assignment of the Committee would be to insure that the maximum resources of the Federal Government are fully engaged

456

in the job of protecting the President, by defining responsibilities clearly and overseeing their execution. Major needs of personnel or other resources might be met more easily on its recommendation than they have been in the past.

The Committee would be able to provide guidance in defining the general nature of domestic and foreign dangers to Presidential security. As improvements are recommended for the advance detection of potential threats to the President, it could act as a final review board. The expert assistance and resources which it could draw upon would be particularly desirable in this complex and sensitive area.

This arrangement would provide a continuing high-level contact for agencies that may wish to consult respecting particular protective measures. For various reasons the Secret Service has functioned largely as an informal part of the White House staff, with the result that it has been unable, as a practical matter, to exercise sufficient influence over the security precautions which surround Presidential activities. A Cabinet-level committee which is actively concerned with these problems would be able to discuss these matters more effectively with the President.

Responsibilities for Presidential Protection

The assignment of the responsibility of protecting the President to an agency of the Department of the Treasury was largely an historical accident.[230] The Secret Service was organized as a division of the Department of the Treasury in 1865, to deal with counterfeiting. In 1894, while investigating a plot to assassinate President Cleveland, the Service assigned a small protective detail of agents to the White House. Secret Service men accompanied the President and his family to their vacation home in Massachusetts and special details protected him in Washington, on trips, and at special functions. These informal and part-time arrangements led to more systematic protection in 1902, after the assassination of President McKinley; the Secret Service, then the only Federal investigative agency, assumed full-time responsibility for the safety of the President. Since that time, the Secret Service has had and exercised responsibility for the physical protection of the President and also for the preventive investigation of potential threats against the President.

Although the Secret Service has had the primary responsibility for the protection of the President, the FBI, which was established within the Department of Justice in 1908, has had in recent years an increasingly important role to play. In the appropriations of the FBI there has recurred annually an item for the "protection of the person of the President of the United States," which first appeared in the appropriation of the Department of Justice in 1910 under the heading "Miscellaneous Objects."[231] Although the FBI is not charged with the physical protection of the President, it does have an assignment, as do other Government agencies, in the field of preventive investigation in regard to the President's security. As discussed above, the Bureau has attempted to meet its responsibilities in this field by spelling out in its Handbook the procedures which its agents are to follow in connection with information received "indicating the possibility of an attempt against the person or safety of the President" or other protected persons.

With two Federal agencies operating in the same general field of preventive investigation, questions inevitably arise as to the scope of each agency's authority and responsibility. As the testimony of J. Edgar Hoover and other Bureau officials revealed, the FBI did not believe that its directive required the Bureau to notify the Secret Service of the substantial information about Lee Harvey Oswald which the FBI had accumulated before the President reached Dallas. On the other hand, the Secret Service had no knowledge whatever of Oswald, his background, or his employment at the Book Depository, and Robert I. Bouck, who was in charge of the Protective Research Section of the Secret Service, believed that the accumulation of the facts known to the FBI should have constituted a sufficient basis to warn the Secret Service of the Oswald risk.

The Commission believes that both the FBI and the Secret Service have too narrowly construed their respective responsibilities. The Commission has the impression that too much emphasis is placed by both on the investigation of specific threats by individuals and not enough on dangers from other sources. In addition, the Commission has concluded that the Secret Service particularly tends to be the passive recipient of information regarding such threats and that its Protective Research Section is not adequately staffed or equipped to conduct the wider investigative work that is required today for the security of the President.

During the period the Commission was giving thought to this situation, the Commission received a number of proposals designed to improve current arrangements for protecting the President. These proposals included suggestions to locate exclusive responsibility for all phases of the work in one or another Government agency, to clarify the division of authority between the agencies involved, and to retain the existing system but expand both the scope and the operations of the existing agencies, particularly those of the Secret Service and the FBI.

It has been pointed out that the FBI, as our chief investigative agency, is properly manned and equipped to carry on extensive information gathering functions within the United States. It was also suggested that it would take a substantial period of time for the Secret Service to build up the experience and skills necessary to meet the problem. Consequently the suggestion has been made, on the one hand, that all preventive investigative functions relating to the security of the President should be transferred to the FBI, leaving with the Secret Service only the responsibility for the physical protection of the President, that is, the guarding function alone.

On the other hand, it is urged that all features of the protection of the President and his family should be committed to an elite and independent corps. It is also contended that the agents should be intimately

458

associated with the life of the Presidential family in all its ramifications and alert to every danger that might befall it, and ready at any instant to hazard great danger to themselves in the performance of their tremendous responsibility. It is suggested that an organization shorn of its power to investigate all the possibilities of danger to the President and becoming merely the recipient of information gathered by others would become limited solely to acts of physical alertness and personal courage incident to its responsibilities. So circumscribed, it could not maintain the esprit de corps or the necessary alertness for this unique and challenging responsibility.

While in accordance with its mandate this Commission has necessarily examined into the functioning of the various Federal agencies concerned with the tragic trip of President Kennedy to Dallas and while it has arrived at certain conclusions in respect thereto, it seems clear that it was not within the Commission's responsibility to make specific recommendations as to the long-range organization of the President's protection, except as conclusions flowing directly from its examination of the President's assassination can be drawn. The Commission was not asked to apply itself as did the Hoover Commission in 1949, for example, to a determination of the optimum organization of the President's protection. It would have been necessary for the Commission to take considerable testimony, much of it extraneous to the facts of the assassination of President Kennedy, to put it in a position to reach final conclusions in this respect. There are always dangers of divided responsibility, duplication, and confusion of authority where more than one agency is operating in the same field; but on the other hand the protection of the President is in a real sense a Government-wide responsibility which must necessarily be assumed by the Department of State, the FBI, the CIA, and the military intelligence agencies as well as the Secret Service. Moreover, a number of imponderable questions have to be weighed if any change in the intimate association now established between the Secret Service and the President and his family is contemplated.

These considerations have induced the Commission to believe that the determination of whether or not there should be a relocation of responsibilities and functions should be left to the Executive and the Congress, perhaps upon recommendations based on further studies by the Cabinet-level committee recommended above or the National Security Council.

Pending any such determination, however, this Commission is convinced of the necessity of better coordination and direction of the activities of all existing agencies of Government which are in a position to, and do, furnish information and services related to the security of the President. The Commission feels the Secret Service and the FBI, as well as the State Department and the CIA when the President travels abroad, could improve their existing capacities and procedures so as to lessen the chances of assassination. Without, therefore, coming to final conclusions respecting the long-range organization of the President's security, the Commission believes that the facts of the assassination of President Kennedy point to certain measures which, while assuming no radical relocation of responsibilities, can and should be recommended by this Commission in the interest of the more efficient protection of the President. These recommendations are reviewed below.

General Supervision of the Secret Service

The intimacy of the Secret Service's relationship to the White House and the dissimilarity of its protective functions to most activities of the Department of the Treasury have made it difficult for the Treasury to maintain close and continuing supervision. The Commission believes that the recommended Cabinet-level committee will help to correct many of the major deficiencies of supervision disclosed by the Commission's investigation. Other measures should be taken as well to improve the overall operation of the Secret Service.

Daily supervision of the operations of the Secret Service within the Department of the Treasury should be improved. The Chief of the Service now reports to the Secretary of the Treasury through an Assistant Secretary whose duties also include the direct supervision of the Bureau of the Mint and the Department's Employment Policy Program, and who also represents the Secretary of the Treasury on various committees and groups.[232] The incumbent has no technical qualifications in the area of Presidential protection.[233] The Commission recommends that the Secretary of the Treasury appoint a special assistant with the responsibility of supervising the Service. This special assistant should be required to have sufficient stature and experience in law enforcement, intelligence, or allied fields to be able to provide effective continuing supervision, and to keep the Secretary fully informed regarding all significant developments relating to Presidential protection.

This report has already pointed out several respects in which the Commission believes that the Secret Service has operated with insufficient planning or control. Actions by the Service since the assassination indicate its awareness of the necessity for substantial improvement in its administration. A formal and thorough description of the responsibilities of the advance agent is now in preparation by the Service.[234] Work is going forward toward the preparation of formal understandings of the respective roles of the Secret Service and other agencies with which it collaborates or from which it derives assistance and support. The Commission urges that the Service continue this effort to overhaul and define its procedures. While manuals and memoranda are no guarantee of effective operations, no sizable organization can achieve efficiency without the careful analysis and demarcation of responsibility that is reflected in definite and comprehensive operating procedures.

The Commission also recommends that the Secret Service consciously set about the task of inculcating and maintaining the highest standard of excellence and esprit for all of its personnel. This involves tight and unswerving discipline as well as the promotion of an outstanding degree of dedication and loyalty to duty. The Commission emphasizes that it finds no causal connection between the assassination and the breach of regulations which occurred on the night of November 21 at Fort Worth. Nevertheless, such a breach, in which so many agents participated, is not consistent with the standards which the responsibilities of the Secret Service require it to meet.

Preventive Intelligence

In attempting to identify those individuals who might prove a danger to the President, the Secret Service has largely been the passive recipient of threatening communications to the President and reports from other agencies which independently evaluate their information for potential sources of danger. This was the consequence of the Service's lack of an adequate investigative staff, its inability to process large amounts of data, and its failure to provide specific descriptions of the kind of information it sought.[235]

The Secret Service has embarked upon a complete overhaul of its research activities.[236] The staff of the Protective Research Section (PRS) has been augmented, and a Secret Service inspector has been put in charge of this operation. With the assistance of the President's Office of Science and Technology, and of the Advanced Research Projects Agency of the Department of Defense, it has obtained the services of outside consultants, such as the Rand Corp., International Business Machines Corp., and a panel of psychiatric and psychological experts. It has received assistance also from data processing experts at the CIA and from a specialist in psychiatric prognostication at Walter Reed Hospital.[237] As a result of these studies, the planning document submitted by the Secretary of the Treasury to the Bureau of the Budget on August 31, 1964, makes several significant recommendations in this field.[238] Based on the Commission's investigation, the following minimum goals for improvements are indicated:

Broader and more selective criteria.—Since the assassination, both the Secret Service and the FBI have recognized that the PRS files can no longer be limited largely to persons communicating actual threats to the President. On December 26, 1963, the FBI circulated additional instructions to all its agents, specifying criteria for information to be furnished to the Secret Service in addition to that covered by the former standard, which was the possibility of an attempt against the person or safety of the President. The new instructions require FBI agents to report immediately information concerning:

> Subversives, ultrarightists, racists and fascists (a) possessing emotional instability or irrational behavior, (b) who have made threats of bodily harm against officials or employees of Federal, state or local government or officials of a foreign government, (c) who express or have expressed strong or violent anti-U.S. sentiments and who have been involved in bombing or bomb-making

461

or whose past conduct indicates tendencies toward violence, and (d) whose prior acts or statements depict propensity for violence and hatred against organized government.[239]

Alan H. Belmont, Assistant to the Director of the FBI, testified that this revision was initiated by the FBI itself.[240] The volume of references to the Secret Service has increased substantially since the new instructions went into effect; more than 5,000 names were referred to the Secret Service in the first 4 months of 1964.[241] According to Chief Rowley, by mid-June 1964, the Secret Service had received from the FBI some 9,000 reports on members of the Communist Party.[242] The FBI now transmits information on all defectors,[243] a category which would, of course, have included Oswald.

Both Director Hoover and Belmont expressed to the Commission the great concern of the FBI, which is shared by the Secret Service, that referrals to the Secret Service under the new criteria might, if not properly handled, result in some degree of interference with the personal liberty of those involved.[244] They emphasized the necessity that the information now being furnished be handled with judgment and care. The Commission shares this concern. The problem is aggravated by the necessity that the Service obtain the assistance of local law enforcement officials in evaluating the information which it receives and in taking preventive steps.

In June 1964, the Secret Service sent to a number of Federal law enforcement and intelligence agencies guidelines for an experimental program to develop more detailed criteria.[245] The suggestions of Federal agencies for revision of these guidelines were solicited. The new tentative criteria are useful in making clear that the interest of the Secret Service goes beyond information on individuals or groups threatening to cause harm or embarrassment to the President.[246] Information is requested also concerning individuals or groups who have demonstrated an interest in the President or "other high government officials in the nature of a complaint coupled with an expressed or implied determination to use a means, other than legal or peaceful, to satisfy any grievance, real or imagined." [247] Under these criteria, whether the case should be referred to the Secret Service depends on the existence of a previous history of mental instability, propensity toward violent action, or some similar characteristic, coupled with some evaluation of the capability of the individual or group to further the intention to satisfy a grievance by unlawful means.[248]

While these tentative criteria are a step in the right direction, they seem unduly restrictive in continuing to require some manifestation of animus against a Government official. It is questionable whether such criteria would have resulted in the referral of Oswald to the Secret Service. Chief Rowley believed that they would, because of Oswald's demonstrated hostility toward the Secretary of the Navy in his letter of January 30, 1962.[249]

I shall employ all means to right this gross mistake or injustice to a boni-fied U.S. citizen and ex-service man. The U.S. government has no charges or complaints against me. I ask you to look into this case and take the necessary steps to repair the damage done to me and my family.[250]

Even with the advantage of hindsight, this letter does not appear to express or imply Oswald's "determination to use a means, other than legal or peaceful, to satisfy [his] grievance" within the meaning of the new criteria.[251]

It is apparent that a good deal of further consideration and experimentation will be required before adequate criteria can be framed. The Commission recognizes that no set of meaningful criteria will yield the names of all potential assassins. Charles J. Guiteau, Leon F. Czolgosz, John Schrank, and Guiseppe Zangara—four assassins or would-be assassins—were all men who acted alone in their criminal acts against our leaders.[252] None had a serious record of prior violence. Each of them was a failure in his work and in his relations with others, a victim of delusions and fancies which led to the conviction that society and its leaders had combined to thwart him. It will require every available resource of our Government to devise a practical system which has any reasonable possibility of revealing such malcontents.

Liaison with other agencies regarding intelligence.—The Secret Service's liaison with the agencies that supply information to it has been too casual. Since the assassination, the Service has recognized that these relationships must be far more formal, and each agency given clear understanding of the assistance which the Secret Service expects.[253]

Once the Secret Service has formulated its new standards for collection of information, it should enter into written agreements with each Federal agency and the leading State and local agencies that might be a source of such information. Such agreements should describe in detail the information which is sought, the manner in which it will be provided to the Secret Service, and the respective responsibilities for any further investigation that may be required.

This is especially necessary with regard to the FBI and CIA, which carry the major responsibility for supplying information about potential threats, particularly those arising from organized groups, within their special jurisdiction. Since these agencies are already obliged constantly to evaluate the activities of such groups, they should be responsible for advising the Secret Service if information develops indicating the existence of an assassination plot and for reporting such events as a change in leadership or dogma which indicate that the group may present a danger to the President. Detailed formal agreements embodying these arrangements should be worked out between the Secret Service and both of these agencies.

It should be made clear that the Secret Service will in no way seek to duplicate the intelligence and investigative capabilities of the agencies now operating in this field but will continue to use the data developed by these agencies to carry out its special duties. Once experience has been gained in implementing such agreements with the Federal and leading State and local agencies, the Secret Service, through its field offices, should negotiate similar arrangements with such other State and local law enforcement agencies as may provide meaningful assistance. Much useful information will come to the attention of local law enforcement agencies in the regular course of their activities, and this source should not be neglected by undue concentration on relationships with other Federal agencies. Finally, these agreements with Federal and local authorities will be of little value unless a system is established for the frequent formal review of activities thereunder.

In this regard the Commission notes with approval several recent measures taken and proposed by the Secret Service to improve its liaison arrangements. In his testimony Secretary of the Treasury C. Douglas Dillon informed the Commission that an interagency committee has been established to develop more effective criteria. According to Secretary Dillon, the Committee will include representatives of the President's Office of Science and Technology, Department of Defense, CIA, FBI, and the Secret Service.[254] In addition, the Department of the Treasury has requested five additional agents for its Protective Research Section to serve as liaison officers with law enforcement and intelligence agencies.[255] On the basis of the Department's review during the past several months, Secretary Dillon testified that the use of such liaison officers is the only effective way to insure that adequate liaison is maintained.[256] As a beginning step to improve liaison with local law enforcement officials, the Secret Service on August 26, 1964, directed its field representatives to send a form request for intelligence information to all local, county, and State law enforcement agencies in their districts.[257] Each of these efforts appears sound, and the Commission recommends that these and the other measures suggested by the Commission be pursued vigorously by the Secret Service.

Automatic data processing.—Unless the Secret Service is able to deal rapidly and accurately with a growing body of data, the increased information supplied by other agencies will be wasted. PRS must develop the capacity to classify its subjects on a more sophisticated basis than the present geographic breakdown. Its present manual filing system is obsolete; it makes no use of the recent developments in automatic data processing which are widely used in the business world and in other Government offices.

The Secret Service and the Department of the Treasury now recognize this critical need. In the planning document currently under review by the Bureau of the Budget, the Department recommends that it be permitted to hire five qualified persons "to plan and develop a workable and efficient automated file and retrieval system." [258] Also the Department requests the sum of $100,000 to conduct a detailed feasibility study; this money would be used to compensate consultants, to lease standard equipment or to purchase specially designed pilot equipment.[259] On the basis of such a feasibility study, the Department hopes to design a practical system which will fully meet the needs of the Protective Research Section of the Secret Service.

The Commission recommends that prompt and favorable consideration be given to this request. The Commission further recommends that the Secret Service coordinate its planning as closely as possible with all of the Federal agencies from which it receives information. The Secret Service should not and does not plan to develop its own intelligence gathering facilities to duplicate the existing facilities of other Federal agencies. In planning its data processing techniques, the Secret Service should attempt to develop a system compatible with those of the agencies from which most of its data will come.*

Protective Research participation in advance arrangements.—Since the assassination, Secret Service procedures have been changed to require that a member of PRS accompany each advance survey team to establish liaison with local intelligence gathering agencies and to provide for the immediate evaluation of information received from them.[260] This PRS agent will also be responsible for establishing an informal local liaison committee to make certain that all protective intelligence activities are coordinated. Based on its experience during this period, the Secret Service now recommends that additional personnel be made available to PRS so that these arrangements can be made permanent without adversely affecting the operations of the Service's field offices.[261] The Commission regards this as a most useful innovation and urges that the practice be continued.

Liaison With Local Law Enforcement Agencies

Advice by the Secret Service to local police in metropolitan areas relating to the assistance expected in connection with a Presidential visit has hitherto been handled on an informal basis.[262] The Service should consider preparing formal explanations of the cooperation anticipated during a Presidential visit to a city, in formats that can be communicated to each level of local authorities. Thus, the local chief of police could be given a master plan, prepared for the occasion, of all protective measures to be taken during the visit; each patrolman might be given a prepared booklet of instructions explaining what is expected of him.

---

*In evaluating data processing techniques of the Secret Service, the Commission had occasion to become informed, to a limited extent, about the data processing techniques of other Federal intelligence and law enforcement agencies. The Commission was struck by the apparent lack of effort, on an interagency basis, to develop coordinated and mutually compatible systems, even where such coordination would not seem inconsistent with the particular purposes of the agency involved. The Commission recognizes that this is a controversial area and that many strongly held views are advanced in resistance to any suggestion that an effort be made to impose any degree of coordination. This matter is obviously beyond the jurisdiction of the Commission, but it seems to warrant further study before each agency becomes irrevocably committed to separate action. The Commission, therefore, recommends that the President consider ordering an inquiry into the possibility that coordination might be achieved to a greater extent than seems now to be contemplated, without interference with the primary mission of each agency involved.

The Secret Service has expressed concern that written instructions might come into the hands of local newspapers, to the prejudice of the precautions described.[263] However, the instructions must be communicated to the local police in any event and can be leaked to the press whether or not they are in writing. More importantly, the lack of carefully prepared and carefully transmitted instructions for typical visits to cities can lead to lapses in protection, such as the confusion in Dallas about whether members of the public were permitted on overpasses.[264] Such instructions will not fit all circumstances, of course, and should not be relied upon to the detriment of the imaginative application of judgment in special cases.

Inspection of Buildings

Since the assassination of President Kennedy, the Secret Service has been experimenting with new techniques in the inspection of buildings along a motorcade route.[265] According to Secretary Dillon, the studies indicate that there is some utility in attempting to designate certain buildings as involving a higher risk than others.[266] The Commission strongly encourages these efforts to improve protection along a motorcade route. The Secret Service should utilize the personnel of other Federal law enforcement offices in the locality to assure adequate manpower for this task, as it is now doing.[267] Lack of adequate resources is an unacceptable excuse for failing to improve advance precautions in this crucial area of Presidential protection.

Secret Service Personnel and Facilities

Testimony and other evidence before the Commission suggest that the Secret Service is trying to accomplish its job with too few people and without adequate modern equipment. Although Chief Rowley does not complain about the pay scale for Secret Service agents, salaries are below those of the FBI and leading municipal police forces.[268] The assistant to the Director of the FBI testified that the caseload of each FBI agent averaged 20–25, and he felt that this was high.[269] Chief Rowley testified that the present workload of each Secret Service agent averages 110.1 cases.[270] While these statistics relate to the activities of Secret Service agents stationed in field offices and not the White House detail, field agents supplement those on the detail, particularly when the President is traveling. Although the Commission does not know whether the cases involved are entirely comparable, these figures suggest that the agents of the Secret Service are substantially overworked.

In its budget request for the fiscal year beginning July 1, 1964, the Secret Service sought funds for 25 new positions, primarily in field offices.[271] This increase has been approved by the Congress.[272] Chief Rowley explained that this would not provide enough additional manpower to take all the measures which he considers required. However, the 1964–65 budget request was submitted in November 1963 and requests for additional personnel were not made because of the studies then being conducted.[273]

The Secret Service has now presented its recommendations to the Bureau of the Budget.[274] The plan proposed by the Service would take approximately 20 months to implement and require expenditures of approximately $3 million during that period. The plan provides for an additional 205 agents for the Secret Service. Seventeen of this number are proposed for the Protective Research Section; 145 are proposed for the field offices to handle the increased volume of security investigations and be available to protect the President or Vice President when they travel; 18 agents are proposed for a rotating pool which will go through an intensive training cycle and also be available to supplement the White House detail in case of unexpected need; and 25 additional agents are recommended to provide the Vice President full protection.

The Commission urges that the Bureau of the Budget review these recommendations with the Secret Service and authorize a request for the necessary supplemental appropriation, as soon as it can be justified. The Congress has often stressed that it will support any reasonable request for funds for the protection of the President.[275]

Manpower and Technical Assistance From Other Agencies

Before the assassination the Secret Service infrequently requested other Federal law enforcement agencies to provide personnel to assist in its protection functions.[276] Since the assassination, the Service has experimented with the use of agents borrowed for short periods from such agencies. It has used other Treasury law enforcement agents on special experiments in building and route surveys in places to which the President frequently travels.[277] It has also used other Federal law enforcement agents during Presidential visits to cities in which such agents are stationed. Thus, in the 4 months following the assassination, the FBI, on 16 separate occasions, supplied a total of 139 agents to assist in protection work during a Presidential visit,[278] which represents a departure from its prior practice.[279] From February 11 through June 30, 1964, the Service had the advantage of 9,500 hours of work by other enforcement agencies.[280]

The FBI has indicated that it is willing to continue to make such assistance available, even though it agrees with the Secret Service that it is preferable for the Service to have enough agents to handle all protective demands.[281] The Commission endorses these efforts to supplement the Service's own personnel by obtaining, for short periods of time, the assistance of trained Federal law enforcement officers. In view of the ever-increasing mobility of American Presidents, it seems unlikely that the Service could or should increase its own staff to a size which would permit it to provide adequate protective manpower for all situations. The Commission recommends that the agencies involved determine how much periodic assistance they can provide, and that each such agency and the Secret Service enter into a formal

467

agreement defining such arrangements. It may eventually be desirable to codify the practice in an Executive order. The Secret Service will be better able to plan its own long-range personnel requirements if it knows with reasonable certainty the amount of assistance that it can expect from other agencies.

The occasional use of personnel from other Federal agencies to assist in protecting the President has a further advantage. It symbolizes the reality that the job of protecting the President has not been and cannot be exclusively the responsibility of the Secret Service. The Secret Service in the past has sometimes guarded its right to be acknowledged as the sole protector of the Chief Executive. This no longer appears to be the case.[282] Protecting the President is a difficult and complex task which requires full use of the best resources of many parts of our Government. Recognition that the responsibility must be shared increases the likelihood that it will be met.

Much of the Secret Service work requires the development and use of highly sophisticated equipment, some of which must be specially designed to fit unique requirements. Even before the assassination, and to a far greater extent thereafter, the Secret Service has been receiving full cooperation in scientific research and technological development from many Government agencies including the Department of Defense and the President's Office of Science and Technology.[283]

Even if the manpower and technological resources of the Secret Service are adequately augmented, it will continue to rely in many respects upon the greater resources of the Office of Science and Technology and other agencies. The Commission recommends that the present arrangements with the Office of Science and Technology and the other Federal agencies that have been so helpful to the Secret Service be placed on a permanent and formal basis. The exchange of letters dated August 31, 1964, between Secretary Dillon and Donald F. Hornig, Special Assistant to the President for Science and Technology, is a useful effort in the right direction.[284] The Service should negotiate a memorandum of understanding with each agency that has been assisting it and from which it can expect to need help in the future. The essential terms of such memoranda might well be embodied in an Executive order.

CONCLUSION

This Commission can recommend no procedures for the future protection of our Presidents which will guarantee security. The demands on the President in the execution of his responsibilities in today's world are so varied and complex and the traditions of the office in a democracy such as ours are so deepseated as to preclude absolute security.

The Commission has, however, from its examination of the facts of President Kennedy's assassination made certain recommendations which it believes would, if adopted, materially improve upon the procedures in effect at the time of President Kennedy's assassination and result in a substantial lessening of the danger.

As has been pointed out, the Commission has not resolved all the proposals which could be made. The Commission nevertheless is confident that, with the active cooperation of the responsible agencies and with the understanding of the people of the United States in their demands upon their President, the recommendations we have here suggested would greatly advance the security of the office without any impairment of our fundamental liberties.

APPENDIX I

IMMEDIATE RELEASE   NOVEMBER 30, 1963

Office of the White House Press Secretary

- -

THE WHITE HOUSE

EXECUTIVE ORDER
NO. 11130
- - - -

APPOINTING A COMMISSION TO REPORT UPON THE
ASSASSINATION OF PRESIDENT JOHN F. KENNEDY

Pursuant to the authority vested in me as President of the United States, I hereby appoint a Commission to ascertain, evaluate and report upon the facts relating to the assassination of the late President John F. Kennedy and the subsequent violent death of the man charged with the assassination. The Commission shall consist of --

The Chief Justice of the United States, Chairman;

Senator Richard B. Russell;

Senator John Sherman Cooper;

Congressman Hale Boggs;

Congressman Gerald R. Ford;

The Honorable Allen W. Dulles;

The Honorable John J. McCloy.

The purposes of the Commission are to examine the evidence developed by the Federal Bureau of Investigation and any additional evidence that may hereafter come to light or be uncovered by federal or state authorities; to make such further investigation as the Commission finds desirable; to evaluate all the facts and circumstances surrounding such assassination, including the subsequent violent death of the man charged with the assassination, and to report to me its findings and conclusions.

The Commission is empowered to prescribe its own procedures and to employ such assistants as it deems necessary.

Necessary expenses of the Commission may be paid from the "Emergency Fund for the President".

All Executive departments and agencies are directed to furnish the Commission with such facilities, services and cooperation as it may request from time to time.

                                    LYNDON B. JOHNSON

THE WHITE HOUSE,

     November 29, 1963.

                        # # #

APPENDIX II

IMMEDIATE RELEASE   November 29, 1963

Office of the White House Press Secretary

- -

THE WHITE HOUSE

The President today announced that he is appointing a Special Commission to study and report upon all facts and circumstances relating to the assassination of the late President, John F. Kennedy, and the subsequent violent death of the man charged with the assassination.

The President stated that the Majority and Minority Leadership of the Senate and the House of Representatives have been consulted with respect to the proposed Special Commission.

The members of the Special Commission are:

> Chief Justice Earl Warren, Chairman
> Senator Richard Russell (Georgia)
> Senator John Sherman Cooper (Kentucky)
> Representative Hale Boggs (Louisiana)
> Representative Gerald Ford (Michigan)
> Hon. Allen W. Dulles of Washington
> Hon. John J. McCloy of New York

The President stated that the Special Commission is to be instructed to evaluate all available information concerning the subject of the inquiry. The Federal Bureau of Investigation, pursuant to an earlier directive of the President, is making complete investigation of the facts. An inquiry is also scheduled by a Texas Court of Inquiry convened by the Attorney General of Texas under Texas law.

The Special Commission will have before it all evidence uncovered by the Federal Bureau of Investigation and all information available to any agency of the Federal Government. The Attorney General of Texas has also offered his cooperation. All Federal agencies and offices are being directed to furnish services and cooperation to the Special Commission. The Commission will also be empowered to conduct any further investigation that it deems desirable.

The President is instructing the Special Commission to satisfy itself that the truth is known as far as it can be discovered, and to report its findings and conclusions to him, to the American people, and to the world.

# # # # #

APPENDIX III

Public Law 88-202
88th Congress, S. J. Res. 137
December 13, 1963

Joint Resolution

Authorizing the Commission established to report upon the assassination of President John F. Kennedy to compel the attendance and testimony of witnesses and the production of evidence.

Resolved by the Senate and House of Representatives of the United States of America in Congress assembled, That (a) for the purposes of this joint resolution, the term "Commission" means the Commission appointed by the President by Executive Order 11130, dated November 29, 1963.

(b) The Commission, or any member of the Commission when so authorized by the Commission, shall have power to issue subpenas requiring the attendance and testimony of witnesses and the production of any evidence that relates to any matter under investigation by the Commission. The Commission, or any member of the Commission or any agent or agency designated by the Commission for such purpose, may administer oaths and affirmations, examine witnesses, and receive evidence. Such attendance of witnesses and the production of such evidence may be required from any place within the United States at any designated place of hearing.

(c) In case of contumacy or refusal to obey a subpena issued to any person under subsection (b), any court of the United States within the jurisdiction of which the inquiry is carried on or within the jurisdiction of which said person guilty of contumacy or refusal to obey is found or resides or transacts business, upon application by the Commission shall have jurisdiction to issue to such person an order requiring such person to appear before the Commission, its member, agent, or agency, there to produce evidence if so ordered, or there to give testimony touching the matter under investigation or in question; and any failure to obey such order of the court may be punished by said court as a contempt thereof.

(d) Process and papers of the Commission, its members, agent, or agency, may be served either upon the witness in person or by registered mail or by telegraph or by leaving a copy thereof at the residence or principal office or place of business of the person required to be served. The verified return by the individual so serving the same, setting forth the manner of such service, shall be proof of the same, and the return post office receipt or telegraph receipt therefor when registered and mailed or telegraphed as aforesaid shall be proof of service of the same. Witnesses summoned before the Commission, its members, agent, or agency, shall be paid the same fees and mileage that are paid witnesses in the courts of the United States, and witnesses whose depositions are taken and the persons taking the same shall severally be entitled to the same fees as are paid for like services in the courts of the United States.

(e) No person shall be excused from attending and testifying or from producing books, records, correspondence, documents, or other evidence in obedience to a subpena, on the ground that the testimony or evidence required of him may tend to incriminate him or subject him to a penalty or forfeiture; but no individual shall be prosecuted or subjected to any penalty or forfeiture (except demotion or removal from office) for or on account of any transaction, matter, or thing concerning which he is compelled, after having claimed his privilege

Marginal notes:
Commission investigating assassination of President John F. Kennedy.
Subpena power.
28 F.R. 12789.

Manner of service.

77 STAT. 362.
77 STAT. 363.

Privilege against self-incrimination.

473

against self-incrimination, to testify or produce evidence, except that such individual so testifying shall not be exempt from prosecution and punishment for perjury committed in so testifying.

Place of service.

(f) All process of any court to which application may be made under this Act may be served in the judicial district wherein the person required to be served resides or may be found.

Approved December 13, 1963.

LEGISLATIVE HISTORY:

CONGRESSIONAL RECORD, Vol. 109 (1963):
   Dec. 9: Passed Senate.
   Dec. 10: Considered and passed House.

Biographical Information and Acknowledgments

MEMBERS OF COMMISSION

The Honorable Earl Warren, Chief Justice of the United States, was born in Los Angeles, Calif., on March 19, 1891. He graduated from the University of California with B.L. and J.D. degrees, and was admitted to the California bar in 1914. Chief Justice Warren was attorney general of California from 1939 to 1943. From 1943 to 1953 he was Governor of California and in September 1953 was appointed by President Eisenhower to be the Chief Justice of the United States.

The Honorable Richard B. Russell was born in Winder, Ga., on November 2, 1897. He received his B.L. degree from the University of Georgia in 1918 and his LL.B. from Mercer University in 1957. Senator Russell commenced the practice of law in Winder, Ga., in 1918, became county attorney for Barrow County, Ga., and was a member of the Georgia House of Representatives from 1921 to 1931. He was Governor of Georgia from 1931 to 1933, was elected to the U.S. Senate in January 1933 to fill a vacancy, and has been Senator from Georgia continuously since that date.

The Honorable John Sherman Cooper was born in Somerset, Ky., on August 23, 1901. He attended Centre College, Kentucky, received his A.B. degree from Yale College in 1923, and attended Harvard Law School from 1923 to 1925. Senator Cooper has been a member of the House of Representatives of the Kentucky General Assembly, a county judge and circuit judge in Kentucky, and is now a member of the U.S. Senate, where he has served, though not continuously, for 12 years. He was a delegate to the Fifth, Sixth, and Seventh Sessions of the General Assembly of the United Nations, an advisor to the Secretary of State in 1950 at meetings of the North Atlantic Treaty Organization, and Ambassador to India and Nepal in 1955–56. He served in the 3d U.S. Army in World War II in Europe, and after the war headed the reorganization of the German judicial system in Bavaria.

The Honorable Hale Boggs was born in Long Beach, Miss., on February 15, 1914. He graduated from Tulane University with a B.A. degree in 1935 and received his LL.B. in 1937. He was admitted to the Louisiana bar in 1937 and practiced law in New Orleans. Representative Boggs was elected to the 77th Congress of the United States and in World War II was an officer of the U.S. Naval Reserve and of the Maritime Service. He has been a Member of Congress since 1946 when he was elected to represent the Second District, State of Louisiana, in the 80th Congress, and he is currently the majority whip for the Democratic Party in the House of Representatives.

The Honorable Gerald R. Ford was born in Omaha, Nebr., on July 14, 1913. He graduated from the University of Michigan with a B.A. degree in 1935 and from Yale University Law School with an LL.B. degree in 1941. Representative Ford was admitted to the Michigan bar in 1941. He was first elected to Congress in 1948 and has been reelected to each succeeding Congress. He served 47 months in the U.S. Navy during World War II. Representative Ford was elected in January 1963 the chairman of the House Republican Conference.

The Honorable Allen W. Dulles was born in Watertown, N.Y., on April 7, 1893. He received his B.A. degree from Princeton in 1914, his M.A. in 1916, his LL.B. from George Washington University in 1926, and LL.D. degrees. Mr. Dulles entered the diplomatic service of the United States in 1916 and resigned in 1926 to take up law practice in New York City. In 1953 Mr. Dulles was appointed Director of Central Intelligence and served in that capacity until 1961.

The Honorable John J. McCloy was born in Philadelphia, Pa., on March 31, 1895. He received an A.B. degree, cum laude, from Amherst College in 1916; LL.B. from Harvard, and LL.D. from Amherst College. He was admitted to the New York bar in 1921 and is now a member of the firm of Milbank, Tweed, Hadley & McCloy. He was Assistant Secretary of War from April 1941 to November 1945. Mr. McCloy was President of the World Bank from 1947 to 1949 and U.S. Military Governor and High Commissioner for Germany from 1949 to 1952. He has been coordinator of U.S. disarmament activities since 1961.

GENERAL COUNSEL

J. Lee Rankin was born in Hartington, Nebr., on July 8, 1907. He received his A.B. degree from the University of Nebraska in 1928 and his LL.B. in 1930 from the University of Nebraska Law School. He was admitted to the Nebraska bar in 1930 and practiced law in Lincoln, Nebr., until January 1953 when he was appointed by President Eisenhower to be the assistant attorney general in charge of the Office of Legal Counsel in the Department of Justice. In August 1956 President Eisenhower appointed Mr. Rankin to be the Solicitor General of the United States. Since January 1961 Mr. Rankin has been in private practice in New York City. He accepted the appointment as General Counsel for the President's Commission on the Assassination of President Kennedy on December 8, 1963.

ASSISTANT COUNSEL

Francis W. H. Adams was born in Mount Vernon, N.Y., on June 26, 1904. He graduated from Williams College with an A.B. degree, and received his LL.B. degree from Fordham Law School in 1928. Mr. Adams has acted as chief assistant U.S. attorney in New York, special assistant to the U.S. Attorney General, and as an arbitrator for the War Labor Board. In 1954 and 1955 he served as police commissioner of New York City. Mr. Adams is a member of the New York and Washington law firm of Satterlee, Warfield & Stephens.

Joseph A. Ball was born in Stuart, Iowa, on December 16, 1902. He received his B.A. degree from Creighton University in Omaha, Nebr., and his LL.B. degree from the University of Southern California in 1927. Mr. Ball teaches criminal law and procedure at the University of Southern California. He is a member of the U.S. Judicial Conference Advisory Committee on Federal Rules of Criminal Procedure. Mr. Ball is a member of the firm of Ball, Hunt & Hart, Long Beach and Santa Ana, Calif.

David W. Belin was born in Washington, D.C., on June 20, 1928. He is a graduate of the University of Michigan, where he earned three degrees with high distinction: A.B. (1951), M. Bus. Adm. (1953), and J.D. (1954). At the University of Michigan he was associate editor of the Michigan Law Review. He is a member of Phi Beta Kappa and the Order of the Coif. He is a member of the law firm of Herrick, Langdon, Sandblom & Belin, Des Moines, Iowa.

William T. Coleman, Jr., was born in Germantown, Philadelphia, Pa., on July 7, 1920. He graduated from the University of Pennsylvania in 1941 with an A.B. degree, summa cum laude, received his LL.B. in 1946, magna cum laude, from Harvard Law School and served as an editor of the Harvard Law Review. From 1947 to 1948 he served as law clerk to Judge Herbert F. Goodrich, U.S. Court of Appeals for the Third Circuit, and during the 1948–49 term of the U.S. Supreme Court, as law clerk to Justice Felix Frankfurter. Mr. Coleman has served as a special counsel for the city of Philadelphia and has been a consultant with the U.S. Arms Control and Disarmament Agency since January 1963. He is a member of the law firm of Dilworth, Paxson, Kalish, Kohn & Dilks, Philadelphia, Pa.

Melvin A. Eisenberg was born in New York City on December 3, 1934. He was graduated from Columbia College, A.B., summa cum laude, in 1956, and from Harvard Law School, LL.B., summa cum laude, in 1959. Mr. Eisenberg is a member of Phi Beta Kappa, and served as an editor of the Harvard Law Review. He is associated with the law firm of Kaye, Scholer, Fierman, Hays & Handler in New York City.

Burt W. Griffin was born in Cleveland, Ohio, on August 19, 1932. He received his B.A. degree, cum laude, from Amherst College in 1954, and LL.B. from Yale University Law School in 1959. He was note and comment editor of the Yale Law Journal. During 1959–60 Mr. Griffin served as law clerk to Judge George T. Washington of the U.S. Court of Appeals for the District of Columbia Circuit. From 1960 to 1962 Mr. Griffin was an assistant U.S. attorney for the northern district of Ohio, and since 1962 he has been associated with the firm of MacDonald, Hopkins & Hardy, Cleveland, Ohio.

Leon D. Hubert, Jr., was born in New Orleans, La., July 1, 1911. He received his A.B. degree from Tulane University in 1932, and

LL.B. from Tulane in 1934. He was associate editor of the Tulane Law Review, and a member of Phi Beta Kappa and the Order of the Coif. Mr. Hubert was assistant U.S. attorney for the eastern district of Louisiana, 1934–46, and a professor of law at Tulane University, 1942–60. He has worked with the Louisiana State Law Institute on the revision of statutes and on the codes of civil and criminal procedure. Mr. Hubert is a member of the law firm of Hubert, Baldwin & Zibilich, New Orleans, La.

Albert E. Jenner, Jr., was born in Chicago, Ill., on June 20, 1907. He received his law degree from the University of Illinois in 1930. He is a member of the Order of the Coif. In 1956 and 1957 Mr. Jenner served as a special assistant attorney general of Illinois in the investigation of fraud in the office of the auditor of public accounts of the State of Illinois. Mr. Jenner is a Commissioner on Uniform State Laws, a member of the U.S. Judicial Conference Advisory Committee on Federal Rules of Civil Procedure and vice chairman of the Joint Committee for the Effective Administration of Justice. He is a former professor of law at the Northwestern University School of Law. Mr. Jenner is a member of the law firm of Raymond, Mayer, Jenner & Block, Chicago, Ill.

Wesley J. Liebeler was born in Langdon, N. Dak., on May 9, 1931. He received his B.A. degree from Macalester College, St. Paul, Minn., in 1953 and graduated, cum laude, from the University of Chicago Law School in 1957. He was a managing editor of the University of Chicago Law Review and is a member of the Order of the Coif. Mr. Liebeler is associated with the law firm of Carter, Ledyard & Milburn, New York City.

Norman Redlich was born in New York City on November 12, 1925. He received his B.A. degree, magna cum laude, from Williams College in 1947, his LL.B., cum laude, from Yale Law School in 1950, and LL.M. (Taxation) in 1955 from the New York University School of Law. He is a member of Phi Beta Kappa and the Order of the Coif, and was executive editor of the Yale Law Journal. Mr. Redlich is Professor of Law at the New York University School of Law, and is editor in chief of the Tax Law Review, New York University.

W. David Slawson was born in, Grand Rapids, Mich., on June 2, 1931. He received his A.B. degree, summa cum laude, from Amherst College in 1953, and M.A. from Princeton University in 1954. Mr. Slawson received his LL.B., magna cum laude, from Harvard University in 1959. He is a member of Phi Beta Kappa and was a note editor of the Harvard Law Review. Mr. Slawson is a member of the law firm of Davis, Graham & Stubbs, Denver, Colo.

Arlen Specter was born in Wichita, Kans., on February 12, 1930. He received his B.A. degree from the University of Pennsylvania in 1951, where he was a member of Phi Beta Kappa, and received his LL.B. from Yale Law School in 1956. He was an editor of the Yale Law Journal. Mr. Specter was an associate of the law firm of Dechert, Price & Rhoads in Philadelphia from 1956 to 1959, and from 1959 to 1964 he was an assistant in the Philadelphia district attorney's office. Mr. Specter is a member of the firm of Specter & Katz, Philadelphia, Pa.

Samuel A. Stern was born in Philadelphia, Pa., on January 21, 1929. He graduated with honors from the University of Pennsylvania with an A.B. in 1949. In 1952 he received his LL.B., magna cum laude, from Harvard Law School, and was developments editor of the Harvard Law Review. Mr. Stern served as law clerk to Chief Judge Calvert Magruder, U.S. Court of Appeals for the First Circuit, during 1954–55 and was law clerk to Chief Justice Earl Warren during 1955–56. He is a member of the law firm of Wilmer, Cutler & Pickering, Washington, D.C.

Howard P. Willens was born in Oak Park, Ill., on May 27, 1931. He received his B.A. degree, with high distinction, from the University of Michigan in 1953 and his LL.B. from Yale Law School in 1956. Mr. Willens is a member of Phi Beta Kappa and was an editor of the Yale Law Journal. He was associated with the law firm of Kirkland, Ellis, Hodson, Chaffetz & Masters, Washington, D.C., until 1961, when he was appointed Second Assistant in the Criminal Division of the U.S. Department of Justice.

STAFF MEMBERS

Philip Barson was born in Philadelphia, Pa., on May 2, 1912. He received his Bachelor of Science of Commerce, from Temple University, Philadelphia, in 1934. Mr. Barson has been employed by the Internal Revenue Service, Intelligence Division, Philadelphia, since September 1948, first as a special agent and since 1961 has been group supervisor. Mr. Barson is a certified public accountant from the Commonwealth of Pennsylvania.

Edward A. Conroy was born in Albany, N.Y., on March 20, 1920. He attended Brooklyn Polytechnical Institute and Benjamin Franklin University, Washington, D.C. Mr. Conroy joined the Internal Revenue Service as a revenue officer in 1946. After acting as executive assistant to the assistant regional inspector, Boston, Mass., Mr. Conroy became senior inspector in the Planning and Programing Branch of the Internal Security Division, Inspection, of the Internal Revenue Service. He currently occupies that position.

John Hart Ely was born in New York City on December 3, 1938. He graduated, summa cum laude, from Princeton University in 1960, and from Yale Law School, magna cum laude, in 1963. He was note and comment editor of the Yale Law Journal. He is a member of the Phi Beta Kappa and the Order of the Coif. During the 1964–65 term Mr. Ely will serve as law clerk to Chief Justice Warren.

Alfred Goldberg was born in Baltimore, Md., on December 23, 1918. He received his A.B. degree from Western Maryland College in 1938, and his Ph. D. from the Johns Hopkins University in 1950. After 4 years' service with the U.S. Army, Dr. Goldberg became historian with the U.S. Air Force Historical Division and later Chief of the Current History Branch. In 1962–63 he was a visiting American fellow, King's College, University of London, and since his return has been senior historian, U.S. Air Force Historical Division. Dr. Goldberg is the author or editor of several publications on historical subjects and is a contributor to Encyclopedia Britannica and the World Book.

Murray J. Laulicht was born in Brooklyn, N.Y., on May 12, 1940. He received his B.A. in 1961 from Yeshiva College, and received his LL.B. degree, summa cum laude, from Columbia University School of Law in 1964. He was notes and comments editor of the Columbia Law Review. During 1964–65 Mr. Laulicht will clerk for Senior Judge Harold R. Medina of the U.S. Court of Appeals for the Second Circuit.

Arthur K. Marmor was born in New York City on December 5, 1915. He received a B.S.S. degree from the College of the City of New York in 1937 and an A.M. degree from Columbia University in 1940. He served in the U.S. Army in World War II. Mr. Marmor has been historian for the Departments of Interior, Army, and Air Force, and Chief, Editorial Services Branch, Department of State. He has also taught for the American University and the University of Maryland. Mr. Marmor has contributed to numerous Government publications and has been in charge of the editing of historical and legal volumes. At present he is a historian for the Department of the Air Force.

Richard M. Mosk was born in Los Angeles, Calif., on May 18, 1939. He graduated from Stanford University, with great distinction, in 1960 and from Harvard Law School, cum laude, in 1963. Mr. Mosk is a member of Phi Beta Kappa. During the 1964–65 term of the California Supreme Court Mr. Mosk will clerk for Justice Mathew Tobriner.

John J. O'Brien was born in Somerville, Mass., on September 11, 1919. Mr. O'Brien received his B.B.A. degree in law and business, cum laude, from Northeastern University, Boston, Mass. He re-received his M.A. degree in the field of governmental administration from George Washington University, Washington, D.C., and in 1941 joined the Bureau of Internal Revenue. After service in the U.S. Coast Guard, Mr. O'Brien resumed his work as an Internal Revenue Service investigator, and is currently the Assistant Chief of the Inspection Services Investigations Branch, in the National Office of Internal Revenue.

Stuart R. Pollak was born in San Pedro, Calif., on August 24, 1937. He received his B.A. degree from Stanford University, with great distinction, in 1959, and was a member of Phi Beta Kappa. Mr. Pollak obtained his LL.B., magna cum laude, from Harvard Law School in 1962, where he was book review and legislation editor of the Harvard Law Review. During the 1963–64 term Mr. Pollak was law clerk to Justices Stanley Reed and Harold Burton. Mr. Pollak is a staff assistant in the Criminal Division of the U.S. Department of Justice.

Alfredda Scobey was born in Kankakee, Ill. She received her A.B. degree from American University, Washington, D.C., in 1933, studied law at John Marshall Law School, Atlanta, Ga., and was admitted to the Georgia bar in 1945. Miss Scobey did graduate study at the National University of Mexïco, at Duke University, and at Emory University, Atlanta. She practiced law from 1945 to 1949 in Atlanta and since 1949 has been a law assistant in the Court of Appeals, Georgia.

Charles N. Shaffer, Jr., was born in New York City on June 8, 1932. He attended Fordham College in 1951 and received his LL.B. from the Fordham University School of Law in 1957. From 1958 to 1959 Mr. Shaffer was associated with the law firm of Chadburn, Parke, Whiteside & Wolff, New York City. He was assistant U.S. attorney in the southern district of New York from 1959 to 1961, when he was appointed Special Trial Attorney in the Criminal and Tax Divisions of the U.S. Department of Justice, Washington, D.C.

Lloyd L. Weinreb was born in New York City on October 9, 1936. He received B.A. degrees from Dartmouth College, summa cum laude, in 1957, and from the University of Oxford in 1959. He received his LL.B., magna cum laude, from Harvard Law School in 1962. He was case editor of the Harvard Law Review. During the 1963–64 term Mr. Weinreb was law clerk to Justice John M. Harlan. Mr. Weinreb is a staff assistant in the Criminal Division of the U.S. Department of Justice.

Acknowledgments

During the taking of testimony in various parts of the United States, the Commission was greatly assisted by the offices of numerous U.S. attorneys of the Department of Justice. The Commission would like to acknowledge its gratitude for this assistance and thank in particular Harold Barefoot Sanders, Jr., U.S. attorney for the northern district of Texas, and his conscientious assistant, Martha Joe Stroud.

In addition the Commission wishes to thank the following lawyers, secretaries, and clerks for their unstinting efforts on behalf of the Commission:

Sheila Adams	Paul Dodyk
Stephen R. Barnett	Charlee Dianne Duke
Thomas D. Barr	Julia T. Eide
Miriam A. Bottum	Josephine M. Farrar
Stephen G. Breyer	William T. Finley, Jr.
Patrick O. Burns	Dennis M. Flannery
Charlene Chardwell	James C. Gaither
Anne M. Clark	Stephen R. Goldstein
Jonathan M. Clark	Patricia E. Gormley
George C. Cochran	Jeanne C. Hauer
Betty Jean Compton	Beverly A. Heckman
Francine Davis	Sadie M. Hennigan
Viola C. Davis	Lela B. Hewlett

Elaine Johnson
Vivian Johnson
Pearl G. Kamber
Sharon Kegarise
Adele W. Lippard
David T. Luhm
Ella M. McCall
Louise S. McKenzie
Michael W. Maupin
Jean H. Millard
Seresa Mintor
Maurice Moore
Mary L. Norton
Vaughnie Perry
Jane W. Peter
Edward R. Pierpoint

James H. Pipkin, Jr.
S. Paul Posner
Douglas Prather
Monroe Price
Lucille Ann Robinson
Suzanne Rolston
Mary Ann Rowcotsky
Carolyn A. Schweinsberg
Ruth D. Shirley
Ray Shurtleff
Helen Tarko
Jane M. Vida
Jay Vogelson
Anne V. Welsh
Margaret C. Yager

List of Witnesses

The following is a list of the 552 witnesses whose testimony has been presented to the Commission. Witnesses who appeared before members of the Commission have a "C" following their names; those questioned during depositions by members of the Commission's legal staff are indicated by a "D"; and those who supplied affidavits and statements are similarly identified with "A" and "S". The brief descriptions of the witnesses pertain either to the time of their testimony or to the time of the events concerning which they testified.

Witness	Description	Testimony
Ables, Don R.[D]	Jail Clerk, Dallas Police Department.	Vol. VII, p. 239.
Abt, John J.[D]	New York City attorney	Vol. X, p. 116.
Adamcik, John P.[D]	Member, Dallas Police Department.	Vol. VII, p. 202.
Adams, R. L.[A D]	Placement interviewer, Texas Employment Commission.	Vol. X, p. 136. Vol. XI, p. 480.
Adams, Victoria Elizabeth [D]	Employee, Texas School Book Depository (TSBD).	Vol. VI, p. 386.
Akin, Gene Coleman [D]	Doctor, Parkland Hospital	Vol. VI, p. 63.
Alba, Adrian Thomas [D]	Acquaintance of Oswald in New Orleans.	Vol. X, p. 219.
Allen, Mrs. J. U.[A]	Secretary, Chamberlin-Hunt Academy.	Vol. XI, p. 472.
Altgens, James W.[D]	Witness at assassination scene.	Vol. VII, p. 515.
Anderson, Eugene D.[D]	Marine Corps markmanship expert.	Vol. XI, p. 301.
Andrews, Dean Adams, Jr.[D]	New Orleans attorney	Vol. XI, p. 325.
Applin, George Jefferson, Jr.[D]	Witness of Oswald arrest	Vol. VII, p. 85.
Arce, Danny G.[D]	Employee, TSBD	Vol. VI, p. 363.
Archer, Don Ray [D]	Member, Dallas Police Department.	Vol. XII, p. 395.
Armstrong, Andrew, Jr.[D]	Acquaintance of Jack Ruby	Vol. XIII, p. 302.
Arnett, Charles Oliver [D]	Member, Dallas Police Department.	Vol. XII, p. 128.
Aycox, James Thomas [D]	Acquaintance of Jack Ruby	Vol. XV, p. 203.
Baker, Marrion L.[A C]	Member, Dallas Police Department.	Vol. III, p. 242. Vol. VII, p. 592.
Baker, Mrs. (Rachley) Donald.[D]	Employee, TSBD	Vol. VII, p. 507.
Baker, T. L.[C]	Member, Dallas Police Department.	Vol. IV, p. 248.
Ballen, Samuel B.[D]	Acquaintance of the Oswalds in Texas.	Vol. IX, p. 45.
Barbe, Emmett Charles, Jr.[A]	Employee, William B. Reily Co.	Vol. XI, p. 473.
Bargas, Tommy [D]	Superintendent, Leslie Welding Co.	Vol. X, p. 160.

Witness	Description	Testimony
Barnes, W. E.[D]	Member, Dallas Police Department.	Vol. VII, p. 270.
Barnett, W. E.[D]	.....do......	Vol. VII, p. 539.
Barnhorst, Colin [D]	Desk Clerk, YMCA, in Dallas..	Vol. X, p. 284.
Bashour, Fouad A.[D]	Doctor, Parkland Hospital....	Vol. VI, p. 61.
Batchelor, Charles [D]	Assistant Chief, Dallas Police Department.	Vol. XII, p. 1. Vol. XV, p. 114.
Bates, Pauline Virginia [D]	P u b l i c stenographer, Fort Worth.	Vol. VIII, p. 330.
Baxter, Charles Rufus [D]	Doctor, Parkland Hospital....	Vol. VI, p. 39.
Beaty, Buford Lee [D]	Member, Dallas Police Department.	Vol. XII, p. 158.
Beavers, William Robert [D]	Psychiatrist, Dallas..........	Vol. XIV, p. 570.
Beers, Ira J. "Jack", Jr.[D]	N e w s p a p e r photographer, Dallas.	Vol. XIII, p. 102.
Bellocchio, Frank [D]	Acquaintance of Jack Ruby...	Vol. XIV, p. 466.
Belmont, Alan H.[C]	Assistant to the Director, Federal Bureau of Investigation (FBI).	Vol. V, p. 1.
Benavides, Domingo [D]	Witness in the vicinity of the Tippit crime scene.	Vol. VI, p. 444.
Benton, Nelson [D]	Television reporter, CBS......	Vol. XV, p. 456.
Bieberdorf, Fred A.[D]	First aid attendant, Dallas Health Department.	Vol. XIII, p. 83.
Biggio, William S.[D]	Member, Dallas Police Department.	Vol. XIV, p. 48.
Blalock, Vance [D]	Observed Oswald in New Orleans.	Vol. X, p. 81.
Bledsoe, Mary E.[D]	Oswald's former landlady in Dallas.	Vol. VI, p. 400.
Bogard, Albert Guy [D]	Automobile salesman, Dallas..	Vol. X, p. 352.
Bookhout, James W.[D]	Agent, FBI.................	Vol. VII, p. 308.
Boone, Eugene [C]	Deputy Sheriff, Dallas County.	Vol. III, p. 291.
Boswell, J. Thornton [C]	Doctor, Bethesda Naval Hospital.	Vol. II, p. 376.
Botelho, James Anthony [A]	Acquaintance of Oswald in Marine Corps.	Vol. VIII, p. 315.
Bouck, Robert Inman [C]	Agent, U.S. Secret Service....	Vol. IV, p. 294.
Boudreaux, Anne [D]	Acquaintance of Oswald during his youth.	Vol. VIII, p. 35.
Bouhe, George A.[D]	Acquaintance of the Oswalds in Texas.	Vol. VIII, p. 355.
Bowers, Lee E., Jr.[D]	Employee, Union Terminal Co.	Vol. VI, p. 284.
Bowron, Diana Hamilton [D]	Nurse, Parkland Hospital.....	Vol. VI, p. 134.
Boyd, Elmer L.[D]	Member, Dallas Police Department.	Vol. VII, p. 119.
Branch, John Henry [D]	Acquaintance of Jack Ruby...	Vol. XV, p. 473.
Brennan, Howard Leslie[AC]	Witness at assassination scene.	Vol. III, pp. 140, 184, 211. Vol. XI, p. 206.
Brewer, E. D.[D]	Member, Dallas Police Department.	Vol. VI, p. 302.
Brewer, Johnny Calvin [D]	Witness of Oswald arrest.....	Vol. VII, p. 1.
Brian, V. J.[C]	Member, Dallas Police Department.	Vol. V, p. 47.
Bringuier, Carlos [D]	Cuban attorney, now a resident of New Orleans.	Vol. X, p. 32.
Brock, Alvin R.[D]	Member, Dallas Police Department.	Vol. XII, p. 171.

Witness	Description	Testimony
Brock, Mary [A]	Witness in the vicinity of the Tippit crime scene.	Vol. VII, p. 593.
Brock, Robert [A]	.....do......	Vol. VII, p. 593.
Brooks, Donald E.[D]	Employment counselor, Texas Employment Commission.	Vol. X, p. 143.
Brown, C. W.[D]	Member, Dallas Police Department.	Vol. VII, p. 246.
Brown, Earle V.[D]	.....do......	Vol. VI, p. 321.
Brown, Peter Megargee [A]	Counsel for Community Service Society, New York.	Vol. XI, p. 470.
Burcham, John W.[A]	Chief of Unemployment Insurance, Texas Employment Commission.	Vol. XI, p. 473.
Burns, Doris [D]	Employee, TSBD	Vol. VI, p. 397.
Burroughs, Warren H.[D]	Employee, Texas Theatre	Vol. VII, p. 14.
Cabell, Earle [D]	Mayor of Dallas	Vol. VII, p. 476.
Cabell, Mrs. Earle [D]	Wife of Mayor Cabell	Vol. VII, p. 485.
Cadigan, James C.[C D]	Questioned document expert, FBI.	Vol. IV, p. 89. Vol. VII, p. 418.
Call, Richard Dennis [A]	Acquaintance of Oswald in the Marine Corps.	Vol. VIII, p. 322.
Callaway, Ted [C]	Witness in the vicinity of the Tippit crime scene.	Vol. III, p. 351.
Camarata, Donald Peter [A]	Acquaintance of Oswald in the Marine Corps.	Vol. VIII, p. 316.
Carlin, Bruce Ray [D]	Acquaintance of Jack Ruby	Vol. XIII, p. 201. Vol. XV, p. 641.
Carlin, Karen Bennett [D]	.....do......	Vol. XIII, p. 205. Vol. XIV, p. 656.
Carr, Waggoner [C]	Attorney general of State of Texas.	Vol. V, p. 258.
Carrico, Charles James [C D]	Doctor, Parkland Hospital	Vol. III, p. 357. Vol. VI, p. 1.
Carro, John [D]	Probation officer, New York City, 1952–54.	Vol. VIII, p. 202.
Carroll, Bob K.[D]	Member, Dallas Police Department.	Vol. VII, p. 17.
Carswell, Robert [C]	Special assistant to Secretary of the Treasury.	Vol. IV, p. 299. Vol. V, p. 486.
Carter, Clifton C.[A]	Assistant to President Johnson.	Vol. VII, p. 474.
Cason, Frances [D]	Telephone clerk, Dallas Police Department.	Vol. XIII, p. 89.
Cason, Jack Charles [A]	President, TSBD	Vol. VII, p. 379.
Caster, Warren [D]	Assistant manager, Southwestern Publishing Co., TSBD.	Vol. VII, p. 386.
Chayes, Abram [C]	Legal Adviser, Department of State.	Vol. V, pp. 307, 327.
Cheek, Bertha [D]	Acquaintance of Jack Ruby	Vol. XIII, p. 382.
Church, George B., Jr.[A]	Passenger with Oswald on SS *Marion Lykes*.	Vol. XI, p. 115.
Church, Mrs. George B., Jr.[A]	.....do......	Vol. XI, p. 116.
Clardy, Barnard S.[D]	Member, Dallas Police Department.	Vol. XII, p. 403.
Clark, Max E.[D]	Acquaintance of the Oswalds in Texas.	Vol. VIII, p. 343.

Witness	Description	Testimony
Clark, Richard L.[D]	Member, Dallas Police Department.	Vol. VII, p. 235.
Clark, William Kemp [D]	Doctor, Parkland Hospital....	Vol. VI, p. 18.
Clements, Manning C.[D]	Agent, FBI.	Vol. VII, p. 318.
Cole, Alwyn [C D]	Questioned document examiner, Treasury Department.	Vol. IV, p. 358. Vol. XV, p. 703.
Combest, B. H.[D]	Member, Dallas Police Department.	Vol. XII, p. 176.
Connally, John Bowden, Jr.[C]	Governor of Texas.	Vol. IV, p. 129.
Connally, Mrs. John Bowden, Jr.[C]	Wife of the Governor of Texas.	Vol. IV, p. 146.
Connor, Peter Francis [A]	Acquaintance of Oswald in the Marine Corps.	Vol. VIII, p. 317.
Conway, Hiram P.[D]	Fort Worth neighbor of the Oswalds in Oswald's youth.	Vol. VIII, p. 84.
Corporon, John [A]	Official of New Orleans radio station.	Vol. XI, p. 471.
Couch, Malcolm O.[D]	TV news cameraman, Dallas.	Vol. VI, p. 153.
Coulter, Harris [C]	State Department interpreter.	Vol. V, p. 408.
Cox, Roland A.[D]	Reserve force, Dallas Police Department.	Vol. XV, p. 153.
Crafard, Curtis LaVerne [D]	Acquaintance of Jack Ruby...	Vol. XIII, p. 402. Vol. XIV, p. 1.
Craig, Roger D.[D]	Witness at assassination scene.	Vol. VI, p. 260.
Crawford, James N.[D]	....do......	Vol. VI, p. 171.
Creel, Robert J.[A]	Employee, Louisiana Department of Labor, New Orleans.	Vol. XI, p. 477.
Crowe, William D., Jr. (a.k.a. Bill DeMar).[D]	Acquaintance of Jack Ruby..	Vol. XV, p. 96.
Crowley, James D.[A]	Specialist in intelligence matters, Department of State.	Vol. XI, p. 482.
Croy, Kenneth Hudson [D]	Reserve force, Dallas Police Department.	Vol. XII, p. 186.
Crull, Elgin E.[D]	City Manager of Dallas......	Vol. XV, p. 138.
Cunningham, Cortlandt [A C]	Firearms identification expert, FBI.	Vol. II, p. 251. Vol. III, p. 451. Vol. VII, p. 591.
Cunningham, Helen P.[A D]	Employment Counselor, Texas Employment Commission.	Vol. X, p. 117. Vol. XI, p. 477.
Curry, Jesse Edward [A C D]	Chief, Dallas Police Department.	Vol. IV, p. 150. Vol. XII, p. 25. Vol. XV, p. 124, 641.
Curtis, Don Teel [D]	Doctor, Parkland Hospital....	Vol. VI, p. 57.
Cutchshaw, Wilbur Jay [D]	Member, Dallas Police Department.	Vol. XII, p. 206.
Daniels, John L.[D]	Employee, Dallas parking lot.	Vol. XIII, p. 296.
Daniels, Napoleon J.[D]	Former member, Dallas Police Department.	Vol. XII, p. 225.
Davis, Barbara Jeanette [C]	Witness in the vicinity of the Tippit crime scene.	Vol. III, p. 342.
Davis, Floyd Guy [D]	Operator, Sports Drome Rifle Range.	Vol. X, p. 356.
Davis, Virginia (Mrs. Charles).[D]	Witness in the vicinity of the Tippit crime scene.	Vol. VI, p. 454.

Witness	Description	Testimony
Davis, Virginia Louise [D]	Wife of Floyd Guy Davis	Vol. X, p. 363.
Day, J. C.[A C]	Lieutenant, Dallas Police Department.	Vol. IV, p. 249. Vol. VII, p. 401.
Dean, Patrick Trevore [C D]	Member, Dallas Police Department.	Vol. V, p. 254. Vol. XII, p. 415.
Decker, J. E. (Bill)[D]	Sheriff, Dallas County	Vol. XII, p. 42.
Delgado, Nelson [D]	Acquaintance of Oswald in Marine Corps.	Vol. VIII, p. 228.
DeMar, William (see Crowe, William D., Jr.).		
De Mohrenschildt, George S.[D]	Acquaintance of the Oswalds in Texas.	Vol. IX, p. 166.
De Mohrenschildt, Jeanne [D]	....do	Vol. IX, p. 285.
Dhority, C. N.[A D]	Member, Dallas Police Department.	Vol. VII, pp. 149, 380.
Dietrich, Edward C.[D]	Guard, Armored Motor Service.	Vol. XV, p. 269.
Dillard, Tom C.[D]	Photographer-Journalist, Dallas.	Vol. VI, p. 162.
Dillon, C. Douglas [C]	Secretary of the Treasury	Vol. V, p. 573.
Dobbs, Farrell [A D]	International Secretary, Socialist Workers Party.	Vol. X, p. 109. Vol. XI, p. 208.
Donabedian, George [D]	Captain, U.S. Navy	Vol. VIII, p. 311.
Donovan, John E.[D]	Acquaintance of Oswald in the Marine Corps.	Vol. VIII, p. 289.
Dougherty, Jack Edwin [D]	Employee, TSBD	Vol. VI, p. 373.
Dowe, Kenneth Lawry [D]	Acquaintance of Jack Ruby	Vol. XV, p. 430.
Dulany, Richard B.[D]	Doctor, Parkland Hospital	Vol. VI, p. 113.
Duncan, William Glenn, Jr.[D]	Employee, radio station, Dallas.	Vol. XV, p. 482.
Dymitruk, Lydia [D]	Acquaintance of the Oswalds in Texas.	Vol. IX, p. 60.
Dziemian, Arthur J.[C]	Wound ballistics expert, U.S. Army.	Vol. V, p. 90.
Eberhardt, A. M.[D]	Member, Dallas Police Department.	Vol. XIII, p. 181.
Edwards, Robert Edwin [D]	Employee, Dallas City Courthouse.	Vol. VI, p. 200.
Euins, Amos Lee [C]	Witness at assassination scene.	Vol. II, p. 201.
Evans, Julian [D]	Husband of Myrtle Evans	Vol. VIII, p. 66.
Evans, Myrtle [D]	Acquaintance of Marguerite Oswald in Oswald's youth.	Vol. VIII, p. 45.
Evans, Sidney, Jr.[D]	Resident of Ruby's apartment house.	Vol. XIII, p. 195.
Fain, John W.[C]	Agent, FBI	Vol. IV, p. 403.
Fehrenbach, George William.[D]	Resident of Ashland, Oreg	Vol. XV, p. 289.
Feldsott, Louis [A]	President, Crescent Firearms, Inc.	Vol. XI, p. 205.
Fenley, Robert Gene [D]	Reporter, Dallas	Vol. XI, p. 314.
Finck, Pierre A.[C]	Doctor, Bethesda Naval Hospital.	Vol. II, p. 377.
Fischer, Ronald B.[D]	Auditor, City of Dallas	Vol. VI, p. 191.
Fleming, Harold J.[D]	Employee, Armored Motor Service, Inc.	Vol. XV, p. 159.

487

Witness	Description	Testimony
Folsom, Allison G., Jr.[D]......	Lt. Col., U.S. Marine Corps..	Vol. VIII, p. 303.
Ford, Declan P.[C]............	Husband of Katherine N. Ford and acquaintance of the Oswalds in Texas.	Vol. II, p. 322.
Ford, Katherine N.[C].........	Acquaintance of the Oswalds in Texas.	Vol. II, p. 295.
Foster, J. W.[D].............	Member, Dallas Police Department.	Vol. VI, p. 248.
Frazier, Buell Wesley [C D]....	Employee, TSBD and neighbor of the Paines in Irving, Tex.	Vol. II, p. 210. Vol. VII, p. 531.
Frazier, Robert A.[A C]........	Firearms Identification Expert, FBI.	Vol. III, p. 390. Vol. V, p. 58. Vol. VII, p. 590.
Frazier, W. B.[D].............	Captain, Dallas Police Department.	Vol. XII, p. 52.
Fritz, John Will [A C D]........	.....do.....................	Vol. IV, p. 202. Vol. VII, p. 403. Vol. XV, p. 145.
Fuqua, Harold R.[D]..........	Parking attendant in basement of city hall.	Vol. XIII, p. 141.
Gallagher, John F.[D].........	Agent, FBI...............	Vol. XV, p. 746.
Gangl, Theodore Frank [A]....	Employee, Padgett Printing Corp.	Vol. XI, p. 478.
Garner, Jesse J.[A]............	Neighbor of the Oswalds in New Orleans.	Vol. X, p. 276.
Garner, Mrs. Jesse [D]........	Landlady of Oswald in New Orleans.	Vol. X, p. 264.
Gauthier, Leo J.[C]............	Inspector, FBI..............	Vol. V, p. 135.
George, M. Waldo [A].........	Landlord of Oswalds in Dallas	Vol. XI, p. 155.
Geraci, Philip, III [D].........	Resident of New Orleans who met Oswald.	Vol. X, p. 74.
Gibson, Mrs. Donald [D].......	Acquaintance of the Oswalds in Texas.	Vol. XI, p. 123.
Gibson, John [D]..............	Witness to Oswald arrest....	Vol. VII, p. 70.
Giesecke, Adolph H., Jr.[D]....	Doctor, Parkland Hospital....	Vol. VI, p. 72.
Givens, Charles Douglas [D]....	Employee, TSBD.............	Vol. VI, p. 345.
Glover, Everett D.[D]..........	Acquaintance of the Oswalds in Texas.	Vol. X, p. 1.
Goin, Donald Edward [D]......	Armored car operator........	Vol. XV, p. 168.
Goldstein, David [A]...........	Owner, Dave's House of Guns.	Vol. VII, p. 594.
Goodson, Clyde Franklin [D]....	Member, Dallas Police Department.	Vol. XV, p. 596.
Graef, John G.[D].............	Oswald's supervisor, Jaggars-Chiles-Stovall, Dallas.	Vol. X, p. 174.
Graf, Allen D.[A].............	Acquaintance of Oswald in Marine Corps.	Vol. VIII, p. 317.
Grant, Eva [D]................	Sister of Jack Ruby..........	Vol. XIV, p. 429. Vol. XV, p. 321.
Graves, Gene [A]..............	Secretary, Leslie Welding Co..	Vol. XI, p. 479.
Graves, L. C.[D]..............	Member, Dallas Police Department.	Vol. VII, p. 251. Vol. XIII, p. 1.
Gravitis, Dorothy [D]..........	Acquaintance of Mrs. Paine in Dallas.	Vol. IX, p. 131.
Gray, Virginia [A].............	Employee, Duke University Library.	Vol. XI, p. 209.
Greener, Charles W.[D]........	Proprietor, Irving Sports Shop.	Vol. XI, p. 245.
Greer, William Robert [C]......	Agent, U.S. Secret Service....	Vol. II, p. 112.

488

Witness	Description	Testimony
Gregory, Charles F.^{C D}........	Doctor, Parkland Hospital....	Vol. IV, p. 117. Vol. VI, p. 95.
Gregory, Paul Roderick ^D....	Son of Peter Paul Gregory and acquaintance of the Oswalds in Texas.	Vol. IX, p. 141.
Gregory, Peter Paul ^C........	Acquaintance of the Oswalds in Texas.	Vol. II, p. 337.
Guinyard, Sam ^D............	Witness in the vicinity of Tippit crime scene.	Vol. VII, p. 395.
Hall, C. Ray ^D...............	Agent, FBI..................	Vol. XV, p. 62.
Hall, Elena A.^D.............	Acquaintance of the Oswalds in Texas.	Vol. VIII, p. 391.
Hall, John Raymond ^D......	Husband of Elena A. Hall and acquaintance of the Oswalds.	Vol. VIII, p. 406.
Hall, Marvin E. "Bert" ^D....	Employee, Armored Motor Service, Dallas.	Vol. XV, p. 174.
Hallmark, Garnett Claud ^D...	Acquaintance of Jack Ruby..	Vol. XV, p. 488.
Hamblen, C. A.^D............	Employee, Western Union Telegraph Co.	Vol. XI, p. 311.
Hankal, Robert L.^D..........	Director, television station, Dallas.	Vol. XIII, p. 112.
Hansen, Timothy M., Jr.^D....	Member, Dallas Police Department.	Vol. XV, p. 438.
Hardin, Michael ^D...........	City ambulance driver........	Vol. XIII, p. 94.
Hargis, Bobby W.^D..........	Member, Dallas Police Department.	Vol. VI, p. 293.
Harkness, D. V.^D............	....do...................	Vol. VI, p. 308.
Harrison, William J.^D........	....do..................	Vol. XII, p. 234.
Hartogs, Renatus ^D..........	Psychiatrist, New York City..	Vol. VIII, p. 214.
Hawkins, Ray ^D.............	Member, Dallas Police Department.	Vol. VII, p. 91.
Haygood, Clyde A.^D..........	....do...................	Vol. VI, p. 296.
Heindel, John Rene ^A........	Acquaintance of Oswald in Marine Corps.	Vol. VIII, p. 318.
Helmick, Wanda Yvonne or Wanda Sweat.^D	Employee of Ralph Paul, an acquaintance of Jack Ruby.	Vol. XV, p. 396.
Helms, Richard M.^{C A}........	Deputy Director for Plans, Central Intelligence Agency.	Vol V, p. 120. Vol. XI, p. 469.
Henchliffe, Margaret M.^D....	Nurse, Parkland Hospital.....	Vol. VI, p. 139.
Henslee, Gerald D.^D..........	Member, Dallas Police Department.	Vol. VI, p. 325.
Herndon, Bell P.^D...........	Polygraph operator, FBI.....	Vol. XIV, p. 579.
Hicks, J. B.^D...............	Member, Dallas Police Department.	Vol. VII, p. 286.
Hill, Clinton J.^C...........	Agent, U.S. Secret Service.....	Vol. II, p. 132.
Hill, Gerald Lynn ^D..........	Member, Dallas Police Department.	Vol. VII, p. 43.
Hill, Jean Lollis ^D...........	Witness at assassination scene.	Vol. VI, p. 205.
Hine, Geneva L.^D...........	Employee, TSBD............	Vol. VI, p. 393.
Hodge, Alfred Douglas ^D.....	Owner, Buckhorn Trading Post.	Vol. XV, p. 494.
Holland, S. M.^D.............	Witness at assassination scene.	Vol. VI, p. 239.
Holly, Harold B., Jr.^D........	Reserve force, Dallas Police Department.	Vol. XII, p. 261.

489

Witness	Description	Testimony
Holmes, Harry D.[D]	U.S. Post Office inspector	Vol. VII, p. 289, 525.
Hoover, J. Edgar [C]	Director, FBI	Vol. V, p. 97.
Hosty, James, P., Jr.[C]	Agent, FBI	Vol. IV, p. 440.
Howlett, John Joe [A][D]	Agent, U.S. Secret Service	Vol. VII, p. 592. Vol. IX, p. 425.
Hudson, Emmett J.[D]	Witness at assassination scene.	Vol. VII, p. 558.
Huffaker, Robert S., Jr.[D]	Newsman, Dallas	Vol. XIII, p. 116.
Hulen, Richard Leroy [D]	Employee of Dallas YMCA	Vol. X, p. 277.
Hulse, C. E.[D]	Member, Dallas Police Department.	Vol. XIII, p. 99.
Humes, James J.[C]	Doctor, Bethesda Naval Hospital.	Vol. II, p. 347.
Hunley, Bobb [A]	Employee, Louisiana Department of Labor, New Orleans.	Vol. XI, p. 476.
Hunt, Jackie H.[D]	Doctor, Parkland Hospital	Vol. VI, p. 76.
Hunter, Gertrude [D]	Witness concerning alleged encounter with Oswald.	Vol. XI, pp. 253, 275.
Hutchison, Leonard Edwin [D]	Owner of grocery store in Irving.	Vol. X, p. 327.
Hutson, Thomas Alexander [D]	Member, Dallas Police Department.	Vol. VII, p. 26.
Isaacs, Martin [D]	Employee, Special Services Welfare Center, New York.	Vol. VIII, p. 324.
Jackson, Robert Hill [C]	News photographer, Dallas	Vol. II, p. 155.
Jackson, Theodore [D]	Attendant at Dallas parking lot.	Vol. XIII, p. 299.
James, Virginia H.[D]	International Relations Officer, Office of Soviet Affairs, State Department.	Vol. XI, p. 180.
Jarman, James, Jr.[C]	Employee, TSBD	Vol. III, p. 198.
Jenkins, Marion T.[D]	Doctor, Parkland Hospital	Vol. VI, p. 45.
Jenkins, Ronald Lee [D]	News editor, radio station, Dallas.	Vol. XV, p. 600.
Jimison, R. J.[D]	Orderly, Parkland Hospital	Vol. VI, p. 125.
Johnson, Arnold Samuel [D]	Director of Information and Lecture Bureau, Communist Party, U.S.A.	Vol. X, p. 95.
Johnson, Arthur Carl [D]	Owner of roominghouse in Dallas where Oswald resided.	Vol. X, p. 301.
Johnson, Mrs. Arthur Carl [D]	Wife of A. C. Johnson	Vol. X, p. 292.
Johnson, Joseph Weldon, Jr.[D]	Acquaintance of Jack Ruby	Vol. XV, p. 218.
Johnson, Lyndon B.[S]	President of the United States.	Vol. V, p. 561.
Johnson, Mrs. Lyndon B.[S]	Wife of the President of the United States.	Vol. V, p. 564.
Johnson, Marvin [D]	Member, Dallas Police Department.	Vol. VII, p. 100.
Johnson, Priscilla Mary Post [D].	Newspaper reporter who interviewed Oswald in Russia.	Vol. XI, p. 442.
Johnson, Speedy [D]	Acquaintance of Jack Ruby	Vol. XV, p. 607.
Johnston, David L.[D]	Justice of the peace, Dallas	Vol. XV, p. 503.
Jones, O. A.[D]	Captain, Dallas Police Department.	Vol. XII, p. 58.
Jones, Ronald C.[D]	Doctor, Parkland Hospital	Vol. VI, p. 51.
Kaiser, Frankie [D]	Employee, TSBD	Vol. VI, p. 341.
Kaminsky, Eileen [D]	Jack Ruby's sister	Vol. XV, p. 275.
Kantor, Seth [D]	Reporter,	Vol. XV, p. 71.

Witness	Description	Testimony
Lovelady, Billy Nolan [D]	Employee, TSBD	Vol. VI, p. 336.
Lowery, Roy Lee [D]	Member, Dallas Police Department.	Vol. XII, p. 271.
Lujan, Daniel Gutierrez [D]	Appeared in lineup with Oswald.	Vol. VII, p. 243.
Lux, J. Philip [A]	Employee, H. L. Green Co.	Vol. XI, p. 206
McClelland, Robert N.[D]	Doctor, Parkland Hospital.	Vol. VI, p. 30.
McCone, John Alex [C]	Director, Central Intelligence Agency.	Vol. V, p. 120.
McCullough, John G.[D]	Reporter, Philadelphia	Vol. XV, p. 373.
McCurdy, Danny Patrick [D]	Acquaintance of Jack Ruby	Vol. XV, p. 529.
McDonald, M. N.[C]	Member, Dallas Police Department.	Vol. III, p. 295.
McFarland, John Bryan [A]	Passenger on bus with Oswald to Mexico City in 1963.	Vol. XI, p. 214.
McFarland, Meryl [A]	....do....	Vol. XI, p. 214.
McKinzie, Louis [D]	Porter, Dallas City Hall	Vol. XIII, p. 147.
McMillon, Thomas Donald [D]	Member, Dallas Police Department.	Vol. XIII, p. 37.
McVickar, John A.[C]	Foreign Service officer stationed at American Embassy in Soviet Union in 1959–61.	Vol. V, pp. 299, 318.
McWatters, Cecil J.[C]	Busdriver, Dallas	Vol. II, p. 262.
Malley, James R.[A]	Inspector, FBI	Vol. XI, p. 468.
Mallory, Katherine [A]	Tourist in Minsk in 1961	Vol. XI, p. 210.
Mamantov, Ilya A.[D]	Member of Russian-speaking community in Dallas.	Vol. IX, p. 102.
Mandella, Arthur [C] (accompanied by Joseph A. Mooney).	Fingerprint expert, New York City Police Department.	Vol. IV, p. 48.
Markham, Helen Louise [C D]	Witness in the vicinity of the Tippit crime scene.	Vol. III, p. 305. Vol. VII, p. 499.
Martello, Francis L.[A D]	Lieutenant, New Orleans Police Department.	Vol. X, p. 51. Vol. XI, p. 471.
Martin, B. J.[D]	Member, Dallas Police Department.	Vol. VI, p. 289.
Martin, Frank M.[D]	Captain, Dallas Police Department.	Vol. XII, p. 277.
Martin, James Herbert [C]	Former business manager for Mrs. Lee Harvey Oswald.	Vol. I, p. 469. Vol. II, p. 1.
Maxey, Billy Joe [D]	Member, Dallas Police Department.	Vol. XII, p. 285.
Mayo, Logan W.[D]	Reserve force, Dallas Police Department.	Vol. XII, p. 291.
Meller, Anna N.[D]	Acquaintance of the Oswalds in Texas.	Vol. VIII, p. 379.
Meyers, Lawrence V.[D]	Acquaintance of Jack Ruby	Vol. XV, p. 620.
Michaelis, Heinz W.[D]	Manager, Seaport Traders, Inc.	Vol. VII, p. 372.
Miller, Austin L.[D]	Witness at assassination scene.	Vol. VI, p. 223.
Miller, Dave L.[D]	Acquaintance of Jack Ruby	Vol. XV, p. 450.
Miller, Louis D.[D]	Member, Dallas Police Department.	Vol. XII, p. 297.
Mitchell, Mary Ann [D]	Witness at assassination scene.	Vol. VI, p. 175.
Molina, Joe R.[D]	Employee, TSBD	Vol. VI, p. 368.
Montgomery, L. D.[D]	Member, Dallas Police Department.	Vol. VII, p. 96. Vol. XIII, p. 21.

Witness	Description	Testimony
Mooney, Luke ^C..............	Deputy Sheriff, Dallas County	Vol. III, p. 281.
Moore, Henry M.^D...........	Member, Dallas Police Department.	Vol. VII, p. 212.
Moore, Russell Lee (Knight)^D	Acquaintance of Jack Ruby...	Vol. XV, p. 251.
Mumford, Pamela ^D.........	Passenger on bus with Oswald to Mexico City in 1963.	Vol. XI, p. 215.
Murphy, Joe E.^D..............	Member, Dallas Police Department.	Vol. VI, p. 256.
Murphy, Paul Edward ^A.....	Acquaintance of Oswald in Marine Corps.	Vol. VIII, p. 319.
Murray, David Christie, Jr.^A.	.....do......................	Vol. VIII, p. 319.
Murret, Charles (Dutz) ^D....	Uncle of Lee Harvey Oswald, New Orleans.	Vol. VIII, p. 180.
Murret, John Martial (Boogie).^D	Cousin of Lee Harvey Oswald, New Orleans.	Vol. VIII, p. 188.
Murret, Lillian ^{A D}...........	Sister of Marguerite Oswald and aunt of Lee Harvey Oswald, New Orleans.	Vol. VIII, p. 91. Vol. XI, p. 472.
Murret, Marilyn Dorothea ^D..	Cousin of Lee Harvey Oswald, New Orleans.	Vol. VIII, p. 154.
Naman, Rita ^A................	Tourist in Minsk in 1961......	Vol. XI, p. 213.
Nelson, Doris Mae ^D.........	Nurse, Parkland Hospital.....	Vol. VI, p. 143.
Newman, William J.^D........	Reserve force, Dallas Police Department.	Vol. XII, p. 314.
Newnam, John ^D..............	Advertising department employee, Dallas newspaper.	Vol. XV, p. 534.
Nichols, Alice Reaves ^D.......	Acquaintance of Jack Ruby...	Vol. XIV, p. 110.
Nichols, H. Louis ^D...........	Former president, Dallas bar association.	Vol. VII, p. 325.
Nicol, Joseph D.^C.............	Firearms identification expert, Bureau of Criminal Identification and Investigation, Illinois Department of Public Safety.	Vol. III, p. 496.
Norman, Harold ^C...........	Employee, TSBD.............	Vol. III, p. 186.
Norton, Robert L.^D...........	Acquaintance of Jack Ruby...	Vol. XV, p. 546.
O'Brien, Lawrence F.^D.......	Assistant to President Kennedy.	Vol. VII, p. 457.
Odio, Sylvia ^D................	Former citizen of Cuba now residing in Dallas.	Vol. XI, p. 367.
O'Donnell, Kenneth ^D.........	Assistant to President Kennedy.	Vol. VII, p. 440.
Odum, Bardwell D.^A..........	Agent, FBI..................	Vol. XI, p. 468.
Ofstein, Dennis Hyman ^D.....	Employee, Jaggers-Chiles-Stovall, Dallas.	Vol. X, p. 194.
Olds, Gregory Lee ^D.........	President, Dallas Chapter, American Civil Liberties Union.	Vol. VII, p. 322.
Oliver, Revilo P.^D...........	Member of the council of the John Birch Society.	Vol. XV, p. 709.
Olivier, Alfred G.^C..........	Wound ballistics expert, U.S. Army.	Vol. V, p. 74.
Olsen, Harry N.^D.............	Former member, Dallas Police Department.	Vol. XIV, p. 624.
Olsen, Kay Helen ^D..........	Acquaintance of Jack Ruby..	Vol. XIV, p. 640.
Osborne, Mack ^A..............	Acquaintance of Oswald in Marine Corps.	Vol. VIII, p. 321.

Witness	*Description*	*Testimony*
O'Sullivan, Frederick S.[D]....	Acquaintance of Oswald at Beauregard Junior High School, New Orleans.	Vol. VIII, p. 27.
Oswald, Marguerite [C]........	Mother of Lee Harvey Oswald.	Vol. I, p. 126.
Oswald, Marina [C D]..........	Widow of Lee Harvey Oswald.	Vol. I, p. 1.
		Vol. V, pp. 387, 410, 588..
		Vol. XI, p. 275.
Oswald, Robert Edward Lee [C]	Brother of Lee Harvey Oswald.	Vol. I, p. 264.
Owens, Calvin Bud [D]........	Member, Dallas Police Department.	Vol. VII, p. 78.
Paine, Michael R.[C D].........	Acquaintance of the Oswalds in Texas.	Vol. II, p. 384.
		Vol. IX, p. 434.
		Vol. XI, p. 398.
Paine, Ruth Hyde [A C D].......	Wife of Michael R. Paine and acquaintance of the Oswalds in Texas.	Vol. II, p. 430.
		Vol. III, p. 1.
		Vol. IX, p. 331.
		Vol. XI, pp. 153, 389.
Palmer, Thomas Stewart [D]..	Acquaintance of Jack Ruby..	Vol. XV, p. 206.
Pappas, Icarus M.[D]..........	Reporter, radio station, New York City.	Vol. XV, p. 360.
Patterson, B. M.[A]...........	Witness in the vicinity of the Tippit crime scene.	Vol. 15, p. 744.
Patterson, Bobby G.[D]........	Member, Dallas Police Department.	Vol. XII, p. 334.
Patterson, Robert Carl [D]....	Acquaintance of Jack Ruby...	Vol. XIV, p. 126.
Paul, Ralph [D]................	.....do.....................	Vol. XIV, p. 134.
		Vol. XV, p. 664.
Pena, Orest [D]...............	Owner, Habana Bar, New Orleans.	Vol. XI, p. 346.
Pena, Ruperto [D].............	Brother of Orest Pena........	Vol. XI, p. 364.
Perry, Malcolm O.[C D]........	Doctor, Parkland Hospital....	Vol. III, p. 366.
		Vol. VI, p. 7.
Perry, W. E.[D]...............	Member, Dallas Police Department.	Vol. VII, p. 232.
Peterman, Viola [D]...........	Neighbor of Oswald family in New Orleans.	Vol. VIII, p. 38.
Peters, Paul C.[D]...........	Doctor, Parkland Hospital....	Vol. VI, p. 68.
Peterson, Joseph Alexander [D]	Acquaintance of Jack Ruby....	Vol. XIV, p. 615.
Phenix, George R.[D]..........	Television cameraman and reporter, Dallas.	Vol. XIII, p. 123.
Pic, Edward John, Jr.[A D].....	First husband of Marguerite Oswald.	Vol. VIII, p. 196.
		Vol. XI, p. 82.
Pic, John Edward [D].........	Half brother of Lee Harvey Oswald.	Vol. XI, p. 1.
Pierce, Edward E.[D]..........	Employee, Dallas City Hall...	Vol. XIII, p. 156.
Pierce, Rio S.[D].............	Lieutenant, Dallas Police Department.	Vol. VII, p. 76.
		Vol. XII, p. 337.
Pinkston, Nat A.[D]............	Employee, TSBD..............	Vol. VI, p. 334.
Piper, Eddie [D]...............	.....do.....................	Vol. VI, p. 382.
		Vol. VII, p. 388.
Pitts, Elnora [D]...............	Acquaintance of Jack Ruby....	Vol. XIII, p. 228.
Pizzo, Frank [D]...............	Assistant manager of auto agency, Dallas.	Vol. X, p. 340.
Poe, J. M.[D]..................	Member, Dallas Police Department.	Vol. VII, p. 66.
Postal, Julia [D]...............	Cashier, Texas Theatre.......	Vol. VII, p. 8.

494

Witness	*Description*	*Testimony*
Potts, Walter E.[D]	Member, Dallas Police Department.	Vol. VII, p. 195.
Powell, Nancy M. (a.k.a. Tammie True).[D]	Acquaintance of Jack Ruby...	Vol. XV, p. 404.
Powers, Daniel Patrick[D]	Acquaintance of Oswald in Marine Corps.	Vol. VIII, p. 266.
Powers, David F.[A]	Assistant to President Kennedy.	Vol. VII, p. 472.
Price, Charles Jack[D]	Administrator, Parkland Hospital.	Vol. VI, p. 148.
Price, Malcolm H., Jr.[D]	Patron, Sports Drome Rifle Range.	Vol. X, p. 369.
Priddy, Hal Jr.[D]	Relief dispatcher, O'Neil Funeral Home in Dallas.	Vol. XIII, p. 239.
Pryor, Roy A.[D]	Acquaintance of Jack Ruby...	Vol. XV, p. 554.
Pugh, Oran[A]	Agent, U.S. Customs	Vol. XV, p. 640.
Pullman, Edward J.[D]	Acquaintance of Jack Ruby...	Vol. XV, p. 222.
Putnam, James A.[D]	Member, Dallas Police Department.	Vol. VII, p. 74. Vol. XII, p. 341.
Quigley, John L.[C]	Agent, FBI	Vol. IV, p. 431.
Rachal, John R.[A]	Employee, Louisiana Department of Labor, New Orleans.	Vol. XI, p. 474.
Rackley, George W., Sr.[D]	Employee, Coordinated RR. Co.	Vol. VI, p. 273.
Raigorodsky, Paul M.[D]	Member of Russian-speaking community in Dallas.	Vol. IX, p. 1.
Randle, Linnie Mae[C]	Buell Wesley Frazier's sister and neighbor of Ruth Paine.	Vol. II, p. 245.
Ray, Natalie (Mrs. Thomas M.).[D]	Acquaintance of the Oswalds in Texas.	Vol. IX, p. 27.
Ray, Thomas M.[D]	Husband of Natalie Ray and acquaintance of the Oswalds in Texas.	Vol. IX, p. 38.
Ray, Valentine A. (Mrs. Frank H.).[D]	Acquaintance of the Oswalds in Texas.	Vol. VIII, p. 415.
Rea, Billy A.[D]	Advertising staff, Dallas newspaper.	Vol. XV, p. 571.
Reeves, Huey[D]	Acquaintance of Jack Ruby...	Vol. XIII, p. 243.
Reid, Mrs. Robert A.[C]	Employee, TSBD	Vol. III, p. 270.
Reilly, Frank E.[D]	Witness at assassination scene.	Vol. VI, p. 227.
Revill, Jack[C D]	Lieutenant, Dallas Police Department.	Vol. V, p. 33. Vol. XII, p. 73.
Reynolds, Warren Allen[D]	Witness in the vicinity of the Tippit crime scene.	Vol. XI, p. 434.
Rheinstein, Frederic[D]	Producer-director, NBC	Vol. XV, p. 354.
Rich, Nancy Perrin[D]	Acquaintance of Jack Ruby...	Vol. XIV, p. 330.
Richey, Marjorie R.[D]	.....do	Vol. XV, p. 192.
Richey, Warren E.[D]	TV engineer, Fort Worth....	Vol. XIII, p. 255.
Riggs, Alfreadia[D]	Porter, City Hall	Vol. XIII, p. 166.
Riggs, Chester Allen, Jr.[A]	Landlord of the Oswalds in Fort Worth.	Vol. X, p. 229.
Ritchie, James L.[D]	Passport Officer, Department of State.	Vol. XI, p. 191.
Roberts, Earlene[A D]	Housekeeper at Oswald's roominghouse in Dallas.	Vol. VI, p. 434. Vol. VII, p. 439.

495

Witness	Description	Testimony
Robertson, Mary Jane [D]	Employee, Dallas Police Department.	Vol. VII, p. 404.
Robertson, Victor F., Jr.[D]	Reporter, Dallas	Vol. XV, p. 347.
Rodriguez, Evaristo [D]	Bartender at Habana Bar, New Orleans.	Vol. XI, p. 339.
Rogers, Eric [D]	Neighbor of the Oswalds in New Orleans.	Vol. XI, p. 460.
Romack, James E.[D]	Witness at assassination scene.	Vol. VI, p. 277.
Rose, Guy F.[D]	Member, Dallas Police Department.	Vol. VII, p. 227.
Ross, Henrietta M.[D]	Technician, Parkland Hospital.	Vol. VI, p. 123.
Rossi, Joseph [D]	Acquaintance of Jack Ruby	Vol. XV, p. 235.
Roussel, Henry J., Jr.[A]	Acquaintance of Oswald in Marine Corps.	Vol. VIII, p. 320.
Rowland, Arnold Louis [C]	Witness at assassination scene.	Vol. II, p. 165.
Rowland, Barbara (Mrs. Arnold L.).[D]	....do	Vol. VI, p. 177.
Rowley, James J.[C]	Chief, U.S. Secret Service	Vol. V, p. 449.
Rubenstein, Hyman [D]	Brother of Jack Ruby	Vol. XV, p. 1.
Ruby, Earl [D]	....do	Vol. XIV, p. 364.
Ruby, Jack [C D]	Convicted slayer of Oswald	Vol. V, p. 181. Vol. XIV, p. 504.
Ruby, Sam [D]	Brother of Jack Ruby	Vol. XIV, p. 488.
Rusk, Dean [C]	Secretary of State	Vol. V, p. 363.
Russell, Harold [A]	Witness in the vicinity of the Tippit crime scene.	Vol. VII, p. 594.
Ryder, Dial D.[D]	Employee, Irving Sports Shop.	Vol. XI, p. 224.
Salyer, Kenneth E.[D]	Doctor, Parkland Hospital	Vol. VI, p. 80.
Saunders, Richard L.[D]	Advertising staff, Dallas newspaper.	Vol. XV, p. 577.
Sawyer, J. Herbert [D]	Inspector, Dallas Police Department.	Vol. VI, p. 315.
Sawyer, Mildred [D]	Neighbor and acquaintance of Oswald as a youth in New Orleans.	Vol. VIII, p. 31.
Schmidt, Hunter, Jr.[D]	City editor, Dallas	Vol. XI, p. 240.
Scibor, Mitchell J.[D]	Employee, Klein's Sports Goods.	Vol. VII, p. 370.
Scoggins, William W.[C]	Witness in the vicinity of the Tippit crime scene.	Vol. III, p. 322.
Seeley, Carroll Hamilton, Jr.[D]	Assistant Chief, Legal Division, Passport Office, Department of State.	Vol. XI, p. 193.
Semingsen, W. W.[D]	Employee, Western Union Telegraph Co.	Vol. X, p. 405.
Senator, George [D]	Roommate of Jack Ruby	Vol. XIV, p. 164.
Servance, John Olridge [D]	Head porter, City Hall and Municipal Building.	Vol. XIII, p. 175.
Shaneyfelt, Lyndal L.[C D]	Photography expert, FBI	Vol. IV, p. 279. Vol. V, p. 138, 176. Vol. VII, p. 410.
Shasteen, Clifton M.[D]	Owner of barbershop in Irving, Tex.	Vol. X, p. 309.
Shaw, Robert Roeder [C D]	Doctor, Parkland Hospital	Vol. IV, p. 101. Vol. VI, p. 83.

496

Witness	*Description*	*Testimony*
Shelley, William H.[D]	Employee, TSBD	Vol. VI, p. 327. Vol. VII, p. 390.
Shields, Edward [D]	Employee, TSBD	Vol. VII, p. 393.
Shires, George T.[D]	Doctor, Parkland Hospital	Vol. VI, p. 104.
Siegel, Evelyn Grace Strickman [D]	Social worker, New York City.	Vol. VIII, p. 224.
Simmons, Ronald [C]	Weapons evaluation expert, U.S. Army Weapons System Division.	Vol. III, p. 441.
Sims, Richard M.[D]	Member, Dallas Police Department.	Vol. VII, p. 158.
Skelton, Royce G.[D]	Witness at assassination scene.	Vol. VI, p. 236.
Slack, Garland Glenwill [D]	Patron, Sports Drome Rifle Range.	Vol. X, p. 378.
Slack, Willie B.[D]	Member, Dallas Police Department.	Vol. XII, p. 347.
Slaughter, Malcolm R.[D]	Resident in Jack Ruby's apartment building.	Vol. XIII, p. 261.
Smart, Vernon S.[D]	Lieutenant, Dallas Police Department.	Vol. XIII, p. 266.
Smith, Bennierita [D]	Acquaintance of Oswald at Beauregard Junior High School in New Orleans.	Vol. VIII, p. 21.
Smith, Edgar Leon, Jr.[D]	Member, Dallas Police Department.	Vol. VII, p. 565.
Smith, Glenn Emmett [D]	Service station attendant in Dallas.	Vol. X, p. 399.
Smith, Hilda L.[A]	Employee, Louisiana Department of Labor, New Orleans.	Vol. XI, p. 474.
Smith, Joe Marshall [D]	Member, Dallas Police Department.	Vol. VII, p. 531.
Smith, John Allison [D]	TV technician, Fort Worth	Vol. XIII, p. 277.
Smith, William Arthur [D]	Witness in the vicinity of the Tippit crime scene.	Vol. VII, p. 82.
Snyder, Richard Edward [C]	Foreign Service officer, stationed in the Embassy in the Soviet Union, 1959–61.	Vol. V, p. 260.
Solomon, James Maurice [D]	Captain, Dallas Police Department.	Vol. XII, p. 87.
Sorrels, Forrest V.[D][A]	Agent, U.S. Secret Service	Vol. VII, pp. 332, 592. Vol. XIII, p. 55.
Standifer, Roy E.[D]	Member, Dallas Police Department.	Vol. XV, p. 614.
Standridge, Ruth Jeanette [D]	Head nurse of operating rooms, Parkland Hospital.	Vol. VI, p. 115.
Staples, Albert F.[A]	Dentist at Baylor University College of Dentistry.	Vol. XI, p. 210.
Statman, Irving [D]	Assistant District Director of Dallas District, Texas Employment Commission.	Vol. X, p. 149.
Steele, Charles Hall, Jr.[D]	Resident of New Orleans who assisted Oswald in distribution of handbills.	Vol. X, p. 62.
Steele, Charles Hall, Sr.[D]	Father of Charles Hall Steele, Jr.	Vol. X, p. 71.

Witness	Description	Testimony
Steele, Don Francis [D]	Member, Dallas Police Department.	Vol. XII, p. 353.
Stevenson, M. W. [D]	Deputy Chief, Dallas Police Department.	Vol. XII, p. 91. Vol. XV, p. 133.
Stombaugh, Paul Morgan [C A]	Hair and fiber expert, FBI	Vol. IV, p. 56. Vol. XV, p. 702.
Stovall, Richard S. [D]	Member, Dallas Police Department.	Vol. VII, p. 186.
Stovall, Robert L. [D]	President, J a g g a r s-Chiles-Stovall, Dallas, Tex.	Vol. X, p. 167.
Strong, Jesse M. [D]	Employee, Western Union Telegraph Co.	Vol. XIII, p. 284.
Stuckey, William Kirk [D]	Radio program director, New Orleans.	Vol. XI, p. 156.
Studebaker, Robert Lee [D]	Member, Dallas Police Department.	Vol. VII, p. 137.
Surrey, Robert Alan [C]	Publisher of handbill attacking President Kennedy.	Vol. V, p. 420.
Tague, James Thomas [D]	Witness at assassination scene.	Vol. VII, p. 552.
Talbert, Cecil E. [D]	Captain, Dallas Police Department.	Vol. XII, p. 108. Vol. XV, p. 182.
Tasker, Harry T. [D]	Taxicab driver in Dallas	Vol. XV, p. 679.
Taylor, Gary E. [D A]	Acquaintance of the Oswalds in Texas.	Vol. IX, p. 73. Vol. XI, p. 470.
Thompson, Llewellyn E. [C]	Former U.S. Ambassador to Russia.	Vol. V, p. 567.
Thornley, Kerry Wendell [D]	Acquaintance of Oswald in Marines.	Vol. XI, p. 82.
Tice, Wilma May [D]	Resident of Dallas	Vol. XV, p. 388.
Tobias, Mahlon F., Sr. [D]	Manager of apartment house where the Oswalds resided, Dallas.	Vol. X, p. 251.
Tobias, Mrs. Mahlon F. [D]	Wife of M. F. Tobias, Sr.	Vol. X, p. 231.
Tomlinson, Darrell C. [D]	Senior engineer, Parkland Hospital.	Vol. VI, p. 128.
Tormey, James J. [D]	Executive secretary, Hall-Davis Defense Commission.	Vol. X, p. 107.
Truly, Roy Sansom [A C D]	Superintendent, TSBD	Vol. III, p. 212. Vol. VII, pp. 380, 591.
Turner, F. M. [D]	Member, Dallas Police Department.	Vol. VII, p. 217.
Turner, Jimmy [D]	TV director, Fort Worth	Vol. XIII, p. 130.
Twiford, Horace Elroy [A]	Member, Socialist Labor Party, Houston, Tex.	Vol. XI, p. 179.
Twiford, Estelle [A]	Wife of Horace Elroy Twiford.	Vol. XI, p. 179.
Underwood, James R. [D]	Assistant news director, TV and radio, Dallas.	Vol. VI, p. 167.
Vaughn, Roy Eugene [D]	Member, Dallas Police Department.	Vol. XII, p. 357.
Vinson, Philip Eugene [D]	Reporter, Fort Worth	Vol. VIII, p. 75.
Voebel, Edward [D]	Acquaintance of Oswald in Beauregard Junior High School, New Orleans.	Vol. VIII, p. 1.
Voshinin, Igor Vladimir [D]	Member of Russian-speaking community in Dallas.	Vol. VIII, p. 448.
Voshinin, Mrs. Igor Vladimir. [D]	Acquaintance of the Oswalds in Texas.	Vol. VIII, p. 425.

Witness	Description	Testimony
Wade, Henry [C]	District attorney, Dallas County.	Vol. V, p. 213.
Waldman, William J.[D]	Vice President, Klein's Sporting Goods, Inc.	Vol. VII, p. 360.
Waldo, Thayer [D]	Reporter, Forth Worth	Vol. XV, p. 585.
Walker, C. T.[D]	Member, Dallas Police Department.	Vol. VII, p. 34.
Walker, Maj. Gen. Edwin A.[D]	Resident of Dallas and object of shooting in April 1963.	Vol. XI, p. 404.
Walker, Ira N., Jr.[D]	Broadcast technician, Fort Worth.	Vol. XIII, p. 289.
Wall, Breck (a.k.a. Billy Ray Wilson).[D]	Acquaintance of Ruby	Vol. XIV, p. 599.
Walthers, Eddy Raymond [D]	Deputy sheriff, Dallas County.	Vol. VII, p. 544.
Warner, Roger C.[A]	Agent, U.S. Secret Service	Vol. XV, p. 619.
Waterman, Bernice [C]	Adjudicator, Passport Office, Department of State.	Vol. V, p. 346.
Watherwax, Arthur William.[D]	Printer, Dallas newspaper	Vol. XV, p. 564.
Watson, James C.[D]	Member, Dallas Police Department.	Vol. XII, p. 372.
Weinstock, Louis [A]	General manager, the Worker.	Vol. XI, p. 207.
Weissman, Bernard [C D]	Codraftsman and signer of November 22, 1963, full-page advertisement.	Vol. V, p. 487. Vol. XI, p. 428.
Weitzman, Seymour [D]	Deputy constable, Dallas County.	Vol. VII, p. 105.
West, Troy Eugene [D]	Employee, TSBD	Vol. VI, p. 356.
Westbrook, W. R.[D]	Captain, Dallas Police Department.	Vol. VII, p. 109.
Wester, Jane Carolyn [D]	Nurse, Parkland Hospital	Vol. VI, p. 120.
Whaley, William Wayne [C D]	Taxicab driver in Dallas	Vol. II, pp. 253, 292. Vol. VI, p. 428.
White, J. C.[D]	Member, Dallas Police Department.	Vol. VI, p. 253.
White, Martin G.[D]	Doctor, Parkland Hospital	Vol. VI, p. 82.
Whitworth, Edith [D]	Manager, used furniture store, Irving, Tex.	Vol. XI, p. 262.
Wiggins, Woodrow [D]	Lieutenant, Dallas Police Department.	Vol. XII, p. 388.
Wilcox, Laurance R.[D]	District manager, Western Union Telegraph Co.	Vol. X, p. 414.
Williams, Bonnie Ray [C]	Employee, TSBD	Vol. III, p. 161.
Willis, Linda Kay [D]	Daughter of Phillip L. Willis.	Vol. VII, p. 498.
Willis, Phillip L.[D]	Witness at assassination scene.	Vol. VII, p. 492.
Wilson, Billy Ray (see Wall, Breck).		
Wittmus, Ronald G.[A]	Fingerprint expert, FBI	Vol. VII, p. 590.
Wood, Homer [D]	Patron, Sports Drome Rifle Range.	Vol. X, p. 385.
Wood, Sterling Charles [D]	Son of Dr. Homer Wood	Vol. X, p. 390.
Wood, Theresa [D]	Wife of Dr. Homer Wood	Vol. X, p. 398.
Worley, Gano E.[D]	Reserve Force, Dallas Police Department.	Vol. XII, p. 378.
Worrell, James Richard, Jr.[C]	Witness at assassination scene.	Vol. II, p. 190.
Wright, Norman Earl [D]	Acquaintance of Jack Ruby	Vol. XV, p. 244.

Commission Procedures for the Taking of Testimony

RESOLUTION GOVERNING QUESTIONING OF WITNESSES BY MEMBERS OF THE COMMISSION STAFF

Pursuant to Executive Order No. 11130, November 29, 1963, which authorizes this Commission "to prescribe its own procedures," it is therefore

Resolved, That the following are hereby adopted as the rules of this Commission for the questioning of witnesses by members of the Commission staff.

I. Sworn Depositions

A. Individual members of the staff are hereby authorized to administer oaths and affirmations, examine witnesses, and receive evidence in the form of sworn depositions on any matter under investigation by the Commission.

B. Such sworn depositions may be taken only from witnesses designated in writing for questioning in this manner by the Commission, by a member of the Commission, or by the General Counsel of the Commission.

C. A stenographic verbatim transcript shall be made of all sworn depositions. Copies of the witness' testimony shall be available for inspection by the witness or his counsel. When approved by the Commission, said copies may be purchased by the witness or his counsel at regularly prescribed rates from the official reporter.

D. Process and papers of the Commission issued under Paragraph (d) of Joint Resolution S.J. 137, 88th Congress, 1st session, shall be returnable no less than three days from the date on which such process or papers are issued, and shall state the time, place, and general subject matter of the deposition. In lieu of such process and papers, the Commission may request the presence of witnesses and production of evidence for the purpose of sworn depositions by written notice mailed no less than three days from the date of the deposition.

E. The period of notice specified in Paragraph D may be waived by a witness.

F. A witness at a sworn deposition shall have the right to be accompanied by counsel of his own choosing, who shall have the right to advise the witness of his rights under the laws and Constitution of the United States, and the state wherein the deposition shall occur, and to make brief objections to questions.

At the conclusion of the witness' testimony, counsel shall have the right to clarify the testimony of the witness by questioning the witness.

G. At the opening of any deposition a member of the Commission's staff shall read into the record a statement setting forth the nature of the Commission's inquiry and the purpose for which the witness has been asked to testify or produce evidence.

H. Any witness who refuses to answer a question shall state the grounds for so doing. At the conclusion of any deposition in which the witness refuses to answer a question the transcript shall be submitted to the General Counsel for review and consideration whether the witness should be called to testify before the Commission.

II. Sworn Affidavits

A. Members of the Commission staff are hereby authorized to obtain sworn affidavits from those witnesses who have been designated in writing by the Commission, a member of the Commission, or the general counsel of the Commission as witnesses whose testimony will be obtained in this manner.

B. A copy of the affidavit shall be provided the affiant or his counsel.

RESOLUTION

Pursuant to Executive Order No. 11130, November 29, 1963, which authorizes this Commission "to prescribe its own procedures," it is therefore

Resolved, That the following are hereby adopted as the rules of this Commission in connection with hearings conducted for the purpose of the taking of testimony or the production of evidence.

1. One or more members of the Commission shall be present at all hearings. If more than one Commissioner is present, the Chairman of the Commission shall designate the order in which the Commissioners shall preside.

2. Any member of the Commission or any agent or agency designated by the Commission for such purpose, may administer oaths and affirmations, examine witnesses, and receive evidence.

3. Process and papers of the Commission issued under Paragraph (d) of Joint Resolution S.J. 137, 88th Congress, 1st session, shall be returnable no less than three days from the date on which such process or papers are issued, and shall state the time, place, and general subject matter of the hearing. In lieu of such process and papers, the Commission may request the presence of witnesses and the production of evidence by written notice mailed no less than 3 days from the date of the hearing.

4. The period of notice specified in paragraph three (3) may be waived by a witness.

5. At the opening of any hearing at which testimony is to be received a member of the Commission shall read into the record a state-

ment setting forth the nature of the Commission's inquiry and the purpose for which the witness has been asked to testify or produce evidence. A copy of this statement shall be given to each witness prior to his testifying.

6. A witness shall have the right to be accompanied by counsel, of his own choosing, who shall have the right to advise the witness of his rights under the laws and Constitution of the United States and to make brief objections to questions. At the conclusion of the witness' testimony, counsel shall have the right to clarify the testimony of the witness by questioning the witness.

7. Every witness who testifies at a hearing shall have the right to make an oral statement and to file a sworn statement which shall be made part of the transcript of such hearing, but such oral or written statement shall be relevant to the subject of the hearing.

8. Rulings on objections or other procedural questions shall be made by the presiding member of the Commission.

9. A stenographic verbatim transcript shall be made of all testimony received by the Commission. Copies of such transcript shall be available for inspection or purchase by the witness or his counsel at regularly prescribed rates from the official reporter. A witness or his counsel shall be permitted to purchase or inspect only the transcript of his testimony before the Commission.

A Brief History of Presidential Protection

In the course of the history of the United States four Presidents have been assassinated, within less than 100 years, beginning with Abraham Lincoln in 1865. Attempts were also made on the lives of two other Presidents, one President-elect, and one ex-President. Still other Presidents were the objects of plots that were never carried out. The actual attempts occurred as follows:

Andrew Jackson_____ Jan. 30, 1835.
Abraham Lincoln_____ Apr. 14, 1865. Died Apr. 15, 1865.
James A. Garfield_____ July 2, 1881. Died Sept. 19, 1881.
William McKinley_____ Sept. 6, 1901. Died Sept. 14, 1901.
Theodore Roosevelt_____ Oct. 14, 1912. Wounded; recovered.
Franklin D. Roosevelt_____ Feb. 15, 1933.
Harry S. Truman_____ Nov. 1, 1950.
John F. Kennedy_____ Nov. 22, 1963. Died that day.

Attempts have thus been made on the lives of one of every five American Presidents. One of every nine Presidents has been killed. Since 1865, there have been attempts on the lives of one of every four Presidents and the successful assassination of one of every five. During the last three decades, three attacks were made.

It was only after William McKinley was shot that systematic and continuous protection of the President was instituted. Protection before McKinley was intermittent and spasmodic. The problem had existed from the days of the early Presidents, but no action was taken until three tragic events had occurred. In considering the effectiveness of present day protection arrangements, it is worthwhile to examine the development of Presidential protection over the years, to understand both the high degree of continuing danger and the anomalous reluctance to take the necessary precautions.

BEFORE THE CIVIL WAR

In the early days of the Republic, there was remarkably little concern about the safety of Presidents and few measures were taken to protect them. They were at times the objects of abuse and the recipients of threatening letters as more recent Presidents have been, but they did not take the threats seriously and moved about freely without protective escorts. On his inauguration day, Thomas Jefferson walked from his boarding house to the Capitol, unaccompanied by any guard, to take the oath of office. There was no police authority in Washington itself until 1805 when the mayor appointed a high constable and 40 deputy constables.[1]

John Quincy Adams received many threatening letters and on one occasion was threatened in person in the White House by a court-martialed Army sergeant. In spite of this incident, the President asked for no protection and continued to indulge his fondness for solitary walks and early morning swims in the Potomac.[2]

Among pre-Civil War Presidents, Andrew Jackson aroused particularly strong feelings. He received many threatening letters which, with a fine contempt, he would endorse and send to the Washington Globe for publication. On one occasion in May 1833, Jackson was assaulted by a former Navy lieutenant, Robert B. Randolph, but refused to prosecute him. This is not regarded as an attempt at assassination, since Randolph apparently did not intend serious injury.[3]

Less than 2 years later, on the morning of January 10, 1835, as Jackson emerged from the east portico of the Capitol, he was accosted by a would-be assassin, Richard Lawrence, an English-born house painter. Lawrence fired his two pistols at the President, but they both misfired. Lawrence was quickly overpowered and held for trial. A jury found him not guilty by reason of insanity. He was confined in jails and mental hospitals for the rest of his life.[4]

The attack on Jackson did not inspire any action to provide protection for the Chief Executive. Jackson's immediate successor, Martin Van Buren, often walked to church alone and rode horseback alone in the woods not far from the White House. In August 1842, after an intoxicated painter had thrown rocks at President John Tyler, who was walking on the grounds to the south of the White House, Congress passed an act to establish an auxiliary watch for the protection of public and private property in Washington. The force was to consist of a captain and 15 men. This act was apparently aimed more at the protection of the White House, which had been defaced on occasion, than of the President.[5]

LINCOLN

Even before he took the oath of office, Abraham Lincoln was thought to be the object of plots and conspiracies to kidnap or kill him. Extremist opponents apparently contemplated desperate measures to prevent his inauguration, and there is some evidence that they plotted to attack him while he was passing through Baltimore on his way to Washington.[6]

For the inauguration, the Army took precautions unprecedented up to that time and perhaps more elaborate than any precautions taken since. Soldiers occupied strategic points throughout the city, along the procession route, and at the Capitol, while armed men in plain clothes mingled with the crowds. Lincoln himself, in a carriage with President Buchanan, was surrounded on all sides by such dense masses of soldiers that he was almost completely hidden from the view of the crowds. The precautions at the Capitol during the ceremony were almost as thorough and equally successful.[7]

Lincoln lived in peril during all his years in office. The volume of threatening letters remained high throughout the war, but little attention was paid to them. The few letters that were investigated yielded no results.[8] He was reluctant to surround himself with guards and often rejected protection or sought to slip away from it. This has been characteristic of almost all American Presidents. They have regarded protection as a necessary affliction at best and contrary to their normal instincts for either personal privacy or freedom to meet the people. In Lincoln these instincts were especially strong, and he suffered with impatience the efforts of his friends, the police, and the military to safeguard him.[9]

The protection of the President during the war varied greatly, depending on Lincoln's susceptibility to warnings. Frequently, military units were assigned to guard the White House and to accompany the President on his travels. Lincoln's friend, Ward H. Lamon, on becoming marshal of the District of Columbia in 1861, took personal charge of protecting the President and provided guards for the purpose, but he became so exasperated at the President's lack of cooperation that he tendered his resignation. Lincoln did not accept it. Finally, late in the war, in November 1864, four Washington policemen were detailed to the White House to act as personal bodyguards to the President. Lincoln tolerated them reluctantly and insisted they remain as inconspicuous as possible.[10]

In the closing days of the war, rumors of attempts on Lincoln's life persisted. The well-known actor, John Wilkes Booth, a fanatical Confederate sympathizer, plotted with others for months to kidnap the President. The fall of the Confederacy apparently hardened his determination to kill Lincoln.[11] Booth's opportunity came on Good Friday, April 14, 1865, when he learned that the President would be attending a play at Ford's Theater that night. The President's bodyguard for the evening was Patrolman John F. Parker of the Washington Police, a man who proved himself unfit for protective duty. He was supposed to remain on guard in the corridor outside of the Presidential box during the entire performance of the play, but he soon wandered off to watch the play and then even went outside the theater to have a drink at a nearby saloon. Parker's dereliction of duty left the President totally unprotected.[12] Shortly after 10 o'clock on that evening, Booth found his way up to the Presidential box and shot the President in the head. The President's wound was a mortal one; he died the next morning, April 15.[13]

A detachment of troops captured Booth on April 26 at a farm near Bowling Green, Va.; he received a bullet wound and died a few hours later. At a trial in June, a military tribunal sentenced four of Booth's associates to death and four others to terms of imprisonment.[14]

Lincoln's assassination revealed the total inadequacy of Presidential protection. A congressional committee conducted an extensive investigation of the assassination, but with traditional reluctance, called for no action to provide better protection for the President in the future. Nor did requests for protective measures come from the President or from Government departments. This lack of concern for the protection of the President may have derived also from the tendency of the time to regard Lincoln's assassination as part of a unique crisis that was not likely to happen to a future Chief Executive.[15]

THE NEED FOR PROTECTION FURTHER DEMONSTRATED

For a short time after the war, soldiers assigned by the War Department continued to protect the White House and its grounds. Metropolitan Washington policemen assisted on special occasions to maintain order and prevent the congregation of crowds. The permanent Metropolitan Police guard was reduced to three and assigned entirely to protection at the White House. There was no special group of trained officers to protect the person of the President. Presidents after Lincoln continued to move about in Washington virtually unattended, as their predecessors had done before the Civil War, and, as before, such protection as they got at the White House came from the doormen, who were not especially trained for guard duty.[16]

This lack of personal protection for the President came again tragically to the attention of the country with the shooting of President James A. Garfield in 1881. The President's assassin, Charles J. Guiteau, was a self-styled "lawyer, theologian, and politician" who had convinced himself that his unsolicited efforts to help elect Garfield in 1880 entitled him to appointment as a consul in Europe. Bitterly disappointed that the President ignored his repeated written requests for appointment to office and obsessed with a kind of megalomania, he resolved to kill Garfield.

At that time Guiteau was 38 years old and had an unusually checkered career behind him. He had been an itinerant and generally unsuccessful lecturer and evangelist, a lawyer, and a would-be politician. While it is true he resented Garfield's failure to appoint him consul in Paris as a reward for his wholly illusory contribution to the Garfield campaign, and he verbally attacked Garfield for his lack of support for the so-called Stalwart wing of the Republican Party, these may not have supplied the total motivation for his crime. At his trial he testified that the "Deity" had commanded him to remove the President. There is no evidence that he confided his assassination plans to anyone or that he had any close friends or confidants. He made his attack on the President under circumstances where escape after the shooting was inconceivable. There were some hereditary mental problems in his family and Guiteau apparently believed in divine inspiration.[17]

Guiteau later testified that he had had three opportunities to attack the President prior to the actual shooting. On all of these occasions, within a brief period of 3 weeks, the President was unguarded. Guiteau finally realized his intent on the morning of July 2, 1881. As Garfield was walking to a train in the Baltimore and Potomac Railroad Station in Washington, Guiteau stepped up and shot him in the back. Garfield did not die from the effects of the wound until September 19, 1881. Although there was evidence of serious abnormality in Guiteau, he was found guilty of murder and sentenced to be hanged. The execution took place on June 30, 1882.[18]

At least one newspaper, the New York Tribune, predicted that the assault on Garfield would lead to the President becoming "the slave of his office, the prisoner of forms and restrictions," in sharp and unwelcome contrast to the splendidly simple life he had been able to live before.

> The bullet of the assassin who lurked in the Washington railway station to take the life of President Garfield shattered the simple Republican manner of life which the custom of nearly a century has prescribed for the Chief Magistrate of the United States. Our Presidents have been the first citizens of the Republic—nothing more. With a measure of power in their hands far greater than is wielded by the ruler of any limited monarchy in Europe, they have never surrounded themselves with the forms and safeguards of courts. The White House has been a business office to everybody. Its occupant has always been more accessible than the heads of great commercial establishments. When the passions of the war were at fever heat, Mr. Lincoln used to have a small guard of cavalry when he rode out to his summer residence at the Soldier's Home; but at no other time in our history has it been thought needful for a President to have any special protection against violence when inside or outside the White House. Presidents have driven about Washington like other people and travelled over the country as unguarded and unconstrained as any private citizen.[19]

The prediction of the Tribune did not come to pass. Although the Nation was shocked by this deed, its representatives took no steps to provide the President with personal protection. The President continued to move about Washington, sometimes completely alone, and to travel without special protection. There is a story that President Chester A. Arthur, Garfield's successor, once went to a ceremony at the Washington Navy Yard on a public conveyance that he hailed in front of the White House.[20]

During Grover Cleveland's second administration (1893–97) the number of threatening letters addressed to the President increased markedly, and Mrs. Cleveland persuaded the President to increase the number of White House policemen to 27 from the 3 who had constituted the force since the Civil War. In 1894, the Secret Service began to provide protection, on an informal basis.[21]

The Secret Service was organized as a division of the Department of the Treasury in 1865, to deal with counterfeiting.[22] Its jurisdiction was extended to other fiscal crimes against the United States in later appropriations acts,[23] but its early work in assisting in protecting the President was an unofficial, stopgap response to a need for a trained organization, with investigative capabilities, to perform this task. In 1894, while investigating a plot by a group of gamblers in Colorado to assassinate President Cleveland, the Secret Service assigned a small detail of operatives to the White House to help protect him. Secret Service men accompanied the President and his family to their vacation home in Massachusetts; special details protected the President in Washington, on trips, and at special functions.[24] For a time, two agents rode in a buggy behind President Cleveland's carriage, but this practice attracted so much attention in the opposition newspapers that it was soon discontinued at the President's insistence.[25] These initially informal and part-time arrangements eventually led to the organization of permanent systematic protection for the President and his family.

During the Spanish-American War the Secret Service stationed a detail at the White House to provide continuous protection for President McKinley. The special wartime protective measures were relaxed after the war, but Secret Service guards remained on duty at the White House at least part of the time.[26]

Between 1894 and 1900, anarchists murdered the President of France, the Premier of Spain, the Empress of Austria, and the King of Italy. At the turn of the century the Secret Service thought that the strong police action taken against the anarchists in Europe was compelling them to flee and that many were coming to the United States. Concerned about the protection of the President, the Secret Service increased the number of guards and directed that a guard accompany him on all of his trips.[27]

Unlike Lincoln and Garfield, President McKinley was being guarded when he was shot by Leon F. Czolgosz, an American-born 28-year-old factory worker and farmhand. On September 6, 1901, the President was holding a brief reception for the public in the Temple of Music at the Pan American Exposition in Buffalo. Long lines of people passed between two rows of policemen and soldiers to reach the President and shake his hand. In the immediate vicinity of the President were four Buffalo detectives, four soldiers, and three Secret Service agents. Two of the Secret Service men were facing the President at a distance of 3 feet. One of them stated later that it was normally his custom to stand at the side of the President on such occasions, but that he had been requested not to do so at this time in order to permit McKinley's secretary and the president of the exposition to stand on either side of McKinley. Czolgosz joined the line, concealed a pistol under a handkerchief, and when he stood in front of the President shot twice through the handkerchief. McKinley fell critically wounded.[28]

Czolgosz, a self-styled anarchist, did not believe in rulers of any kind. There is evidence that the organized anarchists in the U.S.A. did not accept or trust him. He was not admitted as a member to any of the secret anarchist societies. No co-plotters were ever discovered, and there is no evidence that he had confided in anyone. A calm inquiry made by two eminent alienists about a year after Czolgosz was executed found that Czolgosz had for some time been suffering from delusions. One was that he was an anarchist; another was that it was his duty to assassinate the President.[29]

The assassin said he had no grudge against the President personally but did not believe in the republican form of government or in rulers of any kind. In his written confession he included the words, " 'I don't believe one man should have so much service and another man should have none.' " As he was strapped to the chair to be electrocuted, he said: " 'I killed the President because he was the enemy of the good people—the good working people. I am not sorry for my crime.' " [30]

McKinley lingered on for 8 days before he died of blood poisoning early on the morning of September 14. Czolgosz, who had been captured immediately, was swiftly tried, convicted, and condemned to death. Although it seemed to some contemporaries that Czolgosz was incompetent, the defense made no effort to plead insanity. Czolgosz was executed 45 days after the President's death. Investigations by the Buffalo police and the Secret Service revealed no accomplices and no plot of any kind.[31]

DEVELOPMENT OF PRESIDENTIAL PROTECTION

This third assassination of a President in a little more than a generation—it was only 36 years since Lincoln had been killed—shook the nation and aroused it to a greater awareness of the uniqueness of the Presidency and the grim hazards that surrounded an incumbent of that Office. The first congressional session after the assassination of McKinley gave more attention to legislation concerning attacks on the President than had any previous Congress but did not pass any measures for the protection of the President.[32] Nevertheless, in 1902 the Secret Service, which was then the only Federal general investigative agency of any consequence, assumed full-time responsibility for the safety of the President. Protection of the President now became one of its major permanent functions, and it assigned two men to its original full-time White House detail. Additional agents were provided when the President traveled or went on vacation.[33]

Theodore Roosevelt, who was the first President to experience the extensive system of protection that has surrounded the President ever since, voiced an opinion of Presidential protection that was probably shared in part by most of his successors. In a letter to Senator Henry Cabot Lodge in 1906, from his summer home, he wrote:

The Secret Service men are a very small but very necessary thorn in the flesh. Of course, they would not be the least use in preventing any assault upon my life. I do not believe there is any danger of such an assault, and if there were, as Lincoln said, "though it would be safer for a President to live in a cage, it would interfere with his business." But it is only the Secret Service men who render life endurable, as you would realize if you saw the procession of carriages that pass through the place, the procession of people on foot who try to get into the place, not to speak of the multitude of cranks and others who are stopped in the village.[34]

Roosevelt, who had succeeded to the Presidency because of an assassin's bullet, himself became the object of an assassination attempt a few years after he left office and when he was no longer under Secret Service protection. During the Presidential campaign of 1912, just as he was about to make a political speech in Milwaukee on October 14, he was shot and wounded in the breast by John N. Schrank, a 36-year-old German-born ex-tavern keeper. A folded manuscript of his long speech and the metal case for his eyeglasses in the breast pocket of Roosevelt's coat were all that prevented the assassination.[35]

Schrank had had a vision in 1901, induced possibly by McKinley's assassination, which took on meaning for him after Roosevelt, 11 years later, started to campaign for the Presidency. In this vision the ghost of McKinley appeared to him and told him not to let a murderer (i.e., Roosevelt, who according to the vision had murdered McKinley) become President. It was then that he determined upon the assassination. At the bidding of McKinley's ghost, he felt he had no choice but to kill Theodore Roosevelt. After his attempt on Roosevelt, Schrank was found to be insane and was committed to mental hospitals in Wisconsin for the rest of his life.[36]

The establishment and extension of the Secret Service authority for protection was a prolonged process. Although the Secret Service undertook to provide full-time protection for the President beginning in 1902, it received neither funds for the purpose nor sanction from the Congress until 1906 when the Sundry Civil Expenses Act for 1907 included funds for protection of the President by the Secret Service.[37] Following the election of William Howard Taft in 1908, the Secret Service began providing protection for the President-elect. This practice received statutory authorization in 1913, and in the same year, Congress authorized permanent protection of the President.[38] It remained necessary to renew the authority annually in the Appropriations Acts until 1951.

As in the Civil and Spanish-American Wars, the coming of war in 1917 caused increased concern for the safety of the President. Congress enacted a law, since referred to as the threat statute, making it a crime to threaten the President by mail or in any other manner.[39] In 1917 Congress also authorized protection for the President's immediate family by the Secret Service.[40]

As the scope of the Presidency expanded during the 20th century, the Secret Service found the problems of protection becoming more numerous. In 1906, for the first time in history, a President traveled outside the United States while in office. When Theodore Roosevelt visited Panama in that year, he was accompanied and protected by Secret Service men.[41] In 1918–19 Woodrow Wilson broadened the precedent of Presidential foreign travel when he traveled to Europe with a Secret Service escort of 10 men to attend the Versailles Peace Conference.[42]

The attempt on the life of President-elect Franklin D. Roosevelt in 1933 further demonstrated the broad scope and complexity of the protection problems facing the Secret Service. Giuseppe Zangara was a bricklayer and stonemason with a professed hatred of capitalists and Presidents. He seemed to be obsessed with the desire to kill a President. After his arrest he confessed that he had first planned to go to Washington to kill President Herbert Hoover, but as the cold climate of the North was bad for his stomach trouble, he was loath to leave Miami, where he was staying. When he read in the paper that President-elect Roosevelt would be in Miami, he resolved to kill him.[43]

On the night of February 15, 1933, at a political rally in Miami's Bayfront Park, the President-elect sat on the top of the rear seat of his automobile with a small microphone in his hand as he made a short informal talk. Fortunately for him, however, he slid down into the seat just before Zangara could get near enough to take aim. The assassin's arm may have been jogged just as he shot; the five rounds he directed at Roosevelt went awry. However, he mortally wounded Mayor Anton Cermak, of Chicago, and hit four other persons; the President-elect, by a miracle, escaped. Zangara, of course, never had any chance of escaping.[44]

Zangara was electrocuted on March 20, 1933, only 33 days after his attempt on Roosevelt. No evidence of accomplices or conspiracy came to light, but there was some sensational newspaper speculation, wholly undocumented, that Zangara may have been hired by Chicago gangsters to kill Cermak.[45]

The force provided since the Civil War by the Washington Metropolitan Police for the protection of the White House had grown to 54 men by 1922.[46] In that year Congress enacted legislation creating the White House Police Force as a separate organization under the direct control of the President.[47] This force was actually supervised by the President's military aide until 1930, when Congress placed supervision under the Chief of the Secret Service.[48] Although Congress transferred control and supervision of the force to the Secretary of the Treasury in 1962,[49] the Secretary delegated supervision to the Chief of the Secret Service.[50]

The White House detail of the Secret Service grew in size slowly from the original 2 men assigned in 1902. In 1914 it still numbered only 5, but during World War I it was increased to 10 men. Additional men were added when the President traveled. After the war the size of the detail grew until it reached 16 agents and 2 supervisors by 1939. World War II created new and greater protection problems, especially those arising from the President's trips abroad to the Grand Strategy Conferences in such places as Casablanca, Quebec, Tehran, Cairo, and Yalta. To meet the increased demands, the White House detail was increased to 37 men early in the war.[51]

The volume of mail received by the White House had always been large, but it reached huge proportions under Franklin D. Roosevelt. Presidents had always received threatening letters but never in such quantities. To deal with this growing problem, the Secret Service established in 1940 the Protective Research Section to analyze and make available to those charged with protecting the President, information from White House mail and other sources concerning people potentially capable of violence to the President. The Protective Research Section undoubtedly permitted the Secret Service to anticipate and forestall many incidents that might have been embarrassing or harmful to the President.[52]

Although there was no advance warning of the attempt on Harry S. Truman's life on November 1, 1950, the protective measures taken by the Secret Service availed, and the assassins never succeeded in firing directly at the President. The assassins—Oscar Collazo and Griselio Torresola, Puerto Rican Nationalists living in New York—tried to force their way into Blair House, at the time the President's residence while the White House was being repaired. Blair House was guarded by White House policemen and Secret Service agents. In the ensuing gun battle, Torresola and one White House policeman were killed, and Collazo and two White House policemen were wounded. Had the assassins succeeded in entering the front door of Blair House, they would probably have been cut down immediately by another Secret Service agent inside who kept the doorway covered with a submachine gun from his vantage point at the foot of the main stairs. In all, some 27 shots were fired in less than 3 minutes.[53]

Collazo was brought to trial in 1951 and sentenced to death, but President Truman commuted the sentence to life imprisonment on July 24, 1952. Although there was a great deal of evidence linking Collazo and Torresola to the Nationalist Party of Puerto Rico and its leader, Pedro Albizu Campos, the Government could not establish that the attack on the President was part of a larger Nationalist conspiracy.[54]

The attack on President Truman led to the enactment in 1951 of legislation that permanently authorized the Secret Service to protect the President, his immediate family, the President-elect, and the Vice President, the last upon his request. Protection of the Vice President by the Secret Service had begun in January 1945 when Harry S. Truman occupied the office.[55]

In 1962 Congress further enlarged the list of Government officers to be safeguarded, authorizing protection of the Vice President (or the officer next in order of succession to the Presidency) without requiring his request therefor; of the Vice President-elect; and of a former President, at his request, for a reasonable period after his departure from office. The Secret Service considered this "reasonable period" to be 6 months.[56]

Amendments to the threat statute of 1917, passed in 1955 and 1962, made it a crime to threaten to harm the President-elect, the Vice President, or other officers next in succession to either office. The President's immediate family was not included in the threat statute.[57]

Congressional concern regarding the uses to which the President might put the Secret Service—first under Theodore Roosevelt and subsequently under Woodrow Wilson—caused Congress to place tight restrictions on the functions of the Service and the uses of its funds.[58] The restrictions probably prevented the Secret Service from developing into a general investigative agency, leaving the field open for some other agency when the need arose. The other agency proved to be the Federal Bureau of Investigation (FBI), established within the Department of Justice in 1908.[59]

The FBI grew rapidly in the 1920's, and especially in the 1930's and after, establishing itself as the largest, best equipped, and best known of all U.S. Government investigative agencies. In the appropriations of the FBI there recurred annually an item for the "protection of the person of the President of the United States," that had first appeared in the appropriation of the Department of Justice in 1910 under the heading "Miscellaneous Objects." [60] But there is no evidence that the Justice Department ever exercised any direct responsibility for the protection of the President. Although it had no prescribed protection functions, according to its Director, J. Edgar Hoover, the FBI did provide protection to Vice President Charles Curtis at his request, when he was serving under Herbert Hoover from 1929 to 1933. Over the years the FBI contribution to Presidential protection was confined chiefly to the referral to the Secret Service of the names of people who might be potentially dangerous to the President.[61]

In recent years the Secret Service has remained a small and specialized bureau, restricted to very limited functions prescribed by Congress. In 1949, a task force of the Commission on Organization of the Executive Branch of the Government (Hoover Commission), recommended nonfiscal functions be removed from the Treasury Department.[62] The recommendation called for transfer of the White House detail, White House Police Force, and Treasury Guard Force from the Secret Service to the Department of Justice. The final report of the Commission on the Treasury Department omitted this recommendation, leaving the protective function with the Secret Service.[63] At a meeting of the Commission, ex-President Hoover, in a reference to the proposed transfer, expressed the opinion that "the President will object to having a 'private eye' looking after these fellows and would rather continue with the service." [64]

In 1963 the Secret Service was one of several investigative agencies in the Treasury Department. Its major functions were to combat counterfeiting and to protect the President, his family, and other designated persons.[65] The Chief of the Secret Service administered its activities through four divisions: Investigation, Inspection, Administrative, and Security, and 65 field offices throughout the country, each under a special agent in charge who reported directly to Washington. The Security Division supervised the White House detail, the White House Police, and the Treasury Guard Force. During fiscal year 1963 (July 1, 1962–June 30, 1963) the Secret Service had an average strength of 513, of whom 351 were special agents. Average strength of the White House Police during the year was 179.[66]

Medical Reports From Doctors at
Parkland Memorial Hospital, Dallas, Tex.

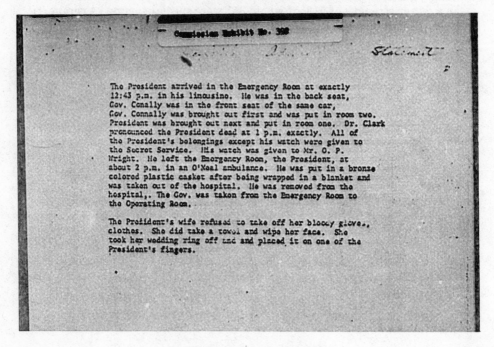

The President arrived in the Emergency Room at exactly
12:43 p.m. in his limousine. He was in the back seat,
Gov. Conally was in the front seat of the same car,
Gov. Connally was brought out first and was put in room two.
President was brought out next and put in room one. Dr. Clark
pronounced the President dead at 1 p.m. exactly. All of
the President's belongings except his watch were given to
the Secret Service. His watch was given to Mr. O. P.
Wright. He left the Emergency Room, the President, at
about 2 p.m. in an O'Neal ambulance. He was put in a bronze
colored plastic casket after being wrapped in a blanket and
was taken out of the hospital. He was removed from the
hospital,. The Gov. was taken from the Emergency Room to
the Operating Room.

The President's wife refused to take off her bloody gloves,
clothes. She did take a towel and wipe her face. She
took her wedding ring off and and placed it on one of the
President's fingers.

COMMISSION EXHIBIT No. 392

516

SUMMARY

The President arrived at the Emergency Room at 12:43 P.M., the 22nd of November, 1963. He was in the back seat of his limousine. Governor Connally of Texas was also in this car. The first physician to see the President was Dr. James Carrico, a Resident in General Surgery.

Dr. Carrico noted the President to have slow, agonal respiratory efforts. He could hear a heartbeat but found no pulse or blood pressure to be present. Two external wounds, one in the lower third of the anterior neck, the other in the occipital region of the skull, were noted. Through the head wound, blood and brain were extruding. Dr. Carrico inserted a cuffed endotracheal tube. While doing so, he noted a ragged wound of the trachea immediately below the larynx.

At this time, Dr. Malcolm Perry, Attending Surgeon, Dr. Charles Baxter, Attending Surgeon, and Dr. Ronald Jones, another Resident in General Surgery, arrived. Immediately thereafter, Dr. M. T. Jenkins, Director of the Department of Anesthesia, and Doctors Giesecke and Hunt, two other Staff Anesthesiologists, arrived. The endotracheal tube had been connected to a Bennett respirator to assist the President's breathing. An Anesthesia machine was substituted for this by Dr. Jenkins. Only 100% oxygen was administered.

A cutdown was performed in the right ankle, and a polyethylene catheter inserted in the vein. An infusion of lactated Ringer's solution was begun. Blood was drawn for type and crossmatch, but unmatched type "O" RH negative blood was immediately obtained and begun. Hydrocortisone 300 mgms was added to the intravenous fluids.

Dr. Robert McClelland, Attending Surgeon, arrived to help in the President's care. Doctors Perry, Baxter, and McClelland began a tracheostomy, as considerable quantities of blood were present from the President's oral pharynx. At this time, Dr. Paul Peters, Attending Urological Surgeon, and Dr. Kemp Clark, Director of Neurological Surgery, arrived. Because of the lacerated

COMMISSION EXHIBIT No. 392—Continued

trachea, anterior chest tubes were placed in both pleural spaces. These were connected to sealed underwater drainage.

Neurological examination revealed the President's pupils to be widely dilated and fixed to light. His eyes were divergent, being deviated outward; a skew deviation from the horizontal was present. No deep tendon reflexes or spontaneous movements were found.

There was a large wound in the right occipito-parietal region, from which profuse bleeding was occurring. 1500 cc. of blood were estimated on the drapes and floor of the Emergency Operating Room. There was considerable loss of scalp and bone tissue. Both cerebral and cereballar tissue were extruding from the wound.

Further examination was not possible as cardiac arrest occurred at this point. Closed chest cardiac massage was begun by Dr. Clark. A pulse palpable in both the carotid and femoral arteries was obtained. Dr. Perry relieved on the cardiac massage while a cardiotachioscope was connected. Dr. Fouad Bashour, Attending Physician, arrived as this was being connected. There was electrical silence of the President's heart.

President Kennedy was pronounced dead at 1300 hours by Dr. Clark.

Kemp Clark, M.D.
Director
Service of Neurological Surgery

KC:aa

cc to Dean's Office, Southwestern Medical School
cc to Medical Records, Parkland Memorial Hospital

COMMISSION EXHIBIT No. 392—Continued

DATE AND HOUR: 11/22/63   1620   DOCTOR: Carrico

When patient entered emergency room on
ambulance carriage had slow agonal respiratory
efforts and some cardiac beats by auscultation.
Two external wounds were noted. One
small penetrating wound of ant. neck in
lower 1/3. The other wound had avulsed
the calvarium and shredded brain tissue
present ē profuse oozing. No pulse or
Blood pressure were present. Pupils bilat, dilated & fixed.

A cuffed endotracheal tube was inserted
and through the laryngo scope a ragged
wound of the trachea was seen immediately
below the larynx. The tube was passed
past the laceration & the cuff inflated.
Respiration using the resp assistor on automatic were instituted. Concurrently an IV
infusion of Lactated Ringer solution was
begun via catheter placed in ® leg & blood
drawn for type and cross match. Type O
Rh negative Blood was obtained as well
as hydrocortisone.

In view of tracheal injury + ↓ BS
on ® tracheotomy was performed by
Dr Perry and Bilat chest tubes inserted.

1033   (OVER)

1767

COMMISSION EXHIBIT No. 392—Continued

A second IV infusion was begun in ① arm. In addition Dr. Jenkins began resp c̄ anesthesia machine, cardiac monitor + defibrillator attached. Solu cortef IV given (300mg), attempt to control slow oozing from cerebral + cerebellar tissue via packs instituted. Despite these measures as well as external cardiac massage BP never returned and EKG evidence of cardiac activity was never obtained.

Charles J. Carrico M.D.

J F Kennedy.

DATE AND HOUR: 22 Nov 1963   DOCTOR: PERRY

Staff Note -

At the time of initial examination, the pt. was noted to be non-responsive. The eyes were deviated and the pupils dilated. A considerable quantity of blood was noted on the patient, the carriage and the floor. A small wound was noted in the midline of the neck, in the lower third anteriorly. It was exuding blood slowly. A large wound the right posterior cranium was noted, exposing severely lacerated brain. Brain tissue was noted in the blood at the head of the carriage.

Pulse or heart beat were not detectable, but slow spasmodic respiration was noted. An endotracheal tube was in place and respiration was being assisted. An intravenous infusion was being placed in the leg.

At this point I noted that respiration was ineffective and while additional venesections were done to administer fluids + blood, a tracheostomy was effected. A right lateral injury to the trachea was noted. The tracheostomy tube was put in place and the cuff inflated and respiration assisted. Closed chest cardiac massage was initiated after placement of sealed-drainage chest tubes, but

1033   (OVER)

1767

COMMISSION EXHIBIT No. 392—Continued

521

without benefit. Electrocardiographic
evaluation ~~confi~~ revealed that no detectable
electrical activity existed in the heart.
Resuscitative attempts were abandoned after
the team of physicians determined that the
patient had expired.

Malcolm O. Perry, M.D.
1630 h 22 Nov 1963

COMMISSION EXHIBIT No. 392—Continued

DATE AND HOUR: Nov 22, 1963   DOCTOR:

Note of Attendance to President Kennedy

I was contacted at approx 12:40 that the President was on the way to the emergency room having been shot. On arrival there, I found an endotracheal tube in place ē assisted respiration, a left chest tube being inserted + cut downs going in one leg + in the left arm. The President had a wound in the mid-line of the neck. On quick observation of the remaining wounds the R temporal + occipital bones were missing + the brain was lying on the table, with extensive maceration + contusion. The pupils were fixed + dilated laterel + dilated. No pulse was obtainable + respirations were (as noted) being supplied. A tracheotomy was performed by Dr Perry + O, + a chest tube inserted into the Rt Chest (2nd interspace anteriorly). Meanwhile I gave O my blood was administered by pump ē respiration. When all of these maneuvers were complete, no heart beat could be detected. Closed chest massage was performed until a cardioscope could be attached which revealed no cardiac activity was obtained. Due to the extensive + irreparable brain damage which was lethal, no further attempt to resuscitate the heart was made.

Charles R. Baxter M.D.
Assoc Prof of Surgery
Southwestern Med School

1033   (OVER)

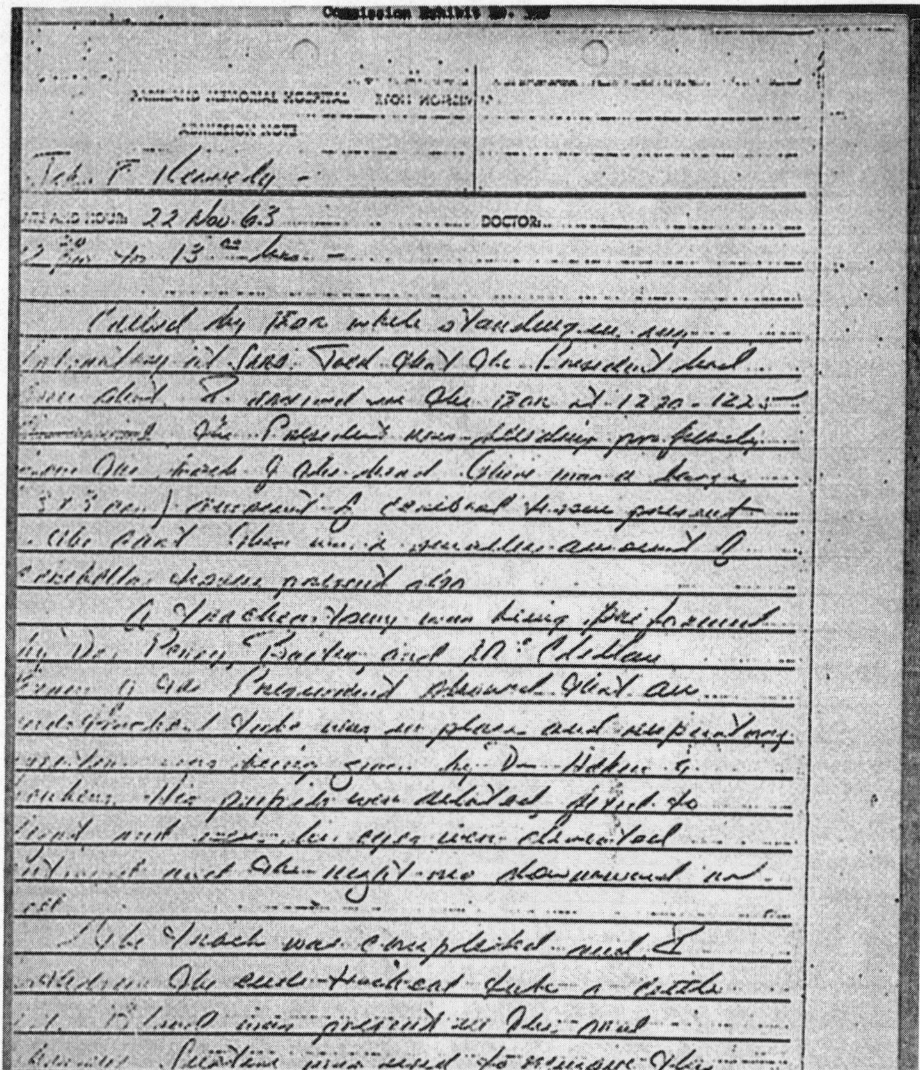

Commission Exhibit No. 392

PARKLAND MEMORIAL HOSPITAL

ADMISSION NOTE

John F. Kennedy –

DATE AND HOUR: 22 Nov 63 DOCTOR:

12:30 pm to 1:00 pm –

Called by Box while standing in surg. [illegible] at [illegible]. Told that the President had been shot. I arrived in the Box at 1220-1225 [illegible]. The President was bleeding profusely from the back of the head. There was a large (3 x 3 cm) amount of cerebral tissue present on the cart. There was a smaller amount of cerebellar tissue present also.

A tracheotomy was being performed by Drs. Perry, Baxter, and McClelland. [illegible] the endotracheal tube was in place and respiratory assistance was being given by Dr. [illegible] & [illegible]. His pupils were dilated, fixed to light and [illegible] eyes were deviated outward and the right [illegible] downward [illegible]

The trach was completed and I suctioned the endo-tracheal tube a little. Blood was present in the [illegible] airway. Suction was used to remove the [illegible] was passed into the stomach [illegible] the [illegible]

(OVER)

561

Commission Exhibit No. 392—Continued

COMMISSION EXHIBIT NO. 392

ADMISSION NOTE

In the meantime it was noted there was no carotid pulse. Immediately I began closed chest massage. A pulse was noted at the carotid and femoral pulse levels.

Dr Perry then took over the cardiac massage so I could evaluate the head wound.

There was a large wound beginning in the right occiput extending into the parietal region. Much of the skull appeared gone at brief examination. The previously described extruded brain was present.

By then an EKG was hooked up. There was no electrical activity of the heart and no respiratory effort —

He was pronounced dead at 1300 hrs by me —

/s/ Kemp Clark MD

22 Nov 1963

1615 hrs —

561

COMMISSION EXHIBIT NO. 392—Continued

DATE AND HOUR: Nov. 22, 1963   4:45 P.M.   DOCTOR: Robert N. M°Clelland

Statement Regarding Assassination of
        President Kennedy

At approximately 12:45 P.M. on the above date
I was called from the second floor of
Parkland Hospital and went immediately to the
Emergency Operating Room. When I arrived
President Kennedy was being attended by Drs.
Malcolm Perry, Charles Baxter, James Carrico and
Ronald Jones. The President was at that time
comatose from a massive gunshot wound of the
head with a fragment wound of the trachea.
An endotracheal tube and assisted respiration
was started immediately by Dr. Carrico on duty
in the EOR when the President arrived. Drs.
Perry, Baxter and I then performed a tracheostomy
for respiratory distress and tracheal injury and
Drs. Jones and Paul Peters inserted bilateral
anterior chest tubes for pneumothoraces secondary
to the tracheomediastinal injury. Simultaneously
Dr. Jones had started 3 cut-downs giving
blood and fluids immediately. In spite of this,
at 12:55 he was pronounced dead by Dr. Kemp
Clark the neurosurgeon and professor of neuro-
surgery who arrived immediately after I did. The

1033

(OVER)

COMMISSION EXHIBIT No. 392—Continued

ADMISSION NOTE I

cause of death was due to massive head and brain injury from a gunshot wound of the left temple. He was pronounced dead after external cardiac massage & intra ECG activity was gone.

Robt. N. McClelland, M.D.
Asst. Prof. of Surgery
Southwestern Med.
School of Univ. of Tex.
Dallas, Texas

COMMISSION EXHIBIT No. 392—Continued

PARKLAND MEMORIAL HOSPITAL

ADMISSION NOTE

DATE AND HOUR: Nov 22 1963 4 45 PM   DOCTOR: Bashour

Statement Regarding Assassination of the President
of the USA, President Kennedy –

At 12⁵⁰ PM, we were called from the 1st Floor of Parkland
Hospital and Told that President Kennedy was shot – Dr. D Seldin
and myself went to the emergency room of Parkland – Upon
examination, the President had no pulsation, no heart beat,
no blood pressure – The oscilloscope showed a complete standstill –
The President was declared dead at 12⁵⁰ PM.

J. Bashour MD
Associate Professor of Medicine
Southwestern Medical School
Dallas – Texas –

COMMISSION EXHIBIT No. 392—Continued

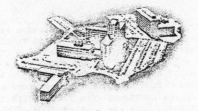

M. T. JENKINS, M. D.
PROFESSOR AND CHAIRMAN
Department of Anesthesiology

Clinical Departments of Anesthesia
PARKLAND MEMORIAL HOSPITAL
CHILDREN'S MEDICAL CENTER

November 22, 1963
1630

To: Mr. C. J. Price, Administrator
    Parkland Memorial Hospital

From: M. T. Jenkins, M.D., Professor and Chairman
    Department of Anesthesiology

Subject: Statement concerning resuscitative efforts for
    President John F. Kennedy

Upon receiving a stat alarm that this distinguished patient was being brought to
the emergency room at Parkland Memorial Hospital, I dispatched Doctors A. H.
Giesecke and Jackie H. Hunt with an anesthesia machine and resuscitative equipment
to the major surgical emergency room area, and I ran down the stairs. On my
arrival in the emergency operating room at approximately 1230 I found that Doctors
Carrico and/or Delaney had begun resuscitative efforts by introducing an orotracheal
tube, connecting it for controlled ventilation to a Bennett intermittent positive
pressure breathing apparatus. Doctors Charles Baxter, Malcolm Perry, and Robert
McClelland arrived at the same time and began a tracheostomy and started the
insertion of a right chest tube, since there was also obvious tracheal and chest
damage. Doctors Paul Peters and Kemp Clark arrived simultaneously and immediately
thereafter assisted respectively with the insertion of the right chest tube and
with manual closed chest cardiac compression to assure circulation.

For better control of artificial ventilation, I exchanged the intermittent positive
pressure breathing apparatus for an anesthesia machine and continued artificial
ventilation. Doctors Gene Akin and A. H. Giesecke assisted with the respiratory
problems incident to changing from the orotracheal tube to a tracheostomy tube, and
Doctors Hunt and Giesecke connected a cardioscope to determine cardiac activity.

During the progress of these activities, the emergency room cart was elevated at the
feet in order to provide a Trendelenburg position, a venous cutdown was performed on
the right saphenous vein, and additional fluids were begun in a vein in the left
forearm while blood was ordered from the blood bank. All of these activities were
completed by approximately 1245, at which time external cardiac massage was still
being carried out effectively by Doctor Clark as judged by a palpable peripheral
pulse. Despite these measures there was no electrocardiographic evidence of cardiac
activity.

COMMISSION EXHIBIT No. 392—Continued

Mr. C. J. Price, Administrator
November 22, 1963
Page 2 - Statement concerning resuscitative
efforts for President John F. Kennedy

These described resuscitative activities were indicated as of first importance, and after they were carried out attention was turned to all other evidences of injury. There was a great laceration on the right side of the head (temporal and occipital), causing a great defect in the skull plate so that there was herniation and laceration of great areas of the brain, even to the extent that the cerebellum had protruded from the wound. There were also fragmented sections of brain on the drapes of the emergency room cart. With the institution of adequate cardiac compression, there was a great flow of blood from the cranial cavity, indicating that there was much vascular damage as well as brain tissue damage.

It is my personal feeling that all methods of resuscitation were instituted expeditiously and efficiently. However, this cranial and intracranial damage was of such magnitude as to cause the irreversible damage. President Kennedy was pronounced dead at 1300.

Sincerely,

M. T. Jenkins, M.D.

COMMISSION EXHIBIT No. 392—Continued

530

PARKLAND MEMORIAL HOSPITAL

OPERATIVE RECORD

ROOM: 220   STATUS: Pvt

NAME: John Connally

UNIT # 26 36 99

DATE: 11-22-63   Thoracic Surg   AGE: RACE: W/M

PRE-OPERATIVE DIAGNOSIS: Gunshot wound of the chest with comminuted fracture of the 5th rib

POST-OPERATIVE DIAGNOSIS: Same with laceration right middle lobe, hematoma lower lobe of lung

OPERATION: Thoracotomy , removal rib fragment, de-   BEGAN: 1335   ENDED: 1520
bridement of wound

ANESTHETIC: General   BEGAN: 1300   ANESTHESIOLOGIST: Giesecke

SURGEON: Robert Shaw, M.D   DRAINS:

ASSISTANTS: Drs. Boland and Duke   APPLIANCES:

SCRUB NURSE: King/Burkett   CIRC. NURSE: Johnson   CASTS/SPLINTS:

SPONGE COUNTS: 1ST Correct   DRUGS   I.V. FLUIDS AND BLOOD
2ND Correct   111-500 cc whole blood
11-1000cc D-5-RL

COMPLICATIONS: None

CONDITION OF PATIENT: Satisfactory

Clinical Evaluation: The patient was brought to the OR from the EOR. In the EOR a sucking wound of the right chest was partially controlled by an occlusive dressing supported by manual pressure. A tube been placed through the second interspace in the mid-clavicular line connected to a waterseal bottle to evacuate the right pneumothorax and hemathorax. An IV infusion of RL solution had already been started. As soon as the patient was positioned on

Operative indication the anesthesia was induced by Dr. Giesecke and an endotracheal tube was in place. As soon as it was possible to control respiration with positive pressure the occlusive dressing was taken from the right chest and the extent of the wound more carefully determined. It was found that the wound of entrance was just lateral to the right scapula close the the axilla yet had passed through the latysmus dorsi muscle shattered approxi-

Description of Operation: the lateral and anterior portion of the right fifth rib and emerged below the right nipple. The wound of entrance was approximately three cm in its longest diameter and the wound of exit was a ragged wound approximately five cm in its greatest diameter. The skin and subcutaneous tissue over the path of the missile moved in a paradoxical manner with respiration indicating softening of the chest. The skin of the whole area was carefully cleansed with Phisohex and Iodine. The entire area including the wound of entrance and wound of exit was draped partially excluding the wound of entrance for the first part of the operation. An elliptical incision was made around the wound of exit removing the torn edges of the skin and the damaged subcutaneous tissue. The incision was then carried in a downward curve up toward the right axilla so as to not have the skin incision over the actual path of the missile been through the chest wall. This incision was carried down through the subcutaneous tissue to expose the Serratus anterior muscle and the anterior border of the latissimus dorsi muscle. The fragmented and damaged portions of the Serratus anterior muscle were excised. Small rib fragments that were adhering to periosteal tags were carefully removed preserving as much periosteum as possible. The fourth intercostal muscle bundle and fifth intercostal muscle bundle were not appreciably damaged.

Dr. Robert Shaw M.D.

RS:bl   (continued)

1747

COMMISSION EXHIBIT No. 392—Continued

531

CONNALLY JOHN G 26739)
WM   11-22-63
John Connally 9115
26 36 99

DESCRIPTION OF OPERATION (Continued): The ragged ends of the damaged fifth rib were cleaned out with the rongeur. The plura had been torn open by the secondary missiles created by the fragmented fifth rib. The wound was open widely and exposure was obtained with a self retaining retractor. The right pleural cavity was then carefully inspected. Approximately 200 cc of clot and liquid blood was removed from the pleural cavity. The middle lobe had a linear rent starting at its peripheral edge going down towards its hilum separating the lobe into two segments. There was an open bronchus in the depth of this wound. Since the vascularity and the bronchial connections to the lobe were intact it was decided to repair the lobe rather then to remove it. The repair was accomplished with a running suture of #000 chromic gut on atraumatic needle closing both plural surfaces as well as two runnin sutures approximating the tissue of the central portion of the lobe. This almost completely sealed off the air leaks which were evident in the torn portion of the lobe. The lower lobe was next examined and found to be engorged with blood and at one point a laceration of allowed the oozing of blood. This laceration had undoubtedly been caused by a rib fragment. This laceration was closed with a single suture of #3-0 chromic gut on atraumatic needle. The right pleural cavity was now carefully examined and small ribs fragments were removed, the diaphram was found to be uninjured. There was no evidence of injury of the mediastinum and its contents. Hemostasis had been accomplished within the pleural cavity with the repair of the middle lobe and the suturing of the laceration in the lower lobe. The upper lobe was found to be uninjured. The drains which had previously been placed in the second interspace in the midclavicular line was found to be longer than necessary so approximately ten cm of it was cut away and the remaining portion was demonstrated with two additional openings. An additional drain was placed through a stab wound in the eighth interspace in the posterior axillary line. Both these drains were then connected to a waterseal bottle. The fourth and fifth intercostal muscles were then approximated with interrupted sutures of #0 chromic gut. The remaining portion of the Serratus anterior muscle was then approximated across the closure of the intercostal muscle. The laceration of the latissimus dorsi muscle on its intermost surface was then closed with several interrupted sutures of #0 chromic gut. The subcutaneus tissue was th Before closing the subcutaneous tissue one million units of Penicillin and one gram of Streptomycin in 100 cc normal saline was instilled into the wound. The stab wound was then made in the most dependent portion of the wound coming out near the angle of the scapula. A large Penrose drain was drawn out through this stab wound to allow drainage of the wound of the chest wall. The subcutaneous tissue was then closed with interrupted #0 chromic gut inverting the knots. Skin closed with interrupted vertical sutures of black silk. Attention was next turned to the wound of entrance. It was excised with an elliptical incision. It was found that the latissimus dorsi muscle although lacerated was not badly damaged so that the opening was closed with sutures of #0 chromic gut in the fascia of the muscle. Before closing this incision the palpation with the index finger the Penrose drain could be felt immediately below in the space beneath the latissimus dorsi muscle. The skin closed with interrupted vertical mattress sutures of black silk. Drainage tubes were secured with safety pens and adhesive tape and dressings applied. As soon as the operation on the chest had been concluded Dr. Gregory and Dr. Shires started the surgery that was necessary for the wounds of the right wrist and left thigh.

RS:bl

Dr Robert Shaw

* There was also a comminuted fracture of the right radius secondary to the same missile and in addition a small flesh wound of the left thigh. The operative notes concerning the management of the right arm and left thigh will be dictated by Dr. Charles Gregory and Dr. Tom Shires.

1767

PARKLAND MEMORIAL HOSPITAL

OPERATIVE RECORD

NAME: Governor John Connally

UNIT # 26 36 99

DATE: 11-22-63   Ortho

AGE: W/M   RACE:

PRE-OPERATIVE DIAGNOSIS: Commimuted fracture of the right distal radius, open secondary to gunshot wound

POST-OPERATIVE DIAGNOSIS: Same

OPERATION: Debridement of gunshot wound of right wrist, reduction of fracture of the radius   BEGAN: 1600   ENDED: 1650

ANESTHETIC: General   BEGAN: 1300   ANESTHESIOLOGIST: Giesecke

SURGEON: Dr. Charles Gregory   DRAINS:

ASSISTANTS: Drs. Osborne and Parker   APPLIANCES:

SCRUB NURSE: Rutherford   CIRC. NURSE: Schroder   CASTS/SPLINTS:

SPONGE COUNTS: 1ST _____ 2ND _____   DRUGS   I.V. FLUIDS AND BLOOD

COMPLICATIONS: None

CONDITION OF PATIENT: Fair

Also a partial transection of the superficial radius

Clinical Evaluation: While still under general anesthesia and following a thoracotomy and repair of the chest injury by Dr. Robert Shaw, the right upper extremity was thoroughly prepped in the routine fashion after shaving. He was draped in the routine fashion using stockinette, the only addition was the use of a debridement pan. The wound of entry on the dorsal aspect of the right wrist over the junction of the distal fourth of the radius and shaft was approximately two cm in length and rather oblique with the loss of tissue with some considerable contusion at the margins of it. There was a wound of exit along the volar surface of the wrist about two cm above the flexion crease of the wrist and in the midline. The wound of entrance was carefully excised and developed through the muscles and tendons from the radial side of that bone to the bone itself where the fracture was encountered. It was noted that the tendon of the abductor palmaris longus was transected, only two small fragments of bone was removed, one approximately one cm in length and consisted of lateral cortex which lay free in the wound and had no soft tissue connections, another much smaller fragment perhaps 3 mm in length was subsequently removed. Small bits of metal were encountered at various levels throughout the wound and these were wherever they were identified and could be picked up were picked up and have been submitted to the Pathology department for identification and examination. Throughout the wound at was not and especially in the superficial layers and to some extent in the tendon and tendon sheaths on the radial side of the arm small fine bits of cloth consistant with fine bits of Mohair. It is our understanding that the patient was wearing a Mohair suit at the time of the injury and this accounts for the deposition of such organic material within the wound. After as careful and complete a debridement as could be carried out and with an apparent integrity of the flexor tendons and the median nerve in the volar side, and after thorough irrigation the wound of exit on the volar surface of the wrist was closed primarily with wire sutures while the wound of entrance on the radial side of the forearm was only partially closed, being left open for the purpose of drainage should any make spontaneous appearance.

Charles Gregory, M.D.

CG:bl   (continued)

11-22-63   . Ortho

DESCRIPTION OF OPERATION (Continued):   This is ~~indistinctness to~~ the presence of Mohair and organic material deep into the wound which is prone to produce tissue reactions and to encourage infection and this precaution of not closing the wound was taken in correspondance with our experience in that regard.

   In view of the urgancy of the Governor's original chest injury it was impossible to definitely ascertain the status of the circulation ~~and~~ the nerve supply to the hand and wrist on the right side. Accordingly, it was determined as best we could at the time of operation and the radial artery was found to be intact and pulsating normally. The integrity of the median nerve and the ulnar nerve is not clearly established but it is presumed to be present. Following closure of the volar wound and partial closure of the radial wound, dry sterile dressings were applied and a long arm cast was then applied with skin tape traction, rubber band variety, attached to the thumb and index finger of the right hand. ~~The rig~~ An attitude of flexon was created at the right elbow, and post operatively the limbus suspended from an overhead frame using tape traction. The post operative diagnosis for the right forearm remains the same and again I suggest that you incorporate this particular dictation together with other dictations which will be given to you by the surgeons concerned with this patient.

Charles Gregory, M.D.

CG:bl

COMMISSION EXHIBIT No. 392—Continued

PARKLAND MEMORIAL HOSPITAL

OPERATIVE RECORD

NAME: Connally, John

UNIT # 263699
A #24842

DATE: Nov. 22, 1963

AGE: RACE: W/M

PRE-OPERATIVE DIAGNOSIS: Gunshot Wound, Right Chest, Right Wrist, Left Thigh

POST-OPERATIVE DIAGNOSIS: Same

OPERATION: Exploration and Debridement of   (*See below)
Gunshot Wound of Left Thigh   BEGAN: 16:00   ENDED: 16:20

ANESTHETIC: General   BEGAN: 13:00   ANESTHESIOLOGIST: Geisecke

SURGEON: Dr. Shires   DRAINS:

ASSISTANTS: Drs. McClelland, Baxter and Patman   APPLIANCES:

SCRUB NURSE: Oliver   CIRC. NURSE: Deming and Schröder   CASTS/SPLINTS:

SPONGE COUNTS: 1ST Correct, PS   DRUGS   I.V. FLUIDS AND BLOOD

2ND

COMPLICATIONS: *This portion of the operation is involved only with the operation on the left thigh. The chest injury has been dictated by Dr. Shaw, the orthopedic injury to the arm by Dr. Gregory.

CONDITION OF PATIENT:

Clinical Evaluation: There was a 1 cm. punctate missile wound over the juncture of the middle and lower third, medial aspect, of the left thigh. X--rays of the thigh and leg revealed a bullet fragment which was imbedded in the body of the femur in the distal third. The leg was prepared with Phisohex and I.O. Prep and was draped in the usual fashion.

Operative Findings: Following this the missile wound was excised and the bullet tract was explored. The missile wound was seen to course through the subcutaneous fat and into the vastus medialis. The necrotic fat and muscle were debrided down to the region of the femur. The direction of the missile wound was judged not to be in the course of

Description of Operation: the femoral vessel, since the wound was distal and anterior to Hunter's canal. Following complete debridement of the wound and irrigation with saline, the wound was felt to be adequately debrided enough so that three simple through-and-through, stainless steel Aloe #28 wire sutures were used encompassing skin, subcutaneous tissue, and muscle fascia on both sides. Following this a sterile dressing was applied. The dorsalis pedis and posterior tibial pulses in both legs were quite good. The thoracic procedure had been completed at this time, the debridement of the compound fracture in the arm was still in progress at the time this soft tissue injury repair was completed.

fs

Tom Shires, M.D.

1767

1679

COMMISSION EXHIBIT No. 392—Continued

PARKLAND MEMORIAL HOSPITAL

OPERATIVE RECORD

NAME: Oswald, Lee Harvey

EOR
~~UNFT~~ # 25260

DATE: 11/24/63   Surg.   AGE: 24 Yr.   RACE: W/M

PRE-OPERATIVE DIAGNOSIS: _____ upper GSW of/abdomen and chest with massive bleeding

POST-OPERATIVE DIAGNOSIS: _____ Major vascular injury in abdomen and chest

OPERATION: Exploratory laparotomy, thoracotomy, efforts to repair aorta   1'15"   BEGAN: 1142   ENDED: 1307

ANESTHETIC: _____ General _____ BEGAN: _____ 1142 _____ ANESTHIOLOGIST: Dr. M.T. Jenkins / Dr. Gene Akin / Dr. Curtis Spier

SURGEON: _____ Dr. Tom Shires _____ DRAINS: _____

ASSISTANTS: Dr. Perry, Dr. McClelland, Dr. Ron Jones _____ APPLIANCES: _____

SCRUB NURSE: Schrader-Lunsford _____ CIRC. NURSE: Schrader-Bell-Burkett-Simpson _____ CASTS/SPLINTS: _____

2 counted sponges missing when body closed. Square pack count correct.

SPONGE COUNTS: 1ST _____

2ND _____

COMPLICATIONS:

CONDITION OF PATIENT: Expired at 1307

DRUGS
Ca chloride - 3 vials
Cedilanid - 12
One molar lactate-6
Isuprel - 24
Adrenalin 1:1000 - 3

I.V. FLUIDS AND BLOOD
3-1000 cc. lactated Ringer's solution
16- 500 cc. whole blood
6-1000 cc. 5% dextrose in lactated Ringer's solution

Measured blood loss - 8,376 cc.

Clinical Evaluation: Previous inspection had revealed an entrance wound over the left lower lateral chest cage, and an exit was identified by subcutaneous palpation of the bullet over the right lower lateral chest cage. At the time he was seen preoperatively he was without blood pressure, heart beat was heard infrequently at 130 beats per minute, and preoperatively had endotracheal tube placed and was receiving oxygen by anesthesia

Operative Findings: at the time he was moved to the operating room.

Description of Operation: Under endotracheal oxygen anesthesia, a long mid-line abdominal incision was made. Bleeders were not apparent and none were clamped or tied. Upon opening the peritoneal cavity, approximately 2 to 3 liters of blood, both liquid and in clots, were encountered. These were removed. The bullet pathway was then identified as having shattered the upper medial surface of the spleen, then entered the retroperitoneal area where there was a large retroperitoneal hematoma in the area of the pancreas. Following this, bleeding was seen to be coming from the right side, and upon inspection there was seen to be an exit to the right through the inferior vena cava, thence through the superior pole of the right kidney, the lower portion of the right lobe of the liver, and into the right lateral body wall. First the right kidney, which was bleeding, was identified, dissected free, retracted immediately, and the inferior vena cava hole was clamped with a partial occlusion clamp of the Satinsky type. Following this immobilization, packing controlled the bleeding from the right kidney. Attention was then turned to the left, as bleeding was massive from the left side. The inspection of the retroperitoneal area revealed

Tom Shires, M.D. (signature)

M.D.

Tom Shires, M.D.

1679

COMMISSION EXHIBIT No. 392—Continued

a huge hematoma in the mid-line. The spleen was then mobilized, as was the left
colon, and the retroperitoneal approach was made to the mid-line structures.
The pancreas was seen to be shattered in its mid portion, bleeding was seen to
be coming from the aorta. This was dissected free. Bleeding was controlled with
finger pressure by Dr. Malcolm O. Perry. Upon identification of this injury, the
superior mesenteric artery had been sheared off of the aorta, there was back
bleeding from the superior mesenteric artery. This was cross-clamped with a
small, curved DeBakey clamp. The aorta was then occluded with a straight DeBakey
clamp above and a Potts clamp below. At this point all major bleeding was controlled, blood pressure was reported to be in the neighborhood of 100 systolic.
Shortly thereafter, however, the pulse rate, which had been in the 80 to 90 range,
was found to be 40 and a few seconds later found to be zero. No pulse was felt
in the aorta at this time. Consequently the left chest was opened through an
intercostal incision in approximately the fourth intercostal space. A Finochietto
retractor was inserted, the heart was seen to be flabby and not beating at all.
There was no hemopericardium. There was a hole in the diaphragm but no hemo-
thorax. A left closed chest tube had been introduced in the Emergency Room
prior to surgery, so that there was no significant pneumothorax on the left side.
The pericardium was opened, cardiac massage was started, and a pulse was
obtainable with massage. The heart was flabby, consequently calcium chloride
followed by epinephrine-Xylocaine® were injected into the left ventricle without
success. However, the standstill was converted to fibrillation. Following
this, defibrillation was done, using 240, 360, 500, and 750 volts and finally
successful defibrillation was accomplished. However, no effective heart beat
could be instituted. A pacemaker was then inserted into the wall of the right
ventricle and grounded on skin, and pacemaking was started. A very feeble,
small, localized muscular response was obtained with the pacemaker but still no
effective beat. At this time we were informed by Dr. Jenkins that there were
no signs of life in that the pupils were fixed and dilated, there was no retinal
blood flow, no respiratory effort, and no effective pulse could be maintained
even with cardiac massage. The patient was pronounced dead at 1:07 P.M.
Anesthesia consisted entirely of oxygen. No anesthetic agents as such were
administered. The patient was never conscious from the time of his arrival in
the Emergency Room until his death at 1:07 P.M. The subcutaneous bullet was
extracted from the right side during the attempts at defibrillation, which were
rotated among the surgeons. The cardiac massage and defibrillation attempts
were carried out by Dr. Robert N. McClelland, Dr. Malcolm O. Perry, Dr. Ronald
Jones. Assistance was obtained from the cardiologist, Dr. Fouad Bashour.

DESCRIPTION OF OPERATION (cont'd.)

COMMISSION EXHIBIT No. 392—Continued

Autopsy Report and Supplemental Report

Standard Form 503
Revised August 1954
Promulgated
By Bureau of the Budget
Circular A—32 (Rev.)

CLINICAL RECORD	AUTOPSY PROTOCOL	A63-272 (JJH:ec)		
DATE AND HOUR DIED	DATE AND HOUR AUTOPSY PERFORMED	CHECK ONE		
		FULL AUTOPSY	HEAD ONLY	TRUNK ONLY
22 November 1963 1300(CST) A.M. P.M.	22 November 1963 2000(EST) A.M. M.			
PROSECTOR (497831)	ASSISTANT (489378)			
CDR J. J. HUMES, MC, USN	CDR "J" THORNTON BOSWELL, MC, USN	X		
CLINICAL DIAGNOSES (Including operations)	LCOL PIERRE A. FINCK, MC, USA (04 043 322)			

Ht. - 72½ inches
Wt. - 170 pounds
Eyes - blue
Hair - Reddish brown

PATHOLOGICAL DIAGNOSES

CAUSE OF DEATH: Gunshot wound, head.

APPROVED-SIGNATURE

J. J. HUMES, CDR, MC, USN

MILITARY ORGANIZATION (When required)	AGE	SEX	RACE	IDENTIFICATION NO.	AUTOPSY NO.
PRESIDENT, UNITED STATES	46	Male	Cauc.		A63-272
PATIENT'S IDENTIFICATION (For typed or written entries give: Name—last, first, middle; grade; date; hospital or medical facility)				REGISTER NO.	WARD NO.
KENNEDY, JOHN F. NAVAL MEDICAL SCHOOL					

AUTOPSY PROTOCOL
Standard Form 503

CLINICAL SUMMARY: According to available information the
                                         deceased, President John F. Kennedy,
was riding in an open car in a motorcade during an official visit to Dallas, Texas
on 22 November 1963. The President was sitting in the right rear seat with Mrs.
Kennedy seated on the same seat to his left. Sitting directly in front of the
President was Governor John B. Connolly of Texas and directly in front of Mrs. Kennedy
sat Mrs. Connolly. The vehicle was moving at a slow rate of speed down an incline
into an underpass that leads to a freeway route to the Dallas Trade Mart wherett the
President was to deliver an address.

                                         Three shots were heard and the President
fell forward bleeding from the head. (Governor Connolly was seriously wounded by the
same gunfire.) According to newspaper reports ("Washington Post" November 23, 1963)
Bob Jackson, a Dallas "Times Herald" Photographer, said he looked around as he heard
the shots and saw a rifle barrel disappearing into a window on an upper floor of the
nearby Texas School Book Depository Building.

                                         Shortly following the wounding of the two
men the car was driven to Parkland Hospital in Dallas. In the emergency room of that
hospital the President was attended by Dr. Malcolm Perry. Telephone communication with
Dr. Perry on November 23, 1963 develops the following information relative to the observations made by Dr. Perry and procedures performed there prior to death.

                                         Dr. Perry noted the massive wound of the
head and a second much smaller wound of the low anterior neck in approximately the
midline. A tracheostomy was performed by extending the latter wound. At this point
bloody air was noted bubbling from the wound and an injury to the right lateral wall
of the trachea was observed. Incisions were made in the upper anterior chest wall
bilaterally to combat possible subcutaneous emphysema. Intravenous infusions of blood
and saline were begun and oxygen was administered. Despite these measures cardiac
arrest occurred and closed chest cardiac massage failed to re-establish cardiac action.
The President was pronounced dead approximately thirty to forty minutes after receiving
his wounds.

                                         The remains were transported via the
Presidential plane to Washington, D.C. and subsequently to the Naval Medical School,
National Naval Medical Center, Bethesda, Maryland for postmortem examination.

GENERAL DESCRIPTION OF BODY: The body is that of a muscular, well-
                                         developed and well nourished adult Caucasia
male measuring 72½ inches and weighing approximately 170 pounds. There is beginning
rigor mortis, minimal dependent livor mortis of the dorsum, and early algor mortis. The
hair is reddish brown and abundant, the eyes are blue, the right pupil measuring 8 mm.
in diameter, the left 4 mm. There is edema and ecchymosis of the inner canthus region
of the left eyelid measuring approximately 1.5 cm. in greatest diameter. There is edem
and ecchymosis diffusely over the right supra-orbital ridge with abnormal mobility of
the underlying bone. (The remainder of the scalp will be described with the skull.)

COMMISSION EXHIBIT No. 387—Continued

There is clotted blood on the external ears but otherwise the ears, nares, and mouth are essentially unremarkable. The teeth are in excellent repair and there is some pallor of the oral mucous membrane.

Situated on the upper right posterior thorax just above the upper border of the scapula there is a 7 x 4 millimeter oval wound. This wound is measured to be 14 cm. from the tip of the right acromion process and 14 cm. below the tip of the right mastoid process.

Situated in the low anterior neck at approximately the level of the third and fourth tracheal rings is a 6.5 cm. long transverse wound with widely gaping irregular edges. (The depth and character of these wounds will be further described below.)

Situated on the anterior chest wall in the nipple line are bilateral 2 cm. long recent transverse surgical incisions into the subcutaneous tissue. The one on the left is situated 11 cm. cephalad to the nipple and the one on the right 8 cm. cephalad to the nipple. There is no hemorrhage or ecchymosis associated with these wounds. A similar clean wound measuring 2 cm. in length is situated on the antero-lateral aspect of the left mid arm. Situated on the antero-lateral aspect of each ankle is a recent 2 cm. transverse incision into the subcutaneous tissue.

There is an old well healed 8 cm. McBurney abdominal incision. Over the lumbar spine in the midline is an old, well healed 15 cm. scar. Situated on the upper antero-lateral aspect of the right thigh is an old, well healed 8 cm. scar.

MISSILE WOUNDS:

1. There is a large irregular defect of the scalp and skull on the right involving chiefly the parietal bone but extending somewhat into the temporal and occipital regions. In this region there is an actual absence of scalp and bone producing a defect which measures approximately 13 cm. in greatest diameter.

From the irregular margins of the above scalp defect tears extend in stellate fashion into the more or less intact scalp as follows:

a. From the right inferior temporo-parietal margin anterior to the right ear to a point slightly above the tragus.

b. From the anterior parietal margin anteriorly on the forehead to approximately 4 cm. above the right orbital ridge.

c. From the left margin of the main defect across the midline antero-laterally for a distance of approximately 8 cm.

d. From the same starting point as c. 10 cm. postero-laterally.

COMMISSION EXHIBIT No. 387--Continued

Situated in the posterior scalp approximately 2.5 cm. laterally to the right and
slightly above the external occipital protuberance is a lacerated wound measuring
15 x 6 mm. In the underlying bone is a corresponding wound through the skull which
exhibits beveling of the margins of the bone when viewed from the inner aspect of
the skull.

                              Clearly visible in the above described
large skull defect and exuding from it is lacerated brain tissue which on close
inspection proves to represent the major portion of the right cerebral hemisphere.
At this point it is noted that the falx cerebri is extensively lacerated with disruption of the superior saggital sinus.

                              Upon reflecting the scalp multiple complete
fracture lines are seen to radiate from both the large defect at the vertex and the
smaller wound at the occiput. These vary greatly in length and direction, the longest
measuring approximately 19 cm. These result in the production of numerous fragments
which vary in size from a few millimeters to 10 cm. in greatest diameter.

                              The complexity of these fractures and the
fragments thus produced tax satisfactory verbal description and are better appreciated
in photographs and roentgenograms which are prepared.

                              The brain is removed and preserved for
further study following formalin fixation.

                              Received as separate specimens from Dallas,
Texas are three fragments of skull bone which in aggregate roughly approximate the
dimensions of the large defect described above. At one angle of the largest of these
fragments is a portion of the perimeter of a roughly circular wound presumably of
exit which exhibits beveling of the outer aspect of the bone and is estimated to
measure approximately 2.5 to 3.0 cm. in diameter. Roentgenograms of this fragment
reveal minute particles of metal in the bone at this margin. Roentgenograms of the
skull reveal multiple minute metallic fragments along a line corresponding with a line
joining the above described small occipital wound and the right supra-orbital ridge.
From the surface of the disrupted right cerebral cortex two small irregularly shaped
fragments of metal are recovered. These measure 7 x 2 mm. and 3 x 1 mm. These are
placed in the custody of Agents Francix X. O'Neill, Jr. and James W. Sibert, of the
Federal Bureau of Investigation, who executed a receipt therefor (attached).

                          2. The second wound presumably of entry
is that described above in the upper right posterior thorax. Beneath the skin there
is ecchymosis of subcutaneous tissue and musculature. The missile path through the
fascia and musculature cannot be easily probed. The wound presumably of exit was
that described by Dr. Malcolm Perry of Dallas in the low anterior cervical region.
When observed by Dr. Perry the wound measured "a few millimeters in diameter", however it was extended as a tracheostomy incision and thus its character is distorted
at the time of autopsy. However, there is considerable ecchymosis of the strap
muscles of the right side of the neck and of the fascia about the trachea adjacent
to the line of the tracheostomy wound. The third point of reference in connecting

COMMISSION EXHIBIT No. 387—Continued

these two wounds is in the apex (supra-clavicular portion) of the right pleural cavity. In this region there is contusion of the parietal pleura and of the extreme apical portion of the right upper lobe of the lung. In both instances the diameter of contusion and ecchymosis at the point of maximal involvement measures 5 cm. Both the visceral and parietal pleura are intact overlying these areas of trauma.

INCISIONS: The scalp wounds are extended in the coronal plane to examine the cranial content and the customary (Y) shaped incision is used to examine the body cavities.

THORACIC CAVITY: The bony cage is unremarkable. The thoracic organs are in their normal positions and relationships and there is no increase in free pleural fluid. The above described area of contusion in the apical portion of the right pleural cavity is noted.

LUNGS: The lungs are of essentially similar appearance the right weighing 320 Gm., the left 290 Gm. The lungs are well aerated with smooth glistening pleural surfaces and gray-pink color. A 5 cm. diameter area of purplish red discoloration and increased firmness to palpation is situated in the apical portion of the right upper lobe. This corresponds to the similar area described in the overlying parietal pleura. Incision in this region reveals recent hemorrhage into pulmonary parenchyma.

HEART: The pericardial cavity is smooth walled and contains approximately 10 cc. of straw-colored fluid. The heart is of essentially normal external contour and weighs 350 Gm. The pulmonary artery is opened in situ and no abnormalities are noted. The cardiac chambers contain moderate amounts of postmortem clotted blood. There are no gross abnormalities of the leaflets of any of the cardiac valves. The following are the circumferences of the cardiac valves: aortic 7.5 cm., pulmonic 7 cm., tricuspid 12 cm., mitral 11 cm. The myocardium is firm and reddish brown. The left ventricular myocardium averages 1.2 cm. in thickness, the right ventricular myocardium 0.4 cm. The coronary arteries are dissected and are of normal distribution and smooth walled and elastic throughout.

ABDOMINAL CAVITY: The abdominal organs are in their normal positions and relationships and there is no increase in free peritoneal fluid. The vermiform appendix is surgically absent and there are a few adhesions joining the region of the cecum to the ventral abdominal wall at the above described old abdominal incisional scar.

SKELETAL SYSTEM: Aside from the above described skull wounds there are no significant gross skeletal abnormalities.

PHOTOGRAPHY: Black and white and color photographs depicting significant findings are exposed but not developed. These photographs were placed in the custody of Agent Roy H. Kellerman of the U. S. Secret Service, who executed a receipt therefore (attached).

COMMISSION EXHIBIT No. 387—Continued

ROENTGENOGRAMS: Roentgenograms are made of the entire body
              and of the separately submitted three
fragments of skull bone. These are developed and were placed in the custody of
Agent Roy H. Kellerman of the U. S. Secret Service, who executed a receipt therefor
(attached).

SUMMARY: Based on the above observations it is our
              opinion that the deceased died as a result
of two perforating gunshot wounds inflicted by high velocity projectiles fired by a
person or persons unknown. The projectiles were fired from a point behind and somewhat above the level of the deceased. The observations and available information
do not permit a satisfactory estimate as to the sequence of the two wounds.

              The fatal missile entered the skull above
and to the right of the external occipital protuberance. A portion of the projectile
traversed the cranial cavity in a posterior-anterior direction (see lateral skull
roentgenograms) depositing minute particles along its path. A portion of the projectile made its exit through the parietal bone on the right carrying with it
portions of cerebrum, skull and scalp. The two wounds of the skull combined with
the force of the missile produced extensive fragmentation of the skull, laceration of
the superior saggital sinus, and of the right cerebral hemisphere.

              The other missile entered the right superior
posterior thorax above the scapula and traversed the soft tissues of the supra-scap-
ular and the supra-clavicular portions of the base of the right side of the neck.
This missile produced contusions of the right apical parietal pleura and of the apical
portion of the right upper lobe of the lung. The missile contused the strap muscles
of the right side of the neck, damaged the trachea and made its exit through the
anterior surface of the neck. As far as can be ascertained this missile struck no
bony structures in its path through the body.

              In addition, it is our opinion that the
wound of the skull produced such extensive damage to the brain as to preclude the
possibility of the deceased surviving this injury.

              A supplementary report will be submitted
following more detailed examination of the brain and of microscopic sections. However,
it is not anticipated that these examinations will materially alter the findings.

J. J. HUMES
CDR, MC, USN (497831)

"J" THORNTON BOSWELL
CDR, MC, USN (489878)

PIERRE A. FINCK
LT COL, MC, USA
(04-043-322)

COMMISSION EXHIBIT No. 387—Continued

/221

SUPPLEMENTARY REPORT OF AUTOPSY NUMBER A63-272
PRESIDENT JOHN F. KENNEDY

11/6/63

PATHOLOGICAL EXAMINATION REPORT   No. A63-272   Page 1

GROSS DESCRIPTION OF BRAIN: Following formalin fixation the brain
weighs 1500 gms. The right cerebral
hemisphere is found to be markedly disrupted. There is a longitudinal laceration
of the right hemisphere which is para-sagittal in position approximately 2.5 cm.
to the right of the of the midline which extends from the tip of the occipital
lobe posteriorly to the tip of the frontal lobe anteriorly. The base of the
laceration is situated approximately 4.5 cm. below the vertex in the white matter.
There is considerable loss of cortical substance above the base of the laceration,
particularly in the parietal lobe. The margins of this laceration are at all
points jagged and irregular, with additional lacerations extending in varying
directions and for varying distances from the main laceration. In addition, there
is a laceration of the corpus callosum extending from the genu to the tail. Exposed in this latter laceration are the interiors of the right lateral and third
ventricles.

When viewed from the vertex the left
cerebral hemisphere is intact. There is marked engorgement of meningeal blood
vessels of the left temporal and frontal regions with considerable associated
sub-arachnoid hemorrhage. The gyri and sulci over the left hemisphere are of
essentially normal size and distribution. Those on the right are too fragmented
and distorted for satisfactory description.

When viewed from the basilar aspect
the disruption of the right cortex is again obvious. There is a longitudinal
laceration of the mid-brain through the floor of the third ventricle just behind
the optic chiasm and the mammillary bodies. This laceration partially communi-
cates with an oblique 1.5 cm. tear through the left cerebral peduncle. There are
irregular superficial lacerations over the basilar aspects of the left temporal
and frontal lobes.

In the interest of preserving the
specimen coronal sections are not made. The following sections are taken for
microscopic examination:

   a. From the margin of the laceration in the right parietal lobe.

   b. From the margin of the laceration in the corpus callosum.

   c. From the anterior portion of the laceration in the right frontal lobe.

   d. From the contused left fronto-parietal cortex.

   e. From the line of transection of the spinal cord.

   f. From the right cerebellar cortex.

   g. From the superficial laceration of the basilar aspect of the left temporal
       lobe.

COMMISSION EXHIBIT No. 391

During the course of this examination seven (7) black and white and six (6) color 4x5 inch negatives are exposed but not developed (the cassettes containing these negatives have been delivered by hand to Rear Admiral George W. Burkley, MC, USN, White House Physician).

MICROSCOPIC EXAMINATION:

BRAIN: Multiple sections from representative areas as noted above are examined. All sections are essentially similar and show extensive disruption of brain tissue with associated hemorrhage. In none of the sections examined are there significant abnormalities other than those directly related to the recent trauma.

HEART: Sections show a moderate amount of subepicardial fat. The coronary arteries, myocardial fibers, and endocardium are unremarkable.

LUNGS: Sections through the grossly described area of contusion in the right upper lobe exhibit disruption of alveolar walls and recent hemorrhage into alveoli. Sections are otherwise essentially unremarkable.

LIVER: Sections show the normal hepatic architecture to be well preserved. The parenchymal cells exhibit markedly granular cytoplasm indicating high glycogen content which is characteristic of the "liver biopsy pattern" of sudden death.

SPLEEN: Sections show no significant abnormalities.

KIDNEYS: Sections show no significant abnormalities aside from dilatation and engorgement of blood vessels of all calibers.

SKIN WOUNDS: Sections through the wounds in the occipital and upper right posterior thoracic regions are essentially similar. In each there is loss of continuity of the epidermis with coagulation necrosis of the tissues at the wound margins. The scalp wound exhibits several small fragments of bone at its margins in the subcutaneous tissue.

FINAL SUMMARY: This supplementary report covers in more detail the extensive degree of cerebral trauma in this case. However neither this portion of the examination nor the microscopic examinations alter the previously submitted report or add significant details to the cause of death.

J. J. HUMES
CDR, MC, USN, 497831

COMMISSION EXHIBIT No. 391—Continued

6 December 1963

From: Commanding Officer, U. S. Naval Medical School
To: The White House Physician
Via: Commanding Officer, National Naval Medical Center

Subj: Supplementary report of Naval Medical School autopsy No. A63-272,
John F. Kennedy; forwarding of

1. All copies of the above subject final supplementary report are forwarded herewith.

J. H. STOVER, JR.

- -

6 December 1963

FIRST ENDORSEMENT

From: Commanding Officer, National Naval Medical Center
To: The White House Physician

1. Forwarded.

C. B. GALLOWAY

COMMISSION EXHIBIT No. 391—Continued

546

APPENDIX X

Expert Testimony

FIREARMS AND FIREARMS IDENTIFICATION

Three experts gave testimony concerning firearms and firearms identification: Robert A. Frazier and Cortlandt Cunningham of the FBI, and Joseph D. Nicol, superintendent of the Bureau of Criminal Identification and Investigation of the State of Illinois. Frazier has been in the field of firearms identification for 23 years, following a 1-year course of specialized training in the FBI Laboratory. Cunningham has been in the field for 5 years, having also completed the FBI course. Nicol has been in the firearms identification field since 1941, having begun his training in the Chicago police crime laboratory. Each has made many thousands of firearms identification examinations.[1] Frazier testified on the rifle, the rifle cartridge cases, and the rifle bullets; Cunningham on the revolver, the revolver cartridge cases, the revolver bullets, and the paraffin test; and Nicol on all the bullets and cartridge cases and the paraffin test.[2] Nicol's conclusions were identical to those of Frazier and Cunningham, except as noted.

General Principles

A cartridge, or round of ammunition, is composed of a primer, a cartridge case, powder, and a bullet. The primer, a metal cup containing a detonable mixture, fits into the base of the cartridge case, which is loaded with the powder. The bullet, which usually consists of lead or of a lead core encased in a higher strength metal jacket, fits into the neck of the cartridge case. To fire the bullet, the cartridge is placed in the chamber of a firearm, immediately behind the firearm's barrel. The base of the cartridge rests against a solid support called the breech face or, in the case of a bolt-operated weapon, the bolt face. When the trigger is pulled, a firing pin strikes a swift, hard blow into the primer, detonating the priming mixture. The flames from the resulting explosion ignite the powder, causing a rapid combustion whose force propels the bullet forward through the barrel.

The barrels of modern firearms are "rifled," that is, several spiral grooves are cut into the barrel from end to end. The purpose of the rifling is to set the bullet spinning around its axis, giving it a stability in flight that it would otherwise lack. The weapons of a given make and model are alike in their rifling characteristics; that is, number of grooves, number of lands (the raised portion of the barrel between the grooves) and twist of the rifling. When a bullet is fired through a barrel, it is engraved with these rifling characteristics. For example, all S. & W. .38/200 British Service Revolvers have five grooves and five lands, which twist to the right, and bullets fired through such a revolver will have five groove and land impressions, right twist.

In addition to rifling characteristics, every weapon bears distinctive microscopic characteristics on its components, including its barrel, firing pin, and breech face. While a weapon's rifling characteristics are common to all other weapons of its make and model (and sometimes even to weapons of a different make or model), a weapon's microscopic characteristics are distinctive, and differ from those of every other weapon, regardless of make and model. Such markings are initially caused during manufacture, since the action of manufacturing tools differs microscopically from weapon to weapon, and since the tools change microscopically while being operated. As a weapon is used, further distinctive microscopic markings are introduced by the effects of wear, fouling, and cleaning. As Frazier testified:

Q. Can you explain how you are able to come to a conclusion that a cartridge case was fired in a particular weapon to the exclusion of all other weapons?

Mr. FRAZIER. Yes, sir; during the manufacture of a weapon, there are certain things done to the mechanism of it, which are by machine or by filing, by grinding, which form the parts of the weapon into their final shape. These machining and grinding and filing operations will mark the metal with very fine scratches or turning marks and grinding marks in such a way that there will be developed on the surface of the metal a characteristic pattern. This pattern, because it is made by these accidental machine-type operations, will be characteristic of that particular weapon, and will not be reproduced on separate weapons. It may be a combination of marks that—the face of the bolt may be milled, then it may be in part filed to smooth off the corners, and then, as a final operation, it may be polished, or otherwise adjusted during the hand fitting operation, so that it does have its particular pattern of microscopic marks.

The bolt face of the 139 rifle I have photographed and enlarged in this photograph [Commission Exhibit No. 558] to show the types of marks I was referring to.

*   *   *   *   *   *   *

The marks produced during manufacture are the marks seen on the bolt face; filing marks, machining marks of the various types, even forging marks or casting marks if the bolt happens to be forged or cast. And then variations which occur in these marks during the life of the weapon are very important in identification, because many of the machining marks can be flattened out, can be changed, by merely a grain of sand between the face of the cartridge case and the bolt at the time a shot is fired, which will itself scratch and dent the bolt face. So the bolt face will pick up a characteristic pattern of marks which are peculiar to it.

*   *   *   *   *   *   *

* * * [T]he marks which are placed on any bolt face are accidental in nature. That is, they are not placed there intentionally in the first place. They are residual to some machining operation, such as a milling machine, in which each cutter of the milling tool cuts away a portion of the metal; then the next tooth comes along and cuts away a little more, and so on, until the final surface bears the combination of the various teeth of the milling cutter. In following that operation, then, the surface is additionally scratched—until you have numerous—we call them microscopic characteristics, a characteristic being a mark which is peculiar to a certain place on the bolt face, and of a certain shape, it is of a certain size, it has a certain contour, it may be just a little dimple in the metal, or a spot of rust at one time on the face of the bolt, or have occurred from some accidental means such as dropping the bolt, or repeated use having flattened or smoothed off the surface of the metal.

    *   *   *   *   *   *   *

* * * [A]s the blade of a milling machine travels around a surface, it takes off actually a dust—it is not actually a piece of metal—it scrapes a little steel off in the form of a dust—or a very fine powder or chip—that tooth leaves a certain pattern of marks—that edge. That milling cutter may have a dozen of these edges on its surface, and each one takes a little more. Gradually you wear the metal down, you tear it out actually until you are at the proper depth. Those little pieces of metal, as they are traveling around, can also scratch the face of the bolt—unless they are washed away. So that you may have accidental marks from that source, just in the machining operation.

Now, there are two types of marks produced in a cutting operation. One, from the nicks along the cutting edge of the tool, which are produced by a circular operating tool—which produce very fine scratches in a circular pattern. Each time the tool goes around, it erases those marks that were there before. And when the tool is finally lifted out, you have a series of marks which go around the surface which has been machined, and you will find that that pattern of marks, as this tool goes around, will change. In one area, it will be one set of marks— and as you visually examine the surface of the metal, these very fine marks will extend for a short distance, then disappear, and a new mark of a new type will begin and extend for a short distance. The entire surface, then, will have a—be composed of a series of circles, but the individual marks seen in the microscope will not be circular, will not form complete circles around the face of the bolt.

Q. Have you had occasion to examine two consecutive bolt faces from a factory?

A. Oh, yes.

Q. And what did you find on that examination?

A. There would be no similarity in the individual microscopic characteristics between the two bolt faces.

Q. There actually was none?

A. No, there was none.[3]

*　　*　　*　　*　　*　　*　　*

Q. How are you able to conclude that a given bullet was fired in a given weapon to the exclusion of all other weapons, Mr. Frazier?

A. That is based again upon the microscopic marks left on the fired bullets and those marks in turn are based upon the barrel from which the bullets are fired.

The marks in the barrel originate during manufacture. They originate through use of the gun, through accidental marks resulting from cleaning, excessive cleaning, of the weapon, or faulty cleaning.

They result from corrosion in the barrel due to the hot gases and possibly corrosive primer mixtures in the cartridges used, and primarily again they result from wear, that is, an eroding of the barrel through friction due to the firing of cartridges, bullets through it.

In this particular barrel the manufacturer's marks are caused by the drill which drills out the barrel, leaving certain marks from the drilling tool. Then portions of these marks are erased by a rifling tool which cuts the four spiral grooves in the barrel and, in turn, leaves marks themselves, and in connection with those marks of course, the drilling marks, being circular in shape, there is a tearing away of the surface of the metal, so that a microscopically rough surface is left.

Then removing part of those marks with a separate tool causes that barrel to assume an individual characteristic, a character all of its own.

In other words, at that time you could identify a bullet fired from that barrel as having been fired from the barrel to the exclusion of all other barrels, because there is no system whatever to the drilling of the barrel. The only system is in the rifling or in the cutting of the grooves, and in this case of rifle barrels, even the cutters wear down as the barrels are made, eventually of course having to be discarded or resharpened.

Q. Have you examined consecutively manufactured barrels to determine whether their microscopic characteristics are identical?

A. Yes, sir; I have three different sets of, you might say, paired barrels, which have been manufactured on the same machine, one after the other, under controlled conditions to make them as nearly alike as possible, and in each case fired bullets from those barrels could not be identified with each other; in fact, they looked nothing at all alike as far as individual microscopic characteristics are concerned. Their rifling impressions of course would be identical, but the individual marks there would be entirely different.[4]

When a cartridge is fired, the microscopic characteristics of the weapon's barrel are engraved into the bullet (along with its rifling characteristics), and the microscopic characteristics of the firing pin and breech face are engraved into the base of the cartridge case. By virtue of these microscopic markings, an expert can frequently match a bullet or cartridge case to the weapon in which it was fired. To make such an identification, the expert compares the suspect bullet or cartridge case under a comparison microscope, side by side with a test bullet or cartridge case which has been fired in the weapon, to determine whether the pattern of the markings in the test and suspect items are sufficiently similar to show that they were fired in the same weapon. This is exemplified by Frazier's examination of Commission Exhibit No. 543, one of the cartridge cases found in the Texas School Book Depository Building after the assassination:

Q. Mr. Frazier, we were just beginning to discuss, before the recess, Commission Exhibit 559, which is a picture, as you described it, of Exhibit No. 543 and a test cartridge under a microscope * * *?

Mr. FRAZIER. Yes, sir.

Q. Could you discuss, by using that picture, some of the markings which you have seen under the microscope and on the basis of which you made your identification?

A. Yes, sir. In the photograph I have drawn some small circles and numbered them, those circles, correspondingly on each side of the photograph. The purpose of the circles is not to point out all the similarities, but to call attention to some of them and to help orient in locating a mark on one with a mark on the opposite side of the photograph. In general the area shown is immediately outside of the firing pin in the bolt of the 139 rifle, on the left side of the photograph, and Commission Exhibit 543 on the right side.

The circles have been drawn around the dents or irregularly shaped ridges, small bumps, and depressions on the surface of the metal in six places on each side of the photograph. It is an examination of these marks, and all of the marks on the face of the breech, microscopically which permits a conclusion to be reached. The photograph itself actually is a substitute to show only the type of marks found rather than their nature, that is, their height, their width, or their relationship to each other, which is actually a mental, visual, comparison on the two specimens themselves.

Q. Referring for a second to this mental, visual, comparison, Mr. Frazier, would a person without firearms training—firearms-identification training—be able to look under a microscope and make a determination for himself concerning whether a given cartridge case had been fired in a given weapon?

A. In that connection that person could look through the microscope. He may or may not see these individual characteristics which are present, because he does not know what to look for in the first place, and, secondly, they are of such a nature that you have to mentally sort them out in your mind going back and forth between one area and the other until you form a mental picture of them in a comparison such as this.

If it was a different type of comparison, of parallel marks or something of that nature, then he could see the marks, but in either instance, without having compared hundreds and hundreds of specimens, he would not be able to make any statement as to whether or not they were fired from the same rifle.

Q. Would you say that this is, then, a matter of expert interpretation rather than a point-for-point comparison which a layman could make?

A. I would say so; yes. I don't think a layman would recognize some of the things on these cartridge cases and some shown in the photographs as actually being significant or not significant, because there will be things present which have nothing whatsoever to do with the firing of the cartridge case in the gun.

There may be a depression in the primer to begin with, and there are no marks registered at that point as a result of the firing. Unless these things are known to occur, someone may actually arrive at a different conclusion, because of the absence of similar marks.

Q. Now having reference to the specific exhibit before you, which is 559——

A. Yes.

Q. Are all the marks shown in both photographs identical?

A. No.

Q. And could you go into detail on a mark which is not identical to explain why you would get such a result?

A. Well, for instance, between what I have drawn here as circle 4 and circle 5, there is a slanting line from the upper left to the lower right on C–6. This line shows as a white line in the photograph.

On the other side there is a rough, very rough ridge which runs through there, having an entirely different appearance from the relatively sharp line on C–6. The significant part of that mark is the groove in between, rather than the sharp edge of the mark, because the sharp corner could be affected by the hardness of the metal or the irregular surface of the primer and the amount of pressure exerted against it, pressing it back against the face of the bolt, at the time the cartridges were fired. So that you would never expect all the marks on one cartridge case to be identical with all the marks on the other cartridge case.

In fact, you would expect many differences. But the comparison is made on the overall pattern, contour, and nature of the marks that are present.

*   *   *   *   *   *   *

Q. Again there are dissimilar marks on these two pictures [of the firing-pin depressions on the cartridge case Commission Exhibit No. 543, and a test cartridge case], Mr. Frazier?

A. Yes; there are, for the same reason, that metal does not flow the same in every instance, and it will not be impressed to the same depth and to the same amount, depending on the type of metal, the blow that is struck, and the pressures involved.

Q. Is your identification made therefore on the basis of the presence of similarities, as opposed to the absence of dissimilarities?

A. No, that is not exactly right. The identification is made on the presence of sufficient individual microscopic characteristics so that a very definite pattern is formed and visualized on the two surfaces.

Dissimilarities may or may not be present, depending on whether there have been changes to the firing pin through use or wear, whether the metal flows are the same, and whether the pressures are the same or not.

So I don't think we can say that it is an absence of dissimilarities, but rather the presence of similarities.[5]

A bullet or cartridge case cannot always be identified with the weapon in which it was fired. In some cases, the bullet or cartridge case is too mutilated. In other cases, the weapon's microscopic characteristics have changed between the time the suspect item was fired and the time the test item was fired—microscopic characteristics change drastically in a short period of time, due to wear, or over a longer period of time, due to wear, corrosion, and cleaning. Still again, the weapon may mark bullets inconsistently—for example, because the bullets are smaller than the barrel, and travel through it erratically.[6]

The Rifle

The rifle found on the sixth floor of the Texas School Book Depository shortly after the assassination was a bolt-action, clip-fed, military rifle, 40.2 inches long and 8 pounds in weight.[7] Inscribed on the rifle were various markings, including the words "CAL. 6.5," "MADE ITALY," "TERNI," and "ROCCA"; the numerals "1940" and "40"; the serial number C2766; the letters "R–E," "PG," and "TNI"; the figure of a crown; and several other barely decipherable letters and numbers.[8] The rifle bore a very inexpensive Japanese four-power sight, stamped "4 x 18 COATED," "ORDNANCE OPTICS INC.," "HOLLYWOOD CALIFORNIA," and "MADE IN JAPAN"[9] and a sling consisting of two leather straps, one of which had a broad patch, which apparently had been inserted on the rifle and cut to length.[10]   The sling was not a standard rifle sling, but appeared to be a musical instrument strap or a sling from a carrying case or camera bag.[11]   A basic purpose of a rifle sling is to enable the rifleman to steady his grip, by wrapping the arm into the sling in a prescribed manner. The sling on the rifle was too short to use in the normal way, but might have served to provide some additional steadiness.[12]

The rifle was identified as a 6.5-millimeter Mannlicher-Carcano Italian military rifle, Model 91/38.[13]   This identification was initially made by comparing the rifle with standard reference works and by the markings inscribed on the rifle.[14]   The caliber was independently determined by chambering a Mannlicher-Carcano 6.5 millimeter cartridge in the rifle for fit, and by making a sulfur cast of the inside of the rifle's barrel which was measured with a micrometer.[15]   (The caliber of a weapon is the diameter of the interior of the barrel, measured between opposite lands. The caliber of American weapons is expressed in inches; thus a .30-caliber weapon has a barrel which is thirty one-hundredths or three-tenths of an inch in diameter. The caliber of continental European weapons is measured in millimeters. A 6.5-millimeter caliber weapon corresponds to an American .257-caliber weapon, that is, its barrel diameter is about one-fourth inch.) [16] The identification was later confirmed by a communication from SIFAR, the Italian Armed Forces Intelligence Service. This communication also explained the markings on the rifle, as follows: "CAL. 6.5" refers to the rifle's caliber; "MADE ITALY" refers to its origin, and was inscribed at the request of the American importer prior to shipment; "TERNI" means that the rifle was manufactured and tested by the Terni Army Plant of Terni, Italy; the number "C2766" is the serial number of the rifle, and the rifle in question is the only one of its type bearing that serial number; the numerals "1940" and "40" refer to the year of manufacture; and the other figures, numbers, and letters are principally inspector's, designer's, or manufacturer's marks.[17]

The Model 91/38 rifle was one of the 1891 series of Italian military rifles, incorporating features designed by Ritter von Mannlicher and M. Carcano. The series originally consisted of 6.5-millimeter caliber rifles, but Model 38 of the series, designed shortly before World War II, was a 7.35-millimeter caliber. Early in World War II, however, the Italian Government, which encountered an ammunition supply problem, began producing many of these rifles as 6.5-millimeter caliber rifles, known as the 6.5-millimeter Model 91/38.[18]   The 91/38 has been imported into this country as surplus military equipment, has been advertised quite widely, and is now fairly common in this country.[19]

Like most bolt-action military rifles, the 91/38 is operated by turning up the bolt handle, drawing the bolt to the rear, pushing the bolt forward, turning down the bolt handle, and pulling the trigger. Bringing the bolt forward and turning down the bolt handle compresses the spring which drives the firing pin, and locks the bolt into place. When the trigger is pulled, the cocked spring drives the firing pin forward and the cartridge is fired. The face of the bolt bears a lip, called the extractor, around a portion of its circumference. As the bolt is pushed forward, this lip grasps the rim of the cartridge. As the bolt is pulled back, the extractor brings the empty cartridge case with it, and as the cartridge case is being brought back, it strikes a projection in the ejection port called the ejector, which throws it out of the rifle. Meanwhile, a leaf spring beneath the clip has raised the next cartridge into loading position. When the bolt is brought forward, it pushes the fresh cartridge into the chamber. The trigger is pulled, the cartridge is fired, the bolt handle is brought up, the bolt is brought back, and the entire cycle starts again. As long as there is ammunition in the clip, one need only work the bolt and pull the trigger to fire the rifle.[20]

The clip itself is inserted into the rifle by drawing back the bolt, and pushing the clip in from the top. The clip holds one to six cartridges.[21] If six cartridges are inserted into the clip and an additional cartridge is inserted into the chamber, up to seven bullets can be fired before reloading.[22] When the rifle was found in the Texas School Book Depository Building it contained a clip [23] which bore the letters "SMI" (the manufacturer's markings) and the number "952" (possibly a part number or the manufacturer's code number).[24] The rifle probably was sold without a clip; however, the clip is commonly available.[25]

Rifle Cartridge and Cartridge Cases

When the rifle was found, one cartridge was in the chamber.[26] The cartridge was a 6.5-millimeter Mannlicher-Carcano cartridge, manufactured by the Western Cartridge Co., at East Alton, Ill. This type of cartridge is loaded with a full metal-jacketed, military type of bullet, weighing 160–161 grains. The bullet has parallel sides and a round nose. It is just under 1.2 inches long, and just over one-fourth inch in diameter.[27] Its velocity is approximately 2,165 feet per second.[28] The cartridge is very dependable; in tests runs by the FBI and the Infantry Weapons Evaluation Branch of the U.S. Army, the C2766 rifle was fired with this Western Cartridge Co. ammunition over 100 times, with no misfires. (In contrast, some of the other ammunition available on the market for this rifle is undesirable or of very poor quality).[29] The cartridge is readily available for purchase from mail-order houses, as well as a few gunshops; some 2 million rounds have been placed on sale in the United States.[30]

The presence of the cartridge in the chamber did not necessarily mean that the assassin considered firing another bullet, since he may have reloaded merely by reflex.[31]

Apart from the cartridge in the rifle, three expended cartridge cases were found in the southeast portion of the sixth floor of the Texas School Book Depository Building, lying between the south

COMMISSION EXHIBIT No. 558

Bolt face of the C2766 rifle.

wall and a high stack of boxes which ran parallel to the wall.[32] The cartridge cases were a short distance to the west of the southeast corner window in that wall.[33] Based on a comparison with test cartridge cases fired from the C2766 rifle, the three cartridge cases were identified as having been fired from the C2766 rifle.[34] (See Commission Exhibit No. 558, p. 556.) A test was run to determine if the cartridge-case-ejection pattern of the rifle was consistent with the assumption that the assassin had fired from the southeast window.[35] In this test, 11 cartridges were fired from the rifle while it was depressed 45° downward, and 8 cartridges were fired from the rifle while it was held horizontally. The elevation of the ejected cartridge cases above the level of the ejection port, and the points on the floor at which the ejection cartridge cases initially landed, were then plotted. The results of these tests are illustrated by the diagrams, Commission Exhibits Nos. 546 and 547. Briefly, Commission Exhibit No. 547 shows that with the weapon depressed at a 45° angle, the cartridge cases did not rise more than 2 inches above the ejection port; with the weapon held horizontally, they did not rise more than 12 inches above the ejection port.[36] Commission Exhibit No. 546 shows that if a circle was drawn around the initial landing points of the cartridge cases which were ejected in the test while the rifle was held depressed at 45°, the center of the circle would be located 86 inches and 80° to the right of the rifle's line of sight; if a circle was drawn around the initial landing points of the cartridge cases ejected while the rifle was held horizontally, the center of the circle would be 80 inches and 90° to the right of the line of sight. In other words, the cartridge cases were ejected to the right of and at roughly a right angle to the rifle.[37] The cartridge cases showed considerable ricochet after their initial landing, bouncing from 8 inches to 15 feet.[38] The location of the cartridge cases was therefore consistent with the southeast window having been used by the assassin, since if the assassin fired from that window the ejected cartridge cases would have hit the pile of boxes at his back and ricocheted between the boxes and the wall until they came to rest to the west of the window.[39]

The Rifle Bullets

In addition to the three cartridge cases found in the Texas School Book Depository Building, a nearly whole bullet was found on Governor Connally's stretcher and two bullet fragments were found in the front of the President's car.[40] The stretcher bullet weighed 158.6 grains, or several grains less than the average Western Cartridge Co. 6.5-millimeter Mannlicher-Carcano bullet.[41] It was slightly flattened, but otherwise unmutilated.[42] The two bullet fragments weighed 44.6 and 21.0 grains, respectively.[43] The heavier fragment was a portion of a bullet's nose area, as shown by its rounded contour and the

character of the markings it bore.[44]   The lighter fragment consisted
of bullet's base portion, as shown by its shape and by the presence of
a cannelure.[45]   The two fragments were both mutilated, and it was
not possible to determine from the fragments themselves whether
they comprised the base and nose of one bullet or of two separate
bullets.[46]   However, each had sufficient unmutilated area to provide
the basis of an identification.[47]   Based on a comparison with test
bullets fired from the C2766 rifle, the stretcher bullet and both bullet
fragments were identified as having been fired from the C2766 rifle.[48]

The Revolver

The revolver taken from Oswald at the time of his arrest was a
.38 Special S. & W. Victory Model revolver.[49]   It bore the serial
No. V510210, and is the only such revolver with that serial number,
since S. & W. does not repeat serial numbers.[50]   The revolver was originally made in the United States, but was shipped to England, as
shown by the English inspection or proof marks on the chambers.[51]
The revolver showed definite signs of use but was in good operating
condition.[52]   The revolver was originally designed to fire a .38 S. & W.
cartridge, whose bullet is approximately 12 or 13 grains lighter than
the .38 Special, and approximately .12 inches shorter, but has a somewhat larger diameter.[53]   In the United States, the .38 Special is considered to be a better bullet than the .38 S. & W.,[54] and the revolver
was rechambered for a .38 Special prior to being sold in the United
States.[55]   The weapon was not rebarreled, although the barrel was
shortened by cutting off approximately 2¾ of its original 5 inches.[56]
The shortening of the barrel had no functional value, except to facilitate concealment.[57]

The weapon is a conventional revolver, with a rotating cylinder
holding one to six cartridges.   It is loaded by swinging out the cylinder
and inserting cartridges into the cylinder's chambers.   If all six chambers are loaded, the weapon can be fired six consecutive times without
reloading.[58]   To extract empty cartridge cases, the cylinder is swung
out and an ejector rod attached to the cylinder is pushed, simultaneously ejecting all the cartridge cases (and cartridges) in the
cylinder.   If both live cartridges and expended cartridge cases are
in the cylinder, before pushing the ejection rod one can tip the cylinder
and dump the live cartridges into his hand.[59]   The cartridge cases will
not fall out, because they are lighter than the cartridges, and when
fired they will have expanded so as to tightly fit the chamber walls.[60]

In a crouched stance a person can fire five shots with the revolver
in 3–4 seconds with no trouble, and would need no training to hit a
human body four times in four or five shots at a range of 8 feet.[61]   A
person who had any training with the weapon would not find its
recoil noticeable.[62]

558

Revolver Cartridges and Cartridge Cases

When Oswald was arrested six live cartridges were found in the revolver.[63] Three were Western .38 Specials, loaded with copper-coated lead bullets, and three were Remington-Peters .38 Specials, loaded with lead bullets.[64] Five additional live cartridges were found in Oswald's pocket,[65] all of which were Western .38 Specials, loaded with copper-coated bullets.[66] The Western and Remington-Peters .38 Special cartridges are virtually identical—the copper coating on the Western bullets is not a full jacket, but only a gilding metal, put on principally for sales appeal.[67]

Four expended cartridge cases were found near the site of the Tippit killing.[68] Two of these cartridge cases were Remington-Peters .38 Specials and two were Western .38 Specials.[69] Based on a comparison with test cartridge cases fired in the V510210 revolver, the four cartridge cases were identified as having been fired in the V510210 revolver.[70]

Revolver Bullets

Four bullets were recovered from the body of Officer Tippit.[71] In Nicol's opinion one of the four bullets could be positively identified with test bullets fired from V510210 revolver, and the other three could have been fired from that revolver.[72] In Cunningham's opinion all four bullets could have been fired from the V510210 revolver, but none could be positively identified to the revolver [73]—that is, in his opinion the bullets bore the revolver's rifling characteristics, but no conclusion could be drawn on the basis of microscopic characteristics.[74] Cunningham did not conclude that the bullets had not been fired from the revolver, since he found that consecutive bullets fired in the revolver by the FBI could not even be identified with each other under the microscope.[75] The apparent reasons for this was that while the revolver had been rechambered for a .38 Special cartridge, it had not been rebarreled for a .38 Special bullet. The barrel was therefore slightly oversized for a .38 Special bullet, which has a smaller diameter than a .38 S. & W. bullet. This would cause the passage of a .38 Special bullet through the barrel to be erratic, resulting in inconsistent microscopic markings.[76]

Based on the number of grooves, groove widths, groove spacing, and knurling on the four recovered bullets, three were copper-coated lead bullets of Western-Winchester manufacture (Western and Winchester are divisions of the same company), and the fourth was a lead bullet of Remington-Peters manufacture.[77] This contrasts with the four recovered cartridge cases, which consisted of two Remington-Peters and two Westerns. There are several possible explanations for this variance: (1) the killer fired five cartridges, three of which were Western-Winchester and two of which were Remington-Peters; one Remington-Peters bullet missed Tippit; and a Western-Winchester cartridge case and the Remington-Peters bullet that missed were simply not found. (2) The killer fired only four cartridges, three of which were Western-Winchester and one of which was Remington-Peters; prior to the shooting the killer had an expended Remington-Peters cartridge case in his revolver, which was ejected with the three Western-Winchester and one Remington-Peters cases; and one of the Western-Winchester cases was not found.   (3) The killer was using hand-loaded ammunition, that is, ammunition which is made with used cartridge cases to save money; thus he might have loaded one make of bullet into another make of cartridge case.[78]   This third possibility is extremely unlikely, because when a cartridge is fired the cartridge case expands, and before it can be reused it must be resized. There was, however, no evidence that any of the four recovered cartridge cases had been resized.[79]

The Struggle for the Revolver

Officer McDonald of the Dallas police, who arrested Oswald, stated that he had struggled with Oswald for possession of the revolver and that in the course of the struggle, "I heard the snap of the hammer, and the pistol crossed my left cheek * * * the primer of one round was dented on misfire at the time of the struggle. * * *"[80]   However, none of the cartridges found in the revolver bore the impression of the revolver's firing pin.[81]   In addition, the revolver is so constructed that the firing pin cannot strike a cartridge unless the hammer (which bears the firing pin) has first been drawn all the way back by a complete trigger pull.[82]   Had the hammer gone all the way back and then hit the cartridge, it is unlikely that the cartridge would have misfired.[83]   It would be possible for a person to interject his finger between the hammer and the cartridge, but the spring driving the hammer is a very strong one and the impact of the firing pin into a finger would be clearly felt.[84]   However, the cylinder and the trigger are interconnected and the trigger cannot be fully pulled back if the cylinder is grasped.[85]   Therefore, if Oswald had pulled on the trigger while McDonald was firmly grasping the cylinder, the revolver would not have fired, and if the gun was grabbed away at the same time the trigger would have snapped back with an audible sound.[86]

The Paraffin Test

During the course of the interrogation of Lee Harvey Oswald following the assassination a paraffin test was performed by the Dallas police on both of his hands and his right cheek. The paraffin cast of Oswald's hands reacted positively to the test. The cast of the right cheek showed no reaction.[87]

To perform the paraffin test, layers of warm liquid paraffin, interleaved with layers of gauze for reinforcement, are brushed or poured on the suspect's skin. The warm sticky paraffin opens the skin's pores and picks up any dirt and foreign material present at the surface. When the paraffin cools and hardens it forms a cast, which is taken off and processed with diphenylamine or diphenylbenzidine, chemicals which turn blue in the presence of nitrates. Since gunpowder residues contain nitrates, the theory behind the test is that if a cast reacts positively, i.e., if blue dots appear, it provides evidence that the suspect recently fired a weapon.[88] In fact, however, the test is completely unreliable in determining either whether a person has recently fired a weapon or whether he has not.[89] On the one hand, diphenylamine and diphenylbenzidine will react positively not only with nitrates from gunpowder residues, but nitrates from other sources and most oxidizing agents, including dichromates, permanganates, hypochlorates, periodates, and some oxides. Thus, contact with tobacco, Clorox, urine, cosmetics, kitchen matches, pharmaceuticals, fertilizers, or soils, among other things, may result in a positive reaction to the paraffin test. Also, the mere handling of a weapon may leave nitrates on the skin.[90] A positive reaction is, therefore, valueless in determining whether a suspect has recently fired a weapon. Conversely, a person who has recently fired a weapon may not show a positive reaction to the paraffin test, particularly if the weapon was a rifle. A revolver is so constructed that there is a space between the cylinder, which bears the chambers, and the barrel. When a revolver is fired, nitrate-bearing gases escape through this space and may leave residues on the hand.[91] In a rifle, however, there is no gap between the chamber and the barrel, and one would therefore not expect nitrates to be deposited upon a person's hands or cheeks as a result of his firing a rifle. As Cunningham testified:

> Mr. CUNNINGHAM. * * * I personally wouldn't expect to find any residues on a person's right cheek after firing a rifle due to the fact that by the very principles and the manufacture and the action, the cartridge itself is sealed into the chamber by the bolt being closed behind it, and upon firing the case, the cartridge case expands into the chamber filling it up and sealing it off from the gases, so none will come back in your face, and so by its very nature, I would not expect to find residue on the right cheek of a shooter.[92]

The unreliability of the paraffin test has been demonstrated by experiments run by the FBI. In one experiment, conducted prior to the assassination, paraffin tests were performed on 17 men who had just fired 5 shots with a .38-caliber revolver. Eight men tested negative in both hands, three men tested positive on the idle hand and negative on the firing hand, two men tested positive on the firing hand and negative on the idle hand, and four men tested positive on both their firing and idle hands.[93] In a second experiment, paraffin tests were performed on 29 persons, 9 of whom had just fired a revolver or an automatic, and 20 of whom had not fired a weapon. All 29 persons tested positive on either or both hands.[94] In a third experiment, performed after the assassination, an agent of the FBI, using the C2766 rifle, fired three rounds of Western 6.5-millimeter Mannlicher-Carcano ammunition in rapid succession. A paraffin test was then performed on both of his hands and his right cheek. Both of his hands and his cheek tested negative.[95]

The paraffin casts of Oswald's hands and right cheek were also examined by neutron-activation analyses at the Oak Ridge National Laboratory. Barium and antimony were found to be present on both surfaces of all the casts and also in residues from the rifle cartridge cases and the revolver cartridge cases.[96] Since barium and antimony were present in both the rifle and the revolver cartridge cases, their presence on the casts were not evidence that Oswald had fired the rifle. Moreover, the presence on the inside surface of the cheek cast of a lesser amount of barium, and only a slightly greater amount of antimony, than was found on the outside surface of the cast rendered it impossible to attach significance to the presence of these elements on the inside surface. Since the outside surface had not been in contact with Oswald's cheek, the barium and antimony found there had come from a source other than Oswald. Furthermore, while there was more barium and antimony present on the casts than would normally be found on the hands of a person who had not fired a weapon or handled a fired weapon, it is also true that barium and antimony may be present in many common items; for example, barium may be present in grease, ceramics, glass, paint, printing ink, paper, rubber, plastics, leather, cloth, pyrotechnics, oilcloth and linoleum, storage batteries, matches and cosmetics; antimony is present in matches, type metal, lead alloys, paints and lacquers, pigments for oil and water colors, flameproof textiles, storage batteries, pyrotechnics, rubber, pharmaceutical preparations and calico; and both barium and antimony are present in printed paper and cloth, paint, storage batteries, rubber, matches, pyrotechnics, and possibly other items. However, the barium and antimony present in these items are usually not present in a form which would lead to their adhering to the skin of a person who had handled such items.[97]

The Walker Bullet

On April 10, 1963, a bullet was recovered from General Walker's home, following an attempt on his life.[98] The bullet, which was severely mutilated, weighed 148.25 grains.[99] This bullet had the rifling characteristics of the C2766 rifle and all its remaining physical characteristics were the same as the Western 6.5 millimeter Mannlicher-Carcano bullet. However, while the bullet could have been fired from the C2766 rifle, it was severely multilated and in Frazier's opinion could not be identified as having been fired or not fired from that rifle.[100] Nicol agreed that a positive identification could not be made, but concluded there was "a fair probability" that the bullet had been fired from the same rifle as the test bullets.[101]

FINGERPRINTS AND PALMPRINTS

Two experts gave testimony concerning fingerprints and palmprints: Sebastian Latona [102] and Arthur Mandella.[103] Latona is the supervisor of the Latent Fingerprint Section of the Identification Division of the FBI. He has been with that Division over 32 years, having begun as a student fingerprint classifier and worked up to his present position. Mandella is a detective and fingerprint instructor with the police department of the city of New York. He has been in the fingerprint field for 19 years. Both have made a vast number of fingerprint examinations and have testified in Federal, State, and military courts.[104] Their conclusions were identical, except as noted.

General Principles [105]

Fingerprints and palmprints are made by the ridges which cover the surface of the fingers and palms. These ridges first appear 2 or 3 months before birth, and remain unchanged until death. Commission Exhibit No. 634–A (p. 564) illustrates several common characteristics or "points" formed by the ridges; a clear fingerprint impression will contain anywhere from 85 to 125 such points. While many of the common points appear in almost every print, no two prints have the same points in the same relationship to each other.

A print taken by a law-enforcement agency is known as an "inked print," and is carefully taken so that all the characteristics of the print are reproduced on the fingerprint card; a print which is left accidentally, such as a print left at the scene of a crime, is known as a latent print. To make an identification of a latent print, the expert compares the points in the latent print with the points in an inked print. If a point appearing in a latent print does not appear in the inked print, or vice versa, the expert concludes that the two prints were not made by the same finger or palm. An identification is made only if there are no inconsistencies between the inked and latent prints, and the points of similarity and their relative positions are sufficiently distinctive, and sufficient in number, to satisfy the expert that an identity exists.[106]

There is some disagreement concerning whether a minimum number of points is necessary for an identification. Some foreign law-enforcement agencies require a minimum number of 16 points. However, in the United States, in which there has been a great deal of experience with fingerprints, expert opinion holds there is no minimum number of points, and that each print must be evaluated on its own merits.[107]

Palmprints are as distinctive as fingerprints, but are not as popularly known. Possibly this is because law enforcement agencies usually record only fingerprints for their identification files, since fingerprints can be much more readily classified and filed than palmprints. Also, latent fingerprint impressions are probably more common than latent palmprint impressions, because persons generally touch objects with their fingers rather than their palms. However,

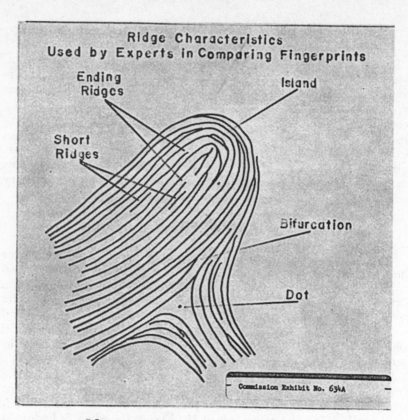

Ridge Characteristics
Used by Experts in Comparing Fingerprints

Ending Ridges

Island

Short Ridges

Bifurcation

Dot

Commission Exhibit No. 634A

135a COMMISSION EXHIBIT NO. 634-A

564

palmprints will frequently be found on heavy objects, since the palms as well as the fingers are employed in handling such objects.[108]

A latent print is the result of perspiration exuded by the sweat pores in the ridges. This perspiration is composed of water, protein or fatty materials, and sodium chloride (salt). A latent print can be developed—made visible—in several ways. Sometimes a latent print can be developed merely by the use of correct lighting. A second method is to brush the print very lightly with a powder, which adheres to its outline. Once a print is powdered it can be photographed, lifted, or both. (In lifting, an adhesive substance, such as scotch tape, is placed over a powdered print. When the adhesive is lifted the powder clings to its surface. The adhesive is then mounted.) However, powder is usually effective only on objects which have a hard, smooth, nonabsorbent surface, such as glass, tile, and various types of highly polished metals and is usually not effective on absorbent materials, such as paper or unfinished wood or metal, which absorb perspiration so that there is nothing on the material's surface to which the powder can adhere. Prints on absorbent materials can sometimes be developed by iodine fumes, which may react with fatty or protein materials which have been absorbed into the object, or by a silver nitrate solution, which may react with sodium chloride which has been absorbed into the object.[109]

Not every contact of a finger or palm leaves a latent print. For example, if the surface is not susceptible to a latent print, if the finger or palm had no perspiration, or if the perspiration was mostly water and had evaporated, no print will be found.[110]

Objects in the Texas School Book Depository Building

A number of objects found in the Texas School Book Depository Building following the assassination were processed for latent fingerprints by the FBI—in some cases, after they had been processed by the Dallas police. These objects included the homemade wrapping paper bag found near the southeast corner window; the C2766 rifle; three small cartons which were stacked near that window (which were marked "Box A," "Box B," and "Box C"),[111] and a fourth carton resting on the floor nearby (marked "Box D"); [112] the three 6.5-millimeter cartridge cases found near the window; and the cartridge found in the rifle. The results were as follows:

The paper bag.—The FBI developed a palmprint and a fingerprint on the paper bag by silver nitrate. These were compared with the fingerprints and palmprints of Lee Harvey Oswald taken by the Dallas police, and were found to have been made by the right palm and the left index finger of Lee Harvey Oswald.[113]

The C2766 rifle.—The wood and metal of the rifle was absorbent, and not conducive to recording a good print.[114] However, the Dallas police developed by powder some faint ridge formations on the metal magazine housing in front of the trigger and also developed by powder and lifted a latent palmprint from the underside of the barrel.[115] The faint ridge formations were insufficient for purposes of effecting an identification,[116] but the latent palmprint was identified as the right palm of Lee Harvey Oswald.[117]

The cartons.—Using the silver nitrate method, the FBI developed nine identifiable latent fingerprints and four identifiable latent palmprints on Box A,[118] seven identifiable fingerprints and two identifiable palmprints on Box B,[119] and two identifiable fingerprints and one identifiable palmprint on Box C.[120] One of the fingerprints on Box A was identified as the right index fingerprint of Lee Harvey Oswald,[121] and one of the palmprints on Box A was identified as the left palmprint of Lee Harvey Oswald.[122] All the remaining prints on Box A were the palmprints of R. L. Studebaker, a Dallas police officer, and Forest L. Lucy, an FBI clerk, who shipped the cartons from Dallas to the FBI Laboratory in Washington, D.C., and fingerprints of Detective Studebaker. All but one of the fingerprints on Box B belonged to Studebaker and Lucy and one palmprint was that of Studebaker. The fingerprints on Box C were those of Studebaker and Lucy and the palmprint was Studebaker's.[123] One palmprint on Box B was unidentified.[124]

The FBI developed two fingerprints on Box D by silver nitrate, and the Dallas police developed a palmprint on Box D by powder.[125] The fingerprints belonged to Lucy. The palmprint was identified as the right palmprint of Lee Harvey Oswald.[126] While the age of a print cannot be generally determined,[127] this palmprint must have been relatively fresh, because the carton was constructed of cardboard, an absorbent material, and if a long period had elapsed between the time the print was made and the time it was powdered, the perspiration would have been absorbed into the cardboard, and the print could not have been developed by powder.[128] Tests run by the FBI show that usually a latent impression on such cardboard cannot be developed by powder more than 24 hours after it is made.[129] Latona felt that the maximum age of the palmprint on Box D at the time of development (which was shortly after the assassination), would have been 3 days;[130] Mandella felt that the maximum time would have been a day and a half.[131]

The three cartridge cases and the cartridge case found in the rifle.— No prints were developed on the cartridge found in the rifle or on the three expended cartridge cases.[132]

QUESTIONED DOCUMENTS

Two experts gave testimony concerning questioned documents: Alwyn Cole [133] and James C. Cadigan.[134] Cole apprenticed as a questioned document examiner for 6 years, from 1929 to 1935, and has been examiner of questioned documents for the U.S. Treasury Department since then. Cadigan has been a questioned document examiner with the FBI for 23½ years, following a specialized course of training and instruction. Both have testified many times in Federal and States courts.[135] Their conclusions were identical, except as noted.

Both experts examined and testified on the following questioned documents: (1) The mail order to Klein's Sporting Goods of Chicago, in response to which Klein's sent the C2766 rifle; the accompanying money order; and the envelope in which the mail order and the money order were sent—all of which bore the name "A. Hidell" and the address "P.O. Box 2915, Dallas, Texas"; [136] (2) the mail order to Seaport Traders, Inc., of Los Angeles, bearing the same name and address, in response to which the Seaport Traders sent the V510210 revolver; [137] (3) part of an application for Post Office Box 2915, Dallas, Tex., opened October 9, 1962 and closed May 14, 1963, and two change-of-address orders relating to that box, dated October 10, 1962 and May 12, 1963—all signed "Lee H. Oswald," and part of an application for Post Office Box 30061, New Orleans, La., naming "A. J. Hidell" as a party entitled to receive mail through the box, signed "L. H. Oswald"; [138] (4) a spurious selective service system notice of classification and a spurious certificate of service in the U.S. Marine Corps, found in Oswald's wallet after his arrest, both in the name "Alek James Hidell"; [139] (5) a spurious smallpox vaccination certificate, found among Oswald's belongings at his room at 1026 North Beckley, purportedly issued to Lee Oswald by "Dr. A. J. Hideel, P.O. Box 30016, New Orleans, La."; [140] and (6) a card, found in Oswald's wallet after his arrest, reading "Fair Play for Cuba Committee New Orleans Chapter," dated "June 15, 1963," bearing the name "L. H. Oswald" and the signature "Lee H. Oswald," and signed "A. J. Hidell" as chapter president.[141] Cadigan also examined (7) the unsigned note, Commission Exhibit No. 1, written almost entirely in Russian, which Marina testified Oswald had left for her prior to his attempt on the life of General Walker; [142] and (8) the homemade paper bag found on the sixth floor of the Texas School Book Depository following the assassination.[143]

General principles.[144]—The area of questioned document examination encompasses many types of inquiries, the most familiar of which is the identification of handwriting. Handwriting identification is based upon the principle that every person's handwriting is distinctive. As Cole testified:

Q. Mr. Cole, could you explain the basis on which you were able to make an identification of a questioned writing as being authored by the person who wrote a standard writing?

Mr. COLE. This is based upon the principle that every handwriting is distinctive, that since the mental and physical equipment for producing handwriting is different in every individual, each person produces his own distinctive writing habits. Of course, everyone learns to write in the beginning by an endeavor to repeat ideal letter forms but, practically no one is able to reproduce these forms exactly. Even though a person might have some initial success during the active period of instruction, he soon departs from these and develops his own habits. It may be said that habit in handwriting is that which makes handwriting possible. Habit is that which makes handwriting efficient. If it were not for the development of habit, one would be obliged to draw or sketch.

Some habit would be included even in those efforts. But the production of handwriting rapidly and fluently always involves a recording of personal writing habit. This has been confirmed by observation of a very large number of specimens over a long period of time, and it has further been demonstrated by, on my part, having a formal responsibility for rendering decisions about the identification of handwriting based upon an agreement of handwriting habit in situations where there would be a rigorous testing of the correctness of these decision by field investigators, for example, of the law-enforcement agencies, and a demonstration that these results were confirmed by other evidence.

This is the basis for identification of handwriting.[145]

The same principles are generally applicable to hand printing,[146] and in the balance of this section the term "handwriting" will be used to refer to both cursive or script writing and hand printing.

Not every letter in a questioned handwriting can be used as the basis of an identification. Most people learn to write letters in a standard or "copybook" form: a handwriting is distinctive only insofar as it departs significantly from such forms.[147] Correspondingly, not every variation indicates nonidentification; no two acts are precisely alike and variations may be found within a single document. Like similarities, variations are significant only if they are distinctive.[148] Moreover, since any single distinctive characteristic may not be unique to one person, in order to make an identification the expert must find a sufficient number of corresponding distinctive characteristics and a general absence of distinctive differences.[149]

The possibility that one person could imitate the handwriting of another and successfully deceive an expert document examiner is very remote. A forger leaves two types of clue. First, he can seldom perfectly simulate the letter forms of the victim; concentrating on the reproduction of one detail, he is likely not to see others. Thus, the forger may successfully imitate the general form of a letter, but get proportions or letter connections wrong. In addition, the forger draws rather than writes. Forged writing is therefore distinguished by defects in the quality of its line, such as tremor, waver, patching, retouching, noncontinuous lines, and pen lifts in awkward and unusual places.[150]

To make a handwriting identification, the handwriting in the document under examination (the questioned document) is compared against the handwriting in documents known to have been prepared by a suspect (the known or standard documents). This is exemplified by Cole's examination of Commission Exhibit No. 773, the photograph of the mail order for the rifle and the envelope in which it was sent:

Q. Now, Mr. Cole, returning to 773, the questioned document, can you tell the Commission how you formed the conclusion that it was prepared by the author of the standards, that is, what steps you followed in your examination and comparison, what things you considered, what instruments or equipment you used, and so forth?

Mr. COLE. I made first a careful study of the writing on Commission Exhibit 773 without reference to the standard writing, in an effort to determine whether or not this writing contained what I would regard as a basis for identification, contained a record of writing habit, and as that—as a result of that part of my examination, I concluded that this is a natural handwriting. By that I mean that it was made at a fair speed, that it doesn't show any evidence of an unnatural movement, poor line quality, tremor, waver, retouching, or the like. I regard it as being made in a fluent and fairly rapid manner which would record the normal writing habits of the person who made it.

I then made a separate examination of the standards, of all of the standard writings, to determine whether that record gave a record of writing habit which could be used for identification purposes, and I concluded that it, too, was a natural handwriting and gave a good record of writing habit.

I then brought the standard writings together with the questioned writing for a detailed and orderly comparison, considering details of letter forms, proportion, pen pressure, letter connections, and other details of handwriting habit * * *.[151]

The standards used by Cole and Cadigan consisted of a wide variety of documents known to be in the handwriting of Lee Harvey Oswald, including indorsements on his payroll checks, applications for employment, for a passport, for membership in the American Civil Liberties Union, and for a library card, and letters to the Immigration and Naturalization Service, the Marine Corps, the State Department, and the American Embassy in Russia.[152]

The Mail Order for the C2766 Rifle, the Related Envelope, and the Money Order

The mail order and envelope for the C2766 rifle were photographed by Klein's on microfilm, and then destroyed.[153] To identify the handwriting an enlarged photograph was made which showed the handwriting characteristics with sufficient clarity to form the basis of an identification.[154] Based on a comparison with the standards, the handwriting on the purchase order and the envelope were identified as Lee Harvey Oswald's.[155] The money order, which was retained by the post office after having been cashed by Klein's,[156] was also identified as being in Oswald's handwriting.[157] These identifications were made on the basis of numerous characteristics in which the writing in both the questioned and standard documents departed from conventional letter forms.[158] For example, in the return address on the envelope, the left side of the "A" in "A. Hidell" was made by a down-stroke followed by an upstroke which almost exactly traced the down-stroke, the "i" showed an elongation of the approach stroke and an exaggerated slant to the right, and the second "l" was somewhat larger than the first; the "B" in "Box" had an upper lobe smaller than the lower lobe; the "D" in "Dallas" exhibited a distinctive construction of the looped form at the top of a letter, and the "s" was flattened and forced over on its side; and the "x" in "Texas" was made in the form of a "u" with a cross bar. These characteristics were also present in the standards.[159] In addition, these items, as well as other questioned documents, resembled the standards in their use of certain erroneous combinations of capital and lowercase letters.[160] For example, in the mail order, "Texas" was printed with a capital "T," "X," "A," and "S," but a lowercase "e"; a similar mixture of capital and lowercase letters in "Texas" was found in the standards.[161]

The writing on the purchase order and envelope showed no significant evidence of disguise (subject to the qualification that the use of hand printing on the mail order, rather than handwriting, may have been used for that purpose).[162] However, it is not unusual for a person using an alias not to disguise his writing. For example, Cole, who is document examiner for the Treasury Department, has frequently examined forgeries evidencing no attempt at disguise.[163]

Mail Order for the V510210 Revolver

Based on a comparison with the standards, the handwriting on the mail order [164] for the V510210 revolver was also identified as Lee Harvey Oswald's.[165]

Post Office Box Applications and Change-of-Address Card

A post office box application consists of three parts: The first contains directions for use. The second provides applicant's name, address, signature space, box number, date of opening and closing. The third part provides instruction space concerning delivery of mail and names of persons entitled to use the box.[166] Under post office regulations [167] the second part was retained by the Dallas Post Office for box 2915; it destroyed the third part after the box was closed. Based on the standards, the signature "Lee H. Oswald," and other handwriting on the application, was identified as that of Lee Harvey Oswald.[168] The postal clerk appeared to have filled in the balance.[169]

The Fort Worth and Dallas post offices retained two change-of-address orders signed "Lee H. Oswald": One to "Postmaster, Fort Worth, Tex.," dated October 10, 1962, to send mail to "Oswald, Lee H" at 2703 Mercedes Av., Fort Worth, Texas" and forward to "Box 2915, Dallas, Texas"; the other to "Postmaster, Dallas, Texas" dated May 12, 1963, requested mail for post office box 2915 be forwarded to "Lee Oswald" at "4907 Magazine St., New Orleans, La." [170] Based on a comparison with the standards, the handwriting on these orders was identified as that of Lee Harvey Oswald.[171]

The New Orleans post office retained the third part of the application for post office box 30061, New Orleans, La., dated June 11, 1963, and signed "L. H. Oswald." [172] Inserted in the space for names of persons entitled to receive mail through the box were written the names "A. J. Hidell" and "Marina Oswald." On the basis of a comparison with the standards, the writing and the signature on the card was identified as the handwriting of Lee Harvey Oswald.[173]

The Spurious Selective Service System Notice of Classification and U.S. Marine Corps Certificate of Service

When Oswald was arrested he had in his possession a Selective Service System notice of classification and a certificate of service in the U.S. Marine Corps in the name of "Alek James Hidell," and a Selective Service System notice of classification, a Selective Service System registration certificate, and a certificate of service in the U.S. Marine Corps in his own name.[174] (See Cadigan Exhibits Nos. 19 and 21, p. 573.) The Hidell cards where photographic counterfeits.[175] After Oswald's arrest a group of retouched negatives were found in Mr. Paine's garage at 2515 West Fifth Street, Irving, Tex.,[176] among which were retouched negatives of the Oswald cards.[177] A comparison of these retouched negatives with the Hidell and Oswald cards showed that the Hidell cards had been counterfeited by photographing the Oswald cards, retouching the resulting negatives, and producing photographic prints from the retouched negatives.

The Hidell Notice of Classification

Face side.—The face of the Hidell notice of classification [178] was produced from the face of the Oswald notice of classification [179] by a two-step process. First, the counterfeiter photographed the Oswald notice, making a basic intermediate negative.[180] He then opaqued out of this intermediate negative all of the information typed or handwritten onto the Oswald notice, including the name "Lee Harvey Oswald," the selective service No., "41–114–39–532," the signature of the official of the local board, and the mailing date. In addition, he made another intermediate negative of the lowermost third of the Oswald notice, which contained a printed legend setting forth various instructions relating to draft board procedures.[181] This negative reproduced the printed material exactly, but reduced it in size.[182] The two intermediate negatives were combined to produce a third negative, substantially identical to the basic intermediate negative except that, by virtue of the reduction in the size of the printed legend, a square space had been created in the lower left-hand corner.[183] The counterfeiter then made a photographic print of this third negative, which contained blanks wherever typed or handwritten material had appeared on the original Oswald notice and a new space in the lower left-hand corner. Finally, new material was inserted into the blanks on the Hidell notice where typed or handwritten material had appeared on the Oswald notice.[184] Thus the name "ALEK JAMES HIDELL," the selective service No. "42–224–39–532," and the mailing date "Feb. 5, 1962," were typed into the appropriate blanks on the Hidell notice. Two typewriters were used in this typing, as shown by differences in the design of the typed figure "4," [185] and by differences in the strength of the typed impression.[186] Probably the counterfeiter switched typewriters when he discovered that the ribbon of his first typewriter was not inked heavily enough to leave a clear impression (a problem which would have been aggravated by the fact that the glossy photographic paper used to make the Hidell notice did not provide a good surface for typewriting).[187] The face of the notice also bore many uninked indentations, which could only be made out under strong side lighting.[188] These indentations were apparently made with the typewriter set at stencil—that is, set so that the typewriter key struck the notice directly, rather than striking it through the inked typewriter ribbon.[189] This may have been done as a dry-run practice, to enable the counterfeiter to determine how to properly center and aline the inserted material.[190] A sidelight photograph showed that the names "ALEK," "JAMES," and "HIDELL" had each been typed in stencil at least twice before being typed in with the ribbon.[191] A capital letter "O" had been stenciled prior to one of the stenciled "ALEK's." [192] A serial number and a date of mailing had also been typed in stencil.[193]

In addition to the typed material, a signature, "Alek J. Hidell," was written in ink in the blank provided for the registrant's signature, and another, somewhat illegible signature, apparently reading "Good Hoffer," was written in ink in the blank provided for the signature of an official of the local board.[194] This name differed from the name written in ink on the Oswald notice, which appeared to consist of a first name beginning with an "E" or a "G" and the surname "Schiffen." [195] However, the legibility of the name on the Oswald notice was also quite poor, and the counterfeiter might have been attempting to duplicate it. A possible reason for deleting the original name and substituting another is that if the name had not been deleted it would have been reproduced on the Hidell notice as a photographic reproduction, which would look less authentic than a pen-and-ink signature.[196]

Based on a comparison with the handwriting in the standards, the signature "Alek J. Hidell" on the Hidell notice was identified as being in the handwriting of Lee Harvey Oswald.[197] The signature "Good Hoffer" could not be positively identified, being almost illegible; however, it was not inconsistent with Oswald's handwriting.[198]

To complete the face of the Hidell notice a picture of Lee Harvey Oswald was inserted into the space in the lower left-hand corner which had been created by reducing the size of the printed legend at the bottom.[199]

In creating the face of the Hidell notice, the counterfeiter left traces which enabled the experts to link together the Hidell notice, the retouched negatives, and the Oswald notice. To retouch the nega-

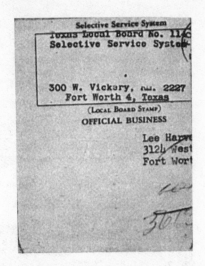

Face and reverse sides of the Oswald Notice of Classification.

CADIGAN EXHIBIT No. 19

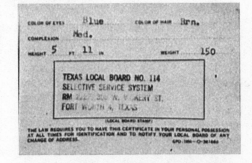
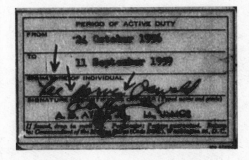

Face and reverse sides of the Oswald Selective Service System Registration Certificate and the Oswald Certificate of Service in the U.S. Marine Corps.

CADIGAN EXHIBIT No. 21

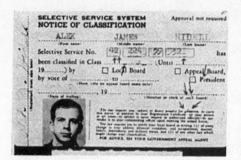
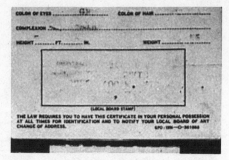

Face and reverse sides of the Hidell Selective Service System Notice of Classification.

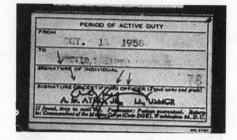

Face and reverse sides of the Hidell Certificate of Service in the U.S. Marine Corps.

CADIGAN EXHIBITS NOS. 15 AND 16

tives the counterfeiter simply painted a red opaque substance on one side of the negative over the material he wished to delete. When the negative was printed, the opaquing prevented light from passing through, so that the print showed blanks wherever the negative had been opaqued. However, the original material was still clearly visible on the negative itself.[200] In addition, at several points the typed or handwritten material in the Oswald notice had overlapped the printed material. For example, the signature of the official of the local board overlapped the letters "re" in the printed word "President," "l" and "a" in the printed word "local," and "viola" in the printed word "violation." When this signature was opaqued out, the portions of the printed material which had been overlapped by the signature were either removed or mutilated. The consequent distortions were apparent on both the retouched negative and the Hidell notice itself. Similarly, the selective service number typed on the Oswald notice overlapped the margins of the boxes into which it was typed. Although the counterfeiter opaqued out the numerals themselves, the margins of the boxes remained thickened at the points where they had been overlapped by the numerals. These thickened margins were apparent on both the retouched negative and the Hidell notice.[201]

Reverse side.—The reverse side of the Hidell notice, which was pasted back-to-back to the face, was actually a form of the reverse side of a Selective Service System registration certificate. Essentially, it was counterfeited the same way as the face of the notice: a photograph was made of the reverse side of the Oswald registration certificate, the material which had been typed or stamped on the Oswald registration certificate was opaqued out of the resulting negative, and a photographic print was made from the retouched negative. This is shown by the negative, in which the opaqued-out information is still visible, and by defects in the printed material on the Hidell notice at point where typed-in material had overlapped printed material on the Oswald registration certificate.[202]

As the final step, new information was typed on the print in the blanks which resulted from the retouching operation.[203] Thus "GR" was substituted for "Blue" under color of eyes; "BROWN" was substituted for "Brn" under color of hair; "FAIR" was substituted for "Med." under complexion; "5" [ft.] "9" [in.] was substituted for "5" [ft.] "11" [in.] under height; and "155" was substituted for "150" under weight. The name and address of the local board on the Oswald registration certificate were opaqued out, but substantially the same name and address were typed back onto the Hidell notice.[204] As in the signature of the local board official on the face of the notice, a possible reason for deleting the original draft board name and the address and substituting substantially similar material in its place is that if the original material had not been deleted it would have reproduced as a photographic reproduction, which would look much less authentic than typed-in material.[205]

A limited number of typed uninked indentations are also present. Thus the indented letters "CT" appear before the letters "GR" (under color of eyes) and the indented letters "EY" follow "GR." An indented "9" appears above the visible "9" for the inch figure of height, and an indented "i" appears before the weight, "155." Much of the typed material on the reverse side of the Hidell notice was not very legible under ordinary lighting, since it was typed with a typewriter which left a very weakly inked impression.[206] In fact, it is difficult to tell whether some of the material, particularly the word "Brown" under color of hair, was put in by stencil or by ribbon.

The Hidell Certificate of Service

The face and reverse side of the Hidell certificate of service were produced from the face and reverse side of the Oswald certificate of service [207] by photographing the Oswald certificate, retouching the resulting negatives to eliminate typed and handwritten material, and making a photographic print from the retouched negative.[208] As in the case of the notice of classification, this is shown by the negative itself, in which the opaqued-out information is still visible, and by defects in the printed material on the Hidell certificate at points where handwritten material had crossed over printed material on the Oswald certificate. Thus, in the Oswald certificate the upper portion of the name "Lee" in Oswald's signature crosses the letter "u" in the printed word "signature." The consequent mutilation of the printed letter "u" can be seen on the Hidell certificate. Similarly, the ending stroke in the letter "y" in the name "Harvey" in Oswald's signature crosses the letter "n" in the printed word "certifying." This stroke was not removed at all, and can be seen as a stroke across the "n" in the Hidell certificate.[209] As the final step in producing the Hidell certificate, new material was typed into the blanks on the photographic print. On the face, the words "ALEK JAMES HIDELL" were typed into the blank where "LEE HARVEY OSWALD 1653230" had appeared. A sidelight photograph shows that these words had been typed in stencil at least twice before being typed in with the ribbon apparently to determine proper centering and alinement.[210] In producing the reverse side of the Hidell certificate, the signature "Lee Harvey Oswald," and the dates "24 October 1956" and "11 September 1959," showing the beginning and end of the period of active service, had been opaqued out. No signature was inserted into resulting blank signature space. However, just below the word "of" in the printed line "signature of individual," there are two vertical indentations which fill about three-fourths of the height of the signature blank, and a diagonal indentation which slants from approximately the base of the left vertical to approximately the midpoint of the right vertical—the total effect being of a printed capital letter "H." Also, just below the second and third "i's" in the printed word "individual" are two more vertical indentations, which could be the vertical strokes of "d's" or "l's"—although the circular portion of the letter "d" is not present.[211] These indentations could have been made by any sharp instrument, such as a ballpoint pen which was not delivering ink, a stylus of the type used in preparing mimeograph forms, or even a toothpick.[212] The indentations are brought out rather clearly in a sidelight photograph, but can also be seen on the card itself if the card is held so that light strikes it at an angle.[213]

Into the space for the beginning of active service was typed the date "OCT. 13 1958." The space for the end of active service contains several light-impression and stencil typewriting operations. It was apparently intended to read "OCT. 12 1961," but because of the lightness of the impression and the many stenciled characters, the date is barely legible.[214] Interestingly, one of the stenciled impressions in the blank for end of active service reads "24 October 1959," as determined under a microscope, while a stenciled impression in the blank for beginning of active service reads "24 October 1957." [215]

The counterfeiting of the Hidell cards did not require great skill, but probably required an elementary knowledge of photography, particularly of the photographic techniques used in a printing plant.[216] A moderate amount of practice with the technique would be required—perhaps half a dozen attempts. Practicing retouching on the balance of the negatives found at the Paine garage would have been sufficient.[217] The retouching of the negatives could have been accomplished without any special equipment. However, the preparation of the negative, apart from retouching, would probably have required a very accurate camera, such as would be found in a photographic laboratory or printing plant.[218]

The Vaccination Certificate

A government-printed form entitled "International Certificates of Vaccination or Revaccination against Smallpox" [219] was found among Oswald's belongings at his room at 1026 Beckley Avenue, Dallas.[220] The form purported to certify that "LEE OSWALD" had been vaccinated against smallpox on "JUNE 8, 1963" by "DR. A. J. HIDEEL, P.O. BOX 30016, NEW ORLEANS, LA." The card was signed "Lee H. Oswald" and "A. J. Hideel," and the name and address "Lee H. Oswald, New Orleans, La." were hand printed on the front of the card. All of this material, except the signatures and the hand printing, had been stamped onto the card. The Hideel name and address consisted of a three-line stamp—"DR. A. J. HIDEEL/P.O. BOX 30016/NEW ORLEANS, LA." A circular, stamped, illegible impression resembling a seal appeared under a column entitled "Approved stamp." [221]

On the basis of a comparison with the standards, Cole identified all of the handwriting on the vaccination certificate, including the signature "A. J. Hideel," as the writing of Lee Harvey Oswald.[222] Cadigan identified all of the writing as Oswald's except for the "A. J. Hideel" signature, which in his opinion was too distorted to either identify or nonidentify as Oswald's handwriting.[223] The stamped material on the certificate was compared with a rubber stamping kit which be-

577

longed to Oswald.[224] In this kit was a rubber stamp with three lines of print assembled: "L. H. OSWALD/4907 MAGAZINE ST/NEW ORLEANS, LA."[225] Cole found a perfect agreement in measurement and design between the letters stamped on the certificate and the letters he examined from Oswald's rubber stamping kit. However, he was unable to determine whether the characteristics of Oswald's rubber stamping kit were distinctive, and therefore, while he concluded that Oswald's rubber stamping kit could have made the rubber stamp impressions on the certificate, he was unable to say that it was the only kit which could have made the impressions.[226] On the basis of the comparison between the words "NEW ORLEANS, LA." set up in the rubber stamp in Oswald's kit, and the words "NEW ORLEANS, LA." on the certificate, Cadigan concluded that these words had been stamped on the certificate with Oswald's rubber stamp. However, he could draw no conclusion as to the remaining stamped material, which was not directly comparable to the remaining lines set up on Oswald's rubber stamp.[227]

On close examination, the circular impression resembling a seal consisted of the words "BRUSH IN CAN," printed in reverse.[228] Apparently, the impression was made with the top of a container of solvent or cleaning fluid which bore these words in raised lettering. In the center of the impression was a mottled pattern which was similar to the blank areas on a date stamp found in Oswald's rubber stamping kit.[229]

The Fair Play for Cuba Committee Card

The Fair Play for Cuba Committee card had two signatures: "L. H. Oswald" and "A. J. Hidell." Based on the standards, both Cole and Cadigan identified "L. H. Oswald" as the signature of Lee Harvey Oswald,[230] but both were unable to identify the "A. J. Hidell" signature.[231] Cadigan noted differences between the Hidell signature and Oswald's handwriting, indicating the possibility that someone other than Oswald had authored the signature.[232] Cole believed that the signature was somewhat beyond Oswald's abilities as a penman.[233] On the basis of a short English interlinear translation written by Marina Oswald, Cole felt that she might have been the author of the signature,[234] but the translation did not present enough of her handwriting to make possible a positive identification.[235] In subsequent testimony before the Commission, Marina stated that she was indeed the author of the Hidell signature on the card.[236] Cadigan confirmed this testimony by obtaining further samples of Marina Oswald's handwriting and comparing these samples with the signature on the card.[237]

The Unsigned Russian-Language Note

Cadigan's examination confirmed Marina's testimony that the handwriting in the unsigned note, Commission Exhibit No. 1, was that of

Lee Harvey Oswald.[238] Since the note was written almost entirely in the Russian language, which uses the Cyrillic alphabet (as opposed to the Latin alphabet used in the English language), in making his examination Cadigan employed not only Oswald's English language standards, but also letters written by Oswald in the Russian language.[239]

The Homemade Wrapping Paper Bag

In the absence of watermarks or other distinctive characteristics, it is impossible to determine whether two samples of paper came from the same manufacturer.[240] The homemade paper bag found on the sixth floor of the Texas School Book Depository following the assassination was made out of heavy brown paper and glue-bearing brown paper tape, neither of which contained watermarks or other distinctive characteristics.[241] However, Cadigan compared the questioned paper and tape in the paper bag with known paper and tape samples obtained from the shipping department of the Texas School Book Depository on November 22, 1963, to see if the questioned items could have come from the shipping room.[242] The questioned and known items were examined visually by normal, incidental, and transmitted natural and electric light, and under ultraviolet light; [243] examined microscopically for surface, paper structure, color, and imperfections; [244] examined for their felting pattern, which is the pattern of light and dark areas caused by the manner in which the fibers become felted at the beginning stages of paper manufacture; [245] measured for thickness with a micrometer sensitive to one one-thousandth of an inch,[246] subjected to a fiber analysis to determine the type of fibers of which they were composed, and whether the fibers were bleached or unbleached; [247] and examined spectrographically to determine what metallic ions were present.[248] The questioned and known items were identical in all the properties measured by these tests.[249] (The width of the tape on the paper sack was 3 inches, while the width of the sample tape was 2.975, or twenty-five thousandths of an inch smaller; however, this was not a significant difference).[250] In contrast, a paper sample obtained from the Texas School Book Depository shipping room on December 1, 1963, was readily distinguishable from the questioned paper.[251]

Examination of the tape revealed other significant factors indicating that it could have come from the Texas School Book Depository shipping room. There were several strips of tape on the bag.[252] All but two of the ends of these strips were irregularly torn; the remaining two ends had machine-cut edges. This indicated that the person who made the bag had drawn a long strip of tape from a dispensing machine and had torn it by hand into several smaller strips.[253] Confirmation that the tape had been drawn from a dispensing machine was supplied by the fact that a series of small markings in the form of half-inch lines ran down the center of the tape like ties on a railroad track. Such lines are made by a ridged wheel in a tape dispenser which is constructed so that when a hand lever is pulled, the wheel, which is connected to the lever, pulls the tape from its roll and dispenses it. Such dispensers are usually found only in commercial establishments. A dispenser of this type was located in the Texas School Book Depository shipping room. The length of the lines and the number of lines per inch on the tape from the paper bag was identical to the length of the lines and the number of lines per inch on the tape obtained from the dispenser in the Texas School Book Depository shipping room.[254]

WOUND BALLISTICS EXPERIMENTS

Purpose of the Tests

During the course of the Commission's inquiry, questions arose as to whether the wounds inflicted on President Kennedy and Governor Connally could have been caused by the Mannlicher-Carcano rifle found on the sixth floor of the Texas School Book Depository Building and Western Cartridge Co. bullets and fragments of the type found on the Governor's stretcher and in the Presidential limousine. In analyzing the trajectory of the bullets after they struck their victims, further questions were posed on the bullet's velocity and penetration power after exiting from the person who was initially struck. To answer these and related questions, the Commission requested that a series of tests be conducted on substances resembling the wounded portions of the bodies of President Kennedy and Governor Connally under conditions which simulated the events of the assassination.

The Testers and Their Qualifications

In response to the Commission's request, an extensive series of tests were conducted by the Wound Ballistics Branch of the U.S. Army Chemical Research and Development Laboratories at Edgewood Arsenal, Md. Scientists working at that branch are engaged in full-time efforts to investigate the wound ballistics of missiles in order to test their effects on substances which simulate live human bodies.[255] The tests for the Commission were performed by Dr. Alfred G. Olivier under the general supervision of Dr. Arthur J. Dziemian with consultation from Dr. Frederick W. Light, Jr.[256] Dr. Olivier received his doctorate in veterinary medicine from the University of Pennsylvania in 1953. Since 1957 he has been engaged in research on wound ballistics at Edgewood Arsenal and is now chief of the Wound Ballistics Branch.[257] His supervisor, Dr. Dziemian, who is chief of the Biophysics Division at Edgewood Arsenal, holds a Ph. D. degree from Princeton in 1939, was a national research fellow in physiology at the University of Pennsylvania and was a fellow in anatomy at Johns Hopkins University Medical School.[258] Since 1947, Dr. Dziemian has been continuously engaged in wound ballistics work at Edgewood Arsenal.[259] In 1930, Dr. Light was awarded an M.D. degree from

Johns Hopkins Medical School and in 1948 received his Ph. D. from the same institution.[260]   After serving a residency in pathology, he worked as a pathologist until 1940 when he returned to Johns Hopkins University to study mathematics.   Since 1951, Dr. Light has been engaged in the study of the pathology of wounding at Edgewood Arsenal.[261]   All three of these distinquished scientists testified before the Commission.

General Testing Conditions

The Commission made available to the Edgewood Arsenal scientists all the relevant facts relating to the wounds which were inflicted on President Kennedy and Governor Connally including the autopsy report on the President, and the reports and X-rays from Parkland Hospital.[262]   In addition, Drs. Olivier and Light had an opportunity to discuss in detail the Governor's wounds with the Governor's surgeons, Drs. Robert R. Shaw and Charles F. Gregory.[263]   The Zapruder films of the assassination were viewed with Governor and Mrs. Connally to give the Edgewood scientists their version.[264]   The Commission also provided the Edgewood scientists with all known data on the source of the shots, the rifle and bullets used, and the distances involved.   For purposes of the experiments, the Commission turned over to the Edgewood testers the Mannlicher-Carcano rifle found on the sixth floor of the Depository Building.[265]   From information provided by the Commission, the Edgewood scientists obtained Western bullets of the type used by the assassin.[266]

Tests on Penetration Power and Bullet Stability

Comparisons were made of the penetrating power of Western bullets fired from the assassination rifle with other bullets.[267]   From the Mannlicher-Carcano rifle, the Western bullet was fired through two gelatin blocks totaling 72½ centimeters in length.[268]   As evidenced by Commission Exhibit No. 844, which is a photograph from a high-speed motion picture, the Western bullets passed through 1½ blocks in a straight line before their trajectory curved.[269]   After coming out of the second gelatin block, a number of the bullets buried themselves in a mound of earth.[270]

Under similar circumstances, a bullet described as the NATO round M–80 was fired from a M–14 rifle.[271]   The penetrating power of the latter is depicted in Commission Exhibit No. 845 which shows that bullet possesses much less penetrating power with a quicker tumbling action.   Those characteristics cause an early release of energy which brings the bullet to a stop at shorter distances.[272]   A further test was made with a 257 Winchester Roberts soft-nosed hunting bullet as depicted in Commission Exhibit No. 846.   That bullet became deformed almost immediately upon entering the block of gelatin and released its energy very rapidly.[273]   From these tests, it was concluded that the Western bullet fired from the Mannlicher-Carcano had "terrific penetrating ability" and would retain substantial velocity after passing through objects such as the portions of the human body.[274]

Tests Simulating President Kennedy's Neck Wound

After reviewing the autopsy report on President Kennedy, the Edgewood scientists simulated the portion of the President's neck through which the bullet passed. It was determined that the bullet traveled through 13½ to 14½ centimeters of tissue in the President's neck.[275] That substance was simulated by constructing three blocks: one with a 20-percent gelatin composition, a second from one animal meat and a third from another animal meat.[276] Those substances duplicated as closely as possible the portion of the President's neck through which the bullet passed.[277] At the time the tests were conducted, it was estimated that the President was struck at a range of approximately 180 feet, and the onsite tests which were conducted later at Dallas established that the President was shot through the neck at a range of 174.9 feet to 190.8 feet.[278] At a range of 180 feet, the Western bullets were fired from the assassination weapon, which has a muzzle velocity of approximately 2,160 feet per second, through those substances which were placed beside a break-type screen for measuring velocity.[279] The average entrance velocity at 180 feet was 1,904 feet per second.[280]

To reconstruct the assassination situation as closely as possible both sides of the substances were covered with material and clipped animal skin to duplicate human skin.[281] The average exit velocity was 1,779 feet from the gelatin, 1,798 feet from the first animal meat and 1,772 feet from the second animal meat.[282] Commission Exhibit No. 847 depicts one of the animal meats compressed to 13½ to 14½ centimeters to approximate the President's neck and Commission Exhibit No. 848 shows the analogous arrangement for the gelatin.[283] The photograph marked Commission Exhibit No. 849 shows the bullet passing through the gelatin in a straight line evidencing very stable characteristics.[284]

Commission Exhibit No. 850 depicts the pieces of clipped animal skin placed on the points of entry and exit showing that the holes of entrance are round while the holes of exit are "a little more elongated."[285] From these tests, it was concluded that the bullet lost little of its velocity in penetrating the President's neck so that there would have been substantial impact on the interior of the Presidential limousine or anyone else struck by the exiting bullet. In addition, these tests indicated that the bullet had retained most of its stability in penetrating the President's neck so that the exit hole would be only slightly different from the appearance of the entry hole.[286]

Tests Simulating Governor Connally's Chest Wounds

To most closely approximate the Governor's chest injuries, the Edgewood scientists shot an animal with the assassination weapon

using the Western bullets at a distance of 210 feet.[287] The onsite
tests later determined that the Governor was wounded at a distance
of 176.9 feet to 190.8 feet from the sixth-floor window at the southeast corner of the Depository Building.[288] The average striking
velocity of 11 shots at 210 feet was 1,929 feet per second and the average exit velocity was 1,664 feet per second.[289]

One of the shots produced an injury on the animal's rib very similar
to that inflicted on Governor Connally.[290] For purposes of comparison with the Governor's wound, the Edgewood scientists studied the
Parkland Hospital report and X-rays, and they also discussed these
wounds with Dr. Shaw, the Governor's chest surgeon.[291] The similar animal injury passed along the animal's eighth left rib causing
a fracture which removed a portion of the rib in a manner very
similar to the wound sustained by the Governor.[292] The X-ray of
that wound on the animal is reproduced as Commission Exhibit No.
852.[293] A comparison with the Governor's chest wound, shown in
X-ray marked as Commission Exhibit No. 681, shows the remarkable
similarity between those two wounds.[294]

The bullet which produced the wound depicted in Commission Exhibits Nos. 851 and 852 was marked as Commission Exhibit No. 853
and possessed characteristics very similar to the bullet marked as
Commission Exhibit No. 399 found on Governor Connally's stretcher
and believed to have been the bullet which caused his chest wound.[295]
Those bullets, identified as Commission Exhibits Nos. 399 and 853,
were flattened in similar fashion.[296] In addition, the lead core was
extruded from the rear in the same fashion on both bullets.[297] One
noticeable difference was that the bullet identified as Commission
Exhibit No. 853, which penetrated the animal, was somewhat more
flat than Commission Exhibit No. 399 which indicated that Commission Exhibit No. 853 was probably traveling at somewhat greater
speed than the bullet which penetrated the Governor's chest.[298] After
the bullet passed through the animal, it left an imprint on the velocity
screen immediately behind the animal which was almost the length
of the bullet indicating that the bullet was traveling sideways or
end over end.[299] Taking into consideration the extra girth on the
Governor, the reduction in the velocity of the bullet passing through
his body was estimated at 400 feet.[300] The conclusions from the animal shots are significant when taken in conjunction with the experiments performed simulating the injuries to the Governor's wrist.

Tests Simulating Governor Connally's Wrist Wounds

Following procedures identical to those employed in simulating
the chest wound, the wound ballistics experts from Edgewood Arsenal
reproduced, as closely as possible, the Governor's wrist wound. Again
the scientists examined the reports and X-rays from Parkland Hospital and discussed the Governor's wrist wound with the attending
orthopedic surgeon, Dr. Charles F. Gregory.[301] Bone structures
were then shot with Western bullets fired from the assassination

weapon at a distance of 210 feet.[302] The most similar bone-structure shot was analyzed in testimony before the Commission. An X-ray designated as Commission Exhibit No. 854 and a photograph of that X-ray which appears as Commission Exhibit No. 855 show a fracture at a location which is very similar to the Governor's wrist wound depicted in X-rays marked as Commission Exhibits Nos. 690 and 691.[303]

The average striking velocity of the shots was 1,858 feet per second.[304] The average exit velocity was 1,786 feet per second for the 7 out of 10 shots from bone structures which could be measured.[305] These tests demonstrated that Governor Connally's wrist was not struck by a pristine bullet, which is a missile that strikes an object before hitting anything else.[306] This conclusion was based on the following factors: (1) Greater damage was inflicted on the bone structure than that which was suffered by the Governor's wrist; [307] and (2) the bone structure had a smaller entry wound and a larger exit wound which is characteristic of a pristine bullet as distinguished from the Governor's wrist which had a larger wound of entry indicating a bullet which was tumbling with substantial reduction in velocity.[308] In addition, if the bullet found on the Governor's stretcher (Commission Exhibit No. 399) inflicted the wound on the Governor's wrist, then it could not have passed through the Governor's wrist had it been a pristine bullet, for the nose would have been considerably flattened, as was the bullet which struck the bone structure, identified as Commission Exhibit No. 856.[309]

Conclusions From Simulating the Neck, Chest, and Wrist Wounds

Both Drs. Olivier and Dziemian expressed the opinion that one bullet caused all the wounds on Governor Connally.[310] The wound to the Governor's wrist was explained by circumstances where the bullet passed through the Governor's chest, lost substantial velocity in doing so, tumbled through the wrist, and then slightly penetrated the Governor's left thigh.[311] Thus, the results of the wound ballistics tests support the conclusions of Governor Connally's doctors that all his wounds were caused by one bullet.[312]

In addition, the wound ballistics tests indicated that it was most probable that the same bullet passed through the President's neck and then proceeded to inflict all the wounds on the Governor. That conclusion was reached by Drs. Olivier and Dziemian based on the medical evidence on the wounds of the President and the Governor and the tests they performed.[313] It was their opinion that the wound on the Governor's wrist would have been more extensive had the bullet which inflicted that injury merely passed through the Governor's chest exiting at a velocity of approximately 1,500 feet per second.

Thus, the Governor's wrist wound indicated that the bullet passed through the President's neck, began to yaw in the air between the President and the Governor, and then lost substantially more velocity than 400 feet per second in passing through the Governor's chest.[314] A bullet which was yawing on entering into the Governor's back would lose substantially more velocity in passing through his body than a pristine bullet.[315]   In addition, the greater flattening of the bullet that struck the animal's rib (Commission Exhibit No. 853) than the bullet which presumably struck the Governor's rib (Commission Exhibit No. 399) indicates that the animal bullet was traveling at a greater velocity.[316]   That suggests that the bullet which entered the Governor's chest had already lost velocity by passing through the President's neck.[317]   Moreover, the large wound on the Governor's back would be explained by a bullet which was yawing although that type of wound might also be accounted for by a tangential striking.[318]

Dr. Frederick W. Light, Jr., the third of the wound ballistics experts, testified that the anatomical findings alone were insufficient for him to formulate a firm opinion on whether the same bullet did or did not pass through the President's neck first before inflicting all the wounds on Governor Connally.[319]   Based on the other circumstances, such as the relative positions in the automobile of the President and the Governor, Dr. Light concluded that it was probable that the same bullet traversed the President's neck and inflicted all the wounds on Governor Connally.[320]

Tests Simulating President Kennedy's Head Wounds

Additional tests were performed on inert skulls filled with a 20 percent gelatin substance and then coated with additional gelatin to approximate the soft tissues overlying the skull.[321]   The skull was then draped with simulated hair as depicted in Commission Exhibit No. 860.[322]   Using the Mannlicher-Carcano rifle and the Western bullets, 10 shots were fired at the reconstructed skulls from a distance of 270 feet which was the estimated distance at the time those tests were conducted.[323]   It was later determined through the onsite tests that President Kennedy was struck in the back of the head at a distance of 265.3 feet from the assassination weapon.[324]

The general results of these tests were illustrated by the findings on one skull which was struck at a point most nearly approximating the wound of entry on President Kennedy's head.[325]   The whole skull, depicted in Commission Exhibit No. 860, was struck 2.9 centimeters to the right and almost horizontal to the occipital protuberance or slightly above it, which was virtually the precise point of entry on the President's head as described by the autopsy surgeons.[326]   That bullet blew out the right side of the reconstructed skull in a manner very similar to the head wounds of the President.[327]   The consequences on that skull are depicted in Commission Exhibits Nos. 861 and 862, which illustrate the testimony of Dr. Alfred G. Olivier, who supervised the experiments.[328]   Based on his review of the autopsy report,

Dr. Olivier concluded that the damage to the reconstructed skull was very similar to the wound inflicted on the President.[329]

Two fragments from the bullet which struck the test skull closely resembled the two fragments found in the front seat of the Presidential limousine. The fragment designated as Commission Exhibit No. 567 is a mutilated piece of lead and copper very similar to a mutilated piece of copper recovered from the bullet which struck the skull depicted in Commission Exhibit No. 860. The other fragment, designated as Commission Exhibit No. 569 which was found in the front seat of the Presidential limousine, is the copper end of the bullet.[330] Commission Exhibit No. 569 is very similar to a copper fragment of the end of the bullet which struck the test skull.[331] The fragments from the test bullet are designated as Commission Exhibit No. 857 and are depicted in a photograph identified as Commission Exhibit No. 858.[332] A group of small lead particles, recovered from the test bullet, are also very similar to the particles recovered under the left jump seat and in the President's head. The particles from the test bullet are a part of Commission Exhibit No. 857 and are depicted in photograph designated as Commission Exhibit No. 859.[333] That skull was depicted as Commission Exhibit No. 862.[334]

As a result of these tests, Dr. Olivier concluded that the Western bullet fired from the Mannlicher-Carcano rifle at a distance of 270 feet would make the same type of wound found on the President's head.[335] Prior to the tests, Dr. Olivier had some doubt that such a stable bullet would cause a massive head wound like that inflicted on the President.[336] He had thought it more likely that such a striking bullet would make small entrance and exit holes.[337] The tests, however, showed that the bones of the skull were sufficient to deform the end of the bullet causing it to expend a great deal of energy and thereby blow out the side of the skull.[338] These tests further confirmed the autopsy surgeons' opinions that the President's head wound was not caused by a dumdum bullet.[339] Because of the test results, Dr. Olivier concluded that the fragments found on and under the front seat of the President's car most probably came from the bullet which struck the President's head.[340] It was further concluded that the damage done to Governor Connally's wrist could not have resulted from a fragment from the bullet which struck President Kennedy's head.[341]

HAIRS AND FIBERS

Testimony on hairs and fibers was given by Paul M. Stombaugh [342] of the FBI. Stombaugh has been a specialist in hairs and fibers since 1960, when he began a 1-year period of specialized training in this field. He has made thousands of hair and fiber examinations, and has testified in Federal and State courts in approximately 28 States.[343] Stombaugh examined and gave testimony on the following objects: (1) The green and brown blanket found in the Paine's garage, Commission Exhibit No. 140; (2) the homemade paper bag found on the sixth floor

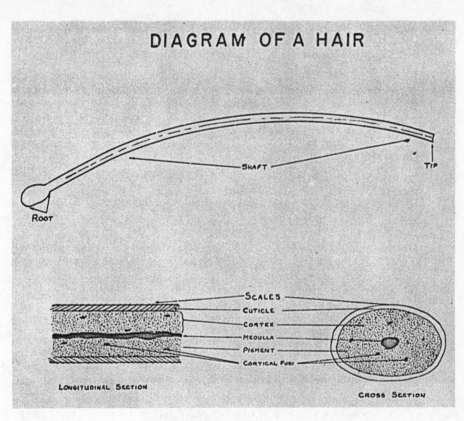

DIAGRAM OF A HAIR

SHAFT

TIP

ROOT

SCALES
CUTICLE
CORTEX
MEDULLA
PIGMENT
CORTICAL FUSI

LONGITUDINAL SECTION

CROSS SECTION

COMMISSION EXHIBIT No. 666

of the Texas School Book Depository following the assassination, Commission Exhibit No. 142; (3) the shirt worn by Oswald on November 22, 1963, Commission Exhibit No. 150; and (4) the C2766 rifle, Commission Exhibit No. 139.

General Principles

Hairs.—As shown in Commission Exhibit No. 666 (p. 587), a hair consists of a central shaft of air cells, known as the medulla; a cortex containing pigment granules (which give the hair its color) and cortical fusi (air spaces); and a cuticle and an outer layer of scales. Unlike fingerprints, hairs are not unique. However, human hairs can be distinguished from animal hairs by various characteristics, including color, texture, length, medullary structure and shape, shape of pigment, root size, and scale size. In addition, hairs of the Caucasian, Negroid, and Mongoloid human races can be distinguished from each other by color, texture, size and degree of fluctuation of diameter, thickness of cuticle, shape and distribution of pigment, and shape of cross-section. Moreover, even though individual hairs are not unique, the expert usually can distinguish the hairs of different individuals. Thus, Stombaugh, who had made approximately 1,000 comparison examinations of Caucasian hairs and 500 comparison examinations of Negroid hairs, had never found a case in which he was unable to differentiate the hairs of two different Caucasian individuals, and had found only several cases in which he could not distinguish, with absolute certainty, between the hairs of two different Negroid individuals.[344]

Fibers.—Like hairs, the various types of natural and artificial fibers can be distinguished from each other under the microscope. Like hairs too, individual fibers are not unique, but the expert usually can distinguish fibers from different fabrics. A major identifying characteristic of most fibers is color, and under the microscope many different shades of each color can be differentiated—for example, 50–100 shades of green or blue, and 25–30 shades of black. The microscopic appearance of three types of fibers—cotton, wool, and viscose—is illustrated in Commission Exhibit No. 665 (p. 589). Two of these, cotton and viscose, were the subject of testimony by Stombaugh. Cotton is a natural fiber. Under the microscope, it resembles a twisted soda straw, and the degree of twist is an additional identifying characteristic of cotton. Cotton may be mercerized or (more commonly) unmercerized. Viscose is an artificial fiber. A delustering agent is usually added to viscose to cut down its luster, and under the microscope this agent appears as millions of tiny spots on the outside of the fiber. The major identifying characteristics of viscose, apart from color, are diameter—hundreds of variations being possible—and size and distribution of delustering agent, if any.[345]

The blanket.—Stombaugh received the blanket, Commission Exhibit No. 140, in the FBI Laboratory at 7:30 a.m., on November 23, 1963.[346] Examination showed that it was composed of brown and green fibers, of which approximately 1–2 percent were woolen, 20–35 percent

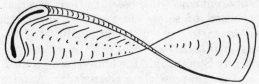

COTTON

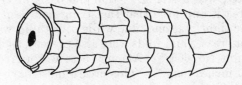

WOOL

VISCOSE

COMMISSION EXHIBIT NO. 665

were cotton, and the remainder were delustered viscose.[347] The viscose fibers in the blanket were of 10–15 different diameters, and also varied slightly in shade and in the size and distribution of the delustering agent. (The apparent cause of those variations was that the viscose in the blanket consisted of scrap viscose.) [348] The cotton also varied in shade, about seven to eight different shades of green cotton being present, but was uniform in twist.[349]

When received by Stombaugh, the blanket was folded into approximately the shape of a narrow right triangle.[350] A safety pin was inserted in one end of the blanket, and also at this end, loosely wrapped around the blanket, was a string.[351] On the basis of creases in the blanket in this area it appeared that the string had been tied around the blanket rather tightly at one time while something was inside the blanket.[352] Other creases and folds were also present, as illustrated in Commission Exhibit No. 663.[353] Among these was a crease or hump approximately 10 inches long.[354] This crease must have been caused by a hard protruding object approximately 10 inches long which had been tightly wrapped in the blanket, causing the yarn to stretch so that the hump was present even when the object had been extracted.[355] The hump was approximately the same length and shape as the telescopic sight on the C2766 rifle, and its position with respect to the ends of the blanket was such (based on the manner in which the blanket was folded when Stombaugh received it) that had the rifle been in the blanket the telescopic sight could have made the hump.[356]

The string wrapped around the blanket was made of ordinary white cotton.[357] It had been tied into a granny knot (a very common knot tied right over right, right over right) and the dangling ends had been further tied into a bow knot (the knot used on shoelaces).[358]

After receiving the blanket, Stombaugh scraped it to remove the foreign textile fibers and hairs that were present.[359] He found numerous foreign textile fibers of various types and colors, and a number of limb, pubic, and head hairs, all of which had originated from persons of the Caucasian race, and had fallen out naturally, as was shown by the shape of their roots.[360] Several of the limb and pubic hairs matched samples of Oswald's limb and pubic hairs obtained by the Dallas police in all observable characteristics, including certain relatively unusual characteristics.[361] For example, in both Oswald's pubic hairs and some of the blanket pubic hairs, the color was a medium brown, which remained constant to the tip, where it changed to a very light brown and then became transparent, due to lack of color pigments; the diameters were identical, and rather narrow for pubic hairs; the hairs were very smooth, lacking the knobbiness characteristic of pubic hairs, and the upper two-thirds were extremely smooth for pubic hairs; the tips of the hairs were sharp, which is unusual for pubic hairs; the cuticle was very thin for pubic hairs; the scales displayed only a very small protrusion; the pigmentation was very fine, equally dispersed, and occasionally chained together, and displayed only very slight gapping; cortical fusi were for the most part absent; the medulla was either fairly continuous or completely absent; and the root area was rather clear of pigment, and contained only a fair amount of cortical fusi, which was unusual.[362] Similarly, in both Oswald's limb hairs and some of the limb hairs from the blanket the color was light brown through its entire length; the diameter was very fine and did not noticeably fluctuate; the tips were very sharp, which is unusual; the scales were of medium size, with very slight protrusion; there was a very slight gapping of the pigmentation near the cuticle; there was an unusual amount of cortical fusi, equally distributed through the hair shaft; and the medulla was discontinuous, granular, very bulbous, and very uneven.[363]

Other limb, pubic, and head hairs on the blanket did not come from Oswald.[364]

The paper bag.—Stombaugh received the paper bag, Commission Exhibit No. 142, at 7:30 a.m. on November 23, 1963.[365] No foreign material was found on the outside of the bag except traces of fingerprint powder and several white cotton fibers, which were of no significance, since white cotton is the most common textile, and at any rate the fibers may have come from Stombaugh's white cotton gloves.[366] Inside the bag were a tiny wood fragment which was too minute for comparison purposes, and may have come from the woodpulp from which the paper was made; a particle of a waxy substance, like candle wax; and a single brown delustered viscose fiber and several light-green cotton fibers.[367]

The fibers found inside the bag were compared with brown viscose and green cotton fibers taken from the blanket. The brown viscose fiber found in the bag matched some of the brown viscose fibers from the blanket in all observable characteristics, i.e., shade, diameter, and size and distribution of delustering agent.[368] The green cotton fibers found in the bag were, like those from the blanket, of varying shades, but of a uniform twist. Each green cotton fiber from the bag matched some of the green cotton fibers from the blanket in all observable characteristics, i.e., shade and degree of twist. Like the blanket cotton fibers, the cotton fibers found in the bag were unmercerized.[369]

The shirt.—Stombaugh received the shirt, Commission Exhibit No. 150, at 7:30 a.m. on November 23, 1963.[370] Examination showed that it was composed of gray-black, dark blue, and orange-yellow cotton fibers.[371] The orange-yellow and gray-black cotton fibers were of a uniform shade, and the dark-blue fibers were of three different shades.[372] All the fibers were mercerized and of substantially uniform degree of twist.[373]

The C2766 rifle.—The rifle, Commission Exhibit No. 139, was received in the FBI Laboratory on the morning of November 23, 1963, and examined for foreign material at that time.[374] Stombaugh noticed immediately that the rifle had been dusted for fingerprints, "and at the time I noted to myself that I doubted very much if there would be any fibers adhering to the outside of this gun—I possibly might find some in a crevice some place—because when the latent fingerprint man dusted this gun, apparently in Dallas, they use a little brush to dust with they would have dusted any fibers off the gun at the same time * * *." [375] In fact, most of the fibers Stombaugh found were either adhering to greasy, oily deposits or were jammed down into crevices, and were so dirty, old, and fragmented that he could not even determine what type of fibers they were.[376] However, Stombaugh found that a tiny tuft of fibers had caught on a jagged edge on the rifle's metal butt plate where it met the end of the wooden stock, and had adhered to this edge, so that when the rifle had been dusted for fingerprints the brush had folded the tuft into a crevice between the butt plate and the stock, where it remained.[377] Stombaugh described these fibers as "fresh," [378] by which he meant that "they were clean, they had good color to them, there was no grease on them and they were not fragmented." [379] However, it was not possible to determine how long the fibers had been on the rifle, in the absence of information as to how frequently the rifle had been used.[380] Examination showed that the tuft was composed of six or seven orange-yellow, gray-black, and dark-blue cotton fibers. These fibers were compared with fibers from the shirt, Commission Exhibit No. 150, which was also composed of orange-yellow, gray-black, and dark-blue cotton fibers. The orange-yellow and gray-black tuft fibers matched the comparable shirt fibers in all observable characteristics, i.e., shade and twist. The three dark-blue fibers matched two of the three shades of the dark-blue shirt fibers, and also matched the dark-blue shirt fibers in degree of twist.[381] Based on these facts, Stombaugh concluded that the tuft of fibers found on the rifle "could easily" have come from the shirt, and that "there is no doubt in my mind that these fibers could have come from this shirt. There is no way, however, to eliminate the possibility of the fibers having come from another identical shirt." [382]

PHOTOGRAPHS

Two photographs of Lee Harvey Oswald holding a rifle were found among Oswald's possessions in Mrs. Ruth Paine's garage at 2515 West Fifth Street, Irving, Tex.[383] In one, Commission Exhibit No. 133–A, Oswald is holding the rifle generally in front of his body; in the other, Commission Exhibit No. 133–B, he is holding the rifle to his right. Also found at Mrs. Paine's garage were a negative of 133–B and several photographs of the rear of General Walker's house.[384] An Imperial reflex camera,[385] which Marina Oswald testified she used to take 133–A and 133–B, was subsequently produced by Robert Oswald, Lee Harvey Oswald's brother.[386] Testimony concerning the photographs, the negative, and the camera was given by Lyndal D. Shaneyfelt of the FBI.[387] Shaneyfelt has been connected with photographic work since 1937. He has made 100–300 photographic examinations, and has testified frequently on the subject in court.[388]

Photographs 133–A and 133–B.—The background and lighting in 133–A and 133–B are virtually identical; the only apparent difference between the two photographs is the pose. However, in 133–A the rifle is held in a position showing many more of its characteristics than are shown in 133–B.[389]   In order to bring out the details in the rifle pictured in 133–A, Shaneyfelt rephotographed 133–A and prepared prints of varying densities from the new negative.[390]   He also took two new photographs of the C2766 rifle itself: one shows the rifle in approximately the same position as the rifle pictured in 133–A.   The other shows a man holding the rifle simulating the pose in 133–A.[391]   Shaneyfelt compared the actual rifle, the photograph 133–A, his rephotographs of 133–A, and the two new photographs to determine whether the rifle pictured in 133–A was the C2766 rifle.   He found it to be the same in all appearances, noted no differences, and found a notch in the stock of the C2766 which also appeared very faintly in 133–A.   However, he did not find enough peculiarities to positively identify the rifle in 133–A as the C2766 rifle, as distinguished from other rifles of the same configuration.[392]

The rifle's position in 133–B is such that less of its characteristics were visible than in 133–A; essentially, 133–B shows only the bottom of the rifle.   However, the characteristics of the rifle visible in 133–B are also similar to the observable characteristics of the C2766 rifle, except that while the C2766 rifle was equipped with a homemade leather sling when it was found after the assassination, the rifle in 133–B seems to be equipped with a homemade rope sling.[393]   The portion of the sling visible in 133–A is too small to establish whether it is rope or leather, but it has the appearance of rope, and its configuration is consistent with the rope sling pictured in 133–B.[394]

The negative.—Shaneyfelt's examination of the negative, Commission Exhibit No. 749, showed that the photograph, 133–B, had been printed directly or indirectly from the negative.   It was Shaneyfelt's opinion that 133–B had been directly from the negative, but he could not absolutely eliminate the possibility of an internegative, that is, the possibility that a print had been produced from the negative 749, a photograph had been taken of that print, and 133–B had been produced from the new negative, rather than from the original negative.[395]   "I think this is highly unlikely, because if this were the result of a copied negative, there would normally be evidence that I could detect, such as a loss of detail and imperfections that show up due to the added process."[396]   In any event, any "intermediate" print would have been virtually indistinguishable from 133–B, so that Shaneyfelt's testimony conclusively established that either 133–B or a virtually indistinguishable print had been produced from the negative 749.

The camera.—The Imperial camera, Commission Exhibit No. 750, was a relatively inexpensive, fixed-focus, one-shutter-speed, box-type camera, made in the United States.[397]   Shaneyfelt compared this camera with the negative, Commission Exhibit No. 749, to determine whether this negative had been taken with the camera.[398]   To make this determination, Shaneyfelt compared the margins of the image on Commission Exhibit No. 749 with the margins of the image on a negative

COMMISSION EXHIBIT No. 751

Oswald's Imperial Reflex camera, with the back removed to show the camera's film-plane aperture.

he himself had taken with the camera. Microscopic examination shows that the margins of a negative's image, although apparently straight, are actually irregular. The irregularities usually do not show on a finished print, because they are blocked out to give the print a neat border.[399] The cause of these irregularities can be best understood by examination of Commission Exhibit No. 751 (p. 594), a photograph of the Imperial camera with the back removed to show the camera's film-plane aperture. When the camera's shutter is opened, light exposes that portion of the film which is not blocked off by this aperture. The edges of the aperture, therefore, define the edges of the image which will appear on the developed negative. In effect, the edge of the image is a shadowgraph of the edge of the aperture. As Shaneyfelt testified:

> * * * the basis of the examination was a close microscopic study of the negative made in the camera to study the shadowgraph that is made of the edge of the aperture.
> As the film is placed across the aperture of the camera, and the shutter is opened, light comes through and exposes the film only in the opening within the edges. Where the film is out over the edges of the aperture it is not exposed, and your result is an exposed negative with a clear edge, and on the negative then, the edges of that exposure of the photograph, are actually shadowgraphs of the edges of the aperture.[400]

The basis of the identification is that the microscopic characteristics of every film-plane aperture, like those of a rifle barrel, are distinctive, for much the same reason; that is, when the camera is manufactured, certain handwork is done which differs microscopically from camera to camera, and further differences accrue as the camera is used. As Shaneyfelt testified:

> Q. Mr. Shaneyfelt, what is the basis of your statement, the theoretical basis of your statement, that every camera with this type of back aperture arrangement is unique in the characteristics of the shadowgraph it makes on the negative?
> Mr. SHANEYFELT. It is because of the minute variations that even two cameras from the same mold will have. Additional handwork on cameras, or filing the edges where a little bit of plastic or a little bit of metal stays on, make individual characteristics apart from those that would be general characteristics on all of them from the same mold.
> In addition, as the film moves across the camera and it is used for a considerable length of time, dirt and debris tend to accumulate a little—or if the aperture is painted, little lumps in the paint will make little bumps along that edge that would make that then individually different from every other camera.
> Q. Is this similar then to toolmark identification?
> Mr. SHANEYFELT. Very similar; yes.[401]

Based on his examination of the shadowgraph on the negative, Commission Exhibit No. 749, Shaneyfelt determined that it had been taken with the Imperial camera.[402]

Three edges of the shadowgraph of the film-plane aperture were also visible on one of the photographs of General Walker's house, not having been blocked out in the making of the print. On the basis of these three margins, Shaneyfelt determined that this photograph had also been taken with Oswald's Imperial Reflex camera. Shaneyfelt could not determine whether 133–A had been photographed with the Imperial camera, because the negative of 133–A had not been found, and the print itself did not show a shadowgraph area.[403]

During his interrogations Oswald had been shown 133–A, and had claimed it was a composite—that the face in the picture was his, but the body was not.[404] Shaneyfelt examined 133–A and 133–B to determine if they were composite pictures. He concluded that they were not:

> * * * it is my opinion that they are not composites. Again with very, very minor reservation, because I cannot entirely eliminate an extremely expert composite. I have examined many composite photographs, and there is always an inconsistency, either in lighting of the portion that is added, or the configuration indicating a different lens used for the part that was added to the original photograph, things many times that you can't point to and say this is a characteristic, or that is a characteristic, but they have definite variations that are not consistent throughout the picture.
>
> I found no such characteristics in this picture.
>
> In addition, with a composite it is always necessary to make a print that you then make a pasteup of. In this instance paste the face in, and rephotograph it, and then retouch out the area where the head was cut out, which would leave a characteristic that would be retouched out on the negative and then that would be printed.
>
> Normally, this retouching can be seen under magnification in the resulting composite—points can be seen where the edge of the head had been added and it hadn't been entirely retouched out.
>
> This can nearly always be detected under magnification. I found no such characteristics in these pictures.
>
> Q. Did you use the technique of magnification in your analysis?
> A. Yes.[405]

Furthermore, the negative, Commission Exhibit No. 749, showed absolutely no doctoring or composition.[406] Since the negative was made in Oswald's Imperial camera, Commission Exhibit No. 750, a composite of 133–B could have been made only by putting two pictures together and rephotographing them in the Imperial camera—all without leaving a discernible trace. This, to Shaneyfelt, was "in the realm of the impossible":

In addition, in this instance regarding 133–B which I have just stated, I have identified as being photographed or exposed in the camera which is Exhibit 750, for this to be a composite, they would have had to make a picture of the background with an individual standing there, and then substitute the face, and retouch it and then possibly rephotograph it and retouch that negative, and make a print, and then photograph it with this camera, which is Commission Exhibit 750, in order to have this negative which we have identified with the camera, and is Commission Exhibit 749.

This to me is beyond reasonable doubt, it just doesn't seem that it would be at all possible, in this particular photograph.[407]

*   *   *   *   *   *   *

Q. You have the negative of this? [Referring to Exhibit 133B.]

A. We have the negative of 133B.

Q. You have the negative of 133B. That negative in itself shows no doctoring or composition at all?

A. It shows absolutely no doctoring or composition.

Q. So that the only composition that could have been made would have been in this process which you have described of picture on picture and negative and then photographing?

A. And then finally rephotographing with this camera.

Q. Rephotographing with this camera, this very camera?

A. That is correct, and this then, to me, becomes in the realm of the impossible.[408]

Following the assassination, photographs similar to 133–A appeared in a number of newspapers and magazines.[409] At least some of these photographs, as reproduced, differed both from 133–A and from each other in minor details.[410] Shaneyfelt examined several of these reproductions and concluded that in each case the individual publisher had taken a reproduction of 133–A and retouched it in various ways, apparently for clarifying purposes, thus accounting for the differences between the reproductions and 133–A, and the differences between the reproductions themselves.[411] Subsequently one of the publishers involved submitted the original photographs which it had retouched. Shaneyfelt's examination of this photograph confirmed his original conclusion.[412] The remaining publishers either confirmed that they had retouched the photographs they had used, or failed to contradict Shaneyfelt's testimony after having been given an opportunity to do so.[413]

Reports Relating to the Interrogation of Lee Harvey Oswald at the Dallas Police Department

As discussed in chapters IV and V, Lee Harvey Oswald was interrogated for a total of approximately 12 hours between 2:30 p.m. on Friday, November 22, 1963, and 11:15 a.m. on Sunday, November 24, 1963. There were no stenographic or tape recordings of these interviews. Several of the investigators present at one or more of the interrogation sessions, prior to testifying before the Commission, had prepared memoranda setting forth their recollections of the questioning of Oswald and his responses. The following are the most important of these reports.

REPORT OF CAPT. J. W. FRITZ, DALLAS POLICE DEPARTMENT

INTERROGATION OF LEE HARVEY OSWALD

We conducted the investigation at the Texas School Book Depository Building on November 22, 1963, immediately after the President was shot and after we had found the location where Lee Harvey Oswald had done the shooting from and left three empty cartridge cases on the floor and the rifle had been found partially hidden under some boxes near the back stairway. These pieces of evidence were protected until the Crime Lab. could get pictures and make a search for fingerprints. After Lt. Day, of the Crime Lab, had finished his work with the rifle, I picked it up and found that it had a cartridge in the chamber, which I ejected. About this time some officer came to me and told me that Mr. Roy S. Truly wanted to see me, as one of his men had left the building. I had talked to Mr. Truly previously, and at that time he thought everyone was accounted for who worked in the building. Mr. Truly then came with another officer and told me that a Lee Harvey Oswald had left the building. I asked if he had an address where this man lived, and he told me that he did, that it was in Irving at 2515 W. 5th Street.

I then left the rest of the search of the building with Chief Lumpkin and other officers who were there and told Dets. R. M. Sims and E. L. Boyd to accompany me to the City Hall where we could make a quick check for police record and any other information of value, and we would then go to Irving, Texas, in an effort to apprehend this man. While I was in the building, I was told that Officer J. D. Tippit had been shot in Oak Cliff.

I 136 A

Immediately after I reached my office, I asked the officers who had brought in a prisoner from the Tippit shooting who the man was who shot the officer. They told me his name was Lee Harvey Oswald, and I replied that that was our suspect in the President's killing. I instructed the officers to bring this man into the office after talking to the officers for a few minutes in the presence of Officers R. M. Sims and E. L. Boyd of the Homicide Bureau and possibly some Secret Service men. Just as I had started questioning this man, I received a call from Gordon Shanklin, Agent in Charge of the FBI office here in Dallas, who asked me to let him talk to Jim Bookhout, one of his agents. He told Mr. Bookhout that he would like for James P. Hosty to sit in on this interview as he knew about these people and had been investigating them before. I invited Mr. Bookhout and Mr. Hosty in to help with the interview.

After some questions about this man's full name I asked him if he worked for the Texas School Book Depository, and he told me he did. I asked him which floor he worked on, and he said usually on the second floor but sometimes his work took him to all the different floors. I asked him what part of the building he was in at the time the President was shot, and he said that he was having his lunch about that time on the first floor. Mr. Truly had told me that one of the police officers had stopped this man immediately after the shooting somewhere near the back stairway, so I asked Oswald where he was when the police officer stopped him. He said he was on the second floor drinking a coca cola when the officer came in. I asked him why he left the building, and he said there was so much excitement he didn't think there would be any more work done that day, and

_I 136 B_

600

that as this company wasn't particular about their hours, that they did not
punch a clock, and that he thought it would be just as well that he left for
the rest of the afternoon. I asked him if he owned a rifle, and he said
that he did not. He said that he had seen one at the building a few days
ago, and that Mr. Truly and some of the employees were looking at it. I
asked him where he went to when he left work, and he told me that he had
a room on 1026 North Beckley, that he went over there and changed his trousers
and got his pistol and went to the picture show. I asked him why he carried
his pistol, and he remarked, "You know how boys do when they have a gun, they
just carry it."

Mr. Hosty asked Oswald if he had been in Russia. He told him, "Yes,
he had been in Russia three years." He asked him if he had written to
the Russian Embassy, and he said he had. This man became very upset and
arrogant with Agent Hosty when he questioned him and accused him of accosting his wife two different times. When Agent Hosty attempted to talk to
this man, he would hit his fist on the desk. I asked Oswald what he meant
by accosting his wife when he was talking to Mr. Hosty. He said Mr. Hosty
mistreated his wife two different times when he talked with her, practically
accosted her. Mr. Hosty also asked Oswald if he had been to Mexico City,
which he denied. During this interview he told me that he had gone to
school in New York and in Fort Worth, Texas, that after going into the
Marines, finished his high school education. I asked him if he won any
medals for rifle shooting in the Marines. He said he won the usual medals.

I asked him what his political beliefs were, and he said he had none
but that he belonged to the Fair Play for Cuba Committee and told me that

I 136 C

they had headquarters in New York and that he had been Secretary for this organization in New Orleans when he lived there. He also said that he supports the Castro Revolution. One of the officers had told me that he had rented the room on Beckley under the name of O. H. Lee. I asked him why he did this. He said the landlady did it. She didn't understand his name correctly.

Oswald asked if he was allowed an attorney and I told him he could have any attorney he liked, and that the telephone would be available to him up in the jail and he could call anyone he wished. I believe it was during this interview that he first expressed a desire to talk to Mr. Abt, an attorney in New York. Interviews on this day were interrupted by showups where witnesses identified Oswald positively as the man who killed Officer Tippit, and the time that I would have to talk to another witness or to some of the officers. One of these showups was held at 4:35 pm and the next one at 6:30 pm. and at 7:55 pm. At 7:05 pm I signed a complaint before Bill Alexander of the District Attorney's office, charging Oswald with the Tippit murder. At 7:10 pm Tippit was arraigned before Judge Johnston. During the second day interviews I asked Oswald about a card that he had in his purse showing that he belonged to the Fair Play for Cuba Committee, which he admitted was his. I asked him about another identification card in his pocket bearing the name of Alex Hidell. He said he picked up that name in New Orleans while working in the Fair Play for Cuba organization. He said he spoke Russian, that he corresponded with people in Russia, and that he received newspapers from Russia.

I 136 D

602

I showed the rifle to Marina Oswald, and she could not positively identify it, but said that it looked like the rifle that her husband had and that he had been keeping it in the garage at Mrs. Paine's home in Irving. After this, I questioned Oswald further about the rifle, but he denied owning a rifle at all, and said that he did have a small rifle some years past. I asked him if he owned a rifle in Russia, and he said, "You know you can't buy a rifle in Russia, you can only buy shotguns." "I had a shotgun in Russia and hunted some while there." Marina Oswlad had told me that she thought her husband might have brought the rifle from New Orleans, which he denied. He told me that he had some things stored in a garage at Mrs. Paine's home in Irving and that he had a few personal effects at his room on Beckley. I instructed the officers to make a thorough search of both of these places.

After reviewing all of the evidence pertaining to the killing of President Kennedy before District Attorney Henry Wade and his assistant, Bill Alexander, and Jim Allen, former First Assistant District Attorney of Dallas County, I signed a complaint before the District Attorney charging Oswald with the murder of President Kennedy. This was at 11:26 pm. He was arraigned before Judge David Johnston at 1:35 am, November 23, 1963.

Oswald was placed in jail about 12:00 midnight and brought from the jail for arraignment, before Judge David Johnston at 1:36 am.

I 137 A

Page 6

On November 23 at 10:25 AM Oswald was brought from the jail for an interview. Present at this time was FBI agent Jim Bookhout, Forrest Sorrells, special agent and in charge of Secret Service, United States Marshall Robert Nash, and Homicide officers. During this interview I talked to Oswald about his leaving the building, and he told me he left by bus and rode to a stop near home and walked on to his house. At the time of Oswald's arrest he had a bus transfer in his pocket. He admitted this was given to him by the bus driver when he rode the bus after leaving the building.

One of the officers had told me that a cab driver, William Wayne Whaley, thought he had recognized Oswald's picture as the man who had gotten in his cab near the bus station and rode to Beckley Avenue. I asked Oswald if he had ridden a cab on that day, and he said, "Yes, I did ride in the cab. The bus I got on near where I work got into heavy traffic and was traveling too slow, and I got off and caught a cab." I asked him about his conversation with the cab driver, and he said he remembered that when he got in the cab a lady came up who also wanted a cab, and he told Oswald to tell the lady to "take another cab".

We found from the investigation the day before that when Oswald left home, he was carrying a long package. He usually went to see his wife of week ends, but this time he had gone on Thursday night. I asked him if he had told Buell Wesley Frazier why he had gone home a different night, and if he had told him anything about bringing back some curtain rods. He denied it.

During this conversation he told me he reached his home by cab and changed both his shirt and trousers before going to the show. He

I 137 B

604

said his cab fare home was 85 cents. When asked what he did with his
clothing, he took off when he got home, he said he put them in the dirty
clothes. In talking with him further about his location at the time the
President was killed, he said he ate lunch with some of the colored boys who
worked with him. One of them was called "Junior" and the other one was
a little short man whose name he did not know. He said he had a cheese
sandwich and some fruit and that was the only package he had brought with
him to work and denied that he had brought the long package described by
Mr. Frazier and his sister.

I asked him why he lived in a room, while his wife lived in Irving.
He said Mrs. Paine, the lady his wife lived with, was learning Russian,
that his wife needed help with the young baby, and that it made a nice
arrangement for both of them. He said he didn't know Mr. Paine very
well, but Mr. Paine and his wife, he thought, were separated a great deal
of the time. He said he owned no car, but that the Paines have two cars,
and told that in the garage at the Paine's home he had some sea bags that
had a lot of his personal belongings, that he had left them there after
coming back from New Orleans in September.

He said he had a brother, Robert, who lived in Fort Worth. We
later found that this brother lived in Denton. He said the Paines were
close friends of his.

I asked him if he belonged to the Communist Party, but he said
that he had never had a card, but repeated that he belonged to the Fair
Play for Cuba organization, and he said that he belonged to the American

I/37C

Civil Liberties Union and paid $5.00 dues. I asked him again why he carried the pistol to the show. He refused to answer questions about the pistol. He did tell me, however, that he had bought it several months before in Fort Worth, Texas.

I noted that in questioning him that he did answer very quickly, and I asked him if he had ever been questioned before, and he told me that he had. He was questioned one time for a long time by the FBI after he had returned from Russia. He said they used different methods, they tried the hard and soft, and the buddy method, and said he was very familiar with interrogation. He reminded me that he did not have to answer any questions at all until he talked to his attorney, and I told him again that he could have an attorney any time he wished. He said he didn't have money to pay for a phone call to Mr. Abt. I told him to call "collect", if he liked, to use the jail phone or that he could have another attorney if he wished. He said he didn't want another attorney, he wanted to talk to this attorney first. I believe he made this call later as he thanked me later during one of our interviews for allowing him the use of the telephone. I explained to him that all prisoners were allowed to use the telephone. I asked him why he wanted Mr. Abt, instead of some available attorney. He told me he didn't know Mr. Abt personally, but that he was familiar with a case where Mr. Abt defended some people for a violation of the Smith Act, and that if he didn't get Mr. Abt, that he felt sure the American Civil Liberties Union would furnish him a lawyer. He explained to me that this organization helped people who needed attorneys and weren't able to get them.

I. 371.

While in New Orleans, he lived at 4907 Magazine Street and at one time worked for the William Riley Company near that address. When asked about any previous arrests, he told me that he had had a little trouble while working with the Fair Play for Cuba Committee and had a fight with some anti-Castro people. He also told me of a debate on some radio station in New Orleans where he debated with some anti-Castro people.

I asked him what he thought of President Kennedy and his family, and he said he didn't have any views on the President. He said, "I like the President's family very well. I have my own views about national policies." I asked him about a polygraph test. He told me he had refused a polygraph test with the FBI, and he certainly wouldn't take one at this time. Both Mr. Bookhout, of the FBI, and Mr. Kelley, and the Marshall asked Oswald some questions during this interview.

Oswald was placed back in jail at 11:33 am. At 12:35 pm Oswald was brought to the office for another interview with Inspector Kelley and some of the other officers and myself. I talked to Oswald about the different places he had lived in Dallas in an effort to find where he was living when the picture was made of him holding a rifle which looked to be the same rifle we had recovered. This picture showed to be taken near a stairway with many identifying things in the back yard. He told me about one of the places where he had lived.

Mr. Paine had told me about where Oswald lived on Neely Street. Oswald was very evasive about this location. We found later that this was the place where the picture was made. I again asked him about his property

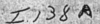

and where his things might be kept, and he told me about the things at
Mrs. Paine's residence and a few things on Beckley. He was placed
back in jail at 1:10 PM.

At 6:00 PM I instructed the officers to bring Oswald back into
the office, and in the presence of Jim Bookhout, Homicide officers,
and Inspector Kelley, of the Secret Service, I showed Oswald an enlarged picture of him holding a rifle and wearing a pistol. This
picture had been enlarged by our Crime Lab from a picture found in
the garage at Mrs. Paine's home. He said the picture was not his,
that the face was his face, but that this picture had been made by
someone superimposing his face, the other part of the picture was
not him at all and that he had never seen the picture before. When
I told him that the picture was recovered from Mrs. Paine's garage,
he said that picture had never been in his possession, and I explained
to him that it was an enlargement of the small picture obtained in
the search. At that time I showed him the smaller picture. He
denied ever seeing that picture and said that he knew all about
photography, that he had done a lot of work in photography himself,
that the small picture was a reduced picture of the large picture,
and had been made by some person unknown to him. He further stated
that since he had been photographed here at the City Hall and that
people had been taking his picture while being transferred from my
office to the jail door that someone had been able to get a picture
of his face and that with that, they had made this picture. He told
me that he understood photography real well, and that in time, he would

I 138 B

608

be able to show that it was not his picture, and that it had been made
by someone else.   At this time he said that he did not want to answer
any more questions and he was returned to the jail about 7:15 pm.

At 9:30 on the morning of November 24, I asked that Oswald be
brought to the office.   At that time I showed him a map of the City of
Dallas which had been recovered in the search of his room on North Peckley.
This map had some markings on it, one of which was about where the President
was shot. He said that the map had nothing to do with the President's
shooting and again, as he had one in the previous interviews, denied knowing anything of the shooting of the President, or of the shooting of
Officer Tippit.   He said the map had been used to locate buildings where
he had gone to talk to people about employment.

During this interview Inspector Kelley asked Oswald about his religious views, and he replied that he didn't agree with all the philosophies on
religion.   He seemed evasive with Inspector Kelley about how he felt about
religion, and I asked him if he believed in a Piety.   He was evasive and
didn't answer this question.

Someone of the Federal officers asked Oswald if he thought Cuba
would be better off since the President was assassinated. To this he replied
that he felt that since the President was killed that someone else would
take his place, perhaps Vice-President Johnson, and that his views would
probably be largely the same as those of President Kennedy.

I again asked him about the gun and about the picture of him
holding a similar rifle, and at that time he again positively

I7380C

denied having any knowledge of the picture or the rifle and
denied that he had ever lived on Neely Street, and when I told
him that friends who had visited him there said that he had
lived there, he said that they were mistaken about visiting
him there, because he had never lived there.

During this interview, Oswald said he was a Marxist. He
repeated two or three times, "I am a Marxist, but not a Leninist-
Marxist. He told me that the station that he had debated on in
New Orleans was the one who carried Bill Stakey's program. He
denied again knowing Alex Hidell in New Orleans, and again reiterated his belief in Fair Play for Cuba and what the committee
stood for.

After some questioning, Chief Jesse E. Curry came to the
office and asked me if I was ready for the man to be transferred.
I told him we were ready as soon as the security was completed in
the basement, where we were to place Oswald in a car to transfer
him to the County Jail. I had objected to the cameras obstructing
the jail door, and the Chief explained to me that these have been
moved, and the people were moved back, and the cameramen were well
back in the garage. I told the Chief then that we were ready to
go. He told us to go ahead with the prisoner, and that he and
Chief Stevenson, who was with him, would meet us at the County Jail.

Oswald's shirt, which he was wearing at the time of arrest,
had been removed and sent to the crime lab in Washington with all
the other evidence for a comparison test. Oswald said he would
like to have a shirt from his clothing that had been brought to the

I 138D

Page 13

office to wear over the T-shirt that he was wearing at the time. We selected the best-looking shirt from his things, but he said he would prefer wearing a black Ivy League type shirt, indicating that it might be a little warmer. We made this change and I asked him if he wouldn't like to wear a hat to more or less camouflage his looks in the car while being transferred as all of the people who had been viewing him had seen him bareheaded. He didn't want to do this. Then Officer J. R. Leavelle handcuffed his left hand to Oswald's right hand, then we left the office for the transfer.

Inasmuch as this report was made from rough notes and memory, it is entirely possible that one of these questions could be in a separate interview from the one indicated in this report. He was interviewed under the most adverse conditions in my office which is 9 feet 6 inches by 14 feet, and has only one front door, which forced us to move this prisoner through hundreds of people each time he was carried from my office to the jail door, some 20 feet, during each of these transfers. The crowd would attempt to jam around him, shouting questions and many containing slurs. This office is also surrounded by large glass windows, and there were many officers working next to these windows. I have no recorder in this office and was unable to record the interview. I was interrupted many times during these interviews to step from the office to talk to another witness or secure additional information from officers needed for the interrogation.

I /38 C

611

REPORTS OF AGENTS OF THE FEDERAL BUREAU OF INVESTIGATION

FD-302 (Rev. 3-3-59)

FEDERAL BUREAU OF INVESTIGATION

Date _____ 11/23/63 _____

1

      LEE HARVEY OSWALD, 1026 North Beckley, Dallas, Texas, was interviewed by Captain WILL FRITZ of the Homicide Bureau, Dallas Police Department. Special Agents JAMES P. HOSTY, JR. and JAMES W. BOOKHOUT were present during this interview. When the Agents entered the interview room at 3:15 p.m., Captain FRITZ had been previously interviewing LEE HARVEY OSWALD for an undetermined period of time. Both Agents identified themselves to OSWALD and advised him they were law enforcement officers and anything he said could be used against him. OSWALD at this time adopted a violent attitude toward the FBI and both Agents and made many uncomplimentary remarks about the FBI. OSWALD requested that Captain FRITZ remove the cuffs from him, it being noted that OSWALD was hand-cuffed with his hands behind him. Captain FRITZ had one of his detectives remove the handcuffs and handcuff OSWALD with his hands in front of him.

      Captain FRITZ asked OSWALD if he ever owned a rifle and OSWALD stated that he had observed a MR. TRULY (phonetic), a supervisor at the Texas Schoolbook Depository on November 20, 1963, display a rifle to some individuals in his office on the first floor of the Texas Schoolbook Depository, but denied ever owning a rifle himself. OSWALD stated that he had never been in Mexico except to Tijuana on one occasion. However, he admitted to Captain FRITZ to having resided in the Soviet Union for three years where he has many friends and relatives of his wife.

      OSWALD also admitted that he was the secretary for the Fair Play for Cuba Committee in New Orleans, Louisiana a few months ago. OSWALD stated that the Fair Play for Cuba Committee has its headquarters in New York City. OSWALD admitted to having received an award for marksmanship while a member of the U.S. Marine Corps. He further admitted that he was living at 1026 N. Beckley in Dallas, Texas, under the name of O. H. LEE. OSWALD admitted that he was present in the Texas Schoolbook Depository on November 22, 1963, where he has been employed since October 15, 1963. OSWALD stated that as a laborer, he has access to the entire building which has offices on the first and second

---

on ___11/22/63___ at ___Dallas, Texas___ File # ___DL 89-43___

by Special Agent S ___JAMES P. HOSTY, JR. and JAMES W. BOOKHOUT___ /wvm Date dictated ___11/23/63___

floors and storage on the third and fourth, as well as the
fifth and sixth floors. OSWALD stated that he went to
lunch at approximately noon and he claimed he ate his lunch
on the first floor in the lunchroom; however he went to the
second floor where the Coca-Cola machine was located and
obtained a bottle of Coca-Cola for his lunch. OSWALD claimed
to be on the first floor when President JOHN F. KENNEDY
passed this building.

After hearing what had happened, he said that
because of all the confusion there would be no work performed that afternoon so he decided to go home. OSWALD
stated he then went home by bus and changed his clothes
and went to a movie. OSWALD admitted to carrying a pistol
with him to this movie stating he did this because he
felt like it, giving no other reason. OSWALD further
admitted attempting to fight the Dallas police officers
who arrested him in this movie theater when he received a
cut and a bump.

OSWALD frantically denied shooting Dallas police
officer TIPPITT or shooting President JOHN F. KENNEDY. The
interview was concluded at 4:05 p.m. when OSWALD was removed
for a lineup.

FD-302 (Rev. 3-3-59)

FEDERAL BUREAU OF INVESTIGA..ON

Date ___11/23/63___

     LEE HARVEY OSWALD, interviewed in offices of the
Dallas Police Department, was advised that he did not have to
make any statement, any statement he made could be used against
him in court and of his right to an attorney. He was requested
to furnish descriptive and biographical data concerning himself.

     The following was obtained from his responses and
examination of contents of his wallet:

     OSWALD declined to explain his possession of a photo-
graph of a Selective Service card in the name of "ALEK JAMES
HIDELL".

     When interview had been substantially completed and
OSWALD was asked as to his present employment, he stated he
thought perhaps interview to obtain descriptive information was
too prolonged, that he had declined to be interviewed by any
other officers previously, and did not desire to be interviewed
by this agent. He remarked "I know your tactics - there is a
similar agency in Russia. You are using the soft touch and, of
course, the procedure in Russia would be quite different."

     OSWALD was advised questions were intended to obtain
his complete physical description and background. Upon repetition of the question as to his present employment, he furnished
same without further discussion.

Race	White
Sex	Male
Date of Birth	October 18, 1939
Place of Birth	New Orleans, Louisiana
Height	5' 9"
Weight	140
Hair	Medium brown, worn medium length, needs haircut -
Eyes	Blue-gray
Scars	No tattoos or permanent scars
Relatives	Mother - MARGUERITE OSWALD, unknown address, Arlington, Texas, practical nurse (has not seen for about one year)

---

on ___11/22/63___ at ___Dallas, Texas___   File # ___89-43___

by Special Agent ___MANNING C. CLEMENTS / mac___ Date dictated ___11/23/63___

9.2-

Relatives (cont'd)   Father - ROBERT LEE OSWALD,
                       deceased, August 31, 1939,
                       New Orleans, Louisiana
                     Wife - MARINA; two infant children
                     Brothers - JOHN OSWALD, address
                       unknown, last known at Fort Worth,
                       Texas, five or six years ago, age
                       about 30, works with pharma-
                       ceuticals, but not graduate
                       pharmacist;
                       ROBERT OSWALD, 7313 Davenport,
                       Fort Worth, Texas (wife - VADA,
                       two small children), works for
                       brick company (believed Acme)

Dress at Time of
  Interview   Black trousers, brown "salt and
                     pepper", long sleeved shirt, bare-
                     headed

Contents of Wallet   Had card in possession, LEE HARVEY
                     OSWALD, Social Security No. 433-54-3937

                     Photo of Selective Service System
                     card with photo of OSWALD, "Notice of
                     Classification" and name "ALEK JAMES
                     HIDELL, SSN 42-224-39-5321". Card
                     shows classification IV___(?). Bears
                     date February 5, 1962, reverse side
                     shows card from Texas Local Board,
                     400 West Vickery, Fort Worth, Texas.
                     Card shows erasures and retyping of
                     the information indicated and bears
                     longhand signature "ALEK J. HIDELL".
                     Signature of member or clerk of local
                     board (indistinct, may be GOOD ___.

                     Local Board 114, Fort Worth, LEE HARVEY
                     OSWALD, SSN 41-114-39-532, address
                     3124 West 5th Street, Fort Worth, Texas,
                     registered September 14, 1959. Date
                     of birth October 18, 1939, New Orleans,
                     5' 11", 150 lbs., blue eyes, brown
                     hair. Mrs. ZOLA Z. BURGER, Clerk.

Snapshot photo of woman, apparently
wife

Snapshot photo of infant

White card with longhand, "Embassy
USSR, 1609 Decatur, NW, Washington,
D. C., Consular REZHUYEHKO" (indistinct)

Department of Defense Identification
No. N4,271,617, issued to LEE H. OSWALD,
expiration date December 7, 1962,
Private First Class, E-2, MCR/INAC,
Service No. 1653230. Card shows date
of birth October 18, 1939, 5' 11", 145
lbs., brown hair, gray eyes.

Dallas Public Library card, undated,
expiration date December 7, 1965,
issued to LEE HARVEY OSWALD, 602 Elsbeth, Dallas, school or business -
Jaggers - Chiles - Stovall, followed
by the name JACK L. BOWEN, 1916 Stevens
Forest Drive, WH 8-8997.

U. S. Forces, Japan Identification card
issued to LEE H. OSWALD, Private,
Service No. 1653230, organization -
MACS-1 MAG-11 1st MAW. Identification
card #00646, issued, May 8, 1958. Date
of birth October 18, 1939, American.

Card, "Compliments GA - JO Enkanko
Hotel, telephone number ED 5-0755 of
reverse side.

Certificate of Service in Armed Forces
of United States, issued to LEE HARVEY
OSWALD, 1653230, reflected honorably
served on active duty, U. S. Marine
Corps, October 24, 1956 - September 11,
1959.

Card of "Fair Play for Cuba Committee,
799 Broadway, New York 3, New York,
telephone ORegon 4-8295", issued to
LEE H. OSWALD, May 28, 1963, filed by
V. T. LEE as Executive Secretary

Card of "Fair Play for Cuba, New
Orleans Chapter", issued to L. H.
OSWALD, June 15, 1963, filed by A. T.(?)
HIDELL, Chapter President (note name
HIDELL on fictitious Selective Service
card)

Selective Service notice of classifi-
cation card to LEE HARVEY OSWALD,
Selective Service No. 41-114-39-532,
IV-A, dated February 2, 1960, from
Local Board 114, Fort Worth, Texas

$13.00 in currency, consisting of one
$5.00 bill and eight $1.00 bills

Residence   2515 West 5th Street, Irving, Texas,
phone BL 3-1628 (residence of wife for
past five weeks)

Room in rooming house, 1026 North
Beckley, for about five weeks. Phone
number unknown.

Previous Residences   4706 Magazine Street, New Orleans,
Louisiana, no phone (about three months)

602 Elsbeth. no phone (about seven
months), Dallas, Texas

Unrecalled street in Fort Worth, Texas,
(a few months), with brother in Fort
Worth, Texas, for a few months.

Previously in Soviet Union, until July,
1962.

Occupations   Photography - Jaggers - Chiles -
Stovall, 522 Browder, Dallas, Texas

Factory worker, William B. Riley
Company (Coffee and Coffee Canisters),
644 Magazine Street, New Orleans,
Louisiana

Unemployed for several months

Employed with Texas State Book
Depository, Dallas, Texas, September,
1963, stock work, filing orders, etc.

FD-302 (Rev. 3-3-59)

FEDERAL BUREAU OF INVESTIGATION

Date _____11/25/63_____

1

LEE HARVEY OSWALD was interviewed at the Homicide and Robbery Bureau, Dallas Police Department, by Captain J. W. FRITZ in the presence of Special Agent JAMES W. BOOKHOUT, Federal Bureau of Investigation. OSWALD was advised of the identity and official capacity of said agent and the fact that he did not have to make any statement, that any statement he did make could be used in a court of law against him, and that any statement made must be free and voluntary and that he had the right to consult with an attorney.

OSWALD stated that he did not own any rifle. He advised that he saw a rifle day before yesterday at the Texas School Book Depository which MR. TRULY and two other gentlemen had in their possession and were looking at.

OSWALD stated that on November 22, 1963, at the time of the search of the Texas School Book Depository building by Dallas police officers, he was on the second floor of said building, having just purchased a Coca-cola from the soft-drink machine, at which time a police officer came into the room with pistol drawn and asked him if he worked there. MR. TRULY was present and verified that he was an employee and the police officer thereafter left the room and continued through the building. OSWALD stated that he took this Coke down to the first floor and stood around and had lunch in the employees lunch room. He thereafter went outside and stood around for five or ten minutes with foreman BILL SHELLY, and thereafter went home. He stated that he left work because, in his opinion, based upon remarks of BILL SHELLY, he did not believe that there was going to be any more work that day due to the confusion in the building. He stated after arriving at his residence, then he went to a movie, where he was subsequently apprehended by the Dallas Police Department.

OSWALD stated that his hours of work at the Texas School Book Depository are from 8 a.m. to 4:45 p.m., but that he is not required to punch a time clock. His usual place of work in the building is on the first floor; however, he frequently is required to go to the fourth, fifth, sixth, and seventh floors of the building in order to get books and

---

on __11/22/63__ at _____Dallas, Texas_____ File # __DL 89-43__

by Special Agent __JAMES W. BOOKHOUT__ /wvm _____ Date dictated __11/24/63__

97

this was true on November 22, 1963, and he had been on all of the floors in the performance of his duties on November 22, 1963.

Date ___11/25/63___

1

         LEE HARVEY OSWALD was interviewed by Captain
J. W. FRITZ, Homicide and Robbery Bureau, Dallas Police
Department. OSWALD was advised of the identity of SA
JAMES W. BOOKHOUT, and his capacity as a Special Agent
of the Federal Bureau of Investigation. He was informed
of his right to an attorney, that any statement he might
make could be used against him in a court of law, and
that any statement which he might make must be free and
voluntary. He furnished the following information in
the presence of T. J. KELLY, U.S. Secret Service; DAVID
B. GRANT, Secret Service; ROBERT I. NASH, United States
Marshall; and Detectives BILLY L. SENKEL and FAY M.
TURNER of the Homicide and Robbery Bureau, Dallas
Police Department.

         Following his departure from the Texas School
Book Depository, he boarded a city bus to his residence
and obtained transfer upon departure from the bus. He
stated that officers at the time of arresting him took
his transfer out of his pocket.

         OSWALD advised that he had only one post office
box which was at Dallas, Texas. He denied bringing any
package to work on the morning of November 22, 1963. He
stated that he was not in the process of fixing up his
apartment and he denied telling WESLEY FRAZIER that the
purpose of his visit to Irving, Texas, on the night of
November 21, 1963, was to obtain some curtain rods from
MRS. RUTH PAINE.

         OSWALD stated that it was not exactly true
as recently stated by him that he rode a bus from his
place of employment to his residence on November 22, 1963.
He stated actually he did board a city bus at his place
of employment but that after about a block or two, due to
traffic congestion, he left the bus and rode a city cab to
his apartment on North Beckley. He recalled that at the time
of getting into the cab, some lady looked in and asked the
driver to call her a cab. He stated that he might have
made some remarks to the cab driver merely for the purpose
of passing the time of day at that time. He recalled that

on __11/23/63__ at ____Dallas, Texas____ File # ___DL 89-43___

by Special Agent ___JAMES W. BOOKHOUT___/cvm   Date dictated ___11/24/63___

his fare was approximately 85 cents. He stated that
after arriving at his apartment, he changed his shirt and
trousers because they were dirty. He described his dirty
clothes as being a reddish colored, long sleeved, shirt
with a button-down collar and gray colored trousers. He
indicated that he had placed these articles of clothing
in the lower drawer of his dresser.

OSWALD stated that on November 22, 1963, he had eaten
lunch in the lunch room at the Texas School Book Depository,
alone, but recalled possibly two Negro employees walking
through the room during this period. He stated possibly
one of these employees was called "Junior" and the other
was a short individual whose name he could not recall but
whom he would be able to recognize. He stated that his
lunch had consisted of a cheese sandwich and an apple which
he had obtained at MRS. RUTH PAINE's residence in Irving,
Texas, upon his leaving for work that morning.

OSWALD stated that MRS. PAINE receives no pay
for keeping his wife and children at her residence. He
stated that their presence in MRS. PAINE's residence is
a good arrangement for her because of her language
interest, indicating that his wife speaks Russian and
MRS. PAINE is interested in the Russian language.

OSWALD denied having kept a rifle in MRS. PAINE's
garage at Irving, Texas, but stated that he did have certain
articles stored in her garage, consisting of two sea bags,
a couple of suitcases, and several boxes of kitchen articles
and also kept his clothes at MRS. PAINE's residence. He stated
that all of the articles in MRS. PAINE's garage had been
brought there about September, 1963, from New Orleans,
Louisiana.

OSWALD stated that he has had no visitors at his
apartment on North Beckley.

OSWALD stated that he has no receipts for purchase
of any guns and has never ordered any guns and does not own
a rifle nor has he ever possessed a rifle.

OSWALD denied that he is a member of the Communist
Party.

OSWALD stated that he purchased a pistol, which
was taken off him by police officers November 22, 1963, about

six months ago. He declined to state where he had purchased
it.

OSWALD stated that he arrived about July, 1962,
from USSR and was interviewed by the FBI at Fort Worth,
Texas. He stated that he felt they overstepped their
bounds and had used various tactics in interviewing him.

He further complained that on interview of RUTH
PAINE by the FBI regarding his wife, that he felt that his
wife was intimidated.

OSWALD stated that he desired to contact Attorney
ABT, New York City, indicating that ABT was the attorney
who had defended the Smith Act case about 1949 - 1950. He
stated that he does not know Attorney ABT personally.
Captain FRITZ advised OSWALD that arrangements would be
immediately made whereby he could call Attorney ABT.

OSWALD stated that prior to coming to Dallas
from New Orleans he had resided at a furnished apartment
at 4706 Magazine Street, New Orleans, Louisiana. While
in New Orleans, he had been employed by WILLIAM B. RILEY
Company, 640 Magazine Street, New Orleans.

OSWALD stated that he has nothing against
President JOHN F. KENNEDY personally; however in view
of the present charges against him, he did not desire to
discuss this phase further.

OSWALD stated that he would not agree to take
a polygraph examination without the advice of counsel.
He added that in the past he has refused to take polygraph
examinations.

OSWALD stated that he is a member of the American
Civil Liberties Union and added that MRS. RUTH PAINE was
also a member of same.

With regard to Selective Service card in the
possession of OSWALD bearing photograph of OSWALD and
the name of ALEK JAMES HIDELL, OSWALD admitted that he
carried this Selective Service card but declined to state
that he wrote the signature of ALEK J. HIDELL appearing
on same. He further declined to state the purpose of
carrying same or any use he has made of same.

OSWALD stated that an address book in his possession
contains the names of various Russian immigrants residing in
Dallas, Texas, whom he has visited with.

OSWALD denied shooting President JOHN F. KENNEDY
on November 22, 1963, and added that he did not know that
Governor JOHN CONNALLY had been shot and denied any
knowledge concerning this incident.

FD-302 (Rev. 3-3-59)

Date ___11/25/63___

1
—

LEE HARVEY OSWALD was interviewed at the Homicide and Robbery Bureau, Dallas Police Department, at 6:35 p.m., by Captain J. W. FRITZ in the presence of Special Agent JAMES W. BOOKHOUT, Federal Bureau of Investigation. OSWALD was advised of the identity and official capacity of said Agent and the fact that he did not have to make any statement, that any statement he did make could be used in a court of law against him, and that any statement made must be free and voluntary and that he had the right to consult with an attorney.

Captain J. W. FRITZ exhibited to LEE HARVEY OSWALD a photograph which had been obtained by the Dallas Police Department in a search, by search warrant, of the garage at the residence of MRS. RUTH PAINE, located at Irving, Texas, which photograph reflects OSWALD holding a rifle and wearing a holstered pistol. OSWALD was asked if this was a photograph of himself. OSWALD stated that he would not discuss the photograph without advice of an attorney. He stated that the head of the individual in the photograph could be his but that it was entirely possible that the Police Department had superimposed this part of the photograph over the body of someone else. He pointed out that numerous news media had snapped his photograph during the day and the possibility existed that the police had doctored up this photograph.

OSWALD denied that he had purchased any rifle from Kleins Store in Chicago, Illinois.

OSWALD complained of a lineup wherein he had not been granted a request to put on a jacket similar to those worn by some of the other individuals in the lineup.

---

on __11/23/63__ at _____Dallas, Texas_____ File # ___DL 89-43___

by Special Agent ____JAMES W. BOOKHOUT____ /wvm ____ Date dictated ___11/24/63___

103

REPORTS OF INSPECTOR THOMAS J. KELLEY, U.S. SECRET SERVICE

FIRST INTERVIEW OF
LEE HARVEY OSWALD

At about 10:30 A.M., November 23, 1963, I attended my first interview with Oswald. Present during the interview at the Homicide Division, Dallas Police Department, were Special Agent Jim Bookhout, FBI; Captain Will Fritz, Homicide Division, Dallas Police Department; U. S. Marshal Robert Nash; SA David Grant and SAIC Sorrels; and Officers Boyd and Hall of Captain Fritz's detail. The interview was not recorded. Mr. Sorrels and my presence was as observers, since Oswald was being held for murder and his custody and interrogation at that time was the responsibility of the Dallas Police Department.

In response to questions put by Captain Fritz, Oswald said that immediately after having left the building where he worked, he went by bus to the theater where he was arrested; that when he got on the bus he secured a transfer and thereafter transferred to other buses to get to his destination. He denied that he brought a package to work on that day and he denied that he had ever had any conversation about curtain rods with the boy named Wesley who drove him to his employment. Fritz asked him if he had ridden a taxi that day and Oswald then changed his story and said that when he got on the bus he found it was going too slow and after two blocks he got off the bus and took a cab to his home; that he passed the time with the cab driver and that the cab driver had told him that the President was shot. He paid a cab fare of 85¢.

In response to questions, he stated that this was the first time he had ever ridden in a cab since a bus was always available. He said he went home, changed his trousers and shirt, put his shirt in a drawer. This was a red shirt, and he put it with his dirty clothes. He described the shirt as having a button down collar and of reddish color. The trousers were grey colored.

He said he ate his lunch with the colored boys who worked with him. He described one of them as "Junior", a colored boy, and the other was a little short negro boy. He said his lunch consisted of cheese, bread, fruit, and apples, and was the only package he had with him when he went to work.

He stated that Mrs. Paine practices Russian by having his wife live with her. He denied that he had ever owned/rifle. He said he does not know Mr. Paine very well but that Paine usually comes by the place where his wife was living with Mrs. Paine on Friday or Wednesday. He stated that Mr. Paine has a car and Mrs. Paine has had two cars. He said in response to questions by Captain Fritz that his effects were in Mrs. Paine's garage and that they consisted of two sea bags with some other packages containing his personal belongings and that he had brought those back from New Orleans with him sometime in September. He stated that his brother, Robert, lived at 7313 Davenport Street, Fort Worth, and that the Paines were his closest friends in town. He denied that he had ever joined the Communist party; that he never had a Communist card. He did belong to the American Civil Liberties Union and had

338

626

paid $5 a year dues. He stated that he had bought the pistol that was found in his possession when he was arrested about seven months ago. He refused to answer any questions concerning the pistol or a gun until he talked to a lawyer.

Oswald stated that at various other times he had been thoroughly interrogated by the FBI; that they had used all the usual interrogation practices and all their standard operating procedure; that he was very familiar with interrogation, and he had no intention of answering any questions concerning any shooting; that he knew he did not have to answer them and that he would not answer any questions until he had been given counsel. He stated that the FBI had used their hard and soft approach to him, they used the buddy system; that he was familiar with all types of questioning and had no intention of making any statements. He said that in the past three weeks when the FBI had talked to his wife, they were abusive and impolite; that they had frightened his wife and he considered their activities obnoxious. He stated that he wanted to contact a Mr. Abt, a New York lawyer whom he did not know but who had defended the Smith Act "victims" in 1949 or 1950 in connection with a conspiracy against the Government; that Abt would understand what this case was all about and that he would give him an excellent defense. He stated in returning a question about his former addresses that he lived at 4907 Magazine Street in New Orleans at one time and worked for the William Riley Company; that he was arrested in New Orleans for disturbing the peace and paid a $10 fine while he was demonstrating for the Fair Play for Cuba Committee; that he had a fight with some anti-Castro refugees and that they were released while he was fined.

Upon questioning by Captain Fritz, he said, "I have no views on the President." "My wife and I like the President's family. They are interesting people. I have my own views on the President's national policy. I have a right to express my views but because of the charges I do not think I should comment further." Oswald said "I am not a malcontent; nothing irritated me about the President." He said that during 1962 he was interviewed by the FBI and that he at that time refused to take a polygraph and that he did not intend to take a polygraph test for the Dallas police. At this time Captain Fritz showed a Selective Service Card that was taken out of his wallet which bore the name of Alex Hidell. Oswald refused to discuss this after being asked for an explanation of it, both by Fritz and by James Bookhout, the FBI Agent. I asked him if he viewed the parade and he said he had not. I then asked him if he had shot the President and he said he had not. I asked him if he had shot Governor Connally and he said he had not. He did not intend to answer further questions without counsel and that if he could not get Abt, then he would hope that the Civil Liberties Union would give him an attorney to represent him. At that point Captain Fritz terminated the interview at about 11:30 A.M., 11-23-63.

Thomas J. Kelley
Inspector

338

627

At about 12:35 P.M., November 23, 1963, Lee Oswald was interviewed in the office of Captain Will Fritz of the Homicide Division, Dallas Police Department. Among those present at this interview were Inspector Kelley, Captain Fritz, Detectives Senkel and Tiernon of the Homicide Division and SA James Bookout, FBI. Captain Fritz conducted the interview which was concerned mostly with Oswald's places of residence in Dallas and was an attempt to ascertain where the bulk of Oswald's belongings were located in Dallas. As a result of the interview, Oswald furnished information to Captain Fritz that most of his personal effects, including a sea bag, were in the garage at the address of Mrs. Paine, 2515 West 5th Street, Irving, Texas.

The interview was concluded about 1:10 P. M. and immediately thereafter members of the Homicide Division secured a search warrant and recovered Oswald's effects from the home of Mrs. Paine. Found among the effects were two different poses in snapshot type photographs taken of Oswald holding a rifle in one hand and holding up a copy of a paper called the Militant and "The Worker" in the other hand. Oswald was wearing a revolver in a holster on his right side. This photograph was enlarged by the Dallas Police Laboratories and was used as a basis of additional questioning of Oswald at approximately 6:00 P.M. that same evening.

On November 23, 1963, at 6:00 P.M., in the office of Captain Fritz, Homicide Division, Dallas Police Department, I was present at an interview with Oswald. Also present were Captain Fritz, FBI Agent Jim Bookhoutt, and four officers from the Homicide Division. This interview was conducted with Oswald for the purpose of displaying to him the blow-ups of photographs showing him holding a rifle and a pistol which were seized as a result of the search warrant for the garage of Mrs. Paine at 2515 West 5th Street, Irving, Texas. When the photographs were presented to Oswald, he sneered at them saying that they were fake photographs; that he had been photographed a number of times the day before by the police and apparently after they photographed him they superimposed on the photographs a rifle and put a gun in his pocket. He got into a long argument with Captain Fritz about his knowledge of photography and asked Fritz a number of times whether the smaller photograph was made from the larger or whether the larger photograph was made from the smaller. He said at the proper time he would show that the photographs were fakes. Fritz told him that the smaller photograph was taken from his effects at the garage. Oswald became arrogant and refused to answer any further questions concerning the photographs and would not identify the photographs as being a photograph of himself. Captain Fritz displayed great patience and tenacity in attempting to secure from Oswald the location of what apparently is the backyard of an address at which Oswald formerly lived, but it was apparent that Oswald, though slightly shaken by the evidence, had no intention of furnishing any information.

The interview was terminated at about 7:15 P.M.

338

Thomas J. Kelley
Inspector

U. S. Secret Service

Chief   November 29, 1963

Inspector Kelley

Preliminary Special Dallas Report # 3
Covers third interview with Oswald and
circumstances immediately following his murder

This interview started at approximately 9:30 AM on Sunday, November 24, 1963.
The interview was conducted in the office of Captain Will Fritz of the Homicide
Bureau, Dallas Police. Present at the interview in addition to Oswald were
Captain Fritz, Postal Inspector Holmes, SAIC Sorrels, Inspector Kelley and four
members of the Homicide Squad. The interview had just begun when I arrived and
Captain Fritz was again requesting Oswald to identify the place where the photograph of him holding the gun was taken. Captain Fritz indicated that it would
save the Police a great deal of time if he would tell them where the place was
located. Oswald refused to discuss the matter. Captain Fritz asked, "Are you
a Communist?" Oswald answered, "No, I am a Marxist but I am not a Marxist
Leninist". Captain Fritz asked him what the difference was and Oswald said it
would take too long to explain it to him. Oswald said that he became interested
in the Fair Play for Cuba Committee while he was in New Orleans; that he wrote
to the Committee's Headquarters in New York and received some Committee literature and a letter signed by Alex Hidell. He stated that he began to distribute
that literature in New Orleans and it was at that time that he got into an
altercation with a group and he was arrested. He said his opinions concerning
Fair Play for Cuba are well known; that he appeared on Bill Stukey's television
program in New Orleans on a number of occasions and was interviewed by the local
press often. He denies knowing or ever seeing Hidell in New Orleans, said he
believed in all of the tenets of the Fair Play for Cuba and the things which the
Fair Play for Cuba Committee stood for, which was free intercourse with Cuba and
freedom for tourists of the both countries to travel within each other's borders.

Among other things, Oswald said that Cuba should have full diplomatic relationship with the United States. I asked him if he thought that the President's
assassination would have any effect on the Fair Play for Cuba Committee. He said
there would be no change in the attitude of the American people toward Cuba with
President Johnson becoming President because they both belonged to the same
political party and the one would follow pretty generally the policies of the
other. He stated that he is an avid reader of Russian literature whether it is
communistic or not; that he subscribes to "The Militant", which, he says, is the
weekly of the Socialist party in the United States (it is a copy of "The Militant"
that Oswald is shown holding in the photograph taken from his effects at Irving
Street). At that time he asked me whether I was an FBI Agent and I said that I
was not that I was a member of the Secret Service. He said when he was standing
in front of the Textbook Building and about to leave it, a young crew-cut man
rushed up to him and said he was from the Secret Service, showed a book of
identification, and asked him where the phone was. Oswald said he pointed toward
the pay phone in the building and that he saw the man actually go to the phone
before he left.   177

I asked Oswald whether as a Marxist he believed that religion was an opiate of the people and he said very definitely so that all organized religions tend to become monopolistic and are the causes of a great deal of class warfare. I asked him whether he considered the Catholic Church to be an enemy of the Communist philosophy and he said well, there was no Catholicism in Russia; that the closest to it is the Orthodox Churches but he said he would not further discuss his opinions of religion since this was an attempt to have him say something which could be construed as being anti-religious or anti Catholic.

Capt. Fritz displayed an Enco street map of Dallas which had been found among Oswald's effect at the rooming house. Oswald was asked whether the map was his and whether he had put some marks on it. He said it was his and remarked "My God don't tell me there's a mark near where this thing happened". The mark was pointed out to him and he said "What about the other marks on the map?- I put a number of marks on it. I was looking for work and marked the places where I went for jobs or where I heard there were jobs".

Since it was obvious to Captain Fritz that Oswald was not going to be cooperative, he terminated the interview at that time.

I approached Oswald then and, out of the hearing of the others except perhaps one of Captain Fritz's men, said that as a Secret Service agent, we are anxious to talk with him as soon as he had secured counsel; that we were responsible for the safety of the President; that the Dallas Police had charged him with the assassination of the President but that he had denied it; we were therefore very anxious to talk with him to make certain that the correct story was developing as it related to the assassination. He said that he would be glad to discuss this proposition with his attorney and that after he talked to one, we could either discuss it with him or discuss it with his attorney, if the attorney thought it was the wise thing to do, but that at the present time he had nothing more to say to me. Oswald was then handed some different clothing to put on. The clothing included a sweater. Captain Fritz made a number of telephone calls to ascertain whether the preparations he had placed into effect for transferring the prisoner to the County Jail were ready and upon being so advised, Captain Fritz and members of the Detective Bureau escorted Oswald from the Homicide Office on the third floor to the basement where Oswald was shot by Jack Ruby.

On the completion of the interview, SAIC Sorrels and I proceeded to the office of the Chief of Police on the third floor and were discussing the interview when we heard that Oswald had been shot. We both ran down the steps to the basement. I arrived in the ante-room where they had dragged Oswald. SAIC Sorrels located and interviewed Ruby. Someone was bending over Oswald with a stethoscope and he appeared to be unconscious in very serious condition at that time. I asked Captain Fritz what had happened and he said Oswald had been shot by one Jack "Rubio" whom the police knew as a tavern operator. Shortly thereafter a stretcher arrived and I accompanied the stretcher to the ambulance which had been hastily backed into the garage. I observed that during the transfer that Oswald was unconscious; when the ambulance drove away from the building, I attempted to board a cruiser that apparently was going to follow the ambulance but I was unable to get into the car before it pulled away. Special Agents Warner and Patterson had heard of the shooting on their radio, proceeded to Parkland Hospital where Oswald was being taken and arrived very shortly after Oswald had arrived at the emergency entrance and was

177

being taken into the emergency treatment room. One or the other of these agents
was in close proximity to Oswald while he was being treated. When I arrived at
the hospital, I rode up on the elevator with Dr. Shaw who had looked at Oswald
as he had come in and was being recalled to the operating room where Oswald had
been taken. While Oswald was in the operating room, no one other than medical
personnel was present but a Dallas policeman who had accompanied Oswald in the
ambulance was standing in the doorway of the operating room in operating room
scrub clothes. No other investigating personnel were in the vicinity. In the
immediate vicinity of the detective was Special Agent Warner. Oswald made no
statements from the time he was shot until the time of his death. He was unconscious during the ambulance run to the hospital which I verified through
Detective Daugherty, who accompanied him. He did not regain consciousness at
any time during the treatment until he died. At the time of his death, myself,
Detective Daugherty and Colonel Garrison of the Texas State Police were on the
fifth floor of the hospital arranging a security room in which to take Oswald,
in the event he survived the operating room treatment. It was never necessary
to use this room and upon learning of his death, I proceeded to the morgue to
arrange for his family to view the body. When the family heard of the death
they were in the process of being interviewed by Special Agents Kunkel and Howard,
and requested to be brought to the hospital. Oswald's brother, Robert, who had
also come to the hospital, was being interviewed by Special Agent Houlett. Before
the post mortem was performed, Oswald's family, with the exception of Robert,
viewed the body. Robert arrived too late to view the body before the autopsy
had started and was not permitted by hospital authorities to view the body. The
family was accompanied during the viewing by the hospital chaplain.

After making arrangements through the chaplain and another clergyman for the
burial of the body, the family was returned to a secluded spot under the protection of Special Agents Kunkel and Howard, and the Irving Texas police. Precaution
was taken to insure their safety in view of the excitement caused by the killing
of Oswald. Special Agents Howard and Kunkel did an excellent job in handling the
security of this family detail and insuring their safety. Thereafter, I was
called by SAIC Bouck who advised me that the President and the Attorney General
were concerned about the safety of this family and instructed that all precautions
should be taken to insure that no harm befell them. SAIC Bouck was advised that
the family was presently under our protection; we would continue providing
protection until further notice.

Later that same day, I was contacted by SA Robertson of the FBI who asked whether
we had someone with the family. He was assured that we had. He requested to be
advised where the family had been taken. Since their ultimate destination was
unknown to me at the time, I assured him that when I learned of their whereabouts
I would relay it to him. He said that they received instructions from the Attorney
General and President Johnson that precaution should be taken to insure the family
safety.

As 11 pm, Sunday, November 24th, I was advised of the location of the family and
immediately notified Robertson and inquired whether they now wished to take over
their protection. He said no they had no such instructions, they merely wished to
be assured that someone was looking out for their safety. I assured them that

177

adequate protection was being provided and that they were available for interviews by the FBI. He stated that they did not wish to interview the family at this time; that they merely wanted to make sure they were in safe hands.

TJK:VS

177

REPORT OF U.S. POSTAL INSPECTOR H. D. HOLMES

Dallas, Texas

December 17, 1963

MEMORANDUM OF INTERVIEW

Informal memorandum furnished by Postal Inspector H. D. Holmes, Dallas, Texas, of an interview he took part in with Lee H. Oswald on Sunday morning, November 24, 1963, between the approximate hours of 9:25 a.m. to 11:10 a.m. Those present, in addition to Inspector Holmes, were Captain Will Fritz, Dallas Police, Forrest V. Sorrels, Local Agent in Charge, Secret Service, and Thomas J. Kelly, Inspector, Secret Service. In addition, there were three Detectives who were apparently assigned to guarding Oswald as none of them took part in the interrogation.

Oswald at no time appeared confused or in doubt as to whether or not he should answer a question. On the contrary, he was quite alert and showed no hesitancy in answering those questions which he wanted to answer, and was quite skillful in parrying those questions which he did not want to answer. I got the impression that he had disciplined his mind and reflexes to a state where I personally doubted if he would ever have confessed. He denied, emphatically, having taken part in or having had any knowledge of the shooting of the policeman Tippitt or of the President, stating that so far as he is concerned the reason he was in custody was because he "popped a policeman in the nose in a theater on Jefferson Avenue."

P. O. BOXES---He was questioned separately about the three boxes he had rented, and in each instance his answers were quick, direct and accurate as reflected on the box rental applications. He stated without prompting that he had rented Box 2915 at the Main Post Office for several months prior to his going to New Orleans, that this box was rented in his own name, Lee H. Oswald, and that he had taken out two keys to the box, and that when he had closed the box, he directed that his mail be forwarded to him at his street address in New Orleans.

He stated that no one received mail in this box other than himself, nor did he receive any mail under any other name than his own true name; that no one had access to the box other than himself nor did he permit anyone else to use this box. He stated it was possible that on rare occasions he may have handed one of the keys to his wife to go get his mail but certainly nobody else. He denied emphatically that he ever ordered a rifle under his name or any other name, nor permitted anyone else to order a rifle to be received in this box. Further, he denied that he had ever ordered any rifle by mail order or bought any money order for the purpose of paying for such a rifle. In fact, he claimed he owned no rifle and had not practiced or shot a rifle other than possibly a .22, small bore rifle, since his days with the Marine Corp. He stated that "How could I afford to order a rifle on my salary of $1.25 an hour when I can't hardly feed myself on what I make."

When asked if he had a post office box in New Orleans he stated that he did, for the reason that he subscribed to several publications, at least two of which were published in Russia, one being the hometown paper published in Minsk where he met and married his wife, and that he moved around so much that it was more practical to simply rent post office boxes and have his mail forwarded from one box to the next rather than going through the process of furnishing changes of address to the publishers. When asked if he permitted anyone other than himself to get mail in box 30061 at New Orleans, he stated that he did not. It will be recalled that on this box rent application he showed that both Marina Oswald and A. J. Hidell were listed under the caption "Persons entitled to receive mail through box". After denying that anyone else was permitted to get mail in the box, he was reminded that this application showed the name Marina Oswald as being entitled to receive mail in the box and he replied "well so what, she was my wife and I see nothing wrong with that, and it could very well be that I did place her name on the application". He was then reminded that the application also showed the name A. J. Hidell was also entitled to receive mail in the box, at which he simply shrugged his shoulders and stated "I don't recall anything about that".

He stated that when he came back to Dallas and after he had gone to work for the Texas School Book Depository, he had rented a box at the nearby Terminal Annex postal station, this being Box 6225, and that this box was also rented in his name, Lee H. Oswald. He stated he had only checked out one key for this box, which information was found to be accurate, and this key was found on his person at the time of his arrest. He professed not to recall the fact that he showed on the box rental application under name of corporation "Fair Play For Cuba Committee" and "American Civil Liberties Union". When asked as to why he showed these organizations on the application, he simply shrugged and said that he didn't recall showing them. When asked if he paid the box rental fee or did the organizations pay it, he stated that he paid it. In answer to another question, he also stated that no one had any knowledge that he had this box other than himself.

ORGANIZATIONS- MEMBERSHIP IN --- With respect to American Civil Liberties Union he was a little evasive stating something to the effect that he had made some effort to join but it was never made clear whether he had or had not been accepted. He stated that he first became interested in the Fair Play for Cuba Committee, after he went to New Orleans, that it started out as being a group of individuals who, like him, who thought and had like political opinions. They did decide to organize, and did organize after a fashion, but denied that they had any president or any elected officers. He stated that he, himself, could probably be considered the secretary since he wrote some letters on their behalf and attempted to collect dues which, if I recall, were $1.00 per month. He also stated that there was a "Fair Play for Cuba Committee" in New York which was better organized. He denied that he was sent to Dallas for the purpose of organizing such a cell in Dallas.

When asked if he was a communist, he stated emphatically not, that he was a Marxist. Someone asked the difference and he stated that a communist is a Lenin-Marxist, that he himself was a pure Marxist, and when someone asked the difference, he stated that it was a long story and if they didn't know, it would take too long to tell them. He stated further that he had read about everything written by or about Karl Marx.

When asked as to his religion, he stated that Karl Marx was his religion, and in response to further questioning he stated that some people may find the Bible interesting reading, but it was not for him, stating further that even as a philosophy there was not much to the Bible.

MARINE CORP SERVICE---Captain Fritz made some mention of his dishonorable discharge from the Marine Corp at which point he bristled noticeably, stating that he had been discharged with an "honorable" discharge and that this was later changed due to his having attempted to denounce his American Citizenship while he was living in Russia. He stated further that since his change of citizenship did not come to pass, he had written a letter to Mr. Connally, then Secretary of the Navy, and after considerable delay, received a very respectful reply wherein Connally stated he had resigned to run for Governor of Texas, and that his letter was being referred to the new Secretary, a Mr. Cork, Kurth, or something like that. He showed no particular animosity toward Mr. Connally while discussing this feature.

MAP---Captain Fritz advised him that among his effects in his room, there was found a map of the City of Dallas that had some marks on it and asked him to explain this map. Oswald said he presumed he had reference to an old City map which he had on which he had made some X's denoting location of firms that had advertised job vacancies. He stated that he had no transportation and either walked or rode a bus and that as he was constantly looking for work, in fact had registered for employment at the Texas Employment Bureau, and that as he would receive leads either from newspaper ads or from the Bureau or from neighbors, he would chart these places on the map to save time in his traveling. He said to the best of his recollection, most of them were out Industrial, presumably meaning Industrial Blvd. When asked as to why the X at the location of the Texas School Book Depository at Elm and Houston, he stated that "Well, I interviewed there for a job, in fact, got the job, therefore the X".

When asked as to how he learned about this vacancy, he stated that "Oh, it was general information in the neighborhood, I don't recall just who told me about it, but I learned it from people in Mrs. Paynes' neighborhood" and that all the people around there were looking out for possible employment for him.

ACTIVITY JUST PRIOR TO AND IMMEDIATELY FOLLOWING ASSASSINATION ATTEMPT---To an inquiry as to why he went to visit his wife on Thursday night, November 21, whereas he normally visited her over the weekend, he stated that on this particular weekend he had learned that his wife and Mrs. Payne were giving a party for the children and that they were having in a "houseful" of neighborhood children and that he just didn't want to be around at such a time. Therefore, he made his weekly visit on Thursday night.

When asked if he didn't bring a sack with him the next morning to work, he
stated that he did, and when asked as to the contents of the sack, he stated
that it contained his lunch. Then, when asked as to the size or shape of the
sack, he said "Oh, I don't recall, it may have a small sack or a large sack,
you don't always find one that just fits your sandwiches." When asked as to
where he placed the sack when he got in the car, he said in his lap, or possibly
the front seat beside him, as he always did because he didn't want to get it
crushed. He denied that he placed any package in the back seat. When advised
that the driver stated that he had brought out a long parcel and placed it in
the back seat, he stated "Oh, he must be mistaken or else thinking about some
other time when he picked me up."

When asked as to his whereabouts at the time of the shooting, he stated that
when lunch time came, and he didn't say which floor he was on, he said one of
the Negro employees invited him to eat lunch with him and he stated "You go
on down and send the elevator back up and I will join you in a few minutes."
Before he could finish whatever he was doing, he stated, the commotion
surrounding the assassination took place and when he went down stairs, a policeman questioned him as to his identification and his boss stated that "he is one
of our employees" whereupon the policeman had him step aside momentarily.
Following this, he simply walked out the front door of the building. I don't
recall that anyone asked why he left or where or how he went. I just presumed
that this had been covered in an earlier questioning.

A. J. HIDELL IDENTIFICATION CARD---Captain Fritz asked him if he knew anyone
by the name of A. J. Hidell and he denied that he did. When asked if he had
ever used this name as an alias, he also made a denial. In fact, he stated
that he had never used the name, didn't know anyone by this name, and never
had heard of the name before. Captain Fritz then asked him about the I.D.
card he had in his pocket bearing such a name and he flared up and stated
"I've told you all I'm going to about that card. You took notes, just read
them for yourself, if you want to refresh your memory." He told Captain Fritz
that "You have the card. Now you know as much about it as I do."
****

About 11:00 a.m. or a few minutes thereafter, someone handed through the door
several hangers on which there were some trousers, shirts, and a couple of
sweaters. When asked if he wanted to change any of his clothes before being
transferred to the County jail, he said "Just give me one of those sweaters."
He didn't like the one they handed him and insisted on putting on a black
slip-over sweater that had some jagged holes in it near the front of the right
shoulder. One cuff was released while he slipped this over the head, following
which he was again cuffed. During this change of clothing, Chief of Police
Curry came into the room and discussed something in an inaudible undertone with
Captain Fritz, apparently for the purpose of not letting Oswald hear what was
being said. I have no idea what this conversation was, but just presume they
were discussing the transfer of the prisoner. I did not go downstairs to
witness the further transfer of the prisoner.

H. D. HOLMES
Postal Inspector
Dallas 22, Texas

Speculations and Rumors

Myths have traditionally surrounded the dramatic assassinations of history. The rumors and theories about the assassination of Abraham Lincoln that are still being publicized were for the most part first bruited within months of his death. Wherever there is any element of mystery in such dramatic events misconceptions often result from sensational speculations.

Lacking the testimony of Lee Harvey Oswald, it has been necessary to reconstruct painstakingly all of the facts that led the Commission to the conclusion that Oswald assassinated President Kennedy, acting alone and without advice or assistance. The Commission has found no credible evidence that he was a member of a foreign or domestic conspiracy of any kind. Nor was there any evidence that he was involved with any criminal or underworld elements or that he had any association with his slayer, Jack Ruby, except as his victim. The evidence on these issues has been set forth in great detail in this report.

In addition the Commission has inquired into the various hypotheses, rumors, and speculations that have arisen from the tragic developments of November 22–24, 1963. It is recognized that the public judgment of these events has been influenced, at least to some extent, by these conjectures.

Many questions have been raised about the facts out of genuine puzzlement or because of misinformation which attended some of the early reporting of the fast-crowding events of these 3 days. Most of the speculation and attempted reconstruction of these events by the public centered on these basic questions: Was Lee Harvey Oswald really the assassin of the President; why did he do it; did he have any accomplices; and why did Ruby shoot Oswald? Many of the theories and hypotheses advanced have rested on premises which the Commission feels deserve critical examination.

Many people who witnessed the assassination and the killing of Oswald or were present in the area were a major source of diverse and often contradictory information. As is easily understood under such circumstances, all of the witnesses did not see and hear the same thing or interpret what they saw and heard the same way and many changed their stories as they repeated them. Moreover, they were interviewed at different times after the event by different people and often under circumstances which made accurate reporting extremely difficult.

Even the occupants of the cars in the Presidential motorcade were not entirely in agreement in their accounts because they, too, saw and heard what happened from different positions. Moreover, those closest to the assassination were subjected to a physical and emotional strain that tended to affect their recollections of what they thought they saw or heard. Consequently, the presentation of the news from Dallas included much misinformation. This, to some extent, was unavoidable, but the widespread and repetitive dissemination of every scrap of information about the President's assassination and its aftermath has helped to build up a large number of erroneous conclusions. The manner in which local authorities released information about the investigation, sometimes before it could be verified in all detail, has further contributed to the fund of ill-founded theories. Typographical mistakes in the press and failure to transcribe sound accurately from tapes resulted in errors, some of which have remained uncorrected in print at the time of the publication of this report.

Much of the speculation that has persisted in one form or another since November 22–24 came from people who usually spoke in good faith. Some of the errors have resulted simply from a lack of complete knowledge at the time of the event. In this category are the statements attributed to doctors at Parkland Memorial Hospital who attended the dying President and described his wounds to the press afterward. It remained for the autopsy in Washington, completed early the next morning, to ascertain the full facts concerning the wounds. The correction of earlier assertions of fact on the basis of later and fuller analysis or investigation is a normal part of the process of accumulation of evidence. But it is not often that the process is conducted in such an intense glare of worldwide publicity, and later corrections have difficulty overtaking the original sensational reports.

There is still another category of speculation and rumor that complicated and broadened the work of the Commission. Numerous people claimed to have seen Oswald or Ruby at various times and places in the United States or abroad. Others insisted that during the days following the assassination, they had detected significant actions on television that were witnessed by no one else. Still others assumed from a widely published picture that Oswald was standing on the steps of the entrance to the Texas School Book Depository at the time the President was shot. Throughout the country people reported overheard remarks, conversations, threats, prophesies, and opinions that seemed to them to have a possible bearing on the assassination. More than a few informants initially told their speculations or professed firsthand information to newspaper and television reporters. Later, many of them changed or retracted their stories in telling them to official investigators.

The U.S. investigative agencies expended much valuable time and effort inquiring into these leads. Investigations of a vast number of rumors and speculations reached into almost every part of the United States and to most of the other continents of the world.

The Commission's work was also handicapped by those witnesses and other persons connected with the investigation who sold for publication evidence pertinent to the investigation. These persons sold pictures and documents and even recollections, sometimes before the

Commission had an opportunity to receive their evidence. Some of the evidence thus published was changed from its original form and gave misleading impressions to the public. The piecemeal release of this evidence, sometimes in distorted or exaggerated form, and often out of context, provided the basis for new speculations and rumors or served to reinforce already current ones. The practice was frequently harmful to the work of the Commission and a disservice to the public.

This appendix is intended to clarify the most widespread factual misunderstandings. False or inaccurate speculations concerning the assassination and related events are set forth below together with brief summary statements of what the Commission has found to be the true facts. The citation following each Commission finding is either to that portion of the report in which the subject is discussed more fully, to the evidence in the record supporting the finding, or to both. For complete answers to these speculations, the sources cited in the footnotes should be consulted. The speculations are considered under the following headings:

1. The source of the shots.
2. The identity of the assassin.
3. Oswald's movements between 12:33 and 1:15 p.m. on November 22, 1963.
4. The murder of Patrolman Tippit.
5. Oswald after his arrest.
6. Oswald in the Soviet Union.
7. Oswald's trip to Mexico City.
8. Oswald and U.S. Government agencies.
9. Conspiratorial relationships.
10. Miscellaneous charges.

THE SOURCE OF THE SHOTS

There have been speculations that some or all of the shots aimed at President Kennedy and Governor Connally came from the railroad overpass as the Presidential automobile approached it, or from somewhere other than the Texas School Book Depository Building. Related speculations maintain that the shots came from both the railroad overpass and the Texas School Book Depository Building. These are supported by a number of assertions that have been carefully examined by the Commission in the course of its investigation and rejected as being without foundation. They are set forth below, together with the results of the Commission's investigation.

Speculation.—The shots that killed the President came from the railroad overpass above the triple underpass.

Commission finding.—The shots that entered the neck and head of the President and wounded Governor Connally came from behind and above. There is no evidence that any shots were fired at the President from anywhere other than the Texas School Book Depository Building.[1]

Speculation.—The railroad overpass was left unguarded on November 22.

Commission finding.—On November 22 the railroad overpass was guarded by two Dallas policemen, Patrolmen J. W. Foster and J. C. White, who have testified that they permitted only railroad personnel on the overpass.[2]

Speculation.—There are witnesses who alleged that the shots came from the overpass.

Commission finding.—The Commission does not have knowledge of any witnesses who saw shots fired from the overpass. Statements or depositions from the 2 policemen and 13 railroad employees who were on the overpass all affirm that no shots were fired from the overpass. Most of these witnesses who discussed the source of the shots stated that they came from the direction of Elm and Houston Streets.[3]

Speculation.—A rifle cartridge was recovered on the overpass.

Commission finding.—No cartridge of any kind was found on the overpass nor has any witness come forward to claim having found one.[4]

Speculation.—A witness to the assassination said that she saw a man run behind the concrete wall of the overpass and disappear.

Commission finding.—Mrs. Jean L. Hill stated that after the firing stopped she saw a white man wearing a brown overcoat and a hat running west away from the Depository Building in the direction of the railroad tracks. There are no other witnesses who claim to have seen a man running toward the railroad tracks. Examination of all available films of the area following the shooting, reexamination of interviews with individuals in the vicinity of the shooting, and interviews with members of the Dallas Police Department and the Dallas County sheriff's office failed to corroborate Mrs. Hill's recollection or to reveal the identity of the man described by Mrs. Hill.[5]

Speculation.—Immediately after the shooting a motorcycle policeman was seen racing up the grassy embankment to the right of the shooting scene pursuing a couple seeking to flee from the overpass.

Commission finding.—There are no witnesses who have ever stated this and there is no evidence to support the claim. A motorcycle policeman, Clyde A. Haygood, dismounted in the street and ran up the incline. He stated that he saw no one running from the railroad yards adjacent to the overpass. Subsequently, at 12:37 p.m., Haygood reported that the shots had come from the Texas School Book Depository Building.[6]

Speculation.—More than three shots, perhaps as many as five or six, were fired at the President and Governor Connally.

Commission finding.—The weight of the evidence indicates that three shots were fired, of which two struck President Kennedy. There is persuasive evidence from the experts that one of these two bullets also struck Governor Connally. Some witnesses claimed that they heard more than three shots but, as fully described in chapter III, the great majority heard only three shots.[7]

Speculation.—At least four or five bullets have been found.

Commission finding.—After the assassination, metal remains of bullets were recovered. These included an almost whole bullet of 158.6 grains, fragments weighing 44.6 grains and 21.0 grains, and other fragments too small to be identified. These metal remains indicate that at least two shots were fired. The Commission believes that three shots were fired.[8]

Speculation.—A bullet was found on the stretcher used for President Kennedy at Parkland Hospital.

Commission finding.—No bullet was found on the stretcher used by President Kennedy. An almost whole bullet was found when it rolled off the stretcher used by Governor Connally.[9]

Speculation.—A bullet was found in the grass near the scene of the assassination shortly afterward by a deputy sheriff of Dallas County, E. R. Walthers.

Commission finding.—Walthers has denied that he found a bullet at any time or that he told anyone that he had found one. With another deputy sheriff he made a diligent search for such a bullet 2 or 3 days after the assassination.[10]

Speculation.—The Presidential car stopped momentarily or almost came to a complete halt after the first shot. This is evidence that the driver had the impression that the first shot came from the front and therefore hesitated to drive closer to the overpass.

Commission finding.—The Presidential car did not stop or almost come to a complete halt after the firing of the first shot or any other shots. The driver, Special Agent William R. Greer, has testified that he accelerated the car after what was probably the second shot. Motion pictures of the scene show that the car slowed down momentarily after the shot that struck the President in the head and then speeded up rapidly.[11]

Speculation.—The Presidential car had a small round bullet hole in the front windshield. This is evidence that a shot or shots were fired at the President from the front of the car.

Commission finding.—The windshield was not penetrated by any bullet. A small residue of lead was found on the inside surface of the windshield; on the outside of the windshield was a very small pattern of cracks immediately in front of the lead residue on the inside. The bullet from which this lead residue came was probably one of those that struck the President and therefore came from overhead and to the rear. Experts established that the abrasion in the windshield came from impact on the inside of the glass.[12]

Speculation.—The throat wound sustained by the President was the result of a shot fired from the front according to doctors at Parkland Hospital.

Commission finding.—Doctors at Parkland Hospital originally believed that the throat wound could have been either an entry or exit wound, but they made no examination to determine entry and exit wounds. Subsequently, when the evidence of the autopsy became available, the doctors at Parkland agreed that it was an exit wound.[13]

Speculation.—It is inconceivable that the doctors at Parkland Hospital did not turn the President over on his face and notice the bullet hole in the back of his neck.

Commission finding.—Doctors at Parkland Hospital have testified that the President remained on his back while he was at Parkland Hospital for treatment and that they did not turn him over at any time; they were busy trying to save his life. Consequently, they were never aware of the hole in the back of his neck until they were notified of it later.[14]

Speculation.—The first shot struck the President in the throat as the car was proceeding along Houston Street toward the Texas School Book Depository. The car then made a left turn on to Elm Street and proceeded for some distance before additional shots were fired at the President.

Commission finding.—Before the autopsy findings made it clear that the shots were fired from the rear, there was speculation that the first shot may have been fired before the Presidential car turned on to Elm Street. As this report demonstrates, all of the shots that struck the President were fired from the rear and in a time period inconsistent with the theory that the first shot struck him while his car was coming down Houston Street. Motion pictures taken at the time show that the first shot struck the President after the car had turned onto Elm Street and was proceeding away from the Depository.[15]

THE ASSASSIN

Speculations tending to support the theory that Oswald could not have assassinated President Kennedy are based on a wide variety of assertions. Among these are statements that Oswald could not have been acquainted with the motorcade route before he came to work on November 22, that he may well have carried curtain rods rather than a rifle in a brown paper package he brought with him, that there may have been other people in the building who could have fired the rifle, that Oswald could not have fired the shots in the time available to him, that he was not a good enough marksman to have scored the hits with the rifle, that there were other people in the lunchroom of the Depository Building when he was confronted by Patrolman M. L. Baker, and that there are no eyewitnesses who could identify Oswald as having been in the window. Each of these speculations is dealt with below in the light of the testimony and evidence considered by the Commission.

Speculation.—Oswald could not have known the motorcade route before he arrived at work on November 22.

Commission finding.—The motorcade route was published in both Dallas papers on November 19 and was therefore available at least 72 hours before Oswald reported for work on November 22.[16]

Speculation.—The route as shown in the newspaper took the motorcade through the Triple Underpass via Main Street, a block away from the Depository. Therefore, Oswald could not have known that the motorcade would pass directly by the Texas School Book Depository Building.

Commission finding.—The motorcade route as published showed the motorcade turning right off Main Street onto Houston for one block and then left on Elm to the access road to the Stemmons Freeway. This route was clearly indicated in published descriptions and maps of the motorcade route. There was no mention of continuing on Main Street through the Triple Underpass.[17]

Speculation.—The motorcade route was changed on November 22 after the map had been printed. The motorcade was shifted from Main Street over to Elm Street to bring it by the Texas School Book Depository Building.

Commission finding.—The motorcade route was decided upon on November 18 and published in the Dallas newspapers on November 19. It was not changed in any way thereafter. The route called for the motorcade to turn off Main Street at Houston, go up to Elm, and then turn left on Elm Street.[18]

Speculation.—The normal and logical route would have been straight down Main Street through the Triple Underpass to the Stemmons Freeway. It is possible to drive from Main onto the access road to the Stemmons Freeway from a point beyond the underpass.

Commission finding.—The normal, direct, and only permissible route to the Stemmons Freeway from Main Street is via Houston and Elm Streets. Any attempt to turn onto the access road to the Stemmons Freeway from Main Street beyond the Triple Underpass would have been extremely difficult because of a concrete strip dividing Elm and Main Streets. Such an attempt would have required making an S-turn beyond the strip at a very tight angle, thereby slowing the Presidential car almost to a stop.[19]

Speculation.—Oswald may well have carried curtain rods to work on November 22 in the brown paper package he was observed to bring into the building because he lived in a room where he needed them.

Commission finding.—According to Oswald's landlady at 1026 North Beckley Avenue, Mrs. A. C. Johnson, the room had venetian blinds, curtain rods, and curtains while Oswald was living there. The curtain rods in the Paine garage that belonged to Mrs. Paine were still there after Oswald went to work on November 22. Mrs. Paine and Marina Oswald testified that Oswald had not spoken to them about curtain rods. After the assassination the empty package was found near the window from which the shots were fired, but no curtain rods were found.[20]

Speculation.—Oswald spent the morning of November 22 in the company of other workers in the building and remained with them until they went downstairs to watch the President go by, no later probably than 12:15.

Commission finding.—Oswald did not spend the morning in the company of other workers in the building, and before the assassination he was last seen in the building on the sixth floor at about 11:55 a.m. by Charles Givens, another employee.[21]

Speculation.—It is probable that the chicken lunch, remains of which were found on the sixth floor, was eaten by an accomplice of Oswald who had hidden on the sixth floor overnight.

Commission finding.—The chicken lunch had been eaten shortly after noon on November 22 by Bonnie Ray Williams, an employee of the Texas School Book Depository, who after eating his lunch went to the fifth floor where he was when the shots were fired. Oswald did not eat the chicken lunch, nor did he drink from the soft drink bottle found near the chicken lunch.[22]

Speculation.—Laboratory tests showed remains of the chicken lunch found on the sixth floor were 2 days old.

Commission finding.—The chicken lunch remains had been left there shortly after noon on November 22 by Bonnie Ray Williams.[23]

Speculation.—An amateur 8-millimeter photograph taken at 12:20 p.m., 10 minutes before the assassination of President Kennedy, showed two silhouettes at the sixth-floor window of the Depository.

Commission finding.—A film taken by an amateur photographer, Robert J. E. Hughes, just before the assassination, shows a shadow in the southeast corner window of the sixth floor. This has been determined after examination by the FBI and the U.S. Navy Photographic Interpretation Center to be the shadow from the cartons near the window.[24]

Speculation.—A picture published widely in newspapers and magazines after the assassination showed Lee Harvey Oswald standing on the front steps of the Texas School Book Depository Building shortly before the President's motorcade passed by.

Commission finding.—The man on the front steps of the building, thought or alleged by some to be Lee Harvey Oswald, is actually Billy Lovelady, an employee of the Texas School Book Depository, who somewhat resembles Oswald. Lovelady has identified himself in the picture, and other employees of the Depository standing with him, as shown in the picture, have verified that he was the man in the picture and that Oswald was not there.[25]

Speculation.—The post office box in Dallas to which Oswald had the rifle mailed was kept under both his name and that of A. Hidell.

Commission finding.—It is not known whether Oswald's application listed the name A. Hidell as one entitled to receive mail at the box. In accordance with U.S. Post Office regulations, the portion of the application listing the names of persons other than the applicant entitled to receive mail was discarded after the box was closed on May 14, 1963. During the summer of 1963, Oswald rented a post office box in New Orleans, listing the name "Hidell" in addition to his own name and that of his wife. Hidell was a favorite alias used by Oswald on a number of occasions. Diligent search has failed to reveal any person in Dallas or New Orleans by that name. It was merely a creation for his own purposes.[26]

Speculation.—The President's car was going at a speed estimated at from 12 to 20 miles per hour, thus presenting a target comparable to the most difficult that a soldier would encounter under battlefield conditions.

Commission finding.—During the period between the time that the first and second shots struck the President, the Presidential car was traveling at an average speed of approximately 11.2 miles per hour. Expert witnesses testified that the target is regarded as a favorable one because the car was going away from the marksman in a straight line.[27]

Speculation.—Oswald could not have fired three shots from the Mannlicher-Carcano rifle in 5½ seconds.

Commission finding.—According to expert witnesses, exacting tests conducted for the Commission demonstrated that it was possible to fire three shots from the rifle within 5½ seconds. It should be noted that the first loaded shell was already in the chamber ready for firing; Oswald had only to pull the trigger to fire the first shot and to work the bolt twice in order to fire the second and third shots. They testified that if the second shot missed, Oswald had between 4.8 and 5.6 seconds to fire the three shots. If either the first or third shot missed, Oswald had in excess of 7 seconds to fire the three shots.[28]

Speculation.—Oswald did not have the marksmanship ability demonstrated by the rifleman who fired the shots.

Commission finding.—Oswald qualified as a sharpshooter and a marksman with the M–1 rifle in the Marine Corps. Marina Oswald testified that in New Orleans her husband practiced operating the bolt of the rifle. Moreover, experts stated that the scope was a substantial aid for rapid, accurate firing. The Commission concluded that Oswald had the capability with a rifle to commit assassination.[29]

Speculation.—The name of the rifle used in the assassination appeared on the rifle. Therefore, the searchers who found the rifle on the sixth floor of the Texas School Book Depository should have been able to identify it correctly by name.

Commission finding.—An examination of the rifle does not reveal any manufacturer's name. An inscription on the rifle shows that it was made in Italy. The rifle was identified by Captain Fritz and Lieutenant Day, who were the first to actually handle it.[30]

Speculation.—The rifle found on the sixth floor of the Texas School Book Depository was identified as a 7.65 Mauser by the man who found it, Deputy Constable Seymour Weitzman.

Commission finding.—Weitzman, the original source of the speculation that the rifle was a Mauser, and Deputy Sheriff Eugene Boone found the weapon. Weitzman did not handle the rifle and did not examine it at close range. He had little more than a glimpse of it and thought it was a Mauser, a German bolt-type rifle similar in appearance to the Mannlicher-Carcano. Police laboratory technicians subsequently arrived and correctly identified the weapon as a 6.5 Italian rifle.[31]

Speculation.—There is evidence that a second rifle was discovered on the roof of the Texas School Book Depository or on the overpass.

Commission finding.—No second rifle was found in either of these places or in any other place. The shots that struck President Kennedy and Governor Connally came from the rifle found on the sixth floor of the Texas School Book Depository.[32]

Speculation.—It is possible that there was a second Mannlicher-Carcano rifle involved in the assassination. The Irving Sports Shop mounted a scope on a rifle 3 weeks before the assassination.

Commission finding.—Dial D. Ryder, an employee of the Irving Sports Shop, has stated that he found on his workbench on November 23 an undated work tag with the name "Oswald" on it, indicating that sometime during the first 2 weeks of November three holes had been bored in a rifle and a telescopic sight mounted on it and bore-sighted. However, Ryder and his employer, Charles W. Greener, had no recollection of Oswald, of his Mannlicher-Carcano rifle, of the transaction allegedly represented by the repair tag, or of any person for whom such a repair was supposedly made. The rifle found on the sixth floor of the Texas School Book Depository had two holes in it bored for the installation of a scope prior to shipment to Oswald in March 1963. The Commission concluded that it is doubtful whether the tag produced by Ryder was authentic. All of the evidence developed proves that Oswald owned only the one rifle—the Mannlicher-Carcano—and that he did not bring it or a second rifle to the Irving Sports Shop.[33]

Speculation.—Ammunition for the rifle found on the sixth floor of the Texas School Book Depository had not been manufactured since the end of World War II. The ammunition used by Oswald must, therefore, have been at least 20 years old, making it extremely unreliable.

Commission finding.—The ammunition used in the rifle was American ammunition recently made by the Western Cartridge Co., which manufactures such ammunition currently. In tests with the same kind of ammunition, experts fired Oswald's Mannlicher-Carcano rifle more than 100 times without any misfires.[34]

Speculation.—The assertion that Oswald's palmprint appeared on the rifle is false. The FBI told newsmen in an off-the-record briefing session that there was no palmprint on the rifle.

Commission finding.—The FBI confirmed that the palmprint lifted by the Dallas police from the rifle found on the sixth floor of the Texas School Book Depository Building was Oswald's palmprint. The FBI informed the Commission that no FBI agent made statements of any type to the press concerning the existence or nonexistence of this print.[35]

Speculation.—If Oswald had been gloveless, he would have left fingerprints on the rifle because he would not have had time to wipe the prints off the rifle after he had fired it.

Commission finding.—An FBI fingerprint expert testified that the poor quality of the metal and wooden parts would cause them to absorb moisture from the skin, thereby making a clear print unlikely. There is no evidence that Oswald wore gloves or that he wiped prints off the rifle. Latent fingerprints were found on the rifle but they were too incomplete to be identified.[36]

Speculation.—Gordon Shanklin, the special agent in charge of the Dallas office of the FBI, stated that the paraffin test of Oswald's face and hands was positive and proved that he had fired a rifle.

Commission finding.—The paraffin tests were conducted by members of the Dallas Police Department and the technical examinations by members of the Dallas City-County Criminal Investigation Laboratory. The FBI has notified the Commission that neither Shanklin nor any other representative of the FBI ever made such a statement. The Commission has found no evidence that Special Agent Shanklin ever made this statement publicly.[37]

Speculation.—Marina Oswald stated that she did not know that her husband owned a rifle nor did she know that he owned a pistol.

Commission finding.—There is no evidence that Marina Oswald ever told this to any authorities. On the afternoon of November 22, she told the police that her husband owned a rifle and that he kept it in the garage of the Paine house in Irving. Later, at Dallas police headquarters, she said that she could not identify as her husband's the rifle shown her by policemen. When Marina Oswald appeared before the Commission she was shown the Mannlicher-Carcano 6.5 rifle found on the sixth floor of the Depository and identified it as the "fateful rifle of Lee Oswald." [38]

Speculation.—The picture of Oswald taken by his wife in March or April 1963 and showing him with a rifle and a pistol was "doctored" when it appeared in magazines and newspapers in February 1964. The rifle held by Oswald in these pictures is not the same rifle that was found on the sixth floor of the Texas School Book Depository Building.

Commission finding.—Life magazine, Newsweek, and the New York Times notified the Commission that they had retouched this picture. In doing so, they inadvertently altered details of the configuration of the rifle. The original prints of this picture have been examined by the Commission and by photographic experts who have identified the rifle as a Mannlicher-Carcano 6.5, the same kind as the one found on the sixth floor of the Texas School Book Depository. FBI experts testified that the picture was taken with Oswald's camera.[39]

Speculation.—The rifle picture of Oswald was a composite one with Oswald's face pasted on somebody else's body.

Commission finding.—Marina Oswald has testified that she took this picture with a camera owned by her husband and subsequently identified as Oswald's Imperial Reflex camera. She identified the man in the picture as her husband. Experts also state the picture was not a composite.[40]

Speculation.—After firing the shots, Oswald could not have disposed of the rifle and descended the stairs to the lunchroom in time to get a drink from a soft drink machine and be there when Patrolman Baker came in.

Commission finding.—A series of time tests made by investigators and by Roy S. Truly and Patrolman M. L. Baker at the request of the Commission, show that it was possible for Oswald to have placed the rifle behind a box and descended to the lunchroom on the second floor before Patrolman Baker and Truly got up there. Oswald did not have a soft drink bottle in his hand at the time he was confronted by Baker and he was not standing by the soft drink machine. He was just entering the lunchroom; Baker caught a glimpse of him through the glass panel in the door leading to the lunchroom vestibule.[41]

Speculation.—There were other people present in the lunchroom at the time that Baker and Truly saw Oswald there.

Commission finding.—Baker and Truly have both stated that there was no one in the lunchroom other than Oswald at the time that they entered. No other witness to this incident has been found.[42]

Speculation.—Police were sealing off all exits from the building by the time Oswald got to the second floor.

Commission finding.—Police may have begun to take up positions at the exits to the building as early as 12:33, but it is unlikely that they had blocked them off completely until 12:37 p.m. at the earliest. Oswald was seen in an office, walking toward an exit leading to the front stairway, at about 12:33 p.m. Oswald probably had at least 7 minutes in which to get out of the building without being stopped.[43]

OSWALD'S MOVEMENTS BETWEEN 12:33 AND 1:15 P.M.

One of the major theses urged in support of the theory that Oswald did not murder Patrolman Tippit was that his known movements after he left the Texas School Book Depository would not have permitted him to have arrived at 10th Street and Patton Avenue in time to encounter Tippit by 1:16 p.m. Careful reenactments by investigative agencies and by members of the Commission staff of Oswald's movements from the time he left the Texas School Book Depository until he encountered Tippit verified that Oswald could reach his roominghouse at 1026 North Beckley Avenue at approximately 1 p.m. or earlier. The housekeeper at the roominghouse testified that Oswald spent only a few minutes at the house, leaving as hurriedly as he had arrived. During police interrogation after his arrest, Oswald admitted to riding both bus and taxi in returning to his roominghouse after the assassination of the President. From 1026 North Beckley Avenue, Oswald could easily have walked the nine tenths of a mile to 10th Street and Patton Avenue where he encountered Tippit.

Speculation.—A detailed and remarkably clear description of Oswald was sent over the police radio in Dallas at 12:36 p.m., November 22, 1963.

Commission finding.—The radio logs of the Dallas Police Department and the Dallas County Sheriff's Office show that no description of a suspect in the assassination of the President was broadcast before 12:45 p.m. on that day. No reference to Oswald by name was broadcast before he was arrested. The description of the suspect that was broadcast was similar to that of Oswald, but it lacked some important specific details such as color of hair and eyes. The information for the initial broadcasts most probably came from Howard Brennan, who saw Oswald in the window when he was firing the rifle.[44]

Speculation.—Oswald did not have time for all of the movements imputed to him between his departure from the Texas School Book Depository and his encounter with Tippit.

Commission finding.—Time tests of all of Oswald's movements establish that these movements could have been accomplished in the time available to him.[45]

Speculation.—Oswald was stopped by police as he left the building and was permitted to pass after he told them he worked in the building.

Commission finding.—The Commission has found no witness who saw Oswald leave the building. This speculation is probably a misinterpretation of the fact that he was stopped in the lunchroom by Patrolman Baker before he left the building and was allowed to proceed after Truly, the Depository superintendent, identified him as an employee there. Police did not seal off the building until at least several minutes after Oswald could have left.[46]

Speculation.—The log of the cabdriver who took Oswald to North Beckley Avenue, William W. Whaley, shows that Oswald entered his cab at 12:30 p.m. Since this occurred at some distance from the point of the President's assassination, Oswald could not have shot the President.

Commission finding.—Whaley's log does show 12:30 p.m., but he has testified that he was not accurate in logging the time that passengers entered his cab, that he usually logged them at 15-minute intervals, and that it was undoubtedly some time later than 12:30 when Oswald entered his cab. Sometimes he did not make entries in his logbook until three or four trips later. The bus transfer in Oswald's possession was issued after 12:36 p.m. The Commission has determined that Oswald probably entered Whaley's cab at about 12:47 or 12:48 p.m.[47]

Speculation.—The distance from the Greyhound terminal in Dallas, where Oswald entered the cab, to North Beckley Avenue, where he probably left the cab, is something over 3 miles—normally a 10-minute cab drive. Given the traffic jam that existed at the time, it is doubtful that Whaley could have made the trip in less than 15 minutes. One estimate has placed the time at 24 minutes from the Greyhound terminal to Oswald's roominghouse.

Commission finding.—The distance from the Greyhound bus terminal at Jackson and Lamar Streets to the 500 block of North Beckley

is 2.5 miles. Oswald actually got out in the 700 block of North Beckley. The distance was, therefore, less than 2.5 miles. Whaley has
testified to the Commission that the trip took 6 minutes. Test runs
made by members of the Commission staff under traffic conditions
somewhat similar to those that existed on November 22, took approximately 5 minutes and 30 seconds. To walk from Beckley and Neely,
which is the 700 block of Beckley, where Oswald probably left the cab,
to 1026 North Beckley, took Commission staff members 5 minutes and
45 seconds.[48]

Speculation.—Oswald was on his way to Jack Ruby's apartment
when he was stopped by Patrolman Tippit.

Commission finding.—There is no evidence that Oswald and Ruby
knew each other or had any relationship through a third party or
parties. There is no evidence that Oswald knew where Ruby lived.
Accordingly, there is neither evidence nor reason to believe that
Oswald was on his way to Ruby's apartment when he was stopped by
Tippit.[49]

MURDER OF TIPPIT

Speculations on the murder of Tippit centered about assertions that
he was elsewhere than he was supposed to be when he was shot, that
he knew the man who shot him, and that the description of the
murderer given by one of the eyewitnesses did not fit Oswald's description.

The Commission found that Tippit was unquestionably patrolling
in an area to which he had been directed by police headquarters.
There was no evidence to support the speculation that Tippit and
Oswald knew each other or had ever seen each other before. The
description of the murderer imputed to one of the witnesses was denied
by her and had no support from any other eyewitness.

Speculation.—Tippit was driving alone in his police car even
though standing orders for police in Dallas were that radio cars of
the type Tippit was driving must have two policemen in them.

Commission finding.—Dallas police officials stated that department
policy required about 80 percent of the patrolmen on the day shift,
7 a.m. to 3 p.m., to work alone. Tippit was one of the patrolmen assigned to work alone that day.[50]

Speculation.—Tippit was violating an order he had received the day
before not to leave the sector to which he had been assigned. This
sector was supposed to be in downtown Dallas at the time he stopped
Oswald.

Commission finding.—A review of Tippit's file in the Dallas Police
Department and the department's radio log revealed that following
the shooting of the President, Tippit was directed to move into and
remain in the central Oak Cliff area available for any emergency.[51]

Speculation.—The police had been withdrawn from the area in
which Tippit found Oswald.

Commission finding.—Other police cars were operating in the Oak Cliff area at the same time as Tippit. They participated in the subsequent search for and apprehension of Tippit's slayer.[52]

Speculation.—Tippit violated a procedure governing radio cars when he failed to notify headquarters that he was stopping to question a suspect.

Commission finding.—The Dallas Police Department had no requirement or regulation for police officers to notify headquarters when stopping to question a suspect. Therefore, Tippit did not violate any police radio procedure in failing to notify the radio dispatcher that he was stopping Oswald.[53]

Speculation.—Tippit could not have recognized Oswald from the description sent out over the police radio.

Commission finding.—There is no certain way of knowing whether Tippit recognized Oswald from the description put out by the police radio. The Dallas Police Department radio log shows that the police radio dispatcher at 1:29 p.m. noted a similarity between the broadcast descriptions of the President's assassin and Tippit's slayer. It is conceivable, even probable, that Tippit stopped Oswald because of the description broadcast by the police radio.[54]

Speculation.—Tippit and his killer knew each other.

Commission finding.—Investigation has revealed no evidence that Oswald and Tippit were acquainted, had ever seen each other, or had any mutual acquaintances. Witnesses to the shooting observed no signs of recognition between the two men.[55]

Speculation.—Mrs. Helen Markham, a witness to the slaying of Tippit, put the time at just after 1:06 p.m. This would have made it impossible for Oswald to have committed the killing since he would not have had time to arrive at the shooting scene by that time.

Commission finding.—The shooting of Tippit has been established at approximately 1:15 or 1:16 p.m. on the basis of a call to police headquarters on Tippit's car radio by another witness to the assassination, Domingo Benavides. In her various statements and in her testimony, Mrs. Markham was uncertain and inconsistent in her recollection of the exact time of the slaying.[56]

Speculation.—Mrs. Helen Markham is the only witness to the killing of Tippit.

Commission finding.—Other witnesses to the killing of Tippit include Domingo Benavides, who used Tippit's car radio to notify the police dispatcher of the killing at 1:16 p.m., and William Scoggins, a cabdriver parked at the corner of 10th Street and Patton Avenue. Barbara Jeanette Davis and Virginia Davis saw a man with a pistol in his hand walk across their lawn immediately after they heard the sound of the shots that killed Tippit. The man emptied the shells from his pistol and turned the corner from 10th Street onto Patton Avenue. All of these witnesses, except Benavides, subsequently picked Oswald out of a lineup as the slayer. Benavides did not feel that he could make a positive identification and never attended a lineup for the purpose.[57]

Speculation.—Mrs. Markham said that the man she saw shooting Tippit was about 30, short, with bushy hair, and wearing a white coat. Since Oswald does not fit this description he could not be the killer.

Commission finding.—In evaluating Helen Markham's testimony the Commission is aware of allegations that she described the killer of Patrolman Tippit as short, stocky, and with bushy hair, · which would not be a correct description of Oswald. It has also been alleged that Mrs. Markham identified Oswald in the lineup because of his clothing rather than his appearance. When Oswald appeared in the lineup at which Mrs. Markham was present, he was not wearing the jacket which he wore at the time of the shooting, and Mrs. Markham has testified that her identification was based "mostly from his face." [58] Moreover, Mrs. Markham has denied that she ever described the man who killed Tippit as short, stocky, and with bushy hair. The Commission reviewed the transcript of a telephone conversation in which Mrs. Markham was alleged to have made such a description. In the transcription Mrs. Markham reaffirmed her positive identification of Oswald and denied having described the killer as short, stocky, and bushy haired.[59]

Speculation.—Another witness to the slaying of Patrolman Tippit, an unidentified woman, was interviewed by the FBI but was never called as a witness by the President's Commission on the Assassination of President Kennedy. This witness is alleged to have stated that she saw two men involved in the shooting and that they ran off in opposite directions afterward.

Commission finding.—The only woman among the witnesses to the slaying of Tippit known to the Commission is Helen Markham. The FBI never interviewed any other woman who claimed to have seen the shooting and never received any information concerning the existence of such a witness. Two women, Barbara Jeanette Davis and Virginia Davis, saw the killer immediately after the shooting as he crossed the lawn at the corner of Patton Avenue and 10th Street, but they did not witness the shooting itself. They were both interviewed by the FBI and appeared before the Commission. The Commission has no evidence that there was any witness to the slaying other than those identified in chapter IV.[60]

Speculation.—No witness saw Oswald between the time he was supposed to have reloaded his gun near the scene of the slaying and his appearance at the shoestore on Jefferson Boulevard.

Commission finding.—Six witnesses identified Oswald as the man they saw in flight after the murder of Tippit. The killer was seen, gun in hand, by Ted Callaway and Sam Guinyard in the block of Patton Avenue between 10th Street and Jefferson Boulevard after the shooting of Tippit. They saw him run to Jefferson and turn right. On the evening of November 22, Callaway and Guinyard picked Oswald out of a police lineup as the man they saw with the gun. Two other men, Warren Reynolds and Pat Patterson, saw a man with a pistol in his hand running south on Patton Avenue. They followed him for a block on Jefferson Boulevard and then lost sight of him. Both men subsequently identified pictures of Oswald as the man they saw with the gun. Harold Russell also saw a man with a gun running south on Patton Avenue and later identified him from pictures as Oswald. Mrs. Mary Brock saw a man she later identified as Oswald walk at a fast pace into the parking lot behind the service station at the corner of Jefferson and Crawford, where Oswald's jacket was found shortly after.[61]

Speculation.—When Oswald left his roominghouse at about 1 p.m. on November 22 he had on a zipper-type tan plaid jacket.

Commission finding.—The jacket that Oswald was wearing at the time of the slaying of Tippit was a light-gray jacket. According to Marina Oswald, her husband owned only two jackets—one blue and the other light gray. The housekeeper at 1026 North Beckley Avenue, Mrs. Earlene Roberts, was not certain about the color of the jacket that Oswald was wearing when he left the house.[62]

Speculation.—Oswald wore an olive-brown plain jacket which is visible in all the pictures of him after his arrest.

Commission finding.—At the time of his arrest, Oswald was not wearing a jacket. The jacket that was subsequently recovered in a parking lot and identified as Oswald's was a light-gray one. There are no witnesses who have stated that Oswald was wearing an olive-brown jacket immediately before or after his arrest. The Commission has seen no pictures of Oswald taken subsequent to his arrest that show him in such a jacket. Pictures taken shortly after his arrest show him in the shirt that Mrs. Bledsoe described him as wearing when she saw him on the bus at approximately 1:40 p.m.[63]

Speculation.—Oswald's landlady, Mrs. A. C. Johnson, said that Oswald never had a gun in the room.

Commission finding.—In her testimony before the Commission, Mrs. Johnson said that he "never brought that rifle in my house. * * * He could have had this pistol, I don't know, because they found the scabbard." [64] As shown in chapter IV, Oswald kept his rifle in the Paine garage in Irving while he was living in Dallas during October and November. The pistol was small and easily concealed.[65]

Speculation.—There was absolutely no place to hide a gun in Oswald's room at 1026 North Beckley Avenue.

Commission finding.—In the search of Oswald's room after his apprehension police found a pistol holster. Oswald's landlady, Mrs. A. C. Johnson, stated that she had not seen the holster before. There is no reason to believe that Oswald could not have had both a pistol and the holster hidden in the room. Oswald's pistol was a small one with the barrel cut down to 2¼ inches. It could have been concealed in a pocket of his clothes.[66]

Speculation.—Oswald did not pick up the revolver from his room at 1 p.m.

Commission finding.—There is reason to believe that Oswald did pick up the revolver from his room, probably concealing it beneath his jacket. This likelihood is reinforced by the finding of the pistol holster in the room after the assassination, since this indicates that

Oswald did not store the pistol at the home of Mrs. Paine where he spent the night before the assassination.[67]

Speculation.—No one saw Oswald enter the Texas Theatre.

Commission finding.—A nearby shoe store manager, Johnny C. Brewer, and the theatre cashier, Julia Postal, saw Oswald enter the lobby of the theatre from where he went on into the theatre proper.[68]

Speculation.—Not a single one of the people in the Texas Theatre at the time of Oswald's arrest has come forward or been brought forward to give an eyewitness account of the arrest.

Commission finding.—Johnny C. Brewer, the shoe store manager, and two patrons of the theatre—John Gibson and George Jefferson Applin, Jr.—were present in the theatre and testified before the Commission on the circumstances of Oswald's arrest at the Texas Theatre. Only 6 or 7 people were seated on the main floor of the theatre.[69]

Speculation.—There is no independent witness aside from the police who testified that Oswald was carrying a gun when arrested by the police.

Commission finding.—Johnny Brewer testified before the Commission that he saw Oswald pull a gun and that he saw it taken away from him by a policeman.[70]

OSWALD AFTER HIS ARREST

The Commission found that assertions that the Dallas police treated Oswald brutally and denied him his constitutional rights to legal counsel had no foundation in fact. Insinuations that Dallas police officials and District Attorney Henry M. Wade fabricated or altered evidence to establish the guilt of Oswald were baseless. It is true that police officials and the district attorney made errors in giving evidential information to the press, but these were clearly the result of misapprehensions or ignorance rather than intent, and at the worst represent bad judgment. At least one imputed fabrication of fact, further embellished by repetition, never really occurred. Sinister connotations were evoked by the attribution to the district attorney of the statement that a taxicab driver named Darryl Click drove Oswald from downtown Dallas to the area of his roominghouse in Oak Cliff. It has been correctly ascertained that no such taxicab driver existed in Dallas. On the other hand, the district attorney, who was quoted in a newspaper transcript as making the statement, never made the statement nor did any one else. Audio tapes of the district attorney's press conference make clear that the person who transcribed the conference rendered a reference to the "Oak Cliff" area of Dallas as a person, "Darryl Click". This error in transcription is the sole source for the existence of a "Darryl Click" as a taxicab driver.

Speculation.—Oswald was the victim of police brutality.

Commission finding.—Oswald resisted arrest in the Texas Theatre and drew a gun. He received a slight cut over his right eye and a

654

bruise under his left eye in the course of his struggles. During the time he was in police custody, he was neither ill-treated nor abused.[71]

Speculation.—Oswald was never formally charged with the assassination of the President; he was charged only with the shooting of Patrolman J. D. Tippit.

Commission finding.—Oswald was arraigned for the murder of President Kennedy before Justice of the Peace David Johnston on the fourth floor of the Police Department building at 1:35 a.m., November 23. Previously, he had been arraigned before Johnston for the murder of Tippit at 7:10 p. m., November 22.[72]

Speculation.—The police questioned Oswald extensively about the Tippit murder on the first day of his detention. They did not question him about the assassination of President Kennedy.

Commission finding.—Dallas police officials stated that they questioned Oswald repeatedly on November 22 about the assassination of President Kennedy and his relationship to it. At the first interrogation, Captain Fritz asked Oswald to account for himself at the time the President was shot. FBI agents who were present also stated that he was questioned about the assassination of the President.[73]

Speculation.—Oswald's attempts to get legal counsel were deliberately thwarted by the police and he was cut off from outside calls that would have permitted him to obtain a lawyer.

Commission finding.—On November 23, Oswald was visited by the president of the Dallas Bar Association, H. Louis Nichols, who offered him help in getting a lawyer; Oswald refused the offer. Oswald was told by the police that he could use the telephone when he wished, and he did make telephone calls. He attempted to call attorney John Abt in New York but was unsuccessful in reaching him. Mrs. Paine testified that at Oswald's request she tried without success to reach Abt. Oswald was also visited by his wife, mother, and brother, to any of whom he could have turned for help in getting counsel.[74]

OSWALD IN THE SOVIET UNION

Oswald's residence in the Soviet Union for more than 2½ years aroused speculation after his arrest that he was an agent of the Soviet Union or in some way affiliated with it. This speculation was supported by assertions that he had received exceptionally favored treatment from the Soviet Government in securing permission to enter and leave the country, especially the latter, because his Russian wife and child were permitted to leave with him. The careful analysis of these speculations in chapter VI of this report led to the Commission's conclusion that there is no credible evidence that Oswald was an agent of the Soviet Government and that he did not receive unusually favorable treatment in entering or leaving the Soviet Union or in returning to the United States.

Speculation.—A young private in the Marine Corps in the 1950's could not study Marxism, learn Russian, and read Soviet newspapers without any adverse repercussions in his unit.

Commission finding.—Although Oswald's interest in the Soviet Union was well known, his interest in Marxism was apparently known to only a few of his fellow marines. While stationed in California, he studied Russian. In February 1959, while still in the Marines, he took an official test on his proficiency in Russian and was rated "Poor." In California at about this time he probably read a Russian-language newspaper. The reactions of his fellow Marines who were aware of his interests in Marxism and the Soviet Union were apparently not antagonistic and did not deter him from pursuing these interests.[75]

Speculation.—Oswald learned Russian during his service in the Marines as part of his military training.

Commission finding.—Oswald never received any training from the Marine Corps in the Russian language. His studies of Russian were entirely on his own time and at his own initiative.[76]

Speculation.—Oswald could not have saved $1,600 from his Marine pay for his trip to Russia in 1959.

Commission finding.—In November 1959, Oswald told an American reporter in Moscow, Aline Mosby, that he had saved $1,500 (not $1,600) while in the Marines. It is entirely consistent with Oswald's known frugality that he could have saved the money from the $3,452.20 in pay he received while he was in the Marines. Moreover, despite his statement to Aline Mosby, he may not actually have saved $1,500, for it was possible for him to have made the trip to Russia in 1959 for considerably less than that amount.[77]

Speculation.—It is probable that Oswald had prior contacts with Soviet agents before he entered Russia in 1959 because his application for a visa was processed and approved immediately on receipt.

Commission finding.—There is no evidence that Oswald was in touch with Soviet agents before his visit to Russia. The time that it took for him to receive his visa in Helsinki for entrance to the Soviet Union was shorter than the average but not beyond the normal range for the granting of such visas. Had Oswald been recruited as a Russian agent while he was still in the Marines, it is most improbable that he would have been encouraged to defect. He would have been of greater value to Russian intelligence as a Marine radar operator than as a defector.[78]

Speculation.—Soviet suspicion of Oswald is indicated by the fact that he was sent off to work in a radio plant in Minsk as an unskilled hand at the lowest rate of pay although he qualified as a trained radar and electronics technician.

Commission finding.—The Soviet Government probably was suspicious of Oswald, as it would be of any American who appeared in Moscow and said he wanted to live in the Soviet Union. Under the circumstances it is to be expected that he would be placed in a position that would not involve national security. Moreover, Oswald had been a radar operator, not a technician, in the Marines. His total income in Russia was higher than normal because his pay was supplemented for about a year by payments from the Soviet "Red Cross," an official agency of the Soviet Government. Oswald believed that these payments really came from the MVD. It is a policy of the Soviet Government to subsidize defectors from Western nations who settle in the Soviet Union, in order that their standard of living may not be too much lower than their previous standard in their own country.[79]

Speculation.—Oswald was trained by the Russians in a special school for assassins at Minsk.

Commission finding.—Commission investigations revealed no evidence to support this claim or the existence of such a school in Minsk during the time Oswald was there. Oswald belonged to a hunting club near Minsk, but there is no evidence that this was other than an ordinary hunting club.[80]

Speculation.—Marina Oswald's father was an important part of the Soviet intelligence apparatus.

Commission finding.—Marina Oswald's father died while she was still an infant. This reference is presumably to her uncle, Ilya Prusakov, who was an executive in the lumber industry, which position carried with it the rank of lieutenant colonel or colonel in the Ministry of Internal Affairs (MVD). Since 1953 the MVD has not been concerned with internal security or other police functions.[81]

Speculation.—It was most exceptional that Oswald was able to bring his wife and child out of the Soviet Union with him.

Commission finding.—There is no reason to believe that the Oswalds received unusually favorable treatment in being permitted or assisted to leave the Soviet Union together. Other American citizens have brought their Russian wives out of the Soviet Union, both before and after Oswald.[82]

Speculation.—Oswald never would have been permitted to return to the United States if Soviet intelligence had not planned to use him in some way against the United States.

Commission finding.—There is no evidence that Oswald had any working relationship with the Soviet Government or Soviet intelligence. The Russians have permitted other American defectors to return to the United States.[83]

Speculation.—Since the exit visa for Marina Oswald was granted so promptly the Soviet authorities must have wanted Marina to accompany her husband.

Commission finding.—Marina Oswald's exit visa application was not acted upon with unusual rapidity. It took at least 5½ months from the time the Oswalds applied until they were notified of permission in December 1961. There have been many instances where visas were granted more quickly to other Soviet wives of American citizens.[84]

Speculation.—Soviet authorities gave Oswald notice a month and a half in advance that they had granted him an exit visa, an unprecedented act for the Soviet Government.

Commission finding.—The Oswalds were notified on December 25, 1961, that their requests for exit visas had been granted by Soviet authorities. Marina Oswald picked up her visa, valid until December 1, 1962, on January 11, 1962, 17 days after receiving notice that it was available. Oswald did not pick up his visa until May 22. The Soviets did not give the Oswalds any advance notice; the visas could have been picked up immediately had the Oswalds so desired. Because his exit visa had a 45-day expiration time after date of issuance, Lee Oswald delayed picking it up until he knew when he was leaving. He could not arrange a departure date until he received permission from the Department of State in May to return to the United States.[85]

OSWALD'S TRIP TO MEXICO CITY

Oswald's trip to Mexico City in late September and early October 1963, less than 2 months before he assassinated President Kennedy, has provoked speculation that it was related in some way to a conspiracy to murder the President. Rumors include assertions that he made a clandestine flight from Mexico to Cuba and back and that he received a large sum of money—usually estimated at $5,000—which he brought back to Dallas with him. The Commission has no credible evidence that Oswald went to Mexico pursuant to a plan to assassinate President Kennedy, that he received any instructions related to such an action while there, or that he received large sums of money from any source in Mexico.

Speculation.—Oswald could not have received an American passport in June 1963 within 24 hours without special intervention on his behalf.

Commission finding.—Oswald's passport application was processed routinely by the Department of State. No person or agency intervened specially on his behalf to speed the issuance of the passport. The passports of 24 other persons, on the same list sent to Washington from New Orleans, were authorized at the same time. The Passport Office of the Department of State had no instructions to delay issuance of or to deny a passport to Oswald.[86]

Speculation.—The Walter-McCarran Act specifically requires anyone who has attempted to renounce his U.S. citizenship to file an affidavit stating why he should receive a U.S. passport. Therefore, Oswald should have been required to file such an affidavit before receiving his passport in June 1963.

Commission finding.—The Internal Security Act of 1950 (Walter-McCarran Act) contains no reference to an affidavit being required of a U.S. citizen who has attempted to expatriate himself.[87]

Speculation.—Oswald did not have money for his trip to Mexico in September 1963.

Commission finding.—An analysis of Oswald's finances by the Commission indicates that he had sufficient money to make the trip to and from Mexico City. There is no evidence that he received any assistance in financing his trip to Mexico. The total cost of his 7-day trip has been reliably estimated at less than $85.[88]

Speculation.—Oswald was accompanied on his trip to Mexico City by a man and two women.

Commission finding.—Investigation has revealed that Oswald traveled alone on the bus. Fellow passengers on the bus between Houston and Mexico City have stated that he appeared to be traveling alone and that they had not previously known him.[89]

Speculation.—While in Mexico, Oswald made a clandestine flight to Havana and back.

Commission finding.—The Commission has found no evidence that Oswald made any flight to Cuba while he was in Mexico. He never received permission from the Cuban Government to enter Cuba nor from the Mexican Government to leave Mexico bound for Cuba. A confidential check of the Cuban airline in Mexico City indicates that Oswald never appeared at its office there.[90]

Speculation.—Oswald came back from Mexico City with $5,000.

Commission finding.—No evidence has ever been supplied or obtained to support this allegation. Oswald's actions in Mexico City and after his return to Dallas lend no support to this speculation.[91]

Speculation.—On November 27, 1963, in a speech at the University of Havana, Fidel Castro, under the influence of liquor, said "The first time that Oswald was in Cuba * * *." Castro therefore had knowledge that Oswald had made surreptitious visits to Cuba.

Commission finding.—Castro's speeches are monitored directly by the U.S. Information Agency as he delivers them. A tape of this speech reveals that it did not contain the alleged slip of the tongue. Castro did refer to Oswald's visit to the "Cuban Embassy" in Mexico which he immediately corrected to "Cuban consulate." The Commission has found no evidence that Oswald had made surreptitious visits to Cuba.[92]

OSWALD AND U.S. GOVERNMENT AGENCIES

Rumors and speculations that Oswald was in some way associated with or used by agencies of the U.S. Government grew out of his Russian period and his investigation by the FBI after his return to the United States. Insinuations were made that Oswald had been a CIA agent or had some relationship with the CIA and that this explained the supposed ease with which he received passports and visas. Speculation that he had some working relationship with the FBI was based on an entry in Oswald's notebook giving the name and telephone number of an agent from the FBI office in Dallas. The Directors of the CIA and the FBI have testified before the Commission that Oswald was never in the employ of their agencies in any capacity. The Commission has concluded on the basis of its own investigations of the files of Federal agencies that Oswald was not and had never been an agent of any agency of the U.S. Government (aside from his service in the Marines) and was not and had never been used by any U.S. Government agency for any purpose. The FBI was interested in him as a former defector and it maintained a file on him.

Speculation.—Oswald was an informant of either the FBI or the CIA. He was recruited by an agency of the U.S. Government and sent to Russia in 1959.

Commission finding.—Mrs. Marguerite Oswald frequently expressed the opinion that her son was such an agent, but she stated before the Commission that "I cannot prove Lee is an agent." [93] The Directors of the CIA and of the FBI testified before the Commission that Oswald was never employed by either agency or used by either agency in any capacity. Investigation by the Commission has revealed no evidence that Oswald was ever employed by either the FBI or CIA in any capacity.[94]

Speculation.—Oswald told Pauline Bates, a public stenographer in Fort Worth, Tex., in June 1962, that he had become a "secret agent" of the U.S. Government and that he was soon going back to Russia "for Washington."

Commission finding.—Miss Bates denied a newspaper story reporting that Oswald had told her that he was working for the U.S. Department of State. She stated that she had assumed incorrectly that he was working with the Department of State when he told her that the State Department had told him in 1959 that he would be on his own while in the Soviet Union.[95]

Speculation.—The FBI tried to recruit Oswald. An FBI agent's name, telephone number, and automobile license number were found among Oswald's papers.

Commission finding.—FBI officials have testified that they had never tried to recruit Oswald to act on behalf of the FBI in any capacity. The Commission's investigation corroborates this testimony. An FBI agent, James P. Hosty, Jr., had given his name and telephone number to Mrs. Ruth Paine so that she could call and give him Oswald's address in Dallas when she learned it. Mrs. Paine and Marina Oswald have stated that Mrs. Paine gave Oswald a slip of paper with the agent's name and telephone number on it. Marina Oswald had taken down the license number of Hosty's car on one of his visits and given it to her husband.[96]

Speculation.—Dallas police must have known where Oswald was living in the city because Mrs. Paine had given the address of Oswald's room on North Beckley Avenue to the FBI some time before the assassination.

Commission finding.—Mrs. Paine had never given the address of Oswald's roominghouse to the FBI, nor had she known the address prior to the assassination. Therefore, the Dallas police could not have learned the address from the FBI which did not know the address before the assassination. The Dallas Police did not know that Oswald was in the city before the assassination.[97]

Speculation.—It has been FBI policy for 20 years to inform employers of Communists or suspected Communists employed by them.

It is a mystery, therefore, how Oswald retained his job at the Texas School Book Depository.

Commission finding.—The FBI advised the Commission that it has never been its policy to inform employers that they have Communists or suspected Communists working for them and that the FBI does not disseminate internal security information to anyone outside the executive branch of the U.S. Government. FBI agents had no contacts with Texas School Book Depository officials until after the assassination.[98]

Speculation.—Municipal and Federal police had observed Oswald closely for some time but had not regarded him as a potential killer.

Commission finding.—The Dallas police had not been aware of Oswald's presence in the city before the assassination. The FBI knew that Oswald was in Dallas from an interview with Mrs. Paine, but no FBI agents had interviewed him there before the assassination. The FBI had not regarded him as a potential killer.[99]

Speculation.—The FBI probably knew that Oswald had the rifle before the President's murder because it was most unlikely that it could have traced the ownership of the rifle within 1 day if it had not already had information on the rifle.

Commission finding.—The FBI successfully traced the purchase of the rifle by Oswald within 24 hours of the assassination. It had had no previous information about the rifle.[100]

Speculation.—The FBI interviewed Oswald 10 days before the assassination.

Commission finding.—The last FBI interview with Oswald, before the assassination, took place in New Orleans in August 1963, when he asked to see an FBI agent after his arrest by police for disturbing the peace, the outcome of his distribution of Fair Play for Cuba handbills. Neither Special Agent Hosty nor any other FBI agent saw or talked with Oswald between his return to Dallas, on October 3, and November 22. Hosty did interview Mrs. Paine at her home about Oswald on November 1 and 5, 1963. He also saw Marina Oswald briefly on November 1 at Mrs. Paine's house, but he did not interview her.[101]

CONSPIRATORIAL RELATIONSHIPS

Rumors concerning accomplices and plots linked Oswald and Ruby with each other, or with others, including Patrolman J. D. Tippit, Gen. Edwin A. Walker, and Bernard Weissman of the nonexistent American Factfinding Committee, in a conspiratorial relationship. The Commission made intensive inquiry into the backgrounds and relationships of Oswald and Ruby to determine whether they knew each other or were involved in a plot of any kind with each other or others. It was unable to find any credible evidence to support the rumors linking Oswald and Ruby directly or through others. The Commission concluded that they were not involved in a conspiratorial relationship with each other or with any third parties.

Speculation.—Lee Harvey Oswald, Jack Ruby, and Patrolman J. D. Tippit lived within a few blocks of each other.

Commission finding.—Oswald's room was 1.3 miles from Ruby's apartment and Tippit lived 7 miles away from Ruby. Tippit's residence was about 7 miles from Oswald's room.[102]

Speculation.—Since Oswald did not have the money to repay the $435.61 he had received from the Department of State to cover part of the expenses of his return from Russia, he must have received help from some other source. Ruby lent Oswald money to pay back the loan and lent him small amounts of money thereafter.

Commission finding.—The Commission has no credible evidence that Oswald received any money from Ruby or anyone else to repay his State Department loan, nor that he received small amounts of money from Ruby at any time. An exhaustive analysis of Oswald's income and expenditures, made for the Commission by an Internal Revenue Service expert, reveals that Oswald had sufficient funds to make the State Department repayments from his earnings.[103]

Speculation.—Just before Oswald was shot by Ruby, he looked directly at Ruby in apparent recognition of him.

Commission finding.—The Commission has been unable to establish as a fact any kind of relationship between Ruby and Oswald other than that Oswald was Ruby's victim. The Commission has examined television tapes and motion picture films of the shooting and has been unable to discern any facial expression that could be interpreted to signify recognition of Ruby or anyone else in the basement of the building.[104]

Speculation.—The Dallas police suspected Oswald and Ruby of being involved in an attack on General Walker and planned to arrest the two when the FBI intervened, at the request of Attorney General Robert F. Kennedy, and asked the police not to do so for reasons of state.

Commission finding.—This allegation appeared in the November 29, 1963, issue (actually printed on November 25 or 26) of a German weekly newspaper, Deutsche National Zeiting und Soldaten Zeitung, published in Munich. The allegation later appeared in the National Enquirer of May 17, 1964. The Commission has been reliably informed that the statement was fabricated by an editor of the newspaper. No evidence in support of this statement has ever been advanced or uncovered. In their investigation of the attack on General Walker, the Dallas police uncovered no suspects and planned no arrests. The FBI had no knowledge that Oswald was responsible for the attack until Marina Oswald revealed the information on December 3, 1963.[105]

Speculation.—Ruby and Oswald were seen together at the Carousel Club.

Commission finding.—All assertions that Oswald was seen in the company of Ruby or of anyone else at the Carousel Club have been investigated. None of them merits any credence.[106]

Speculation.—Oswald and General Walker were probably acquainted with each other since Oswald's notebook contained Walker's name and telephone number.

Commission finding.—Although Oswald's notebook contained Walker's name and telephone number there was no evidence that the two knew each other. It is probable that this information was inserted at the time that Oswald was planning his attack on Walker. General Walker stated that he did not know of Oswald before the assassination.[107]

Speculation.—Patrolman J. D. Tippit, Bernard Weissman, and Jack Ruby met by prearrangement on November 14, 1963, at the Carousel Club.

Commission finding.—Investigation has revealed no evidence to support this assertion. Nor is there credible evidence that any of the three men knew each other.[108]

Speculation.—Ruby's sister, Mrs. Eva Grant, said that Ruby and Tippit were "like two brothers."

Commission finding.—Mrs. Grant has denied ever making this statement or any statement like it, saying it was untrue and without foundation. Ruby was acquainted with another Dallas policeman named Tippit, but this was G. M. Tippit of the special services bureau of the department, not the Tippit who was killed.[109]

Speculation.—Jack Ruby was one of the most notorious of Dallas gangsters.

Commission finding.—There is no credible evidence that Jack Ruby was active in the criminal underworld. Investigation disclosed no one in either Chicago or Dallas who had any knowledge that Ruby was associated with organized criminal activity.[110]

Speculation.—The shooting in Dallas on January 23, 1964, of Warren A. Reynolds, who witnessed the flight of Patrolman Tippit's slayer on November 22 and followed him for a short distance, may have been connected in some way with the assassination of President Kennedy and the slaying of Patrolman Tippit. A man arrested for the attempt on Reynolds, Darrell Wayne Garner, was released as a result, in part, of testimony by Betty (Nancy Jane Mooney) MacDonald, who had allegedly worked at one time as a stripper at Jack Ruby's Carousel Club.

Commission finding.—This rumor, originally publicized by a newspaper columnist on February 23, 1964, was apparently based on the alleged connection between Betty MacDonald and the Carousel Club. Investigation revealed no evidence that she had ever worked at the Carousel Club. Employees of the club had no recollection that she had ever worked there. Betty MacDonald was arrested and charged with disturbing the peace on February 13, 1964. After being placed in a cell at the Dallas city jail, she hanged herself. The Commission has found no evidence that the shooting of Warren Reynolds was in any way related to the assassination of President Kennedy or the murder of Patrolman Tippit.[111]

OTHER RUMORS AND SPECULATIONS

Many rumors and speculations difficult to place in the categories treated above also required consideration or investigation by the Commission. In some way or other, much of this miscellany was related to theories of conspiracy involving Oswald. The rest pertained to peripheral aspects that were of sufficient import to merit attention. The Commission's findings are set forth below.

Speculation.—Oswald was responsible in some way for the death of Marine Pvt. Martin D. Schrand.

Commission finding.—This rumor was mentioned by at least one of Oswald's fellow Marines. Private Schrand was fatally wounded by a discharge from a riot-type shotgun while he was on guard duty on January 5, 1958, near the carrier pier, U.S. Naval Air Station, Cubi Point, Republic of the Philippines. The official Marine investigation in 1958 found that Schrand's death was the result of an accidental discharge of his gun and that no other person or persons were involved in the incident. The rumor that Oswald was involved in Schrand's death in some way may have had its origin in two circumstances: (1) Oswald was stationed at Cubi Point at the time of Schrand's death; (2) on October 27, 1957, while stationed in Japan, Oswald accidentally shot himself in the left elbow with a .22 derringer that he owned. The Commission has found no evidence that Oswald had any connection with the fatal shooting of Private Schrand.[112]

Speculation.—The Texas School Book Depository is owned and operated by the city of Dallas, and Oswald was therefore a municipal employee. Accordingly, he could have secured his job at the Depository only if someone in an official capacity vouched for him.

Commission finding.—The Texas School Book Depository is a private corporation unconnected with the city of Dallas. Oswald therefore was not a municipal employee. He obtained his position at the Depository with the assistance of Mrs. Ruth Paine, who learned of a possible opening from a neighbor and arranged an interview for him with Superintendent Roy S. Truly at the Depository.[113]

Speculation.—Prior to the assassination Dallas police searched other buildings in the area of the Texas School Book Depository but not the School Book Depository itself.

Commission finding.—The Dallas police and the Secret Service both notified the Commission that, other than the Trade Mart, they had searched no buildings along the route of the President's motorcade or elsewhere in Dallas in connection with the President's visit. It was not Secret Service practice to search buildings along the routes of motorcades.[114]

Speculation.—Sheriff E. J. Decker of Dallas County came on the police radio at 12:25 p.m. with orders to calm trouble at the Texas School Book Depository.

Commission finding.—The final edition of the Dallas Times-Herald of November 22 (p. 1, col. 1) reported that "Sheriff Decker came on the air at 12:25 p.m." and stated: "'I don't know what's happened. Take

664

every available man from the jail and the office and go to the railroad yards off Elm near the triple underpass.'" The article in the Times-Herald did not mention the time that the President was shot. The radio log of the Dallas County Sheriff's Office shows that Sheriff Decker came on the air at 40 seconds after 12:30 p.m. and stated: "Stand by me. All units and officers vicinity of station report to the railroad track area, just north of Elm—Report to the railroad track area, just north of Elm." The radio log does not show any messages by Sheriff Decker between 12:20 p.m. and 40 seconds after 12:30 p.m.[115]

Speculation.—Police precautions in Dallas on November 22 included surveillance of many people, among them some who did no more than speak in favor of school integration.

Commission finding.—The Dallas Police Department notified the Commission that on November 22 it had no one under surveillance as a precaution in connection with President Kennedy's visit except at the Trade Mart. The Commission received no evidence that the Dallas police had under surveillance people who spoke in favor of school integration.[116]

Speculation.—Oswald was seen at shooting ranges in the Dallas area practicing firing with a rifle.

Commission finding.—Marina Oswald stated that on one occasion in March or April 1963, her husband told her that he was going to practice firing with the rifle. Witnesses have testified that they saw Oswald at shooting ranges in the Dallas area during October and November 1963. Investigation has failed to confirm that the man seen by these witnesses was Oswald.[117]

Speculation.—Oswald could drive a car and was seen in cars at various places.

Commission finding.—Oswald did not have a driver's license. Marina Oswald and Ruth Paine have testified that he could not drive a car, and there is no confirmed evidence to establish his presence at any location as the driver of a car. Mrs. Paine did give Oswald some driving lessons and he did drive short distances on these occasions.[118]

Speculation.—Oswald received money by Western Union telegraph from time to time for several months before the assassination of President Kennedy.

Commision finding.—An employee in the Western Union main office in Dallas, C. A. Hamblen, made statements that he remembered seeing Oswald there on some occasions collecting money that had been telegraphed to him. In his testimony before the Commission, Hamblen was unable to state whether or not the person he had seen was Lee Harvey Oswald. Western Union officials searched their records in Dallas and other cities for the period from June through November 1963 but found no money orders payable to Lee Oswald or to any of his known aliases. A Western Union official concluded that the allegation was "a figment of Mr. Hamblen's imagination."[119] The Commission has found no evidence to contradict this conclusion.[120]

Speculation.—On his way back from Mexico City in October 1963, Oswald stopped in Alice, Tex., to apply for a job at the local radio station.

Commission finding.—This rumor apparently originated with the manager of radio station KOPY, Alice, who stated that Oswald visited his office on the afternoon of October 4 for about 25 minutes. According to the manager, Oswald was driving a battered 1953 model car and had his wife and a small child in the car with him. Oswald traveled from Mexico City to Dallas by bus, arriving in Dallas on the afternoon of October 3. The bus did not pass through Alice. On October 4, Oswald applied for two jobs in Dallas and then spent the afternoon and night with his wife and child at the Paine residence in Irving. Investigation has revealed that Oswald did not own a car and there is no convincing evidence that he could drive a car. Accordingly, Oswald could not have been in Alice on October 4. There is no evidence that he stopped in Alice to look for a job on any occasion.[121]

Speculation.—Oswald or accomplices had made arrangements for his getaway by airplane from an airfield in the Dallas area.

Commission finding.—Investigation of such claims revealed that they had not the slightest substance. The Commission found no evidence that Oswald had any prearranged plan for escape after the assassination.[122]

Speculation.—One hundred and fifty dollars was found in the dresser of Oswald's room at 1026 North Beckley Avenue after the assassination.

Commission finding.—No money was found in Oswald's room after the assassination. Oswald left $170 in the room occupied by his wife at the Paine residence in Irving. At the time of his arrest Oswald had $13.87 on his person.[123]

Speculation.—After Oswald's arrest, the police found in his room seven metal file boxes filled with the names of Castro sympathizers.

Commission finding.—The Dallas police inventories of Oswald's property taken from his room at 1026 North Beckley Avenue do not include any file boxes. A number of small file boxes listed in the inventory as having been taken from the Paine residence in Irving contained letters, pictures, books and literature, most of which belonged to Ruth Paine, not to Oswald. No lists of names of Castro sympathizers were found among these effects.[124]

Speculation.—Oswald's letters vary so greatly in quality (spelling, grammar, sentence structure) that he must have had help in preparing the better constructed letters or someone else wrote them for him.

Commission finding.—There is no evidence that anyone in the United States helped Oswald with his better written letters or that anyone else wrote his letters for him. His wife stated that he would write many drafts of his more important letters. His mother indicated that he would work hard over the drafts of some of his letters. It is clear that he did take greater pains with some of his letters than with others and that the contrasts in quality were accordingly substantial.

It is also clear that even his better written letters contained some distinctive elements of spelling, grammar, and punctuation that were common to his poorer efforts. Oswald wrote in his diary that he received help from his Intourist Guide, Rima Shirokova, in the preparation of his letter of October 16, 1959, to the Supreme Soviet.[125]

Speculation.—A Negro janitor who was a witness to the shooting and was supposed to be able to identify Oswald as the killer was held in protective custody by the Dallas police until he could appear before the President's Commission on the Assassination of President Kennedy.

Commission finding.—Investigation revealed that this story had no foundation in fact. No such witness was kept in protective custody by the Dallas police for appearance before the Commission. The story had its origin in a newspaper account based on hearsay.[126]

Speculation.—The Secret Service incarcerated Marina Oswald immediately after the assassination.

Commission finding.—Marina Oswald was given protection by the Secret Service for a period of time after the assassination. She had freedom to communicate with others at anytime she desired, to go where she pleased, or to terminate the protection at any time.[127]

Speculation.—Mrs. Marguerite Oswald was shown a photograph of Jack Ruby by an FBI agent the night before Ruby killed her son.

Commission finding.—On the night of November 23, 1963, Special Agent Bardwell D. Odum of the FBI showed Mrs. Marguerite Oswald a picture of a man to determine whether the man was known to her. Mrs. Oswald stated subsequently that the picture was of Jack Ruby. The Commission has examined a copy of the photograph and determined that it was not a picture of Jack Ruby.[128]

Speculation.—The son of the only witness to the Tippit slaying was arrested after talking to some private investigators and soon plunged to his death from an unbarred jail window.

Commission finding.—According to Mrs. Helen Markham, one of the witnesses to the Tippit slaying, Mrs. Marguerite Oswald and two men who claimed to be reporters from Philadelphia sought to interview her on June 27, 1964. Mrs. Markham did not wish to be interviewed and put them off. Afterward, Mrs. Markham's son, William Edward Markham, talked with Mrs. Oswald and the men about the Oswald matter and the shooting of Patrolman Tippit. William Edward Markham had been in Norfolk, Va., at the time of the assassination and had not returned to Dallas until May 7, 1964. He had no personal knowledge of the shooting of Patrolman Tippit. On June 30, 1964, another of Mrs. Markham's sons, James Alfred Markham, was arrested at Mrs. Markham's apartment by Dallas Police on a charge of burglary. While trying to escape, he fell from the bathroom of the apartment to a concrete driveway about 20 feet below. He was taken to Parkland Memorial Hospital, treated for injuries, and after 6½ hours was taken to jail. As of July 31, 1964, he was in Dallas County Jail awaiting trial. There was also a warrant outstanding against him for parole violation.[129]

Speculation.—The headquarters detachment of the U.S. Army, under orders from [Secretary of Defense Robert S.] McNamara's office, began to rehearse for the funeral more than a week before the assassination.

Commission finding.—This assertion is based on an interview with U.S. Army Capt. Richard C. Cloy that appeared in the Jackson, Miss., Clarion-Ledger of February 21, 1964. The newspaper quotes Captain Cloy, who was a member of the Army unit charged with conducting funeral ceremonials in honor of deceased Chiefs of State, as having said that, "we were in a state of readiness and had just finished a funeral rehearsal because there was grave concern for President Hoover's health. But we never expected that our practice was preparing us for President Kennedy." [130]

Speculation.—The ship in which Oswald went to Europe in 1959 stopped in Havana on the way.

Commission finding.—Oswald boarded the SS *Marion Lykes* in New Orleans and it sailed on September 20, 1959. It docked in Le Havre, France, on October 8 with only one previous stop—at another French port, La Pallice.[131]

Biography of Lee Harvey Oswald

EARLY YEARS

Marguerite Claverie, the mother of Lee Harvey Oswald, was born in New Orleans in 1907,[1] into a family of French and German extraction.[2] Her mother died a few years after Marguerite was born, leaving her and five other young children in the care of their father, a streetcar conductor.[3] Although Marguerite describes herself as "a child of one parent," she recalls being "one of the most popular young ladies in the [grammar] school," and thinks of her childhood as a "very full happy" one.[4] Her older sister, Mrs. Lillian Murret, remembers Marguerite as "a very pretty child, a very beautiful girl," [5] as does a former acquaintance, Clem H. Sehrt, who knew the Claveries.[6] The family was poor but, according to Mrs. Murret, was a "happy family * * * singing all the time." [7] Marguerite had 1 year of high school.[8] Shortly before she was 17, she went to work as a receptionist for a law firm in New Orleans.[9]

In August 1929, while she was still working at the law firm, Marguerite married Edward John Pic, Jr.,[10] a quiet man of her own age, who worked as a clerk for T. Smith & Son, a New Orleans stevedoring company.[11] The marriage was not a success, and by the summer of 1931 she and Pic were separated.[12] Marguerite was then 3 months pregnant; she told her family that Pic did not want any children and refused to support her.[13] Pic ascribed the separation simply to their inability to get along together.[14] A boy was born on January 17, 1932, whom Marguerite named John Edward Pic.[15] Pic saw his son occasionally until he was about 1 year old; after that, he did not see the boy again [16] but contributed to his support until he was 18 years old.[17]

During her separation from her first husband, Marguerite saw a great deal of Robert Edward Lee Oswald, an insurance premium collector,[18] who also was married but was separated from his wife.[19] In 1933, Marguerite was divorced from Pic [20] and, Oswald's wife also having obtained a divorce,[12] they were married in a Lutheran church on July 20.[22] Marguerite has described the period of her marriage to Oswald as "the only happy part" of her life.[23] A son was born on April 7, 1934, who was named for his father; [24] Oswald wanted to adopt John Pic, but his mother objected on the ground that John's father might cut off the support payments.[25] In 1938, the Oswalds purchased a new house on Alvar Street for $3,900,[26] in what John remembered as "a rather nice neighborhood." [27] The house was across the street from the William Frantz School,[28] which first John and

later both he and Robert, Jr., attended.[29]   On August 19, 1939, little
more than a year after the Oswalds bought the Alvar Street house,
Robert Oswald died suddenly of a heart attack.[30]

Two months later, on October 18, 1939, a second son was born.[31]
He was named Lee after his father; Harvey was his paternal grandmother's maiden name.[32]   For a while after her husband's death, Mrs.
Oswald remained in the Alvar Street house without working; she
probably lived on life insurance proceeds.[33]   Sometime in 1940, she
rented the house to Dr. Bruno F. Mancuso, the doctor who had delivered Lee.[34]   (Dr. Mancuso continued to rent the house until 1944,[35]
when Marguerite obtained a judgment of possession against him.[36]
She sold the house for $6,500 to the First Homestead and Savings
Association, which resold it to Dr. Mancuso.)[37]   She herself moved to
a rented house at 1242 Congress Street, where she lived for about half
a year.[38]   For part of this period after Oswald's death, the two older
boys were placed in the Infant Jesus College, a Catholic boarding
school in Algiers, La., a suburb of New Orleans.[39]   Neither they nor
their mother liked this arrangement,[40] which John thought was intended to save money;[41] it lasted for less than a year, after which
the boys returned to the school Frantz and then transferred to the
George Washington Elementary School.[42]

On March 5, 1941, Mrs. Oswald purchased a frame [43] house at 1010
Bartholomew Street, for $1,300.[44]   According to John's recollection,
the neighborhood was not as pleasant as Alvar Street; the house had
a backyard, and the family kept a dog named "Sunshine." [45]   A neighbor, Mrs. Viola Peterman, recalls that Mrs. Oswald kept to herself
but appeared to be "a good mother to her children." [46]   She opened
a shop in the front room, where she sold things like sewing supplies
and small groceries.[47]   Oswald's Notion Shop, as it was called,[48]
failed to make money,[49] and on January 16, 1942, Mrs. Oswald sold
the house back to the Third District Home Association, from which
she had purchased it, for a profit of $800.[50]

Probably in contemplation of the sale of the house, Mrs. Oswald
applied in December 1941 to the Evangelical Lutheran Bethlehem
Orphan Asylum Association for the admission of her two older sons
to the orphan asylum, known as the Bethlehem Children's Home;
she stated on the application that she could contribute $20 per month
to their maintenance and would supply shoes and clothing.[51]   She had
inquired also about Lee, who was too young to be admitted.[52]   John
and Robert were accepted and entered the home on January 3, 1942.[53]

Mrs. Oswald moved to an apartment at 831 Pauline Street,[54] and
returned to work.   In December 1942, she listed her occupation as
"telephone operator"; [55] this may be the job she held at the Pittsburgh
Plate Glass Co., a company for which she worked at some point during
this period.[56]   She left Lee for much of this time with his aunt, Mrs.
Murret, who thought him a good looking, friendly child, but could
not devote a great deal of attention to him because she had five children
of her own.[57]   In the late spring of 1942, Lee was watched for several
weeks by Mrs. Thomas Roach, who lived with her husband in the

same house as the Oswalds.[58] Lee evidently did not get along with Mrs. Roach who told the next occupant of the house that Lee was a bad, unmanageable child who threw his toy gun at her.[59] Apparently referring to the Roaches, Mrs. Oswald testified that she had once hired a couple to care for Lee; the couple neglected him, so she "put them out" and cared for Lee herself until Mrs. Murret was able to help her again.[60] Soon after the incident with the Roaches, Mrs. Oswald moved again,[61] this time to 111 Sherwood Forest Drive, near the Murrets.[62]

Mrs. Murret took care of Lee for several months longer. Near Lee's third birthday, Mrs. Oswald again inquired about his admission into the Bethlehem Children's Home,[63] perhaps because a disagreement with her sister made it impossible to leave him with her any longer.[64] He was admitted on December 26.[65] On his application, Mrs. Oswald agreed to contribute $10 per month and to supply shoes and clothing, as for the other boys.[66]

Lee remained in the home for about 13 months, but according to John's testimony, left on several occasions to spend short periods of time with his mother or the Murrets.[67] John and Robert have pleasant memories of the home,[68] which apparently gave the children a good deal of freedom.[69] Robert described it as nondenominational but having "a Christian atmosphere"; "it might have been just a Protestant home." [70] Mrs. Oswald visited them regularly,[71] and they occasionally left the home to visit her or the Murrets.[72]

In July 1943, Mrs. Oswald was hired to manage a small hosiery store.[73] This is probably the store to which she referred in her testimony as the "Princess Hosiery Shop on Canal Street," at which, she testified, she was left by herself and "in 6 days' time * * * hired four girls." [74] Her employer remembers her as a neat, attractive, and hardworking woman, an aggressive person who would make a good manager.[75] She was not good with figures, however, and after several months he discharged her.[76] At about this same time, she met Edwin A. Ekdahl, an electrical engineer older than herself, who was originally from Boston but was then working in the area.[77] They saw each other often. Ekdahl met the boys [78] and, according to John's testimony, on at least one occasion, they all spent a weekend at a summer resort area in Covington, La.[79]

By January 1944, Mrs. Oswald and Ekdahl had decided to marry.[80] She withdrew Lee from the Children's Home [81] and moved with him to Dallas, where Ekdahl expected to be located.[82] They planned to postpone the marriage until the end of the school year so that the older boys could complete the year at the home before they left it.[83] In the meantime, she would care for Ekdahl,[84] who was recovering from a serious illness, probably a heart attack.[85] Mrs. Oswald has testified that when she arrived in Dallas, she decided that she did not want to marry Ekdahl after all.[86] Using part of the proceeds from the sale of the Alvar Street house,[87] she purchased a house at 4801 Victor Street,[88] a portion of which she rented.[89] In June, John and Robert left the Children's Home and joined their mother in

671

Dallas.[90] They entered the nearby Davy Crockett Elementary School the following September.[91]

Ekdahl visited Mrs. Oswald on weekends and stayed at Victor Street.[92] By the following year she had resolved her doubts about marrying him, influenced in part by his substantial income [93] and perhaps by the visit some time earlier of his sister, who favored the marriage because of his ill health.[94] Explaining that she expected to travel a great deal, Mrs. Oswald tried unsuccessfully to return the older boys to the home in February 1945.[95] She and Ekdahl were married in May.[96] After a brief honeymoon, they returned to Victor Street.[97]

Ekdahl got along well with the boys, on whom he lavished much attention.[98] John testified that Ekdahl treated them as if they were his own children and that Lee seemed to find in Ekdahl "the father he never had"; John recalled that on one occasion he told Lee that Ekdahl and his mother had become reconciled after a separation, and that "this seemed to really elate Lee, this made him really happy that they were getting back together." [99]

Because Ekdahl's business required him to make frequent trips, in September, John and Robert were placed in the Chamberlain-Hunt Military Academy at Port Gibson, Miss.; [100] their mother paid the tuition herself, using the proceeds from the sale of the Alvar Street property.[101] They remained at the academy for the next 3 years, returning home only for vacations.[102] Lee accompanied his parents on their travels.[103] Mrs. Myrtle Evans, who had known both Marguerite and Ekdahl before their marriage,[104] testified that Marguerite insisted on keeping Lee with her; Mrs. Evans thought that Marguerite was "too close" to Lee and "spoiled him to death," which hurt her marriage to Ekdahl.[105]

Sometime in the fall after John and Robert were at boarding school, the Ekdahls moved to Benbrook, a suburb of Fort Worth, where they lived on Granbury Road,[106] in a house of stone or brick, set on a large plot of land.[107] Records of the Benbrook Common School show Lee's admission into the first grade on October 31; his birth date is incorrectly given as July 9, 1939, his mother presumably having given that date to satisfy the age requirement.[108] On February 8, 1946, he was admitted to the Harris Hospital in Fort Worth with "acute mastoiditis." [109] A mastoidectomy was performed without complications, and Lee left the hospital in 4 days.[110] (In 1955, Lee indicated on a school form that he had an "abnormal ear drum in left ear," [111] presumably a reference to the mastoidectomy; but when he entered the Marines 1 year later, physical examination disclosed no physical defects.) [112]

The Ekdahls' marriage quickly broke down. Before they had been married a year, Marguerite suspected Ekdahl of infidelity.[113] She thought him stingy,[114] and there were frequent arguments about his insistence that she account for her expenditures and his refusal to share his money with her.[115] In the summer of 1946, she left Ekdahl, picked up John and Robert at Chamberlain-Hunt, and moved with the boys to Covington, La.,[116] where they lived for at least part of the time

672

at 311 Vermont Street.[117]   Mrs. Evans described them at Covington, possibly during this summer, as "really a happy family"; Lee seemed like a normal boy but "kept to himself" and seemed not "to want to be with any other children." [118]   The separation continued after the two boys returned to boarding school, and in September Lee was enrolled in the Covington Elementary School.[119]   His record at Benbrook had been satisfactory—he was present on 82 school days and absent on 15, and received all A's and B's [120]—but he had not completed the work of the first grade, in which he was enrolled for a second time.[121]

Lee received no grades at the Covington School, from which he was withdrawn on January 23, 1947,[122] because his parents, now reconciled, were moving to Fort Worth, where they lived at 1505 Eighth Avenue.[123]   Four days later, he enrolled in the Clayton Public School; he was still in the first grade, which he completed in May with B's in every subject except physical education and health, in which he received A's.[124]   In the fall, he entered the second grade in the same school but, relations between his parents having deteriorated again, was withdrawn before any grades were recorded.[125]

After the move to Fort Worth, the Ekdahls continued to argue frequently; according to John, "they would have a fight about every other day and he would leave and come back." [126]   That summer, Marguerite obtained what she regarded as proof that Ekdahl was having some sort of affair.   According to her testimony, a neighbor told her that Ekdahl had been living on Eighth Avenue with another woman while she was in Covington.[127]   Then, at a time when Ekdahl was supposed to be out of town,[128] she went with John and several of his friends to an apartment in Fort Worth; one of the boys posed as a telegram carrier, and when the door opened she pushed her way into the apartment and found Ekdahl in his shirt sleeves in the company of a woman in a negligee.[129]

Despite this apparent confirmation of her suspicions, Marguerite continued to live with Ekdahl until January 1948.[130]   In January, according to Ekdahl's allegations in the subsequent divorce proceedings, she "directed * * * [him] to leave the home immediately and never to return," which he did.[131]   Ekdahl filed suit for divorce in March.[132]   The complaint alleged that Marguerite constantly nagged Ekdahl and argued "with reference to money matters," accused him of infidelity, threw things at him, and finally ordered him out of the house; that these acts were unprovoked by Ekdahl's conduct toward her; that her acts endangered his already impaired health; and that her "excesses, harsh and cruel treatment and outrages" toward him made it impossible for them to live together.[133]   She denied all these allegations.[134]   After a trial, at which John testified and, he thought, Lee was called to the stand but was excused without testifying,[135] the jury found on special issues that Marguerite was "guilty of excesses, cruel treatment, or outrages" unprovoked by Ekdahl's conduct.[136]   On June 24, the court granted the divorce and approved an agreement between the parties disposing of their property between them and awarding Marguerite $1,500; at her request, the divorce restored to Marguerite her former name, Marguerite C. Oswald.[137]

While the divorce suit was pending, Marguerite moved from Eighth Avenue to a house on 3300 Willing Street, next to railroad tracks.[138] The boys found her there in May when they returned from the military academy; for John, the move signified that they "were back down in the lower class again." [139] Lee's withdrawal from the Clayton School on March 18, 1948,[140] probably coincided with the move to Willing Street. He entered the Clark Elementary School on the following day, and in June completed the second grade with a record mostly of B's and A's.[141] Philip Vinson, a classmate at the Clayton School, has described Lee at that time as "a quiet type of kid," who "didn't make a lot of noise." [142] Lee was "stocky and well built," which made other boys look up to him and regard him as the leader of one of their schoolyard "gangs." [143] Vinson thought that Lee was not a bully and got along with his classmates, but had the impression that he rarely played with them or brought them home after school.[144]

Shortly after the divorce, Mrs. Oswald purchased a small house in Benbrook, on what is now San Saba Street; [145] John has testified that it had a single bedroom, in which Lee slept with his mother, and a screened porch where John and Robert slept.[146] Mrs. Oswald worked at a department store in Fort Worth, and left the three boys home alone.[147] A neighbor, Mrs. W. H. Bell, has stated that Lee seemed to enjoy being by himself and to resent discipline; [148] another neighbor, Otis R. Carlton, stated that he once saw Lee chase John with a knife and throw it at him, an incident which, Carlton said, their mother passed off as a "little scuffle." [149] At the end of the summer, Carlton purchased the property. He stated that he appraised it at $2,750 at Mrs. Oswald's request; she then insisted that he had made an offer to purchase at that price, which he finally agreed to do.[150]

After the house was sold, the family returned to Fort Worth, a move necessitated by Mrs. Oswald's, and now John's, employment.[151] Mrs. Oswald bought a two-bedroom, frame house at 7408 Ewing, from which Robert and Lee could walk to school.[152] John, who was then 16, obtained a job as a shoe stockboy at Everybody's Department Store; he testified that he wanted to finish high school at the military academy, but that his mother advised him to leave school and help to support the family.[153] He gave her $15 per week out of his salary of $25.[154] Robert returned to school.[155]

Lee entered the third grade at the Arlington Heights Elementary School.[156] He remained at Arlington Heights for the entire school year, completing the third grade with a satisfactory record, which included A's in social studies, citizenship, elementary science, art, and music, and a D in spelling.[157] In September 1949, he transferred to the Ridglea West Elementary School, where he remained for the next 3 years.[158] Lee's record at Ridglea is not remarkable in any respect. In the fourth and fifth grades, he received mostly B's; in the sixth grade, B's and C's predominate.[159] He received D's in both the fifth and sixth grades in spelling and arithmetic; in the fourth and sixth grades, C's are recorded for Spanish,[160] which may account for his rudimentary familiarity with that language later on.[161] In the fourth grade his IQ was recorded at 103; on achievement tests in each of the 3 years, he twice did best in reading and twice did worst in spelling.[162]

Lee is generally characterized as an unexceptional but rather solitary boy during these years. His mother worked in a variety of jobs,[163] and, according to her own testimony, told Lee not to contact her at work except in an emergency.[164] He ordinarily returned home alone directly after school, in obedience to his mother's instructions.[165] A fourth grade teacher, Mrs. Clyde I. Livingston, described him as a lonely boy, quiet and shy, who did not easily form friendships with other students.[166] But Richard W. Garrett has stated that he was a classmate of Lee in the fourth or fifth grade and found him easy to get along with; he recalled playing with Lee often at school and sometimes walking home together with him.[167] Mrs. Livingston recalled that at Christmas 1949, Lee gave her a puppy and afterward came to her home to see the puppy and talk to her and her family.[168]

Lee's relationship with his brothers was good but limited by the difference in their ages.[169] He still had a dog,[170] but there were few children of his age in the neighborhood, and he appears to have been by himself after school most of the time.[171] He read a lot,[172] had a stamp collection, and played chess and Monopoly with his brothers.[173] Mrs. Murret remembered that on a visit to her home in New Orleans, Lee refused to play with other children or even to leave the house; he preferred to stay indoors and read (mostly "funnybooks") or listen to the radio.[174] After several weeks with the Murrets, Lee wrote to his mother and asked her to come for him.[175] Hiram Conway, a neighbor on Ewing Street, thought Lee was an intelligent child, who picked things up easily; although he did not recall many specific incidents to support his impressions, Conway regarded Lee as "a bad kid," who was "quick to anger" and "mean when he was angry, just ornery." [176] John's general picture of Lee in these years is that of "a normal healthy robust boy who would get in fights and still have his serious moments."[177]

John returned to high school in January 1949, but continued to work part time.[178] Early in 1950, he entered the Coast Guard.[179] Robert left school soon after John's departure and went to work full time, contributing most of his earnings to the support of his family.[180] He returned to school in 1951–52, and after completing his junior year in high school, joined the Marines in July 1952.[181] In August, Mrs. Oswald and Lee moved to New York, where John was living with his wife and a very young baby in an apartment at 325 East 92d Street; the apartment belonged to John's mother-in-law, who was temporarily away.[182] Mrs. Oswald has explained that with Robert gone she did not want Lee to be alone while she worked and that she went to New York City "not as a venture," but because she "had family" there.[183]

The visit began well. John testified of his meeting with Lee: "We met in the street and I was real glad to see him and he was real glad to see me. We were real good friends." [184] He took about a week of leave and showed Lee the city; he remembered trips to the Museum of Natural History and Polk's Hobby Shop, and a ride on the Staten Island ferry. [185] But when it became obvious that his mother intended to stay, the atmosphere changed. Mrs. Oswald did not get along with John's wife, with whom she quarreled frequently. [186] There was difficulty about her failure to contribute anything towards her own and Lee's support. [187] According to John, his wife liked Lee and would have been glad to have him alone stay with them but felt that his mother set Lee against her; they never suggested that Lee remain with them since they knew that it would not work out. [188] The visit ended when Lee threatened Mrs. Pic with a pocket knife during a quarrel, [189] and she asked Mrs. Oswald to leave. [190] John testified that during this same quarrel Lee hit his mother, who appeared to have lost all control over him. [191] The incident permanently destroyed the good relationship between Lee and his brother. [192]

Mrs. Oswald and Lee moved uptown to a one-room basement apartment [193] in the Bronx, at 1455 Sheridan Avenue. [194] While they were still at the Pics, he had been enrolled at the Trinity Evangelical Lutheran School on Watson Avenue. [195] He was withdrawn on September 26, after several weeks of irregular attendance, and 4 days later enrolled in the seventh grade of Public School 117, a junior high school. [196] Mrs. Oswald found a job at one of the Lerner Shops, a chain of dress shops for which she had worked briefly in Fort Worth several years before. [197] In January, they moved again, to 825 East 179th Street, [198] and a few weeks later, she left the employ of Lerner Shops. [199] In April, she was working at Martin's Department Store in Brooklyn, where she earned $45 per week; [200] in May, she went to work for a chain of hosiery shops, with which she remained until December. [201] Lee was registered at Public School 117 until January 16, 1953, [202] although the move to 179th Street, which took him out of that school district, probably took place before that date. [203] He had been at Public School 117 for 64 schooldays, out of which he had been present on 15 full and 2 half days; [204] he had received failing grades in most of his courses. [205]

Lee's truancy increased after he moved; he was now located in the school district of Public School 44 but refused to go to school there. [206] On one occasion that spring, an attendance officer located Lee at the Bronx Zoo; the officer testified that Lee was clean and well dressed, but was surly and referred to the officer as a "damned Yankee." [207] Several truancy hearings were held in January, at the first of which at least, both Mrs. Oswald and Lee evidently failed to appear. [208] At a hearing on January 27, by which time it was known that Lee was living in the Public School 44 district, it was decided to commence judicial proceedings if his truancy continued. [209] Meanwhile, on January 16, his mother called the Community Service Society, to which she had been referred by the Federation of Protestant Welfare Agencies, and asked for an appointment to discuss the problem.[210] She mentioned that a truancy hearing had been held and said that Lee would not attend school despite the threat of official action; she thought that his behavior was due to difficulty in adjusting to his new environment.[211] An appointment was scheduled for January 30, but she failed to appear, and the case was closed.[212] Sometime in February, the Pics visited the Oswalds. John testified that his mother told him about Lee's truancy and asked how she could get Lee to accept psychiatric aid. Nothing came of these discussions.[213]

On March 12, the attendance officer in charge of Lee's case filed a petition in court which alleged that Lee had been "excessively absent from school" between October and January, that he had refused to register at Public School 44 or to attend school there, and that he was "beyond the control of his mother insofar as school attendance is concerned." [214] On the same day, Mrs. Oswald appeared in court alone and informed the presiding judge that Lee refused to appear in court.[215] Evidently impressed by the proceedings, however, Lee did register at Public School 44 on March 23.[216] Nevertheless, on April 16, Justice Delany declared him a truant, and remanded him to Youth House until May 7 for psychiatric study.[217]

In accordance with the regular procedures at Youth House, Lee took a series of tests and was interviewed by a staff social worker and a probation officer, both of whom interviewed Mrs. Oswald as well.[218] Their findings, discussed more fully in chapter VII of the Commission's report, indicated that Lee was a withdrawn, socially maladjusted boy, whose mother did not interest herself sufficiently in his welfare and had failed to establish a close relationship with him.[219] Mrs. Oswald visited Lee at Youth House and came away with a highly unfavorable impression; she regarded it as unfit for her son.[220] On the basis of all the test results and reports and his own interview with Lee, Dr. Renatus Hartogs, the chief staff psychiatrist, recommended that Lee be placed on probation with a requirement that he seek help from a child guidance clinic, and that his mother be urged to contact a family agency for help; he recommended that Lee not be placed in an institution unless treatment during probation was unsuccessful.[221]

Lee returned to court on May 7. He and his mother appeared before Justice McClancy, who discussed the Youth House reports with them.[222] He released Lee on parole until September 24, and requested that a referral be made to the Community Service Society for treatment.[223] The probation officer called the society on the same day but was told that it would probably not be able to take the case because of its already full case load and the intensive treatment which Lee was likely to require; [224] it confirmed this position 1 week later and closed the case on May 31.[225] An application was made to the Salvation Army also, which turned it down because it could not provide the needed services.[226]

During the few weeks of school which remained, Lee attended school regularly, and completed the seventh grade with low but passing marks in all his academic subjects.[227]   (He received a failing mark in a home economics course.)[228]   His conduct was generally satisfactory and he was rated outstanding in "Social-Participation"; the record indicates that he belonged to a model airplane club and had a special interest in horseback riding.[229]   Robert Oswald visited New York that summer, while he was on leave from the Marines.[230]   Lee did not appear to him to be unhappy or to be acting abnormally, nor did Robert observe that relations between Lee and his mother were strained.[231]   Lee's truancy the previous fall and winter was apparently discussed only in passing, when Mrs. Oswald mentioned that Lee had had to appear before a judge.[232]

On September 14, Lee entered the eighth grade at Public School 44.[233]   His parole was due to end 10 days later.   On September 24, however, Mrs. Oswald telephoned the probation officer and advised that she could not appear in court; she added that there was no need for her to do so, since Lee was attending school regularly and was now well adjusted.[234]   The parole was extended until October 29, before which date the school was to submit a progress report.[235]   The report was highly unfavorable.   Although Lee was attending school regularly, his conduct was unsatisfactory; teachers reported that he refused to salute the flag, did little work, and seemed to spend most of his time "sailing paper planes around the room."[236]   On October 29, Mrs. Oswald again telephoned to say that she would be unable to appear. Justice Sicher continued Lee's parole until November 19 and directed the probation officer to make a referral to the Berkshire Industrial Farm or Children's Village.[237]

Before the next hearing, Mrs. Oswald discussed Lee's behavior with the school authorities, who indicated to the probation officer that Lee's behavior improved considerably after her visit to the school.[238] He did, in fact, receive passing grades in most of his subjects in the first marking period.   His report also contains notations by his teachers that he was "quick-tempered," "constantly losing control," and "getting into battles with others."[239]   Both Lee and his mother appeared in court on November 19.   Despite Mrs. Oswald's request that Lee be discharged, Justice Sicher stated his belief that Lee needed treatment, and continued his parole until January 28, 1954; the probation officer was directed to contact the Big Brothers counseling service in the meantime.[240]

At the request of the probation officer, the Big Brothers office contacted Mrs. Oswald in December, and on January 4 a caseworker visited her and Lee at home.[241]   The caseworker reported that he was cordially received but was told by Mrs. Oswald that continued counseling was unnecessary; she pointed out to him that Lee now belonged to the West Side YMCA, which he attended every Saturday.   The caseworker reported, however, that Lee was plainly "displeased with the idea of being forced to join various 'Y' organizations about which he cared little."   Mrs. Oswald declared her intention to return to New

Orleans and was advised to obtain Lee's release from the court's jurisdiction before she left.[242] On the following day, she called the probation officer, who was away on vacation, and was advised by his office again not to take Lee out of the jurisdiction without the court's consent.[243] The same advice was repeated to her by the Big Brothers caseworker on January 6.[244] Through all these contacts, Mrs. Oswald had evidenced reluctance to bring Lee into court, prompted probably by fear that he would be retained in some sort of custody as he had been at the time of the commitment to Youth House.[245] Without further communication to the court, Mrs. Oswald and Lee returned to New Orleans sometime before January 10.[246] On March 11, the court dismissed the case.[247]

In New Orleans, Lee and his mother stayed with the Murrets at 757 French Street while they looked for an apartment.[248] Lee enrolled in the eighth grade at Beauregard Junior High School on January 13 [249] and completed the school year without apparent difficulty.[250] He entered the ninth grade in September and again received mediocre but acceptable marks.[251] In October 1954, Lee took a series of achievement tests, on which he did well in reading and vocabulary, badly in mathematics.[252] At the end of the school year, on June 2, 1955, he filled out a "personal history." He indicated that the subjects which he liked best were civics, science, and mathematics; those he liked least were English and art. His vocational preferences were listed as biology and mechanical drawing; his plans after high school, however, were noted as "military service" and "undecided." He said that reading and outdoor sports were his recreational activities and that he liked football in particular. In response to the question whether he had "any close friends in this school," he wrote, "no." [253]

Lee is remembered by those who knew him in New Orleans as a quiet, solitary boy who made few friends.[254] He was briefly a member of the Civil Air Patrol,[255] and considered joining an organization of high school students interested in astronomy; [256] occasionally, he played pool or darts with his friend, Edward Voebel.[257] Beyond this, he seems to have had few contacts with other people. He read a lot, starting at some point to read Communist literature which he found at the public library; [258] he walked or rode a bicycle, sometimes visiting a museum.[259] Except in his relations with his mother, he was not unusually argumentative or belligerent, but he seems not to have avoided fights if they came; they did come fairly frequently, perhaps in part because of his aloofness from his fellows and the traces of a northern accent in his speech.[260] His only close friendship, with Voebel, arose when Voebel helped him tend his wounds after a fight.[261] Friends of Mrs. Oswald thought that he was demanding and insolent toward her and that she had no control over him.[262]

While Lee was in the eighth and ninth grades, Mrs. Oswald worked first at Burt's Shoestore [263] and then at the Dolly Shoe Co.[264] One of her employers at Dolly, where she worked as a cashier and salesclerk, remembered her as a pleasant person and a good worker.[265] At her request, the company hired Lee to work part time; he worked there, mostly on Saturdays, for about 10 weeks in 1955.[266]   On the "personal history" record which he filled out in school, he stated that he had been a "retail shoesaleman"; [267] but his employer recalled that they had tried to train him as a salesman without success and that he had in fact been a stockboy.[268]

After a short period with the Murrets, Mrs. Oswald and Lee had moved to an apartment owned by Myrtle Evans at 1454 Saint Mary Street, which she and Mrs. Murret helped to furnish; later they moved to a less expensive apartment in the same building, the address of which was 1452 Saint Mary Street.[269]   Relations between Mrs. Oswald and Mrs. Evans became strained,[270] and in the spring of 1955 the Oswalds moved to a new apartment at 126 Exchange Place in the French Quarter.[271]   Although Lee gave the Exchange Place address on a school form at the end of the ninth grade,[272] the school authorities had apparently not been advised of these moves earlier, because Mrs. Oswald did not want Lee to be transferred from Beauregard, which she considered a good school.[273]   During the summer of 1955, Robert left the Marine Corps and spent a week with his mother and Lee in New Orleans before moving to Fort Worth; he found Lee unchanged.[274]

That fall, Lee entered the 10th grade at Warren Easton High School.[275]   He had been there for about a month when he presented to the school authorities a note written by himself to which he had signed his mother's name.   It was dated October 7, 1955, and read:

> To whom it may concern,
>   Becaus we are moving to San Diego in the middle of this month Lee must quit school now.   Also, please send by him any papers such as his birth certificate that you may have.   Thank you.
>   Sincirely
>
> Mrs. M. Oswald [276]

He dropped out of school a few days later, shortly before his 16th birthday.[277]   After his birthday, he tried to enlist in the Marines, using a false affidavit from his mother that he was 17.[278]   (Some years before, John Pic had joined the Marine Corps Reserve by means of his mother's false affidavit that he was 17.) [279]   The attempt failed, and, according to his mother's testimony, Lee spent the next year reading and memorizing the "Marine Manual," which he had obtained from Robert and "living to when he is age 17 to join the Marines." [280] He worked for the rest of the school year.   Between November 10 and January 14, he was a messenger boy for Gerald F. Tujague, Inc., a shipping company, where he earned $130 per month.[281]   His employer remembers him as a quiet, withdrawn person.[282]   In January he worked briefly as an office boy for J. R. Michels, Inc.[283]   For several months thereafter, he was a messenger for the Pfisterer Dental Laboratory.[284]   His military record subsequently described his prior civilian jobs as follows:

Performed various clerical duties such as distributing mail, delivering messages & answering telephone. Helped file records & operated ditto, letter opening & sealing machines.[285]

Anticipating that Lee would join the Marines as soon as he was 17, Mrs. Oswald moved in July 1956 to Fort Worth,[286] where she took an apartment at 4936 Collinswood for herself, Lee, and Robert.[287] In September, Lee enrolled in the 10th grade at the Arlington Heights High School [288] but attended classes for only a few weeks. He dropped out of school on September 28.[289] A few days later, he wrote the following letter to the Socialist Party of America:

October 3, 1956

Dear Sirs;
    I am sixteen years of age and would like more information about your youth League, I would like to know if there is a branch in my area, how to join, ect., I am a Marxist, and have been studying socialist principles for well over fifteen months I am very interested in your Y.P.S.L.
    Sincerely

/s/   Lee Oswald [290]

Accompanying the letter was an advertisement coupon, on which he had checked the box requesting information about the Socialist Party.[291]

Lee became 17 on October 18. He enlisted in the Marines on October 24.[292]

MARINES

On October 26, 1956, Lee Harvey Oswald reported for duty at the Marine Corps Recruit Depot in San Diego, Calif., where he was assigned to the Second Recruit Training Battalion.[293] He was 68 inches tall and weighed 135 pounds; he had no physical defects.[294] On October 30, he took a series of aptitude tests, on which he scored significantly above the Marine Corps average in reading and vocabulary and significantly below the average in tests in arithmetic and pattern analysis. His composite general classification score was 105, 2 points below the Corps average. He scored near the bottom of the lowest group in a radio code test.[295] His preference of duty was recorded as Aircraft Maintenance and Repair, the duty assignment for which he was recommended.[296]

While he was at San Diego, Oswald was trained in the use of the M-1 rifle.[297] His practice scores were not very good,[298] but when his company fired for record on December 21, he scored 212, 2 points above the score necessary to qualify as a "sharpshooter" on a marksman/sharpshooter/expert scale.[299] He did not do nearly as well when he fired for record again shortly before he left the Marines.[300] He practiced also with a riot gun and a .45-caliber pistol when he was in the Marines but no scores were recorded.[301]

Oswald was given a 4.4 rating in both "conduct" and "proficiency" at the Recruit Depot, the highest possible rating being 5.0 and an average rating of 4.0 being required for an honorable discharge.[302] On January 18, 1957, he reported to Camp Pendleton, Calif., for further training and was assigned to "A" Company of the First Battalion, Second Infantry Training Regiment.[303] He was at Pendleton for a little more than 5 weeks, at the end of which he was rated 4.2 in conduct and 4.0 in proficiency.[304] Allen R. Felde, a fellow recruit who was with Oswald at San Diego and Pendleton, has stated that Oswald was generally unpopular and that his company was avoided by the other men.[305] When his squad was given its first weekend leave from Pendleton, all eight men took a cab to Tijuana, Mexico. Oswald left the others and did not rejoin them until it was time to return to camp. Felde said that this practice was repeated on other trips to Los Angeles; Oswald accompanied the men on the bus to and from camp but did not stay with them in the city.[306] On February 27, he went on leave for 2 weeks,[307] during which he may have visited his mother in Fort Worth.[308]

On March 18, he reported to the Naval Air Technical Training Center at the Naval Air Station in Jacksonville, Fla.[309] For the next 6 weeks he attended an Aviation Fundamental School, in which he received basic instruction in his specialty, including such subjects as basic radar theory, map reading, and air traffic control procedures.[310] This course, as well as his next training assignment at Keesler Air Force Base, required Oswald to deal with confidential material.[311] He was granted final clearance up to the "confidential" level on May 3, "after [a] careful check of local records had disclosed no derogatory data."[312] He completed the course on the same day, ranking 46th in a class of 54 students.[313] On the previous day, he had been promoted to private, first class, effective May 1.[314] At Jacksonville, he received ratings of 4.7 in conduct and 4.5 in proficiency, the highest ratings he ever attained.[315]

Oswald left for Keesler Air Force Base in Biloxi, Miss., on the day his course was completed;[316] he traveled, probably by overnight train, in a group of six marines led by Pfc. Daniel P. Powers, the senior marine in charge.[317] At Keesler, he attended the Aircraft Control and Warning Operator Course, which included instruction in aircraft surveillance and the use of radar.[318] Powers was not sure whether he had met Oswald before the trip to Biloxi [319] but remembers him there as "a somewhat younger individual, less matured than the other boys," who "was normally outside the particular group of marines that were in this attachment to Keesler."[320] (Oswald was in fact 3 years younger than Powers.)[321] Powers testified that Oswald had the nickname "Ozzie Rabbit."[322] Oswald generally stayed to himself, often read-

ing; he did not play cards or work out in the gym with the others.[323]
He spent his weekends alone, away from the base; Powers thought
he left Biloxi and perhaps went "home" to New Orleans, less than
100 miles away.[324] He finished the course seventh in a class of 30
marines on June 17,[325] and on June 25, was given an MOS (military
occupational specialty) of Aviation Electronics Operator.[326] On
June 20, he went on leave,[327] possibly visiting his mother.[328] His
ratings at Keesler were 4.2 in conduct and 4.5 in proficiency,[329] which
Powers thought was "pretty good." [330]

On July 9, Oswald reported at the Marine Corps Air Station at El
Toro, Calif., near Santa Ana.[331] He was classified as a replacement
trainee and attached to the Fourth Replacement Battalion.[332] Six
weeks later, on August 22, he departed from San Diego for Yokosuka,
Japan, on board the U.S.S. *Bexar*.[333] Powers testified that while on
board, Oswald taught him to play chess, which they played frequently,
sometimes for more than 4 hours a day.[334] Like most of the men on
board, Oswald read a lot from the books which were available.
Powers thought he read "a good type of literature," remembering
in particular Whitman's "Leaves of Grass." [335]

The *Bexar* docked at Yokosuka on September 12.[336] Oswald was
assigned to Marine Air Control Squadron No. 1 (MACS–1), Marine
Air Group 11, 1st Marine Aircraft Wing, based at Atsugi, about 20
miles west of Tokyo.[337] Oswald was a radar operator in MACS–1,
which had less than 100 men.[338] Its function was to direct aircraft to
their targets by radar, communicating with the pilots by radio.[339]
The squadron had also the duty of scouting for incoming foreign aircraft, such as straying Russian or Chinese planes, which would be
intercepted by American planes.[340]

On October 27, when Oswald opened his locker to remove some
gear, a derringer .22 caliber pistol fell to the floor and discharged; the
bullet hit him in the left elbow.[341] Paul Edward Murphy, a fellow
marine who was in the next cubicle, heard the shot, rushed in, and
found Oswald sitting on the locker looking at his arm; without emotion, Oswald said to Murphy, "I believe I shot myself." [342] He was
in the naval hospital at Yokosuka until November 15.[343]

The Judge Advocate General concluded that Oswald had "displayed a certain degree of carelessness or negligence" by storing a
loaded revolver in his locker, but that his injury was incurred "in
the line of duty" and was not the result "of his own misconduct." [344]
He was, however, charged with possession of an unregistered privately
owned weapon in violation of general orders. A court-martial followed on April 11, 1958, when Oswald's unit returned from maneuvers,
and on April 29 he was sentenced to be confined at hard labor for 20
days, to forfeit $25 per month for 2 months, and to be reduced to the
grade of private.[345] The confinement was suspended for 6 months,
after which that portion of the sentence was to be remitted.[346]

Five days after Oswald left the hospital, MACS–1 embarked aboard
the *Terrell County*, LST 1157, for maneuvers in the Philippine Islands

area.[347] According to Powers' recollection, the squadron was expected to return to Atsugi after maneuvers were completed, but an international crisis developed; since another operation was scheduled for a few months later, the squadron debarked at Cubi Point (Subic Bay) in the Philippines and set up a temporary installation.[348] While he was in the Philippines, Oswald passed a test of eligibility for the rank of corporal;[349] in a semiannual evaluation, however, he was given his lowest ratings thus far: 4.0 in conduct and 3.9 in proficiency.[350] The unit participated in exercises at Corregidor, from which it sailed for Atsugi on March 7, 1958, aboard the U.S.S. *Wexford County*, LST 1168.[351] The *Wexford County* reached Atsugi 11 days later.[352]

Oswald was court-martialed a second time on June 27, for using "provoking words" to a noncommissioned officer (a sergeant) on June 20, at the Bluebird Cafe in Yamato, and assaulting the officer by pouring a drink on him.[353] The findings were that Oswald spilled the drink accidentally, but when the sergeant shoved him away, Oswald invited the sergeant outside in insulting language.[354] Oswald admitted that he was rather drunk and had invited the sergeant outside but did not recall insulting him.[355] He was sentenced to be confined at hard labor for 28 days and to forfeit $55;[356] in addition, suspension of the previous sentence of confinement was withdrawn.[357] He was in confinement until August 13.[358] Meanwhile, a previously granted extension of oversea duty was canceled,[359] and he was given ratings of 1.9 in conduct and 3.4 in proficiency.[360]

On September 14, Oswald sailed with his unit for the South China Sea area; the unit was at Ping Tung, North Taiwan on September 30, and returned to Atsugi on October 5.[361] On October 6, he was transferred out of MACS–1 and put on general duty, in anticipation of his return to the United States.[362] He spent several days thereafter in the Atsugi Station Hospital.[363] On October 31, he received his last oversea ratings: 4.0 in both conduct and proficiency.[364]

Oswald appears generally to have been regarded by his fellows overseas as an intelligent person who followed orders and did his work well, but who complained frequently.[365] He did not associate much with other marines and continued to read a great deal.[366] Paul Murphy testified that Oswald could speak "a little Russian" while he was overseas.[367] Powers believed that Oswald became more assertive in Japan and thought that he might have had a Japanese girl friend.[368] He departed from Yokosuka on board the USNS *Barrett* on November 2, and arrived in San Francisco 13 days later.[369] On November 19, he took 30 days' leave.[370]

On December 22, Oswald was assigned to Marine Air Control Squadron No. 9 (MACS–9) at the Marine Corps Air Station at El Toro, where he had been briefly before he went overseas.[371] He was one of about seven enlisted men and three officers who formed a "radar crew," engaged primarily in aircraft surveillance.[372] This work probably gave him access to certain kinds of classified material, some of which, such as aircraft call signs and radio frequencies, was changed after his defection to Russia.[373] For part of his time at El Toro, Oswald may have been assigned to clerical or janitorial tasks on the base.[374] Some of his associates believed rumors,[375] incorrect according to official records,[376] that he had lost his clearance to work on radar crews; one recalled hearing that Oswald had once had clearance above the "confidential" level and had lost it because he "had poured beer over a staff NCO's head in an enlisted club in Japan, and had been put in the brig." [377]

The officer in command of the radar crew, Lt. John E. Donovan, found him "competent in all functions," and observed that he handled himself calmly and well in emergency situations.[378] Donovan thought Oswald was not a leader but that he performed competently on occasions when, as the senior man present, he served as crew chief.[379] This estimate was generally shared by his fellows, most of whom thought that he performed his assigned duties adequately but was deficient in disciplinary matters and such things as barracks inspection.[380] One of them recalled that after a number of bad inspections, the other members of Oswald's quonset hut complained about him and secured his transfer to another hut.[381] He was thought to be an intelligent person, somewhat better educated and more intellectually oriented than other men on the base.[382] A few of the men thought it more accurate to describe him as someone who wanted to appear intelligent.[383] He had a pronounced interest in world affairs, in which he appears to have been better informed than some of the officers, whose lack of knowledge amused and sometimes irritated him; he evidently enjoyed drawing others, especially officers, into conversations in which he could display his own superior knowledge.[384]

It seems clear from the various recollections of those who knew him at El Toro that by the time Oswald returned to the United States, he no longer had any spirit for the Marines; the attitudes which had prompted his enlistment as soon as he was eligible were entirely gone, and his attention had turned away from the Marines to what he might do after his discharge. While no one was able to predict his attempt to defect to Russia within a month after he left the Marines, the testimony of those who knew him at El Toro, in contrast to that of his associates in Japan, leaves no doubt that his thoughts were occupied increasingly with Russia and the Russian way of life. He had studied the Russian language enough by February 25, 1959, to request that he be given a foreign language qualification test; his rating was "poor" in all parts of the test.[385] Most of the marines who knew him were aware that he was studying Russian; [386] one of them, Henry J. Roussel, Jr., arranged a date between Lee and his aunt, Rosaleen Quinn, an airline stewardess who was also studying Russian.[387] (Miss Quinn thought that Oswald spoke Russian well in view of his lack of formal training; she found the evening uninteresting.[388] Donovan, with whom she had a date later, testified that she told him that Oswald was "kind of an oddball.") [389] He read, and perhaps subscribed to, a newspaper, possibly printed in Russian, which his associates connected with his Russian bent.[390]

Most of those who knew him were able to recount anecdotes which suggest that he was anxious to publicize his liking for things Russian, sometimes in good humor and sometimes seriously. Some of his fellows called him "Oswaldskovich," apparently to his pleasure.[391] He is said to have had his name written in Russian on one of his jackets;[392] to have played records of Russian songs "so loud that one could hear them outside the barracks";[393] frequently to have made remarks in Russian [394] or used expressions like "da" or "nyet," [395] or addressed others (and been addressed) as "Comrade";[396] to have come over and said jokingly, "You called?" when one of the marines played a particular record of Russian music.[397]

Connected with this Russophilia was an interest in and acceptance of Russian political views and, to a lesser extent, Communist ideology. Less obvious to his fellows generally,[398] it nevertheless led him into serious discussions with some of them. Donovan, who was a graduate of the School of Foreign Service of Georgetown University,[399] thought Oswald was "truly interested in international affairs" [400] and "very well versed, at least on the superficial facts of a given foreign situation." [401] He recalled that Oswald had a particular interest in Latin America [402] and had a good deal of information about Cuba in particular.[403] Oswald expressed sympathy for Castro but, according to Donovan, "what he said about Castro was not an unpopular belief at that time." [404] Donovan believed that Oswald subscribed to the Russian newspaper—which Donovan thought was a Communist newspaper—not only in order to read Russian but also because he thought it "presented a very different and perhaps equally just side of the international affairs in comparison with the United States newspapers." [405] Donovan was clear, on the other hand, that he never heard Oswald "in any way, shape or form confess that he was a Communist, or that he ever thought about being a Communist." [406]

Private Kerry Thornley described himself as a close acquaintance, but not a good friend, of Oswald, whom he met in the spring of 1959; [407] he later wrote an unpublished novel in which he drew heavily on his impressions of Oswald.[408] Thornley generally corroborates Donovan's testimony but thought Oswald definitely believed that "the Marxist morality was the most rational morality to follow" and communism, "the best system in the world." [409] Thornley thought this belief was "theoretical," a "dispassionate appraisal" which did not indicate "any active commitment to the Communist ends"; he described Oswald as "idle in his admiration for communism." [410] He recalled discussions about Marxism in which Oswald criticized capitalism and praised the Soviet economic system.[411] Thornley testified that his association with Oswald ended when, in response to Oswald's criticism of a parade in which they both had to march, he said "Well, comes the revolution you will change all that." Oswald, he said, looked at him "like a betrayed Caesar" and walked away.[412] Thornley attributed Oswald's decision to go to Russia to a growing disillusionment with the United States, especially its role in the Far East, and a conviction that communism would eventually prevail.[413]   He was surprised by the decision but expected Oswald to adjust to Russian life and remain in Russia permanently.[414]

Another marine, Nelson Delgado, met Oswald soon after the latter arrived at El Toro.[415]   They were about the same age and had similar interests; Oswald enjoyed trying to speak Spanish with Delgado, who spoke it fluently.[416]   Delgado regarded him as a "complete believer that our way of government was not quite right," but did not think he was a Communist.[417]   Their discussions were concerned more with Cuba than Russia.[418]   They both favored the Castro government and talked—"dreaming," Delgado said—about joining the Cuban Army or Government and perhaps leading expeditions to other Caribbean islands to "free them too." [419]   Oswald told Delgado that he was in touch with Cuban diplomatic officials in this country; which Delgado at first took to be "one of his * * * lies," [420] but later believed.[421]

Oswald's interest in Russia and developing ideological attachment to theoretical communism apparently dominated his stay at El Toro. He was still withdrawn from most of his fellows, although his special interests appear to have made him stand out more there than he had at other posts and to have given him a source for conversation which he had hitherto lacked.[422]   According to several of the witnesses, names like "Ozzie Rabbit" still clung to him; [423] others recalled no nickname or only shortened versions of his real name.[424]   His reading acquired direction; books like "Das Kapital" and Orwell's "Animal Farm" and "1984" are mentioned in the testimony concerning this period.[425]   He played chess; [426] according to one of his opponents he chose the red pieces, expressing a preference for the "Red Army." [427]   He listened to classical music.[428]   For a short time, he played on the squadron football team.[429]   According to Donovan, who coached the team, Oswald was not very good; he lacked team spirit and often tried to call the plays, which was not his job.[430]   Delgado thought Oswald was a mediocre player.[431]   Donovan did not know whether Oswald quit or was thrown off the team.[432]   He spent most of his weekends alone, as he had at Keesler, and did not leave the post as often as the other men.[433]   Delgado once rode with him on the train to Los Angeles but separated from him there; Oswald returned to the base after one night.[434]   Delgado recalls that on another weekend Oswald accepted his invitation to go to Tijuana; they stayed there for one night.[435]

At the end of January 1959 and at the end of July, Oswald was given his semiannual ratings, scoring 4.0 in conduct both times, and 4.0 and 4.2 in proficiency.[436]   (The July ratings were repeated in September, when he was transferred from MACS-9 in preparation for his discharge.)[437]   On March 9, he was promoted as of March 1, to the rank of private, first class, for the second time.[438]   He took a series of high school level general educational development tests on March 23 and received an overall rating of "satisfactory." His best scores, in the 76th and 79th U.S. percentiles, were in English composition and physical sciences; his worst was English literature, in which he placed in the 34th percentile.[439]

In the spring, Oswald applied to Albert Schweitzer College in Churwalden, Switzerland, for admission to the spring term in 1960; the application is dated March 19.[440] Schweitzer is a small school, which specializes in courses in religion, ethics, science, and literature. He claimed a proficiency in Russian equal to 1 year of schooling [441] and that he had completed high school by correspondence with an average grade of 85 percent.[442] He listed philosophy, psychology, ideology, football, baseball, tennis and stamp-collecting as special interests, and writing short stories "on contemporary American life" as his vocational interest.[443] Jack London, Charles Darwin, and Norman Vincent Peale were listed as favorite authors.[444] He claimed membership in the YMCA and the "A.Y.H. Association," and said that he had participated in a "student body movement in school" for the control of juvenile delinquency.[445] Asked to give a general statement of his reasons for wanting to attend the college, he wrote:

> In order to aquire a fuller understanding of that subject which interest me most, Philosophy. To meet with Europeans who can broaden my scope of understanding. To receive formal Education by Instructers of high standing and character. To broaden my knowlege of German and to live in a healty climate and Good moral atmosphere.[446]

On the basis of these representations, Oswald's application was approved by the college.[447] He enclosed a registration fee of $25 in a letter dated June 19, in which he said that he was "looking forward to a fine stay." [448] Few of the other marines seem to have known about this application. He told Delgado, however, that he planned to attend a Swiss school to study psychology, and Delgado knew that some application had been made.[449] Another marine, Richard Call, also knew something of his plans.[450]

Oswald was obligated to serve on active duty until December 7, 1959 (the date having been adjusted to compensate for the period of confinement).[451] On August 17, he submitted a request for a dependency discharge, on the ground that his mother needed his support.[452] The request was accompanied by an affidavit of Mrs. Oswald and corroborating affidavits from an attorney, a doctor, and two friends, attesting that she had been injured at work in December 1958, and was unable to support herself.[453] Oswald had previously made a voluntary allotment of part of his salary to his mother, under which arrangement she received $40 in August, and had submitted an application for a "Q" allotment (dependency allowance) in her behalf of $91.30; one payment of the "Q" allotment, for the month of August, was made in September.[454] On August 28, the Wing Hardship or Dependency Discharge Board recommended that Oswald's request for a discharge be approved;[455] approval followed shortly.[456] On September 4, he was transferred from MACS-9 to the H. & H. Squadron,[457] and on September 11, he was released from active duty and transferred to the Marine Corps Reserve, in which he was expected to serve until December 8, 1962.[458]   He was assigned to the Marine Air Reserve Training Command at the Naval Air Station in Glenview, Ill.[459]

Almost exactly 1 year later, on September 13, 1960, Oswald was given an "undesirable discharge" from the Marine Corps Reserve,[460] based on:

> reliable information which indicated that he had renounced his U.S. citizenship with the intentions of becoming a permanent citizen of the Union of Soviet Socialist Republics.   Further, that petitioner brought discredit to the Marine Corps through adverse newspaper publicity, which was generated by the foregoing action, and had thereby, in the opinion of his commanding officer, proved himself unfit for retention in the naval service.[461]

SOVIET UNION

On September 4, the day on which he was transferred out of MACS–9 in preparation for his discharge, Oswald had applied for a passport at the Superior Court of Santa Ana, Calif. His application stated that he planned to leave the United States on September 21 to attend the Albert Schweitzer College and the University of Turku in Finland, and to travel in Cuba, the Dominican Republic, England, France, Germany, and Russia.[462]   The passport was routinely issued 6 days later.[463]

Oswald went directly home after his discharge, and arrived in Fort Worth by September 14.[464]   He told his mother that he intended to get a job on a ship or possibly in the "export-import business." [465]   If he stayed in Fort Worth, he said, he would be able to earn only about $30 per week; on a ship, he would earn "big money" and be able to send substantial amounts home.[466]   Three days after he arrived in Fort Worth, he left for New Orleans.[467]   While he was in Fort Worth he had registered his dependency discharge and entry into the Marine Reserve at the Fort Worth Selective Service Board,[468] and visited his brother Robert and his family.[469]   He also gave his mother $100.[470]

. On September 17, Oswald spoke with a representative of Travel Consultants, Inc., a New Orleans travel bureau; he filled out a "Passenger Immigration Questionnaire," on which he gave his occupation as "shipping export agent" and said that he would be abroad for 2 months on a pleasure trip. He booked passage from New Orleans to Le Havre, France, on a freighter, the SS *Marion Lykes*, scheduled to sail on September 18, for which he paid $220.75.[471]   On the evening of September 17, he registered at the Liberty Hotel.[472]

The *Marion Lykes* did not sail until the early morning of September 20.[473]   Before its departure, Oswald wrote his mother a letter, which was her last news of him until she read stories of his defection in Fort Worth newspapers:

Dear Mother:

Well, I have booked passage on a ship to Europe, I would of had to sooner or later and I think it's best I go now. Just remember above all else that my values are very different from Robert's or your's. It is difficult to tell you how I feel, Just remember this is what I must do. I did not tell you about my plans because you could harly be expected to understand.

I did not see aunt Lilian while I was here. I will write again as soon as I land.

Lee [474]

The *Marion Lykes* carried only four passengers.[475] Oswald shared his cabin with Billy Joe Lord, a young man who had just graduated from high school and was going to France to continue his education. Lord testified that he and Oswald did not discuss politics but did have a few amicable religious arguments, in which Oswald defended atheism. Oswald was "standoffish," but told Lord generally about his background, mentioning that his mother worked in a drugstore in Fort Worth and that he was bitter about the low wages which she received. He told Lord that he intended to travel in Europe and possibly to attend school in Sweden or Switzerland if he had sufficient funds.[476] The other two passengers were Lt. Col. and Mrs. George B. Church, Jr., who also found Oswald unfriendly and had little contact with him. Oswald told them that he had not liked the Marine Corps and that he planned to study in Switzerland; they observed some "bitterness" about his mother's difficulties, but did not discuss this with him. No one on board suspected that he intended to defect to Russia.[477]

Oswald disembarked at Le Havre on October 8. He left for England that same day, and arrived on October 9.[478] He told English customs officials in Southampton that he had $700 and planned to remain in the United Kingdom for 1 week before proceeding to a school in Switzerland. But on the same day, he flew to Helsinki, Finland, where he registered at the Torni Hotel; on the following day, he moved to the Klaus Kurki Hotel.[479]

Oswald probably applied for a visa at the Russian consulate on October 12, his first business day in Helsinki.[480] The visa was issued on October 14. It was valid until October 20 and permitted him to take one trip of not more than 6 days to the Soviet Union.[481] He also purchased 10 Soviet "tourist vouchers" which cost $30 apiece.[482] He left Helsinki by train on the following day, crossed the Finnish-Russian border at Vainikkala, and arrived in Moscow on October 16.[483]

He was met at the Moscow railroad station by a representative of "Intourist," the state tourist agency, and taken to the Hotel Berlin, where he registered as a student.[484] On the same day he met the Intourist guide assigned to him during his stay in Russia, a young woman named Rima Shirokova. They went sightseeing the next day. Almost immediately he told her that he wanted to leave the United States and become a citizen of the Soviet Union. According to Oswald's "Historic Diary," she later told him that she had reported his statement to Intourist headquarters, which in turn had notified the "Passport and Visa Office" (probably the Visa and Registration Department of the Ministry of Internal Affairs, the MVD [485]). She was instructed to help Oswald prepare a letter to the Supreme Soviet requesting that he be granted citizenship. Oswald mailed such a letter that same day.[486] (The "Historic Diary" is Oswald's handwritten account of his life in Russia.[487] The earlier entries were written after the events which they describe; later, in Minsk, he probably kept a contemporaneous record of his experiences. [488] The Commission has used the diary, which Oswald may have written with future readers in mind, only as Oswald's record of his private life and personal impressions as he sought to present them and has relied wherever possible on official documents, correspondence, and the testimony of witnesses.)

The diary records that when Oswald told Rima Shirokova that he intended to defect she was "flabbergassted," but agreeed to help.[489] She was "politly sympathetic but . uneasy" when he told her that he wanted to defect because he was "a Communist, ect." [490] As an Intourist guide, Rima toured parts of Moscow with Oswald in the next few days. His primary concern, however, appeared to be his effort to become a Soviet citizen, and she also aided him in his dealings with the Soviet Government.[491] He thought that Rima felt sorry for him and tried to be a friend because he was "someth. new." [492] On his 20th birthday, 2 days after he arrived in Russia, she gave him Dostoevski's "The Idiot," [493] in which she had written: "Dear Lee, Great congratulations! Let all your dreams come true! 18.X 1959" [494]

On October 19, Oswald was probably interviewed in his hotel room by a man named Lev Setyayev, who said that he was a reporter for Radio Moscow seeking statements from American tourists about their impressions of Moscow,[495] but who was probably also acting for the KGB.[496] Two years later, Oswald told officials at the American Embassy that he had made a few routine comments to Setyayev of no political signifiance. The interview with Setyayev may, however, have been the occasion for an attempt by the KGB, in accordance with regular practice, to assess Oswald or even to elicit compromising statements from him; the interview was apparently never broadcast.[497] (As discussed in ch. VI of this report, the Commission is aware that many of the Soviet officials with whom Oswald came into contact were employees of the KGB, the agency which has primary jurisdiction for the treatment of defectors.)

On the following day, Rima Shirokova told him that the "Pass. and Visa Dept." wanted to see him,[498] and on the morning of October 21, he was interviewed by an official concerning his application for citizenship. The official offered little information and no encouragement; he told Oswald only that he would check to see if the visa could be extended. Oswald returned to the Hotel Berlin.[499] That afternoon, he was notified that his visa had expired and that he had to leave Moscow within 2 hours.[500]

Oswald responded to the unfavorable decision by cutting himself above his left wrist, in an apparent suicide attempt. Rima Shirokova found him unconscious in his hotel room and had him taken to the Botkinskaya Hospital. His diary states: "Poor Rimmea stays by my side as interrpator (my Russian is still very bad) far into the night, I tell her 'Go home' (my mood is bad) but she stays, she is 'my friend.' " [501]

For 3 days Oswald was confined in the psychiatric ward of the hospital. He was examined by a psychiatrist, who concluded that he 'was not dangerous to other people and could be transferred to the "somatic" department. Hospital records containing the results of the examination [502] state that Oswald came to Russia in order to apply for citizenship, and that "in order to postpone his departure he inflicted the injury upon himself." [503] They note that Oswald understood some Russian and, presumably based on information which he provided, that he had "graduated from a technical high school in radio technology and radio electronics." [504] The record states: "He claims he regrets his action. After recovering he intends to return to his homeland." [505]

Oswald resented being in the psychiatric ward and told Rima Shirokova that he wanted a transfer.[506] She visited him at the hospital frequently and his diary records that "only at this moment" did he "notice [that] she is preety." [507] Another entry for the hospital period says: "Afternoon I am visited by Roza Agafonova of the hotel tourist office, who askes about my health, very beautiful, excelant Eng., very merry and kind, she makes me very glad to be alive." [508] These entries reflect an attitude gentler and friendlier than his attitude before the suicide attempt, when he seemed to be coldly concerned only with his status in Russia. Once Oswald was out of the psychiatric ward, he found the hospital more pleasant. The new ward, which he shared with 11 other patients, was "airy," and the food was good. His only complaint, according to his diary, was that an "elderly American" patient was distrustful of him because he had not registered at the American Embassy and because he was evasive about the reasons for his presence in Moscow and confinement in the hospital.[509]

He was released from the hospital on October 28,[510] and, accompanied by Rima Shirokova, was driven to the Hotel Berlin in an Intourist car. After he said goodby to Lyudmila Dmitrieva, head of the Intourist office at the Berlin, and to Roza Agafonova, another Intourist employee at the hotel, he checked out of the Berlin and registered at the Metropole, [511] a large hotel under the same administration as the Berlin.[512] The Government had undoubtedly directed him to make the change. His visa had expired while he was in the hospital, and his presence in Russia was technically illegal; he had received no word that the decision that he must leave had been reversed. Later that day, however, Rima told him that the "Pass and Registration Office" wished to talk to him about his future.[513] According to the diary, when Oswald appeared at the office he was asked whether he still wanted to become a Soviet citizen and he replied that he did; he provided his Marine Corps discharge papers for identification. He was told that he could not expect a decision soon, and was dismissed. During this interview, Oswald was apparently questioned about the interview which preceded his hospitalization, which led him to conclude that there had been no communication between the two sets of officials.[514] That evening he met Rima, on whom he vented his frustration at being put off by the authorities.[515]

Oswald ate only once on the following day; he stayed near the telephone, fully dressed and ready to leave immediately if he were summoned. He remained in his room for 3 days, which seemed to him "like three years," [516] until October 31, when he decided to act. He met Rima Shirokova at noon and told her that he was impatient, but did not say what he planned to do; she cautioned him to stay in his room "and eat well." [517] She left him after a short while and, a few minutes later, he took a taxi to the American Embassy, where he asked to see the consul. (See Commission Exhibits Nos. 24, 912, 913, pp. 264, 263, 261.) When the receptionist asked him first to sign the tourist register, he laid his passport on the desk and said that he had come to "dissolve his American citizenship." Richard E. Snyder, the Second Secretary and senior consular official,[518] was summoned, and he invited Oswald into his office.[519]

Oswald's meeting with Snyder, at which Snyder's assistant, John A. McVickar, was also present, is more fully discussed in appendix XV to the Commission's report. Oswald declared that he wanted to renounce his American citizenship; he denounced the United States and praised the Government of the Soviet Union. Over Oswald's objections, Snyder sought to learn something of Oswald's motives and background and to forestall immediate action. Oswald told him that he had already offered to tell a Soviet official what he had learned as a radar operator in the Marines. The interview ended when Snyder told Oswald that he could renounce his citizenship on the following Monday, 2 days later, if he would appear personally to do so. During the interview, Oswald handed to Snyder a note [520] which suggests that he had studied and sought to comply with section 349 of the Immigration and Nationality Act, which provides for loss of American citizenship.[521] The note contains paragraphs which read like inartistic attempts to cast off citizenship in three of the ways specified by the statute. The attempts failed but there is no reason to doubt that they were sincere. Snyder has testified that he believed that Oswald would immediately have formally renounced his citizenship had he been permitted to do so.[522]

The interview lasted for less than an hour. Oswald returned to his hotel angry about the delay but "elated" by the "showdown" and sure that he would be permitted to remain after his "sign of * * * faith" in the Russians.[523] Soon after he returned to the hotel, he was approached by A. I. Goldberg, a reporter for the Associated Press, whom the Embassy had told about Oswald's actions. Oswald refused to speak to him.[524] He answered a few questions for two other reporters, R. J. Korengold and Miss Aline Mosby, but again refused to be interviewed.[525] Thereafter, the news services made repeated unsuccessful attempts to interview him, which he thought was an indirect form of pressure from the Embassy to return to the United States.[526]

On the day after Oswald's meeting with Snyder, his family read in the newspapers about his appearance at the Embassy and tried to contact him. Mrs. Oswald testified that she was shocked at her son's decision to defect but respected his motives for doing so; later she suspected that he had been forcibly removed to Russia.[527] She placed a telephone call to him,[528] but he either refused to speak to her [529] or cut her off very quickly.[530] So too, on November 2, he rejected the Embassy's efforts to deliver or read on the telephone a telegram from his brother Robert.[531] A call from Robert was either canceled before it was completed or was refused.[532] Robert's telegram, along with a message asking Oswald to contact him immediately, which Robert had asked the State Department to deliver,[533] was finally sent to Oswald from the Embassy by registered mail.[534]

A few days later, the Embassy received a letter from Oswald dated November 3 which requested that his citizenship be revoked.[535] The letter stated that he had appeared at the Embassy "for the purpose of signing the formal papers to this effect" and protested against the "conduct of the official" who had refused him "this legal right." Oswald noted that his application for Soviet citizenship was pending and said that if it were granted he would ask the Soviet Government "to lodge a formal protest" on his behalf.[536] The Embassy replied on November 9 that Oswald could renounce his citizenship by appearing at the Embassy and executing the necessary papers.[537]

Oswald's diary describes the period from November 2 to November 15, during which he continued to isolate himself, as "days of utter loneliness." [538] On November 8, he wrote to his brother:

> Dear Robert
>
> Well, what shall we talk about, the weather perhaps? Certainly you do not wish me to speak of my decision to remain in the Soviet Union and apply for citizenship here, since I'm afraid you would not be able to comprehend my my reasons. You really dont know anything about me. Do you know for instance that I have waited to do this for well over a year, do you know that I * * * [phrase in Russian] speak a fair amount of Russian which I have been studing for many months.
>
> I have been told that I will not *have* to leave the Soviet Union if I do not care to. this than is my decision. I will not leave this country, the Soviet Union, under any conditions, I will never return to the United States which is a country I hate.
>
> Someday, perhaps soon, and than again perhaps in a few years, I will become a citizen of the Soviet Union, but it is a very legal

process, *in any event*, I will not have to leave the Soviet Union
and I will never * * * [word missing].

I recived your telegram and was glad to hear from you, only
one word bothered me, the word "mistake." I assume you mean
that I have made a "mistake" it is not for you to tell me that you
cannot understand my reasons for this very action.

I will not speak to anyone from the United States over the telephone since it may be taped by the Americans.

If you wish to corespond with me you can write to the below
address, but I really don't see what we could take about if you
want to send me money, that I can use, but I do not expect to be
able to send it back.

Lee [539]

Oswald's statement that he had been told that he could remain in
Russia was not true. According to his diary, he was not told
until later that he could remain even temporarily in Russia,[540] and
only in January was he told that he could remain indefinitely.[541] The
Embassy tried to deliver a typed copy of a telegram from his brother
John on November 9; Oswald refused to answer the knock on his
door, and the message was then sent to him by registered mail.[542]

Toward the end of this waiting period, probably on November 13,
Aline Mosby succeeded in interviewing Oswald.[543] A reporter for
United Press International, she had called him on the telephone and
was told to come right over, Oswald's explanation being that he thought
she might "understand and be friendly" because she was a woman.[544]
She was the first person who was not a Soviet citizen to whom he
granted an interview since his meeting with Snyder at the Embassy
on October 31. Miss Mosby found him polite but stiff; she said that he
seemed full of confidence, often showing a "small smile, more like a
smirk," and that he talked almost "non-stop." Oswald said to her
that he had been told that he could remain in the Soviet Union
and that job possibilities were being explored; they thought it
probably would be best, he said, to continue his education. He
admitted that his Russian was bad but was confident that it would
improve rapidly. He based his dislike for the United States on his
observations of racial prejudice and the contrast between "the luxuries
of Park Avenue and workers' lives on the East Side," and mentioned
his mother's poverty; he said that if he had remained in the United
States he too would have become either a capitalist or a worker. "One
way or another," he said, "I'd lose in the United States. In my own
mind, even if I'd be exploiting other workers. That's why I chose
Marxist ideology."

Oswald told his interviewer that he had been interested in Communist theory since he was 15, when "an old lady" in New York
handed him "a pamphlet about saving the Rosenbergs." But when
Mosby asked if he were a member of the Communist Party he said
that he had never met a Communist and that he "might have seen"
one only once, when he saw that "old lady." He told her that while

he was in the Marine Corps he had seen American imperialism in action, and had saved $1,500 in secret preparation for his defection to Russia. His only apparent regrets concerned his family: his mother, whom he had not told of his plans, and his brother, who might lose his job as a result of the publicity.[545]

The interview lasted for about 2 hours. According to Oswald's own account, he exacted a promise from Miss Mosby that she would show him the story before publication but she broke the promise; he found the published story to contain distortions of his words.[546] Miss Mosby's notes indicate that he called her to complain of the distortions, saying in particular that his family had not been "poverty-stricken" and that his defection was not prompted by personal hardship but that was "a matter only of ideology." [547]

According to the diary, Oswald was told in mid-November that he could remain temporarily in Russia "until some solution was found with what to do" with him. [548] Armed with this "comforting news," [549] he granted a second interview, again to a woman, on November 16.[550] Miss Priscilla Johnson of the North American Newspaper Alliance knocked on the door of his room at the Metropole, and Oswald agreed to come to her room at the hotel that evening. This interview lasted about 5 hours, from 9 p.m. until about 2 in the morning. During the interview he frequently mentioned the fact that he would be able to remain in Russia, which gave him great pleasure, but he also showed disappointment about the difficulties standing in the way of his request for Soviet citizenship. He repeated most of the information he had given Aline Mosby and again denied having been a member of the Communist Party or even ever having seen a Communist in the United States. When Miss Johnson asked him to specify some of the socialist writers whose works he had read during the past 5 years, he could name only Marx and Engels; the only title he could recall was "Das Kapital." They talked for a long while about Communist economic theory, which Miss Johnson thought was "his language"; she became convinced that his knowledge of the subject was very superficial.[551] He commented that the Russians treated his defection as a "legal formality," neither encouraging nor discouraging it.[552] When she suggested that if he really wished to renounce his American citizenship he could do so by returning to the Embassy, he said that he would "never set foot in the Embassy again," since he was sure that he would be given the "same run-around" as before. He seemed to Miss Johnson to be avoiding effective renunciation, consciously or unconsciously, in order to preserve his right to reenter the United States.[553]

For the rest of the year, Oswald seldom left his hotel room where he had arranged to take his meals, except perhaps for a few trips to museums. He spent most of his time studying Russian, "8 hours a day" his diary records. The routine was broken only by another interview at the passport office; occasional visits from Rima Shirokova; lessons in Russian from her and other Intourist guides; and a New Year's visit from Roza Agafonova, who gave

him a small "Boratin" clown as a New Year's present.[554] He
replied to a letter from Robert in a letter quoted at length in chapter
VII of this report, which contains his most bitter statements against
the United States.[555] Robert received a third letter on December 17,
in which Oswald said that he would not write again and did not wish
Robert to write to him. The letter concluded:

> I am starting a new life and I do not wish to have anything to
> do with the old life.
> I hope you and your family will always be in good health.
>
> Lee [556]

His mother mailed him a personal check for $20 dated December 18.
It was returned to her on January 5 with the notation that he could
not "use this check, of course"; he asked her to send him $20 in cash
and added that he had little money and needed "the rest," presumably
a reference to the $100 he had given her in September. Mrs. Oswald
later sent him a money order for about $25.[557]

On January 4, Oswald was summoned to the Soviet Passport Office
and given Identity Document for Stateless Persons No. 311479.[558] He
was told that he was being sent to Minsk,[559] an industrial city located
about 450 miles southwest of Moscow and with a population in 1959
of about 510,000.[560] His disappointment that he had not been granted
Soviet citizenship was balanced by relief that the uncertainty was
ended; he told Rima Shirokova that he was happy.[561] On the following day, he went to a Government agency which the Russians
call the "Red Cross"; it gave him 5,000 rubles (about 500 new rubles,
or $500 at the official exchange rate).[562] He used 2,200 rubles
to pay his hotel bill and 150 rubles to purchase a railroad ticket to
Minsk.[563]

Oswald arrived in Minsk on January 7. He was met at the station
by two "Red Cross" workers who took him to the Hotel Minsk. Two
Intourist employees, both of whom spoke excellent English, were
waiting for him.[564] One of them, a young woman named Roza Kuznetsova, became his close friend and attended his 21st birthday party
in October 1960.[565] (See Commission Exhibit No. 2609, p. 271.) On
the following day, Oswald met the "Mayor," who welcomed him to
Minsk, promised him a rent-free apartment, and warned him against
"uncultured persons" who sometimes insulted foreigners.[566]

Oswald reported for work at the Belorussian Radio and Television
Factory on January 13.[567] Two days earlier he had visited the factory
and met Alexander Ziger, a Polish Jew who had emigrated to Argentina in 1938 and went to Russia in 1955. Ziger was a department
head at the factory; he spoke English, and he and his family became
good friends of Oswald and corresponded with him after his return
to the United States.[568] The factory, a major producer of electronic
parts and systems, employed about 5,000 persons.[569] Oswald's union
card described him as a "metal worker"; [570] Marina testified that he
fashioned parts on a lathe.[571] As Oswald later described it, the shop in

which he worked, called the "experimental shop,"[572] employed 58 workers and 5 foremen. It was located in the middle part of the factory area in a 2-story building made of red brick. The workday began at 8 o'clock sharp. Work was assigned according to "pay levels," which were numbered from one to five plus a top "master" level. A worker could ask to be tested for a higher level at any time.[573]

Oswald had hoped to continue his education in Russia, and was disappointed by his assignment to a factory.[574] His salary varied from 700 to perhaps as high as 900 rubles per month ($70–$90).[575] Although high compared with the salaries of certain professional groups in Russia, which in some areas have not grown proportionately with the wages of factory workers,[576] his salary was normal for his type of work.[577] It was supplemented, however, by 700 rubles per month, which he received from the "Red Cross," and, according to Oswald, his total income was about equal to that of the director of the factory.[578] In August he applied for membership in the union;[579] he became a dues-paying member in September.[580]

Undoubtedly more noteworthy to most Russians than his extra income was the attractive apartment which Oswald was given in March 1959. It was a small flat with a balcony overlooking the river,[581] for which he paid only 60 rubles a month.[582] (See Commission Exhibit No. 2606, p. 271.) Oswald describes it in his diary as "a Russian dream."[583] Had Oswald been a Russian worker, he would probably have had to wait for several years for a comparable apartment, and would have been given one even then only if he had a family.[584] The "Red Cross" subsidy and the apartment were typical of the favorable treatment which the Soviet Union has given defectors.[585]

Oswald's diary records that he enjoyed his first months in Minsk. His work at the factory was easy and his coworkers were friendly and curious about life in the United States; he declined an invitation to speak at a mass meeting. He took Roza Kuznetsova, his interpreter and language teacher,[586] to the theater, a movie, or an opera almost every night, until he moved into his apartment and temporarily lost contact with her. He wrote in his diary, "I'm living big and am very satisfied."[587] In March or April, he met Pavel Golovachev, a coworker at the factory, whom Oswald described as intelligent and friendly and an excellent radio technician. (See Commission Exhibit No. 2609, p. 271.) Oswald helped Golovachev with English.[588] They became friends,[589] and corresponded after Oswald returned to the United States until at least as late as September 1963.[590]

The spring and summer passed easily and uneventfully. There were picnics and drives in the country, which Oswald described as "green beauty."[591] On June 18, he obtained a hunting license and soon afterward purchased a 16-gage single-barrel shotgun. His hunting license identifies him as "Aleksy Harvey Oswald." (He was called "Alec" by his Russian friends, because "Lee" sounded foreign to them and was difficult for them to pronounce.)[592] He joined a local chapter of the Belorussian Society of Hunters and Fishermen, a hunting club sponsored by his factory, and hunted for small game in the farm regions around Minsk about half a dozen times in the summer and fall. The hunters spent the night in small villages and often left their bag with the villagers; Oswald described the peasant life which he saw as crude and poor.[593] Sometime in June, he met Ella German, a worker at the factory, of whom he later said he "perhaps fell in love with her the first minute" he saw her.[594] (See Commission Exhibit No. 2609, p. 271.)

At the same time, however, the first signs of disillusionment with his Russian life appeared. He noted in his diary that he felt "uneasy inside" after a friend took him aside at a party and advised him to return to the United States.[595] Another entry compared life in Minsk with military life:

> I have become habituatated to a small cafe which is where I dine in the evening. The food is generaly poor and always eactly the same, menue in any cafe, at any point in the city. The food is cheap and I don't really care about quiality after three years in the U.S.M.C.[596]

In an entry for August–September, he wrote that he was becoming "increasingly concious of just what sort of a sociaty" he lived in.[597]

He spent New Year's Day at the home of Ella German and her family. They ate and drank in a friendly atmosphere, and he was "drunk and happy" when he returned home. During the walk back to his apartment he decided to ask Ella to marry him. On the following night, after he had brought her home from the movies, he proposed on her doorstep. She rejected him, saying that she did not love him and that she was afraid to marry an American. She said that the Polish intervention in the 1920's had led to the arrest of all people in the Soviet Union of Polish origin and she feared that something similar might happen to Americans some day. Oswald was "too stunned to think," and concluded that she had gone out with him only because she was envied by the other girls for having an American as an escort.[598] But in one of the entries in the diary he appears to have attributed her failure to love him to "a state of fear which was always in the Soviet Union."[599] His affection for Ella German apparently continued for some time; [600] he had his last formal date with her in February and remained on friendly terms with her as long as he was in Russia.[601]

After he returned to the United States, Oswald often commented on Russian life. He discussed the Soviet systems of public education [602] and medical care.[603] He observed to one acquaintance that everyone in Russia was trained to do something,[604] and discussed with another the system of regular wage and salary increases.[605] His most frequent criticisms concerned the contrast between the lives of ordinary workers and the lives of Communist Party members. He told an acquaintance in Dallas that the working class in the Soviet Union made just about enough to buy clothing and food and that only party members could afford luxuries.[606] On another occasion, he remarked that if he had had as much money as some of the "managers," he could have visited the Black Sea resorts.[607] He complained about the lack of freedom in Russia; [608] the lack of opportunity to travel;[609] inadequate housing; [610] and the chronic scarcity of food products.[611] To one acquaintance, he observed that the party members were all "opportunists," who "shouted the loudest and made the most noise," but who were interested only in their own welfare.[612]

He expressed similar views in a manuscript which he worked on in Russia [613] and probably intended to publish; soon after he returned to the United States, he hired a stenographer to prepare a typed draft from his notes.[614] Oswald described the manuscript, which amounted to 50 typed pages, as "a look into the lives of work-a-day average Russians." [615]

The manuscript describes the factory in which Oswald worked and suggests that political considerations of which Oswald disapproved dominated its operation. He attributed the lack of unemployment to the shortage of labor-saving machinery and the heavy load of bureaucracy, which kept "tons of paper work" flowing in and out of the factory and required a high foreman-worker ratio.[616] In addition, he wrote, there was "a small army of examiners, committees, and supply checkers and the quality-control board." [617]

He described life in Russia, including life at the factory, as centered around the "Kollective." The head of the Kollective in his shop, Comrade Lebizen, saw to it that everyone maintained shop discipline, attended party meetings, and received all the new propaganda as it came out. He hung the walls of the shop with signs and slogans of the Communist Party. Meetings of the Kollective were "so numerous as to be staggering." In a single month, there were scheduled one meeting of the professional union, four political information meetings, two young Communist meetings, one meeting of the production committee to discuss ways of improving work, two Communist Party meetings, four meetings of the "School of Communist Labor," and one sports meeting. All but one of them were compulsory for Communist Party members and all but three were compulsory for everyone.[618] (Marina Oswald testified that her husband did not attend the courses in Marxism and Leninism given in the factory for party members and those who wished to become party members.) [619] They were scheduled so as not to interfere with work, and lasted anywhere from 10 minutes to 2 hours. Oswald said that no one liked the meetings, which were accepted "philosophically"; at the political meetings especially, everyone paid strict attention, and party members were posted in the audience to watch for the slightest sign that anyone's attention might relax, even for a moment.[620]

Oswald wrote that the "spontaneous" demonstrations on Soviet holidays or for distinguished visitors were almost as well organized as the Kollectivist meetings at the factory.[621] He noted that elections were supervised to ensure that everyone voted, and that they voted for the candidates of the Communist Party. The manuscript touches on other aspects of Soviet life—as the housing shortage and the corruption which it evoked, the "rest-homes" where workers had their vacations, television and the omni-present radio, and Russian reading habits.[622] This writing also may include only what Oswald thought might be acceptable.

On January 4, 1961, 1 year after he had been issued his "stateless" residence permit, Oswald was summoned to the passport office in Minsk and asked if he still wanted to become a Soviet citizen. He replied that he did not, but asked that his residence permit be extended for another year.[623] The entry in his diary for January 4–31 reads: "I am stating to reconsider my disire about staying. The work is drab. The money I get has nowhere to be spent. No nightclubs or bowling allys, no places of recreation acept the trade union dances. I have had enough." [624]

The American Embassy in Moscow had not heard from Oswald after it received his letter of November 3, 1959.[625] On February 13, 1961, it received an undated letter from him which had been mailed in Minsk about a week earlier. He asked for the return of his passport and stated that he wanted to return to the United States if he could "come to some agreement [with the American Government] concerning the dropping of any legal proceedings" against him. He noted that he had not become a Soviet citizen and was living in Russia with "nonpermanent type papers for a foreigner," and said that he did not appear personally because he could not leave Minsk without permission. The letter concluded: "I hope that in recalling the responsibility I have to America that you remember yours in doing everything you can to help me, since I am an American citizen." [626] In this letter, Oswald referred to a previous letter which he said had gone unanswered; there is evidence that such a letter was never sent.[627]

The Second Secretary, Richard Snyder, answered on February 28 that Oswald would have to appear at the Embassy personally to discuss his return to the United States.[628] In the meantime, Oswald's mother, who in January had inquired at the Department of State about his whereabouts,[629] had been notified of his letter.[630] A second letter from Oswald, posted on March 5, reached the Embassy on March 20; it reiterated that he was unable to leave Minsk without permission and asked that "preliminary inquiries * * * be put in the form of a questionnaire" and sent to him.[631] His diary entry for this period records his "state of expectation about going back to the U.S.," and adds that a friend had approved his plans but warned him not to discuss them with others.[632] (The Soviet authorities had undoubtedly intercepted and read the correspondence between Oswald and the Embassy and knew of his plans.[633] Soon after the correspondence began, his monthly payments from the "Red Cross" were cut off.)[634] Having informed Washington,[635] the Embassy wrote to Oswald on March 24, stating again that he would have to come to Moscow.[636] Later, the Department of State decided that Oswald's passport should be returned to him only if he appeared at the Embassy for it and the Embassy was satisfied, after exploring the matter with him, that he had not renounced his citizenship.[637]

Sometime in the second week of March, Miss Katherine Mallory, who was on tour in Minsk with the University of Michigan symphonic band, found herself surrounded by curious Russian citizens. A young man who identified himself as a Texan and former marine stepped out of the crowd and asked if she needed an interpreter; he interpreted for her for the next 15 or 20 minutes. Later he told her that he despised the United States and hoped to stay in Minsk for the rest of his life. Miss Mallory is unable to swear that her interpreter was Oswald, but is personally convinced that it was he.[638]

A few days later, probably on March 17, Oswald attended a trade union dance with a friend, Erik Titovyets, at the Palace of Culture for Professional Workers in Minsk.[639] The dance followed a lecture by a Russian woman who had recently returned from a trip to the United States.[640] Marina Nikolayevna Prusakova arrived too late to hear the lecture [641] but was at the dance. Oswald noticed her and asked Yuriy Merezhinskiy, the son of the lecturer and a friend of both Oswald and Marina, to introduce him to her. Oswald asked her to dance. According to the diary, they liked each other immediately and he obtained her telephone number before she left.[642] Marina testified that she told Oswald that she might see him at another dance, but did not give him her telephone number.[643] Oswald was smitten.[644]

Marina Prusakova was 19 years old when she met Oswald. (See Commission Exhibit No. 1395, p. 270.) She was born on July 17, 1941, at Severodvinsk (formerly Molotovsk), Arkhangel Oblast', Russia.[645] A few years later, her mother, Klavdiya Vasilievna Prusakova, married Aleksandr Ivanovich Medvedev, who became the only father Marina knew.[646] While she was still a young girl, Marina went to Arkhangel'sk, Arkhangel Oblast', to live with her maternal grandparents, Tatyana Yakovlevna Prusakova and Vasiliy Prusakov. Her grandfather died when Marina was about 4 years old; she continued to live with her grandmother for some time.[647] When she was not more than 7, she moved to Zguritva, Moldavian SSR (formerly called Bessarabia) to live with her mother and stepfather, who was an electrical worker.[648] In 1952, the family moved to Leningrad,[649] where her stepfather obtained a job in a power station.[650] Marina testified that neither he nor her mother was a member of the Communist Party.[651]

In Leningrad, Marina attended the Three Hundred and Seventy-Fourth Women's School. After she had completed the seventh grade at the school in 1955,[652] she entered the Pharmacy Teknikum for special training, which she had requested on the ground that her mother was ill and Marina might need to have a specialty in order to support herself. While she was at the Teknikum, she joined the Trade Union for Medical Workers [653] and, in her last year there, worked part time in the Central Pharmacy in Leningrad. She graduated from the Teknikum with a diploma in pharmacy in June 1959.

Marina's mother had died in 1957, during Marina's second year at the Teknikum; she continued to live with her stepfather, but had little contact with him. She testified that she did not get along with her stepfather, whom she displeased by her fresh conduct; she said that she was not easily disciplined [654] and was a source of concern to him.[655]   Because of the friction between them, Marina regarded her childhood as an unhappy one.

After her graduation, Marina was assigned to a job preparing and packing orders in a pharmaceutical warehouse in Leningrad; as a new employee she had the right to leave this job within 3 days after the assignment,[656] and she did so after the first day.   She took no job for the next 2 months, at the end of which she went to live in Minsk with an aunt and uncle, the Prusakovs, who had no children.   She had known them since she was a child and there was a mutual affection between her and them.[657]   Her uncle, a member of the Communist Party,[658] was assigned to the Ministry of Internal Affairs and headed the local bureau concerned with lumber.   The Prusakovs had one of the best apartments in a building reserved for MVD employees.[659]

Marina was 18 when she arrived in Minsk.   She had had boyfriends in Leningrad but was not interested in marriage.   In October 1960 she started work in the drug section of the Third Clinical Hospital where she earned about 450 rubles per month;[660] at about the same time she became a member of the local Komsomol, the Communist youth organization.[661]   Her friends were mostly students, whose social life consisted of meeting in cafes to sip coffee, read newspapers, gossip, and carry on discussions.   The group of friends "ran together," and Marina did not attach herself to a particular boyfriend.   She enjoyed this life, which she had been leading for about 7 months when she met Oswald at the dance at the Palace of Culture in March 1961.[662]

When Marina met Oswald, she thought he was from one of the Russian-speaking Baltic countries because he spoke with an accent; later that same evening she learned that he was an American.[663]   She met him again at another dance a week later.[664]   They danced together most of the evening, at the end of which he walked home with her. They arranged to meet again the following week.[665]   Before the scheduled time, Oswald called to say that he was in the hospital and that Marina should visit him there.[666]   Medical records furnished to the Commission by the Russian Government show that Oswald was admitted to the Clinical Hospital—Ear, Nose, and Throat Division, on Thursday, March 30, 1961.[667]   Marina visited him often,[668] taking advantage of her uniform to visit him outside regular visiting hours, which were only on Sunday.[669]   On Easter Sunday, the first Sunday after his admission to the hospital, she brought him an Easter egg.[670] On a subsequent visit, he asked her to be his fiancee, and she agreed to consider it.[671]   He left the hospital on April 11.[672]

During these visits, Marina apparently discussed with Oswald his reasons for coming to Russia and his current status.   According to her later account, he told her that he had surrendered his American documents to the Embassy in Moscow and had told American officials that he did not intend to return to the United States.   He did not say definitely that he was no longer an American citizen, but said in answer

703

to a question about his citizenship that he could not return to the United States.[673]

Oswald visited Marina regularly at her aunt and uncle's apartment; they were apparently not disturbed by the fact that he was an American and did not disapprove of her seeing him. He continued to ask her to marry him and, according to her recollection, she accepted his proposal on April 20;[674] Oswald's diary puts the date 5 days earlier.[675] Marina testified that she believed that Oswald could not return to the United States when she agreed to marry him, and that she had not married him in hope of going to the United States.[676]

After filing notice of their intent to marry at the registrar, obtaining the special consent necessary for an alien to marry a citizen, and waiting the usual 10 days, they were married on April 30.[677] The diary entry for the wedding day reads:

> two of Marinas girl friends act as bridesmaids. We are married. At her aunts home we have a dinner reception for about 20 friends and neboribos who wish us happiness (in spite of my origin and accept [accent?] which was in general rather disquiting to any Russian since for. are very rare in the soviet Union even tourist. After an evening of eating and drinking in which * * * [Marina's uncle] started a fright [fight?] and the fuse blow on an overloaded circite we take our leave and walk the 15 minutes to our home. We lived near each other, at midnight we were home.[678]

They both took 3 days off from their jobs, which they spent in Minsk.[679]

Oswald wrote in his diary for May 1, 1 day after the wedding: "In spite of fact I married Marina to hurt Ella I found myself in love with Marina."[680] The next entry, marked simply "May," reads in part:

> The trasistion of changing full love from Ella to Marina was very painfull esp. as I saw Ella almost every day at the factory but as the days & weeks went by I adjusted more and more [to] my wife mentaly * * * She is maddly in love with me from the very start. Boat rides on Lake Minsk walks through the parks evening at home or at Aunt Valia's place mark May."[681]

And in June: "A continuence of May, except that; we draw closer and closer, and I think very little now of Ella."[682]

Sometime within the first month or two after they were married Oswald told his wife that he was anxious to return to the United States. The diary says that he told her "in the last days" of June and that she was "slightly startled" but encouraged him to do as he wished.[683] Marina's recollection is that she learned of his plan between May and July. Embassy records show that Oswald notified the Embassy in a letter received on May 25 that he was married and his wife would seek to accompany him to the United States.[684] At about this time, the Oswalds began to make inquiries in Soviet offices about exit visas.[685]

While these preparations were being made, the Oswalds apparently enjoyed their new life.[686] They ate most of their meals in cafes or at restaurants where they worked.[687] For amusement, they went boating, attended the opera, concerts, the circus, and films; occasionally, they gathered with a group of friends for a cooperative meal at someone's apartment.[688] His Russian improved, but he retained an accent and never learned to speak grammatically or to write well.[689] He read the English language edition of the Daily Worker and books, also in English, on Marxism and Leninism; he also read some Russian newspapers.[690]

Before he married Marina (and presumably before February, when he had begun his efforts to return to the United States) Oswald had applied for admission to the Patrice Lumumba Friendship University in Moscow. He received a letter dated May 3 apologizing for the delay in responding to his application and turning it down on the ground that the university had been established exclusively for students from the underdeveloped countries of Asia, Africa, and Latin America.[691] Oswald expressed his disappointment at having been turned down to Marina.[692]

Oswald reopened his correspondence with his family on May 5, with a friendly letter to his brother Robert. He said nothing about his contacts with the American Embassy, but mentioned that he had married, and that he had a job as a "metal-smith" and was living well. He asked his brother for their mother's address, and encouraged him to come to Minsk for a visit.[693] Robert answered the letter quickly. On May 31, Oswald wrote again and expressed his pleasure at having heard from Robert after so long. Apparently in response to an offer to send him whatever he needed, Oswald wrote that he needed nothing and thanked Robert for the thought; he suggested, however, that Marina might like a small wedding present. At the end of the letter he said that he did not know whether he would ever return to the United States; he said that before he could return he would have to obtain the permission of the Soviet Union for him and Marina to leave and insure that no charges would be lodged against him in the United States. In this letter, he mentioned that he was in touch with the Embassy in Moscow.[694] At about this time, Oswald wrote also to his mother.[695]

On May 25, the Embassy received a letter mailed in Minsk about 10 days before, in which Oswald asked for assurances that he would not be prosecuted if he returned to the United States, and informed the Embassy that he had married a Russian woman who would want to accompany him.[696] The Embassy communicated this development to Washington [697] and did not answer Oswald immediately. In addition, he had had no word since March concerning the return of his passport. Impatient for action,[698] he appeared without warning at the Embassy on July 8; it was a Saturday and the offices were closed.[699] He used the house telephone to reach Snyder, who came to the office, talked with him briefly, and suggested that he return on the following Monday.[700] Oswald called Marina and asked her to join him in Moscow. She arrived on Sunday, July 9,[701] and they took a room at the Hotel Berlin,[702] where he had stayed when he first arrived in Russia.

Oswald returned to the Embassy on Monday. Marina waited outside during his interview with Snyder,[703] who asked to see Oswald's Soviet papers and questioned him closely about his life in Russia and possible expatriating acts. Oswald stated that he was not a citizen of the Soviet Union and had never formally applied for citizenship, that he had never taken an oath of allegiance to the Soviet Union, and that he was not a member of the factory trade union organization. He said that he had never given Soviet officials any confidential information that he had learned in the Marines, had never been asked to give such information, and "doubted" that he would have done so had he been asked.[704] Some of Oswald's statements during this interview were undoubtedly false. He had almost certainly applied for citizenship in the Soviet Union [705] and, at least for a time, been disappointed when it was denied.[706] He possessed a membership card in the union organization.[707] In addition, his assertion to Snyder that he had never been questioned by Soviet authorities concerning his life in the United States is simply unbelievable.

Oswald showed anxiety, already displayed in his letters, that he might be prosecuted and imprisoned if he returned to the United States. Snyder told him informally that he did not know any grounds on which he would be prosecuted but that he could give no assurances in this regard.[708] Snyder testified that Oswald seemed to have matured while he was in Russia and did not show the bravado and arrogance which characterized his first contacts with the Embassy. Oswald told him that he had "learned a hard lesson the hard way" and had acquired a new appreciation of the United States and the meaning of freedom.[709]

Since Oswald's passport would expire on September 10, 1961,[710] before which date he probably would not be able to obtain Russian exit papers, he filled out an application for its renewal.[711] On a questionnaire attached to the application,[712] he reiterated his oral statements that he had obtained only a residence permit in the Soviet Union and was still an American national. On the basis of Oswald's written and oral statements, Snyder concluded that he had not expatriated himself and returned his passport, stamped valid only for direct travel to the United States,[713] to him. Accompanied by his wife,[714] Oswald came to the Embassy again on the following day,[715] to initiate procedures for her admission to the United States as an immigrant; they had a routine interview with McVickar, Snyder's assistant.[716] Three days later, they returned to Minsk.[717]

On the same day, Oswald wrote to his brother. He told Robert that he had his passport again and that he and Marina were doing everything possible to leave the Soviet Union. Apparently referring to his initial reappearance at the Embassy in quest of his passport, he wrote: "I could write a book about how many feeling have come and gone since that day." The letter closed with an affectionate greeting to his brother and his family.[718] The letter's tone of firm purpose to return to the United States in the face of heavy odds reflected Oswald's attitude thereafter.

As soon as they returned to Minsk, the Oswalds began to work with local authorities for permission to leave the country.[719] His diary entry for July 16 through August 20 reads,

> We have found out which blanks and certificates are nessceary to apply for a exit visa. They number about 20 papers; birth certificates, affidavit, photos, ect. On Aug 20th we give the papers out they say it will be 3½ months before we know wheather they let us go or not. In the meantime Marina has had to stade 4 differant meeting at the place of work held by her boss's at the direction of "someone" by phone. The Young Comm. leauge headquttes also called about her and she had to go see them for 1½ hours. The purpose (expressed) is to disuade her from going to the U.S.A. Net effect: Make her more stubborn about wanting to go. Marina is pregnet. We only hope that the visas come through soon.[720]

In a letter dated July 15, he reported their efforts to the Embassy, and said that he would keep it informed "as to the overall picture." The letter mentioned that Marina was having difficulties at work because of her decision to leave but added that such "tactics" were "quite useless" and that Marina had "stood up well, without getting into trouble." [721] For August 21 through September 1, the diary reads:

> I make repeated trips to the passport & visa office, also to Ministry of For. Affairs in Minsk, also Min. of Internal Affairs, all of which have a say in the granting of a visa. I extrackted promises of quick attention to us.[722]

For September through October 18, "No word from Min. ('They'll call us.')." [723]

Marina testified that when the news of her visit to the American Embassy in July reached Minsk, she was dropped from membership in "Komsomol," the Communist Youth Organization,[724] and that "meetings were arranged" at which "members of the various organizations" attempted to dissuade her from leaving the Soviet Union.[725] Her aunt and uncle did not speak to her for "a long time." [726] Paul Gregory, to whom Marina taught Russian in the United States, testified that she once referred to this period of her life in Minsk as "a very horrible time." [727]

Oswald wrote to the Embassy again on October 4, to request that the U.S. Government officially intervene to facilitate his and his wife's applications for exit visas.[728] He stated that there had been "systematic and concerted attempts to intimidate [Marina] * * * into withdrawing her application for a visa" which had resulted in her being hospitalized for a 5-day period on September 22 for "nervous exhaustion." [729] Marina has denied that she was hospitalized for a nervous disorder [730] and he made no mention of it in his diary or letters to his family; he probably lied to the Embassy. The Embassy replied to his letter on October 12, saying that it had no way of influencing Soviet conduct on such matters and that its experience had been that action on applications for exit visas was "seldom taken rapidly." [731]

In October 1961 Marina took her annual vacation.[732] She and Oswald agreed that she should get a "change of scenery," [733] and she spent about 3 weeks with an aunt in Khar'kov. It is possible that they were not getting along well together during this period.[734] A dairy entry after her return indicates that they were having some quarrels and that she was wavering in her decision to go to the United States, which Oswald attributed to anxiety about their applications for visas and the fact that she was pregnant; he in turn dreaded the approach of the "hard Russian winter." [735] He noted in his dairy that he was lonely while she was gone, but that he and his friend "Erich," presumably Erik Titovyets, went to some dances and other public amusements.[736] On his 22nd birthday he went alone to see his favorite opera, "The Queen of Spades." [737] Marina sent him a gold and silver cup, inscribed "To my dear husband on his birthday, 18/x/61" and other gifts, for which he wrote to thank her.[738] She returned on November 12, in Oswald's words, "radient, with several jars of preserses for me from her aunt." [739]

Sometime after Marina's return Oswald applied for an interview with Col. Nicolay Aksenov, an official in the local MVD, in an effort to expedite their application for exit visas; he was told by the colonel's subordinates that they were competent to handle the matter. Oswald then insisted that Marina seek an interview; she agreed reluctantly. The interview was granted; [740] Marina thought that this might have been due to the fact that her uncle was also a high-ranking official in the Minsk MVD, but she did not believe that he would personally have presumed on his official position to obtain special treatment.[741] Colonel Aksenov questioned her about her reasons for wanting to go to the United States and, noticing that she was pregnant, suggested that she at least delay her departure so that her child could be born in Russia, but did not otherwise try to discourage her. He finally told her that there were many others seeking visas and that she and her husband would have to wait their turn.[742]

Throughout this period, Oswald continued to correspond with his mother and brother. His letters contained the usual chatter among members of a family and occasional references to the progress of the visa applications.[743] He wrote to the Embassy on November 1, saying that if, as he anticipated, his residence permit were renewed in January for another year, it would be over his protest.[744] On November 13 the Embassy replied, telling Oswald that retention of his Soviet passport, which was of the kind issued to persons considered to be stateless, or an extension of it, would not prejudice his claim to American citizenship. The letter added that he could discuss the renewal of his American passport whenever he appeared in person at the Embassy to do so.[745]

Late in December, Oswald wrote a letter to Senator John G. Tower of Texas, which was received in Washington near the end of January. He stated that he was an American citizen and that the Soviet Government refused to permit him and his wife to leave the Soviet Union. He asked Senator Tower to raise "the question of holding by the Soviet Union of a citizen of the U.S., against his will and expressed desires." The letter was referred to the State Department and no further action concerning it was taken.[746] On December 25, Marina was called to the Soviet Passport Office and told that exit visas would be granted to her and her husband; she was surprised, having doubted that she would ever be permitted to leave. Oswald wrote to the Embassy on December 27 that they would be given visas and asked that his passport be extended without another trip to Moscow; he added, however, that he would come to Moscow if this would expedite the processing of his application. In his diary, he wrote, "It's great (I think?)."[747] Before the year ended, Marina went on maternity leave from her job.[748] They spent New Year's Eve at a dinner party given by the Zigers.[749]

Oswald wrote to his mother on January 2, 1962, and told her that he and his wife expected to arrive in the United States sometime around March. He asked her to contact the local Red Cross and request that it put his case before the International Rescue Committee or some other group which aids immigrants to the United States. He told her that he would need about $800 and that she should insist on a gift rather than a loan; he told her not to send any of her own money.[750] Despite his instructions, she requested a loan from the Red Cross.[751] On January 13, Oswald wrote to the International Rescue Committee himself; he asked for $800 with which to purchase two tickets from Moscow to Texas.[752] He wrote to the Committee again on January 26, this time asking for $1,000.[753]

In the meantime, letters of Oswald [754] and the American Embassy,[755] both dated January 5, crossed in the mail. The Embassy's letter suggested that since there might be difficulties in obtaining an American visa for Marina, he consider returning alone and bringing her over later. He replied on the 16th that he would not leave Russia without her.[756] In his letter, Oswald requested that the U.S. Government loan him the money for his and Marina's airplane tickets or arrange a loan from another source. The Embassy replied on January 15 that Marina had not yet obtained an American visa and that no evidence had yet been submitted that she would not become a public charge in the United States.[757] It suggested that Oswald's mother or some other close relative file an affidavit of support in Marina's behalf. Before receiving this letter, Oswald wrote out such a document himself [758] and mailed it to the Embassy.[759]

On January 23, after receiving the Embassy's letter, he wrote that his own affidavit should be sufficient, since he had been away from

709

the United States for more than 2 years and could not be expected to obtain an affidavit from someone else.[760]   But on the same day, he wrote to his mother asking that she file an affidavit of support with the Immigration and Naturalization Service.[761]   On January 24, the Embassy acknowledged receipt of his affidavit, but again suggested that he obtain one from someone else.[762]

Late in January, Oswald received a letter from his mother telling him that he had been given a dishonorable discharge from the Marines.[763]   (The discharge had actually been "undesirable," a less derogatory characterization.) [764]   This apparently revived his fear of prosecution, and on January 30, he wrote to his brother for more information.[765]   On the same day he wrote also to John B. Connally, Jr., then Governor of Texas, who Oswald believed was still Secretary of Navy. The letter read:

> I wish to call your attention to a case about which you may have personal knowlege since you are a resident of Ft. Worth as I am.
>
> In November 1959 an event was well publicated in the Ft. Worth newspapers concerning a person who had gone to the Soviet Union to reside for a short time, (much in the same way E. Hemingway resided in Paris.)
>
> This person in answers to questions put to him by reporteds in Moscow criticized certain facets of american life. The story was blown up into another "turncoat" sensation, with the result that the Navy department gave this person a belated dishonourable discharge, although he had received an honourable discharge after three years service on Sept. 11, 1959 at El Toro, Marine corps base in California.
>
> These are the basic facts of *my* case.
>
> I have and allways had the full sanction of the U.S. Embassy, Moscow USSR. and hence the U.S. goverment. In as much as I am returning to the U.S.A. in this year with the aid of the U.S. Embassy, bring with me my family (since I married in the USSR) I shall employ all means to right this gross mistake or injustice to a boni-fied U.S. citizen and *ex*-service man. The U.S. government has no charges or complaints against me. I ask you to look into this case, and take the neccessary steps to repair the damage done to me and my family. For information I would direct you to consult the American Embassy, Chikovski St. 19/21, Moscow, USSR.[766]

Connally referred the letter to the Department of the Navy,[767] which sent Oswald a letter stating that the Department contemplated no change in the undesirable discharge.[768] On March 22, Oswald wrote to the Department insisting that his discharge be given a further, full review.[769] The Department promptly replied that it had no authority to hear and review petitions of this sort and referred Oswald to the Navy Discharge Review Board.[770] Oswald filled out the enclosed application for review in Minsk but did not mail it until he returned to the United States.[771]

The Department of State had notified Oswald's mother that it would need $900 to make the travel arrangements for her son and daughter-in-law.[772] On February 1, Oswald sent his mother a brief letter rejecting her suggestion that she try to raise money by telling the newspapers about his financial plight.[773] Five days later, the Embassy wrote to Oswald and asked him to make formal application for a loan.[774] Oswald wrote to his mother again on February 9, reminding her to file an affidavit of support and asking that she send him clippings from the Fort Worth newspapers about his defection to Russia, a request which he later repeated to his brother. He told her that he wanted to know what had been written about him, so that he could be "forewarned." [775]

Oswald took Marina to the hospital on the morning of February 15. A baby girl was born at about 10 a.m.[776] He had gone on to the factory where news of the birth awaited him on his arrival.[777] In accordance with regular hospital practice,[778] he did not see the baby until Marina left the hospital.[779] He was excited by the child,[780] who was named "June Lee" in accordance with the Russian custom and law that a child's second name must be the father's first name or a variation of it. He had wanted to name his child "June Marina," and protested the application of the law to her, since he had a United States passport. His diary contains the wry comment, "Po-Russki." [781] His coworkers at the factory gave the Oswalds "one summer blanket, 6 light diapers, 4 warm diapers, 2 chemises, 3 very good warm chemises, 4 very nice suits and two toys" for the baby.[782] Marina came home on February 23.[783]

There was less urgency about the departure for the United States after June Lee was born.[784] Oswald wrote to his mother,[785] and brother,[786] that he would probably not arrive for several months. The Embassy received a letter on March 3, in which Oswald applied for a loan of $800; [787] the Embassy replied that it was authorized to loan him only $500.[788] It had in the meantime decided that his own affidavit of support for Marina would be sufficient under the circumstances.[789] On March 15, he received notification from the Immigration and Naturalization Service that Marina's application for a visa had been approved.[790] By March 28, he had received an affidavit of support in Marina's behalf from his mother's employer, Byron K. Phillips,[791] which he filed although it was no longer necessary to do so.[792] A few days before, Marina, still on maternity leave, had quit her job.[793] Discussions with the Embassy to complete financial and travel arrangements continued in April and May.[794] In a letter to Robert on April 12, Oswald wrote that only "the American side" was holding up their departure, but added that the winter being over, he didn't "really * * * want to leave until the beginning of fall, since the spring and summer * * * [in Russia] are so nice." [795]

On May 10, the Embassy wrote that everything was in order and suggested that Oswald come to the Embassy with his family to sign the final papers.[796] At his request,[797] he was discharged from the factory on about May 18.[798] His work had apparently never been very good. Marina testified that he was rather lazy and resented having to take orders.[799] This estimate is confirmed by a report of the plant director and personnel department chief, filed on December 11, 1961, which was apparently a routine assessment of his work. The report noted that he did not "display the initiative for increasing his skill" in his job, that he was "over–sensitive * * * to remarks from the foremen, and * * * careless in his work"; Oswald took "no part in the social life of the shop" and kept "very much to himself." [800]

Oswald picked up his Soviet exit visa on May 22; [801] at about this time, he also had an interview with an official of the MVD to obtain final clearance for his departure.[802] He wrote to Robert that he and his family would leave for Moscow on the following day and depart for England 10 to 14 days later. He expected to cross the Atlantic by ship, probably docking in New Orleans. Returning to a point which he had made in an earlier letter to his mother, he commented that he knew from the newspaper clippings what Robert had said about him when he left for Russia; he thought that Robert had talked too much at that time, and asked that Robert say nothing to the newspapers now.[803]

The Oswalds arrived in Moscow by May 24 [804] and on that date filled out various documents at the American Embassy; [805] Marina was given her American visa.[806] Final arrangements for their emigration were made with Soviet officials.[807] On June 1, Oswald signed a promissory note at the Embassy for a repatriation loan of $435.71.[808] He and his family boarded a train for Holland,[809] which passed through Minsk that night.[810] They crossed the Soviet frontier at Brest on June 2. Two days later, they departed from Holland on the SS *Maasdam*.[811] Onboard ship, the Oswalds stayed by themselves; Marina testified that she did not often go on deck because she was poorly dressed and Oswald was ashamed of her.[812]

Probably while he was on board the *Maasdam* Oswald wrote some notes on ship stationery, which appear to be a summary of what he thought he had learned by living under both the capitalist and Communist systems. The notes reflect his unhappy and deepening feeling of disillusionment with both the Soviet Union and the United States. Oswald observed that although reform groups may oppose the government in power, they always declare that they are for their people and their country, and he asked what "would happen if somebody was to stand up and say he was utterly opposed not only to the governments, but to the people, too the entire land and complete foundations" of his society. He condemned existing political groups and proposed the formation of a third choice between communism and capitalism. neither of which was acceptable to him. "I have lived," he said, "under both systems, I have *sought* the answers and although it would be very easy to dupe myself into believing one system is better than the other, I know they are not." In these notes, he acknowledged that his "Red Cross" subsidy had been paid by the Soviet Government rather than the international organization, and said, "I shall never sell myself intentionlly, or unintentionlly to anyone again." [813] (Commission Exhibit No. 25, p. 273.) It was probably also onboard ship that Oswald wrote two sets of answers to questions which he anticipated about his decision to go to Russia and later to return to the United States. Although the sets of answers are somewhat similar, but the tone of one is apologetic, while the other suggests that Oswald went to Russia to study the Soviet system, but remained a loyal American and owed no apologies. [814]

The *Maasdam* landed at Hoboken, N.J., on June 13. [815] The Oswalds were met by Spas T. Raikin, a representative of the Traveler's Aid Society, which had been contacted by the Department of State; Raikin had the impression that Oswald was trying to avoid meeting anyone. He told Raikin that he had only $63 and had no plans either for that night or for travel to Fort Worth, and accepted the society's help, according to Raikin, "with confidence and appreciation." [816] They passed through the immigration office without incident, [817] and Raikin helped them through customs. [818]

The society referred the Oswalds to the New York City Department of Welfare, which helped them find a room at the Times Square Hotel. [819] Oswald told both Raikin and representatives of the welfare department that he had been a marine stationed at the American Embassy in Moscow, had married a Russian girl, renounced his citizenship, and worked in Minsk; he soon found out, he said, that the Russian propaganda was inaccurate but had not been able to obtain an exit visa for his wife and child for more than 2 years. He said also that he had paid the travel expenses himself. [820]

The welfare department called Robert Oswald's home in Fort Worth. His wife answered and said that they would help. She contacted her husband who sent $200 immediately. [821] Oswald refused to accept the money and insisted that the department itself should pav the fare to Texas; he threatened that they would go as far as they could on $63 and rely on local authorities to get them the rest of the way. In the end he accepted the money. [822] On the afternoon of June 14, the Oswalds left New York by plane for Fort Worth. [823]

FORT WORTH, DALLAS, NEW ORLEANS

Oswald had originally indicated that he and his family would stay with his mother in Vernon, Tex. [824] His decision to stay with Robert Oswald in Fort Worth apparently had been prompted by his brother's invitation in a letter to him in Russia. [825] Oswald listed only his brother as a relative on an "Intake Interview" form which he prepared for the New York Department of Welfare. [826]

Robert took his wife and children to Love Field, the Dallas airport, to meet Lee and Marina and their baby, June Lee.[827] He testified that the most noticeable change in his brother's appearance was that he had become rather bald; he seemed also to be somewhat thinner than he had been in 1959. Robert thought that his brother had picked up "something of an accent" but, except for these changes was "the same boy" whom he had known before.[828] Lee commented on the absence of newspaper reporters and seemed to Robert to be disappointed that none had appeared.[829] Later on, Lee was anxious to avoid publicity.[830]

Robert drove the Oswalds to his home at 7313 Davenport Street.[831] For a few days, Lee seemed tense,[832] but the brothers got along well,[833] and to Robert it was "more or less * * * [as if Lee] had not been to Russia"; they were "just together again." [834] They did not discuss politics, according to Robert because of a "tacit agreement" between them.[835] Lee indicated to his brother that he hoped to have his undesirable discharge from the Marines corrected.[836] Robert and his wife "took to Marina and June," and enjoyed showing Marina "things that she had never seen before." [837] Marina rested and took care of her baby, and when she could, helped in the household.[838] She testified that, apart from a trip to the library, Lee spent about a week "merely talking." [839]

On June 18, 4 days after he arrived in Fort Worth, Oswald went to the office of Mrs. Pauline Virginia Bates, a public stenographer whose name he had found in the telephone directory,[840] and asked her to type a manuscript from the "scraps of paper," on which he had recorded his impressions of the Soviet Union.[841] Intrigued by his tale that he had just returned from the Soviet Union and had smuggled his notes out of that country, she agreed to type the notes for $1 per page or $2 an hour, 50 cents less than her usual hourly rate.[842] On that day and the succeeding 2 days, Mrs. Bates spent 8 hours typing for Oswald while he remained in her office helping her with the notes and translating portions of them which were in Russian.[843] At the end of each session he collected his notes and as much of the manuscript as she had done and took them away with him.[844] On June 20, he gave Mrs. Bates $10 for the 10 completed pages; he told her that he had no more money and refused to accept her offer to postpone payment or continue the work for nothing.[845]

Oswald told Mrs. Bates that there was an engineer in Fort Worth who wanted to help him publish his notes.[846] On June 19,[847] he had called Peter Gregory, a petroleum engineer who was born in Siberia and taught Russian at the Fort Worth Public Library as a "civic enterprise." [848] He asked if Gregory could give him a letter testifying to his ability to read and speak Russian, so that he could obtain work as an interpreter or translator. Gregory suggested that Oswald come to his office, where Gregory opened a Russian book at random and asked Oswald to read from it. Oswald read well, and Gregory gave him the letter he wanted.[849] Gregory and Oswald had lunch together and discussed Oswald's life in the Soviet Union,[850] but, according to Gregory's testimony, nothing was said about publishing Oswald's manuscript.[851] About a week later, Gregory and his son Paul, a college student, visited the Oswalds at Robert Oswald's home and arranged for Marina to give Paul lessons in Russian during the summer.[852]

On June 26, Oswald was interviewed by FBI agents in Fort Worth.[853] One of the agents who interviewed him described him as tense and "drawn up"; he said that Oswald "exhibited an arrogant attitude * * * and [was] inclined to be just a little insolent." [854] Oswald declined to say why he had gone to Russia, saying that he refused to "relive the past." [855] He said that he had not attempted to obtain Soviet citizenship, had not been approached by Soviet officials for information about his experiences in the Marines, and had not offered them such information. Marina's Soviet passport required her to notify the Soviet Embassy in Washington of her address in this country, and Oswald told the agents that he planned to contact the Embassy for this purpose within a few days.[856] He promised to notify the FBI if he were contacted by Soviet agents "under suspicious circumstances or otherwise." [857] Oswald told his brother about the interview, saying that it had been "just fine." [858]

Oswald and his family remained with Robert for about a month.[859] While they were there his mother moved to Fort Worth from Crowell, Tex.,[860] and, sometime in July they moved into her apartment at 1501 West Seventh Street.[861] Mrs. Oswald testified that she had visited them at Robert's house in June [862] and moved to Fort Worth because she thought that the house was too crowded and wanted to help them.[863] Mrs. Oswald described the period when her son and his family lived with her as "a very happy month"; according to her testimony, she and her son and daughter-in-law got along well. She mentioned that she not only helped Marina keep house and care for the baby but also aided her son in his efforts to find employment.[864] Marina testified, however, that Lee did not get along well with his mother and that he decided after several weeks that they should move to their own apartment.[865] He did not file a change-of-address card at the post office when the family moved to West Seventh Street, as he did when they made their next move,[866] so he may have contemplated from the beginning that they would stay with his mother for only a short while. Around the middle of August,[867] the Oswalds moved to a one-bedroom furnished apartment at 2703 Mercedes Street, for which they paid $59.50 in advance for 1 month's rent.[868]

In the third week in July, Oswald had obtained a job as a sheet metal worker with the Louv-R-Pak Division of the Leslie Welding Co.,[869] a manufacturer of louvers and ventilators,[870] to which he had been referred by the Texas Employment Commission.[871] On his application for employment, filled out several days before, he wrote falsely that he had had experience as a sheet metal worker and machinist in the Marines and had been honorably discharged.[872] He usually worked 8 or 9 hours a day, for which he was paid $1.25 an hour.[873] Marina testified that Oswald did not like his work,[874] but he was regarded as a good employee [875] and remained with the company until October, when he quit.[876]   On the job, he kept to himself and was considered uncommunicative.[877]

Mrs. Oswald visited her son and his family at their apartment and tried to help them get settled; she testified that she bought some clothes for Marina and a highchair for the baby but that Oswald told her that he did not want her to buy "things for his wife that he himself could not buy." [878]   Finally, Oswald apparently decided that he did not want his mother to visit the apartment anymore and he became incensed when his wife permitted her to visit despite his instructions.[879]   After he moved to Dallas in October, Oswald did not see his mother or communicate with her in any way until she came to see him after the assassination.[880]   Witnesses have described the Mercedes Street apartment as "decrepit" and very poorly furnished; [881] there was no telephone service.[882]   Acquaintances observed that Marina and the baby were poorly clothed, that the Oswalds had little food, and that at first there was not a bed for the baby.[883]

On August 16, the FBI again interviewed Oswald. This interview took place in the back seat of a car in front of his home and covered substantially the same material as the previous interview. Oswald again denied having made any deal with representatives of the Soviet Union. He protested his undesirable discharge from the Marines, and stated that his wife was registered at the Soviet Embassy. He still refused to discuss why he had gone to the Soviet Union, but he was less hostile than he had been during the previous interview.[884]   According to his wife, however, he was very upset by the interest the FBI showed in him.[885]

The Oswalds became acquainted with a growing number of people of the Russian-speaking community in the Dallas-Fort Worth area, who were tied together socially by a common origin, language, and religion. The group was not restricted to people from Russia but was composed primarily of people from Eastern European countries.[886]   The Oswalds' initial contact with this group was through Peter Gregory. Marina gave conversational Russian lessons to Paul Gregory 2 days a week during August and early September, for which she was paid $35. Most of the lessons took place at the Mercedes Street apartment and Oswald was generally present.[887]   In addition, Paul Gregory occasionally took the Oswalds shopping; after they became friendly, he had a number of discussions with Oswald, some of them politically oriented.[888]

Sometime around August 25, Peter Gregory invited the Oswalds and several members of the Russian community to his house for dinner. One of the guests was George Bouhe, a Dallas accountant and a leader of the Russian community. He was very interested in meeting and conversing with Marina, because she had spent much of her life in Leningrad, which was his birthplace.[889]   Also present was Mrs. Anna Meller, the Russian-born wife of a Dallas department store employee.[890]   Near the end of August, the Oswalds met Declan Ford, a consulting geologist in the Dallas area, and his Russian-born wife at Mrs. Meller's home. The Oswalds were also introduced to Mrs.

Elena Hall, who was born in Tehran, Iran, of Russian parentage. She worked in a dental laboratory and at this time was divorced from her former husband John Hall, whom she subsequently remarried. In order to obtain dental aid for Marina, George Bouhe had brought her to Mrs. Hall's house.[891] In early September, the Oswalds met Alexander Kleinlerer, another member of the Russian group, who was then courting Mrs. Hall.[892] Mrs. Max Clark was introduced to Marina during this period by George Bouhe and Anna Meller. Max Clark met the Oswalds at a later time.[893] At about the same time, they were visited by George De Mohrenschildt, a petroleum engineer born in Russia,[894] who had heard of them from one of the Russian-speaking group.[895] Later on, the Oswalds met his wife, Jeanne, and his daughter and son-in-law, Gary and Alexandra Taylor.[896]

Most of the members of the Russian community were interested in the Oswalds not only because they needed help, but also because they could provide the latest information about what was happening in Russia.[897] Some members of the group were at first apprehensive about them because the apparent ease with which they had left Russia seemed suspicious.[898] Nevertheless, many of the group provided small amounts of money, groceries, clothing, and furniture for the Oswalds; George Bouhe, Anna Meller, and Elena Hall were the primary contributors, although others provided help in the form of transportation and groceries.[899] These acquaintances occasionally visited the Oswalds, and the Oswalds in turn visited some of them in Dallas.[900]

It was evident that Oswald did not appreciate the help of the Russian community.[901] At least once he flew into a rage and shouted that he did not need any of the things that people were giving to him.[902] Some felt that he resented the gifts because he could not give his wife what the others were providing;[903] he apparently was critical of them also because he felt that they were overly concerned with improving themselves economically.[904]

Oswald became increasingly unpopular with his Russian-speaking acquaintances, partly because of his resentment of their assistance.[905] Alexander Kleinlerer stated that none of them cared for Oswald "because of his political philosophy, his criticism of the United States, his apparent lack of interest in anyone but himself and because of his treatment of Marina."[906] Some of them believed that Oswald was mentally disturbed.[907] However, they felt sorry for Marina and the child and continued to help.[908]

On a weekend afternoon early in October, the Oswalds were visited by his mother and a number of people from the Russian community, including George Bouhe, Anna Meller, the Halls, the De Mohrenschildts, and the Taylors.[909] Oswald had apparently decided to look for a new job, and discussed his lack of job prospects and the fact that his rent was overdue.[910] He was advised to seek employment in the Dallas area.[911] Elena Hall invited Marina to move into her house in Fort Worth until Oswald found a job in Dallas. She accepted the proposal, and Mrs. Hall moved Marina, her daughter June, and the

Oswalds' few household goods in a pickup truck belonging to the dental laboratory where she was employed.[912]

Oswald worked at the Leslie Welding Co. on Monday, October 8, but failed to appear on the following day. He was already in Dallas.[913] He falsely told his wife that he had been discharged,[914] and told George Bouhe that the job had been a temporary one.[915] Sometime later, the company received an undated letter from him stating that he had "moved permanently to Dallas," and asking that the wages due him be forwarded to him at box 2915 in Dallas.[916] He did not tell his mother that he was leaving Fort Worth.[917]

While they were in Fort Worth, the Oswalds were having marital problems.[918] Several people noted that Marina had a blackened eye when they visited her at the Mercedes Street apartment.[919] She told her mother-in-law and George Bouhe that her husband had struck her, but said to Anna Meller that she had walked into a door.[920] It seems clear that Oswald had in fact hit her.[921] People observed friction between the Oswalds on various occasions,[922] although their disputes became more apparent later. Marina has written that this was a difficult period for them and that her husband was "very irritable" and sometimes some completely trivial thing would "drive him into a rage."[923]

She testified that:

> * * * immediately after coming to the United States Lee changed. I did not know him as such a man in Russia. * * * He helped me as before, but he became a little more of a recluse * * * He was very irritable, sometimes for a trifle * * * [924]

She has denied, however, that their separation was the result of quarrels between them.[925]

Marina spent the first few weeks after Oswald's departure at Elena Hall's house in Fort Worth, except for a brief stay at Gary Taylor's house in Dallas after one of her appointments at the Baylor Dental Clinic.[926] While she was in Dallas, Mrs. De Mohrenschildt brought her to the clinic on October 8, October 10, and October 15; [927] George Bouhe had given Mrs. De Mohrenschildt the money to cover the expense of Marina's dental care.[928]

Even before Oswald went to Dallas, some of his acquaintances were helping him in his effort to find a job there.[929] George De Mohrenschildt directed him to Samuel B. Ballen, a Dallas financial consultant, but no employment resulted.[930] George Bouhe recommended that Oswald go to the Texas Employment Commission in Dallas; and Anna Meller had her husband ask Mrs. Helen Cunningham, a counselor in the clerical and sales division of the Dallas office of the employment commission, to help Oswald find a job.[931] Oswald first came into the office of the employment commission on October 9. He was reluctant to accept industrial employment, and was placed in the clerical category and turned over to Mrs. Cunningham for counseling. He indicated that he had an interest in writing. The results of general aptitude tests which he had taken at the Fort Worth employment office had been transmitted to the Dallas office, and indicated that he had some aptitude in this direction and for clerical work. It was noted on his application form that he had "outstanding verbal-clerical potential." He demonstrated ability to perform many skilled and semiskilled jobs, and there was some indication that he could do college work. Mrs. Cunningham gave him three special tests: for general clerical work, work as an insurance claims examiner, and drafting work. He scored high on all three. His application form indicated that he did not have a driver's license, and noted: "well-groomed and spoken, business suit, alert replies—expresses self extremely well." He told Mrs. Cunningham that he hoped to develop qualifications for responsible junior executive employment by a work-study program at a local college but that this must be delayed because of his immediate financial needs and responsibilities.[932]

Mrs. Cunningham concluded that although Oswald would be classified for clerical work, she should try to get him any available job, since he badly needed money. He was referred to an architect for an opening as a messenger but was not hired. On October 11, he was referred to Jaggars-Chiles-Stovall Co., a graphic arts company, in response to a call from John Graef, head of the photographic department of the company, who had told the employment commission that he needed a photoprint trainee. Oswald was enthusiastic about his prospects and apparently made a good impression; Graef picked him over several other applicants.[933] On the following day he began working in his new position as a trainee making prints of advertising material. He worked a 40-hour week at approximately $1.35 per hour; his take-home pay varied from $49 to $74 a week.[934] According to his wife, "he liked his work very much."[935]

Oswald moved into the YMCA on October 15, and stayed there until October 19, paying $2.25 a night.[936] He had used the Taylors' address and telephone number as a place where he could be reached,[937] but on October 9 had also rented post office box 2915 under his own name at the main post office on Ervay Street.[938] On October 10, he filed a change-of-address form indicating that mail for 2703 Mercedes Street should be forwarded to the box.[939] Marina has written that Oswald wrote her letters and telephoned her during the separation.[940]

On October 16, Mrs Hall brought Marina and June to Dallas to have June baptized. Marina apparently did this surreptitiously, because her husband opposed baptism; they did not contact him in Dallas, but left birthday gifts for him at the Taylors. Oswald did not appear very disturbed when he found out about the baptism.[941]

Two days later, Mrs. Hall had an automobile accident and went to the hospital, where she remained until October 26; Marina remained in the Hall house. Mrs. Max Clark and Alexander Kleinlerer, a friend of Mrs. Hall, checked up to make sure that she was getting along without too much trouble.[942]   After Oswald left the YMCA on October 19, he moved to a room or apartment somewhere in Dallas,[943] which has not been located.[944]   It seems likely, however, that during that time he spent several weekends with Marina at the Hall house.[945]

Four days after Mrs. Hall returned from the hospital, she left for New York to visit friends. By the time she returned, Marina had moved to a three-room apartment at 604 Elsbeth Street in Dallas, which Oswald had rented on Saturday, November 3;[946] the landlady stated that he had looked at the apartment about a week before. The monthly rent was $68, in addition to which he had to pay several dollars a month for utilities. He paid the rent plus a $5 deposit on November 3,[947] but probably spent that night with Marina at the Hall house. On Sunday the Taylors helped the Oswalds move their belongings to the Elsbeth Street apartment with a rented trailer.[948]   Oswald had asked Kleinlerer to help them move, and Kleinlerer also was present when they departed.[949]

Soon after the Oswalds were reunited, their marital difficulties started again. While they were moving to Elsbeth Street, Kleinlerer noticed that Oswald slapped his wife for not having the zipper on her dress completely closed.[950]   They argued over his refusal to allow her to smoke.[951]   There was a quarrel also when he told the landlady that Marina was from Czechoslovakia; he was angered when Marina, who disapproved of this deception, told the landlady the truth.[952]

Although several people tried to help Marina improve her scanty knowledge of English, Oswald discouraged this,[953] perhaps because he wanted to keep up his Russian.[954]   Some witnesses testified that she commented about his sexual abilities.[955]   He apparently continued to beat her, and once she suggested to George De Mohrenschildt that she should "get away" from Oswald. When De Mohrenschildt criticized Oswald's conduct, Oswald replied, "It is my business."[956]   Marina testified that when they moved into the Elsbeth Street apartment, her husband became "nervous and irritable" and was very angry over "trifles."[957]   She said that it was sometimes her fault that he beat her,[958] for example when she wrote to an old boyfriend in Russia that she wished she had married him; the letter was returned for postage due, and Oswald read it.[959]

Because of this quarreling, a few of their acquaintances felt that Marina would be better off alone. George Bouhe offered to help her if she promised to leave Oswald permanently.[960]   Finally, in early November, Marina, helped by the De Mohrenschildts, moved into Anna Meller's house with the intention not to return to Oswald. He was apparently quite upset and did not want Marina to leave him.[961]

Oswald did not visit his wife at Anna Meller's house,[962] and for a short time did not even know where she was.[963]   According to Marina, he called her after she moved and they met at De Mohrenschildt's house. He asked her to return home. She insisted that he stop quarreling and that he change his ways. He said that he could not change. Marina would not agree to return home with him and he left.[964]

Marina was uncomfortable at the Meller house, where there was very little room. She moved to Katherine Ford's house [965] where she apparently stayed from November 11 to 17. She indicated that she had decided never to return to her husband; [966] it was Mrs. Ford's impression that Marina was going to stay at other people's houses until a permanent place could be found for her.[967] When Mr. Ford returned from a business trip on November 17, Marina and June moved to the home of Mrs. Frank Ray, where they spent the day. Mrs. Ray, the wife of a Dallas advertising man, was also of Russian origin. Since Mrs. Ray had no baby bed, Marina returned to the Fords that evening. On the next day, however, Marina moved her belongings to the Rays' house. That same day, Oswald called and asked to visit his wife, whom he had called and written. Mr. Ray picked him up and took him to Marina.[968]

Marina testified that at this meeting Oswald professed his love for her. She stated: "I saw him cry * * * [he] begged me to come back, asked my forgiveness, and promised that he would try to improve, if only I would come back." [969] On another occasion she said: "* * * he cried and you know a woman's heart—I went back to him. He said he didn't care to live if I did not return." [970] That same day she decided to return to him. Mr. Ray packed her belongings and took her back to the Elsbeth Street apartment.[971]

Members of the Russian community who had taken care of Marina so that she would not have to live with Oswald felt that their efforts had been in vain. George Bouhe was so irritated that he never again tried to help either of the Oswalds.[972] Contacts between them and members of the Russian community diminished markedly.[973] Oswald did not care for most of these people and made his feelings apparent.[974] Even the De Mohrenschildts, whom he liked most, saw much less of them.[975] Lydia Dymitruk, another Russian born woman in the Dallas-Fort Worth area, testified that she saw the Oswalds on only one occasion, and did not care to see them again. She drove Marina and June, who had a high fever, to the hospital; Oswald told the hospital that he was unemployed in order to avoid paying for June's treatment and later left Mrs. Dymitruk without thanking her.[976] Mrs. Ford testified that Marina had told her that she contemplated suicide during this period because Oswald was treating her badly and she had no friends; she felt that she had "no way out." [977] Marina acknowledged to the Commission that she had had such thoughts.[978]

In an effort to renew family ties, Robert Oswald wrote to Lee and John Pic on November 17, inviting them and their families to Thanksgiving dinner. Lee accepted the invitation. He and Marina traveled to Fort Worth by bus on Thanksgiving Day, and John Pic and Robert met them at the station.[979] Pic had not seen his half-brother for 10 years. He observed, as many others have also attested, that Lee seemed to be a good father and to take an active interest in June.[980] After dinner, Marina phoned Paul Gregory, who later drove the Oswalds to his house for sandwiches and then took them to the bus station for the return trip to Dallas.[981] Thereafter, Robert spoke to his brother once by telephone and received a post card and a letter from him, but he eventually lost contact with Lee and did not see him again until after the assassination.[982]

Despite his disillusionment with Soviet life, Oswald kept up his interest in Russia. He wrote to the Soviet Embassy in Washington for information on how to subscribe to Russian periodicals and for "any periodicals or bulletins which you may put out for the benefit of your citizens living, for a time, in the U.S.A." [983] He subsequently subscribed to several Russian journals.[984] In December 1962, the Soviet Embassy received a card in Russian, signed "Marina and Lee Oswald," which conveyed New Year's greetings and wishes for "health, success and all of the best" to the employees at the Embassy.[985] The Oswalds continued to correspond with acquaintances in Russia.[986]

Soon after his return to this country, Oswald had started to correspond with the Communist Party, U.S.A., and the Socialist Workers Party. He subscribed to the Worker in August 1962.[987] He wrote for additional literature from these organizations, and attempted to join the Socialist Workers Party, which, however, had no branch in Texas.[988] He sent samples of his photographic work to the Socialist Workers Party, the Worker, and the Hall-Davis Defense Committee, and offered to aid them in printing and photographic work in connection with posters; these offers were not accepted.[989]

He continued to read a great deal on a variety of subjects.[990] George Bouhe testified that Oswald's fare consisted of books by Marx, Lenin, "and similar things." [991] Marina said that he read books of a historical nature, including H. G. Wells' two volume "Outline of History," and biographies of Hitler, Kennedy, and Khrushchev.[992]

Despite the Oswalds' break with the Russian community, De Mohrenschildt, knowing that they would be alone during the Christmas season, asked the Fords whether he could bring the Oswalds to a party celebrating the Russian Christmas at the Fords' home; the Fords assented. The party was attended by many members of the Russian community.[993] Oswald spoke at length with Yaeko Okui, a Japanese woman who had been brought to the party by Lev Aronson, first cellist of the Dallas Symphony Orchestra; [994] she told Federal investigators that she never saw Oswald again.[995] The Oswalds were not invited to three other Russian Christmas season gatherings which occurred during the next few days.[996]

Marina visited the De Mohrenschildts several times after Christmas.[997] They invited both Lee and Marina to a small dinner party in February 1963; also present were Everett Glover, a chemist employed in Dallas, and his roommate Volkmar Schmidt.[998] On February 22, Glover had a gathering at his house, one of the purposes of which was to permit his friends, many of whom were studying Russian, to meet the Oswalds.[999] They were the objects of much attention.[1000] Marina conversed at length with another guest named Ruth Paine, who had recently separated from her husband, Michael Paine, a research engineer at the Bell Helicopter plant in Fort Worth. Mrs. Paine, who was studying Russian, obtained Marina's address [1001] and shortly thereafter wrote Marina asking to see her. Marina responded by inviting Mrs. Paine to visit her.[1002]

The Oswalds moved out of their Elsbeth Street apartment on March 3, 1963, to an upstairs apartment several blocks away at 214 West Neely Street. Oswald inquired about the apartment in response to a "For Rent" sign; the rent was $60 per month, not including utilities.[1003] They moved without assistance, carrying their belongings in their hands and in a baby stroller.[1004] Marina preferred the Neely Street apartment because it had a porch and was, she felt, more suitable for June.[1005]

Aware of Oswald's difficulties in obtaining employment, George Bouhe had advised him as early as October 1962 to attend a night school in Dallas.[1006] On January 14, Oswald enrolled in a typing course in the night school of Crozier Technical High School, and started attending on January 28. The class ran from 6:15 to 7:15 p.m. on Mondays, Tuesday, and Thursdays. Although Oswald reviewed a typing textbook at home, he attended the course irregularly and stopped going altogether on about March 28.[1007]

Ruth Paine and Marina started to exchange visits in March. Mrs. Paine invited the Oswalds for dinner, and on April 20 she took them on a picnic. When Oswald was not present, the two women frequently discussed their respective marital problems, and Marina disclosed to Mrs. Paine that she was pregnant.[1008] Marina wrote of these meetings:

> One day we were invited to a friend's house, where I met Ruth Paine, who was studying Russian here in America and wanted to improve her conversational knowledge. We began to see each other. Ruth would come to see me with her children. This was very good for both me and for June. She was growing up alone and becoming terribly wild, so the company of other children was good for her. Sometimes we went out on picnics at a nearby lake. Lee loved to fish, and we would look and rejoice if he caught a little fish. Several times we went to visit Ruth who lived in Irving.[1009]

Using the name of A. J. Hidell, Oswald had ordered a Smith & Wesson .38 revolver from Los Angeles on a form which he dated January 27. On March 12, he ordered a rifle from Klein's Sporting Goods in Chicago under the name of A. Hidell.[1010] Oswald used the name "Alek James Hidell" on identification cards which he probably produced at Jaggars-Chiles-Stovall. One of his fellow employees taught him various photographic techniques, which he could have used to prepare not only these cards, but also the samples of his work which he sent to various organizations.[1011]

Both weapons were shipped on March 20.[1012] Oswald kept the rifle in a small storeroom at the Neely Street apartment. He spent long periods of time in the storeroom, which he told Marina she was not to enter.[1013] He told her that he intended to use the rifle for hunting [1014] and that he practiced with it. She saw him leave with it once, and clean it several times.[1015] He also posed for two pictures, taken by Marina in the backyard of the Neely apartment, in which he held his rifle and copies of the Worker and the Militant and the revolver was strapped to his belt. He gave one of the pictures to his wife and asked her to keep it for June.[1016]

Over the weekend of March 9–10, Oswald photographed the alley which runs behind the home of Gen. Edwin Walker, and probably at about the same time he photographed the rear of Walker's home and a nearby railroad track and right-of-way.[1017] He prepared and studied a notebook in which he outlined a plan to shoot General Walker, and he looked at bus schedules.[1018] He went to the Walker residence on the evening of April 6 or 7, planning to make his attack. However, he changed his plans, hid his rifle nearby, and determined to act on the following Wednesday, April 10, when a nearby church was planning a meeting which, Oswald reasoned, would create a diversion that would help him escape.[1019] On Wednesday, Oswald left a note for Marina telling her what to do if he were apprehended. He retrieved his rifle and fired at Walker, but the bullet narrowly missed Walker's head. Oswald secreted his rifle again and took the bus home.[1020]

When Oswald told Marina what he had done, she became angry and made him promise never to repeat such an act. She testified that she kept his letter, intending to give it to the authorities if he repeated his attempt. He told Marina that he was sorry he had missed Walker and said that the shooting of Walker would have been analogous to an assassination of Hitler.[1021] Several days later, the De Mohrenschildts visited the Oswalds, bringing an Easter present for June. During the visit, Jeanne De Mohrenschildt saw the rifle and told her husband about it. Without any knowledge of the truth, De Mohrenschildt jokingly intimated that Oswald was the one who had shot at Walker. Oswald apparently concluded that Marina had told De Mohrenschildt of his role in the attempt and was visibly shaken.[1022]

On April 6, Oswald was dropped by Jaggars-Chiles-Stovall because, in his supervisor's opinion, he could not do the work, although he was trying; in addition, he did not get along with his fellow employees.[1023] The fact that he brought a Russian newspaper to work may also have been of some significance.[1024] Marina testified that her husband, who had always worried about his job security at Jaggars-Chiles-Stovall,[1025] was quite upset by the loss of his job since he had liked the work.[1026]

Oswald again resorted to the Texas Employment Commission.[1027] On April 8, he informed the Commission that he was seeking employment but was referred to no employers. He stated that he had been laid off at Jaggars-Chiles-Stovall due to lack of work." [1028] On April 12, he made a claim for unemployment benefits; 4 days later the commission mailed him a determination disapproving his claim because of insufficient wage credits.[1029]

For a while after the Oswalds moved into the Neely Street apartment they got along well,[1030] but they soon began to quarrel.[1031]

724

Oswald was apparently still preventing Marina from learning English,[1032] and there is some indication that he continued to beat her.[1033] Since February, he had been urging her to return to Russia.[1034] Marina wrote several letters to the Russian Embassy requesting a visa to return to Russia; [1035] she testified, however, that Oswald forced her to write them, and that she never wanted to return to Russia.[1036]

When Ruth Paine visited the Oswalds at their apartment on April 24, she was surprised to learn that Oswald was packed and ready to leave for New Orleans by bus. He explained that he had been unable to find employment in or around Dallas, and that Marina had suggested that he go to New Orleans since he had been born there.[1037] Marina has testified that the real reason behind her suggestion was that she wanted to get him out of town because of the Walker incident.[1038] Mrs. Paine offered to drive Marina to New Orleans at a later date, and also to have Marina and June stay with her rather than at the apartment in the meantime. Oswald helped the women pack Mrs. Paine's car, and the two women moved everything from the Neely Street apartment to the Paine house in Irving.[1039]

When he arrived at the bus station in New Orleans, Oswald telephoned his aunt, Lillian Murret, to ask if he could stay at her home at 757 French Street while he looked for employment. She had been unaware that he had returned from Russia or that he was married and had a child and was surprised to hear from him. She said that she did not have room to accommodate three guests, but that since he was alone he was welcome.[1040]

Oswald had been born in New Orleans, and on his return showed great interest in finding out what had happened to the other members of his father's family. He visited the cemetery where his father was buried and called all the Oswalds in the telephone book. By this method he located one relative, Mrs. Hazel Oswald of Metairie, La., the widow of William Stout Oswald, his father's brother. He visited her at her home; she gave him a picture of his father and told him that as far as she knew the rest of the family was dead.[1041]

On April 26, Oswald began his search for employment. He went to the employment office of the Louisiana Department of Labor and stated that he was qualified as a commercial photographer, shipping clerk, or "darkroom man." The interviewer noted on Oswald's application card: "Will travel on limited basis. Will relocate. Min. $1.25 hr. Neat. Suit. Tie. Polite." [1042] Although the employment commission made a few referrals, Oswald relied primarily upon newspaper advertisements, and applied for a number of positions.[1043] Mrs. Murret testified that he would spend the day job hunting, return to her home for supper, watch television, and go to bed.[1044]

On April 29, he filed a request for reconsideration of the employment commission's disapproval of his unemployment compensation claim. His complaint that he had not been credited for his employment at Jaggars-Chiles-Stovall was ruled valid on May 8, and he was granted maximum benefits of $369, payable at the rate of $33 per week. He filed interstate claims on May 7 and 15, and received

$33 in response to the latter; the former claim was filed before the expiration of the prescribed waiting period.[1045] Not only had Oswald in fact been working since May 10, but he included on his claim sheet, as concerns with which he had sought work, fictitious employers and employers whom he apparently had not contacted.[1046]

Oswald wrote to Marina: "All is well. I am living with Aunt Lillian. She has very kindly taken us in. I am now looking for work. When I find it I will write you."[1047] And on May 3, he wrote to Marina and Ruth Paine: "Girls, I still have not found work, but I receive money from the unemployment office in the amount 15 to 20 dollars. They were mistaken in the Dallas office when they refused, but I straightened everything out. Uncle 'Dyuz' offered me a loan of $200.00 if needed. Great, eh? !"[1048]

On May 9, responding to a newspaper advertisement, Oswald completed an application for employment with William B. Reily Co., Inc., at 640 Magazine Street, an enterprise engaged in the roasting, grinding, canning, bagging, and sale of coffee. On his application form, Oswald listed as references in addition to John Murret, "Sgt. Robert Hidell" and "Lieut. J. Evans," both apparently fictitious names.[1049] His application was approved and he began work on May 10, at the rate of $1.50 per hour. His task was the lubrication of the company's machinery.[1050] Oswald did not enjoy this work,[1051] and told his wife and Mrs. Paine that he was working in commercial photography.[1052]

Also on May 9, Oswald obtained an apartment at 4905 Magazine Street with the help of Myrtle Evans, who had known him when he was a child. The rent was $65 a month. Oswald moved in on May 10,[1053] after telephoning Marina on the ninth and asking her to come to New Orleans. Ruth Paine testified that the invitation elated Marina: "Papa nas lubet"—"Daddy loves us," she repeated again and again. Mrs. Paine drove Marina and June to New Orleans; they left Dallas on May 10, spent the night in Shreveport, and arrived on the 11th. Mrs. Paine stayed with the Oswalds for 3 days; the three of them, with June and Mrs. Paine's children, toured the French Quarter. On May 14, Mrs. Paine left New Orleans to return to her home.[1054]

The Murrets and the Oswalds exchanged visits from time to time; Marina testified that the Murrets were very good to them.[1055] Mrs. Murret's daughter, Marilyn, took the Oswalds on an outing.[1056] But, according to Marina's testimony, aside from Ruth Paine and Ruth Kloepfer and her daughters, the Murrets were the only social visitors the Oswalds had.[1057] Ruth Kloepfer was a clerk of the Quaker Meeting in New Orleans whom Ruth Paine had written in the hope that she might know some Russian-speaking people who could visit Marina. Mrs. Kloepfer herself visited the Oswalds but made no attempt to direct any Russian-speaking people to them.[1058]

On July 19, Oswald was dismissed by Reily because of inefficiency and inattention to his work. He had spent many of his working hours next door at the Crescent City Garage, where he read gun magazines and discussed guns with one of the owners, Adrian Alba.[1059] On the

726

following Monday, July 22, Oswald again visited the Louisiana employment office to seek new employment and file a claim for unemployment compensation. Thereafter, he collected unemployment compensation weekly and, although apparently making some effort to obtain another job, again listed a number of fictitious job applications on his unemployment compensation claim forms.[1060] He soon gave up his search for employment, and began to spend his days at home reading.[1061] He received another setback on July 25, when he was notified that in response to the request for review which he had made in 1962, his undesirable discharge from the Marine Corps had been affirmed.[1062]

During this period, Oswald began to evidence thoughts of returning to the Soviet Union or going to Cuba. On June 24 he applied for a new passport, which he received on the following day.[1063] Apparently at Oswald's request,[1064] Marina wrote to the Russian Embassy, expressing a desire to return to Russia and indicating that she would be accompanied by her husband. She explained that she wanted to return because of family problems, including the impending birth of her second child.[1065] Accompanying her letter was a letter written by Oswald dated July 1, in which he asked the Embassy to rush an entrance visa for his wife and requested that his visa be considered separately.[1066] Marina believed that Oswald was really planning to go only to Cuba.[1067] She testified that "his basic desire was to get to Cuba by any means, and that all the rest of it was window dressing for that purpose." [1068]

During the early days of the New Orleans period, the Oswalds' marriage was more harmonious than it had been previously. Marina wrote:

> * * * our family life in New Orleans was more peaceful. Lee took great satisfaction in showing me the city where he was born. We often went to the beach, the zoo, and the park. Lee liked to go and hunt crabs. It is true, that he was not very pleased with his job * * * We did not have very much money, and the birth of a new child involved new expenses * * * As before, Lee spent a great deal of time reading.[1069]

Marina testified, however, that after they had been in New Orleans for a while, Oswald became depressed and that she once found him alone in the dark crying.[1070] She wrote to Ruth Paine that his "love" had ceased soon after Mrs. Paine had left New Orleans.[1071] Mrs. Paine testified, however, that she had noticed friction between the Oswalds before she left.[1072] On July 11, Mrs. Paine wrote Marina that if Oswald did not wish to live with her any more and preferred that she return to the Soviet Union, she could live at the Paines' house. Although Mrs. Paine had long entertained this idea, this was the first time she explicitly made the invitation. She renewed the invitation on July 12, and again on July 14; she attempted to overcome any feeling which Marina might have that she would be a burden by stating that

Marina could help with the housework and help her learn Russian, and that she would also provide a tax advantage.[1073]

Marina replied that she had previously raised the subject of a separation and that it had led to arguments. She stated that she was happy and that for a considerable period of time Oswald had been good to her. She attributed this improved attitude to the fact that he was anticipating their second child. Marina turned down Mrs. Paine's invitation but said that she would take advantage of it if things became worse.[1074] Mrs. Paine replied that she was taking a trip north to visit her parents and would visit Marina in New Orleans about September 18. She also suggested that Marina come to her house for the birth of the baby.[1075]

On July 6, Eugene Murret, a cousin of Oswald who was studying to be a Jesuit Priest in Mobile, Ala., wrote and asked if Oswald could come to Mobile and speak at the Jesuit House of Studies about "contemporary Russia and the practice of Communism there." Oswald accepted, and on July 27 he and his family, joined by some of the Murrets, traveled to Mobile; Charles Murret paid the expenses. Oswald spoke concerning his observations in Russia and conducted a question and answer period; he impressed his listeners as articulate. He indicated that he had become disillusioned during his stay in Russia, and that in his opinion the best political system would be one which combined the best points of capitalism and communism.[1076] While he left his listeners with the impression that he was an atheist, he avoided a direct discussion of religion. The group returned to New Orleans on July 28.[1077]

In late May and early June, Oswald had apparently begun to formulate plans for creating a New Orleans branch of the Fair Play for Cuba Committee. Using the name "Lee Osborne" he ordered a number of printed circulars demanding "Hands off Cuba" in large letters, and application forms and membership cards for the proposed chapter.[1078] On August 5, he visited a store managed by Carlos Bringuier, a Cuban refugee and avid opponent of Castro and the New Orleans delegate of the Cuban student directorate. Oswald indicated an interest in joining the struggle against Castro. He told Bringuier that he had been a marine and was trained in guerrilla warfare, and that he was willing not only to train Cubans to fight Castro but also to join the fight himself. The next day Oswald returned to the store and left his "Guidebook for Marines" for Bringuier.[1079]

On August 9, Bringuier saw Oswald passing out Fair Play for Cuba leaflets. Bringuier and his companions became angry and a dispute resulted. Oswald and the three Cuban exiles were arrested for disturbing the peace.[1080] Oswald spent the night in jail and was interviewed the next day by a lieutenant of the New Orleans Police Department. At Oswald's request, an FBI agent also interviewed him. Oswald maintained that he was a member of the New Orleans branch of the Fair Play for Cuba Committee which, he claimed, had 35 members. He stated also that he had been in touch with the president of that organization, A. J. Hidell.[1081] Oswald was in fact the only member of the "New Orleans branch," which had never been chartered by the National Fair Play for Cuba Committee.[1082] Later that day Oswald was released on bail, and 2 days later he pleaded guilty to the charges against him and paid a $10 fine. The charges against the Cuban exiles were dismissed.[1083] Marina testified that the arrest upset Lee and that he "became less active, he cooled off a little" after it.[1084]

On August 16, Oswald, assisted by at least one other person who was a hired helper, again passed out Fair Play for Cuba literature, this time in front of the International Trade Mart. That night, television newscasts ran pictures of Oswald's activities.[1085] (This hindered Oswald's subsequent attempts to obtain employment in New Orleans.)[1086] Bringuier sent one of his friends to Oswald's home to pose as a Castro sympathizer and attempt to obtain information about Oswald, but Oswald apparently saw through the ruse.[1087]

William Stuckey, a radio broadcaster with a program called "Latin Listening Post," had long been looking for a member of the Fair Play for Cuba Committee to appear on his program. He learned about Oswald from Bringuier, and visited Oswald on August 17. Later that day, Stuckey recorded an interview with Oswald which was cut to about 5 minutes and played back on the show that evening.[1088] Two days later, Stuckey asked the news director of the station if he could run the entire tape, but the director felt that a debate with a local opponent of Castro would be of greater public interest. Consequently, Stuckey arranged for a debate between Oswald and Bringuier on a 25-minute daily public affairs program called "Conversation Carte Blanche," which took place on August 21.[1089] Oswald defended the Castro regime and discussed Marxism. He was put on the defensive when his defection to Russia was brought up,[1090] and Stuckey later testified that he thought that the program had finished the Fair Play for Cuba Committee in New Orleans.[1091] However, Stuckey also testified that Oswald seemed to be a clean-cut and intelligent person who conducted himself very well during the interviews and debates.[1092]

Oswald wrote several times to V. T. Lee, then national director of the Fair Play for Cuba Committee, telling him, sometimes in exaggerated terms, of his activities.[1093] He wrote also to the Communist Party and asked whether, in view of his prior defection, he should "continue to fight, handicapped as it were, by * * * [his] past record, [and] compete with anti-progressive forces, above-ground or * * * should always remain in the background, i.e., underground."[1094] The Party replied that "often it is advisable for some people to remain in the background, not underground."[1095] And although Oswald wrote four letters to V. T. Lee during the summer,[1096] there is no evidence that Oswald heard from him after May 29.

Ruth Paine arrived in New Orleans on September 20, and spent three nights with the Oswalds. During this stay, Mrs. Paine found relations between them much improved. Nonetheless, it was decided that Marina would go back with her to Irving for the birth of the baby. Marina and Mrs. Paine toured Bourbon Street while Oswald stayed home and did some packing for Marina's return to Texas.[1097] On Sunday, September 22, Oswald and Mrs. Paine finished loading the station wagon with the Oswalds' household belongings.[1098]

MEXICO CITY

Marina Oswald testified that sometime in August her husband first told her of his plan to go to Mexico and from there to Cuba, where he planned to stay; he had given up a plan to hijack an airplane and fly directly to Cuba, which plan Marina consistently opposed.[1099] On September 17, he obtained from the Mexican consulate general in New Orleans a "Tourist Card," FM-8 No. 24085, good for one journey into Mexico for no longer than 15 days. Typed in the blank, "Appelidos y nombre," was "Lee, Harvey Oswald," "Fotogrofo"; the intended destination was shown as Mexico City.[1100] (The comma between "Lee" and "Harvey" seems to have been an error.)[1101] On the application Oswald stated that he was employed at "640 Rampart"; he was in fact unemployed.[1102] (See Commission Exhibits Nos. 2478, 2481, p. 300.)

Marina and June departed with Mrs. Ruth Paine for Irving on the morning of September 23.[1103] Before she left, Oswald told Marina that she should not tell anyone about his impending trip to Mexico.[1104] Marina kept this secret until after the assassination.[1105] On the previous day, Oswald's landlord had seen Mrs. Paine's car being packed and had asked Oswald, whose rent was about 15 days overdue, whether he was leaving. Oswald told him that Marina was leaving temporarily but that he would remain.[1106] A neighbor testified that on the evening of September 24, he saw Oswald, carrying two pieces of luggage, hurriedly leave the Magazine Street apartment and board a bus.[1107] Though uncertain of the exact date, a city busdriver recalls that at the same time of day and at the same location he picked up a man who was carrying two suitcases of different sizes and helped him place them so that they would not disturb the other passengers. The driver remembers that the man asked directions to the Greyhound bus station. He discharged the passenger at an intersection where he could board a Canal Street car and transfer to another bus which would go past the Greyhound and Continental Trailways stations.[1108] The landlord found Oswald's apartment vacant on September 25.[1109]

Oswald appears to have taken with him a Spanish-English dictionary; [1110] his address book; [1111] his 1963 passport and old passport; [1112] his correspondence with the Communist Party and with the Soviet Embassy in Washington, some of which was in Russian; [1113] proof of his marriage; [1114] newspaper clippings concerning his arrest and his interest in the activities of the Fair Play for Cuba Committee [1115] (activities which, Marina testified, he had undertaken because he thought that they would help him when he got to Cuba) ; [1116] evidence that he was the "Director" of the New Orleans chapter of the Committee; [1117] and various other cards, such as a work card, which he had obtained in Russia.[1118] He took also several sheets of notepaper on which he had written a summary of important events in his life which he presumably intended to call to the attention of Cuban and Soviet officials in Mexico City to convince them to let him enter Cuba. On these sheets he had recorded facts about his Marine service, including the dates of his enlistment and discharge, the places where he had served, and the diplomas that he had received from military school. Recorded also were notes on his stay in the Soviet Union, his early interest in Communist literature, his ability to speak Russian, his organization of the New Orleans chapter of the Fair Play for Cuba Committee, his contact with police authorities in connection with his work for the Committee, and his experience in "street agitation," as a "radio speaker and lecturer," and as a photographer.[1119] The two pieces of luggage which Oswald took with him were a small, blue, zipper bag [1120] and a large, olive-colored bag,[1121] both made of cloth. He carried the smaller bag with him throughout the trip, but, at least from Nuevo Laredo to Mexico City, checked the larger one through to his destination.[1122]

Oswald remained in New Orleans until September 25. His precise whereabouts on the night of September 24 are uncertain, but in view of his limited finances, he probably returned to the apartment to sleep after checking his luggage at a bus station or spent the night at an inexpensive hotel or roominghouse. Some time after 5 a. m. on September 25, he collected a Texas unemployment compensation check for $33 at his New Orleans post office box. He cashed the check between 8 a.m. and noon at a store about six blocks from his apartment on Magazine Street.[1123] This gave him about $200 for the trip to Mexico.[1124]

He left New Orleans by bus,[1125] probably on Continental Trailways Bus No. 5121, departing New Orleans at 12:20 p.m. on September 25, and scheduled to arrive in Houston at 10:50 p.m.; that bus is the only one on which Oswald could have left New Orleans after noon on September 25 [1126] and arrived in Houston before midnight.[1127] Sometime in the evening he called the home of Horace Elroy Twiford, a member of the Socialist Labor Party who had received Oswald's name from the party's headquarters in New York and sent him a copy of its official publication, the "Weekly People." [1128] Mrs. Twiford, who answered the telephone,[1129] believes that the call was made locally, before 10 p.m. It may have been made from Beaumont or some other stop on the route; however, in view of the bus schedule, it probably was made in Houston later than Mrs. Twiford remembered.[1130] Oswald told Mrs. Twiford that he was a member of the Fair Play for Cuba Committee and that he hoped to see her husband for a few hours that evening before he flew to Mexico. He wanted also to find out how Twiford had obtained his name and address. Mrs. Twiford told Oswald that her husband, a merchant seaman, was at sea but would be happy to see him at some other time; she offered to take a message.

Oswald said that he could not await her husband's return because he was flying to Mexico.[1131] The Twifords have stated that they had no other contact with Oswald.[1132]

An employee of the U.S. Selective Service System has stated that an individual calling himself "Harvey Oswald" appeared at her office in Austin, Tex., immediately after lunch on September 25, and discussed with her the possibility of rectifying his undesirable discharge from the Marine Corps.[1133] Despite the employee's reputability and apparent sincerity, all of the information which she furnished with respect to Oswald's appearance and conversation could have been derived from news media, consciously or unconsciously, by the time she told the FBI her story. Other persons in Austin who, according to the employee's testimony, should also have observed Oswald failed to corroborate her testimony.[1134] No other evidence tending to show that Oswald was in Austin at this time has been discovered.

The telephone call which Oswald made to the Twifords on the evening of September 25, indicates that he was either in Houston or on his way there when he made it, since the purpose of the call was to make an appointment to see Twiford in Houston that evening. Oswald could not have left New Orleans on September 25, been in Austin 521 miles away by early afternoon, and returned 162 miles to Houston by night unless he traveled by air; airline records contain no indication that Oswald was on such flights.[1135] It is very unlikely that he had with him enough money beyond what he needed for the trip to Mexico City to take such flights, and the poor state of his finances at this time plus his well-established frugality make it extremely unlikely that he would have considered it worthwhile to do so even if he could. There is no evidence that Oswald was in such a hurry to reach Mexico that he would have felt it necessary to travel by airplane rather than a less expensive means of travel. He took a bus from Houston to Mexico City, lived very inexpensively there, and took a bus back to Dallas; there is no apparent reason why he would have interrupted such an inexpensive trip to fly to Austin and then to Houston. He told a passenger whom he met on the next leg of his trip that he had come from New Orleans, and made no reference to Austin.[1136]

On September 26, Oswald boarded Continental Trailways bus No. 5133 in Houston and departed at 2:35 a.m. for Laredo, Tex., via Corpus Christi and Alice.[1137] Two British tourists, Dr. and Mrs. John B. McFarland, who boarded No. 5133 in Houston, noticed Oswald when they awoke at about 6 a.m. Oswald told them that he was going to Cuba via Mexico City, and they inferred from conversation with him that he had left New Orleans early in the afternoon of September 25 and that he was going to Cuba via Mexico City. He said also that he was secretary of the New Orleans branch of the Fair Play for Cuba Committee and that he hoped to see Fidel Castro in Cuba. The bus was scheduled to arrive in Laredo at approximately 1:20 p.m.[1138]

Oswald crossed the border from Laredo to Nuevo Laredo, Mexico, between 1:30 and 2 p.m.[1139] From Nuevo Laredo, he traveled to Mexico City aboard bus No. 516 of the Flecha Roja Bus Line, which departed at 2:15 p.m. and was scheduled to arrive in Mexico City at 9:45 a.m. on the following day; he held baggage claim check No. 320435.[1140] He was seen on the bus by the McFarlands and by two Australian girls who boarded the bus on the evening of September 26 at Monterrey.[1141] He occupied the seat next to an elderly Englishman, who told the girls that the young man sitting next to him apparently had been to Mexico before.[1142] The man next to Oswald was probably Albert Osborne, a native of the British Isles who has worked as an itinerant preacher in the Southern United States and Mexico for many years. Osborne denied that he sat beside Oswald; but in view of his inconsistent and untrue responses to Federal investigators concerning matters not directly related to Oswald, the Commission believes that his denial cannot be credited. It appeared to the other passengers on the bus that Osborne and Oswald had not previously met; extensive investigation has revealed no other contact between them.[1143]

In the course of the 20-hour bus trip, Oswald initiated two conversations with the Australian girls, during which he mentioned his visit to Russia and recommended the Hotel Cuba in Mexico City as a "clean and cheap" hotel; he told them, apparently falsely, that he had stayed there on previous occasions. He said that when he had seen them board the bus with their heavy suitcases, he had been under the impression that they were Mexican and had therefore asked the man next to him how to say "How can I help you?" in Spanish. From this they inferred that Oswald did not speak Spanish, an impression which is shared by every witness who met Oswald on his trip and is supported by notations which he made on documents that he carried.[1144] He got off the bus at every stop and ate large meals, always eating by himself; the girls thought he ate so much because he could not make himself understood in Spanish and had to order by pointing at the menu.[1145] The bus arrived in Mexico City 15 minutes late, at 10 a.m.[1146] Oswald left the bus station by himself and had no known further contact with any of the people with whom he had spoken on the bus.[1147]

Oswald registered at the Hotel del Comercio within an hour of his arrival in Mexico City. He stayed there throughout his visit.[1148] The hotel, located not far from the commercial heart of the city and within four blocks of the bus station, is one of a group of hotels located near the intercity bus terminals and has perhaps the best appearance of the group.[1149] It is known by personnel in other hotels that the owner of the Hotel del Comercio can understand and speak a little English.[1150] Oswald registered as "Lee, Harvey Oswald," and gave his occupation as "photo."[1151] He had room 18 which cost $1.28 per day.[1152]

After he had registered, Oswald turned promptly to the task of obtaining permission to enter Cuba. Mexican officials would not permit a U.S. citizen without a Cuban visa to board a plane for Cuba even if he had an American passport, but would permit passage if he had a visa even though the passport proscribed travel to Cuba.[1153] Oswald had a 1963 American passport (stamped invalid for travel to Cuba)[1154] but had neither a regular Cuban visa nor an intransit visa which would permit a short stay in Cuba on his way to Russia or some other country. His address book contained the telephone number and address of a Cuban airline, but there is evidence that he never visited its office.[1155]

He visited the Cuban Embassy on Friday, September 27 and spoke with Senora Silvia Tirado de Duran, a Mexican citizen employed there. Senora Duran later made a signed statement to the Mexican police that Oswald:

> * * * applied for a visa to Cuba in transit to Russia and based his application on his presentation of his passport in which it was recorded that he had been living in the latter country for a period of three years, his work permit from that same country written in the Russian language and letters in the same language, as well as proof of his being married to a woman of Russian nationality and being the apparent Director in the city of New Orleans of the organization called "Fair Play for Cuba" with the desire that he should be accepted as a "friend" of the Cuban Revolution * * *.[1156]

He apparently also stated that he was a member of the Communist Party and displayed documents which he claimed to be evidence of his membership.[1157] He said that he intended to go to Cuba on September 30 and to remain there for 2 weeks, or longer if possible, and then go on to Russia.[1158] Senora Duran took down the relevant date and filled out the appropriate application. Oswald left the Embassy but was to return in the afternoon.[1159]

Then, or possibly even before his initial visit to the Cuban Embassy Oswald went to the Soviet Embassy where he spoke with either Pavel Antonovich Yatskov or Valeriy Vladimirovich Kostikov.[1160] They are both consular officials serving also as agents of the KGB.[1161] Oswald later said that he had dealt with "Kostin," [1162] undoubtedly a reference to Kostikov. He was unable to obtain a Soviet visa then. Marina said that the officials at the Soviet Embassy "refused to have anything to do with him." [1163]

Oswald returned to the Cuban Embassy later that afternoon, this time bringing with him passport photographs which he may have obtained in the United States.[1164] Senora Duran telephoned the Soviet Embassy to inquire about the status of Oswald's Russian visa and was told that there would be a delay of about 4 months.[1165] Oswald became "highly agitated and angry," particularly when he learned that he could not obtain an intransit visa to Cuba before he acquired a Russian visa. Senora Duran called the Cuban consul, then Eusibio Azque, to speak to him. The discussion between Oswald and Azque developed into a heated argument, which ended when Azque told Oswald that in his opinion people like Oswald were harming the Cuban Revolution and that so far as Azque was concerned, he would not give Oswald a visa.[1166] Senora Duran wrote her name and the phone number of the Embassy on a piece of paper which she gave to Oswald in case he wished to contact her again. He copied this information into his address book.[1167] Senora Duran forwarded the Cuban visa application to Havana;[1168] the Cuban Ministry of Foreign Affairs replied on October 15 that the visa could be issued only after Oswald had obtained a Russian visa.[1169] (See Commission Exhibit No. 2564, p. 303.)

Oswald contacted the Russian and Cuban Embassies again during his stay in Mexico.[1170] He had no greater success than he had before. Marina testified that when he returned to Texas, he was convinced that his trip had been a failure and disappointed at having been unable to go to Cuba.[1171] A month later, in a painstakingly composed [1172] letter to the Soviet Embassy in Washington, Oswald ascribed his failure to "a gross breach of regulations" on the part of the Cuban Embassy. "Of corse," he wrote, "the Soviet Embassy was not at fault, they were, as I say unprepared." [1173]

The hotel maid said that Oswald generally was gone by the time she arrived at 9 a.m. The night watchman said he usually returned at about midnight,[1174] which is not unusual, in view of the late hour at which Mexico City's evening activities begin. He ate several lunches at a small restaurant immediately adjacent to the hotel, coming to the restaurant shortly after 2 p.m., and ordering food by pointing to the menu, apparently with some consideration of cost; he spent between 40 and 48 cents for each meal. He ate the soup of the day, rice, and either meat or eggs, but refused dessert and coffee; the waitress concluded that Oswald did not realize that the items which he refused were included in the price of the lunch.[1175] He was seen with no other person either at his hotel or at the restaurant.[1176] A hotel guest stated that on one occasion he sat down at a table with Oswald because there was no empty table in the restaurant, but that neither spoke to the other because of the language barrier.[1177]

Although the Soviet and Cuban Embassies are within two blocks of each other, they are some distance from Oswald's hotel.[1178] He must, therefore, have traversed a substantial portion of the city on more than one occasion. Marina testified that he told her that he had seen a bullfight,[1179] which would normally have been on Sunday afternoon, and that he had visited museums [1180] and done some sightseeing.[1181] He apparently also saw one or more motion pictures, either American with Spanish subtitles or Mexican with English subtitles.[1182] From notations in his Spanish-English dictionary and on his guide map of Mexico City, it appears that Oswald intended to attend a jai alai game [1183] but he almost certainly did not do so.[1184]

He purchased several postcards depicting bullfights and tourist attractions, which he brought back to Marina.[1185] She had told him before he left that she would like Mexican silver bracelets as a souvenir, and he brought her a silver bracelet inscribed with her name.[1186] Marina suspected, almost certainly correctly, that the bracelet, of Japanese origin, did not come from Mexico.[1187] No such jewelry is known to be sold in or around Mexico City, because of a high duty [1188] but the bracelet is of a type commonly sold in 5-and-10-cent stores in Dallas.[1189] Oswald did not buy the Mexican phonograph records which Marina had requested, despite the notation, "records," which he had placed in his dictionary.[1190]

On Monday, September 30, Oswald began to prepare for his return to the United States. He appeared at the Agencia de Viages, Transportes Chihuahuenses,[1191] and purchased international exchange orders costing $20.30 for travel on a Transportes del Norte bus from Mexico City to Laredo and by Greyhound bus directly from Laredo to Dallas. The travel agency made a reservation for him on Transportes del Norte bus No. 332, departing Mexico City at 8:30 a.m. on October 2. The seat, No. 12, was reserved in the name of the travel agency, which recorded the reservation in the name of "H. O. Lee." [1192] The employee who made the reservation testified that he probably wrote the name that way because he was copying from Oswald's tourist card, which read "Lee, Harvey Oswald." [1193] (The manifest for Transportes Frontera bus No. 340, leaving Mexico City for Monterrey and Nuevo Laredo at 1 p.m. on Wednesday, October 2, 1963, contains the name "Oswld" [sic], which apparently was added to the manifest after the trip; [1194] in any event, Oswald did not take bus 340.) [1195]

On October 1, Oswald paid his hotel bill through that night.[1196] The hotel night watchman remembers helping Oswald obtain a taxicab at about 6:30 or 7 on the following morning.[1197] Transportes del Norte bus No. 332 left as scheduled at about 8:30 a.m.; at Monterrey the passengers were shifted to a relief bus, No. 373, scheduled to depart for Laredo at 10 p.m. that evening.[1198] Fellow passengers recall that Oswald was pulled off the bus by Mexican officials at the border, because of some alleged irregularity in his Mexican tourist papers; one passenger overheard him mumbling complaints about the Mexican immigration officials when he returned to the bus.[1199] They remember also that Oswald was hurriedly "gulping" down a banana after the bus reached customs, perhaps because he believed that he could not take fruit into the United States.[1200] (Marina has testified that her husband liked bananas and frequently ate them.) [1201] One of the passengers testified that Oswald annoyed him by keeping his overhead light on to read after 10 p.m.[1202] He may have conversed with an elderly woman on the bus, but he was not traveling with her.[1203]

At about 1:35 a.m. on October 3, Oswald crossed the International Bridge from Nuevo Laredo into Texas.[1204] He traveled from Laredo to Dallas via San Antonio, on Greyhound bus No. 1265, substantially following Interstate Route 35 for the entire trip [1205] leaving Laredo at 3 a.m. and arriving in Dallas at about 2:20 p.m. on the same day.[1206]

DALLAS

Oswald did not contact his wife immediately when he returned to Dallas. He went to the office of the employment commission, where he filed an unemployment compensation claim [1207] and announced that he was again looking for work.[1208] He spent the night at the YMCA, where he registered as a serviceman in order to avoid paying the membership fee.[1209] On the following day, he applied for a job as a typesetter trainee at the Padgett Printing Co. He made a favorable impression on the department foreman, but the plant superintendent called Jaggars-Chiles-Stovall and decided not to hire Oswald because of the unfavorable responses which his inquiries produced.[1210] Later that day, Oswald telephoned Marina and asked her to have Mrs. Paine pick him up in Dallas. Marina refused, and he hitchhiked out to the Paine home,[1211] where he spent part or all of the weekend.[1210] Marina testified that although her husband "changed for the better" and treated her better after his Mexican trip,[1213] she did not want to live with him because she was pregnant and thought it would be better "to be with a woman who spoke English and Russian." [1214] On Monday, October 7, Mrs. Paine drove Oswald to the bus station, and he returned to Dallas to look for a job and a place to live.[1215]

Oswald thought that the YMCA was too expensive for him, and intended to rent a room.[1216] He inquired about a room at 1026 North Beckley, where he lived later, but on October 7 there were no vacancies.[1217] He next responded to a "For Rent" sign at a rooming house at 621 Marsalis Street. He obtained a room, for which he paid the weekly rent of $7 in advance, and moved in on the same day.[1218] He immediately resumed his job-hunting, relying partially on referrals by the employment commission.[1219] He spent much of the time when he was not looking for work in his room.[1220] He telephoned his wife daily.[1221] She wrote: "Lee called twice a day, was worried about my health and about June." [1222] On Friday, Oswald told his landlady, Mrs. Mary Bledsoe, that he was going to Irving for the weekend but would return the following week. She refused to rent the room to him for another week because she didn't like him.[1223]

Oswald spent the weekend of October 12–13 at Mrs. Paine's home, during which time she gave him a driving lesson.[1224] He told her that he had received the last of the unemployment checks due him, and that it had been smaller than the previous ones. Mrs. Paine testified that Oswald was extremely discouraged because his wife was expecting a baby, he had no job prospects in sight, and he no longer had any source of income.[1225]

On Monday, Mrs. Paine drove Oswald into Dallas, since she had other business there.[1226] He picked up his bag from Mrs. Bledsoe's roominghouse [1227] and later that day rented a room at 1026 North Beckley Avenue from Mrs. A. C. Johnson for $8 a week. He registered as O. H. Lee and moved in immediately.[1228] Oswald felt that this room was more comfortable than the previous one, particularly because he had television and refrigerator privileges.[1229]   He apparently continued to spend most of his evenings in his room.[1230]   He borrowed books from the library [1231] and had subscriptions to various periodicals, including Time, the Worker, the Militant, and some Russian periodicals.[1232]

On that Monday, Mrs. Paine mentioned the Oswalds' financial and employment problems to neighbors whom she was visiting.   Mrs. Linnie Mae Randle, who was also present, remarked that she thought that her younger brother, Buell Wesley Frazier, who worked at the Texas School Book Depository, had said that there was a job opening there. When Marina heard of this, she asked Mrs. Paine to call the Depository to see if there was an opening.[1233]   Mrs. Paine called Roy S. Truly, superintendent of the Depository, who indicated that he would talk to Oswald if he would apply in person.[1234]   When Oswald telephoned the Paine house on Monday evening, Mrs. Paine told him about this possibility.[1235]   On the next day, Oswald was interviewed by Truly and hired in a temporary capacity.   He began work on Wednesday, October 16.   His duties were to fill book orders; his hours were 8 a.m. to 4:45 p.m., for which he received $1.25 an hour.[1236]

Both the Oswalds were elated with the new job,[1237] although it apparently required little skill or experience [1238] and he indicated that he still hoped to obtain a better job.[1239]   He did a satisfactory job at the Depository,[1240] but he kept to himself and very few of his fellow employees got to know him.[1241]

During his first week at work, Oswald became acquainted with Frazier, with whom he arranged to ride to Irving on weekends.[1242] On Friday, October 18, Frazier drove him from work to the Paine home; [1243] since it was his birthday, Marina and Ruth Paine had arranged a small celebration.[1244]   On Sunday, he stayed with June and the Paine children, while Mrs. Paine drove Marina to Parkland Hospital where she gave birth to a second daughter, Rachel.[1245]   He went to work on Monday, but that evening visited Marina in the hospital and spent the night in Irving.[1246]   Marina wrote:

> Monday evening Lee visited me in the hospital.   He was very happy at the birth of another daughter and even wept a little. He said that two daughters were better for each other—two sisters.   He stayed with me about two hours.[1247]

Oswald returned to Dallas the next morning.[1248]

Oswald wrote to Arnold Johnson of the Communist Party, U.S.A., that on the evening of October 23, he had attended an "ultra right" meeting headed by Gen. Edwin A. Walker.[1249]   Two evenings later, he accompanied Michael Paine to a meeting of the American Civil Liberties Union, held at Southern Methodist University.[1250]   At this meeting, a statement was made to the effect that members of the John Birch Society should not be considered anti-Semitic; Oswald rose and stated that at the meeting which he had attended 2 days earlier, he had heard a number of anti-Semitic and anti-Catholic statements.

738

Later in the evening, Oswald became involved in a discussion with several people, including Frank Krystinik, who was employed with Paine at the Bell Helicopter plant. During this conversation, Oswald expressed Marxist views and declared that he was a Marxist, although denying that he was a Communist. He admitted that the United States was superior to the Soviet Union in the area of civil liberties and praised President Kennedy for his work in that connection.[1251] Krystinik testified that he got the impression that Oswald did not fully understand the views he was expounding.[1252]

Throughout that week Oswald telephoned his wife to inquire about her health and that of the baby. He spent the weekend at the Paine home, to which Marina and Rachel had returned during the week.[1253] On Friday, November 1, he obtained post office box No. 6225 at the Terminal Annex Post Office Station. He indicated that the box would also be used to receive mail for the Fair Play for Cuba Committee and the American Civil Liberties Union.[1254] Once again he spent the weekend in Irving.[1255]

Throughout this period, the FBI had been aware of the whereabouts of the Oswalds. There was a record in the Dallas office of the FBI that Oswald subscribed to the Worker, engaged in Fair Play for Cuba Committee activities and had traveled to Mexico.[1256] An FBI agent visited the Paine home on November 1 and, accompanied by another agent, again on November 5, and spoke briefly with Mrs. Paine. On neither occasion was Oswald present.[1257] Ruth Paine noted the agent's name and telephone number and, in accordance with her husband's instructions, Marina noted the license number of the agent's automobile, all of which was subsequenty reported to Oswald.[1258] Both Mrs. Paine and Marina testified that Oswald was troubled by the FBI's interest in him.[1259] He declared that the FBI was "trying to inhibit" his activities,[1260] and wrote the Soviet Embassy in Washington:

> The Federal Bureau of Investigation is not now interested in my activities in the progressive organization "Fair Play for Cuba Committee" of which I was secretary in New Orleans (state Louisiana) since I no longer reside in that state. However, the F.B.I. has visted us here in Dallas, Texas, on November 1st. Agent James P. Hasty warned me that if I engaged in F.P.C.C. activities in Texas the F.B.I. will again take an "interest" in me.
>
> This agent also 'suggested' to Marina Nichilayeva that she could remain in the United States under F.B.I. 'protection', that is, she could defect from the Soviet Uion, of couse, I and my wife strongly protested these tactics by the notorious F.B.I.
>
> Please inform us of the arrival of our Soviet entrance visa's as soon as they come.[1261]   (See Commission Exhibit 15, p. 311.)

Marina testified that the statements, both by and to the FBI agents, to which her husband referred in this letter, were in fact never made.[1262]

The following Friday, November 8, Oswald as usual drove to the Paine house with Frazier.[1263]   On Saturday Mrs. Paine took him to the Texas Drivers' License Examining Station, but because it was an election day the station was closed.   Oswald stayed at the Paines through Monday, November 11, which was Veterans Day.   During the weekend, Mrs. Paine gave Oswald a second driving lesson.[1264]

Oswald did not go to Irving on the next weekend.   His wife had asked him not to come because Michael Paine, with whom Oswald did not get along, would be there to celebrate his daughter's birthday.   Also, she felt that because he had stayed for 3 days the preceding weekend, he would abuse Mrs. Paine's hospitality if he returned so soon.   Oswald telephoned Marina on Saturday afternoon and said that he had returned to the drivers' license examining station that morning but had not waited because there was a long line.[1265]

On Sunday, November 17, at Marina's request, Ruth Paine telephoned Oswald at the Beckley Avenue number, which he had given to Marina.   When she asked for him, she was told that no one by that name lived at the address, which greatly surprised her. On the next day, Oswald telephoned his wife.   When she indicated that she had been upset by the fact that there had been no Lee Oswald at the number which she had asked Mrs. Paine to call, Oswald became angry; he said that he was using a fictitious name and that she should not have called the Beckley Avenue number.[1266]   He did not telephone on the following day, which was unusual.[1267]

On the morning of Thursday, November 21, Oswald asked Frazier to take him to Irving when he went home that evening, saying that he wanted to pick up some curtain rods.[1268]   His arrival was a surprise because he generally asked Mrs. Paine's permission before arriving for a visit.[1269]   The women thought that he had come to Irving because he felt badly about arguing with his wife about the use of the fictitious name.[1270]   He said that he was lonely, because he had not come the preceding weekend, and told Marina that he "wanted to make his peace" with her.[1271]   He spent the time before dinner on the lawn playing with his daughter.[1272]   However, when he attempted to talk to his wife she would not answer, which upset him.   He asked her to live with him in Dallas, and she refused.[1273]   After supper, Oswald watched television while the women cleaned the house and prepared their children for bed.[1274]   He retired early in the evening at about 9.[1275]

Analysis of Lee Harvey Oswald's Finances
From June 13, 1962,
Through November 22, 1963

The following analysis of Lee Harvey Oswald's receipts and expenditures for the period June 13, 1962, through November 22, 1963, contains a complete record of all funds that he and his wife are reported to have received and disbursed from all known sources. It also contains an estimate for food, clothing, and incidental expenses, which include telephone calls, money order and check cashing fees, postage, local transportation costs, personal care goods and services, local newspapers, and similar small items. Oswald's expenditures for food, clothing, and incidentals were estimated at $100 per month, except for those months in which his wife and children resided with relatives or acquaintances. The estimate reflects Oswald's frugal living habits during this period, as described in chapter VI of this report. The Commission has been advised by the Bureau of Labor Statistics of the U.S. Department of Labor that this estimate is a little higher than would be normal for a family in Oswald's income class residing in the southern region of the United States. (See Commission Exhibit No. 1169.)

Lee Harvey Oswald Receipts and Expenditures
June 13, 1962, to Nov. 22, 1963

	Receipts	Expenditures	Balance
June 1962:			
On hand on arrival, New York City [1]	$63.00		
Received from Robert Oswald [2]	200.00		
Received from Marguerite Oswald [3]	10.00		
Transportation in New York City [4]		$10.35	
Plane fare, New York City to Dallas, including luggage [5]		201.04	
Hotel bill, New York City [6]		15.21	
Estimated cost of food, clothing, and incidental expenses [7]		5.00	
Public stenographer [8]		10.00	
Estimated repayment, Robert Oswald [9]		30.00	
Total	273.00	271.60	
Cash on hand, June 30, 1962			$1.40
July 1962:			
Net salary [10]	46.82		
Estimated repayment, Robert Oswald [11]		10.00	
Subscription for Time magazine [12]		3.87	
Total	46.82	13.87	
Cash on hand, July 31, 1962			34.35

August 1962:	Receipts	Expenditures	Balance
Net salary [13]	$207. 31		
Repayment, State Department loan [14]		$10. 00	
Estimated repayment, Robert Oswald [15]		50. 00	
Rent and utilities [16]		71. 50	
Subscription for the Worker [17]		2. 00	
Estimated cost of food, clothing, and incidental expenses [18]		75. 00	
Total	207. 31	208. 50	
Cash on hand, Aug. 31, 1962			$33. 16

September 1962:			
Net salary [19]	187. 59		
Received from Paul Gregory [20]	35. 00		
Rent and utilities [21]		71. 50	
Repayment, State Department loan [22]		9. 71	
Estimated repayment, Robert Oswald [23]		50. 00	
Subscription for the Russian humor magazine "Krokodil" [24]		2. 20	
Estimated cost of food, clothing, and incidental expenses		100. 00	
Total	222. 59	233. 41	
Cash on hand, Sept. 30, 1962			22. 34

October 1962:			
Net salary [25]	228. 22		
Received from George Bouhe [26]	5. 00		
Repayment, State Department loan [27]		10. 00	
Rent, room in YMCA [28]		9. 00	
Post office box rental [29]		4. 50	
Estimated repayment, Robert Oswald [30]		60. 00	
Estimated cost of food, clothing, and incidental expenses [31]		50. 00	
Total	233. 22	133. 50	
Cash on hand, Oct. 31, 1962			122. 06

November 1962:			
Net salary [32]	315. 71		
Rent [33]		73. 00	
Rental of U-Haul Trailer [34]		5. 00	
Repayment, State Department loan [35]		10. 00	
Bus fare, Dallas to Fort Worth and return [36]		4. 60	
Estimated cost of food, clothing, and incidental expenses [37]		50. 00	
Total	315. 71	142. 60	
Cash on hand, Nov. 30, 1962			295. 17

December 1962:	Receipts	Expenditures	Balance
Net salary [38]	$243. 13		
Rent [39]	--------	$68. 00	
Post office box rental [40]	--------	4. 50	
Repayment, State Department loan [41]	--------	190. 00	
Subscription for the Militant [42]	--------	1. 00	
Estimated cost of food, clothing, and incidental expenses	--------	100. 00	
Total	243. 13	363. 50	
Cash on hand, Dec. 31, 1962			$174. 80

January 1963:			
Net salary [43]	247. 12		
Rent and utilities [44]	--------	75. 13	
Repayment, State Department loan [45]	--------	206. 00	
Deposit, Smith & Wesson revolver [46]	--------	10. 00	
Fee paid Crozier Tech High School [47]	--------	9. 00	
Subscription for Ogonek, Agitator, Sovetskaya Belorussiya [48]	--------	13. 20	
Estimated cost of food, clothing, and incidental expenses	--------	100. 00	
Total	247. 12	413. 33	
Cash on hand, Jan. 31, 1963			8. 59

February 1963:			
Net salary [49]	256. 95		
Rent and utilities [50]	--------	71. 64	
Subscription for the Worker [51]	--------	7. 00	
Estimated cost of food, clothing, and incidental expenses	--------	100. 00	
Total	256. 95	178. 64	
Cash on hand, Feb. 28, 1963			86. 90

March 1963:			
Net salary [52]	327. 55		
Rent and utilities [53]	--------	78. 76	
Post office box rental [54]	--------	4. 50	
Cost of rifle [55]	--------	21. 45	
Subscription for Time magazine [56]	--------	3. 82	
Balance due on revolver and freight charge [57]	--------	21. 22	
Estimated cost of food, clothing, and incidental expenses	--------	100. 00	
Total	327. 55	229. 75	
Cash on hand, Mar. 31, 1963			184. 70

743

April 1963:	Receipts	Expenditures	Balance
Net salary [58]_____	$108. 86		
Income Tax refund [59]_____	57. 40		
Rent and utilities [60]_____	--------	$62. 97	
Bus fare from Dallas to New Orleans [61]_____	--------	13. 85	
Estimated cost of food, clothing, and incidental expenses [62]_____	--------	100. 00	
Total_____	166. 26	176. 82	
Cash on hand, Apr. 30, 1963_____			$174. 14
May 1963:			
Net salary [63]_____	107. 44		
Unemployment compensation check [64]_____	33. 00		
Rent and utilities [65]_____	--------	75. 00	
Subscription for the Militant [66]_____	--------	1. 00	
Dues and printing—Fair Play for Cuba [67]_____	--------	9. 00	
Estimated cost of food, clothing, and incidental expenses [68]_____	--------	100. 00	
Total_____	140. 44	185. 00	
Cash on hand, May 31, 1963_____			129. 58
June 1963:			
Net salary [69]_____	216. 00		
Rent and utilities [70]_____	--------	67. 85	
Post office box rental [71]_____	--------	4. 00	
Printing—Fair Play for Cuba [72]_____	--------	15. 23	
New alien registration card [73]_____	--------	5. 00	
Estimated cost of food, clothing, and incidental expenses _____	--------	100. 00	
Total_____	216. 00	192. 08	
Cash on hand, June 30, 1963_____			153. 50
July 1963:			
Net salary [74]_____	224. 97		
Rent and utilities [75]_____	--------	72. 22	
Printing—Fair Play for Cuba [76]_____	--------	3. 50	
Estimated cost of food, clothing, and incidental expenses _____	--------	100. 00	
Total_____	224. 97	175. 72	
Cash on hand, July 31, 1963_____			202. 75
August 1963:			
Unemployment compensation payments [77]_____	165. 00		
Rent and utilities [78]_____	--------	73. 54	
Fine [79] _____	--------	10. 00	
Distribution, Fair Play for Cuba circulars [80]___	--------	2. 00	
Estimated cost of food, clothing, and incidental expenses _____	--------	100. 00	
Total_____	165. 00	185. 54	
Cash on hand, Aug. 31, 1963_____			182. 21

Sept. 1–24, 1963:	Receipts	Expenditures	Balance
Unemployment compensation payments [81]_____	$132.00		
Estimated cost of food, clothing, and incidental expenses [82] _____	_____	$100.00	
Total_____	132.00	100.00	
Cash on hand, Sept. 24, 1963_____			[83]$214.21
Sept. 25–Oct. 2, 1963:			
Mexican trip:			
Estimated transportation cost [84]_____	_____	50.55	
Hotel plus estimated food cost [85]_____	_____	18.70	
Estimated cost of entertainment and miscellaneous items [86]_____	_____	15.20	
Total_____	_____	84.45	
Cash on hand, Oct. 2, 1963_____			[87] 129.76
Oct. 3–31, 1963:			
Unemployment compensation payments [88]_____	39.00		
Net salary [89]_____	104.41		
Rent, rooms and YMCA [90]_____	_____	33.25	
Estimated cost of food, clothing, and incidental expenses [91]_____	_____	75.00	
Total_____	143.41	108.25	
Cash on hand, Oct. 31, 1963_____			164.92
Nov. 1–22, 1963:			
Net salary [92]_____	104.41		
Room rent [93]_____	_____	24.00	
Post office box rental [94]_____	_____	3.00	
American Civil Liberties Union dues [95]_____	_____	2.00	
Bus and taxi fares Nov. 22, 1963 [96]_____	_____	1.23	
Estimated cost of food, clothing, and incidental expenses [97] _____	_____	75.00	
Total_____	104.41	105.23	
Cash on hand, Nov. 22, 1963_____			164.10
Grand total, June 13, 1962–Nov. 22, 1963_____	3,665.89	3,501.79	164.10
Contents of Oswald's wallet_____	170.00		
Cash taken from Oswald when arrested_____	13.87		
Total_____	[98] 183.87		

745

Transactions Between Lee Harvey Oswald and Marina Oswald, and the U.S. Department of State and the Immigration and Naturalization Service of the U.S. Department of Justice

From September 4, 1959, when he applied for his first passport, until shortly before the assassination, Lee Harvey Oswald had numerous dealings with the U.S. Department of State in Washington and with the American Embassy in Moscow. In connection with Marina Oswald's entry into the United States, the dealings also extended to the Immigration and Naturalization Service of the Department of Justice. During the course of these dealings, the Department of State and the Immigration and Naturalization Service were called upon to decide a series of legal and administrative questions which arose under the laws of this country. In order to determine whether Lee Harvey Oswald or his wife received any treatment not accorded others in similar positions, the Commission has examined the manner in which the transactions with the Oswalds were handled and the manner in which the relevant legal questions were resolved. In light of the facts then available and the applicable statutes, regulations, and practices in force at the time, the Commission has found no indication that the treatment accorded the Oswalds was illegal or different in any respect from the treatment that other persons similarly situated would have received.

ISSUANCE OF PASSPORT IN 1959

On September 4, 1959, while on active duty with the U.S. Marine Corps, Oswald applied for a passport before a clerk of the superior court at Santa Ana, Calif.[1] On the application Oswald stated that he intended to leave the United States for 4 months on approximately September 21, 1959, by ship from New Orleans, La., and that the purposes of his trip would be to attend the Albert Schweitzer College in Switzerland[2] and the University of Turku in Finland, and to visit Cuba, the Dominican Republic, England, France, Switzerland, Germany, Finland and Russia as a tourist. With the application, Oswald submitted a statement signed by a Marine officer that he was to be discharged from the Corps on September 11, 1959.[3] The passport, No. 1733242, was routinely issued on September 10, 1959.[4] At the time, the United States proscribed travel to none of the countries named in Oswald's application.

OSWALD'S ATTEMPTS TO RENOUNCE HIS U.S. CITIZENSHIP

American officials in Moscow had no knowledge that Oswald was in Russia until October 31, 1959,[5] more than 2 weeks after he had arrived, since he failed to register at the U.S. Embassy, as Americans traveling through Russia normally did.[6]   However, on October 31, 1959, a Saturday, Oswald presented himself at the American Embassy in Moscow.[7]   He placed his passport on the receptionist's desk and informed her that he had come to "dissolve his American citizenship." [8] She immediately summoned the consul, Richard E. Snyder, who invited Oswald into his office.[9]   In the room with Snyder was his assistant, John A. McVickar, who observed what ensued.[10]   Snyder recalled Oswald as "neatly and very presentably dressed," [11] but he also remembered his arrogance.   Oswald seemed to "know what his mission was.   He took charge, in a sense, of the conversation right from the beginning." [12]

Oswald stated at once that he was there to renounce his citizenship [13] and that "his allegiance was to the Soviet Union." [14]   He said he had already applied for Soviet citizenship.[15]   He said he knew the provisions of American law on loss of citizenship and did not want to hear them reviewed by Snyder.[16]   Having taken his passport back from the receptionist, Oswald put it on Snyder's desk.[17]   Snyder noticed that Oswald had inked out the portion which would have shown his address in the United States.[18]   Oswald also presented Snyder with a note [19] which he had prepared in advance, which reads:

> I Lee Harey Oswald do herby request that my present citizenship in the United States of america, be revoked.
>
> I have entered the Soviet Union for the express purpose of appling for citizenship in the Soviet Union, through the means of naturalization.
>
> My request for citizenship is now pending before Suprem Soviet of the U.S.S.R.
>
> I take these steps for political reasons.   My request for the revoking of my American citizenship is made only after the longest and most serious considerations.
>
> I affirm that my allegiance is to the Union of Soviet Socialist Republics.[20]

Oswald told Snyder that he had not mentioned his intent to remain in the Soviet Union to the Soviet Embassy in Helsinki at the time he had applied for his tourist visa.[21]   Oswald's passport, upon which his Soviet visa was stamped, shows that by the 31st of October he had already overstayed his visa, despite a 1-day extension which he had received.[22]

Oswald gave as his "principal reason" for wanting to renounce his citizenship, "I am a Marxist." [23]   He stated that he admired the system and policies of the Soviet Union and desired to serve the Soviet

State, and that his intent to defect to the Soviet Union had been formed long before he was discharged from the Marine Corps.[24] Shortly after the interview, Snyder observed that Oswald had "displayed all the airs of a new sophomore partyliner." [25] At one point, Oswald alluded to hardships endured by his mother as a "worker" and said he did not intend to let this happen to him.[26] He stated that his Marine service in Okinawa and elsewhere had given him a chance "to observe American imperialism," and he displayed some resentment at not having been given a higher rank in the Marine Corps.[27] Oswald stated to Snyder that he had voluntarily told Soviet officials that he would make known to them all information concerning the Marine Corps and his specialty therein, radar operation, as he possessed.[28]

Snyder did not permit Oswald to renounce his citizenship at that time. He told Oswald that his renunciation could not be effected on a Saturday, but that if he would return on a day when the Embassy was open for business, the transaction could then be completed.[29] Snyder testified that his real reason for delaying Oswald was that he believed, as a matter of sound professional practice, that no one should be permitted to renounce his American citizenship precipitously; such an act has extremely serious consequences, and, once accomplished, it is irrevocable.[30] Snyder noticed that Oswald was young, apparently not well educated and obviously in a highly emotional state.[31] Snyder testified: "particularly in the case of a minor, I could not imagine myself writing out the renunciation form, and having him sign it, on the spot, without making him leave my office and come back at some other time, even if it is only a few hours intervening." [32] Snyder's decision was also influenced by his familiarity with a recent unfavorable incident in which an American citizen by the name of Petrulli had been allowed to renounce his citizenship hastily, without awareness that Petrulli was mentally ill at the time.[33] Snyder was able to persuade Oswald to tell him his home address and the name of his mother, however, by saying that no progress on his renunciatiton could be made without this information.[34] The State Department has advised that Snyder's treatment of Oswald "was in line * * * with the general policy of the Department to discourage expatriation of American citizens." [35]

The same day, the Embassy sent a telegram to the Department of State, advising that Oswald had appeared there in an attempt to renounce his American citizenship, and setting out most of the details of the interview with Snyder.[36] Copies were immediately furnished to the FBI [37] and the CIA.[38] The telegram was followed on November 2, 1959, by an Embassy report addressed to the Department of State,[39] which concluded:

> * * * in view of the Petrulli case and other considerations, the Embassy proposes to delay action on Oswald's request to execute an oath of renunciation to the extent dictated by developments and subject to the Department's advice.[40]

Copies of this memorandum were also furnished both Federal security agencies.[41]

After having received the telegram of October 31, 1959,[42] but not the Embassy Despatch of November 2, 1959, the State Department on November 2, 1959, sent a telegram to the Moscow Embassy which read in part:

> If Oswald insists on renouncing U.S. citizenship, Section 1999 Revised Statutes precludes Embassy withholding right to do so regardless status his application pending Soviet Government and final action taken Petrulli case.[43]

This telegram, like most of the communications from the Department regarding Oswald, was prepared in the Passport Office and cleared by the Office of Eastern European Affairs and the Office of Soviet Union Affairs.[44]

Oswald never returned to the Embassy.[45] On November 6, 1959, the Embassy received[46] a handwritten letter from Oswald on the stationery of the Metropole Hotel, dated November 3, 1959, which read:

> I, Lee Harvey Oswald, do hereby request that my present United States citizenship be revoked.
>
> I appeered in person, at the consulate office of the United States Embassy, Moscow, on Oct. 31st, for the purpose of signing the formal papers to this effect. This legal right I was refused at that time.
>
> I wish to protest against this action, and against the conduct of the official of the United States consular service who acted on behalf of the United States government.
>
> My application, requesting that I be considered for citizenship in the Soviet Union is now pending before the Surprem Soviet of the U.S.S.R. . In the event of acceptance, I will request my government to lodge a formal protest regarding this incident.[47]

The Embassy immediately informed the Department of the receipt of this letter and advised that it intended to reply to Oswald by letter telling him that, if he wished, he could appear at the Embassy on any normal business day and request that the necessary expatriation documents be prepared.[48] On the same day, November 6, the Embassy sent Oswald a letter so advising him.[49] From then until November 30 the Embassy attempted to communicate with Oswald on several occasions to deliver messages from his relatives in the United States urging him to reconsider, but he refused to receive the messages or talk to anyone from the Embassy.[50] The messages were therefore sent to him by registered mail.[51]

On November 16, 1959, Priscilla Johnson, an American newspaperwoman stationed in Moscow, interviewed Oswald at the Metropole

Hotel.[52] On November 17, 1959, she informed the Embassy of her interview, and the information was recorded in a file memorandum.[53] Oswald told Miss Johnson that he was scheduled to leave Moscow within a few days. She thought that Oswald "may have purposely not carried through his original intent to renounce [citizenship] in order to leave a crack open." [54] The Embassy accordingly informed the Department of State about 2 weeks later that Oswald had departed from the Hotel Metropole within the last few days.[55] According to his "Historic Diary" [56] and other records available to the Commission,[57] however, Oswald probably did not in fact leave Moscow for Minsk until about January 4, 1960. Miss Johnson's report of her interview with Oswald was the last information about him which the U.S. Government was to receive until February 13, 1961.[58]

On March 6, 1960, Oswald's mother asked Representative James C. Wright, Jr., of Texas to help her locate her son. The Congressman forwarded her inquiry to the Department of State, which in turn sent it to the Embassy.[59] In response, the Embassy in Moscow informed the Department on March 28, 1960, that they had had no contact with Oswald since November 9, 1959.[60] The Embassy went on to say that it had no evidence that Oswald had expatriated himself "other than his announced intention to do so." It believed, therefore, that since Oswald was presumably still an American citizen, the American Government could properly make inquiry concerning him through a note to the Soviet Foreign Office. The Embassy went on to suggest, however, that it would be preferable if Oswald's mother wrote a letter to her son which could then be forwarded by the Department to the Soviet Government.[61]

The Department replied on May 10, 1960, that no action should be taken in the case other than on a request voluntarily submitted by a member of Oswald's family.[62] On June 22, a second communication was dispatched, asking whether the Embassy had been able to contact Oswald.[63] On July 6, 1960, the Embassy replied that it had received no further communication with anyone on the subject of Oswald and that in view of the Department's memorandum of May 10, 1960, it intended to take no further action in the matter.[64] Mrs. Oswald apparently took no steps to follow up on her original inquiry.

Under the procedures in effect in 1960, a "refusal sheet" was prepared in the Department of State Passport Office whenever circumstances created the possibility that a prospective applicant would not be entitled to receive an American passport.[65] The records section of the Passport Office, on the basis of the refusal sheet, would prepare what was known as a lookout card [66] and file it in the lookout file in the Passport Office. Whenever anyone applied for a passport from any city in the world, his application was immediately forwarded to this office, and his name and date of birth checked against the lookout file.[67] If a lookout card was found, appropriate action, including the possible refusal of a passport, was taken.[68] Passport Office procedures also provided that the lookout card would be removed from a prospective applicant's file whenever facts warranted an unquestioned passport grant.[69]

On March 25, 1960, the Passport Office had made up a "refusal sheet" on Lee Harvey Oswald, typed across which was the explanation that Oswald "may have been naturalized in the Soviet Union or otherwise * * * expatriated himself." [70] An Operations Memorandum stating the reasons for which the card had been prepared was drawn up on March 28 and also put on file [71] and a copy sent to the Embassy. It advised the Embassy to take no further action on the Oswald case unless it came into possession of evidence upon which to base the preparation of a certificate of loss of nationality. Included in the operations memorandum was the following:

> An appropriate notice has been placed in the lookout card section of the Passport Office in the event that Mr. Oswald should apply for documentation at a post outside the Soviet Union.[72]

Despite these indications that a lookout card was prepared, the Department of State on May 18, 1964, informed the Commission that "investigations, to date, failed to reveal any other indication or evidence that a lookout card was ever prepared, modified or removed." No such card was ever located, and certain file entries indicate that such a card was never prepared.[73]

The State Department has advised the Commission that as of October 1959 the Department had "developed information which might reasonably have caused it to prepare * * * a lookout card for Lee Harvey Oswald." [74] The Passport Office employee who prepared the refusal sheet for Oswald has suggested as a possible explanation of the failure to prepare a lookout card that between the day she prepared the refusal sheet and the time the records section would normally have prepared the lookout card, Oswald's file was temporarily pulled from its place because the Department received some additional correspondence from the Embassy. When the file was returned, she suggested, it may have been assumed that the card had already been prepared.[75]

Had a lookout card been prepared on the ground of possible expatriation, it would have been removed and destroyed after the decision was made in 1961 that Oswald had not expatriated himself and thus prior to the time that he applied for a second passport in June 1963. Hence, the Department's apparent failure to prepare a lookout card on Oswald had no effect on its future actions. As of February 20, 1964, the Department issued additional regulations regarding the manner in which the lookout file is to be handled.[76] On March 14, 1964, a category was established for returned defectors, so that these persons automatically have lookout cards in their files, and on July 27, 1964, the Office of Security of the Department of State issued a procedural study of the lookout-card system, with recommendations.[77]

RETURN AND RENEWAL OF OSWALD'S 1959 PASSPORT

Negotiations Between Oswald and the Embassy

On February 1, 1961, as a result of a visit by Oswald's mother to the Department of State on January 25, 1961,[78] the Department sent a request to the Moscow Embassy as follows:

> The Embassy is requested to inform the [Soviet] Ministry of Foreign Affairs that Mr. Oswald's mother is worried as to his present safety, and is anxious to hear from him.[79]

The inquiry went to the Embassy by diplomatic pouch and was received in Moscow on February 10 or 11.[80] On February 13, before the Embassy had acted on the Department's request,[81] the Embassy received an undated letter from Oswald postmarked Minsk, February 5. The letter stated:

> Since I have not received a reply to my letter of December 1960, I am writing again asking that you consider my request for the return of my American passport.
> I desire to return to the United States, that is if we could come to some agreement concerning the dropping of any legal proceedings against me. If so, than I would be free to ask the Russian authorities to allow me to leave. If I could show them my American passport, I am of the opinion they would give me an exit visa.
> They have at no time insisted that I take Russian citizenship. I am living here with non-permanent type papers for a foreigner.
> I cannot leave Minsk without permission, therefore I am writing rather than calling in person.
> I hope that in recalling the responsibility I have to america that you remember your's in doing everything you can to help me since I am an american citizen.[82]

Despite Oswald's reference to his letter of December 1960, there is no indication that he had written to the Embassy previously.[83] Furthermore, his diary refers to his February 1 letter as his "first request" concerning his return to the United States.[84]

On February 28, 1961, the Embassy wrote Oswald that he would have to come to Moscow to discuss the passport and expatriation matters.[85] Then on March 20, 1961, a second letter from Oswald, dated March 12, was received by the Embassy. It read:

> In reply to your recent letter. I find it inconvenient to come to Moscow for the sole purpose of an interview.
> In my last letter I believe I stated that I cannot leave the city of Minsk without permission.

I believe there exist in the United States also a law in regards to resident foreigners from Socialist countries, traveling between cities.

I do not think it would be appropriate for me to request to leave Minsk in order to visit the American Embassy. In any event, the granting of permission is a long drawn out affair, and I find that there is a hesitation on the part of local officials to even start the process.

I have no intention of abusing my position here, and I am sure you would not want me to.

I see no reasons for any preliminary inquires not to be put in the form of a questionnaire and sent to me.

I understand that personal interviews undobtedly make to work of the Embassy staff lighter, than written correspondence, however, in some cases other means must be employed.[86]

After receiving the first letter postmarked February 5, the Embassy on February 28 forwarded a despatch to the Department informing it of Oswald's letter and its reply to Oswald. At that time, the Embassy also inquired of the Department whether Oswald would be subject to prosecution on any grounds if he should return to the United States and, if so, whether Oswald should be so informed. The Department was also asked whether there was any objection to returning Oswald's 1959 passport to him by mail, since that might facilitate his application for a Soviet exit visa.[87] Upon receiving Oswald's March 20 letter, the Embassy again consulted with Washington. The Embassy proposed that it write Oswald repeating that he must come to Moscow if he wanted to discuss reentering the United States and pointing out that the Soviet government did not object to such visits by American citizens.[88] Such a letter was mailed to Oswald on March 24.[89]

In the meantime, the State Department was considering the Embassy despatch of February 28, 1961.[90] Although a different response was originally recommended by a staff member in the Passport Office,[91] the Department instructed the Embassy on April 13 that for security reasons Oswald's passport should be given to him only if he personally appeared at the Embassy and that even then he was to receive the document only after a full investigation had been made and the Embassy was satisfied that he had not renounced his American citizenship. Also, he was to present evidence that he had made arrangements to depart from the Soviet Union to travel to the United States, and his passport was to be stamped valid for direct return to the United States only. The Department also told the Embassy that Oswald could not be advised whether or not he would be prosecuted for any possible offenses should he return to the United States.[92] Matters remained in this posture for over a month. During the interim, Oswald met and married Marina Nikolaevna Prusakova.[93]

On May 26, 1961, the Embassy sent a despatch to the Department [94] advising that on May 25, 1961, it had received a letter from Oswald postmarked Moscow, May 16, 1961.[95] In his latest letter Oswald said he wanted "to make it clear" that he was asking for full guarantees that he would not be prosecuted "under any circumstances" should he return to the United States. Oswald went on to say that if the Embassy could not give him these assurances, he would "endeavor to use my relatives in the United States, to see about getting something done in Washington." He also informed the Embassy that he was married to a Russian woman who would want to accompany him back to his native country, and he once again repeated his reluctance to come to Moscow. The Embassy suggested that it reply to Oswald by repeating that the question of citizenship could only be made on the basis of a personal interview, and by advising Oswald of the requirements and procedures pertaining to his wife's immigration. The despatch noted that Oswald's letter referred to his present Soviet internal passport in which he claimed to be designated as "without citizenship," and observed: "It would appear on this basis that Oswald has not yet expatriated himself under Section 349(a)(1) of the Immigration and Nationality Act." The Embassy inquired whether the Department considered Oswald entitled "to the protection of the United States Government while he continues to reside abroad under present circumstances in the absence of reasonable evidence that he has committed an expatriating act?"

The Department answered the despatch under date of July 11, 1961. It said that it was not entirely clear what the description "without citizenship" means, i.e., "whether he is without Soviet citizenship or without any citizenship." The instructions continued:

> In any event in the absence of evidence showing that Mr. Oswald has definitely lost United States citizenship he apparently maintains that technical status. Whether he is entitled to the protection of the United States pending any further developments concerning his precise status is a matter which will be left to the Embassy's discretion in the event an emergency situation should arise. In a situation of this kind, not of an emergency nature, the facts should be submitted to the Department.
>
> It is noted that the Embassy intends to seek the Department's prior advice before granting Mr. Oswald documentation as a United States citizen upon any application he may submit.
>
> The Embassy's careful attention to the involved case of Mr. Oswald is appreciated * * * [96]

However, on Saturday, July 8, 1961, before the Embassy had received the response from Washington, Oswald appeared without warning at the Embassy in Moscow. Snyder came down to meet Oswald after Oswald called him on the house telephone, and after a brief talk, asked Oswald to return on Monday, July 10.[97] Later that day Oswald telephoned his wife and told her to come to Moscow, which she did the next day.[98] Oswald returned alone to the American Embassy on Monday, where Snyder questioned him about his life in Russia.

According to a memorandum which Snyder prepared shortly afterwards:

> Twenty months of the realities of life in the Soviet Union have clearly had a maturing effect on Oswald. He stated frankly that he learned a hard lesson the hard way and that he had been completely relieved about his illusions about the Soviet Union * * * Much of the arrogance and bravado which characterized him on his first visit to the Embassy appears to have left him.[99]

Oswald told Snyder that despite the statement he had given him in October 1959, he had never applied for Soviet citizenship, but only for permission to reside in the Soviet Union. He presented his Soviet internal passport, which described him as without citizenship of any kind. Oswald said that he had been employed since January 13, 1960, as a metal worker in the research shop in the Byelorussian Radio and Television Factory in Minsk. He claimed that he had taken no oath of allegiance of any kind, and that he had not been required to sign any papers in connection with this employment. He added that he was not a member of the factory trade union organization. Oswald said that he was earning 90 rubles ($90) a month and that he had saved about 200 rubles ($200) toward travel expenses to the United States. He denied that he had made any derogatory statements concerning the United States to radio, press, or TV in the Soviet Union, and he denied that he had turned over any information to the Russians as he had threatened to do in the 1959 interview with Snyder.[100]

During the course of the interview Oswald filled out an application for renewal of his American passport.[101] The renewal application was required since Oswald's existing passport would expire on September 10, 1961,[102] and it was extremely unlikely that he would be able to obtain the requisite Soviet departure documents before that time. The renewal application contained a printed statement which set forth, in the disjunctive, a series of acts which, if committed by the applicant, would either automatically disqualify him from receiving a passport on the ground that he had lost his American citizenship, or would raise a question whether he might be so disqualified. The printed statement was preceded by two phrases, "have," and, "have not," the first phrase being printed directly above the second. One carbon copy of the application indicates Oswald signed the document after the second phrase, "have not," had been typed over, thereby apparently admitting that he had committed one or more of the acts which would at least raise a question as to whether he had expatriated himself. Snyder was not able to remember with certainty to which of the acts listed on the statement Oswald's mark was intended to refer, but believed it may have been to "swearing allegiance to a foreign state." [103] He points out that the strikeout of "have not" may also have been a clerical error.[104] On the actual signed copy of the application kept in the files of the Moscow Embassy, which is not a carbon copy of the copy sent to the Department, the strikeout is slightly above the "have;" therefore, since the "have" is itself printed above the "have not," the strikeout may have been intended to obliterate the "have." [105]

In any event, Oswald filled out the supplementary questionnaire which was required to be completed if the applicant admitted he had performed one or more of the possibly expatriating acts. He signed the questionnaire under oath.[106] Snyder testified that it was routine for any kind of "problem case" to fill out the supplementary questionnaire.[107] The Passport Office employee who processed the Oswald case in Washington testified that she routinely regarded the questionnaire rather than the application itself as the controlling document for expatriation purposes, so that she probably paid no attention to the strikeout.[108]

The pertinent questions included on the questionnaire, with Oswald's answers, read as follows:

2.(a) Are you known or considered in your community to be a national of the country in which you are residing? *No.* (Yes or No)

(b) If your answer to 2(a) is "No," explain why not. *On my document for residence in the USSR my nationality is American.*

3.(a) Have you ever sought or obtained registration as a national of a foreign country, applied for or obtained a passport, certificate, card document or other benefit therefrom in which you were described as a national of a country other than the United States? *No.* (Yes or No)

(b) If your answer to 3(a) is "Yes," did you voluntarily seek or claim such benefits? (Yes or No) If "No," please explain.
I recived a document for residence in the USSR but I am described as being "Without citizenship."

4.(a) Have you ever informed any local or national official of a foreign state that you are a national of the United States? *No.* * * *

(b) If your answer to 4(a) is "No," explain why not. *On my document for residence in the USSR, my nationality is American.*

6.(a) Have you ever taken an oath or made an affirmation or other formal declaration of allegiance to a foreign state? *No.* * * *

8. Have you ever accepted, served in, or performed the duties of any office, post or employment under the government of a foreign state or political subdivision thereof? *No.* * * * *I do not regard factory employment as state employment, as is meant in the question above.*[109]

On the basis of these answers, and on the basis of the statements Oswald made orally during the interview, Snyder concluded that Oswald had not lost his citizenship. Snyder therefore handed him back his passport. Pursuant to the instructions from Washington, it was stamped, "This passport is valid only for direct travel to the United States." [110]

In a despatch dated July 11, 1961,[111] the Embassy informed the Department of State of its conclusion that Oswald had not lost his American citizenship and requested that, if Washington agreed with the conclusion, "the Embassy be authorized to renew Oswald's passport at its discretion." The despatch, with which Oswald's application and supplemental questionnaire [112] were enclosed, informed the Department that Oswald was questioned at length at the Embassy and that no evidence was revealed of any act which might be considered as having caused the loss of his American citizenship.

The Embassy added in the despatch—

> It is our intention not to renew it [the passport] without the Department's prior approval of the enclosed renewal application, and then only upon evidence of a present need for the renewal in connection with his efforts to return to the United States.[113]

Oswald appeared at the Embassy once again on July 11, 1961, this time accompanied by Marina, in order to complete the papers necessary to obtain permission for his wife to enter the United States.[114] In a letter dated July 16, 1961, Oswald informed the American Embassy about his and Marina's application to the Soviet officials for permission to leave Russia, and described the harassment which Marina was allegedly undergoing because of her attempts to leave the country.[115]

Based upon Snyder's recommendation and the information in its files, the Passport Office on August 18, 1961, concluded that Oswald had not expatriated himself.[116] Therefore, on that date, the Department of State sent a despatch to the Embassy in Moscow stating that they concurred in the Embassy's recommendation of July 11, 1961, with respect to Oswald's citizenship:

> We concur in the conclusion of the Embassy that there is available no information and/or evidence to show that Mr. Oswald has expatriated himself under the pertinent laws of the United States.
> The renewal of Mr. Oswald's passport, issued on September 10, 1959, is authorized upon his referenced application if no adverse reason is known, to take place upon his presentation of evidence that he needs such renewal in connection with his efforts to return to the United States as indicated in the final sentence on page 2 of Despatch 29. As requested in the final paragraph of the Despatch the Embassy may perform this citizenship function for Mr. Oswald at its discretion.

Any passport renewal granted to Mr. Oswald should be limited to his passport needs and, as stated in the second paragraph of the Department's A–173, April 13, 1961 his passport should be made valid for direct return to the United States. The additional precaution set forth in the same paragraph should be observed and his passport should be delivered to him on a personal basis only. When available, a report of his travel data should be submitted, as well as a report of any intervening developments.[117]

On October 12, 1961, the Embassy wrote the Department to inform it of four letters it had received from Oswald dated July 15, August 8, and October 4, and an undated letter received in August. With reference to these letters, the despatch noted:

* * * that Oswald is having difficulty in obtaining exit visas for himself and his Soviet wife, and that they are subject to increasing harassment in Minsk. In replying to Oswald's latest letter, the Embassy pointed out that it has no way of influencing Soviet action on exit visas. It informed him that the question of his passport renewal could be discussed with him personally at the Embassy. In answer to Oswald's question, the Embassy notified him that the petition to classify his wife's status had not yet been approved.[118]

The Department on December 28, 1961, informed the Embassy that the Passport Office approved the manner of the Embassy's reply to Mr. Oswald with respect "to his receiving further passport facilities." [119] After a further exchange of correspondence between Oswald and the Embassy, dealing primarily with Oswald's difficulties in obtaining the necessary Soviet clearance, his impatience in receiving American approval for Marina's entry into the United States, and his efforts to obtain a repatriation loan,[120] the passport problem was finally concluded on May 24, 1962, when the Embassy renewed Oswald's passport for 30 days, stamped it valid for direct return to the United States only and handed it to him.[121] A week later he used it to return to the United States.[122]

The decision that Oswald was entitled to a new passport because he had not expatriated himself was made for the Embassy by the consul, Richard E. Snyder.[123] For the Department it was made initially by Miss Bernice L. Waterman, a worker in the Passport Office for 36 years, and was then approved by her area chief, by the head of the Foreign Operations Division, and by the Legal Division of the Passport Office.[124] Snyder and Miss Waterman have both testified that they reached their decisions independently and without influence from any other person.[125] The Director of the Passport Office and the Legal Adviser to the State Department both stated that after a review of the record they concluded that Oswald had not expatriated himself and that Snyder and Waterman, therefore, acted correctly.[126]

Legal Justification for the Return and Reissue of Oswald's Passport

Since he was born in the United States, Oswald was an American citizen.[127] However, Congress has provided that by performing certain acts, a person may forfeit his American citizenship. Thus Oswald would have become expatriated while in Russia if he obtained naturalization in the Soviet Union, renounced U.S. nationality, took an oath of allegiance to the Soviet Union, or voluntarily worked for the Soviet Government in a post requiring that the employee take an oath of allegiance.

Naturalization in a foreign state.—Section 349(a)(1) of the Immigration and Nationality Act of 1952 provides that a U.S. citizen shall lose his nationality by "obtaining naturalization in a foreign state upon his own application * * *."[128] Although Oswald applied for Soviet citizenship, he never received it.[129] Thus, Oswald did not expatriate himself under section 349(a)(1).

Formal renunciation of U.S. nationality.—Section 349(a)(6) of the act provides that a U.S. citizen shall lose his citizenship by:

> * * * making a formal renunciation of nationality before a diplomatic or consular officer of the United States in a foreign state, in such form as may be prescribed by the Secretary of State.[130]

In accordance with this statute, the Secretary has promulgated regulations prescribing the manner in which renunciation is to be effected.[131] The regulations provide, among other things, that 4 copies of the renunciation form are to be executed and the original and one copy sent to the Department. The Department must then approve the form and advise the appropriate consular official, who may then furnish a copy of the form to the person to whom it relates. The form itself requires the person to subscribe it in the presence of a consular official, and it must also be signed by this official.[132]

Though in 1959 Oswald clearly stated to officials at the American Embassy, both orally and in writing, that he desired to renounce his U.S. citizenship, he at no time took the steps required by the statute and regulations to effect his renunciation. Oswald did not execute the proper forms, he did not sign his letter of October 31 or November 3, 1959, in the presence of a consular official, and neither letter was signed by such an official.[133] Because section 349(a)(6) in terms requires compliance with the form prescribed by the Secretary of State, Oswald did not expatriate himself under that section.

Oath of allegiance to a foreign state.—Section 349(a)(2) of the act provides that a U.S. citizen shall lose his nationality by:

> * * * taking an oath or making an affirmation or other formal declaration of allegiance to a foreign state or a political subdivision thereof.[134]

759

In his letter of October 31, 1959, Oswald wrote: "I affirm that my allegiance is to the union of Soviet Socialist Republics." [135]   Both in this letter and in his letter of November 3, 1959, he stated that his application for citizenship in the Soviet Union was pending before the Supreme Soviet of the U.S.S.R.[136]

Oswald's letters no doubt were intended to express allegiance to the Soviet Union in a manner inconsistent with continued allegiance to the United States, as the statute has been held to require.[137]   However, since 1940, it has been well established that in order for an oath of allegiance to a foreign state to work an expatriation from the United States, it must be given to an official of the foreign state, and not to a party unconnected with the foreign state.[138]   This requirement can be viewed as a necessary corollary of the broader, but less clearly established, principle that the oath must be taken in accord with the requirements of the foreign state.[139]   Although Lee Harvey Oswald wrote that his allegiance was to the Soviet Union,[140] there is no indication that he had ever actually taken an oath or declaration or that any such oath was taken before an official of the Soviet Government. He, therefore, did not expatriate himself under section 349(a)(2).

Employment under the government of a foreign state.—Section 349(a)(4) of the Immigration and Nationality Act of 1952 provides that a U.S. citizen shall lose his nationality by:

> (a) accepting, serving in, or performing the duties of any office, post, or employment under the government of a foreign state or a political subdivision thereof, if he has or acquires the nationality of such foreign state; or (b) accepting, serving in, or performing the duties of any office, post of employment under the government of a foreign state or a political subdivision thereof, for which office, post, or employment an oath, affirmation, or declaration of allegiance is required. * * * [141]

While Oswald was employed in a state-owned factory in Minsk, he did not acquire Russian nationality, and there is no indication that he had to take any oath when he obtained this employment.[142]   Furthermore, prior judicial decisions indicate that merely working in a government-owned factory does not result in expatriation even if an oath was required to be taken in connection with such employment.[143]   Several cases decided under an earlier but similar statutory provision held that where a person took a government job in order to subsist, such employment was considered involuntary since it was based on economic duress, and thus it did not result in expatriation.[144]   Thus, Oswald did not expatriate himself under section 349(a)(4).

The Commission therefore concludes that Lee Harvey Oswald had not expatriated himself by any acts performed between October 16, 1959, and May 1962, and concurs in the opinion of the State Department that his passport was properly returned to him in July 1961 and properly reissued in May 1962.

AUTHORIZATION FOR MARINA OSWALD TO ENTER THE UNITED STATES

Negotiations Between Oswald and the Embassy

On July 11, 1961, Oswald and his wife appeared at the Embassy in Moscow before John A. McVickar.[145] Together they executed papers to set in motion the procedures for her admittance to the United States as a nonquota immigrant under the provisions applicable to the wife of an American citizen.[146] The interview was routine. McVickar asked Marina whether she was a member of any Communist organization and she replied that she was a member of the Trade Union of Medical Workers [147] but she denied she was or ever had been a member of the Komsomol,[148] the Communist youth organization, or any other Communist organization.[149] Marina Oswald has since admitted to the Commission that at one time she was a member of The Komsomol, but was expelled, according to her testimony, when it was learned that she intended to accompany her husband to the United States.[150] The Embassy forwarded the papers pertaining to her application to the State Department on August 28, 1961.[151]

Marina Oswald's ability to obtain a nonquota immigrant visa depended on the favorable resolution of 3 questions. First, it had to be determined that she was the wife of an American citizen,[152] which depended on whether her husband had expatriated himself. Second, it was necessary to determine that she was not and had not been affiliated with a Communist organization on other than an involuntary basis.[153] Third, it had to be determined that she was not likely to become a public charge after she was admitted to the United States.[154] Section 243(g) of the Immigration and Nationality Act [155] presented a fourth issue. This section of the act prohibits the issuance of immigrant visas by American Consuls stationed in countries which have refused to accept or have unduly delayed accepting the return of persons sought to be deported from the United States. The Soviet Union had been designated as such a country in 1953. However, the sanctions of section 243(g) are often waived; and even if they were not waived in Marina's case, she could obtain her visa at an American Embassy in some other country on her way from the Soviet Union to the United States, if she were otherwise entitled to the visa.[156]

In a despatch dated August 28, 1961, the Embassy requested from the Department a security advisory opinion on Marina Oswald's application to enter the United States. The Embassy wrote:

> A favorable advisory opinion and approval of * * * [Mrs. Oswald's] petition is recommended together with a waiver of the sanctions imposed by section 243(g) of the Act. * * *
>
> In connection with her employment and her professional training, she has been a member of the Soviet Trade Union for Medical Workers since 1957. Such membership is routinely considered to be involuntary. * * * [157]

The Department initiated a check on Marina Oswald with the CIA, the FBI, the Department's own Office of Security, and Passport Office.[158] The security check turned up no derogatory information on her, so that in early October 1961 the Department cabled Moscow that the available information concerning the applicant established her eligibility to enter the country as a nonquota immigrant.[159]

The Department's decision assumed that prior to obtaining her visa to enter the United States, Marina Oswald would provide some reasonable assurance that she was not likely to become a public charge after she had arrived there. The Department later encountered some difficulty in deciding that she had met this requirement. She knew no one in the United States other than the members of her husband's family, and they lacked the means to furnish any substantial financial guarantees. After considerable correspondence on the matter with Oswald [160] and with the Department,[161] the Embassy decided to accept Oswald's own affidavit to support his wife as sufficient assurance that she would not become a public charge. The Embassy's reasons were set forth in a memorandum dated March 16, 1962:

It appears that * * * [Oswald] can find no one in the United States who is able and willing to execute an affidavit of support for his wife. Furthermore, Oswald has been able to obtain no concrete offer of employment in the United States. On the other hand, he is trained in a trade which should make him readily employable and he and his family will be able to live with his mother in Texas until he has found work and become otherwise settled. Taking into consideration the latter factors, Oswald's legal obligation to support his wife, and the unusual circumstances of the case which make it difficult for Oswald to provide the usual financial evidence, the responsible consular officer * * * [is] willing to accept Oswald's unsubstantiated affidavit as sufficient to overcome the public charge provisions of the law.[162]

The necessity of relying solely upon Oswald's own affidavit, however, was eliminated somewhat later when the Department received an affidavit of support from the employer of Oswald's mother in Vernon, Tex.[163]

By law the Attorney General must also pass upon an applicant's eligibility, and this responsibility has been delegated to the District Directors of the Immigration and Naturalization Service.[164] The machinery to get approval of the Immigration and Naturalization Service for Marina Oswald's admission to the United States was set in motion on October 6, 1961. On that date the Visa Office of the Department of State sent a letter to the District Director of the Immigration and Naturalization Service in Dallas, Tex., requesting the Service to take action on her immigrant visa.[165] The letter transmitted her marriage certificate, a check for $10 from Lee Harvey Oswald, and a "Petition to Classify Status of Alien For Issuance of Immigrant Visa." The petition was signed by Oswald and was on behalf of Marina, asking that she be classified in "the status of the alien beneficiary for issuance of an immigrant visa as * * * the spouse of a United States citizen."[166]   The letter from the Visa Office stated:

> Mrs. Oswald has been the object of an investigation by the Department and has been found, in the Department's opinion, not ineligible to secure a visa.[167]

On the basis of this communication, the Immigration and Naturalization Service at its Dallas, Tex., office instituted a field investigation on Lee Harvey Oswald.[168]   Routine checks with the Federal security agencies and with local law enforcement authorities turned up no new derogatory information, and no evidence was uncovered that Oswald was ever a member of the Communist Party or other subversive groups.[169]   A record check was made in New Orleans, La., and a birth certificate was found for Lee Harvey Oswald, proving that he was an American citizen by birth.[170]   On October 17, 1961, an investigator from the Dallas office interviewed Oswald's brother, Robert, who expressed the view that Lee was just a "mixed up kid" who had emigrated to Russia because he had become embittered, possibly over something that had happened while he was in the Marine Corps.[171]

On January 25, 1962, the results of the field investigation in Dallas were consolidated in a report [172] which, with a covering memorandum,[173] was sent to the District Director of the Service in San Antonio the next day.   The accompanying memorandum noted that the immigrant inspector who processed the case had endorsed it "approved," but the author of the memorandum overruled the decision of the inspector on the grounds that the sanctions under section 243(g) should not be waived.[174]   The reasons for denying the waiver were stated as follows:

> OI [Operations Instructions] 205.3, as you know, provides that the District Director may waive sanctions in an individual meritorious case for a beneficiary of a petition filed by a reputable relative where no substantial derogatory security information is developed.   I am of the opinion that both of these restrictions are present in this case.[175]

On January 30, 1962, the District Director at San Antonio affirmed the decision of the Dallas office, including the decision that the sanctions imposed under section 243(g) not be waived.[176]   He concluded that Oswald's recent statements to the American Embassy in Moscow to the effect that he had learned from his experiences in Russia were not sufficient to relieve the doubts which were raised regarding his loyalty to the United States by the arrogant, anti-American statements he made when he entered Russia in 1959.[177]

San Antonio forwarded its decision to Washington in a letter dated January 31, 1962, in which Marina Oswald's petition and all the

763

aforementioned memoranda and reports were included.[178] However, because Washington had previously indicated its impatience at not yet having received anything on the Oswald case, the San Antonio office also telegraphed its decision to Washington about a week later,[179] the telegram presumably being received by Washington before the letter of January 31. The Washington copy of this telegram has a handwritten note on the lower portion which indicates that on February 12 an officer in the Visa Office of the State Department informed the Immigration and Naturalization Service by telephone: "Political desk of opinion, we're better off with subject in U.S. than in Russia." [180]

Nonetheless, the Washington office of the Service concurred in the field decision that the provisions of section 243(g) should not be waived.[181] However, the Washington office pointed out that the correct disposition should be not to deny the visa petition as the field offices had proposed, but to grant the petition and indorse it to read, "Waiver of sanctions imposed under section 243(g) of the Act is not authorized." [182]

On February 28, 1962, the Dallas office of the Immigration and Naturalization Service notified the Department of State in Washington and the American Embassy in Moscow of this disposition. The communication from the Dallas office noted that Oswald "has been notified at his Minsk, Russia, address of the approval of the petition in his wife's behalf." [183] Oswald later told the Embassy that he had received the notice on March 15.[184] On March 9, 1962, the Department of State also notified the Embassy in Moscow that Oswald's wife was entitled to nonquota status but that the Immigration and Naturalization Service would not waive section 243(g) of the Act. The Embassy was told to inform Oswald of this fact if he asked about it. The memorandum indicated that the Embassy might suggest that Marina could proceed to some other country to file her visa application and thus avoid the sanction.[185]

The Moscow Embassy on March 16, 1962, asked the Embassy at Brussels if Mrs. Oswald could obtain her visa in Brussels.[186] The Brussels Embassy replied affirmatively and said a visa could be issued to Marina within 2 or 3 days of her arrival.[187] The Marina Oswald file accordingly was sent to the Embassy at Brussels.[188]

The plan to obtain the visa in Belgium was rendered unnecessary, however, when the Immigration and Naturalization Service reversed its position regarding the waiver of section 243(g). On March 16, the Soviet desk at the Department of State took initial action to attempt to secure such a change by sending a memorandum to the Visa Office within the Department, urging that the Immigration and Naturalization Service be asked to reconsider its decision.[189] According to this memorandum:

SOV believes it is in the interest of the U.S. to get Lee Harvey Oswald and his family out of the Soviet Union and on their way to this country as soon as possible. An unstable character, whose actions are entirely unpredictable, Oswald may well refuse to leave the USSR or subsequently attempt to return there if we should make it impossible for him to be accompanied from Moscow by his wife and child.

Such action on our part also would permit the Soviet Government to argue that, although it had issued an exit visa to Mrs. Oswald to prevent the separation of a family, the United States Government had imposed a forced separation by refusing to issue her a visa. Obviously, this would weaken our Embassy's position in encouraging positive Soviet action in other cases involving Soviet citizen relatives of U.S. citizens.[190]

Soon thereafter, however, the Department of State notified its Moscow Embassy that the decision was under review and instructed it to withhold action pending the outcome of the reconsideration.[191]

The Visa Office first contacted the Washington office of the Immigration and Naturalization Service informally, and was advised, according to a contemporaneous notation:

* * * that case had been carefully considered and decision made at Assistant or Deputy Associate Commissioner level. Therefore, although not wishing to comment on likelihood of reversal, [INS officer] felt that any letter requesting a review of the case should come from the Director or Acting Administrator.[192]

On March 27, 1962, such a letter was written from an acting administrator in the Department of State to the Commissioner of Immigration and Naturalization. The letter read in part:

I appreciate the difficulty this case presents for your Service, because of Mr. Oswald's background, and the fact that granting a waiver of the sanction makes it appear that this Government is assisting a person who is not altogether entitled to such assistance. However, if the Embassy at Moscow is unable to issue Mrs. Oswald a visa, it would appear that she and indirectly the Oswalds' newborn child are being punished for Mr. Oswald's earlier indiscretions. I might also point out that this Government has advanced Mr. Oswald a loan of $500.00 for repatriation.

More important, however, is the possibility that if Mrs. Oswald is not issued a visa by the Embassy, the Soviet Government will be in a position to claim that it has done all it can to prevent the separation of the family by issuing Mrs. Oswald the required exit permission, but that this Government has refused to issue her a visa, thus preventing her from accompanying her husband and child. This would weaken the Embassy's attempts to encourage positive action by the Soviet authorities in other cases involving Soviet relatives of United States citizens.

Because of these considerations and because I believe it is in the best interests of the United States to have Mr. Oswald depart from the Soviet Union as soon as possible, I request that the section 243(g) sanction be waived in Mrs. Oswald's case.[193]

The Immigration and Naturalization Service ultimately reversed its original position and granted the waiver on May 9, 1962. The letter reversing its initial decision states that the matter has been "carefully reviewed in this office" and that "in view of the strong representations" made in the letter of March 27, the sanctions imposed pursuant to section 243(g) were thereby waived in behalf of Mrs. Oswald.[194]

Actually, the Office of Soviet Affairs had informally learned on May 8 that the May 9 letter would be signed by the Immigration and Naturalization Service.[195] On the strength of the assurance that a written reversal would be forthcoming immediately, the State Department quickly telegraphed the Moscow Embassy reporting that the waiver had been granted.[196] Marina Oswald completed her processing when she, her husband, and daughter came to Moscow in May 1962 on their way from Minsk to the United States.[197]

Legal Justification for the Decisions Affecting Marina Oswald

Wife of a citizen of the United States.—Section 205 of the Immigration and Nationality Act of 1952 provides for the admission into the United States of persons married to American citizens.[198] Once it was determined that Lee Harvey Oswald was born in the United States [199] and had not expatriated himself, his American citizenship was established. Marina Oswald submitted a marriage certificate to show that she was his wife.[200] This requirement was, therefore, satisfied.

Assurance that Marina Oswald would not become a public charge.—Section 212(a)(15) of the act provides that aliens will not be admitted to the United States if, in the opinion of the responsible Government official, they "are likely at any time to become public charges." [201] The pertinent Department of State regulations provide that a determination to exclude an alien for this reason must be "predicated upon circumstances which indicate that the alien will probably become a charge upon the public after entry into the United States." [202]

In 1962, Oswald was 22 years old and in good health. He had lived in the United States for 17 years before joining the Marine Corps and was, therefore, familiar with its language and customs. He had gained job experience by working 2½ years in a factory which produced electronic equipment. Under these circumstances the Department was not unreasonable in concluding that Oswald's own affidavit that he would support his wife was sufficient assurance that she was not likely to become a charge upon the public after her entry into the United States. The receipt of the affidavit from Marguerite Oswald's employer provided a possible alternative basis for reaching this decision, but since a favorable ruling had already been made on the basis of Oswald's affidavit, the Embassy had no reason to consider the sufficiency of the second affidavit.

Membership in a Communist organization.—Under section 212(a) (28) of the Immigration and Nationality Act, an alien will not be admitted to the United States if he is or was a member of, or affiliated with, a Communist organization unless:

> * * * such an alien establishes to the satisfaction of the consular officer when applying for a visa and the consular officer finds that (i) such membership or application is or was involuntary, or is or was solely when under sixteen years of age, by operation of law, or for purposes of obtaining employment, food rations, or other essentials of living and where necessary for such purposes * * *" 203

At the time Marina Oswald applied for a visa she was a member of the Soviet Trade Union for Medical Workers.204 According to the Department of State, the

> * * * long-standing interpretation [of the statute] concurred in by the State and Justice Departments [is] that membership in a professional organization or trade union behind the Iron Curtain is considered involuntary unless the membership is accompanied by some indication of voluntariness, such as active participation in the organization's activities or holding an office in the organization.205

Since there was no evidence that Marina Oswald actively participated in the union's activities or held an office in the organization, her union membership was properly held not to bar her admission to this country.

Although Marina Oswald declared that she was not a member of the Komsomol or any other Communist organization, she was in fact a member of the Komsomol, the Communist youth organization.206 If this fact had been known to the State Department, Marina Oswald would not necessarily have been denied a visa, although a careful investigation into the nature of the membership would have been required.207 However, had her membership in the Komsomol become known to the Department after her denial of such membership, it is possible that she would have been excluded from the United States on the ground of having willfully misrepresented a material fact.208

Judicial decisions are not in agreement as to what constitutes a "material fact" such that its intentional misrepresentation warrants exclusion of the alien.209 Some cases indicate that a misrepresentation in an application for a visa involves a material fact even if the alien would not definitely have been excluded on the true facts; 210 others hold that a misstatement is material only if it referred to such facts as would have justified refusing the visa had they been disclosed.211 The Visa Office of the Department of State has announced that it applies a "rule of probability" under which a misstatement will be deemed material only if it concealed facts which probably would have resulted in a denial of a visa.[212]

Waiver of the provisions of section 243(g).—Section 243(g) of the Immigration and Nationality Act of 1952, by its terms, prevented issuance of a visa to Marina Oswald by the Moscow Embassy. The section provides that upon notification of the Secretary of State by the Attorney General that a country has refused or unduly delayed the acceptance of a deportable alien from the United States who is a subject or was a resident of that country, consular officers in such country are not to issue visas to citizens of the country. The section had been invoked against Russia on May 26, 1953. Nonetheless, although section 243(g) does not contain an express provision for waiver, the Justice Department has concluded that the Attorney General possesses such waiver powers.[213] Pursuant to this decision, the Department has granted waivers in over 600 cases from the Soviet Union since 1953.[214] The waiver procedures followed in 1962 were prescribed by the Immigration and Naturalization Service. The relevant provision reads:

> Before adjudicating a petition for an eligible beneficiary residing in the USSR, Czechoslovakia or Hungary, against which sanctions have been imposed, the district director shall obtain a report of investigation regarding the petitioner which shall include an affiliation of a subversive nature disclosed by a neighborhood investigation, local agency records and responses to Form G-135a. * * * If no substantial derogatory security information is developed, the district director may waive the sanctions in an individual meritorious case for a beneficiary of a petition filed by a reputable relative to accord status under Section 101(a)(27) (A) or Section 203(a) (2), (3) or (4). * * * If substantial adverse security information relating to the petitioner is developed, the visa petition shall be processed on its merits and certified to the regional commissioner for determination whether the sanctions should be waived. The assistant commissioner shall endorse the petition to show whether the Waiver is granted or denied, and forward it and notify the appropriate field office of the action taken. * * *[215]

State Department regulations are much less explicit.[216] The State Department's visa instructions for the guidance of consular officers provide, "The sanctions will be waived only in individual meritorious cases in behalf of a beneficiary of a petition filed by a reputable relative pursuant to [sections] of the act." [217]

Because Lee Harvey Oswald signed the petition on Marina's behalf, his character was relevant to whether the sanctions of section 243(g) could be waived for her. The file on Lee Harvey Oswald which was maintained by the Department of State and made available to the Department of Justice for purposes of passing on his wife's application contained the facts relating to Oswald's attempted expatriation. However, despite the derogatory material in the Oswald file, the Immigration and Naturalization Service regulations did not require automatic denial of the waiver; they provided only that if adverse security information were developed, "the visa petition shall be processed on its merits and certified to the regional commissioner for determination whether the sanctions should be waived." This procedure was followed in Marina's case and the factors considered in reaching the decision do not appear to be inappropriate. The State Department successfully urged that the original decision of the Immigration and Naturalization Service be reversed because this would be in the best interests of future United States dealings with the Soviet Union on behalf of American citizens, and because it seemed unfair to punish Lee Harvey Oswald's wife and baby for his own earlier errors.[218] Prevention of the separation of families is among the most common reasons underlying the frequent waivers of section 243(g).[219]

OSWALD'S LETTER TO SENATOR TOWER

Sometime shortly before January 26, 1962, an undated letter from Lee Harvey Oswald was received in the office of the U.S. Senator from Texas, John G. Tower.[220] The letter reads as follows:

My name is Lee Harvey Oswald, 22, of Fort Worth up till October 1959, when I came to the Soviet Union for a residenaul stay. I took a residenual document for a non-Soviet person living for a time in the U S S R. The American Embassy in Moscow is familier with my case

Since July 20th 1960, I have unsucessfully applied for a Soviet Exit Visa to leave this country, the Soviets refuse to permit me and my Soviet wife, (who applied at the U.S. Embassy Moscow, July 8, 1960 for immigration status to the U.S.A.) to leave the Soviet Union. I am a citizen of the United States of America (passport No. 1733242, 1959) and I bessech you, Senator Tower, to rise the question of holding by the Soviet Union of a citizen of the U.S., against his will and expressed desires.[221]

The letter was read in Senator Tower's office by a caseworker on his staff. According to the caseworker and the Senator's press secretary, the letter was forwarded as a matter of routine on January 26 to the Assistant Secretary for Congressional Relations, Department of State. The letter was forwarded with a cover letter, machine signed by the Senator, stating that he did "not know Oswald, or any of the facts concerning his reasons for visiting the Soviet Union; nor what action, if any, this Government can or should take on his behalf." The cover letter pointed out that Oswald's inquiry should have gone to the executive branch of the Government and that for this reason the Senator was forwarding it "for whatever action the Department may consider appropriate." [222] On February 1 an officer at the Department of State telephoned the Senator's office and spoke briefly with the caseworker on the Oswald case. She made a memorandum of the call which notes, "Senator should not become involved in such case—therefore State will report to us the course which they follow regarding Lee Harvey Oswalt [sic]." [223] About a week later the Department of State forwarded to Senator Tower copies of some of the correspondence which the Department had had with Oswald and informed the Senator that if he wished to be kept informed on further developments regarding Oswald he could contact the Department of State.[224] Neither the Senator nor any member of his staff contacted the Department again nor did they take any other action in respect to the matter.[225]

THE LOAN FROM THE STATE DEPARTMENT

In a letter dated January 5, 1962, Oswald said that he would like to make arrangements for a loan from the Embassy or some private organization for part of the airplane fares.[226] The Embassy on February 6, 1962, replied that he would have to supply certain personal and financial data.[227] The letter also said that after repatriation he would not be furnished a passport for travel abroad until he had repaid the money.

Between February 6, 1962, and May 1, 1962, Oswald attempted to secure a loan from the Red Cross [228] and the International Rescue Committee [229] in the United States. The State Department on February 1 wrote Oswald's mother a letter asking whether she could advance the money.[230] Oswald later wrote both his mother and the Department advising each that his mother should not be bothered in reference to the loan.[231] Ultimately, after an exchange of communications between the Embassy and Washington,[232] the Department approved a loan to Oswald for passage to New York only, directing the Embassy to "Keep cost minimum." [233] On June 1 Oswald signed a promissory note for $435.71.[234]

Statutory authority for making such a loan was conferred by title 5, section 170(a), of the U.S. Code, which authorizes the Secretary of State to "make expenditures, from such amounts as may be specifically appropriated therefor, for unforeseen emergencies arising in the diplomatic and consular service." Since 1947, the Department of State's annual appropriation act has included a sum for expenses necessary "to enable the Secretary of State to meet unforeseen emergencies arising in the Diplomatic and Consular Service. * * *" [235] In recent years, the accompanying reports submitted by the Appropriations Committee of the House of Representatives have stated, "These funds are used for relief and repatriation loans to the U.S. citizens abroad and for other emergencies of the Department." [236] Out of the amount appropriated to meet unforeseen emergencies arising in the Diplomatic and Consular Service, the Secretary of State has annually allotted approximately $100,000 to meet the expenses of indigent U.S. nationals, including those in the Soviet Union, who request repatriation loans. From 1959 to 1963, 2,343 such loans were granted.[237]

Section 423.2–1 of the Department's regulations provides that repatriation loans may be granted only to destitute U.S. nationals:

    a. Who are in complete and unquestioned possession of their citizenship rights;

    b. Who are entitled to receive United States passports;

    c. Whose loyalty to the United States Government is beyond question, or to whom the provisions of Section 423.1–2(b) apply.[238]

Oswald undoubtedly satisfied the requirements of paragraphs (a) and (b), since he was determined to have been a U.S. citizen at the time the loan was granted and he had been issued a passport to return to the United States. There is a serious question whether he could have qualified under the first clause of paragraph (c). The Commission is of the opinion that in its application of this clause the Department should exercise great care in determining whether an applicant's loyalty to the U.S. Government is beyond question, particularly in the case of a defector like Oswald who has expressed hostility and disloyalty to our government and manifested a desire to renounce his citizenship. The Department chose instead to exercise its judgment under the second clause of paragraph (c), which refers to section 423.1–2(b). This section provides that loans to destitute nationals are authorized when:

    b. The United States national is in or the cause of a situation which is damaging to the prestige of the United States Government or which constitutes a compelling reason for extending assistance to effect his return.[239]

The Department decided that the provisions of section (b) were applicable to Oswald because his "unstable character and prior criticism of the United States" would make his continued presence in the Soviet Union damaging to the prestige of the United States.[240] In acting under this section, the Department was acting within its competence and the law. As required by another section of the regulations, the Department sought to obtain funds for the Oswalds' repatriation from private sources—his mother and the International Rescue Committee—before using Government funds.[241]

Regulations further provide that repatriation loans are authorized for the alien, wife, and children of the U.S. national receiving a repatriation loan in order to avoid the division of families.[242] However, loans are limited

    To the minimum amount required to cover transportation and subsistence while enroute to the nearest continental United States port. * * * When necessary, loans may include: expenses incident to embarkation, such as fees for documentation and minimum subsistence from the date of application for a loan to the date of departure by the first available ship. * * * The cost of transportation shall be limited to third-class passage by ship.[243]

Oswald's loan was sufficient to cover no more than the least expensive transportation from Moscow to New York. His passport was stamped as valid only for return to the United States.[244] Oswald completed all necessary forms and affidavits to obtain the loan.[245]

According to its own procedures the Department of State should have prepared a lookout card for Oswald in June 1962 when he received the proceeds of the loan.[246] The promissory note which he signed contained a provision stating,

> I further understand and agree that after my repatriation I will not be furnished a passport for travel abroad until my obligation to reimburse the Treasurer of the United States is liquidated.[247]

However, a lookout card was never in fact prepared. With respect to this failure the State Department has informed the Commission as follows:

> On receipt of notice of the loan from the Embassy in Moscow, the Department's procedures provided that Miss Leola B. Burkhead of the Revenues and Receipts Branch of the Office of Finance should have notified the Clearance Section in the Passport Office of Oswald's name, date, and place of birth. If the Passport Office received only the name and not the date and place of birth of a borrower, it would not have prepared a lookout card under its established procedures because of lack of positive identification. (Among the Passport Office's file of millions of passport applicants, there are, of course, many thousands of identical names.) Mr. Richmond C. Reeley was the Chief of the Revenues and Receipts Branch of the Office of Finance and Mr. Alexander W. Maxwell was Chief of the Clearance Section. If the notice was received in the Clearance Section it would have been delivered to the Carding Desk for preparation of a lookout card on Oswald. It appears, however, that such a lookout card was not prepared. It may have been that the Finance Office did not notify the Clearance Section of Oswald's loan. One reason for this might have been the Finance Office's lack of information concerning Oswald's date and place of birth. On the other hand, the Finance Office may have notified the Clearance Section of Oswald's name only, in which case this Section would not have prepared a lookout card under its procedures. Since Oswald began repaying the loan in installments immediately after his return to the United States, it is also possible that the Office of Finance decided that it was un-

necessary to pursue the matter further. In any event, Oswald's loan was repaid in full on January 29, 1963, five months prior to his application for a new passport.[248]

OSWALD'S RETURN TO THE UNITED STATES AND REPAYMENT OF HIS LOAN

On June 1, 1962, the same day that Oswald received his loan from the State Department, he and his family left Moscow by train destined for Rotterdam, The Netherlands.[249] They boarded the SS *Maasdam* at Rotterdam on June 4 and arrived in New York on June 13, 1962.[250] The Embassy sent word of the Oswalds' departure to the Department of State in Washington on May 31.[251] Consistent with its prior practice of keeping the Federal security agencies informed of Oswald's activity,[252] the Department notified the FBI.[253]

Frederick J. Wiedersheim, an officer of the Immigration and Naturalization Service in New York, interviewed the Oswalds upon their entry into the United States at Hoboken, N.J., on June 13, 1962, but made no written report. Mr. Wiedersheim recalled that he asked the Oswalds various questions which would determine the eligibility of both Oswald and Marina to enter the United States. The questions included whether Oswald had expatriated himself and whether Marina belonged to any Communist organization which would bar her entry. These questions were answered in ways which did not appear to raise any problems and therefore the Oswalds were admitted.[254]

After his reentry, Oswald repaid his loan without having to be reminded by the Department to do so. The early payments were very small because he first repaid the approximately $200 he had borrowed from his brother Robert to apply against the expenses of his travel from New York to Fort Worth, Tex.[255] The schedule of payments is as follows:

Aug. 13, 1962	$10.00
Sept. 5, 1962	9.71
Oct. 10, 1962	10.00
Nov. 19, 1962	10.00
Dec. 11, 1962	190.00
Jan. 9, 1963	100.00
Jan. 29, 1963	106.00
Total	[256]435.71

ISSUANCE OF A PASSPORT IN JUNE 1963

On June 24, 1963, Oswald applied for a U.S. passport at the Passport Office in New Orleans, La.[257] He said he was planning to visit England, France, Holland, U.S.S.R., Finland, Italy, and Poland, and that he intended to leave the country sometime during November or December 1963 by ship from New Orleans.[258] He stated further that

773

he was married to a person born in Russia who was not an American citizen. For occupation, the word "Photographer" was inserted on the application.[259]

On the same day a teletype was sent to Washington containing the names of 25 of the persons who applied for passports on that date in New Orleans, Oswald's name among them. On the right side of the Washington Passport Office copy of the teletype message, approximately parallel to his name, are the letters, "NO," written in red pencil.[260] Oswald was issued a passport on June 25, 1963.[261]

Since there was no lookout card on Oswald, the passport was processed routinely. Twenty-four hours is the usual time for routinely granted passports to be issued.[262] The handwritten notation, "NO," which appeared beside Oswald's name on the list of applicants from New Orleans, is a symbol for the New Orleans Passport Office that is routinely placed on incoming teletype messages by anyone of a group of persons in the teletype section of the Passport Office.[263] No one looked at Oswald's file previously established with the Department.[264] The Department, however, has informed the Commission that at the time the passport was issued there was no information in its passport or security files which would have permitted it to deny a passport to Oswald.[265] No lookout card should have been in the file based upon the Moscow Embassy's memorandum of March 28, 1960, which drew attention to Oswald's intention to expatriate himself, because the subsequent determination that Oswald had not expatriated himself would remove expatriation as a possible ground for denying him a passport.[266] And by January 29, 1963, the repatriation loan had been repaid, so a lookout card should not have been in the file on that basis.[267]

Oswald was entitled to receive a passport in 1963 unless he came within one of the two statutory provisions authorizing the Secretary of State to refuse to issue it.[268] Section 6 of the Subversive Activities Control Act of 1950, which has recently been declared unconstitutional,[269] then provided:

> * * * it shall be unlawful for any member of [an organization required to register], with knowledge or notice that such organization is so registered and that such order has become final—(1) to make application for passport, or the renewal of a passport, to be issued or renewed by or under the authority of the United States; or (2) to use or attempt to use any such passport.[270]

Pursuant to section 6, the State Department promulgated a regulation which denied passports to

> * * * any individual who the issuing officer knows or has reason to believe is a member of a Communist Organization registered or required to be registered under Section 7 of the Subversive Activities Control Act of 1950 as amended.[271]

Since there is no evidence that Lee Harvey Oswald was a member of the American Communist Party or any other organization which had been required to register under section 7 of the Subversive Activities Control Act,[272] a passport could not have been denied him under section 6.

Section 215 of the Immigration and Nationality Act provides that, while a Presidential proclamation of national emergency is in force,

> * * * it shall, except as otherwise provided by the President, * * * be unlawful for any citizen of the United States to depart from or enter * * * the United States unless he bears a valid passport.[273]

Because a proclamation of national emergency issued by President Truman during the Korean war had not been revoked by 1963, the Government has taken the position that the statute remains in force.[274] Pursuant to section 215, the State Department has issued regulations setting forth the circumstances under which it will refuse a passport:

> In order to promote and safeguard the interests of the United States, passport facilities, except for direct and immediate return to the United States, shall be refused to a person when it appears to the satisfaction of the Secretary of State that the person's activity abroad would: (a) violate the laws of the United States; (b) be prejudicial to the orderly conduct of foreign relations; or (c) otherwise be prejudicial to the interests of the United States.[275]

The State Department takes the position that its authority under this regulation is severely limited. In a report submitted to the Commission, the Department concluded that "there were no grounds consonant with the passport regulations to take adverse passport action against Oswald prior to November 22, 1963." [276] Although Oswald's statement in 1959 that he would furnish the Russians with information he had obtained in the Marine Corps may have indicated that he would disclose classified information if he possessed any such information, there was no indication in 1963 that he had any valuable information.[277] Moreover, Oswald's 1959 statement had been brought to the attention of the Department of the Navy [278] and the FBI [279] and neither organization had initiated criminal proceedings. The Department therefore had no basis for concluding that Oswald's 1959 statement was anything more than rash talk.[280] And the State Department's files contained no other information which might reasonably have led it to expect that Oswald would violate the laws of the United States when he went abroad.

The most likely ground for denying Oswald a passport in 1963, however, was provided by subsection (c) of the regulation quoted above, which requires the denial of a passport when the Secretary of

State is satisfied that the applicant's "activity abroad would * * * otherwise be prejudicial to the interests of the United States." In 1957 the State Department described to the Senate Foreign Relations Committee one category of persons to whom it denied passports under this provision:

> Persons whose previous conduct abroad has been such as to bring discredit on the United States and cause difficulty for other Americans (gave bad checks, left unpaid debts, had difficulties with police, etc.).[281]

In light of the adverse publicity caused the United States by Oswald's prior defection to the Soviet Union, he could have been considered a person "whose previous conduct abroad had been such as to bring discredit on the United States." Indeed, the State Department itself had previously been of the opinion that Oswald's continued presence in Russia was damaging to the prestige of the United States because of his unstable character and prior criticisms of the United States.[282]

However, in 1958 the Supreme Court had decided two cases which restricted the Secretary of State's authority to deny passports. In *Kent* v. *Dulles* [283] and *Dayton* v. *Dulles*,[284] the Supreme Court invalidated a State Department regulation permitting the denial of passports to Communists and to those "who are going abroad to engage in activities which will advance the Communist movement for the purpose, knowingly and willfully of advancing that movement," on the ground that the regulation exceeded the authority Congress had granted the Secretary. The *Kent* opinion stressed the importance to be attached to an individual's ability to travel beyond the borders of the United States:

> The right to travel is a part of the "liberty" of which the citizen cannot be deprived without due process of law under the Fifth Amendment * * * Freedom of movement across frontiers in either direction, and inside frontiers as well, was a part of our heritage. Travel abroad, like travel within the country, may be necessary for a livelihood. It may be as close to the heart of the individual as the choice of what he eats, or wears, or reads. Freedom of movement is basic in our scheme of values.[285]

The *Kent* opinion also suggested that grounds relating to citizenship and allegiance to illegal conduct might be the only two upon which the Department could validly deny a passport application.

The Department, though publicly declaring that these decisions had little effect upon its broadly worded regulation,[286] in practice denied passports only in limited situations. In 1963 the Department denied passports only to those who violated the Department's travel restrictions, to fugitives from justice, to those involved in using passports fraudulently, and to those engaged in illegal activity abroad or in conduct directly affecting our relations with a particular country.[287]   Passports were granted to people who the Department might have anticipated would go abroad to denounce the United States, and to a prior defector.[288]   State Department officials believed that in view of the Supreme Court decisions, the Department was not empowered to deny anyone a passport on grounds related to freedom of speech or to political association and beliefs.[289]

Since Oswald's citizenship was not in question and since there was no indication that he would be involved in illegal activity abroad, the only grounds upon which a passport might have been denied Oswald would have fallen within the area of speech or political belief and association.   The Commission therefore concludes that the Department was justified in granting a passport to Oswald on June 25, 1963.

VISIT TO THE RUSSIAN EMBASSY IN MEXICO CITY

In October 1963, the Passport Office of the State Department received a report from the Central Intelligence Agency that Oswald had visited the Soviet Embassy in Mexico City.[290]   The report said nothing about Oswald's having visited the Cuban Embassy in Mexico City, a fact which was not known until after the assassination.   Upon receipt of the information the passport file on Lee Harvey Oswald was reviewed by the Passport Office.[291]   The CIA communication and the passport file were read by an attorney and a supervisory attorney in that office who found no basis for revoking Oswald's passport or for notifying the FBI or CIA that Oswald had been issued a new passport in June 1963.[292]   The Department has informed the Commission that, "since the report indicated no grounds for determining Oswald was ineligible for a passport, a determination was made that no action by the passport office was required." [293]   Travel to Russia was not proscribed in 1963.   Moreover, the Soviet Union was one of the countries Oswald had listed on his passport application.   Hence, the Commission agrees that Oswald's taking steps to enter the Soviet Union in 1963 was not a sufficient reason to revoke his passport.

Later, on November 14, 1963, the FBI sent the Department a report on Oswald's arrest in New Orleans, La. during August in connection with a fistfight in which he became engaged when passing out pamphlets entitled "Hands Off Cuba."   No action was taken on the basis of the Bureau's report.[294]   The Commission agrees that this incident was not grounds for revoking Oswald's passport.

CONCLUSION

Investigation of Oswald's complete dealings with the Department of State and the Immigration and Naturalization Service reveals no irregularity suggesting any illegal actions or impropriety on the part of government officials.   The Commission believes, however, that in applying its own regulations the Department should in all cases exercise great care in the return to this country of defectors such as Oswald who have evidenced disloyalty or hostility to this country or who have expressed a desire to renounce their U.S. citizenship and that, when such persons are returned, procedures should be adopted for the better dissemination of information concerning them to the intelligence agencies of the Government. The operation of the "lookout card" system in the Department of State was obviously deficient, but since these deficiencies did not affect Oswald or reflect any favoritism or impropriety, the Commission considers them beyond the scope of its inquiry.

Especially while he was in the Soviet Union, Oswald's manner to Government personnel was frequently insulting and offensive. As one 1962 communication between the Embassy and the Department of State observed, "It is not that our hearts are breaking for Oswald. His impertinence knows no bounds." [295] Nonetheless, the officials of the U.S. Government respected Oswald as a troubled American citizen and extended to him the services and assistance for which the agencies of government have been created. Though Oswald was known to be "an unstable character, whose actions are highly unpredictable," [296] there was no reasonable basis in 1961 and 1962 for suspecting that upon his readmittance to the country he would resort to violence against its public officials. The officers of the Department of State and the Immigration and Naturalization Service, acting within the proper limits of their discretion, concluded that Oswald's return to the United States was in the best interests of the country; it is only from the vantage of the present that the tragic irony of their conclusion emerges.

A Biography of Jack Ruby

In this appendix the Commission presents a biography of Jack Ruby. Although criminal proceedings involving its subject are pending in the State of Texas, the Commission has decided to include this rather detailed account of Ruby's life and activities for several reasons. Most importantly, the Commission believes it will permit a better evaluation of the evidence on the question whether Ruby was involved in any conspiracy. Furthermore, the Commission believes that in view of the many rumors concerning Ruby the public interest will be served by an account which attempts to give sufficient material to provide an impression of his character and background. The Commission's desire not to interfere in the pending proceedings involving Ruby necessarily limits the scope of this appendix, which does not purport to discuss the legal issues raised during Ruby's trial or his possible motive for shooting Oswald.

FAMILY BACKGROUND

Jack Ruby, born Jacob Rubenstein, was the fifth of his parents' eight living children. There is much confusion about his exact birth date. School records report it as June 23, April 25,[1] March 13, and, possibly, March 3, 1911.[2] Other early official records list his date of birth as April 21 and April 26, 1911.[3] During his adult life the date Ruby used most frequently was March 25, 1911.[4] His driver's license, seized following his arrest, and his statements to the FBI on November 24, 1963, listed this date.[5] However, the police arrest report for November 24 gave his birth date as March 19, 1911.[6] Since the recording of births was not required in Chicago prior to 1915, Ruby's birth may never have been officially recorded.[7] No substantial conflict exists, however, about whether Jack Ruby was born in 1911.[8]

Ruby has one older brother and three older sisters. The oldest children, Hyman and Ann, were born shortly after the turn of the century,[9] before their parents arrived in the United States.[10] The other children were born in Chicago. Ruby's sister Marion was born in June 1906 [11] and his sister Eva in March 1909.[12] Ruby also has two younger brothers and a younger sister. Sam was born in December 1912,[13] Earl in April 1915.[14] The youngest child, Eileen, was born in July 1917.[15] At least one and possibly two other children died during infancy.[16]

Jack Ruby's father, Joseph Rubenstein, was born in 1871 in Sokolov, a small town near Warsaw, Poland, then under the rule of Czarist Russia.[17] He entered the Russian artillery in 1893.[18] There he learned the carpentry trade, which had been practiced by his father and at least one brother [19] and he picked up the habit of excessive drinking that was to plague him for the rest of his life.[20] While in the army,[21] he married Jack's mother, Fannie Turek Rutkowski; [22] the marriage was arranged, as was customary, by a professional matchmaker.[23] According to his oldest son, Joseph Rubenstein served in China, Korea, and Siberia, detesting these places and army life. Eventually, in 1898, he simply "walked away" from it and about 4 years later he went to England and Canada, entering the United States in 1903.[24]

Settling in Chicago, Joseph Rubenstein joined the carpenters union in 1904 and remained a member until his death in 1958.[25] Although he worked fairly steadily until 1928, he was unemployed during the last 30 years of his life.[26] The only other group which Joseph Rubenstein joined consisted of fellow immigrants from Sokolov. His daughter Eva described this group as purely social and completely nonpolitical.[27]

Jack Ruby's mother, Fannie Rubenstein, was probably born in 1875 near Warsaw, Poland.[28] She followed her husband to the United States in 1904 or 1905, accompanied by her children Hyman and Ann.[29] An illiterate woman, she went to night school in about 1920 to learn how to sign her name.[30] She apparently failed in this endeavor, however, for an alien registration form, filed after about 35 years in the United States, was signed by an "X".[31] Although she apparently learned some English, her speech was predominantly Yiddish, the primary language of the Rubenstein household.[32] Still, Mrs. Rubenstein felt strongly that her children required an education in order to better themselves. She frequently argued about this with her husband, who had received little, if any, formal education and firmly believed that grammar school training was sufficient for his children.[33]

CHILDHOOD AND YOUTH (1911–33)

In 1911, when Jack Ruby was born, his family resided near 14th and Newberry Streets in Chicago, the first in a series of Jewish neighborhoods in which the Rubensteins lived during his childhood.[34] In 1916, the Rubensteins lived at 1232 Morgan Street, where they apparently remained until 1921.[35] This was the fourth residence in the first 5 years of Jack Ruby's life.[36] Earl Ruby described one typical neighborhood in which the family lived as a "ghetto" with "pushcarts on the streets." [37] His sister Eva characterized it as "below the middle class but yet it wasn't the poorest class." [38] The family generally lived near Italian sections, where there were frequent fights along ethnic lines.[39]

The Rubenstein home was marked by constant strife and the parents were reported to have occasionally struck each other.[40] Between 1915 and 1921, Joseph Rubenstein was frequently arrested because of disorderly conduct and assault and battery charges, some filed by his wife.[41] In the spring of 1921, Jack Ruby's parents separated.[42]   In 1937 Mrs. Rubenstein reported that she had desired a divorce 15 years earlier, but her husband had been opposed to it.[43]   The predominant causes of the separation were apparently Joseph Rubenstein's excessive drinking and Fannie Rubenstein's uncontrollable temper.   She resented her numerous pregnancies, believed her husband to be unfaithful, and nagged him because he failed to make enough money.[44]

Psychiatric Report

Young Jack soon showed the effects of parental discord.   On June 6, 1922, at the age of 11, he was referred to the Institute for Juvenile Research by the Jewish Social Service Bureau.   The reason for the referral was "truancy and incorrigible at home." [45]   On July 10, 1922, the institute recommended to the bureau that Jack be placed in a new environment where his characteristics might be understood and where he might be afforded the supervision and recreation that would end his interest in street gangs.[46]   In March 1923, the institute advised the bureau that "placement in a home, where intelligent supervision and discipline can be given" was appropriate.[47]

The institute's psychiatric examination, which served as a basis for these recommendations, took place in 1922, prior to the advent of many techniques and theories of modern psychiatry,[48] but it is the most objective evidence of Jack Ruby's childhood character.   According to the psychiatric report, Jack was "quick tempered" and "disobedient." [49]   He frequently disagreed openly with his mother, whom he considered an inferior person with whose rules he did not have to comply.[50]   Jack told the institute's interviewer that he ran away from home because his mother lied to him and beat him.[51]   Although Mrs. Rubenstein was severe with her children, she was described as totally incapable of coping with them "because of their delinquencies, i.e., principally their destructive tendencies and disregard for other people's property." [52]   His mother's "extreme temperament" and quarrelsomeness were cited as possible causes of Jack's "bad behavior." [53]

Self-administered questionnaires revealed that Jack felt his classmates were "picking" on him and that he could not get along with his friends.[54]   They also indicated that, although Jack described himself as a good ballplayer, he did not belong to any clubs and was not a member of any athletic teams.[55]   Jack's psychiatric interviewer reported:

> He could give no other good reason for running away from school except that he went to amusement parks.   He has some sex knowledge and is greatly interested in sex matters.   He stated that the boys in the street tell him about these things.   He also claims that he can lick everyone and anybody in anything he wants to do.[56]

The interviewer noted that during "mental tests" he reacted quickly, often carelessly, and his attention was apt to wander so that he had to be reprimanded.[57]

A letter recommending the boy's placement in a more wholesome environment stated:

> He is egocentric and expects much attention, but is unable to get it as there are many children at home. His behavior is further colored by his early sex experiences, his great interest [in sex] and the gang situation in the street. From a superficial examination of his mother who was here with him, it is apparent that she has no insight into his problem, and she is thoroughly inadequate in the further training of this boy.[58]

Recognizing that the sketchiness of the case record precluded complete diagnosis, Dr. Raymond E. Robertson, currently the superintendent of the institute, reported nonetheless that it seems "firmly established * * * [that] his unstable and disorganized home could not provide Jack with the necessary controls and discipline." [59]

Placement in Foster Homes

On July 10, 1923, a dependency hearing involving Jack, his younger brothers Sam and Earl, and his sister Eileen, was held in Chicago's juvenile court.[60] The petition alleged that the children were not receiving proper parental care. They had, until then, been in their mother's custody, living on Roosevelt Road, the border between Jewish and Italian districts.[61] The juvenile court made a finding of dependency. It appointed the Jewish Home Finding Society guardian with the right to place the children in foster homes, and it ordered Joseph Rubenstein to pay the court clerk $4 per week for the support of each child. On November 24, 1924, this order was vacated, which apparently signified the termination of the guardianship and the return of the children to their mother. On April 8, 1925, the case was continued "generally," meaning that it was inactive but could be reactivated if the court so desired.[62]

Despite court records, the exact circumstances and length of time that Jack Ruby lived away from home are not entirely clear. Records indicate that Jack, Sam, Earl, and Eileen Rubenstein were wards of the Jewish Home Finding Society "for a short time in 1922–23." [63] However, Jack and Eileen stated they spent about 4 or 5 years in foster homes.[64] Earl testified that he and Sam were originally sent to a private foster home and then lived on a farm for a little more than a year, while Jack was on a different farm "some distance away." Subsequently the three brothers lived together in another foster home.[65]

Subsequent Home Life

When Jack Ruby returned to his family, the unit was still disordered. His father remained apart from the children at least until 1936 and perhaps until a few years later.[66] Mrs. Rubenstein's inability to manage her home, which had been reported by the Institute for Juvenile Research in 1922, apparently continued. For example, in 1937 Marion Rubenstein observed that her mother "has never been any kind of a housekeeper, was careless with money, and never took much interest in the children's welfare * * * she was selfish, jealous, disagreeable, and never cared to do anything in the home but lie around and sleep." [67] Dr. Hyman I. Rubenstein, the son of Joseph Rubenstein's brother, recalled that Jack Ruby's mother ran "an irregular household" and appeared to be "a rather disturbed person of poor personal appearance with no incentive for cleaning or cooking." [68]

Mrs. Rubenstein's domestic shortcomings were accompanied by symptoms of mental disease. In about 1913, 2 years after Jack was born, Mrs. Rubenstein began to develop a delusion that a sticking sensation in her throat was caused by a lodged fishbone.[69] Each month Hyman, her oldest child, took her to a clinic. And each month the examining doctor, finding no organic cause for discomfort, informed her that there was nothing in her throat and that the sensation was but a figment of her imagination. According to Hyman, this practice continued for a number of years until Mrs. Rubenstein tired of it.[70]

In 1927, Mrs. Rubenstein once again began to visit clinics in connection with her fishbone delusion. Three years later, a thyroidectomy was performed, but she subsequently said it did nothing to relieve her discomfort.[71] According to the Michael Reese Hospital, whose clinic she had visited since 1927, Mrs. Rubenstein was suffering from psychoneurosis with marked anxiety state.

By order of the county court of Cook County, Mrs. Rubenstein was committed to Elgin State Hospital on July 16, 1937.[72] She was paroled on October 17, 1937, 3 months after her commitment.[73] On January 3, 1938, the Chicago State Hospital informed Elgin State that the family desired that she be readmitted to the mental hospital. The family reported that she was uncooperative, caused constant discord, was very noisy, and used obscene language.[74] A State social worker observed that Mrs. Rubenstein refused ever to leave the house, explaining that her children would have thrown her things out had she left. Mrs. Rubenstein rebuffed a suggestion by the social worker that she help with the dishes by stating that she would do nothing as long as her "worthless" husband was in the house.[75] She was readmitted on January 14, 1938.[76]

Mrs. Rubenstein was again paroled on May 27, 1938, and was discharged as "improved" on August 25, 1938.[77] She stayed in an apartment with Marion, and her separation from the rest of the family apparently ended most of the difficulties.[78] Subsequently, Jack Ruby's parents were apparently reconciled, since their alien registration forms, filed in late 1940, indicated that they both resided at Marion's address.[79]

Fannie Rubenstein was admitted to Michael Reese Hospital on April 4, 1944, as a result of a heart ailment. Her condition was complicated by an attack of pneumonia and she died at the hospital on April 11, 1944.[80] Hyman testified that, perhaps because she favored the education of her children and they recognized her difficulties in rearing them during a turbulent marriage, they all remembered Mrs. Rubenstein with warmth and affection.[81] The evidence also indicates that Jack, notwithstanding his earlier attitudes, became especially fond of his mother.[82] Following his wife's death, Joseph Rubenstein stayed with the children in Chicago, where he died at the age of 87, on December 24, 1958.[83]

Education

Records provided by the Chicago Board of Education revealed that Jack Ruby attended Smyth Grammar School from October 24, 1916, through the 1920–21 term, completing kindergarten to grade 4B.[84] He repeated the third grade.[85] During the 1921–22 school year Jack finished the fourth grade at the Clarke School; he attended Schley School for the 1924–25 term, when he completed the sixth grade. Ruby's relationship with the Institute for Juvenile Research and the Jewish Home Finding Society may explain the lack of academic records for the 1922–23 and 1923–24 school years. While there is some uncertainty about Ruby's education subsequent to September 1925,[86] it seems likely that he completed the eighth grade in 1927, when he was 16. Although Jack Ruby and others have stated that he attended at least 1 year of high school,[87] the Chicago Board of Education could not locate any record of Ruby's attending Chicago high schools.[88] Considering the absence of academic records and Jack's apathetic attitude toward school,[89] the Commission deems it unlikely that his education extended into high school.

Records of the Institute for Juvenile Research revealed that, as of June 1922, Ruby had no religious education outside the public school system.[90] However, according to their children, Jack's parents made some effort to inculcate in them a desire to adhere to the tenets of Orthodox Judaism. Jewish dietary and festival laws were observed and several of the children accompanied Joseph Rubenstein to the synagogue.[91] Earl Ruby stated that all the boys received some Hebrew school training until the breakup of the Rubenstein home in 1921.[92] However, Hyman Rubenstein testified that the instability and economic necessities of the household and the children's relationships outside the home frustrated the religious efforts of Ruby's parents.[93]

Activities

Born in a home that disintegrated when he was 10 and boasting no substantial educational background, Jack Ruby early found himself on Chicago streets attempting to provide for himself and other members of his family. An avid sports fan, he, together with many of his friends, "scalped" tickets to various sporting events.[94] He also sold numerous novelty items and knickknacks, particularly those connected with professional and collegiate athletics. Even in his youth, Ruby declined to work on a steady basis for someone else.[95]

According to his brother Hyman, Jack Ruby's only legal difficulty as a youth resulted from an altercation with a policeman about ticket scalping. Hyman, then active in local politics, was able to have charges arising out of the incident dropped.[96] Ruby has indicated that during the depression he served a short jail sentence for the unauthorized sale of copyrighted sheet music.[97]

The only other member of the Rubenstein family who appears to have had any difficulty with the law while a youth was Hyman. On May 1, 1916, Chicago's juvenile court declared Hyman incorrigible, a term covering a wide range of misbehavior. Because of the absence of informative court records and the lapse of time, the misconduct that occasioned this proceeding could not be ascertained, but Hyman is not known to have encountered subsequent difficulty.[98] Some of Ruby's childhood friends eventually became criminals;[99] however, Hyman Rubenstein, his sister Mrs. Eva Grant, and virtually all of Ruby's friends and acquaintances who were questioned reported that he was not involved with Chicago's criminal element.[100]

The evidence indicates that young Jack was not interested in political affairs.[101] Hyman was the only Rubenstein to participate actively in politics. Sponsored by various political officials, he became a sidewalk inspector and warehouse investigator for 8 years. On one occasion, he obtained a permit for Jack to sell novelties from a pushcart located in a business district during the pre-Christmas buying rush. Eventually the complaints of enraged businessmen led licensing authorities to declare that a mistake had been made and to revoke Ruby's permit.[102]

Temperament

The evidence reveals striking differences of opinion among childhood friends and acquaintances of Jack Ruby about whether he possessed violent tendencies. Many persons stated that he was mild mannered, quiet, and even tempered.[103] Former welterweight champion Barney Ross, whom Jack Ruby idolized from the inception of his boxing career,[104] stated that Ruby was "well behaved," was never a troublemaker, and was never involved with law-enforcement agencies.[105] Another friend, who became a successful businessman on the west coast, said that, as a youth, Ruby never started fights even though he was adept with his fists.[106] Other friends declared that he would, if at all possible, avoid clashes.[107]

But many other friends and acquaintances recalled that he had a hot temper and was quickly moved to violent acts or words.[108] One friend explained that in the "tough" Chicago neighborhood where they lived, self-defense was vitally important and added that Ruby was fully capable of defending himself.[109]   Another friend described Ruby as quick tempered and, though unlikely to pick fights, willing to accept any challenge without regard to the odds against him.[110] Young Jack also interfered in fights, particularly when the person he was aiding appeared to be taking a severe beating or in a disadvantageous position.[111]   Others reported that he had the reputation of being a good street brawler.[112]   One school friend recalled that when Jack argued vehemently about sports, he occasionally used a stick or other available weapon.   He reported, however, that after Ruby's anger subsided, he reverted to his normal, likable character.[113]

From early childhood, Jack Ruby was called "Sparky" by those who knew him.[114]   According to his sister Eva Grant, the nickname derived from the way Jack wobbled when he walked.   He was thought to resemble the slow-moving horse called "Sparky" or "Sparkplug" depicted in a contemporary comic strip.   Mrs. Grant testified that her brother became incensed when called "Sparky" and that from the time he was about 8 years old he would strike anyone calling him by that name.[115]   A childhood friend also recalled that Jack hated the nickname and would fight when called by it.[116]   Mrs. Grant was unsure whether the nickname "Sparky" did not also result from his quick reaction to the taunts of young friends.[117]   Hyman Rubenstein thought that the nickname derived from Jack's speed, aggressiveness, and quick thinking.   The many accounts of Ruby's lightninglike temper lend credence to the theory, widely held, that his nickname was connected with his volatility.[118]

YOUNG MANHOOD (1933–43)

San Francisco (1933–37)

Jack Ruby reported that in about 1933, he and several Chicago friends went to Los Angeles and, shortly thereafter, to San Francisco.[119]   Although there is evidence that he stayed there until 1938, 1939, or 1940,[120] Ruby stated that he returned to Chicago in about 1937,[121] and this appears to have been the case.[122]   Eva Grant testified that Ruby went to the west coast because he believed employment would be available there.[123]

Eva, who married Hyman Magid in Chicago in 1930,[124] was divorced in early 1934, and in about June of that year joined her brother Jack in San Francisco.   She and her son, Ronald, shared an apartment with him.   In 1936, Eva married Frank Granovsky, also known as Frank Grant, in San Francisco, and Ruby shared a four-room apartment with them and Ronald for a short while.[125]

Occupations and Activities

Ruby stated that when he and his friends arrived in Los Angeles, they sold a handicapper's tip sheet for horseraces at Santa Anita racetrack which had just opened.[126]   Eva Grant testified that Ruby also worked as a singing waiter in Los Angeles, but made very little money.[127]

When the group moved to San Francisco, Ruby continued to sell "tip" sheets at Bay Meadows racetrack.[128]   Subsequently, he became a door-to-door salesman of subscriptions to San Francisco newspapers.[129]   Although there is some evidence that he ultimately became chief of his crew and had several people working under him,[130] other reports indicate that this is unlikely.[131]   Eva Grant testified that she also sold newspaper subscriptions but was less proficient than her brother and relied upon him for advice and support.[132]

Although virtually all his San Francisco acquaintances knew Jack Ruby as "Sparky," [133] there is no evidence that he engaged in violent activities in San Francisco or was reputed to possess a vicious temper. One friend, who stated that he resided with Ruby and Eva for about a year, described him as a "well-mannered, likable individual who was soft spoken and meticulous in his dress and appearance." [134]   Another friend described him as a "clean-cut, honest kid," [135] and the manager of a crew with which Ruby worked stated that he had a good reputation and appeared to be an "honest, forthright person." The crew manager reported that Ruby associated with a sports crowd, some of whose members were involved with professional boxing, but not with criminals.   He added that Ruby had a personal liking for law enforcement and would have wanted to become a police officer had he been larger physically.[136]

One friend reported that although Ruby always associated with Jewish people, he never exhibited great interest in religion.[137]   Ruby met Virginia Belasco, granddaughter of the prominent playwright and actor, David Belasco, in about 1936 at a dance at the Jewish community center in San Francisco.   Miss Belasco stated that while a teenager she saw Ruby socially on several occasions between 1936 and 1941.[138]   The only other evidence concerning Ruby's social activities while in San Francisco is his statement to his long-time girl friend, Alice Nichols of Dallas,[139] that while in San Francisco he met the only other woman, Virginia Fitzgerald or Fitzsimmons, that he ever considered marrying.[140]

Chicago (1937–43)

Jack Ruby stated that following his return to Chicago, he was unemployed for a considerable period.[141]   However, when his mother was admitted to Elgin State Hospital in 1937,[142] she reported that he was employed as a "traveling salesman" apparently living away from home.[143]   Although there is conflicting evidence about his ability to earn a comfortable living,[144] he apparently was able to maintain a normal existence [145] and required no financial assistance from his family or friends.   He continued to be a so-called "hustler," scalping tickets and buying watches and other small items for resale at discount prices.[146]   One of his closest Chicago friends stated that Ruby's sales and promotions were "shady" but "legitimate."[147]

Labor union activities.—Ruby reported that in "about 1937" he became active in Local 20467 of the Scrap Iron and Junk Handlers Union.[148]   At this time, his friend, attorney Leon Cooke, was the local's financial secretary.[149]   Records provided by the Social Security Administration indicate that Ruby was employed by the union from late 1937 until early 1940;[150] he worked as a union organizer and negotiated with employers on its behalf.[151]

On December 8, 1939, the union's president, John Martin, shot Cooke, who died of gunshot wounds on January 5, 1940; Martin was subsequently acquitted on the ground of self-defense.[152]   Although a Jack Rubenstein is mentioned in the minutes of a union meeting on February 2, 1940,[153] and Ruby is reported to have said after Cooke's death that he wanted to "take over" the union,[154] the evidence indicates that Ruby was so upset by Cooke's death that he was unable to devote himself further to union activities and left its employ.[155]   Ruby reported that after Cooke's death he adopted the middle name "Leon," which he used only infrequently, in memory of his friend.[156]

Since Ruby was the ultimate source of all but one of these accounts,[157] other descriptions of Ruby's separation from the union cannot with certainty be deemed inaccurate. These reports indicated that Ruby might have been forced out of the union by a criminal group, or might have left because he lacked the emotional stability necessary for successful labor negotiations[159] or because he felt he was not earning enough money with the union.[160]

Although the AFL–CIO investigated the ethical practices of local 20467 in 1956, placed the local in trusteeship, and suspended Paul Dorfman, who succeeded Martin and Cooke, there is no evidence that Ruby's union activities were connected with Chicago's criminal element.[161]   Several longtime members of the union reported that it had a good reputation when Ruby was affiliated with it[162] and employers who negotiated with it have given no indication that it had criminal connections.[163]

Subsequent employment.—In 1941, Ruby and Harry Epstein organized the Spartan Novelty Co., a small firm that sold in various northeastern States small cedar chests containing candy and gambling devices known as punchboards.[164]   Earl Ruby and two of Jack Ruby's friends, Martin Gimpel and Martin Shargol, were also associated in this venture. The group had no fixed addresses, living in hotels.[165]

Late in 1941, Jack Ruby returned to Chicago, where he continued his punchboard business through the mails.[166]   Following the December 7, 1941, attack on Pearl Harbor, he and several friends decided to design and sell plaques commemorating the Day of Infamy. However, the venture was impeded by Ruby's perfectionistic approach to details of design which resulted in numerous production delays.[167]   By the time Ruby's copyrighted plaque[168] was finally ready for sale, the market was flooded with similar items.[169]   At about this time,

Ruby also sold busts of Franklin Delano Roosevelt.[170]   In late 1942 and 1943, Ruby was employed by the Globe Auto Glass Co.[171] and Universal Sales Co.[172]

Although one of Ruby's acquaintances at this time described him as a cuckoo nut on the subject of patriotism,[173] the evidence does not indicate that Ruby's promotion of "Remember Pearl Harbor" plaques and Roosevelt busts was motivated by patriotic or political considerations.   Rather, the sale of these items was, to Ruby, just another commercial venture, but he might also have considered these sales "a good thing." [174]   Numerous friends reported that Ruby had no interest in political affairs during this period,[175] although he greatly admired President Roosevelt.[176]

Other activities.—The evidence indicates that Ruby led a normal social life during these years.   Virginia Belasco stated that while Ruby was selling punchboards in New York during November 1941, he entertained her each weekend.[177]   Other reports indicate that Ruby fancied himself a "ladies' man," enjoyed dancing, almost always had female accompaniment and was "very gentlemanly" with women.[178]

Ruby, with several friends, frequently attempted to disrupt rallies of the German-American Bund.[179]   One acquaintance reported that Ruby was responsible for "cracking a few heads" of Bund members.[180] Apparently he joined in this activity for ethnic rather than political reasons.   The young men in the group were not organized adherents of any particular political creed, but were poolhall and tavern companions from Ruby's Jewish neighborhood who gathered on the spur of the moment to present opposition when they learned that the pro-Nazi and anti-Semitic Bund movement was planning a meeting.[181] Hyman Rubenstein testified that Ruby would fight with any person making derogatory comments about his ethnic origins, and others have stated that Ruby would fight with anyone he suspected of pro-Nazi or anti-Semitic tendencies.[182]

During this period Ruby, though temperamental, apparently engaged in no unusual acts of violence.   However, he did interfere on several occasions when he thought someone was treated unfairly.   A friend who described Ruby as "somewhat overbearing regarding the rights and feelings of others," reported that Ruby fought two college students who insulted a Negro piano player.[183]   Another friend reported that Ruby had a "bitter" fight with a man who was abusing an older woman.[184]

Maintaining his friendship with Barney Ross, and still an ardent sports fan, Ruby associated with various figures in the boxing world and regularly attended the fights at Marigold Gardens.[185]   He frequented the Lawndale Poolroom and Restaurant, a rallying point for the anti-Bundists and chief "hangout" of many of Ruby's friends.[186] In addition, Ruby, described as a "health nut" [187] who earnestly contended that he could hit harder than Joe Louis,[188] exercised at several athletic clubs.[189]

Despite Ruby's participation in "shady" financial enterprises, his association with a labor union subsequently disciplined by the AFL–

CIO, his participation in violent anti-Bund activities, and his connection with a poolroom, the evidence falls short of demonstrating that Ruby was significantly affiliated with organized crime in Chicago. Virtually all of Ruby's Chicago friends stated he had no close connection with organized crime.[190] In addition, unreliable as their reports may be, several known Chicago criminals have denied any such liaison.[191] The Commission finds it difficult to attach credence to a newspaper reporter's contrary statement that his undisclosed "syndicate sources" revealed Ruby was connected with organized crime and confidence games.[192] Ruby was unquestionably familiar, if not friendly, with some Chicago criminals,[193] but there is no evidence that he ever participated in organized criminal activity.

MILITARY ACTIVITIES (1943–46)

In September 1941, Jack Ruby was apparently classified 1–A [194] and declared eligible for the draft. Subsequently he appeared before a local board and was reclassified 1–H or 3–A.[195] Between August 31, 1941, and November 19, 1942, when it was abolished, the 1–H classification applied to registrants who had reached their 28th birthday and were, therefore, no longer liable for service.[196] The 3–A deferment applies to persons whose entry into military service presents financial hardship to dependents. Because of the length of time involved and the destruction of local draft board records, Ruby's precise status or the reason for his deferment could not be ascertained.[197] According to one somewhat unreliable report, Ruby, immediately prior to his physical examination, feigned a hearing disability and occasionally wore a hearing aid.[198] Hyman Rubenstein, who testified that Jack was deferred because of economic hardship since he was "the only one home," specifically denied the truthfulness of this allegation.[199] Early in 1943, Ruby was again classified 1–A, and, following an unsuccessful appearance before his appeal board, he was inducted into the U.S. Army Air Forces on May 21, 1943.[200] Jack was the last of the Rubenstein brothers to enter the service. Previously, Earl had enlisted in the Navy, Sam was in Army Air Force Intelligence and Hyman was in the field artillery.[201]

Except for 5 weeks in Farmingdale, N.Y., Ruby spent his military days at various airbases in the South.[202] He received the basic training given all recruits and advanced training as an aircraft mechanic.[203] On August 2, 1943, he passed marksmanship tests with the .30 caliber carbine and the .45 caliber submachinegun, but failed with the .30 caliber rifle. On February 10, 1944, he earned a sharpshooter's rating for his firing of an M1 .30 caliber carbine. His character and efficiency ratings, when determined, were excellent.[204] After attaining the rank of private first class and receiving the good conduct medal, Ruby was honorably discharged on February 21, 1946.[205]

Two persons who recalled Ruby while he was in the Army Air Forces asserted that he was extremely sensitive to insulting remarks about

Jews.[206]   When, during an argument, a sergeant called Ruby a "Jew bastard," Ruby reportedly attacked him and beat him with his fists.[207]

There is conflicting evidence about the zeal with which Ruby performed his military duties.   One associate indicated that Ruby, who at 34 was the oldest in his group, always worked harder than the others to prove that he could keep up with them.[208]   Another recalled, by contrast, that Ruby had "no liking for work" and carefully avoided situations requiring him to dirty his hands.[209]   However, there is no basis in the record for the inference that Ruby was in any way anti-American.

Ruby frequently expressed to some fellow soldiers his high regard for Franklin Delano Roosevelt.[210]   Two independent sources reported that he cried openly when informed of Roosevelt's death in April 1945.[211]   This did not indicate any sudden political interest, however, since none of his known military associates reported such an interest, and Ruby's admiration for President Roosevelt anteceded his military days.[212]

While in service, Ruby is reported to have continued his promotional ventures.   One person recalled that in 1944, Jack received punchboards and chocolates from someone in Chicago and peddled these items through the base to make extra money.   This person also indicated that Ruby enjoyed card and dice games in or near the barracks.[213]

POSTWAR CHICAGO (1946–47)

Following his discharge from the Army Air Forces in February 1946, Jack Ruby returned to Chicago.   He joined his three brothers, who had previously been discharged from the service,[214] in the Earl Products Co.   Earl Ruby testified that he was the sole investor in the enterprise, but each brother received an equal ownership interest on his return from the service.[215]   The company manufactured and sold small cedar chests and distributed punchboards.[216]   In addition, it made aluminum salt and pepper shakers, key chains, bottle openers, screwdrivers, and small hammers.[217]   Sam supervised the manufacturing end of the business, while Earl managed the office and advertising.[218]   Jack was in charge of sales, but the company was small and he had no subordinates.[219]

Because insufficient profits led to frequent arguments, Hyman soon left Earl Products.[220]   Jack, who stayed with the company through most of 1947, had many disputes with his brothers because he insisted on selling the products of other companies, such as costume jewelry, and he did not like traveling outside the Chicago area.   Earl and Sam finally purchased Jack's interest, paying him more than $14,000 in cash.[221]

Although there is some evidence to the contrary,[222] it is unlikely that Ruby was in the nightclub business in Chicago during the postwar period.   Many who have reported this may have mistaken him for Harry Rubenstein,[223] who was convicted of manslaughter and operated several such establishments.[224] None of Jack Ruby's close friends or relatives indicated that he was in the nightclub business.

Following his return from the Army, Ruby was described as ready to fight with any person who insulted Jews or the military.[225] Earl Ruby testified that on one occasion in 1946, Jack returned from downtown Chicago with his suit covered with blood. He explained at that time that he had fought with a person who had called him a "dirty Jew or something like that." [226]

Other evidence indicates that Ruby's personality was not substantially changed by his military experience. One person who met him in 1947, reported that Ruby was a "fashionable" dresser.[227] He continued to be described as soft spoken,[228] although he was also known as hot-tempered.[229] Ruby worked out regularly at an athletic club,[230] and one friend regarded him as a "Romeo," who was quite successful in attracting young women.[231]

DALLAS (1947–63)

The Move to Dallas

During World War II, Ruby's sister, Eva Grant, visited Dallas.[232] Having operated a restaurant on the west coast and considering it a lucrative business, she arranged, near the end of 1945, to lease a building under construction in Dallas, which she ran as a nightclub.[233] Part of the financing for this establishment, the Singapore Supper Club, was provided by her brothers. Jack Ruby, who apparently obtained the money from Earl Products, sent $1,100 as a downpayment on the lease, Earl contributed about $1,500, and Hyman paid for more than $2,000 worth of equipment.[234]

Before she opened the Singapore in 1947, Eva Grant engaged in the sale of metal products.[235] In that year she met Paul Roland Jones, who allegedly was seeking customers for iron pipe and whom she referred to Hyman Rubenstein.[236] Jones had, at about that time, been convicted of attempting to bribe the newly elected sheriff of Dallas.[237] On October 24, 1947, he was arrested for violating Federal narcotics statutes.[238] Jack Ruby had visited Dallas early in 1947 to help Eva Grant manage the Singapore,[239] and 5 days after Jones' arrest, Jack and Hyman Rubenstein were interrogated in Chicago by agents of the Bureau of Narcotics.[240] The brothers admitted knowing Jones but denied awareness of his connection with narcotics. During the 2 years in which Jones was appealing his conviction he and other criminals frequented the Singapore Club, then operated by Jack Ruby.[241]

Intensive investigation to determine whether Jack Ruby was criminally or otherwise connected with Jones' narcotics violation leads the Commission to conclude Ruby probably was not involved.[242] A search of the files of the Bureau of Narcotics disclosed no record that either Hyman or Jack had been prosecuted by Federal authorities in 1947.[243] Jack, Hyman, and Eva denied participating in any narcotics activities.

Jones and his coconspirators also denied that Jack was a participant.[244] One of Jones' confederates reported after the shooting of Oswald that although Jones "propositioned" the two brothers concerning narcotics, they refused to participate.[245] Moreover, when one of the conspirators was arrested with 48 pounds of raw opium in his possession, he implicated Jones and another person, both of whom were convicted, but he did not implicate Jack Ruby or his brother.[246]

Late in 1947, Ruby established permanent residence in Dallas.[247] Shortly after shooting Oswald, Ruby stated that he returned to Dallas at Eva Grant's request, to help her operate the Singapore Supper Club.[248] However, on December 21, 1963, he reported that although association with his sister had been the purpose of his initial visit to Dallas, he returned there because of the failure of his "merchandising deals" in Chicago.[249] These factors, in conjunction with his separation from Earl Products,[250] probably motivated Ruby's move to Dallas.

A different reason has been given by Steve Guthrie, former sheriff of Dallas. Guthrie reported that shortly after his election as sheriff in July 1946, Paul Roland Jones, representing other Chicago criminals, offered him a substantial amount of money to permit them to move in and manage illegal activities in Dallas. Although he never met Ruby, Guthrie asserted that these criminals frequently mentioned that Ruby would operate a "fabulous" restaurant as a front for gambling activities.[251]

Despite its source, the Commission finds it difficult to accept this report. A member of the Dallas Police Department, Lt. George E. Butler, who was present during virtually all the conversations between Guthrie and Jones and who performed considerable investigative work on the case, stated that Ruby was not involved in the bribery attempt and that he had not heard of Ruby until the investigation and trial of Jones had been completed. He explained that Ruby's connection with the case stemmed from the fact that, as mentioned previously, Jones and other criminals frequented the Singapore Supper Club.[252] And 22 recordings of the conversations between Guthrie, Butler, and Jones not only fail to mention Ruby, but indicate that Jones was to bring from outside the Dallas area only one confederate, who was not to be Jewish.[253]

The Change of Name

Sometime in 1947, Jack Ruby's brothers Earl and Sam, pursuant to a joint understanding, legally changed their names from Rubenstein to Ruby.[254] Earl testified that he changed his name because everyone called him Ruby and because a former employer advised him that it was preferable not to use a "Jewish name" on mail orders for Earl Products.[255]

On December 30, 1947, Jack changed his name to Jack L. Ruby by securing a decree from the 68th Judicial District Court of Dallas. His petition alleged that he sought the change because the name Rubenstein was misunderstood and too long and because he was "well known" as Jack L. Ruby.[256] The Bureau of Narcotics report of his relationship with Paul Roland Jones indicates that as of October 29, 1947, Jack was known as Ruby;[257] however, several persons in Dallas knew him as Rubenstein.[258]

Nightclub Operations

Except for a brief period in about 1953, when Ruby managed the Ervay Theater, a motion picture house,[259] the operation of nightclubs and dancehalls was his primary source of income, and his basic interest in life during the 16 years he spent in Dallas prior to shooting Lee Oswald. When Ruby first arrived in Dallas in 1947, he and Eva Grant jointly managed the Singapore Supper Club.[260] Shortly thereafter, she returned to the west coast. Except for sporadic trips to Dallas, she remained there until 1959, leaving Ruby a power of attorney.[261] Ruby, who had received $14,000 from the sale of his interest in Earl Products,[262] invested a substantial amount in the club, which Mrs. Grant described as "too nice a club for that part of town." [263] Ruby changed the Singapore's name to the Silver Spur Club. It was operated primarily as a dancehall, serving beer to its patrons.[264] In about 1952, Ruby borrowed $3,700 from a friend, Ralph Paul, to purchase the Bob Wills Ranch House [265] with Martin Gimpel, a former associate in the Spartan Novelty Co.[266] The Ranch House was run as a western-type nightclub.[267]

With two establishments to run, Ruby experienced substantial financial reversals in 1952. He abandoned his interest in the Ranch House and, on July 1, 1952, transferred the Silver Spur to Gimpel and Willie Epstein, who assumed some of its debts.[268] Disappointed by these setbacks, Ruby stated that he had a "mental breakdown," and "hibernated" in the Cotton Bowl Hotel in Dallas for 3 or 4 months, declining to see his friends.[269] Still depressed, he then returned to Chicago, apparently intending to remain there permanently.[270] However, he stayed only 6 weeks. Gimpel and Epstein were anxious to be rid of the Silver Spur and Ruby once again became its owner.[271]

In 1953, Ruby obtained an interest in the Vegas Club, which he operated with Joe Bonds until September 1953.[272] At that time he informed Irving Alkana, who had retained a prior ownership interest, that he was unable to meet his obligations with respect to the club. Alkana then assumed management of the Vegas until June 19, 1954, when, following numerous disagreements with him, he sold Ruby his interest.[273]

Ruby still owned the Vegas Club at the time of his arrest on November 24, 1963. However, when Eva Grant returned from San Francisco in 1959, she assumed management of the club, receiving a salary but no ownership interest.[274] The Vegas, which occasionally featured striptease acts,[275] employed a dance band and served beer, wine, soft drinks, and some prepared foods.[276]

In 1954, Ruby's Vegas associate, Joe Bonds, was convicted of sodomy and sent to a Texas penitentiary to serve an 8-year sentence.[277] In 1955,

Ruby sold the Silver Spur to Roscoe "Rocky" Robinson; however, Robinson could not obtain a license to operate the club and it was subsequently closed.[278]   For a few months during this period, Ruby also operated Hernando's Hideaway, but this venture proved unsuccessful.[279]

Sam Ruby testified that shortly after he sold his interest in Earl Products in mid-1955 and moved to Dallas, he loaned Jack $5,500 to enable him to pay Federal excise taxes on the Vegas.   As security for the loan, Sam required Jack to execute a bill of sale of the Vegas. Upon Jack's default in payment, Sam instituted suit, claiming that he owned the Vegas and that Jack had breached his promise to repurchase it.   The case was ultimately settled, with Jack retaining his ownership interest in the club.[280]

In late 1959, Jack Ruby became a partner of Joe Slatin in establishing the Sovereign Club, a private club that was apparently permitted by Texas law to sell liquor to members.[281]   Since Slatin was troubled about Dallas news stories describing police raids on a private club that permitted gambling, he felt he needed more capital.[282]   Ruby invested about $6,000 which he borrowed from his brother Earl and perhaps some of his own money.[283]

The Sovereign was described as a "plush" and exclusive club, and Ruby was apparently very anxious to attract a wealthy "carriage" trade.[284]   The venture was not successful, however.   The two men could not work together, and Slatin withdrew in early 1960.[285]   Ruby turned for new capital to Ralph Paul,[286] who had operated a Dallas club with Joe Bonds.[287]   Ruby still owed Paul $1,200 of the $3,700 loan made in connection with the Bob Wills Ranch House, but Paul advanced him another $2,200, which allowed him to pay the Sovereign's rent for 4 months.   Subsequently, Ruby spontaneously gave Paul a stock certificate representing 50 percent of the equity of the corporation owning the club.   Ruby told Paul that if the venture failed, the Sovereign's fixtures and other physical property would belong to Paul.[288]

Experiencing difficulty in recruiting sufficient members, Ruby soon found himself again unable to pay the Sovereign's monthly rent of $550.   Again he turned to Paul, who loaned him $1,650 on the condition that he change the club's method of operation.   Paul insisted that Ruby discontinue club memberships, even though this would prevent the sale of liquor, and offer striptease shows as a substitute attraction. Ruby agreed, and the Sovereign's name was changed to the Carousel Club.[289]   It became one of three downtown Dallas burlesque clubs [290] and served champagne, beer, "setups" and pizza, its only food.[291]   The Carousel generally employed four strippers, a master of ceremonies, an assistant manager, a band, three or four waitresses, and a porter or handyman.[292]   Net receipts averaged about $5,000 per month,[293] most of which was allocated to the club's payroll.[294]   Late in 1963, Ruby began to distribute "permanent passes" to the Carousel; [295] however, the cards were apparently designed solely for publicity and did not affect the club's legal status.

Employee Relationships

Ruby's employees displayed a wide range of personal reactions to him. Those associated with Ruby long enough to grow accustomed to his violent temper and constant threats of discharge generally portray him sympathetically.[296] They reported he was genuinely interested in their welfare and happiness. In addition, many former employees stated that he was a pleasant or unobjectionable employer.[297]

There is also considerable evidence that Ruby tended to dominate his employees, frequently resorted to violence in dealing with them, publicly embarrassed them,[298] sometimes attempted to cheat them of their pay,[299] and delayed paying their salaries.[300] Other employees reported Ruby continually harassed his help,[301] and used obscene language in their presence.[302] However he frequently apologized, sought to atone for his many temper tantrums,[303] and completely forgot others.[304]

One of the many violent incidents that were reported took place in 1950, when Ruby struck an employee over the head with a blackjack.[305] In 1951, after his guitarist, Willis Dickerson, told Ruby to "go to hell," Ruby knocked Dickerson to the ground, then pinned him to a wall and kicked him in the groin. During the scuffle, Dickerson bit Ruby's finger so badly that the top half of Ruby's left index finger was amputated.[306] In approximately 1955, Ruby beat one of his musicians with brass knuckles; the musician's mouth required numerous stitches.[307]

During 1960, Ruby and two entertainers, Breck Wall and Joe Peterson, entered into an agreement that the performers would produce and star in a revue at the Sovereign in exchange for a 50-percent interest in the club.[308] After performing for 2 months, the entertainers complained that they had received neither a share of the profits nor evidence of their proprietary interest. Ruby responded by hitting Peterson in the mouth, knocking out a tooth. The two men left the Sovereign's employ, but they subsequently accepted Ruby's apology and resumed their friendship with him.[309]

In September 1962, Frank Ferraro, the Carousel's handyman, became involved in a dispute at a nearby bar. Ruby told him not to get into a fight, and Ferraro told Ruby to mind his own business. Ruby then followed Ferraro to another club and beat him severely. Ferraro required emergency hospital treatment for his eye, but he decided not to press charges since Ruby paid for his hospital care.[310] In March 1963, during an argument about wages, Ruby threatened to throw a cigarette girl down the stairs of the Carousel.[311]

Ruby's relationship with his employees commanded much of his attention during the months preceding the assassination. The Carousel's comparatively high turnover rate [312] and Ruby's intense desire to succeed [313] required him to meet numerous prospective employees, patrons, and other persons who might help improve his business.

Ruby frequently encountered difficulties with the American Guild of Variety Artists (AGVA), the union which represented Carousel entertainers.[314] For several years, starting in about 1961, he unsuccessfully sought modification of AGVA's policy permitting "amateur" strippers,[315] inexperienced girls paid less than union-scale wages,[316] to perform at union houses. Ruby apparently believed his two competitors, the Weinstein brothers, were scheduling amateur shows in a manner calculated to destroy his business.[317] Ruby's discontent with AGVA grew particularly acute during the late summer and early fall of 1963 when, in addition to meeting with AGVA officials,[318] he called upon several acquaintances, including known criminals, who, he thought, could influence AGVA on his behalf.[319] Other problems with AGVA arose because of his policy of continuous shows, which did not give masters of ceremonies enough time off,[320] and his alleged use of AGVA members to mingle with patrons to promote the consumption of liquor.[321]

In June 1963, Ruby visited New Orleans, where he obtained the services of a stripper known as "Jada," [322] who became his featured performer.[323] Jada and Ruby had numerous contract disputes and he was concerned about her high salary, recurrent absenteeism, and diminishing drawing power.[324] Moreover, he thought that Jada had deliberately exceeded even the Carousel's liberal standards of decency in order to cause him to lose his license or to obtain publicity for herself.[325] On several occasions Ruby excitedly turned off the spotlights during her act, and at the end of October 1963, he fired her.[326] However, after Jada sued out a peace bond, she apparently recovered a week's salary from Ruby.[327]

In addition to problems with its star stripper, the Carousel was required to employ three masters of ceremonies in rapid succession following the departure in about September 1963, of Wally Weston, who worked there about 15 months.[328] And in early November, the band that had played at the Vegas Club for about 8 years left the Vegas to accept the offer of another Dallas club.[329]

Financial Data and Tax Problems

Jack Ruby's pockets and the trunk of his car served as his bank. With a few exceptions, Ruby and his clubs rarely employed bank accounts.[330] Instead, Ruby carried his cash with him, paying the bulk of his expenses and debts directly out of club receipts.[331]

During the latter half of 1963, the Carousel, the Vegas, and Ruby each maintained checking accounts at the Merchants State Bank in Dallas. Balances of the latter two accounts never exceeded $275. In July 1963, the Carousel's account had more than $500; after August 8, its maximum balance was less than $300. Between May 31 and November 24, 1963, 53 checks were drawn on the three accounts; with the exception of one check for $129.47, all were for less than $100.[332] He generally purchased cashier's checks at the Merchants State Bank to pay his monthly rental of $550 for the Carousel and $500 for the Vegas.[333] He also purchased cashier's checks during the 3 months prior to the assassination to pay about $1,500 to the Texas State treasurer, $110 to Temple Shearith Israel, apparently for Jewish high holy day tickets, and $60 to the American Society of Authors and Publishers.[334]

Records of the more than 50 banking institutions checked during the investigation of Ruby's financial affairs [335] revealed that he had three other dormant accounts, all with small balances.[336] Two safety deposit boxes belonging to Ruby, opened by Texas officials pursuant to search warrants, were empty and unused for more than a year prior to the assassination.[337] Although Ruby negotiated several loans at the Merchants State Bank,[338] there is no evidence that he was the maker or co-maker of other loans,[339] and, after investigation, the Dallas Police Department found no record that Ruby cosigned the note of any policeman at any time.[340]

Ruby's financial records were chaotic. One accountant abandoned efforts to prepare income tax returns and other financial statements because of the hopeless disarray of Ruby's data.[341] The record indicates that Ruby was frequently weeks, if not months, late in filing Federal tax forms and that he held numerous conferences with Internal Revenue agents who attempted to obtain the delinquent statements.[342]

Ruby encountered serious difficulties with respect to State franchise and Federal excise and income taxes. The Texas charter of the corporation controlling the Sovereign and Carousel clubs was canceled in 1961, because Ruby failed to pay Texas franchise taxes.[343] And, only after numerous conferences, did Ruby and representatives of the Internal Revenue Service reach agreements on installment payments of various Federal tax liabilities, to which Ruby more or less adhered.[344]

Ruby's primary difficulty concerned Federal excise taxes. Advised by an attorney that the Vegas Club, a dance hall providing food, was not subject to Federal excise taxes because it was not a "cabaret," Ruby charged Vegas patrons on the assumption that no excise taxes were due. However, his attorney reported, when Federal courts ruled that dance halls providing "incidental" food were subject to excise taxes as "cabarets," [345] Ruby became liable to the Federal Government for more than 6 years of taxes, amounting, with interest, to almost exactly $40,000.[346]

Ruby also fell behind on his personal income tax payments. At the time of his arrest he owed more than $4,400 for 1959 and 1960.[347] Remittances accompanied his 1961 and 1962 tax forms, the latter received by the office of the Dallas District Director on September 18, 1963.[348] The following table summarizes amounts which Ruby reported as gross and net income from the Vegas Club from 1956 to 1962; and the taxes due: [349]

Year	Gross income	Net income	Tax
1962	$41,462.77	$5,619.65	[1] $1,217.75
1961	40,411.00	6,255.29	[1] 1,200.00
1960	44,482.41	9,703.90	2,221.39
1959	50,981.95	14,060.86	3,778.17
1958	37,755.65	3,274.64	586.52
1957	33,671.60	2,619.52	438.41
1956	30,695.27	7,437.01	1,527.10

[1] Estimated.

On his income tax forms, Ruby did not itemize personal deductions and claimed only his own exemption. For 1962, Ruby reported salary income of $650 from the corporation controlling the Carousel, and $900 for 1961.[350]

Ruby and officers of the Internal Revenue Service frequently discussed methods of satisfying his large excise and income tax liability.[351] In 1960, the Government filed tax liens for more than $20,000.[352] In November 1962, the Government rejected Ruby's offer to pay $8,000 to compromise the assessed taxes of more than $20,000 because he had not filed returns for other Federal taxes and had not paid these taxes as they became due. These other taxes, for the period September 1959 through June 1962, amounted to an additional $20,000.[353] In June 1963, Ruby submitted an offer of $3,000 to compromise all past assessments; the offer was not acted upon prior to November 24, 1963.[354]

Other Business Ventures

In addition to nightclub management and ownership, Ruby participated in numerous other commercial ventures. He was able to do so primarily because work at the clubs consumed few of his daytime hours. Many of Ruby's ventures related to show business, others were somewhat speculative promotions; almost all ended unsuccessfully. While operating the Silver Spur Club, Ruby sold costume jewelry at discount rates,[355] and, in about 1951, he sold sewing machine attachments at the Texas State Fair.[356] Approximately a year later, he managed a talented young Negro boy, "Little Daddy" Nelson. The boy appeared at the Silver Spur, the Vegas Club, and the Bob Wills Ranch House. In about 1953 or 1954, Ruby took "Little Daddy" and his parents to Chicago to obtain a television appearance for him. However, shortly after their arrival, Ruby was confronted by a second woman claiming to be "Little Daddy's" mother. Upon advice of counsel, Ruby decided to abandon the venture.[357]

In 1954, Ruby became interested in the sale of pizza crusts to Dallas restaurants.[358] He is also reported to have sold an arthritic preparation [359] and to have manufactured and sold "Miniron," a liquid vitamin formula.[360] In about 1958 or 1959, Ruby attempted to build and sell log cabins at a Texas lake resort.[361] In early 1959, he investigated the possibility of selling jeeps to Cuba.[362] He is also reported to have furnished entertainment for a Dallas hotel,[363] to have promoted records for musicians [364] and to have sold English stainless steel razor blades.[365]

In October 1963 Ruby assisted the producers of a carnival show, "How Hollywood Makes Movies," appearing at the Texas State Fair.[366] At about this time Ruby also sought to open a new club in Dallas. He conferred with numerous persons and placed advertisements in Dallas newspapers in an attempt to obtain financial backing.[367] Assuming that he would be occupied by the new club, Ruby offered his oldest brother, Hyman, a managerial post at the Carousel. However, Hyman, who had recently lost his sales territory, declined the offer because he felt he was too old for the nightclub business.[368]

799

Ruby unsuccessfully attempted to sell "twistboards," an exercising device consisting of two square fiberboards separated by ball bearings. Despite the contrary advice of his brother Earl,[369] Jack ordered several dozen twistboards and had 2,000 promotional flyers published.[370] He had one of his strippers demonstrate the twistboards at the Texas Products Show during the first week of November 1963.[371]

Arrests and Violations

Between 1949 and November 24, 1963, Ruby was arrested eight times by the Dallas Police Department. The dates, charges, and dispositions of these arrests are as follows:[372] February 4, 1949, Ruby paid a $10 fine for disturbing the peace. July 26, 1953, Ruby was suspected of carrying a concealed weapon; however, no charges were filed and Ruby was released on the same day. May 1, 1954, Ruby was arrested for allegedly carrying a concealed weapon and violating a peace bond; again no charges were filed and Ruby was released on the same day. December 5, 1954, Ruby was arrested for allegedly violating State liquor laws by selling liquor after hours; the complaint was dismissed on February 8, 1955.[373] June 21, 1959, Ruby was arrested for allegedly permitting dancing after hours; the complaint was dismissed on July 8, 1959. August 21, 1960, Ruby was again arrested for allegedly permitting dancing after hours; Ruby posted $25 bond and was released on that date. February 12, 1963, Ruby was arrested on a charge of simple assault; he was found not guilty February 27, 1963. Finally, on March 14, 1963, Ruby was arrested for allegedly ignoring traffic summonses; a $35 bond was posted.

When Ruby applied for a beer license in March 1961, he reported that he had been arrested "about four or five times" between 1947 and 1953.[374] Between 1950 and 1963, he received 20 tickets for motor vehicle violations, paying four $10 fines and three of $3.[375] In 1956 and 1959, Ruby was placed on 6 months' probation as a traffic violator.

Ruby was also frequently suspended by the Texas Liquor Control Board. In August 1949, when he was operating the Silver Spur, he was suspended for 5 days on a charge of "Agents—Moral Turpitude." In 1953 Ruby received a 5-day suspension because of an obscene show, and, in 1954, a 10-day suspension for allowing a drunkard on his premises.[376] On February 18, 1954, he was suspended for 5 days because of an obscene striptease act at the Silver Spur and for the consumption of alcoholic beverages during prohibited hours.[377] On March 26, 1956, Ruby was suspended by the liquor board for 3 days because several of his checks were dishonored.[378] On October 23, 1961, he received another 3-day suspension because an agent solicited the sale of alcoholic beverages for consumption on licensed premises.[379]

Police Associations

Although the precise nature of his relationship to members of the Dallas Police Department is not susceptible of conclusive evaluation, the evidence indicates that Ruby was keenly interested in policemen and their work.[380] Jesse Curry, chief of the Dallas Police Department, testified that no more than 25 to 50 of Dallas' almost 1,200 policemen were acquainted with Ruby.[381] However, the reports of present and past members of the Dallas Police Department as well as Ruby's employees and acquaintances indicate that Ruby's police friendships were far more widespread than those of the average citizen.[382]

There is no credible evidence that Ruby sought special favors from police officers or attempted to bribe them.[383] Although there is considerable evidence that Ruby gave policemen reduced rates,[384] declined to exact any cover charge from them,[385] and gave them free coffee and soft drinks,[386] this hospitality was not unusual for a Dallas nightclub operator.[387] Ruby's personal attachment to police officers is demonstrated by reports that he attended the funeral of at least one policeman killed in action and staged a benefit performance for the widow of another.[388] Ruby regarded several officers as personal friends, and others had worked for him.[389] Finally, at least one policeman regularly dated, and eventually married, one of the Carousel's strippers.[390]

Underworld Ties

From the time that Ruby arrived in Dallas in 1947, he was friendly with numerous underworld figures. One of his earliest Dallas acquaintances was Paul Roland Jones, who was convicted of attempting to bribe the sheriff of Dallas and engaging in the sale of narcotics.[391] Joe Bonds, one of Ruby's partners in the Vegas Club, had a criminal record.[392]

Ruby, who enjoyed card playing [393] and horse racing,[394] was friendly with several professional gamblers. In 1959, he visited Cuba at the invitation and expense of Lewis McWillie, a professional gambler.[395] Alice Nichols reported that Ruby's refusal to give up gambling was one reason why she never seriously considered marrying him.[396] When Sidney Seidband, a Dallas gambler, was arrested in Oklahoma City, his list of gambling acquaintances included Jack Ruby.[397] And other friends of Ruby have been identified as gamblers.[398] Finally, two persons of questionable reliability have reported that Ruby's consent was necessary before gambling or narcotics operations could be launched in Dallas.[399]

Based on its evaluation of the record, however, the Commission believes that the evidence does not establish a significant link between Ruby and organized crime. Both State and Federal officials have indicated that Ruby was not affiliated with organized criminal activity.[400] And numerous persons have reported that Ruby was not connected with such activity.[401]

Travels

Despite reports that Ruby visited Havana, Las Vegas, New York, Chicago, Honolulu, and Mexican border towns, most of his time subsequent to 1947 was spent in Dallas. Some of his travels, including his efforts in behalf of "Little Daddy" Nelson and his visit to New Orleans in June 1963 have been discussed.[402]   Ruby stated that he went to Chicago in 1952, in 1958 when his father died, and in August 1963 when he met members of his family at O'Hare International Airport while en route from New York to Dallas.[403] His August trip to New York motivated by his difficulties with the American Guild of Variety Artists and his desire to obtain talent, has been completely established by hotel records.[404] Early in 1963 Ruby also traveled to Wichita, Kans., because of his interest in stripper Gail Raven,[405] and on May 25, 1963, he apparently registered in an Oklahoma motel.[406]

Although Ruby denies being in Las Vegas after 1937,[407] there are unsupported rumors that he was in that city in late 1962,[408] and the early part of November 1963.[409] Reports that he was in Las Vegas during the weekend prior to the assassination [410] appear similarly unfounded.[411]

There is some uncertainty about Ruby's trip to Havana, Cuba, in 1959. The evidence indicates that he accepted an invitation from gambler Lewis J. McWillie, who subsequently became a violent anti-Castroite, to visit Havana at McWillie's expense.[412] Ruby apparently met McWillie in about 1950, when McWillie operated a Dallas nightclub.[413] McWillie, whom Ruby said he idolized,[414] supervised gambling activities at Havana's Tropicana Hotel in 1959 and later was employed in a managerial capacity in a Las Vegas gambling establishment.[415] Ruby testified that he went to Havana for 8 days in August 1959 and left because he was not interested in its gambling activities.[416] McWillie corroborated this story except that he stated only that Ruby visited Havana "sometime in 1959." [417] Three Chicagoans reported seeing Ruby in Havana during the Labor Day weekend in 1959.[418] Meyer Panitz, an acquaintance of McWillie, reported that when he met Ruby in Miami during the "summer of 1959" Ruby stated that he was returning from a pleasure trip to Cuba.[419] The theory that the trip to Havana had conspiratorial implications is discussed in chapter VI. There is no reliable evidence that Ruby went to Havana subsequent to September 1959.[420]

Although Ruby denied ever being in Hawaii,[421] there is some evidence that during the summer of 1961 he was in Honolulu seeking dancing talent.[422] While it is unlikely that Ruby would forget a trip to Honolulu in 1961, there is no other indication that such a trip, if it occurred, had any sinister motives.

CHARACTER AND INTERESTS

Family Relationships

As mentioned previously,[423] Eva Grant was the only member of the family living in Dallas when Ruby returned to that city in late 1947. In 1948, she returned to the west coast, visiting Dallas sporadically until 1959, when she assumed management of the Vegas.[424] Despite their recurring arguments, during which they sometimes came to blows,[425] Ruby was closer to Eva than any of his brothers or sisters. In the summer of 1963, Eva complained bitterly to Ruby because he gave a friend about $800 instead of paying Vegas Club bills. Eva, citing her poor health, stated that she should be hospitalized. Ruby rejoined that he had provided her money to enter a hospital. He then shoved her, causing her to fall back about 8 feet and hurt her arm and shoulder. At this point Ruby insisted he wanted her to leave the Vegas Club.[426]

Ruby frequently told Eva to submit to an operation and in early November 1963 she consented. She was hospitalized for a week, leaving about November 13.[427] While she was in the hospital, Jack called Earl and Sam, requesting them to convey their concern to Eva.[428] According to Eva, Jack visited her at the hospital two or three times a day. He kept in constant touch with her throughout the weekend of November 22.[429]

Sam Ruby moved to Dallas from Chicago in July 1955, after selling his interest in the Earl Products Co.[430] His son's asthma and Eva's suggestion that he work as a builder in Dallas prompted the move.[431] Apparently as a result of difficulties in collecting the $5,500 Sam loaned Jack in 1955 to pay Federal excise taxes, [432] Jack and Sam were never particularly close to each other. However, Sam entered into a partnership in an unsuccessful ice cream business with Jack's close friend, Ralph Paul.[433] Jack visited Sam and his family occasionally, especially on Jewish holidays, and from time to time they spoke to each other by telephone.[434]

Jack had sporadic contacts with his brother Earl, who remained in Chicago until about 1960, when he moved to Detroit.[435] The most successful of the brothers, Earl often gave Jack business advice and capital.[436] He estimated, perhaps conservatively, that, when arrested, Jack owed him $15,000.[437] The evidence also indicates that Jack borrowed at least $1,000, and probably more, from his sister Marion in Chicago.[438]

Social Relationships

There have been statements that Ruby was a homosexual. The available evidence does not support the allegation. There is no evidence of homosexuality on his part; Ruby did not frequent known gathering places for homosexuals,[439] many of the reports were inherently suspect or based upon questionable or inaccurate premises,[440] and Ruby and most of his associates and employees denied the charge.[441] All the allegations were based on hearsay or derive from Ruby's lisp or a "feeling" that Ruby was a "sissy," seemed "weird," acted effeminately, and sometimes spoke in a high-pitched voice when angry.[442] Some proceeded upon the erroneous theory that Ruby did not date women.[443]

For the better part of 11 years, Ruby dated Mrs. Alice Reaves Nichols, a blonde divorcee, 4 years younger than he. Mrs. Nichols, secretary to a Dallas life insurance company executive,[444] testified that she saw Ruby twice a week between 1948 and 1956, and once a week from then until about 1959.[445] Ruby discussed marriage with Mrs. Nichols,[446] but Mrs. Nichols stated that while dating Ruby she was seeing other men and he was taking out other women.[447] Although there are sharply conflicting reports about whether Ruby dated women who worked for him,[448] the record indicates that Ruby sought and enjoyed feminine company.[449]

Affection for Dogs

Ruby was extremely fond of dogs. Numerous persons stated that he was constantly accompanied by several of the dogs he owned.[450] Testimony at Ruby's trial in March 1964 indicated that he referred to his dogs as his "children." [451] He also became extremely incensed when he witnessed the maltreatment of any of his dogs.[452]

Religious Interests

Reared in the Jewish faith, Jack Ruby was not especially devout. Rabbi Hillel Silverman, whose conservative temple Ruby favored, reported that when Ruby's father died in 1958, Ruby came to services twice daily for the prescribed period of 11 months to recite the traditional memorial prayer.[453] Ruby normally attended services only on the Jewish high holy days and he was quite unfamiliar with the Hebrew language.[454]

Ruby was apparently somewhat sensitive to his identity as a Jew. He forbade his comedians to tell stories directed at Jews or Jewish practices [455] and, on several occasions after 1947, he fought with persons making derogatory remarks about his ethnic origins.[456] The evidence also indicates that he was deeply upset that an advertisement insulting President Kennedy appeared above a Jewish-sounding name.[457]

Physical Activities and Violence

While in Dallas, Ruby continued attempts to keep in excellent physical condition. He frequently exercised at the YMCA, the Carousel, and his apartment, where he maintained a set of weights.[458] Ruby was extremely concerned about his weight and health, including his baldness,[459] and about his appearance in general.[460]

Ruby's concern for his physical well-being was partially motivated by practical considerations, for he was his own unofficial club bouncer. On about 15 occasions since 1950, he beat with his fists, pistol whipped, or blackjacked patrons who became unruly.[461] At other times, he ejected troublesome customers without a beating,[462] in many instances, justifiably.[463] However, many people stated that he employed more force than necessary, particularly because he often ended a fracas by throwing his victim down the stairs of the Carousel.[464]

Besides acting as a bouncer, Ruby on numerous other occasions severely beat people who were not club patrons, usually employing only his fists. Several of these episodes have been discussed in connection with Ruby's relationship with his employees.[465] In 1951, Ruby attacked a man who had called him a "kike Jew" and knocked out a tooth.[466] At about that time Ruby is also reported to have knocked a man down from behind and then to have kicked him in the face.[467] In about 1958, Ruby disarmed a man who had drawn a gun on him at the Vegas, beat him almost to death, put the gun back in the man's pocket, and threw him down the stairs.[468] In 1958, Ruby reportedly knocked down a man at the Vegas who was 6'3'' tall and weighed 230 pounds. Ruby was approximately 5'9'' tall and weighed about 175 pounds.[469] Ruby then made the man, who had slapped his date, crawl out of the club.[470] In a fight at the Vegas, reportedly witnessed by policemen, Ruby severely beat a heavyweight boxer who had threatened him.[471]

During 1962, several violent episodes occurred. Ruby beat a man who refused to pay admission or leave and then shoved him down the stairs.[472] He "jostled" a woman down the stairs of the Carousel and struck her escort, who was "much smaller" than he.[473] On one occasion, Ruby picked up a man who was arguing with his date, knocked him to the floor, cursed him, and then removed him from the Vegas.[474] When a cabdriver entered the Carousel and inquired about a patron who had neglected to pay his fare, Ruby struck the cabdriver.[475]

In February 1963, Ruby badly beat Don Tabon, who had made some remarks about Ruby's lady companion, injuring Tabon's eye.[476] Ruby was acquitted of a charge of assault and Tabon sought no monetary relief because he believed Ruby financially incapable of satisfying any resulting judgment. A doctor who went to the Carousel several times between August and November 1963, stated that on each occasion Ruby ejected someone from the club.[477]

Buddy Turman, a prizefighter and Ruby's friend, stated that Ruby "picked his shots." [478] According to Turman, a bouncer at the Vegas for about a year, Ruby's victim was frequently drunk, female, or otherwise incapable of successfully resisting Ruby's attack. The evidence indicates that, unlike his youthful escapades, Ruby was often malicious. He frequently felt contrite, however, when his anger had passed or when his victim was an old acquaintance, and he would seek to make amends for his violent temper.[479]

With two exceptions, there is no evidence that Ruby settled disputes with firearms. Shortly before Joe Bonds' conviction in 1954, Ruby is reported to have chased Bonds with a pistol.[480] And, Larry Crafard reported that about a week before the assassination, Ruby told him to get Ruby's gun so that an AGVA official and former employee, Earl Norman, could be ejected.[481] Although Ruby did not often use his gun, it was frequently accessible when he was carrying large amounts of money.[482]

Generosity to Friends and the Need for Recognition

While Ruby often flared up and acted aggressively, he seemed to calm down or forget his anger quickly, and there is also a great deal of evidence that he was extremely generous to his friends. He loaned money to them and apparently cared little whether the loans would be repaid.[483] He was quick to offer employment to persons desperately in need of a job [484] and he lent considerable aid to persons seeking work elsewhere.[485] Moreover, when friends or new acquaintances had no roof over their heads, Ruby's apartment was frequently theirs to share.[486]

Ruby's unusual generosity may be explained in part by his extremely emotional reaction to persons in distress, which may have resulted from his firsthand familiarity with poverty, and by his unusual craving to be recognized and relied upon.[487] Many of Ruby's acquaintances described him as a "publicity hound," "glad hander," and "name dropper," one always seeking to be the center of attention.[488] Apparently the "egocentrism" of his youth [489] never left Ruby. Yet, frequently he sought reassurance from persons he admired.[490]

Polygraph Examination of Jack Ruby

PRELIMINARY ARRANGEMENTS

As early as December of 1963, Jack Ruby expressed his desire to be examined with a polygraph, truth serum, or any other scientific device which would test his veracity.[1] The attorneys who defended Ruby in the State criminal proceedings in Texas agreed that he should take a polygraph examination to test any conspiratorial connection between Ruby and Oswald.[2] To obtain such a test, Ruby's defense counsel filed motions in court and also requested that the FBI administer such an examination to Ruby.[3] During the course of a psychiatric examination on May 11, 1964, Ruby is quoted as saying: "I want to tell the truth. I want a polygraph * * *."[4] In addition, numerous letters were written to the President's Commission on behalf of Ruby requesting a polygraph examination.[5]

When Ruby testified before the Commission in Dallas County Jail on June 7, 1964, his first words were a request for a lie detector test. The Commission hearing commenced with the following exchanges:

Mr. JACK RUBY. Without a lie detector test on my testimony, my verbal statements to you, how do you know if I am telling the truth?

Mr. TONAHILL [Defense Counsel]. Don't worry about that, Jack.

Mr. RUBY. Just a minute, gentlemen.

Chief Justice WARREN. You wanted to ask something, did you, Mr. Ruby?

Mr. RUBY. I would like to be able to get a lie detector test or truth serum of what motivated me to do what I did at that particular time, and it seems as you get further into something, even though you know what you did, it operates against you somehow, brain washes you, that you are weak in what you want to tell the truth about and what you want to say which is the truth.

Now Mr. Warren, I don't know if you got any confidence in the lie detector test and the truth serum, and so on.

Chief Justice WARREN. I can't tell you just how much confidence I have in it, because it depends so much on who is taking it, and so forth.

But I will say this to you, that if you and your counsel want any kind of test, I will arrange it for you. I would be glad to do that, if you want it. I wouldn't suggest a lie detector test to testify the truth.

We will treat you just the same as we do any other witness, but if you want such a test, I will arrange for it.

Mr. Ruby. I do want it. Will you agree to that, Joe?
Mr. Tonahill. I sure do, Jack.[6]

Throughout Ruby's testimony before the Commission, he repeated his request on numerous occasions that he be given an opportunity to take a lie detector test.[7] Ruby's insistence on taking a polygraph examination is reflected right to the end of the proceedings where in the very last portion of the transcribed hearings Ruby states:

Mr. Ruby. All I want to do is to tell the truth, and the only way you can know it is by the polygraph, as that is the only way you can know it.
Chief Justice Warren. That we will do for you.[8]

Following Ruby's insistence on a polygraph test, the Commission initiated arrangements to have the FBI conduct such an examination.[9] A detailed set of questions was prepared for the polygraph examination, which was set for July 16, 1964.[10] A few days before the scheduled test, the Commission was informed that Ruby's sister, Eva Grant, and his counsel, Joe H. Tonahill, opposed the polygraph on the ground that psychiatric examinations showed that his mental state was such that the test would be meaningless.[11]

The Commission was advised that Sol Dann, a Detroit attorney representing the Ruby family, had informed the Dallas office of the FBI on July 15, 1964, that a polygraph examination would affect Ruby's health and would be of questionable value according to Dr. Emanuel Tanay, a Detroit psychiatrist.[12] On that same date, Assistant Counsel Arlen Specter discussed by telephone the polygraph examination with Defense Counsel Joe H. Tonahill, who expressed his personal opinion that a polygraph examination should be administered to Ruby.[13] By letter dated July 15, 1964, Dallas District Attorney Henry Wade requested that the polygraph examination cover the issue of premeditation as well as the defensive theories in the case.[14]

Against this background, it was decided that a representative of the Commission would travel to Dallas to determine whether Jack Ruby wanted to take the polygraph test. Since Ruby had had frequent changes in attorneys and because he was presumed to be sane, the final decision on the examination was his, especially in view of his prior personal insistence on the test.[15] In the jury conference room at the Dallas jail on July 18, Assistant Counsel Arlen Specter, representing the Commission, informed Chief Defense Counsel Clayton Fowler, co-Counsel Tonahill and Assistant District Attorney William F. Alexander that the Commission was not insisting on or even requesting that the test be taken, but was merely fulfilling its commitment to make the examination available.[16] In the event Ruby had changed his mind and would so state for the record, that would conclude the issue as far as the Commission was concerned.[17]

Chief Defense Counsel Fowler had objected to the test. He conferred with Jack Ruby in his cell and then returned stating that

Ruby insisted on taking the examination.[18] Mr. Fowler requested that (1) Dr. Tanay, the Detroit psychiatrist, be present; (2) the results of the test not be disclosed other than to the Commission; (3) the questions to be asked not be disclosed to the District Attorney's office; and (4) the results of the test be made available to defense counsel.[19] Sheriff William Decker announced his intention to have Allan L. Sweatt, his chief criminal deputy who was also a polygraph operator, present to maintain custody of Jack Ruby while the examination was being administered.[20] Assistant District Attorney Alexander requested a list of questions, a copy of the recording made by the polygraph machine and a copy of the report interpreting the test.[21] In response to the numerous requests, the procedure was determined that the questions to be asked of Ruby would be discussed in a preliminary session in the presence of defense counsel, the assistant district attorney and Chief Jailer E. L. Holman, who was to replace Sweatt.[22] The assistant district attorney would not be present when Ruby answered the questions, but Jailer Holman was allowed to remain to retain custody of Ruby.[23] No commitment was made on behalf of the Commission as to what disclosure would be made of the results of the examination.[24] Since Dr. Tanay was not in Dallas and therefore could not be present,[25] arrangements were made to have in attendance Dr. William R. Beavers, a psychiatrist who had previously examined and evaluated Ruby's mental state.[26]

At the conclusion of the lengthy preliminary proceedings, Ruby entered the jury conference room at 2:23 p.m. and was informed that the Commission was prepared to fulfill its commitment to offer him a polygraph examination, but was not requesting the test.[27] On behalf of the Commission, Assistant Counsel Specter warned Ruby that anything he said could be used against him.[28] Chief Defense Counsel Fowler advised Ruby of his objections to the examination.[29] Ruby then stated that he wanted the polygraph examination conducted and that he wanted the results released to the public as promptly as possible.[30] Special Agent Bell P. Herndon, polygraph operator of the FBI, obtained a written "consent to interview with polygraph" signed by Jack Ruby.[31] Herndon then proceeded to administer the polygraph examination by breaking the questions up into series which were ordinarily nine questions in length and consisted of relevant interrogatories and control questions.[32]

ADMINISTRATION OF THE TEST

During the course of the polygraph examination Jack Ruby answered the relevant questions as follows:

Q. Did you know Oswald before November 22, 1963?
A. No.[33]
Q. Did you assist Oswald in the assassination?
A. No.[34]
Q. Are you now a member of the Communist Party?

A. No.[35]

Q. Have you ever been a member of the Communist Party?

A. No.[36]

Q. Are you now a member of any group that advocates the violent overthrow of the United States Government?

A. No.[37]

Q. Have you ever been a member of any group that advocates violent overthrow of the United States Government?

A. No.[38]

Q. Between the assassination and the shooting, did anybody you know tell you they knew Oswald?

A. No.[39]

Q. Aside from anything you said to George Senator on Sunday morning, did you ever tell anyone else that you intended to shoot Oswald?

A. No.[40]

Q. Did you shoot Oswald in order to silence him?

A. No.[41]

Q. Did you first decide to shoot Oswald on Friday night?

A. No.[42]

Q. Did you first decide to shoot Oswald on Saturday morning?

A. No.[43]

Q. Did you first decide to shoot Oswald on Saturday night?

A. No.[44]

Q. Did you first decide to shoot Oswald on Sunday Morning?

A. Yes.[45]

Q. Were you on the sidewalk at the time Lieutenant Pierce's car stopped on the ramp exit?

A. Yes.[46]

Q. Did you enter the jail by walking through an alleyway?

A. No.[47]

Q. Did you walk past the guard at the time Lieutenant Pierce's car was parked on the ramp exit?

A. Yes.[48]

Q. Did you talk with any Dallas police officers on Sunday, November 24, prior to the shooting of Oswald?

A. No.[49]

Q. Did you see the armored car before it entered the basement?

A. No.[50]

Q. Did you enter the police department through a door at the rear of the east side of the jail?

A. No.[51]

Q. After talking to Little Lynn did you hear any announcement that Oswald was about to be moved?

A. No.[52]

Q. Before you left your apartment Sunday morning, did anyone tell you the armored car was on the way to the police department?

A. No.[53]

Q. Did you get a Wall Street Journal at the Southwestern Drug Store during the week before the assassination?

A. No.[54]

Q. Do you have any knowledge of a Wall Street Journal addressed to Mr. J. E. Bradshaw?

A. No.[55]

Q. To your knowledge, did any of your friends or did you telephone the FBI in Dallas between 2 or 3 a.m. Sunday morning?

A. No.[56]

Q. Did you or any of your friends to your knowledge telephone the sheriff's office between 2 or 3 a.m. Sunday morning?

A. No.[57]

Q. Did you go to the Dallas police station at any time on Friday, November 22, 1963, before you went to the synagogue?

A. No.[58]

Q. Did you go to the synagogue that Friday night?

A. Yes.[59]

Q. Did you see Oswald in the Dallas jail on Friday night?

A. Yes.[60]

Q. Did you have a gun with you when you went to the Friday midnight press conference at the jail?

A. No.[61]

Q. Is everything you told the Warren Commission the entire truth?

A. Yes.[62]

Q. Have you ever knowingly attended any meetings of the Communist Party or any other group that advocates violent overthrow of the Government?

A. No.[63]

Q. Is any member of your immediate family or any close friend, a member of the Communist Party?

A. No.[64]

Q. Is any member of your immediate family or any close friend a member of any group that advocates the violent overthrow of the Government?

A. No.[65]

Q. Did any close friend or any member of your immediate family ever attend a meeting of the Communist Party?

A. No.[66]

Q. Did any close friend or any member of your immediate family ever attend a meeting of any group that advocates the violent overthrow of the Government?

A. No.[67]

Q. Did you ever meet Oswald at your post office box?

A. No.[68]

Q. Did you use your post office mailbox to do any business with Mexico or Cuba?

A. No.[69]

Q. Did you do business with Castro-Cuba?

A. No.[70]

Q. Was your trip to Cuba solely for pleasure?

A. Yes.[71]

Q. Have you now told us the truth concerning why you carried $2,200 in cash on you?

A. Yes.[72]

Q. Did any foreign influence cause you to shoot Oswald?

A. No.[73]

Q. Did you shoot Oswald because of any influence of the underworld?

A. No.[74]

Q. Did you shoot Oswald because of a labor union influence?

A. No.[75]

Q. Did any long-distance telephone calls which you made before the assassination of the President have anything to do with the assassination?

A. No.[76]

Q. Did any of your long-distance telephone calls concern the shooting of Oswald?

A. No.[77]

Q. Did you shoot Oswald in order to save Mrs. Kennedy the ordeal of a trial?

A. Yes.[78]

Q. Did you know the Tippit that was killed?

A. No.[79]

Q. Did you tell the truth about relaying the message to Ray Brantley to get McWillie a few guns?

A. Yes.[80]

Q. Did you go to the assembly room on Friday night to get the telephone number of KLIF?

A. Yes.[81]

Q. Did you ever meet with Oswald and Officer Tippit at your club?

A. No.[82]

Q. Were you at the Parkland Hospital at any time on Friday?

A. No.[83]

Q. Did you say anything when you shot Oswald other than what you've testified about?

A. No.[84]

Q. Have members of your family been physically harmed because of what you did?

A. No.[85]

Q. Do you think members of your family are now in danger because of what you did?

(No response.)[86]

Q. Is Mr. Fowler in danger because he is defending you?

(No response.)[87]

Q. Did "Blackie" Hanson speak to you just before you shot Oswald?

A. No.[88]

INTERPRETATION OF THE TEST

A polygraph examination is designed to detect physiological responses to stimuli in a carefully controlled interrogation. Such responses may accompany and indicate deception.[89] The polygraph instrument derives its name from the Greek derivative "poly" meaning many and the word "graph" meaning writings.[90] The polygraph chart writings consist of three separate markings placed on a graph reflecting three separate physiological reactions.[91] A rubber tube is placed around the subject's chest to record his breathing pattern on a pneumograph.[92] That device records the respiratory ratio of inhalation and exhalation strokes.[93] The second component is called a galvanic skin response which consists of electrodes placed on the examinee's fingers, through which a small amount of electrical current is passed to the skin.[94] The galvanometer records the minute changes in electrical skin response.[95] The third component consists of a cardiograph which is a tracing obtained by attaching a pneumatic cuff around the left arm in a manner very similar to an apparatus which takes blood pressure.[96] When the cuff is inflated, that device records relative blood pressures or change in the heart rate.[97]

From those testing devices, it is possible to measure psychological or emotional stress.[98] This testing device is the product of observation by psychologists and physiologists who noted certain physiological responses when people lie.[99] In about 1920 law enforcement officials with psychological and physiological training initiated the development of the instrument to serve as an investigative aid.[100]

The polygraph may record responses indicative of deception, but it must be carefully interpreted.[101] The relevant questions, as to which the interrogator is seeking to determine whether the subject is falsifying, are compared with control questions where the examiner obtains a known indication of deception or some expected emotional response.[102] In evaluating the polygraph, due consideration must be given to the fact that a physiological response may be caused by factors other than deception, such as fear, anxiety, nervousness, dislike, and other emotions.[103] There are no valid statistics as to the reliability of the polygraph.[104] FBI Agent Herndon testified that, notwithstanding the absence of percentage indicators of reliability, an informed judgment may be obtained from a well-qualified examiner on the indications of deception in a normal person under appropriate standards of administration.[105]

Ordinarily during a polygraph examination only the examiner and the examinee are present.[106] It is the practice of the FBI, however, to have a second agent present to take notes.[107] It is normally undesirable to have other people present during the polygraph examina-

813

tion because the examinee may react emotionally to them.[108] Because of the numerous interested parties involved in Ruby's polygraph examination, there were present individuals representing the Commission and the Dallas district attorney, as well as two defense counsel, two FBI agents, the chief jailer, the psychiatrist, and the court reporter, although the assistant district attorney and one defense counsel left when Ruby was actually responding to questions while the instrument was activated.[109] Ruby was placed in a position where there was a minimum of distraction for him during the test.[110] He faced a wall and could not see anyone except possibly through secondary vision from the side.[111] Agent Herndon expressed the opinion that Ruby was not affected by the presence of the people in the room.[112]

Answer by Ruby to certain irrelevant control questions suggested an attempt to deceive on those questions. For example, Ruby answered "No" to the question "While in the service did you receive any disciplinary action?"[113] His reaction suggested deception in his answer.[114] Similarly, Ruby's negative answer to the query "Did you ever overcharge a customer?" was suggestive of deception.[115] Ruby further showed an emotional response to other control questions such as "Have you ever been known by another name"[116] "Are you married?"[117] "Have you ever served time in jail?"[118] "Are your parents alive?"[119] "Other than what you told me, did you ever hit anyone with any kind of a weapon?"[120] Herndon concluded that the absence of any physiological response on the relevant questions indicated that there was no deception.[121]

An accurate evaluation of Ruby's polygraph examination depends on whether he was psychotic. Since a psychotic is divorced from reality, the polygraph tracings could not be logically interpreted on such an individual. A psychotic person might believe a false answer was true so he would not register an emotional response characteristic of deception as a normal person would.[122] If a person is so mentally disturbed that he does not understand the nature of the questions or the substance of his answers, then no validity can be attached to the polygraph examination.[123] Herndon stated that if a person, on the other hand, was in touch with reality, then the polygraph examination could be interpreted like any other such test.[124]

Based on his previous contacts with Ruby and from observing him during the entire polygraph proceeding, Dr. William R. Beavers testified as follows:

> In the greater proportion of the time that he answered the questions, I felt that he was aware of the questions and that he understood them, and that he was giving answers based on an appreciation of reality.[125]

Dr. Beavers further stated that he had previously diagnosed Ruby as a "psychotic depressive."[126]

814

Based on the assumption that Ruby was a "psychotic depressive," Herndon testified:

> There would be no validity to the polygraph examination, and no significance should be placed upon the polygraph charts.[127]

Considering other phases of Dr. Beavers' testimony, Herndon stated:

> Well, based on the hypothesis that Ruby was mentally competent and sound, the charts could be interpreted, and if those conditions are fact, the charts could be interpreted to indicate that there was no area of deception present with regard to his response to the relevant questions during the polygraph examination.[128]

In stating his opinion that Ruby was in touch with reality and understood the questions and answers, Dr. Beavers excepted two questions where he concluded that Ruby's underlying delusional state took hold.[129] Those questions related to the safety of Ruby's family and his defense counsel.[130] While in the preliminary session Ruby had answered those questions by stating that he felt his family and defense counsel were in danger, he did not answer either question when the polygraph was activated.[131] Dr. Beavers interpreted Ruby's failure to answer as a reflection of "internal struggle as to just what was reality." [132] In addition, Dr. Beavers testified that the test was not injurious to Ruby's mental or physical condition.[133]

Because Ruby not only volunteered but insisted upon taking a polygraph examination, the Commission agreed to the examination. FBI Director J. Edgar Hoover commented on the examination as follows:

> It should be pointed out that the polygraph, often referred to as "lie detector" is not in fact such a device. The instrument is designed to record under proper stimuli emotional responses in the form of physiological variations which may indicate and accompany deception. The FBI feels that the polygraph technique is not sufficiently precise to permit absolute judgements of deception or truth without qualifications. The polygraph technique has a number of limitations, one of which relates to the mental fitness and condition of the examinee to be tested.
>
> During the proceedings at Dallas, Texas, on July 18, 1964, Dr. William R. Beavers, a psychiatrist, testified that he would generally describe Jack Ruby as a "psychotic depressive." In view of the serious question raised as to Ruby's mental condition, no significance should be placed on the polygraph examination and it should be considered nonconclusive as the charts cannot be relied upon.[134]

Having granted Ruby's request for the examination, the Commission is publishing the transcript of the hearing at which the test was conducted [135] and the transcript of the deposition of the FBI polygraph operator who administered the test.[136]   The Commission did not rely on the results of this examination in reaching the conclusions stated in this report.

Footnotes

For references to the testimony of witnesses before the Commission, the following citation form is used: number of volume, "H" (for "Hearings before the President's Commission on the Assassination of President Kennedy"), page number, and the name of the witness in parentheses, e.g., 7 H 441 (O'Donnell). Commission exhibits are referred to by the capital letters "CE" and number; deposition exhibits by the name of the witness, the capital letters "DE," and the number or letter of his exhibit, e.g., CE 705; Sorrels DE 1. References to audiovisual sources for one Dallas broadcasting station (WFAA) are cited as follows: PKT for video tapes, PKF for films, and PKA for audio tapes. The video and audio reels and tapes of other stations are cited by number, e.g., WFAA–TV reel PKT 10; KRLD–TV reel 13.

FOREWORD

1. Executive Order No. 11130 is set forth as app. I.
2. The White House press release is set forth as app. II.
3. Senate Joint Resolution 137 (Public Law 88–202) is set forth as app. III.

4. The names of all witnesses are set forth in app. V.
5. The procedures of the Commission are set forth as app. VI.

CHAPTER II

1. 4 H 130 (Gov. John B. Connally, Jr.); 7 H 441 (Kenneth O'Donnell).
2. Id. at 441, 442.
3. Id. at 442–443.
4. Id. at 442.
5. Ibid.
6. 7 H 475 (Clifton C. Carter).
7. Ibid.
8. Ibid.
9. 4 H 145–146 (Connally).
10. Ibid.; CE 1367.
11. 4 H 130 (Connally); CE 2960.
12. 7 H 442 (O'Donnell).
13. 4 H 146 (Connally).
14. Ibid.
15. 7 H 443 (O'Donnell).
16. Ibid.
17. 4 H 319–325 (Winston G. Lawson); 7 H 334–341 (Forrest V. Sorrels). Governor Connally testified that he was not consulted about the security arrangements in Dallas, and that he did not expect to be. 4 H 145 (Connally).
18. 4 H 319 (Lawson); 7 H 334 (Sorrels).
19. CE 769, p. 1; 4 H 320 (Lawson).
20. Details of the advance work done by Agent Lawson are set forth in his contemporaneous memoranda; CE 767, 768, 769.

21. 4 H 321–322 (Lawson); 2 H 107 (Roy H. Kellerman).
22. 4 H 322–324, 344–346 (Lawson).
23. CE 768, p. 9; see also 7 H 339 (Sorrels).
24. CE 770.
25. 4 H 323–324 (Lawson).
26. 7 H 334 (Sorrels).
27. See id. at 335; Sorrels DE 4, p. 1.
28. CE 769, p. 2.
29. CE 1360; 4 H 336–337 (Lawson).
30. CE 768, pp. 6–13; CE 769, p. 5; 4 H 338 (Lawson).
31. Id. at 325.
32. Ibid.
33. CE 769, p. 2; 7 H 337 (Sorrels).
34. CE 768, p. 4.
35. Ibid.
36. CE 769, p. 3.
37. 7 H 338 (Sorrels); 4 H 326 (Lawson); CE 1022, p. 2; CE 769, p. 3.
38. 4 H 341 (Lawson); CE 1022, p. 3.
39. 7 H 333 (Sorrels).
40. Id. at 337.
41. Ibid.
42. 4 H 326 (Lawson).
43. CE 876 is an aerial view of Dealey Plaza and the Triple Underpass; see also CE 2188.
44. 7 H 337 (Sorrels); CE 2114–2116.

45. Ibid.
46. CE 2967 ; see 7 H 337 (Sorrels) ; 4 H 333 (Lawson).
47. Id. at 326.
48. CE 769, p. 4 ; 4 H 326 (Lawson).
49. Id. at 326–327.
50. 5 H 465–466 (James J. Rowley) ; 4 H 329, 333 (Lawson).
51. Id. at 327–329. The adequacy of these arrangements is considered in ch. VIII 447–449.
52. CE 1022, p. 2.
53. CE 1361.
54. CE 1362.
55. CE 1363.
56. CE 1364.
57. CE 1365.
58. CE 1366.
59. CE 1367, 1368.
60. CE 1369.
61. CE 1370.
62. CE 1371.
63. CE 1372, 1373.
64. Ibid.
65. CE 1374.
66. CE 1375, 1376.
67. 4 H 323 (Lawson) ; 7 H 339 (Sorrels) ; CE 769, p. 8.
68. CE 1377, 1378.
69. CE 1379.
70. CE 1380.
71. CE 996 ; see also 5 H 534 (Robert G. Klause).
72. CE 1031 ; 5 H 504 (Bernard W. Weissman).
73. CE 1031.
74. 4 H 130 (Connally) ; 7 H 444–445 (O'Donnell).
75. Id. at 445.
76. 4 H 130 (Connally) ; 7 H 445 (O'Donnell).
77. 7 H 472 (David F. Powers).
78. Ibid.
79. 4 H 130 (Connally) ; 7 H 445 (O'Donnell).
80. 2 H 63–64 (Kellerman) ; 7 H 459 (Lawrence F. O'Brien).
81. 7 H 443–444 (O'Donnell).
82. Id. at 456.
83. Ibid.
84. 4 H 349 (Lawson) ; 2 H 67 (Kellerman).
85. 5 H 561 (Pres. Lyndon B. Johnson) ; 4 H 130 (Connally) ; CE 2526.
86. 5 H 560 (Johnson) ; 7 H 474 (Clifton C. Carter) ; 2 H 146 (Rufus W. Youngblood).
87. 7 H 461 (O'Brien) ; 2 H 67 (Kellerman) ; 4 H 339, 350 (Lawson).
88. Id. at 350 ; CE 1024.
89. 4 H 339–340 (Lawson).
90. 5 H 560–561 (Johnson) ; CE 1024, statement of Rufus W. Youngblood.
91. 5 H 561 (Johnson) ; 2 H 115 (Greer).
92. See 4 H 335–336 (Lawson).
93. 4 H 132 (Connally) ; 2 H 135 (Clinton J. Hill) ; 2 H 70 (Kellerman) ; 4 H 326, 351 (Lawson).
94. 2 H 135–136 (Hill) ; 4 H 351 (Lawson).
95. CE 768, p. 5.
96. 2 H 67 (Kellerman) ; 4 H 327 (Lawson).
97. CE 768, p. 5 ; 2 H 67 (Kellerman).
98. Id. at 68 ; 4 H 327–328 (Lawson) ; 2 H 116 (Greer).
99. CE 344, 345, 346.
100. 2 H 65 (Kellerman) ; 2 H 114 (Greer).
101. 4 H 349 (Lawson) ; 2 H 66–67 (Kellerman).
102. Id. at 67.
103. Id. at 64–65.
104. CE 345.

105. 2 H 136–137 (Hill) ; CE 1025.
106. 4 H 130–131 (Connally) ; 2 H 68 (Kellerman) ; 2 H 115 (Greer).
107. Ibid.
108. Ibid.
109. 2 H 70 (Kellerman).
110. 4 H 338–339 (Lawson).
111. 2 H 135 (Hill).
112. Id. at 134.
113. Id. at 134–135.
114. 7 H 446 (O'Donnell) ; 7 H 473 (Powers).
115. 4 H 327, 329 (Lawson).
116. Ibid. ; 7 H 342 (Sorrels).
117. 4 H 327 (Lawson) ; 2 H 135–136 (Hill).
118. Id. at 136.
119. 2 H 147 (Youngblood).
120. Id. at 148.
121. Id. at 147 ; 5 H 561 (Johnson) ; 7 H 439 (Senator Ralph W. Yarborough).
122. 2 H 147 (Youngblood).
123. 7 H 474 (Carter) ; 2 H 69 (Kellerman).
124. CE 767, attachment 3 ; CE 1126.
125. 2 H 70 (Kellerman) ; 4 H 336 (Lawson).
126. CE 768, pp. 9–10.
127. 4 H 130–131 (Connally) ; 2 H 67, 70 (Kellerman) ; 2 H 115 (Greer).
128. 4 H 132 (Connally) ; 2 H 135 (Hill) ; 2 H 70 (Kellerman).
129. Ibid.
130. 4 H 132 (Connally).
131. 7 H 447 (O'Donnell) ; 7 H 473 (Powers) ; 4 H 131 (Connally).
132. 2 H 135–136 (Hill) ; CE 398 ; CE 1024, statement of Clinton J. Hill, p. 2.
133. 2 H 135 (Hill).
134. 2 H 71 (Kellerman).
135. 2 H 147 (Youngblood).
136. CE 876 ; 2 H 71 (Kellerman).
137. CE 878 ; 2 H 71–72 (Kellerman).
138. 5 H 561 (Johnson) ; 4 H 132 (Connally).
139. 7 H 447 (O'Donnell) ; 7 H 463 (O'Brien) ; 7 H 473 (Powers).
140. 4 H 147 (Mrs. John B. Connally, Jr.) ; 4 H 131 (Connally).
141. 2 H 151 (Youngblood).
142. 7 H 473 (Powers).
143. 2 H 120 (Greer).
144. CE 1974, p. 163.
145. 2 H 119 (Greer).
146. 4 H 134 (Connally) ; 4 H 149 (Mrs. Connally) ; 7 H 448 (O'Donnell) ; 7 H 473 (Powers) ; 7 H 474 (Carter) ; 2 H 73 (Kellerman) ; 2 H 139 (Hill) ; 3 H 245 (Baker).
147. 5 H 160–161 (Lyndal L. Shaneyfelt).
148. 5 H 179–180 (Mrs. John F. Kennedy).
149. 4 H 132–133 (Connally).
150. Id. at 135–136.
151. 4 H 147 (Mrs. Connally).
152. 2 H 73–74 (Kellerman).
153. 2 H 117 (Greer).
154. 2 H 74–77 (Kellerman).
155. 4 H 147 (Mrs. Connally).
156. 4 H 133 (Connally).
157. 4 H 147 (Mrs. Connally).
158. 4 H 133 (Connally).
159. Ibid. ; 4 H 147 (Mrs. Connally).
160. Ibid. ; 4 H 133 (Connally).
161. 2 H 138 (Hill).
162. Ibid.
163. Id. at 138–139.
164. Ibid.
165. 7 H 473 (Powers).
166. 5 H 180 (Mrs. Kennedy).
167. CE 1024, statement of John D. Ready.
168. CE 1024, statement of George W. Hickey, Jr.

169. CE 1024, statement of Emory P. Roberts.
170. Ibid.
171. 2 H 148–149 (Youngblood).
172. Id. at 149.
173. 5 H 561 (Johnson).
174. 7 H 475 (Carter).
175. 4 H 325 (Lawson).
176. 7 H 347 (Sorrels).
177. 2 H 74 (Kellerman) ; 2 H 120 (Greer) ; 2 H 141 (Hill) ; 2 H 149 (Youngblood).
178. 4 H 353–354 (Lawson).
179. 4 H 161 (Jesse E. Curry).
180. CE 1974, pp. 163–164.
181. Ibid. ; 2 H 151 (Youngblood) ; 2 H 141 (Hill) ; 7 H 450 (O'Donnell) ; 7 H 475 (Carter).
182. 2 H 151 (Youngblood) ; CE 1126, p. 2.
183. 6 H 144 (Doris M. Nelson) ; 6 H 116 (Ruth J. Standridge).
184. 3 H 358 (Dr. Charles J. Carrico).
185. 6 H 144 (Nelson).
186. 3 H 363 (Carrico) ; 3 H 369–371 (Dr. Malcolm O. Perry).
187. 4 H 354 (Lawson) ; 6 H 135 (Diana H. Bowron).
188. 2 H 142 (Hill) ; 2 H 82 (Kellerman).
189. 4 H 143 (Connally).
190. 6 H 116 (Standridge).
191. 2 H 79 (Kellerman) ; 2 H 124 (Greer) ; 4 H 354 (Lawson).
192. 3 H 359 (Carrico) ; 6 H 141 (Margaret M. Henchliffe) ; 6 H 136 (Bowron).
193. 3 H 358 (Carrico).
194. Ibid.
195. Id. at 359.
196. Ibid.
197. Id. at 361–362 : 6 H 3 (Carrico).
198. 3 H 361 (Carrico).
199. Id. at 359–360.
200. Ibid.
201. Id. at 360.
202. Ibid. ; 6 H 3 (Carrico).
203. 3 H 360 (Carrico) ; 3 H 368 (Perry).
204. Ibid.
205. Id. at 368–370.
206. Id. at 370.
207. Id. at 370, 372.
208. Id. at 370.
209. Id. at 371.
210. Id. at 370.
211. Id. at 371 ; 3 H 360 (Carrico).
212. 3 H 371 (Perry) ; 6 H 20 (Dr. William Kemp Clark).
213. Ibid.
214. Id. at 25.
215. Id. at 20 ; 3 H 371 (Perry).
216. CE 1126, p. 3.
217. 6 H 20 (Clark) : 3 H 372 (Perry) ; 6 H 41 (Dr. Charles R. Baxter).
218. 6 H 20 (Clark).
219. 3 H 372 (Perry) ; 2 H 360 (Comdr. James J. Humes).
220. 3 H 359 (Carrico).
221. 3 H 363 (Carrico) ; 3 H 382 (Perry) ; 6 H 25 (Clark).
222. 6 H 3 (Carrico).
223. 3 H 382 (Perry) ; 6 H 29 (Clark) ; 6 H 48–49 (Dr. Marion T. Jenkins).
224. 4 H 103–104 (Dr. Robert R. Shaw).
225. 3 H 358 (Carrico).
226. Ibid. ; 6 H 77–78 (Dr. Jackie H. Hunt) ; 6 H 74–75 (Dr. A. H. Giesecke, Jr.) : 4 H 103 (Shaw).
227. Id. at 102–103.
228. Id. at 103.
229. Id. at 104–105 ; CE 392 ; 6 H 85, 87 (Shaw).
230. Id. at 88.
231. Id. at 85.
232. 4 H 135 (Connally).

233. 6 H 97 (Dr. Charles F. Gregory).
234. 4 H 126–127 (Gregory).
235. 6 H 105–106 (Dr. George T. Shires).
236. Id. at 106.
237. 5 H 561 (Johnson) ; 2 H 149 (Youngblood).
238. Ibid.
239. Id. at 152 : 7 H 475 (Carter).
240. 5 H 564–565 (Mrs. Lyndon B. Johnson) ; 7 H 475 (Carter).
241. 5 H 561–562 (Johnson) ; 2 H 152 (Youngblood) ; 7 H 475 (Carter).
242. 2 H 152 (Youngblood).
243. 5 H 562 (Johnson) ; 7 H 451 (O'Donnell).
244. 2 H 154–155 (Youngblood).
245. Id. at 152 ; 7 H 451 (O'Donnell) ; 5 H 561 (Johnson).
246. Ibid.
247. CE 1026 ; CE 1024, statement of Emory P. Roberts, p. 5.
248. 5 H 562 (Johnson) ; 2 H 153 (Youngblood).
249. Ibid.
250. 2 H 96 (Kellerman) ; 2 H 126 (Greer) ; CE 1026.
251. 2 H 80 (Kellerman) ; 2 H 142 (Hill).
252. 2 H 96 (Kellerman) ; CE 1024, statements of David B. Grant, Samuel E. Sulliman, Ernest E. Olsson, Jr.. John J. Howlett, Andrew E. Berger, Robert A. Steuart, and Richard E. Johnsen.
253. CE 772, p. 3.
254. CE 2554, statements of Donald J. Lawton, Roger C. Warner, Henry J. Rybka, and William H. Patterson.
255. CE 2554, statement of Roger C. Warner, p. 2.
256. 2 H 153 (Youngblood).
257. 7 H 474 (Powers) ; 3 H 382 (Perry) ; CE 1126.
258. 7 H 452 (O'Donnell).
259. Ibid. ; 2 H 142 (Hill).
260. 7 H 453–454 (O'Donnell) ; 7 H 468–470 (O'Brien).
261. 7 H 453 (O'Donnell) ; 2 H 96–97 (Kellerman).
262. 7 H 454 (O'Donnell).
263. 5 H 562–563 (Johnson).
264. 7 H 454 (O'Donnell) ; 2 H 154 (Youngblood).
265. 2 H 143 (Hill) ; 2 H 98 (Kellerman).
266. 5 H 563 (Johnson) ; 5 H 566 (Mrs. Johnson) ; 7 H 470 (O'Brien).
267. 2 H 143 (Hill) ; 2 H 98 (Kellerman).
268. 7 H 454 (O'Donnell) ; 7 H 471 (O'Brien).
269. 2 H 98 (Kellerman) ; 2 H 143 (Hill).
270. 2 H 98 (Kellerman).
271. 2 H 154 (Youngblood).
272. 7 H 454–455 (O Donnell).
273. 2 H 99 (Kellerman) ; 2 H 143 (Hill).
274. Ibid. ; 7 H 455 (O'Donnell).
275. 2 H 143 (Hill).
276. CE 1024, statement of Clinton J. Hill, p. 5.
277. 2 H 349 (Comdr. James J. Humes).
278. Ibid.
279. CE 387.
280. 2 H 351 (Humes).
281. Id. at 354.
282. Id. at 353–354.
283. 5 H 73 (Robert A. Frazier).
284. 2 H 361–362 (Humes).
285. Id. at 349 : 2 H 100 (Kellerman) ; 2 H 143–144 (Hill).
286. 7 H 455 (O'Donnell) ; 2 H 144 (Hill).

CHAPTER III

1. 3 H 142–143 (Howard L. Brennan); CE 477, 478.
2. 3 H 149 (Brennan); CE 1437.
3. CE 479.
4. 3 H 142 (Brennan).
5. See id. at 142–143.
6. Id. at 143.
7. Ibid.
8. Id. at 143–144.
9. Id. at 144.
10. Ibid.
11. Ibid.
12. Id. at 145.
13. 2 H 204 (Amos Lee Euins).
14. Ibid.; see CE 365, 366.
15. 2 H 204 (Euins).
16. 6 H 310–311 (D. V. Harkness); 6 H 170 (James R. Underwood).
17. 6 H 313 (Harkness).
18. Id. at 310; CE 1974, p. 165.
19. 6 H 313 (Harkness) (Euins' description of the man he saw is discussed in ch. IV, p. 147).
20. 2 H 157–158 (Robert H. Jackson).
21. Id. at 158–159.
22. Id. at 159.
23. 6 H 164 (Tom C. Dillard); 6 H 156–157 (Malcolm D. Couch); 6 H 169 (Underwood).
24. 6 H 164 (Dillard).
25. Id. at 164–165; CE 480, 481, 482.
26. 6 H 156–157 (Couch).
27. Id. at 157.
28. 7 H 485–486 (Mrs. Earle Cabell).
29. Id. at 486.
30. Ibid.
31. Ibid.
32. Ibid.; 7 H 478 (Earle Cabell).
33. 7 H 487 (Mrs. Cabell).
34. 6 H 172–173 (James N. Crawford).
35. Ibid.
36. Id. at 173.
37. Ibid.
38. 6 H 176 (Mary Ann Mitchell).
39. Ibid.
40. 3 H 202–203 (James Jarman, Jr.).
41. 3 H 190 (Harold Norman).
42. 3 H 169–173 (Bonnie R. Williams).
43. Id. at 173; 3 H 190 (Norman); 3 H 202, 203 (Jarman).
44. 3 H 195 (Norman).
45. Id. at 191.
46. 3 H 175 (Williams).
47. Ibid.
48. 3 H 204 (Jarman).
49. Ibid.
50. Ibid.
51. Id. at 204–205.
52. Id. at 211.
53. Ibid.
54. Id. at 207, 211.
55. 3 H 196 (Norman).
56. Id. at 195.
57. See, e.g., the statements of eyewitnesses in CE 1428, 1432, 1433, 1435, 1436, 2084.
58. See e.g. CE 1428, 1432, 2087, 2088, 2098, 2099.
59. 6 H 249 (J. W. Foster); 6 H 254 (J. C. White).
60. 6 H 256–257 (Joe E. Murphy); Murphy DE A.
61. 6 H 257 (Murphy).
62. 6 H 250 (Foster); 6 H 255 (White); see 6 H 256 (Murphy).
63. Id. at 257.
64. 6 H 250 (Foster).
65. 6 H 241 (S. M. Holland).
66. See 6 H 224 (Austin L. Miller); 6 H 228 (Frank E. Reilly); 6 H 236–237 (Royce G. Skelton); 6 H 240–242 (Holland); CE 1416–1424 (statements of James L. Simmons, Walter Luke Winborn,

Nolan H. Potter, Curtis Freeman Bishop, Richard Calvin Dodd, Thomas J. Murphy, Clemon Earl Johnson, Ewell William Cowsert, and George A. Davis).
67. 6 H 239–241 (Holland).
68. 6 H 253 (Foster).
69. 7 H 516 (James W. Altgens); 6 H 226 (Miller).
70. 6 H 284–285 (Lee H. Bowers, Jr.).
71. Id. at 285.
72. Id. at 285–286.
73. Id. at 287.
74. 6 H 229 (Reilly); 6 H 241–242 (Holland); 6 H 258 (Murphy); Murphy DE A.
75. 6 H 250 (Foster); see 6 H 229 (Reilly).
76. 4 H 351 (Winston G. Lawson); 7 H 346 (Forrest V. Sorrels).
77. 4 H 351 (Lawson).
78. See 6 H 258 (Murphy).
79. 6 H 251 (Foster).
80. Id. at 251–252.
81. 6 H 225 (Miller).
82. 6 H 237–238 (Skelton).
83. 6 H 230 (Reilly).
84. 6 H 243–245 (Holland).
85. CE 1421.
86. 6 H 287 (Bowers).
87. See 6 H 251–252 (Foster).
88. 6 H 244 (Holland).
89. 6 H 225 (Miller); see also CE 1416, 1417.
90. 6 H 287–288 (Bowers); CE 1416–1419, 1423.
91. 6 H 298 (Clyde A. Haygood).
92. 5 H 67 (Robert A. Frazier); 3 H 432 (Frazier); CE 567.
93. 5 H 67 (Frazier); 3 H 435 (Frazier); CE 569.
94. 5 H 66, 71 (Frazier); CE 840.
95. 5 H 68 (Frazier).
96. Ibid.; CE 350; see 2 H 85–86, 87–89 (Roy H. Kellerman).
97. 5 H 70 (Frazier); CE 349.
98. 5 H 67–69, 72–74 (Frazier).
99. Ibid.
100. Id. at 68; 3 H 399 (Frazier).
101. 5 H 68 (Frazier).
102. 2 H 86 (Kellerman); CE 351.
103. 5 H 69 (Frazier).
104. 2 H 84–85 (Kellerman); 2 H 122 (William Robert Greer).
105. 5 H 70 (Frazier).
106. Ibid.
107. Ibid.
108. 4 H 204–205 (Jesse W. Fritz); 3 H 283–284 (Luke Mooney).
109. Id. at 284–285; CE 508.
110. 3 H 285 (Mooney); CE 510, 1974, p. 176.
111. 4 H 205 (Fritz).
112. 3 H 285 (Mooney).
113. 4 H 249–250 (J. C. Day); CE 715, 716.
114. 3 H 293–294 (Eugene Boone); 7 H 107 (Seymour Weitzman); CE 514, 515.
115. 3 H 293 (Boone); 4 H 205 (Fritz); 4 H 257 (Day); CE 718; see 7 H 161 (Richard M. Sims).
116. 4 H 258–259 (Day); 4 H 205 (Fritz); CE 141.
117. 4 H 260 (Day); 4 H 206 (Fritz).
118. 3 H 294 (Boone); 4 H 260 (Day); see 7 H 108–109 (Weitzman).
119. 6 H 116–117 (Ruth J. Standridge).
120. 6 H 121–122 (Jane C. Wester); 6 H 126 (R. J. Jimison).
121. 6 H 129–131 (Darrel C. Tomlinson).
122. Id. at 130.

123. 3 H 363 (**Dr.** Charles J. Carrico) ; 6 H 137 (Diana H. Bowron).
124. Id. at 137–138 ; 6 H 141 (Margaret M. Henchcliffe) ; 6 H 145 (Doris M. Nelson).
125. Id. at 145–146 ; 6 H 142 (Henchcliffe) ; 6 H 137–138 (Bowron).
126. 3 H 392–394 (Frazier) ; 4 H 260 (Day) ; CE 139.
127. 3 H 393–394 (Frazier) ; CE 541.
128. 3 H 392–393 (Frazier).
129. Id. at 392 ; CE 540.
130. 3 H 392–393 (Frazier).
131. 7 H 108–109 (Weitzman).
132. 3 H 395 (Frazier).
133. Ibid.
134. Id. at 395–396 ; 4 H 260 (Day).
135. 3 H 397 (Frazier).
136. Id. at 391.
137. Id. at 391, 421.
138. 3 H 496 (Joseph D. Nicol).
139. See generally 3 H 417–419, 429–430 (Frazier).
140. Id. at 424.
141. See app. X.
142. 3 H 429, 432, 435 (Frazier) ; 3 H 498, 500–502 (Nicol) ; CE 399, 567, 569.
143. 3 H 502 (Nicol) ; 3 H 434, 436 (Frazier).
144. 3 H 497 (Nicol) ; 3 H 435 (Frazier).
145. 5 H 73–74 (Frazier).
146. 3 H 415 (Frazier) ; 3 H 505 (Nicol) ; CE 543–545.
147. 3 H 440 (Frazier) ; 7 H 591 (Cortlandt Cunningham) ; 7 H 591 (Charles L. Killion).
148. 2 H 352–353 (Comdr. James J. Humes) ; 2 H 377 (Comdr. J. Thornton Boswell) ; 2 H 380 (Lt. Col. Pierre A. Finck).
149. 2 H 352 (Humes).
150. Id. at 357–359.
151. Id. at 359–361.
152. CE 400.
153. 2 H 379–380 (Finck).
154. 2 H 352 (Humes).
155. Ibid.
156. Ibid.
157. Ibid. ; 2 H 377 (Boswell) ; CE 388.
158. 5 H 75–77 (Dr. Alfred G. Olivier).
159. Id. at 89 ; CE 861, 862.
160. 5 H 87 (Olivier).
161. Id. at 89.
162. 2 H 361 (Humes) ; CE 387, 391.
163. 2 H 364 (Humes) ; 2 H 380 (Finck).
164. Ibid. ; 2 H 364 (Humes) ; 2 H 377 (Boswell).
165. 2 H 363 (Humes).
166. Id. at 367–368.
167. Id. at 364.
168. Ibid. ; 2 H 380 (Finck) ; CE 385.
169. 2 H 368–369 (Humes).
170. Id. at 367.
171. Id. at 363.
172. Id. at 361–362.
173. 3 H 361 (Carrico).
174. 3 H 388 (Dr. Malcolm O. Perry) ; id. at 372.
175. 3 H 362 (Carrico).
176. 3 H 373 (Perry).
177. 3 H 362 (Carrico).
178. 3 H 373 (Perry).
179. 6 H 42–43 (Dr. Charles R. Baxter) ; 6 H 35 (Dr. Robert N. McClelland) ; 6 H 48–50 (Dr. Marion T. Jenkins) ; 6 H 55 (Dr. Ronald C. Jones).
180. 3 H 369 (Perry).
181. Id. at 375.
182. Id. at 375–376.
183. Id. at 375.
184. Id. at 368, 372, 375.
185. Id. at 375.
186. CE 1415. "The Doctors' Hard Fight To Save Him," New York Herald Tribune, Nov. 23, 1963.

187. 5 H 76–78 (Olivier).
188. Id. at 78 ; CE 850.
189. See 3 H 362 (Carrico) ; 3 H 368 (Perry).
190. 2 H 364 (Humes) ; CE 385 ; see 5 H 60–61 (Frazier) ; CE 394.
191. 2 H 375 (Humes).
192. 5 H 77–78 (Olivier) ; CE 849.
193. 5 H 59–62 (Frazier) ; CE 393, 394, 395.
194. 5 H 59–62 (Frazier).
195. Id. at 59.
196. Ibid.
197. Id. at 59–60.
198. Id. at 60.
199. Ibid.
200. Ibid.
201. Ibid.
202. Ibid.
203. Ibid.
204. Id. at 61.
205. Ibid.
206. CE 395.
207. 5 H 62 (Frazier).
208. Ibid.
209. 4 H 104 (Dr. Robert R. Shaw).
210. Id. at 104–105 ; CE 679, 680.
211. 4 H 104 (Shaw) ; 6 H 85 (Shaw).
212. 4 H 136–138 (Gov. John B. Connally, Jr.).
213. Id. at 135.
214. 4 H 118, 124 (Dr. Charles F. Gregory).
215. Id. at 118–119.
216. Id. at 119–120.
217. Id at 120–121.
218. Id at 124.
219. 6 H 89 (Shaw).
220. 4 H 109 (Shaw).
221. 4 H 138 (Connally) ; 6 H 106 (Dr. George T. Shires).
222. See 5 H 87 (Olivier) ; 6 H 106 (Shires).
223. Ibid. ; 4 H 125 (Gregory).
224. 6 H 106, 109 (Shires) ; 4 H 113 (Shaw) ; 4 H 125 (Gregory).
225. CE 684 ; 5 H 63 (Frazier).
226. Ibid.
227. Ibid. ; CE 683.
228. 5 H 64 (Frazier).
229. Id. at 63–64.
230. Id. at 64 ; CE 685.
231. 5 H 64 (Frazier).
232. Ibid.
233. Ibid. ; CE 686.
234. 5 H 64–65 (Frazier).
235. Ibid.
236. Id. at 65.
237. Ibid.
238. CE 687, 688 ; 5 H 65–66 (Frazier).
239. Ibid.
240. 5 H 93 (Dr. Arthur J. Dziemian).
241. Ibid.
242. Ibid. ; see 5 H 82–83 (Olivier).
243. Id. at 81.
244. Ibid. ; CE 854, 855.
245. 5 H 82 (Olivier) ; CE 856.
246. 5 H 82 (Olivier).
247. Id. at 82–83.
248. Ibid.
249. 4 H 121–122 (Gregory).
250. See id. at 124.
251. See 5 H 82 (Olivier).
252. Id. at 87 ; see id. at 82.
253. 3 H 430 (Frazier).
254. 6 H 98 (Gregory).
255. Id. at 98–99.
256. 6 H 91 (Shaw) ; 6 H 101–102 (Gregory) ; 6 H 109–110 (Shires).
257. 4 H 139–140 (Connally).
258. Id. at 138–139 ; CE 689.
259. 5 H 92 (Dziemian) ; see 5 H 84–87 (Olivier) ; 5 H 95–97 (Dr. F. W. Light, Jr.).
260. 2 H 71–73 (Kellerman) ; 2 H 116–117 (Greer) ; 4 H 132–133 (Connally).

261. CE 347, 354, 699.
262. 5 H 137 (Leo J. Gauthier) ; CE 884 ; see 5 H 138–165 (Lyndal L. Shaneyfelt).
263. Id. at 139–141.
264. Id. at 153–154.
265. Id. at 142.
266. Id. at 153–154 ; 3 H 407 (Frazier).
267. See 5 H 93 (Dziemian).
268. 5 H 130–132 (Thomas J. Kelley) ; see CE 871–874.
269. 5 H 132–134 (Kelley).
270. 5 H 147 (Shaneyfelt).
271. Id. at 162.
272. 5 H 134 (Kelley) ; 5 H 167 (Frazier).
273. 5 H 139 (Shaneyfelt).
274. Id. at 149.
275. Id. at 147–148.
276. See id. at 145.
277. Id. at 147–149.
278. Id. at 149–150.
279. Id. at 150–151.
280. Id. at 152.
281. Id. at 151.
282. Id. at 151–152.
283. Id. at 152.
284. Id. at 157.
285. Id. at 153, 156–157.
286. 5 H 168–169 (Frazier).
287. Id. at 71, 169.
288. Id. at 70, 169 (Frazier) ; 5 H 77 (Olivier).
289. 5 H 70–71 (Frazier).
290. Ibid.
291. Ibid.
292. Id. at 174.
293. CE 697, 698.
294. 5 H 131–132 (Kelley).
295. 3 H 359 (Carrico) ; 4 H 147 (Mrs. John B. Connally, Jr.) ; see 4 H 138–140 (Connally).
296. 5 H 169–171 (Frazier).
297. Id. at 170 ; 4 H 145 (Connally).
298. 5 H 170 (Frazier).
299. Ibid.
300. Id. at 167.
301. 5 H 153 (Shaneyfelt) ; 5 H 137 (Gauthier).
302. 5 H 153, 162 (Shaneyfelt).
303. Ibid.
304. Id. at 162.
305. Id. at 162–163.
306. Id. at 163 ; CE 902, 903.
307. 5 H 133 (Kelley).
308. 5 H 163 (Shaneyfelt).
309. 4 H 137–138 (Connally).
310. See 4 H 104–105 (Shaw).
311. 5 H 164 (Shaneyfelt).
312. CE 385.
313. 5 H 78–80 (Olivier).
314. CE 399, 853 ; 5 H 80 (Olivier).
315. Id. at 80, 86.
316. Id. at 86.
317. Id. at 86–87 ; 5 H 91–92 (Dziemian).
318. Id. at 92 (Dziemian).
319. Ibid. ; 5 H 83–84 (Olivier).
320. Id. at 86.
321. Id. at 80.
322. Id. at 84 ; 6 H 95 (Shaw).

323. 5 H 94, 97 (Light).
324. Id. at 97.
325. CE 389, 390, 885.
326. CE 388, 389.
327. See 5 H 159–160 (Shaneyfelt).
328. Ibid.
329. Ibid.
330. Id. at 145, 160.
331. Id. at 160.
332. E.g. 4 H 147 (Mrs. Connally) ; 2 H 76 (Kellerman) ; 2 H 118 (Greer) ; 2 H 149–150 (Rufus W. Youngblood) ; 7 H 448 (Kenneth O'Donnell) ; 7 H 440 (Senator Ralph W. Yarborough) ; see also the reports of numerous eyewitnesses in CE 1416–1419, 1425, 1427, 1430–1432, 1434–1436, 2084, 2087, 2090, 2098–2107.
333. E.g. 2 H 139 (Clinton J. Hill) ; CE 1421, 1429.
334. E.g. 2 H 194 (James R. Worrell, Jr.) ; 6 H 207 (Jean L. Hill) ; 6 H 238 (Skelton).
335. Hatcher, Jury & Weller, *Firearms Investigations, Identification and Evidence,* 418 (1957).
336. See supra at p. 85.
337. CE 1024, statement of Agent Glen A. Bennett.
338. CE 2112.
339. 4 H 132–133 (Connally).
340. 4 H 147 (Mrs. Connally) ; 5 H 152 (Shaneyfelt).
341. 4 H 147 (Mrs. Connally).
342. 7 H 517, 520–521 (Altgens).
343. 5 H 158 (Shaneyfelt).
344. 7 H 493 (Phillip L. Willis) ; 15 H 696–697 (Shaneyfelt) ; Shaneyfelt DE 25, 4 H 133, 135 (Connally).
345. 4 H 133, 135 (Connally).
346. 5 H 160 (Shaneyfelt).
347. Id. at 153–154 ; 3 H 407 (Frazier).
348. For recollection that the second and third shots were closer together see e.g. 2 H 73–74 (Kellerman) ; 2 H 118 (Greer) ; 2 H 150 (Youngblood) ; 2 H 159 (Jackson) ; CE 2084, 2098, 2100.
For recollection that the shots were evenly spaced see e.g. 7 H 495 (Willis).
For recollection that the first and second shots were closer together see the statement of Cecil Ault, CE 2103.
349. 7 H 518 (Altgens).
350. 7 H 560 (Emmett J. Hudson).
351. 5 H 180 (Mrs. John F. Kennedy).
352. 6 H 238 (Skelton).
353. Ibid.
354. 6 H 252 (J. W. Foster).
355. See CE 2111.
356. 7 H 553 (James T. Tague).
357. 7 H 546 (Eddy R. Walthers).
358. Ibid. ; 7 H 553 (Tague).
359. Ibid.
360. Id. at 555.
361. CE 1974, p. 166 ; see 6 H 298 (Haygood).
362. 15 H 700 (Shaneyfelt).
363. Ibid.
364. Ibid.
365. E.g. 2 H 76 (Kellerman) ; 2 H 118 (Greer) ; 2 H 139 (Clinton J. Hill) ; 2 H 150 (Youngblood) ; 2 H 182–183 (Arnold L. Rowland) ; 2 H 160 (Jackson).

CHAPTER IV

1. See ch. III.
2. 11 H 207 (Albert Yeargan) ; 11 H 206 (J. Philip Lux) ; 7 H 364 (William Waldman).
3. 11 H 205 (Louis Feldsott).
4. 7 H 364–365 (Waldman) ; 7 H 370–371 (Mitchell Scibor).

5. 7 H 420 (James Cadigan) ; 4 H 373 (Alwyn Cole).
6. 7 H 420 (Cadigan) ; 4 H 359–362 (Cole).
7. 7 H 365–368 (Waldman) ; Waldman DE 7, 8, 9, 10 ; CE 773, 788.
8. CE 788, 789 ; 7 H 295 (Harry

Holmes) ; 4 H 373 (Cole) ; 7 H 423 (Cadigan) ; Cadigan DE 11.

9. 7 H 366–368 (Waldman) ; Waldman DE 7, 10 ; CE 2957.

10. 7 H 365–368 (Waldman) ; Waldman DE 7, 8, 9, 10 ; CE 773, 788.

11. 7 H 361–364 (Waldman) ; Waldman DE 1, 3, 4.

12. Waldman DE 7.

13. 3 H 393 (Robert Frazier) ; CE 1977.

14. Holmes DE 3 ; Cadigan DE 13 ; 7 H 295 (Holmes) ; CE 2011, p. 17 ; see also CE 791, 792.

15. 4 H 377–378 (Cole) ; CE 791, 792.

16. 4 H 379 (Cole) ; 7 H 425–426 (Cadigan) ; CE 793.

17. 2 H 457–459 (Ruth Paine) ; 1 H 18–19 (Marina Oswald) ; 5 H 388 (Marina Oswald).

18. Cadigan DE 13 ; CE 791 ; 7 H 527 (Holmes).

19. Id. at 528.

20. 3 H 300–301 (M. N. McDonald) ; CE 143 ; 7 H 54 (Gerald Hill) ; 7 H 21–22 (Bob Carroll) ; Cadigan DE 12.

21. 7 H 376 (Heinz Michaelis) ; CE 135, 790 ; 7 H 594 (David Goldstein) ; Cadigan DE 12.

22. 4 H 375 (Cole) ; 7 H 424 (Cadigan).

23. CE 801, 802 ; 7 H 187–188 (Richard Stovall) ; 7 H 228 (Guy Rose) ; CE 1986, 1989, 1990 ; CE 2011, p. 20.

24. CE 2011, p. 21.

25. CE 795, 1986, 1989, 1990 ; 7 H 187–188 (Stovall) ; 7 H 228 (Rose) ; CE 2011, pp. 22–23.

26. Compare CE 801 with 795 ; For a detailed description of additional steps in the creation of the forged card, see 4 H 386–387 (Cole).

27. CE 795, 800–801, 806–812 ; 4 H 380–382, 385–387, 389–391 (Cole) ; 7 H 427 (Cadigan) ; 7 H 195 (Stovall).

28. CE 813, 2004 ; CE 2011, p. 25.

29. 4 H 394–396 (Cole).

30. CE 1838, 2012.

31. 7 H 296 (Holmes).

32. CE 817 ; Cadigan DE 22 ; 7 H 296 (Holmes) ; CE 1799, p. 3 ; CE 2011, p. 19.

33. 4 H 397–398 (Cole) ; 7 H 431–432 (Cadigan).

34. 1 H 64 (Marina Oswald).

35. 5 H 401 (Marina Oswald).

36. See e.g., CE 819 ; CE 1413, pp. 19, 35.

37. 1 H 64 (Marina Oswald) ; 5 H 401, 403 (Marina Oswald).

38. Ibid ; 1 H 65 (Marina Oswald).

39. CE 1398.

40. CE 1945.

41. CE 2014.

42. 1 H 91 (Marina Oswald). When translated from the Russian, the name was spelled "Alec". Oswald himself spelled the name "Alek" in correspondence. See note 43, infra.

43. See, e.g., CE 38, 55–56.

44. 3 H 289 (Luke Mooney) ; 3 H 292–293 (Eugene Boone).

45. 4 H 258 (J. C. Day) ; cf. 3 H 295 (Boone).

46. 4 H 259 (Day).

47. Id. at 261 ; 4 H 20 (Sebastian Latona).

48. Id. at 21.

49. Ibid.

50. Ibid.

51. Id. at 22, 29 ; see also 4 H 258–259 (Day).

52. Id. at 260–261.

53. 4 H 24 (Latona).

54. Ibid.

55. 4 H 261–262 (Day).

56. 7 H 23 (Latona) ; 4 H 261 (Day).

57. CE 2637.

58. 4 H 24 (Latona) ; CE 637–639.

59. 4 H 50 (Arthur Mandella) ; 15 H 745–746 (Mandella).

60. 4 H 47 (Latona) ; 7 H 590 (Ronald Wittmus).

61. 4 H 30 (Latona) ; 4 H 54 (Mandella) ; 7 H 590 (Wittmus).

62. 4 H 2 (Latona) ; 4 H 262 (Day).

63. 4 H 260 (Day).

64. 4 H 82, 85 (Paul Stombaugh) ; CE 674.

65. 4 H 56, 74 (Stombaugh).

66. CE 150, 673–676 ; 3 H 302 (McDonald) ; see CE 2011, p. 13. 15 H 695 (Lyndal Shaneyfelt).

67. 4 H 83–87 (Stombaugh).

68. Id. at 88.

69. Id. at 87.

70. Id. at 87–88.

71. 1 H 121 (Marina Oswald).

72. 3 H 252 (T. L. Baker) ; 3 H 276 (Mrs. Robert Reid) ; 2 H 259 (William Whaley).

73. 6 H 412–413 (Mrs. Mary Bledsoe).

74. 7 H 173 (Richard Sims) ; 2 H 287 (Cecil McWatters) ; 4 H 223 (J. W. Fritz) ; CE 381, 381–A ; CE 2005, p. I 137–B.

75. Ibid.

76. 4 H 84 (Stombaugh).

77. Id. at 83.

78. 3 H 41 (Ruth Paine) ; see app. XIII.

79. See footnotes 107–114, infra.

80. See ch. VI, pp. 318–321.

81. See footnotes 107–114, infra.

82. CE 712, 713 ; 4 H 237, 241 (Fritz) ; 11 H 155–156 (M. Waldo George).

83. 1 H 15–16, 117–118 (Marina Oswald) ; CE 134.

84. CE 133–A.

85. CE 748 ; 4 H 281 (Lyndal Shaneyfelt).

86. Ibid.

87. CE 133–A, 133–B, 134 ; 1 H 117–118 (Marina Oswald) ; 5 H 405, 410 (Marina Oswald) ; CE 750.

88. CE 749 ; 7 H 194 (Stovall) ; 7 H 231 (Rose) ; CE 2011, p. 26. The recovered negative was of the picture introduced as CE 133–B.

89. 4 H 284–288 (Shaneyfelt).

90. Id. at 284.

91. Id. at 289 ; 15 H 693 (Shaneyfelt).

92. 4 H 237, 241 (Fritz) ; CE 712, 713, 714.

93. 4 H 288 (Shaneyfelt).

94. Id. at 290–294 ; 15 H 687–690 (Shaneyfelt).

95. 4 H 292–294 (Shaneyfelt) ; 15 H 689–690 (Shaneyfelt) ; Shaneyfelt DE 13, 14, 18.

96. See footnote 4, 82, 83, supra.

97. CE 1406 ; 15 H 690–692 (Shaneyfelt) ; Shaneyfelt DE 20, 21, 22, 22–A.

98. 1 H 15, 118 (Marina Oswald) ; see p. 182, infra.

99. Michaelis DE 5 ; Waldman DE 7.

100. 1 H 119 (Marina Oswald).

101. Id. at 14.

102. Id. at 21 ; CE 1403, p. 735.

103. 1 H 21–22, 54 (Marina Oswald) ; but see Id. at 65 ; contra CE 1403, p. 736.

104. 1 H 26 (Marina Oswald) ; 3 H 4–5, 7, 10–11, 19 (R. Paine).

105. 1 H 26 (Marina Oswald).

106. 3 H 20–21, 25 (R. Paine) ; 2 H 507–508 (R. Paine).

107. 1 H 26, 52, 53, 61, 67–78, 74 (Marina Oswald) ; CE 2003, p. 46.

108. 1 H 26, 52 (Marina Oswald).

109. 3 H 21–25 (R. Paine) ; 9 H 436–443 (M. Paine).

110. 2 H 414–416 (M. Paine) ; 9 H 437–440 (M. Paine).

111. 9 H 436 (M. Paine).

112. 2 H 417 (M. Paine) ; 9 H 442–443 (M. Paine).
113. 7 H 229 (Rose) ; 7 H 548 (Eddy Walthers).
114. 4 H 57–58 (Stombaugh).
115. 3 H 27–39 (R. Paine) ; 1 H 51 (Marina Oswald) ; 6 H 401–402 (Bledsoe) ; 10 H 293–294 (Mrs. A. C. Johnson) ; 6 H 436 (E. Roberts).
116. 2 H 212–213, 217 (Frazier) ; 1 H 51, 124 (Marina Oswald) ; 3 H 40, 67, 127 (R. Paine).
117. 1 H 51 (Marina Oswald) ; 2 H 222 (Frazier) ; 3 H 40 (M. Paine) ; see 3 H 28–46 (M. Paine).
118. 2 H 222–223 (Frazier) ; CE 2003, p. 25.
119. Ibid.
120. 2 H 247–248 (Mrs. Linnie Mae Randle) ; 2 H 224 (Frazier).
121. 10 H 297 (Mrs. A. C. Johnson).
122. CE 2046.
123. 3 H 72–73 (R. Paine) ; 9 H 424 (R. Paine) ; R. Paine DE 275, 276 ; CE 449.
124. 3 H 75–76 (R. Paine).
125. 1 H 68–69 (Marina Oswald).
126. CE 2640.
127. 3 H 46, 56–57 (R. Paine) ; 1 H 65 (Marina Oswald).
128. 3 H 48, 59–61 (R. Paine) ; 9 H 418 (R. Paine) ; 1 H 71 (Marina Oswald).
129. 3 H 48, 52, 60 (R. Paine) ; 9 H 397, 418 (R. Paine) ; CE 430.
130. CE 429, 430, 434 ; 3 H 29, 52–53 (R. Paine) ; 9 H 402 (R. Paine).
131. 9 H 408, 410 (R. Paine) ; 3 H 20–22 (R. Paine) ; 1 H 26, 52–53, 67, 119 (Marina Oswald) ; CE 140 ; 2003, p. 46.
132. 3 H 47 (R. Paine).
133. Id. at 47, 62–63.
134. Id. at 48–49, 65.
135. 1 H 66–67 (Marina Oswald).
136. Ibid ; 3 H 58–59, 67 (R. Paine).
137. Compare photos in CE 1305 and 1304.
138. 2 H 252 (Cortlandt Cunningham).
139. 1 H 73–74 (Marina Oswald) ; 3 H 68–69 (R. Paine).
140. Ibid ; 3 H 78–79 (R. Paine) ; 7 H 229–230 (Rose).
141. 1 H 119 (Marina Oswald).
142. 3 H 79 (R. Paine).
143. Ibid ; 1 H 74 (Marina Oswald).
144. Ibid ; 7 H 305 (Holmes) ; Holmes DE 4, p. 3–4 ; see also 4 H 223, 229 (Fritz).
145. 1 H 72–73 (Marina Oswald) ; 3 H 68, 112 (R. Paine) ; 2 H 224–226 (Frazier).
146. 1 H 66, 72–73 (Marina Oswald) ; 3 H 68 (R. Paine).
147. 2 H 248 (Randle) ; CE 144, 446.
148. 2 H 251 (Randle) ; CE 144, 446.
149. 2 H 248–249 (Randle).
150. Id. at 249–250.
151. Id. at 249.
152. 2 H 225–226 (Frazier).
153. Id. at 226.
154. Ibid.
155. Ibid.
156. Id. at 228.
157. Id. at 220.
158. Id. at 228.
159. Id. at 230.
160. 6 H 376–377 (Jack Dougherty).
161. See e.g. 6 H 383 (Eddie Piper) ; 3 H 164–165 (Bonnie Ray Williams) ; 3 H 188 (Harold Norman) ; 3 H 200 (James Jarman, Jr.) ; 3 H 218–219 (Roy Truly) ; 6 H 328 (William Shelley) ; 6 H 348–349 (Charles Givens) ; 6 H 358–359 (Troy West) ; 6 H 364–365 (Danny Arce) ; 6 H 337 (Billy Lovelady) ; CE 1381, pp. 2, 9, 12, 13, 18, 20, 25, 33–34, 37, 39, 43, 50, 58, 59, 67, 71, 77, 82, 86, 89, 96, 97, 105.
162. 2 H 226 (Frazier) ; 2 H 249–250 (Randle).

163. 3 H 395 (Frazier) ; CE 139.
164. CE 1304 ; 2 H 240 (Frazier).
165. Id. at 241.
166. Id. at 243.
167. CE 2009.
168. 2 H 249–250 (Randle).
169. 2 H 239 (Frazier).
170. 2 H 248–249 (Randle) ; see CE 2008.
171. Ibid.
172. 2 H 243 (Frazier).
173. Id. at 229.
174. See CE 142 ; 4 H 266 (Day).
175. 4 H 266–267 (Day) ; 7 H 143–145 (Robert Lee Studebaker) ; Studebaker DE F ; CE 1302.
176. 3 H 395 (Frazier) ; CE 142, 626.
177. CE 1301, 1302.
178. See CE 508, 723, 726 ; 4 H 265–266 (Day) ; 3 H 285–286, 289 (Luke Mooney).
179. 4 H 267 (Day).
180. See app. X, pp. 565–566 ; 4 H 3–8 (Latona).
181. Id. at 4–5, 8.
182. Id. at 7.
183. Id. at 47 ; 7 H 590 (Wittmus).
184. 4 H 50–51 (Mandella).
185. 4 H 5, 47 (Latona) ; 4 H 50–51 (Mandella) ; 15 H 745–746.
186. 4 H 44–45 (Latona).
187. Id. at 7 ; 2 H 228 (Frazier).
188. See CE 677 which indicates it was picked up by R. L. Studebaker of the Dallas Police Force on November 22, 1963 ; 4 H 89–90 (Cadigan).
189. Id. at 93.
190. Id. at 95.
191. Id. at 93, 94, 97.
192. Id. at 93–94, 97, 99, 100.
193. CE 1077, 364 ; 4 H 93 (Cadigan).
194. Id. at 94–96, 99–100.
195. Ibid.
196. Id. at 96 ; CE 1965.
197. 3 H 215–218 (Truly).
198. 4 H 77–78 (Stombaugh).
199. Id. at 81.
200. Id. at 78.
201. Ibid.
202. Id. at 81.
203. Ibid.
204. 3 H 214 (Truly).
205. Id. at 214–215 ; 6 H 328 (Shelley).
206. Id. at 215 ; 6 H 328 (Shelley).
207. See infra, p. 143.
208. 4 H 269, 272, 277 (Day) ; CE 654, 733, 734 ; 7 H 147 (Studebaker) ; Studebaker DE J ; CE 1309.
209. 4 H 269, 270–271, 277 (Day) ; CE 641, 733, 734 ; 7 H 141–143, 147 (Studebaker) ; Studebaker DE A, B, C, D, E, J ; CE 1306, 1308.
210. 4 H 251, 277 (Day) ; CE 481, 482, 653, 733, 734 ; 7 H 141–143, 147 (Studebaker) ; Studebaker DE A, B, D, E, J.
211. 7 H 141 (Studebaker) ; 7 H 391 (Shelley) ; 3 H 232, 236 (Truly).
212. 7 H 149 (Studebaker).
213. CE 733 ; 734 ; 1312 ; 7 H 147 (Studebaker) ; Studebaker DE J.
214. CE 1302 ; see pp. 134–135 supra.
215. 4 H 31, 38, 42 (Latona).
216. Id. at 42.
217. Id. at 32, 34.
218. 3 H 231 (Truly) ; 7 H 391–392 (Shelley).
219. 3 H 232 (Truly) ; 7 H 149 (Studebaker) ; 7 H 392 (Shelley).
220. 7 H 391 (Shelley) ; 3 H 236 (Truly).
221. 7 H 391–392 (Shelley).
222. 4 H 269 (Day) ; CE 1302.
223. 4 H 39 (Latona).
224. Id. at 38, 39 (Latona).
225. Id. at 39.
226. Ibid.

227. Id. at 38–39.
228. 4 H 269–270 (Day) ; 4 H 31, 38–39, 42 (Latona).
229. CE 313 ; pp. 17–18.
230. 4 H 51, 52, 54 (Mandella) ; 15 H 745–746 (Mandella) ; CE 662.
231. Id. at 47 ; 7 H 590 (Wittmus).
232. 4 H 42–44 (Latona) ; CE 1980, 3135.
233. 6 H 347, 349 (Givens).
234. Id. at 354.
235. Id. at 349.
236 Ibid.
237. Id. at 349–350, 353.
238. Id. at 350–351.
239. Id. at 351 ; 3 H 223 (Truly).
240. 6 H 351 (Givens).
241. CE 1381.
242. 6 H 342–345 (Frankie Kaiser) ; 6 H 332 (Shelley) ; 6 H 335 (Nat Pinkston) ; 3 H 233–235 (Truly) ; Kaiser DE A ; CE 506.
243. CE 1966, 3141, 6 H 344 (Kaiser) ; 6 H 335 (Pinkston).
244. 6 H 344 (Kaiser) ; 6 H 335 (Pinkston).
245. Ibid ; 6 H 332–333 (Shelley) ; 3 H 215 (Truly).
246. 6 H 332–333 (Shelley).
247. See ch. III.
248. 6 H 144–148 (Howard Brennan) ; 7 H 354 (Forrest Sorrels).
249. 3 H 141–144 (Brennan) ; CE 477–479.
250. 3 H 149–157 (Brennan) ; CE 479.
251. 3 H 142 (Brennan).
252. Id. at 143.
253. Id. at 143–144.
254. Id. at 145 ; 6 H 322–323 (J. Herbert Sawyer) ; 3 H 197 (Norman) ; 3 H 207 (Jarman) ; 7 H 349 (Sorrels) ; 7 H 540–544 (W. E. Barnett).
255. 6 H 321 (Sawyer) ; Sawyer DE A ; CE 1974, p. 24–25.
256. CE 2005.
257. 3 H 144 (Brennan).
258. CE 1991.
259. CE 1945, 1950, 1951 ; CE 1944, p. 3.
260. 11 H 471 (Francis Martello) ; CE 1413, pp. 19, 35.
261. CE 1981.
262. CE 1974, p. 59.
263. Id. at 181.
264. Id. at 74.
265. 3 H 144 (Brennan).
266. CE 481, 715, 733, 734.
267. CE 715, 733, 734.
268. See 5 H 167 (Frazier) ; CE 1301.
269. 3 H 144 (Brennan).
270. See e.g., CE 481, 482, 485.
271. 3 H 174 (Williams) ; 3 H 190–191 (Norman) ; 3 H 204 (Jarman) ; CE 485, 486, 494.
272. CE 485, 486, 494.
273. See CE 485, 486, 494, 715, 733, 734, 1312.
274. 3 H 146, 156 (Brennan) : 3 H 197 (Norman) ; but see, 7 H 349 (Sorrels).
275. 3 H 184–185 (Brennan).
276. 3 H 197 (Norman) ; 3 H 207 (Jarman).
277. 3 H 197 (Norman).
278. 3 H 207 (Jarman).
279. 3 H 147–148 (Brennan) ; 7 H 355 (Sorrels).
280. 3 H 148 (Brennan) ; but see 7 H 354–355 (Sorrels).
281. 3 H 155 (Brennan).
282. CE 2006 : 3 H 155–156 (Brennan).
283. Id. at 155.
284. Id. at 148.
285. Ibid ; see also id. at 155.
286. Id. at 148 ; 7 H 354 (Sorrels).
287. 6 H 193–194 (Ronald Fischer) ; 6 H 203–205 (Robert Edwards).

288. 6 H 192 (Fischer) ; 6 H 202–203 (Edwards).
289. 3 H 141 (Brennan).
290. 6 H 193 (Fischer).
291. Ibid.
292. Ibid.
293. Ibid.
294. Id. at 194.
295. Ibid.
296. Ibid.
297. Ibid.
298. Id. at 197–198.
299. Id. at 197.
300. Id. at 198.
301. Ibid.
302. Id. at 198–199.
303. 6 H 203 (Edwards).
304. Id. at 203–204.
305. See ch. III, p. 64.
306. 2 H 203 (Amos Euins) ; CE 365.
307. 2 H 204–207 (Euins).
308. CE 367.
309. 6 H 170 (James Underwood).
310. 2 H 208 (Euins).
311. 7 H 349 (Sorrels).
312. 7 H 519 (James Altgens).
313. Ibid ; CE 369, 203.
314. 5 H 158–159 (Shaneyfelt) ; 7 H 519 (Altgens) ; CE 900.
315. CE 1408.
316. 6 H 338–339 (Lovelady) ; CE 1407.
317. 2 H 233 (Frazier) ; 6 H 328 (Shelley).
318. Ibid ; CE 369.
319. 3 H 244 (Baker).
320. Id. at 245.
321. Ibid.
322. Ibid.
323. Id. at 246.
324. Ibid.
325. Id. at 247.
326. Ibid.
327. Id. at 248.
328. Ibid.
329. Id. at 248–249.
330. Id. at 249.
331. CE 1118.
332. 3 H 249 (Baker).
333. Ibid.
334. 3 H 223 (Truly).
335. Ibid.
336. 3 H 249–250 (Baker).
337. Id. at 255–256 ; 3 H 222–223 (Truly).
338. CE 1118.
339. 7 H 591 (Truly).
340. 3 H 224 (Truly) ; 3 H 250 (Baker) ; CE 498.
341. 3 H 250, 255 (Baker).
342. Ibid.
343. Id. at 250 : CE 1118.
344. 3 H 223–224 (Truly).
345. 3 H 255 (Baker).
346. Id. at 250.
347. Ibid.
348. Ibid.
349. Id. at 255.
350. Id. at 251.
351. 3 H 225 (Truly).
352. Ibid. : 3 H 251 (Baker).
353. 3 H 225 (Truly) ; 3 H 251 (Baker).
354. Id. at 252 (Baker).
355. 3 H 225 (Truly).
356. Ibid.
357. 3 H 247–248 (Baker).
358. 3 H 228 (Truly).
359. 3 H 252 (Baker).
360. Id. at 254 ; see also 3 H 240 (Truly).
361. 3 H 254 (Baker) ; Truly, however stated that the second run was timed at 1 minute 15 seconds, 3 H 240 (Truly).
362. 7 H 592 (John Howlett).
363. 7 H 592–593 (Baker) ; 3 H 247–248 (Baker).
364. Id. at 253.

365. Id. at 252; accord, 3 H 228 (Truly).
366. Id. at 223.
367. Ibid.
368. 3 H 254 (Baker).
369. 3 H 226 (Truly); see also 3 H 254 (Baker).
370. 3 H 226–227 (Truly).
371. 6 H 379 (Dougherty); see also 3 H 229 (Truly).
372. 6 H 380 (Dougherty).
373. 6 H 382–386 (Piper).
374. 3 H 180 (Williams).
375. Ibid; 3 H 193 (Norman); 3 H 206 (Jarman); 3 H 231 (Truly); CE 490, 492.
376. 3 H 201–206 (Jarman); 3 H 89–97 (Norman); 3 H 171–176 (Williams).
377. 3 H 201–206 (Jarman); 3 H 89–97 (Norman); 3 H 171–176 (Williams); 6 H 378 (Dougherty); CE 1381, pp. 27, 49, 70, 101–102.
378. 6 H 388 (Victoria Adams).
379. Ibid.
380. 6 H 329 (Shelley); 6 H 339 (Lovelady).
381. Ibid.; 6 H 329 (Shelley).
382. 6 H 329 (Shelley).
383. Id. at 329–330; 6 H 338–340 (Lovelady).
384. Id. at 340.
385. 3 H 273 (Mrs. Reid).
386. Ibid.
387. Id. at 274.
388. Ibid.
389. Ibid.
390. Ibid.
391. Id. at 278; CE 1118.
392. 3 H 276 (Mrs. Reid).
393. I H 122 (Marina Oswald).
394. Ibid.
395. 6 H 345 (Kaiser).
396. 3 H 275 (Mrs. Reid).
397. Id. at 275, 279.
398. Id. at 279.
399. CE 1118.
400. 7 H 542–543 (Barnett).
401. See ch. III, p. 63.
402. 7 H 543 (Barnett).
403. Ibid.
404. 6 H 310 (D. V. Harkness); CE 1974, p. 165.
405. 6 H 311 (Harkness).
406. Id. at 312.
407. CE 1974, p. 165; 6 H 316–317 (Sawyer).
408. Id. at 317–318.
409. Id. at 320.
410. Id. at 318, 320.
411. Id. at 320.
412. 7 H 348 (Sorrels).
413. 3 H 238 (Truly).
414. 3 H 230, 238 (Truly).
415. Id. at 230.
416. Id. at 239.
417. 4 H 206 (Fritz).
418. Id. at 211; 7 H 173 (Sims); CE 381.
419. Compare CE 381–A and 372; 2 H 268 (McWatters).
420. 2 H 263–264, 286 (McWatters).
421. Id. at 271.
422. Id. at 264, 271.
423. Id. at 264–265.
424. Id. at 271.
425. Id. at 279–280, 282; CE 377.
426. 2 H 280–283 (McWatters).
427. CE 2641.
428. 2 H 270 (McWatters).
429. 6 H 401, 402 (Mrs. Bledsoe).
430. Id. at 406.
431. Ibid.
432. Id. at 408–409.
433. Id. at 409.
434. Ibid.

435. CE 150; 7 H 33–34 (Thomas Hutson); 1 H 121–122 (Marina Oswald); 15 H 695 (Shaneyfelt).
436. 6 H 412–413 (Mrs. Bledsoe).
437. CE 1985.
438. Ibid; CE 1984.
439. 6 H 411 (Mrs. Bledsoe).
440. 2 H 275 (McWatters); CE 376.
441. 2 H 276 (McWatters).
442. Id. at 275–276.
443. 10 H 292–293 (Mrs. A. C. Johnson).
444. CE 2017.
445. 2 H 283 (McWatters).
446. CE 1987.
447. Ibid.
448. 6 H 266, 270 (Roger Craig); CE 1967, 1992, 1993.
449. Ibid.; 6 H 266–267 (Craig).
450. Ibid.
451. 6 H 270 (Craig).
452. Ibid.
453. 4 H 245 (Fritz).
454. Ibid., 7 H 404 (Fritz).
455. 2 H 260 (Whaley).
456. Ibid.
457. Id. at 260–261.
458. Id. at 261.
459. Ibid.
460. 2 H 260 (Whaley); 6 H 432 (Whaley); CE 2003, p. 293.
461. 2 H 294 (Whaley); 6 H 430, 432 (Whaley).
462. CE 1054, 2003, p. 293.
463. CE 370, 382.
464. 2 H 254 (Whaley).
465. Id. at 255.
466. Ibid.
467. Id. at 256.
468. Ibid.
469. Id. at 258, 371.
470. 2 H 258 (Whaley).
471. CE 1119–A.
472. 6 H 428–429 (Whaley).
473. Id. at 429.
474. Ibid.
475. Id. at 434.
476. Ibid.
477. 2 H 260 (Whaley).
478. 6 H 345 (Kaiser).
479. 6 H 409 (Mrs. Bledsoe).
480. 2 H 259 (Whaley).
481. 2 H 256–257, 292 (Whaley).
482. CE 383–A, 2003, p. 289.
483. 4 H 214 (Fritz).
484. Id. at 211, 223; CE 2003, p. 289.
485. 4 H 223 (Fritz).
486. CE 1119–A.
487. 6 H 440 (Mrs. Roberts).
488. Id. at 435–436.
489. Id. at 436; 10 H 294–295 (Mrs. A. C. Johnson); Mrs. A. C. Johnson DE A.
490. 6 H 438–440 (Mrs. Roberts); 7 H 439 (Mrs. Roberts); CE 2017.
491. CE 1119–A.
492. CE 1974, pp. 52–53.
493. CE 1995.
494. 4 H 177 (Jesse Curry).
495. 3 H 297 (McDonald); CE 1976, p. 8; 522.
496. 7 H 77 (Rio Pierce); Sawyer DE B, p. 1; CE 1974, p. 24.
497. 4 H 179 (Curry); CE 1974, p. 26.
498. CE 1974, pp. 36–37; Sawyer DE A; 4 H 179, 184 (Curry); 7 H 75 (James Putnam).
499. Id. at 76; 4 H 179 (Curry).
500. Ibid; CE 1974, pp. 24–25, 28, 37.
501. 4 H 179 (Curry); CE 1974, pp. 24–25, 28, 37.
502. Ibid.
503. CE 1305.
504. 3 H 322–327 (William Scoggins); CE 1305.
505. 3H 333–334 (Scoggins); 7 H 265–266 (James Leavelle); CE 2003, p. 293.

506. 3 H 334–335 (Scoggins).
507. 6 H 446–449 (Domingo Benavides).
508. Id. at 449: CE 1974, p. 52.
509. 6 H 450–451 (Benavides) ; 7 H 68 (J. M. Poe) ; CE 2011, pp. 7–8.
510. 6 H 451–452 (Benavides) ; 7 H 263–264 (Leavelle).
511. 3 H 306–307, 313 (Helen Markham).
512. Id. at 307.
513. Id. at 307–308, 313–316 ; 3 H 343 (Barbara Davis) ; 6 H 456–457 (Virginia Davis).
514. 3 H 308 (Markham).
515. Id. at 308–309, 316, 321.
516. Id. at 309, 320.
517. 7 H 68 (Poe).
518. CE 1974, p. 58–59.
519. CE 2002 ; 3 H 310 (Markham).
520. Id. at 311 ; see 4 H 176 (Curry) ; 4 H 212 (Fritz) ; 7 H 253–254 (L. C. Graves) ; 7 H 263 (Leavelle) ; CE 2003, p. 293.
521. 7 H 252 (Graves).
522. Id. at 254.
523. 3 H 311 (Markham).
524. 2 H 51 (Mark Lane).
525. Markham, DE 1.
526. Id. at 3–4, 8.
527. Id. at 3, 7.
528. 7 H 68 (Poe) ; CE 1974, p. 59.
529. 3 H 317 (Markham).
530. 7 H 500–506 (Markham).
531. 3 H 343–344 (B. Davis) ; 6 H 455–458 (V. Davis).
532. 3 H 344–345 (B. Davis).
533. Id. at 345–346 ; 6 H 458, 460, 463–464 (V. Davis) ; 7 H 153 (C. N. Dhority) ; CE 2011, pp. 7–8.
534. CE 2003, p. 293 ; 6 H 461–462 (V. Davis) ; 3 H 349 (B. Davis) ; 7 H 153–154 (Dhority) ; 7 H 250 (C. W. Brown).
535. 3 H 348 (B. Davis).
536. Id. at 349.
537. 6 H 461 (V. Davis).
538. CE 2003, p. 293 ; 6 H 462 (V. Davis) ; 3 H 350 (B. Davis) ; 7 H 153–154 (Dhority) ; 7 H 250 (Brown).
539. 6 H 462 (V. Davis).
540. Ibid ; 3 H 350 (B. Davis).
541. Ibid ; 6 H 462 (V. Davis).
542. 7 H 83–84 (William Smith).
543. Id. at 84.
544. Id. at 84–85.
545. Id. at 85.
546. 3 H 351–352 (Ted Callaway) ; 7 H 395–396 (Sam Guinyard).
547. 3 H 352–353 (Callaway) ; 7 H 396–397 (Guinyard).
548. 3 H 353–354 (Callaway).
549. 7 H 398 (Guinyard).
550. Ibid ; 3 H 354 (Callaway).
551. Ibid.
552. Ibid ; 3 H 332 (Scoggins).
553. 7 H 264 (Leavelle) ; 3 H 355 (Callaway) ; 7 H 399–400 (Guinyard) ; CE 2003, p. 293.
554. 3 H 355 (Callaway).
555. 7 H 400 (Guinyard).
556. Ibid. ; 3 H 355 (Callaway).
557. CE 1054.
558. Ibid. ; 7 H 253 (Graves) ; 1 H 167–168 (Sims) ; 4 H 166, 175 (Curry) ; 7 H 262–266 (Leavelle).
559. CE 1305.
560. CE 2523 ; 11 H 434, 436–437. (Warren Reynolds).
561. 7 H 594 (Harold Russell).
562. 15 H 744–745 (B. M. Patterson) ; B. M. Patterson DE A, B.
563. 15 H 703 (L. J. Lewis) ; L. J. Lewis DE A.
564. CE 2523 ; 11 H 435 Reynolds) ; 15 H 744–745 (B. M. Patterson) ; B. M. Patterson DE A, B.

565. 7 H 594 (Russell).
566. 15 H 744–745 (B. M. Patterson) ; B. M. Patterson DE A, B.
567. CE 2523 ; 11 H 435–437 (Reynolds).
568. 15 H 703 (L. J. Lewis) ; L. J. Lewis DE A.
569. 3 H 300–301 (McDonald) ; 7 H 54–55 (Gerald Hill) ; 7 H 24–25 (Carroll).
570. 6 H 449–450 (Benavides) ; 3 H 345–346 (B. Davis) ; 6 H 463–464 (V. Davis).
571. 3 H 465–466, 468 (Cunningham).
572. Id. at 466.
573. 3 H 511 (Joseph Nicol).
574. CE 2011, p. 9.
575. 3 H 475–476 (Cunningham).
576. Id. at 475, 485 ; 3 H 512 (Nicol).
577. 3 H 475 (Cunningham).
578. Id. at 483.
579. CE 603.
580. 3 H 512 (Nicol).
581. 3 H 465 (Cunningham).
582. 3 H 352 (Callaway).
583. 7 H 372–374 (Michaelis).
584. Id. at 373–375 ; Michaelis DE 1.
585. 7 H 375 (Michaelis).
586. 7 H 376 (Michaelis) ; CE 135, 790.
587. 7 H 367–377 (Michaelis) ; CE 135, 790.
588. 7 H 376–378 (Michaelis) ; Michaelis DE. 2–5.
589. 4 H 361, 375 (Cole) ; 7 H 424 (Cadigan).
590. 1 H 118 (Marina Oswald).
591. Id. at 120.
592. Id. at 118, 120 ; 11 H 405 (Edwin Walker).
593. CE 144, 2003, p. 286 ; 7 H 213–214 (Henry Moore) ; Moore DE 1 ; 7 H 222–223 (F. M. Turner), 7 H 197–199 (Walter Potts) ; Potts DE A–1.
594. 1 H 120 (Marina Oswald).
595. 6 H 440 (Roberts) ; CE 1974, p. 52.
596. 6 H 439–440 (Roberts).
597. Hill DE B ; 3 H 302 (MacDonald) ; 7 H 53 (Hill).
598. CE 705, pp. 10, 22, 82.
599. CE 1974, p. 59.
600. 7 H 68–70 (Poe).
601. 7 H 593 (Alvin Brock).
602. CE 1974, p. 60.
603. 7 H 116–118 (Capt. W. R. Westbrook).
604. Ibid.
605. Ibid.
606. Id. at 118.
607. CE 1843.
608. 6 H 345 (Kaiser) ; CE 163.
609. 1 H 122 (Marina Oswald).
610. Ibid ; 7 H 117–118 (Westbrook).
611. 6 H 439 (Roberts).
612. 3 H 356 (Callaway).
613. 3 H 312 (Markham) ; 3 H 347 (B. Davis) ; 3 H 328 (Scoggins).
614. Ibid.
615. CE 1119–A. See pp. 168–169, supra.
616. 7 H 2 (Johnny Brewer).
617. Id. at 3.
618. Ibid.
619. Ibid.
620. Id. at 4.
621. 7 H 10–11 (Mrs. Julia Postal).
622. Id. at 11.
623. Ibid.
624. Ibid.
625. Ibid.
626. Ibid.
627. Ibid.
628. CE 1974, p. 83.
629. Id. at 83–84 ; 3 H 298–299 (McDonald) ; CE 2003, p. 75.
630. 3 H 299 (McDonald).
631. 7 H 19 (Carroll) ; 7 H 49 (Hill).
632. CE 2003, p. 77.

633. 7 H 6 (Brewer) ; 3 H 299 (McDonald) ; 7 H 30 (Hutson) ; 7 H 37 (C. T. Walker).
634. 7 H 5–6 (Brewer) ; 3 H 299 (McDonald) ; 7 H 37 (C. T. Walker).
635. Id. at 38.
636. 7 H 49 (Hill) ; 7 H 31 (Hutson).
637. 3 H 299 (McDonald).
638. Ibid.
639. Id. at 300.
640. Ibid.
641. Ibid.
642. Ibid.
643. Ibid.
644. Ibid.
645. Ibid ; 7 H 93 (Ray Hawkins).
646. 3 H 300 (McDonald).
647. Ibid.
648. Id. at 300–301 ; 7 H 20 (Carroll).
649. 7 H 547–548, 551 (Walthers).
650. 7 H 39 (Walker) ; 7 H 93–94 (Hawkins).
651. 7 H 32 (Hutson) ; 7 H 39–40 (Walker) ; see also 7 H 94 (Hawkins).
652. 3 H 461 (Cunningham).
653. Id. at 464–465.
654. 7 H 87–88 (George Applin Jr.).
655. Id. at 88–90.
656. 7 H 547 (Walthers).
657. 7 H 94–95 (Hawkins).
658. 7 H 72 (John Gibson).
659. Id. at 73.
660. 7 H 6 (Brewer).
661. Ibid.
662. 7 H 40 (C. T. Walker) ; 7 H 52 (G. Hill) ; CE 1974, p. 181.
663. 3 H 301 (McDonald).
664. CE 1974, p. 88.
665. 4 H 206 (Fritz) ; 7 H 163 (Sims).
666. 7 H 59 (Hill).
667. Ibid.
668. Ibid.
669. 4 H 275–276 (Day).
670. 3 H 514 (Nicol) ; 3 H 495 (Cunningham).
671. Id. at 487.
672. For testimony relating to the interrogation sessions, see 4 H 152–153, 157 (Curry) ; 4 H 207–211, 217, 221–231, 239–240 (Fritz) ; 4 H 355–357 (Winston Lawson) ; 4 H 466–470 (James Hosty, Jr.) ; 7 H 123–127 (Elmer Boyd) ; 7 H 164–182 (Sims) ; 7 H 309–318 (James Bookhout) ; 7 H 320–321 (Manning Clements) ; 13 H 58–62 (Sorrels) ; 7 H 590 (Kelley) ; 7 H 296–306 (Holmes) ; CE 1982.
673. 4 H 214, 217, 230–231 (Fritz) ; 7 H 299 (Holmes).
674. 7 H 215 (Moore) ; 7 H 193–194 (Stovall) ; 7 H 231 (Rose) ; 7 H 203–205 (John Adamcik).
675. CE 1982 ; p. 137 ; 4 H 226 (Fritz) ; CE 2003, p. I 138–B, 138–C.
676. 4 H 226–231 (Fritz) ; CE 2003, p. I 138–B, 138–C ; 7 H 298–299 (Holmes).
677. See pp. 126–127, supra.
678. 4 H 214 (Fritz).
679. Id. at 224, 230.
680. See pp. 172–173, supra.
681. CE 795, 1986, 1989, 1990 ; 7 H 187–188 (Stovall) ; 7 H 228 (Rose) ; CE 2011, p. 20.
682. 4 H 222 (Fritz).
683. Ibid.
684. Ibid ; 7 H 299 (Holmes) ; Holmes DE 4.
685. Ibid ; 7 H 299 (Holmes).
686. Ibid.
687. 4 H 211 (Fritz) ; CE 2003, p. I 136–D ; 7 H 311–312 (Bookhout).
688. Mrs. A. C. Johnson DE A ; see 10 H 294–295 (Mrs. A. C. Johnson).
689. CE 2003, p. 137–B.
690. 7 H 305 (Holmes).
691. 3 H 41 (R. Paine).
692. 7 H 305 (Holmes) ; Holmes DE 4, pp. 3–4 ; see also 4 H 223, 229 (Fritz).

693. Id. at 218, 223.
694. 2 H 220 (Frazier).
695. 4 H 467–468 (Hosty) ; see also 4 H 213–214 (Fritz) ; CE 2003, p. I 136–B, 136–C.
696. 6 H 328–329 (Shelley) ; see also 3 H 230 (Truly).
697. CE 1988 ; 4 H 224 (Fritz) ; CE 2005, p. I 137–C ; Holmes DE 4, (Kelley).
698. 3 H 201 (Jarman) ; CE 1980.
699. 3 H 201 (Jarman).
700. 11 H 405 (Walker).
701. CE 2958.
702. 5 H 446 (Surrey).
703. CE 1997.
704. CE 1785, 2525 ; 9 H 393–394 (R. Paine) ; 1 H 18 (Marina Oswald).
705. CE 1 ; 1 H 17, 37 (Marina Oswald).
706. 7 H 437 (Cadigan).
707. CE 1130.
708. 1 H 16 (Marina Oswald).
709. Ibid.
710. Id. at 17.
711. 11 H 155 (Waldo George).
712. 7 H 292 (Holmes).
713. CE 1979.
714. 1 H 16–17 (Marina Oswald) ; 11 H 292–294 (Marina Oswald).
715. Ibid ; 1 H 18 (Marina Oswald).
716. Id. at 38 ; see CE 2, P–2 ; CE 3, P–1 ; CE 5.
717. CE 3, P–1 ; CE 5.
718. CE 1397.
719. CE 1006–1009, 1011–1012.
720. CE 2, P–2 ; see CE 1397.
721. CE 2001, p. 3.
722. CE 1351, p. 8.
723. Waldman DE 7.
724. 15 H 692 (Shaneyfelt) ; Shaneyfelt DE 20.
725. CE 4, P–5 ; 1 H 39 (Marina Oswald).
726. CE 1953, pp. 23–24, CE 4, P–5.
727. CE 1824–A, p. 385 ; 1953, pp. 24–25 ; CE 1953–A, P–1.
728. 1 H 16 (Marina Oswald) ; CE 1403, pp. 733–734.
729. CE 1953, pp. 2–4.
730. Id. at 4–5.
731. CE 2524, 2011, p. 5.
732. 3 H 439 (Frazier).
733. Id. at 434.
734. Id. at 440.
735. 3 H 503 (Nicol).
736. Ibid.
737. 1 H 17 (Marina Oswald) ; CE 1403, p. 733.
738. CE 1953, p. 14.
739. CE 2521, 1790.
740. CE 1953, pp. 27–31 ; CE 1979.
741. 1 H 334–335 (Robert Oswald) ; CE 323, p. 27.
742. 1 H 123 (Marina Oswald).
743. CE 1357.
744. 1 H 334–340 (Robert Oswald).
745. 5 H 392 (Marina Oswald).
746. Id. at 389–390.
747. Id. at 390.
748. Ibid.
749. Michaelis DE 2.
750. 1 H 18–19 (Marina Oswald) ; 2 H 457–459 (R. Paine).
751. CE 1795, 1975.
752. CE 1973.
753. CE 2522, 1795, 1975.
754. CE 1972.
755. 5 H 390 (Marina Oswald).
756. Id. at 397.
757. Ibid.
758. CE 1972.
759. 5 H 395 (Marina Oswald).
760. Id. at 389 (Marina Oswald).
761. 11 H 305–306 (Maj. Eugene D. Anderson).

762. 11 H 305–306 (Anderson) ; 11 H 309 (Sgt. James A. Zahm).
763. 11 H 310 (Zahm).
764. 11 H 305–306 (Anderson).
765. 3 H 413 (Frazier).
766. 3 H 450 (Ronald Simmons).
767. 11 H 306–307 (Zahm).
768. Id. at 307.
769. Ibid.
770. Id. at 308.
771. Id. at 307, 309.
772. 11 H 310 (Zahm).
773. 11 H 302–303 (Anderson).
774. Ibid.
775. Ibid.
776. Ibid.
777. Id. at 304 ; Anderson DE 1.
778. Ibid ; 3 H 304 (Anderson).
779. Id. at 305 ; Anderson DE 1.
780. Ibid.
781. 11 H 304 (Anderson).
782. Id. at 305.
783. 11 H 308 (Zahm).
784. Ibid.
785. 1 H 327 (Robert Oswald).
786. Id. at 325–327.
787. Ibid.
788. CE 1402, 2007 ; CE 1403, p. 731 ; 1 H 327–328 (R. Oswald) ; 1 H 96 (Marina Oswald) ; 2 H 465–466 (R. Paine).
789. 1 H 327 (R. Oswald).
790. 1 H 14–15 (Marina Oswald) ; CE 1156, p. 442.
791. CE 1404, pp. 446–448.

792. 9 H 249 (George De Mohren-schildt) ; 9 H 315–317 (Jeanne De Mohren-schildt).
793. 1 H 21–22, 53–54, 65 (Marina Oswald) ; CE 1814, p. 736.
794. CE 2964.
795. See discussion, ch. III, p. 117, supra.
796. 3 H 399, 437–438 (R. A. Frazier) ; 3 H 449 (Simmons).
797. Id. at 444.
798. Id. at 445–447.
799. Id. at 445.
800. Id. at 446.
801. Ibid.
802. Id. at 444 ; See discussion Chapter III, p. 115, supra.
803. See ch. III, pp. 64–68, supra.
804. 3 H 446 (Simmons).
805. Id. at 447.
806. Id. at 447, 449.
807. Id. at 450 ; See also fn 794, supra.
808. 3 H 403–404 (R. A. Frazier).
809. Id. at 404.
810. Ibid.
811. Id. at 404–405.
812. Id. at 405–407.
813. Id. at 406–407.
814. Id. at 411, 443 (Simmons).
815. 3 H 413–414 (R. A. Frazier).
816. 11 H 309, 310 (Zahm) ; 11 H 305, 306 (Anderson).
817. 11 H 309 (Zahm).
818. Id. at 309–310.

CHAPTER V

1. 4 H 152 (Jesse E. Curry) ; CE 701, 2139, 2140.
2. 4 H 209 (J. W. Fritz) ; 7 H 22 (Bob K. Carroll) ; 7 H 59–60 (Gerald Hill) ; 7 H 123 (Elmer L. Boyd) ; 7 H 164 (Richard Sims).
3. 7 H 125 (Boyd) ; 7 H 166 (Sims).
4. 7 H 126 (Boyd) ; 7 H 173 (Sims).
5. 7 H 128 (Boyd) ; 7 H 168 (Sims).
6. 7 H 128–129 (Boyd) ; 7 H 169–170 (Sims) ; 7 H 264 (James R. Leavelle) ; 7 H 151 (C. N. Dhority).
7. 4 H 216–217 (Fritz) ; 7 H 129 (Boyd) ; CE 2003, p. 104 ; 15 H 506–508 (David L. Johnston) ; see also sources cited in footnote 45.
8. 4 H 217 (Fritz) ; 7 H 130 (Boyd) ; 7 H 171–172 (Sims).
9. 4 H 218 (Fritz) ; 7 H 278–285 (W. E. Barnes) ; 7 H 288–289 (J. B. Hicks) ; CE 2003, pp. 167, 206, 283.
10. CE 2003, p. 168 ; 15 H 507 (Johnston).
11. WFAA–TV reel PKT 11 ; see infra, p. 208.
12. 7 H 132 (Boyd) ; 7 H 177 (Sims) ; CE 2003, pp. 238–239 ; 4 H 153 (Curry) ; see 4 H 219 (Fritz) ; 7 H 266 (Leavelle).
13. 4 H 153 (Curry) ; 12 H 96 (M. W. Stevenson) ; 12 H 389–391 (Woodrow Wiggins) ; 7 H 328 (H. Nichols).
14. 4 H 155 (Curry) ; 4 H 221 (Fritz) ; CE 2003, p. 104 ; 15 H 507–508 (Johnston).
15. 4 H 222, 226 (Fritz) ; 7 H 133 (Boyd).
16. Ibid.
17. CE 2003, pp. 207, 393 ; 1 H 77–79 (Marina Oswald) ; 1 H 149–150 (Marguerite Oswald).
18. CE 1999, 2187.
19. 4 H 227 (Fritz) ; 7 H 265 (Leavelle).
20. CE 2023.

21. CE 2003, pp. 207–208, 393 ; 1 H 461–462 (Robert Oswald).
22. 3 H 85–86 (Ruth Paine).
23. 7 H 328 (H. Nichols) ; CE 2165.
24. CE 2003, p. 142 ; 4 H 228 (Fritz) ; 7 H 178 (Sims).
25. 3 H 87–88 (R. Paine).
26. CE 2003, p. 142 ; 7 H 258 (L. C. Graves) ; 7 H 266 (Leavelle).
27. 4 H 230 (Fritz) ; CE 2003, p. 320.
28. CE 2003, p. 301.
29. CE 2024.
30. For testimony relating to the interrogation sessions, see 4 H 152–153, 157 (Curry) ; 4 H 207–211, 217, 222–231, 239–240 (Fritz) ; 4 H 355–357 (Winston G. Lawson) ; 4 H 444–470 (James P. Hosty) ; 7 H 123–137 (Boyd) ; 7 H 164–182 (Sims) ; 7 H 309–318 (James W. Bookhout) ; 7 H 320–321 (Manning C. Clements) ; 13 H 58–62 (Forrest V. Sorrels) ; 7 H 297–301 (Harry Holmes) ; CE 2003, pp. 136a–138b, CE 2060, 2061.
31. CE 2003, pp. 141–142.
32. 4 H 207 (Fritz) ; CE 2003, p. 125.
33. CE 2003, pp. 136d–138e, 161 ; 5 H 218 (Henry Wade).
34. 4 H 215 (Fritz).
35. CE 2003, pp. 173, 184, 208.
36. 4 H 215 (Fritz) ; 7 H 318 (Bookhout).
37. 4 H 231–232, 246 (Fritz) ; 7 H 133, 135 (Boyd) ; 7 H 180–182 (Sims) ; 7 H 266–267, 269 (Leavelle) ; 7 H 259–260 (L. Graves).
38. 4 H 239 (Fritz).
39. 7 H 310 (Bookhout).
40. 4 H 152 (Curry) ; see also 4 H 232 (Fritz).
41. 4 H 238 (Fritz) ; 7 H 311 (Bookhout).
42. 4 H 153, 175–176 (Curry) ; 15 H

129 (Curry); 4 H 238 (Fritz); 7 H 128, 134–135 (Boyd); 7 H 330 (Nichols); 7 H 311, 316–317 (Bookhout); 7 H 321 (Clements); 7 H 297 (Holmes); 15 H 512–513 (Johnston); see WFAA–TV reel PKT 21; KRLD–TV reel 20; WFAA–TV reel PKT 25.

43. 7 H 59 (G. Hill); 7 H 21 (Carroll); 7 H 134–135 (Boyd); 7 H 330 (Nichols).

44. 4 H 216 (Fritz); 7 H 314, 316–317 (Bookhout).

45. 4 H 216–217, 221 (Fritz); 15 H 506–508 (Johnston).

46. CE 2166.

47. See supra, p. 182.

48. 7 H 323 (Gregory L. Olds).

49. CE 2073, see CE 1999.

50. 3 H 88–89 (R. Paine); 10 H 116 (John J. Abt).

51. 7 H 325–332 (Nichols); 7 H 322–325 (Olds); CE 2165.

52. 7 H 299–300 (Holmes).

53. 12 H 30 (Curry); Glen King DE 4, 5; 15 H 55 (King); NBC–TV reel 3.

54. CE 1359, p. 4.

55. 5 H 218 (Wade).

56. For testimony describing conditions on third floor see, e.g., 4 H 152, 153, 158, 160 (Curry); 4 H 231–232 (Fritz); 4 H 355 (Lawson); 4 H 462–463 (Hosty); 7 H 277 (Barnes); 7 H 318 (Bookhout); 7 H 322 (Clements); 13 H 40 (Thomas D. McMillon); 13 H 58–59 (Sorrels); 15 H 54–55 (King); Seth Kantor DE 4; CE 1353; 7 H 157 (Dhority); 15 H 512 (Johnston); WFAA–TV reel PKT 21; WFAA–TV reel PKT 14; KRLD–TV reel 9.

57. 4 H 463 (Hosty).

58. 4 H 151 (Curry); 12 H 30 (Curry); 15 H 55 (King); Kantor DE 4; Leo Sauvage, "The Oswald Affair," *Commentary* 64 (March 1964); CE 2176.

59. 12 H 30 (Curry).

60. 4 H 151 (Curry).

61. 4 H 355 (Lawson).

62. 7 H 157 (Dhority); 4 H 151 (Curry); 12 H 30 (Curry); 5 H 218 (Wade); CE 1359.

63. 5 H 218 (Wade).

64. 4 H 355 (Lawson).

65. 2 H 260 (William W. Whaley).

66. King DE 5, p. 7; WFAA–TV reel PKF–5; WFAA–TV reel PKT–8.

67. 15 H 55 (King).

68. 7 H 269 (Leavelle).

69. 7 H 358–359 (Sorrels).

70. 12 H 96 (Stevenson); CE 1353.

71. 12 H 34 (Curry); CE 1353.

72. 15 H 54 (King); 12 H 112 (Cecil E. Talbert).

73. 15 H 54 (King); see 12 H 112 (Talbert).

74. 12 H 96 (Stevenson); 12 H 135–138 (Charles O. Arnett); 15 H 590–591 (Thayer Waldo); CE 1757, 2037–2043, 2047–2059; John G. McCullough DE 2; CE 2062, 2066; Waldo DE 1; Icarus N. Pappas DE 3.

75. 13 H 58–59 (Sorrels).

76. See, e.g., Waldo DE 1; CE 1757, 2044, 2048, 2052, 2053.

77. 13 H 40 (McMillon); 13 H 131 (Jimmy Turner); 15 H 591–592 (Waldo); CE 2040, 2074; 15 H 373–377 (McCullough); WBAP–TV reel FW 2.

78. KRLD–TV reel 23.

79. CE 2074.

80. 7 H 64 (G. Hill); WFAA–TV reel PKT 24–27:28; CE 2160.

81. CE 2003, pp. 125, 141–142, 293.

82. 4 H 232, 246 (Fritz); 12 H 33 (Curry).

83. For testimony describing Oswald's passage through the third-floor corridor, see, e.g., 12 H 33 (Curry); 4 H 231–232 (Fritz); 7 H 181 (Sims); 7 H 268–269 (Leavelle); Kantor DE 4, pp. 10–19; WFAA–TV reel PKT 14.

84. For testimony describing the Friday evening press conference, see 4 H 166–167 (Curry); 12 H 96 (Stevenson); 5 H 221–222 (Wade); 15 H 510–512 (Johnston); 15 H 591–593 (Waldo); 13 H 115–116 (Robert L. Hankal); 7 H 132–133 (Boyd); 7 H 175–176 (Sims); 7 H 322 (Clements); 7 H 323–324 (Olds); 4 H 219 (Fritz); 4 H 357–358 (Lawson); 13 H 189–192 (A. M. Eberhardt); CE 2173.

85. 12 H 32 (Curry); Waldo DE 1; CE 2040; 15 H 592 (Waldo); 15 H 510–511 (Johnston); CE 2052; 7 H 324 (Olds); WFAA–TV reel PKF 5; KRLD–TV reel 23.

86. 4 H 219 (Fritz).

87. CE 2173.

88. 12 H 34 (Curry); 7 H 132 (Boyd); 7 H 176 (Sims).

89. 4 H 219 (Fritz).

90. 4 H 167, 175 (Curry); 4 H 219 (Fritz).

91. 15 H 131 (Curry).

92. 4 H 175 (Curry); KRLD–TV reel 23.

93. 4 H 175 (Curry).

94. 12 H 44–46 (J. E. Decker); see also 4 H 180–181 (Curry); 12 H 35 (Curry); 15 H 116 (Charles O. Batchelor).

95. 12 H 2 (Batchelor).

96. 12 H 35 (Curry).

97. CE 2013, 2018, 2021; W. B. Frazier DE 5087; Talbert DE 5065; 12 H 53–55 (W. B. Frazier).

98. 12 H 37 (Curry); 15 H 125 (Curry); 12 H 6–7 (Batchelor); 15 H 116–118 (Batchelor).

99. 12 H 36–37 (Curry); see 12 H 6–7 (Batchelor); 15 H 116 (Batchelor).

100. 12 H 7–8, 12 (Batchelor); 15 H 116–118 (Batchelor); 12 H 37 (Curry); 12 H 99–100 (Stevenson).

101. 12 H 35–36 (Curry); 15 H 128, 132 (Curry); 15 H 115, 122–123 (Batchelor); 15 H 134, 137 (Stevenson).

102. 13 H 17 (Leavelle).

103. Ibid.

104. 13 H 63 (Sorrels).

105. 12 H 91 (James M. Solomon); 12 H 138 (Arnett); 12 H 292 (Logan W. Mayo); 12 H 317–318 (Wm. J. Newman).

106. 12 H 112 (Talbert); 12 H 421–422, 426 (Patrick T. Dean).

107. 12 H 208 (Wilbur J. Cutchshaw); R. L. Lowery DE 5083; 12 H 307 (L. Miller); 12 H 396 (Don R. Archer); 13 H 268 (Vernon S. Smart).

108. 12 H 47–49 (Decker).

109. 12 H 117 (Talbert); 15 H 184 (Talbert); 12 H 16 (Batchelor); 12 H 100 (Stevenson).

110. See, e.g., B. H. Combest DE 5100; Robert S. Huffaker DE 5333.

111. 12 H 113–117 (Talbert); 15 H 183–184 (Talbert); 12 H 141–143 (Arnett); 12 H 166 (Buford L. Beaty); 12 H 173–175 (Alvin R. Brock); 12 H 319 (Newman); 12 H 338–340 (R. Pierce); 12 H 354 (D. F. Steele); 12 H 384–386 (Gano G. Worley); 12 H 421–426 (Dean); 13 H 118 (Huffaker); 13 H 85–88 (Fred A. Bieberdorf); 13 H 143 (Hal Fuqua); 13 H 146–147 (Edward Kelly); 13 H 149–156 (Louis McKinzie); 13 H 166–175 (A. Riggs); 13 H 175–181 (John O. Servance); 13 H 156–166 (E. Pierce); James A. Putnam DE 5071; CE 2010, 2032, 2066.

112. 13 H 159–160 (E. Pierce) ; 13 H 180 (J. O. Servance) ; 12 H 422–423 (Dean) ; 12 H 173–174 (Brock) ; 12 H 141–144 (Arnett).

113. CE 2027, 2062 ; KRLD–TV reel 13 ; but see CE 2029.

114. 12 H 67 (O. A. Jones) ; 12 H 112 (Talbert) ; 13 H 131 (J. Turner) ; 12 H 335–336 (Bobby G. Patterson) ; 12 H 183–184 (Combest) ; 12 H 360 (Roy E. Vaughn) ; 12 H 422 (Dean) ; CE 2051, 2069 ; Hankal DE 5337 ; CE 2037, 2039, 2043, 2047, 2050, 2055, 2056, 2057.

115. 12 H 36 (Curry) ; 12 H 10–15 (Batchelor) ; 12 H 97–98 (Stevenson) ; 15 H 134 (Stevenson) ; 15 H 125–127 (Curry) ; 15 H 115, 119 (Batchelor).

116. 12 H 164–168 (Beaty) ; 12 H 180 (Combest) ; 12 H 313 (L. Miller) ; 12 H 409–411 (Barnard S. Clardy) ; 12 H 428 (Dean) ; 12 H 209 (Cutchshaw) ; CE 2028.

117. 13 H 43 (McMillon).

118. 12 H 66 (O. A. Jones) ; 12 H 191 (Kenneth H. Croy) ; 12 H 209–210 (Cutchshaw) ; 12 H 270 (Harry M. Kriss) ; 15 H 119–120 (Batchelor) ; 15 H 135 (Stevenson).

119. In addition to the testimony cited in footnotes 114 and 115, see 12 H 119 (Talbert) ; 12 H 150–157 (Arnett) ; 12 H 181 (Combest) ; 12 H 189 (Croy) ; 12 H 275–276 (Lowery) ; 13 H 45 (McMillon) ; 12 H 287 (Billy J. Maxey) ; 12 H 345–346 (Putnam) ; 12 H 17 (Batchelor) ; 15 H 120 (Batchelor) ; 12 H 102 (Stevenson) ; 15 H 135 (Stevenson) ; 13 H 8 (L. Graves) ; 13 H 109 (Ira J. Beers) ; 13 H 121 (Huffaker) ; 13 H 127 (George R. Phenix) ; CE 2002 ; WFAA–TV reel PKT 17–38 :00–47 :18.

120. CE 2052, 2053.

121. 12 H 8, 15 (Batchelor) ; 12 H 426 (Dean) ; CE 2070, pp. 9, 10 ; KRLD–TV reel 13 ; WBAP–TV reel FW 1.

122. 13 H 6 (L. Graves) ; 13 H 28 (L. D. Montgomery) ; CE 2054 ; 15 H 594–596 (Waldo) ; CE 2052, 2053, 2059 ; Pappas DE 4.

123. 12 H 15 (Batchelor) ; 15 H 117 (Batchelor) ; 12 H 118 (Talbert) ; 12 H 167 (Beaty).

124. 4 H 188–189 (Curry) ; 12 H 37–38 (Curry) ; 15 H 125 (Curry) ; 4 H 233 (Fritz) ; 12 H 100 (Stevenson) ; 15 H 136 (Stevenson) ; 13 H 61–63 (Sorrels).

125. 7 H 155–156 (Dhority) ; 12 H 339 (R. Pierce) ; CE 2003, pp. 312, 314.

126. 12 H 16 (Batchelor) ; 12 H 68 (O. A. Jones) ; 12 H 100 (Stevenson).

127. 13 H 5 (L. Graves) ; Leavelle DE 5088 ; 13 H 27 (Montgomery) ; CE 2064 ; CE 2003, pp. 220–221.

128. 15 H 137 (Stevenson) ; CE 2003, p. 171 ; CE 2060 12 H 391 (Wiggins) ; 13 H 28 (Montgomery).

129. 12 H 145–146 (Arnett) ; 12 H 287–288 (Maxey) ; 12 H 339–340 (R. Pierce) ; 12 H 345–347 (Putnam) ; 12 H 361–362 (Vaughn) ; 12 H 377 (James G. Watson) ; 12 H 427–428 (Dean) ; 13 H 134–135 (J. Turner).

130. 7 H 155–156 (Dhority) ; CE 2003, pp. 312, 314 ; WFAA–TV reel PKT 16.

131. WFAA–TV reel PKT 10 ; CE 2038, 2039, 2042.

132. CE 2039.

133. CE 2038, 2042, 2059, 2062.

134. McMillon DE 5018 ; see also 13 H 7 (L. Graves) ; 13 H 16–17 (Leavelle).

135. See sources cited in footnote 129. WFAA–TV reel PKT–16 ; WFAA–TV reel PKT–10 ; NBC–TV reel 66 ; KRLD–TV reel 13.

136. 13 H 29 (Montgomery) ; see reels cited in footnote 135.

137. 12 H 183 (Combest) ; see also 12 H 169 (Beaty) ; 12 H 376–377 (Watson) ; 13 H 7, (L. Graves) ; 13 H 115 (Hankal) ; CE 2052.

138. For testimony describing the final seconds culminating in the shooting of Oswald, see, e.g., 4 H 234–235, 243 (Fritz) ; 13 H 137 (J. Turner) ; see also WFAA–TV reel PKF–10 ; KRLD–TV reel 13 ; NBC–TV reel 66.

139. 12 H 434–438 (Dean) ; 15 H 188–189 (Talbert) ; Dean DE 5009, p. 2 ; McMillon DE 5018 ; see Sorrels DE 1.

140. 12 H 433 (Dean) ; 12 H 412 (Clardy).

141. C. R. Hall DE 2.

142. 13 H 71 (Sorrels) ; 5 H 181–213 (Jack Ruby) ; C. R. Hall DE 3, p. 11.

143. CE 2025 ; 13 H 221–226 (D. Lane).

144. KRLD–TV reel 13.

145. 12 H 348–349 (Willie B. Slack) ; 12 H 392 (Wiggins) ; 13 H 90–91 (Frances Cason) ; 13 H 96 (Hardin) ; 13 H 101 (Hulse) ; 13 H 239–243 (Priddy) ; Michael Hardin DE 5125, 5126, 5127 ; F. Cason DE 5135 ; CE 2022 ; see also reels cited in footnote 138.

146. CE 2002, pp. 112–113 ; CE 2026.

147. Compare Dean DE 5009, p. 2 and 12 H 228–234 (N. J. Daniels) with 12 H 434 (Dean) and 12 H 412 (Clardy). See also 12 H 347 (Putnam) and KRLD–TV reel 13 ; C. R. Hall DE 3, pp. 11, 12, which suggests that the Pierce car may have passed Ruby before Putnam entered the car, which would have been at the bottom, rather than the top, of the Main Street ramp.

148. 13 H 135–137 (J. Turner).

149. 12 H 323–329, 332–334 (Newman) ; 12 H 192–193 (K. H. Croy). Cf. 12 H 262–264 (Howard B. Holly) ; 12 H 89–90 (Solomon).

150. 12 H 232 (N. J. Daniels).

151. 12 H 228–234 (Daniels) ; Daniels DE 5325 ; Compare 12 H 362–363 (Vaughn) ; Vaughn DE 5335, p. 2.

152. N. J. Daniels DE 5325, pp. 1–2 ; 12 H 369 (Vaughn).

153. 12 H 359–362 (Vaughn) ; CE 2034, 2035, 2043, 2058.

154. 12 H 359–362 (R. Pierce) ; 12 H 346–347 (Putnam) ; 12 H 287 (Maxey) ; see also CE 2035, 2063 ; 15 H 681–685 (Harry T. Tasker).

155. 12 H 212, 215–216 ; Cutchshaw) ; Lowery DE 5083.

156. KRLD–TV reel 13.

157. 13 H 132–136 (J. Turner).

158. KRLD–TV reel 13.

159. CE 2071.

160. KRLD–TV reel 13 ; 15 H 117–118 (Batchelor).

161. See sources in note 112.

162. CE 2003 pp. 260–261a ; 13 H 49–50 (McMillon) ; C. R. Hall DE 3, pp. 11, 12 ; CE 2182.

163. KLIF reel 75 (Duncan interview with Sergeant Dean), Nov. 24, 1963.

164. See supra, p. 212.

165. CE 2030 ; Vaughn DE 5335 ; Putnam DE 5071.

166. See sources in footnote 152. 12 H 190 (Croy).

167. CE 2002.

168. 5 H 198–199 (Jack Ruby) ; 14 H 545 (Jack Ruby).

169. See Commission Exhibits in footnote 74.

170. See app. XVI.

171. 14 H 167, 191–192 (Curry).

172. 12 H 427, 430 (Dean).

173. 12 H 156–157 (Arnett) ; 12 H 192–194 (Croy) ; 12 H 252–253 (Wm. J. Harrison) ; King DE 3.

174. KRLD–TV reel 13.

175. E.g., 12 H 182–183 (Combest); 12 H 211 (Cutchshaw); 12 H 249, 251 (Harrison); 12 H 275–276 (Lowery); 12 H 399 (Archer); KRLD–TV reel 13.

176. See infra, pp. 353–354; CE 2019; 5 H 199 (J. Ruby); C. R. Hall DE 3. Cf. 13 H 244 (George Senator); Senator DE 5401.

177. 5 H 199 (J. Ruby); 13 H 244 (Senator); Senator DE 5401.

178. CE 2068.

179. CE 1982, 2072; 12 H 30 (Curry); 4 H 241 (Fritz); 12 H 94 (Stevenson).

180. Talbert DE 1; 12 H 112 (Talbert).

181. Talbert DE 2; 15 H 123 (Batchelor); King DE 4, p. 9.

182. 15 H 55 (King).

183. 12 H 39 (Curry). See also 15 H 54–55 (King).

184. 15 H 55 (King).

185. 15 H 53 (King); Talbert DE 2.

186. King DE 4, p. 9; 15 H 55, 58 (King); 15 H 127 (Curry).

187. 4 H 152 (Curry).

188. See supra, pp. 202–206.

189. CE 1359, p. 4.

190. King DE 4, p. 10; 15 H 54 (King).

191. CE 1353; King DE 4, 5; KRLD–TV reel 9; WFAA–TV reel PKT 21; CE 2052.

192. 15 H 55–56 (King).

193. See supra, p. 208.

194. See supra, 208; CE 2052.

195. 15 H 188–191 (Talbert); WFAA–TV PKT–30–35:01–36:21; 15 H 128 (Curry).

196. CE 2018; 4 H 187–188 (Curry).

197. See supra, p. 212.

198. This judgment is shared by the officials of the Dallas Police Department. See, e.g., 15 H 127–128 (Curry); 15 H 122 (Batchelor).

199. King DE 4, pp. 8–9.

200. See supra, p. 201.

201. 15 H 125 (Curry); 15 H 120–121 (Batchelor).

202. 12 H 40; see also 4 H 186 (Curry).

203. 4 H 233 (Fritz).

204. 12 H 53–54 (W. B. Frazier); 15 H 153 (Fritz).

205. 13 H 17 (Leavelle); 13 H 63 (Sorrels).

206. 4 H 233 (Fritz); 12 H 35 (Curry); see sources cited in footnote 101.

207. 12 H 69 (O. A. Jones).

208. See supra, p. 213.

209. 12 H 155 (Arnett); 12 H 247 (Harrison); 12 H 281, 284 (Frank M. Martin); 12 H 428 (Dean); CE 2031.

210. 4 H 187 (Curry); 12 H 35 (Curry); 12 H 9–10, 13 (Batchelor); 12 H 390 (Wiggins).

211. See sources in footnote 133.

212. See supra, p. 215.

213. 7 H 156 (Dhority); 4 H 233–234 (Fritz); WFAA–TV reel PKT–16; 13 H 17 (Leavelle); see supra, p. 216.

214. 13 H 17 (Leavelle).

215. 12 H 69 (O. A. Jones).

216. 15 H 53 (King).

217. CE 1353, p. 3.

218. 4 H 152, 181 (Curry); 12 H 30–31 (Curry); 5 H 218 (Wade).

219. See CE 2142 through 2152 and CE 2168 through 2173.

220. WFAA audio reel 2, Nov. 23, 1963; KRLD audio reel 33–1, –9, Nov. 23, 1963; WFAA–TV reels PKT 12 10:16; PKT 7; PKT 21 48:30; see also 4 H 160, 199–200 (Curry).

221. CE 2153, 2155.

222. CE 2157, 2159, 2160, 2162, 2163, 2164, 2167.

223. 5 H 238–239 (Wade).

224. 5 H 238–240 (Wade); see, for instance, CE 2168 through 2173.

225. 5 H 223 (Wade); KRLD–TV reel 23; CE 2169.

226. 5 H 227 (Wade); CE 2170.

227. 5 H 250 (Wade); CE 2169, 2172.

228. 7 H 108 (Weitzman).

229. 3 H 169 (B. R. Williams); CE 2160.

230. CE 2146.

231. CE 2178.

232. 5 H 239 (Wade).

233. 5 H 228 (Wade); see sources cited in footnote 219.

234. 5 H 115 (J. Edgar Hoover).

235. 5 H 115–116 (Hoover); 15 H 58 (King); CE 2072; cf. 15 H 129 (Curry).

236. CE 2148.

237. 5 H 237 (Wade).

238. 5 H 237–238 (Wade).

239. CE 2168; 5 H 237–238 (Wade).

240. See supra, pp. 165, 174.

241. CE 2180.

242. WBAP Fort Worth audio reel 12 "A," Nov. 24, 1963; CE 2168.

243. 6 H 368–370 (Joe R. Molina); CE 2036, pp. 12–14.

244. CE 2146, 2147, 2162, 2181.

245. KRLD–TV audio reels 21 "B"–11, 22 "A"–5, 24 "A," 25 "A," Nov. 23, 1963; 6 H 370 (Molina).

246. 6 H 372 (Molina).

247. CE 2186.

248. 6 H 370 (Molina); CE 3132.

249. 6 H 371 (Molina); CE 2036, pp. 14–16, CE 2049, 2065, 1970.

250. 5 H 223 (Wade); CE 2169; see Vernon's (Tex.) Ann. C. P. art. 714.

251. CE 2144; see *Washburn* v. *State,* 165 Crim. Rep. 125, 318 S.W. 2d 627, 637 (Tex. Ct. Crim. App. 1958), certiorari denied, 359 U.S. 965 (1958).

252. CE 2168; see supra, pp. 179–180.

253. CE 2153, 2172, 2152; see also WBAP–TV reel FW 2.

254. CE 2146, 2172; WBAP–TV reel FW 2.

255. CE 2183.

256. CE 2184.

257. 4 H 201 (Curry); see also 12 H 39 (Curry).

258. King DE 5, p. 5.

259. CE 1353, 2052; Waldo DE 1.

260. 4 H 153 (Curry).

261. See supra, p. 208.

262. 13 H 17 (Leavelle); 13 H 63 (Sorrels).

263. 4 H 166 (Curry); King DE 4, 5. Felix McKnight, executive editor of the Dallas-Times-Herald, discussed this pressure in an address at Northwestern University in February 1964. See CE 2185.

264. King DE 5, p. 6.

265. Elgin E. Crull DE 1.

266. King DE 4; CE 1359.

CHAPTER VI

1. CE 2768, 2772, 2444, 3042, pp. 59, 65.

2. See pp. 31–40, supra.

3. 10 H 152 (Irving Statman); Helen Cunningham DE 1–A; 11 H 477–478 (H. Cunningham).

4. See app. XIV, p. 745.

5. Burcham DE 1, p. 1; 11 H 473 (John Burcham).

6. 3 H 37 (Ruth Paine); CE 401.

7. See footnote 3, supra.

8. CE 1871; Gangl DE 1; 11 H 478–479 (Theodore Gangl).
9. CE 427; 11 H 478–479 (Gangl).
10. Gangl DE 1; 11 H 478–479 (Gangl).
11. Ibid.
12. 3 H 33–34 (R. Paine); 2 H 246–247 (Linnie Mae Randle); see 1 H 29 (Marina Oswald).
13. 2 H 246 (Randle).
14. 3 H 33–34 (R. Paine); 3 H 213 (Roy Truly).
15. 3 H 34–35 (R. Paine).
16. 3 H 214 (Truly).
17. 10 H 132 (H. Cunningham); H. Cunningham DE 1–A.
18. 10 H 132 (H. Cunningham).
19. Ch. II, p. 31.
20. Ibid.
21. Id. at 40.
22. Ch. IV, p. 131–137.
23. 2 H 216 (Buell Wesley Frazier).
24. Ibid; CE 3118.
25. 2 H 222 (B. W. Frazier).
26. Id. at 226.
27. 1 H 65 (Marina Oswald); 3 H 46 (R. Paine); see app. XIII, p. 740.
28. Ch. IV, pp. 130–131.
29. Id. at pp. 135–136.
30. 1 H 73 (Marina Oswald); 3 H 49 (R. Paine).
31. CE 142, 626; 1, 304.
32. See 3 H 232 (Truly).
33. Id. at 231; CE 483.
34. 3 H 231 (Truly).
35. Id. at 232.
36. Ibid.
37. Ch. IV, pp. 137–140.
38. CE 1131; 1301; see 3 H 231–232 (Truly).
39. 3 H 232, 236 (Truly); CE 1131.
40. See 3 H 232 (Truly).
41. Ch. IV, footnotes 217, 223; p. 140–146.
42. Id. at footnote 215, p. 140.
43. CE 3135.
44. Ch. IV, footnote 232, p. 141.
45. CE 3131, pp. 17–18.
46. Ibid.
47. See 4 H 2–3 (Sebastian Latona).
48. See CE 3155 representing the FBI opinion based on Sebastian Latona's findings.
49. 6 H 349–351 (Charles Givens).
50. Ibid.
51. 3 H 169–170 (Bonnie Ray Williams).
52. Id. at 169.
53. Id. at 170–171.
54. Id. at 169.
55. Id. at 169, 171.
56. Id. at 171–172.
57. Ch. IV, pp. 143–147.
58. Ibid.
59. 2 H 167–168 (Arnold Rowland); CE 354.
60. Id. at 169, 171.
61. Id. at 172.
62. Id. at 169, 182, 185; CE 357.
63. Id. at 175–176.
64. Id. at 188.
65. Id. at 178; CE 357.
66. 2 H 183–184 (A. Rowland).
67. Id. at 184; CE 2782.
68. 6 H 185–188 (Barbara Rowland).
69. Id. at 188.
70. CE 2783. This statement constitutes an amendment to the original testimony; see 6 H 188 (B. Rowland).
71. Id. at 181–182, 185–186.
72. Id. at 190.
73. Compare 2 H 165, 166, 179, 188 (A. Rowland), with CE 2644.
74. 6 H 263–264 (Roger D. Craig).
75. Id. at 264.
76. Id. at 272.
77. CE 1381, pp. 74, 96.
78. CE 1381.
79. Id. at 5.
80. Ch. IV, pp. 156–164.
81. Id. at 155–163.
82. 7 H 543 (W. E. Barnett).
83. Ibid.
84. Ch. IV, pp. 149–156.
85. 2 H 195–196 (James Worrell).
86. 6 H 276 (George Rackley); 6 H 282 (James Romack).
87. Ch. IV, p. 160.
88. Id. at 163.
89. 6 H 443, 7 H 439 (Earlene Roberts).
90. Ibid.
91. Id. at 443–444.
92. CE 2781.
93. CE 2645.
94. Id. at 3; CE 2045.
95. 7 H 439 (E. Roberts).
96. See also CE 3106 and CE 3107.
97. 5 H 364–365 (Dean Rusk).
98. E.g., 9 H 242–243 (George De Mohrenschildt); 11 H 172–173 (William Stuckey); 8 H 323 (Erwin Donald Lewis); 8 H 316–317 (Donald Camarata); 322–323 (Richard Call); 8 H 315–316 (James Botelho); 8 H 320–321 (Henry Roussel, Jr.); 8 H 319–320 (Paul Murphy); 8 H 319 (David Murray, Jr.); 8 H 321–322 (Mack Osborne). But see 8 H 285 (Daniel Powers). For Oswald's Marine service, see app. XIII, pp. 681–689.
99. Priscilla Johnson DE 1, pp. 3, 7–8; CE 1385, p. 10 (Aline Mosby); CE 908.
100. 9 H 242–243 (G. De Mohrenschildt).
101. CE 1385, p. 7 (Mosby); Johnson DE 1, p. 11.
102. See e.g., 2 H 399 (Michael R. Paine); 11 H 172–173 (Stuckey).
103. CE 295, p. 4.
104. CE 2767.
105. CE 2716.
106. CE 2767; 1 H 203 (Marguerite Oswald).
107. CE 3099.
108. CE 2673.
109. 11 H 444–446, 459–460 (P. Johnson); and P. Johnson DE 1, pp. 6, 8.
110. CE 24, entry for Nov. 17 to Dec. 30, 1959; see also CE 206, 202 (Oswald running out of money); CE 24, entry for Nov. 17 to Dec. 30, 1959, in which Oswald says he has only $28 left.
111. CE 1385, p. 11; see also P. Johnson DE 1, p. 3; 11 H 455 (P. Johnson).
112. E.g., 8 H 323 (Lewis); 8 H 316–317 (Camarata); 8 H 322–323 (Call); 8 H 315–316 (Botelho); 8 H 320–321 (Roussel); 8 H 319–320 (Murphy); 8 H 319 (Murray); 8 H 321–322 (Osborne); but see 8 H 285 (Powers).
113. 8 H 307 (Allison Folsom); Folsom DE 1, p. 7.
114. 5 H 291 (Richard E. Snyder); 11 H 455–456 (P. Johnson).
115. CE 24, entry of Nov. 17 to Dec. 30, 1959.
116. CE 24, entry of Jan. 7 to Mar. 16, 1960; CE 93, p. 4 (reference to "Rosa Agafanova" probably should be to "Rosa Kuznetsova.").
117. CE 1401, p. 277.
118. CE 2945 (Felkner).
119. Folsom DE 1, pp. 11, 28.
120. CE 2676, 2711; CE 946, p. 7.
121. CE 2677; app. XIII, p. 690.
122. See CE 946, p. 7.
123. CE 946, p. 9 (translated, CE 2776).
124. CE 946, p. 8 (translated, CE 2775); CE 2676.
125. CE 2769.
126. CE 2780.
127. Ibid.
128. CE 2773.
129. CE 908
130. CE 24.
131. E.g., CE 92, 101, 827.
132. E.g., CE 24, entry of Oct. 31, 1959,

refers to a reporter named "Goldstene" whose name is A. I. Goldberg, see CE 2719; CE 24, entry for Nov. 15, 1959, records an interview with Aline Mosby which appeared in the Fort Worth Star Telegram on Nov. 15, datelined Nov. 14 (CE 2716).

133. 1 H 30, 104–105 (Marina Oswald).

134. E.g., CE 18, 1438.

135. CE 2774, 3096.

136. E.g., compare CE 931, 251–256 with V. T. Lee DE 1, 2, 4–7 and CE 2779.

137. CE 24.

138. The files have been assigned CD 1114, 1115.

139. 5 H 260–299 (Snyder); 5 H 299–306, 318–326 (John A. McVickar).

140. CE 1385.

141. 11 H 442–460 (P. Johnson).

142. CE 985.

143. CE 24, entry of Oct. 16, 1959.

144. CE 24, entry of Oct. 21, 1959.

145. CE 24, entries of Oct. 20 and 21, 1959; 5 H 617; and CE 935, p. 2; CE 1438 and CE 827 indicate that Oswald was interviewed by "Leo Setyaev" (perhaps Lev Setyayev, an English-speaking commentator for Radio Moscow), a "Radio Moscow Reporter," probably also working for the KGB on this occasion. The interview was apparently never broadcast. 2 H 274 (Richard E. Snyder); but see CE 25, p. 3.

146. CE 2760.

147. CE 24, entry of Oct. 21, 1959.

148. CE 2778.

149. CE 985, doc. 1C–2, 1C–3.

150. CE 2776.

151. 1 H 91 (Marina Oswald).

152. E.g., 8 H 382, 384, 386 (Anna N. Meller); 9 H 240 (G. De Mohrenschildt); 9 H 309, 311 (Jeanne De Mohrenschildt); 11 H 474 (Hilda Smith); and see comments of fellow Marines in app. XIII, pp. 681–689, and discussion of his character in ch. VII; see also 2 H 318 (Katherine Ford), relating an incident in which Oswald reacted violently to a suggestion that Marina Oswald may have contemplated suicide.

153. CE 908.

154. 5 H 270 (Snyder).

155. Id. at 262.

156. Id. at 295–296.

157. CE 908.

158. 5 H 290 (Snyder).

159. Id. at 289.

160. CE 913; 5 H 263 (Snyder).

161. CE 2774.

162. 5 H 280 (Snyder); but see 8 H 287–288 (Powers).

163. CE 908, p. 2.

164. CE 912. See app. XV, pp. 747–751, for further details regarding Oswald's attempted expatriation.

165. 5 H 287–288 (Snyder); CE 941, p. 3; 5 H 302–303 (McVickar).

166. 11 H 453–455 (P. Johnson); see also CE 1385; CE 911, p. 1 (contemporaneous observation that Oswald used words as though he had learned them out of a dictionary).

167. 5 H 279, 287, 290 (Snyder); CE 941, 958; 5 H 300–301 (McVickar); and see 11 H 447–460 (P. Johnson).

168. App. XIII, pp. 675, 679, 683, 685–688, 722.

169. See ch. VII, pp. 384, 388–390; app. XIII, pp. 679, 686–687.

170. See, e.g., CE 24, entry of Oct. 16, 1959; 5 H 616 (Marina Oswald).

171. See CE 1385, pp. 15–17 (Mosby): 5 H 272, 287–288 (Snyder); CE 908 (Snyder); CE 941, p. 3, 5 H 302–303 (McVickar); 11 H 453 (P. Johnson).

172. CE 24, entry of Oct. 31, 1959.

173. 5 H 287 (Snyder); but see 5 H 272 (Snyder).

174. P. Johnson DE 6, p. 1; 11 H 444 (P. Johnson).

175. Id. at 452.

176. CE 913.

177. CE 912.

178. 8 U.S.C., sec. 1481.

179. 5 H 269, 290 (Snyder).

180. See Johnson DE 5, passim, and especially p. 13; 11 H 447, 456, 458–459 (Johnson).

181. CE 24, entries of Nov. 16, 1959, and Jan. 4, 1960.

182. CE 985, doc. Nos. 1A, 2A, and 3A (1).

183. CE 1385, p. 4.

184. 11 H 456–457 (P. Johnson); P. Johnson DE 1, pp. 3–4.

185. CE 24, entry of Nov. 16, 1959.

186. CE 297.

187. CE 202; CE 206; 1 H 204 (Marguerite Oswald).

188. See also CE 297 (Oswald seemed to associate acceptance by Soviet authorities with leaving the hotel in Moscow).

189. CE 3125.

190. P. Johnson DE 5, p. 7.

191. CE 985, doc. Nos. 1A, 2A, and 3A (1).

192. CE 2762, p. 2.

193. CE 960, question 2.

194. CE 2762, p. 2.

195. CE 960, question 2.

196. CE 2760.

197. CE 24, entries of Oct. 28, 1959, and Nov. 17 to Dec. 30, 1959.

198. CE 24.

199. CE 985.

200. M. Kramer DE 1, 2.

201. 11 H 213 (Rita Naman); 11 H 212 (Monica Kramer).

202. 11 H 211–212 (Katherine Mallory).

203. See generally app. XV.

204. E.g., CE 298, 315, 184.

205. E.g., CE 1392–1395.

206. E.g., 9 H 171, 229, 241–242 (G. de Mohrenschildt); see also 8 H 359 (George A. Bouhe) (conversation about Leningrad, Marina's native city).

207. E.g., 1 H 92 (Marina Oswald); CE 2761, 104; CE 1401, pp. 275–276; CE 994, p. 1.

208. CE 2761.

209. CE 24, entries of Jan. 4, 5, 7, and 13, 1960, and see CE 25, pp. 1B–2B.

210. CE 24, entry of Jan. 8, 1960.

211. CE 24, entry of Mar. 16, 1960.

212. CE 24, entries of Jan. 11 and 13, 1960; CE 1109 (union membership booklet) and 1108 (workbook); CE 24, entry of Jan. 13, 1960 (700 rubles); CE 1110 (750–850 rubles); CE 1401, p. 270 (800–900 rubles).

213. 1 H 95 (Marina Oswald).

214. CE 1401, p. 271.

215. CE 2720.

216. CE 24, entry of Jan. 13, 1960; CE 25, pp. 1B–2B; see generally 5 H 293–294 (Snyder).

217. CE 24, entry of Jan. 4–31, 1961.

218. 1 H 93.

219. CE 2721; see also 5 H 293–294 (Snyder).

220. CE 2760.

221. 10 H 203 (Dennis Hyman Ofstein).

222. CE 25, pp. 1B–2B.

223. Ibid.

224. 5 H 407 (Marina Oswald).

225. 5 H 616 (Marina Oswald).

226. E.g., 8 H 360 (Bouhe); 9 H 145 (Paul Gregory); 9 H 79 (Gary E. Taylor); 2 H 339 (Peter Gregory).

227. E.g., 8 H 350 (Max E. Clark); 2 H 397 (R. Paine).

228. CE 1401, p. 275; 1 H 93 (Marina Oswald); 5 H 590 (Marina Oswald).

229. CE 985, doc. No. 8A.

230. 9 H 114 (Ilya Mamantov); but see 8 H 362 (Bouhe) (commenting that there is nothing unusual about hunting in Soviet Union).

231. CE 2670.

232. Ibid.

233. Ibid.

234. CE 2770.

235. 1 H 96 (Marina Oswald).

236. CE 1964, pp. 2–3, 5.

237. CE 24, entry of Apr. 30, 31 [sic], 1961.

238. 1 H 327–328 (Robert Oswald); 2 H 466 (R. Paine); 8 H 385 (Meller); 8 H 362 (Bouhe).

239. CE 2649.

240. CE 303.

241. CE 1964.

242. Id. at 6.

243. CE 2733.

244. CE 24, entry of Apr. 31 [sic], 1961; CE 1111.

245. CE 960, attachment 2, p. 2.

246. See, e.g., 1 H 25 (Marina Oswald); 2 H 342 (Peter Gregory); 10 H 59 (Lt. Francis Martello).

247. CE 931.

248. 5 H 277 (Snyder).

249. CE 930.

250. CE 2757.

251. 5 H 276 (Snyder); moreover, it arrived too late to have prompted Oswald's letter even if it had been delivered, see CE 2757 and date stamped on CE 2681.

252. CE 931.

253. CE 933.

254. CE 940.

255. CE 251, 252.

256. CE 1074.

257. 5 H 252–254 (Waterman); CE 970, 971; and see CE 934.

258. CE 24, entry of July 8, 1961; CE 935.

259. CE 24, entry of July 9, 1961; 1 H 96–97 (Marina Oswald); CE 1401, pp. 278, 280.

260. CE 2762, p. 1.

261. CE 2762, p. 1.

262. Ibid.

263. CE 960.

264. CE 24, entry of July 8, 1961.

265. The factual and legal basis of this decision is set forth and evaluated in app. XV, pp. 747–751.

266. CE 935, p. 2.

267. CE 938, 946.

268. CE 935.

269. 5 H 318–319 (McVickar).

270. CE 946, 979.

271. CE 246–247, 249, 251–256, 931, 1083, 1093.

272. CE 2774.

273. E.g., V. T. Lee DE 1, 2, 4–7.

274. 5 H 287–288 (Snyder).

275. CE 2687, 2688; 5 H 280 (Snyder).

276. Id. at 278, 288; see also CE 2687, 2688.

277. CE 1401, pp. 277–278, 280.

278. CE 985, Docs. Nos. 1B–4B; CE 1122.

279. CE 24, entry of Dec. 25, 1961; CE 1403, p. 725.

280. 5 H 591, 604–605, 617–619 (Marina Oswald).

281. CE 1403, p. 745.

282. CE 246, 255.

283. CE 29.

284. CE 316.

285. CE 824, p. 4.

286. 5 H 604, 617–618 (Marina Oswald).

287. CE 2722.

288. CE 960; 5 H 340 (Abram Chayes).

289. CE 2756.

290. CE 2762, p. 3; CE 2771.

291. CE 301.

292. CE 24, entry of July 15 to Aug. 20, 1961.

293. E.g., 9 H 147, 151 (Paul Gregory).

294. CE 1122.

295. 1 H 89–90, 97 (Marina Oswald).

296. Ibid. (Marina Oswald); but see 5 H 604–605 (Marina Oswald). (In a later interview, the official did not try to discourage her.)

297. 1 H 89–90, 97 (Marina Oswald); 5 H 608–609 (Marina Oswald); in an earlier interview with the FBI Marina Oswald said she was "thrown out" because she failed to pick up her membership card, CE 1401, p. 276; this was probably only the ostensible reason, however; 5 H 608–609 (Marina Oswald).

298. 9 H 147 (Paul Gregory).

299. 5 H 598, 604 (Marina Oswald).

300. See CE 960.

301. 1 H 7 (Marina Oswald); 8 H 358 (George H. Bouhe); 9 H 224–226 (George De Mohrenschildt); id. at 306–311 (Jeanne De Mohrenschildt); 2 H 297–299 (Katya Ford); 2 H 323–324, 328–330 (Declan P. Ford); 8 H 344–345, 353 (Max E. Clark); 9 H 64–69 (Lydia Dymitruk); id. at 142–143 (Paul Gregory); 2 H 338–341 (Peter Gregory); 8 H 393–399 (Elena Hall); id. at 407–409 (John R. Hall); 11 H 119–123 (Alexander Kleinlerer); 8 H 381–385 (Anna Meller); id. at 416–419 (Valentina Ray); 9 H 77–78, 82–83 (Gary E. Taylor); id. at 29–30 (Natalie Ray); id. at 22 (Paul M. Raigorodsky); id. at 39–42 (Thomas M. Ray); id. at 46–48 (Samuel B. Ballen); id. at 107 (Ilya A. Mamantov); id. at 134–135 (Dorothy Gravitis); id. at 161–162 (Helen Leslie); 8 H 435 (Mrs. Igor Voshinin); id. at 466–468 (Igor Voshinin); CE 1858, pp. 12–13; 11 H 125–128, 130–133 (Alexandra De Mohrenschildt Gibson); CE 1861; 10 H 16–17 (Everett D. Glover); 2 H 435–437 (R. Paine).

302. See e.g., 9 H 2 (Raigorodsky); id. at 46 (Ballen); id. at 103 (Mamantov); id. at 199, 202–203, 210, 280–282 (G. De Mohrenschildt); 10 H 3, 13 (Glover).

303. 1 H 134–135 (Marguerite Oswald); id. at 7 (Marina Oswald); 8 H 372–373 (Bouhe); id. at 345–346 (M. Clark); 9 H 228–231 (G. De Mohrenschildt); id. at 306–310 (J. De Mohrenschildt); 2 H 299–300 (K. Ford); id. at 329 (D. Ford); 9 H 64–65 (Dymitruk); id. at 144 (Paul Gregory); 8 H 393–395 (E. Hall); id. at 407–408, 411 (J. Hall); 11 H 118–123 (Kleinlerer); 8 H 382–384 (A. Meller); id. at 422–423 (V. Ray); 11 H 147–149 (A. Gibson).

304. 8 H 373 (Bouhe); 9 H 228 (G. De Mohrenschildt); id. at 306, 324 (J. De Mohrenschildt); 8 H 387–388 (A. Meller); 11 H 118–123 (A. Kleinlerer); 2 H 329 (D. Ford); 9 H 65–68 (Dymitruk); 11 H 125–128, 130–134, 135–139, 140, 143–145, 147–149, 150–151 (A. Gibson).

305. 1 H 11–12, 31 (Marina Oswald); 11 H 118–123 (Kleinlerer); 8 H 365 (Bouhe); id. at 394 (E. Hall); 9 H 82, 84 (G. Taylor); id. at 310 (J. De Mohrenschildt); id. at 231–233 (G. De Mohrenschildt); 2 H 298–299 (K. Ford); 2 H 325 (D. Ford); 9 H 64 (Dymitruk); 8 H 345 (M. Clark); id. at 394–395, 403 (E. Hall); id. at 407 (J. Hall); id. at 416–417 (V. Ray).

306. App. XIII, pp. 673–675.

307. CE 2692; 1 H 318, 372, 330–331, 380–381 (R. Oswald); id. at 131–132 (Marguerite Oswald); id. at 4 (Marina Oswald).

308. 1 H 133, 135 (Marguerite Oswald); id. at 4–5 (Marina Oswald).

309. 1 H 134 (Marguerite Oswald) ; id. at 5 (Marina Oswald).
310. See 1 H 7 (Marina Oswald) ; see the accounts of how members of the community met Oswald in footnote 301, supra.
311. 8 H 344–345 (M. Clark) ; CE 1389 ; cf. 2 H 338 (Peter Gregory).
312. 8 H 344–345 (M. Clark).
313. 2 H 338, 340 (Peter Gregory) ; 9 H 142–144 (Paul Gregory).
314. 2 H 341 (Peter Gregory) ; 8 H 358–359, 372–373 (Bouhe) ; id. at 381–385 (A. Meller).
315. See e.g., 9 H 224–226 (G. De Mohrenschildt) ; 2 H 297 (Katya Ford) ; see also footnote 301, supra.
316. Those testifying include G. Bouhe, G. De Mohrenschildt, J. De Mohrenschildt, K. Ford, D. Ford, M. Clark, L. Dymitruk, Paul Gregory, Peter Gregory, E. Hall, J. Hall, E. Glover, A. Meller, V. Ray, G. Taylor, N. Ray, P. Raigorodsky, T. Ray, S. Ballen, I. Mamantov, D. Gravitis, H. Leslie, Mrs. I. Voshinin, I. Voshinin. A. Gibson. See also e.g., CE 1857 (Mrs. Max Clark) ; CE 1858 (Mrs. Tatiana Biggers) ; CE 1860 (Charles Edward Harris, Jr.) ; CE 1861 (Mrs. Charles Edward Harris) ; CE 1865 (Leo Aronson) ; 11 H 118 (Kleinlerer).
317. E.g., 8 H 367, 377 (Bouhe) ; 2 H 309–310 (K. Ford) ; 9 H 238, 252–253 (G. De Mohrenschildt) ; 1 H 34–35 (Marina Oswald).
318. 1 H 11–12, 31 (Marina Oswald) ; 8 H 365–367 (Bouhe) ; 11 H 118–123 (Kleinlerer) ; 8 H 393–394 (E. Hall) ; 9 H 82–83 (G. Taylor) ; id. at 310, 325 (J. De Mohrenschildt) ; id. at 231–233 (G. De Mohrenschildt) ; 2 H 298–299, 304 (K. Ford) ; 2 H 325 (D. Ford) ; 8 H 345 (M. Clark) ; id. at 394–395, 403 (E. Hall) ; id. at 412 (J. Hall) ; id. at 386–388 (A. Meller) ; id. at 416–417 (V. Ray).
319. 1 H 31 (Marina Oswald) ; 8 H 394–395, 403 (E. Hall) ; id. at 412 (J. Hall) ; 11 H 119–121 (Kleinlerer).
320. 1 H 11–12 (Marina Oswald) ; 8 H 365 (Bouhe) ; 2 H 298–299, 304 (K. Ford) ; 2 H 325 (D. Ford) ; id. at 386–388 (A. Meller) ; id. at 416–417 (V. Ray) ; 9 H 310. 325 (J. De Mohrenschildt) ; id. at 231–233 (G. De Mohrenschildt) ; id. at 64 (Dymitruk).
321. 1 H 10 (Marina Oswald) ; see app. XIII, pp. 717–722.
322. 8 H 365–367 (Bouhe) ; 2 H 307 (K. Ford).
323. 2 H 307 (K. Ford) ; see 8 H 367, 377 (Bouhe) ; 2 H 309–310 (K. Ford) ; 9 H 252–253 (G. De Mohrenschildt) ; 1 H 34–35 (Marina Oswald).
324. 2 H 459–462, 468–469, 3 H 4–11, 28–30 (R. Paine) ; 1 H 18–19, 23, 27–28, 46 (Marina Oswald) ; 8 H 133–134, 139 (Lillian Murret) ; 8 H 184–186 (Charles Murret).
325. 9 H 273 (G. De Mohrenschildt) ; 2 H 473 (R. Paine) ; 9 H 69 (Dymitruk).
326. See e.g., 8 H 388–389 (A. Meller) ; id. at 401 (E. Hall) ; id. at 419, 422 (V. Ray) ; 2 H 305–310 (K. Ford) ; 9 H 248, 250 (G. De Mohrenschildt) ; id. at 317 (J. De Mohrenschildt) ; 8 H 410–411 (J. Hall).
327. CE 1781, pp. 546–547 ; CE 1929. pp. 192–193 ; 2 H 499 (R. Paine) ; CE 419–421 ; CE 409–B, p. 2.
328. See footnote 326, supra ; 9 H 106–107 (Mamantov).
329. See 9 H 224–266, 309, 313 (G. De Mohrenschildt) ; 9 H 306–327 (J. De Mohrenschildt) ; 1 H 11 (Marina Oswald) ; 10 H 260–261 (M. F. Tobias) ; 10 H 245–246 (Mrs. Tobias) ; 9 H 93 (G. Taylor).
330. 9 H 248–249 (G. De Mohrenschildt) ; id. at 314–315 (J. De Mohrenschildt).
331. Id. at 315–317 (J. De Mohren-

schildt) ; see id. at 249–250 (G. De Mohrenschildt).
332. Id. at 317 (J. De Mohrenschildt) ; see id. at 249 (G. De Mohrenschildt).
333. Id. at 249 (G. De Mohrenschildt).
334. 1 H 18 (Marina Oswald).
335. 9 H 249–250 (G. De Mohrenschildt) ; see id. at 317 (J. De Mohrenschildt).
336. Id. at 248, 250 (G. Mohrenschildt) ; id. at 317 (J. De Mohrenschildt).
337. Id. at 299, 317–318 (J. De Mohrenschildt).
338. Id. at 318.
339. Id. at 272, 276 (G. De Mohrenschildt).
340. In addition to the testimony and exhibits included in the record to this report, additional data relative to the background of the De Mohrenschildts is included in the files of the Commission.
341. 9 H 168–179 (G. De Mohrenschildt) ; CE 3100.
342. 9 H 179–180, 190–191 (G. De Mohrenschildt).
343. Id. at 191–192, 195, 201–203, 211–212 ; id. at 300–302 (J. De Mohrenschildt).
344. Id. at 213–216 (G. De Mohrenschildt) ; id. at 302–303 (J. De Mohrenschildt).
345. Id. at 216 (G. De Mohrenschildt).
346. Id. at 276, 280–282, 217 (G. De Mohrenschildt) ; see id. at 305 (J. De Mohrenschildt).
347. Id. at 296–297 (J. De Mohrenschildt) ; 8 H 352–353 (Max E. Clark) ; id. at 377 (Bouhe) ; id. at 431–433 (Mrs. Voshinin) ; id. at 467–469 (Igor Voshinin) ; 9 H 99–100 (G. Taylor) ; id. at 120–121 (Ilya Mamantov) ; id. at 164–165 (Helen Leslie) ; 10 H 10–12 (Everett Glover).
348. 9 H 222 (G. De Mohrenschildt) ; and see id. at 296 (J. De Mohrenschildt).
349. Id. at 285–286, 291–295.
350. CE 3116, 3117. See CE 869, footnote 340, supra.
351. 2 H 433–436, 438–439 (R. Paine).
352. 10 H 16, 18–19, 24–26 (Glover) ; 9 H 256, 258 (G. De Mohrenschildt).
353. 2 H 440 (R. Paine) ; 9 H 435 (M. Paine).
354. 2 H 459–462, 468–469 ; 3 H 9 (R. Paine).
355. 2 H 468–469 ; 3 H 9 (R. Paine).
356. CE 408, 409, 409–B, 410, 411, 412, 415, 416 ; 2 H 483–498 (R. Paine) ; cf. CE 422 ; 2 H 501–502 (R. Paine).
357. 3 H 4–5, 9 (R. Paine) ; 1 H 26 (Marina Oswald) ; CE 461.
358. See app. XIII, pp. 730–731.
359. See note 356, supra ; CE 421.
360. 3 H 10 (R. Paine) ; 1 H 23 (Marina Oswald).
361. 3 H 10 (R. Paine).
362. CE 461 ; 9 H 345–346 (R. Paine).
363. 3 H 29–30 (R. Paine).
364. 1 H 37 (Marina Oswald).
365. 3 H 27–41, 84–85 (R. Paine).
366. Id. at 33–39 ; 9 H 345–346 (R. Paine) ; 1 H 46, 51–52, 63–65 (Marina Oswald).
367. 4 H 451–452 (Hosty) ; 3 H 38, 92, 96 (R. Paine).
368. 4 H 452 (Hosty) ; 3 H 38, 96 (R. Paine).
369. 3 H 97 (R. Paine) ; 4 H 450, 452 (Hosty).
370. CE 103 ; 2 H 405–406 (M. Paine) ; 3 H 13–18 (R. Paine) ; 9 H 395 (R. Paine). See pp. 309–310 infra.
371. 3 H 13–18, 97 (R. Paine) ; 2 H 406 (M. Paine).
372. 3 H 15, 18, 100–102 (R. Paine).
373. 4 H 459 (Hosty).
374. 3 H 44–45 (R. Paine).
375. Id. at 44.

376. 2 H 431 (R. Paine) ; 9 H 331–332, 339 (R. Paine) ; CE 1831, pp. 4–5.
377. Ibid.
378. 9 H 332 (R. Paine).
379. 2 H 432 (R. Paine) ; 3 H 133–134 (R. Paine).
380. 3 H 133–134 (R. Paine).
381. 2 H 387–388 (M. Paine).
382. 3 H 134 (R. Paine).
383. 2 H 387 (M. Paine) ; 9 H 338 (R. Paine) ; 3 H 135 (R. Paine).
384. Ibid. ; 9 H 338–339 (R. Paine) ; 9 H 134 (Gravitis).
385. 2 H 508 (R. Paine).
386. 2 H 385 (M. Paine) ; CE 1830, pp. 4–5.
387. 2 H 390–392 (M. Paine) ; CE 1830, pp. 4–5.
388. 2 H 389–390 (M. Paine) ; CE 1830, p. 6.
389. 2 H 389–392 (M. Paine).
390. Id. at 385, 386 ; 2 H 432 (R. Paine).
391. 2 H 385 (M. Paine) ; 4 H 448 (Hosty).
392. 2 H 387–388 (M. Paine).
393. Id. at 389.
394. 3 H 9–10, 93, 129 (R. Paine) ; 9 H 343 (R. Paine), see CE 429–440.
395. 3 H 15–18, 43–46, 96–105 (R. Paine) ; 2 H 405–406 (M. Paine) ; CE 103.
396. 3 H 21–25, 79, 81 (R. Paine) ; 9 H 393–394, 408–410 (R. Paine).
397. 3 H 17–18 (R. Paine) ; 4 H 462, 473 (Hosty).
398. Id. at 450–454 ; CE 830, p. 11.
399. R. Paine DE 277, 278, 278–A, 469 ; CE 404–424.
400. CE 401, 402.
401. E.g., 9 H 342 (R. Paine).
402. CE 3116, 3117 ; in addition to the testimony and exhibits included in the record to this report, additional data relative to the background of the Paines is included in the files of the Commission.
403. CE 3116, 3117, 821–824, 826, 829, 830, 833, 836 ; 4 H 403–430 (John W. Fain) ; 4 H 431–440 (John L. Quigley) ; 4 H 440–476 (James P. Hosty, Jr.).
404. CE 1172 ; cf. A. Johnson DE 1 ; see 9 H 455 (M. Paine) ; 3 H 118 (R. Paine) ; CE 1145, p. 1.
405. A. Johnson DE 1–3 ; 10 H 97–98, 100 (Arnold S. Johnson) ; CE 93 ; see also 10 H 209–210 (Dennis H. Ofstein) ; CE 1799 ; Oswald also subscribed to several Russian periodicals. CE 1147 ; 8 H 370–371 (Bouhe).
406. A. Johnson DE 1, 3–4 ; 10 H 98–100 (A. Johnson).
407. A. Johnson DE 2 ; 10 H 99–100 (A. Johnson).
408. A. Johnson DE 6, 4–A.
409. A. Johnson DE 4, 4–A ; cf. Johnson DE 3, 7.
410. A. Johnson DE 7 ; 10 H 103–104 (A. Johnson).
411. Weinstock DE 1 ; 11 H 207–208 (Louis Weinstock) ; A. Johnson DE 5, 5–A ; Tormey DE 1, 2 ; 10 H 107–108 (James J. Tormey).
412. See pp. 299–307, infra.
413. CE 2564.
414. See app. XIII, notes 1110–1119, infra. When questioned by Mexican police shortly after the assassination, Señora Duran did not recall whether or not Oswald had in fact told her he was a member of the Communist Party. CE 2120, p. 5.
415. See ch. V, p. 201, supra ; 10 H 116–117 (Abt).
416. Dobbs DE 9, 11 ; see also Dobbs DE 10, 13.
417. Dobbs DE 12 ; 10 H 113–114 ; 11 H 208–209 (Farrell Dobbs).

418. Dobbs DE 1–8 ; 10 H 109–110, 113 (Dobbs) ; CE 1799 ; see 3 H 119 (R. Paine).
419. Dobbs DE 13 ; 10 H 114–115 ; 11 H 209 (Dobbs).
420. CE 3153, 824, p. 7 ; CE 826, p. 12 ; CE 869, 2973, 3037, 3038, 3041 ; see also 5 H 28 (Alan H. Belmont) ; 4 H 411 (Fain) ; 4 H 302 (Robert I. Bouck).
421. 10 H 97, 102–105 (A. Johnson) ; 10 H 108 (Tormey) ; 10 H 110–111, 114–116 (Dobbs) ; 11 H 208–209 (Dobbs) ; 11 H 207–208 (Weinstock).
422. H. Twiford DE 1 ; 11 H 179 (Horace Twiford) ; CE 3085 ; CE 2335, pp. 6–7.
423. 11 H 179 (H. Twiford) ; 11 H 179–180 (Estelle Twiford).
424. CE 3085.
425. Ibid., in 1956, when Oswald was 16 years old, he apparently obtained information about the Socialist Party of America. Gray DE 1 ; 11 H 209–210 (V. Gray).
426. V. T. Lee DE 1 ; 10 H 87–88 (Vincent T. Lee).
427. Lee DE 2, 3 ; CE 828 ; 11 H 93 (Lee).
428. Lee DE 2.
429. Lee DE 3.
430. Lee DE 4 ; CE 1410, 1411, 2349, 2542, 2543, 2544, 1413, pp. 28–31 ; CE 2545.
431. Lee DE 5–7.
432. Lee DE 5.
433. 10 H 37–42 (Bringuier) ; Pizzo DE 453–A, 453–B ; CE 1413, pp. 19–30 ; CE 1412, 2548, 2546, 3029 ; 10 H 64–66 (Steele) ; Bringuier DE 1. See also 11 H 475 (Rachal) ; see app. XIII, pp. 728–729.
434. 10 H 37–39 (Bringuier) ; CE 1413, pp. 19–30, 34, 42 ; CE 826, pp. 5–10 ; 10 H 53–57 (Martello) ; Lee DE 6 ; 1 H 21 (Marina Oswald) ; CE 1412, 2210, 2216, 2520, 2860, 2895, 3032 ; CE 3119, pp. 12–14 ; CE 826, pp. 9–10.
435. 10 H 35–37 (Bringuier) ; see app. XIII, p. 728.
436. CE 826, pp. 5–10 ; 10 H 53–57 (Martello).
437. Lee DE 6, 7 ; Bringuier DE 1 ; 11 H 158–171 (Stuckey) ; 10 H 39–43 (Bringuier) ; Stuckey DE 2, 3 ; Pizzo DE 453–A, 453–B.
438. Holmes DE 1.
439. 10 H 90, 93 (Lee).
440. See pp. 407–412, infra.
441. See CE 826, p. 7 ; CE 1413, p. 31 ; CE 1414 ; CE 3119, pp. 14–15 ; CE 3120. The Cuban Revolutionary Council, an anti-Castro organization, at one time did maintain an office at 544 Camp St., but it vacated the building early in 1962, before Oswald had returned from the Soviet Union, CE 1414.
442. CE 1410, 1411, 2542–2544 ; 10 H 90 (Lee).
443. 5 H 401–402 (Marina Oswald).
444. 10 H 62–71 (C. Steele, Jr.) ; see 10 H 93–94 (Lee) ; cf. Lee DE 5.
445. CE 826, p. 12 ; CE 2952, p. 3 ; CE 2973, 3037 ; cf. 5 H 9 (Belmont) ; 4 H 444–445 (Hosty) ; 4 H 432–436 (Quigley) ; compare, e.g., CE 3029, 3128.
446. 2 H 403, 407 (M. Paine) ; CE 783, 2213 ; 7 H 325 (Gregory L. Olds).
447. 2 H 403, 407–408 (M. Paine) ; 9 H 462–464 (Raymond F. Krystinik).
448. 11 H 424–425 (Maj. Gen. Edwin A. Walker, Jr., Resigned, U.S. Army).
449. A. Johnson DE 7 ; 10 H 96, 103–104 (A. Johnson).
450. See pp. 182–187, supra.
451. In addition to the preceding discussion, see ch. VII, infra.
452. 5 H 489–500 (Bernard Weissman) ; CE 1811, pp. 4–15 ; CE 1815, pp. 710–714 ; CE 1034.

453. 5 H 496 (Weissman).
454. CE 1033, p. 1.
455. 5 H 497 (Weissman).
456. CE 1815, 1032, 1033, 1035, 1037, 1042, 1044, 1047, 1049; 5 H 498 (Weissman).
457. CE 1041, 1042; cf. CE 1049; see 5 H 526 (Weissman); see also note 458, infra.
458. CE 1032, 1033, 1037, 1038, 1040, 1044, 1047, 1049.
459. CE 1033, p. 2.
460. 5 H 491 (Weissman).
461. CE 1032; see CE 3112.
462. 5 H 490, 514, 519–520 (Weissman); CE 1811, pp. 6–7; CE 1813.
463. CE 1811, p. 8; CE 1878; 5 H 501, 505, 511, 519–520 (Weissman).
464. 5 H 506; 11 H 429 (Weissman); CE 1811, p. 9.
465. 5 H 505 (Weissman); see also CE 1815, p. 711; CE 1811, p. 9.
466. Id. at 505–508 (Weissman); CE 1815, p. 2; CE 1878, p. 298; CE 1811, p. 9.
467. 5 H 507–508 (Weissman), CE 1031, 1811, p. 9.
468. 5 H 504 (Weissman); CE 1878, 1882, 1811, p. 10; CE 1815, p. 712.
469. 5 H 506, 509, 511 (Weissman); CE 1878, p. 298; CE 1885, 1883, p. 306; CE 1884, p. 307.
470. CE 1882–1885.
471. 5 H 507–509 (Weissman).
472. 5 H 510–512 (Weissman); CE 1815, p. 712.
473. Ibid.; CE 1882, pp. 1–2.
474. 5 H 509 (Weissman); CE 1811, p. 11; CE 1815, p. 711; CE 1878, p. 298.
475. Ibid.; CE 1031.
476. 5 H 509 (Weissman).
477. 5 H 508–509 (Weissman); CE 1811, p. 11; CE 1815, p. 711.
478. 5 H 507 (Weissman).
479. Ibid.
480. Ibid.
481. Id. at 511, 517.
482. Id. at 511, 520; CE 1815, p. 713.
483. 5 H 511 (Weissman).
484. Ibid.
485. Ibid.
486. Id. at 515–516, 521–524; CE 1811, p. 12; CE 1815, p. 713; 3139.
487. 2 H 60 (Mark Lane).
488. 5 H 553–555 (Lane); see CE 2510–2518.
489. 5 H 522–524 (Weissman).
490. CE 996.
491. CE 2473, 2474, 1837, 5 H 541 (Robert G. Klause).
492. CE 1835.
493. 5 H 536–537, 539–544 (Klause); CE 1836, 2474, 1835.
494. 5 H 425–426, 429, 431 (Surrey); 11 H 412 (Walker).
495. 5 H 428 (Surrey).
496. Ibid.
497. Ibid.
498. CE 1835, p. 2; 5 H 537–539 (Klause).
499. Id. at 537 (Klause); CE 2473.
500. 5 H 536 (Klause).
501. Id. at 537–538.
502. Id. at 539.
503. Id. at 537; CE 1836, p. 2.
504. 5 H 539 (Klause); CE 1836, p. 2.
505. 5 H 538 (Klause).
506. Id. at 538–539 (Klause); CE 1836, p. 2; CE 2473, pp. 1–2; CE 2474.
507. 5 H 539 (Klause); CE 1836, p. 2.
508. 5 H 539 (Klause); CE 1836, pp. 1–2; CE 2473, p. 1; CE 2474, p. 6.
509. 5 H 539–540 (Klause).
510. Id. at 546; CE 1836, p. 2.
511. CE 2473, p. 2.
512. Id. at p. 3.
513. CE 1836, p. 2.
514. CE 2473, p. 2.

515. 5 H 530–531 (Weissman).
516. CE 1835–1836, 2473–2474, 3103.
517. 5 H 531 (Weissman).
518. 5 H 542 (Klause); 5 H 447–448 (Surrey); 11 H 424–425 (Walker).
519. 1 H 23, 28, 45 (Marina Oswald).
520. Id. at 28, 45.
521. CE 2478.
522. 1 H 22–24, 44–47 (Marina Oswald).
523. Id. at 45.
524. Id. at 22–23; CE 1404, pp. 451–453.
525. 11 H 214–215 (Dr. and Mrs. John B. McFarland); and see 11 H 179–180 (Estelle Twiford) (Oswald told her in Houston, Tex. that he was a member of the Fair Play for Cuba Committee and on his way to Mexico.)
526. 1 H 23, 46–47 (Marina Oswald).
527. 1 H 24–25 (Marina Oswald); see also ch. VII, pp. 412–413; app. XIII, p. 730. (One purpose of Oswald's Fair Play for Cuba activities was to get him into Cuba.)
528. See app. XIII, pp. 731–733, for time of departure from New Orleans; see CE 2121, p. 47; CE 2566, p. 2, for arrival in Mexico City.
529. CE 2121, p. 39.
530. Ibid.
531. Ibid.
532. See app. XIII, pp. 730–731.
533. CE 2121, p. 39.
534. 1 H 24–25 (Marina Oswald); and see CE 2121, p. 39.
535. CE 2121, pp. 39–40.
536. See CE 2121, pp. 39–40; CE 2564.
537. See app. XIII, pp. 734–736.
538. 1 H 27–28, 50 (Marina Oswald).
539. CE 2121, pp. 35–41.
540. CE 2120, pp. 4–6.
541. CE 2121, p. 42; CE 2120, p. 3. The official report of the Government of Mexico is set out in CE 2120 and CE 2123.
542. CE 2121, p. 38 (Silvia Duran).
543. CE 2123, attachment 5, p. 3.
544. Ibid.; CE 2121, p. 35.
545. See app. XIII, pp. 730–731, for documents Oswald took with him; CE 2121, pp. 39–40 (Silvia Duran's statement); 1 H 24–25 (Marina Oswald); CE 18, p. 54 (the "notation" of the address Silvia Duran gave Oswald).
546. CE 2445.
547. CE 2564.
548. CE 2564.
549. E.g., compare CE 2564 with CE 1969.
550. CE 3127.
551. Compare 2564 with CE 155, 161.
552. CE 2121, pp. 26–28.
553. CE 2121, pp. 53, 58.
554. 11 H 214–15 (Dr. and Mrs. John B. McFarland); 11 H 217 (Pamela Mumford); CE 2121, pp. 72–78.
555. CE 2121, pp. 53–58.
556. CE 2121, pp. 57–58. The only witness who places Oswald with anyone else during the trip was thoroughly discredited. See CE 2450, 2451, 2569, 2570, 2571, 2572, 2573, 2574, 2575, 3095.
557. CE 2450.
558. 11 H 217 (Mumford); CE 2195, pp. 2–3, 40–42.
559. CE 2195, pp. 44–46.
560. 11 H 220–221 (Mumford); 11 H 214 (McFarland); CE 2195, pp. 5–6.
561. CE 2195 passim.
562. CE 2121, p. 59.
563. Id. at 48–59; CE 3074.
564. CE 18, p. 54.
565. CE 2568.
566. CE 2567, p. 3.
567. This is the case of "D" treated at 55, infra.
568. CE 2949.

569. CE 2948.
570. CE 2676.
571. CE 2950.
572. CE 2952, 2953, 2954, 2955, p. 5.
573. CE 2959.
574. E.g., CE 2951.
575. CE 2946.
576. CE 3047.
577. CE 2952, p. 2 ; CE 2955, pp. 1–4.
578. CE 3152, 1161.
579. 5 H 365 (Dean Rusk).
580. CE 986, pp. 1–3 ; CE 29.
581. CE 6 ; CE 986.
582. CE 8.
583. CE 986.
584. CE 2768, 2772, 2444, 3042, pp. 59, 65.
585. CE 15.
586. CE 16.
587. 3 H 13–18, 51–52 (R. Paine).
588. 1 H 45 (Marina Oswald).
589. CE 2764.
590. CE 2764.
591. CE 3126.
592. 1 H 44, 49.
593. Oswald entered Mexico on Sept. 26 and his tourist card was good for 15 days thereafter ; CE 2478, reproduced in report, p. 300.
594. CE 792 ; 7 H 295 (Harry Holmes) ; Holmes DE 3.
595. 7 H 527 (Holmes) ; see Holmes DE 1–A.
596. See pp. 118–122, 172–174, supra.
597. CE 1158.
598. CE 817 ; 7 H 296 (H. Holmes).
599. Holmes DE 1 ; 7 H 292–293 (H. Holmes).
600. Holmes DE 4, pp. 1, 2 ; app. XIII, pp. 713–730, 737–740.
601. 10 H 294 (Mrs. A. C. Johnson) ; 6 H 435–437 (Earlene Roberts).
602. CE 1160, 1158, 1152, 1178.
603. CE 1799, p. 1.
604. See footnotes 594, 597, 599, supra.
605. CE 791 ; 11 H 136, 149 (Gibson).
606. CE 817 ; 8 H 91 (L. Murret).
607. Holmes DE 1 ; 10 H 292–293 (Mrs. A. C. Johnson).
608. 1 H 350, 356, 392 (R. Oswald) ; CE 322 ; Cunningham DE 3, 3–A ; Hunley DE 2, 5 ; Creel DE 1 ; Rachal DE 1 ; CE 427 ; 10 H 198 (Dennis H. Ofstein) ; CE 1167, p. 489. See also, e.g., Holmes DE 3–A ; Arnold Johnson DE 5 ; V. T. Lee DE 7, 8–A, 8–B, 8–C, 9 ; Dobbs DE 6, 9, 10 ; R. Watts DE 1, 4, 5.
609. See pp. 121–122, supra.
610. See, e.g., CE 1135, 2973, 2971–2972, 3113 ; Semingson DE 3001.
611. See CE 796, 815, 809, 806, 819, 1398 ; see 4 H 380–399 (Alwyn Cole).
612. Id. at 387.
613. Id. at 387–388 ; 10 H 184–186 (John J. Graef), 196–197 (Ofstein), 169 (Robert L. Stovall).
614. 10 H 186 (Graef), 198, 201 (Ofstein).
615. 4 H 378–389 (Cole).
616. 10 H 186–187 (Graef), 198 (Ofstein), 172 (Stovall).
617. CE 800 ; CE 115.
618. CE 2478.
619. CE 2539, p. 1.
620. CE 2121, p. 47 ; CE 2480.
621. CE 2463 ; 11 H 217, 220 (Pamela Mumford) ; CE 2120, pp. 39–41 ; cf. 11 H 179–180 (Mrs. E. Twiford).
622. See footnote 601, supra.
623. 6 H 401 (Mary E. Bledsoe).
624. CE 1410, 1411.
625. CE 135 ; 7 H 377 (Heinz W. Michaelis) ; CE 3088.
626. CE 1398.
627. 11 H 226–231 (Dial D. Ryder) ; CE 1333 ; Greener DE 1 ; CE 1334.

628. 11 H 226 (Ryder), 251 (Charles W. Greener) ; see p. 119, supra.
629. See pp. 118–122, 172–174, supra.
630. 11 H 231–233 (Ryder) ; CE 1334, p. 4.
631. CE 2454, p. 6 ; 7 H 224–225 (F. M. Turner) ; CE 1334, p. 24 ; 11 H 246–247 (Greener).
632. CE 1325 ; 11 H 227 (Ryder).
633. CE 1334, pp. 1–2, 13.
634. 11 H 226, 230–231, 234 (Ryder), 246, 251 (Greener).
635. 11 H 234, 226, 230–231 (Ryder) ; CE 1333, p. 2.
636. 11 H 225–226, 233, 235–238 (Ryder).
637. CE 1330, p. 2.
638. 11 H 241–242, 244, 237 (Schmidt), 464–467 (Lehrer).
639. CE 1334, pp. 14–20 ; CE 3030.
640. 11 H 254–259 (Gertrude Hunter) ; 11 H 263–275 (Edith Whitworth).
641. 11 H 261–262, 282, 284 (Mrs. Hunter), 11 H 272, 283 (Mrs. Whitworth).
642. 11 H 277, 300–301 ; 5 H 399–400 (Marina Oswald).
643. CE 1337, 2974.
644. 11 H 226, 228–229 (Ryder) ; CE 2974.
645. 11 H 264, 274, 286–288 (Mrs. Whitworth) ; 11 H 257 (Mrs. Hunter).
646. CE 1327.
647. 11 H 263, 265–266 (Mrs. Whitworth) ; see CE 1327, 3089.
648. 11 H 254, 280, 289 (Mrs. Hunter).
649. 11 H 280 (Marina Oswald) ; see footnotes 707, 708, infra.
650. 11 H 256 (Mrs. Hunter) ; 11 H 266 (Mrs. Whitworth) ; CE 2454 ; 11 H 290–292 (Marina Oswald), 11 H 155 (R. Paine).
651. 11 H 154 (R. Paine).
652. See ibid. ; 11 H 277 (Marina Oswald).
653. 11 H 255, 280, 288 (Mrs. Hunter).
654. CE 2976.
655. CE 2976.
656. CE 2977.
657. CE 2975.
658. CE 2977, p. 3.
659. E.g., compare CE 2903 and CE 2446 with app. XIII, pp. 730–736 ; compare CE 2944 with CE 2448, CE 3049, 3 H 214 (Roy Truly), and CE 2454 ; compare CE 2447 with CE 2904 and CE 3049 : see CE 2547 ; compare CE 3110 with CE 2925 ; compare CE 2926, 2927, 2928 with CE 3049 ; see CE 2933, 2908 ; see also, e.g., 10 H 309–327 (Clifton M. Shasteen) ; CE 2209, 3130.
660. 10 H 372 (Malcolm H. Price, Jr.).
661. 10 H 380 (Garland G. Slack).
662. 10 H 392 (Sterling C. Wood), 10 H 385–390 (Homer Wood).
663. 10 H 375–376 (M. Price), 10 H 383–384 (Slack), 10 H 388–389 (H. Wood), 10 H 394–395 (S. Wood).
664. CE 2934, 2935.
665. 10 H 356–363 (Floyd G. Davis), 10 H 363–369 (Virginia Davis) ; CE 2916, 2919.
666. CE 2915, 2917.
667. CE 2930, 2923, 2924, 2919, 2898, 2922, 2906, 3077 ; see 10 H 381 (Slack).
668. CE 2909, p. 238.
669. CE 2910.
670. 10 H 370 (M. Price) ; see app. XIII, pp. 730–736 infra.
671. 10 H 371 (M. Price), 10 H 380 (Slack), 10 H 361 (F. Davis).
672. 10 H 380 (Slack) ; but see 10 H 361 (F. Davis).
673. 11 H 154–155 (R. Paine) ; see also 2 H 515, 3 H 41 (R. Paine) ; 1 H 58, 62 (Marina Oswald).
674. 10 H 370 (M. Price), 10 H 365 (V. Davis).

675. See footnotes 707, 708 infra; cf. CE 2209.
676. 10 H 365 (V. Davis); CE 2941.
677. 10 H 393 (S. Wood), 10 H 381–382 (Slack); CE 2909; 10 H 358 (F. Davis).
678. Ibid.; 10 H 365–366 (V. Davis), 373 (M. Price); CE 2909, 3077.
679. CE 2897; CE 2898, pp. 116–117.
680. 10 H 373–374 (M. Price), 10 H 392, 395–397 (S. Wood), 10 H 381–383 (Slack); CE 2913.
681. CE 139; 3 H 392–396 (Robert A. Frazier).
682. 10 H 370 (M. Price), 10 H 386 (H. Wood), 10 H 391–392 (S. Wood); cf. 10 H 380 (Slack).
683. 10 H 374 (M. Price), 10 H 382 (Slack); 10 H 392 (S. Wood); see also CE 2916, 2935, 2915.
684. 10 H 374 (M. Price), 10 H 382 (Slack).
685. 10 H 386 (H. Wood), 392 (S. Wood); CE 2924, 2915.
686. CE 139, 3133; 3 H 392–296 (Frazier), 154 (Howard L. Brennan).
687. 10 H 374 (M. Price), 10 H 382 (Slack); 4 H 257 (J. C. Day); CE 139; 10 H 395 (S. Wood).
688. 10 H 374 (M. Price); 3 H 394 (Frazier); CE 541, pp. 3, 4.
689. 10 H 372–373 (M. Price).
690. See pp. 315–316, supra, ch IV. pp. 113–122.
691. 10 H 395 (S. Wood), 10 H 382 (Slack).
692. 10 H 370–371 (M. Price), 10 H 391 (S. Wood), 10 H (F. Davis); but cf. CE 2910.
693. CE 2921, 2918, 2905, 2920, 3049.
694. See, e.g., 2 H 226–229, 241 (Buell W. Frazier); 10 H 297 (Mrs. A. C. Johnson); 6 H 426 (Mary Bledsoe); CE 2932.
695. See 10 H 352–356 (Albert Guy Bogard).
696. In addition to the corroborating evidence discussed in text. it is to be noted that on Feb. 24, 1964, Mr. Bogard was interviewed by the FBI in regard to his allegation with the use of a polygraph. No significant emotional responses were recorded by the polygraph when Bogard was asked relevant questions concerning his report. The responses recorded were those normally expected of a person telling the truth. CE 3031. However, because of the uncertain reliability of the results of polygraph tests, see app. XVII, pp. 813–816, infra. the Commission has placed no reliance upon these results.
697. 10 H 342–345 (Frank Pizzo); CE 3078, p. 7.
698. CE 3091, 3092.
699. CE 3071, p. 365.
700. 10 H 344 (Pizzo); CE 3078, p. 7.
701. Ibid.
702. See 10 H 354 (Bogard); CE 3071, 2969.
703. 10 H 346, 350 (Pizzo); CE 3071 p. 2.
704. CE 3091.
705. 10 H 347–351 (Pizzo); CE 2970.
706. CE 3078, p. 7.
707. 1 H 112–113, 5 H 402, 11 H 280 (Marina Oswald); 8 H 142–143 (L. Murret); id. at 185 (C. Murret); 2 H 292–293 (R. Oswald); 8 H 399 (E. Hall); 9 H 87 (G. Taylor); 10 H 126–127 (Cunningham); 11 H 56–57 (J. Pic).
708. 2 H 502–517, 11 H 153–154 (R. Paine).
709. 2 H 515, 3 H 41, 11 H 153–154 (R. Paine); 1 H 58, 62 (Marina Oswald).
710. 11 H 368–369, 373, 375, 377, 379 (Sylvia Odio).
711. Id. at 370–372.
712. Id. at 370, 382.
713. Id. at 370–371.

714. Id. at 372.
715. Ibid.
716. Id. at 372–373, 377.
717. Id. at 373.
718. Id. at 382, 385.
719. CE 2907.
720. 11 H 370, 374 (S. Odio); CE 2942.
721. 1 H 26 (Marina Oswald); CE 2124, p. 383; CE 405, 1156, pp. 443–444; CE 2125, pp. 475, 477; CE 2479; 10 H 276–277 (Jesse J. Garner).
722. CE 2131; 2939.
723. CE 2938, 2939, 2940, 3109, 2131, 2476.
724. CE 2131, 2939.
725. CE 2961, 2132, pp. 10–14; CE 2533, 2962.
726. 1 H 27 (Marina Oswald); 11 H 214 (McFarland); 179–180 (Estelle Twiford); 11 H 179 (Horace E. Twiford).
727. CE 2191, pp. 5–7.
728. 11 H 214–215 (McFarland).
729. CE 2193, pp. 1–2; CE 2123, 2566, pp. 2–3; CE 2534.
730. CE 2138, pp. 12–14; CE 3075, 3086. But see 11 H 179 (Estelle Twiford).
731. CE 3090.
732. CE 2534.
733. 11 H 214–215 (McFarland); CE 2534, 2732.
734. 11 H 214–215 (McFarland); see also 1 H 27 (Marina Oswald).
735. 11 H 179–180 (E. Twiford).
736. CE 3045.
737. Ibid.; see 11 H 372 (S. Odio).
738. See note 736, supra.
739. CE 3148.
740. Ibid.
741. Ibid.; 11 H 375 (S. Odio).
742. CE 2390.
743. CE 3147.
744. CE 3146.
745. Ibid.
746. Ibid.
747. 11 H 370 (S. Odio).
748. 11 H 341–346 (Rodriguez).
749. Compare 11 H 341–342 (Rodriguez) with 11 H 370, 382–383 (S. Odio).
750. 11 H 343 (Rodriguez).
751. 11 H 350–351 (Orest Pena).
752. CE 2902.
753. Id. at 15; compare 11 H 355–356 (O. Pena).
754. 11 H 342 (Rodriguez); 351 (O. Pena); CE 2477, p. 10.
755. 1 H 35, 83, 100 (Marina Oswald); 2 H 487 (R. Paine); 8 H 389 (A. Meller); 9 H 244 (G. De Mohrenschildt); 11 H 150 (D. Gibson).
756. 11 H 325–339 (Dean Andrews).
757. Id. at 331; CE 3094; CD 2899.
758. CE 2900, 2901, 3104.
759. 1 H 142, 191–193, 195–196, 200 (Marguerite Oswald); but see e.g., 1 H 20, 83 (Marina Oswald); 3 H 108 (R. Paine).
760. CE 1138, p. 3; 1 H 206 (Marguerite Oswald).
761. CE 821; 4 H 408–409 (John W. Fain).
762. 1 H 214 (Marguerite Oswald); see generally footnote 865.
763. CE 2580 p. 4; 2581.
764. 8 H 341 (Pauline Bates).
765. Ibid.
766. 5 H 120–121 (John A. McCone); 5 H 121–122 (Richard M. Helms); see also CE 3138 (Department of Defense).
767. CE 870.
768. 5 H 105–106 (J. Edgar Hoover); 5 H 14–15, 26–27 (Alan H. Belmont); 4 H 429 (Fain); 4 H 440 (John L. Quigley); 4 H 469 (James P. Hosty).
769. CE 825.
770. CE 835.
771. CE 18, address book, p. 76.

772. 4 H 451 (James P. Hosty) ; 3 H 18, 103–104 (Ruth Paine).
773. 1 H 48 (Marina Oswald) ; 3 H 18, 99 (R. Paine).
774. 1 H 48 (Marina Oswald).
775. Ibid.
776. See generally CE 1135, 1141, 1150, 1152, 1158, 1159, 1160, 1161, 1162, 1163, 1164, 1165, 1166, 1167, see CE 1169.
777. 1 H 82–83 (Marina Oswald).
778. CE 1148, 1149, 1155.
779. CE 1169, 1 H 62 (Marina Oswald).
780. 10 H 230 (Chester A. Riggs, Jr.) ; CE 1160 ; 10 H 237–241 (Mrs. Mahlon Tobias) ; CE 1133, 1134 ; 11 H 155 (M. Waldo George) ; 10 H 265 (Mrs. Jesse Garner) ; CE 1139 ; see 1 H 10 (Marina Oswald) see CE 1160.
781. 11 H 140–141 (Mrs. Donald Gibson) ; 2 H 470–472 (R. Paine) ; 9 H 225–226 (G. De Mohrenschildt), 308 (J. De Mohrenschildt), 77 (Gary E. Taylor) ; 1 H 134–135 (Marguerite Oswald).
782. See app. XIII, pp. 713–715.
783. 1 H 7–8 (Marina Oswald) ; 8 H 394–395 (Elena Hall) ; 11 H 120 (Alexander Kleinlerer).
784. 2 H 299, 304 (Katherine Ford) ; 8 H 386–387 (Anna N. Meller) ; 1 H 11–12 (Marina Oswald) ; 8 H 416 (Valentina Ray).
785. 10 H 288–290 (Colin Barnhorst) ; id. at 281–283 (Richard L. Hulen) ; CE 1160, p. 3 ; 10 H 307 (A. C. Johnson) ; 6 H 401–402 (Mary Bledsoe) ; cf. CE 1166, p. 3.
786. 8 H 133–135, 138–139 (Lillian Murret) ; 2 H 459–468 (R. Paine).
787. 3 H 9, 12–13, 18, 32, 39–41 (R. Paine) ; 1 H 26, 51, 53–55, 79 (Marina Oswald) ; 2 H 217 (Buell W. Frazier).
788. 1 H 8 (Marina Oswald) ; 8 H 394 (E. Hall) ; 2 H 299 (Katherine Ford) ; 3 H 9 (R. Paine).
789. 3 H 93 (R. Paine) ; 1 H 62, 69, 70 (Marina Oswald) ; 1 H 134 (Marguerite Oswald) ; see e.g., 1 H 134 (Marguerite Oswald) ; 1 H 6 (Marina Oswald) ; see also note 304, supra. Oswald purchased a TV set on credit, but it was returned without any payment having been made on it ; CE 1165, pp. 17–21 ; CE 1167, pp. 490–495 ; 11 H 210 (Albert F. Staples) ; 9 H 360, 361, 362, 363 (R. Paine).
790. 1 H 135–136 (Marguerite Oswald) ; 8 H 372–373 (Bouhe), 382 (Meller), 394 (E. Hall) ; 9 H 324–325 (J. De Mohrenschildt) ; 11 H 119 (Kleinlerer) ; see also 9 H 66–68 (Dymitruk) ; 8 H 416 (V. Ray).
791. 2 H 487 (R. Paine) ; 1 H 35 (Marina Oswald) ; 8 H 153 (L. Murret) ; 8 H 418 (V. Ray).
792. E.g., 1 H 5, 5 H 416 (Marina Oswald).
793. 1 H 134 (Marguerite Oswald).
794. 2 H 217 (B. W. Frazier).
795. 11 H 171 (William K. Stuckey) ; 8 H 133, 135, 148 (L. Murret), 193 (John Murret) ; CE 146, 148, 149, 150, 151, 152, 153, 154, 155, 157, 158, 159, 160, 161, 162, 163.
796. 9 H 144 (Paul Gregory).
797. 1 H 134–135 (Marguerite Oswald) ; 1 H 7 ; 8 H 382–385 (A. Meller) ; 8 H 393–394 (E. Hall) ; 8 H 416 (V. Ray) ; 8 H 372–373 (Bouhe) ; see 9 H 144 (Paul Gregory) ; cf. 8 H 369 (Bouhe) ; id. at 387 (Meller).
798. 1 H 69–70 (Marina Oswald).
799. 1 H 318 (R. Oswald).
800. CE 1138, pp. 11–12.
801. 1 H 30 (Marina Oswald).
802. 7 H 376 (Heinz W. Michaelis) ; Michaelis DE 2 ; CE 1137 ; see app. XIV, p. 743.
803. CE 1410, 1411.

804. 10 H 64–66 (C. Steele, Jr.). It is not known whether the second person who assisted Oswald was also paid by him. CE 2216 ; see generally, note 434, supra.
805. See app. XIV, p. 744.
806. 2 H 468–469 ; 9 H 343 (R. Paine) ; 1 H 19 (Marina Oswald).
807. 3 H 9–12 (R. Paine).
808. 8 H 186–187 (Charles Murret).
809. 1 H 27 (Marina Oswald) ; CE 2131, 2476 ; see app. XIII, p. 731.
810. See app. XIII, pp. 730–736 ; app. XIV, p. 745.
811. 10 H 334–336, 340 (Leonard A. Hutchison).
812. CE 3121 ; CE 1165, pp. 5–6 ; 1 H 58 (Marina Oswald), CE 3129, p. 4
813. 10 H 328–333, 340 (Hutchison).
814. 11 H 155 (R. Paine), 290–291 (Marina Oswald) ; 10 H 296 (Mrs. A. C. Johnson) ; 6 H 404–405 (Mary Bledsoe) ; CE 2454, pp. 2–4.
815. CE 2789, pp. 630–631.
816. 10 H 328–329, 336–338 (Hutchison) ; but see CE 2789, pp. 629–630.
817. See note 814, supra ; 2 H 213, 222–225 (B. W. Frazier) ; 10 H 328 (Hutchison) ; see CE 3129, p. 6.
818. 10 H 328, 338 (Hutchison).
819. CE 3129, p. 1 ; see also 1 H 58 (Marina Oswald).
820. Compare. 10 H 338 (Hutchison) with CE 1132 ; 1 H 348 (R. Oswald).
821. 10 H 414–415, 422–423 (L. Wilcox).
822. 11 H 315–318 (Robert G. Fenley), 311–312 (C. A. Hamblen) ; Wilcox DE 3005. Hamblen repeated the story to a second journalist the following day. 11 H 316 (Fenley).
823. Wilcox DE 3005 ; see also Wilcox DE 3007 ; 11 H 312 (Hamblen) ; 10 H 415–417 (L. Wilcox).
824. 11 H 311–314 (Hamblen).
825. 11 H 318–325 (A. Lewis) ; Wilcox DE 3006 ; 10 H 417–421 (L. Wilcox).
826. Wilcox DE 3008 ; 10 H 412–413 (Semingsen), 423 (L. Wilcox).
827. 10 H 419–425 (L. Wilcox), 407–413 (Semingsen) ; Semingsen DE 3001.
828. 11 H 313 (Hamblen) ; 10 H 424 (L. Wilcox), 413 (Semingsen).
829. 10 H 424 (L. Wilcox), 412–413 (Semingsen).
830. See 13 H 436 (Curtis LaVerne Crafard).
831. Crafard DE 5226, p. 150 ; CE 2319.
832. Crafard DE 5226, pp. 147–148, 150 : but see CE 2322.
833. CE 2270, 2291.
834. CE 1669.
835. CE 2265.
836. CE 2251.
837. CE 2269, 2288 ; see also CE 2319.
838. CE 2245.
839. Newnam DE 2 ; see also CE 2265.
840. Crafard DE 5226, p. 150 ; 15 H 323 (Eva L. Grant) ; 15 H 283 (Eileen Kaminsky).
841. 15 H 626, 628 (Lawrence V. Meyers), CE 1606, 2267.
842. CE 2259, 2274 ; 14 H 153 (Ralph Paul) ; C. Ray Hall DE 3, p. 3 ; 5 H 183 (Jack Ruby) ; CE 2405, p. 26.
843. CE 2434, 2435.
844. 15 H 629 (Meyers) ; CE 2268.
845. Id. at 627 ; 15 H 667 (Paul) ; see also CE 2266, 13 H 326 (Armstrong).
846. 15 H 183 (J. Ruby) ; C. Ray Hall DE 3, p. 3.
847. Crafard DE 5226, p. 150.
848. Ibid.
849. 5 H 183 (J. Ruby) ; 13 H 330 (Armstrong) ; C. Ray Hall DE 3, p. 4 ; CE 2436 ; see also 15 H 539 (John W. Newnam) ; CE 2438.

850. C. Ray Hall DE 3, p. 4: see also CE 1479, 2321.

851. 5 H 183 (J. Ruby).

852. CE 2405, pp. 17–18; CE 2436.

853. 15 H 183 (J. Ruby); CE 2405, p. 26; CE 2436; see also 13 H 319–320 (Armstrong); 15 H 219–220 (Joseph Weldon Johnson, Jr.).

854. CE 2405, pp. 24, 26; CE 2436; cf. 5 H 184 (J. Ruby).

855. 15 H 535–539 (Newnam); Newnam DE 4; CE 2405, pp. 17–20; see also CE 3050.

856. CE 1031; 15 H 544–545 (Newnam); 5 H 184 (J. Ruby).

857. 15 H 323 (Grant).

858. 15 H 540–541 (Newnam).

859. Id. at 541.

860. 5 H 184 (J. Ruby).

861. Ibid.; 15 H 541 (Newnam); 15 H 575 (Billy A. Rea); CE 2264.

862. 15 H 579–580 (Richard L. Saunders).

863. 15 H 580–581 (Saunders).

864. Id. at 581; see also 15 H 575 (Rea); CE 2408, p. 49; CE 2264.

865. 13 H 330 (Armstrong).

866. 15 H 542, 545 (Newnam); see 15 H 324 (Grant).

867. 5 H 184 (J. Ruby).

868. Id. at 184–185.

869. 14 H 542–544 (Newnam); 15 H 583–584 (Saunders); see also CE 2408, p. 49; CE 2264.

870. 15 H 79–81 (Seth Kantor); see also 15 H 388–396 (Wilma May Tice).

871. See 15 H 388–396 (Tice); CE 2290; CE 2293; CE 2437.

872. 14 H 561–563 (J. Ruby); 5 H 185 (J. Ruby).

873. See KRLD–TV Reel 5: compare 15 H 81 (Kantor).

874. CE 2303, p. 27; 13 H 331–332 (Armstrong); 13 H 208–209 (Karen B. Carlin); see also 5 H 185 (Ruby); but see 13 H 452 (Crafard).

875. 15 H 75–76 (Kantor); CE 2301.

876. 15 H 76–82 (Kantor).

877. CE 2303, p. 27; 13 H 333–335 (Armstrong); 13 H 208–209 (K. Carlin).

878. CE 2068.

879. 15 H 579 (Saunders); 15 H 419 (Nancy M. Powell).

880. See pp. 340–342, infra.

881. 15 H 81–82 (Kantor).

882. 15 H 79, 81–82, 87–88 (Kantor); pp. 342–343, infra: see CE 2441, 2442.

883. 5 H 185 (Ruby); 13 H 333–335 (Armstrong); see 14 H 85 (Crafard); see also 15 H 195 (Marjorie R. Richey).

884. 13 H 452–453 (Crafard); 14 H 42 (Crafard); 13 H 331–335 (Armstrong): see CE 2414.

885. 14 H 151 (Paul); 5 H 185 (J. Ruby); CE 2303, p. 27; 13 H 331–332 (Armstrong).

886. CE 2303, p. 27; 15 H 282–283 (Eileen Kaminsky); 14 H 123 (Alice R. Nichols).

887. Ibid.; see also 13 H 331 (Armstrong).

888. 14 H 123–124 (A. Nichols); 15 H 283 (Kaminsky).

889. 14 H 113–115, 123–124 (A. Nichols).

890. CE 2243; 2303, p. 27; CE 2284.

891. CE 2284; 5 H 185 (J. Ruby); see also 13 H 423–424 (Crafard).

892. 5 H 185 (J. Ruby); CE 2284.

893. CE 2303, p. 27; 14 H 151–152 (Paul).

894. 15 H 325 (Grant); CE 2296; 13 H 333 (Armstrong); see also 13 H 454 (Crafard) cf. 14 H 318–319 (Senator).

895. 13 H 455–457 (Crafard); see also CE 2427, 2273; 14 H 433 (Grant); 13 H 336 (Armstrong); but see 14 H 86–87 (Crafard).

896. 15 H 325 (Grant); 13 H 456 (Crafard).

897. 5 H 186 (J. Ruby); CE 2260, 2296.

898. 15 H 325–331 (Grant); 5 H 186 (J. Ruby).

899. Ibid.

900. 15 H 327 (Grant); CE 2262.

901. CE 2261, 15 H 330 (Grant).

902. 5 H 186–187 (J. Ruby); 15 H 330 (Grant); see also CE 2242, 2275.

903. 14 H 124–125 (Nichols); Nichols DE 5356; 15 H 330 (Grant).

904. 13 H 457 (Crafard); but see 14 H 86 (Crafard).

905. 15 H 332 (Grant).

906. 5 H 186–187 (J. Ruby).

907. 13 H 187 (Augustus M. Eberhardt); 15 H 612 (Roy G. Standifer); 15 H 601–602 (Ronald L. Jenkins); CE 2254, pp. 424–425; compare CE 2410, p. 106, with CE 2249, p. 13; compare 15 H 351–352 (Victor F. Robertson, Jr.); CE 2439 with 15 H 599 (Clyde F. Goodson); CE 2439; see CE 2423; pp. 342–343, 347; KRLD–TV reel 23, 45; 16–23; see also CE 2289; 15 H 375–376 (John G. McCullough); 15 H 455 (Dave L. Miller); 13 H 335–336 (Armstrong).

908. Compare 15 H 601–603 (Jenkins); 15 H 375–376, 380–381 (McCullough); with CE 2790, 2415, 2423, 2424, 2439.

909. 15 H 351–352 (Robertson).

910. 15 H 588–599 (Goodson); CE 2289; see also CE 2440; but cf. CE 2423, 2439.

911. 13 H 187 (Eberhardt); CE 2410, pp. 106–108; 15 H 617 (Standifer); but see 5 H 188 (J. Ruby); see also, pp. 342–343, infra.

912. 5 H 188 (J. Ruby): see also 15 H 327 (Grant).

913. 14 H 152 (Paul); CE 2302, p. 14.

914. CE 2302, p. 14; CE 2300.

915. 15 H 31–32 (Hyman Rubenstein).

916. 5 H 187 (J. Ruby); CE 2281.

917. CE 2281; see also CE 2282.

918. CE 2281.

919. CE 2282, 2283.

920. 5 H 187 (J. Ruby).

921. Ibid.

922. CE 2252.

923. 5 H 187 (J. Ruby); CE 2248.

924. 5 H 187–188 (J. Ruby); see also 14 H 434 (Grant).

925. CE 2247, 2277, 2278, 2279, 2280.

926. CE 2252.

927. 5 H 188 (J. Ruby).

928. KRLD–TV reel 23 0:00–0:19; CE 2423, 2439; see 5 H 188 (J. Ruby); C. Ray Hall DE 3, p. 5.

929. CE 2410, pp. 104–105; see CE 2424; 5 H 188 (J. Ruby).

930. 13 H 187–189 (Augustus M. Eberhardt); see CE 2424.

931. KRLD–TV reel 23, 0:00–3:00; CE 2423, 2439; 5 H 188 (J. Ruby).

932. Ibid.; KRLD–TV; reel 23; WFAA–TV, PKT 11 6:50–6:55; see C. Ray Hall DE 2 p. 13–14.

933. CE 2424; 13 H 189–190 (Eberhardt); 5 H 223 (Wade); 15 H 616–617 (Standifer); CE 2244, 2249, 2256, 2257, 2272, 2276, see also McMillon DE 5017, p. 3; CE 2258.

934. CE 2424, 5 H 188–195 (J. Ruby); 13 H 189–190 (Eberhardt).

935. KRLD–TV reel 23, CE 2169; NBC–TV reel 43.

936. KRLD–TV reel 23; NBC–TV reel 43; 5 H 189 (J. Ruby); 5 H 223–224 (Wade); CE 2295.

937. 5 H 223–224 (Wade); KRLD–TV reel 23, 45; 16–23; CE 2439, 2441, 2442, 5 H 189 (J. Ruby).

938. 15 H 505–506, 508–509 (Johnston); CE 2272.

939. 15 H 346 (Icarus M. Pappas) ; see also CE 2257 ; 15 H 588–589 (Thayer Waldo).

940. CE 2257 ; see also CE 2256.

941. 15 H 531–532 (Danny Patrick McCurdy) ; 15 H 485 (William G. Duncan, Jr.) ; see also CE 2295.

942. 15 H 364–365 (Pappas) ; 5 H 224 (Wade).

943. 15 H 485–486 (Duncan) ; 15 H 254 (Russell Lee Moore, also known as Russell Knight).

944. Id. at 254–255, 267.

945. 15 H 483 (Duncan) ; see also 15 H 256–259 (Knight) ; 15 H 532 (McCurdy).

946. 15 H 257 (Knight) ; CE 2294 ; see also 14 H 318 (Senator).

947. 15 H 530–531 (McCurdy) ; 15 H 259 (Knight).

948. 15 H 530–531 (McCurdy).

949. 15 H 487–488 (Duncan).

950. 15 H 259–260 (Knight) ; 15 H 224–225, 228 (Edward J. Pullman) ; CE 2285 ; see also 15 H 339 (Grant).

951. CE 2285.

952. 15 H 260, 264–265 (Knight).

953. Ibid.

954. 5 H 191 (J. Ruby) ; see also CE 2318 ; 14 H 631 (Harry N. Olsen) ; 14 H 647 (Kay Helen Olsen).

955. C. Ray Hall DE 1, 2, 3.

956. 5 H 191 (J. Ruby).

957. 14 H 632 (H. Olsen) ; 14 H 648 (K. Olsen).

958. 14 H 632 (H. Olsen) ; 14 H 647 (K. Olsen).

959. Ibid.

960. 15 H 555–559 (Roy A. Pryor) ; see also 5 H 194 (J. Ruby).

961. 15 H 558–562 (Pryor) ; CE 2297 ; see also 5 H 206–207 (J. Ruby).

962. 15 H 566–568 (Arthur W. Watherwax) ; see CE 2297 ; CE 2816, pp. 1508–1509.

963. CE 2816, p. 1509.

964. CE 2816, p. 1506 ; 5 H 194 (J. Ruby) ; 15 H 569–570 (Watherwax) ; CE 2791.

965. App. XVI, at p. 800, infra ; 13 H 437–448 (Crafard) ; CE 2791.

966. 15 H 570 (Watherwax).

967. 5 H 193–194 (J. Ruby).

968. CE 2816, p. 1510.

969. 5 H 203 (J. Ruby) ; 15 H 569 (Watherwax) ; see also 14 H 218 (Senator) ; 14 H 87 (Crafard).

970. 15 H 568 (Watherwax) ; CE 2816, pp. 1507–1508 ; CE 2297.

971. 14 H 219–220 (Senator).

972. Id. at 218–219 ; 13 H 463 (Crafard).

973. 5 H 203 (J. Ruby) ; 13 H 463 (Crafard).

974. 5 H 203 (J. Ruby) ; CE 2286 ; see also 14 H 90 (Crafard) ; 13 H 464–466 (Crafard) ; 14 H 219 (Senator).

975. 14 H 222 (Senator) ; see also 13 H 503–504 (Crafard) ; but see 14 H 567–568 (J. Ruby).

976. 5 H 203 (J. Ruby) ; 14 H 220 (Senator) ; 15 H 336 (Grant).

977. 14 H 220–224 (Senator).

978. C. Ray Hall DE 3, p. 9 ; 14 H 224 (Senator) ; see also 13 H 466 (Crafard).

979. C. Ray Hall DE 3, p. 9 ; 13 H 466–468 (Crafard).

980. Ibid. ; C. Ray Hall DE 3, p. 9.

981. 13 H 337–339 (Armstrong) ; 13 H 468–469 (Crafard).

982. 5 H 198 (J. Ruby) ; C. Ray Hall DE 2, p. 14, DE 3, p. 12.

983. 5 H 198 (J. Ruby).

984. 15 H 196 (Marjorie R. Richey).

985. C. Ray Hall DE 3, p. 9 ; CE 2324, 2413, p. 83 ; see also CE 2330, 2340.

986. C. Ray Hall DE 3, p. 9 ; CE 2324.

987. CE 2413, pp. 82–83, 89, 92 ; CE 3039, see CE 2324 ; C. Ray Hall DE 3, p. 9.

988. C. Ray Hall DE 3, p. 9.

989. CE 2341 ; see 15 H 490 (Garnett Claud Hallmark).

990. 15 H 489–490 (Hallmark) ; G. C. Hallmark DE 1, p. 1.

991. 15 H 491 (Hallmark).

992. Ibid.

993. 15 H 434 (Kenneth L. Dowe) ; Dowe DE 2, p. 2 ; see 15 H 491 (Hallmark).

994. Id. at 492–493.

995. 15 H 587–588 (Thayer Waldo) ; 15 H 355–357 (Frederic Rheinstein) ; CE 2276, 2326, 2327.

996. CE 2327 ; see also 15 H 82–83 (Seth Kantor).

997. 15 H 587–589 (Waldo) ; see also CE 2276.

998. 15 H 357 (Rheinstein).

999. CE 2276 ; 2326.

1000. 15 H 386–387 (Abraham Kleinman) ; see also C. Ray Hall DE 3, p. 9.

1001. 15 H 468–469 (Frank Bellochio) ; 15 H 383–386 (Kleinman) ; CE 3043, 3044, 3045, 3046 ; see also 15 H 610–613 (Speedy Johnson).

1002. 15 H 470 (Bellochio) ; 5 H 203–204 (J. Ruby) ; 15 H 336 (Grant).

1003. 15 H 470 (Bellochio).

1004. Id. at 470–471.

1005. Id. at 471.

1006. Ibid.

1007. Id. at 470–472 ; CE 3043, 3044.

1008. Id. at 472.

1009. C. Ray Hall DE 3, p. 9 ; 15 H 519 (Stanley M. Kaufman) ; see also 15 H 337–338 (Grant).

1010. 15 H 520 (Kaufman).

1011. 15 H 519–520 (Kaufman) ; see also 15 H 337–338 (Grant).

1012. 15 H 337 (Grant).

1013. C. Ray Hall DE 3, pp. 9–10.

1014. CE 2329.

1015. 13 H 339–340 (Armstrong) ; see 15 H 454 (Dave L. Miller).

1016. 15 H 338–339 (Grant).

1017. 15 H 262 (Knight) ; cf. 14 H 222 (Senator) ; but see 15 H 337 (Grant).

1018. 15 H 339, 341 (Grant).

1019. CE 2325, 2407.

1020. 13 H 209–210 (Karen B. Carlin) ; 15 H 421–423 (Nancy M. Powell) ; see 15 H 342 (Grant) ; compare 15 H 474 (John Henry Branch) with Branch DE 1 ; 15 H 334 (Grant) ; CE 2336.

1021. 15 H 421–423 (Powell) ; 15 H 647, 652 (Bruce R. Carlin) ; 13 H 209 (K. Carlin).

1022. 13 H 209–210 (K. Carlin) ; see C. Ray Hall DE 3, p. 10 ; 15 H 69–70 (C. Ray Hall) ; 13 H 204–205 (B. Carlin).

1023. 15 H 210 (K. Carlin).

1024. 15 H 342 (Grant).

1025. 15 H 626–635 (Meyers) ; see p. 334, supra.

1026. 15 H 631–634 (Meyers).

1027. Id. at 633–635 ; see 14 H 265 (Senator).

1028. 15 H 632 (Meyers).

1029. 13 H 210 (K. Carlin) ; 13 H 203–204 (B. Carlin).

1030. Id. at 204 ; see also 13 H 210 (K. Carlin).

1031. 13 H 204 (B. Carlin).

1032. 15 H 422 (Powell).

1033. 15 H 211 (K. Carlin) ; see 13 H 205 (B. Carlin) ; 15 H 423–424 (N. Powell).

1034. 13 H 246–247 (Huey Reeves) ; CE 1476, 2334 ; 13 H 210–211 (K. Carlin).

1035. 15 H 336, 339, 342–343 (Grant).

1036. CE 2300, 2306 ; see also CE 2310.

1037. CE 2300.

1038. 15 H 339 (Grant).

1039. 14 H 153 (Paul) ; 15 H 671, 673 (Paul).

1040. 15 H 397, 399 (Wanda Y. Helmick) ; CE 2834.
1041. 15 H 399 (Helmick).
1042. Id. at 400, but see 15 H 672, 678–679 (Paul) ; CE 2339.
1043. 15 H 671–672, 675, 678–679 (Paul).
1044. 15 H 399 (Helmick) ; 14 H 153 (Paul) ; 15 H 671–672 (Paul).
1045. 13 H 247 (Reeves) ; see C. Ray Hall DE 3, p. 10 ; see CE 1476.
1046. 14 H 635 (H. Olsen) ; 14 H 649 (K. Olsen).
1047. CE 2307.
1048. Ibid.
1049. Ibid.
1050. Ibid. ; 14 H 605 (Breck Wall).
1051. CE 2307.
1052. 14 H 532–533, 543, 559, 564 (J. Ruby) ; 5 H 197 (J. Ruby) ; see also C. Ray Hall DE 3, p. 12.
1053. Paul DE 5319, p. 7.
1054. 14 H 153 (Paul) ; 15 H 671–673 796–797, 805 (Paul).
1055. 14 H 605–607 (Wall).
1056. See app. XVI, pp. 796–797, 805 ; CE 2344.
1057. CE 2302, p. 14 ; CE 2303. p. 26 ; 2328, 2331, 2333.
1058. 14 H 605–606 (Wall).
1059. CE 2068.
1060. CE 2337.
1061. C. Ray Hall DE 3, p. 10 ; 15 H 552 (Robert L. Norton) ; 5 H 198 (J. Ruby).
1062. 15 H 552–553 (Norton).
1063. Id. at 553 ; see 5 H 198 (J. Ruby) ; see CE 2836.
1064. 5 H 198 (J. Ruby) ; see 15 H 551 (Norton) ; CE 2836.
1065. 14 H 529 (J. Ruby) ; 5 H 198 (J. Ruby).
1066. 14 H 236 (Senator).
1067. 15 H 343 (Grant).
1068. 14 H 236 (Senator).
1069. 15 H 199 (J. Ruby) ; 14 H 236–240 (Senator).
1070. 13 H 256–261 (Warren E. Richey) ; 13 H 279–283 (John A. Smith) ; 13 H 292–294 (Ira N. Walker).
1071. 13 H 256–258 (W. Richey) ; 13 H 279–282 (J. A. Smith) ; 13 H 291–294 (I. Walker).
1072. 13 H 256–258 (W. Richey) ; 13 H 278–282 (J. A. Smith) ; 13 H 292 (I. Walker).
1073. 13 H 283 (J. A. Smith).
1074. 13 H 257 (W. Richey).
1075. 13 H 283 (J. A. Smith) ; see also 13 H 257 (W. Richey).
1076. App. XVI, pp. 787, 792 ; CE 2424, 1478 ; see 15 H 523 (Kaufman) ; see also 15 H 332 (E. Grant).
1077. 14 H 236, 238–239 (Senator) ; Pappas DE 1.
1078. 13 H 257 (W. Richey).
1079. CE 2790, 2415 ; Pappas DE 1 ; but see 15 H 508 (Johnston) ; 15 H 603 (Ronald L. Jenkins).
1080. Compare 13 H 292–293 (I. Walker) with 13 H 278–280 (J. A. Smith).
1081. 13 H 292 (Walker) ; 13 H 278–281, 283 (J. A. Smith).
1082. KRLD–TV reel 13 ; CE 3072.
1083. 14 H 236 (Senator) ; Senator DE 5402, p. 4.
1084. 13 H 232–233 (Elnora Pitts) ; see 14 H 239–240 (Senator).
1085. 13 H 231–232 (Pitts).
1086. Id. at 230–232.
1087. 13 H 197–198, 200 (Sidney Evans, Jr.) ; see also 13 H 263–264 (Malcolm R. Slaughter).
1088. 14 H 232–233 (Senator) ; see also Senator DE 5402.
1089. 14 H 236–239 (Senator) ; CE 2298.

1090. 13 H 210–211 (K. Carlin).
1091. Id. at 210–212.
1092. 14 H 239 (Senator).
1093. 14 H 236 (Senator) ; see also 14 H 532 (J. Ruby).
1094. 5 H 198–199 (J. Ruby) ; .see 14 H 532 (J. Ruby) ; see also 13 H 502 (Crafard) ; 14 H 207 (Senator).
1095. 14 H 210–211, 240 (Senator) ; C. Ray Hall DE 2, p. 15 ; 5 H 198–199 (J. Ruby).
1096. C. Ray Hall DE 2, p. 15 ; 5 H 199 (J. Ruby) ; 14 H 83–85 (Crafard) ; 13 H 311–312 (Armstrong) ; 14 H 147 (Paul) ; 14 H 211, 312 (Senator).
1097. C. Ray Hall DE 3, pp. 10–11 ; 5 H 199 (Paul).
1098. CE 2068 ; KRLD–TV reel 12, 38 : 20 ; WBAP–TV reel FW No. 2.
1099. 13 H 272–274 (Smart) ; Smart DE 5021 ; CE 1322, pp. 732, 747–751 ; see 13 H 501 (Crafard) ; 14 H 329–330 (Senator).
1100. C. Ray Hall DE 2, p. 15 ; CE 1322, pp. 726–731 ; 15 H 199 (J. Ruby) ; see also 14 H 327 (Senator).
1101. 13 H 226 (Doyle E. Lane).
1102. Id. at 224 ; D. Lane DE 5118, 5119 ; CE 2420, 2421, 1322, p. 726.
1103. Id. at 225.
1104. Ch. V at pp. 216–225 ; KRLD–TV reel No. 13 ; KRLD–TV reel No. 59 ; WBAP–TV reel FW No. 1.
1105. See 15 H 369–371 (Pappas) ; Pappas DE 1, 2 ; C.D. 1314–A (tape recording in Commission files) ; J. R. Leavelle DE 5088, 5089 ; 13 H 8–9 (L. C. Graves) ; 12 H 308, 313–314 (Louis D. Miller) ; L. D. Miller DE 5013, 5014 ; 13 H 29 (L. D. Montgomery) ; McMillon DE 5016 ; 12 H 179 (B. H. Combest) ; Combest DE 5101, p. 3 ; Kantor DE 3, pp. 3S, 3T ; W. J. Harrison DE 5029, pp. 2–3 ; CE 2002, p. 45 ; NBC–TV reel No. 66, Nov. 24, 1963. But see CE 2409, p. 300 ; 5 H 199 (J. Ruby) ; 14 H 562 (J. Ruby).
1106. KRLD–TV reel 13 ; CE 3072.
1107. See app. XVI at 787, 788–789, 793–795, 798–799 ; see 15 H 258 (Knight) ; 15 H 636 (Meyers).
1108. 13 H 469 (Crafard).
1109. 14 H 39–40 (Crafard) ; see Crafard DE 5226, p. 147.
1110. CE 2429.
1111. Crafard DE 5226, p. 152 ; see also 13 H 469 (Crafard).
1112. CE 2793 ; Crafard DE 5227.
1113. 14 H 92–93 (Crafard).
1114. Crafard DE 5226, pp. 148–149 ; 13 H 420–422 (Crafard) ; see 14 H 23–25 (Crafard).
1115. 13 H 466–468 (Crafard) ; C. Ray Hall DE 3, p. 9.
1116. CE 2429 ; see 13 H 471–472 (Crafard) ; see also CE 2792.
1117. 13 H 404–408 (Crafard).
1118. Id. at 407–410, 413–416.
1119. Id. at 470 (Crafard) ; see 14 H 38–39 (Crafard).
1120. CE 2302, 2303, 2307 ; 14 H 152–153 (Paul) ; 15 H 665, 670–673 (Paul) ; app. XVI at 795.
1121. 14 H 153–154 (Paul) ; 15 H 672–673 (Paul).
1122. CE 2311, 2316.
1123. CE 3026, 2980, 3034 ; 15 H 677 (Paul) ; CE 2817.
1124. CE 2823 ; 15 H 401–402 (Helmick).
1125. Id. at 401 ; CE 2338.
1126. CE 2338, 2339.
1127. CE 2431 ; 15 H 399 (Helmick).
1128. 14 H 605–606 (Wall) ; see 15 H 671–672, 675, 678–679 (Paul) ; 14 H 532–533, 543, 559, 564 (J. Ruby) ; 5 H 197 (J. Ruby).
1129. CE 2300.

1130. CE 2314.
1131. CE 2317.
1132. CE 2306, 2433.
1133. 7 H 286 (W. E. Barnes) ; see ch. V, pp, 216, 224, 230.
1134. See, e.g., CE 2794, 2795, 2797, 2798, 2799, 2804, 2806, 2808, 2809, 2810, 2822, 1481, 2824, 2826, 2875, 2814 ; 15 H 48–51 (William S. Biggio).
1135. See, e.g., CE 2796, 2800, 2801, 2802, 2803, 2813, 2818, 2819, 2821, 2825, 2829, 2878, 1818, 2383.
1136. See, e.g., CE 2805, 2812, 2827, 2828, 2874, 2877, 2879.
1137. CE 2830, 2884.
1138. CE 2830.
1139. CE 2884, 2885, 2886.
1140. Crafard DE 5226, p. 149.
1141. 3 H 595 (Paine) ; see also CE 1949, p. 5 ; app. I at notes 1253–1255.
1142. Crowe DE 2 ; 15 H 97–100 (William D. Crowe, Jr.) ; see also CE 2372.
1143. 15 H 104–105 (Crowe).
1144. Id., at 106.
1145. Id. at 105 ; CE 2983.
1146. 15 H 106 (Crowe) ; see KRLD–TV reel 43–a.
1147. 15 H 106 (Crowe).
1148. Crafard DE 5205, 5206 ; CE 2991.
1149. 15 H 113 (Crowe).
1150. Id. at 107–109 ; CE 2995, pp. 207–209.
1151. 15 H 107–109 (Crowe).
1152. CE 2995, p. 212.
1153. CE 2367.
1154. CE 2370, 2432.
1155. 2 H 515 (R. Paine) ; 3 H 41 (R. Paine).
1156. CE 2414.
1157. CE 2998 ; 15 H 658 (K. Carlin).
1158. See, e.g., CE 1479, 1623, 1652, 2362, 2380, 2401, 2403 ; Armstrong DE 5310–A ; Crafard DE 5226, p. 152.
1159. 14 H 102, 104–106 (Wilbryn Waldon Litchfield II).
1160. Compare CE 3149, 2991, 2243, 2284.
1161. CE 3149, p. 270.
1162. Pizzo DE 453–C ; Shaneyfelt DE 24 ; see also CE 3002.
1163. CE 3149, p. 271.
1164. 14 H 96–97 (Litchfield).
1165. Id. at 102–104.
1166. Id. at 102.
1167. CE 2889 ; see also CE 3194, p. 267.
1168. CE 2999, 369.
1169. CE 3004, 3005 ; see also CE 3003.
1170. CE 2807, 2820, 3010, 3027 ; see also CE 2876, 2877, 2880.
1171. 3 H 214 (R. Truly) ; see also CE 1949.
1172. CE 2302 ; 13 H 421 (Crafard) ; 14 H 192, 216 (Senator).
1173. CE 371, 3150.
1174. See p. 321 supra ; app. XIII, footnote 1224 infra.
1175. See CE 371, 376, 1979.
1176. 6 H 437 (E. Roberts) ; see 6 H 404–406 (Bledsoe) ; see also CE 2833.
1177. See app. XIII at pp. 737–740 ; CE 2833.
1178. CE 2303 ; see Crafard DE 5226, pp. 148, 150 ; CE 2319.
1179. CE 3000, 3001, 3006, 3009.
1180. CE 3001, 3006, 3009.
1181. 4 H 240 (Fritz) ; CE 1490, 1491, 3020, 3021, 3022.
1182. Holmes DE 1 ; see pp. 312–314, supra ; app XIII, p. 739, infra.
1183. CE 1322, p. 727 ; CE 3146, 2791, 1567 ; 14 H 560 (Ruby).
1184. CE 2882.
1185. CE 2883.
1186. 13 H 383, 385–389, 400–401 (Bertha Cheek) ; Cheek DE 5353.
1187. CE 2386, 3011.

1188. CE 1509 ; 14 H 91–92 (Crafard) ; 15 H 237–238 (Joseph Rossi).
1189. Cheek DE 5353 ; CE 2996, 2997.
1190. CE 2831.
1191. CE 2832, 2862, 2881.
1192. 14 H 203, 312–313 (Senator) ; CE 3012 ; 14 H 158 (Paul) ; 13 H 322 (Armstrong) ; app. XVI at pp. 803–804 ; 8 H 265 (Delgado) ; 8 H 300 (Donovan) ; see also 13 H 438–440 (Crafard) ; 8 H 270–271 (Powers) ; 8 H 319 (Murray) ; CE 1339.
1193. See CE 3013 ; 15 H 246 (Wright).
1194. 1 H 152–154, 237–238 (Marguerite Oswald).
1195. Id. at 237–238 ; CE 3028, 237.
1196. 11 H 468 (Bardwell D. Odum) ; 11 H 469 (Richard Helms) ; Odum DE 1.
1197. CE 237 ; Compare Odum DE 1 ; see 11 H 469 (Malley) ; 11 H 468 (Odum) ; 11 H 469 (Helms).
1198. Compare CE 237 ; Odum DE 1 ; with CE 2422, 2425.
1199. 11 H 470 (Helms) ; 5 H 208 (J. Ruby) ; see p. 373, infra.
1200. CE 2243 ; CE 1237, p. 5 ; 15 H 10 (Rubenstein) ; cf. app. XVI, p. 783–784.
1201. App. XVI, pp. 792, 794–795, 802–803.
1202. Id. at pp. 784–785, 786–790, 791–792, 794–795, 799–800.
1203. Id. at pp. 794–795, 802–803 ; 14 H 143 (Paul) ; 14 H 383 (E. Ruby).
1204. App. XVI at 797–799.
1205. 14 H 396–407 (Earl Ruby) ; 14 H 473–476, 483 (Grant) ; 15 H 35–36 (Hyman Rubenstein) ; see CE 3070.
1206. 15 H 11–14, 43–44 (Rubenstein) ; Rossi DE 1 ; CE 3052.
1207. CE 1322. p. 763.
1208. See 15 H 229 (Pullman) ; 14 H 209 (Senator).
1209. E.g., 14 H 206–210 (Senator) ; 15 H 241 (Rossi) ; 15 H 492 (Hallmark) ; CE 1512, 1515, p. 554 : CE 1500, 1621, 1748, 2414.
1210. App. XVI, at 791.
1211. CE 1485.
1212. 5 H 206, 209 (J. Ruby) ; 14 H 567–568 (J. Ruby) ; 14 H 468, 484 (Grant) ; 15 H 624 (L. Meyers) ; C. Ray Hall DE 2, p. 14 ; CE 3053 ; CE 1515, p. 554 ; CE 2161 ; 1508, 1540, 1542, 1711, 2392, 3052, 3142, 3143, 3144.
1213. 14 H 437–439 (Grant) ; 15 H 16–17 (Rubenstein).
1214. CE 3033 ; see also CE 2980, 2863, 2864, 2866, 2867, 2868, 2869, 2870, 2871, 2872, 2873 ; cf. Cumulative Index, 1938–1954, Committee on Un-American Activities, U.S. House of Representatives, p. 730.
1215. CE 3034.
1216. 15 H 306–308 (George W. Fehrenbach) ; CE 2837, 2838, 2843.
1217. CE 2848, 2849 ; see CE 2850, 2851, 2856.
1218. CE 2853, 2854 ; see CE 2855.
1219. Compare 15 H 308 (Fehrenbach) and CE 2838, with CE 1189.
1220. Compare 15 H 307 (Fehrenbach) with app. XVI, pp. 787–790, 791–792.
1221. 15 H 301–303 (Fehrenbach) ; CE 2838, 2835.
1222. CE 2835.
1223. 15 H 311, 316, 319 (Fehrenbach).
1224. CE 2835, pp. 1–2 ; see also CE 2861, 3008.
1225. CE 2839, 2840 : see also CE 2844, 2845, 2846.
1226. CE 3151. p. 10–14 ; CE 2847, 2852, 2841.
1227. CE 2842, 2845, 2835, pp. 4–6 ; CE 2858, 2859, 2860.
1228. 15 H 303–304 (Fehrenbach).
1229. 15 H 225 (Pullman) ; CE 1322, p. 734 ; CE 2285.

1230. 15 H 259–261, 264–265 (Knight).
1231. CE 2270, 2888.
1232. CE 2890, 2981, pp. 1, 3, 8; CE 2982; see also CE 305).
1233. 2 H 57–58, 60 (M. Lane).
1234. 14 H 69 (Crafard); CE 2984, cf. 13 H 353 (Armstrong); 15 H 662 (Mrs. Carlin).
1235. 14 H 559–561 (Ruby); 5 H 515–516, 522–525 (Weissman); CE 2985, p. 7; CE 3115.
1236. CE 1620; 14 H 559–560 (J. Ruby); see CE 2430; compare id. at 3.
1237. CE 2430.
1238. Ibid.
1239. Ibid.
1240. Ibid.
1241. See pp. 335, 347–348, supra.
1242. See pp. 344–345, supra.
1243. CE 2985, pp. 7, 9, 10, 12, 14; cf. CE 2986.
1244. See CE 2985, pp. 6–7.
1245. CE 2987.
1246. CE 2985, p. 10.
1247. Id. at 6–7.
1248. CE 2985, pp. 15–17.
1249. See ch. IV at 163–164.
1250. Sawyer CE A; 4 H 179, 184 (Jesse E. Curry); 7 H 75–76 (James Putnam); see ch. IV at 163–164.
1251. Compare ch. IV at 143–144 with CE 3002.
1252. CE 3054, 3055, 3056, 3057; 14 H 330–364 (Nancy Perrin Rich); Nancy Perrin Rich DE 1–4; CE 3058, 3059, 3060, 3061, 3062, 3063, 3064, 3065, 1688, 1689, 3067, 3068.
1253. 5 H 202 (J. Ruby); C. Ray Hall DE 3, p. 15; CE 1688, 1689, 3069; see also 14 H 506 (J. Ruby); CE 2414.
1254. CE 2988, 3069; see CE 1748, 1752.
1255. CE 2303, p. 19.
1256. See CE 2988, 3069.
1257. CE 2989.
1258. See 5 H 200–201 (J. Ruby); CE 1697, 1545, 1690, 1691.
1259. CE 2993, 2994, 1697, 1546.
1260. CE 2978, pp. 4–5.
1261. 14 H 384–385 (Earl Ruby).
1262. See app. XVI at 803.
1263. CE 2980, 2979, pp. 13–14.
1264. CE 2428.
1265. CE 2980.
1266. See app. XVI at p. 801; CE 2988.
1267. See app. XVI at pp. 785, 790, 801.

1268. 14 H 565–566 (J. Ruby); 5 H 103 (J. Edgar Hoover); CE 1353, 1628, 1760; cf. CE 2332, 2333, 3012, 2328, 2331, 1697, 1221, 1500.
1269. 14 H 165–168 (Senator).
1270. 14 H 168–172, 181–182, 185–186 (Senator).
1271. 14 H 175–178, 181–184, 304–305, 309–310 (Senator).
1272. Senator DE 5400, p. 297; CE 3027; 14 H 165–210, 310–311 (Senator); CE 3014, 3026, 3028.
1273. 14 H 249–250 (Senator).
1274. See 14 H 244–245, 302–303 (Senator); Senator DE 5400, 5401, 5402, 5403.
1275. Ibid.
1276. CE 2419.
1277. See 14 H 217–218, 230–235, 261–262, 299–300, 314–315 (Senator).
1278. CE 3015.
1279. 14 H 216, 314–315 (Senator).
1280. 14 H 532 (J. Ruby).
1281. Ibid.
1282. CE 2419; Senator DE 5401; see 14 H 245–246, 302–304, 316–317 (Senator).
1283. CE 3023, pp. 17–18; 14 H 245 (Senator); see Senator DE 5401.
1284. CE 3023; Senator DE 5401; but compare CE 2419; 14 H 245–246, 252–253, 303–304 (Senator).
1285. CE 3024; see also CE 3015, p. 196.
1286. 14 H 246–251, 253 (Senator); CE 3024.
1287. CE 2344, 2302, 2303, 2345.
1288. Ibid.
1289. See, e.g., CE 3036, see also 5 H 208 (J. Ruby).
1290. 14 H 150 (Paul); C. Ray Hall DE 3, pp. 15–16.
1291. CE 2344, 3018, 1695, 3019, 1567.
1292. CE 1561, p. 302; 15 H 248–249 (Wright).
1293. 14 H 216–217 (Senator); 13 H 447 (Crafard).
1294. See CE 1322, pp. 733–751.
1295. See app. XVI at pp. 794, 796–797, 804–806.
1296. 5 H 372 (Dean Rusk); CE 3025 (Robert F. Kennedy); 5 H 585–586 (C. Douglas Dillon); CE 3138 (Robert S. McNamara); 5 H 103 (J. Edgar Hoover); CE 2980 (John A. McCone); 5 H 485 (James J. Rowley).

CHAPTER VII

1. 5 H 394 (Marina Oswald); 2 H 400 (Michael Paine); 10 H 56 (Francis L. Martello); see discussion of Fair Play for Cuba Committee activities, infra.
2. 1 H 91 (Marina Oswald); 5 H 394, 408 (Marina Oswald); 9 H 145 (Paul R. Gregory); 10 H 56 (Martello).
3. 1 H 10–12, 21–22, 66 (Marina Oswald).
4. Id. at 22; see authority at notes 125 and 314, infra.
5. 8 H 150 (Lillian Murret); see authority at notes 125 and 314, infra.
6. 1 H 22 (Marina Oswald).
7. Id. at 22–23; see 11 H 100 (Kerry Thornley); 11 H 402 (Michael Paine).
8. See 8 H 272 (Daniel P. Powers); 11 H 96–97 (Thornley) and discussion, infra.
9. 11 H 96, 99; authority at note 151, infra.
10. 11 H 170 (William Kirk Stuckey); Stuckey DE 2, p. 2; CE 1385, p. 7.
11. 1 H 96, 123 (Marina Oswald); 10 H 97 (Arnold Johnson); CE 100; CE 2564.

12. 1 H 225 (Marguerite Oswald); see 8 H 104–105 (L. Murret).
13. 11 H 4, 10, 20 (John Edward Pic); 1 H 253 (Marguerite Oswald).
14. Id. at 253–254; 1 H 94 (Marina Oswald); 11 H 12, 74 (J. Pic); 8 H 48 (Myrtle Evans); 1 H 271 (Robert Oswald).
15. 11 H 12 (J. Pic); J. Pic DE 3, 5.
16. 1 H 254 (Marguerite Oswald); 8 H 47–48, 63–64 (M. Evans); 8 H 36, 37 (Anne Boudreaux); 8 H 112 (L. Murret).
17. J. Pic DE 2–A; 1 H 255 (Marguerite Oswald).
18. J. Pic DE 2, p. 4; 1 H 272 (R. Oswald); 11 H 15, 22 (J. Pic).
19. 11 H 23 (J. Pic); 8 H 53 (M. Evans); 1 H 255 (Marguerite Oswald); see CE 1960 A, p. 1.
20. 1 H 275–277 (R. Oswald); 11 H 23–25, 28–30 (J. Pic); 11 H 472 (Mrs. J. U. Allen).
21. 8 H 51 (M. Evans); 8 H 68–69 (Julian Evans); 8 H 117 (L. Murret); see 1 H 277–278 (R. Oswald).

22. 11 H 27 (J. Pic).
23. 1 H 250–252 (Marguerite Oswald) ; 11 H 27–29 (J. Pic) ; CE 1960–C.
24. 11 H 75 (J. Pic).
25. Id. at 30–32.
26. Id. at 32.
27. Id. at 32–34.
28. Id. at 33.
29. Id. at 73–74.
30. 1 H 298 (R. Oswald) ; 11 H 31–32 (J. Pic) ; see 1 H 253–254 (Marguerite Oswald).
31. 1 H 298 (R. Oswald) ; Evelyn Strickman Siegel DE 1, p. 1.
32. 8 H 119, 121 (L. Murret) ; 11 H 31 (J. Pic) ; 8 H 87 (Hiram Conway).
33. 8 H 121–122 (L. Murret) ; J. Pic DE 9.
34. 11 H 17, 28, 31 (J. Pic) ; J. Pic DE 23 ; Siegel DE 2, p. 1.
35. 1 H 225–226 (Marguerite Oswald) ; 11 H 37 (J. Pic).
36. 1 H 226, 229 (Marguerite Oswald) ; 11 H 37–41 (J. Pic).
37. 1 H 227 (Marguerite Oswald) ; 11 H 37 (J. Pic).
38. Id. at 38, 39, 42 ; CE 1382, p. 1 ; see John Carro DE 1, p. 1 : Siegel DE 2, p. 2.
39. 11 H 38–39 (J. Pic) ; see CE 1382.
40. 1 H 227 (Marguerite Oswald) ; see CE 1384.
41. See 8 H 208 (Carro) ; Carro DE 1, p. 3.
42. Carro DE 1, p. 2 ; Siegel DE 1, p. 1.
43. 1 H 227 (Marguerite Oswald) ; see Siegel DE 1, p. 2.
44. Carro DE 1, p. 1.
45. Ibid. ; see 8 H 218 (Renatus Hartogs).
46. Carro DE 1, pp. 1, 5.
47. Hartogs DE 1 ; Carro DE 1 ; Siegel DE 1.
48. 1 H 228 (Marguerite Oswald).
49. Ibid.
50. Ibid.
51. Ibid.
52. Carro DE 1, p. 3.
53. Siegel DE 2, p. 3.
54. "Oswald : Evolution of an Assassin," Life, Feb. 21, 1964, p. 72.
55. Hartogs DE 1, p. 1.
56. Ibid.
57. Ibid.
58. Id. at 2.
59. Ibid.
60. Siegel DE 1, p. 1.
61. Ibid.
62. Ibid.
63. Siegel DE 1, p. 2.
64. Siegel DE 2, p. 2.
65. Siegel DE 1, pp. 2, 3.
66. CE 1339.
67. Ibid.
68. Ibid.
69. Ibid.
70. Carro DE 1, p. 2.
71. See Carro DE 1, pp. 3, 6 ; Siegel DE 1, p. 3.
72. Siegel DE 1, pp. 2, 3.
73. Id. at 3, 6.
74. Hartogs DE 1, pp. 1–2.
75. Carro DE 1, p. 2.
76. 11 H 75 (Pic).
77. Compare Carro DE 1, Hartogs DE 1, and Siegel DE 1.
78. Carro DE 1, p. 4 ; see 8 H 206, 210 (Carro).
79. Id. at 212.
80. Siegel DE 1, p. 6.
81. See Carro DE 1, pp. 6–8.
82. CE 1413, pp. 14–15 ; 1 H 196–197, 198–199 (Marguerite Oswald).
83. Allison G. Folsom DE 1, pp. 2, 3.
84. 8 H 124 (L. Murret) ; see 8 H 159 (Marilyn Murret).
85. Id. at 124, 128.

86. Ibid. ; see 1 H 196–197 (Marguerite Oswald).
87. See e.g., 8 H 55, 56, 65 (M. Evans) ; 8 H 70, 71 (J. Evans) ; 8 H 159 (M. Murret).
88. 8 H 125, 131 (L. Murret).
89. Id. at 131 ; see 1 H 199 (Marguerite Oswald) ; 8 H 15 (Edward Voebel).
90. Ibid.
91. Id. at 5 ; see 8 H 159 (M. Murret) ; 8 H 124 (L. Murret).
92. Ibid.
93. 8 H 2–3 (Voebel).
94. Id. at 5, 9–10.
95. CE 1352 ; CE 1387 ; CE 1413, p. 10.
96. CE 3134.
97. 1 H 198 (Marguerite Oswald) ; CE 1386 ; CE 1385, pp. 5–6 ; CE 93, p. 3.
98. CE 1386.
99. Ibid.
100. 8 H 18 (William E. Wulf).
101. 1 H 196–198 (Marguerite Oswald).
102. CE 199 ; see 1 H 196–197 (Marguerite Oswald).
103. Id. at 197–198.
104. 1 H 375–376 (R. Oswald).
105. 1 H 198, 200 (Marguerite Oswald).
106. Id. at 198.
107. 11 H 4 (J. Pic).
108. See 8 H 22–23 (Bennierita Smith) ; 8 H 6–7 (Voebel).
109. See note 97, supra.
110. 11 H 95, 106 (Thornley).
111. 8 H 270 (Powers).
112. 8 H 258 (Nelson Delgado) ; 8 H 315 (James A. Botelho) ; 8 H 316 (Donald P. Camarata).
113. CE 1383 ; Folsom DE 1, p. 1.
114. 11 H 89, 101 (Thornley) ; 8 H 318 (Allen D. Graf) ; 8 H 318 (John Rene Heindell) ; 8 H 321 (Mack Osborne).
115. Folsom DE 1, p. 5.
116. See 8 H 292–293 (John E. Donovan).
117. Id. at 295.
118. Id. at 292–293, 297 ; see 11 H 105–106 (Thornley).
119. 8 H 293 (Donovan).
120. 8 H 265 (Delgado).
121. 11 H 89 (Thornley).
122. Id. at 90.
123. Id. at 100.
124. Ibid.
125. 8 H 270 (Powers).
126. Id. at 272.
127. Id. at 287.
128. Id. at 270.
129. Id. at 277.
130. Id. at 278.
131. Id. at 283.
132. Id. at 285–286.
133. Id. at 275.
134. Id. at 283.
135. See Folsom DE 1, pp. 9, 31–34.
136. Ibid. ; 8 H 308 (Folsom).
137. See Folsom DE 1, pp. 4, 10, 17, 23, and 30.
138. See id. at pp. 77–104.
139. See id. at pp. 10, 14–16, 18–22, 38–43, 48, 50–55, 61, 67–79.
140. Id. at 65.
141. Id. at 63.
142. See 1 H 22, 31, 70–72, 123 (Marina Oswald) ; 1 H 450 (R. Oswald) ; 8 H 374 (George Bouhe) ; 9 H 148–149, 158 (Paul Gregory).
143. 1 H 71 (Marina Oswald) ; but see 5 H 605 (Marina Oswald).
144. Id. at 72.
145. 1 H 385–386, 450 (R. Oswald) ; 11 H 79 (J. Pic).
146. See 1 H 220–222 (Marguerite Oswald) ; Folsom DE 1, pp. 19, 21.
147. Id. at pp. 38–39, 45–47.
148. 5 H 605 (Marina Oswald).
149. See discussion in ch. III, supra.

150. Ibid.
151. 1 H 198 (Marguerite Oswald) ; CE 1385, pp. 5–6 ; CE 1386 ; see 8 H 18 (Wulf).
152. CE 1385, p. 5.
153. 8 H 321 (Henry J. Roussel, Jr.).
154. 8 H 323 (Richard Dennis Call) ; 8 H 315 (Botelho).
155. 8 H 323 (Call).
156. 8 H 319 (David Christie Murray) ; 8 H 315 (Botelho) ; 8 H 321 (Osborne) ; 8 H 323 (Erwin Donald Lewis).
157. 8 H 315 (Botelho) ; 8 H 321 (Osborne).
158. 11 H 93–94 (Thornley).
159. Id. at 99.
160. Id. at 95.
161. Ibid.
162. 8 H 292–293 (Donovan).
163. 8 H 233, 240 (Delgado).
164. 11 H 97–98 (Thornley).
165. Id. at 98.
166. See 8 H 18 (Wulf) ; 8 H 81 (Philip E. Vinson) ; 1 H 94 (Marina Oswald).
167. 11 H 172–173 (Stuckey).
168. 2 H 308 (Mrs. Katherine Ford).
169. CE 295, pp. 4, 7, 8.
170. CE 294, p. 1.
171. See discussion supra pp. 256–257.
172. CE 295, p. 1.
173. Id. at 2–3, 4.
174. Id. at 6–7.
175. See CE 24, pp. 1–2 ; note 178, infra.
176. Ibid.
177. Id. at 2.
178. CE 985, doc. 1 C 3 ; CE 24, pp. 1–2.
179. 5 H 263 (Richard E. Snyder).
180. CE 913.
181. CE 908, p. 2.
182. Ibid.
183. Ibid.
184. Ibid.
185. Ibid.
186. Ibid.
187. CE 24, p. 4.
188. See id. at pp. 4, 5.
189. See id. at 5–6 ; CE 985, doc. 9A.
190. CE 72 ; 5 H 589 (Marina Oswald) ; see 9 H 147 (Paul Gregory).
191. CE 24, p. 6 ; see CE 25, p. 1B.
192. See CE 24, p. 6 ; 5 H 407–408 (Marina Oswald).
193. See CE 24, p. 6 ; 1 H 93 (Marina Oswald).
194. Ibid ; see discussion at pp. 269, supra.
195. 1 H 93 (Marina Oswald).
196. 10 H 56 (Martello) ; 9 H 145 (Paul Gregory) ; see 5 H 408 (Marina Oswald).
197. 1 H 95, 100 (Marina Oswald).
198. 2 H 302 (Mrs. Ford).
199. 9 H 312 (Jeanne De Mohrenschildt).
200. 9 H 234 (George De Mohrenschildt).
201. CE 24, p. 7.
202. Ibid.
203. Id. at 9.
204. See ibid. ; CE 245.
205. 1 H 10 (Marina Oswald).
206. Id. at 10–11.
207. CE 994, p. 25.
208. CE 92 ; see also CE 94 (earlier manuscript) ; 8 H 333 (Pauline V. Bates).
209. CE 94, p. 1.
210. Compare CE 92 and CE 94 with CE 25, CE 97, CE 98.
211. CE 25, p. 3.
212. Ibid.
213. CE 97, p. 8.
214. See CE 98.
215. CE 25, p. 3A.
216. Id. at 1A.
217. Id. at 2A.
218. Id. at 2A–3A.
219. Id. at 3A.
220. CE 97, p. 3.
221. Ibid.
222. Id. at 5.
223. Ibid.

224. Id. at 6.
225. Arnold Johnson DE 4, p. 3.
226. CE 97, p. 1.
227. Id. at 1–2.
228. CE 25, p. 1.
229. CE 100, p. 1.
230. Id. at 3.
231. Id. at 1.
232. Id. at 4.
233. Id. at 2.
234. See id. at 4.
235. CE 986, p. 6.
236. 10 H 209–210 (Denis H. Ofstein) ; CE 1147.
237. See CE 7, 9 ; CE 986. pp. 1–2, 6 ; 1 H 35 (Marina Oswald).
238. See CE 12 ; CE 13.
239. 10 H 56 (Martello).
240. See CE 2464, pp. 4–6.
241. CE 15.
242. 1 H 11 (Marina Oswald) ; see 8 H 377 (Bouhe).
243. 9 H (Paul M. Raigorodsky) ; see 9 H 166–284 passim (G. De Mohrenschildt).
244. CE 1389, p. 3 ; but see 2 H 338 (Peter P. Gregory).
245. 8 H 383–385 (Anna Meller) ; see id. at 372–373, 376 (Bouhe) ; 9 H 309 (J. De Mohrenschildt).
246. 1 H 10–11 (Marina Oswald).
247. See 8 H 376 (Bouhe) ; 8 H 384 (Meller) ; 1 H 11 (Marina Oswald).
248. 9 H 309 (J. De Mohrenschildt).
249. Ibid.
250. 9 H 240 (G. De Mohrenschildt).
251. Id. at 232.
252. Ibid.
253. Id. at 233.
254. See 1 H 11 (Marina Oswald) ; 2 H 305 (Mrs. Ford).
255. 9 H 252–253 (G. De Mohrenschildt) ; 2 H 307, 309 (Mrs. Ford).
256. 1 H 133, 141 (Marguerite Oswald) ; 1 H 312, 387 (R. Oswald).
257. CE 295, p. 7 ; CE 908, p. 2 ; CE 909, p. 2.
258. 1 H 94–95 (Marina Oswald).
259. 1 H 312, 314 (R. Oswald).
260. 1 H 134–136 (Marguerite Oswald).
261. Id. at 136.
262. 1 H 6 (Marina Oswald) ; 2 H 300 (Mrs. Ford).
263. 1 H 140–141 (Marguerite Oswald) ; see 8 H 394–395 (Elena Hall) ; discussion in appendix XIII.
264. 8 H 135–136 (L. Murret).
265. 8 H 165–166 (M. Murret).
266. Priscilla Johnson DE 6.
267. See 9 H 47 (Samuel B. Ballen).
268. CE 1861, p. 3.
269. See, e.g. Helen P. Cunningham DE 1–A ; John Rachal DE 1, 2 ; CE 1398.
270. 10 H 163, 165 (Tommy Bargas).
271. See 1 H 5–7 (Marina Oswald) ; 10 H 166 (Bargas) ; CE 1405.
272. 10 H 144 (Donald Brooks).
273. 10 H 121 (Cunningham) ; Cunningham DE 1–A.
274. 10 H 121–124, 127 (Cunningham).
275. Cunningham DE 1–A, p. 3 ; see 10 H 126 (Cunningham).
276. 11 H 478 (Cunningham).
277. Ibid. ; see 10 H. 177 (John G. Graef).
278. 10 H 176 (Graef) ; CE 427.
279. 1 H 68 (Marina Oswald).
280. 10 H 172 (Robert Stovall) ; 10 H 186–187 (Graef).
281. See id. at 187–189.
282. See id. at 188.
283. See id. at 187, 189.
284. Id. at 189 ; see 10 H 170–171 (Stovall).
285. 2 H 457–459, 468–469, 271 (R. Paine).
286. 11 H 474 (Emmett C. Barbe, Jr.) ; CE 1398.

287. 2 H 468–469 (R. Paine).
288. Id. at 517.
289. 11 H 474 (Barbe).
290. Ibid.; 10 H 220, 225–226 (Adrian Alba).
291. 3 H 6 (R. Paine).
292. See 10 H 53 (Martello); 10 H 37–38 (Carlos Bringuier); discussion FPCC activities, infra.
293. 11 H 476 (Rachal).
294. 10 H 170–171 (Stovall).
295. 11 H 479 (Theodore R. Gangl).
296. See 3 H 216, 218 (Roy S. Truly).
297. See CE 1351, pp. 7–8.
298. 1 H 16 (Marina Oswald).
299. See id. at 17; 11 H 292 (Marina Oswald).
300. 1 H 17 (Marina Oswald).
301. Id. at 15–16, 117–118; 11 H 296 (Marina Oswald).
302. See CE 133; CE 134; CE 1406.
303. 1 H 15–16 (Marina Oswald); 11 H 296 (Marina Oswald).
304. See discussion in ch. IV, supra.
305. 1 H 16 (Marina Oswald); see CE 1.
306. Id. at 17–18.
307. Id. at 18.
308. 11 H 294 (Marina Oswald).
309. Id. at 292–294, 295–296.
310. See 1 H 37–39 (Marina Oswald); 11 H 294–295 (Marina Oswald).
311. 11 H 293 (Marina Oswald).
312. See, e.g. Life, Feb. 21, 1964.
313. See 1 H 22–23 (Marina Oswald); 8 H 354 (Max E. Clark); 9 H 150, 155 (Paul Gregory); 11 H 97–98 (Thornley).
314. See e.g. 8 H 376–377 (Bouhe); 8 H 390 (Mrs. Meller); 8 H 405 (Elena Hall); 8 H 411 (John R. Hall).
315. 1 H 16 (Marina Oswald); see 2 H 315 (Mrs. Ford).
316. See CE 1409; Vincent T. Lee DE 1.
317. See CE 1410; CE 1411.
318. CE 1412.
319. See 10 H 37–39 (Bringuier).
320. CE 1413; 10 H 53 (Martello); see discussion in ch. VIII, infra.
321. 11 H 165–166 (Stuckey).
322. Ibid.
323. 10 H 35–36 (Bringuier).
324. 1 H 24 (Marina Oswald); see 10 H 57 (Martello); 10 H 90, 94 (Lee).
325. Id. at 64–65; see CE 820.
326. See discussion in ch. IV, supra.
327. 5 H 401 (Marina Oswald); see 1 H 64 (Marina Oswald).
328. 5 H 401 (Marina Oswald).
329. 10 H 90, 94 (Lee).
330. 10 H 54 (Martello).
331. Lee DE 5.
332. Ibid.
333. Ibid.
334. Ibid.
335. CE 1413, p. 19.
336. See 10 H 32–51 (Bringuier).
337. See CE 1412; CE 1413, pp. 19–35.
338. Lee DE 6.
339. CE 1414.
340. CE 1410; see Lee DE 4, p. 2; Lee DE 5, p. 2; 10 H 87–89 (Lee); Lee DE 5.
341. Lee DE 7.
342. 11 H 471 (John Corporon).
343. 11 H 162, 165 (Stuckey).
344. 10 H 41 (Bringuier); see 1 H 25 (Marina Oswald); 11 H 268–270 (Mrs. Jesse J. Garner).
345. Stuckey DE 3, p. 2; see 11 H 167 (Stuckey).
346. See 11 H 168 (Stuckey).
347. Stuckey DE 3, p. 8.
348. 11 H 171 (Stuckey).
349. Ibid.
350. Id. at 162.
351. Ibid.
352. Id. at 171.
353. Arnold Johnson DE 4.

354. See Louis Weinstock DE 1; Arnold Johnson DE 5–A.
355. Weinstock DE 1.
356. Arnold Johnson DE 5.
357. Arnold Johnson DE 1 and 3.
358. Arnold Johnson DE 2.
359. 1 H 23 (Marina Oswald).
360. Ibid.
361. Arnold Johnson DE 4, p. 1.
362. Id. at 1–2.
363. Id. at 2–3.
364. Arnold Johnson DE 4–A.
365. 1 H 20 (Marina Oswald); 11 H 474 (Barbe).
366. See CE 409; CE 415; 2 H 490, 493 (R. Paine).
367. 1 H 24 (Marina Oswald).
368. 10 H 91 (Lee); see Lee DE 3.
369. Lee DE 4–7.
370. Lee DE 8–A, 8–B, 8–C.
371. CE 781.
372. 1 H 21, 68 (Marina Oswald).
373. Id. at 21.
374. Ibid.; see CE 7, 12.
375. CE 12.
376. CE 13.
377. See 1 H 23 (Marina Oswald).
378. Id. at 47.
379. Id. at 24.
380. Id. at 25.
381. Id. at 22, 23.
382. Id. at 21–22, 54; but see 5 H 605 (Marina Oswald).
383. 1 H 49–50 (Marina Oswald) see CE 17.
384. 3 H 5 (R. Paine).
385. See id. at 3–4.
386. 2 H 507 (R. Paine); see 3 H 9 (R. Paine).
387. 1 H 23 (Marina Oswald).
388. 3 H 10, 27 (R. Paine); see id. at 29.
389. See CE 2464, p. 2; CE 2121, p. 39.
390. Ibid.
391. Id. at 40.
392. 1 H 50 (Marina Oswald).
393. CE 2695.
394. See Farrell Dobbs DE 1, 2; 11 H 398 (R. Paine).
395. See CEs 1340–1347; discussion of Fair Play for Cuba Committee activities, supra; CE 25, p. 5; 9 H 249 (G. De Mohrenschildt); Arnold Johnson DE 5–A.
396. CE 1343, p. 1.
397. CE 1350; CE 1172; 11 H 398 (R. Paine).
398. 2 H 418 (M. Paine); see 9 H 455 (M. Paine).
399. Stuckey DE 3, p. 9.
400. 9 H 465 (Raymond F. Krystinik).
401. 1 H 50 (Marina Oswald).
402. See app. XIV; 1 H 69 (Marina Oswald).
403. See e.g. CE 2647; CE 2696; CE 2697; CE 2698; CE 2699.
404. See CE 1031; CE 996; discussion in ch. VI, supra.
405. Arnold Johnson DE 7, pp. 2–3.
406. 11 H 424 (Maj. Gen. Edwin A. Walker).
407. 1 H 51–58, 63 (Marina Oswald); 3 H 138–139 (R. Paine).
408. Id. at 50.
409. Ibid.; see id. at 54.
410. Id. at 68.
411. CE 24, p. 10; see id. at 9; 2 H 302 (Mrs. Ford); 1 H 90–91 (Marina Oswald).
412. See e.g. 2 H 302 (Mrs. Ford); 8 H 362 (Bouhe); 8 H 386 (Mrs. Meller); 8 H 422 (Mrs. Frank Ray); but see 9 H 153 (Paul Gregory); see also CE 1401, p. 269.
413. 1 H 10 (Marina Oswald).
414. 2 H 413–414 (R. Paine); CE 410.
415. CE 415.
416. 1 H 12 (Marina Oswald).
417. Id. at 10, 12.

418. See CE 415; 1 H 66 (Marina Oswald).
419. Ibid.
420. See 8 H 150 (L. Murret); 9 H 313 (J. De Mohrenschildt).
421. 1 H 25 (Marina Oswald).
422. 2 H 342 (Peter Gregory).
423. 10 H 59 (Martello).
424. 1 H 33 (Marina Oswald); 5 H 596 (Marina Oswald); 2 H 303–304 (Mrs. Ford); 8 H 365 (Bouhe); 8 H 387 (Mrs. Meller).
425. See 1 H 35 (Marina Oswald); 9 H 259 (G. De Mohrenschildt); 9 H 311 (J. De Mohrenschildt).
426. See 2 H 422 (M. Paine).
427. 2 H 300 (Mrs. Ford).
428. Ibid.; see also 5 H 597 (Marina Oswald).
429. 1 H 33 (Marina Oswald).
430. See ibid.
431. Ibid.
432. Id. at 12.
433. 5 H 593–594 (Marina Oswald); 9 H 233 (G. De Mohrenschildt); see 9 H 309 (J. De Mohrenschildt); 1 H 66 (Marina Oswald).
434. 9 H 233 (G. De Mohrenschildt).
435. Ibid.; see also 9 H 311, 313 (J. De Mohrenschildt).
436. See 8 H 396 (Mrs. Hall).
437. 11 H 396 (R. Paine).
438. 1 H 23 (Marina Oswald).
439. Ibid.
440. Id. at 22 (Marina Oswald).
441. 9 H 314 (J. De Mohrenschildt).
442. Id. at 313.
443. Id. at 309.
444. Id. at 312.
445. Ibid.
446. Ibid.
447. See 2 H 422 (M. Paine).
448. 1 H 54, 63 (Marina Oswald).
449. 2 H 515–516 (R. Paine); 3 H 41 (R. Paine).
450. See ibid.; 3 H 43–44 (R. Paine).
451. 10 H 294 (Mrs. A. C. Johnson).
452. See 1 H 65 (Marina Oswald).
453. Id. at 63.
454. Id. at 46.
455. Ibid.

456. Stuckey DE 3, p. 2; see 11 H 167 (Stuckey).
457. See 1 H 20, 49 (Marina Oswald); 3 H 18, 102 (R. Paine); see discussion of employment relations, supra; ch. VIII, infra.
458. 1 H 48 (Marina Oswald); see also discussion in ch. VIII, infra.
459. CE 15.
460. See discussion in ch. VIII, infra.
461. See CE 15; 1 H 48–49 (Marina Oswald); 3 H 15–16 (Ruth Paine).
462. See CE 15; 1 H 49 (Marina Oswald).
463. Ibid.
464. Id. at 48; discussion in ch. VIII, infra.
465. See discussion at footnote 347, supra.
466. 1 H 63 (Marina Oswald).
467. Ibid.
468. Id. at 65.
469. Id. at 65–66.
470. Id. at 66.
471. Id. at 73.
472. See app. XIV.
473. 2 H 226, 228 (Buell Wesley Frazier); 2 H 248 (Linnie Mae Randle).
474. 2 H 222 (Frazier).
475. CE 2743.
476. CE 1361.
477. CE 1362; CE 1363; CE 1364; CE 1365; see discussion at footnote 52, ch. III, supra.
478. 5 H 595 (Marina Oswald); see 1 H. 54 (Marina Oswald); 2 H 341 (Peter Gregory); 10 H 311 (J. De Mohrenschildt).
479. 1 H 28 (Marina Oswald).
480. 1 H 65 (Marina Oswald); 3 H 46, 66 (R. Paine); 11 H 392 (R. Paine).
481. 3 H 300 (M. N. McDonald); 7 H 551 (Eddy Raymond Walthers).
482. 4 H 217 (J. W. Fritz); 7 H 353, 357 (Forrest V. Sorrels).
483. See discussion in ch. IV, supra.
484. See 4 H 240 (Fritz); 7 H 321 (Manning C. Clements); 7 H 310 (James W. Bookhout).
485. See discussion in ch. IV, supra.

CHAPTER VIII

1. See app. VII for a fuller discussion of prior assassination attempts.
2. C. Rossiter, "The American Presidency" 18 (1960).
3. 30 "Writings of George Washington" 496 (Fitzpatrick ed. 1939).
4. Rossiter at 17, 92–93.
5. M. Smith, "A President Is Many Men" 232 (1948).
6. 7 H 442 (Kenneth O'Donnell); see 7 H 460 (Lawrence F. O'Brien).
7. CE 866; see 5 H 106–107, 116–119 (J. Edgar Hoover).
8. See app. VII.
9. 4 H 295–297 (Robert I. Bouck).
10. CE 761; 4 H 299 (Bouck).
11. Id. at 301.
12. Statistical data set forth in CE 762, p. 1.
13. Ibid.
14. 4 H 303 (Bouck).
15. CE 763.
16. See 4 H 302 (Bouck).
17. CE 1021, p. 1.
18. 4 H 307 (Bouck).
19. Id. at 310–311.
20. Id. at 307–308.
21. CE 762.

22. Ibid.
23. 4 H 306 (Bouck).
24. Id. at 309.
25. Ibid.
26. Ibid.
27. Id. at 310.
28. Ibid.
29. Ibid.
30. Ibid.
31. Id. at 309; see CE 765.
32. 4 H 308–309 (Bouck); see 18 U.S.C. sec. 871. The Secret Service prepared for the Commission abstracts of several cases illustrating the achievement of the goal of eliminating risks by imprisonment or hospitalization, CE 766.
33. 5 H 466 (James J. Rowley).
34. See p. 30 supra.
35. 4 H 304 (Bouck).
36. Ibid.
37. Id. at 303–304.
38. CE 836, attachment 2.
39. See CE 1354, p. 1.
40. See CE 1355.
41. 4 H 304 (Bouck).
42. Id. at 316.
43. CE 836, p. 2.
44. CE 1356.

45. 4 H 403 (John W. Fain) ; 4 H 431 (John L. Quigley) ; 4 H 440 (James P. Hosty, Jr.) ; 5 H 97 (Hoover) ; 5 H 1 (Alan H. Belmont).
46. 5 H 120 (John A. McCone) ; 5 H 121 (Richard M. Helms).
47. CE 834 is a list of each item in the FBI's file on Oswald from the opening of the file until the assassination.
48. CE 833, p. 1.
49. Ibid.
50. Id. at pp. 1–2 of attachment ; see also CE 821 ; 4 H 405–409 (Fain).
51. CE 822, 834.
52. CE 833, p. 1, p. 2 of attachment.
63. 4 H 428 (Fain) ; id. at 441–442 of the text of Oswald's letter appears at p. 463 infra.
54. 4 H 415 (Fain).
55. Id. at 417.
56. CE 823, p. 13 ; 4 H 416–417 (Fain).
57. Id. at 419.
58. CE 824 ; 4 H 418–424 (Fain).
59. 1 H 20 (Marina Oswald).
60. 4 H 422 (Fain) ; CE 824, p. 6.
61. 4 H 423–426 (Fain).
62. Id. at 424 ; relevant administrative procedures are described at 5 H 2–6 (Belmont).
63. 4 H 428 (Fain) ; Id. at 441–442 (Hosty).
64. Ibid.
65. CE 829, pp. 1–2 ; 4 H 441–442 (Hosty).
66. Id. at 442.
67. Id. at 441–442.
68. See id. at 444.
69. Ibid.
70. Ibid.
71. Id. at 444–445 ; see pp. 406–407 supra, where the possibility that Oswald had been distributing pamphlets in Dallas for the Fair Play for Cuba Committee is discussed.
72. 4 H 442 (Hosty).
73. Id. at 443.
74. CE 833, p. 6.
75. Id. at 9.
76. Details regarding the issuance of the passport are set forth in app. XV.
77. CE 833, p. 13.
78. Ibid.
79. 4 H 432 (Quigley).
80. Ibid.
81. Id. at 435.
82. Ibid.
83. Id. at 438 ; Agent Quigley's memorandum of his interview with Oswald appears at pp. 6–10 of the report on Oswald of Agent Milton R. Kaack, CE 826.
84. See CE 833, p. 8.
85. 4 H 434 (Quigley).
86. Id. at 437.
87. CE 833, p. 8.
88. Ibid ; CE 826, p. 11.
89. See 4 H 435–438 (Quigley) ; see also 5 H 9–10 (Belmont).
90. Id. at 9.
91. CE 834, p. 7.
92. CE 826, p. 12.
93. CE 834, p. 7 ; 4 H 445–446 (Hosty).
94. CE 833, p. 12.
95. Ibid ; 4 H 446–447 (Hosty).
96. Ibid.
97. Ibid.
98. CE 834, p. 8.
99. 4 H 447 (Hosty) ; CE 833, pp. 12–13.
100. Id. at 13.
101. CE 952, 2075 ; 11 H 203 (Carroll H. Seeley, Jr.).
102. Id. at 203–204 ; 11 H 192–193 (James L. Ritchie) ; CE 948, "Question 16." See app. XV at p. 777.
103. CE 826, p. 2.
104. 4 H 448 (Hosty).

105. Id. at 448–449.
106. Id. at 450.
107. Ibid ; see also CE 830.
108. 4 H 450 (Hosty).
109. Ibid.
110. Id. at 451.
111. Id. at 450.
112. Id. at 452.
113. Ibid.
114. Id. at 453–454 (Hosty).
115. Id. at 453.
116. 3 H 95–109 (Ruth Paine).
117. CE 826.
118. 4 H 459 (Hosty).
119. Ibid.
120. Ibid.
121. See CE 834, pp. 9–10.
122. 4 H 459 (Hosty).
123. 4 H 311–314 (Bouck).
124. Id. at 312–313.
125. Ibid.
126. 4 H 460 (Hosty).
127. Id. at 459–461.
128. Id. at 460.
129. Id. at 473–474.
130. Id. at 473.
131. Id. at 472–473.
132. Id. at 461–462.
133. Id. at 462.
134. Agent Hosty's testimony appears at 4 H 463–465 ; Lieutenant Revill's at 5 H 34–39.
135. Id. at 34–35.
136. Id. at 35.
137. CE 709.
138. 7 H 405 (Mary Jane Robertson).
139. 4 H 194 (Jesse E. Curry) ; 5 H 216 (Henry Wade).
140. CE 831 ; 4 H 463–464 (Hosty).
141. 5 H 58 (V. J. Brian).
142. 5 H 112 (Hoover).
143. Id. at 104.
144. Id. at 111 ; 5 H 10 (Belmont).
145. Id. at 28–29.
146. See pp. 747–749, 778 infra (regarding his dealings with officials at the Embassy in Moscow) ; pp. 710–711 infra supra (regarding protests of his discharge from the Marine Corps Reserve) ; pp. 434–435 supra (regarding his antipathy for the FBI).
147. CE 833.
148. CE 836, attachment 2.
149. See p. 441 supra.
150. See pp. 461–462 infra.
151. CE 836, pp. 3–4 ; CE 1021, p. 4.
152. CE 836, attachment 4.
153. See p. 30 supra.
154. See pp. 29, 31 supra.
155. 4 H 329 (Winston G. Lawson).
156. Agent Lawson's interim and final reports on the Dallas trip are CE 767 and 768.
157. See 4 H 346–347 (Lawson).
158. CE 1021, p. 5 ; see also 4 H 348–349 (Lawson).
159. 7 H 333–334 (Forrest V. Sorrels).
160. CE 768, p. 11.
161. Ibid.
162. For the Commission's recommendations on this point, see pp. 465–466 infra.
163. 12 H 22–23 (Charles Batchelor) ; 6 H 250–251 (J. W. Foster) ; 4 H 327 (Lawson). See the discussion in ch. III at pp. 71–72.
164. 12 H 22 (Batchelor).
165. 4 H 329 (Lawson).
166. Id. at 333.
167. 5 H 467 (Rowley).
168. See ch. II at p. 42, supra.
169. 7 H 338 (Sorrels).
170. 5 H 578 (C. Douglas Dillon).
171. 4 H 329 (Lawson) ; 5 H 459 (Rowley).
172. 4 H 328 (Lawson).

173. WFAA–TV reel PKT 24.
174. CE 1358, p. 1.
175. Id., attachment 2.
176. Ibid.
177. 7 H 580–581, 584 (P. W. Lawrence).
178. 7 H 532–535 (J. M. Smith) ; 540–541 (W. E. Barnett) ; 566–567 (E. L. Smith, Jr.).
179. 7 H 343 (Sorrels).
180. Id. at 342.
181. 4 H 330 (Lawson).
182. Ibid.
183. 2 H 110–111 (Kellerman).
184. 5 H 451 (Rowley).
185. CE 1020. This exhibit covers the complete investigation by the Secret Service, and includes statements of each agent involved, statements by their supervisors, statements and voluntary reports by witnesses, and the final report of the investigation. In addition to furnishing the Commission the results of the investigation, the Secret Service responded to the Commission's request for information about this occurrence in its letter of May 5, 1964. CE 1019. Chief James J. Rowley, the head of the Secret Service, gave testimony before the Commission concerning this incident. 5 H. 451–462 (Rowley).
186. CE 1020, tab E.
187. CE 1020, tab F (statement of Richard J. Mackie).
188. CE 1020, tabs B and E; see CE 1020, tab G, which explains liquor practices at the Cellar Coffee House.
189. CE 1020, tab E.
190. See 5 H 460–461 (Rowley).
191. Ibid.
192. CE 1020, tab E (statement of Paul A. Burns).
193. 5 H 460 (Rowley).
194. CE 1020, tab D.
195. 5 H 452–453, 459–460 (Rowley).
196. CE 1020, tab D.
197. 5 H 452–453 (Rowley).
198. CE 1018.
199. Ibid.
200. 5 H 453–454 (Rowley).
201. Testimony and other evidence regarding Love Field arrangements appear at 4 H 339–341 (Lawson) ; CE 768, pp. 4–5 ; CE 769.
202. Television tapes of the arrival at Love Field furnished to the Commission by Dallas television stations provide a good record of the security measures at Love Field. See KRLD–TV reels 1 and 8 ; WFAA–TV reel PKT 4.
203. See p. 46 supra.
204. See p. 43 supra.
205. CE 1021, p. 5.
206. CE 2067 ; 5 H 579 (Dillon). J. Edgar Hoover, Director of the FBI, has recommended that the President never ride in an open car, 5 H 107, 117 (Hoover) ; CE 866.
207. CE 1021, p. 6.
208. See pp. 51–52 supra.
209. 15 H 699 (Lyndal L. Shaneyfelt).
210. Ibid.
211. CE 1021, p. 7.
212. 18 U.S.C. sec. 372.
213. 18 U.S.C. sec. 871.
214. 18 U.S.C. sec. 2385.
215. 18 U.S.C. sec. 1114.
216. 18 U.S.C. sec. 3056 ; *United States v. Sheba Bracelets, Inc.*, 248 F. 2d 134 (2d Cir. 1957), *cert. denied*, 355 U.S. 904.
217. CE 1030, pp. 4–5.
218. 18 U.S.C. secs. 3052, 3053.
219. S. 3653, 57th Cong., 1st sess. (1902) ; H.R. 10386, 57th Cong., 1st sess. (1901) ; H.R. 3896, 73d Cong., 1st sess. (1933).

220. 36 Cong. Rec. 2961–2964 (1902).
221. E.g., S. 2330, 88th Cong., 1st sess. (1963). (Introduced by all members of the Senate Committee on the Judiciary).
222. Even in the failure of the House and the Senate to agree, in 1902, as to whether this "line of duty" element was a constitutional requisite to covering officers in the line of succession, there was agreement in conference that this test need not be applied in the case of the President or Vice President, 36 Cong. Rec. 2407 (1902).
223. See "Report on Bills To Make Assassination of the President a Federal Crime," The Association of the Bar of the City of New York, Reports of Committees Concerned With Federal Legislation, vol. 3, Bulletin No. 2, pp. 54–55 (July 1964).
224. 35 Cong. Rec. 2431 (1902).
225. See CE 1030.
226. 5 H 115 (Hoover).
227. See id. at 115–116.
228. 50 U.S.C. sec. 402.
229. See 5 H 583 (Dillon).
230. See generally the discussion in app. VII.
231. Id. at 514.
232. CE 1021, pp. 9–11.
233. Id. at p. 10.
234. 5 H 481 (Rowley).
235. See pp. 429–433 supra.
236. 5 H 464–469, 478 (Rowley).
237. See id. at 466 ; see also 5 H 580 (Dillon).
238. The planning document is CE 1053A and the transmittal letter to the Director of the Bureau of the Budget is 1053B.
239. CE 836, attachment 5, p. 2.
240. 5 H 18 (Belmont).
241. Ibid.
242. 5 H 465 (Rowley).
243. 5 H 12, 21 (Belmont).
244. 5 H 113–114 (Hoover) ; 5 H 18–21 (Belmont).
245. 5 H 465 (Rowley).
246. CE 1023.
247. Ibid.
248. 5 H 465–469 (Rowley).
249. Id. at 469 (Rowley).
250. Folsom DE 1, p. 65.
251. See 5 H 467–469 (Rowley).
252. See app. VII.
253. 5 H 464–466 (Rowley) ; 5 H 585 (Dillon).
254. Id. at 581.
255. Id. at 577.
256. Ibid ; CE 1053A, pp. 6–7.
257. CE 1053C.
258. CE 1053A, p. 5 ; see 5 H 576–577 (Dillon).
259. CE 1053A, pp. 7–8.
260. CE 1027, p. 4.
261. CE 1053A, pp. 3–4.
262. 5 H 480–481 (Rowley).
263. Ibid.
264. See p. 447 supra.
265. CE 1027, p. 5.
266. 5 H 578 (Dillon).
267. Ibid ; CE 1027, p. 1.
268. 5 H 482 (Rowley).
269 5 H 24–25 (Belmont).
270. 5 H 483 (Rowley).
271. CE 1027, p. 5 ; 5 H 478 (Rowley).
272. CE 2765.
273. 5 H 475–478 (Rowley).
274. CE 1053A, 1053B.
275. E.g., hearings before Subcommittee of the House Committee on Appropriations, Treasury Department Appropriations for 1963, 87th Cong., 2d sess., p. 448 (1962).
276. CE 1027, p. 1 ; 5 H 473 (Rowley).
277. CE 1027, p. 1.
278. CE 836, p. 5.
279. 5 H 24–25 (Belmont).

280. 5 H 579 (Dillon).
281. 5 H 24–25 (Belmont) ; CE 1027, pp. 1–2.

282. See 5 H 474–475 (Rowley)
283. See id. at 475–476.
284. CE 1053D.

APPENDIX VII

1. N. Schachner, "Thomas Jefferson" 661 (1957) ; CE 2549, p. 22.
2. S. F. Bemis, "John Quincy Adams and the Union" 120–121 (1956) ; CE 2549, p. 23.
3. M. James, "Andrew Jackson" 636–637 (1938) : CE 2549, p. 23.
4. James at 684–688.
5. M. Smith. "A President Is Many Men" 225 (1948) ; C. M. Green, "Washington: Village and Capitol, 1800–1878" 160 (1962) ; CE 2549, p. 25.
6. B. P. Thomas, "Abraham Lincoln" 242–244 (1952) ; G. S. Bryan, "The Great American Myth" 13–18, 20–48 (1940).
7. Thomas at 245 : Bryan at 54.
8. Bryan at 55–73.
9. Id. at 60–69.
10. Thomas at 454–455, 474–475 ; L. Lewis, "Myths After Lincoln" 167–173. 293–294 (1941).
11. Thomas at 519 ; Bryan at 114–125, 138–144 ; Lewis at 167–173.
12. Thomas at 519 ; Bryan at 149–155, 165–166, 221.
13. Thomas at 520–521 ; Bryan at 173–184, 188–189.
14. Bryan at 262–266, 268 ; B. Pitman, "The Assassination of President Lincoln and the Trial of the Conspirators" 242–249 (facsimile ed. 1954).
15. H.R. Rept. No. 104, 39th Cong., 1st sess. (1865) ; R. G. Tugwell "The Enlargement of the Presidency" 265 footnote 5 (1960).
16. W. B. Hesseltine, "Ulysses S. Grant" 301 (1935) ; CE 2550, p. 37.
17. Ogilvie, "Life and Death of James A. Garfield," 100–131 (1881) ; R. J. Donovan, "The Assassins," 17, 35–42 (1952).
18. Ogilvie at 30–31, 45, 47 ; R. G. Caldwell, "James A. Garfield" 350–351 (1931) ; Donovan at 42–44, 58–61.
19. New York Tribune, July 3, 1881.
20. M. Smith at 229 (1948).
21. CE 2550, pp. 36–37.
22. 13 Stat. 351 : Holverstott. "Preliminary Inventory of the Records of the United States Secret Service in the National Archives" 4–19 (1949) ; Bowen, "United States Secret Service, a Chronicle" 4, unpublished manuscript in the files of the Secret Service.
23. E.g., 20 Stat. 384 ; 22 Stat. 313.
24. CE 2550, pp. 36–37.
25. New York Evening Post, Sept. 7, 1901.
26. M. Leech, "In the Days of McKinley" 231–232, 559–562 (1959).
27. Id. at 559–561 ; C. Dawes, "A Journal of the McKinley Years" 239–240 (1950).
28. Leech at 594–596.
29. Id. at 592–594 ; Donovan at 88–89.
30. Donovan at 85, 107.
31. Id. at 85–88.
32. See supra, p. 455 for a discussion of such legislation.
33. "Hearings Before the Subcommittee of House Committee on Appropriations in Charge of Sundry Civil Appropriations Bill for 1911," 61st Cong., 2d sess. at 176

(1910) ; Records of U.S. Secret Service, Record Group 87, Daily Reports of Agents on White House detail, 1902–36, National Archives ; W. S. Bowen and H. E. Neal, "The United States Secret Service" 11, 126 (1960).
34. 2 "Selections From the Correspondence of Theodore Roosevelt and Henry Cabot Lodge, 1884–1918" 224 (1925).
35. Donovan at 142–147.
36. Id. at 128–129, 146–147.
37. 34 Stat. 708 (1906) ; "Hearings Before Subcommittee of House Committee on Appropriations in Charge of Sundry Civil Appropriations Bill for 1910," 61st Cong., 1st sess. at 225–226 (1909).
38. 38 Stat. 23 (1913).
39. 39 Stat. 919, now 18 U.S.C. 871.
40. 40 Stat. 120.
41. 2 J. B. Bishop, "Theodore Roosevelt and His Times" 451–453 (1920).
42. E. W. Starling, "Starling of the White House" 117 (1946).
43. Donovan at 153–157.
44. Id. at 158–163.
45. Id. at 164–168.
46. S. Rept. No. 760, 67th Cong., 2d sess. (1922) ; CE 2550, p. 37.
47. 42 Stat. 841.
48. 46 Stat. 328.
49. 76 Stat. 95.
50. CE 2553.
51. Starling at 42 ; CE 1029.
52. Baughman, "Secret Service Chief" 54–69 (1961) ; Bowen and Neal at 132–133. The functions of Protective Research Section are discussed supra at pp. 429–433.
53. CE 2549, pp. 113, 115 ; Donovan at 201.
54. Donovan at 202–207 ; CE 2551, p. 116.
55. 65 Stat. 122, 18 U.S.C. 3056.
56. 76 Stat. 956, 18 U.S.C. 3056 (Cum. Supp. 1962) ; S. Rept. No. 836, 87th Cong. 1st sess. (1961).
57. 18 U.S.C. 871.
58. 35 Stat. 328 ; 42 Cong., Rec. 5553–5560, 60th Cong., 2d sess. (1908) ; 35 Stat. 986 ; 41 Stat. 174 (1919).
59. CE 2551.
60. 36 Stat. 748 (1910) ; CE 867.
61. 5 H 102, 119 (J. Edgar Hoover) ; CE 2552.
62. Commission on Organization of the Executive Branch of the Government [hereafter cited as Hoover Commission] "Task Force Report on Fiscal, Budgeting, and Accounting Activities" [app. F] 2, 17 (January 1949).
63. Hoover Commission "Treasury Department" (1949).
64. Hoover Commission transcript of meeting at 39 (Dec. 20, 1948) in Record Group 264, Box 29, National Archives.
65. 18 U.S.C. 3056.
66. "Hearings on Treasury—Post Office Departments and Executive Office Appropriations Before the Subcommittee of the House Committee on Appropriations" 88th Cong., 2d sess. 434, 449 (1964).

APPENDIX X

1. 3 H 390–391 (Robert A. Frazier);
3 H 452 (Cortlandt Cunningham); 3 H 496
(Joseph D. Nicol).
2. 3 H 390–441 (Frazier); 3 H 451–496
(Cunningham); 3 H 496–515 (Nicol).
Frazier and Ronald Simmons of the U.S.
Army Infantry Weapons Evaluation
Branch also testified on rifle capability.
This subject is discussed on pp. 188–194.
3. 3 H 390–515, passim; Hatcher, Jury
& Weller, "Firearms Identification, Investigation, and Evidence," chs. 13–14 (1957).
4. 3 H 415–419 (Frazier).
5. Id. at 429–430.
6. Id. at 421–422, 424.
7. CE 139; 3 H 289 (Joseph A. Mooney);
3 H 292–293 (Eugene Boone); 3 H 392,
395 (Frazier).
8. CE 139, 541; 3 H 393–394 (Frazier).
9. CE 139; 3 H 395–396 (Frazier).
10. CE 139, 541; 3 H 397 (Frazier).
11. Ibid.
12. Ibid.
13. Id. at 392, 396.
14. Id. at 392.
15. Ibid.; CE 540.
16. 3 H 392 (Frazier).
17. CE 1977; 3 H 393–394 (Frazier).
18. Id. at 392–393; W. H. B. Smith,
"Small Arms of the World" (6th ed. 1960).
19. 3 H 416 (Frazier).
20. Id. at 397–398 (Frazier); W. H. B.
Smith, "The Book of Rifles," 298–307 (3d
ed. 1963); W. H. B. Smith, "Mannlicher
Rifles and Pistols" (1947), pp. 84–87.
21. 3 H 397–398 (Frazier).
22. Ibid.
23. 4 H 205 (John Will Fritz); 4 H 258
(J. C. Day).
24. CE 575; 3 H 398 (Frazier).
25. Ibid.
26. CE 141; 4 H 205–206 (Fritz); 4 H
258 (Day).
27. 3 H 399 (Frazier).
28. Id. at 400.
29. Id. at 437–438; 3 H 443, 449 (Ronald Simmons).
30. 3 H 400, 416 (Frazier).
31. Id. at 400–401.
32. CE 512; 3 H 284 (Mooney).
33 CE 510.
34. 3 H 414–428 (Frazier); 3 H 505–507
(Nicol).
35. 3 H 401–402 (Frazier); CE 2724.
36. CE 546, 547; 3 H 401–402 (Frazier).
37. CE 547; 3 H 401–402 (Frazier).
38. Id. at 402.
39. Ibid.
40. CE 399, 567, 569, 2011, pp. 2–4;
6 H 129–130 (Darrell C. Tomlinson).
41. 3 H 430 (Frazier).
42. Ibid.
43. Id. at 432, 435.
44. Id. at 432.
45. Id. at 435.
46. Id. at 435, 437; 3 H 497 (Nicol).
47. 3 H 430, 432, 434, 436–437 (Frazier).
48. Id. at 428–437; 3 H 497–502
(Nicol).
49. CE 143; 3 H 300–301 (M. N. McDonald); 7 H 45–55 (Gerald Hill); 7 H
24–25 (Bob K. Carroll); 3 H 453 (Cunningham).
50. Id. at 458.
51. Id. at 453.
52. Id. at 456.
53. Id. at 455.
54. Ibid.
55. Ibid.
56. Id. at 455–456.
57. Id. at 456.
58. Id. at 457.
59. Ibid.

60. Ibid.
61. Id. at 458.
62. Id. at 459.
63. CE 145, 518; 3 H 301 (McDonald);
7 H 26 (Carroll); 7 H 55 (Hill).
64. 3 H 459 (Cunningham).
65. CE 592; 7 H 126 (Elmer L. Boyd).
66. 3 H 459 (Cunningham).
67. Id. at 453–454.
68. CE 594; 3 H 345 (Barbara Jeannette Davis); 6 H 463–464 (Virginia
Davis); 6 H 449–451 (Domingo Benavides).
69. 3 H 465–466 (Cunningham).
70. Id. at 466–473 (Cunningham); 3 H
511 (Nicol).
71. CE 602–605, 2011, p. 9.
72. 3 H 511–513 (Nicol).
73. 3 H 474–475, 482–483 (Cunningham).
74. Ibid.
75. Id. at 475, 482.
76. Id. at 475–476, 482.
77. Id. at 475–476, 489–491.
78. Id. at 476–478.
79. Id. at 479, 481.
80. CE 2003, pp. 92–93. This was an affidavit, the substance of which was repeated
in the testimony of Officer McDonald, id. at
300–301.
81. 3 H 461, 463 (Cunningham).
82. Id. at 463–464.
83. Ibid.
84. Id. at 464.
85. Id. at 463.
86. Id. at 465.
87. 4 H 275–276 (Day).
88. 3 H 486 (Cunningham).
89. Id. at 486, 495; 3 H 514 (Nicol).
90. 3 H 486–487, 494–495 (Cunningham); 3 H 514 (Nicol).
91. 3 H 492–493 (Cunningham).
92. Id. at 492.
93. Id. at 487.
94. Id. at 487–489.
95. Id. at 494; 15 H 747–748 (Gallagher).
96. CE 2455.
97. Gallagher DE 1; 15 H 748–751
(Gallagher).
98. CE 573; CE 2011, p. 6.
99. 3 H 452 (Cunningham).
100. 3 H 439–440 (Frazier).
101. 3 H 502–503 (Nicol).
102. 4 H 1–48 (Sebastian F. Latona).
103. 4 H 48–56; 15 H 745–746 (Arthur
Mandella).
104. 4 H 1–2 (Latona); 4 H 48–49
(Mandella).
105. 4 H 1–56, passim; see generally
Bridges, Burtis C.; "Practical Fingerprinting," revised by Charles F. O'Hara (1963);
Cummins and Midlow "Fingerprints,
Palms, and Soles," 2d. ed. (1961).
106. 4 H 2–14 (Latona).
107. Id. at 13–14; 4 H 53 (Mandella).
108. 4 H 2–3, 44–45 (Latona).
109. Id. at 3–5.
110. Id. at 22, 39–40.
111. 4 H 251, 269, 272 (Day); CE 733,
734, 1301, 2011, p. 16 (see ch. IV, pp. 122–
123, 134–135, 137, 140).
112. 4 H 269 (Day); 7 H 145 (Studebaker); CE 733, 734, 1302.
113. 4 H 3–20 (Latona); 4 H 50–51
(Mandella).
114. 4 H 22, 29 (Latona).
115. 4 H 259–261 (Day); 4 H 20–21,
23–24 (Latona).
116. Ibid.
117. 4 H 23–27 (Latona). 4 H 50 (Mandella).
118. Id. at 31.

119. 4 H 30–37 (Latona) ; 4 H 51–52 (Mandella).
120. Ibid.
121. Ibid.
122. 4 H 41–43 (Latona).
123. CE 3131, pp. 17–18.
124. 4 H 41–42 (Latona) ; CE 3131, p. 18.
125. 4 H 37–38 (Latona) ; 4 H 267–268 (Day).
126. 4 H 37–41 (Latona) ; 4 H 52 (Mandella).
127. 4 H 30 (Latona).
128. Id. at 38 ; 4 H 55 (Mandella).
129. 4 H 39 (Latona).
130. Id. at 39.
131. 4 H 55 (Mandella).
132. 4 H 23 (Latona) ; 4 H 253–258 (Day) ; CE 2011, pp. 1, 5.
133. 4 H 358–403 ; 15 H 703–709.
134. 7 H 418–438 (James C. Cadigan).
135. 4 H 359 (Alwyn Cole) ; 7 H 419 (Cadigan).
136. 7 H 364–366 (Waldman) ; CE 733 ; Cadigan DE 1 ; CE 788.
137. 7 H 375–378 (Heinz Michaelis) ; CE 135.
138. CE 791, 793, 817, 2342, 2727.
139. 7 H 187–188 (Stovall) ; 7 H 228 (Guy F. Rose) ; CE 795, 806, 1986, 1989, 1990, 2011, pp. 22, 23.
140. 7 H 197–199 (Walter Potts) ; 7 H 222 (F. M. Turner) ; 213–215 (Henry Moore) ; Moore DE 1 ; CE 813, 2003, p. 281 ; CE 2011, p. 25.
141. CE 819, 820, 2011, p. 24.
142. 1 H 16 (Marina Oswald).
143. 4 H 266–267 (Day) ; CE 142.
144. 4 H 358–403, 7 H 418–438, passim ; see also Osborne, Questioned Documents (2d ed., 1940).
145. 4 H 364 (Cole).
146. Ibid.
147. 4 H 366 (Cole).
148. Id. at 368–370.
149. Id. at 364–372.
150. Id. at 372 ; 7 H 436–437 (Cadigan).
151. 4 H 363 (Cole).
152. CE 774–783 ; Cadigan DE 2–3 ; 4 H 360–361 (Cole) ; 7 H 419–420 (Cadigan).
153. CE 3137.
154. 4 H 373 (Cole) ; 7 H 420 (Cadigan).
155. 4 H 361–370 (Cole) ; 7 H 420–422 (Cadigan).
156. 7 H 293–295 (Harry D. Holmes).
157. 4 H 373–375 (Cole) ; 7 H 423–424 (Cadigan).
158. 4 H 366–370 (Cole) ; 7 H 420–422 (Cadigan).
159. 4 H 366–368 (Cole) ; 7 H 421–422 (Cadigan).
160. 4 H 369–370 (Cole) ; 7 H 422 (Cadigan).
161. Ibid.
162. 4 H 371 (Cole).
163. Ibid.
164. CE 135.
165. 4 H 375–377 (Cole) ; 7 H 424 (Cadigan).
166. 7 H 527 (Holmes).
167. Ibid.
168. 4 H 377–378 (Cole) ; 7 H 424–425 (Cadigan).
169. 4 H 377 (Cole) ; 7 H 527 (Holmes).
170. 7 H 527 (Holmes) : CE 2342, 2727.
171. CE 793 ; 4 H 379–380 (Cole) ; 7 H 425–426 (Cadigan) ; CE 2342, 2727.
172. CE 817.
173. 4 H 397–398 (Cole) ; 7 H 431–432 (Cadigan).
174. CE 795, 866, 801, 802 ; Cole DE 1 ; CE 1986, 1989, 1990, 2079, 2483, 2011, pp. 20–24 ; 7 H 187–188 (Richard S. Stovall) ; 7 H 228 (Rose).
175. 4 H 380–381, 389 (Cole) ; 7 H 427–429 (Cadigan).

176. CE 2077, 2011, p. 26; 7 H 195 (Stovall).
177. 7 H 195 (Stovall).
178. CE 795.
179. CE 801.
180. CE 803.
181. CE 805.
182. 4 H 387 (Cole).
183. CE 804 ; 4 H 385–387 (Cole) ; 7 H 427–429 (Cadigan).
184. 4 H 381 (Cole) ; 7 H 427–428 (Cadigan).
185. Id. at 381–382.
186. Ibid.
187. Id. at 382.
188. Ibid ; 7 H 427–428 (Cadigan).
189. 4 H 382 (Cole).
190. 4 H 383, 390–391 (Cole).
191. CE 798 ; 4 H 382–383 (Cadigan).
192. Ibid.
193. Ibid.
194. 4 H 391–392 (Cole) ; 15 H 707 (Cole).
195. 15 H 707 (Cole).
196. 15 H 707–708 (Cole).
197. 4 H 392–393 (Cole) ; CE 3105.
198. 4 H 392–393 (Cole).
199. CE 795.
200. 7 H 427–428 (Cadigan) ; 15 H 703–705 : CE 803, 804 : Cole DE 5, 6.
201. 7 H 428–429 (Cadigan) ; 15 H 703–705 (Cole) ; CE 801, 795, 803, 804, 805.
202. CE 795, 802, 811 ; 7 H 427 (Cadigan) ; 4 H 384 (Cole).
203. Ibid.
204. CE 802, 795 ; 15 H 708 (Cole).
205. Ibid.
206. CE 799 ; 4 H 382 (Cole).
207. Cole DE 1.
208. CE 812.
209. 7 H 430 (Cadigan) ; 15 H 706–707 (Cole).
210. CE 809 ; 4 H 390 (Cole).
211. 15 H 707 (Cole).
212. Ibid.
213. Ibid.
214. CE 808 ; 4 H 389–390 (Cole).
215. CE 810 ; 4 H 390 (Cole).
216. Id. at 387.
217. Id. at 387–388.
218. Id. at 388.
219. CE 813.
220. CE 3097, 2003, p. 281 ; CE 2011, p. 25.
221. CE 813, 814, 815.
222. 4 H 395–396 (Cole).
223. 7 H 432–433 (Cadigan).
224. CE 115 ; 1 H 113 (Marina Oswald).
225. CE 816 ; 4 H 396 (Cole).
226. 4 H 396 (Cole).
227. CE 3105, 3136.
228. 4 H 397 (Cole).
229. Ibid.
230. Id. at 399 ; 7 H 436 (Cadigan).
231. Ibid. ; 4 H 399 (Cole).
232. 7 H 436 (Cadigan).
233. 4 H 399 (Cole).
234. Id. at 399–400.
235. Ibid.
236. 5 H 401 (Marina Oswald).
237. CE 2726.
238. 7 H 437–438 (Cadigan).
239. Ibid.
240. CE 2723.
241. Ibid.
242. CE 677 ; 4 H 89–90 (Cadigan).
243. Id. at 90, 92–93.
244. Id. at 90.
245. Id. at 93.
246. Ibid.
247. Id. at 95–97.
248. Id. at 97.
249. Id. at 93, 97, 100–101.
250. Id. at 98.
251. CE 364 ; 4 H 93–94 (Cadigan).

855

252. CE 677 ; 4 H 75–76 (Paul Morgan Stombaugh).
253. Ibid.
254. 4 H 90–92 (Cadigan).
255. 5 H 74 (Dr. Alfred G. Olivier) ; 5 H 91 (Dr. Arthur J. Dziemian).
256. 5 H 74 (Dr. Olivier) ; 5 H 91 (Dr. Dziemian) ; 5 H 94 (Dr. Frederick W. Light, Jr.).
257. 5 H 75 (Dr. Olivier) ; 5 H 94 (Dr. Light).
258. 5 H 91 (Dr. Dziemian).
259. Ibid.
260. 5 H 94 (Dr. Light).
261. Ibid.
262. 5 H 76, 78–79, 81 (Dr. Olivier).
263. Id. at 78 ; 5 H 96 (Dr. Light).
264. Ibid.
265. 5 H 75 (Dr. Olivier).
266. Ibid.
267. Ibid.
268. Id. at 75, 78.
269. Id. at 75.
270. Id. at 78.
271. Id. at 76.
272. Ibid.
273. Ibid.
274. Id. at 78.
275. Id. at 76.
276. Id. at 76–77.
277. Id. at 77.
278. Ibid. ; 5 H 164 (Lyndal L. Shaneyfelt) ; CE 893, 895.
279. 5 H 75, 77 (Dr. Olivier).
280. Id. at 77.
281. Ibid.
282. Ibid.
283. Ibid.
284. Id. at 78.
285. Ibid.
286. Ibid.
287. Id. at 79–80.
288. 5 H 164 (Shaneyfelt) ; CE 893, 895.
289. 5 H 80 (Dr. Olivier).
290. Id. at 79.
291. Id. at 78–79.
292. Id. at 79.
293. Ibid.
294. Ibid.
295. 5 H 80 (Dr. Olivier).
296. Ibid.
297. Ibid.
298. Ibid.
299. Ibid.
300. Id. at 86.
301. Id. at 81.
302. Ibid.
303. Ibid.
304. Id. at 82.
305. Ibid.
306. Ibid.
307. Ibid.
308. Id. at 82–83.
309. Id. at 82.
310. Id. at 83–87 ; 5 H 92–93 (Dr. Dziemian).
311. 5 H 86 (Dr. Olivier).
312. 6 H 90–91 (Dr. Robert R. Shaw) ; 6 H 101–102 (Dr. Charles F. Gregory) ; 6 H 109–110 (Dr. George T. Shires).
313. 5 H 83–87 (Dr. Olivier) ; 5 H 92–93 (Dr. Dziemian).
314. 5 H 86 (Dr. Olivier).
315. Id. at 83.
316. Id. at 86.
317. Ibid.
318. Id. at 84 ; 5 H 93 (Dr. Dziemian).
319. 5 H 95 (Dr. Light).
320. Ibid.
321. 5 H 87 (Dr. Olivier).
322. Id. at 89.
323. Id. at 87–88.
324. 5 H 160 (Shaneyfelt) ; CE 902.
325. 5 H 89 (Dr. Olivier).

326. Ibid. ; 2 H 351 (Comdr. James J. Humes).
327. 5 H 89 (Dr. Olivier).
328. Ibid.
329. Ibid.
330. 5 H 67 (Frazier).
331. 5 H 88 (Dr. Olivier).
332. Ibid.
333. Ibid.
334. Id. at 89.
335. Ibid.
336. Id. at 87.
337. Ibid.
338. Ibid.
339. 2 H 356 (Comdr. Humes) ; 2 H 380–381 (Lt. Col. Pierre A. Finck).
340. 5 H 89 (Dr. Olivier).
341. Id. at 90 ; 5 H 93 (Dr. Dziemian).
342. 4 H 56–88 (Stombaugh).
343. Id. at 56.
344. Id. at 61–64, 69–70.
345. Id. at 60–61, 78–80, 87 ; 15 H 702 (Stombaugh).
346. 4 H 57 (Stombaugh).
347. Id. at 60.
348. Id. at 78, 15 H 702 (Stombaugh).
349. 4 H 79–80 (Stombaugh)
350. CE 663 ; 4 H 57–58 (Stombaugh).
351. Ibid.
352. 4 H 58 (Stombaugh).
353. Id. at 57–58.
354. Id. at 58.
355. Ibid.
356. Id. at 84.
357. Id. at 59.
358. Ibid.
359. Id. at 61.
360. Id. at 61, 68, 72.
361. Id. at 61, 64, 67, 68 ; CE 2011, p. 14 ; CE 2404.
362. 4 H 64–67 (Stombaugh).
363. Id. at 67–68.
364. Id. at 68.
365. Id. at 75.
366. Id. at 76–77.
367. Ibid.
368. Id. at 77–78.
369. Id. at 78–80 ; 15 H 702 (Stombaugh).
370. 4 H 74 (Stombaugh).
371. Ibid.
372. Id. at 85–87 ; 15 H 702 (Stombaugh).
373. Ibid.
374. 4 H 81 (Stombaugh).
375. Ibid.
376. Id. at 82.
377. Id. at 82–83, 85.
378. Id. at 82.
379. Id. at 83.
380. Id. at 83–84.
381. Id. at 85–87 ; 15 H 702 (Stombaugh).
382. 4 H 87–88 (Stombaugh).
383. CE 135–A, 135–B ; CE 2011, p. 27 ; 7 H 209 (John P. Adamcik) ; 7 H 231 (Rose).
384. CE 3, 5, 749, 2011, p. 26 ; 7 H 194 (Stovall) ; 7 H 231 (Rose).
385. CE 750.
386. 1 H 117–118 (Marina Oswald) ; 5 H 406 (Marina Oswald) ; CE 2083.
387. 4 H 279–294 (Shaneyfelt) ; 7 H 410–418 (Shaneyfelt) ; 15 H 686–702 (Shaneyfelt).
388. 4 H 279 (Shaneyfelt).
389. CE 133–A, 133–B ; 4 H 289 (Shaneyfelt).
390. CE 746 A–E ; 4 H 279–280 (Shaneyfelt).
391. CE 747, 748 ; 4 H 280–281 (Shaneyfelt).
392. Id. at 281.
393. Id. at 289.
394. Ibid.

395. Id. at 283.
396. Ibid.
397. Id. at 284.
398. Ibid.
399. Id. at 285–286, 289.
400. Id. at 285.
401. Id. at 286.
402. Id. at 284–288.
403. Id. at 289 ; 15 H 692–693 (Shaney-felt).
404. 4 H 226 (Fritz).

405. 4 H 288 (Shaneyfelt).
406. Id. at 293.
407. Id. at 288–289.
408. Id. at 293.
409. Shaneyfelt DE 2, 3, 4, 5, 6, 7 ; 15 H 689–690 (Shaneyfelt).
410. 4 H 290–293 (Shaneyfelt) ; 7 H 410–418 (Shaneyfelt).
411. Ibid.
412. 15 H 687–689 (Shaneyfelt).
413. Id. at 687, 689–690.

APPENDIX XII

1. See supra, pp. 61–71.
2. See supra, pp. 71–72.
3. See supra, pp. 72–73.
4. See supra, p. 79.
5. CE 2582, p. 2 ; 6 H 210–216 (Jean L. Hill) ; CE 2594.
6. See supra, p. 76.
7. See supra, pp. 110–117.
8. See supra, pp. 76–77, 79–80.
9. See supra, pp. 79–80.
10. 7 H 550 (Eddy R. Walthers) ; CE 2580, p. 2.
11. See supra, p. 50.
12. See supra, p. 77.
13. See supra, pp. 87–91.
14. See supra, pp. 55–56.
15. See supra, pp. 96–109.
16. See supra, p. 140.
17. Ibid.
18. See supra, pp. 32, 40.
19. See supra, pp. 32, 39.
20. See supra, p. 130.
21. See supra, pp. 141–142.
22. See supra, p. 250.
23. Ibid.
24. CE 2585, p. 3 ; 2591, p. 6.
25. See supra, p. 147.
26. See supra, pp. 312–315.
27. See supra, pp. 49, 189–190, 194.
28. See supra, p. 117.
29. See supra, pp. 188–195.
30. See supra, pp. 79, 553–554 ; CE 2585, p. 4.
31. See supra, pp. 79, 81.
32. See supra, pp. 71–72, 76, 79, 248–251.
33. See supra, pp. 315–318.
34. See supra, p. 555.
35. See supra, pp. 123–124 ; CE 2584.
36. See supra, p. 123.
37. CE 2584, 3087.
38. See supra, pp. 15, 128 ; 3 H 79, 81–82 (Ruth Paine) ; CE 2580, p. 3 ; CE 2003, p. 137a.
39. See supra, pp. 125–128 ; Lyndal Shaneyfelt DE 10, 11, 12, 16, 17.
40. See supra, p. 127.
41. See supra, pp. 151–153.
42. See supra, p. 151 ; CE 3035, 3076.
43. See supra, pp. 155–156.
44. See supra, pp. 143–144 ; CE 2580, p. 3.
45. See supra, pp. 156–163.
46. See supra, pp. 155–156.
47. See supra, pp. 161–163.
48. See supra, pp. 162–163 ; CE 2592.
49. See supra, pp. 359–365.
50. See supra, p. 163.
51. See supra, pp. 163–164.
52. CE 1974, pp. 8, 20, 21.
53. CE 2583.
54. See supra, pp. 144, 165.
55. See supra, p. 369.
56. See supra, pp. 166–167.
57. See supra, pp. 165–168.

58. See supra, p. 167.
59. See supra, pp. 166–167 ; Helen Markham DE 1, pp. 295–299.
60. See supra, pp. 166–168 ; CE 2593.
61. See supra, pp. 168–169, 174.
62. See supra, pp. 174–175.
63. Ibid ; WFAA–TV reels PKT 5—56 :05 and PKF 10—8 :43, 9 :47.
64. 10 H 297 (Mrs. A. C. Johnson).
65. See supra, p. 128.
66. See supra, p. 174 ; 10 H 297 (Johnson).
67. See supra, p. 174.
68. See supra, p. 176.
69. See supra, pp. 178–179.
70. See supra, p. 179.
71. See supra, pp. 178–179, 200.
72. See supra, p. 198.
73. See supra, p. 182 ; see app. XI.
74. See supra, pp. 200–201.
75. See infra, pp. 685–687.
76. See infra, pp. 257, 685.
77. See supra, pp. 256–257.
78. See supra, pp. 257–258.
79. See supra, pp. 267, 269, 272, 274.
80. See supra, pp. 272, 274.
81. See supra, pp. 703, 708.
82. See supra, pp. 274, 280.
83. See supra, pp. 272–280.
84. See supra, pp. 278–279.
85. See supra, p. 278.
86. See infra, pp. 773–774 ; CE 952, 2754.
87. CE 2785.
88. See supra, p. 331 ; app. XIV.
89. See supra, p. 305 ; see infra, 731–733, 736.
90. See supra, p. 305.
91. See supra, pp. 307–309.
92. See supra, p. 307 ; CE 2952, 2953, 2954.
93. 1 H 191 (Marguerite Oswald).
94. See supra, pp. 325–327.
95. CE 2580, p. 3 ; CE 2581.
96. See supra, pp. 327, 437–440.
97. See supra, pp. 438–439 ; CE 2582, p. 5.
98. CE 2583.
99. See supra, pp. 438–439 ; CE 2582, p. 5.
100. See supra, pp. 118–122.
101. See supra, pp. 436–440.
102. CE 2585, p. 6.
103. See supra, pp. 328–333 ; see app. XIV.
104. See supra, p. 359.
105. CE 2585, p. 10.
106. See supra, pp. 359–362.
107. CE 2585, p. 10 ; 11 H 416 (E. Walker).
108. See supra, pp. 297–298.
109. See supra, p. 369 : CE 2585, p. 6.
110. See supra, pp. 370–371 ; see infra, p. 801.
111. 11 H 434–442 (Warren A. Reynolds) ; 8 H 2579, 2587, 2588.

857

112. 8 H 316 (Donald P. Camarata) ; 8 H 281 (Daniel P. Powers) ; CE 2586, pp. 2–12.
113. See supra, pp. 246–247 ; CE 2585, p. 8.
114. See supra, pp. 447–449 ; CE 2583.
115. CE 705, p. 27.
116. CE 2583, pp. 2–3.
117. See supra, pp. 192, 318–320.
118. See supra, pp. 320–321.
119. 10 H 424 (Laurance R. Wilcox).
120. See supra, pp. 332–333.
121. See infra, pp. 736–737 ; Dallas Morning News, Nov. 28, 1963, p. 20, cols. 1–2.
122. See supra, p. 254.

123. See supra, p. 328.
124. 7 H 549–559 (Walthers) ; CE 2003, pp. 295–299.
125. 1 H 45, 109–110 (Marina Oswald) ; 1 H 247–249 (Marguerite Oswald) ; 3 H 13–17, 51–52 (Ruth Paine) ; 4 H 365, 369, 402 (Alwyn Cole).
126. CE 2578 ; CE 2579, pp. 171–180.
127. 1 H 59–60 ; 125–126 (Marina Oswald).
128. See supra, pp. 364–365.
129. CE 3122.
130. Revilo P. Oliver DE 8 ; 15 H 738–740 (Oliver).
131. CE 2711.

APPENDIX XIII

1. Allison G. Folsom, Jr., DE 1, p. 98 ; see CE 2205, p. 569.
2. 1 H 252 (Marguerite Oswald) ; 8 H 92 (Lillian Murret).
3. 1 H 252–253 (Marguerite Oswald) ; 8 H 95–96 (L. Murret).
4. 1 H 252 (Marguerite Oswald).
5. 8 H 98 (L. Murret).
6. CE 2207, p. 50.
7. 8 H 97 (L. Murret).
8. 1 H 252 (Marguerite Oswald).
9. Id. at 252–253 ; see 8 H 93 (L. Murret).
10. John Pic DE 1.
11. 8 H 197–198 (Edward John Pic Jr.) ; see 8 H 92–93 (L. Murret). Mrs. Murret described Pic at that time as "a person who did not talk unless you spoke to him" ; id. at 93.
12. 1 H 253 (Marguerite Oswald) ; see 8 H 95, 99 (L. Murret).
13. 8 H 95, 99 (L. Murret), 162–163 (Marilyn Dorothea Murret) ; 11 H 5 (J. Pic) cf. 8 H 46 (Myrtle Evans). For Mrs. Oswald's testimony to the same effect before the Commission, see 1 H 253.
14. 8 H 198 ; 11 H 82 (E. Pic).
15. 11 H 2 (J. Pic) ; CE 2208 ; see 8 H 198 (E. Pic).
16. 8 H 201 (E. Pic) ; see 8 H 47 (M. Evans), 101 (L. Murret) ; 11 H 5 (J. Pic).
17. Compare 8 H 199 (E. Pic) with 1 H 253 (Marguerite Oswald) ; cf. 8 H 47 (M. Evans).
18. 8 H 104 (L. Murret) ; 11 H 5 (J. Pic) ; see 1 H 253 (Marguerite Oswald).
19. Ibid.
20. CE 1958.
21. CE 1959.
22. CE 2000 ; 1 H 253 (Marguerite Oswald) ; 8 H 104 (L. Murret).
23. 1 H 253 (Marguerite Oswald).
24. CE 2208 ; 1 H 267 (Robert Edward Lee Oswald).
25. 1 H 253 (Marguerite Oswald) ; 8 H 105 (L. Murret).
26. CE 2197, p. 79.
27. 11 H 12 (J. Pic) ; see 8 H 105 (L. Murret) ; see generally CE 2198, pp. 65–67, 69.
28. 1 H 269 (R. Oswald) ; 8 H 105 (L. Murret).
29. CE 2199 ; 8 H 269–270 (R. Oswald) ; 11 H 7 (J. Pic).
30. CE 2211, p. 618–1 ; see 1 H 225 (Marguerite Oswald), 268 (R. Oswald) ; 8 H 47 (M. Evans).
31. 1 H 225 (Marguerite Oswald) ; Folsom DE 1, p. 123.
32. 1 H 225 (Marguerite Oswald).

33. See 8 H 47 (M. Evans), 106 (L. Murret).
34. CE 2200.
35. Ibid.
36. CE 2197, p. 79 ; see CE 2207, p. 51.
37. CE 2197, p. 79.
38. See CE 2201, p. 63 ; CE 2202.
39. 1 H 270 (R. Oswald) ; 11 H 7, 8–9, 11 (J. Pic) ; cf. 8 H 107 (L. Murret).
40. Ibid. ; 11 H 7 (J. Pic) ; but see id., at 17.
41. Id. at 9 ; cf. 8 H 107 (L. Murret).
42. See CE 2199, 2203.
43. 8 H 40 (Viola Peterman).
44. CE 2197.
45. 11 H 12 (J. Pic).
46. 8 H 43 (Peterman).
47. Ibid. ; 11 H 11, 12 (J. Pic) ; see 8 H 48 (M. Evans).
48. 11 H 11 (J. Pic).
49. Id. at 12.
50. CE 2197, p. 80.
51. Pic DE 5. The record contains also a separate application for the admission of Robert, dated Jan. 3, 1942 ; J. Pic DE 3.
52. J. Pic DE 2, p. 3 ; see 1 H 272 (R. Oswald).
53. J. Pic DE 2, p. 4.
54. CE 2201, p. 63 ; see 8 H 35–36 (Anne Boudreaux).
55. J. Pic DE 2, p. 1.
56. 8 H 46, 51 (M. Evans) ; 11 H 18 (J. Pic).
57. 8 H 106–107 (L. Murret).
58. 8 H 36–37 (Boudreaux) ; see CE 2204.
59. 8 H 37 (Boudreaux).
60. 1 H 254 (Marguerite Oswald) ; cf. 8 H 47, 63 (M. Evans).
61. 8 H 36 (Boudreaux).
62. J. Pic DE 2, p. 1 ; 11 H 13, 14 (J. Pic).
63. See J. Pic DE 2, p. 2.
64. See 8 H 112–113 (L. Murret).
65. J. Pic DE 2, p. 4.
66. Id. at 1.
67. 11 H 15 (J. Pic).
68. 11 H 17, 20 (J. Pic) ; see 1 H 271 (R. Oswald) cf. id. at 273.
69. 11 H 20 (J. Pic) ; see 1 H 271 (R. Oswald) ; 8 H 108–109 (L. Murret).
70. 1 H 271 (R. Oswald).
71. 1 H 254 (Marguerite Oswald), 272, 273 (R. Oswald) ; 11 H 20–21 (J. Pic).
72. 1 H 272, 273 (R. Oswald) ; 11 H 18, 20 (J. Pic).
73. CE 2213, p. 27.
74. 1 H 255 (Marguerite Oswald) ; see also 11 H 18 (J. Pic) ("Princess Hosiery") ; 8 H 48, 51 (M. Evans) ("Jean's Hosiery Shop"), 109 (L. Murret) ("Jean's

Hosiery Shop"). It is unclear whether all these references are to the same job or to different jobs.
75. CE 2213, p. 27.
76. Ibid.
77. For descriptions of Ekdahl, see 1 H 250 (Marguerite Oswald), 274 (R. Oswald) ; 8 H 66–67 (Julian Evans), 110–111 (L. Murret) ; 11 H 21–22 (J. Pic). Marguerite testified that she was working at a hosiery shop when she met Ekdahl ; 1 H 255 ; cf. CE 2213, p. 27 ; but cf. 11 H 18 (J. Pic).
78. See 11 H 21 (J. Pic) ; but see 1 H 274 (R. Oswald).
79. 11 H 21 (J. Pic) ; see 8 H 66 (J. Evans).
80. 1 H 255 (Marguerite Oswald) ; see 11 H 21 (J. Pic).
81. Pic DE 2–A.
82. 1 H 255 (Marguerite Oswald).
83. Ibid. The home's rules did not permit children with two living parents to remain there ; see 11 H 21 (J. Pic) ; cf. 8 H 107 (L. Murret).
84. 1 H 255 (Marguerite Oswald).
85. Ibid. ; 8 H 50 (M. Evans), 110 (L. Murret).
86. 1 H 255 (Marguerite Oswald).
87. See p. 670, supra.
88. CE 1963, p. 543 ; 1 H 255 (Marguerite Oswald) ; see J. Pic DE 4, p. 1.
89. 1 H 269 (R. Oswald) ; 8 H 49–50 (M. Evans) ; 11 H 22, 23 (J. Pic).
90. J. Pic DE 2, p. 4 ; 1 H 272, 273 (R. Oswald) ; 11 H 21, 22 (J. Pic).
91. 1 H 274 (R. Oswald) ; 11 H 23 (J. Pic).
92. 1 H 255 (Marguerite Oswald) ; see 1 H 275 (R. Oswald) ; 11 H 22 (J. Pic). Robert believed, apparently incorrectly, that Ekdahl was already living in Dallas when the family moved there ; 1 H 274 (R. Oswald).
93. See 1 H 250, 251 (Marguerite Oswald) ; 8 H 113 (L. Murret).
94. 8 H 53 (M. Evans), 110 (L. Murret).
95. J. Pic DE 4.
96. CE 2211, p. 618–1 ; 11 H 23 (J. Pic).
97. Ibid.
98. 1 H 281 (R. Oswald) ; 11 H 27 (J. Pic) ; see id. at 21, 24.
99. Id. at 27.
100. 1 H 275 (R. Oswald) ; 11 H 23–24 (J. Pic) ; see 1 H 255 (Marguerite Oswald).
101. Ibid. ; 1 H 276 (R. Oswald) ; see 8 H 50–51 (M. Evans), 111 (L. Murret) ; see p. 670, supra.
102. 1 H 277 (R. Oswald) ; 11 H 23–30 (J. Pic).
103. 1 H 277–278 (R. Oswald) ; 8 H 50–51 (M. Evans), 68–69 (J. Evans), 111 (L. Murret).
104. 8 H 45, 49 (M. Evans).
105. Id. at 50–51.
106. CE 2218 ; 11 H 25 (J. Pic). Robert testified that his recollection is that the family did not move to Benbrook until after Christmas 1945, which he and John spent with school friends because the Ekdahls (and Lee) were in Boston. 1 H 278.
107. Ibid. 11 H 25 (J. Pic).
108. CE 1874, pp. 5–6.
109. CE 2218.
110. Ibid.
111. CE 1413, p. 10.
112. Folsom DE 1, p. 1.
113. See 11 H 24–25 (J. Pic).
114. 1 H 251 (Marguerite Oswald) ; 8 H 111 (L. Murret) ; cf. 8 H 50–51 (M. Evans).
115. 1 H 251 (Marguerite Oswald) ; see 11 H 73 (J. Pic).

116. 1 H 251 (Marguerite Oswald) ; 11 H 25–26 (J. Pic).
117. CE 1963, pp. 543–544 ; CE 1413, p. 18 ; CE 2217.
118. 8 H 52 (M. Evans).
119. CE 1413, p. 18.
120. CE 1874, p. 6.
121. CE 1413, p. 18.
122. Ibid.
123. 11 H 26 (J. Pic) ; CE 2206 ; see 1 H 251 (Marguerite Oswald) ; CE 2211, p. 618–6.
124. Ibid.
125. Id. at 618–5.
126. 11 H 27 (J. Pic) ; compare 1 H 251 (Marguerite Oswald).
127. Ibid.
128. Id. at 250.
129. Id. at 250–251 ; 11 H 27–28 (J. Pic) ; see 8 H 112 (L. Murret).
130. See CE 1960–A, p. 1 ; 11 H 28 (J. Pic) ; cf. 1 H 251 (Marguerite Oswald) ; for one explanation of Mrs. Oswald's conduct, see 8 H 112 (L. Murret).
131. CE 1960–A, p. 3.
132. CE 1960–A.
133. Id. at 1–4.
134. CE 1960–B ; see 1 H 251–252 (Marguerite Oswald).
135. 11 H 29 (J. Pic) ; see 1 H 252 (Marguerite Oswald).
136. CE 1960–C, p. 2.
137. Id. at 3–5.
138. CE 1963, p. 544 ; CE 2212 ; 11 H 28 (J. Pic).
139. Ibid.
140. CE 2211, p. 618–6.
141. Id. at 618–5.
142. 8 H 78 (Philip Eugene Vinson).
143. Id. at 77.
144. Id. at 77–78, 79.
145. CE 1874, p. 6 ; CE 2219 ; see 1 H 279 (R. Oswald) ; 11 H 29 (J. Pic).
146. Ibid.
147. Id. at 30–31.
148. CE 2219.
149. CE 1874, p. 7.
150. Id. at 6–7.
151. 11 H 30 (J. Pic).
152. CE 1873–D ; 1 H 292 (R. Oswald) ; 8 H 85 (Hiram Conway) ; 11 H 30 (J. Pic).
153. Ibid.
154. Ibid.
155. 1 H 296 (R. Oswald).
156. CE 1873–D.
157. Ibid.
158. CE 1873–E, –F, –G ; Robert Oswald testified that Ridglea West was newly built, which probably explains the transfer ; 1 H 297.
159. CE 1873–D ; see CE 1873–E, –F, –G.
160. CE 1873–D.
161. See p. 687, infra, but see p. 733 infra.
162. CE 1873–D.
163. 1 H 297, 298 (R. Oswald) (insurance agent) ; 11 H 31, 32 (J. Pic) (department stores) ; CE 2213, pp. 25–26 (assistant store manager, Lerner Shops ; department store sales representative, Literary Guild).
164. 1 H 225 (Marguerite Oswald).
165. 8 H 119 (L. Murret) ; 11 H 31 (J. Pic) ; see 8 H 163 (M. Murret).
166. CE 2220, p. 241.
167. CE 2221.
168. CE 2220, p. 241.
169. 1 H 281 (R. Oswald) ; 11 H 31, 34, 40, 80 (J. Pic).
170. 8 H 87 (Conway) ; 11 H 30–31 (J. Pic).
171. See id. at 31.
172. Ibid. ; see 1 H 225 (Marguerite Oswald) ; 8 H 163 (M. Murret).

173. 1 H 225 (Marguerite Oswald) ; 11 H 81 (J. Pic). Hiram Conway testified that he taught the game of chess to John and another boy, from whom Lee learned it. 8 H 90.
174. 8 H 122 (L. Murret).
175. Ibid.
176. 8 H 86 (Conway) ; see id. at 89–90.
177. 11 H 80 (J. Pic).
178. Id. at 32–33.
179. Id. at 34.
180. 1 H 297–298 (R. Oswald).
181. Id. at 298–299.
182. 1 H 225–226 (Marguerite Oswald) ; 11 H 36–37 (J. Pic).
183. 1 H 225–226 (Marguerite Oswald).
184. 11 H 37 (J. Pic).
185. Ibid.
186. 1 H 226 (Marguerite Oswald) ; 11 H 37–39 (J. Pic).
187. Id. at 38.
188. Id. at 38–39.
189. Marguerite and John gave different accounts of the origins of the quarrel. Compare 1 H 226–227 (Marguerite Oswald) with 11 H 38–39 (J. Pic).
190. Id. at 39.
191. Id. at 38, 39.
192. Id. at 39–40.
193. 1 H 227 (Marguerite Oswald).
194. CE 1384 ; CE 2205, p. 570 ; CE 2222.
195. CE 1384.
196. Ibid.
197. CE 2213, p. 25.
198. CE 1384, 2224, p. 4.
199. CE 2213, p. 25.
200. John Carro DE 1, p. 1.
201. CE 2213, p. 28.
202. CE 1384.
203. See CE 2224, p. 4.
204. CE 1384.
205. Ibid.
206. Ibid. ; cf. CE 2224, p. 4.
207. CE 2225.
208. CE 1384, 2226.
209. Id. at 7.
210. CE 2224, p. 4.
211. Ibid.
212. Id. at 5.
213. 11 H 42, 43–44, (J. Pic).
214. Carro DE 1, p. 1. Concerning this and subsequent truancy proceedings, see generally 8 H 202–214 (Carro).
215. Carro DE 1, p. 1.
216. CE 1384.
217. Carro DE 1, p. 1 ; see 1 H 227 (Marguerite Oswald).
218. Youth House is described by members of its staff at the time Lee was sent there at 8 H 215–218 (Dr. Renatus Hartogs), 225–226 (Evelyn Grace Strickman Siegel).
219. Carro DE 1, pp. 1–4 ; Siegel DE 1. p. 2 : see generally ch. VII, pp. 379–382, supra.
220. 1 H 228 (Marguerite Oswald).
221. Hartogs DE 1, p. 2. Dr. Hartogs' recommendations are discussed more fully in ch. VII, pp. 379–380.
222. Carro DE 1, p. 5.
223. Ibid.
224. CE 2224, p. 7.
225. Ibid.
226. Carro DE 1, p. 5 ; see CE 2213, p. 18.
227. CE 1384.
228. Ibid.
229. Ibid.
230. 1 H 301–302 (R. Oswald). John places this visit much earlier, probably in October or November of 1952 ; 11 H 40 (J. Pic).
231. 1 H 308–309 (R. Oswald).
232. Id. at 309–310.
233. CE 1384.

234. Carro DE 1, p. 5.
235. Id. at 6.
236. Ibid.
237. Ibid.
238. Ibid.
239. CE 1384.
240. Carro DE 1, pp. 6–7.
241. CE 2223, p. 4.
242. Ibid.
243. Carro DE 1, p. 7 ; CE 2223, p. 5.
244. Ibid.
245. See ibid.
246. Ibid ; see Carro DE 1, p. 7.
247. Id. at 8.
248. 1 H 231 (Marguerite Oswald) ; 8 H 122–123 (L. Murret). The address was later changed to 809 French Street ; id. at 122.
249. CE 1413, pp. 12, 14.
250. Id. at 3–5, p. 14.
251. Id. at 6–8, 13, 14.
252. Id. at 17.
253. Id. at 9–10 ; see ch. VII, p. 383.
254. See 8 H 6–7, 12–13 (Edward Voebel), 63, 65 (M. Evans), 71 (J. Evans), 131 (L. Murret), 159–160 (M. Murret) ; CE 2233, 2235, 2236.
255. 1 H 199–200 (Marguerite Oswald) ; 8 H 14 (Voebel), 28–29 (Frederick S. O'Sullivan), 151 (L. Murret). Lillian Murret testified that Lee belonged to the Sea Scouts also, probably a confusion with the Civil Air Patrol ; Cf 8 H 131, 151 (L. Murret).
256. 8 H 16–19 (William E. Wulf).
257. 8 H 3–4, 6, 8 (Voebel).
258. 1 H 198 (Marguerite Oswald) ; 8 H 70–71 (J. Evans) ; cf. 8 H 18 (Wulf). Edward Voebel, who thought Lee was not a "great reader," didn't see him read anything except "comic books and the normal things that kids read" ; 8 H 12 (Voebel).
259. 8 H 125, 131 (L. Murret).
260. 8 H 2–3, 5 (Voebel), 22–25 (Bennierita Smith), 124 (L. Murret), 159–160 (M. Murret) ; cf. CE 2232, 2234.
261. 8 H 2–3 (Voebel).
262. 8 H 55–57 (M. Evans), 70 (J. Evans) ; cf. 8 H 10–11 (Voebel).
263. CE 2201, p. 63.
264. CE 2238, p. 2.
265. Ibid.
266. Ibid. ; see 1 H 198 (Marguerite Oswald) ; CE 1413, p. 9.
267. Ibid.
268. CE 2238, p. 2.
269. 8 H 53–54, 56–57 (M. Evans) ; see 8 H 123 (L. Murret).
270. See 8 H 56–57 (M. Evans).
271. 1 H 197 (Marguerite Oswald) ; see 8 H 57 (M. Evans), 123 (L. Murret), 158–159 (M. Murret) ; CE 2231.
272. CE 1413, p. 9.
273. 8 H 56 (M. Evans) ; 8 H 151 (L. Murret).
274. 1 H 310–311 (R. Oswald).
275. CE 1413, p. 15 ; see CE 1873–I, –J.
276. CE 1413, p. 11 ; see generally 1 H 196–197 (Marguerite Oswald).
277. CE 1413, p. 15 ; see CE 1873–H.
278. 1 H 196–198 (Marguerite Oswald) ; 8 H 130–131 (L. Murret).
279. 11 H 32 (J. Pic).
280. 1 H 200 (Marguerite Oswald) ; see 8 H 64–65 (M. Evans).
281. CE 2227, 2237 ; see 1 H 198–199 (Marguerite Oswald).
282. CE 2227.
283. CE 2228 ; see 1 H 224 (Marguerite Oswald).
284. CE 1386, p. 251 ; CE 2229, 2230 ; see 1 H 198–199 (Marguerite Oswald).
285. Folsom DE 1, p. 7.
286. 1 H 199 (Marguerite Oswald).
287. CE 2205, p. 571 ; CE 2239 ; CE 1873–I, –K.

288. CE 1873–J, –K.
289. Ibid.
290. CE 2240, p. 2.
291. Id. at 2–3.
292. Folsom DE 1, p. 123.
293. Id. at 3. The abbreviations used on the official record to designate Lee's units and duty stations are explained in CE 1961, pp. 3–5.
294. Folsom DE 1, p. 1; see 8 H 304 (Folsom).
295. Folsom DE 1, p. 7; see 8 H 307–308 (Folsom).
296. Folsom DE 1, p. 7.
297. See CE 239; 8 H 310–311 (Folsom).
298. CE 239; see 8 H 311 (Folsom).
299. Folsom DE 1, p. 6; see 8 H 311 (Folsom); see generally 11 H 104 (Kerry Wendell Thornley).
300. Folsom DE 1, p. 6; see generally 8 H 233, 234–236 (Nelson Delgado).
301. Folsom DE 1, p. 6.
302. Id. at 3; see 8 H 305 (Folsom).
303. Folsom DE 1, p. 3.
304. Ibid.
305. CE 1962, p. 3.
306. Id. at 4.
307. Folsom DE 1, p. 36.
308. See CE 1963, p. 546.
309. Folsom DE 1, p. 3.
310. CE 1961, pp. 1–2.
311. See id., at 2–3.
312. Folsom DE 1, p. 10.
313. Id. at 120.
314. Id. at 118.
315. Id. at 3.
316. Ibid.; see 8 H 305 (Folsom); cf. 8 H 268 (Daniel Patrick Powers).
317. Folsom DE 1, p. 119; 8 H 267–268 (Powers).
318. CE 1961, p. 2; see 8 H 269 (Powers).
319. Id. at 267.
320. Id. at 268.
321. Ibid.
322. Id. at 270.
323. Id. at 277–278, 279; see generally id., at 269–271.
324. Id. at 272–273.
325. Folsom DE 1, p. 116.
326. Id. at 7.
327. Id. at 3, 36.
328. See 8 H 274 (Powers); CE 1963, p. 546; see note 308, supra.
329. Folsom DE 1, p. 3.
330. 8 H 274 (Powers).
331. Folsom DE 1, p. 3.
332. Ibid.
333. Id. at 13.
334. 8 H 277 (Powers).
335. Ibid.
336. Folsom DE 1, p. 13.
337. Id. at 3; CE 1961, p. 4.
338. 8 H 278–279 (Powers).
339. Id. at 279.
340. Ibid.
341. Folsom DE 1, p. 111.
342. 8 H 320 (Paul Edward Murphy).
343. Folsom DE 1, p. 3; CE 1961, p. 4.
344. Folsom DE 1, pp. 111–112.
345. Id. at 8.
346. Ibid.
347. CE 1961, p. 4.
348. 8 H 279–280 (Powers).
349. Folsom DE 1, p. 5.
350. Id. at 3.
351. CE 1961, p. 4.
352. Ibid.
353. Folsom DE 1, p. 9.
354. Id. at 32; see 8 H 322 (Mack Osborne); 11 H 84, 85 (Thornley).
355. Folsom DE 1, p. 32.
356. Id. at 9.
357. Id. at 8; see 8 H 308 (Folsom).
358. Folsom DE 1, p. 3.
359. Id. at 10.

360. Id. at 3.
361. CE 1961, p. 5.
362. Folsom DE 1, p. 3.
363. CE 1961, p. 5; see generally 8 H 313–314 (George Donabedian).
364. Folsom DE 1, p. 3.
365. 8 H 317 (Peter Francis Connor), 318 (John Rene Heindel), 320 (Murphy).
366. See authorities cited in note 365 supra.
367. 8 H 320 (Murphy); cf. 8 H 285 (Powers).
368. Id. at 275, 283.
369. Folsom DE 1, p. 13; CE 1961, p. 5.
370. Folsom DE 1, p. 36.
371. Id. at 3; CE 1961, p. 5.
372. 8 H 290 (John E. Donovan); see generally 8 H 231–232 (Delgado).
373. 8 H 297–298 (Donovan); but see CE 1961, p. 3.
374. 8 H 316 (James Anthony Botelho); 11 H 84 (Thornley).
375. 8 H 316 (Botelho); 11 H 84–85 (Thornley).
376. See CE 1961, p. 3; Folsom DE 1, p. 10.
377. 11 H 84 (Thornley).
378. 8 H 291, 292 (Donovan).
379. Id. at 298–299.
380. See 8 H 233–234, 258, 262 (Delgado), 316 (Botelho), 318 (Allen D. Graf), 319 (David Christie Murray, Jr.), 320 (Murphy), 321–322 (Osborne), 323 (Richard Dennis Call); 11 H 85, 89–91, 100–101 (Thornley).
381. 8 H 233 (Delgado); see 8 H 291 (Donovan).
382. See 8 H 245 (Delgado), 297 (Donovan), 316 (Botelho), 319 (Murray), 321 (Henry J. Roussel, Jr.); 11 H 92 (Thornley); but see 8 H 320 (Murphy).
383. 8 H 317 (Donald Camarata), 322 (Osborne), 323 (Call).
384. 8 H 265 (Delgado), 292–293, 297 (Donovan); 11 H 106–107 (Thornley); but see 8 H 322 (Call).
385. Folsom DE 1, p. 7; see 8 H 307.
386. 8 H 244 (Delgado), 292 (Donovan), 315 (Botelho), 316 (Camarata), 319 (Murray), 320 (Murphy), 321 (Roussel), 321 (Osborne), 322 (Call), 323 (Erwin Lewis); 11 H 87 (Thornley).
387. 8 H 321 (Roussel).
388. CE 2015.
389. 8 H 293 (Donovan).
390. 8 H 242 (Delgado), 292 (Donovan), 315 (Botelho), 317 (Camarata), 11 H 87–88 (Thornley); cf. id. at 320 (Murphy).
391. 8 H 315 (Botelho), 323 (Call); but see 8 H 257–258 (Delgado).
392. 8 H 316 (Camarata).
393. Ibid.; see 8 H 321 (Roussel).
394. 8 H 319 (Murray).
395. 8 H 315 (Botelho).
396. 8 H 257–258 (Delgado), 321 (Roussel).
397. 8 H 323 (Call).
398. 8 H 317 (Camarata), 317 (Connor), 318 (Graf), 321 (Roussel), 322 (Osborne), 322–323 (Call).
399. 8 H 290 (Donovan).
400. Id. at 297.
401. Id. at 292.
402. Id. at 295.
403. Id. at 293.
404. Ibid.
405. Id. at 292.
406. Id. at 293.
407. 11 H 85 (Thornley).
408. Id. at 97.
409. Id. at 87.
410. Ibid.
411. Id. at 93.
412. Id. at 94–95.
413. Id. at 98.
414. Id. at 94, 98.

415. 8 H 232 (Delgado).
416. Id. at 233, 241, 246–248.
417. Id. at 233.
418. See id. at 240–241, 243–244, 255.
419. Id. at 240.
420. Id. at 241.
421. Id. at 241–243.
422. See 8 H 233, 240–241, 243–244, 246, 254–255 (Delgado), 292–295, 297, 300 (Donovan), 315 (Botelho), 320 (Murphy), 322–323 (Call); 11 H 86–87, 90–95, 105–108 (Thornley).
423. 11 H 108 (Thornley); see 8 H 320 (Murphy) ("Harvey" after "Harvey the Rabbit").
424. 8 H 234, 264 (Delgado), 300 (Donovan), 317 (Camarata), 318 (Graf), 319 (Murray).
425. 8 H 244, 254 (Delgado); 11 H 90 (Thornley); see id. at 105 ("something * * * by Dostoievsky").
426. 8 H 300 (Donovan), 316 (Botelho), 319 (Murray), 320 (Murphy), 322 (Osborne), 322–323 (Call).
427. Id. at 323.
428. 8 H 251 (Delgado), 315–316 (Botelho).
429. 8 H 251 (Delgado), 295 (Donovan).
430. Id. at 295–296.
431. 8 H 252 (Delgado).
432. 8 H 295 (Donovan); cf. 8 H 251 (Delgado).
433. See id. at 241, 251 (Delgado), 316 (Camarata), 320 (Murphy), 322 (Osborne), 323 (Call).
434. 8 H 241 (Delgado).
435. Id. at 253–254; cf. 8 H 301 (Donovan).
436. Folsom DE 1, p. 3.
437. Ibid.
438. Id. at 105.
439. Id. at 106; see 8 H 309 (Folsom).
440. CE 228, p. 1.
441. Ibid.; see id. at 3.
442. Id. at 2.
443. Ibid.
444. Ibid.
445. Ibid.
446. Id. at 3.
447. See CE 229, 232.
448. CE 234.
449. 8 H 243 (Delgado).
450. 8 H 323 (Call).
451. Folsom DE 1, pp. 27, 79; see 8 H 304 (Folsom).
452. Folsom DE 1, p. 84.
453. Id. at 86–91; cf. CE 2241.
454. Id. at 6, 75, 76, 83.
455. Id. at 79–80.
456. Id. at 10, 78.
457. Id. at 4.
458. Ibid.; id. at 28.
459. Ibid.
460. Id. at 10.
461. CE 2016, p. II–13.
462. CE 1114.
463. CE 946.
464. 1 H 201–202 (Marguerite Oswald); CE 1135, p. 172.
465. 1 H 201–202, 212 (Marguerite Oswald); CE 1396, p. 6.
466. Ibid.
467. 1 H 201–202, 212 (Marguerite Oswald).
468. CE 1135, p. 172.
469. 1 H 329 (R. Oswald); 1 H 212 (Marguerite Oswald).
470. 1 H 203 (Marguerite Oswald).
471. CE 2673, 2665, p. 305.
472. CE 2712.
473. CE 2665, p. 305.
474. CE 200.
475. CE 2665, p. 305; see CE 2674.
476. CE 2675, p. 2.

477. Id. at 2–3; 11 H 116 (George B. Church, Jr.), 117 (Mrs. George B. Church, Jr.).
478. CE 2711, p. 39; CE 946, p. 7; CE 2676, p. 1.
479. Id. at 1, 3.
480. CE 2677. Oswald could have arrived at 5:05 p.m., flying via Copenhagen, or at 5:35 p.m., via Stockholm. See Official Airline Guide, North American Edition, October 1959, p. C–721. But he would have been too late to visit the Russian consulate that day. See CE 2714.
481. CE 946, p. 9.
482. Priscilla Johnson DE 1, p. 8; P. Johnson DE 5, p. 8.
483. CE 946, p. 8; CE 24, entry of Oct. 16, 1959; CE 985, document No. 1A.
484. CE 24, entry of Oct. 16, 1959.
485. CE 3124.
486. CE 24, entry of Oct. 16, 1959.
487. CE 24.
488. CE 18; see, e.g., pp. 3, 7, 22, 23, 27, 29, 31, 35, 61, 81; see also CE 827; 1 H 30, 104 (Marina Oswald).
489. CE 24, entry of Oct. 16, 1959.
490. CE 24, entry of Oct. 17, 1959.
491. CE 24, entries of Oct. 17–21, 1959.
492. CE 24, entry of Oct. 17, 1959.
493. CE 24, entry of Oct. 18, 1959.
494. CE 1399.
495. 5 H 617 (Marina Oswald); CE 935, 827, 1438 (name misspelled by Oswald).
496. CE 2760; cf. CE 25, pp. 1B–2B.
497. 5 H 274 (Richard Edward Snyder).
498. CE 24, entry of Oct. 20, 1959.
499. CE 24, entry of Oct. 21, 1959.
500. Ibid.
501. Ibid, see ch. VII, p. 392.
502. CE 985, documents 1C–1—1C–4.
503. CE 985, document 1C–3, p. 10.
504. Id. at 11.
505. Id. at 10.
506. CE 24, entry of Oct. 23, 1959.
507. CE 24, entry of Oct. 21, 1959.
508. CE 24, entry of Oct. 23, 1959.
509. CE 24, entry of Oct. 23–26, 1959.
510. CE 985, document 1C–2, pp. 1, 8–9.
511. CE 24, entry of Oct. 28, 1959.
512. CE 3123.
513. CE 24, entry of Oct. 28, 1959.
514. Ibid.
515. Ibid.
516. CE 24, entries of Oct. 29–31, 1959.
517. CE 24, entry of Oct. 31, 1959.
518. See CE 908, p. 1; CE 909, p. 1; 5 H 260–261 (Snyder).
519. See generally 5 H 262–265, 269–270, 287–291 (Snyder); 300–304, 322–324 (John A. McVickar); CE 908, 909, 910.
520. CE 913.
521. 8 USC sec. 1481 (1958); CE 101, 941, 958.
522. 5 H 269 (Snyder); see CE 101, 941.
523. CE 24, entry of Oct. 31, 1959.
524. Ibid.; CE 2719.
525. CE 24, entry of Oct. 31, 1959; CE 3098.
526. CE 24, entry of Oct. 31, 1959; CE 3098.
527. 1 H 201, 203 (Marguerite Oswald); CE 1396, pp. 8–9.
528. CE 24, entry of Nov. 1, 1959.
529. CE 2672; P. Johnson DE 5, p. 15.
530. 1 H 323 (R. Oswald); see 11 H 458 (P. Johnson).
531. CE 2715, p. 61; CE 2684; 1 H 322 (R. Oswald).
532. CE 2683, p. 29; CE 2672; CE 24, entry of Nov. 1, 1959; see 1 H 323 (R. Oswald).
533. CE 2715; 1 H 323 (R. Oswald).
534. CE 2715, p. 61.
535. CE 912; see CE 919, 920; 5 H 267–269 (Snyder).
536. CE 912.

537. CE 919.
538. CE 24, entry of Nov. 2–15, 1959.
539. CE 294.
540. CE 24, entry of Nov. 16, 1959.
541. CE 24, entry of Jan. 4, 1960 ; CE 985, documents 1A, 2A.
542. CE 942, 943, 2683, p. 29 ; 5 H 302 (McVickar).
543. See Fort Worth Star Telegram, Nov. 15, 1959, "Fort Worth Defector Confirms Red Beliefs" ; CE 24, entry of Nov. 15, 1959 ; CE 1385 ; see also CE 1438.
544. CE 1385, p. 2.
545. Id. at 1–12.
546. CE 2717 ; CE 24, entry for Nov. 15, 1959.
547. CE 1385, p. 16.
548. CE 24, entry of Nov. 16, 1959.
549. Ibid.
550. 11 H 446–447 (P. Johnson).
551. The interview is described in P. Johnson DE 1, 5, 6 ; 11 H 444–460. Oswald told Aline Mosby that he had read the Communist Manifesto. CE 1385, p. 6.
552. P. Johnson DE 1, p. 6.
553. 11 H 447, 459 (P. Johnson) ; CE 911.
554. CE 24, entries of Nov. 17–Dec. 30, Dec. 31, 1959 ; 5 H 616 (Marina Oswald).
555. CE 295.
556. CE 297.
557. CE 202, 206 ; 1 H 204 (Marguerite Oswald).
558. CE 24, entry of Jan. 4, 1960 ; cf. CE 985, documents 1A, 2A, 3A (1) ; CE 935.
559. CE 24, entry of Jan. 4, 1960.
560. In 1963, the population of Minsk was about 650,000.
561. CE 24, entry of Jan. 4, 1960.
562. CE 24, entry of Jan. 4–5, 1960 ; 5 H 292–293 (Snyder).
563. CE 24, entries of Jan. 5 and 7, 1960.
564. CE 24, entry of Jan. 7, 1960.
565. CE 24, entry of Oct. 18, 1960.
566. CE 24, entry of Jan. 8, 1960.
567. CE 1108.
568. CE 24, entries of Jan. 11 and 13, 1960 ; CE 33.
569. CE 92, p. 3 ; see CE 2669.
570. CE 1128, p. 1 ; CE 1109, p. 2.
571. 5 H 616 (Marina Oswald) ; see 8 H 360 (George A. Bouhe) ; 9 H 145 (Paul Roderick Gregory) ; 9 H 79–80 (Gary E. Taylor) ; 2 H 339 (Peter Paul Gregory) ; CE 2669.
572. CE 1108.
573. CE 92, pp. 8–9.
574. 5 H 590 (Marina Oswald) ; 8 H 347, 350 (Max Clark) ; 9 H 81 (Taylor), 147 (Paul Gregory) ; see P. Johnson DE 1, pp. 1, 6 ; P. Johnson DE 5, p. 7 ; CE 1385, p. 16.
575. 8 H 360 (Bouhe) (900 rubles), 385 (Anna N. Meller) (800 rubles) ; 5 H 407–408 (Marina Oswald) (800 rubles) ; CE 1401, p. 271 (800–900 rubles) ; CE 1110 (700–850 rubles) ; CE 1128 ; CE 24, entry of Jan. 13, 1960 (700 rubles) ; 2 H 339 (Peter Gregory) (800 rubles) ; 8 H 348 (Clark) (800–900 rubles).
576. CE 2720 ; see CE 1401, p. 271.
577. 1 H 95 (Marina Oswald) ; CE 1401, p. 275.
578. CE 24, entry of Jan. 13, 1960.
579. CE 1109.
580. CE 1110, 1128.
581. 1 H 92–93 (Marina Oswald) ; CE 1401, p. 275.
582. CE 24, entry of Mar. 16, 1960 ; cf. 1 H 92 (Marina Oswald).
583. CE 24, entry of Mar. 16, 1960 ; see also 1 H 92 (Marina Oswald).
584. See id. at 93.
585. CE 2721 ; CE 25, pp. 1B–2B.
586. CE 24, entries Jan. 7 to Mar. 17, 1960 ; see CE 93, p. 4 (erroneously referring to "Roza Agafonava").

587. CE 24, entry of Jan. 13, 1960.
588. CE 24, entry of Mar. 17, 1960 ; CE 2693.
589. CE 1403, p. 729 ; CE 42, 79.
590. Ibid.
591. CE 24, entry of June–July 1960.
592. 1 H 91 (Marina Oswald) ; CE 993, p. 5.
593. 1 H 96 (Marina Oswald) ; 2 H 396–397 (M. Paine) ; 5 H 405–406 (Marina Oswald) ; 8 H 362 (Bouhe) ; CE 2678, pp. 13–14 ; CE 2679.
594. CE 2759 ; CE 24, entry of Jan. 1, 1961.
595. CE 24, entry of May 1, 1960.
596. CE 24, entry of June–July 1960.
597. CE 24, entry of Aug.–Sept. 1960.
598. CE 24, entries of Jan. 1, Jan. 2, 1961.
599. CE 24, entry of Jan. 3, 1961.
600. CE 24, entry of May 1, 1961.
601. CE 2759.
602. 11 H 142 (Mrs. Donald Gibson) ; 9 H 79 (Taylor).
603. Ibid.
604. 11 H 142 (Gibson).
605. 9 H 79 (Taylor).
606. 10 H 203 (Dennis Hyman Ofstein).
607. 8 H 348 (Clark).
608. 9 H 80 (Taylor) ; 5 H 590 (Marina Oswald).
609. Ibid. ; see 8 H 348 (Clark).
610. 11 H 142 (Gibson) ; 8 H 60 (M. Evans) ; 5 H 590 (Marina Oswald).
611. 9 H 145, 151 (Paul Gregory).
612. Id. at 145, 154, 156.
613. 1 H 30 (Marina Oswald) ; CE 92, 94.
614. 8 H 330–332 (Pauline Virginia Bates).
615. CE 92, p. 1.
616. Id. at 5.
617. Ibid.
618. Id. at 6–7.
619. 5 H 407 (Marina Oswald), but see CE 25, p. 3.
620. CE 92, pp. 7–8.
621. Id. at 12.
622. Id., passim.
623. CE 985, documents 3A (1)–(2) ; cf. CE 24, entry of Jan. 4, 1961.
624. Ibid.
625. 5 H 277 (Snyder).
626. Id. at 276–277 ; CE 931.
627. 5 H 277 (Snyder) ; CE 24, entries of Feb. 1–Mar. 6, 1961.
628. CE 933, 1084.
629. CE 930, 2681.
630. CE 2666.
631. CE 940.
632. CE 24, entry of Mar. 1–16, 1961.
633. 5 H 278 (Snyder) ; CE 1403, p. 727.
634. CE 25, pp. 1B–2B ; see 5 H 407–408 (Marina Oswald).
635. CE 940.
636. Ibid. ; CE 1085.
637. CE 970, 971 ; 5 H 352–354 (Bernice Waterman).
638. 11 H 210–212 (Katherine Mallory).
639. CE 24, entry of Mar. 17, 1961. Marina thought that the date was Mar. 4. 1 H 90 (Marina Oswald) ; CE 994, p. 1.
640. CE 1401, p. 260.
641. Ibid.
642. CE 24, entry of Mar. 17, 1961.
643. 1 H 90–91 (Marina Oswald) ; CE 1401, p. 267 ; CE 994, p. 7.
644. CE 24, entries of Mar. 17, 18–31, Apr. 1–30, 1961.
645. This and the succeeding paragraphs about Marina's life before she met Oswald are based primarily on CE 1401, pp. 256–261. Additional sources are indicated where appropriate.
646. See also 1 H 84 (Marina Oswald).

647. See id. at 84–85.
648. Marina is unclear about her age at the time of this move; cf. 1 H 84 (Marina Oswald) ("approximately five"), with CE 1401, p. 256 ("about seven").
649. CE 49.
650. 1 H 84 (Marina Oswald).
651. Id. at 85.
652. Id. at 87; CE 49.
653. CE 21; see 1 H 89 (Marina Oswald).
654. Id. at 85.
655. Ibid.
656. Id. at 87.
657. See CE 51, 57.
658. 1 H 89 (Marina Oswald).
659. Ibid.
660. Id. at 87–89.
661. Id. at 89; 5 H 608–609 (Marina Oswald); 5 H 305 (McVickar).
662. 1 H 88, 89 (Marina Oswald).
663. CE 1401, p. 261; CE 994, p. 5.
664. 1 H 91 (Marina Oswald); CE 1401, pp. 267–268; CE 993, p. 7.
665. Cf. ibid, with CE 1401.
666. 1 H 91 (Marina Oswald); CE 1401, p. 268.
667. CE 985, document 1C–1, p. 1.
668. 1 H 91 (Marina Oswald); CE 1401, p. 269.
669. Ibid.
670. CE 994, pp. 8–9; 2 H 302 (Katherine Ford).
671. CE 1401, p. 270; cf. CE 994, p. 9.
672. CE 985, document 1C–1, pp. 19–20.
673. CE 1401, p. 269.
674. Id. at 269–270.
675. CE 24, entry of Apr. 1–30, 1961.
676. CE 1401, p. 269; but see 2 H 302 (K. Ford).
677. CE 1111; CE 24, entry of Apr. 31 [sic], 1961.
678. Ibid.
679. CE 1401, p. 274.
680. CE 24, entry of May 1, 1961.
681. CE 24, entry of May 1961.
682. CE 24, entry of June 1961.
683. Ibid.
684. CE 252.
685. CE 1401, p. 277; CE 1403, p. 725.
686. CE 1401, pp. 274–276.
687. Id. at 274.
688. Id. at 276; CE 993, p. 12.
689. CE 1401, p. 277.
690. 1 H 101 (Marina Oswald).
691. CE 72.
692. 5 H 590 (Marina Oswald).
693. CE 298.
694. CE 299.
695. CE 180.
696. CE 252.
697. CE 936.
698. CE 1403, p. 727.
699. CE 24, entry of July 8, 1961; CE 24, entry of July 1961.
700. See app. XV, p. 754, infra.
701. CE 24, entry of July 9, 1961; see 1 H 96–97 (Marina Oswald); CE 1401, p. 280.
702. Id at 290; CE 1403, p. 726.
703. CE 1401, p. 278.
704. CE 935.
705. CE 24, entries of Oct. 16, 1959, through Jan. 4, 1960; CE 908.
706. CE 1385, p. 4; P. Johnson DE 1, pp. 3, 6, 14; P. Johnson DE 2, pp. 1–2; 11 H 456 (P. Johnson); CE 985, document 1C–2, p. 6.
707. CE 1109, 1110, 1128.
708. CE 909, 935, p. 2.
709. Id. at 3.
710. CE 946, p. 2–3; 5 H 284 (Snyder).
711. CE 935, p. 2.
712. CE 938.

713. 5 H 284 (Snyder); CE 946, p. 6.
714. 5 H 319 (McVickar); CE 1401, pp. 278–279.
715. 5 H 319 (McVickar).
716. CE 944; 5 H 304–306, 318–319 (McVickar); CE 959.
717. CE 24, entry of July 14, 1961; CE 301.
718. Ibid.
719. CE 935, p. 1; CE 985, documents 1B, 2B, 3B, 4B; see CE 1401, pp. 277–278, 280.
720. CE 24, entry of July 16–Aug. 20, 1961.
721. CE 1122, p. 1.
722. CE 24, entry of Aug. 21–Sept. 1, 1961.
723. CE 24, entry of Sept.–Oct. 18, 1961.
724. 1 H 90, 97 (Marina Oswald); but see CE 1401, p. 276.
725. 1 H 97 (Marina Oswald).
726. Ibid.; 5 H 591–592 (Marina Oswald).
727. 9 H 147 (Paul Gregory); see also CE 301; CE 24, entry of July 15–Aug. 20, 1961.
728. CE 1122, pp. 2–3.
729. Ibid.
730. 1 H 97 (Marina Oswald).
731. CE 1087.
732. 1 H 98 (Marina Oswald); CE 1403, p. 740.
733. CE 306.
734. CE 55; but see 1 H 98 (Marina Oswald).
735. CE 24, entry of Nov.–Dec. 1961; see also CE 1401, p. 269.
736. CE 24, entry of Sept.–Oct. 18, 1961; see CE 66(I).
737. CE 24, entry of Sept.–Oct. 18, 1961.
738. CE 56, 306, CE 1315, pp. 1–2.
739. CE 24, entry of Nov. 12, 1961.
740. 5 H 591, 618 (Marina Oswald).
741. CE 1403, p. 745; 5 H 592 (Marina Oswald).
742. Id. at 591–592, 604–605, 617–619 (Marina Oswald).
743. CE 181, 182, 183, 184, 185 (letters to Marguerite Oswald); CE 303, 305, 306, 307, 308, 309 (letters to R. Oswald).
744. CE 253.
745. CE 1076.
746. CE 1058.
747. CE 24, entry of Dec. 25, 1961; 5 H 592, 598, 604–605 (Marina Oswald); see also CE 1403, p. 725.
748. CE 1401, p. 267.
749. CE 24, entry for "New Years" 1962; CE 313.
750. CE 189.
751. CE 2731; cf. CE 2660.
752. CE 2680, pp. 7–8.
753. Id., at 3–4.
754. CE 246.
755. CE 1078.
756. CE 256.
757. CE 1079.
758. CE 2692.
759. CE 247.
760. Ibid.
761. CE 190.
762. CE 1080, p. 2; CE 1101.
763. CE 314.
764. Folsom DE 1, p. 10; see p. 689, supra.
765. CE 314.
766. Folsom DE 1, p. 65.
767. Id. at 63.
768. Id. at 61.
769. Id. at 45–46.
770. CE 2658.
771. CE 2661.
772. CE 222.
773. CE 192.
774. CE 1082, 1102.
775. CE 193.

776. CE 24, entry of Feb. 15, 1962; CE 993, pp. 15–16; CE 1112.
777. CE 994, p. 16.
778. Ibid.; but see CE 60, 61, 64.
779. CE 24, entry of Feb. 23, 1962.
780. CE 40, 52, 58, 59, 60, 61, 63, 194.
781. CE 24, entries of Feb. 28–29, 1962; 1 H 95 (Marina Oswald); CE 316.
782. CE 59, 61.
783. CE 24, entry of Feb. 23, 1961.
784. CE 316.
785. CE 195.
786. CE 316.
787. CE 1093, 2682.
788. CE 1086.
789. CE 1095.
790. CE 249, 1103.
791. CE 196, 2653.
792. CE 2656; see app. XV, p. 762, infra.
793. CE 24, entry of Mar. 24, 1962; CE 22.
794. CE 249, 1083, 1088, 2687, 2688.
795. CE 317.
796. CE 1313.
797. CE 985, document 9A; CE 1108, 1314.
798. CE 1108, 1109, 1128, p. 3.
799. CE 1401, p. 275; 1 H 93 (Marina Oswald); see also 5 H 590 (Marina Oswald).
800. CE 985, document 8A.
801. CE 946, p. 11.
802. 5 H 604, 617–618 (Marina Oswald); CE 2722.
803. CE 318.
804. CE 946, pp. 11, 15; see CE 1401, p. 280.
805. CE 2654, 2662, 2690, 2704.
806. CE 2656.
807. CE 34.
808. CE 1098. After his return to the United States, Oswald repaid the loan in full. See app. XV, p. 773, infra.
809. CE 1099, 1401, p. 280.
810. CE 57.
811. CE 29, 946, 1099.
812. 1 H 101 (Marina Oswald).
813. CE 25.
814. CE 100.
815. CE 946, p. 15.
816. CE 2655.
817. CE 1060, p. 10; CE 2656, 2718, pp. 2–3.
818. CE 2655; CE 2657.
819. CE 2213, pp. 19–20; CE 2657.
820. CE 2655, 2657.
821. CE 2213, pp. 18–24.
822. Ibid.; CE 2657.
823. CE 2213, p. 24.
824. CE 2692.
825. 1 H 372 (R. Oswald).
826. Martin Isaacs DE 1.
827. 1 H 331 (R. Oswald); 1 H 4 (Marina Oswald).
828. 1 H 330–331 (R. Oswald).
829. Id. at 331; see id. at 464.
830. Ibid.; 2 H 343 (Peter Gregory); 1 H 30 (Marina Oswald); 4 H 415 (John W. Fain).
831. CE 2189, p. 1; 1 H 331 (R. Oswald).
832. Id. at 330.
833. 1 H 4 (Marina Oswald); 312 (R. Oswald).
834. Ibid.
835. Ibid.
836. Id. at 385–386.
837. Id. at 313–314.
838. 1 H 4 (Marina Oswald).
839. Ibid.
840. 8 H 331–332 (Bates).
841. Id. at 332–333; see pp. 700–701, supra.
842. 8 H 332–333 (Bates).
843. Id. at 334–336.
844. Id. at 336.

845. Ibid.
846. Ibid.
847. See 2 H 338 (Peter Gregory); CE 384.
848. 2 H 337–338 (Peter Gregory).
849. Id. at 338; CE 384.
850. 2 H 338–339 (Peter Gregory).
851. See id. at 342, 343.
852. Id. at 339–340; 9 H 143 (Paul Gregory).
853. CE 823, p. 11; 1 H 315 (R. Oswald); 4 H 415 (Fain).
854. Id. at 418.
855. CE 823, p. 11.
856. Id. at 12; see CE 29.
857. Id. at 13.
858. 1 H 315, 389 (R. Oswald).
859. See 1 H 133 (Marguerite Oswald), CE 1943, 2189, p. 2; 1 H 4 (Marina Oswald); 312 (R. Oswald).
860. 1 H 132–133 (Marguerite Oswald).
861. CE 2189, p. 2; 1 H 133–135 (Marguerite Oswald).
862. 1 H 131–132 (Marguerite Oswald).
863. Id. at 133.
864. Ibid.
865. 1 H 5 (Marina Oswald).
866. CE 2189, pp. 2, 18.
867. See 4 H 419 (Fain); CE 2189, pp. 2, 18; see 1 H 4–5 (Marina Oswald); 1 H 135 (Marguerite Oswald).
868. CE 2189, pp. 2–3; 1 H 5 (Marina Oswald), 134–135 (Marguerite Oswald); 10 H 230 (Chester Allen Riggs, Jr.).
869. Graves DE 1; CE 2189, p. 12; 10 H 163 (Tommy Bargas).
870. 10 H 161 (Bargas).
871. CE 1943; 10 H 162–163 (Bargas).
872. CE 1943.
873. Graves DE 1.
874. 1 H 5 (Marina Oswald).
875. 10 H 165 (Bargas); CE 2189, p. 13.
876. Ibid.; 10 H 165–166 (Bargas).
877. Id. at 165.
878. 1 H 136 (Marguerite Oswald).
879. See 1 H 6 (Marina Oswald); 2 H 300 (K. Ford).
880. 1 H 141 (Marguerite Oswald).
881. 9 H 226 (George De Mohrenschildt); see 9 H 77 (Taylor), 308 (J. De Mohrenschildt).
882. 10 H 230 (Riggs).
883. 11 H 119 (Alexander Kleinlerer); 8 H 384 (Meller), 393 (Elena A. Hall); 2 H 341 (Peter Gregory); 9 H 225–226 (G. De Mohrenschildt); cf. 5 H 419 (Marina Oswald).
884. CE 824, pp. 4–6; 4 H 419–424 (Fain).
885. 1 H 20 (Marina Oswald).
886. 8 H 357–358 (Bouhe), 452–455 (Igor Vladimir Voshinin); see generally 9 H 4–12 (Paul M. Raigorodsky); 8 H 354–355 (Clark); 9 H 305–306 (J. De Mohrenschildt).
887. 9 H 143–144, 158 (Paul Gregory).
888. See id. at 144–151, 157.
889. See 8 H 358–359 (Bouhe), 2 H 341 (Peter Gregory).
890. Ibid.; 8 H 358 (Bouhe), 379, 381–382 (Meller).
891. 2 H 297 (K. Ford), 323 (Declan P. Ford); 8 H 392–393 (E. Hall); 1 H 7 (Marina Oswald).
892. 11 H 119 (Kleinlerer).
893. 8 H 344–346 (Clark).
894. 9 H 168, 217, 281 (G. De Mohrenschildt).
895. Id. at 224–226; see 1 H 7 (Marina Oswald).
896. See 9 H 308 (J. De Mohrenschildt); 9 H 76–77 (Taylor); 11 H 125–127 (Gibson).
897. 9 H 236 (G. De Mohrenschildt); see 8 H 359, 371–372 (Bouhe).

898. Id. at 368–369 (Bouhe) ; 8 H 351–352, 354–355 (Clark) ; 11 H 122 (Kleinlerer) ; see 8 H 383 (Meller), 404 (E. Hall), 435–436 (Mrs. Voshinin).

899. 8 H 371–373 (Bouhe), 383–385 (Meller), 393–395 (E. Hall), 422–423 (Valentina Ray) ; 11 H 119 (Kleinlerer) ; 9 H 307, 324–325 (J. De Mohrenschildt).

900. See 1 H 7 (Marina Oswald) ; 9 H 231 (G. De Mohrenschildt) ; 11 H 119 (Kleinlerer).

901. E.g., 9 H 309, 311 (J. De Mohrenschildt) ; 8 H 366, 372 (Bouhe), 382, 384 (Meller), 394 (E. Hall).

902. See 8 H 384 (Meller) ; see also 8 H 394 (E. Hall).

903. 9 H 309 (J. De Mohrenschildt) ; 2 H 300 (K. Ford).

904. 1 H 10–11 (Marina Oswald).

905. See, e.g., 8 H 445 (Mrs. Voshinin), 376 (Bouhe).

906. 11 H 123 (Kleinlerer).

907. E.g., 2 H 308 (K. Ford) ; 8 H 374 (Bouhe), 381 (Meller).

908. 11 H 123 (Kleinlerer).

909. E.g., 9 H 77 (Taylor) ; 8 H 366 (Bouhe), 407 (John Hall) ; 1 H 137–138 (Marguerite Oswald).

910. 8 H 366 (Bouhe) ; see 8 H 407 (J. Hall).

911. Ibid, 9 H 230 (G. De Mohrenschildt) ; see 1 H 6 (Marina Oswald).

912. 11 H 120 (Kleinlerer) ; 8 H 394 (E. Hall) ; see 8 H 366 (Bouhe).

913. Helen Cunningham DE 1–A ; 10 H 120 (Cunningham).

914. 1 H 5 (Marina Oswald) ; see also 9 H 230 (G. De Mohrenschildt) ; 10 H 135 (Cunningham).

915. 8 H 366 (Bouhe).

916. CE 820–A ; see 10 H 166 (Bargas).

917. 1 H 141 (Marguerite Oswald).

918. 8 H 345–346 (Clark), 364–365 (Bouhe).

919. 1 H 140 (Marguerite Oswald) ; 8 H 365 (Bouhe), 383 (Meller).

920. 1 H 140 (Marguerite Oswald) ; 8 H 365 (Bouhe), 383 (Meller).

921. 8 H 395–396 (E. Hall), 365 (Bouhe) ; see 2 H 300 (K. Ford).

922. E.g., 11 H 119–120 (Kleinlerer).

923. CE 994, p. 25.

924. 1 H 10 (Marina Oswald) ; see id. at 32, 34.

925. 1 H 32 (Marina Oswald) ; 11 H 296 (Marina Oswald).

926. 1 H 7–8, 31 (Marina Oswald) ; 8 H 394–395 (E. Hall) ; 9 H 324 (J. De Mohrenschildt).

927. 9 H 324, 327 (J. De Mohrenschildt) ; Albert Staples DE 1.

928. 8 H 373 (Bouhe) ; 9 H 306, 324–325 (J. De Mohrenschildt).

929. See 8 H 407 (J. Hall).

930. 9 H 46–47 (Samuel B. Ballen), 230 (G. De Mohrenschildt).

931. 8 H 388 (Meller), 366 (Bouhe) ; 10 H 119 (Cunningham).

932. 10 H 120–130 (Cunningham) ; Cunningham DE 1, 1–A, 2, 2–A, 4 ; 11 H 477–478 (Cunningham) ; 10 H 144–146 (Donald E. Brooks) ; 150 (Irving Statman).

933. 11 H 477 (Cunningham) ; Cunningham DE 4 ; 10 H 175–177 (John G. Graef).

934. 10 H 181 (Graef), 172 (Robert Stovall) ; CE 1144, p. 13.

935. 1 H 8 (Marina Oswald).

936. 10 H 281–282 (Richard Leroy Hulen), 290 (Colin Barnhorst).

937. Cunningham DE 2, 4 ; 11 H 124, 149 (Gibson).

938. CE 792 ; 7 H 295 (Harry D. Holmes) ; CE 1152.

939. CE 1390, p. 177.

940. CE 994, p. 26.

941. 11 H 143–144 (Gibson) ; 8 H 399 (E. Hall) ; 1 H 33 (Marina Oswald) ; CE 1957–A.

942. 8 H 394–395 (E. Hall) ; 11 H 120–121 (Kleinlerer) ; 8 H 345–346 (Clark).

943. 1 H 8, 32 (Marina Oswald) ; 9 H 88–89 (Taylor).

944. Ibid ; 11 H 138–139 (Gibson).

945. 1 H 8 (Marina Oswald) ; 11 H 120 (Kleinlerer), 137 (Gibson).

946. 8 H 395 (E. Hall) ; 11 H 120–121 (Kleinlerer) ; 10 H 232, 234, 237–238 (Mrs. Mahlon F. Tobias) ; see also 1 H 8 (Marina Oswald).

947. 10 H 237–238 (Mrs. Tobias) ; CE 1160, p. 2 ; see also 1 H 8 (Marina Oswald).

948. 9 H 89–91 (Taylor) ; 11 H 470 (Taylor), 120–121 (Kleinlerer), 139–140 (Gibson) ; 1 H 8 (Marina Oswald).

949. 11 H 120–121 (Kleinlerer).

950. Id. at 120.

951. 9 H 244 (G. De Mohrenschildt), 313 (J. De Mohrenschildt) ; 1 H 35 (Marina Oswald).

952. 5 H 415 (Marina Oswald) ; CE 994, p. 26 ; 10 H 242–243 (Mrs. Tobias), 258 (M. F. Tobias).

953. 2 H 309–310 (K. Ford) ; 8 H 375–376 (Bouhe), 382 (Meller) ; see 9 H 226 (G. De Mohrenschildt) ; CE 994, p. 22.

954. 2 H 309–310 (K. Ford) ; 9 H 240 (G. De Mohrenschildt) ; 11 H 128 (Gibson).

955. 9 H 233, 252 (G. De Mohrenschildt), 311, 313 (J. De Mohrenschildt) ; 8 H 396 (E. Hall).

956. 9 H 231–232 (G. De Mohrenschildt).

957. 1 H 32 (Marina Oswald).

958. Id. at 33.

959. Ibid.

960. 11 H 298 (Marina Oswald) ; 9 H 240 (G. De Mohrenschildt).

961. Id. at 232–233 (G. De Mohrenschildt), 310 (J. De Mohrenschildt) ; 8 H 386 (Meller) ; 10 H 245–246 (Mrs. Tobias) ; 1 H 11 (Marina Oswald) ; 5 H 416 (Marina Oswald) ; 11 H 296 (Marina Oswald) ; CE 1817.

962. 8 H 388 (Meller).

963. 1 H 11 (Marina Oswald) ; 11 H 297 (Marina Oswald).

964. 1 H 11–12 (Marina Oswald), cf. 11 H 297–298 (Marina Oswald).

965. 1 H 11–12 (Marina Oswald) ; 2 H 299–300 (K. Ford) ; 8 H 388 (Meller), 365 (Bouhe) ; 11 H 296 (Marina Oswald).

966. 2 H 299 (K. Ford) ; but see CE 994, p. 27.

967. 2 H 299 (K. Ford).

968. 8 H 416 (V. Ray) ; 2 H 304 (K. Ford), 325 (D. Ford) ; 1 H 11–12 (Marina Oswald).

969. CE 994, p. 27–28.

970. 11 H 299 (Marina Oswald).

971. 2 H 304 (K. Ford), 325 (D. Ford) ; 8 H 416 (V. Ray), see 1 H 11 (Marina Oswald).

972. 11 H 298 (Marina Oswald) ; see also 2 H 307 (K. Ford) ; 9 H 252 (G. De Mohrenschildt).

973. 9 H 238, 266 (G. De Mohrenschildt).

974. 8 H 372 (Bouhe) ; 9 H 238, 266 (G. De Mohrenschildt) ; 1 H 35 (Marina Oswald).

975. 5 H 419 (Marina Oswald) ; 9 H 266 (G. De Mohrenschildt) ; 1 H 34–35 (Marina Oswald).

976. 9 H 65–69 (Lydia Dymitruk) ; 5 H 419 (Marina Oswald) ; 10 H 247–248 (Mrs. Tobias).

977. 2 H 318 (K. Ford).

978. 11 H 299 (Marina Oswald).

979. 1 H 386–389 (R. Oswald) ; CE 320 ; 11 H 52–60 (J. Pic).

980. Id. at 53–54, 81.   Accord, 2 H 341 (Peter Gregory); 8 H 423 (V. Ray); 9 H 311 (J. De Mohrenschildt); 1 H 36 (Marina Oswald).
981. 9 H 143–144 (Paul Gregory); 11 H 58–59 (J. Pic); 1 H 389 (R. Oswald).
982. Id. at 389–391; CE 322, 324.
983. CE 986, p. 2748–A.
984. See e.g., CE 93, p. 3; 1147; 8 H 370–371 (Bouhe).
985. CE 986, p. 2757–A.
986. E.g., CE 31, 32, 33, 57.
987. CE 1172.
988. Farrell Dobbs DE 1, 9, 10, 11; 3 H 118 (R. Paine).
989. James J. Tormey DE 1; Arnold Johnson DE 5; Dobbs DE 12.
990. 1 H 5 (Marina Oswald); CE 2642.
991. 8 H 371 (Bouhe); see id. at 382 (Meller); 9 H 150 (Paul Gregory).
992. 1 H 5 (Marina Oswald); 5 H 392–393, 416 (Marina Oswald); CE 1404, p. 456; CE 2652.
993. 9 H 243, 253 (G. De Mohrenschildt); 2 H 326 (D. Ford); 305–307 (K. Ford); 9 H 29–33 (Natalie Ray), 39–41 (Thomas Ray).
994. 9 H 245–246 (G. De Mohrenschildt), 319–320 (J. De Mohrenschildt); 2 H 306, 308 (K. Ford), 329 (D. Ford); 8 H 369–370 (Bouhe), 389 (Meller).
995. CE 1866, p. 573.
996. 2 H 307 (K. Ford); 8 H 389–390 (Meller), 370 (Bouhe); 9 H 33 (Natalie Ray).
997. See 9 H 256 (G. De Mohrenschildt).
998. 10 H 19–20 (Everett D. Glover).
999. Id. at 21–25.
1000. Id. at 24–29; 2 H 435–444 (R. Paine).
1001. Ibid.; 2 H 385–386 (M. Paine); 1 H 35–36 (Marina Oswald).
1002. Id. at 36; 2 H 443–445 (R. Paine); CE 404.
1003. 11 H 155–156 (M. Waldo George); see CE 1133, 1134, 1167, pp. 465–467.
1004. 10 H 241 (Mrs. Tobias), 258–259 (M. F. Tobias).
1005. 1 H 10 (Marina Oswald); see 9 H 94 (Taylor).
1006. 8 H 370 (Bouhe).
1007. CE 2699; 1130; 1 H 9 (Marina Oswald); 9 H 94 (Taylor).
1008. 2 H 445–457 (R. Paine).
1009. CE 994, p. 32.
1010. See ch. IV, pp. 118–120, 172–174, supra.
1011. See ch. IV, p. 121, supra; app. X, pp. 571–577, supra; 10 H 198–199, 201 (Ofstein).
1012. 7 H 365 (William J. Waldman), 376–377 (Heinz W. Michaelis).
1013. 5 H 396 (Marina Oswald).
1014. 1 H 13 (Marina Oswald).
1015. Id. at 14–15, 93–94; 5 H 396–398 (Marina Oswald); CE 1156, p. 442; CE 2694.
1016. 1 H 15–16 (Marina Oswald).
1017. See ch. IV, pp. 184–185, supra.
1018. 1 H 17–18, 38 (Marina Oswald).
1019. Id. at 16–17.
1020. Ibid.; 11 H 404–405 (Edwin A. Walker).
1021. 1 H 16–18 (Marina Oswald).
1022. Id. at 18; 9 H 249–250 (G. De Mohrenschildt), 317 (J. De Mohrenschildt).
1023. 10 H 187–189 (Graef), 198–199, 204–205 (Ofstein), 172–173 (Stovall); 11 H 479 (Theodore F. Gangl).
1024. 10 H 189 (Graef); 11 H 479 (Gangl); Gangl DE 1.
1025. 8 H 409 (John Hall).
1026. 1 H 18 (Marina Oswald); 2 H 517 (R. Paine).

1027. Cunningham DE 1–A; 11 H 478 (Cunningham).
1028. John W. Burcham DE 1.
1029. Ibid.
1030. 1 H 10 (Marina Oswald).
1031. 11 H 155–156 (George); 2 H 470, 472 (R. Paine).
1032. Id. at 447, 472.
1033. 11 H 155–156 (George).
1034. 1 H 10 (Marina Oswald).
1035. CE 7, 9, 986.
1036. 1 H 35, 68 (Marina Oswald); 2 H 448 (R. Paine).
1037. Id. at 457–458; 1 H 18 (Marina Oswald).
1038. Id. at 18–19.
1039. 2 H 459 (R. Paine); 1 H 19 (Marina Oswald).
1040. 8 H 133–134 (Lillian Murret), 164 (Marilyn Murret).
1041. 8 H 135–136 (L. Murret), 165–166 (M. Murret); CE 1919.
1042. 11 H 474–476 (John Rachal); Rachal DE 1.
1043. Ibid.; Rachal DE 2; 8 H 135 (L. Murret); CE 1893, 1946, 1951; Bobb Hunley DE 3.
1044. 8 H 135 (L. Murret).
1045. Burcham DE 1.
1046. CE 1911.
1047. CE 68–A.
1048. CE 69–A.
1049. CE 1398; 11 H 473–474 (Emmett Charles Barbe, Jr.).
1050. 10 H 214–219 (Charles Joseph LeBlanc); 11 H 473–474 (Barbe).
1051. 8 H 137 (L. Murret).
1052. 2 H 517 (R. Paine).
1053. 8 H 58 (M. Evans), 72–73 (J. Evans), 186 (Charles Murret); 10 H 265–266 (Mrs. Jesse Garner).
1054. 2 H 468–469, 475–477, 484–485 (R. Paine); 8 H 139–141 (L. Murret), 186 (C. Murret); 1 H 19 (Marina Oswald).
1055. Id. at 25.
1056. 8 H 172 (M. Murret).
1057. 1 H 25 (Marina Oswald).
1058. 2 H 499–500 (R. Paine); 3 H 5, 8–9 (R. Paine); CE 421, 1929.
1059. 11 H 473–474 (Barbe); 10 H 214–219 (LeBlanc), 220–229 (Adrian Alba).
1060. Burcham DE 1; Rachal DE 1; Hunley DE 2, 5; CE 421, 1911.
1061. CE 1781, p. 550.
1062. Folsom DE 1, pp. 38–41.
1063. CE 1969.
1064. 1 H 10, 68 (Marina Oswald); 2 H 448 (R. Paine); CE 408.
1065. CE 12.
1066. CE 13.
1067. 1 H 44 (Marina Oswald).
1068. Id. at 47.
1069. CE 994, pp. 34–35; see also CE 415; but see CE 408.
1070. 1 H 68 (Marina Oswald).
1071. CE 408.
1072. 2 H 470–472 (R. Paine).
1073. 2 H 449, 491–496 (R. Paine); CE 410, 411, 412.
1074. CE 415.
1075. CE 416.
1076. CE 2649; 8 H 147–148 (L. Murret); 8 H 186–187 (C. Murret); CE 421, 2648.
1077. CE 2649; 8 H 186, 187 (C. Murret); CE 2648.
1078. Lee DE 2, 4; CE 1410, 1411, 1413, pp. 28–31; CE 2542, 2543, 2544, 2545.
1079. 10 H 34–37 (Bringuier).
1080. Id. at 37–38; CE 1413, pp. 19–27. He had probably passed out such leaflets on another occasion in June, near a U.S. naval vessel.   CE 1412.
1081. CE 826, pp. 5–10; 10 H 53–57 (Francis L. Martello).

1082. 10 H 90 (Vincent T. Lee) ; 1 H 64-65 (Marina Oswald) ; 5 H 402-403 (Marina Oswald).
1083. CE 1413, pp. 19, 21, 34 ; Lee DE 6 ; 10 H 38-39 (Bringuier).
1084. 1 H 24 (Marina Oswald).
1085. 10 H 39-41 (Bringuier), 64-66 (Charles Hall Steele, Jr.) ; Garner DE 1 ; Frank Pizzo DE 453A, 453B ; Bringuier DE 1, 2.
1086. 11 H 474-476 (Rachal).
1087. 10 H 41-42 (Bringuier) ; 1 H 25 (Marina Oswald).
1088. 11 H 158-165 (William Kirk Stuckey).
1089. Id. at 166-169 ; 10 H 42-43 (Bringuier).
1090. 11 H 169-171 (Stuckey) ; Stuckey DE 3 ; Bringuier DE 3, 4.
1091. 11 H 171 (Stuckey).
1092. 11 H 162, 168-171 (Stuckey).
1093. Lee DE 1, 2, 4, 5, 6, 7.
1094. Arnold Johnson DE 4.
1095. Arnold Johnson DE 4-A.
1096. Lee DE 4, 5, 6, 7.
1097. 3 H 4-7 (R. Paine) ; 1 H 26 (Marina Oswald) ; CE 1929, p. 193.
1098. 1 H 26 (Marina Oswald) ; 3 H 9 (R. Paine).
1099. 1 H 22-23, 37, 46-47 (Marina Oswald) ; CE 1404, pp. 451-453.
1100. CE 2478 ; CE 1143, p. 1 ; CE 2119, pp. 20-21 ; CE 2120 ; CE 2563, p. 1.
1101. See ch. VI, p. 314, supra.
1102. See CE 2481, 2478 ; app. XIV, p. 745, infra.
1103. CE 2124, p. 383 ; CE 2125, pp. 475, 477-478 ; CE 2479 ; cf. 10 H 276-277 (Jesse J. Garner).
1104. 1 H 37, 45 (Marina Oswald).
1105. Id. at 23. CE 1156, p. 444.
1106. 10 H 276 (Jesse J. Garner), 274 (Mrs. Jesse Garner).
1107. 11 H 460-464 (Eric Rogers).
1108. CE 2126.
1109. 10 H 276 (Jesse J. Garner).
1110. CE 116.
1111. CE 18.
1112. CE 1969 ; CE 946 ; 11 H 217 (Pamela Mumford) ; CE 2121, p. 39.
1113. CE 93, 986, 2121, p. 39 ; CE 2564.
1114. CE 2121, p. 39.
1115. 1 H 25 (Marina Oswald) ; CE 2121, p. 39 ; CE 93.
1116. 1 H 24-25 (Marina Oswald).
1117. CE 2121, p. 39.
1118. Ibid.
1119. CE 93.
1120. CE 126
1121. Rogers DE 1.
1122. 11 H 214 (John Bryan and Meryl McFarland), 221-222 (Mumford) ; CE 2127, p. 1 ; CE 2128, 2121, pp. 8, 9, 55, 119 ; CE 2129, pp. 18-19 ; CE 2532, pp. 12-13 ; 2460, p. 5 : but see 11 H 462-463 (Rogers).
1123. When he picked up the check, he apparently also filed a change of mailing address. CE 2131, 2476.
1124. App. XIV, p. 745, infra ; but cf. CE 2481.
1125. 1 H 27 (Marina Oswald).
1126. CE 2533.
1127. 11 H 179-180 (Estelle Twiford), 179 (Horace E. Twiford) ; CE 2533 ; CE 2961, 2962.
1128. 11 H 179 (H. Twiford), 179-180 (E. Twiford).
1129. Ibid.
1130. CE 2134.
1131. 11 H 179-180 (E. Twiford), 179 (H. Twiford).
1132. Ibid. ; 11 H 179-180 (E. Twiford).

1133. CE 2137, pp. 8-12 ; CE 2138, p. 15.
1134. CE 2137, pp. 14-15, 17 ; CE 2138, p. 3.
1135. Id. at 12-14.
1136. 11 H 214 (McFarland).
1137. Ibid. ; CE 1143, p. 4 ; CE 2191, pp. 5-7 ; CE 2534.
1138. 11 H 214-215 (McFarland) ; CE 2534.
1139. CE 2193, pp. 1-2 ; CE 2123, 2566, pp. 2-3.
1140. CE 2463, pp. 10-12 ; CE 2566, p. 2.
1141. 11 H 214-215 (McFarland), 215-224 (Mumford).
1142. Id. at 220.
1143. CE 2195.
1144. 11 H 217-218 (Mumford) ; CE 2121, pp. 114-115.
1145. 11 H 219 (Mumford) ; CE 116.
1146. CE 2566, p. 2.
1147. 11 H 220 (Mumford), 214-215 (McFarland).
1148. CE 2121, p. 54 ; CE 2120, 3073, p. 7.
1149. CE 1400, 2121, pp. 46, 54, 59 ; CE 2488.
1150. CE 2121, p. 59.
1151. Id. at 47 ; CE 2444, p. 53 ; CE 2480.
1152. CE 2121, pp. 47. 54.
1153. CE 2568.
1154. CE 1969, 2121, p. 1.
1155. CE 18, p. 54 ; CE 2567.
1156. CE 2121, p. 39 ; CE 3073, p. 7.
1157. CE 2564 ; see CE 93.
1158. CE 2445, p. 2.
1159. CE 2121, p. 39.
1160. CE 2764, 3073, p. 6 ; see 1 H 28 (Marina Oswald).
1161. CE 2764.
1162. CE 15. He appears to have attempted to record Kostikov's name in his guide book. CE 2486.
1163. 1 H 28 (Marina Oswald).
1164. CE 2121, p. 39 ; CE 2449.
1165. CE 2121, p. 39.
1166. Id. at 39-40 ; CE 2120 ; cf. CE 2445.
1167. CE 2121, p. 40 ; CE 2465 ; CE 18, p. 54 ; CE 2445, p. 2 ; CE 2120.
1168. CE 2121, p. 39.
1169. CE 2445, p. 3 ; CE 2121, p. 40.
1170. Confidential information.
1171. 1 H 27-28, 50 (Marina Oswald) ; CE 1156, p. 445.
1172. 3 H 13-18, 51-52 (R. Paine) ; 9 H 395 (R. Paine).
1173. CE 15.
1174. CE 2121, pp. 55, 57.
1175. Id. at 57.
1176. Id. at 54-55, 57. One Juarez has said he saw Oswald talking to some Cubans, but an intensive investigation indicates that this is a case of mistaken identity. CE 2450, 2451, 2569, 2570, 2571, 2572, 2573, 2574, 2575, 2787, 3095.
1177. CE 2450.
1178. CE 1400. Oswald marked them on his map of Mexico City. CE 2488, p. 5.
1179. See CE 1166, pp. 6-8 ; CE 2489 ; 1 H 27 (Marina Oswald) ; CE 3073, p. 8.
1180. Ibid. Oswald marked several museums, art galleries, and parks on his guide map, CE 2488, pp. 1-2 ; see CE 1166, pp. 9-10 ; CE 2576, 3073, pp. 1, 6, 10.
1181. 1 H 27 (Marina Oswald) ; CE 3073, p. 10.
1182. CE 2486, 3073, pp. 4-5.
1183. CE 116, 2488, p. 2 ; CE 3073, pp. 1, 6.
1184. CE 2121, pp. 116-118.
1185. CE 2190 ; see CE 1166, p. 13.
1186. CE 2484.
1187. 1 H 27 (Marina Oswald) ; CE 3042, p. 59 ; CE 2484, 2121, pp. 124-128.

1188. Ibid.
1189. CE 2467, pp. 152, 156–157; see also 1 H 27 (Marina Oswald).
1190. Ibid; CE 116.
1191. See CE 1400.
1192. CE 2530, 2531, 2537, 2536, 2458, 2121, pp. 64–69; CE 1166, pp. 2–3; CE 2469, pp. 1–2; CE 2538, 2532, p. 5; CE 2638, 3073, pp. 2, 3.
1193. CE 2639, 2539, p. 1.
1194. CE 2452, 2121, pp. 99–103; CE 2470, 2471, pp. 1–2; CE 2527.
1195. CE 2121, pp. 99–105; CE 2535, pp. 1–2; CE 1143, p. 3.
1196. CE 2540, p. 9.
1197. CE 2121, pp. 56, 119.
1198. Id. at 72–78; CE 2459, 2460, 2535, pp. 10–11.
1199. CE 2121, pp. 61, 76; CE 2456, p. 3; CE 2459, pp. 2–3; CE 2460, p. 6; CE 2532, p. 9.
1200. CE 2121, p. 61; CE 2456, p. 4.
1201. 1 H 70 (Marina Oswald).
1202. CE 2456, p. 5.
1203. CE 2461.
1204. CE 2129, p. 6; CE 2121, pp. 8, 60, 75–77.
1205. CE 2577, 2121, pp. 61, 77–78; CE 2130, 2456, p. 6.
1206. CE 2129, p. 2; CE 2130, 2577.
1207. Burcham DE 1.
1208. Cunningham DE 1–A; 11 H 478 (Cunningham).
1209. Hulen DE 7, 11; 10 H 281–283 (Hulen), 285–290 (Barnhorst); 1 H 27 (Marina Oswald).
1210. 11 H 479 (Gangl); Gangl DE 1.
1211. 3 H 26, 28–29 (R. Paine); 1 H 27 (Marina Oswald).
1212. 3 H 26–31, 33 (R. Paine); 1 H 27–28, 50 (Marina Oswald).
1213. Id. at 50.
1214. Id. at 28.
1215. 3 H 30–31 (R. Paine).
1216. Id at 31.
1217. 10 H 293 (Gladys J. Johnson).
1218. 6 H 401–402 (Mary E. Bledsoe).
1219. Id. at 404; 10 H 139–140 (R. L. Adams); 11 H 480–481 (R. L. Adams).
1220. 6 H 404–406 (Bledsoe).
1221. Id. at 404; 3 H 45 (R. Paine); CE 1401 p. 262.
1222. CE 994, p. 38.
1223. 6 H 405–406 (Bledsoe).
1224. 3 H 12, 32, 35 (R. Paine).
1225. Id. at 5, 33–34.
1226. 3 H 32 (R. Paine); 9 H 428–429 (R. Paine).
1227. 6 H 407 (Bledsoe).
1228. 10 H 294 (G. Johnson); 6 H 436–437 (E. Roberts).
1229. 3 H 38–39 (R. Paine); 10 H 294 (G. Johnson).
1230. 6 H 437 (Roberts).
1231. CE 2642.
1232. 2 H 418–419 (M. Paine); 3 H 117–119 (R. Paine); 9 H 455 (M. Paine); 7 H 293 (Holmes).
1233. 3 H 33–34 (R. Paine); 1 H 29 (Marina Oswald); CE 994, p. 38.
1234. 3 H 34 (R. Paine); CE 994, p. 38; 3 H 213 (Roy S. Truly).

1235. 3 H 34–35 (R. Paine); CE 994, p. 38.
1236. 3 H 214, 216 (Truly); CE 1949, p. 4.
1237. 3 H 37 (R. Paine); CE 994, p. 38.
1238. 3 H 214–216 (Truly).
1239. 1 H 68 (Marina Oswald).
1240. 3 H 214–216 (Truly); 6 H 328 (William H. Shelley).
1241. 3 H 217–218 (Truly); 6 H 375 (Jack E. Dougherty), 394 (Geneva L. Hine), 382–383 (Eddie Piper); 2 H 219 (Buell W. Frazier).
1242. Id. at 216.
1243. Id. at 217.
1244. 3 H 40 (R. Paine); 1 H 52 (Marina Oswald); CE 994, p. 40.
1245. 3 H 39 (R. Paine); 1 H 54 (Marina Oswald).
1246. 3 H 39–40 (R. Paine); CE 994, p. 40.
1247. Ibid.
1248. 3 H 40 (R. Paine).
1249. Arnold Johnson DE 7.
1250. 1 H 55 (Marina Oswald); 2 H 407–408 (M. Paine); 9 H 462–468 (Raymond F. Krystinik).
1251. Ibid; 2 H 407–412 (M. Paine).
1252. 9 H 465 (Krystinik).
1253. 1 H 54–55 (Marina Oswald); 3 H 40–41 (R. Paine).
1254. Holmes DE 1.
1255. 3 H 41 (R. Paine).
1256. 4 H 441–448 (James A. Hosty), 432–440 (John L. Quigley); see CE 834, p. 8; see generally ch. VIII, pp. 434–440. supra.
1257. 4 H 449–454 (Hosty); 1 H 48, 56–57 (Marina Oswald); 3 H 92, 96–104 (R. Paine).
1258. 1 H 48 (Marina Oswald).
1259. 3 H 101–102 (R. Paine); 1 H 57 (Marina Oswald).
1260. 3 H 102 (R. Paine).
1261. CE 15.
1262. 1 H 48–49 (Marina Oswald).
1263. 2 H 217 (Frazier).
1264. 2 H 514 (R. Paine); 3 H 41 (R. Paine); 11 H 153–154 (R. Paine); 1 H 62 (Marina Oswald).
1265. Id. at 54, 63; 2 H 515–516 (R. Paine); 3 H 41 (R. Paine).
1266. 1 H 53, 54, 63, 65–66 (Marina Oswald); 3 H 43–46 (R. Paine). Mrs. Paine thought she had placed the call to Oswald on Monday, November 18. Id. at 43.
1267. 3 H 45–46 (R. Paine).
1268. 2 H 222–223 (Frazier).
1269. 2 H 508 (R. Paine); 3 H 46, 56–57 (R. Paine); 9 H 414 (R. Paine); 1 H 65 (Marina Oswald).
1270. 2 H 508 (R. Paine); 3 H 46 (R. Paine); 1 H 64–65 (Marina Oswald).
1271. Id. at 65.
1272. 3 H 46–47, 56–60 (R. Paine); 1 H 65 (Marina Oswald).
1273. Id. at 65–66; but see 3 H 47 (R. Paine).
1274. 1 H 66 (Marina Oswald); 3 H 60 (R. Paine); 9 H 418 (R. Paine).
1275. 3 H 47–49 (R. Paine); 1 H 66 (Marina Oswald).

APPENDIX XIV

1. Martin Isaacs DE 1, but see footnote 9.
2. Ibid., 1 H 318 (Robert Oswald).
3. 1 H 132 (Marguerite Oswald).
4. Isaacs DE 1; CE 1159.
5. Isaacs DE 1; CE 1159.
6. CE 1159; 1 H 3 (Marina Oswald).
7. Isaacs DE 1.
8. 8 H 336 (Pauline Bates).
9. 1 H 318 (R. Oswald). Robert Oswald testified that Lee paid him back a little less than $100 upon Lee's arrival.

If this is so, Lee Harvey Oswald had more money than he reported to the Welfare Department when he arrived in New York. The $30 figure is an estimate based upon reported funds available to Lee Harvey Oswald when he arrived in Fort Worth and upon Robert Oswald's statement as to later payments.

10. CE 1165, 1173.
11. 1 H 318 (R. Oswald).
12. CE 1170, 1171, see footnote 56. There is no record of initial subscription. This represents an estimate of cost based on subscription rates in July 1962.
13. CE 1165, 1173.
14. CE 1120.
15. 1 H 318 (R. Oswald).
16. 10 H 230 (Chester Riggs).
17. CE 1172.
18. Estimate based on approximate time Oswalds resided on Mercedes Ave., Fort Worth in August. 4 H 419 (John W. Fain) ; 1 H 134 (Marguerite Oswald).
19. CE 1165, 1173.
20. 9 H 144 (Paul R. Gregory) ; 2 H 340 (Peter P. Gregory) ; 5 H 419 (Marina Oswald).
21. 10 H 230 (C. Riggs) ; CE 1160.
22. CE 1120.
23. 1 H 318 (R. Oswald).
24. CE 1147.
25. CE 1165, 1167, 1173, 1174.
26. 8 H 372 (George H. Bouhe).
27. CE 1120.
28. 10 H 288 (Colin Barnhorst) ; 10 H 281 (Richard L. Hulen) ; CE 1160.
29. CE 1160.
30. 1 H 318 (R. Oswald).
31. Marina Oswald lived at the Hall's for part of the month. 1 H 7, 31 (Marina Oswald). She also received assistance from other people. See e.g. 11 H 119–120 (A. Kleinlerer) ; 8 H 345–346 (Clark) ; 5 H 419 (Marina Oswald) ; 1 H 8 (Marina Oswald).
32. CE 1167, 1174.
33. 10 H 238–240 (Mrs. Mahlon F. Tobias) (included $5 key deposit which was never returned).
34. 11 H 470 (Taylor).
35. CE 1120.
36. 9 H 143 (Paul R. Gregory) ; 1 H 387 (R. Oswald) ; CE 1168.
37. Marina Oswald lived with the Mellers, the Fords, and the Rays during part of this month. 2 H 299 (Ford) ; 8 H 386–387 (Meller) ; 8 H 416–417 (Ray) ; 1 H 11–12 (Marina Oswald).
38. CE 1167, 1174.
39. 10 H 240 (Tobias).
40. CE 1160.
41. CE 1120.
42. Farrell Dobbs DE 1 ; 3 H 118 (Ruth Paine).
43. CE 1167, 1174.
44. 10 H 240 (Tobias) ; CE 1160.
45. CE 1120.
46. 7 H 376 (Heinz W. Michaelis) ; Michaelis DE 2 ; CE 1137.
47. CE 1130.
48. CE 1147.
49. CE 1167, 1174.
50. 10 H 240 (Tobias) ; CE 1160.
51. 2 H 418, 9 H 455 (Michael Paine) ; 3 H 118 (R. Paine) ; CE 1145, 1172.
52. CE 1167, 1174.
53. CE 1133, 1134, 1160 ; 11 H 155 (M. Waldo George).
54. CE 1160.
55. CE 1136 ; William J. Waldman DE 7.
56. CE 1152, 1170, 1171.
57. 7 H 376–378 (Michaelis) ; Michaelis DE 5 ; CE 1137.
58. CE 1167, 1174.
59. CE 1165.

60. 11 H 155 (George) ; CE 1134.
61. 2 H 459 (R. Paine) ; CE 1168.
62. Although Oswald spent part of this month at the Murrets, 8 H 133, 139 (Lillian Murret), and Marina Oswald spent part of the time at Ruth Paine's, 2 H 457–461 (R. Paine), he left money with his wife, 3 H 9 (R. Paine).
63. CE 1161, 1175.
64. CE 1157, 1161.
65. 10 H 265, 274, 276 (Mrs. Jesse Garner) ; CE 1139.
66. Dobbs DE 2. Oswald received copies of the Militant after September 1963, but there is no record he paid for a subscription, 3 H 118, 119 (R. Paine).
67. 10 H 93 (Vincent T. Lee) ; V. T. Lee DE 3–4 ; CE 1140, 1410.
68. Although Oswald spent part of the time at the Murrets, 8 H 139 (L. Murret), and his wife spent part of the time at Ruth Paine's, 2 H 468 (R. Paine), this would be offset by the fact that Ruth Paine and her children spent time at the Oswald apartment, and the expenses involved in moving into an apartment in another city, 9 H 343 (R. Paine).
69. CE 1161, 1175.
70. See footnote 65.
71. CE 1158.
72. CE 1410, 1411.
73. CE 1176.
74. CE 1161, 1175.
75. See footnote 65.
76. CE 1411.
77. CE 1157, 1161.
78. See footnote 65.
79. CE 1177 ; V. T. Lee DE 6.
80. 10 H 64–66 (Charles H. Steele, Jr.) There is evidence that two people were handing out literature, but it is not known if both were paid $2.
81. CE 1157, 1161.
82. Although Oswald left for Mexico and his wife stayed with Ruth Paine during the latter part of the month, this is offset by additional expenses incurred in preparing for the Mexican trip.
83. Marina Oswald testified that just before she left New Orleans, her husband had told her that he had a little over $100 which would be sufficient for his Mexican trip, 1 H 27 (Marina Oswald). Later she stated he told her he had between $160–$180, CE 1156. Oswald received $33 in unemployment compensation after his wife left New Orleans. Oswald failed to pay his rent for September 9. 10 H 274–275 (Mrs. Jesse Garner).
84. CE 1146, 1166 ; 1 H 27 (Marina Oswald).
85. CE 1166.
86. CE 1156 ; 1 H 27 (Marina Oswald) ; CE 1166.
87. Marina Oswald testified that her husband returned from Mexico with about $50 or $70, 1 H 51 (Marina Oswald) ; CE 1156. She later said he had about $70.
88. CE 1157, 1165.
89. CE 1129.
90. 10 H 283 (Hulen) ; 10 H 290 (Barnhorst) ; 6 H 401 (Mary L. Bledsoe) ; 10 H 294 (Mrs. A. C. Johnson).
91. During this time Marina Oswald was living with Ruth Paine. Oswald spent weekends there also, 9 H 344 (R. Paine) ; 1 H 69–70 (Marina Oswald) ; 2 H 216, 219 (Buell W. Frazier).
92. CE 1129.
93. 10 H 294 (Mrs. Johnson).
94. CE 1152, 1178.
95. CE 1151.
96. 2 H 256 (William W. Whaley) ; 2 H 268 (Cecil J. McWatters) ; CE 1168.
97. See footnote 91.
98. CE 1148, 1155.

APPENDIX XV

1. CE 1114.
2. He had made out his application for admission on Mar. 19, 1959. See CE 228, p. 1.
3. CE 1114.
4. CE 946.
5. 5 H 262 (Richard E. Snyder).
6. 5 H 295–296.
7. 5 H 262, 288–289.
8. CE 101.
9. Oswald's appearance at the Embassy has been reconstructed from the testimony of Richard E. Snyder, 5 H 262–265, 269–270, and 287–291, and of John A. McVickar, 5 H 300–304 and 322–324, from memoranda and communications made at the time, CE 908, 909, 910, 941, and 958 and from Oswald's own notes, CE 24 and 101.
10. 5 H 300 (McVickar) ; 5 H 289 (Snyder).
11. 5 H 262 (Snyder).
12. 5 H 263 (Snyder).
13. 5 H 263 (Snyder).
14. 5 H 289 (Snyder).
15. 5 H 270 (Snyder) ; CE 101.
16. 5 H 263 ; 289–290 (Snyder).
17. 5 H 289 (Snyder) ; CE 908, p. 1 ; CE 101.
18. 5 H 289 (Snyder) ; see passport, CE 946, p. 1.
19. 5 H 263 (Snyder).
20. CE 913 ; 5 H 263, 289 (Snyder).
21. CE 908, p. 2.
22. CE 946, pp. 8–9 ; CE 908, p. 2.
23. CE 908, p. 2.
24. CE 908, p. 1.
25. CE 908, p. 2.
26. CE 908, p. 2.
27. Ibid.
28. Ibid.
29. 5 H 290 (Snyder) ; see CE 908, p. 3.
30. 5 H 264, 290–291 (Snyder).
31. CE 908, p. 2 ; CE 909, pp. 2–3 ; 5 H 264, 290–291 (Snyder).
32. 5 H 291 (Snyder) ; see CE 910.
33. 5 H 266–267 (Snyder) ; CE 910.
34. CE 908, p. 2.
35. CE 950, p. 3 ; 5 H 341 (Abram Chayes).
36. CE 910.
37. CE 2750 (see stamp) ; CE 834, p. 1.
38. CE 2752 ; and see CE 2750.
39. CE 908.
40. Id. at p. 3.
41. CE 2749 (see stamp) ; CE 834, p. 2 (FBI) ; CE 2752 and enclosure.
42. CE 910.
43. CE 916, 961.
44. Ibid. ; 5 H 347–348 (Waterman).
45. CE 909, p. 3 ; CE 911, p. 2 ; CE 920.
46. CE 919, 920.
47. CE 912.
48. CE 920.
49. CE 919.
50. CE 942, 943, 2683, 2684, 2715.
51. Ibid.
52. 11 H 444 (Johnson).
53. CE 911.
54. CE 911, p. 2 ; 11 H 446–447, 450–451 (Priscilla Johnson).
55. CE 921.
56. CE 24, entry of Jan. 4, 1960.
57. CE 985, Doc. Nos. 1(A), 2(A) and 3(A)(1).
58. CE 921 ; 5 H 274 (Snyder).
59. CE 923.
60. CE 927.
61. Ibid.
62. CE 928.
63. CE 925.
64. CE 926.
65. 5 H 348–349 (Bernice Waterman).

66. 5 H 349 (Waterman) ; CE 948, question No. 12, pp. 1–2, and regulations attached thereto.
67. CE 950, pt. 2, pp. 204 ; 5 H 317 (Chayes).
68. 5 H 80 (Knight) ; CE 950, pt. 2, pp. 3–4 ; and see CE 948, question No. 12 and all attachments thereto for a general description of the lookout card procedure.
69. CE 948, question No. 12, pp. 1–2 and regulations attached thereto.
70. CE 962 ; 5 H 348–349 (Waterman).
71. CE 963 ; 5 H 349 (Waterman).
72. CE 963, 929.
73. CE 948, question No. 13, pp. 2–3 ; 5 H 313 (Chayes).
74. CE 948, question No. 13, p. 1.
75. 5 H 349–351.
76. Passport Office Instruction No. 2300.3 (reproduced in CE 948, question No. 12).
77. 5 H 380 (Frances Knight) ; CE 948, Question 12, p. 3 ; CE 3111.
78. CE 2748.
79. CE 930.
80. See date stamped on CE 2681 and see CE 2757.
81. 5 H 276 (Snyder).
82. CE 931 ; 5 H 276–277 (Snyder).
83. 5 H 277 (Snyder).
84. CE 24, entry of Feb. 1, 1961.
85. CE 933.
86. CE 251, 940.
87. CE 932.
88. CE 940.
89. CE 1085.
90. 5 H 352–354 (Waterman).
91. Ibid ; CE 970. See CE 934.
92. CE 971, 5 H 353–354 (Waterman).
93. CE 1111 ; CE 24, entry of Apr. 31 [sic], 1961.
94. CE 936.
95. CE 252.
96. CE 937.
97. 5 H 281 (Snyder) ; CE 24, entry of July 8, 1961.
98. CE 24, entry of July 8, 1961 ; and see 1 H 96–97 (Marina Oswald), and CE 1401.
99. CE 935, p. 3
100. CE 935, pp. 1–2.
101. 5 H 281 (Snyder) ; CE 938.
102. CE 946 ; 5 H 284 (Snyder).
103. 5 H 283 (Snyder).
104. 5 H 283 (Snyder).
105. CE 947 ; 5 H 282–283, 286 (Snyder).
106. CE 938.
107. 5 H 283 (Snyder).
108. 5 H 359–360 (Waterman).
109. CE 938, pp. 3–4.
110. CE 946, p. 6 ; 5 H 284 (Snyder).
111. CE 935 ; 5 H 283–285 (Snyder).
112. CE 935, p. 3.
113. CE 935, p. 2.
114. 5 H 318–319 (McVickar).
115. CE 1122 (letter of July 15, 1961).
116. CE 979 ; 5 H 357–358 (Waterman) ; 11 H 198 (Carroll Hamilton Seeley, Jr.).
117. CE 939.
118. CE 2747.
119. CE 981 ; 5 H 361–362 (Waterman).
120. CE 253–255, 246, 249, 256, 247, 1083, and 1093 (Oswald to Embassy, from Embassy files) ; CE 1076–1082, 1086, 1088 (Embassy to Oswald, from Embassy files) ; CE 1085, 1087, 1094, 1124 ; and 1100–1106 (Embassy to Oswald, found among his effects).
121. CE 946.
122. CE 1061, 1098.
123. 5 H 283 (Snyder).
124. CE 979 ; 5 H 347, 357 (Waterman) ; CE 948, question No. 11, pp. 1–2.

125. 5 H 362 (Waterman); 5 H 286 (Snyder).

126. CE 989; 5 H 372–376 (Knight); 5 H 308–312 (Chayes).

127. Fourteenth amendment; *United States* v. *Wong Kim Ark* 169 U.S. 649 (1898).

128. 12 U.S.C., sec. 1481(a)(1).

129. See pp. 1, 2, 7, 9–12, supra.

130. 12 U.S.C., sec. 1481(a)(6).

131. 22 CFR, secs. 50.1–50.2; 8 Foreign Affairs Manual sec. 225.6.

132. CE 955; 5 H 263–265 (Snyder).

133. See pp. 2–4, supra.

134. 12 U.S.C., sec. 1481(a)(2).

135. CE 913.

136. CE 244, 913.

137. III Hackworth, "Digest of International Law," 219–220 (1942); see *Jalbuena* v. *Dulles,* 254 F. 2d 379, 381 footnote 2 (3d Cir. 1958).

138. In re Bautista, 183 f. Supp. 271, 274 (D.C. Guam, 1960); see also, Department of State to consul at Guadalajara, May 27, 1937, at 218; Department of State consular official in charge at Birmingham, May 10, 1938; Director of Consular Service to Counsel Glazbrooke, Oct. 30, 1914; Department of State to consul general in Berlin, Mar. 21, 1934; Roche, "The Loss of American Nationality—The Development of Statutory Expatriation," 99 U. Pa. L. Rev. 25, 33 (1950); III Hackworth, op. cit. supra, footnote 138, at 218–219.

139. III Hackworth, op. cit. supra, footnote at 138 at 218; In the Matter of L., 1 Dec. Imm. & Nat. Laws 317, 320, (B.I.A., 1942).

140. See e.g. CE 913.

141. 12 U.S.C., 1481(a)(4).

142. 5 H 310 (Chayes).

143. Cf. *Fletes-Mora* v. *Rogers,* 160 F. Supp. 215 (S.D. Cal. 1958); *Kenji Kamada* v. *Dulles,* 145 F. Supp. 457, 459 (N.D. Cal. 1956) (both arising under sec. 401 of the Nationality Act of 1940); Roche, supra, footnote 138, at 51.

144. *Insogna* v. *Dulles* 116 F. Supp. 473 (D.D.C. 1953); *Stipa* v. *Dulles,* 233 F. 2d 551 (3d Cir. 1956).

145. 5 H 304–306, 318–319 (McVickar).

146. CE 944, 959.

147. CE 944.

148. CE 945; 5 H 305 (McVickar).

149. CE 944; 5 H 305 (McVickar).

150. 1 H 89–90, 97; 5 H 607–608 (Marina Oswald).

151. CE 944.

152. 8 U.S.C., sec. 1155 (1953).

153. 8 U.S.C., sec. 1182(a)(28)(C); 8 U.S.C., sec. 1182(a)(28)(I) (1953).

154. 8 U.S.C., sec. 1182(a)(15) (1953).

155. 8 U.S.C., sec. 1253(g).

156. CE 950, pt. IV, pp. 3–5; 5 H 339–340 (Chayes).

157. CE 944.

158. See CE 2746.

159. 11 H 184–185 (Virginia James); CE 2745 (code phrase used).

160. CE 190, 193, 247, 256, 1081, 1093, 1100, 1101, 1102, 1104, 1124; CE 2692.

161. CE 2740, 2742, 2743, 2744.

162. CE 1095, pp. 1–2.

163. CE 2653 (taken from the Immigration and Naturalization Service file on Marina Oswald, p. 17 of CD 363); CE 196.

164. 8 U.S.C., sec. 1155; 8 CFR, sec. 9.5 a, b.

165. CE 1073.

166. CE 1072.

167. CE 1073.

168. CE 1071.

169. CE 1069, 1070, 2751.

170. CE 1070, pp. 3–4.

171. CE 1070, p. 3.

172. CE 1070.

173. CE 1068.

174. Ibid.

175. Ibid.

176. CE 1067.

177. Ibid.

178. CE 1121.

179. CE 1066.

180. CE 1055, 1066, and see also **11 H** 185–188 (James).

181. CE 1065.

182. Ibid.

183. CE 1064.

184. CE 249; see also CE 1103 (the notice itself).

185. CE 2735.

186. CE 1095.

187. CE 1096.

188. See CE 1095, p. 1, and CE 2734.

189. 11 H 186 (James).

190. CE 1123, p. 1.

191. CE 2741.

192. CE 1123, p. 2.

193. James DE 6.

194. CE 1777; James DE 4.

195. James DE 5.

196. James DE 7.

197. CE 2653, 2654, 2689, 2690, 2702, 2704, 2705.

198. 8 U.S.C., sec. 1155.

199. CE 1070, pp. 3–4.

200. See CE 1073.

201. 8 U.S.C., sec. 1182(a)(15).

202. 22 CFR, sec. 42.91(a)(15) (1963 Supp.).

203. 8 U.S.C., sec. 1182(a)(28)(I) (1953).

204. CE 944; 5 H 607–608.

205. CE 950, pt. 4, pp. 203.

206. 1 H 89–90, 97; 5 H 607–608 H (Marina Oswald).

207. 5 H 321 (McVickar); Cf. *Galvan* v. *Press,* 347 U.S. 522, 527 (1954); *Rowoldt* v. *Perfetto,* 355 U.S. 115, 120 (1957) (cases arising under sec. 22 of the Internal Security Act of 1950 as amended in 1951).

208. Immigration and Nationality Act, sec. 212(a)(19); 8 U.S.C., sec. 1182(a)(19) (1953).

209. See generally, Gordon and Rosenfield, "Immigration Law and Procedure," 229, 424–427 (1959); Appleman, "Misrepresentation in Immigration Law: Materiality." 22 Fed. B.J. 267 (1962).

210. *Langhammer* v. *Hamilton,* 295 F. 2d 642, 648 (1st Cir. 1961); see also *Chaunt* v. *United States,* 364 U.S. 350, 355 (1960) (denaturalization proceeding).

211. E.g., *Calvillo* v. *Robinson,* 271 F. 2d 249 (7th Cir. 1959).

212. Visa Office Bulletin 90, Mar. 2, 1962.

213. CE 950, pt. 4, p. 4.

214. Ibid.

215. Operation Instructions of the Immigration and Naturalization Service 205.3. (This revised instruction was effective Feb. 15, 1962–June 30, 1962. Other versions which may have been considered during Oswald's case were different only in irrelevant respects.)

216. 22 CFR, 42, 120 (1964 Supp.).

217. 22 CFR., sec. 42.120 (1964 Supp.). Procedural note 2 (reproduced in CE 950, pt. 4, p. 5).

218. 11 H 184, 186, 190–191 (James).

219. CE 950, pt. 4, p. 10; 11 H 190–191 (James).

220. CE 1058, pp. 1–2.

221. CE 1058, p. 11.

222. Id. at 4.

223. Id. at 5.

224. Id. at 6–11.

225. Id. at 2.

226. CE 246.

227. CE 1102.

228. CE 189, 2660, 2731.

229. CE 1138, 2660, 2680, 2760.

230. CE 223.
231. CE 197, 1086.
232. CE 2737, 2738, 2739.
233. CE 2736.
234. CE 1098.
235. CE 950, pt. 5, pp. 1–2. E.g., 60 Stat. 452, 79th Cong., 2d sess. (1946); 75 Stat. 546, 87th Cong., 1st sess. (1961).
236. CE 950, pt. 5, pp. 1–2. E.g., H. Rept. 442, 87th Cong., 1st sess. (1961) 4; H. Rept. 1996, 87th Cong., 2d sess. (1962) 4; H. Rept. 388, 88th Cong., 1st sess. (1963) 4.
237. CE 950, pt. 5, exhibit 2.
238. 7 Foreign Affairs Manual sec. 423, 2–1.
239. 7 Foreign Affairs Manual, sec. 423, 1–2.
240. CE 950, pt. 5, p. 3.
241. 7 Foreign Affairs Manual sec. 423, 3–2.
242. 7 Foreign Affairs Manual sec. 423, 3–5; CE 223, 2660, 2766.
243. 7 Foreign Affairs Manual sec. 423, 3–3.
244. See supra, p. 758; cf. 7 Foreign Affairs Manual sec. 423, 7–1.
245. CE 950, pt. 5, p. 6; 7 Foreign Affairs Manual sec. 423.5; CE 950 (repatriation loan, p. 7); 7 Foreign Affairs Manual sec. 423.6.
246. CE 948, question No. 13, p. 3.
247. CE 1098.
248. CE 948, question No. 13, pp. 3–4.
249. CE 1099, 1401.
250. CE 29, 946, 1099.
251. CE 1099.
252. See generally CE 834 (communications to FBI) and CE 2752 (communications to CIA).
253. CE 1059.
254. CE 1060, 1776.
255. CE 2657.
256. CE 1120.
257. CE 781, 952, 1969.
258. CE 781.
259. CE 781.
260. CE 952; 5 H 335 (Chayes).
261. CE 1969.
262. CE 2754, 2755; and see CE 952 (all applications that were made on June 24 for New Orleans in same teletype as Oswald's were authorized within 24 hours).
263. CE 948, question No. 1; 5 H 335 (Chayes). The accuracy of their statement was confirmed, see CE 1057.
264. 5 H 334–335 (Chayes).
265. CE 950, pt. 2, p. 8.
266. CE 948, question No. 13, pp. 1–3.
267. Id. at question No. 13, pp. 3–4.
268. *Kent* v. *Dulles*, 357 U.S. 116 (1958).
269. *Aptheker* v. *Secretary of State*, 378 U.S. 500 (1964).
270. 64 Stat. 993; 50 U.S.C. 785.
271. 22 CFR 51.135 (1964 Supp.).
272. See ch. VI, pp. 287–290.
273. 66 Stat. 190 (1952); 8 U.S.C. sec. 1185(b).

274. Proclamation No. 2914 (Dec. 16, 1950), 64 Stat. A454; Proclamation No. 2974 (Apr. 18, 1952), set out preceding 50 U.S.C. app. 1; Proclamation No. 3004 (Jan. 21, 1953), 18 Fed. Reg. 489.
275. 22 CFR sec. 51.136 (1964 Supp.).
276. CE 948, question No. 17; 5 H 327–328, 337 (Chayes).
277. 5 H 333 (Chayes).
278. CE 2750; Folsom DE 1.
279. CE 834, pp. 1–2; CE 2749, 2750; 5 H 333 (Chayes).
280. 5 H 333 (Chayes) and see 11 H 200 (Seeley) and 5 H 383 (Knight).
281. Hearings before the Senate Foreign Relations Committee on Department of State Passport Policies, 85th Cong., 1st sess., pp. 38–39 (1957).
282. 11 H 186–187 (James); 5 H 332 (Chayes); CE 950 (Repatriation Loan, p. 3); see Comment, "Passport Refusals for Political Reasons: Constitutional Issues and Judicial Review," 61 Yale L.J. 171, 174–178 (1952), for examples of passport refusals prior to *Kent* v. *Dulles*.
283. 357 U.S. 116 (1958).
284. 357 U.S. 144 (1958).
285. 357 U.S. 116, 125–126.
286. Hearings before the Senate Committee on Foreign Relations on S. 2770, et al., 85th Cong., 2d sess., p. 35 (1958); id. at 41 (Roderic O'Connor, Administrator, Bureau of Security and Consular Affairs of the Department of State); id. at 22; hearings before the Senate Committee on Foreign Relations on S. 806 et al. 86th Cong., 1st sess., p. 58 (1959); see also testimony of John W. Hanes, Jr., Administrator, Bureau of Security and Consular Affairs, Department of State; Hearings before a special subcommittee of the Senate Committee on Government Operations on S. 2095, 86th Cong., 1st sess. 157 (1959); compare id. at 369. The regulation was reenacted in 1962. 22 CFR sec. 51.136 (1964 Supp.).
287. CE 949; 5 H 327–328, 331–332 (Chayes); 5 H 379–380 (Knight).
288. 5 H 327–329, 333 (Chayes); id. at 338–339; CE 2756, attachment pp. 2–3. However, the Department had stamped Oswald's passport valid for direct return to the United States only, prior to granting him a repatriation loan. CE 946, p. 6, and 5 H 284 (Snyder).
289. 5 H 327–329, 333 (Chayes).
290. Copy of communication cannot be shown for security reasons.
291. CE 948, question No. 16.
292. 11 H 201–203 (Carroll Hamilton Seeley, Jr.) 11 H 191–193 (James L. Ritchie); CE 948, question No. 16.
293. CE 948, question No. 16; see 5 H 382–383 (Knight).
294. 11 H 482 (James D. Crowley).
295. CE 2688; cf. 5 H 278, 280, 288.
296. James DE 9.

APPENDIX XVI

1. See also CE 1286.
2. See CE 1290.
3. CE 1254; CE 1297, p. 1.
4. See Mrs. Alice Nichols DE 5355, p. 285; CE 1234, 1274, 1654.
5. C. Ray Hall DE 2, pp. 13, 16; C. Ray Hall DE 1; CE 1322, p. 748.
6. CE 1232.
7. CE 1181.
8. But cf. Sam Ruby DE 1, p. 185.

9. 15 H 15 (Hyman Rubenstein); CE 1252; CE 1281, p. 20; CE 1285.
10. See generally CE 1283, 1284.
11. See CE 1186.
12. CE 1254; see 14 H 439 (Eva Grant).
13. 1254; see 14 H 488 (Sam Ruby).
14. 14 H 366 (Earl Ruby); but see CE 1286.
15. 15 H 276 (Eileen Kaminsky); CE 1698, p. 1.

16. See CE 1281, p. 20; cf. 15 H 19 (Rubenstein) and CE 1297, p. 3, with CE 1185.

17. CE 1283; see 15 H 14 (Rubenstein).

18. CE 1283; cf. 15 H 14 (Rubenstein).

19. Id. at 14–15; CE 1297, pp. 3–4.

20. 15 H 18 (Rubenstein); see 14 H 439 (Grant); CE 1281, pp. 20, 42; CE 1297, p. 3.

21. 15 H 15 (Rubenstein); cf. CE 1281, pp. 11, 20.

22. See CE 1284; 14 H 437–438 (Grant); 15 H 17 (Rubenstein).

23. CE 1281, p. 20.

24. 15 H 15 (Rubenstein); cf. CE 1283.

25. See CE 1283.

26. See CE 1281, pp. 11–12.

27. 14 H 438–439 (Grant).

28. CE 1284; see CE 1281, pp. 11, 20; cf. CE 1238.

29. See CE 1252; CE 1281, pp. 11, 20; CE 1284, 1285, p. 2; see also 15 H 2, 3 (Rubenstein).

30. CE 1281, p. 11.

31. CE 1284; CE 1281, p. 11.

32. See CE 1281, pp. 11, 14, 20, 23; 15 H 17–18 (Rubenstein); 14 H 418 (Earl Ruby); 14 H 285 (Kaminsky).

33. See 15 H 8, 19–20 (Rubenstein).

34. CE 1185.

35. CE 1290.

36. CE 1185.

37. 14 H 366 (Earl Ruby).

38. 14 H 441 (Grant).

39. 14 H 367 (Earl Ruby).

40. 15 H 18 (Rubenstein).

41. CE 1256.

42. 14 H 439 (Grant); CE 1281, p. 11; see CE 1297, pp. 3, 8.

43. CE 1281, p. 21.

44. Id. at 42; see also 15 H 18–19 (Rubenstein).

45. CE 1291, p. 1.

46. CE 1297, p. 2; CE 1291, pp. 4–5.

47. CE 1297, p. 13; see CE 1291, pp. 5–6.

48. CE 1291, pp. 6–7.

49. CE 1297, p. 3; CE 1291, p. 1.

50. CE 1297, p. 1.

51. CE 1291, p. 4; see CE 1297, p. 2; see also id. at 7.

52. CE 1297, p. 9; see CE 1291, p. 2.

53. CE 1291, p. 2; see CE 1297, p. 9.

54. CE 1291, p. 2; see CE 1297, p. 22.

55. CE 1297, pp. 11, 16; CE 1291, p. 3.

56. CE 1291, p. 4; see CE 1297, p. 7.

57. CE 1291, p. 4.

58. CE 1297, p. 2; see CE 1291, p. 5.

59. CE 1291, p. 6.

60. CE 1254, 1286.

61. CE 1254; CE 1291, p. 1; see 14 H 367 (Earl Ruby).

62. CE 1254, 1255.

63. CE 1256.

64. C. Ray Hall DE 3, p. 12; 15 H 276–277 (Kaminsky).

65. 14 H 366–367 (Earl Ruby).

66. 15 H 9–10 (Rubenstein); 15 H 277–278 (Kaminsky); CE 1281, pp. 11–12.

67. Id. at 12.

68. CE 1188.

69. CE 1281, p. 23.

70. 15 H 19 (Rubenstein).

71. CE 1281, pp. 11, 13, 20, 23.

72. Id. at 3–8.

73. Id. at 35.

74. Id. at 43.

75. Id. at 42–44; see also id. at 40–41.

76. Id. at 28.

77. Id. at 36, 34.

78. Id. at 47–48.

79. CE 1283, 1284; cf. p. 780 supra.

80. CE 1238.

81. 15 H 19–20 (Rubenstein).

82. 14 H 120 (Alice Nichols); see 15 H 278 (Kaminsky).

83. CE 1253.

84. CE 1290.

85. See CE 1297, pp. 17, 22, 26.

86. See CE 1290; cf. CE 1202, and Earl Ruby DE 4, p. 174, with CE 1276.

87. See 15 H 10 (Rubenstein); 14 H 439 (Grant); 14 H 416, 420 (Earl Ruby); Sam Ruby DE 1, p. 185; C. Ray Hall DE 2, p. 13; C. Ray Hall DE 1; CE 1185.

88. See CE 1290.

89. See 15 H 10 (Rubenstein); CE 1297, pp. 2, 8.

90. CE 1297, pp. 12, 17; see CE 1291, p. 4.

91. 15 H 18 (Rubenstein); 14 H 418 (Earl Ruby); see 15 H 284–285 (Kaminsky).

92. 14 H 418 (Earl Ruby).

93. See 15 H 18 (Rubenstein).

94. 15 H 10 (Rubenstein); Sam Ruby DE 1, p. 185; C. Ray Hall DE 1; CE 1195, 1197, 1200, 1282.

95. 15 H 26 (Rubenstein); C. Ray Hall DE 1; CE 1193, 1195, 1204, 1282.

96. 15 H 12 (Rubenstein).

97. 15 H 533–534 (Jack Ruby).

98. See 15 H 9 (Rubenstein); CE 1254, 1255, 1699.

99. 14 H 443–445 (Grant); 15 H 21 (Rubenstein).

100. 15 H 21 (Rubenstein); 14 H 444–445 (Grant); see, e.g., CE 1193, 1194, 1195, 1196, 1197, 1200, 1202, 1205; Joseph Rossi DE 1; CE 1219.

101. Sam Ruby DE 1, p. 185; C. Ray Hall DE 3, p. 15; CE 1195, 1196, 1197, 1205, 1219; but cf. CE 1217, 1218.

102. See 15 H 11–14 (Rubenstein); CE 1193.

103. CE 1200, 1216.

104. 15 H 21 (Rubenstein); CE 1288; CE 1289, p. 4.

105. CE 1244.

106. CE 1195.

107. CE 1200, 1242.

108. CE 1194, 1197, 1246, 1289, p. 3; see also p. 781 supra.

109. CE 1267.

110. CE 1193; see also CE 1282.

111. CE 1282; CE 1289, p. 3.

112. E.g., CE 1208, 1266, 1267.

113. CE 1191.

114. See, e.g., CE 1191, 1194, 1198, 1261; cf. CE 1297, pp. 17, 23.

115. 14 H 440 (Grant).

116. CE 1191.

117. 14 H 440 (Grant).

118. 15 H 28 (Rubenstein); see, e.g., CE 1185, 1191, 1193, 1194, 1215, 1217.

119. C. Ray Hall DE 1; C. Ray Hall DE 3, p. 13; see also 14 H 44 (Grant); CE 1239.

120. See CE 1195, 1198, 1231, 1241, 1263, 1278.

121. C. Ray Hall DE 1; C. Ray Hall DE 3, p. 13.

122. See CE 1318.

123. 14 H 441–442 (Grant).

124. 14 H 441 (Grant); CE 1239.

125. 14 H 442 (Grant); see also CE 1225, 1237, p. 5; CE 1239, 1249.

126. C. Ray Hall DE 3, p. 13; see C. Ray Hall DE 1.

127. 14 H 442 (Grant).

128. C. Ray Hall DE 3, p. 13.

129. 14 H 442 (Grant); CE 1195, 1198, 1231, 1237, p. 5; CE 1239, 1249, 1263, 1323, 1324.

130. Sam Ruby DE 1, p. 185; CE 1195, 1323.

131. C. Ray Hall DE 1; CE 1239, 1249, 1263; C. Ray Hall DE 3, p. 13.

132. 14 H 442 (Grant); see also CE 1198, 1237, p. 5; CE 1263, 1278, 1324.

133. See CE 1195, 1198, 1231, 1249, 1263, 1323, 1324.

134. CE 1249.

135. CE 1195.
136. CE 1263.
137. CE 1195.
138. CE 1248.
139. Alice Nichols DE 5355, p. 285.
140. See also Sam Ruby DE 1, p. 185.
141. C. Ray Hall DE 3, p. 13.
142. See p. 783 supra.
143. CE 1281, p. 10.
144. Cf. CE 1217, with CE 1205; cf. CE 1266.
145. CE 1241.
146. See CE 1200, 1203, 1207, 1208, 1246, 1261, 1299.
147. CE 1241.
148. C. Ray Hall DE 3, p. 15; cf. C. Ray Hall DE 1.
149. See CE 1293, p. 1; CE 1292, p. 1; see also 14 H 419–420 (Earl Ruby).
150. CE 1318; see also 14 H 420 (Earl Ruby).
151. See 14 H 445 (Grant); CE 1190, 1206, 1279, 1289, pp. 2–3.
152. See CE 1236, 1279; but cf. CE 1235.
153. CE 1293, p. 4.
154. CE 1211.
155. See C. Ray Hall DE 1; CE 1190.
156. 14 H 523 (Jack Ruby); C. Ray Hall DE 1; see also Alice Nichols DE 5355, p. 285; CE 1187.
157. CE 1190, p. 1.
158. See CE 1206, 1211; 5 H 200 (Jack Ruby).
159. CE 1206, 1279.
160. CE 1279, 1289, p. 3.
161. See CE 1292, p. 3; CE 1293, p. 4.
162. See CE 1292, pp. 7–8.
163. See CE 1190, 1206, 1289, pp. 2–3; but cf. CE 1184, pp. 26–27.
164. See C. Ray Hall DE 1; C. Ray Hall DE 3, p. 13; 14 H 442 (Grant); 14 H 368 (Earl Ruby).
165. C. Ray Hall DE 3, p. 13.
166. Ibid.
167. CE 1702, p. 1; see also 14 H 443 (Grant).
168. See CE 1280.
169. CE 1702.
170. CE 1702; 14 H 443 (Grant); CE 1237, p. 8.
171. C. Ray Hall DE 3, p. 13; but cf. CE 1192.
172. CE 1274.
173. CE 1319.
174. See CE 1237, p. 8.
175. See, e.g., CE 1192, 1193, 1194, 1196, 1197, 1205, 1217, 1243, 1245, p. 44.
176. See CE 1192, 1204, 1208, 1217.
177. CE 1248.
178. CE 1245, p. 46; CE 1246, 1299; cf. CE 1205.
179. See, e.g., 14 H 409–410 (Earl Ruby); 15 H 20 (Rubenstein); CE 1192, 1203, 1208, 1246, 1289, pp. 2, 5.
180. CE 1257.
181. See CE 1289, p. 5.
182. 14 H 411 (Earl Ruby); 14 H 20 (Rubenstein); CE 1192.
183. CE 1241; CE 1289, p. 3.
184. CE 1703; see also CE 1319.
185. See 15 H 21 (Rubenstein); CE 1191, 1199, 1205, 1220, 1239, 1244, 1246.
186. See CE 1193, 1203, 1207, 1217, 1239, 1244, 1289, p. 3.
187. CE 1193.
188. CE 1299.
189. See CE 1193, 1216, 1258.
190. See CE 1193, 1196, 1200, 1201, 1202, 1203, 1207, 1208, 1241; CE 1245, p. 8; CE 1246.
191. See CE 1202, 1210, 1212, 1321.
192. See CE 1321.
193. See, e.g., 5 H 200, 204 (Jack Ruby); 15 H 21, 28–29 (Rubenstein); 14 H 443–444 (Grant); CE 1288; CE 1289, p. 3.
194. CE 1274.
195. Ibid.

196. CE 1704.
197. See CE 1296, 1705.
198. Cf. CE 1245, pp. 44–45 with p. 10 supra. Cf. CE 1245, p. 45, with the next paragraph in text, cf. CE 1245, p. 46, with p. 791 infra; see also CE 1245, p. 47.
199. 15 H 44 (Rubenstein); see also CE 1287.
200. CE 1274; see CE 1189.
201. See 14 H 366, 368–369 (Earl Ruby); 14 H 443 (Grant); 15 H 4, 44 (Rubenstein); 14 H 497–498, 502–503 (Sam Ruby).
202. CE 1189.
203. See CE 1707, pp. 2, 14–15; CE 1706, p. 15.
204. CE 1706, p. 15, insert (2) to p. 15, 16–22.
205. CE 1707, p. 2.
206. CE 1287, 1295; see also 14 H 411 (Earl Ruby).
207. CE 1295.
208. Ibid.
209. CE 1294.
210. See CE 1294, 1287.
211. See CE 1294, 1295.
212. See p. 789 supra.
213. CE 1294.
214. See 14 H 370 (Earl Ruby); 15 H 3 (Rubenstein); Sam Ruby DE 1, p. 185; but cf. C. Ray Hall DE 2, p. 16.
215. 14 H 370 (Earl Ruby).
216. Id. at 369–370.
217. Id. at 371; see CE 1268.
218. 14 H 371 (Earl Ruby).
219. Id. at 422–423.
220. Id. at 370.
221. Id. at 370, 422–423; 14 H 493 (Sam Ruby); C. Ray Hall DE 1; C. Ray Hall DE 3, p. 14; see also CE 1200, 1207, 1241.
222. See, e.g., CE 1213, 1240, 1245, p. 4; CE 1247, 1277.
223. CE 1262; see CE 1209, 1211, 1214, 1247, 1320, 1321.
224. CE 1321.
225. CE 1241; see also CE 1289, p. 5.
226. 14 H 411 (Earl Ruby).
227. CE 1708.
228. See CE 1259.
229. See CE 1245, p. 7.
230. CE 1259.
231. CE 1268.
232. Cf. 14 H 436 (Grant) with id. at 447.
233. Id. at 436, 453.
234. Id. at 453; see 15 H 22–23 (Rubenstein).
235. 14 H 449 (Grant).
236. Ibid.; 15 H 23 (Rubenstein).
237. See p. 793 infra.
238. CE 1271, p. 274.
239. C. Ray Hall DE 1; C. Ray Hall DE 3, p. 14.
240. CE 1708; see CE 1250.
241. CE 1265, 1708, 1709.
242. See 14 H 449–451 (Grant); 14 H 23–24 (Rubenstein); CE 1250, 1710, 1711, 1271, 1272, 1273, 1300.
243. CE 1271, p. 279; CE 1708, 1711.
244. See footnote 242 supra.
245. CE 1710; cf. CE 1711.
246. CE 1271, p. 274.
247. C. Ray Hall DE 2, p. 13.
248. C. Ray Hall DE 1.
249. C. Ray Hall DE 3, p. 14.
250. See p. 791 supra.
251. CE 1251; see also CE 1298.
252. CE 1184, p. 21; CE 1265; see also CE 2887.
253. CE 2416.
254. 14 H 371 (Earl Ruby); 14 H 493 (Sam Ruby).
255. 14 H 371, 423 (Earl Ruby).
256. CE 1182; cf. C. Ray Hall DE 2, p. 13.
257. CE 1708.

258. CE 1224, 1229, 1264, 1712; but cf. 15 H 516 (Stanley M. Kaufman).

259. See C. Ray Hall DE 3, p. 14; CE 1318; see also CE 1230, p. 593.

260. 14 H 453 (Grant); C. Ray Hall DE 1.

261. 14 H 453–454 (Grant).

262. See p. 791 supra.

263. 14 H 453 (Grant).

264. Id. at 454; CE 1222, 1269, 1270; see CE 1190.

265. 14 H 138–139 (Ralph Paul); see Alice Nichols DE 5355, p. 238; C. Ray Hall DE 1; cf. Ralph Paul DE 5319, p. 471.

266. See p. 788 supra.

267. 14 H 115–116 (Alice Nichols); CE 1221, 1223.

268. 14 H 116 (Alice Nichols); C. Ray Hall DE 1.

269. C Ray Hall DE 3, p. 14.

270. 14 H 117 (Alice Nichols); 14 H 417, 426 (Earl Ruby).

271. 14 H 117 (Alice Nichols); C. Ray Hall DE 1.

272. C. Ray Hall DE 1; CE 1227, 1228.

273. CE 1228; see C. Ray Hall DE 1.

274. 14 H 455 (Grant); see 15 H 220 (Joseph W. Johnson, Jr.).

275. Ibid.; 15 H 415 (Nancy Powell).

276. CE 1230, p. 593.

277. CE 1696; see C. Ray Hall DE 1, CE 1227.

278. Sam Ruby DE 1, p. 187; C. Ray Hall DE 1; CE 1538; cf. 14 H 117 (Alice Nichols); C. Ray Hall DE 3, p. 14.

279. Sam Ruby DE 1, p. 187; C. Ray Hall DE 1, p. 3; C. Ray Hall DE 3, p. 14; see 14 H 454 (Grant).

280. 14 H. 496–497 (Sam Ruby).

281. 14 H 142 (Paul); CE 1675; but see CE 1569, 1656.

282. CE 1500, 1569.

283. 14 H 382 (Earl Ruby); C. Ray Hall DE 3, p. 14; cf. CE 1500, and CE 1549, with 14 H 382–383 (Earl Ruby) and 14 H 456–457 (Grant).

284. CE 1653, 1656, 1677.

285. CE 1500, 1569; 14 H 141 (Paul).

286. 14 H 141 (Paul); see C. Ray Hall DE 1.

287. 14 H 136 (Paul); CE 1504.

288. 14 H 139, 141 (Paul).

289. Id. at 142–143.

290. See 13 H 319 (Andrew Armstrong, Jr.); 15 H 212 (Thomas S. Palmer).

291. 13 H 436 (Curtis Laverne Crafard).

292. CE 1322, pp. 744–745; see 15 H 193 (Marjorie Richey).

293. Cf. CE 1322, pp. 12–13; 14 H 458 (Grant); 13 H 320 (Armstrong).

294. See CE 1322, pp. 12–13; 14 H 458 (Grant); 13 H 320 (Armstrong).

295. See, e.g., CE 1514, 1616, 1629, 1630, 1631, 1634.

296. E.g., 15 H 414, 416–417 (Powell); 13 H 134 (Armstrong); 15 H 219, 221–222 (J. Johnson); 14 H 642 (Kay Olsen); CE 1530.

297. CE 1222, 1512, 1527, 1529, 1541, 1542, 1623, 1624, 1647, 1649, 1650, 1670, 1685.

298. CE 1502, 1532, 1533, 1651, 1653, 1657.

299. CE 1517, 1561, p. 297; CE 1656, 1682, 1683, 1637; cf. CE 1565, 1681.

300. CE 1515, p. 549; CE 1635.

301. CE 1648, 1657.

302. 12 H 216 (Karen Carlin); CE 1561, p. 300; CE 1653.

303. E.g., CE 1512, 1648; CE 1653.

304. CE 1530; 15 H 413 (Powell).

305. CE 1556.

306. See CE 1548, 1568, 1676, 1633; 15 H 440 (T. M. Hansen).

307. CE 1674.

308. 14 H 616–619 (Joseph L. Peterson); CE 1564, 1566; but cf. 14 H 601–602 (Breck Wall).

309. Cf. 14 H 617 (Peterson) and CE 1564 and 1566, with 14 H 614 (Wall); see also CE 1657.

310. See CE 1514, 1554, 1672.

311. CE 1683.

312. 15 H 209 (Palmer).

313. E.g., CE 1530.

314. See 15 H 208 (Palmer).

315. Id. at 211–214; CE 1543, 1544.

316. 15 H 415–416 (Powell).

317. 14 H 459 (Grant).

318. See CE 1543, p. 191; CE 1562.

319. See 5 H 200 (Jack Ruby); 15 H 28–29 (Rubenstein); 14 H 458–460 (Grant); 13 H 500 (Crafard).

320. 15 H 209 (Palmer); see 14 H 605 (Wall).

321. 15 H 208, 214 (Palmer); 15 H 199 (Marjorie Richey); CE 1648; but cf. 15 H 415 (Powell); CE 1540, 1541, 1542.

322. CE 1261, 1521, 1522, 1523, 1524, 1525, 1526.

323. See 15 H 211 (Palmer); CE 1322, pp. 744–45.

324. See 15 H 211 (Palmer); 15 H 200 (Marjorie Richey); 15 H 410 (Powell); CE 1561, p. 297.

325. 15 H 410–411 (Powell); CE 1561, p. 301.

326. See 15 H 210–211 (Palmer); 15 H 411–412 (Powell); 15 H 199 (Marjorie Richey); CE 1561, p. 299.

327. Cf. 15 H 412 (Powell) and CE 1501, and 1557 with CE 1550, and CE 1561, p. 300.

328. See 13 H 368–369 (Armstrong); 14 H 67–68 (Crafard); 15 H 99–100 (William D. Crowe, Jr.); 15 H 200–201 (Marjorie Richey); CE 1508, 1530, 1563.

329. See 14 H 456 (Grant); 15 H 219–220 (J. Johnson); CE 1560.

330. See 15 H 518 (Kaufman); CE 1519, 1571, 1572, 1573, 1574, 1575, 1662, 1664, 1665, 1666, 1667, 1668, 1669, 1680, 1686, 1687.

331. See 12 H 184 (August M. Eberhardt); 13 H 309–311 (Armstrong); 14 H 455 (Grant); CE 1735, 1748.

332. CE 1575.

333. See 13 H 310 (Armstrong); 14 H 455 (Grant); CE 1570, 1667, 1668, 1669, 1673.

334. CE 1669.

335. See CE 1574, 1662, 1664, 1665, 1680.

336. See CE 1519, 1574, 1679,

337. See CE 1571, 1572, 1573, 1686, 1687.

338. See CE 1519.

339. See footnote 335 supra; CE 1666.

340. CE 1660, 1661.

341. See CE 1678; cf. 15 H 385 (Abraham Kleinman); CE 1218, 1226.

342. See CE 1713, p. 3; CE 1719, p. 1; see generally CE 1720.

343. CE 1539.

344. See CE 1720, 1721, 1723, 1724; cf. CE 1722, 1725, 1726.

345. See CE 1720, p. 29; CE 1727, pp. 1–4; CE 1728, p. 2.

346. CE 1727, 1728, 1729, 1730, 1731.

347. CE 1729, 1730, 1731; cf. CE 1715, 1716.

348. CE 1713, p. 3; CE 1714.

349. See CE 1713, pp. 3, 9; CE 1714 pp. 1, 3; CE 1715, pp. 1, 4; CE 1716, pp. 1, 6; CE 1717, pp. 1, 2; CE 1718, pp. 1, 3; CE 1719, pp. 1, 5.

350. CE 1713, pp. 1, 3; CE 1714, p. 1.

351. See generally CE 1720.

352. See CE 1732, 1733.

353. See CE 1727, 1729, 1730, 1731.

354. CE 1728, pp. 2, 4.
355. CE 1516.
356. CE 1619.
357. See 15 H 26 (Rubenstein) ; Alice Nichols DE 5355, p. 287 ; CE 1613.
358. CE 1552 ; see CE 1742.
359. CE 1531.
360. Sam Ruby DE 1, p. 187 ; 14 H 391 (Earl Ruby) ; 15 H 27 (Rubenstein) ; CE 1478, p. 4.
361. See Sam Ruby DE 1, p. 187 ; CE 1555, 1638, 1639, 1640, 1641, 1642, 1694 ; cf. CE 1720, p. 19.
362. 5 H 202 (Jack Ruby) ; C. Ray Hall DE 3, p. 15 ; CE 1688, 1689.
363. CE 1534 ; cf. CE 1746.
364. 14 H 129–130 (Robert C. Patterson) ; CE 1503, 1507.
365. 15 H 224 (Edward J. Pullman) ; see also CE 1507.
366. 13 H 416–417 (Crafard) ; CE 1535, 1606.
367. See 13 H 386–388 (Bertha Cheek) ; 14 H 457–458 (Grant) ; 15 H 230 (Pullman) ; 15 H 237–238 (Joseph P. Rossi) ; CE 1509, 1551, 1617, 1643, 1644.
368. 15 H 24–25 (Rubenstein).
369. Id. at 25 ; 14 H 390–391 (Earl Ruby).
370. CE 1567, 1695 ; see 15 H 237 (Rossi).
371. 15 H 224–227 (Pullman) ; 15 H 413 (Powell).
372. See CE 1528.
373. See CE 1607, 1608, 1609, 1610, 1611, 1612.
374. CE 1233, 1654.
375. CE 1518.
376. CE 1510.
377. Ibid. ; CE 1233.
378. CE 1233.
379. Ibid.
380. See, e.g., CE 1505, 1537. 1632, 1736.
381. 4 H 167, 191–192 (Jesse Curry).
382. See 4 H 240 (J. W. Fritz) ; 12 H 193–195 (Eberhardt) ; 14 H 626 (Harry N. Olsen) ; Nancy Powell DE 3 ; CE 1180, 1224, 1511, pp. 152–153 ; CE 1512, 1542, 1592, 1615, 1621, 1622, 1632, 1646, 1735, 1743, 1744, 1745, 1748, 1749.
383. See, e.g., CE 1229, 1547, 1549, 1620, 1648, 1736, p. 2 ; Pullman DE 1.
384. 13 H 324 (Armstrong) ; see C. Ray Hall DE 3, p. 17.
385. 13 H 434 (Crafard) ; 14 H 213–214 (George Senator) ; Pullman DE 1 ; C. Ray Hall DE 3, p. 17 ; CE 1502, 1663.
386. See 14 H 213–214 (Senator) ; 15 H 228 (Pullman) ; Pullman DE 1 ; C. Ray Hall DE 3, p. 17 ; CE 1505, 1513 ; CE 1515, p. 551 ; CE 1632, 1636, 1646 ; CE 1659, p. 198 ; CE 1663, 1739, 1741, 1744, 1747, 1749.
387. See CE 1615, 1636, 1684, 1740.
388. See 13 H 193 (Eberhardt) ; 14 H 485 (Grant).
389. 13 H 193 (Eberhardt) ; 15 H 447–448 (Hansen) ; CE 1592, 1646, 1736, 2325.
390. See 14 H 626 (Harry Olsen) ; 14 H 641–642 (Kay Olsen) ; but cf. CE 1749.
391. See pp. 792–793 supra.
392. See p. 794 supra.
393. See CE 1505, 1536, 1559, 1742, 1745, 1748, 1750, 1751, 1752, 1758 ; but see 5 H 201 (Jack Ruby) ; CE 1697, pp. 2–5.
394. C. Ray Hall DE 3, p. 16.
395. See p. 802 infra.
396. Alice Nichols DE 5355, p. 289 ; cf. 14 H 115. 122–123 (Alice Nichols).
397. CE 1693.
398. See CE 1754, 1755 ; CE 1748, 1752.
399. CE 1506, 1520, 1585, 1618, 1652 ; C. Ray Hall DE 3, p. 16 ; cf. CE 1757, 1758.
400. 5 H 103 (J. Edgar Hoover) ; CE 1353, 1628, 1760.

401. R. C. Patterson DE 5358 ; CE 1229, 1467, 1514, 1469, 1470 ; CE 1543, p. 195 ; CE 1449, 1748 ; CE 1511, p. 151 ; CE 1741, 1473, 1474, 1742, 1223, 1745.
402. See pp. 797, 799 supra.
403. C. Ray Hall DE 3, p. 16 ; see 5 H 200 (Jack Ruby).
404. See 5 H 200 (Jack Ruby) ; CE 1580, 1581, 1582, 1583, 1765 ; Pullman DE 1 ; cf. 1543, p. 193.
405. See CE 1576, 1577, 1578, 1579, 1625, 1626, 1627.
406. CE 1584.
407. C. Ray Hall DE 3, p. 16.
408. CE 1588.
409. CE 1600, 1601.
410. CE 1586.
411. CE 1587, 1588, 1589, 1590, 1591, 1593, 1594, 1595, 1596, 1597, 1598, 1599, 1602, 1603, 1604, 1605.
412. 5 H 200–202 (Jack Ruby) ; CE 1545, 1690, 1691, 1697.
413. See CE 1546, 1655 ; CE 1692, pp. 2–5.
414. 5 H 200–201 (Jack Ruby).
415. CE 1697, pp. 1, 4.
416. See 5 H 201–202 (Jack Ruby).
417. CE 1546 ; CE 1697, pp. 1–2.
418. CE 1440, 1767, 1768, 1769 1770, 1771, 1772, 1773, 1774, 1775 ; see also CE 1766 ; 14 H 114–115 (Alice Nichols) ; CE 1471.
419. CE 1441.
420. Cf. CE 1444, pp. 8–15.
421. C. Ray Hall DE 3, p. 15.
422. CE 1445, 1446, 1447.
423. See p. 792 supra ; Sam Ruby DE 1, p. 186.
424. See p. 794 supra.
425. 14 H 462 (Grant) ; CE 1448, 1648, 1744 ; CE 1561, p. 302 ; CE 1585.
426. 14 H 463–464 (Grant).
427. Id. at 465–466.
428. 14 H 391 (Earl Ruby) ; 14 H 499–500 (Sam Ruby).
429. 14 H 466 (Grant).
430. 14 H 493–494 (Sam Ruby) ; see 14 H 114 (Alice Nichols) ; 14 H 371–372 (Earl Ruby) ; pp. 791, 793 supra.
431. 14 H 494 (Sam Ruby).
432. See p. 798 supra.
433. 14 H 137 (Paul) ; 14 H 498 (Sam Ruby).
434. 14 H 498–499 (Sam Ruby).
435. 14 H 371, 373 (Earl Ruby) ; Earl Ruby DE 4, p. 177 ; see C. Ray Hall DE 3, pp. 14–15.
436. 14 H 378, 382–384, 390–391, 417, 426 (Earl Ruby) ; C. Ray Hall DE 3, pp. 14–15 ; see 14 H 457 (Grant) ; 14 H 491 (Sam Ruby).
437. 14 H 383 (Earl Ruby).
438. CE 1185 ; 14 H 491 (Sam Ruby).
439. CE 1458, 1542, 1556.
440. 13 H 438–440 (Crafard) ; CE 1459, 1460, 1453, 1454, 1461, 1462, 1463, 1180, 1464, 1504, 1465, 1663, 1224.
441. CE 1180 ; 15 H 638 (Lawrence V. Meyers) ; 14 H 158 (Paul) ; 15 H 446 (Hansen) ; 14 H 203 (Senator) ; 13 H 194 (Eberhardt) ; 15 H 563 (Roy A. Pryor) ; 14 H 319 (Armstrong) ; Powell DE 3 ; CE 1515, p. 553 ; CE 1742 ; CE 1478, p. 86 ; cf. 13 H 215–216 (Karen Carlin).
442. E.g., CE 1452, 1454, 1457, 1461, 1663.
443. See CE 1454.
444. 14 H 111 (Alice Nichols).
445. 14 H 113–114 (Alice Nichols).
446. 14 H 535 (Jack Ruby) ; 14 H 113 (Alice Nichols) ; 15 H 516 (Kaufman) ; see 14 H. 463 (Grant).
447. Alice Nichols DE 5355, p. 289.
448. Cf. 14 H 203–205 (Senator) and Powell DE 3, and Paul DE 5319, p. 473, and CE 1479, 1480, 1541, with 13 H 215

(Karen Carlin), and 13 H 318 (Armstrong), and CE 1481, 1482, 1505, 1512, 1739.

449. 14 H 203–205 (Senator); Powell DE 3; Paul DE 5319, p. 473; Wright DE 1; CE 1260, 1466, 1487, 1748.

450. 13 H 318 (Armstrong); 14 H 194–195 (Senator); 14 H 125 (Alice Nichols); CE 1449, 1450, 1485, 1542, 1592, 1663, 1740, 1748.

451. CE 2406, p. 650; CE 2411, pp. 621–626; see 14 H 195 (Senator).

452. CE 1451, 1591.

453. CE 1483; see 14 H 152 (Paul); 14 H 503 (Sam Ruby); 14 H 552 (Jack Ruby); 15 H 516 (Kaufman); CE 1484.

454. CE 1483, 1485; see 14 H 152 (Paul); 14 H 205–206 (Senator); 14 H 552 (Jack Ruby).

455. See 13 H 347 (Armstrong); 13 H 441 (Crafard); 14 H 205 (Senator); CE 1486, 1478, p. 83; CE 1512, 1542, 1740; cf. 14 H 311 (Senator); 15 H 209–210 (Palmer); but see 15 H 441–442 (Hansen).

456. See 15 H 446 (Hansen); Hansen DE 1; CE 1478, p. 83; CE 1488, 1542.

457. See ch. VI, pp. 335, 345, 348.

458. See, e.g., 14 H 196 (Senator); CE 1472, 1477, 1489, 1490, 1491, 1492, 1493, 1542, 1738.

459. See CE 1494.

460. See 15 H 240 (Rossi); CE 1449; but see CE 1511, p. 150.

461. See CE 1250, 1483, 1496, 1497, 1498, 1499, 1548, 1671, 2243, 2414.

462. CE 1645, 2243.

463. CE 1497, 1548, 1645, 1671, 1711.

464. CE 1496, 1497, 1499, 1671, 2414.

465. See p. 796 supra.

466. CE 1488, 1542.

467. CE 2495.

468. CE 1624, p. 2.

469. CE 2342, p. 748.

470. CE 1624.

471. CE 2243.

472. CE 2414.

473. CE 1499, 1671.

474. CE 1671.

475. CE 1499.

476. See 14 H 197–198 (Senator); CE 2492, 2493, 2503.

477. CE 2494.

478. CE 1467.

479. See 14 H 202 (Senator); 14 H 562 (Pryor); CE 1223, 1512, 1515, p. 551; CE 1653, 1624.

480. CE 1502.

481. Cf. Crafard DE 5226, p. 149, and 13 H 444–445 (Crafard) with 15 H 248–249 (Earl Wright), and 15 H 412–413 (Powell).

482. See 13 H 312, 349 (Armstrong); 14 H 147 (Paul); 14 H 122 (Alice Nichols); Wright DE 1; CE 1470, 1623, 1624, 2243, 2509.

483. CE 1229; CE 1511, p. 150; CE 2499, 2500, 2505.

484. CE 1491, 1511, 2502.

485. CE 2497.

486. CE 1491, 2491, 1511, p. 150; 14 H 184, 188 (Senator).

487. See generally 15 H 413–414 (Powell). Paul DE 5319, p. 473; CE 1512; 15 H 441 (Hansen).

488. See, e.g., 1469, 1735, 1737, 1738, 1742, 1765, 2498, 2502, 2504, 2506.

489. See p. 782 supra.

490. See 15 H 522 (Kaufman).

APPENDIX XVII

1. 14 H 507 (Jack Ruby).
2. Ibid.
3. Ibid.
4. CE 2785, p. 4 statement of Dr. R. L. Stubblefield, M.D.
5. 14 H 508 (Ruby).
6. 5 H 181–182 (Ruby).
7. Id. at 190, 192–193, 196, 211–212.
8. Id. at 123.
9. See CE 2728.
10. CE 2729.
11. CE 2730.
12. CE 2786.
13. 14 H 507–508 (Ruby).
14. CE 2784.
15. 14 H 504–505 (Ruby).
16. Id. at 512.
17. Id. at 504.
18. Ibid.
19. Id. at 504–506, 510.
20. Id. at 507, 509.
21. Id. at 510.
22. Id. at 506–507, 509, 511.
23. Id. at 509; see id. at 514.
24. Id. at 505, 510.
25. Id. at 505.
26. Id. at 508; 14 H 571 (Dr. William R. Beavers).
27. Id. at 511–512.
28. Id. at 512.
29. Id. at 513.
30. Ibid.
31. Id. at 515.
32. See id. at 517–524; see 14 H 581–582 (Bell P. Herndon).
33. 14 H 523 (Ruby).
34. Ibid.
35. Id. at 526.
36. Ibid.

37. Ibid.
38. Ibid.
39. Id. at 534.
40. Ibid.
41. Ibid.
42. Id. at 536.
43. Ibid.
44. Ibid.
45. Ibid.
46. Id. at 540.
47. Ibid.
48. Ibid.
49. Ibid.
50. Id. at 546.
51. Id. at 547.
52. Ibid.
53. Id. at 551.
54. Id. at 551.
55. Ibid.
56. Ibid.
57. Ibid.
58. Id. at 553.
59. Ibid.
60. Ibid.
61. Ibid.
62. Ibid.
63. Id. at 556.
64. Ibid.
65. Ibid.
66. Ibid.
67. Ibid.
68. Id. at 560.
69. Ibid.
70. Ibid.
71. Id. at 560–561.
72. Id. at 561.
73. Ibid.
74. Ibid.
75. Ibid.

76. Ibid.
77. Ibid.
78. Ibid.
79. Ibid.
80. Ibid.
81. Ibid.
82. Ibid.
83. Id. at 563.
84. Ibid.
85. Ibid.
86. Ibid.
87. Ibid.
88. Ibid.
89. 14 H 580 (Herndon).
90. Ibid.
91. Ibid.
92. Ibid.; 14 H 520 (Ruby).
93. 14 H. 580 (Herndon).
94. Ibid.; 14 H 520 (Ruby).
95. 14 H 580 (Herndon).
96. Id. at 581; 14 H 520 (Ruby).
97. Ibid.
98. 14 H 581 (Herndon).
99. Ibid.
100. Ibid.
101. Id. at 581–582.
102. Id. at 581.
103. Ibid.
104. Ibid.
105. Ibid.
106. Id. at 583.

107. Ibid.
108. See id. at 583.
109. Id. at 582–583; see 5 H 520, 523 (Ruby).
110. Id. at 583.
111. Ibid.
112. Ibid.
113. Id. at 590.
114. Ibid.
115. Id. at 593.
116. Id. at 588.
117. Id. at 590.
118. Id. at 591.
119. Id. at 592.
120. Ibid.
121. Id. at 584.
122. Id. at 582.
123. Id. at 585.
124. Ibid.
125. 14 H 572 (Beavers).
126. Id. at 571.
127. 14 H 584 (Herndon).
128. Ibid.
129. 14 H 572 (Beavers).
130. Ibid.
131. Ibid.
132. Ibid.
133. Id. at 573–574 (Beavers).
134. CE 2651.
135. 14 H 504–570 (Ruby).
136. 14 H 579–598 (Herndon).

Index

De Mohrenschildt, Jeanne, 282–283, 394, 400–401, 418, 717–718, 721, 724.
Department of Defense, 461, 464, 468.
Department of Justice, 238, 457.
Department of State, 13, 26, 244, 258, 266, 267, 275, 276, 277, 279, 326, 327, 330, 331, 432–434, 436, 438, 456, 459, 748.
Department of the Treasury, 454, 457, 460, 464.
Dhority, C. N., 215.
Dickerson, Willis, 796.
Dillon, Hon. C. Douglas, 374, 425, 464, 466, 468.
Dmitrieva, Lyndmila, 692.
Dobbs, Farrell, 289.
Donovan, John E., 385, 389, 685–687.
Dougherty, Jack Edwin, 133, 153.
Dowe, Kenneth Lawry, 346.
Downey, (Mrs.) William, 371.
Downey, William, 372.
Drittal, D. F. (See Oswald, Lee Harvey.)
Duff, William McEwan, 368.
Dulany, Dr. Richard B., 56.
Duncan, William Glenn, Jr., 343.
Duran, Senora Silvia Tirado de, 288–289, 301–302, 304–305, 309–310, 734–735.
Dymitruk, Lydia, 721.
Dziemian, Dr. Arthur J., 109, 580, 584.

E

Eberhardt, Augustus M., 342.
Edwards, Robert Edwin, 145–146.
Eisenhower, President Dwight D., 384.
Ekdahl, Edwin A., 9, 10, 377–378, 671–673.
Epstein, Harry, 788.
Epstein, Ruby, 788.
Epstein, Willie, 794.
Euins, Amos Lee, 64, 147, 155.
Evans, Lt. J. (See Oswald, Lee Harvey.)
Evans, (Mrs.) Myrtle, 672–673, 680, 726.
Evans, Sidney, Jr., 353.
Executive Order No. 11130, 501–502.

F

Fain, John W., 326, 434.
Fair Play for Cuba Committee, 19, 21–22, 122, 244, 287–292, 301–302, 312–313, 315, 326, 331, 342–344, 390, 402, 404, 406–408, 410–413, 419, 435–436, 441–442, 567, 578, 661, 728–732, 734, 739, 744.

Federal Bureau of Investigation, 13–14, 16, 22, 24, 26, 30, 60, 76, 81, 84–85, 96–97, 105, 118–119, 121, 123, 125, 131, 134–135, 140, 168–170, 172, 179, 185–186, 193, 199–200, 209, 224, 232, 235, 238, 244–245, 249, 251, 262, 284, 285–287, 289, 292, 309, 315–318, 320, 325–328, 344, 350, 358–359, 362, 364–365, 367–368, 407, 419–420, 429, 431, 433–444, 455–459, 461–464, 466, 514, 547, 555, 561, 565–566, 588, 591, 644, 646, 652, 659–662, 667, 715–716, 732, 739, 748, 762, 775, 777, 779, 807–808, 811.
Felde, Allan R., 682.
Ferraro, Frank, 796.
Finck, Lt. Col. Pierre A., 86, 88.
Fischer, Ronald B., 145–146.
Fisher, Deputy Chief N. T., 32, 206.
Fitgerald (or Fitzsimmons), Virginia, 787.
Folsom, Lt. Col. Allison G., Jr., 191.
Ford, Declan P., 722.
Ford, Katherine N., 282, 394, 417, 722.
Foster, J. W., 71–72, 76, 116, 640.
Fowler, Clayton, 808–809, 812.
Frazier Buell Wesley, 15, 129, 131, 133–134, 137, 147, 181, 247, 332, 421, 738, 740.
Frazier, Robert A., 77, 84–85, 92, 105–106, 171, 185–186, 189, 193–194, 547–553.
Frazier, Capt. W. B., 229.
Fritz, Capt. J. Will, 8, 9, 16, 79, 122, 155, 160, 162, 179–182, 198–201, 208–210, 215–216, 229–230, 232, 234, 239, 241, 346, 645.

G

Gadash, Clyde, 344–345.
Garfield, President James A., 425, 507, 509.
Garner, Darrell Wayne, 663.
Garrett, Richard W., 675.
German, Ella, 699, 704.
Gibson, John, 179, 654.
Giesecke, Dr. Adolph H., Jr., 53–54.
Gimpel, Martin, 788, 794.
Givens, Charles Douglas, 141, 142, 250, 644.
Glover, Everett D., 722.
Goldberg, A. I., 694.
Golovachev, Pavel, 698.
Gonzalez, Representative Henry B., 57.
Graef, John G., 719.
Grant, David B., 445.
Grant, Eva, 334–336, 338, 348–350, 352, 663, 779, 785–787, 792–794, 802–803, 808.
Granovsky, Frank, 786.

Kennedy, President John F.—Con.
53–61, 68–69, 79, 81, 85–87, 89, 90–
91, 96–98, 105–107, 109–111, 115–118,
129, 173, 179–180, 182–183, 186, 188–
190, 194–196, 198, 200–201, 228, 233,
236, 239–240, 242–248, 250, 254, 255,
284–285, 287, 292, 296–298, 304, 309,
316, 321, 322, 325, 333, 335–336, 338,
342, 344–346, 348–352, 354, 364, 366,
368, 370, 373–377, 387, 414–415, 422,
424–429, 431–433, 440, 443, 445, 447–
450, 452–456, 459–460, 466, 580–582,
584–586, 637, 639–642, 644–646, 652,
655, 658, 663, 665, 667–668, 722, 739,
804.
Kennedy, (Mrs.) John F., 1–4, 40, 42,
43, 45, 49–51, 57–59, 116, 344, 349,
354, 372, 452–453, 812.
Kennedy, Hon. Robert F., 59, 374, 662.
Khrushchev, Nikita, 255, 722.
Kiev, 276.
Kilduff, Malcolm, 57, 335.
Killom, Wanda Joyce, 363–364.
Killion Charles L., 171.
King, Capt. Glen D., 205, 224, 226, 228,
231, 239, 241.
Klause, Robert G., 298–299.
Klein's Sporting Goods Co., 118–119,
127, 566, 569, 723.
Kleinlerer, Alexander, 717, 719–720.
Kloepfer, Ruth, 726.
Knapp, David, 161.
Knight, Russell. (See Moore, Russell
Lee.)
Komsomol, 280, 761, 767.
Korengold, R. J., 694.
Kostikov, Valeriy Vladimirovich, 285,
309, 734.
Krystinik, Raymond Franklin, 739.
Kuznetsova, Roza, 697–698.

L

Lamon, Ward H., 506.
Lane, Mark R., 297–298, 368.
Larkin, James, 347.
Latona, Sebastian F., 123, 135, 140,
249, 563, 566.
Lawrence, Capt. Perdue W., 448–449.
Lawrence, Richard, 505.
Lawson, Winston G., 29, 30, 31, 32, 39,
43, 53, 57, 72, 202, 204, 431, 445–449,
452.
Leavelle, James R., 215–216, 230.
Lee, H. O. (See Oswald, Lee Har-
vey.)
Lee, O. H. (See Oswald, Lee Har-
vey.)
Lee, Vincent T., 291, 407–408, 729.
Lewis, L. J., 169.

Light, Dr. Frederick W., Jr., 109, 580,
581, 585.
Lincoln, President Abraham, 425, 504–
506, 508–510, 637.
"Little Lynn." (See Carlin, Karen
Bennett.)
Livingston (Mrs.) Clyde I., 675.
Lodge, Senator Henry Cabot, 510.
Lord, Billy Joe, 690.
Louis, Joe, 789.
Louisiana Department of Labor, 404,
725.
Louisiana State Unemployment Com-
mission, 292, 309.
Love Field, 1–2, 4, 24, 30–31, 39–40,
42–43, 46, 58, 202, 245, 422, 445, 447,
450, 452, 665, 714.
Lovelady, Billy Nolan, 147, 153–154,
644.
Lucy, Forest L., 566.
Lujan, Daniel Gutierrez, 161.

M

McBride, Palmer, 384.
McChann, Rev. Walter J., 324.
McClelland, Dr. Robert N., 53–54, 56.
McCone, Hon. John Alex, 327, 374,
433.
McCurdy, Danny Patrick, 343.
McDonald, M. N., 8, 176, 178–179, 560.
McFarland, John Bryan, 323, 732.
McKinley, President William, 425,
455, 457, 504, 509–511.
McKnight, Felix, 201.
McMillon, Thomas Donald, 213.
McNamara, Hon. Robert S., 374.
McVickar, John A., 693, 706, 747, 761.
McWatters, Cecil J., 157, 159, 252.
McWillie, Louis J., 370, 801–802, 812.
MacDonald, Betty, 663.
Magia, Hyman, 786.
Mallory, Katherine, 702.
Mamantov, Ilya A., 282.
Mancuso, Dr. Bruno F., 670.
Mandella, Arthur, 123, 135, 141, 563.
Marine Corps, 11, 12, 180, 189–192, 194,
244, 256–258, 262, 322, 326, 376–378,
383–386, 388, 390–391, 393, 395, 397,
402, 422, 434, 440, 569, 571, 645, 656,
660, 672, 675, 678, 680–682, 685, 689–
690, 693, 696, 706, 710, 714, 716, 727,
731–732, 746, 748, 763, 766, 775.
Markham, Helen Louise, 7, 166–167,
169, 174–175, 651–652, 667.
Markham, James Alfred, 667.
Markham, William Edward, 667.
Martello, Francis L., 417.
Martin, James Herbert, 187, 372.
Martin, John, 788.

Matthews, R. D., 369.
Maxey, Billy Joe, 215.
Maxwell, Alexander W., 772.
Medvedev, Aleksandr, 702.
Meller, Anna N., 281, 716–718, 720.
Mexico, 246, 285, 288, 299, 301–302, 304–305, 307–310, 324, 331, 362, 372, 413, 416, 419, 422, 438, 441, 443, 639, 658–659, 666, 730, 732–733, 736, 739, 777, 811.
Meyers, Lawrence V., 334–335, 349, 358.
Michaelis, Heinz W., 172.
Miller, Austin L., 76.
Minsk, 12, 257–258, 267, 269, 272, 274–275, 277–278, 280, 393 –394, 402, 656–657, 711, 713, 752, 755, 758, 760, 764, 766.
Mitchell, Mary Ann, 68.
Molina, Joe R., 237–238.
Montgomery, L. D., 216.
Mooney, Deputy Sheriff Luke, 8, 79.
Moore, Henry M., 180.
Moore, Russell Lee, 343, 344, 349.
Mosby, Aline, 256, 259, 265, 656, 694–696.
Muchmore, Mary, 97, 109–110.
Murphy, Joe E., 71–72.
Murphy, Paul Edward, 683.
Murphy, Thomas J., 76.
Murret, Charles, 331, 728.
Murret, Eugene, 728.
Murret, Lillian, 313, 378, 383, 669–671, 675, 679–680, 690, 725–726.

N

National Naval Medical Center, 4, 59.
National Security Agency, 244.
Navarro, Horacio Duran, 304.
Nelson, "Little Daddy," 799, 802.
Newnam, John, 334–336.
Nichilayeva, Marina. (*See* Oswald, Marina.)
Nichols, Alice R., 337–338, 787, 801, 803–804.
Nichols, H. Louis, 201, 655.
Nicol, Joseph D., 84–85, 171, 186, 547, 562.
Nix, Orville O., 97, 109–110.
Nixon, Richard M., 187–188.
Norman, Earl, 805.
Norman, Harold, 68, 70–71, 144–145, 153, 250.
Norton, Robert L., 352.

O

O'Brien, Lawrence F., 59.
Odio, Sylvia, 321–324.

O'Donnell, Kenneth, 2, 31, 42, 45, 48, 49, 57–59, 427.
Odum, Bardwell D., 364–365, 667.
Office of Naval Intelligence, 433–434.
Office of Science and Technology, 464.
O'Grady, Thomas J., 348.
Okui, Yaeko, 722.
Olivier, Dr. Alfred G., 87, 109, 580–581, 584–586.
Olsen, Harry N., 343–344, 350.
Olsen, (Mrs.) Harry N., 344.
Osborne. (*See* Oswald, Lee Harvey.)
Osborne, Albert, 305, 733.
Osborne, Dr. William, 56.
Oswald, Lee Harvey, 6, 9–17, 19–22, 24, 30, 118–119, 121–125, 127–131, 133–137, 140–141, 143–147, 149, 151–157, 159–163, 165–169, 171–172, 174–176, 178–196, 198–202, 204, 206, 208–210, 212–213, 215–216, 219, 221–222, 224–231, 233–250, 252–254, 256–260, 262, 265–267, 269, 272, 274–293, 295, 297, 299, 301–302, 304–305, 307–310, 312–334, 342–345, 347, 350, 353–354, 357–365, 367–424, 428, 433–444, 456, 458, 462–463, 558–560, 562, 565–567, 569–572, 575–579, 590, 592, 596, 637–639, 642–701, 703–713, 716, 719, 720, 722, 724–728, 731–734, 736, 739–740, 746, 748–751, 753–766, 768–779, 794, 807, 809–811.
Oswald, Marina, 13–15, 122, 124, 127–131, 154, 175, 180–181, 184–188, 198, 235, 238, 246–248, 257, 260, 267, 269, 272, 274–284, 287, 292, 301–302, 309–310, 312, 317–318, 322–323, 328–332, 364, 376, 387, 394–395, 401–402, 404–407, 411–424, 435, 437–440, 567, 571, 578, 592, 643, 645, 647, 653, 657–658, 660–663, 665, 667, 697, 700, 702–709, 711–712, 714–730, 734–740, 746, 753, 757–758, 761–769, 773.
Oswald, Hazel, 725.
Oswald, June Lee, 711, 714, 721, 724, 725, 726, 730, 737.
Oswald, Marguerite Claverie, 9, 10, 256, 275, 326–327, 329–330, 364–365, 377–381, 384, 401–402, 434, 667, 669–681, 688–689, 694, 697, 711, 741, 766.
Oswald, Rachel, 317, 738–739.
Oswald, Robert Edward Lee, 9, 13, 187, 199, 265, 274, 281, 329–331, 377–378, 384, 390–392, 401, 434, 669–671, 678, 680, 690, 694, 697, 705–706, 711–715, 721, 741–742, 763, 773.
Oswald, Robert Edward Lee (deceased), 669–670.
Oswald, William Stout, 725.

Rusk, Hon. Dean, 255–256, 309, 374, 456.
Russell, Harold, 169, 653.
Rutkowski, Fannie Turek, 780.
Rutledge, John, 340.
Ryder, Dial D., 315–316, 646.

S

Saffran, Don, 337–338.
Sawyer, Inspector J. Herbert, 8, 76, 155, 253.
Schmidt, Larrie H., 295–297.
Schmidt, Volkmar, 722.
Schrand, Martin D., 664.
Schrank, John N., 463, 511.
Scoggins, Williams W., 7, 165–166, 169, 175, 651.
Secret Service, 2, 16, 23–26, 28, 30, 32, 39, 43, 45, 52, 57, 71, 96–97, 116, 179, 199, 245, 247, 316, 326, 374, 425, 427–433, 440–444, 446–461, 468, 508–515, 664, 667.
Seidband, Sidney, 801.
Senator, George, 344–346, 352–354, 371–372, 810.
Setyayev, Lev, 691.
Shaneyfelt, Lyndal L., 98, 125–126, 592–593, 595–597.
Shanklin, J. Gordon, 440, 647.
Shargol, Martin, 788.
Shaw, Dr. Robert Roeder, 56, 92–93, 581, 583.
Shelley, William H., 147, 153–154, 182.
Shires, Dr. George T., 56.
Shirokova, Rima, 259, 667, 690–693, 696–697.
Siegel, Evelyn G. S., 379–382.
Silverman, Rabbi Hillel, 340, 804.
Simmons, Ronald, 189, 194.
Simmons, William F., 364.
Skelton, Royce G., 76, 116.
Slack, Garland Glenwill, 318–320.
Slatin, Joe, 795.
Slaughter, Malcolm R., 353.
Smith, John Allison, 352–353.
Smith, William Arthur, 168, 175.
Snyder, Richard Edward, 262, 265, 277–278, 392, 693–695, 701, 705–706, 747–748, 754–758.
Sokolow, Irving, 381.
Sorrels, Forrest V., 29, 31–32, 39, 43, 52, 155, 204, 206, 210, 446, 448, 452.
Soviet Union, 11–13, 21, 23, 128, 192, 243–244, 254–259, 262, 265–267, 269, 272, 274–279, 285, 287, 289, 299, 301, 307, 309–310, 312, 326, 329–330, 374, 376–377, 387–388, 390–395, 397–399, 401–402, 408, 410, 412–414, 417, 420, 422, 434, 436–437, 442, 639, 655–657,

Soviet Union—Continued
660, 662, 690, 693–695, 698–699, 706, 709, 711, 714, 716, 727, 731, 747–751, 753, 755–757, 759–761, 764–766, 768–769, 771, 776, 778.
Stevenson, Hon. Adlai, 30, 41, 292, 295, 415–416, 433.
Stevenson, Deputy Chief M. W., 208–210, 213.
Stombaugh, Paul M., 124–125, 128, 136, 586, 588, 590–591.
Stovall, Richard S., 180.
Stovall, Robert L., 246.
Stuckey, William Kirk, 390, 408, 437, 729.
Studebaker, Robert Lee, 566.
Surrey, Robert Alan, 298–299.
Sweatt, Allan L., 809.

T

Tabon, Don, 805.
Taft, President William Howard, 426, 511.
Tague, James Thomas, 116.
Talbert, Capt. Cecil E., 210, 212–213, 230.
Tanay, Dr. Emanuel, 808–809.
Taylor, Alexander, 717.
Taylor, Gary E., 717–718.
Taylor, Robert Adrian, 318.
Texas Employment Commission, 246–247, 281, 308, 332, 400, 402–403, 715, 724.
Texas School Book Depository—3–6, 8–9, 14–16, 18–19, 21, 25, 32, 48, 52, 61, 63–65, 68, 71–72, 76, 79, 81, 84–85, 87, 95–98, 112, 115, 117–118, 122, 125, 128, 129–130, 133, 135–137, 140, 144, 146–147, 149, 153–155, 157, 159–160, 175, 179, 182, 185, 189–190, 192, 195, 198, 233–235, 237–238, 245–248, 250–253, 285, 318, 335, 360, 370, 378, 404, 421–422, 438, 441, 443, 448–449, 458, 551, 553, 555, 557, 565–567, 579–580, 583, 588, 638–640, 642–649, 661, 664, 738.
Texas Theatre, 8, 9, 124, 159, 176, 198, 200, 206, 234, 423, 654.
Thomas, Representative Albert, 1, 42, 57–58.
Thornberry, Hon. Homer, 57–58.
Thornley, Kerry Wendell, 385–386, 388–389, 686.
Tippit J. D., 6–8, 16, 20, 22, 118, 144, 156, 165–168, 173–176, 179–180, 195, 198, 200–201, 240, 252, 254, 297, 330, 368–370 376, 423, 639, 648–653, 655, 661–663, 667, 812.
Titovyets, Erik, 702, 708.
Tobias, (Mrs.) M. F., 435.

Tomlinson, Darrell C., 81.
Tonahill, Joe H., 807–808.
Tormey, James J., 289.
Torresola, Griselio, 513.
Tower, Senator John G., 769–770.
Trade Mart, 1–3, 24, 30–32, 39–40, 46, 53, 58, 245, 247, 422, 445, 447, 450, 729.
Trammel, Connie, 368.
Treasury Department, 119, 121, 314, 328, 433.
Truly, Roy S., 5, 6, 9, 149, 151–156, 247–248, 252, 648, 664, 738.
Truman, President Harry S., 425, 513.
Turman, Buddy, 805.
Turner, F. M., 221.
Twiford, Horace Elroy, 289, 731–732.
Tyler, President John, 505.

U

Underwood, James R., 64–65.

V

Van Buren, President Martin, 505.
Vaughn, Roy Eugene, 215, 221–222.
Vinson, Philip Eugene, 674.
Voebel, Edward, 383, 679.
Volpert, Ann, 338.

W

Wade, Henry, 201, 205, 208, 234–237, 342–343 346–347, 441, 654.
Waldman, William J., 119.
Walker, C. T., 176.
Walker, Maj. Gen. Edwin A., 13, 15, 20, 23, 118, 128, 182–187, 195, 282–283, 286, 288, 298–299, 368, 376–377, 404–406, 416, 442–443, 562, 567, 592, 596, 661–663, 738.
Walker, Ira N., Jr., 352–353.
Wall, Breck, 350, 352, 358–359, 796.
Walthers, Eddy Raymond, 116, 178, 641.
Washington, President George, 426–427.

Waterman, Bernice L., 758.
Watherwax, Arthur William, 344–345.
Weinstein, Abe, 349, 352, 358.
Weinstein, Barney, 349, 350, 359.
Weissman, Bernard, 293–299, 335, 344, 347, 357, 368–369, 661, 663.
Weitzman, Seymour, 79, 81, 645.
Westbrook, Capt. W. R., 175.
Weston, Wally, 797.
Whaley, William Wayne, 160–162, 252, 649–650.
White, J. C., 71, 640.
White House, 1–2, 29–31, 40, 42, 57, 59–60, 90, 245, 429, 431, 445–446, 450–452, 457, 460, 466–467, 505–506, 508–509, 510, 512–515.
Whitworth, Edith, 316.
Wiedersheim, Frederick J., 773.
Wiggins, Lt. Woodrow, 230.
Williams, Bonnie Ray, 68, 70–71, 153, 250, 644.
Willis, Billy Joe, 361.
Willis, Phillip L., 112.
Wilson, President Woodrow, 512, 514.
Wittmus, Ronald G., 123, 135, 141.
Wood, Dr. Homer, 318–319.
Wood, Sterling Charles, 319–320.
Worrell, James Richard, Jr., 253.
Wright, James C., Jr., 750.
Wulf, William E., 384.

Y

Yarborough, Senator Ralph W., 2, 42, 46, 52.
Yatskov, Antonovich, 734.
Young, Arthur, 286.
Young, Ruth Forbes, 286.
Youngblood, Rufus W., 3, 46, 48, 51–52, 57–58, 453.

Z

Zahn, James A., 189–191, 194.
Zangara, Guiseppe, 463.
Zapruder, Abraham, 49, 63, 97–98, 105, 109–110, 112, 115, 453.
Ziger, Alexander, 697, 709.
Zoppi, Tony, 334.